Intermediate Structured Finance Modeling

T0305274

Intermediate Structured Finance Modeling

Leveraging Excel, VBA, Access and PowerPoint

WILLIAM PREINITZ

WITH MATTHEW NIEDERMAIER

WILEY

John Wiley & Sons, Inc.

Published by John Wiley & Sons, Inc., Hoboken, New Jersey.
Published simultaneously in Canada.

For general information on our other products and services or for technical support, please contact our Customer Care Department within the United States at (800) 762-2974, outside the United States at (317) 572-3993 or fax (317) 572-4002.

Wiley also publishes its books in a variety of electronic formats. Some content that appears in print may not be available in electronic books. For more information about Wiley products, visit our web site at www.wiley.com.

Library of Congress Cataloging-in-Publication Data

Preinitz, William, 1950–
  Intermediate structured finance modeling : fast track VBA and access / William Preinitz and Matthew Niedermaier.
      p.   cm. – (Wiley finance series)
   Includes index.
   ISBN 978-0-470-56239-0 (cloth); ISBN 978-0-470-92875-2 (ebk);
ISBN 978-0-470-92877-8 (ebk); ISBN 978-0-92878-3 (ebk)
   1. Finance–Computer simulation.   2. Finance–Mathematical models.
3. Microsoft Visual BASIC.   I. Niedermaier, Matthew, 1981–   II. Title.
   HG106.P745 2011
   332.0285'5133–dc22
                                                2010027041

10   9   8   7   6   5   4   3   2   1

Contents

PART FIVE

Financing the CLTS and the LWM 655

CHAPTER 33

Running the Models

Preface

The preface of a book is where the author tries to make a good first impression on the reader. It is here that the author tries to entice and inform the reader as to the utility and attractiveness of the subject matter or story line. It is hoped there will be a meeting of the minds and the content of the book will meet your specific interests. The question of royalty payments aside, it is abundantly clear that authors want you to be interested because they themselves are interested in the subject matter. They have found it so interesting that they have spent a considerable amount of time and emotional and psychological energy, and have endured sore fingers and stiff wrists composing, editing, and reediting the manuscript that became the book you have before you! Get ready! I am now going to try to make that first good impression with a dual approach and try to convince you of both the practical and esthetic merits of this book.

Let us deal with the practical issues first.

GOALS OF THE BOOK

The goal of this book is to provide you with a set of examples of how to maximize the combined synergy of the four Microsoft products: the Excel spreadsheet tool, Visual Basic Application (VBA) language, the Access database, and the PowerPoint presentation software.

A set of immediately applicable modeling approaches, techniques, skills, and examples that can be employed to address a wide range of commercial and financial problems will be presented. Although the main example in the book is a structured finance application, the book itself is not intended or developed to be a text on structured finance per se. Every technique and approach that you see in this book can be widely generalized for almost any commercial activity. This is especially true of the data selection and reporting techniques. The book also discusses how to organize your development effort, keep your models coherent and flexible, and build a strong base for future work. As such, it contains valuable information, no matter what the type or scope of business application you are interested in creating.

The focus will be on the development of a set of financial models. The development effort will concentrate on the construction of a series of models to perform the cash flow evaluation and structuring activities supporting a deal financing a portfolio of residential mortgage loans. As such, it will make use of a data and computationally intense model with a developed user interface. The most important goal of this book is to teach you intermediate levels of financial modeling skills, not to train you in financial deal structuring techniques. Once you learn these modeling skills and the products used to implement them, you can apply them to a wide range of financial, or nonfinancial, problems. The best way to think about this is to conceptualize this combination of skills and product knowledge as sort of an intellectual Swiss Army knife. For the range of tasks that the knife is designed to address, there are very few that will not succumb to some combination of the available attachments!

Specifically you will learn:

- To organize and build a set of directories to contain the model system you will develop.
- To take an existing large model and separate its two main functional components. This division will separate the Asset Pool portion of the model that calculates the collateral cash flows (the sources of funds) from the Liabilities Structure of the model (the uses of funds). From this starting point we will then develop each of the two pieces into more sophisticated analytical platforms. We will call the first model, the sources of funds model, the Collateral Cash Flow Generator (CCFG). The second model, the uses of funds model, will be called the Liabilities Waterfall Model (LWM).
- How to expand the capabilities of the CCFG. Doing this will involve enhancements to the model that will allow it to amortize additional mortgage types and apply improved collateral selection techniques. It will also update the model's ability to perform prepayment and default analysis based on Geographic and Demographic Methodologies.
- How to expand the capabilities of the LWM by introducing a multiple tranche bond class structure and to employ other various liability structuring features.
- How to expand the existing reporting package to produce a series of more varied and complicated reports and to combine PowerPoint with VBA and Excel to produce reports directly in a PowerPoint format.
- To employ Access to handle large sets of input data for the models, such as collateral characteristics and modeling assumptions including prepayment, default, and market value decline inputs to the model.
- To use Access to store the results of both the models.
- To use Outlook to improve the messaging capabilities of the model.

WHAT YOU SHOULD KNOW

Keeping all of the above in mind, note that the word "Intermediate" is prominent in the title of the book. This is *not* a beginning-level book. Those of you who would like an introductory-level work on modeling are strongly encouraged to consult *A Fast Track Guide to Structured Finance Modeling, Monitoring, and Valuation: Jump Start VBA* by William Preinitz (Hoboken, NJ: John Wiley & Sons, 2009). The models that we will work with in this book are a direct extension of the models used to teach basic modeling skills in my earlier book. If you have some modeling experience and are confident in your mastery of the fundamental features of VBA and Excel, you can plunge right into this book.

This book is designed to address readers who have some experience under their belts already. To wit:

- You have designed a basic model or two or, for better or worse, have inherited someone else's model and modified it.
- You are familiar with Excel functionality in the form of functions and add-in features.
- You are familiar with all the basic VBA computational symbols, data types, and logical operators.
- You are familiar with decision structures, such as "If..Then..Else". You are comfortable with both "For..Next" and "Do..While" or "Do..Until" loops and know when to use one rather than the other.
- You understand VBA variable types, give your variables reasonable names, and know how to declare their scopes.
- You comment your code, especially those subroutines and user-written functions that are either complex or lengthy.
- You can write subroutines that make sense and place these subroutines in VBA modules that organize them in a logical, obvious manner.
- You can run the VBA Debugger and use the 15 to 20 most commonly employed features.
- You know how to build a basic menu interface using VBA and Excel.
- You can design and implement a basic report package using Excel template files and VBA report-writing subroutines.

If you can answer an enthusiastic "YES!" to all, or most, of the above, you know the basics. The basics, however, are no longer enough! You are itching for more! There has to be a better way to do things! You are enthusiastic enough or dissatisfied enough to want to take a significant step forward.

Expanding your modeling skills now and quickly are the orders of the day. This effort will, it is hoped, not only improve the look and feel of your models but allow them to tackle problems that they cannot readily encompass now. This will mean developing the skills to make your models more capable, more effective, and at the same time more efficient, more understandable, and easier to use. Well, that is quite a to-do list! How are we going to get *that* done?

This book will teach you how to take the basic Excel/VBA model that was introduced in my earlier book and significantly enhance its speed, power, clarity, flexibility, and scope by taking you to the next level of model development. As specifically listed above, doing this will not only involve using the Excel and VBA products that we are familiar with but also Access, PowerPoint, and Outlook. That is not to say that you will not also improve your Excel and VBA skills. The backbone and guts of the models we will develop here are firmly Excel and VBA based. It is the creation of a much more powerful synergy by including the data handling power of Access, the presentation and communication capabilities of PowerPoint, and the messaging and monitoring aspects of Outlook that will allow you to immediately boost your models to a higher level of effectiveness and efficiency.

SETTING THE CONTEXT FOR LEARNING

This book is a companion volume to the previously mentioned *Fast Track Guide to Structured Finance Modeling, Monitoring, and Valuation: Jump Start VBA*. In that book we assumed that the reader was a financial analyst who had been recently assigned to a structured finance group in an investment bank. The first task was to work with someone who would be rotating out of the department at the end of the following month. This person would be handing off a nearly complete Excel waterfall model spreadsheet. The assets in the deal were a portfolio of small business loans and represented the part of the financing that was comprised of an owner note with no guarantee from the federal government. The challenge before our newcomer was to turn the waterfall spreadsheet into a fully completed model equipped with menus, a collateral cash flow generator, and a report package. The need was immediate, and fortunately several things were working in favor of a successful conclusion to the exercise. The loan portfolio was small and fairly straightforward. It consisted of approximately 2,800 loans each of which had only 26 data fields. The collateral selection process was limited, unchanging, and specifically expressed. The reports that were needed were, for the most part, working reports, and were relatively limited in both sophistication of the informational content and presentation format. The greatest factor in favor of success was that the reader had the *Fast Track* book that showed him or her, in a clear and heavily illustrated manner, what to do and how to do it.

In this book we will assume that the passage of time, one year, has brought both success and additional responsibility. Our newcomer is now becoming a seasoned structured finance modeler with a basic skill set sufficient unto the routine tasks at hand. The modeler probably, however, needs more information to be successful in attacking the next big step up the ladder of more complex and computationally burdensome potential future modeling.

The first issue that concerns our modeler is the number of apparent shortcomings in the current model and its environment that now need to be addressed. These issues initially centered around the limited capability of the model to change demand. The model users are not able to create custom collateral selection criteria or rules. They are unable to create specialized reports. The report package the model currently produces still requires significant additional effort to reformat its appearance to produce presentation-quality material. The demand for these presentation-quality reports for either internal management or external groups such as regulators, investors, or rating agencies is growing. There also appears to be growing dissatisfaction with the model's execution speed. Although it is sufficient for small portfolios, say 1,000 to 3,000 loans, it has proven less satisfactory for a larger portfolio the department was asked to bid on that contained over 5,000 loans. To evaluate even the smallest changes to the Liabilities Structure, the entire collateral portfolio needs to be recalculated for each model run. Doing this proved frustrating to the structuring personnel and consumed large amounts of machine run time, spent mostly watching progress messages churn to completion.

You have recently been informed that the department routinely will be looking at a set of much larger portfolios, each loan of which will contain significantly more data. These portfolios are collections of current issuance mortgages on single-family residential properties. It is clear that you will also need to segregate the collateral cash flow generator from the liabilities waterfall functionality in the model to improve the efficiency of both. Doing this will also allow you to expand the capabilities of both, now separated, pieces of the original model, without the whole becoming too large and unwieldy. You will need to provide for a more flexible and interactive model. You will need to be able to sort through these larger collections of collateral using interactively specified collateral selection criteria. The reporting requirements will also change, and a much more flexible report package able to produce a wider range of report package configurations will be needed. The appearance and formats of these reports will become more sophisticated and more targeted to specific audiences. As the model becomes more complex, you will need to improve the messaging capabilities of the model.

The department is looking to you to come up with the Next New Great Solution. Fortunately you have some time, approximately three months, to get ready for the next onslaught. You will obviously need to consider a design to meet these challenges, which are beyond the limits of the current model's framework.

Despite these challenges, you are both eager and optimistic! You have the current model to use as a base development platform. While much of the code will have to be broken down, examined, revised, and then subsequently rebuilt in an expanded form, the model is a firm base from which to proceed. You have recently been advised that you will also be able to draw on the time and expertise of another member of the department who has experience building Access databases. Last, but (I hope) not least, you have this book. Opportunity beckons!

I am sympathetic to your situation. I have been there myself on numerous occasions! Expectations run high, especially if you have been successful in the past.

THE STRUCTURE OF THE BOOK

Part One: First Steps

Part One contains Chapters 1 through 7.

Chapter 1, "Introduction," is designed to impart the spirit and approaches that will be employed in the book. It lists the reasons the book was written, which are threefold. The first is to educate the reader regarding the challenges of developing larger-scale models. The second is to describe a real-world solution that many analysts will face in their careers. The third is to discuss the evolutionary paths of models and to present an example of significant evolution from a more simple model to a more sophisticated one. This chapter will also describe the intended audience of the book and the Excel/VBA skills you will need to be comfortable with the material.

In Chapter 2, "The Existing Model," we review the state of the current model that forms the basis of the instructional plan of the remainder of the book. In this scenario you have previously written a model that has performed well for some period of time. A new business opportunity has arisen that is simply beyond the capabilities of the current model. You need to use the existing model as a base from which to develop a more powerful model that addresses the requirements of this new analytical task. You need to conduct a review of the current model to determine what you are going to be able to salvage from it. You will also need to review the current model directory system to determine it is also adequate.

In Chapter 3, "Conventions and Advice," we step away from the modeling process for a moment. We have completed our initial assessment of the existing model and will now give some thought to *how* we will work before we begin the rebuilding/construction process. In this chapter there are five pieces of hard-won general advice. Take the time to avail yourself of these little nuggets. They are useful admonitions and can save you both headaches and heartaches as you proceed about your task.

In Chapter 4, "Segregation of the Existing Model's Functionality," we discuss the organization of the base model. We examine its structure, menus, data, and modular organization. In the next two chapters we break this model into two parts. The first is the cash-generating portion, the sources of funds side, which we will call the Base Asset Model (BAM). The second model is the liabilities structure portion, the uses of funds side, which we will call the Base Liabilities Model (BLM), that applies those cash flows to a liability structure.

In Chapter 5, "Creating the Base Asset Model," we start with the original small business model and strip out everything not related to the evaluation of the collateral. It contains all the model functionality that screens and selects the collateral that will be eligible to be included in the asset portfolio of the deal. It also contains the calculation routines that produce sets of cash flow projections based on various prepayment and default methodologies.

In Chapter 6, "Building the Base Liabilities Model," we find ourselves back at the start again, working from a second copy of the original model. In this instance we focus on segregating and discarding all portions of the model not related to the liabilities side of the deal. When we complete this exercise, we will have a pair of compiled working models that will replicate the earlier, original model's complete functionality. These two new models serve as the springboard for the subsequent modeling development for the rest of the book. The Base Asset Model will be developed into the Collateral Cash Flow Generator Model. The Base Liabilities Model will be developed into the Liabilities Waterfall Model.

Finally in Chapter 7, "Establishing the Model Environment," we design and implement the directory environment to accommodate the new models once they are written. We also create other portions of the environment to accommodate the sources of data, the template files of the reports, and preservation and organization of all of the output of the model.

Thus by the end of Part One we have split two complete models from the original. This pair of models forms the departure points for the new development efforts to follow. We have also created the environment to house and organize these future models and all of their supporting files and data bases.

Part Two: Building the New Assets Model

Part Two consists of Chapters 8 through 13. In this part we design and implement the new Asset model. The name of this model is the Collateral Cash Flow

Generator (CCFG). This model performs the tasks of collateral screening, selection, and amortization.

In Chapter 8, "Designing the New Collateral Cash Flow Generator," we do just that. With the BAM as out point of departure, we consider what changes we need to prepare the model for the asset class that we next analyze, that of residential mortgage loans. We look at the different types of collateral that we need to amortize. We develop a new approach to organizing and applying assumptions regarding collateral performance. We also look at the construction of a collateral pool from all or parts of other collateral pools. We also address the subject of using aggregated collateral data known as representative lines. Last we revise and expand the collateral reporting capabilities of the model.

Chapter 9, "Writing the CCFG Menus and Data Sheets," addresses the design and implementation of the new menus of the CCFG, their supporting VBA code (including extensive error checking), and first appearance of UserForms in menus.

In Chapter 10, "Writing the Collateral Data Handling Code," we describe the changes needed to read, merge, select, and report on either single or combinations of multiple collateral portfolios.

Chapter 11, "Writing the Collateral Selection Code," focuses on changes to the process of determining eligible collateral on both a loan-by-loan and a portfolio basis. These eligibility tests can be based on the financial, demographic, or geographic characteristics of the collateral or any combination of those factors. This chapter will also discuss the issue and treatment of geographic concentration issues.

Chapter 12, "Writing the Collateral Cash Flow Amortization Code," addresses writing the VBA code that performs the amortization calculations for all the types of loans found in the collateral pool. These include a number of new mortgage types that the earlier model was incapable of handling. The chapter also introduces the concepts of geographic and demographic prepayment and default calculation methodologies.

Chapter 13, "Writing the CCFG Reporting Capability," addresses changes to the cash flow reporting process. Here we implement the capability to produce everything from simple working group reports, to stratification and cross-tabulation reports, and later presentation reports in the same model run.

At the conclusion of Part Two we will have completed the CCFG.

Part Three: Building the New Liabilities Model

Part Three consists of Chapters 14, 15, and 16. These chapters are the mirror image of Chapters 9 to 13 described above. They describe the design and construction of the Liabilities Model that will be the consumer of the collateral cash flows of Part Two.

In Chapter 14, "Designing the Liabilities Waterfall Model," we examine the wish list of additional capabilities we would like to see on the structuring side. These will include a multiple tranche bond structure and the concept of subordination in which some tranches of the debt absorb the effects of collateral underperformance to preserve the performance of senior notes. We also look at revisions to the reporting package to detail the performance of each of these now very different bonds.

In Chapter 15, "Writing the Liabilities Waterfall Model Spreadsheet," we structure and construct the Liabilities Waterfall spreadsheet and several menus to accommodate both inputs and outputs to the spreadsheet.

In Chapter 16, "Writing the LWM VBA Code," we write all the supporting code needed to manage both the input and output activities of the LWM. This includes finding, opening, and reading collateral cash flow files; managing the run operations of the model; and specifying and producing various structure performance reports.

At the conclusion of Part Three we will have completed the Liabilities Waterfall Model.

Part Four: Access, PowerPoint, and Outlook

Part Four consists of Chapters 17, 18, and 19. These chapters announce the introduction of the Access Database product into the modeling process.

Chapter 17, "Access: An Introduction," provides a concise but firm grounding in the basics of the product, its forms and commands, and a foreshadowing of the specific areas of the model we apply it to.

Chapter 18, "Implementing Access in the CCFG and LWM," illustrates the areas where we employ database technology to improve both the CCFG and the LWM. A partial list includes the management of collateral data, the collection and reporting of collateral selection results, and the capture and storage of amortized collateral cash flows. We also apply Access to the task of supplying the collateral cash generated by the CCFG to the LWM and to record the performance of the liabilities of the deal under various scenarios.

Chapter 19, "Implementing PowerPoint and Outlook in the CCFG," addresses the use of Excel and VBA in combination with PowerPoint to produce presentation appearance reports directly from a model run. It also introduces the use of MS Outlook to improve the communications of the model with the outside world.

Part Five: Running the CCFG and the LWM

Part Five consists of Chapter 20.

Chapter 20, "Running the Models," presents a step-by-step model run employing both the CCFG and the LWM. This model run starts with a collateral cash flow file, a set of collateral selection constraints, and various collateral performance assumptions. From these the CCFG generates a series of cash flow files. These files, in conjunction with a file containing inputs describing the Liabilities Structure, are used to run the LWM.

Indices

This book also contains an Exhibits Index and a Subject Index. The former is an index of all exhibits in the book by their financial, functional, and computational contents. We hope this index will quickly and painlessly provide the reader with a reference to any exhibit seen in the journey through the book. Under the auspice of "A single picture is worth 1,000 words," this index will serve as a fast reference to that one picture that you need to see!

A FISH STORY

These are very difficult times for the global financial markets. The need for trained people to model, measure, and manage financial risk has never been greater. The needs of governments to understand and quantify existing risk in the holdings of their financial communities, whether they are investors, issuers, or sellers of assets, has never been greater. The need for competent modelers has never been greater. The skills that you will learn in this book will be applicable to all forms of financial products and activities. Keeping the above in mind, I wish to reemphasize that while this book uses a structured finance example, it is not a book primarily concerned with structured finance theory or practice. It is a book designed to show you how to apply the skills and techniques you will learn here to any large data and computationally intense problem. The goal of the book is to provide you with a broad-based design and implementation skills, not to teach you how to finance the receivables from a revolving credit card portfolio.

My grandfather was an avid freshwater fisherman. He had a sign on the garage wall of our summer cottage in Illinois that read "God does not subtract from a man's allotted time the number of hours that he spends fishing."

One day when I was quite young, he was in the process of cleaning his equipment in preparation of renewing the struggle with the fish for the upcoming summer season. It was the first time that I had seen the full panoply of hooks, lines, bobbers, sinkers, and the complete battery of artificial lures. All was now fully revealed! Among the lures was one fully 9 inches long that mounted five sets of razor-sharp hooks. It was his "muskie" (muskellunge) lure. The muskellunge is the largest and most ferocious member of the pike family. Looking in awe at the size of this lure, I asked why it was so much bigger than anything else he had in the box.

My grandfather said simply, "If you want to catch big fish, you need big bait."

It is the same with modeling. The ideas, the techniques, and above all the combination of the five products—Excel, VBA, Access, PowerPoint, and Outlook—will allow you to confront the most forbidding of modeling assignments. I am here to give you the "big bait" and the right tackle. The combination of programming techniques and software products will allow you to take on the large, complex, and time-critical problems that you will face in the marketplace today.

A PERSPECTIVE ON MODELING

Each one of us is an individual, and we all experience the world through the lens of our own personal viewpoints and desires. The ancient adage from Aesop's Fables, "One man's meat is another man's poison," is a universal truth.

Having said that, one of the first things that I would like to convey to you is the tremendous intellectual pleasure and challenge that I have experienced over the last 30 years of my time spent in this pursuit. Modeling can be stimulating in a number of different ways and is one of the few activities that are both creative and analytical at the same time. As we humans over time have employed ever more complex methodologies to understand the world around us, modeling has grown from the simple yet elegant geometry of the Euclidian Greeks, through the calculus of Newton and Leibnitz, to Descartes and the founders of probability theory, and on to Turing and the advent of electronic computing. The current combination of easily learned software products and high-capacity hardware allow us to combine both sophisticated computational and logical structures and apply them to large amounts of data. This capability has exponentially expanded the scope of problems that we can now model.

In the 1970s we lived in a world where most of the structured finance analysis we perform today would have been impossible. Data entry was slow and tedious; the amount of available memory to hold information and results was limited. Processing speeds of the machines themselves were snail-like compared with even the most bargain basement laptop available today. We are now able to command far more power and carry it around with us wherever we go!

One of the fascinating things about modeling is that once you learn how to do it, and do it in an organized and rigorous manner, the numbers of problems you can investigate are almost unlimited. I have personally modeled over 70 different types of cash flow–producing asset types and have managed people who have added 50 to 60 types to that list.

APPROACHING THIS MATERIAL

The teaching approach I employ is based on achieving the goals of the above scenario. This is especially true when it comes to use of the existing model as the base for development. It is extremely rare that a modeling exercise is begun without any reference to the existing software resident in either the firm as a whole or your own department. All models share a large degree of functional commonality. Data moves into the model in a variety of formats from the environment. The model goes through a computational assessment process and the results of the process are produced.

It is by far the most likely circumstance that the base of a new development effort will be the corpus of an existing model. This is not as straightforward a procedure as it might seem. Modeling is a skill that needs to be developed along with the other skills you will learn here. To this end, the new model development we embark on here starts by using as much as is possible from the existing model. General George Patton once said, "I never pay for the taking the same ground twice!" and neither should you. Use your earlier development efforts to accelerate the progress of the model.

Learning to create new and different applications, or creating new features and capabilities within the context of existing models, is an exercise that will prove valuable. The responsibility for undertaking an incremental or substantial enhancement to a new or existing models is a circumstance that you will find yourself in over and over again. By the way, in case you think that statement is made in a pejorative context, it is not! As you accumulate a larger and larger body of code, you will integrate more techniques and products into your work. You will find that reuse of this code will allow you to become more and more productive with each successive assignment. If the code is well designed, you can reuse greater and greater portions of it, saving yourself quite a lot of work!

I hope that this approach will prove to be both clear and productive. You will notice that I did not say easy. If you find it easy, well, all the better! Remember that you will get out of this book what you put into it. There is a lot of material, both in the form of code and explanatory material on the Web site. Although there are many ways to utilize this material, the effort can be summarized in three simple levels:

1. Low. Do nothing.
2. Medium. Download the code and run it.
3. High. Make an effort to replicate the design and application efforts in each chapter. Think hard about the best way to do things, study the examples closely, and run the code to replicate and understand all the results.

If you download each of the code samples from the Web site and simply run them, you will get far less out of the material than if you try to replicate the work first on your own and then compare your results. Try to understand not just the line-by-line content of the examples; also read the chapters with the specific intention of understanding the design and implementation concepts behind the selection of these products and techniques. Read, think, and then code.

STYLE

One of the biggest challenges when two authors contribute to a single work is insuring the book has a cohesive voice. I, Bill Preinitz, took on the role of being the primary writer of this book. I am also solely responsible for the small interjections in the material that you will see from time to time, such the "A Fish Story" above. Please feel free to blame me exclusively for any of the humor or personal observations, such as all the material in Chapter 3, that does not meet with your approval! I would like to thank Matt for his critical assistance in several key areas of the work. He designed and built the Liabilities Waterfall spreadsheet in Chapter 15, which is the foundation of the Liabilities Waterfall Model. He also designed and built the Access code in Chapters 17 and 18. His early drafts of these chapters shaped their contents and exhibits. He is also responsible for the Outlook application in Chapter 19. In addition, Matt provided a current market perspective as an industry practitioner.

A PARTING REMARK

It is never easy to look at someone else's code. It is, however, more often the case that that is the situation in which you will find yourself. If you have some initial difficulty, try to treat it as an exercise in decryption, a decipherment of a lost language, or any other framework to lend interest and novelty to the exercise.

I will close with this thought. It is verbatim from my earlier work:

"Modeling can be real fun. It can instill in you a sense of accomplishment and self-worth. There is nothing so satisfying as a job well done, especially if none of your peers can accomplish as much! I have had a lot of fun modeling over the years and I would like you to share in the experience."

To the extent that I can help you down the path, avoiding the potholes and the speed bumps (and sometimes the other crazy drivers), I will consider the time I spent on this book quite worthwhile!

Just remember one thing. No model, no matter how sophisticated, efficient, and informative, can ever replace human judgment and insight. All models have limitations. These limitations are inherent in the quality and completeness of their assumptions, data, and analytical perspective. Do not produce results merely to see numbers on a piece of paper or graphs on a presentation slide. You must, first and foremost, seek to understand all aspects of the business situation you are to analyze. Be cognizant of both its quantitative and the qualitative aspects. It is also imperative that you, as an analyst, recognize that any model is merely a tool and not a means unto itself. It is your intelligence and creativity that, in conjunction with the judicious use of the model, produces the final intellectual product you offer.

WILLIAM PREINITZ
December 2010

On the Web Site

OVERVIEW

With this book you get access to a Web site (www.wiley.com/go/vba02).

The Web site for this book contains supplemental material that corresponds to the contents of the chapters. Each chapter section will describe the files on the Web site and their relationship to the chapter material.

Form of the Material

The material in support of a book chapter on the Web site can take the form of any or all of the following content:

- Models and auxiliary programs (either partially or fully developed).
- Input files needed by the model. These files could contain such items as the assumptions needed to run the model, data files containing raw or processed information, or files saved from previous runs that will allow you use the models more efficiently.
- Any report files produced by the model. These files are especially useful if you are replicating the model runs with the downloaded software and wish to check your results against those in the book.
- Economic performance information relating to the collateral of the deal. The assets used by the models of this book are residential mortgages. In this case, such information will be various prepayment and default estimates.
- Access databases created to support the modeling efforts.
- Web chapter comments files that explain the material of the particular chapter. These comments files guide the reader in utilizing the Web site material. This is especially true of chapters that contain developed models and/or other programs and their supporting files. The comments files tells you where you are in the development process and how to correctly deploy and organize the models to be able to run them on your own.
- Independent Web chapters that cover background or auxiliary subject matter. An example of this is a Web chapter on the securitization process or one on bond or mortgage math. These chapters contain information whose inclusion in the book is precluded by size and page count constraints.

Web Chapter Comment Files

Of all of these, the comments files are the most important. It is imperative that you read and understand the contents of the comments file of each chapter before you attempt to download material from the site. These files, entitled "Chapter‑NN‑Comments.doc", are divided into four sections:

1. **"Where We Are in the Process"** places the contents of the Web material in the overall context of the book.
2. **"New Material for This Chapter"** describes the specific activities and developments of the chapter.
3. **"File Names and Their Functions"** lists each of the files for that chapter, its name, type, and role.
4. **"What You Should Do"** contains specific instructions on how to make the files available for use. It will precisely guide you on how to establish the directory system needed to support the models and on the correct placement of the files within the directories.

Following the instructions contained in the comments files, you will be able to download, unzip, and correctly place each of the files pertinent to the chapter. At that point you can run the models and auxiliary programs and they will perform just as they do in the book. The Web site will also contain errata files for each of the chapters as necessary. Take note: This Web site is dynamic, and additional material will be added to it as time or circumstances dictate.

Web Site Contents by Chapter

What follows is a general discussion of the contents of the Web site as it will exists at the time of the publication of the book. I have individually listed those items on the Web site that are immediately recognizable. As you have not yet read the book in its entirety, my listing each and every file in full detail is a waste of your time and energy. Instead I will give an overview of the material, with the exception of general background material that would be understood by almost all the readers.

Just a note on the Web site comments files addressed above. Each chapter that has Web site material associated with it will have a comments file. The file name of the comments file will be in the following format: "ChapterXX‑Comments". Thus the comments file for Chapter 2 will be "Chapter02‑Comments" and the one for Chapter 19 will be "Chapter19‑Comments".

Not all chapters have Web site material associated with them. There tends to be more material with chapters associated with software development and the chapters where we run the models and produce sets of report files. Just remember that there is complete and very detailed discussion of the Web site material in the comment files and in the "On the Web Site" section that concludes each chapter that has material associated with it.

Preface   There is no material on the Web site for this chapter.

Chapter 1: Introduction   There is no material on the Web site for this chapter.

Chapter 2: The Existing Model   There are five Web chapters that cover the following topics:

- **"Web_Chapter02_1"**. This Web chapter, "Securitizing a Loan Portfolio," contains a description of the steps in the securitization process. It also discusses who is involved in the process and what role each of the parties plays in the transaction.
- **"Web_Chapter02_2"**. This Web chapter, "Understanding the Structuring Model Excel Waterfall," contains a detailed description of the Liabilities Waterfall Spreadsheet.
- **"Web_Chapter02_3"**. This Web chapter, "Mortgage Math," contains a discussion of the basic financial mathematics of amortizing mortgages.
- **"Web_Chapter02_4"**. This chapter, "Bond Math," contains a discussion of the basic financial mathematics of the concepts of present and future value and how they relate to the valuation of fixed income liabilities.
- **"Web_Chapter02_5"**. This chapter, Running the Model", walks the reader through a step-by-step conceptual process of a typical model run of the Base Model.

  This Web chapter also contains the basic structuring model that we will use as the basis for almost all future software development in the book. The Base Model is the one that we will later divide into two parts. These parts will separate the asset side of the deal (sources of funds) from the liabilities side of the deal (the uses of funds).

In addition to this base model there are:

- Four collateral files, containing the initial collateral, and the final eligible collateral used to structure the deal.
- Four sets of reports that delineate the results of each stage of the collateral selection process.
- Four base cash result cash flow and liabilities performance files.
- Seven report template files for the various reports of the model.

Chapter 3: Conventions and Advice   This is a chapter of general good advice on model development, VBA coding conventions, and how to be a professional. There is no material on the Web site for this chapter.

Chapter 4: Segregation of the Existing Model's Functionality   In this chapter we discuss the advantages and justifications for bifurcating the base model. There is no material on the Web site for this chapter.

Chapter 5: Creating the Base Asset Model   In this chapter we begin the process of bifurcating the Base Model into the two pieces, assets (sources of funds) and liabilities (uses of funds). We will begin with the asset side of the model. In the chapter there is a 12-step editing process that creates an asset-specific model. The Web site material for this chapter contains a set of 12 model files that mirror each of these step-by-step actions from the beginning to the end of the process. There are also:

- Two data files so that you can test the completed model.
- Seven report template files that now reflect only asset information. These files are modified versions of the report files found in Chapter 2.

Chapter 6: Building the Base Liabilities Model   Chapter 6 mirrors the activities of Chapter 5. We now repeat the process, with the goal of producing a liabilities- (uses of funds) only model. There are 12 individual files that contain the step-by-step modifications to the Base Model that results in the creation of the Base Liabilities Model (BLM). These 12 files are contained in a set of three zip files.

There is also a collection of three LWM output report template files you can use to run the model and produce the results displayed in the chapter.

There are three sets of output reports, each in its own zip file. These reports are from the Base Model the newly created assets-only model, and the newly created liabilities model. These reports are provided as an example of the verification process that you would undertake to confirm that the work performed in Chapters 5 and 6 was both accurate and complete.

Chapter 7: Establishing the Model Environment   In this chapter we set up the directory structure to house the new models. There is no material on the Web site for this chapter.

Chapter 8: Designing the New Collateral Cash Flow Generator   In this chapter we design the major improvements we need to add to the CCFG. There is a file containing the framework for one of the major menus in the file "Chapter08_MenuGeographic". The template file for the collateral data information "Chapter08_CollateralDataFile" is also presented.

Chapter 9: Writing the CCFG Menus and Data Sheets   In Chapter 8 we completed the design of the new and improved asset model. We will call this model the Collateral Cash Flow Generator model or CCFG for short. In this chapter, starting with the asset-specific model created in Chapter 5, we will begin the coding development of the model. From this chapter until Chapter 13, we will incrementally add large blocks of function-specific code to the model. In this chapter you will find the following material on the Web site:

- The finished chapter version of the CCFG containing new menus and data sheets. Data sheets are worksheets in the model that contain information used by the model for various purposes and that allow the developer more flexibility in creating the interface. For each chapter from 9 to 13, the finished model files will be identified as "CCFG_ChapterXX". The CCFG model file for this chapter is therefore "CCFG_Chapter09".
- There is also a Excel file that serves as a stand-alone example containing a simple UserForm that acts as a menu.

Chapter 10: Writing the Collateral Data Handling Code   In Chapter 10 we signifi- cantly enhance the ability of the CCFG to read and process the collateral information of the mortgage portfolio that will constitute the assets of the deal. In this Web chap- ter you will find:

- The completed version of the CCFG, "CCFG_Chapter10".
- A collateral data file containing 5,000 mortgage loans, each with 50 data fields. This represents slightly less than a 100% increase in information the CCFG will process as opposed to its predecessor the Base Asset Model,

■ Three report template files for reports in the initial data screening processes. These processes assess how complete and accurate each of the collateral records is and the scope of analysis that can be performed on each one.

■ A stand-alone program named the Representative Line Generator. This program will produce aggregated collateral records of similar collateral types. Please see the chapter for a full discussion of this process.

Chapter 11: Writing the Collateral Selection Code   In Chapter 11we significantly expand the abilities of the CCFG to perform various selection activities on the collateral of the deal. The Web chapter contains:

■ The completed version of the CCFG, "CCFG_Chapter11".

■ Two data files that the analyst can produce to specify the contents of a multiple report stratification package and the geographic regions that reports are to be produced for.

■ Two report templates that are used by reports that save financial and geographic selection criteria. This ability to save the prior specifications relieves the analyst of the burden of reentering long and involved selection criteria sets.

■ Five report template files for output reports. These reports are the collateral stratification report, a pair of geographic selection reports, and a pair of reports listing the eligible collateral and ineligible collateral on a loan-by-loan basis.

Chapter 12: Writing the Collateral Cash Flow Amortization Code   In Chapter 12 we expand the ability of the CCFG to amortize additional mortgage types. These are hybrid adjustable rate mortgages and fixed and adjustable rate balloon mortgages. The Web chapter contains:

■ The completed version of the CCFG, "CCFG_Chapter12".

■ A set of four files that contain input and various amortization assumptions for the Demographic Methodology and the Geographic Methodology of prepayment and default analysis. These methodologies are explained in the chapter.

■ Two output report template files. The first contains detailed cash flows that will form the basis of the sources of funds inputs to the liabilities model. The second is a statistical and graphic summary of the cash flows performance of the collateral

Chapter 13: Writing the CCFG Reporting Capability   In Chapter 13 we complete the development of the CCFG by expanding its reporting capabilities. In this chapter you will find:

■ The completed version of the CCFG, "CCFG_Chapter13".

■ Six output report template files. These files are for stratification reports, cross tabulation reports, geographic reports are the state and local levels, a report containing the assumptions of the model run, and a "presentation" report that summarizes the collateral performance and characteristics using graphic displays.

■ Two zip files containing state flags and maps used by the PowerPoint presentation report mentioned above.

- Two templates used to specify the composition of the stratification or cross tabulation report packages. These files allow the analyst to create standardized report groups for any number of purposes.

Chapter 14: Designing the Liabilities Waterfall Model In this chapter we design the new liabilities-only model. There is no material on the Web site for this chapter.

Chapter 15: Writing the Liabilities Waterfall Model Spreadsheet In this chapter we develop the liabilities waterfall Excel spreadsheet. The name for this model is the Liabilities Waterfall Model (LWM). In this chapter we write the complete liabilities (uses of funds) waterfall. You will find:

- The Excel spreadsheet version, "LWM_Chapter15".

Chapter 16: Writing the WLM VBA Code In this chapter we add the VBA infrastructure to the LWM. This allows the LWM to read cash flow files produced by the CCFG and to run multiple cases (with multiple scenarios in each case). We will also build all the UserForm menus of the LWM and their supporting code. The Web chapter contains:

- The completed LWM, "LWM_Chapter16".
- Thirteen output report template files that display the various performance aspects of the liabilities structure, including reporting of single tranches and comparative performance reports across multiple tranches.
- One input template file that will hold all the structuring assumptions needed for a single run of the LWM.

Chapter 17: Access: An Introduction In this chapter we introduce the reader to the use of the Access database product. We examine how Access can be used to more efficiently and effectively organize and move large amounts of data around for our models.

The Web chapter contains a series of files that teach those new to Access how to build tables, move information to and from databases, and import needed information into the models.

Chapter 18: Implementing Access in the CCFG and the LWM In this chapter we apply the Access lessons learned in Chapter 17. We implement a number of features to both the CCFG and the LWM using Access. This Web chapter contains:

- A version of the CCFG with Access "CCFG_Access".
- A version of the LWM with Access "LWM_Access".
- A database containing all output reports from the LWM developed in Chapter 16.
- One portfolio-size collateral data file.
- Five sub-portfolio-size data files. These are smaller files that can be incrementally added to the Asset Pool of the model to address various size or asset concentration issues.

Chapter 19: Implementing PowerPoint and Outlook in the CCFG   In Chapter 19 we turn to the integration of PowerPoint and Outlook into the model. We will confine our attentions to the last version of the CCFG prior to the addition of the Access code. We will modify the model to do the following:

■ Produce a ready-to-present multiple-page PowerPoint presentation automatically from menu inputs of the CCFG. This report will examine various demographic, financial, and geographic characteristics of the Collateral Pool.
■ Build into the CCFG the ability to use Outlook to automate the distribution of report packages to various audiences.

The Web chapter contains the following files:

■ The completed version of the CCFG, "CCFG_Chapter19".
■ Two PowerPoint output report template files.
■ 7 CCFG-completed Excel report files used in the production of the PowerPoint report.
■ Four completed PowerPoint presentation report examples. One is a complete report, and the others are examples of diagnostic reports.

Chapter 20: Running the Models   After all the hard work of Chapters 1 to 19, we finally see the models in action. In this chapter we will start with an unfiltered data collateral file, run the collateral through all aspects of the CCFG, produce a series of base and stressed cash flows, load a liability structure and the collateral cash flows into the LWM, produce the base case LWM results, produce the stress case LWM results, and arrive at a finished deal. In the Web chapter you will find:

■ Four Collateral Pool files that represent the eligible collateral at each stage of the collateral selection process performed by the CCFG.
■ Two sets of amortization assumptions for the Demographic Prepayment/Default Methodology, a base case and a stress case.
■ Two sets of amortization assumptions for the Geographic Prepayment/Default Methodology, a base case and a stress case.
■ One geographic concentration assumptions file and one geographic concentration limits file.
■ The final collateral selection file that has passed all financial, geographic, and demographic tests.
■ Two report package specification files, one for the base stratification reports and the other for a set of state level geographic files.
■ A set of six groups of CCFG output files for each of the collateral selection phases. See "On the Web Site" in Chapter 20 for more complete information.
■ The structural inputs file for the LWM.
■ Four sets of report output files, each consisting of 13 LWM performance files (52 total). These files represent the output report packages of the Base and Stress Demographic Methodology files and the Base and Stress Geographic Methodology files.

In Conclusion

As you can see, there is quite a bit of material here to guide you and to augment the material in the book! As indicated in the Preface, you will learn quite a bit more, and retain more of what you learn, if you go through the process of trying to replicate the analysis presented in the chapters.

I hope you find this material helpful.

The password for the Web site is: "preinitz02".

Acknowledgments

We would like to acknowledge Nancy Wilt, who read the entire manuscript and offered many helpful insights that improved the clarity and content of the book. Our thanks to Kevin Ays at Markit for conversations early in the process.

At Wiley, we would like to thank our editor, Sheck Cho, for his patience throughout the entire process. Also, we would like to commend the efforts of Joe Ruddick, the technical proofreader, and the cheerful enthusiasm of the production team of Natasha Andrews-Noel and Leigh Camp.

First Steps

Chapter 1: Introduction

This chapter introduces the reader to the organization of the book and a broad survey of the types of subjects that we will cover. The book is designed to present the reader with a problem in large model development. We define the target audience and state the purpose of the book. This purpose is threefold:

1. Improve your software skills in Excel, Visual Basic for Applications (VBA), Access, PowerPoint, and Outlook.
2. Expand your model design skills by addressing the issues in the planning and execution of large models.
3. Expand your finance knowledge by presenting other asset types and a multiple class liabilities structure.

We will close by discussing how the chapters are structured and the general content and function of each of the major chapter sections.

Chapter 2: The Existing Model

This chapter reviews the existing Structuring Model from which we will launch our later development efforts.

Chapter 3: Conventions and Advice

This chapter is divided into two sections. The first deals with a series of practices that we encourage you to adhere to as you develop the VBA code, build Access data bases, and employ Outlook and PowerPoint in the new models.

The second section of the chapter consists of a few pieces of commonsense advice that many people have found useful and that we hope will save you time and trouble in the future.

Chapter 4: Segregation of the Existing Model's Functionality

In this chapter we examine the advantages of splitting the existing model into two different models. The first of these models will focus exclusively on the activities of modeling the assets of the model. These activities relate to the:

- Screening and selection of collateral.
- Generation of collateral cash flows under various default and prepayment assumptions.

The second of the models will deal exclusively with the application of the output of the asset model (the collateral cash flows) to the liabilities structure. The liabilities structure receives these cash flows as inputs and then applies them to the payment rules of the deal to retire the notes of the structure.

Chapter 5: Building the Base Asset Model

In this chapter we will start with the original model of Chapter 2 and proceed to remove all Excel/VBA related to the liabilities functions. When we are complete we will have produced a model exclusively focused on processing the asset side of the deal.

Chapter 6: Building the Base Liabilities Model

In this chapter we will perform the reverse of the processes we engaged in Chapter 5. Here we will remove all of the asset-focused functionality of the model, leaving us with a liabilities-only model.

Chapter 7: Establishing the New Model Environment

Before we begin to develop the two successor models to those that we created in Chapters 5 and 6, we will lay out the new modeling environment within which this development will take place. This chapter contains a schema for a set of new directories into which we will place the various models, data files, assumption files, databases, report template files, and model inputs and outputs that will become the different parts of the model environment.

A Note to Readers

The activities in Chapters 5 and 6 are designed to serve these purposes:

- Familiarize the reader with working on a model of intermediate size that they did not write themselves. In doing so this process requires them to read the model, understand its basic structure, and add or remove code to achieve the desired ending configuration.

- Acquaint the reader with the types of subroutines and functions that perform the core functionalities of menu management, error checking, data management, collateral selection, and cash flow generation and reporting.
- Introduce the reader to the systemic organization of a large model by applying a specific approach to creating and naming VBA modules to hold the various model elements.

Everyone will, at some point in their career, have to undertake a task similar to the activity covered in this chapter. We hope you will not need to do this more than once or twice. This is because while instructive the first time you have to perform these tasks, you will learn almost everything you need to know by doing this once and only once.

Future repetition of these activities carries a dramatically diminishing incremental value.

Therefore, if in your experience you have already walked the walk, you need not do it again here. Jump from Chapter 4 to Chapter 7 with my blessing. For those of you that have not had experience with this process, studying Chapters 5 and 6 will make it significantly quicker and less painful when you are called on to do so.

## CHAPTER 1

Introduction

OVERVIEW

The purpose of this chapter is to give you a view from 100,000 feet in the air as to the goals of the book, how I will present the material, the general organization of that material, and, along the way, a helping of model-building philosophy.

I will also give you a punch list as to what skills we expect you to have. If you do not have these skills, you may need to reconsider buying this book as it will not address a number of fundamental VBA or VBE skills, and that might end up making the work more frustrating than fun. "Fun" seems to be a neglected word when it comes to technical books. It seems that everyone has to be very matter of fact, declamatory, and serious. I think this is overdoing it. I really do not know anyone who is a competent model builder who does not think that a good portion of the intellectual and computational challenges of building sophisticated models is not fun. There may be elements of frustration (see the story at the end of this chapter about a FORTRAN compiler). There may be boredom, or pressure (some of it extreme), but in the end the feelings of accomplishment and validation are worth the effort. In total, the experience is a positive one, and I certainly think fun too.

In this vein, the voice of this book will be a conversational one. We would like you to think of it as an extended chat along the lines of Franklin Delano Roosevelt's series of radio broadcasts that become known as the "Fireside Chats." An even better analogy is sitting with a somewhat more experienced coworker on a joint project. The mentor genuinely wants to share his experiences. He hopes that you can avoid the traps and travails he himself had encountered working his way from novice to journeyman and finally to mastery of these specific skills.

WHY WAS THIS BOOK WRITTEN?

This book is written to address a need for an intermediate-level guide to model building in the primary context of the Excel/VBA environment but with incremental inclusions of other Microsoft products to enhance productivity and performance. There are any numbers of books that deal with Excel spreadsheet development. There are also many that teach the elements of and how to program in the VBA language. The same can be said for Access, PowerPoint, and Outlook. There are also books that will show you how to develop single-purpose financial applications in these languages.

Where there is a dearth of information is how to build models that combine the collective functionality of a number of Microsoft products. Each of these products is employed to optimize its particular strengths in the finished model and to bring the synergy of this combination to bear on the problems the model is intended to address. Most programming or model examples covered in other books are very narrow, single-purpose programs of limited sophistication and scope. They almost always are presented as a start-from-scratch effort. This is a low-probability scenario for a new analyst or associate joining a department with a developed software infrastructure. A person in that situation will need to assess what has already been developed and will face time, cost, and perhaps even personal pressures to make do with what is already in place.

This book seeks to set out a representative real-world development challenge that calls for the analyst to have or acquire an intermediate-level mastery of both model design and development and of software that can adequately address a more robust set of requirements.

Addresses a Need for Large Program Programming

The key element in the aforementioned approach is the use of a large application. Many books shy away from this particular class of problem. Some of this avoidance is legitimate. The book in question may wish to cover a variety of other subjects, or the authors or publishers may feel that a large application consumes too much space and that its value is too limited. Other authors approach the subject but limit themselves to the use of Excel spreadsheets with minimal or no use of the other available software products. Several others deal with large program development but do so in a fragmentary manner. In these works only portions of the corpus of the application code is available. The code presented tends to be either mostly unavailable to the reader or unavailable in a sufficiently critical mass to provide a firm understanding of the practical challenges and full scope of such a development effort.

An earlier book[1] by Preinitz, addressed this issue by developing a rudimentary moderate-size model that was used to securitize a portfolio of small business loans. This model was developed, using VBA, from the starting base of an Excel spreadsheet application.

The finished model application was comprised of several parts. The first was an Excel file, composed of a single spreadsheet. The contents of the spreadsheet represented all the information regarding a portfolio of small business loans that we would need to conduct a cash flow analysis. This Excel file contained the financial and demographic information on approximately 2,000 individual loans. A model was developed to transfer the information from this collateral portfolio file, determine through a user-described selection process the collateral that was usable in the deal, purge the ineligible collateral, and then amortize the eligible collateral under a variety of economic conditions. The model then applied the resultant cash flows to a liability structure. The results of the collateral selection process, the cash flow generation processes, and the liabilities waterfall performance were all captured and displayed in a series of reports. These reports were produced using preconfigured Excel spreadsheets that served as template report files. The model execution options, file selection, and reporting options were specified and controlled by user entries to a series of menus.

This model, which will become that starting point for the case study exercise in this book, is reviewed in Chapter 2, "The Existing Model."

A Real-World Problem

The issue most beginning developers face is that, like it or not, they usually end up working with someone else's code. This is especially true of those areas that use proprietary applications. These applications are more likely than not the backbones of the analytical framework of the business units that have developed them.

In this environment the situation most commonly faced by the modeler is to produce a series of modifications to the existing model. The first assignment may be something small: adding additional fields to a report, changing the format of an existing report, adding a relatively straightforward calculation to an easily identifiable place in the program. Just as often, however, these changes are not simple. This is especially true when the prior person jealously guarded the code as a form of job security. Depending on the timing and reasons for the person's departure, the severity of the resultant crisis may range from a merely annoying level all the way up to a drop-dead, heart-attack level. Now the lucky man or woman has to read and understand the application immediately, under economic and time pressures. Having the experience of picking up a moderately large application, reading it, understanding it, and then significantly modifying it is under these circumstances a critical job skill.

Thus you can see that aside from whatever other information or skills you acquire from this work, being prepared for such an eventuality can be a real career lifesaver. Not only can it save you immense amount of pain and suffering, but it can be the springboard to better things. There is nothing so valuable as to be viewed as the solution to a crisis, and the more severe and hopeless the crisis initially appears, the better.

Steps in Model Evolution

The subject of Darwinian evolution is still held in contention by a regrettably significant number of people. One form of evolution that cannot be disputed, however, is the evolutionary pathway of models. Not all models pass through the stages detailed below. Many models never evolve past simple self-contained Excel spreadsheets (nor do they need to). Some rise to a higher level of sophistication and become stable. Some models relentlessly evolve, becoming ever more intricate, complex, or massive, or, in rare cases, all three.

You are a person who will, it is highly probable (possibly sooner rather than later), be called upon to work on the dreaded someone else's model (SEM). This SEM should be approached prudently. One of the first things you should be able to assess is where it is on the evolutionary scale of model development. Still floating aimlessly in the sea, has it just developed into a multi-cellular structure? Has it just crawled onto the land? Is it, even now, sitting in the cockpit of an F-22 jet fighter, zooming down on you with all guns blazing? It is good to have the answer.

Evolutionary Hierarchy   Although we can always argue how many angels can dance on the head of a pin, in a nutshell, there are roughly nine stages of model evolution:

> **Level 1.** A single-purpose Excel spreadsheet application, an equivalent of an electronic scratchpad.
>
> **Level 2.** An Excel spreadsheet with recorded macros that address repetitive or onerous tasks. The macros serve as labor-saving devices and perform tasks such as data importation or report formatting.
>
> **Level 3.** An Excel spreadsheet with VBA subroutines and functions. The blocks of VBA code may or may not be organized into task-specific VBA modules. They are, however, purpose designed and are significantly more complex and powerful than recorded code. All output is contained within the model.
>
> **Level 4.** An Excel/VBA model that uses menus and external files to input data and template files to output the results. The main computational and analytical burden of the model is now preponderantly seated in the VBA code. The VBA code is interpreted, not compiled.
>
> **Level 5.** A Level 4 model with Access to address more onerous data management issues. The model may or may not make use of online data sources, such as Bloomberg, or private client Web sites to import data into the model.
>
> **Level 6.** A Level 4 or 5 model with a more sophisticated and/or intensive user interface. This usually occurs when the model has reached a stable state of development, usually correlated to the maturation or decline of its product line.
>
> **Level 7.** A Level 4, 5, or 6 model with compiled VBA code in separate libraries linked to the model. This VBA-compiled code addresses those functionalities of the model earmarked by timing software that measure the highest-use portions of the program. Object-oriented programming may now be introduced or may have already appeared as early as Level 4.
>
> **Level 8.** A Level 7 model with a preponderance of compiled code replaces almost all of the VBA modules. This compiled code is most often C++, Java, or many other general-purpose programming languages based on the particular suitability of the product and the expertise or organizational platforms already in place.
>
> **Level 9.** The final extension of a Level 8 model, which uses compiled code only. The role of Excel is restricted to the user interface, and VBA has been completely eliminated from the model.

Generally the trend is that the higher the evolutionary level, the greater the support requirements of the model. A good rule of thumb is a factor of 2 for each level over Level 4. This is because as the models grow in size and sophistication, they may require extensive hardware support as well as increasingly burdensome software management. In addition, models with lives of five years or more are usually deemed mission critical to the business unit and are therefore subject to such activities as periodic audits, release control procedures, third-party validation, and valuation methodology reviews.

Where We Are Now   The model that we will inherit and be asked to improve is a solid Level 4 model. We will review its characteristics in Chapter 2. (The model and its supporting files will be available on the Web site.)

Where We Will Be at the End of the Book   When the smoke clears at the end of the book, we will be as close to Level 7 as we can get without using another compiled language to augment the calculation subroutines. Before we get too far ahead of ourselves, let us examine the fundamental work to be done.

The first thing that we are going to do is break down the existing model into its two natural functionalities. The first functional portion that we will segregate from the initial model will be the code that handles the assets and generates cash flows from them. Upon completion we will call this the Base Asset Model (BAM). The second functional portion of the original model that we will segregate will focus exclusively on calculation the performance of the liabilities when the cash flow streams produced by the BAM are applied to them. We will call this the Base Liabilities Model (BLM). Once this segregation has been accomplished, we will separately develop each of these models from its current Level 4 form to a Level 6 configuration. This will be enough work to keep everyone, especially you, gentle readers, more than busy.

WHO IS THE TARGET AUDIENCE?

In order of immediacy, this book is aimed at these people:

- Those working in the financial industry, especially at the levels of vice president and below, who want or need to develop their modeling skills beyond a fundamental competency.
- Members of regulatory, governmental, or audit functions seeking to be able to investigate and understand intermediate-level models and modern modeling techniques.
- Intermediate-level managers who supervise these people but have little or no knowledge of, or experience with, modeling. They want to know what is possible, how difficult the task is, and how to go about accomplishing it.
- Anyone wishing to develop intermediate-level modeling skills using a combination of Microsoft application software.
- Students in graduate or undergraduate programs wishing to enter the financial community in the near future and interested in trading or banking positions requiring analytical skills.
- Anyone who wants to have the ability to intensively explore problems that require a quick, fluid medium of analysis. This includes anyone in the financial world dealing in risk and especially those who seek to measure it and evaluate risk through modeling.
- Anyone in any commercial, nonprofit, or military function who needs a tool to assist in dynamic problem solving.
- Anyone who is a regular Excel/VBA user and wants to significantly expand the power of the applications by integrating other Microsoft products in the models.

■ Anyone who thinks he or she knows and is good at Excel, VBA, Access, or PowerPoint. I am certain that you will find many useful techniques here that you may have overlooked.

WHAT IS THE PURPOSE OF THE BOOK?

The thrust of the book is to expand your skills and knowledge in three distinct but interrelated areas:

1. Your software and application skills
2. Your modeling skills
3. Your financial knowledge

EXPANDING YOUR SOFTWARE SKILLS

The expansion of your software skills will fall mainly along the lines of the five Microsoft products we will be working with:

1. **Improving your Excel,** especially as it relates to UserForms and the user interface portions of the model.
2. **Improving your VBA techniques.** This will span the subjects of supporting the UserForm menu additions, to financial amortization calculation of the collateral, to reporting techniques.
3. **Expanding your Access knowledge** by building databases to support the model by storing, retrieving, managing, and outputting data and results.
4. **Expanding your PowerPoint skills** by learning to harness the combination of Excel, VBA, and PowerPoint to improve model reporting activities.
5. **Expand your Outlook skills** by giving your model the ability to communicate with you and the rest of the world.

Excel Skills

Two of the areas that you will expand your Excel knowledge are UserForms embedded in the menus of the model and working with Excel graphs/charts for augmenting reports.

Employing UserForms in Menus You will learn how to enhance the appearance and functionality of the model by the employment of UserForms in the menus. These forms will allow us to develop a significantly more dynamic model interface. They will also allow us to use a series of lists to control and direct the operation sequence of the model. In addition, they will serve to decrease the chance of model operator errors by limiting the possible choices to valid and meaningful ones.

Improving Reports with Graphs and Charts We will make aggressive use of charts and graphics in both the presentation and working-level reports produced by the model.

VBA Skills

This book also seeks to expand your mastery of the various uses of VBA in model building.

The Real World: New Models from Old Models   As discussed above, one of the most important lessons you will learn is how to work with someone else's model. You will be presented with a model of moderate complexity and size, a Level 4 model, and will have to significantly alter it to create the desired model, a Level 6 model. You will start by learning to identify and understand the significant functionalities of the initial model. You will then split this model into two self-contained entities along these functionalities. In the process you will either retain or discard portions the existing code. You will, however, try to preserve as much of that code as possible to accelerate and streamline the production of the follow-on application.

We cannot overemphasize the importance of having experience in this type of activity at least once early in your career. You will find over and over again that it is more often the rule than the exception in model building.

Expanding the Scope and Variety of Inputs   We will significantly expand the scope of data inputs and the ability of the user to specify what selection actions the model is to perform on this information. This includes the ability to dynamically build selection and sorting criteria conditions and report formatting options. The size of the collateral portfolios will be significantly larger and more complex. The number of data per loan will increase by a factor of 2 and the number of initial loans in the portfolio by even more than that over the requirements of the base model.

Access Skills

The Access database product will be employed as a part of both the models we will build in the later chapters of this book. Access will serve to more efficiently facilitate the movement of significantly larger amounts of data than the existing first model we will encounter in Chapters 4, 5, and 6. These databases will hold loan level data for the collateral portfolio, collateral selection criteria sets, prepayment, default, market value decline, recovery lag period curves, the portfolio and sub-portfolio collateral cash flows, and the performance metrics of the liability tranches.

PowerPoint Skills

PowerPoint will be used to produce specialized reports to be used in regulatory, rating or investor presentations. We will use VBA and Excel to automatically populate and format PowerPoint template files. This will result in PowerPoint presentation reports without any other need to transcribe, copy, or import the data manually.

Outlook Skills

Outlook will be employed to improve the messaging capabilities of the program, allowing the model to communicate directly to the users of the model. This communication can take several forms, such as calculation progress, data import facilitation, or any other significant events that occur in the course of the operation of the model. It can also be used to create automated report distribution systems that can dramatically reduce the time and effort of disseminating the output of the model to critical parties.

EXPANDING YOUR MODEL DESIGN SKILLS

This book will seek to integrate all of the above items into an improved model engineering expertise. We will show you how to think of a model as more than a specific single program entity.

It Is a Modeling System, Not a Model

As the model is bifurcated into the Collateral Cash Flow Generator (CCFG) and the Liabilities Waterfall Model (LWM), we will make use of an ever-increasing number of Microsoft products to build a modeling system versus a single stand-alone model. The integration of these various products in such a model, along with its template files, databases, and associated programs, now begins to resemble a system more than an individual model. The flexibility of this approach will give you experience in thinking in a more general and fluid manner about how to combine various program and products to achieve results you desire.

Improving Reporting Flexibility   Models are worthless if you cannot effectively communicate their results in a manner that is intelligible to the intended audience. Keeping this critical fact in mind, we will look at improving your modeling knowledge by significantly overhauling both the content and the appearance of the model's report package. We will target specific report packages to specific audiences. On one end of the spectrum, we will have the basic working reports that are designed to support the day-to-day work on the deal. On the opposite end, we will have reports that are narrowly targeted to the particular requirements of a specific audience.

More Complex Report Formats   The complexity of the report packages will increase to encompass the increasing amounts of information available to the model. This information will take the form of both collateral data analysis,the composition of geographically adjusted prepayment and default assumptions,and the performance of the various components of the liability structure.

Tiered and Specialized Reporting   In addition to the increase in complexity noted above, we will tier our reports depending on the degree of detail and the level of complexity appropriate to the target audience. This specialization will be reflected in report packages designed for both internal and external target audiences.

EXPANDING YOUR FINANCE KNOWLEDGE

The financial knowledge, like the model itself, is divided between the asset side and the liability side of the deal. A broader understanding of the behaviors of collateral is key as these assets are the preponderant source of cash flows entering the deal. As you expand your knowledge of various liability structures you will improve your understanding of how structured finance attempts to segregate and identify risk.

On the Asset Side

The concepts we will cover regarding the asset side of the model fall into the four broad concepts discussed below.

Using Residential Mortgages in the Structure   Residential mortgages have been selected as the asset collateral because of their ongoing relevance in the current economic crisis. They have another advantage. The securitization of mortgages has long been an important part of the financial landscape. They are a data-rich asset class and because of this fact are excellent training tools. They will present you with a variety of risk issues, the conceptual knowledge of which is immediately transferable to practically any other asset producing a stream of payments. There is a saying, "If you can do mortgages, you have a good foundation for everything else."

Different Amortization Patterns   The plethora of mortgage products that have evolved in the last 30 years is truly astounding. We can expect to encounter any number of very interesting amortization patterns, including standard adjustable rate mortgages, hybrid adjustable rate mortgages, and both fixed and adjustable rate balloon mortgages.

Pool Level Prepayment and Default Assumptions   The current trend in prepayment and default analysis, especially given the wide range of economic conditions nationwide, is to employ geographically specific prepayment and loss curves. This analysis may also be augmented by an analysis of the particular demographic, credit, property, loan type, and servicing capacity for each individual loan in the portfolio.

Loan Level Market Value Decline and Recovery Lag Period Assumptions   Market value decline (MVD) is the amount of value loss experienced since the purchase of the property by the current owner until its liquidation sale. This is a factor that is strongly determined by local real estate market conditions and therefore modeled with geographically distinct assumptions. It is the prime determinant in the amount of recoveries generated by a liquidation sale. The recovery lag period (RLP) is the amount of time since the initial foreclosure to the receipt of the recovery amount.

On the Liability Side

Two additional concepts will be introduced when we develop the LWM. The first is the use of multiple bond classes. The second is the use of other mechanisms to preserve the creditworthiness of the liabilities structure.

Multiple Tranche Structure   We will introduce the concept of the tranche. The term "tranche" means "slice" in French. Bond tranches allow the deal structure to custom-design liabilities of differing risk characteristics, weighted average life, and duration to meet specific investor requirements.

The liabilities structure that we will model in the LWM will consist of two bond classes. The first bond class, the A class, will consist of two tranches of bonds, the A-1 and A-2 tranches. The second bond class, the B class, will consist of four bond tranches, B-1 to B-4. There are very important distinctions between these two bond classes. The class A bond classes will have seniority over the class B bond classes. This "seniority" will take the form of preferential treatment in regard to the receipt of the cash flows available from the collateral payments. If an interest rate swap is included in the liabilities structure, the class A bonds will be first in line to receive payments from that source as well. In addition to the priority of payment privilege the class A bonds enjoy, they will also enjoy an enhanced immunity to principal losses. In certain prepayment and default conditions there may be insufficient collateral cash flows to fully retire the principal balances of all tranches of the bond classes. In this case the class B tranches will absorb the losses until the point of their complete devaluation, thus protecting the class A bonds to the extent they can.

Both tranches of the class A bonds will also solely receive principal payments for a certain initial period of the deal. No principal will be retired from any of the class B bond tranches during this initial lockout period.

Additional Structural Enhancements   Additional structural enhancements will also be employed in the LWM. One of the most common is an interest rate swap (IRS). This type of derivative is used to negate to a significant (but not perfect) extent the fluctuations between fixed and floating rate interest cash flows. In the case of the model, an IRS may be purchased and included in the deal if we are faced with the task of immunizing the deal from the effects of a potential fixed/floating interest rate match. The collateral of the mortgage portfolio that supports the deal could be comprised of fixed-rate mortgages while the class A and B bonds may have floating-rate coupon payments. If the dollar weighted fixed rate collateral coupon rates always exceed the floating rate debt service payments of the bond classes, things are fine. If, however, the reverse becomes the case, over time the deal structure could find itself in dire straits. All the collateral interest cash flows would be paid out in the form of debt service on the bonds and still not be sufficient to meet the expenses. An IRS allows two parties to agree that one will pay the other a fixed rate of interest while the other pays a floating rate of interest based on a predefined principal balance schedules. This allows, for a fee, the "swapping" of a fixed-rate interest flow for a floating-rate interest flow.

In addition to an IRS, the deal will also employ overcollateralization as a credit enhancement for the bond classes.

ORGANIZED TO TEACH

A certain amount of thought has gone into the organization of this book, its chapters, and its accompanying Web site. An understanding of some of the common features in each chapter will help frame your understanding of the contents more clearly. These common features are designed to present the initial concepts to the reader, reinforce them with the body of the chapter content, and recapitulate the material in a summary section at the end of the chapter. This approach is based on an old saw about effective instruction. The steps of effective teachings are as follows:

1. Tell the students what you are going to tell them.
2. Tell them what you told them you would tell them.
3. Tell them what you have told them.

CHAPTER ORGANIZATION

Each chapter contains a number of common section headers. These sections, such as "Overview," "Deliverables," "Under Construction," and "On the Web Site," are prospective in nature. They have been included with the intention of focusing your attention on specific upcoming events.

Overview Section

This section gives a one- to two-paragraph introduction about what major subjects to expect in the chapter. It is meant to alert you to the broad concepts and, it is hoped, whet your appetite for the upcoming material. If you are looking through the book after having read it once, this section will concisely inform you if you are looking in the correct chapter for that piece of, as Poe put it so succinctly, "forgotten lore."

Deliverables Section

This section, usually in the form of a list or two, is designed to delineate the specific concepts, skills, or facts that you need to learn from the chapter. This serves as a sort of a punch list in waiting. Keep your eyes glued for these items and be ready to jump on them when they appear later in the chapter.

Under Construction Section

This section lists any changes to the model environment, the model, or any of its supporting template files or databases that we will be making in the chapter. Anytime you see items in this section, the model or its environment will be undergoing significant change. The section will list the names of the specific files or directory elements, the types of changes we will be making, what the form of these changes will be, and why we will be making them. If we are going to be adding significant amounts of VBA code or any new VBA modules to house them, they will be listed here. The section is designed to give you a view as to the incremental changes to the model or models that we will be working on in the chapter.

Chapter Material

This section contains the particular subject and its supporting concepts. We have tried to make extensive use of both diagrams and code samples. We are willing to bet that there are very few books concerning modeling and VBA that have anywhere near this amount of code exhibits or, in many cases, entire modules and subroutines.

The reasoning behind this approach is twofold. The first is that while many may argue that programming is an art, just as many will argue that it is a skill that can be learned by following specific examples. Literally, the more well-organized, well-documented, and well-implemented VBA code you see, the higher the chances are that your code will grow to look more and more like the code in the examples. It is only natural for you to adopt and employ the techniques as you see them presented (at least in the beginning), then to go off on a tangent. You will find that if you follow this book's examples, you will be able to develop better code faster. You will also have a *much* easier time when the day comes that you need to look at your code again after a substantial time away from it. There is no worse feeling in the world than picking up a piece of code that you wrote three years back and not being able to understand what you did or why you did it.

The second reason is that a gradual incremental approach is the best way to approach these subjects. Start with simple and straightforward examples and move on from there. The approach that we find infuriating is to see a nine-step process presented in a book in the following manner:

Step 1 is fully explained.

Step 2 is fully explained.

Steps 3 through 8: "These steps are left to the reader."

Step 9 is the solution.

In most of these cases I immediately ask myself why I bought the book. If I already knew how to do it on my own, I wouldn't need the book in the first place. I promise to never leave you hanging for those interim steps. That is why you will see 20, 25, 30, or more exhibits in some of the more detailed and technical of the chapters.

These issues aside, you almost always find that the first section of the chapter after the "Under Construction" section contains a brief outline of the chapter material to follow. You will know the subject material portion of the chapter has been concluded when you hit the "Deliverables Checklist" section.

On the Web Site Section

This section describes the contents of the section of the Web site that pertains to the material in this chapter. Some chapters will have nothing while others may have many, many files. This section will give you a brief description of each piece of the material and its relevance to the chapter contents. Usually a large "Under Construction" section is highly correlated to a large "On the Web Site" section.

ACCOMPANYING WEB SITE

This book comes with a Web site www.wiley.com/go/modeling. On this Web site you will find a variety of material. This material can take the form of models in progress, data files, report template files, Web site chapter files, and last but not least Web chapters.

Web Site Organization

The Web site is organized on a chapter-by-chapter basis with a section for each chapter that contains material. Placeholder notations for chapters without Web site content simply state: There is no material for this chapter.

Content

The content of the Web site falls broadly into five types of files.

1. **Blurbs.** Blurbs are sections of descriptive text that describe the Web site content for the chapter. They are meant to be a reminder of where we are in the book, what are the current concepts, and how the files or other material on the Web site directly relate to the book. There is generally a comment or explanation for each file, placing it in the chapter context.
2. **Comment files.** Comment files for each chapter provide a guide for downloading the software and any modifications to the model environment that have to be made based on the activities in the chapter. Each of these files is divided into four sections. These sections give an overview of the material, the specific file-by-file descriptions, what you need to do with the files, and any changes to the environment needed to accommodate their use. *It is imperative that you read this file before downloading any web site files containing code.* This file contains critical instructions that are placed there to make your life easier and to minimize the chance of errors in running the models.
3. **Chapter files.** These files are essentially the same as the chapters in the book. Often they are organized along the same lines, having an "Overview," "Deliverables," and other sections you will become familiar with in the chapters of the book. These chapters contain a wide range of explanatory text and examples. All in all they amount to several hundred pages of additional material that the authors thought you might need to look at. Why were these chapters not included in the book? Much of the material is subject matter that we thought you should know but could not be sure you would know. We have provided it to provide a crib if you need to check on a particular subject. Some of the material is extensions of the material in the book that was just too lengthy to include.
4. **Code files.** These files are the model, data, database, report template, or any other application files featured in the associated chapter.
5. **Errata files.** As time progresses, there is a high probability that errors will be discovered in the text of the book or in the code. In this event, I will post errata files before sitting down to a tasty meal of crow.

LEARNING THE "HARD" WAY

I believe that there are two ways to learn how to program—the smart way and the hard way. I hope I am providing you with a valuable tool to learn the smart way. A lot of thought and a lot of work has been put into the book and the Web site. They are designed to work in tandem. The more you use them in this manner, by downloading the models, data, and reports from the Web site and combining this material with the contents of the book, the smarter you will be.

Or you can do it the hard way. . .

"The FORTRAN Compiler Is Broken!"

There is one final thought we would like to leave with you before you leave the Web site section. You can approach the material on the Web site in a number of different ways. On one extreme you can ignore it entirely. On the other you can download the material and painstakingly replicate each of the exhibited code and design changes. Which approach do you think will give you the greater understanding of the principles and practices we are trying to communicate to you?

In 1977 I was enrolled in an MBA program that required all its candidates to take a course entitled "Fundamentals of Business Systems." The purpose of the course was to expose the MBA generalist to the problems faced by the computer specialist. The professor wanted the students to take one additional but voluntary step: to write and compile a simple program. The reward was a significant credit toward the final class grade that all but guaranteed passing the course. I thought I would give it a try. The language was FORTRAN, now nearly extinct in the United States. I bought a basic guide to programming in FORTRAN, studied it closely for about three days, and wrote my first program. The program consisted of 20 statements inside a simple loop. The program was intended to calculate various wage and tax amounts for a six-person employee payroll. Using a keypunch machine, I entered the statements on a set of Hollerith cards and ran them through the card reader. I expected to receive back a report with all the sums in nice neat columns, accurately calculated. What I got back from the FORTRAN compiler instead was an error listing 26 items long. Dumbfounded, I surveyed the, to me, almost unintelligible messages, immediately noting that there were more errors on the listing than I had statements in the program. Coming out of my stupor, I realized the extreme seriousness of the situation. There were hundreds if not thousands of students' work at risk, and it seemed that I was the only one aware of the scope of the impending catastrophe. I immediately made a beeline for the small office containing the three graduate Computer Science students who were on duty to help the uninitiated heathens such as myself. Not wishing to cause a panic, I shut the door before informing them of my terrifying discovery.

"The FORTRAN compiler is broken!" I said.

"Really?" they replied, staring at each other in amazement.

"Yes. Really! I just wanted to bring this to your attention before things got much worse!" I said with a note of panic seeping into my voice.

Needless to say, after their rather embarrassing hilarity subsided, they pointed out to me that what I had mistaken as evidence of a broken compiler was, in fact, an error in my program of my own making. It was in fact what is known as a cascading error. This was a type of FOTRAN syntax error that triggered the compiler to misinterpret many if not all of the succeeding program statements following the location of the error and report additional errors that were not actually present. Six sets of changes, many new Hollerith cards and four hours later I had a working program.

The moral is: The compiler isn't broken, you moron! You can read about model development all day long, but until you get down and dirty in the code yourself, you aren't going to learn a thing.

NOTE

1. William Preinitz, *A Fast-Track to Structured Finance Modeling, Monitoring, and Valuation: Jump Start VBA* (Hoboken, NJ: John Wiley & Sons, 2009).

## CHAPTER 2

The Existing Model

OVERVIEW

In this chapter we will review the structure, contents, and functionality of the current Structuring Model. We will conduct this review with the aim of using portions of this model in our effort to build the next set of models. We would be foolish not to do so! There certainly will be significant portions of the existing model that will prove unusable for the next application, but there will be surprisingly large amounts that will be immediately useful almost without modification.

As mentioned in Chapter 1, it is by far more likely that you will adopt this approach when building new models. As you gain experience, you will find that there are major commonalities between models in the way they load their data, the base cash flow amortization assumptions, and their report content. This is not to say that any two models will be virtually identical or even highly similar. Having made that statement, it is, however, obvious that the approach to the forecasting of cash flows—and their subsequent impact on the financing structure, the metrics of risk, and the need for decision makers to be able to frame the results in a comparable and cogent manner—all argue for broad similarities in both structure and appearance of models and the reports they produce. This is a process, like many other processes, that becomes more effective and efficient through experience and repetition. It is difficult the first time, less so the second, and quite a bit easier the fifth, sixth, or seventh time you have done it. By the tenth time you build a model, you will find yourself able to do most of the planning during your shower the day you are going to start the project! Better yet, you will have most if not all of the concept fully formulated by the time you have gotten your morning coffee and arrived at your desk.

We are particularly fortunate that the next model we have been asked to build needs to analyze assets that have many similarities to the assets in our existing model. It has, however, a much larger data requirement, 50 data per record versus the 26 data per record of the current model. This will require a number of significant departures in design and implementation from schema of the current model. We will need to create an initial data screening capability for illegible or illegal records. The additional data fields will require a more flexible and robust selection process. We will work with collateral portfolios that have a wider range of both fixed rate and adjustable rate mortgages. Some, such as hybrid mortgage types, are characterized by irregular payment patterns. The increase in information about each piece of collateral will allow us to employ prepayment and default methodologies not found in the existing model. Nevertheless, we may find the underlying structure of the existing model to be robust enough to support an evolutionary rather than a revolutionary approach to writing the next application.

So let us conduct a review that will firmly establish what our starting position is, always keeping in mind the following options:

- What features, structures, and code can be retained almost intact?
- What analytical features such as cash flow calculation subroutines can serve as a base for further model development?
- What features would we need to modify so extensively that our time is better spent creating something new?
- What features can we discard all together?

I will leave you with one last thought. The passage of time affects all models in a fundamentally inalterable way. The evolution and metamorphosis of existing models is a continual ongoing process that you will experience throughout your modeling career. As time passes many changes will naturally occur that will alter the requirements of even the most carefully designed and best-constructed models. New financial products and opportunities arise from the environment. New technologies become available to the modeler. Faster, more powerful computers with greater storage capabilities are marketed. New capabilities are created for existing software, and new software packages are developed. Last of all, your personal abilities will expand with experience and training. You should expect to rework your current collection of models in response to any of these stimuli and several that I may have missed. That is why the exercise that I will pursue over the next several chapters is an important one. It is one that you will find yourself performing as part of your basic responsibilities and one you should greet as an opportunity to showcase your skills. Time flies by, so we might as well have fun while it does.

DELIVERABLES

The modeling knowledge deliverables for this chapter are:

- Understanding the layout and relationship of the components of the model, the data input file, the analytical engine, and the report template files.
- Understanding the number, composition, and role of the menus of the model.
- Understanding the structure of the current model's VBA modules and their task specialization.
- Understand the existing reporting package, the nature of the reports, and their intended audiences.
- Understanding the process of reviewing an existing application with the goal of salvaging as much as possible as a framework for the next application.

UNDER CONSTRUCTION

We will not be manipulating either the Excel or the VBA of the existing model in this chapter. We will be *thinking* very hard about doing that, but today we do not have to put our coding hats on; we have the day off!

CRISIS DU JOUR

It has now been the better part of a year since we constructed the original model. We have used it to structure about half a dozen deals. While it is functional enough, we have begun to notice that there are some modifications that we should make to it. These modifications relate to the greater availability of data, some awkwardness in the collateral handling processes, and a need to overhaul many of the reports.

We are about to begin this task when we are informed of a new project that has significant economic potential. The firm has been approached with a proposal to purchase a series of residential mortgage loan portfolios.

The question is, can we utilize the functionality of the existing model to develop a new model that will meet the analytical requirements of this new opportunity?

New Project

We are asked to create a residential mortgage model that will, within the constraints of our resources, replicate much of the current risk assessment theory used in the marketplace. The challenges in the process to value a portfolio comprised of these assets will require a much more robust model. We will need to meet the following requirements:

- We will probably have to work with collateral pools that have more loans than we have seen in the past. In addition the loans may be obtained from several sources and we may need to segregate the collateral in a series of identifiable sub-portfolios as opposed to the single pool we are currently used to.
- Each loan in the pool will have almost two times as much individual descriptive data. This data will include not only additional financial data but also geographic data and demographic data related to the borrower population.
- There will be a number of different mortgage amortization patterns that the model cannot currently perform.
- The collateral selection process will have to be significantly more robust. We will need to be able to interactively build our sorting criteria using all the data fields available to us.
- To transfer the purchased risk, we will need to sell the liabilities into the marketplace. This will require the use of several different types of liabilities, each with different payment priorities and risk characteristics.
- We will need to produce a wider range of reports. Many of these reports will be considerably more complex than the existing reports and will incorporate much of the additional data that will available to us. These reports will be needed not

only by ourselves but by other constituencies, such as rating agencies, our own management, and, most important, investors.

We are also working under, as of now, a poorly determined time constraint. Right now we need to tell the management how feasible this project is and provide a rough time frame.

We think that it should be possible to employ much of the code of the existing model; how much we do not yet know. How many other features we will have to add to the new model, what its interface requirements will be, whether we will need to consider other software products in addition to the Excel/VBA platform now in use, and how extensively the report package will have to change are still to be determined.

We do have one ray of light in the fog of uncertainty. We are going to get some help. One of the most significant challenges will be the greatly increased amount of data associated with analyzing mortgages. We have been told that we can draw on the services of another individual who will help us with the project. This help will come in the form of Access database expertise that we can apply specifically to the data-expanded requirements of the model.

(By the way, if you need to brush up on securitization in general, see Web Chapter 2.1.)

You Are the Man or Woman!

Before we start preparing our mental estimate of how long all of this is going to take and what form of model we will try to end up with, it will be a good idea to review what we have to work with.

We realize we can kill two birds with one stone if we invite our new coworker to join us as we review the existing model. There is a wonderful phenomenon related to having to sit down and explain your work to another person, especially if they are another modeler as well. All of a sudden, those quirky little issues of the model seem to jump out. You are immediately, and sometimes painfully, aware of dozens of small, medium, and large improvements that you now *just have* to put into the model. It is also hardly necessary to point out that you were perfectly happy to live without the aforementioned changes forever up until one minute before the review began.

Keeping all this in mind, let us review the model that will be the initial point of departure for our upcoming effort!

OVERVIEW OF THE CURRENT MODEL

The current model was designed to securitize portfolios of loans to small businesses. These loans were the nonguaranteed portion of a financing for chattel and brick-and-mortar assets. The portfolios generally ranged in size from 500 up to 2,000 loans with aggregate current balances of from $100 million to $500 million. The loans of the larger portfolios were nationally distributed with concentrations in the seven to ten most populous states. The issuer supplied all the financial parameters necessary to amortize the loans and some, additional mostly geographic, information.

There were 26 data per loan. The initial terms of the loans ranged from 10 to 30 years. The portfolios were seasoned on average between 2 to 3 years. The portfolios were comprised exclusively of floating-rate notes, indexed off of one-month London Interbank Offered Rate (LIBOR) with spreads between 1% and 4.25%. The amortization characteristics of the loans did not allow for optional payments, negative amortization, or any other exotic features.

The model needed to perform the following functions:

- Read the data from data files.
- Perform eligibility testing both on the loan-by-loan basis and a portfolio level basis (geographic location only).
- Produce an ineligible collateral report package.
- Produce an eligible report package in the form of various stratification reports.
- Amortize the collateral and feed the resultant cash flows into the liabilities waterfall.
- Calculate the liabilities waterfall and capture the performance of the notes created in the securitization issuance.
- Produce a series of cash flow and structural performance reports for both the collateral portfolio and the issued liabilities.

General Design Elements

To accomplish these tasks, the system was designed around a model that performed both the asset and liability calculations in a single program. This program relied on an Excel data file containing the portfolio information and a series of preconfigured report template files. A schematic of the system is given in Exhibit 2.1.

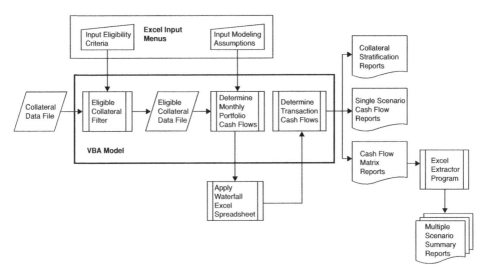

EXHIBIT 2.1 Schematic of the small business loan model

Collateral Data Files In that we have had to deal with relatively small, 500 to 2,000 loan, portfolios up until this time, the existing model uses Excel to house collateral files. For portfolios of this size, with smaller record formats, the current Structuring Model is adequate. Using the current model to address larger portfolios with twice the amount of information per loan but may later become problematic however.

The Structuring Model The Structuring Model consists of a combination of Excel worksheets and VBA modules. The Excel worksheets serve three functions:

1. **Menus.** In the first and most visible function, they serve as the menus of the model. There are a total of eight menus. These menus accept information from the analyst as to the run options the model is to perform, the financial and geographic selection criteria, the information on interest rates and days counts, default and prepayment assumptions, reporting options, and inputs for a multiple-scenario Batch Mode.
2. **Template files.** They serve as the template files for all of the reports produced directly by the model as well as the reports of other associated programs that directly support the model. They also serve as the framework for the internal reports of the model. These are reports that appear in the model itself. There are two such reports: a Coupon Trace Graph report that can be used to display the monthly coupon levels for any eligible loan in the portfolio and the Collateral Selection Results report that will tell us how many loans were deemed eligible and how many were not. The Collateral Selection Results report also lists how many loans were collectively ineligible due to each selection criteria.
3. **Waterfall structure layout.** The third role of Excel spreadsheets in the model is that they hold the entire deal structure and cash flow waterfall of the model. This worksheet is named the "CFWaterfall" and contains the Liabilities Waterfall spreadsheet. This spreadsheet is a 60-column waterfall spreadsheet that contains the entire structural framework of the deal. A VBA module produces the portfolio level cash flows using a loan-by-loan analysis approach and copies these resultant cash flows into the "CFWaterfall" spreadsheet. The spreadsheet is then triggered, producing the liabilities performance of the deal for that cash flow scenario, and the results are captured in a series of VBA arrays for later presentation.

The VBA code that supports the model consists of 22 modules containing a total of 176 subroutines. These modules are segregated by functional task. The main tasks are program management (run options), menu and data error checking, data input, collateral selection, collateral cash flow amortization on a loan-by-loan basis, management of the liabilities waterfall structure, and the reporting function.

Report Template Files The last major design component involves the use of a series of report template files that comprise the reporting package. There are seven of these template files, each producing a unique report that serves a particular reporting function:

- Three of these template files support the collateral selection and reporting process. The first is the ineligible report package and the second is the eligible collateral stratification report package. The third report is a data file format that allows the analyst to save the eligible collateral in a separate portfolio.

- One report template file serves to report the entire contents of the Liabilities Waterfall worksheet for each scenario in the model run.
- One report template file serves a detailed summary single-scenario report.
- One report template file serves as a summary report package for all scenarios of the model run.
- One report template file serves as a cash flow trace report that allows the analyst to examine the monthly cash flow components of all loans in the portfolio, by each scenario.

Collateral Data File

The collateral data file is one of the most important files in the entire group of files that support the model. Without the information in the collateral data file, we would be unable to assess the demographic and credit characteristics of the collateral portfolio. This file contains all the information we need to create a loan-by-loan credit and cash flow analysis of the portfolio. It contains the information we need both to screen the portfolio for ineligible loans and to produce the cash flows of the loans that have successfully passed all of the eligibility tests for inclusion in the deal.

File Format   Exhibit 2.2 shows the information contained in and the layout and form at of the current data file.

#	Item Name	Format
1	Original Balance	$
2	Current Balance	$
3	Current Coupon	% 3 digits
4	Original Term	#
5	Remaining Term	#
6	Seasoning	#
7	Fixed or Floating Coupon	1=Fix, 2=Float
8	Floating Rate Index	Alpha
9	Spread to Index	% 3 digits
10	Coupon Reset Frequency	#
11	Payment Reset Frequency	#
12	Lifetime Coupon Floor	% 3 digits
13	Lifetime Coupon Cap	% 3 digits
14	Coupon Reset Cap	% 3 digits
15	Coupon Reset Floor	% 3 digits
16	Day Count Method	# code 1-3
17	Stated Monthly Payment	$
18	Appraisal Value	$
19	Original Equity	$
20	Current Equity	$
21	Business Location State	2 digit Alpha Postal
22	Business Location Zip Code	#
23	Origination Date – Year	YY
24	Origination Date – Month	MM
25	Maturity Date – Year	YY
26	Maturity Date – Month	MM

EXHIBIT 2.2   Contents and formats of the collateral data file

Need for Additional Information   The contents of the file are first type checked by the model and then read into a series of VBA arrays and vectors. We have been told that the typical loan file will consist of up to 60 data fields, and a portfolio may consist of as many as 10,000 loans. This information will consist of both personal information such as Fair Isaac's Corporation (FICO) credit scores, household consumer debt levels, delinquency history (if any), and specialized loan amortization information. We will also need to analyze most of the data based from the standpoint of geographic MSA (Metropolitan Statistical Area) data requirements.

Loan Structuring Model

The existing loan structuring model performs the following tasks:

1. **Collateral selection process.** The process that determines what collateral pieces meet all constraints needed to be included in the deal portfolio pool.
2. **Collateral amortization process.** Applies the prepayment, default, market value decline, and recovery lag assumptions to amortize each individual piece of collateral.
3. **Transfer collateral cash flows to the liabilities waterfall structure.**
4. **Run the liabilities waterfall** spreadsheet and capture the results.
5. **Produce the collateral and liabilities reports.**

   With the exception of the collateral data file, all of the inputs to the model are made through a series of menus. All reports are generated by the use of preformatted template files.

   A Batch Mode is provided, should the analyst wish to have the model run repeatedly across entire scenario sets, each of which can evaluate up to 100 scenarios.

Menus

The menus that serve as the primary input vehicle to the existing Structuring Model are listed below.

Main Menu   The Main Menu (Exhibit 2.3) is the entry point to the program. There are four major subdivisions to this menu. If we start at the top and work our way downward, we will see that these sections are the Run Time Options section, the Data section, the Report File section, and Report Template section.

   The uppermost section of the menu contains a listing of the eight Run Time Options of the model. The first four of these pertain to the collateral selection process, the next three govern the production of the structural performance reports, and the last option produces an in-depth, period-by-period cash flow report by loan.

   The middle section of the menu asks the analyst for the main directory pathway, the name of the portfolio data file, and the number of loans from that file the model is to process as the starting collateral set.

   The lower left section of the menu accepts inputs for names to be assigned to the various output reports. The first field in this group is a common prefix that will be attached to each of the files as they are produced. This will allow them to be more easily recognized as belonging to a given scenario set. The lower-right-hand section

Loan Securitization Model Main Menu

Program Execution Options	(Y=YES; N=NO)	
Y	Perform the Collateral Eligibility Test ?	*Run the Model*
Y	Write out Ineligible Collateral Reports ?	
Y	Write out Eligible Collateral Reports ?	*Run the Batch Model*
Y	Write out Eligible Collateral Loan File ?	
Y	Write out Cash Flow Waterfall Reports ?	
Y	Write out Matrix Summary Reports ?	
Y	Write out Single Scenario Reports ?	
N	Write out Cash Flow Trace files? *(Caution: can generate VERY LENGTHY run times!)*	

Input File Information

C:\VBAInf\Code\	
portfolio_comb.xls	Collateral Data File Name
0	# of Loans *Enter "0" to read all available, otherwise enter the number of loans that you want to have read from the top of the file.*

	BTest04 MVD70 L24 S100	Report Group Prefix (attached to all output files)	Template File Names
View	Ineligibles.xls	Ineligible Collateral Reports File Name <======	ac_inelig_template.xls
View	Collateral.xls	Eligible Collateral Reports File Name <======	ac_collat_template.xls
View	Waterfall.xls	Cash Flow Waterfalls Report File Name <======	ac_waterfall_template.xls
View	Matrix.xls	Summary Matrix Reports Files <======	ac_matrix_template.xls
View	Eligibles.xls	Eligible Collateral File <======	ac_datafile_template.xls
View	Scenario.xls	Scenario Summary Reports File <======	ac_scenario_template.xls
	CFTrace.xls	Cash Flow Trace Report File <======	cf_trace_template.xls

EXHIBIT 2.3   Main Menu

of the menu contains the names of the template files to be used in the preparation of the report.

Collateral Selection Criteria Menu   The Collateral Selection Criteria Menu is shown in Exhibit 2.4.

This menu allows the analyst to input selection parameters for a total of ten collateral selection tests. The parameters and formats of the tests are fixed. The first five of the tests are two condition minimum/maximum tests. The last two tests are single condition tests.

Collateral Selection Criteria Menu

Minimum	Maximum		
12	360	Original Term (Months)	*Run the Model*
12	360	Remaining Term (Months)	
$25,000	$2,000,000	Original Balance	
$25,000	$1,100,000	Remaining Balance	
7.000%	11.000%	Gross Coupon	
	80.000%	Maximum Total Project LTV%	
	$5	Difference Stated-Calculated Pmt	

Indices & Minimum Spreads		
Index Code	Min Spread	
PRIME	2.250%	Index #1 and Minimum Spread
		Index #2 and Minimum Spread
		Index #3 and Minimum Spread
		Index #4 and Minimum Spread
		Index #5 and Minimum Spread
		Index #6 and Minimum Spread

EXHIBIT 2.4   Collateral Selection Criteria Menu

Geographic Selections Menu

X	AK	Alaska	X	MA	Massachusettes	X	OR	Oregon	National	Include	Exclude
X	AL	Alabama	X	MD	Maryland	X	PA	Pennsylvania	New England	Include	Exclude
X	AR	Arkansas	X	ME	Maine	X	RI	Rhode Island	Mid-Atlantic	Include	Exclude
X	AZ	Arizona	X	MI	Michigan	X	SC	South Carolina	South East	Include	Exclude
X	CA	California	X	MN	Minnesota	X	SD	South Dakota	Midwest	Include	Exclude
X	CO	Colorado	X	MO	Missouri	X	TN	Tennessee	South West	Include	Exclude
X	CT	Connecticut	X	MS	Mississippi	X	TX	Texas	North West	Include	Exclude
X	DE	Delaware	X	MT	Montana	X	UT	Utah			
X	FL	Florida	X	NC	North Carolina	X	VA	Virginia			
X	GA	Georgia	X	ND	North Dakota	X	VT	Vermont			
X	HI	Hawaii	X	NE	Nebraska	X	WA	Washington			
X	IA	Iowa	X	NH	New Hampshire	X	WI	Wisconsin	*Run the*		
X	ID	Idaho	X	NJ	New Jersey	X	WV	West Virginia	*Model*		
X	IL	Illinois	X	NM	New Mexico	X	WY	Wyoming			
X	IN	Indiana	X	NV	Nevada	X	DC	Dist of Col			
X	KS	Kansas	X	NY	New York	X	VI	US Virgin Is			
X	KY	Kentucky	X	OH	Ohio	X	GM	US Marians Is			
X	LA	Louisana	X	OK	Oklahoma	X	PR	Puerto Rico			

EXHIBIT 2.5 Geographic Selections Menu

The next section allows the analyst to specify a minimum spread to index for any of the floating rate collateral.

Geographic Selections Menu The Geographic Selections Menu of Exhibit 2.5 is used to include or exclude collateral at the state level.

The states can be individually selected or deselected by placing any symbol in the box to the immediate left of the state's postal code field. There is also a collection of buttons on the right-hand side of the menu. The button "Exclude" in the National line at the upper right hand corner of the menu is used when the analyst wants to blank out most if not all of the states and perform a collateral analysis on a single state. If one wanted to analyze only Florida, one could exclude the National portfolio and then simply include Florida by checking a single box. This would be more efficient that excluding the 53 other choices manually.

Default and Prepayment Assumptions Menu The Default and Prepayment Assumptions Menu, see Exhibit 2.6, is designed to accept both prepayment and default assumptions. These assumptions are applied uniformly across all of the loans in the portfolio.

This menu allows the analyst to specify both the default and the prepayment rates along with static market value decline value and recovery lag period value. The prepayments can be specified in either Public Securities Administration (PSA) methodology or the constant prepayment rate (CPR) methodology. There are three alternatives for specifying the default pattern to be applied to the collateral. The defaults can be specified in either Public Securities Administration Standard Default Assumptions Curve (SDA) or expressed in the same form as the CPR methodology used for prepayments above or in a pattern defined by the analyst. In the User Defined pattern, the analyst enters a percentage rate into the default rate. The default rate is then calculated as a percentage of the period 1 beginning principal balance of the loan at the time of the deal. These losses are then spread over as many years in the

Default Rates		
Default Rate	400.00%	Default Methodology Codes
Default Rate Step	50.00%	1=CPR, 2=PSA
# Default Steps	5	3=User Defined
Methodology	2	

Prepayment Rates		
Prepay Base Rate	200.00%	Prepay Method
Prepay Rate Step	50.00%	Codes
# Prepay Steps	5	1=CPR, 2=PSA,
Methodology	2	

Distribution of Portfolio Lifetime Annual Defaults					
Year 1		Year 11		Year 21	
Year 2		Year 12		Year 22	
Year 3		Year 13		Year 23	
Year 4		Year 14		Year 24	
Year 5		Year 15		Year 25	
Year 6		Year 16		Year 26	
Year 7		Year 17		Year 27	
Year 8		Year 18		Year 28	
Year 9		Year 19		Year 29	
Year 10		Year 20		Year 30	

Percentage Sum for all Years=> 0.00%

Run the Model

Mkt Value Decline	70.00%	
Recovery Lag	24	Months

Clear All

EXHIBIT 2.6 Default and Prepayment Assumptions Menu

percentage proportions specified in the section "Distribution of Portfolio Lifetime Annual Defaults." The sum of the distribution factors must equal 100% or an error message is generated. Below this block there are two entry fields for the market value decline (MVD) percentage and the recovery lag period (RLP), in months. The first of these parameters, MVD, is applied as a percentage of the original appraisal value of the property to determine the severity of loss for the loan. The second factor, RLP, is the delay in months between when the loan is deemed in default and the receipt of any recovery amounts.

Index, Spread, and Date Count Menu   The Index, Spread, and Date Count Menu, see Exhibit 2.7, contains a series of index rate levels, spread rate levels, and the day count decimal equivalents.

Day Count Factors and Rates																	
	Rates Used in Model Run					Alternative LIBOR Pathways						Alternative Conduit Financing Spreads			Alternative Prim		
	Prime	Libor	Spread	Conduit		1	2	3	4	5				1	2	3
	2	1	1	Fund Rate												
1	6.000%	2.750%	1.000%	3.750%	1	2.750%	2.900%	3.000%	3.250%	3.500%	1	1.000%	1	5.250%	6.000%	6.25
2	6.000%	2.750%	1.000%	3.750%	2	2.750%	2.900%	3.000%	3.250%	3.500%	2	2.000%	2	5.250%	6.000%	6.25
3	6.000%	2.750%	1.000%	3.750%	3	2.750%	2.900%	3.000%	3.250%	3.500%	3	0.650%	3	5.250%	6.000%	6.25
4	6.000%	2.750%	1.000%	3.750%	4	2.750%	2.900%	3.000%	3.250%	3.500%	4	4.000%	4	5.250%	6.000%	6.25
5	6.000%	2.750%	1.000%	3.750%	5	2.750%	2.900%	3.000%	3.250%	3.500%	5	5.000%	5	5.250%	6.000%	6.25
6	6.000%	2.750%	1.000%	3.750%	6	2.750%	2.900%	3.000%	3.250%	3.500%			6	5.250%	6.000%	6.25
7	6.000%	2.750%	1.000%	3.750%	7	2.750%	2.900%	3.000%	3.250%	3.500%			7	5.250%	6.000%	6.25
8	6.000%	2.750%	1.000%	3.750%	8	2.750%	2.900%	3.000%	3.250%	3.500%			8	5.250%	6.000%	6.25
9	6.000%	2.750%	1.000%	3.750%	9	2.750%	2.900%	3.000%	3.250%	3.500%			9	5.250%	6.000%	6.25
10	6.000%	2.750%	1.000%	3.750%	10	2.750%	2.900%	3.000%	3.250%	3.500%			10	5.250%	6.000%	6.25
11	6.000%	2.750%	1.000%	3.750%	11	2.750%	2.900%	3.000%	3.250%	3.500%			11	5.250%	6.000%	6.25
12	6.000%	2.750%	1.000%	3.750%	12	2.750%	2.900%	3.000%	3.250%	3.500%			12	5.250%	6.000%	6.25

EXHIBIT 2.7 Index, Spread, and Date Count Menu

Program Costs Menu

Program Expenses
0.75%	Servicer Fee (off of Asset Balance)
0.20%	Program Fees (off of Note Balance)

Principal Reallocation Triggers
10.00%	Clean Up Call Level
5.00%	Rolling 3 Month Default Rate

Advance Rate
95.00%	Conduit Percentage

1	Conduit Spread Choice
1	Libor Pathway
2	Prime Rate Pathway

Run the Model

EXHIBIT 2.8   Program Costs Menu

The analyst can select any of five interest rate paths for LIBOR and prime. The base rate and the spread for the conduit financing rate can also be specified. The day count tables for 30/360, 30/Actual, and Actual/Actual are to the right of the interest rate calculations. One selects the options by entering the numeric pathway code on the Program Costs Menu.

Program Costs Menu   The Program Costs Menu, see Exhibit 2.8, allows the analyst to specify the costs associated with running the deal, the thresholds for two deal triggers, the advance rate of the deal, and the selection of the interest rate vectors to use for LIBOR and prime and the financing spread for the conduit borrowing.

Report Selection Menu   The Reporting Selection Menu, see Exhibit 2.9, allows the analyst to select specific eligible collateral (stratification) reports from the Eligible Collateral report package and individual reports from the Summary Matrix report package.

Batch Mode Menu   The Batch Mode Menu, see Exhibit 2.10, allows the analyst to specify a number of inputs in a columnar list by scenario. The column report allows for the input of the following parameters:

- Market value decline percentage
- Recovery lag period
- Conduit financing spread
- Base file name prefix label
- Conduit financing spread choice
- LIBOR path selection
- Prime rate path selection

Report Selection Menu

Run? "X"	Report Code	PORTFOLIO STRATIFICATION REPORTS Report Name
X	Elig-1	Current Balances by Original Term Structure
X	Elig-2	Current Balances by Remaining Term Structure
X	Elig-3	Current Balances by Loan Seasoning
X	Elig-4	Current Balances by Yield
X	Elig-5	Current Balance by Spread
X	Elig-6	Current Balances by Owners Equity %
X	Elig-7	Current Balances by LTV %
X	Elig-8	Current Balances by $ Current Balances
X	Elig-9	Current Balances by $ Original Balances
X	Elig-10	Geographic Concentration -- State Code
X	Elig-11	Geographic Concentration -- Zip Code
		(reserved for future use)
		(reserved for future use)
		(reserved for future use)
		(reserved for future use)
		(reserved for future use)
		(reserved for future use)
		(reserved for future use)

Run? "X"	Report Code	MULTIPLE SCENARIO MATRIX RESULTS Report Name
X	Matrix-1	Conduit Tenor Report
X	Matrix-2	Collateral Cash Flows Report
X	Matrix-3	Conduit Note Performance
X	Matrix-4	Seller Interest Performance
		(reserved for future use)

Run the Model

EXHIBIT 2.9 Report Selection Menu

The model then constructs a file name prefix that uses a standard format that incorporates some of the assumptions used to produce the scenarios contained in the file.

The Batch Mode Menu allows the analyst to specify as many as 50 different scenarios. When the "Run the Batch Model" button is pushed, a separate module calls the main structuring program as a subroutine and systemically replaces the current inputs of the structuring model with the entries from the Batch Mode Menu. There are no prepayment or default specification fields on the Batch Mode Menu, however, so these fields are assumed from the Defaults and Prepayment Menu at their last specified values.

Liabilities Waterfall Spreadsheet

This spreadsheet contains the calculation structure of the liabilities waterfall. It receives from the VBA collateral cash flow generator the five component streams of cash flows. It passes these streams of cash flows through the waterfall and captures

Batch Output File Menu

	Select	Market Value Decline	Recovery Period Lag	Conduit Finance Spread	File Name Prefix ID	Time Prefix Code	Conduit Spread Choice	Libor Rates Path	Prime Rates Path	File Name Prefix
1	X	50%	6	1.000%	BTest01		1	1	2	BTest01 MVD50_L6_S100
2	X	55%	12	1.000%	BTest02		1	1	2	BTest02 MVD55_L12_S100
3	X	60%	18	1.000%	BTest03		1	1	2	BTest03 MVD60_L18_S100
4	X	70%	24	1.000%	BTest04		1	1	2	BTest04 MVD70_L24_S100
5										
6										
7										
8										
9										
10										

EXHIBIT 2.10 Batch Mode Menu

the structural performance results in a summary section to the left of the waterfall that we will affectionately call the "Box Score" section. The sections below capture the entire waterfall from the initial receipt of cash flows to the determination of trigger status at the end of the period. A detailed description of all fields, including their cell formulas, is available in a Web Chapter 2.2, "Understanding the Structuring Model Excel Waterfall."

Box Score and Collateral Cash Flows Section   The Box Score section contains a summary of all major cash flow and liability performance metrics. The upper portion of the Box Score contains Sources and Uses statement for the deal. The next section contains performance statistics for the conduit financing and the seller interest components of the deal. The final section displays the terminal state of the three deal triggers: one for 3-month default rates and the other two for shortfalls in either servicing fees or interest payments to the conduit financing. See Exhibit 2.11.

To the immediate right of the Box Score section is the Collateral Cash Flows section of the Liabilities Waterfall. This is the beginning of the structural waterfall, and it accepts the five component streams of the collateral cash flows from the VBA program.

Deal Expenses Section   The second section of the liabilities waterfall is the deal expenses section. In this section, the total cash from the collateral is displayed and the two main expenses of the deal, the program expense and the servicing expense, is paid. See Exhibit 2.12

Conduit Interest, Conduit Principal, and the Excess Cash Available Sections   This section displays the third portion of the waterfall that pays the interest to and retires the principal of the conduit financing. After these payments are made, the amount remaining is designated excess cash. This excess cash can be used to fund the delinquency reserve fund, or, if that reserve fund is complete, released to the seller interest. See Exhibit 2.13.

Conduit Summary Section   This section displays the current state of the conduit financing. It indicates the current balance outstanding in dollars, the percentage of the original principal amount outstanding, the amount of the principal retired each period, and the per-period interest payment made to the conduit. See Exhibit 2.14.

Delinquent Reserve Activity and Deal Triggers Section   This section displays the funding, current balance, and cash flows released from the delinquent reserve fund. The section that tracks the performance of the deal triggers displays the current status of the event, clean-up and default level triggers of the deal. See Exhibit 2.15.

Default Test Section and Present Value Calculation Section   The final section of the Liability Waterfall displays the calculation of those inputs needed to determine if any of the deal triggers (which accelerate principal payments to the conduit financing) have been activated. It also contains a series of columns that are used to calculate

Single Scenario Cash Flow Waterfall Report

600.00%	PSA	✓ = Default Rate
400.00%	PSA	✓ = Prepayment Rate

Summary Report

Collateral Cash Flows
- Scheduled Amortization: 116,093,912 — 23.62%
- Prepayments to Principal: 325,968,243 — 66.33%
- Total Principal Retired: 442,062,154
- Defaulted Principal: 49,358,223 — 10.04%
- Recoveries of Principal (& rate): 26,429,173 — 53.55%
- Coupon Income: 162,769,568
- **Total Cash Sources: 631,260,896**

Debt Cash Flows
- Program Fees: 3,256,678
- Servicing Fee: 13,269,401
- Conduit Debt Service: 61,062,714
- Conduit Principal Payments: 466,849,358
- Released to Seller: 86,822,744
- **Total Cash Uses: 631,260,896**

Performance	Conduit	Seller Interest
Structuring		
Beginning Balance	466,849,358	24,571,019
Ownership Interest	95.00%	5.00%
Performance		
Principal Outstanding	$0	0.00%
Severity of Loss	0.000%	0.00%
IRR	3.750%	40.264%
Tenor		
Average Life (yrs)	3.488	
Final Maturity (yrs)	11.167	
Modified Duration	3.186	
Macauley Duration	3.071	
Checks		
Program Fee Shortfall	FALSE	.
Servicing Fee Shortfall	FALSE	.
Interest Shortfall	FALSE	.

Collateral Cashflows

1	Beginning Principal Balance	Pool Factor	Regular Amort Principal	Prepaid Principal	Defaulted Principal	Ending Principal Balance Outstanding	Total Principal Retired	Coupon Income	Recoveries of Principal
			116,093,912	325,968,243	49,358,223		442,062,154	162,769,568	26,429,173
1	491,420,377	1.00000	1,834,955	327,090	751,542	488,506,789	2,162,045	3,784,129	.
2	488,506,789	0.99407	1,844,885	652,631	788,377	485,220,895	2,497,517	3,761,087	.
3	485,220,895	0.98738	1,853,468	975,870	823,489	481,568,068	2,829,338	3,735,188	.
4	481,568,068	0.97995	1,860,677	1,296,055	856,976	477,554,361	3,156,732	3,706,473	.
5	477,554,361	0.97178	1,866,486	1,612,443	888,805	473,186,627	3,478,929	3,674,931	.
6	473,186,627	0.96290	1,870,877	1,924,239	918,715	468,472,737	3,795,176	3,640,795	.
7	468,472,737	0.95330	1,873,830	2,230,899	946,717	463,421,291	4,104,729	3,603,949	.
8	463,421,291	0.94302	1,875,334	2,531,538	972,292	459,042,127	4,406,872	3,564,522	.
9	459,042,127	0.93208	1,875,376	2,825,526	995,769	452,345,455	4,700,903	3,522,590	.
10	452,345,455	0.92049	1,873,951	3,112,196	1,016,864	446,342,444	4,986,147	3,478,232	.
11	446,342,444	0.90827	1,871,054	3,390,904	1,035,505	440,044,980	5,261,958	3,431,538	.
12	440,044,980	0.89546	1,866,687	3,661,036	1,051,324	433,465,933	5,527,723	3,382,601	.
13	433,465,933	0.88207	1,860,852	3,922,007	1,064,483	426,618,592	5,782,859	3,331,520	.
14	426,618,592	0.86813	1,853,559	4,173,270	1,074,087	419,517,676	6,026,829	3,278,406	.
15	419,517,676	0.85368	1,844,817	4,414,306	1,081,172	412,177,381	6,259,123	3,223,363	.
16	412,177,381	0.83875	1,834,640	4,644,627	1,085,920	404,612,194	6,479,267	3,166,501	.
17	404,612,194	0.82335	1,823,044	4,863,792	1,087,721	396,837,638	6,686,835	3,107,936	.
18	396,837,638	0.80753	1,810,050	5,071,395	1,086,744	388,869,449	6,881,445	3,047,788	.
19	388,869,449	0.79132	1,795,682	5,267,069	1,083,387	380,723,310	7,062,751	2,986,174	.
20	380,723,310	0.77474	1,779,969	5,450,490	1,077,537	372,415,314	7,230,459	2,923,217	.
21	372,415,314	0.75783	1,757,068	5,621,466	1,069,164	363,967,616	7,378,534	2,859,041	.
22	363,967,616	0.74064	1,738,821	5,779,683	1,058,147	355,390,965	7,518,504	2,793,819	.
23	355,390,965	0.72319	1,719,334	5,924,950	1,044,661	346,702,020	7,644,285	2,727,633	.
24	346,702,020	0.70551	1,698,648	6,057,124	1,028,681	337,917,567	7,755,772	2,660,611	.
25	337,917,567	0.68763	1,676,806	6,176,119	1,009,736	329,054,905	7,852,925	2,592,986	435,768
26	329,054,905	0.66960	1,653,858	6,281,908	987,194	320,131,946	7,935,766	2,524,596	453,882
27	320,131,946	0.65144	1,629,848	6,374,470	963,343	311,164,284	8,004,319	2,455,862	471,034
28	311,164,284	0.63319	1,604,825	6,453,845	937,492	302,168,121	8,059,671	2,386,809	487,282

EXHIBIT 2.11 Liabilities Waterfall Box Score section

	T	U	V	W	X	Y	Z	AA	AB	AC	AD	AE
5	11	12	13	14	15	16	17	18	19	20	21	22
6				Expenses								
7–11		Total Cash Available For Waterfall		Program Fees Due	Program Fees Paid	Program Fees Unpaid	Cash Available	Servicing Fee Due	Servicing Fee Paid	Servicing Fee Unpaid	Cash Available	
12		638,505,640		3,256,678	3,256,678	-		13,269,401	13,269,401	-	621,979,561	
14	1	5,946,175	1	77,808	77,808	-	5,868,366	307,138	307,138	-	5,561,229	1
15	2	6,258,604	2	77,347	77,347	-	6,181,257	305,317	305,317	-	5,875,940	2
16	3	6,564,526	3	76,827	76,827	-	6,487,699	303,263	303,263	-	6,184,436	3
17	4	6,863,205	4	76,248	76,248	-	6,786,957	300,980	300,980	-	6,485,977	4
18	5	7,153,920	5	75,613	75,613	-	7,078,307	298,471	298,471	-	6,779,836	5
19	6	7,435,971	6	74,921	74,921	-	7,361,050	295,742	295,742	-	7,065,308	6
20	7	7,708,678	7	74,175	74,175	-	7,634,503	292,795	292,795	-	7,341,707	7
21	8	8,047,667	8	73,375	73,375	-	7,974,292	289,638	289,638	-	7,684,653	8
22	9	8,304,851	9	72,523	72,523	-	8,232,328	286,276	286,276	-	7,946,052	9
23	10	8,550,669	10	71,621	71,621	-	8,479,048	282,716	282,716	-	8,196,332	10
24	11	8,784,548	11	70,671	70,671	-	8,713,877	278,964	278,964	-	8,434,913	11
25	12	9,005,955	12	69,674	69,674	-	8,936,281	275,028	275,028	-	8,661,253	12
26	13	9,214,396	13	68,632	68,632	-	9,145,764	270,916	270,916	-	8,874,848	13
27	14	9,409,430	14	67,548	67,548	-	9,341,882	266,637	266,637	-	9,075,245	14
28	15	9,590,643	15	66,424	66,424	-	9,524,220	262,199	262,199	-	9,262,021	15
29	16	9,757,673	16	65,261	65,261	-	9,692,412	257,611	257,611	-	9,434,801	16
30	17	9,910,199	17	64,064	64,064	-	9,846,135	252,883	252,883	-	9,593,252	17
31	18	10,047,946	18	62,833	62,833	-	9,985,113	248,024	248,024	-	9,737,090	18
32	19	10,170,688	19	61,571	61,571	-	10,109,117	243,043	243,043	-	9,866,073	19
33	20	10,278,247	20	60,281	60,281	-	10,217,966	237,952	237,952	-	9,980,014	20
34	21	10,364,708	21	58,966	58,966	-	10,305,742	232,760	232,760	-	10,072,982	21
35	22	10,441,721	22	57,628	57,628	-	10,384,092	227,480	227,480	-	10,156,613	22
36	23	10,503,326	23	56,270	56,270	-	10,447,055	222,119	222,119	-	10,224,936	23
37	24	10,549,591	24	54,894	54,894	-	10,494,697	216,689	216,689	-	10,278,008	24
38	25	11,016,326	25	53,504	53,504	-	10,962,822	211,198	211,198	-	10,751,624	25
39	26	11,050,259	26	52,100	52,100	-	10,998,158	205,659	205,659	-	10,792,499	26
40	27	11,068,238	27	50,688	50,688	-	11,017,550	200,082	200,082	-	10,817,468	27
41	28	11,070,549	28	49,268	49,268	-	11,021,281	194,478	194,478	-	10,826,803	28

EXHIBIT 2.12   Deal Expenses section

the yield, price, average life, and durations of the conduit financing portion of the debt structure. See Exhibit 2.16.

Before we leave the discussion of the components of the Liabilities Waterfall, I strongly urge any reader who does not feel comfortable with the elements of this spreadsheet to consult Web Chapter 2.2, "Understanding the Structuring Model Excel Waterfall." This Web chapter contains a column-by-column description of the entire waterfall and the calculations for each of the cells.

Program Reports Screens

There are two reports that are internal to the model. That is, the reports are contained in the Structuring Model. These reports are written to spreadsheets contained in the Structuring Model and reside there. This is very different from the more extensively employed method of report writing that uses report template files that reside outside of the model. These template files are opened, saved under a different file name, and then written to from the Structuring Model. Once the output process is finished, the file is saved and the report is complete.

In contrast, even if no external report files were produced, as long as the most current model run had produced the information to populate these two internal reports, they would appear inside the model.

IRR=> 3.36%

Totals: Interest Due **61,062,714** · Interest Covered By Available Cash **61,062,714** · Principal Paid **466,849,358** · Cash Available **94,067,488** · Funding of Delinquent Reserve Balance **7,244,744** · Release of Delinquent Reserve **7,244,744** · Cash Released to Seller **86,822,744**

	Conduit Interest							Conduit Principal				Excess Cash Treatment		
Row	Interest Due	Interest Covered By Available Cash	Interest Due	Interest Covered By Delinquency Reserve	Interest Unpaid	Cash Available	Row	Principal Due	Principal Paid	Cash Available	Row	Funding of Delinquent Reserve Balance	Release of Delinquent Reserve (next period waterfall)	Cash Released to Seller
						.								(24,571,019)
1	1,458,904	1,458,904	.	.	.	4,102,324	1	2,767,909	2,767,909	1,334,416	1	1,334,416	.	.
2	1,450,255	1,450,255	.	.	.	4,425,685	2	3,121,599	3,121,599	1,304,086	2	1,304,086	.	.
3	1,440,500	1,440,500	.	.	.	4,743,937	3	3,470,186	3,470,186	1,273,751	3	1,273,751	.	.
4	1,429,655	1,429,655	.	.	.	5,056,322	4	3,813,022	3,813,022	1,243,299	4	1,243,299	.	.
5	1,417,740	1,417,740	.	.	.	5,362,096	5	4,149,347	4,149,347	1,212,749	5	1,212,749	.	.
6	1,404,773	1,404,773	.	.	.	5,660,535	6	4,478,196	4,478,196	1,182,340	6	876,443	.	305,897
7	1,390,778	1,390,778	.	.	.	5,950,929	7	4,798,874	4,798,874	1,152,055	7	.	76,273	1,152,055
8	1,375,782	1,375,782	.	.	.	6,308,872	8	5,110,205	5,110,205	1,198,666	8	.	81,359	1,198,666
9	1,359,813	1,359,813	.	.	.	6,586,239	9	5,411,838	5,411,838	1,174,401	9	.	86,290	1,174,401
10	1,342,901	1,342,901	.	.	.	6,853,431	10	5,702,861	5,702,861	1,150,571	10	.	91,052	1,150,571
11	1,325,079	1,325,079	.	.	.	7,109,834	11	5,982,590	5,982,590	1,127,243	11	.	95,631	1,127,243
12	1,306,384	1,306,384	.	.	.	7,354,870	12	6,250,095	6,250,095	1,104,775	12	.	100,017	1,104,775
13	1,286,852	1,286,852	.	.	.	7,587,996	13	6,504,974	6,504,974	1,083,022	13	.	104,195	1,083,022
14	1,266,524	1,266,524	.	.	.	7,808,721	14	6,745,870	6,745,870	1,062,851	14	.	108,157	1,062,851
15	1,245,443	1,245,443	.	.	.	8,016,578	15	6,973,280	6,973,280	1,043,298	15	.	111,905	1,043,298
16	1,223,652	1,223,652	.	.	.	8,211,149	16	7,186,927	7,186,927	1,024,222	16	.	115,427	1,024,222
17	1,201,192	1,201,192	.	.	.	8,392,060	17	7,385,829	7,385,829	1,006,231	17	.	118,713	1,006,231
18	1,178,112	1,178,112	.	.	.	8,558,978	18	7,569,779	7,569,779	989,199	18	.	121,763	989,199
19	1,154,456	1,154,456	.	.	.	8,711,617	19	7,738,832	7,738,832	972,785	19	.	124,571	972,785
20	1,130,272	1,130,272	.	.	.	8,849,741	20	7,892,596	7,892,596	957,145	20	.	127,132	957,145
21	1,105,608	1,105,608	.	.	.	8,967,374	21	8,025,313	8,025,313	942,061	21	.	129,397	942,061
22	1,080,529	1,080,529	.	.	.	9,076,084	22	8,147,818	8,147,818	928,265	22	.	131,408	928,265
23	1,055,067	1,055,067	.	.	.	9,169,869	23	8,254,498	8,254,498	915,371	23	.	133,209	915,371
24	1,029,272	1,029,272	.	.	.	9,248,736	24	8,345,230	8,345,230	903,506	24	.	134,747	903,506
25	1,003,193	1,003,193	.	.	.	9,748,431	25	8,419,528	8,419,528	1,328,903	25	.	136,015	1,328,903
26	976,882	976,882	.	.	.	9,815,617	26	8,476,812	8,476,812	1,338,805	26	.	137,024	1,338,805
27	950,392	950,392	.	.	.	9,867,076	27	8,519,279	8,519,279	1,347,797	27	.	137,787	1,347,797
28	923,769	923,769	.	.	.	9,903,034	28	8,546,355	8,546,355	1,356,680	28	.	138,301	1,356,680

EXHIBIT 2.13 Conduit Interest, Conduit Principal, and Excess Cash treatment sections

37

	AP	AQ	AR	AS	AT	AU	AV	AW	AX	AY	AZ
3								Avg Life =:	3.49	0.00	
4			IRR=>	3.36%		7,016,010		Fin Mat =>	11.17	0.00	
5	33	34	35	36	37	38	39	40	41	42	43
6		Excess Cash Treatment				Conduit Summary					
7–11		Funding of Delinquent Reserve Balance	Release of Delinquent Reserve (next period waterfall)	Cash Released to Seller		Conduit Beginning Balance 95.00%	Conduit Position as Percentage Original Balance	Conduit Position as Percentage Current Balance	Conduit Principal Paydown	Conduit Debt Service	
12		7,244,744	7,244,744	86,822,744		0.00%			466,849,358	61,062,714	
13				(24,571,019)							
14	1	1,334,416	-	-	1	466,849,358	95.00%	95.00%	2,767,909	1,458,904	1
15	2	1,304,086	-	-	2	464,081,450	94.44%	95.00%	3,121,599	1,450,255	2
16	3	1,273,751	-	-	3	460,959,850	93.80%	95.00%	3,470,186	1,440,500	3
17	4	1,243,299	-	-	4	457,489,665	93.10%	95.00%	3,813,022	1,429,655	4
18	5	1,212,749	-	-	5	453,676,643	92.32%	95.00%	4,149,347	1,417,740	5
19	6	876,443	-	305,897	6	449,527,295	91.48%	95.00%	4,478,196	1,404,773	6
20	7	-	76,273	1,152,055	7	445,049,100	90.56%	95.00%	4,798,874	1,390,778	7
21	8	-	81,359	1,198,666	8	440,250,226	89.59%	95.00%	5,110,205	1,375,782	8
22	9	-	86,290	1,174,401	9	435,140,021	88.55%	95.00%	5,411,838	1,359,813	9
23	10	-	91,052	1,150,571	10	429,728,182	87.45%	95.00%	5,702,861	1,342,901	10
24	11	-	95,631	1,127,243	11	424,025,322	86.29%	95.00%	5,982,590	1,325,079	11
25	12	-	100,017	1,104,775	12	418,042,731	85.07%	95.00%	6,250,095	1,306,384	12
26	13	-	104,195	1,083,022	13	411,792,636	83.80%	95.00%	6,504,974	1,286,852	13
27	14	-	108,157	1,062,851	14	405,287,662	82.47%	95.00%	6,745,870	1,266,524	14
28	15	-	111,905	1,043,298	15	398,541,792	81.10%	95.00%	6,973,280	1,245,443	15
29	16	-	115,427	1,024,222	16	391,568,512	79.68%	95.00%	7,186,927	1,223,652	16
30	17	-	118,713	1,006,231	17	384,381,584	78.22%	95.00%	7,385,829	1,201,192	17
31	18	-	121,763	989,199	18	376,995,756	76.72%	95.00%	7,569,779	1,178,112	18
32	19	-	124,571	972,785	19	369,425,977	75.18%	95.00%	7,738,832	1,154,456	19
33	20	-	127,132	957,145	20	361,687,145	73.60%	95.00%	7,892,596	1,130,272	20
34	21	-	129,397	942,061	21	353,794,548	71.99%	95.00%	8,025,313	1,105,608	21
35	22	-	131,408	928,265	22	345,769,235	70.36%	95.00%	8,147,818	1,080,529	22
36	23	-	133,209	915,371	23	337,621,417	68.70%	95.00%	8,254,498	1,055,067	23
37	24	-	134,747	903,506	24	329,366,919	67.02%	95.00%	8,345,230	1,029,272	24
38	25	-	136,015	1,328,903	25	321,021,688	65.33%	95.00%	8,419,528	1,003,193	25
39	26	-	137,024	1,338,805	26	312,602,160	63.61%	95.00%	8,476,812	976,882	26
40	27	-	137,787	1,347,797	27	304,125,348	61.89%	95.00%	8,519,279	950,392	27
41	28	-	138,301	1,356,680	28	295,606,070	60.15%	95.00%	8,546,355	923,769	28

EXHIBIT 2.14 Conduit Summary section

Collateral Selection Results Report   The Collateral Selection Result report screen in the model displays the results of the last collateral selection performed on the portfolio. See Exhibit 2.17.

It displays the total composition of the portfolio prior to selection, and the composition of the eligible and ineligible collateral components after the selection has been performed. In addition to summary statistics. The report also displays the number of loans that have failed each of the individual eligibility tests. Remember that a single loan can fail more than one eligibility test and therefore be listed in two or more categories simultaneously. (This is the reason that the balance and loan counts do not make the portfolio ineligible loan totals in the second left hand section of the report.)

Coupon Trace Report   This report was introduced into the model to allow for the examination of the coupon levels for any floating rate loan in the portfolio. It serves as a validation mechanism to ensure that the stated characteristics of the loan such

	AZ	BA	BB	BC	BD	BE	BF	BG	BH	BI	BJ	BK	BL	BM	BN
5	43	44	45	46	47	48	49	50	51	52	53	54	55	56	57
6		Delinquent Reserve Activity							Triggers					Debt Costs	
		Delinquent Account Reserve Cap	Beginning Delinquent Account Reserve Balance	Draws to Delinquent Account Reserve Account	Deposits to Delinquent Reserve Account Balance	Delinquent Reserve Account Release	Ending Delinquent Account Reserve Balance		Test 1 Event Trigger	Test 2 Clean-up Trigger	Test 3 Default Trigger	Global Global Trigger		Conduit Funding Coupon Rate	
12					7,244,744	7,244,744			10.00%	5.00%				3.750%	
14	1	7,545,216	-	-	1,334,416	-	1,334,416	1	FALSE	FALSE	FALSE	FALSE	1	3.750%	1
15	2	7,496,275	1,334,416	-	1,304,086	-	2,638,502	2	FALSE	FALSE	FALSE	FALSE	2	3.750%	2
16	3	7,441,661	2,638,502	-	1,273,751	-	3,912,253	3	FALSE	FALSE	FALSE	FALSE	3	3.750%	3
17	4	7,381,464	3,912,253	-	1,243,299	-	5,155,552	4	FALSE	FALSE	FALSE	FALSE	4	3.750%	4
18	5	7,315,786	5,155,552	-	1,212,749	-	6,368,301	5	FALSE	FALSE	FALSE	FALSE	5	3.750%	5
19	6	7,244,744	6,368,301	-	876,443	-	7,244,744	6	FALSE	FALSE	FALSE	FALSE	6	3.750%	6
20	7	7,168,471	7,244,744	-	-	76,273	7,168,471	7	FALSE	FALSE	FALSE	FALSE	7	3.750%	7
21	8	7,087,112	7,168,471	-	-	81,359	7,087,112	8	FALSE	FALSE	FALSE	FALSE	8	3.750%	8
22	9	7,000,822	7,087,112	-	-	86,290	7,000,822	9	FALSE	FALSE	FALSE	FALSE	9	3.750%	9
23	10	6,909,770	7,000,822	-	-	91,052	6,909,770	10	FALSE	FALSE	FALSE	FALSE	10	3.750%	10
24	11	6,814,139	6,909,770	-	-	95,631	6,814,139	11	FALSE	FALSE	FALSE	FALSE	11	3.750%	11
25	12	6,714,121	6,814,139	-	-	100,017	6,714,121	12	FALSE	FALSE	FALSE	FALSE	12	3.750%	12
26	13	6,609,926	6,714,121	-	-	104,195	6,609,926	13	FALSE	FALSE	FALSE	FALSE	13	3.750%	13
27	14	6,501,769	6,609,926	-	-	108,157	6,501,769	14	FALSE	FALSE	FALSE	FALSE	14	3.750%	14
28	15	6,389,864	6,501,769	-	-	111,905	6,389,864	15	FALSE	FALSE	FALSE	FALSE	15	3.750%	15
29	16	6,274,437	6,389,864	-	-	115,427	6,274,437	16	FALSE	FALSE	FALSE	FALSE	16	3.750%	16
30	17	6,155,724	6,274,437	-	-	118,713	6,155,724	17	FALSE	FALSE	FALSE	FALSE	17	3.750%	17
31	18	6,033,961	6,155,724	-	-	121,763	6,033,961	18	FALSE	FALSE	FALSE	FALSE	18	3.750%	18
32	19	5,909,390	6,033,961	-	-	124,571	5,909,390	19	FALSE	FALSE	FALSE	FALSE	19	3.750%	19
33	20	5,782,258	5,909,390	-	-	127,132	5,782,258	20	FALSE	FALSE	FALSE	FALSE	20	3.750%	20
34	21	5,652,861	5,782,258	-	-	129,397	5,652,861	21	FALSE	FALSE	FALSE	FALSE	21	3.750%	21
35	22	5,521,452	5,652,861	-	-	131,408	5,521,452	22	FALSE	FALSE	FALSE	FALSE	22	3.750%	22
36	23	5,398,244	5,521,452	-	-	133,209	5,398,244	23	FALSE	FALSE	FALSE	FALSE	23	3.750%	23
37	24	5,253,496	5,398,244	-	-	134,747	5,253,496	24	FALSE	FALSE	FALSE	FALSE	24	3.750%	24
38	25	5,117,482	5,253,496	-	-	136,015	5,117,482	25	FALSE	FALSE	FALSE	FALSE	25	3.750%	25
39	26	4,980,458	5,117,482	-	-	137,024	4,980,458	26	FALSE	FALSE	FALSE	FALSE	26	3.750%	26
40	27	4,842,671	4,980,458	-	-	137,787	4,842,671	27	FALSE	FALSE	FALSE	FALSE	27	3.750%	27
41	28	4,704,370	4,842,671	-	-	138,301	4,704,370	28	FALSE	FALSE	FALSE	FALSE	28	3.750%	28

EXHIBIT 2.15 Delinquent Reserve Activity and Deal Triggers section

	BH	BI	BJ	BK	BL	BM	BN	BO	BP	BQ	BR	BS	BT	BU	BV
5	51	52	53	54	55	56	57	58	59	60	61	62	63	64	63
6	Triggers					Debt Costs		Default Tests							
	Test 1 Event Trigger	Test 2 Clean-up Trigger	Test 3 Default Trigger	Global Global Trigger		Conduit Funding Coupon Rate		Rolling 3 Month Default Rate	Lifetime Default Rate	Conduit Funding Period PV Factor	Conduit Funding Cum PV Factor	Total Conduit CFs	NPV Conduit CFs		Vinddown Triggers Activated
12	10.00%	5.00%				3.750%						527,912,073	466,849,358		
13												(466,849,358)			
14	FALSE	FALSE	FALSE	FALSE	1	3.750%	1		0.153%	0.996885	0.996895	4,226,813	4,213,645	1	FALSE
15	FALSE	FALSE	FALSE	FALSE	2	3.750%	2		0.313%	0.996885	0.993779	4,571,954	4,543,413	2	FALSE
16	FALSE	FALSE	FALSE	FALSE	3	3.750%	3		0.481%	0.996885	0.990683	4,910,685	4,864,934	3	FALSE
17	FALSE	FALSE	FALSE	FALSE	4	3.750%	4	0.481%	0.655%	0.996885	0.987597	5,242,677	5,177,653	4	FALSE
18	FALSE	FALSE	FALSE	FALSE	5	3.750%	5	0.505%	0.836%	0.996885	0.984520	5,567,097	5,480,911	5	FALSE
19	FALSE	FALSE	FALSE	FALSE	6	3.750%	6	0.530%	1.023%	0.996885	0.981453	5,882,969	5,773,859	6	FALSE
20	FALSE	FALSE	FALSE	FALSE	7	3.750%	7	0.553%	1.216%	0.996885	0.978396	6,189,652	6,055,930	7	FALSE
21	FALSE	FALSE	FALSE	FALSE	8	3.750%	8	0.577%	1.414%	0.996885	0.975348	6,485,987	6,326,094	8	FALSE
22	FALSE	FALSE	FALSE	FALSE	9	3.750%	9	0.600%	1.616%	0.996885	0.972309	6,771,651	6,584,140	9	FALSE
23	FALSE	FALSE	FALSE	FALSE	10	3.750%	10	0.622%	1.823%	0.996885	0.969280	7,045,761	6,829,319	10	FALSE
24	FALSE	FALSE	FALSE	FALSE	11	3.750%	11	0.644%	2.034%	0.996885	0.966261	7,307,669	7,061,115	11	FALSE
25	FALSE	FALSE	FALSE	FALSE	12	3.750%	12	0.665%	2.248%	0.996885	0.963251	7,556,478	7,278,783	12	FALSE
26	FALSE	FALSE	FALSE	FALSE	13	3.750%	13	0.686%	2.464%	0.996885	0.960250	7,791,826	7,482,101	13	FALSE
27	FALSE	FALSE	FALSE	FALSE	14	3.750%	14	0.706%	2.683%	0.996885	0.957259	8,012,394	7,669,932	14	FALSE
28	FALSE	FALSE	FALSE	FALSE	15	3.750%	15	0.725%	2.903%	0.996885	0.954276	8,218,723	7,842,934	15	FALSE
29	FALSE	FALSE	FALSE	FALSE	16	3.750%	16	0.743%	3.124%	0.996885	0.951304	8,410,579	8,001,014	16	FALSE
30	FALSE	FALSE	FALSE	FALSE	17	3.750%	17	0.760%	3.345%	0.996885	0.948340	8,587,021	8,143,416	17	FALSE
31	FALSE	FALSE	FALSE	FALSE	18	3.750%	18	0.776%	3.566%	0.996885	0.945386	8,747,891	8,270,131	18	FALSE
32	FALSE	FALSE	FALSE	FALSE	19	3.750%	19	0.791%	3.787%	0.996885	0.942441	8,893,288	8,381,396	19	FALSE
33	FALSE	FALSE	FALSE	FALSE	20	3.750%	20	0.805%	4.006%	0.996885	0.939505	9,022,869	8,477,027	20	FALSE
34	FALSE	FALSE	FALSE	FALSE	21	3.750%	21	0.818%	4.224%	0.996885	0.936579	9,130,921	8,551,818	21	FALSE
35	FALSE	FALSE	FALSE	FALSE	22	3.750%	22	0.831%	4.439%	0.996885	0.933660	9,228,347	8,616,140	22	FALSE
36	FALSE	FALSE	FALSE	FALSE	23	3.750%	23	0.842%	4.652%	0.996885	0.930752	9,309,565	8,664,892	23	FALSE
37	FALSE	FALSE	FALSE	FALSE	24	3.750%	24	0.852%	4.861%	0.996885	0.927852	9,374,502	8,698,150	24	FALSE
38	FALSE	FALSE	FALSE	FALSE	25	3.750%	25	0.860%	5.067%	0.996885	0.924961	9,422,721	8,715,654	25	FALSE
39	FALSE	FALSE	FALSE	FALSE	26	3.750%	26	0.868%	5.267%	0.996885	0.922080	9,453,693	8,717,062	26	FALSE
40	FALSE	FALSE	FALSE	FALSE	27	3.750%	27	0.873%	5.463%	0.996885	0.919207	9,469,671	8,704,592	27	FALSE
41	FALSE	FALSE	FALSE	FALSE	28	3.750%	28	0.876%	5.654%	0.996885	0.916344	9,470,124	8,677,890	28	FALSE

EXHIBIT 2.16 Default Tests section and Present Value Factor calculation sections

Collateral Selection Results

Portfolio Totals	
2,368	Number of Loans
$537,852,271	Current Balances

Ineligible Collateral	
88	Number of Loans
$46,431,894	Current Balances
8.633%	% Balances

Eligible Collateral Summary	
2,279	Number of Loans
$491,420,377	Current Balances
91.367%	% Balances
8.505%	Wght Avg Coupon
191.62	Wght Avg Rem Term (months)
15.19	Wght Avg Seasoning (months)

Ineligible Collateral Detail		
		Min/Max Remaining Term
		Min/Max Original Term
25	$2,111,171	Min/Max Original Balance
83	$43,656,065	Min/Max Remaining Balance
		Exceeded Max LTV
5	$2,775,829	Min Floater Spread
		Excluded Geographic Region
		Inconsistent Orig vs. Rem Term
		Inconsistent Orig vs. Rem Balance
		Exceeded Calc vs. Stated Pmt
1	$429,347	Unacceptable Gross Coupon

EXHIBIT 2.17   Collateral Selection Results report

as lifetime interest rate floors and caps, periodic floors and caps, and the current coupon of the loan are been correctly determined by the program.

The various floor and cap levels are displayed and the calculated coupon rate is also plotted. To select a loan for display, merely enter its number and set the trace switch field to "Y". See Exhibit 2.18.

Coupon Trace Graph

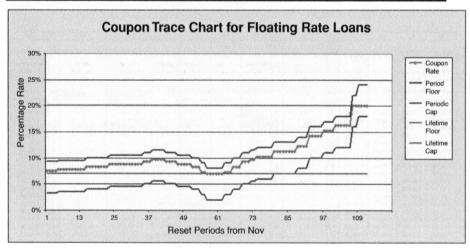

Period	Coupon Level	Index Level	Periodic Floor	Period Cap	Lifetime Floor	Lifetime Cap
1	7.50%	5.25%	3.25%	9.25%	7.00%	20.00%
2	7.50%	5.25%	3.25%	9.25%	7.00%	20.00%
3	7.50%	5.25%	3.25%	9.25%	7.00%	20.00%
4	7.50%	5.25%	3.25%	9.25%	7.00%	20.00%
5	7.75%	5.50%	3.50%	9.50%	7.00%	20.00%
6	7.75%	5.50%	3.50%	9.50%	7.00%	20.00%
7	7.75%	5.50%	3.50%	9.50%	7.00%	20.00%

Plot Coupon Pathway

Coupon Trace Switch	Y
Loan Numer	5

EXHIBIT 2.18   Coupon Trace report

VBA Modules

The code of the VBA model is organized into a set of 21 modules. An additional module, that does not contain any VBA code, is also provided so that the developers of the model can maintain a change log for the benefit of themselves and others.

This module structure is displayed in Exhibits 2.19a and 2.19b. The modules are grouped by task. Modules containing subroutines and functions used for input activities start with the prefix "Read_", those concerned with output, the prefix "Write". The main program is in its own module, as are the declarations of the global and Constant variables. The list below groups all the modules by the major function that they perform within the model. The degree of specialization of the modules within the group varies widely, and we should expect that given the wide range of dissimilar tasks they need to perform in the course of a single run of the model. We can however readily glimpse the broad underlying pattern of their grouping. The first set group containing the Main Model Module and the module that will hold the vast majority of the variable establishes the infrastructure framework of the model. The second group is focused on the receipt of the analyst's inputs, its verification, and finally acceptance into the model. The third grouping performs the collateral selection process. The fourth calculates the cash flows from the portion of the original portfolio deemed eligible for inclusion in the deal. The fifth group writes all of the external reports of the model. The sixth handles the Batch Mode function. The seventh and last module group consists of the modules that contain the miscellaneous support subroutines of the model and a change log.

Set #1. Main Model Module and the Global and Constant variable module group

"A_MainProgram". Contains the Main Program. This is the highest-level subroutine in the Structuring Model when it is being run in single scenario mode. In Batch Mode, the Batch Model calls the Main Program subroutine.

"A_Constants". All Constant global variables are declared in this module.

"A_Globals". All global variables are declared in this module.

Set #2. Menu Support module group

"MenusErrorChecking". Contains error checking subroutines for each of the menus and the code to construct and display the error messages.

"MenusReadInputs". Reads the post–error-tested menu contents into VBA arrays for use by the program.

"CollateralReadDataFile". Reads the designated collateral portfolio data file in VBA arrays for use by the model.

Set #3. Collateral Selection module group

"CollateralSelectionSubs". Performs the collateral selection based on the collateral selection criteria entered by the analyst.

Set #4. Cash Flow Generator module group

"CollateralCFGenerator". Computes the collateral cash flows for the portfolio on a loan-by-loan basis.

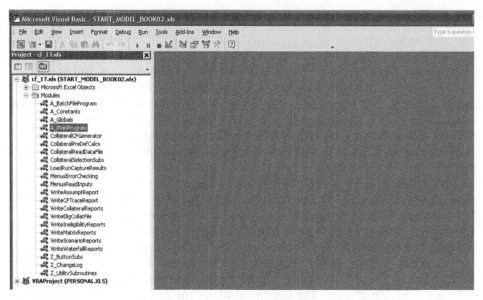

EXHIBIT 2.19   (a) Display of modules in the Visual Basic Editor

Name Prefix	Core Name	Function
A_	BatchFileProgram	Holds all code to run the Structuring Model in a Batch Mode
A_	Constants	Holds all the Constants variables declarations
A_	Globals	Holds all the Global variables declarations
A_	MainProgram	The Main Program of the model
Collateral	CFGenerator	Calculates collateral cash flows
Collateral	PreDefCals	Performs specialty prepayment and default calculations
Collateral	ReadDataFile	Finds, opens and reads collateral data file contents into VBA
Collateral	SelectionSubs	Performs the collateral eligibility selection process
Load	RunCaptureResults	Loads the collateral cash flows, calculates the waterfall, captures the results
Menus	ErrorChecking	Performs all menu input error checking, prints error messages
Menus	ReadInputs	Reads all menu inputs of the model into VBA variables
Write	AssumptReport	Outputs a set of assumptions pages into other reports
Write	CFTraceReports	Outputs cash flow loan-by-loan validation trace report
Write	CollateralReports	Outputs eligible collateral report package
Write	EligCollatFile	Outputs a file of that contains eligible collateral only
Write	IneligibleReports	Outputs ineligible collateral reports
Write	MatrixReports	Outputs summary reports of multiple scenario model runs
Write	ScenarioReports	Outputs the single page scenario report
Write	WaterfallReports	Outputs the complete waterfalls of all scenarios
Z_	ButtonSubs	Code that controls macro buttons on the menus
Z_	ChangeLog	Module to hold comments of changes over time
Z_	UtilitySubroutines	Code that performs various non calculation functions

EXHIBIT 2.19   (b) Table of module names and their functional descriptions

"CollateralPreDefCals". Sets up the prepayment and default factor vectors for each loan in the portfolio.

"LoadRunCaptureResults". Loads the collateral cash flows into the Liabilities Waterfall report, triggers the calculation of the waterfall, and captures the collateral cash flow sources and uses as well as the performance metrics of the debt.

Set #5. Report Package module group

"WriteAssumptReport". Writes the Assumptions Report.

"WriteCollateralReports". Writes the Eligible Collateral report package.

"WriteCFTraceReport". Writes the period-by-period, loan-by-loan, scenario-by-scenario cash flow trace file.

"WriteEligCollatFile". Opens and writes a collateral data file that contains only eligible loans based on the selection criteria last applied to the portfolio.

"WriteIneligibleReports". Writes the Ineligible Collateral report package that consists of the individual ineligible loan listing reports by test, the listing of all individual loans displaying each of their failed criteria, and a list of all unique ineligibility condition combinations and the number of loans that fell into each category.

"WriteMatrixReports". Writes the Matrix Summary report package.

"WriteScenarioReports". Writes a file of single-page summary Scenario reports.

"WriteWaterfallReports". Writes the complete Liabilities Waterfall report for each scenario of the model run that contains the Box Score and the waterfall in full detail.

Set #6. Batch Mode Run Option module

"A_BatchFileProgram". Contains all the subroutines necessary to run the Structuring Program in batch mode.

Set #7. Miscellaneous-purpose module group

"Z_ButtonSubs". Contains the code activated by the use of the button of the menus of the model.

"Z_ChangeLog". A blank module containing no VBA code used only to record changes to the model as an at-hand history of the development of the model, the people who worked on it, and contact information for them.

"Z_UtilitySubroutines". Utility and miscellaneous VBA code mostly used to map geographic codes, sort arrays, and other utilitarian purposes.

Report Template Files

The report template files are a critical component of the collection of files that, while external to the model itself, provide an indispensable role in the running of the model. These are the files that contain all the information concerning what inputs we entered into the model and the specific results that we obtained when we ran it. These reports fall into three groups by function:

1. **Assumptions report.** This report restates all of the inputs used in the run.
2. **Eligible and Ineligible Collateral reports.** These reports list the disposition of the collateral used in the deal.
3. **Structural Performance reports.** These reports inform us as to the performance of the collateral when subjected our amortization criteria. They also display the subsequent performance of the liabilities of the deal when those cash flows were applied to it.

Assumptions Page   A common feature to each of the report packages is the inclusion of an Assumptions Page report. This is a single-spreadsheet report that appears at the beginning (leftmost) position of the reports package workbook. It lists all the assumptions of the run for both the asset and liability side of the model. It may also include a summary of the collateral selection process if such a process was performed as part of the model run. See Exhibit 2.20.

Collateral Report Files   If a collateral selection process has been included in the modeling run, the analyst may elect to produce the Ineligible Collateral reports package. This package consists of three different reports. The first set of reports, one for each of the eligibility tests, consists of a list of all loans that have failed that individual test.

Not all loans fail only a single test. The much more likely situation is that the loan has failed multiple tests. Using the first set of reports only, there would be no way of detecting this fact without a laborious cross-tabulation of each loan on any of the tests. To address this situation, a second report contains a list, on a loan-by-loan basis, of all ineligible loans. This report displays all of the ineligible conditions for each loan.

The final report lists each of the unique patterns of ineligibility features for the loan. This allows the analyst to examine the portfolio to determine if there are any common trends in the collateral defects. It is also extremely useful in determining if there are any systemic data errors in the portfolio information. A large number of loans exhibiting an unusual combination of ineligibility factors may be the result of errors in the data-gathering process rather than in the true characteristics of the loans themselves.

Ineligible Collateral Report Package   The first report is the Individual Exception report. It lists all loans that have failed single eligibility criteria. See Exhibit 2.21.

The next report in the Ineligible Collateral report package lists each ineligible loan and displays any of the tests it has failed. See Exhibit 2.22.

Assumptions Page

Program Expenses

0.75%	Servicier Expense
0.20%	Program Expenses
1.00%	Conduit Spread

Seller Interest

5.000%	Initial Seller Interest

Principal Acceleration Triggers

5.000%	Rolling 3-Month Delinquency Rate
	Cumulative Default Trigger
10.000%	Clean-Up Call Level

Collateral Selection Criteria

Minimum	Maximum	
12	360	Original Term (Months)
12	360	Remaining Term (Months)
$25,000	$2,000,000	Original Balance
$25,000	$2,000,000	Remaining Balance
7.000%	11.000%	Gross Coupon
	80.000%	Maximum Total Project LTV%
	$5	Difference Stated-Calculated Pmt

Indices & Minimum Spreads

Index Code	Min Spread	
LIBOR	2.250%	Index #1 and Minimum Spread
	0.000%	Index #2 and Minimum Spread
	0.000%	Index #3 and Minimum Spread
	0.000%	Index #4 and Minimum Spread
	0.000%	Index #5 and Minimum Spread
	0.000%	Index #6 and Minimum Spread

Collateral Data File

C:\WBA_Class\WBA_Book\data\portfolio_orig_sprd.xls

Default Sensitivity

100.00%	Base Portfolio Default Rate
100.00%	Scenario Default Rate Step Increase
5	Scenarios
2	Default Methodology 1=CPR, 2=PSA, 3=User Defined

Prepayment Sensitivity

100.00%	Base Prepayment Rate Rate
50.00%	Scenario Prepayment Rate Step Increase
5	Scenarios
2	Prepayment Methodology 1=CPR, 2=PSA

Loss & Recovery

50.00%	Market Value Decline
36	Recovery Period (months)

Distribution of Defaulted Principal

Year 1	Year 11	Year 21
Year 2	Year 12	Year 22
Year 3	Year 13	Year 23
Year 4	Year 14	Year 24
Year 5	Year 15	Year 25
Year 6	Year 16	Year 26
Year 7	Year 17	Year 27
Year 8	Year 18	Year 28
Year 9	Year 19	Year 29
Year 10	Year 20	Year 30

Geographic Selection

TRUE	AK	Alaska
TRUE	AL	Alabama
TRUE	AR	Arkansas
TRUE	AZ	Arizona
TRUE	CA	California
TRUE	CO	Colorado
TRUE	CT	Connecticut
TRUE	DE	Delaware
TRUE	FL	Florida
TRUE	GA	Georgia
TRUE	HI	Hawaii
TRUE	IA	Iowa
TRUE	ID	Idaho
TRUE	IL	Illinois
TRUE	IN	Indiana
TRUE	KS	Kansas
TRUE	KY	Kentucky
TRUE	LA	Louisana
TRUE	MA	Massachusettes
TRUE	MD	Maryland
TRUE	ME	Maine
TRUE	MI	Michigan
TRUE	MN	Minnesota
TRUE	MO	Missouri
TRUE	MS	Mississippi
TRUE	MT	Montana
TRUE	NC	North Carolina

EXHIBIT 2.20 The Assumptions Page report

Collateral Selection Portfolio Exception Report
INELIGIBLE-3 Minimum/Maximum Original Bank Balance

	Loan Number	Selection Criteria	Obligor Number	Obligor Name	Current Yield	Current Bank Balance	Current Bank LTV	Current Equity Balance	Current Equity LTV	Original Appraisal Value
24				Averages/Totals		356,258	47.501%	393,742	52.499%	750,000
1	3	15,000			10.000%	11,617	38.72%	18,383	61.28%	30,000
2	58	24,400			10.000%	19,859	49.65%	20,141	50.35%	40,000
3	61	22,000			10.000%	17,476	43.69%	22,524	56.31%	40,000
4	240	24,800			10.000%	18,704	46.76%	21,296	53.24%	40,000
5	268	20,100			11.000%	17,402	58.01%	12,598	41.99%	30,000
6	375	24,000			10.000%	19,064	47.66%	20,936	52.34%	40,000
7	453	13,600			11.000%	11,273	56.36%	8,727	43.64%	20,000
8	456	21,000			11.000%	17,406	58.02%	12,594	41.98%	30,000
9	742	22,200			9.000%	16,128	53.76%	13,872	46.24%	30,000
10	1183	21,600			10.000%	18,805	47.01%	21,195	52.99%	40,000
11	1422	19,200			11.000%	15,550	51.83%	14,450	48.17%	30,000
12	1551	15,000			9.000%	11,211	37.37%	18,789	62.63%	30,000
13	1691	24,800			10.000%	18,193	45.48%	21,807	54.52%	40,000
14	1704	20,700			11.000%	18,656	62.19%	11,344	37.81%	30,000
15	1822	21,300			9.000%	15,474	51.58%	14,526	48.42%	30,000
16	1828	20,100			11.000%	17,219	57.40%	12,781	42.60%	30,000
17	1879	19,800			9.000%	17,525	58.42%	12,475	41.58%	30,000
18	1955	10,800			11.000%	6,838	34.19%	13,162	65.81%	20,000
19	2026	18,600			11.000%	12,396	41.32%	17,604	58.68%	30,000
20	2142	18,000			10.000%	12,443	41.48%	17,557	58.52%	30,000
21	2143	22,400			10.000%	15,484	38.71%	24,516	61.29%	40,000
22	2165	15,000			9.000%	10,417	34.72%	19,583	65.28%	30,000
23	2185	10,400			11.000%	7,702	38.51%	12,298	61.49%	20,000
24	2252	12,600			9.000%	9,418	47.09%	10,582	52.91%	20,000

EXHIBIT 2.21   Single Exception report

The last report in the package lists all unique combinations of ineligibility conditions and the number of loans having that particular pattern of ineligibility. See Exhibit 2.23.

Eligible Collateral Report Package (Stratification Reports)   Having dispensed with the Ineligible report package, let us move on to those loans that have passed all the eligibility tests. The first report in this package is a simple list of each loan in the portfolio, its eligibility status, either "Accepted" or "Rejected", and its basic information. See Exhibit 2.24.

The second set of reports is a series of standard stratification reports that describe the eligible loans along a number of characteristics such as balance, type, loan to value (LTV), term, seasoning, and coupon. See Exhibit 2.25.

Structural Performance Reports   These reports display both the performance of the collateral cash flows generated using our prepayment, default, MVD and recovery assumptions, and the performance of the liability structure.

Waterfall Report Package   The Waterfall report file consists of a series of spreadsheets, one for each of the cash flow scenarios generated in the model run, that display the entire liabilities waterfall and its attendant Box Score summary. See Exhibit 2.26.

Loan Listing Exception Report
Individual Loan Ineligibility Conditions

Ineligibility Condition Reference

1 = Min/Max Remaining Term	7 = Excluded State or Geographic Region
2 = Min/Max Original Term	8 = Inconsistent Original vs Remaining Term
3 = Min Max Original Balance	9 = Inconsistent Original vs Remaining Balance
4 = Min/Max Current Balance	10 = Calculated vs. Stated Payment Differences
5 = Exceeds Maximum LTV	11 = Unacceptable Gross Coupon
6 = Unacceptable Floater Indice/Spread	

Total Loans Rejected	Loan Number	Ineligibility Condition											Loan Yield	Current Balance
		1	2	3	4	5	6	7	8	9	10	11		
56		0	0	24	52	0	4	0	0	0	0	1	7.940%	3,024,285
1	3			1	1								10.000%	11,617
2	58			1	1								10.000%	19,859
3	61			1	1								10.000%	17,476
4	76				1								10.000%	20,587
5	175				1								10.000%	22,014
6	196				1								10.000%	20,136
7	222				1								10.000%	21,094
8	224				1								10.000%	22,931
9	230			1	1								10.000%	20,826
10	240				1								10.000%	18,704
11	268			1	1								11.000%	17,402
12	283				1								9.000%	24,306
13	308				1								10.000%	21,742
14	375			1	1								10.000%	19,064
15	453			1	1								11.000%	11,273
16	456			1	1								11.000%	17,406
17	563						1						7.000%	539,480

EXHIBIT 2.22 Loan Listing Exception report

Summary Exception Report
Contracts Grouped By Unique Ineligibility Combinations

Ineligibility Condition Reference	
1 = Min/Max Remaining Term	7 = Excluded State or Geographic Region
2 = Min/Max Original Term	8 = Inconsistent Original vs Remaining Term
3 = Min Max Original Balance	9 = Inconsistent Original vs Remaining Balance
4 = Min/Max Current Balance	10 = Calculated vs. Stated Payment Differences
5 = Exceeds Maximum LTV	11 = Unacceptable Gross Coupon
6 = Unacceptable Floater Indice/Spread	

Unique Ineligibility Code	Ineligibility Condition											Number of Loans	Total Current Balance	Total Equity Position
	1	2	3	4	5	6	7	8	9	10	11			
	0	0	1	2	0	2	0	0	0	0	1	56	3,024,285	646,065
8				1								28	620,496	25,150
12		1	1									24	356,258	10,582
32						1						3	1,618,184	69,679
1056						1					1	1	429,347	540,653

EXHIBIT 2.23 Summary Exception report

Eligible Collateral—All Loans
Final Securitization Status of all Loans of the Portfolio

Loan Number	Obligor Name	Current Bank Loan Balance	Original Term	Remain Term	Current Yield	Index if Floating Rate	Spread to Index	Current Equity Balance
Totals	Totals	461,898,460	202.47	187.11	8.511%		3.261%	365,601,540
1	Accepted	29,569	84	59	9.000%	LIBOR	3.7500%	40,431
2	Accepted	50,137	84	61	9.000%	LIBOR	3.7500%	69,863
3	Rejected	11,617	84	59	10.000%	LIBOR	4.7500%	18,383
4	Accepted	55,317	84	58	9.000%	LIBOR	3.7500%	44,683
5	Accepted	201,825	120	114	9.000%	LIBOR	3.7500%	78,175
6	Accepted	53,980	84	76	9.000%	LIBOR	3.7500%	46,020
7	Accepted	320,030	120	113	7.750%	LIBOR	2.5000%	239,970
8	Accepted	25,224	84	58	10.000%	LIBOR	4.7500%	34,776
9	Accepted	60,494	84	76	9.000%	LIBOR	3.7500%	39,506
10	Accepted	53,871	83	77	9.000%	LIBOR	3.7500%	26,129
11	Accepted	32,223	83	51	9.000%	LIBOR	3.7500%	47,777
12	Accepted	50,428	84	60	9.000%	LIBOR	3.7500%	39,572
13	Accepted	39,652	84	71	9.000%	LIBOR	3.7500%	30,348
14	Accepted	70,752	84	56	9.000%	LIBOR	3.7500%	49,248
15	Accepted	59,140	84	74	9.000%	LIBOR	3.7500%	60,860
16	Accepted	67,290	84	58	9.000%	LIBOR	3.7500%	52,710
17	Accepted	47,311	84	59	9.000%	LIBOR	3.7500%	62,689
18	Accepted	29,117	83	73	10.000%	LIBOR	4.7500%	30,883
19	Accepted	36,211	119	98	9.000%	LIBOR	3.7500%	33,789
20	Accepted	31,530	84	55	9.000%	LIBOR	3.7500%	38,470
21	Accepted	558,321	276	274	7.750%	LIBOR	2.5000%	421,679
22	Accepted	51,109	83	73	9.000%	LIBOR	3.7500%	28,891
23	Accepted	44,461	84	55	9.000%	LIBOR	3.7500%	45,539
24	Accepted	59,597	84	61	9.000%	LIBOR	3.7500%	60,403

EXHIBIT 2.24 Final Securitization Status report

Eligible Collateral Report #2
Current Balances Distribution by Remaining Terms

	4	5	6	7	8	9	10	11	12	13	14	15	16
Remaining Term Range	Number of Loans	Current Loan Balance	Current Loan LTV	% Current Balances	Cum % Current Balances	Average Loan Balance	WtAvg Current Yield	WtAvg Original Term	WtAvg Remain Term	WtAvg Current Seasoning	Equity Balance	Equity % Appraisal	Total Appraisal
	2,199	458,874,175									362,915,825		821,790,000
13 to 24	1	134,158	43.277%	0.029%	0.029%	134,158	8.500%	60.00	20.00	40.00	175,842	56.723%	310,000
25 to 36	3	266,669	40.404%	0.058%	0.087%	88,890	9.000%	74.03	33.51	40.52	393,331	59.596%	660,000
37 to 48	35	2,482,623	42.366%	0.541%	0.628%	70,932	8.927%	81.44	43.97	37.47	3,377,377	57.634%	5,860,000
49 to 60	140	9,346,263	48.301%	2.037%	2.665%	66,759	8.925%	83.53	54.77	28.76	10,003,737	51.699%	19,350,000
61 to 72	175	13,747,882	55.257%	2.996%	5.661%	78,559	8.913%	85.04	66.53	18.51	11,132,118	44.743%	24,880,000
73 to 84	213	19,320,271	57.347%	4.210%	9.872%	90,705	8.911%	92.31	78.17	14.14	14,369,729	42.653%	33,690,000
85 to 96	148	20,167,543	51.619%	4.395%	14.267%	136,267	8.711%	114.85	90.99	23.86	18,902,457	48.381%	39,070,000
97 to 108	257	41,680,023	56.955%	9.083%	23.350%	162,179	8.693%	118.54	102.89	15.65	31,499,977	43.045%	73,180,000
109 to 120	336	68,123,225	62.665%	14.846%	38.195%	202,748	8.654%	120.19	114.17	6.02	40,586,775	37.335%	108,710,000
121 to 132	16	3,759,259	54.880%	0.819%	39.015%	234,954	8.652%	140.98	126.61	14.37	3,090,741	45.120%	6,850,000
133 to 144	27	8,858,919	50.192%	1.931%	40.945%	328,108	8.555%	158.84	137.36	21.48	8,791,081	49.808%	17,650,000
145 to 156	25	7,931,193	53.698%	1.728%	42.674%	317,248	8.585%	169.86	151.23	18.64	6,838,807	46.302%	14,770,000
157 to 168	28	10,047,532	58.861%	2.190%	44.863%	358,840	8.495%	179.08	162.37	16.70	7,022,468	41.139%	17,070,000
169 to 180	27	10,247,186	52.388%	2.233%	47.096%	379,525	8.665%	190.82	173.86	16.96	9,312,814	47.612%	19,560,000
181 to 192	28	7,716,822	46.487%	1.682%	48.778%	275,601	8.479%	213.78	187.05	26.73	8,883,178	53.513%	16,600,000
193 to 204	50	12,307,482	46.217%	2.682%	51.460%	246,150	8.482%	225.50	198.40	27.11	14,322,518	53.783%	26,630,000
205 to 216	63	17,344,535	50.100%	3.780%	55.240%	275,310	8.446%	235.73	211.29	24.43	17,275,465	49.900%	34,620,000
217 to 228	70	20,141,202	55.424%	4.389%	59.629%	287,731	8.478%	240.80	223.01	17.79	16,198,798	44.576%	36,340,000
229 to 240	58	17,424,144	58.119%	3.797%	63.426%	300,416	8.366%	243.90	234.55	9.35	12,555,856	41.881%	29,980,000

EXHIBIT 2.25 Sample Stratification report

49

Single Scenario Cash Flow Waterfall Report

| 100% | PSA | <= Default Rate |
| 100% | PSA | <= Prepayment Rate |

Summary Report

Collateral Cash Flows		
Scheduled Amortization	300,605,088	
Prepayments to Principal	178,508,881	36.33%
Total Principal Retired	479,113,970	
Defaulted Principal	12,306,408	2.50%
Recoveries of Principal (& rate)	10,518,849	85.47%
Coupon Income	293,712,379	
Total Cash Sources	783,345,198	
Debt Cash Flows		
Program Fees	6,527,841	
Servicing Fee	26,128,463	
Conduit Debt Service	122,397,021	
Conduit Principal Payments	466,849,358	
Released to Seller	161,442,514	
Total Cash Uses	783,345,198	

Performance	Conduit	Seller Interest
Structuring		
Beginning Conduit Balance	466,849,358	24,571,019
Ownership Interest	95.00%	5.00%
Performance		
Principal Outstanding	$ -	0.00%
Severity of Loss	0.000%	0.00%

Collateral Cash Flow

1	2	3	4	5	6	7
	Beginning Principal Balance	Pool Factor	Regular Amort Principal	Prepaid Principal	Defaulted Principal	Ending Principal Balance Outstanding
			300,605,088	178,508,881	12,306,408	
1	491,420,377	1.00000	1,924,713	81,637	124,057	489,289,971
2	489,289,971	0.99566	1,937,728	162,706	130,387	487,059,150
3	487,059,150	0.99113	1,950,480	243,155	136,520	484,728,994
4	484,728,994	0.98638	1,962,960	322,935	142,483	482,300,616
5	482,300,616	0.98144	1,975,164	401,993	148,279	479,773,179
6	479,773,179	0.97630	1,987,084	480,282	153,872	477,153,941
7	477,153,941	0.97097	1,998,715	557,750	159,272	474,438,204
8	474,438,204	0.96544	2,010,051	634,350	164,399	471,629,403
9	471,629,403	0.95973	2,021,086	710,036	169,312	468,728,969
10	468,728,969	0.95382	2,031,815	784,759	173,968	465,738,428
11	465,738,428	0.94774	2,042,232	858,474	178,355	462,659,367
12	462,659,367	0.94147	2,052,332	931,137	182,414	459,493,484
13	459,493,484	0.93503	2,062,111	1,002,704	186,169	456,242,500
14	456,242,500	0.92842	2,071,563	1,073,133	189,463	452,908,342
15	452,908,342	0.92163	2,080,684	1,142,382	192,469	449,492,807
16	449,492,807	0.91468	2,089,470	1,210,412	195,214	445,997,711
17	445,997,711	0.90757	2,097,916	1,277,183	197,584	442,425,027

EXHIBIT 2.26 Waterfall report package

Single Scenario Report   The Single Scenario Summary report package contains a summarized version of all the information on a waterfall report spreadsheet. Here the intent is to reduce the size of the report to a single sheet that contains all of the assumptions of the run and the collateral and liabilities cash flows in a summarized form and a small graphic display. See Exhibit 2.27.

Summary Matrix Report   The Summary Matrix report is intended to present a summary of up to 100 different scenarios that comprise a single model run. Each cell in the matrix of the report body lists between five and six results. The Summary Matrix report allows these results to be quickly and easily compared across a wide number of scenarios and has the added advantage of being a single-page report. See Exhibit 2.28.

CURRENT MODEL ENVIRONMENT

This is the directory structure you need to establish prior to downloading the material from the Web site. Place the files as indicated and the program will run:

```
C:\VBABook_2
   \Code
      \data
          portfolio_comb.xls
      \model
          STRUCTURING_MODEL_Ver0.xls
      \output
      \templates
          ac_inelig_template.xls
          ac_collat_template.xls
          ac_waterfall_template.xls
          ac_matrix_template.xls
          ac_datafile_template.xls
          ac_scenario_template.xls
```

ON THE WEB SITE

There are four Web chapters that cover the following topics:

- **Web Chapter 2.1.** This Web chapter, "Securitizing a Loan Portfolio," contains a description of the steps in the securitization process. It also discusses who is involved in the process and what role each of the parties plays in the transaction.
- **Web Chapter 2.2.** This Web chapter, "The Liability Waterfall Spreadsheet," contains a detailed description of the liabilities waterfall spreadsheet.
- **Web Chapter 2.3.** This Web chapter, "Mortgage Math," contains a discussion of the basic financial mathematics of amortizing mortgages.
- **Web Chapter 2.4.** This Web chapter, "Bond Math," contains a discussion of the basic financial mathematics of the concepts of present and future value and how they relate to the valuation of fixed income liabilities.
- **Web Chapter 2.5.** This Web Chapter "Running the Model" contains a step-by-step for running the original model.

Single-Scenario Summary Report

SCENARIO ASSUMPTIONS

Program Expenses

Servicer Expense	0.750%
Program Expenses	0.200%
Conduit Coupon	1.000%

Principal Acceleration Triggers

Rolling 3M Doling Rate	5.00%
Clean Up Call	10.00%
Non-Quant Perfomance	0

Collateral Selection Criteria

Collateral Data File

Data3.xls

Minimum	Maximum	Criteria
0	0	Orig Term
0	0	Remain Term
0	0	Orig Balance
0	0	Remain Bal
0.000%	0.000%	Gross Coupon
	0.00%	Maximum LT
	0.00	Pmt Difference

Floating Rate Index and Min Spre

Index	Min Spread
	0.00%
	0.00%
	0.00%
	0.00%
	0.00%

Loss & Recovery Parameters

Market Value Decline	50.00%
Recovery Period (months)	12

Prepayment Assumptions

Rate	200.00%
Methodology	PSA

Default Assumptions

Rate	400.00%
Methodology	PSA

stribution of USER Defined Defaul

Years 1-10	Years 11-20	Years 21-30

SOURCES AND USES

Collateral Cash Flows		
Scheduled Amortization	197,427,612	
Prepayments to Principal	252,247,689	51.33%
Total Principal Retired	449,675,300	
Defaulted Principal	41,745,077	8.49%
Principal Recoveries	35,765,295	85.68%
Coupon Income	216,235,379	
Total Cash Sources	**701,675,975**	
Debt Cash Flows		
Program Fees	4,739,182	
Servicing Fee	19,216,364	
Conduit Debt Service	88,859,663	
Conduit Principal Paymen	466,849,358	
Released to Seller	122,011,408	
Total Cash Uses	**701,675,975**	

Performance	**Conduit**	**Seller**
Structuring		
Beginning Balance	466,849,358	24,571,019
Ownership Interest	95.00%	5.00%
Performance		
Principal Outstanding	$ -	0.00%
Severity of Loss	0.000%	0.00%
IRR	3.750%	49.880%
Tenor (yrs)		
Average Life	5.076	
Final Maturity	17.000	
Modified Duration	4.418	
Macauley Duration	4.259	
Structural Triggers		
Program Fee Shortfall	FALSE	
Servicing Fee Shortfall	FALSE	
Interest Shortfall	FALSE	

	1	2	3	4	5	6	7	8	9	10	11
	Collateral Cashflows						Expenses		Conduit Performance		
YEAR	Beginning Principal Balance	Regular Amort Principal	Prepaid Principal	Defaulted Principal	Coupon Paid	Recoveries of Principal	Program Fee	Servicing Fees	Balance	Interest Expense	Principal Paid
		197.4	252.2	41.7	216.2	35.8	4.7	19.2		88.9	466.8
1	452.6	23.6	12.3	7.4	40.2	0.0	0.9	3.6	430.0	16.9	41.2
2	389.2	24.0	31.7	9.1	35.6	6.6	0.8	3.1	369.7	15.0	61.6
3	315.6	23.1	42.0	8.3	29.6	7.9	0.7	2.6	299.8	12.4	69.7
4	251.5	21.4	35.3	6.4	23.7	7.1	0.5	2.1	239.0	10.0	59.9
5	199.0	19.1	28.0	4.5	18.7	5.4	0.4	1.7	189.0	7.9	49.0
6	156.8	16.4	22.1	2.8	14.8	3.8	0.3	1.3	149.0	6.2	39.3
7	123.3	13.9	17.4	1.6	11.6	2.4	0.3	1.0	117.2	4.9	31.2
8	96.7	11.7	13.7	0.8	9.1	1.3	0.2	0.8	91.8	3.9	24.8
9	75.9	9.3	10.7	0.3	7.1	0.7	0.2	0.6	72.1	3.0	19.3
10	60.8	6.0	8.5	0.1	5.6	0.3	0.1	0.5	57.8	2.4	13.9
11	49.6	4.1	6.9	0.1	4.6	0.1	0.1	0.4	46.7	1.9	11.2
12	40.2	3.7	5.6	0.1	3.7	0.1	0.1	0.3	35.3	1.5	11.2
13	32.2	3.3	4.5	0.0	3.0	0.0	0.1	0.3	25.7	1.1	9.5
14	25.5	3.0	3.6	0.0	2.4	0.0	0.0	0.2	17.5	0.8	8.0
15	19.9	2.6	2.8	0.0	1.9	0.0	0.0	0.2	10.7	0.5	6.7
16	15.3	2.4	2.2	0.0	1.4	0.0	0.0	0.1	5.0	0.3	5.7
17	11.4	2.1	1.6	0.0	1.1	0.0	0.0	0.1	0.2	0.1	4.5
18	8.3	1.8	1.2	0.0	0.8	0.0	0.0	0.1	0.0	0.0	0.0
19	5.8	1.6	0.9	0.0	0.6	0.0	0.0	0.1	0.0	0.0	0.0
#	3.9	1.3	0.6	0.0	0.4	0.0	0.0	0.0	0.0	0.0	0.0
21	2.4	1.1	0.4	0.0	0.3	0.0	0.0	0.0	0.0	0.0	0.0
#	1.3	0.9	0.2	0.0	0.1	0.0	0.0	0.0	0.0	0.0	0.0
#	0.5	0.6	0.1	0.0	0.1	0.0	0.0	0.0	0.0	0.0	0.0
#	0.1	0.4	0.0	0.0	0.0	0.0	0.0	0.0	0.0	0.0	0.0
#	0.0	0.1	0.0	0.0	0.0	0.0	0.0	0.0	0.0	0.0	0.0
#	0.0	0.0	0.0	0.0	0.0	0.0	0.0	0.0	0.0	0.0	0.0
#	0.0	0.0	0.0	0.0	0.0	0.0	0.0	0.0	0.0	0.0	0.0
#	0.0	0.0	0.0	0.0	0.0	0.0	0.0	0.0	0.0	0.0	0.0
#	0.0	0.0	0.0	0.0	0.0	0.0	0.0	0.0	0.0	0.0	0.0
#	0.0	0.0	0.0	0.0	0.0	0.0	0.0	0.0	0.0	0.0	0.0

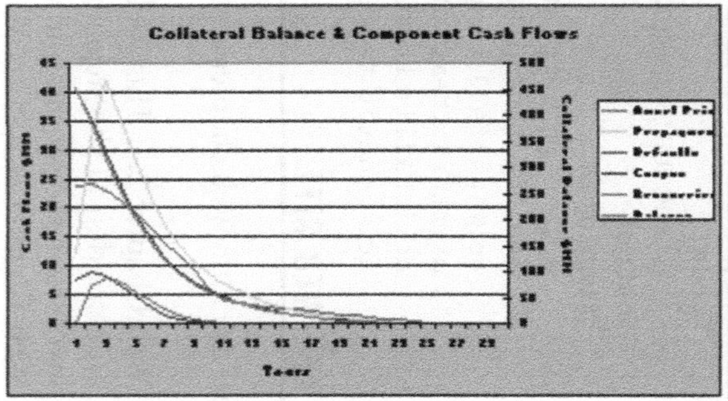

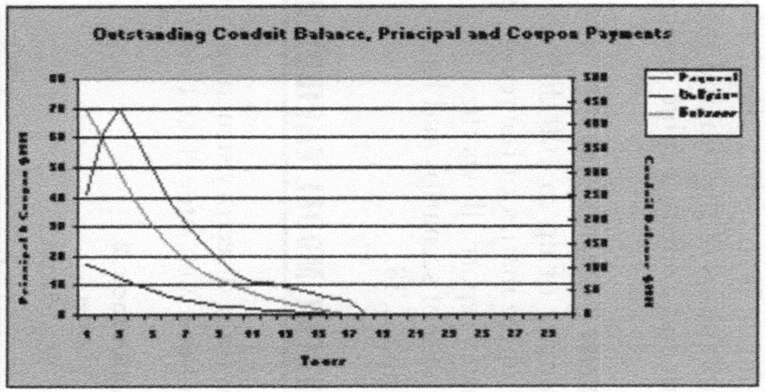

EXHIBIT 2.27 Single Scenario Summary report package

Summary Matrix Report #2
Collateral Cash Flow Report

> Total Scheduled Amortization
> Total Prepayment to Principal
> Total Principal Retired
> Total Defaults of Principal
> Total Recoveries of Principal
> Total Coupon Cash Flows

Default Levels	PSA Prepayment Methodology				
	1	2	3	4	5
	100.00%	125.00%	150.00%	175.00%	200.00%
1 100.00% PSA	305,611,089 173,668,115 479,279,203 12,141,174 10,378,710 237,462,260	278,134,403 201,541,716 479,676,119 11,744,258 10,044,703 221,851,254	254,692,895 225,358,804 480,051,699 11,368,678 9,728,578 208,071,926	234,565,599 245,842,068 480,407,666 11,012,711 9,428,888 195,858,979	217,171,836 263,573,700 480,745,535 10,674,842 9,144,361 184,989,584
2 150.00% PSA	301,788,990 171,536,413 473,325,403 18,094,974 15,469,001 234,955,170	274,779,344 199,134,678 473,914,022 17,506,355 14,973,664 219,596,597	251,730,701 222,740,410 474,471,111 16,949,266 14,504,754 206,036,858	231,935,753 243,063,456 474,999,209 16,421,168 14,060,138 194,015,595	214,824,781 260,675,768 475,500,549 15,919,828 13,637,939 183,314,115
3	298,017,063	271,467,280	248,805,541	229,337,968	212,505,616

EXHIBIT 2.28　Summary Matrix report package

The following models, data files, and report template files are also on the Web site:

- "STRUCTURE_MODEL_Ver0.xls". This is the current structuring model.
- "portfolio_orig.xls". This is the initial collateral file.
- "portfolio_add.xls". This is a file of additional collateral available for inclusion in the deal.
- "portfolio_comb.xls". This is the combined portfolio of "porfolio.org" and "portfolio.add" above.
- "Select00_Collateral.xls". The original collateral pool.
- "Select01_Collateral.xls" and "Select01_Ineligible.xls". Collateral after initial financial screening.
- "Select02_Collateral.xls" and "Select02_Ineligible.xls". Eligible and ineligible collateral after geographic selection and concentration tests.
- "Select03_Collateral.xls" and "Select03_Ineligible.xls". Final eligible and ineligible collateral files.
- "Select03_CollateralData.xls". This is the file containing the final eligible collateral pool.
- "portfolio_comb.xls". This is a portfolio of unguaranteed small business loans. You will need to perform the collateral selection process on these loans when you run the model.

- "ac_inelig_template.xls". The template report file for the Ineligible Collateral report package.
- "ac_collat_template.xls". The template report file for the Eligible Collateral report package.
- "ac_waterfall_template.xls". The template report file for the waterfall report package.
- "ac_matrix_template.xls. The report template file for the Matrix Summary report package".
- "ac_datafile_template.xls". The template of the portfolio data file of Eligible Collateral Data file.
- "ac_scenario_template.xls". The template report file of the Single Scenario report package.
- "ac_cf_trace_template.xls". The template report file for the Cash Flow Trace report.
- **"BaseEC_Waterfall", "BaseEC_Collateral", "BaseEC_Matrix", and "BaseEC_Scenario".** These files are the ouput files of the Expected Case run of the model.

## CHAPTER 3

Conventions and Advice

OVERVIEW

This chapter addresses two different topics. This is the last chapter that is general in nature; the remaining chapters are very focused on a particular topic and explore that topic within a tightly specified framework. The two topics of this chapter are VBA coding conventions and general advice.

Beginning with Chapter 5 and ending with Chapter 20, only three chapters do not contain a discussion of VBA or Access code in one form or another. In Chapters 5 and 6 you will divide the existing base model into an asset side model and a liabilities side model. In Chapters 8 to 13 you will rebuild and expand the asset side model. In Chapters 14 to 16 you will expand the liabilities side model. In Chapters 17 and 18 you will learn how to integrate VBA with Access and employ it in both the new asset and the new liabilities model. In Chapter 19 you will integrate MS Outlook and PowerPoint with VBA. You will see VBA, VBA, and more VBA.

As you peruse the 750+ exhibits in this book, you will notice that over 80% of them involve VBA code in one form or another. Not long into your reading, you will probably notice recurrent patterns in the manner and style of the VBA code. These recurrent patterns are a result of a predetermined set of rules that are helpful in developing VBA that is clear, supportable, and sustainable over the foreseeable life of the average application. Some of these guidelines are at the application level. This is to say that they affect the form and content of the entire model. An example of this type of feature would be a specific practice as to how VBA modules are organized and named. Another set of guidelines relate to the appearance of the code. These determine how the code is visibly configured. An example of this is commenting and indentation. Finally we address such seemingly mundane subjects such as naming conventions.

Collectively we refer to these sections as the "Conventions" section of the chapter. The term "conventions" is used instead of "standards" because "standards" tend to imply a degree of enforcement and conformation to a guideline that is altogether too stringent for these recommendations. Instead we will use "conventions," which implies agreement between free parties of their own consent. These practices are just common ideas and usages that we and many other people have found useful over time. It is assumed that anyone reading this book already has some experience programming in VBA. In fact, some readers will have considerable experience. My message to both groups of readers is this: Read the sections. If you find the material useful, all the better; if you do not, that is up to you.

This short list of guidelines is neither exhaustive nor unequivocal. Take the time to read it, however. You may find something useful!

The second part of the chapter is completely subjective in nature. It is a section of advice. Six short topics are presented. These observations on experience. The definition of "experience" is :

Experience is what you get when you don't get what you want!

Readers are advised that they can, as with the first section of the chapter, take it or leave it as they see fit.

DELIVERABLES

The modeling knowledge deliverables for this chapter are:

- A brief set of guidelines and examples of various VBA code development practices.
- Some advice.

VBA CONVENTIONS

The following is a list of practices that we have found useful over time and will discuss below.

- Application level practices
  - Modules
    - Use of modules
    - Naming of modules
  - Declaring global Constants and variables
  - Form of the Main Program subroutine
  - Subroutines
    - Suggested length
    - Naming conventions
    - Use of utility subroutines
- Code level practices
  - Use and abuse of continuation statements
  - If..Then..EndIf statements
  - Select..Case statements and loops
  - Abbreviation of module, subroutine and variable names
  - Use of comments statements
    - Worse than useless commenting practices
    - Commenting subroutine mastheads
    - Commenting variables
    - Explanatory comments in the body of the code

Application-Level Practices

May you be blessed with small applications! However, sometimes we do not have that luxury. You certainly do *not* have it in this book. When you are faced with building a larger application, you need to spend some time and thought as to how you are going to organize it. You need to impose a structure to make it easier for anyone, especially you, to understand how the code will work. This structure will make it easy to identify where the various functional tasks of the code are performed. It will also help you when the time comes for changing the code (as it surely will).

Modules   VBA modules should be used to hold related collections of VBA subroutines that perform the same tasks. They are *not* meant simply to perform the role of buckets that you dump your code into without any thought to structure or organization.

Each module should hold the related code that performs a major task. This task may be to perform a set of calculations or manipulate information needed by the model. Typical major tasks or data handling requirements are:

- Global Constant variables used by the model.
- Global variables used by the model.
- Main program of the model.
- Menu handling and Menu support code (especially menu input error checking code).
- Major data handling tasks (reading data files or assumption files into the model).
- Calculation sequences.
- Report writing for a specific report or related collection of reports.

Grouping the task-related subroutines in a module is only the first step of the process. You must name the module so that it is immediately apparent to you, and anyone else, what role the module performs and what type of code it contains. This allows you not only to identify where the code is but to segregate the code by function.

If you attach a functional prefix to the names of the modules, you are off to a good start in establishing a meaningful identification system. For example:

- "Calc_" for modules performing calculations.
- "Menu_" or "MenuSupport_" for menu handling and menu error checking code.
- "Data_", "DataInput_", "DataFile_", or the like for the data input or output tasks.
- "DBase_" for code that interacts with databases.
- "Report_" for report writing functions.
- "Constant_" for global Constant variables.
- "Global_" for global variables.

Using a naming convention system is a subject either omitted entirely or mentioned only in passing by most VBA development books. However, taking a small amount of effort each time you develop a module in your model will save you lots of time and trouble in the future. A list of the final modules names for the expanded

Asset side of the model follows this type of module naming convention. It is readily apparent where the global variables and the global Constant variables are declared. The "A-" prefix is used so that they appear at the top of the module list. Calculation, menu support, data, and reporting modules are all clearly identified by both a group prefix and a functional suffix. Thus:

```
CollatCFs_CalcFactorsCoupon
```

is a module containing the calculation subroutines for coupon income from the collateral.

```
Report_Assumptions
```

is the module that produces the model run time assumptions report file. The full list of module names for the finished asset-side model, the "Collateral Cash Flow Generator," is shown in Exhibit 3.1.

Global Constants and Global Variables   Global Constant variables and all other global variables should be grouped in their own modules. The module names should be prefixed by the letter "A-". The VBA Project Explorer window lists modules alphabetically. Modules with the "A-" prefix will appear at the top of the module list. Each global variable and global Constant in either module should have a descriptive in-line comment at the end of its declaration. Related items should be grouped, and the group should be identified.

   To the extent that there is a strongly related collection of variables or constants the names should have functional prefixes (mirroring the practice for naming VBA modules). Constant variables should be spelled out in all-capital letters. All global variables should have the prefix "g" before any other part of the name. All variables that have a modular scope, except for utility variables such as loop counters, should be prefixed with an "m". For example, a modular variable that aggregates the number of loans by loan type might be named "mLoanNumByType". See Exhibit 3.2 for an example of constant variables and Exhibit 3.3 for examples of the declaration and naming of global variables.

Main Program   The main program should be short and concise. It should call only the highest-level subroutines that trigger the most major blocks of model activity. All housekeeping and other auxiliary functional should be placed well clear of the code of the main program. You should be able to read down the list of subroutine calls from the main program and be able to determine the precise sequence of major activities performed by the model in a typical run.

   The main program should be placed in its own module and named "A_MainProgram" or "A_(Application Name)". See Exhibit 3.4.

Subroutines   Subroutines should be tightly focused to perform a single action. Subroutines that work on a major task should be grouped together in a module that is clearly identified as holding the VBA for that task.

EXHIBIT 3.1 Modules of the Collateral Cash Flow Generator

Length An excellent rule of thumb is that if a subroutine does not fit easily on a single screen display, say less than 40 lines of VBA code, it is probably too long. It is highly likely that there are identifiable subtasks being performed in the subroutine. These subtasks themselves would be candidates for their *own* subroutines.

Names Subroutines should contain a prefix in their name that identifies the module in which they reside. The suffix of the name should inform the reader what function

```
'==================================================================================
'FINANCIAL AND DEMOGRAPHIC SELECTION CRITERIA
'==================================================================================
Public Const NUM_FINANCIAL_ITEMS = 53    'number of financial items in data file
'financial criteria test parameteres
Public Const NUM_OPERATOR_ITEMS = 6      '# of logical comparison operators
Public Const NUM_SEL_SETS = 5            '# of selection test sets
Public Const NUM_SEL_TESTS = 20          '# of collateral selection tests per set
Public Const MAX_SEL_ITEMS = 3           'maximum number of criteria
Public Const MAX_SEL_OPERS = 10          'maximum number of operators
Public Const MAX_SEL_VALUE = 10          'maximum number of comparison values
'constants for the isNumeric tests for the Set and Test fields of the menu
Public Const ISNUMERIC_TEST_ONLY = 1     'isNumeric for the Test Field Only
Public Const ISNUMERIC_SET_ONLY = 2      'isNumeric for the Set Field Only
Public Const ISNUMERIC_TEST_SET = 3      'isNumeric for the Set and Test Fields
'read the financial selection criteris from a data file
Public Const FINSEL_MAX_RECORDS = NUM_SEL_TESTS * NUM_SEL_SETS
Public Const FINSEL_REC_START = 6        'start row fin criteria selection test file
Public Const MAX_LABELS = 10             'data labels (appraisal types, etc)
'==================================================================================
'COLATERAL POOL MENU
'==================================================================================
Public Const COLLAT_STARTROW = 3
Public Const COLLAT_ENDCOL = 55
'mortgage amortization types
Public Const NUM_MORT_TYPES = 6
Public Const MORTTYPE_FIXED_RATE = 1
Public Const MORTTYPE_STAND_ARM = 2
Public Const MORTTYPE_HYBRID_ARM = 3
Public Const MORTTYPE_OPTION_ARM = 4
Public Const MORTTYPE_BALLOON_FIXED = 5
Public Const MORTTYPE_BALLOON_ARM = 6
```

EXHIBIT 3.2   Constant variable declarations

```
'==================================================================================
'RUN OPTIONS MENU
'==================================================================================
Public gPortActive(0 To NUM_PORTS)   As Boolean  'is this portfolio active?
Public gROInitDataTest               As Boolean  'apply base collat screening
Public gROApplyFinDemo()             As Boolean  'apply fin/demo test
Public gROApplyGeoSelect()           As Boolean  'apply geo test
Public gROTestSetFinDemo()           As Integer  'apply fin/demo test
Public gROTestSetGeoSelect()         As Integer  'apply geo test set
Public gROApplyGeoConcen             As Boolean  'apply geo concentration?
Public gROReportElig()               As Boolean  'report eligible collateral
Public gROReportInelig()             As Boolean  'report ineligible collateral
Public gRODataFileElig()             As Boolean  'write elig collat data file
Public gRODataFileInelig()           As Boolean  'write inelig collat data file
Public gROCFWaterfall                As Boolean  'write cf waterfall file


'==================================================================================
'GEOGRAPHIC CONCENTRATION TESTS VARIABLES
'==================================================================================
'the final concentration levels
Public gConLevel                              As Double   'concen level from UForm
Public gFinalConcenStates(1 To NUM_STATES)    As Double   'limits at state
Public gFinalConcenMSASet1(1 To NUM_MSA_SET1) As Double   'limits MSA set 1
Public gFinalConcenMSASet2(1 To NUM_MSA_SET2) As Double   'limits MSA set 2
Public gMSAIndex()                            As Integer  'MSA index
Public gTestConcenOutput                      As Boolean  'test concen?
Public gWriteConcenReport                     As Boolean  'write concen?
Public gSheetIsHere(1 To NUM_GEO_TESTS)       As Boolean  'if found true
```

EXHIBIT 3.3   Public variable declarations

```
Sub CCFG_Model()

        Application.DisplayAlerts = False                    'turn off the warning messages
        gPrintAssumptionsReport = False
        Call MainProgram_ReadAllDataFileLabels
        Call MainProgram_FindActivePoolOrSubPorts            'Pool Level/Sub-Portfolio Level?
        Call MainProgram_errCheck_AllMenus                   'error check each menu
        Call MainProgram_ReadAllMenuInputs                   'read menu inputs into model
        Call CollatData_ReadCollateralFiles                  'read collat data into the model
        Call InitScreen_BasicScreeningMain                   'initial data screening
        Call FinSelect_FinancialCriteriaSelectionMain        'apply fin/demo screening
        Call GeoSelect_GeographicEligibilityTesting          'apply geographical screening
        Call GeoConcen_ApplyConcentrationLimits              'apply concentration limits
        Call RepGeoCon_CalcPortTotal                         'aggregates total port amount
        Call CollatCF_ComputeCollateralCashflows             'compute the collateral cfs
        'reporting routines
        If gCashFlowWriteCFFileName <> "" Or _
            gCashFlowWriteCFFileName <> "No File Selected" Then
            Call RepInitScreen_MainWriteReport               'intial data screening reports
            Call RepDemoRisk_MainWriteReport                 'demographic risk factors report
            Call RepCollatCF_MainWriteReport                 'collateral cash flows
            Call RepCrossTab_MainWriteReports                'cross tabulations reports
            Call RepBaseStrat_MainWriteReports               'base stratification reports
            Call RepUserInelig_MainWriteReports              'user criteria ineligibles
            Call RepGeoCon_MainWriteReports(0)               'initial geo concentrations
            Call RepGeoCon_MainWriteReports(1)               'final geo concentrations
            Call RepGeoLoanList_MainWriteReports             'geo loan listings
            Call RepGeoStrat_MainWriteReports                'geo stratification reports
            Call RepLoanListing_MainWriteReports             'loan list, elig/inelig collat
            Call RepPortPresent_MainWriteReports             'portflio presentation reports
            Call RepSingleScen_MainWriteReports              'single scenario CF reports
            If gPrintAssumptionsReport Then
                Call RepAssumptions_WriteAllAssumptions
            End If
        End If

End Sub
```

EXHIBIT 3.4   Main program

they perform. Thus the subroutine:

```
Sub MainProgram_FindActivePoolOrSubPorts()
```

identifies this subroutine as residing in the "A_MainProgram" module and performing the task of determining which collateral pools or sub-portfolios are active. "Active" in this context means "selected for inclusion in the deal." Whereas:

```
Sub RepPortPresent_MainWriteReports()
```

is the main subroutine in the module that writes the portfolio presentation report. Exhibit 3.5 is typical of a small, very focused subroutine that reads a Collateral Pool level data file.

Utility Subroutines   A special type of subroutines are "utility" subroutines. Utility subroutines perform tasks that are for the most part simple, mind-numbingly boring, tedious to write, and *absolutely essential* to the model. An example of such a subroutine is a subroutine that when given a numeric code returns the string value of a member of a list. We will use such subroutines to return:

- The two-letter postal code of a state from a array that contains the alphabetized list of all 50 states followed by the four United States territories.

```
Sub CollatData_ReadPoolDataFile()

    'open the Pool Level file
    iloan = 0
    Workbooks.Open FileName:=gfnPoolName
    current_row = FIRST_DATA_ROW
    Sheets("LoanInformation").Select
    Range("A1").Select
    'count the number of loans in the file
    Do While Cells(current_row, 1).Value <> ""
        current_row = current_row + 1
    Loop
    gTotalLoans = current_row - 3   '2 header rows and 1 false count
    'redimension the data arrays based on the number of total loans
    ReDim gLoanOK(1 To gTotalLoans) As Boolean
    ReDim gLoanData(1 To gTotalLoans, 1 To DATA_FILE_FIELDS) As Double
    ReDim gLoanScreen(1 To gTotalLoans, 1 To TOTAL_SCREEN_SCORES) As Long
    ReDim gLoanSelect(1 To gTotalLoans, 1 To TOTAL_SELECT_SCORES) As Long
    Call CollatData_ReadDataFileContents(gTotalLoans + 2, iloan)
    ActiveWorkbook.Close

End Sub
```

EXHIBIT 3.5   CollatData_ReadPoolDataFile subroutine

- The name of a Metropolitan Statistical Area (MSA) from a number that repre-sents the position of the MSA on an array containing all 150 MSAs
- The MSA code number. The value of the MSA identification number will be determined in one of two ways. The first is by determining its location on one of the four MSA lists in which the MSAs are ranked by population. The second would be the position of the MSA in the overall list of the total 150 MSA if such list is available at that point in the execution sequence of the model.
- The ordinal ranking of a column in the Excel spreadsheet given the letter of the column. An example would be put in "E" returns numeric 5.
- The letter of the column given the ordinal ranking of the column. An example would be put in a numeric 5 gets back "E".

It is clear that these subroutines can be called from almost any module of the application. They collectively perform mundane, ubiquitous, and irreplaceable tasks. They are the little nondescript worker bees. Gather them together and place them in a separate module named "Z_Utilities". As when we used the "A_" module prefix to move the modules to the top of the Project Explorer window list in the VBA Editor, here we use "Z_" to move the utilities to the bottom of the list.

Code Level Practices

The following are a collection of other practices that make VBA code more legible and easier to understand. Remember you may be called upon to work on code that you have written weeks, months or years after you last looked at it. By making your code as structured, clear, and orderly as possible you will be in essence writing yourself an insurance policy for the future. There is nothing worse than being asked

```
If set_num = gPriorSet And test_num = gPriorTest Then
    'this test has the same set and test number as the last entered test
    'ask if this is intended, if not capture new values for the variables
    msgTitle = "SET AND TEST NUMBERS MATCH PREVIOUS TEST"
    msgPrompt = "                           TEST SET = " & set_num & vbCrLf & _
                "                           TEST NUMBER = " & test_num & vbCrLf & _
                "Select OK to overwrite the previous test" & vbCrLf & _
                "or CANCEL to return to the Financial Selection Menu" & _
                vbCrLf
    msgResult = MsgBox(msgPrompt, gMsgButtonCode1, msgTitle)
    If msgResult = 1 Then gFinOK = True
    If msgResult = 2 Then gFinOK = False
Else
    gPriorSet = Range("m09CollatSelectSet")
    gPriorTest = Range("m09CollatSelectTest")
    gFinOK = True
End If
```

EXHIBIT 3.6   Components of a complex error message

to help add to or fix a model that you have written some time ago and being lost when you reenter the code *you know you wrote*! Build your code with the understanding that you will be responsible for it for the rest of the life of the application. Build the kind of applications and models that will reflect well on your personal reputation. To this end the following suggestions will save you many hours of confusion and distress if you follow them as best you can.

Continuation Statements   The continuation statement allows you to carry a VBA statement that is too long to fit on to a single line of the screen display onto the next screen line. Use continuation lines judiciously! Do not just drop them in when you think the line is too long. Most lines that require continuation statements have some internal structure to them. They have multiple groups of factors in a calculation or execute a complex report format. If you cannot break the line into one or more precursor statements to make it more readable, employ the continuation symbol to align these subsections of the longer line. An example of a formatting statement employing multiple continuation symbols would involve the assembly of a complex error message from a series of smaller component ones. See Exhibit 3.6.

Aligning the multiple components of logic test, one over the other, in a column is a similar use of a continuation symbol that adds to clarity and legibility. See Exhibit 3.7.

"If..Then..Endif" Statements   When using a simple "If..Then..EndIf" test where there is no alternative action to be taken, simply write the test and resultant action on one line instead of the "If..Then..Else..EndIf" form of the statement.

```
If test_condition > test_value Then sum = sum + gCurrentBalance
    (iloan)
```

instead of

```
If test_condition > test_value Then
    sum = sum + gCurrentBalance(iloan)
Endif
```

```
'Remember!! gLoanScreen of "ALL_OK", DEMO_OK" do NOT contain error
'   scores. if these items are equal to 0 it means the record is unusable
'   for these tasks, if it contains a 1 the record has suffecent and
'   correct data for the task at hand.
If gLoanScreen(iloan, FD_SCREEN_FORMAT) = 0 And _
   gLoanScreen(iloan, FD_SCREEN_AMORT) = 0 And _
   gLoanScreen(iloan, FD_SCREEN_STRAT) = 0 And _
   gLoanScreen(iloan, FD_SCREEN_FOF) = 0 And _
   gLoanScreen(iloan, FD_SCREEN_MVD) = 0 And _
   gLoanScreen(iloan, FD_SCREEN_GEO) Then
        gLoanScreen(iloan, FD_SCREEN_ALL_OK) = 1      'good all purposes!
        gLoanOK(iloan) = True
End If
```

EXHIBIT 3.7   Components of a complex logic test

Select Case and Loops   An extension of the last principle is to use the end-of-line symbol ":" at the end of the individual case statement in a "Select..Case" statement block. This format is both more compact and clearer than placing the resultant action on the next line. It has the simple virtue of saving a lot of space on the page when there are many case statements. It helps keep the subroutine legible by displaying as much of it as possible in the least number of lines. It also more clearly conveys the sense of "This Case = This Action". It is especially useful for "Select..Case" statements inside of looping structures. This is especially true of "For..Next" loops. Each repetition of the loop often triggers a different "Case" consequence for each successive loop. See Exhibit 3.8.

Clear Code Rather than Clever Code   Write your code as if you will be struck with a form of application-specific amnesia ten minutes after the model is put into production. *The simple truth of the matter is that you will!*

Any useful application that you write will, it is hoped, be indelibly linked to you personally. (Let us hope fervently that this is the case so that you get full credit for all the hard work you have contributed!) But attribution of authorship has an unfortunate element attached to it. People without application development experience will assume that you will be able to instantly recall every nuance along with every idiosyncratic feature of every application you have ever written.

Your challenge is to make it appear that this is indeed the case. In your own best interests remember that there is a 50%/3 months extinction curve for any code that you write (without exception). Write your code with this in mind and you will never regret it! Simplify and strive for clarity. Organize your applications in a logical and well-labeled manner. Lastly, do yourself and everyone who will ever come in contact with your application a BIG favor. Comment your applications extensively and effectively! (Much more on this later.)

Try to make things as easy on yourself as you can in that sure-to-come future when you are called to return to your earlier efforts.

Abbreviate (with Caution)   If you take care in using abbreviations you can both simplify your code and make it more understandable. The following code is a typical

```
'populates the gCTOutputArray, and if the data item in the body of the report
' needs to be dollar weighted, (which most do), builds the numerator by
' multiplying the statistic by the current balance, and the denominator by
' accumulating the current balance amouts in the gCTOutputDollar.
For iloan = 1 To gTotalLoans
    irow = gCTOutputLoc(iloan, 1)    'find the row location of the loan data
    icol = gCTOutputLoc(iloan, 2)    'find the column location of the loan data
    'add loan data to the Cross Tabs matrix based on mRow and MCol values
    Select Case gCTBodyItem(irep)
        Case Is = 1: amt = 1       'loan count per grid square
        Case Is = FD_ORIGBAL:    amt = gLoanData(FD_ORIGBAL, iloan)
        Case Is = FD_CURRBAL:    amt = gLoanData(FD_CURRBAL, iloan)
        Case Is = FD_ORIGLTV:    amt = gLoanData(FD_ORIGLTV, iloan)
        Case Is = FD_CURRLTV:    amt = gLoanData(FD_CURRLTV, iloan)
        Case Is = FD_ORIGTERM:   amt = gLoanData(FD_ORIGTERM, iloan)
        Case Is = FD_REMTERM:    amt = gLoanData(FD_REMTERM, iloan)
        Case Is = FD_SEASON:     amt = gLoanData(FD_SEASON, iloan)
        Case Is = FD_CURRRATE:   amt = gLoanData(FD_CURRRATE, iloan)
        Case Is = FD_ORIGAPP:    amt = gLoanData(FD_ORIGAPP, iloan)
        Case Is = FD_CURRAPP:    amt = gLoanData(FD_CURRAPP, iloan)
        Case Is = FD_FICO:       amt = gLoanData(FD_FICO, iloan)
        Case Is = FD_MDBTTOINC:  amt = gLoanData(FD_MDBTTOINC, iloan)
        Case Is = FD_TDBTTOINC:  amt = gLoanData(FD_TDBTTOINC, iloan)
        Case Is = FD_THIRDPARTY: amt = gLoanData(FD_THIRDPARTY, iloan)
        Case Is = FD_SERVERATE:  amt = gLoanData(FD_SERVERATE, iloan)
    End Select
    'if the data item that makes up the body of the report needs to be dollar
    ' weighted do so at this time
    If gCTDolWght(mCTBItem) Then
        'building the numerator for dollar weighted statistics
        amt = amt * gLoanData(FD_CURRBAL, iloan)
        'building the demoninator for dollar weighted statistics
        gCTOutputDollar(irow, icol) = _
            gCTOutputDollar(irow, icol) + gLoanData(iloan, FD_CURRBAL)
    End If
    'building the denominator
    gCTOutputArray(irow, icol) = gCTOutputArray(irow, icol) + amt
Next iloan
```

EXHIBIT 3.8   "Select..Case" inside a "For..Next" with inline results

example of an instance in which the use of an abbreviated working variable will improve both the legibility and the clarity of your code. These situations pertain:

1. You need to assign a value from an array named "gOrigLTVRatio" to the variable "amt" based on the result of two other values that will determine which row and column of the array you will read.
2. The row value will come from an array "gLoanData(iloan, FD_CURRAPPTYPE)" field.
3. The column value will come from a combination of the two other arrays, "gOrig AdjValue(iloan, FD_VALUE)" and "gOrigAdjType(ivalue, FD_TYPE)".

The unabbreviated equation looks like this:

```
amt = gOrigLTVRatio(gLoanData(iloan, FD_CURRAPPTYPE), _
    gOrigAdjType(gOrigAdjType(ivalue, FD_TYPE), FD_TYPE))
```

This assignment statement is both messy and difficult to read. Instead we try to break it up into the various pieces that will help us understand where the inputs for the value we will assign are read from:

```
'find the column value
irow = gOrigAdjType(ivalue, FD_TYPE)
icol = gOrigAdjType(irow, FD_TYPE))
'find the row value
irow = gLoanData(iloan, FD_CURRAPPTYPE)
'assign on basis of irow, icol combination
amt = gOrigLTVRatio(irow, icol)
```

While somewhat tedious, this approach allows us to deconstruct the various portions of the assignment. This can be a tremendous help if we need to debug when we revisit the code at a later date or when someone else is assigned to support it. Another application of this principle is when we assign the value of a variable with a long name to a working variable with a much shorter name: in this example, we can shorten "gLoanData(iloan,FD_CURRBAL)" to "Cbal" (Exhibit 3.9). In this exhibit

```
Sub RepGeoStrat_AccumPropTypeInfo(istate As Integer, iMSA As Integer)

Dim ptype      As Integer   'property type code
Dim otype      As Integer   'occupancy type
Dim stype      As Integer   'servicer rating
Dim etype      As Integer   'escrow agreement
Dim cBal       As Double    'current balance of the loan

    For iloan = 1 To gTotalLoans
        go_ok = False
        If gLoanOK(iloan) Then
            Call RepGeoStrat_DetermineIfLoanIsAMatch(istate, iMSA)
        End If
        If go_ok Then
            'loan is data suffucent, eligible collateral from the target state
            ptype = gLoanData(iloan, FD_PROPTYPE)
            cBal = gLoanData(iloan, FD_CURRBAL)
            'schedule 1 - property type distribution
            mPropType(ptype, 1) = mPropType(ptype, 1) + 1
            mPropType(ptype, 2) = mPropType(ptype, 2) + cBal
            'schedule 9 - occupancy code
            otype = (gLoanData(iloan, FD_OCCPCODE) * 2) - 1
            mOccupancy(ptype, otype) = mOccupancy(ptype, otype) + 1
            mOccupancy(ptype, otype + 1) = mOccupancy(ptype, otype + 1) + cBal
            'schedule 10 - loan servicer rating
            stype = gLoanData(iloan, FD_SERVERATE)
            mServicerRate(ptype, stype) = mServicerRate(ptype, stype) + 1
            mServicerRate(ptype, stype + 1) = mServicerRate(ptype, stype + 1) + cBal
            'schedule 11 - escrow servicing agreement
            etype = gLoanData(iloan, FD_ESCROW)
            mEscrowAgree(ptype, etype) = mEscrowAgree(ptype, etype) + 1
            mEscrowAgree(ptype, etype + 1) = mEscrowAgree(ptype, etype + 1) + cBal
        End If
    Next iloan

End Sub
```

EXHIBIT 3.9　"gloanData(iloan,FD_CURRBAL)" to "Cbal"

we see no less than five different abbreviations used to make both the indexing of the assignments statements and the values being assigned more compact and legible.

Commenting Your Code   Commenting is critical; just do it! Having said that, how does one comment effectively? All comments are *not* equal. A comment needs to have content. Comments do not have to be of any specific length or form, but they do need to be informative. They need to tell you or anyone else something about the code that will help you understand the portion of the application that holds the comment. Comments can fulfill a variety of different tasks, as we will see in the next discussion.

Useless Comments Are Worse than Useless!   Useless comments are worse than no comments at all! Comments that you place in your code because someone, like me, told you to do so do not help if you are writing them only to be able to say you wrote them. You or the next person called on to support your application will read these useless comments expecting to find guidance and will become either confused or frustrated at their lack of content. This is especially true of the next example. Exhibit 3.10 provides two examples of the same subroutine with different sets of comments; one set useful and one completely set useless.

The purpose of the subroutine is to find the correct location of each piece of data for a given cross tabulation report and correctly report the dollar weighted statistic and the sum of all principal balances represented by the items in each cell of the report. The tasks that the subroutine needs to perform are as follows:

1. Determine the row location of the cell into which to place the data based on value of the first data item of the cross tabulation report.
2. Determine the column location of the cell into which to place the data based on the value of the second data item of the cross tabulation report.
3. Loop through all loans of the portfolio.
4. Test if the loan is an eligible piece of collateral prior to including it in the statistics of the report.
5. Use a "Select..Case" statement to determine the type of data item is in the body of the report (these lines have been omitted from the Exhibit for the sake of brevity).
6. Test if the data in the body of the report needs to be dollar weighted.
7. If the statistic needs to be dollar weighted multiple the value of the variable "amt" but the current balance of the loan. Note the value of "amt" was set in the "Select..Case" statements that are hidden. This gives us the contribution to the numerator of the weighted dollar calculation.
8. Accumulate the current balance of the loan in the array "gCTOutputDollar" array. This will later serve as the denominator of the dollar weighted calculation for the cell.
9. Accumulate the number calculated in step 7 above to the total running balance of the cell numerator. This is stored in the array "gCTOutputArray".

Once these operations are complete all we have to do in the reporting subroutine that calls this subroutine is to divide "gCTOutputArray" by the corresponding row/column match of the "gCTOutputDollar" and we will have the result we desire.

```
'====================================================================
Sub RepCrossTab_PopulateOutputArray()
    'sets the row  locations for every piece of loan data
    Call RepCrossTab_FindLoanDataRowLocation
    'sets the column locations for every piece of loan data
    Call RepCrossTab_FindLoanDataColLocation
    'populates the gCTOutputArray, if the data item in the body of the report
    ' needs to be dollar weighted, (which most do), builds the numerator by
    ' multiplying the statistic by the current balance, and the denominator by
    ' accumulating the current balance amouts in the gCTOutputDollar.
    For iloan = 1 To gTotalLoans
      If gLoanOK(iloan) Then                    'eligible loans only
          irow = gCTOutputLoc(iloan, ROW_LOC) 'row location to add loan data
          icol = gCTOutputLoc(iloan, COL_LOC) 'col location to add loan data
          'add loan data to the Cross Tabs matrix based on mRow and MCol values
          Select Case gCTBodyItem(irep)
              [14 lines of code not shown]
          End Select
          'check if the data item that makes up the body of the report
          ' needs to be dollar weighted. if yes, do so at this time.
          If gCTDolWght(mCTBItem) Then
              'accumulate the numerator for dollar weighted statistics
              amt = amt * gLoanData(iloan, FD_CURRBAL)
              'accumulate the demoninator for dollar weighted statistics
              gCTOutputDollar(irow, icol) = _
                  gCTOutputDollar(irow, icol) + gLoanData(iloan, FD_CURRBAL)
          End If
          'accumulate this item's numerator to the total cross tab cell numerator
          gCTOutputArray(irow, icol) = gCTOutputArray(irow, icol) + amt
      End If
    Next iloan
End Sub
'====================================================================
Sub RepCrossTab_PopulateOutputArray()
    'find location
    Call RepCrossTab_FindLoanDataRowLocation
    Call RepCrossTab_FindLoanDataColLocation
    For iloan = 1 To gTotalLoans                    'loan by loan
      If gLoanOK(iloan) Then
          irow = gCTOutputLoc(iloan, ROW_LOC)
          icol = gCTOutputLoc(iloan, COL_LOC)
          Select Case gCTBodyItem(irep)
              [14 lines of code not shown]
          End Select
          If gCTDolWght(mCTBItem) Then              'dollar weighting
              amt = amt * gLoanData(iloan, FD_CURRBAL)
              gCTOutputDollar(irow, icol) = _
                  gCTOutputDollar(irow, icol) + gLoanData(iloan, FD_CURRBAL)
          End If
          gCTOutputArray(irow, icol) = gCTOutputArray(irow, icol) + amt
      End If
    Next iloan
End Sub
```

EXHIBIT 3.10 Useful and useless comments

If we look at the upper example of commenting it is very easy to understand the steps of the process. In the lower example, although we are greatly helped by the names of the variables and the subroutines called, the comments are essentially useless. They are both too short and too non-descriptive of the steps of the process that they are trying to tell us about. This is a clear case of a situation where you cannot see the forest because the trees are in the way. This subroutine is perfectly

```
' =========================================================================
' 10/04/2010   L. Clark    Added "Percent20" and "State" cases
' =========================================================================
Sub RepBaseStrat_PopulateStratArrays()

    Select Case mRFTemplate(irep)
        Case Is = "Label":      Call RepBaseStrat_WriteLabelReport
        Case Is = "Dollar":     Call RepBaseStrat_WriteDollarReport
        Case Is = "Percent20":  Call RepBaseStrat_WritePercent20Report
        Case Is = "Percent100": Call RepBaseStrat_WritePercent100Report
        Case Is = "Percent150": Call RepBaseStrat_WritePercent150Report
        Case Is = "Month1":     Call RepBaseStrat_WriteMonth1Report
        Case Is = "Month3":     Call RepBaseStrat_WriteMonth3Report
        Case Is = "Month12":    Call RepBaseStrat_WriteMonth12Report
        Case Is = "State":      Call RepBaseStrat_WriteStateReport
        Case Is = "MSA":        Call RepBaseStrat_WriteMSAReport
    End Select

End Sub
```

EXHIBIT 3.11 Change comment in the subroutine masthead

clear to the person who wrote it at the time that he or she did write it. With three short and unhelpful comments versus the virtually line-by-line commenting in the upper example a person reading the lower version will be left to puzzle out many issues on their own.

With the three-month 50% extinction curve operating, you will find the first set of comments helpful, possibly even invaluable. You will find the second comment more of an annoyance than anything else.

Commenting Subroutine Mastheads All code changes with time. Once the original code has been written, it is only a matter of time—sometimes weeks, but in many cases only days—before the first changes take place. If you are *not* using a code change tracking system that keeps a record of all changes to the VBA code, you will want to know when the changes occurred and who placed them into the code.

An easiest way to facilitate this in-model change documentation is to place a masthead of three comment lines at the top of each subroutine. Besides performing the role of a visual break between subroutines, these lines can serve as a repository for change information. Once any change occurs, the author of the change places his or her name, the date, and a brief description of the change in the masthead. See Exhibit 3.11.

Commenting Variables Every, and I mean *every*, variable needs to have an in-line comment at the end of its declaration statement. Always identify variables and what role they perform. Do this even if it is a loop counter variable, such as the ever-present "irow" and "icol". Why? What would you rather do, read a brief and easily located comment line or be forced to puzzle out what that variable is doing by looking at the code? Even if the comment is trivial (notice I did not say "useless," just "trivial"), put it in variable declaration line. An example of such a comment is:

```
Dim irow    As Integer    'generic loop counter
```

versus commenting variables that are more specific and important, such as the next collection of modular scope report formatting variables:

```
'report formatting and content variables
Dim mRFName()       As String    'data item name
Dim mRFValues()     As Integer   '# values vertical axis of report
Dim mRFStart()      As Double    'value of starting criteria
Dim mRFStep()       As Double    'interval step vertical values
Dim mRFType()       As String    'type of stratification data
Dim mRFTemplate()   As String    'type of template file for this data
Dim mRFTitle1()     As String    'title line one for sort column
Dim mRFTitle2()     As String    'title line two for sort column
Dim mRFRepTitle()   As String    'main report title
Dim mRFLastRow      As Integer   'last row of the report
Dim mRFMSACodes()   As Double    'list of MSA numbers
```

Explanatory Comments Explanatory comments tell you and others exactly what is transpiring in the application. We have already seen an example of an explanatory comment in Exhibit 3.10. Explanatory comments are especially useful to keep the developer informed as to the progress of multistep processes. In this manner you can help yourself or someone else walk through a process in an informed and guided manner. Exhibit 3.12 is the subroutine that calculates the principal payment factors for a hybrid adjustable rate mortgage (HARM). The HARM has a 1, 3, 5, 7 or 10 year interest-only payment period. During this period of time, there is, of course, no principal payable by the mortgagor. Thereafter the interest-only period principal payments are calculated based on the remaining term of the loan, its current coupon rate and the balance. The comments of this subroutine clearly delineate each phase of the process including any recalculation of principal amortization caused by the reset of the adjustable coupon rate of the note. See Exhibit 3.12.

COMMON SENSE

We have now arrived at the "Common Sense" section of the chapter. My advice is:

1. **Measure twice, cut once.**
   "A stitch in time, saves nine (stitches later)."
   "An ounce of prevention is worth a pound of cure."
   Do not just rush off and start writing code, no matter how excited you are about the project. Sit down and figure what you will need to develop to launch the application, how you are going to structure the application, and how you are going to get the necessary information and expertise to help you. A reasonable amount of planning is time that is never wasted. What is "reasonable"? It will depend on the size of the application, your experience, and the amount of technical, financial, and referential resources you can draw on. No matter what the situation, even if it is a ten-minute chat with someone else, take the time to plan.

```
Sub CollatCF_CalcHybridARMSchPrin(iloan As Long)

Dim RemPeriods      As Double    'remaining term periods
Dim IOPeriods       As Integer   'interest only periods


    IOPeriods = gLoanData(iloan, FD_HBAIOPERIODS)
    'INTEREST ONLY PHASE
    'test if the loan is in the I/O period. if it is there is no principal
    '   payment, set factors to 0.
    If gLoanData(iloan, FD_SEASON) < IOPeriods Then
        For mPeriods = 1 To (IOPeriods - gLoanData(iloan, FD_SEASON))
            gLoanAmortFactors(iloan, mPeriods) = 0#   'no principal component!
        Next mPeriods
    End If
    'PRINCIPAL AMORTIZATION PHASE
    'first we need to determine the starting position of the amortization
    '   sequence. Is the loan at the very beginning of the full payment phase
    '   (having just finished the I/O period assignments above), or is it
    '   already into the full payment phase?
    If gLoanData(iloan, FD_SEASON) < IOPeriods Then
        'we just filled the I/O period months with zeros above therefore
        '   advance the starting period to first principal pay month.
        mStart = IOPeriods + 1
        RemPeriods = gLoanData(iloan, FD_REMTERM) - IOPeriods
        mResetStart = IOPeriods
        Else
        'the loan is already out of the I/O periods, amortize principal
        '   as if it were a Standard ARM the reset sequence will start with
        '   the seasoning.
        mStart = 1
        RemPeriods = gLoanData(iloan, FD_REMTERM)
        mResetStart = gLoanData(iloan, FD_SEASON)
    End If
    'with the starting time period in place we can calculate the remaining
    '   principal amortization factors
    For mPeriods = mStart To RemPeriods
      If mPeriods = 1 Then Call CollatCF_CalcDiscountFactors(RemPeriods)
      'if its a reset period recalculate the factor sets
      If (mResetStart + mPeriods - 1) Mod gLoanData(iloan, FD_ARMPERRESET) = 0 Then
        Call CollatCF_CalcDiscountFactors(RemPeriods - mPeriods)
      End If
      mBaseDiscFactor = mDiscFactors(RemPeriods)
      gLoanAmortFactors(iloan, mPeriods) = _
            1 - ((mBaseDiscFactor - mDiscFactors(mPeriods)) / _
                 (mBaseDiscFactor - mDiscFactors(mPeriods - 1)))
    Next mPeriods

End Sub
```

EXHIBIT 3.12 Calculation of monthly principal payments factors for a HARM loan

2. **Divide and conquer.**

   Once you have your plan, break it into manageable pieces. Set intermediate goals and make a very serious effort to stick to them. Make lists and cross off the items as you complete them. A recent study asserted that people who were list makers were happier than those who were not. I think this fact is so self-evident that a study is not needed. This is because there is a small but measureable satisfaction in completing a task. You can see the incremental progress more clearly as the line of checked-off items or crossed-out lines marches down the page over the course of the day.

Lists also make the prioritization process easier, or if not any easier, at least clearer.

3. **Give yourself a break (or reward!).**

    Give yourself short-term rewards. Be careful to self-reinforce. Napoleon said: "The morale is to the physical as three is to one."

    One way to insure following this practice to have a To Do List with one or several of the times in the list written as "Take 15 minute break." Generally, if you are involved in intense activity, especially debugging code, frequent breaks are best. I highly recommend that you do not work for more than two hours at a stretch without taking at least a 15 minute break. (This is not to say that in a crunch time you can't just throw this piece of advice out the window, I have myself on many occasions.) Also if you have been staring at a screen from a distance of 12–18 inches refocus you eyes on a far object, or just close them.

    One last warning about working in "emergency" mode. Remember that you will at some point, if you work hard enough and long enough, become so tired you will make an abnormal amount of fatigue induced errors. It is then time to stop no matter what. Taking even a small break at this time may help you gain a better perspective and outlook on the work.

4. **Stay focused.**

    Stay with the task until it is completed. Don't fragment your efforts.

    This is really a way of saying "effectively combine items 2 and 3 above!"

5. **Be safe, not sorry.**

    Test and document your project. Do not think that when you are done writing your application you are finished with it. Testing, and then, depending on the complexity of the application and the financial importance it is to the business, some form of documentation is absolutely necessary.

6. **Do unto others as you would have done to you.**

    Be a professional! Write your applications in a manner that you would want to see if you had to open a model that you were unfamiliar with. Use a functionally recognizable module and variable naming convention. Comment your code as outlined above. Strive to simple and clear. Remember, if you look at your own work two years later you may feel that you are looking at something entirely new written by someone else. This is especially true when the application is over several thousands of VBA lines long. Remember, every aid and help that you can build into the structure and syntax of the application may be the critical clue, that *you*, not someone else, needs in the future!

Well at this point you probably feel as if you have just sat through a lecture from your mother! That feeling is probably justified. Just remember it is your decision to benefit from the "experience" as defined above of others or not. I hope this is of value to you and that you will avail yourself of it.

ON THE WEB SITE

There is no material on the Web site for this chapter.

## CHAPTER 4

Segregation of the Existing Model's Functionality

OVERVIEW

In this chapter we examine the advantages to splitting the Structuring Model that we spent time poring over in Chapter 2 into two distinct entities.

As we add more and more functionality to the model, we will need to effect this division of labor along the natural divide of the model. We will segregate that portion of the model that deals with the collateral and its cash flows—the asset side—from the side of the model that deals with the debt structure—the liabilities side. Another way to think of it is to categorize the two components as the "sources" side and the "uses" side of the transaction.

In this chapter we cover the reasons for making the split. The process of splitting the model will be a tedious exercise, and the time and effort of undertaking this work should be clearly justified by the benefits we will realize.

This is a short chapter but an important one. Here we lay the groundwork that we will build on for the rest of the book.

DELIVERABLES

The modeling knowledge deliverables for this chapter are:

- Understanding the benefits of splitting the model.
- Laying out the high-level approach we will use to achieve this goal.

UNDER CONSTRUCTION

We will not be doing any coding in this chapter. In Chapters 5 and 6 we will be up to our necks in the Visual Basic Editor as we bifurcate the model. There we create the two models that will become our departure points for the development effort in the rest of the book.

DELIVERABLES CHECKLIST

The modeling concept that is the takeaway for this chapter is:

- The advantages of splitting the model along its two main functionalities, the asset side and the liabilities side of the model.

BREAKING UP IS HARD TO DO

In the words of the 1962 pop classic by Neil Sedaka, "Breaking Up Is Hard to Do," and it is. It's not as hard as some modeling tasks, but it is harder than many. The challenges facing the modeler fall into two basic and interrelated concepts. The first challenge is to clearly determine where in the product the conceptual fault line lies that we are going to use as our guide to the process. The second lies in ending up with a working basic version when the smoke clears at the end of the coding process. Keep in mind that as we work our way from the original Structuring Model to produce the two specialized models, most of what we will be doing is *deleting* VBA code. Also keep in mind that at the end of the process, we may well have to add code to one or the other portions to allow them to communicate with each other. We need to have a clear plan before we start and then carefully execute it as we proceed with the bifurcation process.

What is more important is that we also have a clear vision of what tasks these two models, the Base Asset Model (BAM) and the Base Liabilities Model (BLM), will have to solve moving forward. If we can establish a firm conceptual foundation at the start, our future work will be much easier.

To wit, we will quickly review where we want to be at the very end of the model development process and then, working backward, set up a systemic approach to the editing process.

Where We Want to Be When the Smoke Clears

This would be a good time to refresh ourselves as to where we are now and where we want to be. We definitely know that, in the near future, there will be a significant increase in complexity in both the asset and liability analysis expected of the finished models.

The BAM will have to evolve into a model that must:

- Process much larger collateral portfolios. The portfolios we are currently working with are comprised of several thousand loans, but we may need to deal with several tens or hundreds of thousand loans. These sizes may occur in the aggregate portfolio or in sub-portfolios.
- Deal with assets that exhibit amortization patterns that the model is not currently capable of calculating. These may include such collateral as hybrid adjustable rate mortgages (HARMs) or other exotic mortgage types.
- Deal with collateral sets organized into multiple portfolios or sub-portfolios or both.
- Provide pool level and sub-portfolio level collateral selection reporting.

- Provide pool level and sub-portfolio level eligible collateral reporting (stratification reports).
- Have the ability to condense and combine loans of similar amortization characteristics into micro-portfolios (the creation of representative lines).
- Be able to merge cash flows from different portfolios.
- Be able to provide the BLMs models with sub-portfolio segregated cash flows.
- Move from pool level prepayment, default, market value decline, and recovery lag period assumptions to assumptions derived from the Metropolitan Statistical Area (MSA) that the loan resides within.
- Move from a scalar representation of prepayment and default rate behaviors to a vector representing their effects over time.
- Make loan type adjustment factors to prepayment and default rate modeling vectors based on the amortization pattern of the collateral.

As for the BLM, eventually it will have to:

- Read one or more cash flow files that have been produced by the BAM.
- Use multiple tranche structures to address the need for a difference in investor risk characteristics and tenor.
- Produce a tiered series of reports ranging from very broad single-page summaries to highly detailed working papers.
- Allow the user to select between very basic report appearances or to produce presentation-level formats directly into PowerPoint slides or files.

Regardless of whether we are addressing issues of the BAM or the BLM, we will extensively implement the Access database product to manage these data flows to and from the model:

- The input of the collateral data
- The criteria and results of the collateral selection process
- The output of the ineligible loan report package
- The output of the eligible collateral reports, data files, and databases
- The input of the MSA based delinquency, default, curtailment, prepayment, market value decline, and recovery curves
- The output of the collateral cash flows by either single or combined collateral portfolios as desired
- The output of the performance of the liabilities structure, including the amortization schedules of the various tranches of the structure and sensitivity tables

Where We Are on the Evolutionary Scale

If we return to the description of the model evolutionary scale in Chapter 1, we can see from our examination of the current model that it is definitely a Level 4 model. We will want to end up with a Level 6 model when we are finished. To review, the definition of a Level 4 to Level 6 models are:

Level 4. An Excel/VBA model that uses menus and external files to input data and template files to output the results. The blocks of VBA code are organized into very task-specific modules. They are purpose designed and are significantly more complex and powerful than recorded code. The main computational and analytical burden of the model is now preponderantly seated in the VBA code. The VBA code is interpreted, not compiled.

In this book we expand the model through Levels 5 and 6.

Level 5. Starts with a Level 4 model and then introduces the use of Access to address more onerous data management issues. The model may or may not make use of online data sources, such as Bloomberg, or private client Web sites to import data into the model.

Level 6. Usually is developed directly from a Level 4 or Level 5 model and is characterized by a more flexible, sophisticated, and/or technologically intensive user interface. This evolution is most likely to occur when the model has reached a stable state of development and when it makes sense to spend more time on improving the interface because the rate of change in both the financial product and the modeling approach has stabilized. This activity is highly correlated to the maturation of the financial instrument or a long-term consensus on standardized risk metrics or both.

You will have to wait for the next book for a discussion of Level 7 models listed below. We are in the predicament of J.R.R. Tolkien who said of the "Lord of the Rings" trilogy, "The tale grew in the telling."

ACCOMMODATING OUR DESIGN NEEDS

We now have our wish list laid out. It is reasonable to ask one more question before we just start hacking away at the current model. That question is:

"Is this trip really necessary?"

This saying came into popularity among the bomber crews of the U.S. Air Force during World War II. Before the advent and widespread use of fighter aircraft to escort the bombers to and from their targets, the average life expectancy of an aircrew in 1941–1942 was 12 missions. A crewmember was rotated home after 20 missions, so the outlook for survival could be termed bleak at best. As these men entered their aircraft, they wanted to know if what they were doing was worth the risk they were taking. They wanted to know if someone, somewhere, had thought of all the alternatives before arriving at the decision to send them onward.

So let us build the case for making this trip.

ADVANTAGES OF FUNCTIONAL SEGREGATION

We will find that there are six major advantages of a segregated model:

1. We will recognize operational and computational efficiencies in the operation of the model.
2. By splitting the model in two, we will have two smaller models that should be easier to maintain and manage.

3. We will be able to conduct independent validation and audits of each of the new models.
4. We will be able to increase the complexity of the models and increase the specialization of their functionality with less concern about whether the model will become too large and unwieldy.
5. We will be able to develop each of the two new models independently if circumstances demand it. We do need to be careful that each model can still effectively communicate with the other!
6. We will reduce key person dependence if we train more than one person to work on each side of the model.

More Efficient Model

One of the main inefficiencies of the current model configuration is that its execution and processing operations are entirely sequential in nature. The only exception to this condition is the fact that the analyst can run the collateral selection criteria against a portfolio and then save the results into a portfolio data file. This file can then be used directly in subsequent model runs, bypassing the selection process altogether.

The limitation of this sequential operation becomes strikingly obvious under these circumstances: Let us say we need to run the model in Batch Mode, evaluating 10 cases of 100 scenarios each. Let us also assume that the conditions are identical in regard to those inputs that govern the generation of the collateral cash flows. In these circumstances the current model will perform a set of identical recalculations of the cash flows 100 times. A far better alternative would be to calculate them once and then read them from a file or database for use by the remaining cases. An even better solution would be to read the first set of cash flows into the appropriate VBA arrays and then determine if the scenario had changed. If the collateral amortization conditions have not changed, we would not even need to read the collateral information into the model a second time. We could simply utilize the cash flows that had already been produced in the previous run.

Another opportunity for efficiency and effectiveness also exists. If we need to run the model 50 times (the maximum capacity in Batch Mode), the current model will perform an asset amortization calculation followed by a structural performance assessment. If the first part of the operation takes place in 4 minutes and the second in 1 minute, the total run time of the model will be 50 times 5 minutes, or 4 hours and 10 minutes. A more effective approach would be to have the model generate a cash flow file or database entry and allow the now-segregated liabilities waterfall to independently process each of the 50 files as they became available. If the timing sequences are as previously stated, the Collateral Cash Flow Generator (CCFG) will finish in 200 minutes, or 3 hours and 20 minutes. The last run of the Liabilities Waterfall model will now, however, finish 1 minute later, and the processing time will be cut by 25%. This time-saving effect will be recognized with absolutely no other changes to the model other than that of the bifurcation process.

Ease of Maintenance

Given that all other things are equal, smaller models are much easier to understand and support than larger models. These "other things" are clear, legible, and concise code. A forward-looking and logically developed module structure that holds the main program, the subroutines, the functions, the global variables, the Constant variables, and the Objects of the model is a must. General and widespread use of commenting and a set of either online or offline documents are also critical to lowering the barriers to understanding and learning a model. Therefore, with all these considerations equal, the smaller model is the clear choice.

Ease of Validation and Audit

Splitting up the functionality of the model will also ease the burdens associated with the validation process and any attendant auditing requirements. Smaller, properly designed, structured, and commented models are easier to validate and audit. This is due primarily to their absolute size and the fact that by separating the functionalities, you have, de facto, reduced the amount of code that has to be looked at if not its absolute complexity.

Specialization of Function

If you find that as your business unit grows, the model continues to expand, you may wish to consider assigning different people to specialize in the different parts of the model. This specialization generally improves efficiency and effectiveness and creates a sense of "ownership" over the code. Often the use of the term "ownership" of code has a strong negative connotation. Ownership is often construed in a negative sense in which a person jealously guards a critical piece of code and limits others from accessing it. The type of ownership being referred to here is the positive sense of the term. It is where a person takes individual responsibility for the improvement and expansion of critical software. This type of ownership can lead to productivity enhancement through specialization and, if properly managed, can at the same time significantly lower your exposure to key person risk, as discussed later.

Separate Development Schedules

Another advantage to bifurcation is that the development schedules of the two models can now proceed independently. There will no longer need to be a model release of only the combined model. Though not true in all cases (few things are), you will find that many changes will affect either the asset side or the liabilities side of the model more times than they will affect both simultaneously.

If the CCFG is modified, there will be no needed to revalidate the Liabilities Waterfall model as well. In addition, teams can work on each division of the model independently.

Decreases Key Person Dependence Issues

Larger models, especially large models developed by a single person or in a particularly idiosyncratic manner, create an environment that may foster the problem of key person dependence.

Obviously it is easier to organize, comment, and support a model of 1,000 lines of code than it is one of 10,000 lines of code, and far easier than one of 100,000 lines of code. If we know that the size and complexity of the model will definitely increase over time, then it is imperative that we take what steps we prudently can to avoid development and maintenance burdens.

By reducing the model to a series of more manageable, more specialized, and initially smaller components, the now-separated portions of the model will be easier to learn. The specialization will allow the person to concentrate on either the asset or liability aspect of the model. It is a given that each of the two portions of the now-divided model will grow over time; that is one of the reasons we advanced for doing the separation exercise. Nevertheless, it is highly unlikely that either will grow to a size of the original combined model.

This division also allows us the luxury of training people on either of the two model components. This significantly lessens the possibility that all the critical knowledge of the model's intricacies do not reside in a single person. Some people manipulate their personal model knowledge and ownership into a form of short-term job insurance. They then hold themselves out as irreplaceable based on this specific knowledge. Generally this form of zero-sum game has a limited payoff horizon. Your greatest value as a model developer is to be the tide that lifts all the boats simultaneously. Your key role is to leverage up the efforts of as many of your coworkers and others as you can, thus creating more value than you alone could ever create through your own individual efforts.

DISADVANTAGES OF FUNCTIONAL SEGREGATION

We have just listed the advantages of dividing the Structuring Model into separate parts. Are there any disadvantages to taking this course of action?

More Management of the Environment Needed

There will be a marginal increase in the amount of environment management needed. By the end of the development effort, we will manage the code of:

- The CCFG model.
- The Liabilities Waterfall model.
- A series of Access databases containing the delinquency, default, curtailment, prepayment, market value, and recovery period assumptions.
- A series of databases containing ineligible and eligible collateral results.
- A series of databases containing the collateral cash flows.
- A database containing the performance results of the structure.
- A larger number of report template files, some in Excel and some in PowerPoint.
- A few extra auxiliary support programs, such as the Collateral Representative Line Generator.

More Management of the Code Needed

Obviously when your model is comprised of separate programs with a degree of interdependence, the models may become somewhat more problematic to administer.

This is especially true if the interface between the pieces is changing as fast or faster than the pieces themselves.

In this case we will be able to overcome the main bottleneck of information transfer through the eventual use of the Access database project. The final configuration of the Liabilities Waterfall model will be developed from the BLM created in Chapter 6. As long as the content of the cash flow database is correctly and completely populated, the Liabilities model should be indifferent to how the cash flows got there in the first place. The two sides of the model will then achieve semi-independence. The two divisions of the original model can be developed independently as long as the database contents are synchronized.

ON THE WEB SITE

There is no material on the Web site for this chapter.

## CHAPTER 5

Creating the Base Asset Model

OVERVIEW

In this chapter we will create an asset handling–specific model from the Structuring Model. This model will retain only the functionalities associated with the collateral selection and cash flow amortization portions of the Structuring Model. We will eliminate any of the model interface and VBA language that deals specifically with the liability side of the deal.

As we work our way systemically through the model, we will start first with the menus, editing each in turn, and then move on to the VBA code. The task of creating a "cut-down" version of one model from another is straightforward in concept but can be tricky in practice.

To avoid any major irreversible mistakes, we will break the process into 12 steps. We will work our way through the model by starting at the Main Program subroutine and simply following each of the major subroutine calls from that point down through their calling hierarchies to the end. This approach will assure us that we have visited all of the VBA code of the model.

DELIVERABLES

The following are the deliverables for the chapter:

- An understanding of and familiarity with the code of the Structuring Model. By going through the code on an almost line-by-line basis, we will be thoroughly (and possibly painfully) familiar with it by the end of the chapter. This familiarity will also make our task in Chapter 6 easier when we have to perform the mirror image of this process and segregate a Base Liabilities Model (BLM) also using the Structuring Model as a departure point.
- A set of report template files specific to the Base Asset Model (BAM). These template files will produce the Eligible and Ineligible Collateral report packages and the cash flow reports of the Waterfall, the Matrix Summary, and the Single Scenario report packages.
- A working BAM that will be the working platform for all of our future development effort in Chapters 8 through 13 and 18 and 19. In these chapters we will create the more capable Collateral Cash Flow Generator model (CCFG) that will be the direct successor to the BAM.

UNDER CONSTRUCTION

We will successively strip out of the Structuring Model all functionalities related to the liabilities side of the deal, leaving only the BAM. We will also edit and reconfigure its associated report template files. In that this chapter contains such a large number of modifications and code changes to the Structuring Model, we will not list them here as we would in the case of a task-specific model modification. We will be working inside of almost every single module of the Structuring Model to achieve the final BAM. Including a detailed list of these changes would be both tedious and cumbersome.

In future chapters where we are making a series of more localized enhancements and modifications to the model, we will use this section of the chapter to discuss each enhancement in turn. Within each of those discussions we will then list every menu, external file, or VBA code module affected by the changes. This discussion will be accompanied by a module-specific list of changes to the code.

For now we will simply set about the work at hand.

THE BIG PICTURE: "JUST THE ASSETS, MA'AM"

In the 1950s–1960s television show *Dragnet*, the two detective characters, Sergeants Friday and Gannon, often had scenes in which they were interviewing a witness to a crime. In the course of the interview, there would inevitably come a time when the witness would become excited or began expressing opinions about the matter at hand. At that point one of the two officers would stop the witness and say:

"Just the facts, ma'am!"

What we have to do in the upcoming process is to end up with "just the assets." To do this we will first take a step back and view the larger elements of the model and determine where these changes are likely to occur. From there we can work our way from the reports, through the menus, and finally into the VBA modules, subroutines, and functions themselves.

What to Take Out: The Liability Support Components of the Model

The Structuring Model has a well-organized menu, report, and module system. The menus and reports are clearly labeled, and, fortunately, there are not too many of them. The modules are well defined and, even more important, have meaningful names. This is vital because it will allow us to quickly zero in on the areas of these items that contain liability content. I will tell you at this point that segregating the asset side from the Structuring Model will be the less difficult of the two tasks. Ironically this is due to the fact that there are entire modules that contain nothing but VBA code supporting the asset side. It is also the case that a number of special purpose menus can be completely eliminated at a stroke. In addition, keep in mind that at the time that we run the liability side of the model, we will have already calculated all the collateral cash flows separately. We will still want to report them alongside the liability in any case. In that we will retain all the collateral information, there will be very little change to the configuration of the original Structuring Model reports as they appear in the BLM.

Liabilities Information in the Waterfall Spreadsheet   The first and obvious place to start is the Liabilities Waterfall spreadsheet. Here we will remove a vast majority of the columns of the worksheet. For the purposes of the BAM, we need only retain the first 13 columns of the spreadsheet dealing with the components of the cash flows and the balances of the collateral pool over time.

With all the rest of the liabilities portion of the waterfall removed, the Box Score section that summarizes the contents of the worksheet will also dramatically contract. The remaining Box Score section now needs only to summarize the surviving collateral cash flow section. The first seven lines of the Box Score section are now all we need.

Structuring Assumptions on the Menus   Our next stop will be the Program Costs Menu, where we can eliminate the input fields of the liability side expenses. With the expense input fields deleted, all that remains are the input fields for the amortization triggers and the index selection fields. It should also be possible to move the index pathways of the menu to the Rates and Dates Menu. The triggers are also liability side inputs as they govern the allocation of principal payments to the conduit financing. With these removed, we have eliminated the need for this menu altogether!

Liabilities Menus Input and Error Checking Subroutines   Having eliminated the liabilities fields from the various menus, we will also need to remove the references to these fields from the input and error checking code of various menu support subroutines.

Liabilities Reports and Their Associated Subroutines   Starting with the menus, we can see one immediate alteration. On the Reports Menu, we can remove three of the four Summary Matrix reports as they deal exclusively with the liability performance.

Moving on to the other reports, we will need to remove the portions dealing with the presentation of liability information as well. In the case of the Waterfall report, we will simply delete the liability columns and match the report template to the newly reconfigured "CFWaterfall" spreadsheet of the model.

In the case of the Single Scenario report, we will have to adjust and collapse the Assumptions section to elimination assumptions specific to the liability structure. Next we will eliminate the last five columns of the Annual Cash Flows section and the lower-right-hand graph as they deal exclusively with the expenses associated with and the repayment of the financing.

Liabilities Fields Range Names   When all of the above chores have been accomplished, all that remains will be a last quick clean-up measure to purge all the spreadsheet Range names that we have deleted from the Names Directory of the model.

What to Leave In: The Collateral Cash Flow Components of the Model

Having completed the tasks just listed, we should be left with the Base Asset Model, right? Yes and no. It would be expedient to quickly review what we are going to leave in, so we are all clear, and the concept of what we are going to do is fixed in our minds before we start. This is not an operation where we want to have doubts halfway through!

Menu Inputs Support Code   We can safely ignore all the menus that are exclusive property of the asset side. These menus are the Collateral Selection Criteria Menu, the Defaults/Prepayment Menu, and the Geographic Menu. These menus are focused solely on performing the collateral selection process and are in no way related to the liabilities side of the model. That means that we can also ignore 100% of the VBA code supporting those menus.

The Main Menu will also be unchanged in that all the functions are transferable to an asset-only function. We will review this in more detail below.

Other menus, such as the Reports Menu and the Program Costs Menu, will need to be sifted through on a line-by-line basis.

Later we will expand the asset side model to amortize more complex mortgage types. It would be only prudent to retain the Coupon Trace Chart worksheet and its VBA support code. This will allow us to more easily verify that the model is performing the new amortization patterns.

Collateral Selection and Reporting Code   Any VBA module that is designed to perform the collateral selection process and the reporting of its results can also be safely ignored.

Eligible Collateral Data File Creation   What was said concerning the collateral selection process is equally true for the code that aggregates the eligible collateral and produces the eligible collateral file. This file, the process of the selection process based on the conditions of the Assumptions Page contained with the file, is exclusively as asset side functionality.

Cash Flow Generation   All cash flow generation code will be retained. This includes not only the VBA modules that perform the cash flow calculations. It also includes all the menu input and error checking VBA modules that function to make the amortization assumptions available to those calculators. This focuses on defaults, prepayments, recoveries, and market value decline assumptions.

Cash Flow Trace and Validation   As mentioned in passing earlier, we will need to preserve whatever cash flow calculation trace and validation software is now contained in the model. This is especially true as we contemplate the introduction into our collateral pools of other specialty mortgage types, specifically hybrid adjustable rate mortgages (HARMs) and other mortgages with variable rate, or variable payment features.

STEPPING THROUGH THE MODEL

The most straightforward and methodical approach to finding and removing all of the liabilities side elements of the Structuring Model is simply to start with the Main Program subroutine and work our way through it in order of its execution hierarchy.

Before we embark on the exercise, we should quickly visit the issue of carving out a set of exclusively asset side reports from the existing report package. Due to space constraints in this chapter and the large number of exhibits necessary to illustrate the VBA code changes, we will place the reports material on the Web site for this book.

In the section of the Web site pertaining to this chapter, you will find a set of template files for the BAM. The matching files for the Structuring Model can be found in the Chapter 6 Web site material.

We will present an overview of these changes in the section named "Step 0: The Reports" in this chapter. All the information, in excruciating detail, refers to the changes file mentioned above.

From that point on, we will review the Structuring Model from the outside in starting with the menus of the model. Progressing inward we will walk through each of the VBA modules in the order that the Main Program subroutine utilizes them. The one exception to this execution order-based approach will be the "A_Globals" variables module and the "A_Constants" variables module. These modules are independent of the execution sequence and will be visited after we have weeded out the menus a bit.

We will then progress through the rest of the VBA modules, finishing with the report-writing subroutines. Finally we will delete all references to the unused post-edit Range names of the spreadsheet and rename the Main Program.

Remember the adage of Virgil, the Roman poet, "Fortune favors the brave!"

Step 0: The Reports

Here we will quickly overview the changes to the report package. These reports will be presented, keeping with the methodology described above, in the order in which they are produced by the model in a normal course of operation.

There will be no changes to the Ineligible Collateral report package, the Eligible Collateral report package, and the format of the Eligible Collateral Portfolio file.

Waterfall Report   We will remove the "Debt Cash Flows" section and the "Performance" section of the Box Score on the left of the report. We will also remove columns "U" through "BV" of the spreadsheet. These columns are numbers 12 through 65 in the report itself.

Matrix Summary Report   We can delete in their entirety three of the four reports: the Tenor, Conduit Note Performance, and Seller Interest Performance reports. We will retain the Cash Flows report in that its contents are the collateral cash flows of the scenario.

Single-Scenario Report   In the "Assumptions" section in the left hand corner of the report, we will remove the "Program Costs" and the "Principal Acceleration Triggers" sections. We will then slide up the remaining portion of that column.

In the "Sources and Uses" section, we will eliminate all items below the "Collateral Cash Flows" section that ends on line 12.

We will eliminate the last five columns of the annual cash flows schedule. These are the two expense columns, "S" and "T," and the "Conduit Performance" section, columns "U," "V," and "W."

The last three columns of this table populate the graph at the lower right of the report entitled "Outstanding Conduit Balance, Principal, and Coupon Payments." With the data sources for the graph deleted from the table, we can now drop it from the report.

Step 1: The Menus

Working our way from the outside in and then down the execution sequence of the program, our first stop is the menus.

Main Menu   We do not need to make *any* changes whatsoever to the Main Menu. Why? At first glance it would appear impossible to NOT change something here; the entire Main Menu contents cannot be focused exclusively on the asset side of the model. You are right, they are not *exclusively* focused on the asset side, but every item on the Main Menu is at least partially focused on the asset side.

In the uppermost segment of the menu—see Exhibit 5.1—we will observe that the first four and the eighth of the Program Execution Options are exclusively asset model functions. The first four options relate to the collateral selection function, either performing the selection itself or producing the resultant reports or the final portfolio file of the eligible collateral. The eighth Program Execution Option turns on the trace function of the collateral cash flows calculation sequence. This function allows the user to specify the creation of a diagnostic file for each of the loans of the portfolio, at an individual cash flow component level, on a month-to-month basis, for each of the scenarios of the model run.

What about the fifth through the seventh options? These options relate to the production the Waterfall, Matrix Summary, and Single Scenario reports. All of these reports contain critical asset information. We have removed the liability structure

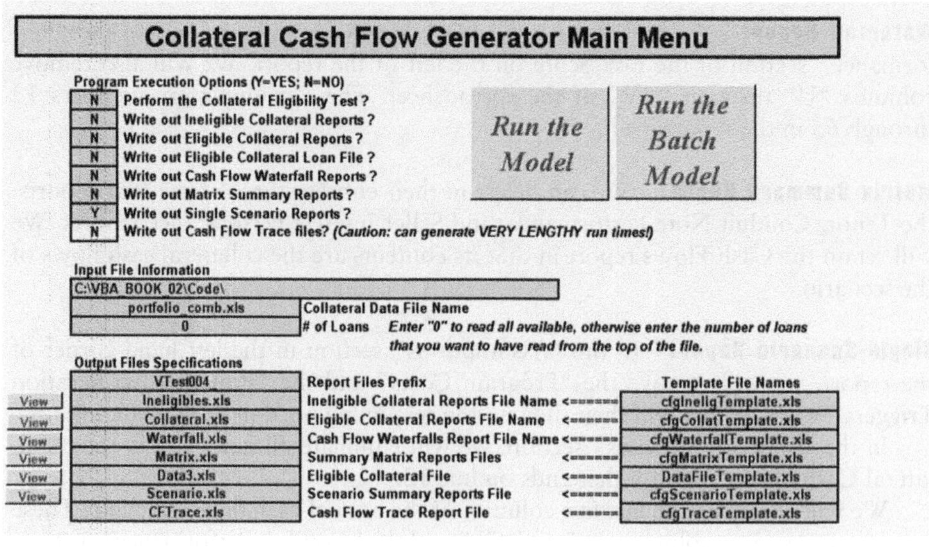

EXHIBIT 5.1   Main Menu will be unchanged

elements of the reports, but the necessity of producing them remains as they contain critical information about the timing and magnitude of the cash stream components. The Waterfall report will also serve as the input file to the Base Liability Model.

The second section of the Main Menu, the Input File Information section, is 100% asset side in function. This is the section that tells the model where to find the portfolio collateral file and how many records to process. We will leave it untouched.

Finally the two lower sections, the Output File Specifications and the Template File Names, will be unchanged as well. Why? These reports and the template files from which they are originated all contain asset information and therefore need to be retained.

Default and Prepayments Menu The Default and Prepayments Menu contains 100% asset side information related to the specification of the portfolio level inputs as to the collateral amortization conditions. There is no need to modify it. In the interest of space we will not present an exhibit of it at this time.

Rates and Dates Menu In the Rates and Dates Menu, shown in Exhibit 5.2, we can see that the only information that is *not* related to the asset side is the reference to the conduit pricing spread. The conduit pricing spread, the risk premium that in combination with the underlying index becomes the coupon of the liabilities, is set once at the beginning of the deal and is not changed thereafter. It is for that reason that the table in the Structuring Model contains a single value for each of the five scenarios. This piece of information, the spread over the base conduit financing rate of the liabilities is displayed in a small table in column "N" of the menu. This rate is used only in the liabilities side of the model. We can therefore remove that column and the two immediately to each side of it.

Program Costs Menu The Program Costs Menu contains a mix of both asset- and liabilities side information. The first five fields in this menu, the two deal expense

	Rates				Alternative LIBOR Pathways					Alternative Prime Rate Pathways							
	Prime	LIBOR		1	2	3	4	5	1	2	3	4	5		Month	D
	1	1														
1	5.250%	2.750%	1	2.750%	2.900%	3.000%	3.250%	3.500%	5.250%	6.000%	6.250%	7.000%	8.000%	1	1-Jan-08	0.I
2	5.250%	2.750%	2	2.750%	2.900%	3.000%	3.250%	3.500%	5.250%	6.000%	6.250%	7.000%	8.000%	2	1-Feb-08	0.I
3	5.250%	2.750%	3	2.750%	2.900%	3.000%	3.250%	3.500%	5.250%	6.000%	6.250%	7.000%	8.000%	3	1-Mar-08	0.I
4	5.250%	2.750%	4	2.750%	2.900%	3.000%	3.250%	3.500%	5.250%	6.000%	6.250%	7.000%	8.000%	4	1-Apr-08	0.I
5	5.250%	2.750%	5	2.750%	2.900%	3.000%	3.250%	3.500%	5.250%	6.000%	6.250%	7.000%	8.000%	5	1-May-08	0.I
6	5.250%	2.750%	6	2.750%	2.900%	3.000%	3.250%	3.500%	5.250%	6.000%	6.250%	7.000%	8.000%	6	1-Jun-08	0.I
7	5.250%	2.750%	7	2.750%	2.900%	3.000%	3.250%	3.500%	5.250%	6.000%	6.250%	7.000%	8.000%	7	1-Jul-08	0.I
8	5.250%	2.750%	8	2.750%	2.900%	3.000%	3.250%	3.500%	5.250%	6.000%	6.250%	7.000%	8.000%	8	1-Aug-08	0.I
9	5.250%	2.750%	9	2.750%	2.900%	3.000%	3.250%	3.500%	5.250%	6.000%	6.250%	7.000%	8.000%	9	1-Sep-08	0.I
10	5.250%	2.750%	10	2.750%	2.900%	3.000%	3.250%	3.500%	5.250%	6.000%	6.250%	7.000%	8.000%	10	1-Oct-08	0.I
11	5.250%	2.750%	11	2.750%	2.900%	3.000%	3.250%	3.500%	5.250%	6.000%	6.250%	7.000%	8.000%	11	1-Nov-08	0.I
12	5.250%	2.750%	12	2.750%	2.900%	3.000%	3.250%	3.500%	5.250%	6.000%	6.250%	7.000%	8.000%	12	1-Dec-08	0.I
13	5.250%	2.750%	13	2.750%	2.900%	3.000%	3.250%	3.500%	5.250%	6.000%	6.250%	7.000%	8.000%	13	1-Jan-09	0.I
14	5.250%	2.750%	14	2.750%	2.900%	3.000%	3.250%	3.500%	5.250%	6.000%	6.250%	7.000%	8.000%	14	1-Feb-09	0.I
15	5.250%	2.750%	15	2.750%	2.900%	3.000%	3.250%	3.500%	5.250%	6.000%	6.250%	7.000%	8.000%	15	1-Mar-09	0.I
16	5.250%	2.750%	16	2.750%	2.900%	3.000%	3.250%	3.500%	5.250%	6.000%	6.250%	7.000%	8.000%	16	1-Apr-09	0.I
17	5.250%	2.750%	17	2.750%	2.900%	3.000%	3.250%	3.500%	5.250%	6.000%	6.250%	7.000%	8.000%	17	1-May-09	0.I
18	5.250%	2.750%	18	2.750%	2.900%	3.000%	3.250%	3.500%	5.250%	6.000%	6.250%	7.000%	8.000%	18	1-Jun-09	0.I
19	5.250%	2.750%	19	2.750%	2.900%	3.000%	3.250%	3.500%	5.250%	6.000%	6.250%	7.000%	8.000%	19	1-Jul-09	0.I

Floating Rate Mortgage Index Rates and Day Counts

EXHIBIT 5.2 New Rates and Dates Menu less the conduit pricing table

rates, the two amortization triggers, and the deal financing advance rate are exclusively liability side parameters. The two expense items are entirely irrelevant to the asset side of the model. They are used to assess fees in the liability section of the waterfall once the notes have been issued and the deal is under way. Their use lies in the future, once the deal is up and running. We should not be particularly concerned what they are when we are in the process of selecting and amortizing the collateral. It can be argued that one of the accelerated conduit note amortization triggers relates to asset performance (the three-month default rate trigger). This trigger has no relevance whatsoever if we are concerned with the asset side of the model only. It serves to accelerate the pay down of the liability upon the advent of default rates that are higher than expected. In that the trigger therefore only affects the "Uses" side of the deal equation, it can be ignored. The last field, the "Advance Rate", is the percentage of financing in relationship to the initial balance of the collateral pool and is entirely a liability side item.

There are three fields remaining. The first of these, the "Conduit Spread Choice" is used to indicate which vector of spreads that we will select from the Rate and Dates Menu to determine the financing rate for the conduit debt. It is therefore an exclusively liability side item. The next two fields, the "Libor Pathway" field and the "Prime Rate Pathway" field are used by both the asset and the liability side of the model. We can however move both of these fields from the Program Costs Menu to the Rates and Dates Menu. We will place these fields at the tops of column "C" and "D" respectively.

This change effectively clears the menu of all input fields, and we can delete the Program Costs Menu altogether.

Report Selection Menu The Reports Selection Menu, shown in Exhibit 5.3, allows the analyst to select an individual report from either the Eligible Collateral report package, the column to the left, or the Matrix Summary report package, the column on the right. We will obviously want to retain the entire contents of the left column as

Report Selection Menu

Run ? "X"	Report Code	PORTFOLIO STRATIFICATION REPORTS Report Name	Run ? "X"	Report Code	MULTIPLE SCENARIO MATRIX RESULTS Report Name
X	Elig-1	Current Balances by Original Term Structure	X	Matrix-1	Collateral Cash Flows Report
X	Elig-2	Current Balances by Remaining Term Structure			(reserved for future use)
X	Elig-3	Current Balances by Loan Seasoning			(reserved for future use)
X	Elig-4	Current Balances by Yield			(reserved for future use)
X	Elig-5	Current Balance by Spread			(reserved for future use)
X	Elig-6	Current Balances by Owners Equity %			
X	Elig-7	Current Balances by LTV %			
X	Elig-8	Current Balances by $ Current Balances			*Run the*
X	Elig-9	Current Balances by $ Original Balances			*Model*
X	Elig-10	Geographic Concentration -- State Code			
X	Elig-11	Geographic Concentration -- Zip Code			
		(reserved for future use)			
		(reserved for future use)			
		(reserved for future use)			
		(reserved for future use)			
		(reserved for future use)			
		(reserved for future use)			
		(reserved for future use)			

EXHIBIT 5.3 New Report Selection Menu

it allows us to perform a limited customization of the eligible collateral stratification reports produced.

Of the Matrix Summary reports, three of them, the "Tenor" report, the "Conduit Note Performance" report, and the "Seller Interest Performance" report, are designed to display the liability performance. These three reports will be eliminated, and the sole surviving report, the "Collateral Cash Flows" report, will be advanced to the initial position in the list. The vacated list positions two through four will be marked "(reserved for future use)," allowing us to create and list additional BAM reports at a future time if necessary without reconfiguring the menu.

Waterfall Report Spreadsheet The Waterfall Report Spreadsheet, shown in Exhibit 5.4, will now be edited to conform to the format that we created for the Waterfall Report template file. We will eliminate all the contents of the leftmost Box Score section that lie below the initial Collateral Cash Flows Summary section. In addition, we will also delete all columns of the spreadsheet to the right of column "U," eliminating the liability portion of the waterfall.

There is an advantage to retaining the first ten columns of the report. We will avoid the task of designing, and programming the production of, an eligible collateral cash flow file. Remember that we will need a file containing the cash flows as a bridge between the BAM and the BLM. The cash flows will not magically leap from one model to the next! We do not need to reinvent this file, as the surviving portions of the "CFWaterfall" spreadsheet will meet all the requirements for holding the cash flow components of a single scenario. A simple subroutine or two in the BLM will suffice to read the contents of this file and its summary amounts. This file also has the added advantage of having all of the assumptions used in its creation, including the file name of the original collateral portfolio file, written to the accompanying Assumptions Page report. The various scenarios written to separate worksheets are each identified by the unique prepayment and default conditions used to generate their cash flows.

Single Scenario Cash Flow Waterfall Report

600.00%	PSA	<= *Defaults*
400.00%	PSA	<= *Prepays*

Summary Report

Collateral Cash Flows		
Scheduled Amortization	105,136,955	24.28%
Prepayments to Principal	284,395,478	65.68%
Total Principal Retired	389,532,433	
Defaulted Principal	43,492,316	10.04%
Recoveries of Principal	38,043,165	87.47%
Coupon Income	130,943,161	
Total Cash Sources	**558,518,759**	

1	2	3	4	5	6	7	8	9	10	12	13
	Collateral Cash Flow										
	Beginning Principal Balance	Pool Factor	Regular Amort Principal	Prepaid Principal	Defaulted Principal	Ending Principal Balance Outstanding	Total Principal Retired	Coupon Income	Recoveries of Principal	Total Cash Available For Waterfall	
			105,136,955	284,395,478	43,492,316		389,532,433	130,943,161	38,043,165	558,518,759	
1	433,024,749	1.00000	1,705,717	288,138	699,284	430,331,610	1,993,855	3,067,388	-	5,061,243	1
2	430,331,610	0.99378	1,713,741	574,743	730,636	427,312,490	2,288,484	3,047,805	-	5,336,289	2
3	427,312,490	0.98681	1,720,504	859,155	760,352	423,972,478	2,579,660	3,025,922	-	5,605,582	3
4	423,972,478	0.97910	1,725,986	1,140,717	788,554	420,317,222	2,866,702	3,001,775	-	5,868,477	4
5	420,317,222	0.97065	1,730,164	1,418,775	815,213	416,353,070	3,148,940	2,975,404	-	6,124,343	5
6	416,353,070	0.96150	1,733,025	1,692,690	840,101	412,087,254	3,425,714	2,946,856	-	6,372,571	6
7	412,087,254	0.95165	1,734,553	1,961,828	863,326	407,527,547	3,696,381	2,916,184	-	6,612,565	7
8	407,527,547	0.94112	1,734,742	2,225,575	884,338	402,682,893	3,960,317	2,883,447	-	6,843,763	8
9	402,682,893	0.92993	1,733,583	2,483,331	903,412	397,562,567	4,216,914	2,848,706	-	7,065,619	9
10	397,562,567	0.91811	1,731,072	2,734,516	920,280	392,176,699	4,465,589	2,812,030	-	7,277,619	10
11	392,176,699	0.90567	1,727,211	2,978,574	934,909	386,536,005	4,705,785	2,773,492	-	7,479,277	11
12	386,536,005	0.89264	1,722,003	3,214,972	946,979	380,652,051	4,936,976	2,733,170	-	7,670,145	12
13	380,652,051	0.87905	1,715,455	3,443,206	956,669	374,536,721	5,158,661	2,691,145	636,393	8,486,199	13
14	374,536,721	0.86493	1,707,578	3,662,806	963,061	368,203,276	5,370,383	2,647,510	662,696	8,680,589	14
15	368,203,276	0.85031	1,698,384	3,873,326	967,144	361,664,422	5,571,710	2,602,350	687,507	8,861,566	15
16	361,664,422	0.83520	1,687,888	4,074,350	969,154	354,933,031	5,762,238	2,555,755	710,954	9,028,947	16
17	354,933,031	0.81966	1,676,108	4,265,500	968,476	348,022,946	5,941,609	2,507,821	733,012	9,182,442	17
18	348,022,946	0.80370	1,663,067	4,446,433	965,433	340,948,013	6,109,500	2,458,645	753,478	9,321,624	18
19	340,948,013	0.78736	1,648,790	4,616,835	960,404	333,721,984	6,265,625	2,408,321	772,470	9,446,416	19
20	333,721,984	0.77068	1,633,303	4,776,431	953,285	326,358,965	6,409,735	2,356,949	789,483	9,556,167	20

EXHIBIT 5.4 New "CFWaterfall" spreadsheet

Batch Output File Menu

	Select	Market Value Decline	Recovery Period Lag	Conduit Finance Spread	File Name Prefix ID	Libor Rates Path	Prime Rates Path	File Name Prefix
1	X	50%	12	2.000%	Test_06_01	3	1	Test_06_01_MVD50_RPL12_S200
2	X	50%	12	2.000%	Test_06_02	3	1	Test_06_02_MVD50_RPL12_S200
3	X	50%	12	2.000%	Test_06_03	3	1	Test_06_03_MVD50_RPL12_S200
4	X	50%	12	2.000%	Test_06_04	3	1	Test_06_04_MVD50_RPL12_S200
5	X	50%	12	2.000%	Test_06_05	3	1	Test_06_05_MVD50_RPL12_S200
6	X	60%	12	2.000%	Test_06_06	3	1	Test_06_06_MVD60_RPL12_S200
7	X	60%	12	2.000%	Test_06_07	3	1	Test_06_07_MVD60_RPL12_S200
8	X	60%	12	2.000%	Test_06_08	3	1	Test_06_08_MVD60_RPL12_S200
9	X	60%	12	2.000%	Test_06_09	3	1	Test_06_09_MVD60_RPL12_S200
10	X	70%	12	2.000%	Test_06_10	3	1	Test_06_10_MVD70_RPL12_S200
11	X	70%	12	2.000%	Test_06_11	3	1	Test_06_11_MVD70_RPL12_S200
12	X	70%	12	2.000%	Test_06_12	3	1	Test_06_12_MVD70_RPL12_S200
13	X	70%	12	2.000%	Test_06_13	3	1	Test_06_13_MVD70_RPL12_S200
14	X	70%	12	2.000%	Test_06_14	3	1	Test_06_14_MVD70_RPL12_S200
15	X	70%	12	2.000%	Test_06_15	3	1	Test_06_15_MVD70_RPL12_S200
16								
17								
18								

Run the Batch Model

EXHIBIT 5.5   New Batch Mode Menu

Batch Mode Menu   The Structuring Model contains a feature that allows the analyst who to input a series of entries that will trigger successive runs of the model. The input for each of these runs is determined by the entries to a single line in the Batch Mode Menu as seen in Exhibit 5.5.

The set of inputs related to the liabilities side of the model is our old friend the conduit spread financing rate in columns "F" and "I." We will delete these columns. One of these columns, however, is used to produce the compound file name in the rightmost column. When we delete the Range name from a worksheet, we get a "#REF" error message in the menu field. This means that Excel can no longer identify the cells the formula was formerly referencing. We will need to eliminate the reference to the conduit financing spread in the formula of this field. We can simply modify the formula in the first row of the table and then copy the change to the successive rows.

The preservation of this function will be very useful in the future if we want to explore large numbers of collateral combinations. We can simply run the pool amortizations on a single machine while we are busy doing something else! This is a great way to leverage your productivity on deals such as these.

Pausing before the Descent into the Code

Having completed the modifications to the menus of what will become the BAM, we will now enter the VBA modules of the program. We are fortunate that these modules contain task-related, and logically grouped, subroutines and functions. Each of the modules is clearly labeled, and the module names are easily understood. The module names reflect the roles that the subroutines within them perform during the execution sequence of the model. You might think this is a trivial and self-evident issue and that all the someone else's models (SEMs) that you see will look broadly like this one.

Don't kid yourself! I was once shown a very simple, barely Level 3 model that had these six module names:

1. ABSAuto06_898_CVD
2. VariablesAndOtherStuff
3. NewCode
4. OldCode
5. VeryOldCode
6. CodeNotUsed

I have to admit I was stunned. To make matters even worse, its author, who said, "VBA is limited in its modeling usefulness. Besides it's so simple, I learned it in a weekend!" was in the process of proudly presenting this model as an example of a well-ordered application!

So there you have it. Tread lightly into the SEMs you encounter! Although I hope that you never see anything as obscure, obtuse, ill planned, and obstructionist as the example above, some SEMs will assuredly *not* be as transparent as the look of either the Structuring Model or the BAM and BLM we will derive from it.

Let us step backward for a minute and get the lay of the land. In Exhibit 5.6 we have a listing of the main program of the "Loan_Financing_Model". This is the topmost subroutine in the Structuring Model. Unless the model is operating in a Batch Mode method, no other subroutines call the "Loan_Financing_Model" subroutine while all other subroutines can trace their call trees back to this point of origin. As in the old saying "All roads lead to Rome," all subroutines can trace their calling trees back to this starting point.

If we therefore start at the top of this code and trace it, call by call, from the first higher-level calls in this Main Program subroutine to the lowest-level calls below it, we will exhaustively visit all the code of the model. Even at the highest level we can

```
Sub Loan_Financing_Model()

    Application.DisplayAlerts = False            'temporarily turn off the warning me
    Call Display PrepayDefault ProgressMsg(99)   'display program progress msg (null)
    Call ErrCheck_All_Menus                      'error check all menu entries
    Call Read_All_Menu_Input                     'transfer the menu entries to variab
    Call Read_Portfolio_Data_File                'read in the loan information to var
    Call Select_Deal_Collateral                  'select collateral, print eligibilit
    gMainFileName = ActiveWorkbook.Name
    'run the cash flow waterfall model
    Call Compute_Collateral_Cashflows            'generate the cash flows
    Call Load_and_Run_the_Waterfall              'loads scenario cfs and runs the wat
    'write the report package
    Call Write_Waterfall_Report_Package          'package of waterfall reports in det
    Call Write_Matrix_Report_Package             'package of 4 matrix reports
    Call Write_Scenario_Report_Package           'package of single scenario reports
    'exit the program
    Sheets("Main Menu").Select
    Application.DisplayAlerts = True              'turn message displays back on
    Application.StatusBar = False

End Sub
```

EXHIBIT 5.6 "Loan_Financing_Model" subroutine

see that there are several sections of the code that we will be involved in, but more important, there are several we can ignore. Fortunately, there are only ten calls to other subroutines. One of these is a call to a trivial message subroutine. The names of the others explicitly state what they do. We can now review these in turn and see where our work will be focused.

In that we have made changes to the menus, we will certainly have to visit the first two calls, "ErrCheck_All_Menus" and "Read_All_Menu_Input". The subroutines under the third call of the program, "Read_Portoflio_Data_File", will probably not require any modification whatsoever, as we are not, at the present time, changing the asset types being modeled. The sole purpose of the subroutines below this call is to open the collateral data file, error check the contents, and transfer them to VBA arrays. This is clearly and exclusively an asset side function. Likewise the call to the subroutine "Select_Deal_Collateral" is also obviously an exclusively asset side activity. This is immediately followed by the subroutine "Compute_Collateral_Cashflows", an asset side functionality if there ever was one!

Having cash flows in hand, we will now load them into the "CFWaterfall" spreadsheet and capture the results. This function is performed by the subroutines call from "Load_and_Run_the_Waterfall". This is an obvious place where we will need to remove the code that records the performance of the liabilities structure. From this point on, the rest of the model is involved solely in the reporting function. The next three subroutine calls are specific to the report packages that they produce. The Collateral Eligibility reports were produced earlier. These calls all produce reports that have elements of the liability structure results within their contents. We will need to examine each of these and eliminate the references to the liability structure performance of those elements. Having completed that task, we will be almost done with the transformation. All that will remain will be to purge all unused liability structure Range names from the program, rename the Main Program subroutine to "Base_Asset_Model", and relink any of the "Run Program" buttons reflecting the change in the newly renamed Main Program subroutine name.

We will shortly be looking at a lot of code samples. Wherever possible I have indicated in the exhibits the lines of code that will be changed by highlighting them. I used the "Insert Breakpoint" feature that works on executable statements only. For variable declarations and other non-executable lines in the program, I will specifically reference them as the nth line from the top or bottom of the exhibit (whichever is closer).

So let us start at the top of the "Loan_Financing_Model" subroutine and get to work!

Step 2: Menu Error Checking Module

All subroutines visited in this step are contained in the module "MenusError Checking" unless otherwise indicated.

"ErrCheck_All_Menus" Subroutine   Our first stop is the subroutine "ErrCheck_All_Menus" shown in Exhibit 5.7. In this subroutine we see calls to seven other subroutines. The first of these calls performs a check for numeric format entries on all of the menus. The next six perform error checks on the individual input fields of

```
Sub ErrCheck_All_Menus()

    'Set up of message title
    msgTitle = "MODEL MENUs Input Error"
    Call errAllMenus_for_IsNumerics
    Call errMainMenu
    Call errProgramCostsMenu
    Call errReportsMenu
    Call errGeographicMenu
    Call errSelectionCriteriaMenu
    Call errDefaultsMenu

End Sub
```

EXHIBIT 5.7   "ErrCheck_All_Menus" subroutine

the Main, Program Costs, Report Selection, Geographic Selection Criteria, Collateral Selection Criteria, and the Defaults Menus in that order.

We have not made any changes to the Main, Geographic Selection Criteria, Collateral Selection Criteria, and Defaults Menus. We will therefore ignore the error checking subroutines for this code.

The Program Costs Menu has been eliminated in its entirety. We can therefore delete the call to "errProgramCostsMenu" and the subroutine itself. We have modified the content of the Reports Menu, so we will need to modify the VBA that reads the menu on our visit to that code.

Last we will take a look at the "errAllMenu_Is_Numerics" subroutine to eliminate references to the Program Costs menu that it contains.

"errProgramCostsMenu" Subroutine   The subroutine "errProgramCostsMenu", shown in Exhibit 5.8, is now no longer required as the entire menu that it supports has been deleted from the BAM. We will remove it in its entirety.

"errAllMenus_for_IsNumerics" Subroutine   The subroutine "errAllMenus_for_IsNumerics", shown in Exhibit 5.9, contains calls to four other subroutines. These subroutines error check the numeric entries of the Program Costs, Collateral Select Criteria, Defaults, and Rates and Dates Menus.

If any of the called subroutines find errors on their respective menus, a variable, "mErrCase(n)", is set to TRUE. This will later trigger the display of an error message concerning that particular menu. The Program Costs Menu has been deleted so the call to perform an error check on its numeric fields should be deleted from this subroutine as well. Due to this fact we will need to delete one of the four "mErrCase" array members from the fifth line of the subroutine. We only have three menus to check now so that line will become:

```
MsgTotal = mErrCase(1) + mErrCase(2) + mErrCase(3)
```

We notice a little lower in this subroutine that there is a loop that runs from 1 to "MENU_CHECK_NUMERIC", a Constant variable that is currently defined in the "A_Constants" module and set to a value of 4. With the elimination of the Program

```
Sub errProgramCostsMenu()

    'menu location masthead statement for top of error message
    msgTotal = "Program Cost Menu    => " & Chr(13)
    'group error conditions
    msgInfo(1) = "   These costs must be between 0% and 5%" & Chr(13)
    msgInfo(2) = "   Notes Clean Up percentage must be between 0% and 10%" & Chr(13)
    msgInfo(3) = "   Delinquency Rate Trigger must be between 0% and 10%" & Chr(13)
    msgInfo(4) = "   Advance Rate must be between 0% and 100%" & Chr(13)
    msgInfo(5) = "   Pathway Choice must be between 1 and 5" & Chr(13)
    'individual field error conditions
    msgComp(1) = "        Servicing Expense rate" & Chr(13)
    msgComp(2) = "        Program Expense charge rate" & Chr(13)
    msgComp(3) = "        Note Clean Up percentage" & Chr(13)
    msgComp(4) = "        Rolling 3 Month Delinquency rate" & Chr(13)
    msgComp(5) = "        Conduit Advance rate" & Chr(13)
    msgComp(6) = "        Conduit Spread Pathway Choice" & Chr(13)
    msgComp(7) = "        LIBOR Rate Pathway Choice" & Chr(13)
    msgComp(8) = "        Prime Rate Pathway Choice" & Chr(13)

    'test the values of each of the fields of the menu
    For itest = 1 To PROG_COSTS_FIELDS
        mErrResult(itest) = False
        Select Case itest
            Case Is = 1: x = Range("m2ServicerExp")
            Case Is = 2: x = Range("m2ProgramExpenses")
            Case Is = 3: x = Range("m2TrigCleanUpPct")
            Case Is = 4: x = Range("m2Trig3MDelRate")
            Case Is = 5: x = Range("m2AdvanceRate")
            Case Is = 6: x = Range("m2SpreadChoice")
            Case Is = 7: x = Range("m2LiborPathway")
```

EXHIBIT 5.8 "errProgramCostsMenu" subroutine

Costs Menu, we will need to adjust its value to 3. We will make a note of this and adjust it at a later date when we visit that module.

"IsNumeric_ProgramCostsInfo" Subroutine   The "IsNumeric_ProgramCostsInfo" subroutine, shown in Exhibit 5.10, can be eliminated entirely as it supports a menu that now no longer exists.

```
Sub errAllMenus_for_IsNumerics()

    Call IsNumeric_ProgramCostsInfo    'populates msgInfo(1) & mErrCase
    Call IsNumeric_CriteriaInfo        'populates msgInfo(2) & mErrCase
    Call IsNumeric_DefaultPrepayInfo   'populates msgInfo(3) & mErrCase
    Call IsNumeric_RatesDatesInfo      'populates msgInfo(4) & mErrCase

    'If there are errors to print -- print them!
    mErrTotal = mErrCase(1) + mErrCase(2) + mErrCase(3) + mErrCase(4)
    If mErrTotal > 0 Then
        'Error box title -- displayed above any errors
        msgTotal = "Non-numeric Inputs for the following Tables" & Chr(13) & Chr(13)
        'Print the combination of errors based on the error code value
        For iloop = 1 To MENU_CHECK_NUMERIC
            If mErrCase(iloop) > 0 Then msgTotal = msgTotal & msgInfo(iloop)
        Next iloop
        msgPrompt = msgTotal
        msgResult = MsgBox(msgPrompt, cMsgButtonCode1, msgTitle)
        End
    End If

End Sub
```

EXHIBIT 5.9 "errAllMenus_for_IsNumerics" subroutine

```
Sub IsNumeric_ProgramCostsInfo()

    msgInfo(1) = "Program Cost Menu    => non-numeric entry in inputs" & Chr(13)
    msgComp(1) = "     Servicing Expense rate" & Chr(13)
    msgComp(2) = "     Program Expense charge rate" & Chr(13)
    msgComp(3) = "     Note Clean Up Trigger percentage" & Chr(13)
    msgComp(4) = "     3 Month Rolling Delinquency Rate" & Chr(13)
    msgComp(5) = "     Conduit Advance Rate" & Chr(13)
    msgComp(6) = "     Conduit Spread Pathway Choice" & Chr(13)
    msgComp(7) = "     Conduit LIBOR Rate Pathway Choice" & Chr(13)
    msgComp(8) = "     Conduit Prime Rate Pathway Choice" & Chr(13)
    'set all IsNumeric tests to OK
    For itest = 1 To ISNUMERIC_TESTS_PROG_COSTS
        mErrResult(itest) = False
    Next itest
    'check each of the fields for non numerics
    mErrResult(1) = (IsNumeric(Range("m2ServicerExp")) = False)
    mErrResult(2) = (IsNumeric(Range("m2ProgramExpenses")) = False)
    mErrResult(3) = (IsNumeric(Range("m2TrigCleanUpPct")) = False)
    mErrResult(4) = (IsNumeric(Range("m2Trig3MDelRate")) = False)
    mErrResult(5) = (IsNumeric(Range("m2AdvanceRate")) = False)
    mErrResult(6) = (IsNumeric(Range("m2SpreadChoice")) = False)
    mErrResult(7) = (IsNumeric(Range("m2LiborPathway")) = False)
    mErrResult(8) = (IsNumeric(Range("m2PrimePathway")) = False)
    'combine any or all of the above messages into a compound message
    'the compound message will be sent to the calling sub for display
    mErrCase(1) = False          'no non numerics detected
    For itest = 1 To ISNUMERIC_TESTS_PROG_COSTS
        If mErrResult(itest) = True Then              'got one!
            mErrCase(1) = mErrCase(1) + 1               'tell calling sub to print out
            msgInfo(1) = msgInfo(1) & msgComp(itest)  'add detail msg to general header
        End If
    Next itest

End Sub
```

EXHIBIT 5.10   "IsNumeric_ProgramCostsInfo" subroutine

"IsNumeric_RatesDatesInfo" Subroutine   Due to its length, the "IsNumerics_RatesDatesInfo" subroutine is shown in Exhibits 5.11 and 5.12. If you recall, we removed the conduit financing spread from this menu as it was an item related solely to the liability side of the model. We therefore now need to remove those portions of this subroutine that checked the contents of that Range.

In Exhibit 5.11 we will remove the variable declaration of "condt_value":

```
Dim condt_value   as String
```

We will also delete the assignment statement to the array element "msgComp(3)" that pertains to the conduit spread:

```
MsgComp(3) = ''Conduit Spread Table in Entry ''
```

We will renumber the initialization of the "mErrCase" array element from 4 to 3 because the Rates and Dates Menu check has moved up a notch in the queue upon the elimination of the Program Costs Menu, thus:

```
MErrCase(3) = 0
```

This ends our changes to the top portion of the subroutine.

```
Sub IsNumeric_RatesDatesInfo()

Const NUM_TABLES = 2                    'number of rates tables
Const NUM_COLS = 5                      'number of columns per table
Dim libor_value        As String       'test value for the libor rate
Dim condt_value        As String       'test value for the conduit spread
Dim prime_value        As String       'test value for the prime rate
Dim column_err(1 To NUM_COLS, 1 To NUM_TABLES + 1) As Double 'number of errors in co
Dim table_total(1 To NUM_TABLES + 1)                As Double 'number of errors in ta
Dim rtable             As Integer      'counter for looping through tables

    msgInfo(4) = "Rates & Dates Menu   => non-numeric entry in table" & Chr(13)
    msgComp(1) = "    LIBOR Rate Table in Pathway "
    msgComp(2) = "    Prime Spread Table in Pathway "
    msgComp(3) = "    Conduit Spread Table in Entry "
    msgComp(4) = Chr(13)
    mErrCase(4) = 0                     'tells the calling subroutine we have error if = 1

    'set all error counts for the columns and tables to zero
    For itest = 1 To NUM_TABLES + 1
        table_total(itest) = 0
        For icase = 1 To 5
            column_err(icase, itest) = 0#
        Next icase
    Next itest
```

EXHIBIT 5.11 "IsNumeric_RatesDatesInfo" subroutine (first half)

In the second half of the subroutine, we will drop the entire section under the comment "conduit spread table in Entry". This checks the values of this now-defunct table.

In the section immediately following we need to renumber all the references to "msgInfo(4)" and "msgComp(4)" to "msgInfo(3)" and "msgComp(3)". This reflects the elimination of the conduit spread table above.

```
    'Conduit Spread Table
    For icase = 1 To 5
        condt_value = Range("m11AltConduitSpreads").Cells(icase)
        'if the cell is not blank then test the value for numeric
        mErrResult(3) = False:
        If condt_value <> "" Then mErrResult(3) = (IsNumeric(condt_value) = False)
        'if we find an error, increment the counter and table of the error
        If mErrResult(3) Then
            column_err(icase, 3) = column_err(icase, 3) + 1
            table_total(3) = table_total(3) + 1
            mErrCase(4) = 1                      'error of this type detected
        End If
    Next icase

    'assemble the error message
    For itest = 1 To NUM_TABLES + 1                        '1=Libor, 2=Prime, 3=Condui
        If table_total(itest) > 0 Then                    'got one!
            msgInfo(4) = msgInfo(4) & msgComp(itest)      'add detail msg to general
            For icase = 1 To 5
                If column_err(icase, itest) > 0 Then      'add the pathway(s) numbers
                    msgInfo(4) = msgInfo(4) & " " & icase & ","
                End If
            Next icase
            msgInfo(4) = msgInfo(4) & msgComp(4)          'close with a line return
        End If
    Next itest

End Sub
```

EXHIBIT 5.12 "IsNumeric_RatesDatesInfo" subroutine (second half)

```
Option Explicit
' ================================================================================
'MODULE LEVEL CONSTANTS
' ================================================================================
'Number of numeric entry tests by menu
Const ISNUMERIC_TESTS_SEL_CRIT = 13     '# isnumeric? test Selection Criteria menu
Const ISNUMERIC_TESTS_PROG_COSTS = 8    '# isnumeric? test Program Costs menu
Const ISNUMERIC_TESTS_PRE_DEF = 8       '# isnumeric? test Prepayment/Defaults menu
'Number of input field value tests by menu
Const VALUE_TESTS_SEL_CRIT = 4          '# value tests of Selection Criteria menu input
Const VALUE_TESTS_PROG_COSTS = 8        '# value tests of Program Costs menu inputs
Const VALUE_TESTS_DEFAULT_PREPAY = 5    '# value tests of Prepay/Defaults menu inputs
'Number of output file sets we need to check to prevent overwritting of existing files
Const OUTPUT_FILE_TESTS = 7             '# types of output file election tests
Const OUTPUT_FILE_EXISTS = 7            '# tests for overwritting existing output files

Const cMsgButtonCode1  As Integer = vbOKOnly + vbCritical
Const cMsgButtonCode2  As Integer = vbOKOnly + vbExclamation
```

EXHIBIT 5.13   Module scope Constant variable declarations (prior to editing)

"IsNumeric_CriteriaInfo" Subroutine   In this subroutine we need to renumber all the references to "msgInfo(2)" and "msgComp(2)" to "msgInfo(1)" and "msg-Comp(1)". This reflects the elimination of the conduit spread table above.

"IsNumeric_DefaultPrepay" Subroutine   In this subroutine we need to renumber all the references to "msgInfo(3)" and "msgComp(3)" to "msgInfo(2)" and "msg-Comp(2)". This reflects the elimination of the conduit spread table above.

Module Scope Constant Variable Declarations   In Exhibit 5.13 we see the declaration of module level Constant variables that support these error checking subroutines. To correctly ripple through the changes we have made to the error checking of the Program Costs Menu and the Rates and Dates Menu, we need to make two changes here.

This first change is to eliminate the declaration for the Constant variables "ISNMERIC_TEST_PROG_COSTS". The second is to eliminate the Constant variable "VALUE_TEST_PROG_COSTS". These variables were used exclusively in handling inputs for the Program Costs Menu that we have deleted in the steps above.

Step 3: Menu Input Module

The next step that the model performs after error checking the contents of the menus is to move the now-verified information from the menus into its VBA variables and arrays.

This process starts with a call to the subroutine "Read_All_Menu_Input". This subroutine in turn calls eight additional menu specific subroutines that read the contents of their respective menus into the VBA arrays that have been declared to receive them.

All the subroutines in this section are contained in the module "MenusRead Inputs".

"Read_All_Menu_Input" Subroutine   In the "Read_All_Menu_Input" subroutine, shown in Exhibit 5.14, we can see a direct and transparent correspondence

```
Sub Read_All_Menu_Input()

    Call Read_Main_Menu                    'Read Main Menu -- set program run options
    Call Read_Program_Costs_Menu           'Reads the program costs and credit enhance
    Call Read_Selection_Criteria_Menu      'Read tenor, coupon & balance selection cri
    Call Read_Report_Selection_Menu        'Read menu for report selections
    Call Read_Geographic_Menu              'Read state code geographic selection crite
    Call Read_Prepay_Defaults_Menu         'Read prepayment and default schedule to ap
    Call Read_Rates_and_Dates_Menu         'Read the rates and dates menu
    Call Read_Coupon_Trace_Screen          'Read the Coupon Trace report switch

End Sub
```

EXHIBIT 5.14   "Read_All_Menu_Input" subroutine

between each of the calls and the menus of the model. As noted when we took our first look at the error checking double of this subroutine earlier, there are several subroutines called here that are exclusively asset side functions. We will not need to review or modify any of this code if the names of the subroutines are accurate in describing the function of the code within them.

We can make the same observations that we made of the error checking code above. We have not made any changes to the Main, Geographic Selection Criteria, Collateral Selection Criteria, and the Defaults Menus. We will ignore these subroutines as they are exclusively asset side in nature, and their menus are unchanged.

The Program Costs Menu has been eliminated in its entirety. We can therefore delete the call to "ReadProgram_Costs_Menu". We have modified the content of the Reports Menu, so we will visit the "Read_Report_Selection_Menu". We have also modified the Rates and Dates Menu, necessitating a review of the "Read_Rates_and_Dates_Menu" subroutine.

"Read_Program_Costs_Menu" Subroutine   With the elimination of this menu, we can delete the entire subroutine as well. It is shown in Exhibit 5.15.

"Read_Rates_and_Dates_Menu" Subroutine   On this menu we have eliminated the two columns and the small table of conduit financing spreads. We must therefore adjust the menu-reading subroutine to align with the new menu configuration and

```
Sub Read_Program_Costs_Menu()

    Sheets("Program Costs Menu").Select
    Range("A1").Select
    ' Read program costs section of the menu
    gExpenseService = Range("m2ServicerExp") / 12#      'servicing fee
    gExpenseProgram = Range("m2ProgramExpenses") / 12#  'program expenses
    gTriggerCleanup = Range("m2TrigCleanUpPct")         'principal reallocation trigger
    gTrigger3MDefaults = Range("m2Trig3MDelRate")       'principal reallocation trigger
    gAdvanceRate = Range("m2AdvanceRate")               'conduit advance rate
    gSpreadPath = Range("m2SpreadChoice")               'spread pathway elected
    gLIBORPath = Range("m2LiborPathway")                'libor pathway elected
    gPrimePath = Range("m2PrimePathway")                'prime rate pathway elected

End Sub
```

EXHIBIT 5.15   "Read_Program_Costs_Menu" subroutine

contents. We will first change the "icol" counter terminus from 3 to 2 in the 12th line of the subroutine. This will now read only the LIBOR (London Interbank Offered Rate) and prime rate pathways.

The second change is to eliminate the statement that reads the choice of the conduit funding spread:

```
gConduitSpread = Range(''m11IndexLevels'').Cells(1,3)
```

We will also delete the entire "For..Next" loop immediately below it that reads the funding rates from the conduit spread table. See Exhibit 5.16.

"Read_Report_Selection_Menu" Subroutine   To bring this subroutine in line with the changes we made to the Reports Menu Matrix Summary report list, we need only change the value of the "MATRIX_REPORTS" variable from its previous value of 4 to its current value of 1, reflecting our elimination of three of the initial four reports.

"Redim_All_MatrixSummaryReport_Vectors" Subroutines   Although we did not modify the Defaults and Prepayment Menu, some of the menu inputs are used to determine the total number of cases in each scenario. The total number of cases is determined by the product of the number of default scenarios multiplied by the number of prepayment scenarios.

The "Redim_All_MatrixSummaryReport_Vectors" subroutine shown in Exhibit 5.17 uses these values to re-dimension a number of previously declared vectors holding liability side performance statistics. These statistics include average life,

```
Sub Read_Rates_and_Dates_Menu()

    Sheets("Rates Dates Menu").Select
    Range("A1").Select
    Sheets("Rates Dates Menu").Calculate
    'read the day count factors for 30/360, Act/360, Act/Act
    For irow = 1 To PAY_DATES
        For icol = 1 To 3
            gDayFactors(irow, icol) = Range("m11DayCntFactors").Cells(irow, icol)
        Next icol
        gMonths(irow) = Range("m11Months").Cells(irow)
    Next irow
    'index interest level; Prime, LIBOR, spread
    For irow = 1 To PAY_DATES
        For icol = 1 To 3
            gIndexLevels(irow, icol) = Range("m11IndexLevels").Cells(irow, icol)
        Next icol
    Next irow
    gConduitSpread = Range("m11IndexLevels").Cells(1, 3)

    'funding rates for the conduit
    For irow = 1 To PAY_DATES
        gFundConduit(irow) = Range("m11FundConduit").Cells(irow)
    Next irow

End Sub
```

EXHIBIT 5.16   "Read_Rates_and_Dates_Menu" subroutine

```
Sub Redim_All_SummaryMatrixReport_Vectors()

    'If we are going to produce the summary matrix cashflows
    If gOutputMatrixReport Then
        ReDim gOutAverageLife(1 To gPrepayLevels, 1 To gDefaultLevels) As Double
        ReDim gOutFinalMaturity(1 To gPrepayLevels, 1 To gDefaultLevels) As Double
        ReDim gOutModDuration(1 To gPrepayLevels, 1 To gDefaultLevels) As Double
        ReDim gOutMacDuration(1 To gPrepayLevels, 1 To gDefaultLevels) As Double
        ReDim gOutAmt10yrs(1 To gPrepayLevels, 1 To gDefaultLevels) As Double
        ReDim gOutTotalDefaults(1 To gPrepayLevels, 1 To gDefaultLevels) As Double
        ReDim gOutRecoveries(1 To gPrepayLevels, 1 To gDefaultLevels) As Double
        ReDim gOutPctPaidExcess(1 To gPrepayLevels, 1 To gDefaultLevels) As Double
        ReDim gOutPctPaidSeller(1 To gPrepayLevels, 1 To gDefaultLevels) As Double
        ReDim gOutTotalSchPrincipal(1 To gPrepayLevels, 1 To gDefaultLevels) As Double
        ReDim gOutTotalPrepayments(1 To gPrepayLevels, 1 To gDefaultLevels) As Double
        ReDim gOutTotalCoupIncome(1 To gPrepayLevels, 1 To gDefaultLevels) As Double
        ReDim gOutConduitRepay(1 To gPrepayLevels, 1 To gDefaultLevels) As Double
        ReDim gOutConduitDebtService(1 To gPrepayLevels, 1 To gDefaultLevels) As Double
        ReDim gOutConduitSOL(1 To gPrepayLevels, 1 To gDefaultLevels) As Double
        ReDim gOutConduitCoverage(1 To gPrepayLevels, 1 To gDefaultLevels) As Double
        ReDim gOutConduitIRR(1 To gPrepayLevels, 1 To gDefaultLevels) As Double
        ReDim gOutSellerIRR(1 To gPrepayLevels, 1 To gDefaultLevels) As Double
        ReDim gOutSellerExcessSprd(1 To gPrepayLevels, 1 To gDefaultLevels) As Double
        ReDim gOutSellerCoverage(1 To gPrepayLevels, 1 To gDefaultLevels) As Double
        ReDim gOutProgramShortfall(1 To gPrepayLevels, 1 To gDefaultLevels) As Double
        ReDim gOutServicerShortfall(1 To gPrepayLevels, 1 To gDefaultLevels) As Double
        ReDim gOutCoupExpShortfall(1 To gPrepayLevels, 1 To gDefaultLevels) As Double
    End If

End Sub
```

EXHIBIT 5.17 "Redim_All_MatrixSummaryReport_Vectors" subroutine

maturity, duration returns, and coverage performance information of both the conduit financing portion of the deal and the seller interest portion. The initialization of these vectors can now be deleted from the subroutine. Once within the "If..Then..Endif" test that checks to see if we have elected to produce the "Matrix-Summary Report" package, we will delete the 1st to the 4th, 7th, 8th, and 12th to the 23rd lines of the subroutine. The highlighted lines of the subroutine will be deleted.

Step 4: Constant Variables Module

We have now edited all of the menus and the entire menu input and error checking portions of the Structuring Model. Having completed this task, we have, along the way, noted various Constant variables that need to be adjusted to make these changes complete. We will now enter the "A_Constants" module to effect them.

Program Costs Menu Support Constants   In Exhibit 5.18 we see a portion of the "A_Constants" module that contains the Constant variable declarations supporting the menu activities. From this listing we will remove one and modify one of these declarations.

The first declaration to be removed was used exclusively within the newly deleted Program Costs Menu and was used to set the number of fields on that menu that were to be error checked by the subroutines.

```
Public Const PROG_COST_FIELDS = 8
```

```
'=========================================================================
'Menu Support Constants
'=========================================================================
'Geographic Selection Menu and support code
Public Const STATES = 54                     'number of states and territories
Public Const STATES_PER_COL = 18             'territories per col on menu
Public Const STATES_NUM_COLS = 3             'number of columns on geographic menu
'Zip Code matrix limit
Public Const TOTAL_ZIP_CODES = 2000          'size of zip code sorting array
'Reports Selection Menu Row/Column
Public Const PORTFOLIO_REPORTS = 11          'number of stratification reports
Public Const REPORT_MENU_ROW = 7
Public Const REPORT_MENU_COL = 2
'Selection Criteria Menu
Public Const SEL_CRIT_FIELDS = 11            '# selection criteria parameter fields
Public Const SEL_CRIT_INDEX_SPREADS = 6      '# spread/index fields to check
'Program Costs Menu
Public Const PROG_COSTS_FIELDS = 8           '# fields on Program Costs menu
'Defaults and Prpeayment Menu
Public Const DEFAULT_PREPAY_FIELDS = 8       '# fields in Default/Prepayment menus
Public Const MAX_RECOVERY_PERIOD = 60        'maximum recovery lag period
Public Const MAX_MRKT_VAL_DECLINE = 1#       'maximum market value decline
Public Const MAX_CONDUIT_SPREAD = 0.1        'maximum conduit spread
Public Const USER_DEFAULT_COL_COUNT = 10     'years per column in the User default table
'Main Menu
Public Const MAIN_MENU_TEMPLATE_FILE_NAMES = 7    'names of output files

'Number of menus checked for IsNumerics
Public Const MENU_CHECK_NUMERIC = 4                'number of menu checked for IsNumerics
```

EXHIBIT 5.18 "A_Constants" module (menu support section)

The second declaration to be removed is the declaration of the number of menus that required numeric form entry inputs checking. With the elimination of the Program Costs Menu, this number decreased by 1 from 4 to 3

```
Public Const MENU_CHECK_NUMERIC = 3
```

Reports Selection Menu Support Constants We also eliminated three of the four Matrix Summary reports, leaving only the Collateral Cash Flows report. We will therefore need to modify the Constant variable declarations for these reports.

We will change the "MATRIX_REPORTS" variable to a value of 1.

We will also delete the variables "MATRIX_TENOR_REPORT", "MATRIX_CONDUIT_REPORT", and the "MATRIX_SELLER_INT_REPORT".

This will leave, after editing, Exhibit 5.19 as follows:

```
Public Const MATRIX_REPORTS = 1
Public Const MATRIX_CFS_REPORT = 1
```

A Few Other Changes We will also reset the value of the Constant variable "PAY_COLS" from 63, the full extent of the liability "CFWaterfall" spreadsheet, to 12, the number of columns necessary to accommodate only the collateral cash flow components of the first section.

```
' =====================================================================
'Matrix Summary Report Package Constants
' =====================================================================
Public Const MATRIX_REPORTS = 4                    'total # of reports
Public Const MATRIX_TENOR_REPORT = 1
Public Const MATRIX_CFS_REPORT = 2
Public Const MATRIX_CONDUIT_REPORT = 3
Public Const MATRIX_SELLER_INT_REPORT = 4
```

EXHIBIT 5.19 Matrix Summary report Constant variables

We will also change the assignment of the "SCEN_ITEMS" variable from 11 to 6 to reflect the exclusion of the deal expenses and conduit financing performance information in the table portion of the Single Scenario report. As you may recall, these are the columns in the Annual Cash Flows report section of the page in the upper-right-hand quadrant. It is these columns that originally populated the second graphic of the report on the lower right of the page. The corrected entry is:

```
Public Const SCEN_ITEMS = 6 'cols on the single scenario rep
```

We are now finished with the Constant variables module.

Step 5: Global Variables Module

We now move to the VBA module that contains the listing of all global variables for the model. This module is named, not unsurprisingly, "A_Globals".

We will now seek to remove all global variables not required by the asset side model. Some of these variables will relate to our old friend the Program Expenses Menu while others will be the working variables that we saw earlier in the "Redim_All_MatrixSummaryReport_Vectors" subroutine that we edited earlier in Step 3. Finally there will be the variables that we no longer need in that their purpose was to carry the information displayed in those portions of the Waterfall, Matrix Summary, and Single Scenario reports we reformatted to delete the liability side information.

Program Costs Menu Variables In Exhibit 5.20 we find the listing of the variables of the extinct Program Costs Menu. These can be now deleted.

```
' PROGRAM COST MENU VARIABLES
Public gExpenseService         As Double      'Percentage rate for servicing
Public gExpenseProgram         As Double      'Percentage for program expense f
Public gTriggerCleanup         As Double      'percentage for clean up call of
Public gTrigger3MDefaults      As Double      'percentage of rolling 3 month de
Public gAdvanceRate            As Double      'conduit advance rate
Public gConduitSpread          As Double      'conduit financing spread
```

EXHIBIT 5.20 Program Costs Menu global variables declarations

```
'RATES & DATES MENU
Public gIndexLevels(1 To PAY_DATES, 1 To 3) As Double    'index levels
Public gFundConduit(1 To PAY_DATES)          As Double    'funding rate to conduit
Public gDayFactors(1 To PAY_DATES, 1 To 3)   As Double    'decimal days counts 30/360, Ac
Public gMonths(1 To PAY_DATES)               As Date      'beginning month dates
```

EXHIBIT 5.21   Rates and Dates Menu global variables declarations

Rates and Dates Menu Variables   In Exhibit 5.21 we see some of the declarations of the variables supporting the Rates and Dates Menu. We have eliminated the conduit financing spread from this menu and can therefore delete the vector

```
Public gFundConduit(1 to PAY_DATES) as Double
```

Liabilities Waterfall Results Global Variables   The variables listed in Exhibit 5.22 capture the results of the liability waterfall. As you recall, in Step 0 we removed over 50 columns of material from the "CFWaterfall" spreadsheet. What remained were the first 12 columns of the "CFWaterfall" spreadsheet that listed the period-by-period cash flows of beginning period balance, scheduled principal, prepaid principal, coupon income, and recoveries. All following columns of the Waterfall report were removed.

We therefore need to remove from the global variables declaration listing in Exhibit 5.22 all variables beginning with and including the variable "gOutAverageLife"

```
' ==============================================================================
'
'  Waterfall results
'
' ==============================================================================
Public gOutAverageLife()          As Double    'scenario average life
Public gOutFinalMaturity()        As Double    'scenario final maturity
Public gOutModDuration()          As Double    'modified duration
Public gOutMacDuration()          As Double    'macauley duration
Public gOutAmt10yrs()             As Double    'scenario principal remaining after
Public gOutRecoveries()           As Double    'recoveries
Public gOutPctPaidExcess()        As Double    'Excess collections
Public gOutPctPaidSeller()        As Double    'Paid to the seller
Public gOutTotalSchPrincipal()    As Double    'scenario total scheduled amortizatc
Public gOutTotalPrepayments()     As Double    'scenario total prepaid principal
Public gOutTotalCoupIncome()      As Double    'scenario total coupon cashflows
Public gOutTotalDefaults()        As Double    'scenario total defaults
Public gOutConduitRepay()         As Double    'conduit principal repayment
Public gOutConduitDebtService()   As Double    'conduit debt service
Public gOutConduitSOL()           As Double    'conduit severity of loss
Public gOutConduitCoverage()      As Double    'conduit finance coverage
Public gOutConduitIRR()           As Double    'conduit internal rate of return
Public gOutSellerIRR()            As Double    'beg seller interest
Public gOutSellerExcessSprd()     As Double    'excess spread released to seller
Public gOutSellerCoverage()       As Double    'coverage of the seller interets
Public gOutProgramShortfall()     As Double    'program fee shortfall
Public gOutServicerShortfall()    As Double    'servicer fee shortfall
Public gOutCoupExpShortfall()     As Double    'coupon shortfall
```

EXHIBIT 5.22   Waterfall results global variable declarations

```
' Waterfall file
Public gWaterfallFile                       As String   'waterfall file for scenario outputs
Public gWaterfallWrkshtName(1 To MAX_SCEN)           As String   'worksheet names in cf outpu
Public gWaterfallCFs(1 To MAX_SCEN, 1 To PAY_DATES, 1 To PAY_COLS) As Double
Public gWaterfallMisc(1 To MAX_SCEN, 1 To 2)    As Double   'prepay and default info for scene
Public gWaterfallMethod(1 To MAX_SCEN, 1 To 2) As String   'prepay and default method
Public gWaterfallBoxscore1(1 To MAX_SCEN, 1 To 14, 1 To 2)    As Double   'box score field gro
Public gWaterfallBoxscore2(1 To MAX_SCEN, 1 To 11, 1 To 2)    As Double   'box score field gro
Public gWaterfallBoxscore3(1 To MAX_SCEN, 1 To 3)            As Double   'box score field gro
' Single Scenario file
Public gScenarioFile                     As String   'waterfall file for scenario outputs
Public gScenarioName(1 To MAX_SCEN)           As String   'worksheet names in cf output file
Public gScenarioInfo(1 To MAX_SCEN, 1 To MAX_YEARS, 1 To SCEN_ITEMS) As Double
Public gScenarioMisc(1 To MAX_SCEN, 1 To 2)    As Double   'prepay and default info for scenar
Public gScenarioMethod(1 To MAX_SCEN, 1 To 2) As String   'prepay and default method
Public gScenBoxScore1(1 To MAX_SCEN, 1 To 14, 1 To 2)    As Double   'box score field group 1
Public gScenBoxScore2(1 To MAX_SCEN, 1 To 11, 1 To 2)    As Double   'box score field group 2
Public gScenBoxScore3(1 To MAX_SCEN, 1 To 3)            As Double   'box score field group 3
```

EXHIBIT 5.23   Waterfall and Single Scenario report global variables

and ending with and including the variable "gOutPctPaidSeller". We will follow this action by then deleting all the declarations starting with and including the variable "gOutConduitRepay" to the end of the list.

Waterfall Report Variables and the Single Scenario Report Variables   In Exhibit 5.23 we see the global variable declarations that hold the information for the Waterfall report package and the Single Scenario report package.

In regard to the Waterfall Report package declarations, we have already changed the dimensions of the "gWaterfallCFS" array by our reduction in the value of the Constant variable "PAY_COLS" from its initial value of 63 to its current value of 12 in Step 4. This effectively reduces the size of the array to conform with our reformatted now asset-only cash flow report.

Next we will alter the dimensions of the "gWaterfallBoxScore1" variable to:

```
Public gWaterfallBoxScore1(1 to MAX_SCEN, 1 to 7, 1 to 2)
```

This change reflects the deletion of the "Sources" portion of the Box Score. Following this we will delete both the "gWaterfallBoxScore2" and "gWaterfall-BoxScore3" arrays as they contain information related exclusively to the liabilities performance.

Moving on to the next block of global variable declarations, we find the global variables employed to produce the Single Scenario report package. Here as before we have already effected some changes by altering the value of the "SCEN_ITEMS" Constant variable in Step 4 from its original value of 11 to its current 6. This change reflects the deletion of the five report columns that presented conduit performance information in the upper-right-hand table of the Scenario report.

As with the Waterfall report package, we will alter the Box Score variables to conform to the asset-only configuration. First we will alter the dimensions of the "gScenBoxScore1" variable to:

```
Public gScenBoxScore1(1 to MAX_SCEN, 1 to 7, 1 to 2)
```

This change reflects the deletion of the "Sources" portion of the Box Score. Following this we will delete both the "gScenBoxScore2" and "gScenBoxScore3" arrays, as we did with the Waterfall reports above. These sections contain information related exclusively to the liabilities performance.

A Pause in the Action

If we review the contents of Step 0, reformatting the reports, up to the current Step 5, finishing up with the global variables declarations of the program, we can see we have accomplished quite a bit!

If we refer back to Exhibit 5.6, we will see that we have now hit a stretch of the program where the model is 100% asset side. We are finished with the portion of the model that error checks the menu inputs and reads their contents into the VBA arrays. Making use of this information, the next steps in the Structuring Model execution sequence are to:

- Open and read the contents of the collateral data file. This function is performed by the "Read_Portfolio_Data_File" subroutine that is called directly from the main model subroutine. We do not have to modify any of this code because it is clearly and exclusively asset side code.
- Perform the collateral selection process using the criteria we have read from the Collateral Selection Criteria Menu and the Geographic Selection Menu. Again, this is an exclusively asset side function.
- Report the results of the selection process in the Ineligible and the Eligible Collateral report packages. Again, there is not even a whiff of liabilities; this is a pure asset operation and reporting function.
- Compute of the eligible collateral portfolio cash flows. This is the final portion of the model that is, in its current configuration, a 100% asset function. Once the cash flows have been calculated, we are going to read them from the VBA arrays where they reside into the liabilities waterfall. This is the first place where we begin again to run into liabilities side code and functionality.

It is as if we were just given a free pass to jump over the middle part of the model in one bound! Landing on the other side, we again pick up the modification process as we put the collateral cash flows to work in the liability "CFWaterfall" worksheet.

Step 6: Load and Run the Waterfall

Our next stop is the point at which the model feeds the freshly calculated collateral cash flows into the liability waterfall. All VBA code in the subroutines in this step is found in the "LoadRunCaptureResults" module.

"Load_and_Run_the_Waterfall" Subroutine In Exhibit 5.24 the "Load_and_Run_the_Waterfall" subroutine code first checks to see if we have elected to produce any of the report packages. If we have it will begin the process of sequentially loading the "CFWaterfall" spreadsheet with the contents of up to 100 cash flow scenarios.

```
Sub Load_and_Run_the_Waterfall()

    If gOutputMatrixReport Or gOutputWaterfallReport Or gOutputScenarioReport Then
        i_scenario = 0
        For i_prepay = 1 To gPrepayLevels
            For i_default = 1 To gDefaultLevels
                i_scenario = i_scenario + 1
                Call Load Collateral Cashflows(i_prepay, i_default)
                Call Load Funding Rate Levels
                Calculate
                If gOutputWaterfallReport Then Call Capture_Waterfall_Results(i_scenari
                If gOutputScenarioReport Then Call Capture_Scenario_Results(i_scenario)
                If gOutputMatrixReport Then Call Capture_Matrix_Report_Results
                Call Display_Waterfall_ProgressMsg(i_scenario, 2)
            Next i_default
        Next i_prepay
    End If

End Sub
```

EXHIBIT 5.24 "Load_and_Run_the_Waterfall" subroutine

In the BAM we will be using the Waterfall report as our main period-by-period collateral cash flow component output report. We may want to run the model only to perform the collateral selection function. In that case, it makes sense to leave the test for the cash flow reports in place.

The call to the "Load_Funding_Rate_Levels" is, however, a 100% liability side support function. This subroutine loads the user-selected conduit financing spread into the "CFWaterfall" spreadsheet. It is therefore completely unneeded as the conduit financing portion of the "CFWaterfall" spreadsheet no longer exists. It should be noted that we should retain the "Calculate" command in the subroutine as it triggers the column headers in the surviving collateral cash flows section of the waterfall.

Continuing downward, we will need to examine all three of the "Capture subroutines" that grab their report contents from the waterfall for later use.

"Load_Funding_Rate_Levels" Subroutine This subroutine loads the calculated funding rates for the conduit financing. The funding rate for the period is the rate of the index selected and the conduit funding spread. No longer needed, the entire subroutine can be deleted. See Exhibit 5.25.

```
Sub Load_Funding_Rate_Levels()

    Application.Calculation = xlCalculationManual
    Sheets("CFWaterfall").Select
    Range("cfFundConduit").ClearContents
    For irow = 1 To PAY_DATES
        Range("cfFundConduit").Cells(irow) = gFundConduit(irow)
    Next irow

End Sub
```

EXHIBIT 5.25 "Load_Funding_Rate_Levels" subroutine

```
Sub Get_Waterfall_Box_Score(scen)

    For irow = 1 To 14
        For icol = 1 To 2
            gWaterfallBoxscore1(scen, irow, icol) = Range("WaterfallBox1").Cells(irow,
        Next icol
    Next irow
    For irow = 1 To 11
        For icol = 1 To 2
            If IsNumeric(Range("WaterfallBox2").Cells(irow, icol)) Then
                gWaterfallBoxscore2(scen, irow, icol) = Range("WaterfallBox2").Cells(ir
            End If
        Next icol
    Next irow
    'trigger conditions
    For irow = 1 To 3
        gWaterfallBoxscore3(scen, irow) = Range("WaterfallBox3").Cells(irow)
    Next irow

End Sub
```

EXHIBIT 5.26 "Get_Waterfall_Box_Score" subroutine

"Get_Waterfall_Box_Score" Subroutine This subroutine is called from the "Capture_Waterfall_Results" subroutine. Here we need to modify the code to eliminate that portion of it that seeks to read information from the Box Score section of the "CFWaterfall" spreadsheet. We deleted this section when we revised the worksheet back in Step 1.

In Exhibit 5.26 you will note that we will change the terminus of the first "For..Next" loop from its current value of 14 (capturing both the "Sources" and the "Uses" sections) to 7, which captures the "Sources" section only. As this task is now complete, we can delete the following second and third "For..Next" loops. These loops serve to capture the liability structure performance information in the two remaining sections of the Box Score.

"Capture_Matrix_Report_Results" Subroutine This subroutine is shown in Exhibit 5.27. We should expect this subroutine to be *crawling* with liability structure performance data. Earlier in Step 0 we removed three out of four Matrix Summary reports from the original package. We no longer need to capture the data items of those reports; therefore, the code that captures them can be eliminated.

As a result, when we have removed all the noncollateral cash flow items, this will be a greatly diminished subroutine. We will preserve only the lines of code that capture the five cash flow stream components. Those components are defaulted principal, prepaid principal, amortized principal, coupon income, and recovered principal amounts.

Step 7: Write Assumptions Report

This marks the first point at which we will be working with the VBA code of the model that produces the report packages or portions thereof. It also means that if we are this far along, the process is well advanced and the end may be in sight! All code in this section is contained in the "WriteAssumptionsReport" module.

```
Sub Capture_Matrix_Report_Results()
    gOutAverageLife(i_prepay, i_default) = Range("AvgLifeConduit")
    gOutFinalMaturity(i_prepay, i_default) = Range("FinalMaturityConduit")
    gOutModDuration(i_prepay, i_default) = Range("ConduitModDurat")
    gOutMacDuration(i_prepay, i_default) = Range("ConduitMacDurat")
    gOutAmt10yrs(i_prepay, i_default) = Range("Conduit10yrBalance")
    gOutRecoveries(i_prepay, i_default) = Range("sumPrinRecoveries")
    gOutTotalSchPrincipal(i_prepay, i_default) = Range("sumPrinRegAmort")
    gOutTotalPrepayments(i_prepay, i_default) = Range("sumPrinPrepayments")
    gOutTotalCoupIncome(i_prepay, i_default) = Range("sumCoupon")
    gOutTotalDefaults(i_prepay, i_default) = Range("sumPrinDefaults")
    gOutConduitRepay(i_prepay, i_default) = Range("sumConduitPrinPaid")
    gOutConduitDebtService(i_prepay, i_default) = Range("sumConduitDebtServic
    gOutConduitSOL(i_prepay, i_default) = Range("SolConduit")
    If gOutConduitSOL(i_prepay, i_default) > 0.00001 Then
        gOutConduitCoverage(i_prepay, i_default) = 0#
    Else
        gOutConduitCoverage(i_prepay, i_default) =
            Range("CFExSprdReleased") / Range("TotalBeginPrincipal")
    End If
    If IsNumeric(Range("CFConduitIRR")) Then
        gOutConduitIRR(i_prepay, i_default) = Range("CFConduitIRR")
    Else
        gOutConduitIRR(i_prepay, i_default) = 999999#
    End If
    If IsNumeric(Range("CFSellerIRR")) Then
        gOutSellerIRR(i_prepay, i_default) = Range("CFSellerIRR")
    Else
        gOutSellerIRR(i_prepay, i_default) = 999999#
    End If
    gOutSellerExcessSprd(i_prepay, i_default) = Range("CFExSprdReleased")
    gOutSellerCoverage(i_prepay, i_default) =
        (Range("CFExSprdReleased") / Range("CFSellerBegBal")) - 1#
    gOutProgramShortfall(i_prepay, i_default) = Range("CFProgFeeShortAmt")
    gOutServicerShortfall(i_prepay, i_default) = Range("CFServiceFeeShortAmt"
    gOutCoupExpShortfall(i_prepay, i_default) = Range("CFCouponShortAmt")
End Sub
```

EXHIBIT 5.27   "Capture_Matrix_Report_Results" subroutine

Each of the three report packages, the Waterfall, the Matrix Summary, and the Single Scenario, contains as its first page an Assumptions Page report. This report displays all of the inputs of the menus and the results of the collateral selection process available for use in the Structuring Model.

The format used by the Structuring Model also contains a smattering of liability assumptions. These relate to the expense and trigger items that formerly resided on the now-extinct Program Costs Menu. It also contains one of the rates vectors from the Rates and Dates Menu.

The inputs from the Program Costs Menu are grouped together at the top left of the report. We can see in Exhibit 5.28 the code statements we need to remove from the report.

Lower in the same subroutine, we find the section of the code that reproduces the information for the Rates and Dates Menu. In this section we need to remove the conduit funding level column, as shown in Exhibit 5.29.

```
Sub Write_Assumptions_Page()

    Sheets("Assumptions").Select

    'SECTION I - Program Costs, Selection Critera, Spread Information
    'load the program costs section
    Cells(4, 2).Value = gExpenseService * 12#       'servicing fee
    Cells(5, 2).Value = gExpenseProgram * 12#       'program expenses
    Cells(6, 2).Value = gConduitSpread              'condit financing spread
    Cells(8, 2).Value = 1 - gAdvanceRate            'seller interest percentage
    Cells(10, 2).Value = gTrigger3MDefaults         'principal reallocation trigger
    Cells(12, 2).Value = gTriggerCleanup            'principal reallocation trigger
    'load the collateral selelction criteria
    Cells(15, 2).Value = gCriteriaMinOrigTerm       'min original term in months
    Cells(15, 4).Value = gCriteriaMaxOrigTerm       'max original term in months
    Cells(16, 2).Value = gCriteriaMinRemTerm        'min remaining term in months
    Cells(16, 4).Value = gCriteriaMaxRemTerm        'max remaining term in months
    Cells(17, 2).Value = gCriteriaMinOrigBal        'min original balance
    Cells(17, 4).Value = gCriteriaMaxOrigBal        'max original balance
    Cells(18, 2).Value = gCriteriaMinRemBal         'min remaining balance
    Cells(18, 4).Value = gCriteriaMaxRemBal         'max remaining balance
    Cells(19, 2).Value = gCriteraMinCoupon          'min gross coupon
    Cells(19, 4).Value = gCriteraMaxCoupon          'max gross coupon
    Cells(20, 4).Value = gCriteriaMaxLTV            'max LTV ratio
    Cells(21, 4).Value = gCriteraMaxPmtDiff         'allowable difference stated/calc p
```

EXHIBIT 5.28 "Write_Assumptions_Page" subroutine (upper portion)

Step 8: Writing the Waterfall Report

We now move to the production of the Waterfall report. The code we will be looking at is contained in the "WriteWaterfallReports" module.

"Write_Single_Case_Waterfall" Subroutine   The creation of a single scenario of the Waterfall report is contained in the "Write_Single_Case_Waterfall" subroutine. Note that one of the first calls in this subroutine is to the "Write_Waterfall_Box_Score" subroutine. Given the drastic surgery that we have performed on this section of the "CFWaterfall" spreadsheet, we can expect to see a major modification to this subroutine that will reflect the exclusion of the liabilities structure performance statistics. This is indeed the case. Earlier, in Exhibit 5.27, we looked at modifications to the VBA code to *capture* this information from the spreadsheet. Now we will be outputting the results of those activities back to the report. The modifications are mirror images of each other. See Exhibit 5.30.

```
            'SECTION V - Rates and Dates Schedule
            For irow = 1 To PAY_DATES
                Cells(irow + 5, 20).Value = gIndexLevels(irow, 1)
                Cells(irow + 5, 21).Value = gIndexLevels(irow, 2)
                Cells(irow + 5, 22).Value = gFundConduit(irow)
                Cells(irow + 5, 24).Value = gMonths(irow)
                Cells(irow + 5, 25).Value = gDayFactors(irow, 1)
                Cells(irow + 5, 26).Value = gDayFactors(irow, 2)
                Cells(irow + 5, 27).Value = gDayFactors(irow, 3)
            Next irow
```

EXHIBIT 5.29   "Write_Assumptions_Page" subroutine (lower portion)

```
Sub Write_Waterfall_Box_Score(scen)

    'Box Score Section 1 -- Cash Flow Summary
    For irow = 1 To 14
        For icol = 1 To 2
            If irow = 8 Then Exit For
            Cells(irow + 8, icol + 5).Value = gWaterfallBoxscore1(scen, irow, icol)
            If irow = 1 Or irow = 3 Or irow > 5 Then Exit For
        Next icol
    Next irow
    'Box Score Section 2 -- Performance of the Notes and Seller Interest
    For irow = 1 To 11
        For icol = 1 To 2
            If irow = 3 Or irow = 7 Then Exit For
            Cells(irow + 25, icol + 5) = gWaterfallBoxscore2(scen, irow, icol)
            If irow >= 8 Then Exit For
        Next icol
    Next irow
    'Box Score Section 3 -- Triggers
    For irow = 1 To 3
        Cells(irow + 37, 6) = "TRUE"
        If gWaterfallBoxscore3(scen, irow) = 0 Then Cells(irow + 37, 6) = "FALSE"
    Next irow

End Sub
```

EXHIBIT 5.30   "Write_Waterfall_Box_Score" subroutine

First we will change the loop terminus on Box Score section 1 from 14 to 7 to reflect the output of only the Sources portion of the cash flows. Next we delete all code related to the remaining content of the Box Score, sections 2 and 3, as these field relate to liability side performance only.

"Write_Single_Case_Waterfall" Subroutine   With the Assumptions Page report within the Waterfall report package corrected, we can now turn out attention to the series of worksheets that will display the collateral cash flows from each of the scenarios of the model run. The "Write_Single_Case_Waterfall" subroutine, as seen in Exhibit 5.31, produces the Waterfall report page of a single scenario. The calls in the upper part of the subroutine write the Assumption Page report, and the headers of the report as well as producing a progress message to reassure the person running the model as to the continuing progress of the model. In long model runs it is vitally important to inform the analyst that interim progress is in fact being made. In this case the messages produce various indications that a particular phase or portion of a phase has been completed. The next "For..Next" loop outputs the period-by-period cash flow components.

The last "For..Next" loop is the one that concerns us now. It checks to see the state of the Triggers section of the scenario results, and then, based on the numerical value of the trigger, prints out either "True" or "False" in the report grid. In that the liabilities entries that are the basis for the determination of whether these triggers should be activated have been removed from the model, this code should join them on the cutting room floor.

Step 9: Writing the Matrix Summary Reports

The subroutines that produce the Matrix Summary report package are next in line.

```
Sub Write_Single_Case_Waterfall(scen)

    Sheets(gWaterfallWrkshtName(scen)).Select
    'write the rest of the report
    Call Write_Waterfall_Box_Score(scen)
    Call Write_Waterfall_PrepayDefault_Headers(scen)
    Call Display_Waterfall_ProgressMsg(scen, 1)
    'write out the waterfall contents
    irow = 14
    For iloop = 1 To PAY_DATES
        For icol = 1 To PAY_COLS
            Cells(irow, icol + 10).Value = gWaterfallCFs(scen, iloop, icol)
        Next icol
        irow = irow + 1
    Next iloop
    'rewrite the contents of the "Triggers" section
    irow = 14
    For iloop = 1 To PAY_DATES
        For icol = 50 To 53
            If gWaterfallCFs(scen, iloop, icol) = 0 Then
                Cells(irow, icol + 10).Value = "FALSE"
            Else
                Cells(irow, icol + 10).Value = "TRUE"
            End If
        Next icol
        irow = irow + 1
    Next iloop
    Call Trim_the_Waterfall_Report

End Sub
```

EXHIBIT 5.31   "Write_Single_Case_Waterfall" subroutine

"Write_Matrix_Reports" Subroutine   As we recall from Step 0, where we were working on reconfiguring the reports of the BAM, we elected to dispose of three of the four reports in the Matrix Summary report package. To that end we will now delete the calls to the subroutines that produce those three reports. We will, however, retain the "Select..Case" statement structure, even if there is now only a single choice within it. Remember, the model is not a static entity, and we may need to add other Matrix Summary reports at a later date. See Exhibit 5.32.

"Delete_UnSelected_Matrix_Report" Subroutine   This alternative choice to producing one of the Matrix Summary reports is to not produce it. If the user of the model does not select a particular report it will be deleted from the report file. If we are no longer allowing the selection of these reports, we no longer have to worry about their de-selection and the three report choices can be removed from this subroutine as well. See Exhibit 5.33.

Finishing Touches to the Process   Having eliminated the three reports, we will also delete the subroutines that produce them. These subroutines are:

- "Write_Matrix_Tenor_Report" subroutine
- "Write_Conduit_Financing_Performance" subroutine
- "Write_SellerInterest_Report" subroutine

```
Sub Write_Matrix_Reports(mSumPrincipal)

    Call Write_Assumptions_Page
    For i_report = 1 To MATRIX_REPORTS
        If gSumMatrixReports(i_report) Then
            Select Case i_report
                    Case Is = MATRIX_TENOR_REPORT:      Call Write_Matrix_Tenor_Report(mSum
                    Case Is = MATRIX_CFS_REPORT:        Call Write_Matrix_CFs_Report
                    Case Is = MATRIX_CONDUIT_REPORT:    Call Write_Conduit_Financing_Perfor
                    Case Is = MATRIX_SELLER_INT_REPORT: Call Write_Matrix_SellerInterest_Re
            End Select
            Call Load_Prepay_Levels     'loads the prepayment rates in the header
            Call Load_Default_Levels    'loads the default rates in the header
            Call Trim_Matrix_Report     'removes unused cells of the matrix
        Else
            Call Delete_UnSelected_Matrix_Report(i_report)
        End If
    Next i_report

End Sub
```

EXHIBIT 5.32 "Write_Matrix_Reports" subroutine

Step 10: Writing the Single Scenario Report

The final report package of the Structuring Model is the Single Scenario report package. The code for this report package is contained in the "WriteScenarioReports" module. As this report was added in the final development phases of the Structuring Model, the subroutine that captures the information from the "CFWaterfall" spreadsheet was included in the reporting module itself. We will start at that point.

"Capture_Scenario_Results" Subroutine   This subroutine captures the data needed for the output of the Single Scenario report from the waterfall results. The report originally contained a number of assumption items and cash flow columns that derived from the liability structure. Also, the original report produced end-of-year balances in the table rather than beginning-of-year balances. These beginning-year balances make the impacts of prepayments, defaults, and amortization much clearer, and we want to use them going forward into the BAM.

Thus the first change we will make to the subroutine is to replace the term "iend" with the term "ibeg" in the first IF test inside the second "For..Next" loop. The test

```
Sub Delete_UnSelected_Matrix_Report(i_report)

    Select Case i_report
            Case Is = MATRIX_TENOR_REPORT:      Sheets("Tenor").Delete
            Case Is = MATRIX_CFS_REPORT:        Sheets("Cashflows").Delete
            Case Is = MATRIX_CONDUIT_REPORT:    Sheets("ConduitNotePerformance").Delete
            Case Is = MATRIX_SELLER_INT_REPORT: Sheets("SellerInterestPerformance").Delete
    End Select

End Sub
```

EXHIBIT 5.33 "Delete_UnSelected_Matrix_Report" subroutine

```
Sub Capture_Scenario_Results(scen)

Dim ip                     As Integer    'period counter
Dim ibeg                   As Integer    'beginning period
Dim iend                   As Integer    'ending period
Dim scen_sum(1 To SCEN_ITEMS)   As Double    'annual sum or end balance
Dim isum                   As Double     'item counter

    'write out the waterfall contents
    ibeg = 1
    iend = 12
    For iloop = 1 To MAX_YEARS
        'get the year end balances or sum the yearly cash flows
        For ip = ibeg To iend
            'collateral balance
            If ip = iend Then
                scen_sum(1) = Range("WaterfallCFS").Cells(ip, 1)
            'sum the cash flows, scheduled amortization of principal,
            ' prepayments, defaults, coupon, recoveries
            scen_sum(2) = scen_sum(2) + Range("WaterfallCFS").Cells(ip, 3)
            scen_sum(3) = scen_sum(3) + Range("WaterfallCFS").Cells(ip, 4)
            scen_sum(4) = scen_sum(4) + Range("WaterfallCFS").Cells(ip, 5)
            scen_sum(5) = scen_sum(5) + Range("WaterfallCFS").Cells(ip, 8)
            scen_sum(6) = scen_sum(6) + Range("WaterfallCFS").Cells(ip, 9)
            'program, servicing, and conduit coupon expenses
            scen_sum(7) = scen_sum(7) + Range("WaterfallCFS").Cells(ip, 14)
            scen_sum(8) = scen_sum(8) + Range("WaterfallCFS").Cells(ip, 18)
            'conduit balance outstanding and conduit principal paid
            If ip = iend Then
                scen_sum(9) = Range("WaterfallCFS").Cells(ip, 37)
            scen_sum(10) = scen_sum(10) + Range("WaterfallCFS").Cells(ip, 23)
            scen_sum(11) = scen_sum(11) + Range("WaterfallCFS").Cells(ip, 30)
        Next ip
```

EXHIBIT 5.34 "Capture_Scenario_Results" subroutine

should now read:

```
For iloop = 1 To MAX_YEARS
  'get the year end balances or sum the yearly cash flows
  For ip = ibeg To iend
    'collateral balance
    If ip = ibeg Then scen_sum(1) = Range (''WaterfallCFS'').
      Cells(ip, 1)
```

Next we will delete all the code that captures the liability structure performance. The subroutine is shown in Exhibit 5.34.

"Write_Single_Case_Scenario_File" Subroutine   Earlier in Step 0 we removed five columns of liability structure performance statistics from a table in the Single Scenario report page. With these columns removed, the size of the table can be expanded to allow for wider rows. We no longer need to display the annual cash flow totals in the form of millions; we can express them as full dollar amounts, although without the cents. Here, in Exhibit 5.35, we remove the "/1000000".

"Get_Scenario_Box_Score" and "Write_Scenario_Box_Score" Subroutines   We will make the same adjustments to these subroutines as we did to the ones that

```
Sub Write_Single_Case_Scenario_File(scen)

    Sheets(gScenarioName(scen)).Select
    'write the rest of the report
    Call Write_Scenario_Box_Score(scen)
    Call Write_Scenario_PrepayDefault_Headers(scen)
    Call Write_Scenario_Assumptions_Section
    'write out the waterfall contents
    irow = 11
    For iloop = 1 To MAX_YEARS
        For icol = 1 To SCEN_ITEMS
            Cells(irow, icol + 12).Value =
                gScenarioInfo(scen, iloop, icol) / 1000000#
        Next icol
        irow = irow + 1
    Next iloop

End Sub
'================================================================================
'
'
'================================================================================
Sub Write_Scenario_PrepayDefault_Headers(scen)
    'prepayment and default headers
    Cells(41, 4).Value = gScenarioMisc(scen, 2)      'prepay rate
    Cells(42, 4).Value = gScenarioMethod(scen, 2)    'prepay method
    Cells(45, 4).Value = gScenarioMisc(scen, 1)      'default rate
    Cells(46, 4).Value = gScenarioMethod(scen, 1)    'default method
End Sub
```

EXHIBIT 5.35   "Write_Single_Case_Scenario_File" subroutine

produced the Box Scores for the Waterfall reports. The changes are identical to the waterfall box score subroutines. See the revised subroutines in the "WriteScenarioReport" module if you have any questions.

"Write_Scenario_Assumptions_Section" Subroutine   As with the two subroutines mentioned in the section immediately above, we will allow you to notice the changes without presenting them here. Needless to say, we will delete references to the program expenses, the servicing expenses, and the conduit funding spread levels. We will also delete the presentation of the conduit financing rapid amortization triggers. With the elimination of a large part of the original Box Score region of the report, most of the changes to the Assumptions section of the single page report are due to changes in formatting as the information is moved higher up in the right-hand column of the reports to fill the void.

Step 11: Batch Mode Function

We are almost there! The last major module of code that we have to address is the "A_BatchModeProgram". In a sense this is the most important of the changes we will make. After all is said and done, this is the critical functionality that we want to incorporate into the BAM.

The ability to run large numbers of portfolio cash flows is a necessary building block of the future model development we are about to undertake. All the changes that we have made up until now can be seen as directly integral to getting a working batch mode operation up and running. Remember, as far as the "Big Bad Batch Mode Model" is concerned, the entire Structuring Model is just another subroutine call!

```
'====================================================================
'Batch File Modular Constants
'====================================================================
Public Const NUM_OF_BATCH_FILES = 50    'max number of files
Public Const BATCH_RANGE_TESTS = 6      'error tests for columns
Const cMsgButtonCode1    As Integer = vbOKOnly + vbCritical
Const cMsgButtonCode2    As Integer = vbOKOnly + vbExclamation
```

EXHIBIT 5.36 Module-level Constant variable declarations

All of the subroutines and code we will be examining are located in the "A_BatchModeProgram" module.

Module-Level Constant Variables of the Batch Mode We need to change one of the two Constant variables declared in the "A_BatchModeProgram" module. This Constant variable refers to the number of columns that we are going to perform input reasonableness tests on in the Batch Model Menu. The two deleted columns were the Conduit Finance Spread in column "F" and the Conduit Spread Choice in column "I." With the elimination of these two input columns, the number of tests drops from six to four. We will therefore initialize the value of the Constant variable "BATCH_RANGE_TESTS = 4". See Exhibit 5.36.

Module-Level Variable Declarations With the two columns from the menu gone, we can delete the variable declarations created to hold the menu information. See Exhibit 5.37. To this end we can delete the two variables "mBatchCondSpread" and "mBatchCondSpreadPath".

"Read_Batch_Program_Menu" Subroutine We will now remove the references to the two variables, "mBatchCondSpreadPath" and "mBatchCondSpread", from the subroutine that reads them from the Batch Mode Menu. We need to delete both the statements in which the variables are re-dimensioned and the statements inside the loop where the program reads them from the menu fields. See Exhibit 5.38.

"Load_and_Run_Loan_Financing_Model" Subroutine The role of the "Load_and_Run_Loan_Financing_Model" subroutine is to place the inputs of the Batch Mode

```
'====================================================================
'Batch File Modular Variables
'====================================================================
Dim i_file                  As Integer   'scenario loop counter
Dim num_file                As Integer   'number of files requested

'menu input vectors
Dim mBatchMvdFactor()        As Double    'market value decline vector
Dim mBatchLagFactor()        As Integer   'recovery lag period in months
Dim mBatchCondSpread()       As Double    'conduit financing spread
Dim mBatchFileName()         As String    'name of the inidividual file
Dim mBatchSpreadPath()       As Integer   'conduit spread pathway
Dim mBatchLIBORPath()        As Integer   'libor spread pathway
Dim mBatchPrimePath()        As Integer   'prime rate pathway
```

EXHIBIT 5.37 Module-level variable declarations

```
Sub Read_Batch_Program_Menu()

    'read the contents of the ranges
    ReDim mBatchMvdFactor(1 To num_file) As Double     'market value decline vector
    ReDim mBatchLagFactor(1 To num_file) As Integer    'recovery lag period in months
    ReDim mBatchCondSpread(1 To num_file) As Double    'conduit financing spread
    ReDim mBatchFileName(1 To num_file) As String      'name of the inidividual file
    ReDim mBatchSpreadPath(1 To num_file) As Integer   'conduit spread pathway
    ReDim mBatchLIBORPath(1 To num_file) As Integer    'libor spread pathway
    ReDim mBatchPrimePath(1 To num_file) As Integer    'prime rate pathway
    For i_file = 1 To num_file
        mBatchMvdFactor(i_file) = Trim(Range("m10MktValueDecline").Cells(i_file).Va.
        mBatchLagFactor(i_file) = Trim(Range("m10RecPeriodLag").Cells(i_file).Value)
        mBatchCondSpread(i_file) = Trim(Range("m10ConduitSpread").Cells(i_file).Val
        mBatchFileName(i_file) = Trim(Range("m10FilePrefixName").Cells(i_file).Valu
        mBatchSpreadPath(i_file) = Trim(Range("m10SpreadPathway").Cells(i_file).Val
        mBatchLIBORPath(i_file) = Trim(Range("m10LiborPathway").Cells(i_file).Value)
        mBatchPrimePath(i_file) = Trim(Range("m10PrimePathway").Cells(i_file).Value)
    Next i_file

End Sub
```

EXHIBIT 5.38   "Read_Batch_Program_Menu" subroutine

Model into the appropriate menus of the Structuring Model. When that process is complete, it calls what would be in other circumstances the Main Program of the Structuring Model. This call runs the Structuring Model as if it had been initiated in any other manner, such as using a "Run Model" button. Here we will make several changes:

- Move the Sheets ("Defaults Menu"). Calculate statement up to be the fourth statement in the loop. This change is made for clarity. We have just finished placing the new information into the menu, we are done, initiate the calculation to finish.
- Delete the Sheets ("Program Costs Menu"). Calculate line. The Program Cost Menu no longer exists. We have moved the entry points for the Index choice information to the Rates and Dates Menu. We will enter the pathway choices there and then calculate the sheet. The replacement statement will now calculate the Rates and Dates Menu.
- Replace the call to the "Loan_Financing_Model" with a call to our now almost complete "Base_Asset_Model".

   See Exhibit 5.39.

"ErrCheck_IsNumeric_BatchMenu" Subroutine   This subroutine tests that the inputs to the Batch Mode Menu that should be numeric are numeric. Unfortunately for us, both of the liability entries, one for the conduit pricing spread and the other for the conduit pricing index pathway, are numeric. (If they were not numeric, we could just skip over this subroutine.) As it is, we will need to do the following:

- Delete the assignments to variables "msgInfo(3)" and "msgInfo(4)", as they relate to the two entries that are about to be deleted.
- With these two error messages gone we need to renumber the remaining error message assignments to "msgInfo" array positions 1 through 4.

```
Sub Load_and_Run_Loan_Financing_Model()

    For i_file = 1 To num_file
        Sheets("Defaults Menu").Select
        Cells(23, 4).Value = mBatchMvdFactor(i_file)
        Cells(24, 4).Value = mBatchLagFactor(i_file)
        Sheets("Program Costs Menu").Select
        Cells(16, 3).Value = mBatchSpreadPath(i_file)
        Cells(17, 3).Value = mBatchLIBORPath(i_file)
        Cells(18, 3).Value = mBatchPrimePath(i_file)
        Sheets("Defaults Menu").Calculate
        Sheets("Main Menu").Select
        Cells(19, 3).Value = mBatchFileName(i_file)
        Call Loan_Financing_Model
    Next i_file

End Sub
```

EXHIBIT 5.39   "Load_and_Run_Loan_Financing_Model" subroutine

- Next we delete the "IsNumerics" test for these two variables inside the "Select..Case" statement. Once they are gone, we will renumber the "Case Is = N:" statements to be 1 through 4.
- Finally, at the very bottom of the subroutine, we will change the number in the argument of the "Produce_Error_Box_Message" subroutine from 6 to 4. The argument sets the loop terminus for testing and printing the combined error conditions in a message box.

See Exhibit 5.40.

"ErrCheck_MaximumValues" Subroutine   The task of the "ErrCheck_Maximum Values" subroutine, shown in Exhibit 5.41, is to ensure that the user does not enter a number greater than the largest legitimate response. For example, if there are five possible LIBOR pathways to choose from, seven is not an acceptable answer. We are already eliminated the conduit financing spread input field and its accompanying conduit financing index pathway choice. We now need to correct this subroutine to reflect those changes. To do so we will follow the steps that we just performed in the "ErrCheck_IsNumeric_BatchMenu" subroutine. We will:

- Delete the two error messages and renumber the survivors.
- Delete the two tests, cases 3 and 4 in the "Select..Case" statement and renumber the remaining cases.
- Change the argument number in the call to the subroutine "Produce_Error_Box_Message" from 6 to 4.

These changes complete the modifications needed to the BAM

Step 12: Finishing Touches

We still have two more things to do and then we can count ourselves truly finished.

```
Sub ErrCheck_IsNumeric_BatchMenu()

Dim num_test                   As Boolean  'holding variable
    'Error box title -- displayed above any errors
    msgTotal = "Non-numeric Inputs for the Batch Menu Columns" & Chr(13) & Chr(13)
    msgInfo(1) = "Market Value Decline non-numeric entry in scenarios" & Chr(13)
    msgInfo(2) = "Recovery Period non-numeric entry in scenarios" & Chr(13)
    msgInfo(3) = "Conduit Financing Spread non-numeric entry in scenarios" & Chr(13)
    msgInfo(4) = "Conduit Spread Pathway non-numeric entry in scenarios" & Chr(13)
    msgInfo(5) = "Libor Rate Pathway non-numeric entry in scenarios" & Chr(13)
    msgInfo(6) = "Prime Rate Pathway non-numeric entry in scenarios" & Chr(13)
    err_total = False          'any errors at all?
    'check each of the fields for non numerics
    For i_type = 1 To BATCH_RANGE_TESTS
        'set the accumulator to zero or null
        err_string = ""                'numer of non-numeric scenarios
        scen_count = 0                 'running count of errors
        err_case(i_type) = False     'case trigger to print error message
        For i_scen = 1 To num_file
            'test each cell location over the effective scenario range
            Select Case i_type
                Case Is = 1: num_test = (IsNumeric(Trim(Range("m10MktValueDecline")
                Case Is = 2: num_test = (IsNumeric(Trim(Range("m10RecPeriodLag")).Ce.
                Case Is = 3: num_test = (IsNumeric(Trim(Range("m10ConduitSpread")).C
                Case Is = 4: num_test = (IsNumeric(Trim(Range("m10SpreadPathway")).C
                Case Is = 5: num_test = (IsNumeric(Trim(Range("m10LiborPathway")).Ce.
                Case Is = 6: num_test = (IsNumeric(Trim(Range("m10PrimePathway")).Ce.
            End Select
            err_result = (num_test = False)
            If err_result Then Call Build_The_Scenario_List
        Next i_scen
        If err_case(i_type) Then Call Build_The_Error_Message_List
    Next i_type
    'If err total is TRUE print the messages
    Call Produce_Error_Box_Message(6)

End Sub
```

EXHIBIT 5.40   "ErrCheck_IsNumeric_BatchMenu" subroutine

Deleting all Unused Range Names   There is nothing more annoying then someone who does not clean up when they are finished doing a chore. It is the same here. We need to invoke the Names Editor function and delete all the Range names associated with the Ranges we have deleted from the menus and spreadsheets of the original Structuring Model over the course of our edits that produced the BAM.

To see the existent list of current Range names, we will pull down the Insert menu from the Microsoft Excel Toolbar. Following the

Insert->Name->Define

path, the Define Name box appears. All we need to do now is to click on each Range name in turn. Those that are no longer valid will display the "#Ref" symbol somewhere in the pathway shown in the "Refers to:" window at the bottom of the form. When you locate such a Range name, click the "Delete" button to remove both the Range name and its definition from the program. There will be several dozen of these names so be careful not to get sloppy and miss one or, worse, yet delete an active Range. Save your work after removing every five Range names as insurance against frustration and heartache. See Exhibit 5.42.

Renaming the Main Program   We will now go to the "A_MainProgram" module and rename the main subroutine of the model "Base_Asset_Model". Once we do this,

```
Sub ErrCheck_MaximumValues()

Dim num_test   As String  'holding variable

     'Error box title -- displayed above any errors
     msgTotal = "Maximum Values Exceeded in the Batch Menu Columns" & Chr(13) & Chr(:
     msgInfo(1) = "Exceedes MAXIMUM Market Value Decline scenarios = " & Chr(13)
     msgInfo(2) = "Exceedes MAXIMUM Recovery Lag Period scenarios = " & Chr(13)
     msgInfo(3) = "Exceedes MAXIMUM Conduit Spread Level scenarios = " & Chr(13)
     msgInfo(4) = "Exceedes MAXIMUM Conduit Spread Pathway choice = " & Chr(13)
     msgInfo(5) = "Exceedes MAXIMUM LIBOR Pathway choice = " & Chr(13)
     msgInfo(6) = "Exceedes MAXIMUM Prime Pathway Choice = " & Chr(13)
     'check each of the fields for non numerics
     err_total = False         'any errors at all?
     For i_type = 1 To BATCH_RANGE_TESTS
          'set the accumulator to zero or null
          err_string = ""                 'numer of non-numeric scenarios
          scen_count = 0                  'running count of errors
          err_case(i_type) = False        'case trigger to print error message
          For i_scen = 1 To num_file
               err_result = False
               'test each cell location over the list of active scenarios
               Select Case i_type
                    Case Is = 1     'test for maximum market value decline
                         err_result = ((Trim(Range("m10MktValueDecline").Cells(i_scen)))
                    Case Is = 2     'test for maximum recovery lag period value
                         err_result = ((Trim(Range("m10RecPeriodLag").Cells(i_scen))) > )
                    Case Is = 3     'test for maximum conduit spread value
                         err_result = ((Trim(Range("m10ConduitSpread").Cells(i_scen))) >
                    Case Is = 4     'test for maximum conduit spread pathway choice
                         err_result = ((Trim(Range("m10SpreadPathway").Cells(i_scen))) >
                    Case Is = 5     'test for maximum LIBOR pathway choice
                         err_result = ((Trim(Range("m10LiborPathway").Cells(i_scen))) > )
                    Case Is = 6     'test for maximum Prime pathway choice
                         err_result = ((Trim(Range("m10PrimePathway").Cells(i_scen))) > )
               End Select
               If err_result Then Call Build_The_Scenario_List
```

EXHIBIT 5.41   "ErrCheck_MaximumValues" subroutine

remember to reconnect all the "Run the Model" buttons of the various menus (there are a total of five). Right click on each of the buttons and select the option "Assign Macro, then pick out the "Base_Asset_Model" and left click on the "OK" button. See Exhibit 5.43.

TESTING THE COMPLETED BASE ASSET MODEL

So you think you are done? Not so fast there! We only said that to build up a false sense of security! In all seriousness we now need to run a few simple tests to make sure the new Base Asset Model will perform as we expect it to. We can conduct two tests.

1. **Run the BAM in a Single Scenario Mode and then run it again in Batch Mode.** If our asset side model is fully functional, we should have identical collateral selection results, a Waterfall report with the collateral cash flows that match the Structuring Model, a single report Matrix Summary report package, and a Single Scenario report package that has everything except the liabilities cash flows, the second graphic, and the liabilities assumptions.

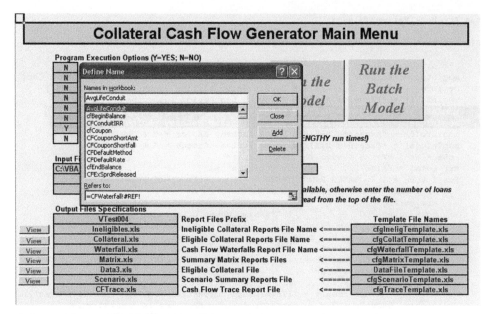

EXHIBIT 5.42   Deleting the defunct Range names

2. **Set up identical Batch Mode runs in both the Structuring Model and the Base Asset Model Ver12 and run them.** The best way to make this comparison would be a set of runs where only one variable changed, say market value decline or recovery period lag, by small amounts to see that the runs were also consistent across scenario sets. The second approach would be, in the Batch Mode Menu, to make each run as dissimilar as possible, widely varying the range of inputs

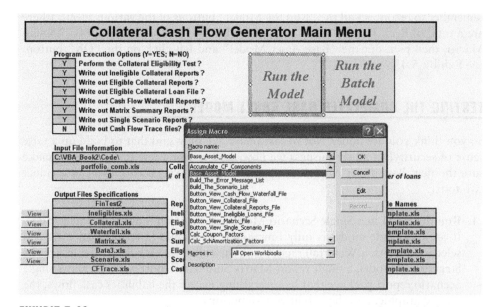

EXHIBIT 5.43   Reassigning the new Main Program name to the "Run the Model" buttons

from one run to the next. This would make sure that all the variable inputs were being correctly furnished to the BAM when it was being called in Batch Mode.

The control program will be the Structuring Model.xls. Our test platform will be BaseAssetModel12.xls.

ON THE WEB SITE

There is a "Chapter_05_Comments.doc" file for the chapter.

There are 12 interim versions of the work in progress Base Asset Model, named "BaseAssetModel01.xls" through "BaseAssetModel12.xls".

The data file that should be used in conjunction with "BaseAssetModel_12.xls" is "portfolio_comb.xls".

The report template files that have been edited for the BAM are:

- "bamIneligibleTemplate.xls". Ineligible Collateral report package
- "bamEligibleTemplate.xls". Eligible Collateral report package
- "bamDataFile.xls". Eligible Collateral Data file template
- "bamWaterfallTemplate.xls". Waterfall report package template
- "bamMatrixTemplate.xls". Matrix Summary report package template
- "bamScenarioTemplate.xls". Single Scenario report package template
- "bamTraceTemplate.xls". Cash Flow Trace report template

## CHAPTER 6

Building the Base Liabilities Model

OVERVIEW

In this chapter we will start with the current Structuring Model and, applying the same techniques used in Chapter 5, judiciously edit the model into a single-purpose Base Liabilities Model (BLM).

Using the same approach, our starting point will be the various existing report packages of the current model. We will examine each of them in reference to the BLM for suitability and content. Some reports that are clearly asset side reports, such as the Ineligible Collateral report package, will be discarded. Others, such as the Waterfall report package, will be retained.

Following the same methodology as we did in Chapter 5, we will start at the Main Program, the subroutine named "Loan_Financing_Program". Working our way from top to bottom, we will trace the execution steps of the program, editing or eliminating code that exclusively supports the asset side of the model.

At the conclusion of the exercise, we will have to write some new code to bridge the gap between the Base Asset Model (BAM) and the BLM. This code will allow them to pass the collateral cash flows and the assumptions under which they were created from the BAM to the BLM. This code will take the form of a set of subroutines to read a file written by the BAM containing the assumptions used to produce the cash flows and the cash flows themselves. We will then test the BLM to see that we have something that can produce results identical to those of the Structuring Model.

When this chapter is complete, we will have the platform from which to launch the development of the new model.

DELIVERABLES

The modeling knowledge deliverables for this chapter are:

- Understanding the process of separating out the liabilities side of the current Structuring Model.

The VBA development deliverables for this chapter are:

- Producing a working BLM from which we can launch the development of the next phase of our model building. This development will occur in Chapters 14 to 16 and 19.

- A set of report template files specific to the BLM. These template files will produce the Waterfall, the Matrix Summary, and the Single Scenario report packages.

UNDER CONSTRUCTION

In this chapter we will be building the BLM from the current Structuring Model. In the process we will modify in one form or another or delete:

- **Main Menu.** We will remove any run options that are exclusively related to the asset side of the model. The name of the collateral file and the number of records it contains will be removed. Any output file name entry field and the names of the templates for those reports that are exclusively asset side in nature will be deleted.
- **Defaults and Prepayment Menu.** This menu will be deleted.
- **Collateral Selection Menu.** This menu will be deleted.
- **Geographic Selection Menu.** This menu will be deleted.
- **Cash Flow Trace report worksheet.** This worksheet will be deleted.
- **Collateral Eligibility report worksheet.** This worksheet will be deleted.
- **Reports Menu.** This menu will contain only the references to the Matrix Summary reports; the Eligible Collateral reports will be deleted.
- **Batch Run Menu.** We will eliminate the asset amortization inputs from this menu.

We will be modifying the following VBA modules:

- **"A_BatchFileProgram" module.** We will eliminate the asset amortization inputs from this module.
- **"A_Constants" module.** We will modify or eliminate all Constant variables that relate exclusively to the asset side. We will also change the value of all Constant variables that serve as loop counters or other control limits to reflect the removal of any asset side functionalities.
- **"A_Globals" module.** We will modify or eliminate all variables that deal with the descriptive characteristics of the collateral, its amortization parameters, the interim cash flow calculation variables, the collateral selection process and its results, and any of the reports generated that are exclusively asset side in nature.
- **"A_MainProgram" module.** We will delete all calls that are to the collateral selection and its resultant reports. We will also delete the call to the cash flow calculation processes.
- **"LoadRunCaptureResults" module.** We will modify the subroutines that load the cash flows into the liabilities waterfall to take their input from files generated by the BAM.
- **"MenusErrorChecking" and "MenusReadInputs" modules.** The subroutines in these modules will be modified to reflect the deletion of the asset side input fields they contained.
- **"WriteAssumptionsReport" module.** The format of the Assumptions page will reflect whether collateral selection criteria information was available in the cash flows file. If it is available, it will be displayed; if not, the format of the report will be changed to reflect its absence.

- **"Z_ButtonSubs" module.** Button support code for the Main Menu that supports the "View" buttons for deleted reports will be removed. The button support code for the Geographic Selection menu will be deleted.
- **"Z_UtilitySubroutines".** Utility subroutines that service the Geographic reports in both the Eligible and Ineligible Collateral reports will be removed.

We will be deleting the following modules in their entirety as they exclusively support asset side model functions of collateral selection and cash flow generation:

- "CollateralCFGenerator" module
- "CollateralPreDefClacs" module
- "CollateralReadDataFile" module
- "CollateralSelectionSubs" module
- "WriteCFTraceReport" module
- "WriteCollateralReports" module
- "WriteEligibleCollateralFile" module
- "WriteIneligibilityReports" module

LIABILITIES SIDE OF THE MODEL

We will now perform the functional obverse of the process that we just completed in Chapter 5. Fortunately, there are a few things that will make this task more straightforward than the one just completed. First, although there is more, in fact much more, asset side code, most of it is heavily concentrated in a limited number of modules. Unlike the process of building the BAM, we will be able to delete entire modules at a stroke. Again, we are lucky that the code of the current Structuring Model is both clearly labeled and segregated by function. If it were not, we might end up mucking through each of the modules on a subroutine-by-subroutine basis. The calculations of the liabilities side of the model are almost exclusively contained in the Excel Waterfall spreadsheet, not in the VBA code itself. We will not have to hunt through the modules to find it. Once we have loaded the collateral cash flows into the "WaterfallCF" spreadsheet, the remaining calculations are completed in Excel. We then need only capture the results of the spreadsheet calculations. With those results in VBA arrays, we are ready to produce the various liabilities side report packages.

View from the Main Program

We will once again use the approach of starting from the Main Program and working down the chain of senior subroutine calls. This is an easy, organized way to make sure that we exhaustively visit all parts of the model. When we are at the Main Program and come across very high-level functionality that is exclusively asset side, we can delete the senior subroutines and all of the subroutines called by them.

View from the Project Explorer

Unlike the work we did in Chapter 5, we will be able to delete entire VBA modules. We could do this all at once at the beginning of the task, but it is more instructive to follow the game plan and take a more methodical approach. Doing this will allow you to once again peruse the code and gain more familiarity with it. We will find that time well spent when we begin to develop the new Liabilities Waterfall Model from the BLM we will create here.

WHAT TO LEAVE IN

Let us take a few moments and review what will be left when we are finished.

Menu Support Code

We want to retain all the menu support VBA and its associated error checking functionality for the Main, the Program Costs, the Reports, the Rates and Dates, and the Batch Run Menus.

There will be a lot of menu input and menu error checking code that we will be deleting in this process. Several menus—the Collateral Selection, the Geographic Selection, and the Defaults and Prepayment Menus—will be eliminated. In addition, the Main Menu, the Reports, and the Batch Run Menus will be significantly altered in content and appearance.

Results Extraction Code

We will need to preserve all the code that deals with the capture of the structural performance of the deal. Equally, but not so obviously, we will also need to capture the *collateral cash flow* information from the "WaterfallCF" spreadsheet. Why? Unlike the BAM, which can stand completely isolated from the BLM, the reverse is not the case. We can generate collateral cash flows knowing and caring nothing about whatever structure they are to be applied to. The same is definitely not the case in reverse. The performance, behaviors, and sensitivities of the liabilities structure are intimately intertwined with the magnitude and timing of the cash flows it receives.

Liabilities Reporting Code

We need to retain not only the VBA code that creates the liabilities performance information but at the same time retain as much of the original report configurations that also capture the asset side performance for the reasons stated above.

We also need to provide for the capture of any remnants of the collateral selection process, when such data are available. That information, when combined with the original collateral file or files used in the analysis, will allow us to precisely replicate the collateral portfolio in the future if we ever need to. Without it, we would be guessing as to what contents and criteria were used to generate the cash flows that are driving the structural cases we are seeing.

STEPPING THROUGH THE MODEL

As with any development activity, it is always best to look first at those activities that will occur last: the results. Once these results are clearly fixed in our mind, it is simply a matter of starting at the beginning and walking the path that brings us to our desired conclusion.

We will therefore start with defining the number and appearance of the reports that we wish the BLM to produce. Once we have defined these reports, we can return to the very beginning of the model and work our way from start to finish to achieve the goal. When we move onto the model itself, we will start with the menus first and then follow the code execution from beginning to end.

Step 0: The Reports

Let us get the easy work done first! We can completely eliminate the two collateral report packages, the Ineligible Collateral report package and the Eligible Collateral report package. We can also eliminate from the BLM any of the code that produces the Eligible Collateral file. Since we will not be concerned with the production of any of the cash flows in this model, we can also eliminate the Cash Flow Trace report and all of its supporting logic.

We will retain as much as possible—in fact, all—of the content of the Waterfall, Summary Matrix, and the Single Scenario report packages. If the BAM had performed a collateral selection process prior to the generation of the cash flows, the criteria of the selection process and its results would be available in the Assumptions page of the report. We would therefore be able to include this information in the subsequent Assumption pages of the BLM's reports. We would thus have presented all the data that were available.

It is for this reason that we will retain the sections of these reports that contain any asset information. Should the information not be available, we will delete the unused portions of the Assumptions page at the time of its preparation.

If we think about this a bit further, we will see that we have a completely binary situation. Either a report is discarded in its entirety or it is preserved without change!

Step 1: The Menus

We will next turn to the task of reconfiguring the menus of the model. This reconfiguration effort will eliminate some menus in their entirety (those dealing exclusively with the collateral selection process) and modify the appearance of the others.

Main Menu The Main Menu will be extensively reconfigured. In the uppermost input block on the left hand side of the menu, the first four and the eighth Run options will be deleted. These are:

- Perform the Collateral Eligibility Test?
- Write out the Ineligible Collateral Reports?
- Write out the Eligible Collateral Reports?
- Write out the Eligible Collateral Loan File?
- Write out the Cash Flow Trace Reports?

In the next block, the Input File Information block, we will retain the Base Directory field and change the Collateral Data File field to the Cash Flow File field.

Liabilities Structuring Model Main Menu

Program Execution Options	(Y=YES; N=NO)		
Y	Write out Cash Flow Waterfall Reports ?		
Y	Write out Matrix Summary Reports ?	*Run the Model*	*Run the Batch Model*
Y	Write out Single Scenario Reports ?		

Input File Information

C:\VBA_Book2\Code\

Cash Flow Source File

CF_Source_01.xls	Cash Flow Scenarios File

Results File and Associated Templates

	BTest04 MVD70_L24_S100		Report Group Prefix (attached to all output files)	Template File Names
View	Waterfall.xls		Cash Flow Waterfalls Report File Name <======	ac_waterfall_template.xls
View	Matrix.xls		Summary Matrix Reports Files <======	ac_matrix_template.xls
View	Scenario.xls		Scenario Summary Reports File <======	ac_scenario_template.xls

EXHIBIT 6.1   Revised Main Menu

We will delete the "# of Loans" field; it is no longer required since we do not read collateral files any longer.

In the final, lowermost pair of output file names and template file names, we will delete the second, third, sixth, and eighth pairs of fields. These fields are for the Ineligible Collateral report package, the Eligible Collateral report package, the Eligible Collateral Data file, and the Cash Flow Trace file.

When we have complete the process the Main Menu should appear as shown in Exhibit 6.1.

Reports Menu   We will remove the left column of this menu. It had been used for the selection of individual Eligible Collateral stratification reports. We will retain the full set of Matrix Summary reports. Three of these reports, Matrix-1, -3, and -4, are exclusively liabilities side reports. The fourth, Matrix-2, is an asset side report that displays summary statistics of the components of the collateral cash flows. Why should we retain this report? We will retain it keeping in mind our policy of preserving as much of the available information as possible. This report is very useful when trying to understand the performance of the liabilities structure. We can, at a glance, compare the magnitude (but not the timing) of each of the cash flow components for each of the scenarios. See Exhibit 6.2.

Report Selection Menu

Run ? "X"	Report Code	MULTIPLE SCENARIO MATRIX RESULTS Report Name
X	Matrix-1	Conduit Tenor Report
X	Matrix-2	Collateral Cash Flows Report
X	Matrix-3	Conduit Note Performance
X	Matrix-4	Seller Interest Performance
		(reserved for future use)

EXHIBIT 6.2   Revised Reports Menu

	Select	Conduit Finance Spread	File Name Prefix ID	Time Prefix Code	Conduit Spread Choice	Libor Rates Path	Prime Rates Path	File Name Prefix
								Batch Output File Menu
1	X	1.000%	BTest01		1	1	2	BTest01 MVD_L_S100
2	X	1.000%	BTest02		1	1	2	BTest02 MVD_L_S100
3	X	1.000%	BTest03		1	1	2	BTest03 MVD_L_S100
4	X	1.000%	BTest04		1	1	2	BTest04 MVD_L_S100
5								
6								
7								
8								
9								
10								

Run the Batch Model

EXHIBIT 6.3   Revised Batch Run Menu

Batch Run Menu   We will delete from the Batch Run Menu the following columns, which are inputs for the cash flow amortization calculations and are therefore irrelevant to the BLM (front left to right):

- Market Value Decline assumption
- Recovery Period Lag assumption

We will retain all the other columns in the menu. Why are we retaining the Prime Rate column when it is only used, at present, in the current Structuring Model, to provide the base index for the floating rate loans of the portfolio? We do so because we may need it for a particular type of bond or some other use that is unforeseen at this time. Here we will err on the side of caution. Remember, it is generally easier to delete than to add code. See Exhibit 6.3.

Rates and Dates Menu, Program Costs Menu   These menus will remain unchanged as they concern input items that are exclusively in the liabilities side of the model.

Defaults Menu, Collateral Selection Criteria Menu, Geographic Selection Menu, Eligibility Results Spreadsheet, and Coupon Trace Report Spreadsheet   All these menus or in-program reports will be deleted, as they are exclusively asset side oriented.

Step 2: Menu Error Checking Module

We will now examine all of the subroutines that perform the menu error checking functions. We will start with the "ErrCheck_All_Menus" subroutine and work our way through all the subroutines that it calls.

All the code for these changes resides in the "MenusErrorChecking" module.

"ErrCheck_All_Menus" Subroutine   The "ErrCheck_All_Menus" subroutine shown in Exhibit 6.4 contains a series of seven calls to other subroutines. The first of these calls performs a check on a number of the menus containing numeric data. The remaining six calls are menu specific. Each checks a particular menu for completeness and consistency. We will be retaining the Main, Program Costs, and Rates and Dates

```
Sub ErrCheck_All_Menus()

    'Set up of message title
    msgTitle = "MODEL MENUs Input Error"
    Call errAllMenus_for_IsNumerics
    Call errMainMenu
    Call errProgramCostsMenu
    Call errReportsMenu
    Call errGeographicMenu
    Call errSelectionCriteriaMenu
    Call errDefaultsMenu

End Sub
```

EXHIBIT 6.4   "ErrCheck_All_Menus" subroutine

Menus. The Collateral Selection Criteria, Geographic Selection, and Defaults Menus will be deleted from the BLM. We can therefore delete the call to them here and then delete the subroutines themselves.

"errAllMenus_for_IsNumerics" Subroutine   If we proceed down the list of the subroutine calls in the order they appear in the "ErrCheck_All_Menus" subroutine, the first call is to the "errAllMenus_for_IsNumerics" subroutine, shown in Exhibit 6.5. The role of this subroutine is to check all entries to any menu that need to be in a numeric in format and confirm that they are in that format.

There are four such menus. Of the four, two—the Collateral Selection Criteria Menu and the Defaults Menu—have been deleted from the BLM. This relieves the program of error checking these menus for numeric inputs, and the calls to the two subroutines here that do so can be deleted. The two subroutines are:

1. "IsNumeric_CriteriaInfo"
2. "IsNumeric_DefaultsPrepaysInfo"

```
Sub errAllMenus_for_IsNumerics()

    Call IsNumeric_ProgramCostsInfo      'populates msgInfo(1) & mErrCase
    Call IsNumeric_CriteriaInfo          'populates msgInfo(2) & mErrCase
    Call IsNumeric_DefaultPrepayInfo     'populates msgInfo(3) & mErrCase
    Call IsNumeric_RatesDatesInfo        'populates msgInfo(4) & mErrCase

    'If there are errors to print -- print them!
    mErrTotal = mErrCase(1) + mErrCase(2) + mErrCase(3) + mErrCase(4)
    If mErrTotal > 0 Then
        'Error box title -- displayed above any errors
        msgTotal = "Non-numeric Inputs for the following Tables" & Chr(13) & Chr(13)
        'Print the combination of errors based on the error code value
        For iloop = 1 To MENU_CHECK_NUMERIC
            If mErrCase(iloop) > 0 Then msgTotal = msgTotal & msgInfo(iloop)
        Next iloop
        msgPrompt = msgTotal
        msgResult = MsgBox(msgPrompt, cMsgButtonCode1, msgTitle)
        End
    End If

End Sub
```

EXHIBIT 6.5   "errAllMenus_for_IsNumerics" subroutine

We will also delete the subroutines themselves. With these two subroutines gone, we also need to change the line:

```
mErrTotal = mErrCase(1)+ mErrCase(2)+ mErrCase(3)+ mErrCase(4)
```

to read:

```
mErrTotal = mErrCase(1)+ mErrCase(2)
```

We make this change to reflect the fact that we now have only two menus that can generate error messages, not four. We will also have to change the subscript of the "mErrCase" and the "mMsgInfo" variables in the Rates and Dates menu from 4, its previous location in the queue, to 2, its current position.

The subscripting of the above variables in the subroutine "IsNumeric_Program CostsInfo" will remain unchanged since this subroutine position is still first in the list.

The last thing we will need to remember to do is to change the value of the Constant variable "MENU_CHECK_NUMERIC" from "4" to "2", again reflecting the decrease in the number of menus checked for numeric content.

"errMainMenu" Subroutine   The next subroutine call from "ErrCheck_All_Menus" is the call to the subroutine "errMainMenu". This subroutine calls three subroutines in turn:

1. "errMainMenu_FilesCheckTemplate". This subroutine checks that if a program Run option, such as "Write out Matrix Summary Reports?" is "Yes", there is a template file name in the appropriate field of the Template File Names box.
2. "errMainMenu_FilesCheckOutput". This subroutine checks that if a program Run option, such as "Write out Matrix Summary Reports?" is "Yes", the user has entered an output file name in the appropriate field of the Results Files box.
3. "errMainMenu_FieldsFilledIn". This subroutine checks that there is some form of input into other fields of the Main Menu, such as the root directory pathway field.

We will not be making any changes to this subroutine, but we will to each of the three subroutines that are called by it. These are the modifications that will be displayed in Exhibits 6.6 to 6.13.

"errMainMenu_FilesCheckTemplate" Subroutine   The first subroutine called by the "errMainMenu" subroutine in the "errMainMenu_FilesCheckTemplates" subroutine seen in Exhibits 6.6 and 6.7. As we enter the top of this subroutine, we see a series of assignment statements to the array "msgInfo". These assignments are used to build individual error messages concerning each of the Template File Names fields in the lower right of the Main Menu. The subroutine checks if there is a template file available in the "Templates" directory that matches the name that has been entered in the field. If the model cannot find a template file with the name that has been entered, an error message is issued.

We have eliminated four of these files and need to adjust the subroutine to reflect this reduction in the number of template files. In the assignment statement in Exhibit 6.7, we will delete the assignments to "msgInfo"(1), (3), (6), and (7), which are the Eligible Collateral report, Ineligible Collateral report, Eligible Collateral

```
Sub errMainMenu_FilesCheckTemplate()

Dim iblock                      As Integer   'counter for number of file checks
Dim errFileMissing(1 To MAIN_MENU_TEMPLATE_FILE_NAMES)      As Boolean
                                             'code for missing file
Dim a                           As String    'abbreviation for pathway
Dim template_pathway            As String    'pathway to the template directory
Dim template_file_name          As String    'current file being tested
Dim template_file_target        As String    'expected file name
Dim output_pathway              As String    'pathway to the results directory
Dim output_file_name            As String    'current output file being tested
Dim output_file_target          As String    'expected output file name
Dim iFileNumber                 As Integer   'error code number from Excel
Dim count_miss                  As Integer   'how many files are missing?
Dim go_ok_03                    As Boolean   'trigger that a file is missing

      msgTotal = "MAIN MENU INPUT ERROR MESSAGES " & Chr(13) & Chr(13)
      'Missing entry error messages
      msgInfo(1) = "   OUTPUT TEMPLATE FILES are missing" & Chr(13)
      msgInfo(2) = "      Collateral Report template file missing" & Chr(13)
      msgInfo(3) = "      Exceptions Report template file missing" & Chr(13)
      msgInfo(4) = "      Cash Flow Waterfall template file missing" & Chr(13)
      msgInfo(5) = "      Matrix Summary template file missing" & Chr(13)
      msgInfo(6) = "      Eligible Collateral Data File template missing" & Chr(13)
      msgInfo(7) = "      Single Scenario template missing" & Chr(13)
      msgInfo(8) = "      Cash Flow Trace File template missing" & Chr(13)
      'set up the pathway to the template directory
      a = Range("m1DirectoryPath")
      template_pathway = a & "template\"
      count_miss = 0          'number of missing template files
```

EXHIBIT 6.6   "errMainMenu_FilesCheckTemplate" subroutine (top)

Data file, and the Cash Flow Trace report, respectively. We will then renumber the surviving assignments to the Waterfall, Matrix Summary, and Single Scenario reports numbered (2), (3), and (4), respectively.

In Exhibit 6.7 we will also delete the corresponding cases in the "Select..Case" statement that correspond to these four template files and renumber the remaining

```
      go_ok_03 = True
      For iblock = 1 To MAIN_MENU_TEMPLATE_FILE_NAMES
          Select Case iblock
              Case Is = 1: template_file_name = Range("templateCollat")
              Case Is = 2: template_file_name = Range("templateIneligible")
              Case Is = 3: template_file_name = Range("templateWaterfall")
              Case Is = 4: template_file_name = Range("templateMatrix")
              Case Is = 5: template_file_name = Range("templateEligCollat")
              Case Is = 6: template_file_name = Range("templateScenario")
              Case Is = 7: template_file_name = Range("templateCFTrace")
          End Select
          template_file_target = template_pathway & template_file_name
          'open template file and set err message
          errFileMissing(iblock) = False
          On Error GoTo TemplateFileErr
          iFileNumber = FreeFile()
          Open template_file_target For Input As iFileNumber
      Next iblock
```

EXHIBIT 6.7   "errMainMenu_FilesCheckTemplate" subroutine (bottom)

...

```
Sub errMainMenu_FilesCheckOutput()

Dim iblock                   As Integer      'loop counter
Dim directory_pathway        As String       'root directory pathway
Dim output_pathway           As String       'reports output directory
Dim output_file_name         As String       'report output file name
Dim output_file_target       As String       'full pathway to output file
Dim iFileNumber              As Integer      'VBA error code
Dim count_exist              As Integer      'number of files found to exist
Dim print_message            As Boolean      'print the error message box
Dim errFileExist(1 To OUTPUT_FILE_EXISTS) As Boolean 'found this file

    msgTotal = "MAIN MENU INPUT ERROR MESSAGES " & Chr(13) & Chr(13)
    msgInfo(1) = "  OUTPUT FILES already exist under these file names" & Chr(13)
    msgInfo(2) = "      Collateral Report output file exists" & Chr(13)
    msgInfo(3) = "      Exceptions Report output file exists" & Chr(13)
    msgInfo(4) = "      Cash Flow Waterfall output file exists" & Chr(13)
    msgInfo(5) = "      Matrix Summary output file exists" & Chr(13)
    msgInfo(6) = "      Portfolio Collateral file exists" & Chr(13)
    msgInfo(7) = "      Single Scenario output file exists" & Chr(13)
    msgInfo(8) = "      Cash Flow Trace output file exists" & Chr(13)
    msgInfo(9) = "  Try changing the output file prefix code" & Chr(13)
    'set up the pathway to the output directory
    directory_pathway = Range("m1DirectoryPath")
    output_pathway = directory_pathway & "output\"
    count_exist = 0          'number of existing output files found
    print_message = False    'no errors found yet
```

EXHIBIT 6.8   "errMainMenu_FilesCheckOutput" subroutine (top)

choices 1 to 3. We will also have to remember to adjust the declaration of the value of the Constant variable "MAIN_MENU_TEMPLATE_FILE_NAMES" in the "A_Constants" module from 7 to 3 to reflect the deleted template reports.

"errMainMenu_FilesCheckOutput" Subroutine   The subroutine "errMainMenu_FilesCheckTemplate" discussed immediately above checked for the presence of a template file name. The "errMainMenu_FilesCheckOutput" subroutine, shown in Exhibits 6.8 and 6.9, performs the same task for the output file names in the lower

```
    For iblock = 1 To OUTPUT_FILE_EXISTS
        Select Case iblock
            Case Is = 1: output_file_name = Range("m1FilePrefix") & Range("m1CollatFileNam
            Case Is = 2: output_file_name = Range("m1FilePrefix") & Range("m1ExceptRepName
            Case Is = 3: output_file_name = Range("m1FilePrefix") & Range("m1CFFileName")
            Case Is = 4: output_file_name = Range("m1FilePrefix") & Range("m1MatrixRepName
            Case Is = 5: output_file_name = Range("m1FilePrefix") & Range("m1EligCollatNam
            Case Is = 6: output_file_name = Range("m1FilePrefix") & Range("m1ScenarioName"
            Case Is = 7: output_file_name = Range("m1FilePrefix") & Range("m1CFTraceName")
        End Select
        output_file_target = output_pathway & output_file_name
        'open output file and set error condition, default: output file is present
        errFileExist(iblock) = True     'found the output file
        On Error GoTo OutputFileErr
        iFileNumber = FreeFile()
        Open output_file_target For Input As iFileNumber
        'the file exists, increment the found file count
        If errFileExist(iblock) Then count_exist = count_exist + 1
    Next iblock
```

EXHIBIT 6.9   "errMainMenu_FilesCheckOutput" subroutine (bottom)

```
Sub errMainMenu_FieldsFilledIn()

Dim msgs(1 To 2)           As String    'error message components
Dim option_test            As Boolean   'results of testing the input filed
Dim print_message          As Boolean   'if true, print error message block
Dim r_field                As String    '1=file name, 2=template file name
Dim iblock                 As Integer   'loop counter

    msgTotal = "MAIN MENU INPUT ERROR MESSAGES " & Chr(13) & Chr(13)
    'Missing entry error messages for center block, directory pathway,
    '   collateral data file, and the record count for the file
    msgInfo(1) = "   No root directory information specified" & Chr(13)
    msgInfo(2) = "   No collateral input data file name specified" & Chr(13)
    msgInfo(3) = "   Missing beginning loan input file loan count" & Chr(13) & _
               "     must be a record count, or 0 to read all records"
    'three center fields, directory pathway, collateral file name, # of records
    print_message = False
    If Trim(Range("m1DirectoryPath")) = "" Then  'test for the main directory pathway
        msgTotal = msgTotal + msgInfo(1)
        print_message = True
    End If
    If Trim(Range("m1CollatRepName")) = "" Then  'test for the collateral input file n
        msgTotal = msgTotal + msgInfo(2)
        print_message = True
    End If
    If Trim(Range("m1CollatNumLoans")) = "" Then  'test for the number of loans
        msgTotal = msgTotal + msgInfo(3)
        print_message = True
    End If
```

EXHIBIT 6.10 "errMainMenu_FieldsFilledIn" subroutine (top)

right hand side of the Main Menu. This subroutine looks for a match in the output directory and issues a warning that a file name with the specified name already exists.

The changes are virtually identical to those just performed. We will drop the references to the four deleted reports and renumber the "msgInfo" array positions to reflect these deletions.

Lower in the subroutine we will now delete the specific cases from the "Select..Case" statement and renumber the "Case Is = N" numbers from 1 to 7 to 1 to 3, to reflect the deleted output file names.

"errMainMenu_FieldsFilledIn" Subroutine The next subroutine called from the "errMainMenu" is the "errMainMenu_FieldsFilledIn" subroutine, shown in Exhibits 6.10, 6.11, and 6.12. This subroutine checks three fields: the root directory pathway, the field containing the name of the collateral data file, and the number of records in that field. It then checks the selection of the run options against the number of required file names.

In Exhibit 6.10, the upper portion of the subroutine is displayed. Here we see the assignments to the "msgInfo" array for three conditions. The first error message is that no root directory is specified; the second is that the collateral data file name is missing; and the third is that the number of loans in the data file is not specified. In that we have eliminated the "# of loans" field entirely, we can delete the assignment to "msgInfo"(3). We will, at a later time, need to use this field to serve as the input

```
'Error messages for the various output file names, and their associated
'   template files.  Messages print when option choice selected but the
'   file specifications are missing
msgInfo(1)  = "  WRITE OUT Ineligible Collateral Reports = TRUE, but," & Chr(13)
msgInfo(2)  = "        No exceptions report file name specified" & Chr(13)
msgInfo(3)  = "  WRITE OUT Collateral Reports = TRUE, but" & Chr(13)
msgInfo(4)  = "        No collateral reports file name specified" & Chr(13)
msgInfo(5)  = "  WRITE OUT Cash Flow Waterfall Reports = TRUE, but," & Chr(13)
msgInfo(6)  = "        No cfs waterfall report file name specified" & Chr(13)
msgInfo(7)  = "  WRITE OUT Matrix Summary Cash Flow Reports = TRUE, but," & Chr(13)
msgInfo(8)  = "        No summary cfs report file name specified" & Chr(13)
msgInfo(9)  = "  WRITE OUT Eligible Collateral File = TRUE, but," & Chr(13)
msgInfo(10) = "        No eligible collateral file name specified" & Chr(13)
msgInfo(11) = "  WRITE OUT Single Scenario Report = TRUE, but," & Chr(13)
msgInfo(12) = "        No single scenario report file name specified" & Chr(13)
msgInfo(13) = "  WRITE OUT Cash Flow Trace Report = TRUE, but," & Chr(13)
msgInfo(14) = "        No cash flow trace report file name specified" & Chr(13)
```

EXHIBIT 6.11 "errMainMenu_FieldsFilledIn" subroutine (middle)

field for the name of the Collateral Cash Flow file that was generated by the BAM. This is as good a place as any to enter it, so we will retain that field on the Main Menu. We will, however, change the error message from:

''No collateral loan data file name specified''

to

''No cash flow file specified''.

```
For iblock = 1 To OUTPUT_FILE_TESTS

    'load the appropriate messages and conditions for error checking by report
    Select Case iblock
        Case Is = 1:    'Ineligible collateral report file
            option_test = (UCase(Trim(Range("m1WriteCollatInelig"))) = "Y")
            r_field = "m1ExceptRepName"        'output report file name
        Case Is = 2:    'Eligible collateral report file
            option_test = (UCase(Trim(Range("m1WritePortReps"))) = "Y")
            r_field = "m1CollatFileName"
        Case Is = 3:    'Cash Flow Waterfall report file
            option_test = (UCase(Trim(Range("m1WriteCFDetail"))) = "Y")
            r_field = "m1CFFileName"
        Case Is = 4:    'Summary Matrix report file
            option_test = (UCase(Trim(Range("m1WriteCFSummary"))) = "Y")
            r_field = "m1MatrixRepName"
        Case Is = 5:    'Eligible collateral data file
            option_test = (UCase(Trim(Range("m1WriteEligCollatFile"))) = "Y")
            r_field = "m1EligCollatName"
        Case Is = 6:    'Single Scenario report file
            option_test = (UCase(Trim(Range("m1WriteScenSummary"))) = "Y")
            r_field = "m1ScenarioName"
        Case Is = 7:    'Cash Flow Trace
            option_test = (UCase(Trim(Range("m1WriteCFTrace"))) = "Y")
            r_field = "m1CFTraceName"
    End Select
```

EXHIBIT 6.12 "errMainMenu_FieldsFilledIn" subroutine (bottom)

We will need to assign a different Range name to the field and place it in the "If..Then" test immediately below. We can also eliminate the third "If..Then" test, as it is no longer needed due to the disappearance of the "# of loans" field on the Main Menu.

As we progress farther down the subroutine, see Exhibit 6.11, we find that a second set of values are now being assigned to the "msgInfo" array to alert us to mismatches between the Program Run options and the requested report file names. We can eliminate assignments to the array elements of "msgInfo"(1) and (2), (3) and (4), (9) and (10), and (13) and (14). These assignments are used to assemble the components of error messages for the deleted reports.

In Exhibit 6.12 we see the "Select..Case" block that prints each of the error messages in turn, if they are needed. Here we need to delete cases 1, 2, 5, and 7. We will then renumber the remaining cases 1 to 3, for the surviving liability report packages. These are the Waterfall, Matrix Summary, and Single Scenario report packages.

"errReportsMenu" Subroutine   The next call in order of appearance in "ErrCheck_All_Menus" is the call to the "errReportsMenu" subroutine. This subroutine checks the contents of the Report Menu. It makes two calls to subordinate subroutines, one that checks the section of the menu that deals with the Eligible Collateral report package, which produces the collateral stratification reports, and another that deals with the Matrix Summary report package. Because in the Eligible Collateral report package, fields have been eliminated from the Reports menu, we can delete the first call to this subroutine. See Exhibit 6.13.

Module-Level Constant Variables   Based on all the changes we have made in this module, we need to adjust the values of some of the module-level Constant variables at the top of the module. See Exhibit 6.14.

We will delete the following Constant variables:

- **"ISNUMERIC_TEST_SEL_CRIT"**. Number of "IsNumeric" tests that need to be performed on the collateral selection criteria test inputs.
- **"ISNUMERIC_TEST_PRE_DEF"**. Number of "IsNumeric" tests that need to be performed on the inputs to the Defaults and Prepayments Menu.
- **"VALUE_TESTS_SEL_CRIT"**. Number of value limits test to the inputs of the collateral selection process.
- **"VALUE_TESTS_DEFAULT_PREPAY"**. Number of value limits test to the inputs of the Defaults and Prepayments Menu inputs.

```
Sub errReportsMenu()

    Call errCollateralReports
    Call errMatrixReports

End Sub
```

EXHIBIT 6.13   "errReportsMenu" subroutine

```
Option Explicit
'==============================================================================
'MODULE LEVEL CONSTANTS
'==============================================================================
'Number of numeric entry tests by menu
Const ISNUMERIC_TESTS_SEL_CRIT = 13      '# isnumeric? test Selection Criteria menu
Const ISNUMERIC_TESTS_PROG_COSTS = 8     '# isnumeric? test Program Costs menu
Const ISNUMERIC_TESTS_PRE_DEF = 8        '# isnumeric? test Prepayment/Defaults menu
'Number of input field value tests by menu
Const VALUE_TESTS_SEL_CRIT = 4           '# value tests of Selection Criteria menu inpu
Const VALUE_TESTS_PROG_COSTS = 8         '# value tests of Program Costs menu inputs
Const VALUE_TESTS_DEFAULT_PREPAY = 5     '# value tests of Prepay/Defaults menu inputs
'Number of output file sets we need to check to prevent overwrtting of existing files
Const OUTPUT_FILE_TESTS = 7              '# types of output file election tests
Const OUTPUT_FILE_EXISTS = 7             '# tests for overwriting existing output file
```

EXHIBIT 6.14 Module level Constant variables of the "MenusErrorChecking" module

We will change the values of the following Constant variables:

- "OUTPUT_FILE_TESTS". From 7 to 3 to reflect the deletion of four reports. These are the Ineligible and Eligible Collateral report packages, the Eligible Collateral data file, and the Cash Flow Trace report.
- "OUTPUT_FILE_EXISTS". From 7 to 4. For the reasons stated above.

We have finally finished with all the error checking subroutines in what will become the BLM. We will now proceed to the subroutines that read the information from the menus and assign it to the VBA arrays and variables of the model.

Step 3: Menu Input Module

After we have error checked the information coming into the model from the menus, we can load it into the VBA variables and arrays. We have, however, eliminated three major menus and have extensively edited two of the surviving menus. We need therefore to follow up the effects of the changes to the menus through these subroutines. The pattern will be broadly similar to the edits we have just seen in the error checking code.

All the code for these changes resides in the "MenusReadInputs" module.

"Read_All_Menu_Input" Subroutine In the "Read_All_Menu_Input" subroutine, shown in Exhibit 6.15, we will delete the subroutines that read information from the

```
Sub Read_All_Menu_Input()

    Call Read_Main_Menu               'Read Main Menu -- set program run options
    Call Read_Program_Costs_Menu      'Reads the program costs and credit enhancemen
    Call Read_Selection_Criteria_Menu 'Read tenor, coupon & balance selection criter
    Call Read_Report_Selection_Menu   'Read menu for report selections
    Call Read_Geographic_Menu         'Read state code geographic selection criteria
    Call Read_Prepay_Defaults_Menu    'Read prepayment and default schedule to apply
    Call Read_Rates_and_Dates_Menu    'Read the rates and dates menu
    Call Read_Coupon_Trace_Screen     'Read the Coupon Trace report switch

End Sub
```

EXHIBIT 6.15 "Read_All_Menu_Input" subroutine

```
Sub Read_Main_Menu()
    Sheets("Main Menu").Select
    Range("A1").Select
    ' Read the program runtime options selections
    gRunIneligiblesReport = UCase(Range("m1CollatElig")) = "Y"           'run exceptio
    gWriteIneligiblesReport = UCase(Range("m1WriteCollatInelig")) = "Y"  'write out ex
    gWriteEligiblesReport = UCase(Range("m1WritePortReps")) = "Y"        'write out po
    gOutputMatrixReport = UCase(Range("m1WriteCFSummary")) = "Y"         'write out ma
    gOutputWaterfallReport = UCase(Range("m1WriteCFDetail")) = "Y"       'write out de
    gOutputCFTraceReport = UCase(Range("m1WriteCFTrace")) = "Y"          'write out th
    gOutputEligCollatFile = UCase(Range("m1WriteEligCollatFile")) = "Y"  'write out a
    gOutputScenarioReport = UCase(Range("m1WriteScenSummary")) = "Y"     'write out a
    ' Read deal name and number of loans in the collateral file
    gPathwayMain = Range("m1DirectoryPath")          'name of root directory for th
    gPathwayTemplate = gPathwayMain & "template\"     'complete for the template dir
    gPathwayOutput = gPathwayMain & "output\"         'complete for the output file
    gTotalLoans = Range("m1CollatNumLoans")           'total loans in the portfolio
    'names of the output report files
    gfnOutputPrefix = Range("m1FilePrefix")           'output files prefix
    gfnCollateralFileName = Range("m1CollatRepName")  'data file of collateral infor
    gfnEligiblesFile = Range("m1CollatFileName")      'output file for collateral re
    gfnWaterfallCFsFile = Range("m1CFFileName")       'output file for cashflow repo
    gfnIneligiblesFile = Range("m1ExceptRepName")     'output file for ineligible co
    gfnSumMatrixFile = Range("m1MatrixRepName")       'output file for matrix report
    gfnEligibleOutDataFile = Range("m1EligCollatName") 'output file for eligible coll
    gfnScenarioFile = Range("m1ScenarioName")         'output file for single scenar
    gfnCFTraceFile = Range("m1CFTraceName")           'output file Cash Flow Trace r
    'names of the template files
    gTemplateEligibles = Range("templateCollat")      'template file collateral sele
    gTemplateWaterfall = Range("templateWaterfall")   'template file cash flow water
    gTemplateIneligibles = Range("templateIneligible")'template file ineligible coll
    gTemplateSumMatrix = Range("templateMatrix")      'template file summary matrix
    gTemplateEligDataFile = Range("templateEligCollat")'template for the eligible col
    gTemplateScenario = Range("templateScenario")     'template for the single scena
    gTemplateCFTrace = Range("templateCFTrace")       'template for the cash flow tr
End Sub
```

EXHIBIT 6.16   "Read_Main_Menu" subroutine

menus and reports that we have dropped from the BLM. We will also delete these subroutines from the module as well.

"Read_Main_Menu" Subroutine   We have extensively modified the Main menu. We must now go through this subroutine and delete all references to the input fields that we have removed. The first five deleted lines in the subroutine are those of the "Run Options" section of the menu. All relate to the collateral selection and reporting process. The sixth and seventh deleted lines of the subroutine refer to the "# of loans" field and the Portfolio Data File Name field. In the "Read_Main_Menu" subroutine shown in Exhibit 6.16, we complete this task.

"Read_Report_Selection_Menu" Subroutine   In the "Read_Report_Selection_Menu" subroutine, shown in Exhibit 6.17, we will delete references to the report selection fields for the Eligible Collateral report package.

Step 4: Constant Variables Module

We have made a large number of changes up to this point. We will now visit the "A_Constants" module, which contains the complete listing of all global Constant variables of the model. Due to its size, we will look at this module in four sections.

```
Sub Read_Report_Selection_Menu()

    Sheets("Reports Menu").Select
    Range("A1").Select

    'collateral reports
    For i_rep = 1 To PORTFOLIO_REPORTS
        gStratReports(i_rep) = False
        If Range("m4ReportsSelected").Cells(i_rep) = "X" Then gStratReports(i_rep) = T
    Next i_rep
    'summary reports
    For i_rep = 1 To MATRIX_REPORTS
        gSumMatrixReports(i_rep) = False
        If Range("m4MatrixRepsSelected").Cells(i_rep) = "X" Then gSumMatrixReports(i_r
    Next i_rep

End Sub
```

EXHIBIT 6.17 "Read_Report_Selection_Menu" subroutine

In the first section, shown in Exhibit 6.18, we will delete the variables "FIXED_RATE" and "FLOAT_RATE", as they are used exclusively in the collateral amortization portions of the model.

In the second section, shown in Exhibit 6.19, we will delete the first two sets of variables used in the geographic selection and reporting processes. These are the variables "STATES", "STATES_PER_COL", "STATES_NUM_COLS", and "TOTAL_ZIP_CODES".

In the next group of variables related to the Reports Selection Menu, we will delete the three declarations beginning with the "PORTFOLIO_REPORTS" variable. These are the Constants used to manage the production of the Eligible Collateral stratification reports. In the following group, we can eliminate both "SEL_CRIT_FIELDS" and "SEL_CRIT_INDEX_SPREADS" as they are used in the collateral selection process only.

In the "Defaults and Prepayments Menu" section we can delete all of the Constant variables, as this menu itself has been deleted earlier in the editing process.

We will change the value assigned to the MENU_CHECK_NUMERIC from 7 to 4 to reflect the reduction in the number of menus surviving in the BLM.

In the third section, shown in Exhibit 6.20, we will delete all the variables shown, as they are used solely in the collateral selection and reporting process.

In the fourth section, shown in Exhibit 6.21, we will delete the first seven declarations, starting with the variable "PREPAYS" and ending with the variable

```
Option Explicit
'==============================================================================
' Public Constants and Variables Declaration block
'==============================================================================
Public Const FIXED_RATE = 1
Public Const FLOAT_RATE = 2

Public Const MAX_YEARS = 30              'maximum Excel model years
Public Const PAY_DATES = 360             'maximum Model months
Public Const PAY_COLS = 63               'maximum Excel model columns
Public Const SCEN_ITEMS = 11             'columns on the single scenario rep
```

EXHIBIT 6.18 "A_Constants" variable module (section 1)

```
'=====================================================================================
'Menu Support Constants
'=====================================================================================
'Geographic Selection Menu and support code
Public Const STATES = 54                          'number of states and territories
Public Const STATES_PER_COL = 18                  'territories per col on menu
Public Const STATES_NUM_COLS = 3                  'number of columns on geographic menu
'Zip Code matrix limit
Public Const TOTAL_ZIP_CODES = 2000               'size of zip code sorting array
'Reports Selection Menu Row/Column
Public Const PORTFOLIO_REPORTS = 11               'number of stratification reports
Public Const REPORT_MENU_ROW = 7
Public Const REPORT_MENU_COL = 2
'Selection Criteria Menu
Public Const SEL_CRIT_FIELDS = 11                 '# selection criteria parameter fields
Public Const SEL_CRIT_INDEX_SPREADS = 6           '# spread/index fields to check
'Program Costs Menu
Public Const PROG_COSTS_FIELDS = 8                '# fields on Program Costs menu
'Defaults and Prpeayment Menu
Public Const DEFAULT_PREPAY_FIELDS = 8            '# fields in Default/Prepayment menus
Public Const MAX_RECOVERY_PERIOD = 60             'maximum recovery lag period
Public Const MAX_MRKT_VAL_DECLINE = 1#            'maximum market value decline
Public Const MAX_CONDUIT_SPREAD = 0.1             'maximum conduit spread
Public Const USER_DEFAULT_COL_COUNT = 10          'years per column in the User default ta
'Main Menu
Public Const MAIN_MENU_TEMPLATE_FILE_NAMES = 7    'names of output files

'Number of menus checked for IsNumerics
Public Const MENU_CHECK_NUMERIC = 4                        'number of menu checked for IsNumeric

'Batch Menu pathway maximum
Public Const MAX_SPREAD_PATH_CHOICE = 5           'maximum counduit spread choice
Public Const MAX_LIBOR_PATH_CHOICE = 5            'maximum Libor pathway choice
Public Const MAX_PRIME_PATH_CHOICE = 5            'maximum Prime choice
```

EXHIBIT 6.19   "A_Constants" variable module (section 2)

"DEFAULTS_USR". Finally we will delete all the variables used in the Cash Flow Trace functions, as it is no longer part of the model. These are the final two variables of the exhibit: "COUP_TRACE_ITEMS" and "COUP_TRACE_ROWS".

Step 5: Global Variables Module

We now move to the global variables of the program. All global variables are declared in the module "A_Globals". As many of these are related to holding collateral, prepayment, and default information, we should expect to delete large numbers of them from the BLM. Again, as with the "A_Constants" module above, we will break this module into a number of sections.

In the first section, shown in Exhibit 6.22, we will delete the global variables that correspond on a one-to-one basis with the input fields we deleted from the Main Menu earlier. We have already eliminated them from the "Read_Main_Menu" subroutine above. From the top down, we will delete the variable declarations for "gRunIneligibleReport", "gWriteIneligibleReport", "gWriteEligibleReport", "gfnEligibleFile", "gfnIneligibleFile", "gfnEligibleOutDataFile", "gfnCFTraceFile", "gTemplateIneligibles", "gTemplateEligibles", "gTemplateEligibleFile", "gTemplateCFTrace", "gOutputCFTraceReport", and "gOutputEligibleFile".

```
' ================================================================================
' EXCEPTION REPORTING CONSTANTS
' ================================================================================
Public Const INELIG_SINGLE_REPS = 11                    'Single cause reports
Public Const INELIG_LISTING_REP = INELIG_SINGLE_REPS + 1 'Loan Listing inelig repor
Public Const INELIG_SUMMARY_REP = INELIG_SINGLE_REPS + 2 'Summary inelig reports
' ================================================================================
' Loan selection criteria test conditions
Public Const EXCEPT_REMAINING_TERM = 1        'Over/Under remaining term range
Public Const EXCEPT_ORIGINAL_TERM = 2         'Over/Under original term range
Public Const EXCEPT_ORIGINAL_BALANCE = 4      'Over/Under original balance range
Public Const EXCEPT_CURRENT_BALANCE = 8       'Over/Under remaining balance range
Public Const EXCEPT_MAX_LTV = 16              'Exceeeds maximum LTV
Public Const EXCEPT_INDEX = 32                'Under minimum spread
Public Const EXCEPT_STATE_CODE = 64           'Excluded state code
Public Const EXCEPT_TENOR_TEST = 128          'Orig Term / Rem Term Relationship
Public Const EXCEPT_BAL_TEST = 256            'Orig Bal / Rem Bal Relationship
Public Const EXCEPT_PMT_TEST = 512            'Calculated Payment vs. Stated Payment
Public Const EXCEPT_COUPON = 1024             'Acceptable range of gross coupon values
' ================================================================================
' These variables correspond one-to-one with the exception conditions above
' They are used to indicate the index location in the gSelectionTag vector.  When a
'   piece of collateral fails one of the tests, the nth position of the gSelectionTa
'   vector is set to "1" based on the value of the constant below.
' ================================================================================
Public Const TEST_REM_TERM = 1
Public Const TEST_ORIG_TERM = 2
Public Const TEST_ORIG_BAL = 3
Public Const TEST_REM_BAL = 4
Public Const TEST_MAX_LTV = 5
Public Const TEST_INDEX = 6
Public Const TEST_STATE_CODE = 7
Public Const TEST_TENOR_CODE = 8
Public Const TEST_BAL_CODE = 9
Public Const TEST_PMT_CODE = 10
Public Const TEST_COUPON_CODE = 11
```

EXHIBIT 6.20   "A_Constants" variable module (section 3)

In the second section, shown in Exhibit 6.23, we will retain all of the variables. Why should we seek to retain the variables pertaining to the collateral selection process? We want to retain this information to serve as a basis for analysis if we ever have to replicate the collateral selection process. Knowing the criteria that produced the portfolio from which we form the incoming cash flow files is therefore quite important!

In the third section, shown in Exhibit 6.24, we will delete the "gStratReports" array, all of the Geographic Section variables and arrays, and the Collateral Selection variables and arrays.

In the fourth section, shown in Exhibit 6.25, we will delete all of the variables as they serve to hold loan-by-loan collateral information not needed in the BLM.

There are a block of variables that start after the end of Exhibit 6.25 and end prior to the start of Exhibit 6.26. These variables are those that capture the results of the waterfall calculations. They are declared immediately under a masthead named "Waterfall Results". There are 23 variables in this block, starting with "gOutAverageLife" and ending with "gOutCoupExpShortfall". They are critical to the process of capturing the performance of the liability structure. Therefore, we will retain them all.

```
' ==============================================================================
' MODELING INPUTS
' ==============================================================================
'Prepayment and Default Table Constants
' ==============================================================================
'Switch between prepayments and defaults
Public Const PREPAYS = 1
Public Const DEFAULTS = 2
'Prepayment Methodologies
Public Const PREPAY_CPR = 1                    'Constant Percentage Rate
Public Const PREPAY_PSA = 2                    'Public Securities Admin
'Default Methodologies
Public Const DEFAULTS_CPR = 1                  'Constant Percentage Rate
Public Const DEFAULTS_PSA = 2                  'Public Securities Admin
Public Const DEFAULTS_USR = 3                  'User Defined Rate
'Maximum Number of Steps
Public Const MAX_STEPS_PREPAY = 10
Public Const MAX_STEPS_DEFAULT = 10


'day count conventions
Public Const DAYS_30_360 = 1
Public Const DAYS_ACT_360 = 2
Public Const DAYS_ACT_ACT = 3
'Cash Flow Waterfall Report Package Constants
Public Const MAX_SCEN = MAX_STEPS_PREPAY * MAX_STEPS_DEFAULT
'Matrix Summary Report Package Constants
Public Const MATRIX_REPORTS = 4                      'total # of reports
Public Const MATRIX_TENOR_REPORT = 1
Public Const MATRIX_CFS_REPORT = 2
Public Const MATRIX_CONDUIT_REPORT = 3
Public Const MATRIX_SELLER_INT_REPORT = 4
' =========================================================================
'Coupon Trace Constants  --  Floating Rate Loans Only
'    1 = computed coupon level   2 = index level
'    3 = periodic floor          4 = periodic cap
Public Const COUP_TRACE_ITEMS = 4       'data we need to store by reset period
Public Const COUP_TRACE_ROWS = 120      'quarterly for 30 years
```

EXHIBIT 6.21   "A_Constants" variable module (section 4)

In the fifth section, shown in Exhibit 6.26, we will delete the top two blocks of variables, those related to the Cash Flow Trace report and to the Loan Coupon Level Trace report. We will retain all the other global variables from this point onward to the bottom of the module.

Step 6: Collateral Selection and Cash Flow Calculation Modules

We will now proceed to the portion of the model that performs the collateral eligibility selection process. From the results of this process, we arrive at the Eligible Collateral for the deal. The loans of the portfolio that have been deemed eligible for inclusion in the deal can be written to a file. This allows subsequent model runs to bypass the selection process and use this collateral directly. (This assumes that the original portfolio and the selection criteria have not changed in the interim!) This collateral portfolio is then amortized using a variety of assumption to determine the range of possible cash flows.

```
Option Explicit
' ================================================================================
'
' Public Variables
'
' ================================================================================
'MAIN MENU VARIABLES
Public gMainFileName              As String   'Name of main model workbook
Public gfnCollateralFileName      As String   'Name of the INPUT collateral data file
Public gRunIneligiblesReport      As Boolean  'Run the selection criteria exceptions re
Public gWriteIneligiblesReport    As Boolean  'Write the selection criteria exceptions
Public gWriteEligiblesReport      As Boolean  'Write portfolio collateral reports
Public gPathwayMain               As String   'Directory level pathway
Public gPathwayTemplate           As String   'Report templates directory pathway
Public gPathwayOutput             As String   'Outputs directory pathway
Public gfnOutputPrefix            As String   'Prefix label concatenated to all output
Public gfnEligiblesFile           As String   'Name of OUTPUT collateral reports file
Public gfnWaterfallCFsFile        As String   'Name of OUTPUT collateral cashflows file
Public gfnIneligiblesFile         As String   'Name of OUTPUT exceptions reports file
Public gfnSumMatrixFile           As String   'Name of OUTPUT matrix summary file
Public gfnEligibleOutDataFile     As String   'Name of OUTPUT eligible collateral data
Public gfnScenarioFile            As String   'Name of OUTPUT single scenario report fi
Public gfnCFTraceFile             As String   'Name of OUTPUT single scenario report fi
Public gTotalLoans                As Long     'Number of loans in the portfiolio
Public gTemplateIneligibles       As String   'template file ineligible collateral
Public gTemplateEligibles         As String   'template for the collateral reports
Public gTemplateWaterfall         As String   'template for the waterfall reports
Public gTemplateSumMatrix         As String   'template file summary matrix reports
Public gTemplateEligDataFile      As String   'template file name for eligibile collate
Public gTemplateScenario          As String   'template file name for single scenarios
Public gTemplateCFTrace           As String   'template for the Cash Flow Trace report
Public gOutputMatrixReport        As Boolean  'Switch to output the cashflow matrix rep
Public gOutputWaterfallReport     As Boolean  'Switch to output the detailed period by
Public gOutputCFTraceReport       As Boolean  'Switch to produce file of monthly indivi
Public gOutputEligCollatFile      As Boolean  'Switch to output the eligible collateral
Public gOutputScenarioReport      As Boolean  'Switch to output the eligible collateral
```

EXHIBIT 6.22   "A_Globals" variable module (section 1)

We can therefore delete the following four modules that are specifically devoted to this process. See Exhibit 6.27.

After we have deleted the module "CollateralReadDataFile", we will use the same set of actions to delete the following modules:

- ■ **"CollateralSelectionSubs".** This module contains all the code that performs the collateral eligibility selection process.
- ■ **"CollateralCFGenerator".** This module contains the general collateral cash flow generation code.
- ■ **"CollateralPreDefCalcs".** This module contains all the specialized prepayment and default calculation subroutine code.

Step 7: Remove Collateral Reporting Modules

The next step in the process is to remove all of the specialized reporting that accompanies the collateral selection process. The first module that we will delete is the Cash Flow Trace report. See Exhibit 6.28.

```
' PROGRAM COST MENU VARIABLES
Public gExpenseService          As Double          'Percentage rate for servicing
Public gExpenseProgram          As Double          'Percentage for program expens
Public gTriggerCleanup          As Double          'percentage for clean up call
Public gTrigger3MDefaults       As Double          'percentage of rolling 3 month
Public gAdvanceRate             As Double          'conduit advance rate
Public gConduitSpread           As Double          'conduit financing spread
' DEFAULTS AND PREPAYMENTS MENU VARIABLES
Public gPrepayLevels            As Integer         'Number of prepayment rate sce
Public gPrepayBaseLevels        As Double          'Base prepayment rate (CPR met
Public gPrepayIncrement         As Double          'Increment to base prepayment
Public gPrepayMethod            As Integer         '1=CPR, 2=PSA, 3=SMM
Public gDefaultLevels           As Integer         'Number of default rates used
Public gDefaultBaseRate         As Double          'Starting default rate
Public gDefaultIncrement        As Double          'Increment by which base rate
Public gRecoveryLagPeriod       As Integer         'Recovery lag of defaults in m
Public gLossSeverityPct         As Double          'Market value decline for reco
'Public gDefaultFactor(1 To PAY_DATES) As Double       'Default rate for the year of a
Public gDayFactors(1 To PAY_DATES, 1 To 3)    As Double    'decimal days counts 30/36
Public gMonths(1 To PAY_DATES)    As Date          'beginning month dates
' SELECTION CRITERIA MENU VARIABLES
Public gCriteriaMinOrigTerm     As Double          'Min original term in months
Public gCriteriaMaxOrigTerm     As Double          'Max original term in months
Public gCriteriaMinRemTerm      As Double          'Min remaining term in months
Public gCriteriaMaxRemTerm      As Double          'Max remaining term in months
Public gCriteriaMinOrigBal      As Double          'Min original balance
Public gCriteriaMaxOrigBal      As Double          'Max original balance
Public gCriteriaMinRemBal       As Double          'Min remaining balance
Public gCriteriaMaxRemBal       As Double          'Max remaining balance
Public gCriteriaMaxLTV          As Double          'Max loan LTV
Public gCriteriaMinSpread(1 To 6)   As Double      'Min spread to floating rate i
Public gCriteriaOKIndex(1 To 6)     As String      'Min spread to floating rate i
Public gCriteraMinCoupon        As Double          'Min current yield
Public gCriteraMaxCoupon        As Double          'Max current yield
Public gCriteraMaxPmtDiff       As Double          'Max diff between stated/calcu
```

EXHIBIT 6.23 "A_Globals" variable module (section 2)

We will also delete the following collateral and collateral cash flow reporting modules:

- **"WriteCollateralReports".** This module produces the Eligible Collateral stratification reports.
- **"WriteIneligibilityReports".** This module produces the Ineligible report package.
- **"WriteEligCollatFile".** This module writes a portfolio data file of all loans that have passed the eligibility tests.

Step 8: Button and Utility Library

In the process of removing the collateral eligibility testing and report functions, we deleted the Geographic Selection Menu. This menu contained a series of buttons that allowed the user of the program to either select or de-select either the entire National set of states or any set of states contained in one of the six smaller regions. With the removal of the menu, we need to clean up the model by removing these button support subroutines. This code is contained in the "Z_Buttons" module. See Exhibit 6.29.

```
' ---------------------------------------------------------------------------
' REPORT SELECTION MENU
' ---------------------------------------------------------------------------
Public gStratReports(1 To PORTFOLIO_REPORTS)      As Boolean      'Report selection vec
Public gSumMatrixReports(1 To MATRIX_REPORTS) As Boolean      'Summary selection vecto
' ---------------------------------------------------------------------------
' GEOGRAPHIC REGION SELECTION MENU
' ---------------------------------------------------------------------------
Public gNumSelectStates                        As Integer      'The number of codes in th
Public gStateSelect(1 To STATES)               As Boolean      'Array of which states are
Public gStatePostal(1 To STATES)               As String       'A compressed list of the
Public gStateName(1 To STATES)                 As String       'Full name of the state
Public gStateIDNumber(1 To STATES)             As Integer      'Number in list order of t
' ---------------------------------------------------------------------------
'Collateral Selection Results variables
' ---------------------------------------------------------------------------
Public gSelectionTag()                         As Boolean      'Vector of 1's and 0'
Public gSelectionTotal()                       As Double       'Expression of gSelec
Public gExceptionReports(INELIG_SINGLE_REPS)   As Boolean      'checks if there are ANY ex
Public gSelectionMaxScore                      As Double       'value of the highest
' ---------------------------------------------------------------------------
' Default and prepayment variables
' ---------------------------------------------------------------------------
Public gPrepayRate()                           As Double       'user input prepay levels fo
Public gMonthlyPrepayRate()                    As Double       'monthly prepayment factors
Public gDefaultRate()                          As Double       'user input default levels f
Public gMonthlyDefaultRate()                   As Double       'monthly default factors
Public gAnnualDefaultDists(1 To MAX_YEARS)     As Double       'annual default rates
Public gIndexLevels(1 To PAY_DATES, 1 To 3)    As Double
Public gFundConduit(1 To PAY_DATES)            As Double       'funding rate to conduit
Public gDefaultMethod                          As Integer      '1=CPR,2=PSA,3=UserDefined
Public gLoanAmortFactors()                     As Double
```

EXHIBIT 6.24   "A_Globals" variable module (section 3)

A related set of subroutines contained in the "Z_UtilitySubroutines" module processed state postal codes and matched these to the full name of the state or its numeric ranking in an alphabetical list. We can now delete these subroutines. See Exhibit 6.30.

With the changes to the Main Menu, a number of button support subroutines that are no longer needed should be eliminated from the model. These buttons allow the user to open and view any report file directly from the Main Menu. With the elimination of the "Ineligible Collateral Reports", the "Eligible Collateral Reports", the "Eligible Data File", and the "CF Trace Report", we can dispense with their buttons! See Exhibit 6.31.

Step 9: Batch Mode Model

The last VBA module we need to edit is the Batch Mode Model. The changes to this module have been minor. We have needed only to delete a pair of collateral behavior assumption fields from the menu. These fields were the Market Value Decline and the Recovery Period Lag assumptions. We will now review the code to reflect these changes in the VBA.

All of the code in these subroutines is contained in the module named "A_BatchFileProgram".

```
'-----------------------------------------------------------------------
' Portfolio data in the data file
'    This data is, with a very few exceptions read into the program from the "Loan In
'    worksheet of the data file.  The exceptions are:
'          state_code      Mapped to a numeric from the 2 alpha postal abbreviation
'          obligor_code    Assinged to track multiple loans to the same obligor
'-----------------------------------------------------------------------
Public gLoanOK()              As Boolean    'Loan accepted for securitization ? (0=ye
Public gLoanNumber()          As String     'Loan number
Public gLoanOrigBalance()     As Double     'Original loan balance
Public gLoanRemBalance()      As Double     'Current loan balance
Public gLoanCoupon()          As Double     'Implicit yield of the loan
Public gLoanOrigTerm()        As Double     'Original term of the loan (months)
Public gLoanRemTerm()         As Double     'Remaining term of the loan (months)
Public gLoanSeason()          As Double     'Seasoning
Public gLoanFixedFloat()      As Integer    'Fixed or floating rate 1=Fixed,2=Float
Public gLoanIndex()           As String     'Floater underlying index for variable pa
Public ggLoanFloaterCode()    As Integer    'numeric code 1=prime, 2=LIBOR, 3=10yrTSY
Public gLoanSpread()          As Double     'Floater spread
Public gLoanResetRate()       As String     'Frequency of coupon adjustment
Public gLoanResetPmt()        As String     'Frequency of payment adjustment
Public gLoanLifeCap()         As Double     'Lifetime interest rate cap
Public gLoanLifeFloor()       As Double     'Lifetime interest rate floor
Public gLoanResetCap()        As Double     'Quarterly interest rate reset cap
Public gLoanResetFloor()      As Double     'Quarterly interest rate reset floor
Public gLoanDayCount()        As Integer    'Day count convention
Public gLoanCalcPmt()         As Double     'Calculated loan payment
Public gLoanStatedPmt()       As Double     'Stated payment
'Project Information & Demographics
Public gLoanAppraisal()       As Double        'Appraisal value of project
Public gLoanOrigEquity()      As Double        'Original owners equity
Public gLoanCurrEquity()      As Double        'Current owners equity (estimated)
Public gLoanPostalCode()      As String        '2 letter state postal code
Public gLoanNumericCode()     As Integer       'Numeric state code for reporting
Public gLoanZipCode()         As Double        'Zip code
Public gLoanObligorCode()     As Integer       'Lender assigned obligor code number
Public gMonthlyCoupLevels()   As Double        'monthly coupon level, index+spread
```

EXHIBIT 6.25　"A_Globals" variable module (section 4)

```
'CASH FLOW TRACE REPORT VARIABLES
Public gValidateDefaults(1 To PAY_DATES)      As Double    'monthly defaults per loan
Public gValidateCoupIncome(1 To PAY_DATES)    As Double    'monthly coupon per loan
Public gValidatePrinRetired(1 To PAY_DATES)   As Double    'monthly princpal per loan
Public gValidatePrepayments(1 To PAY_DATES)   As Double    'monthly prepays per loan
'LOAN COUPON LEVEL TRACE REPORT
Public gValidateCoupTrace()       As Double        'coupon pathway trace informatio
Public gValidateCoupTraceSwitch   As Boolean       'turn trace on or off
'WATERFALL REPORT VARIABLES
' Cashflow components
Public gPrepaidPrin()             As Double        'per period prepayments of principal
Public gDefaultPrin()             As Double        'per period defaulted principal
Public gAmortPrin()               As Double        'per period amortized principal
Public gCoupIncome()              As Double        'per period coupon payments
Public gRecoverPrin()             As Double        'per period recoveries of defaulted
Public gRecover                   As Double        'per loan recovery of defaulted prin
' Collateral cashflow components
Public gBeginCollateral           As Double        'beginning balances of loans
```

EXHIBIT 6.26　"A_Globals" variable module (section 5)

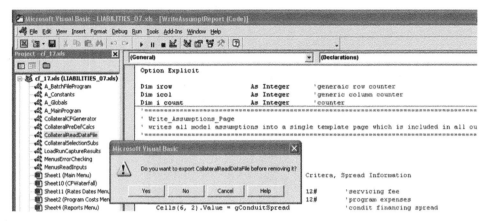

EXHIBIT 6.27 Deleting the "CollateralReadDataFile" module

Module-Level Variables Declarations In Exhibit 6.32, we see the module-level variables declarations for this module. We will delete the variables "mBatchMVD-Factor" and "mBatchLagPeriod".

"Count_Number_Of_Scenarios" Subroutine The task of the subroutine "Count_Number_Of_Scenarios", shown in Exhibit 6.33, is to test that a scenario has been selected. In addition the subroutine also tests that there is *some* information in the input line of the selected scenario. We were using as our test criteria the Market Value Decline factor for the scenario. Having eliminated this field Range from the menu, it would be wise to replace it with a field of something that *is* there. We will use the "m10ConduitSpread" Range as a replacement test criteria.

"ErrCheck_IsNumeric_BatchMenu" Subroutine In the "ErrCheck_IsNumeric_BatchMenu" subroutine, shown in Exhibit 6.34, we see that we can immediately

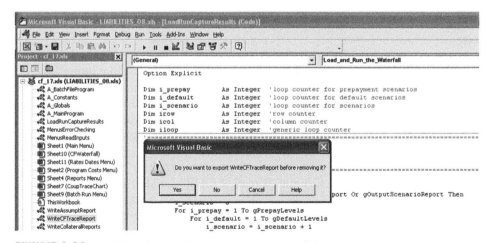

EXHIBIT 6.28 Deleting the "WriteCFTraceReport" module

```
'    GEOGRAPHIC MENU BUTTON SUBROUTINES
'
'
'
'================================================================================
Sub Include_National_Portfolio()
    For i_state = 1 To STATES_PER_COL
        Range("m6States1").Cells(i_state) = "X"
        Range("m6States2").Cells(i_state) = "X"
        Range("m6States3").Cells(i_state) = "X"
    Next i_state
End Sub
Sub Exclude_National_Portfolio()
    For i_state = 1 To STATES_PER_COL
        Range("m6States1").Cells(i_state) = ""
        Range("m6States2").Cells(i_state) = ""
        Range("m6States3").Cells(i_state) = ""
    Next i_state
End Sub
Sub Include_New_England()
    Cells(10, 2).Value = "X"       ' Connecticut
    Cells(4, 6).Value = "X"        ' Massachusetts
    Cells(6, 6).Value = "X"        ' Maine
    Cells(15, 6).Value = "X"       ' New Hampshire
    Cells(6, 10).Value = "X"       ' Rhode Island
    Cells(13, 10).Value = "X"      ' Vermont
End Sub
Sub Exclude_New_England()
    Cells(10, 2).Value = ""        ' Connecticut
    Cells(4, 6).Value = ""         ' Massachusetts
    Cells(6, 6).Value = ""         ' Maine
    Cells(15, 6).Value = ""        ' New Hampshire
    Cells(6, 10).Value = ""        ' Rhode Island
    Cells(13, 10).Value = ""       ' Vermont
End Sub
```

EXHIBIT 6.29   Removing the Geographic Selection Menu button support code

eliminate the error checking for the Market Value Decline and Recovery Period Lag inputs. We will delete the assignments to "msgInfo"(1) and (2). We will then drop down to the "Select..Case" and delete the first two tests there! We now renumber the assignments to "msgInfo" from 1 to 4 and the corresponding cases below from 1 to 4. After we have completed that task, the only thing we need to do is change the argument in the "Produce_Error_Message_Box" subroutine. It currently has a value of 6, which needs to be reduced to 4 to reflect the lesser number of test cases we now have.

"ErrCheck_MaximumValues" subroutine   In the "ErrCheck_MaximumValues" subroutine, shown in Exhibit 6.35, we need to delete the first two assignments to the "msgInfo" array that relate to the Market Value Decline and the Recovery Period Lag. With this task accomplished, we also need to delete the first two cases in the "Select..Case" statement below that tests the inputs against the maximum allowable values.

We now note that we are missing three error messages for the pathway values that can be chosen for the Conduit Spread, LIBOR (London Interbank Offering Rate), and Prime.

While we round up the guilty parties, we can add these error messages and renumber the "msgInfo" array from 1 to 4. This will leave us with a corrected subroutine in the final form we need it to be in!

```
Option Explicit

Dim i_state          As Integer              'generic state loop counter
'=================================================================================
'  Assign_State_Name
'=================================================================================
Function Assign_State_Name(i)
    Assign_State_Name = gStateName(i)
End Function
'=================================================================================
'  Assign_State_Number
'=================================================================================
Function Assign_State_Number(state_id)

    For i_state = 1 To STATES
        If state_id = gStatePostal(i_state) Then
            Assign_State_Number = i_state
            Exit For
        End If
    Next i_state

End Function
'=================================================================================
'  Assign_State_Number
'=================================================================================
Function Assign_State_Name_From_Postal(state_id)

    For i_state = 1 To STATES
        If state_id = gStatePostal(i_state) Then
            Assign_State_Name_From_Postal = gStateName(i_state)
            Exit For
        End If
    Next i_state

End Function
```

EXHIBIT 6.30 Removing the Geographic Utility subroutines

```
'=================================================================================
'    Open Output reports
'=================================================================================
Sub Button_View_Collateral_Reports_File()
    Workbooks.Open Filename:=gPathwayOutput & gfnOutputPrefix & gfnEligiblesFile
End Sub

Sub Button_View_Ineligible_Loans_File()
    Workbooks.Open Filename:=gPathwayOutput & gfnOutputPrefix & gfnIneligiblesFile
End Sub

Sub Button_View_Cash_Flow_Waterfall_File()
    Workbooks.Open Filename:=gPathwayOutput & gfnOutputPrefix & gfnWaterfallCFsFile
End Sub
Sub Button_View_Matrix_File()
    Workbooks.Open Filename:=gPathwayOutput & gfnOutputPrefix & gfnSumMatrixFile
End Sub
Sub Button_View_Collateral_File()
    Workbooks.Open Filename:=gPathwayOutput & gfnOutputPrefix & gfnEligibleOutDataFi
End Sub
Sub Button_View_Single_Scenario_File()
    Workbooks.Open Filename:=gPathwayOutput & gfnOutputPrefix & gfnScenarioFile
End Sub
```

EXHIBIT 6.31 Removing the "View" button support code

```
'=====================================================================
'Batch File Modular Variables
'=====================================================================
Dim i_file                   As Integer    'scenario loop counter
Dim num_file                 As Integer    'number of files requested
Dim mBatchMVDFactor()        As Double     'market value decline vector
Dim mBatchLagPeriod()        As Integer    'recovery lag period in months
Dim mBatchConduitSpread()    As Double     'conduit financing spread
Dim mBatchFileName()         As String     'name of the inidividual file
Dim mBatchSpreadPathway()    As Integer    'conduit spread pathway
Dim mBatchLIBORPathway()     As Integer    'libor spread pathway
Dim mBatchPrimePathway()     As Integer    'prime rate pathway
```

EXHIBIT 6.32   Module-level variables declarations

Read the Batch Menu Inputs   As shown in Exhibit 6.36, we will need to adjust the subroutine that reads the contents of the Batch Menu. We will eliminate the lines that read the Market Value Decline and the Recovery Lag Period information.

"Load_and_Run_Loan_Financing_Model" Subroutine   In the "Load_and_Run_Loan_Financing_Model" subroutine, shown in Exhibit 6.37, we will delete the lines containing the references to the "mBatchMVDFactor" and the "mBatchLagPeriod" variables. Since we have deleted the Defaults Menu, we should also remove the statements referencing it, as they are no longer necessary. We were loading these inputs to the Defaults Menu to provide inputs for the collateral amortization process that we are no longer performing in this model.

Step 10: Purging the Menu Range Names

We now need to purge the deleted Range names from the BLM. Consult Step 12 in Chapter 5 if you need to review the procedure for doing so.

Remember to be very careful here! Also remember that many of the deleted Ranges will be on the menus that we eliminated, and most of the remainder will be concentrated in the Main Menu.


```
Sub Count_Number_Of_Scenarios()

    'count the number of designated scenarios
    For i_file = 1 To NUM_OF_BATCH_FILES
        If Range("m10SelectScenario").Cells(i_file) <> "" And _
           Range("m10MktValueDecline").Cells(i_file) <> "" Then
            num_file = i_file
        Else
            Exit For
        End If
    Next i_file

End Sub
```

EXHIBIT 6.33   "Count_Number_Of_Scenarios" subroutine

```
Sub ErrCheck_IsNumeric_BatchMenu()

Dim num_test                  As Boolean  'holding variable
    'Error box title -- displayed above any errors
    msgTotal = "Non-numeric Inputs for the Batch Menu Columns" & Chr(13) & Chr(13)
    msgInfo(1) = "Market Value Decline non-numeric entry in scenarios" & Chr(13)
    msgInfo(2) = "Recovery Period non-numeric entry in scenarios" & Chr(13)
    msgInfo(3) = "Conduit Financing Spread non-numeric entry in scenarios" & Chr(13)
    msgInfo(4) = "Conduit Spread Pathway non-numeric entry in scenarios" & Chr(13)
    msgInfo(5) = "Libor Rate Pathway non-numeric entry in scenarios" & Chr(13)
    msgInfo(6) = "Prime Rate Pathway non-numeric entry in scenarios" & Chr(13)
    err_total = False          'any errors at all?
    'check each of the fields for non numerics
    For i_type = 1 To BATCH_RANGE_TESTS
        'set the accumulator to zero or null
        err_string = ""                'numer of non-numeric scenarios
        scen_count = 0                 'running count of errors
        err_case(i_type) = False    'case trigger to print error message
        For i_scen = 1 To num_file
            'test each cell location over the effective scenario range
            Select Case i type
                Case Is = 1: num_test = (IsNumeric(Trim(Range("m10MktValueDecline").Ce
                Case Is = 2: num_test = (IsNumeric(Trim(Range("m10RecPeriodLag").Cells
                Case Is = 3: num_test = (IsNumeric(Trim(Range("m10ConduitSpread").Cell
                Case Is = 4: num_test = (IsNumeric(Trim(Range("m10SpreadPathway").Cell
                Case Is = 5: num_test = (IsNumeric(Trim(Range("m10LiborPathway").Cells
                Case Is = 6: num_test = (IsNumeric(Trim(Range("m10PrimePathway").Cells
            End Select
            err_result = (num_test = False)
            If err_result Then Call Build_The_Scenario_List
        Next i_scen
        If err_case(i_type) Then Call Build_The_Error_Message_List
    Next i_type
    'If err_total is TRUE print the messages
    Call Produce_Error_Box_Message(6)
End Sub
```

EXHIBIT 6.34   "ErrCheck_IsNumeric_BatchMenu" subroutine

READING THE CASH FLOWS AND ASSUMPTIONS FROM A FILE

To complete the BLM, we will have to create a couple of subroutines that will open the Collateral Cash Flow file computed by the BAM and read its contents. We have already discussed the reasons why we will want to preserve as much information as possible about the selection criteria that resulted in the collateral portfolio used to create the cash flows. Being clear as to the conditions of the origin of these cash flows is vital if we ever need to re-create them.

To meet this need we will not only have to write a subroutine to extract the cash flows from the file but along with them all of the information that is also available in the Assumptions page of the report. The cash flow file that we will use will be the Collateral Waterfall report.

To finish off the BLM, we therefore need to do the following six things:

1. Create a field on the Main Menu for the entry of the target Waterfall report file from which we will we read the cash flows.
2. Write the appropriate VBA code in the subroutines that perform the error checking for the Collateral Cash Flow file name entry field of the Main Menu.

```
Sub ErrCheck_MaximumValues()

Dim num_test    As String  'holding variable

    'Error box title -- displayed above any errors
    msgTotal = "Maximum Values Exceeded in the Batch Menu Columns" & Chr(13) & Chr(13)
    msgInfo(1) = "Exceeds MAXIMUM Market Value Decline scenarios = " & Chr(13)
    msgInfo(2) = "Exceeds MAXIMUM Recovery Lag Period scenarios = " & Chr(13)
    msgInfo(3) = "Exceedes MAXIMUM Conduit Spread Level scenarios = " & Chr(13)
    'check each of the fields for non numerics
    err_total = False            'any errors at all?
    For i_type = 1 To BATCH_RANGE_TESTS
        'set the accumulator to zero or null
        err_string = ""                'numer of non-numeric scenarios
        scen_count = 0                 'running count of errors
        err_case(i_type) = False          'case trigger to print error message
        For i_scen = 1 To num_file
            err_result = False
            'test each cell location over the list of active scenarios
            Select Case i_type
                Case Is = 1    'test for maximum market value decline
                    err_result = ((Trim(Range("m10MktValueDecline").Cells(i_scen))) >
                Case Is = 2    'test for maximum recovery lag period value
                    err_result = ((Trim(Range("m10RecPeriodLag").Cells(i_scen))) > MAX
                Case Is = 3    'test for maximum conduit spread value
                    err_result = ((Trim(Range("m10ConduitSpread").Cells(i_scen))) > MA
                Case Is = 4    'test for maximum conduit spread pathway
                    err_result = ((Trim(Range("m10SpreadPathway").Cells(i_scen))) > MA
                Case Is = 5    'test for maximum LIBOR pathway choice
                    err_result = ((Trim(Range("m10LiborPathway").Cells(i_scen))) > MAX
                Case Is = 6    'test for maximum Prime pathway choice
                    err_result = ((Trim(Range("m10PrimePathway").Cells(i_scen))) > MAX
            End Select
            If err_result Then Call Build_The_Scenario_List
        Next i_scen
```

EXHIBIT 6.35 "ErrCheck_MaximumValue" subroutine

```
Sub Read_Batch_Program_Menu()

    'read the contents of the ranges
    ReDim mBatchMVDFactor(1 To num_file) As Double       'market value decline vector
    ReDim mBatchLagPeriod(1 To num_file) As Integer      'recovery lag period in months
    ReDim mBatchConduitSpread(1 To num_file) As Double   'conduit financing spread
    ReDim mBatchFileName(1 To num_file) As String        'name of the inidividual file
    ReDim mBatchSpreadPathway(1 To num_file) As Integer  'conduit spread pathway
    ReDim mBatchLIBORPathway(1 To num_file) As Integer   'libor spread pathway
    ReDim mBatchPrimePathway(1 To num_file) As Integer   'prime rate pathway
    For i_file = 1 To num_file
        mBatchMVDFactor(i_file) = Trim(Range("m10MktValueDecline").Cells(i_file).Value
        mBatchLagPeriod(i_file) = Trim(Range("m10RecPeriodLag").Cells(i_file).Value)
        mBatchConduitSpread(i_file) = Trim(Range("m10ConduitSpread").Cells(i_file).Val
        mBatchFileName(i_file) = Trim(Range("m10FilePrefixName").Cells(i_file).Value)
        mBatchSpreadPathway(i_file) = Trim(Range("m10SpreadPathway").Cells(i_file).Val
        mBatchLIBORPathway(i_file) = Trim(Range("m10LiborPathway").Cells(i_file).Value
        mBatchPrimePathway(i_file) = Trim(Range("m10PrimePathway").Cells(i_file).Value
    Next i_file

End Sub
```

EXHIBIT 6.36 "Read_Batch_Program_Menu" subroutine

```
Sub Load_and_Run_Loan_Financing_Model()

    For i_file = 1 To num_file
        Sheets("Defaults Menu").Select
        Cells(23, 4).Value = mBatchAVDFactor(i_file)
        Cells(24, 4).Value = mBatchLagPeriod(i_file)
        Sheets("Program Costs Menu").Select
        Cells(16, 3).Value = mBatchSpreadPathway(i_file)
        Cells(17, 3).Value = mBatchLIBORPathway(i_file)
        Cells(18, 3).Value = mBatchPrimePathway(i_file)
        Sheets("Defaults Menu").Calculate
        Sheets("Main Menu").Select
        Cells(19, 3).Value = mBatchFileName(i_file)
        Call Loan_Financing_Model
    Next i_file

End Sub
```

EXHIBIT 6.37 "Load_and_Run_Loan_Financing_Model" subroutine

3. Create a VBA module named "ReadCashFlowFiles" to hold the new subroutines.
4. Write a subroutine to open the cash flow file. This subroutine will need to be able to determine how many scenarios are in the file, read each of the worksheets in turn, and place the information in the appropriate positions of the VBA arrays. We will also write a subroutine to read the Assumptions page of the Waterfall file and transfer all available data from that page to the Assumptions pages of any subsequent reports that are generated by the BLM.
5. Once all this code is written, we need to call it from the BLM main program at an appropriate place in its operational sequence.
6. Last, but not least, we need to test the BLM and see if we can replicate its results against those of the combined current Structuring Model using the same inputs. We will start with a Waterfall Cash Flow file and run the cash flows for each of its scenarios through the newly created BLM. If we have performed the split between the original Structuring Model that we started with and our newly completed BLM correctly, the results between the BLM and the original model runs will be identical.

Step 11: Reading the Collateral Cash Flow File

We will next turn to the task of preparing the model to read the collateral cash flows that the BAM has generated. Remember that this capability was not required in the combined model. The cash flows were originally placed in arrays and were therefore immediately available to the portion of the combined model that loaded them into the waterfall spreadsheet. Here we will need to find a file designated by the modeler (or print an error message if we cannot), open it, and transfer the cash flows into the preexisting arrays. At that point we will be ready to evaluate the performance of the structure as before.

Adding the File Input Field to the Main Menu We will need an entry field on the Main Menu of the BLM to direct the program to the appropriate cash flow file previously produced by the BAM. Once we have the name of the file in hand, we

```
Sub errMainMenu()

    Call errMainMenu_FilesCheckCFFile
    Call errMainMenu_FilesCheckTemplate
    Call errMainMenu_FilesCheckOutput
    Call errMainMenu_FieldsFilledIn

End Sub
```

EXHIBIT 6.38　"errMainMenu" subroutine with the call to the "errMainMenu_FilesCheck CFFile" subroutine added

can open it and read the cash flows into the model, completely obviating the need for any collateral computations whatsoever.

We are fortunate to have just such a field in place! We can put the Cash Flow file name field in the position formerly occupied by the Collateral Data file field in the Main Menu of the Structuring Model.

We will assign the Range name "m1CollatCFFile" to the input field. If we review Exhibit 6.1, the Main Menu, we will see this field in cells C15 to C16.

Error Checking the File Entry　We next need to have whatever file name the user enters into the field run through an error checking program. This file entry is on the Main Menu. It will therefore be checked by the "errMainMenu" subroutine that is called by the "errCheck_All_Menus" subroutine. We will need to add a subroutine call to "errMainMenu" to check if the Collateral Cash Flow file is present in the "cffiles" directory. But wait! Why can we just not add an additional file check on one of the subroutines that checked for the output files or the template files? We cannot for one very good reason: The cash flow file is neither a template file nor is it an output file; it is an input file, and we need to keep this distinction intact. We may find ourselves in a situation in which we may want to add several more input files to this menu. If we begin the practice of intermixing the file types now, we could end up with unnecessary confusion later on!

We will call this subroutine "errMainMenu_FilesCheckCFFile". It will be called from the "errMainMenu" subroutine, as shown in Exhibit 6.38. The error-checking subroutine itself is shown in Exhibit 6.39. We will add this code to the module "MenusErrorChecking".

Reading the File Name into a VBA Variable　Once we have verified that this file name is valid, we can read it into a VBA variable created to hold the name until we need to access the file. We will create a global variable named "gfnCollatCFFileName" and declare it in the "Main Menu Variables" section of the "A_Globals" module. We next need to add a single line of code in the "Read_Main_Menu" subroutine in the "MeanusReadInputs" module:

```
'input file for cash flows

gfnCollatCFFileName = Range(''m1CollatCFFileName'')
```

We now have the file name verified and stored in a variable for future use.

```
Sub errMainMenu_FilesCheckCFFile()

Dim cffile_target    As String        'full pathway to output file
Dim iFileNumber      As Integer       'VBA error code
Dim errFileExist     As Boolean       'found this file

    msgTotal = "MAIN MENU INPUT ERROR MESSAGES " & Chr(13) & Chr(13)
    msgInfo(1) = "  COLLATERAL CASH FLOW file is missing" & Chr(13)
    'set up the pathway to the output directory
    cffile_target = Range("m1DirectoryPath") & "cffiles\" & _
        Range("m1CollatCFFileName")
    errFileExist = False 'False means NO ERROR!
    On Error GoTo OutputFileErr
    iFileNumber = FreeFile()
    Open cffile_target For Input As iFileNumber
    'If the value of errFileExist=True print the error message
    If errFileExist Then
        msgTotal = msgTotal & msgInfo(1)
        Sheets("Main Menu").Select
        msgPrompt = msgTotal
        msgResult = MsgBox(msgPrompt, cMsgButtonCode1, msgTitle)
        End
    End If
    On Error GoTo 0
    Exit Sub

OutputFileErr:
    Select Case Err
        Case Is = 52, 53, 75, 76
            'ERROR CONDITION did not find the file!
            errFileExist = True
    End Select
    Resume Next

End Sub
```

EXHIBIT 6.39   "errMainMenu_FilesCheckCFFile" subroutine

Create a New Module Named "ReadCashFlowFiles"   The subroutines we are about to create to open and read the cash flows and their accompanying Assumptions page are special-purpose activities. They will replace the cash flow generator subroutines of the current Structuring Model that we removed earlier in the editing process. As such, this code will be placed in a separate VBA module.

We will name this module "ReadCashFlowFile". Using the

"Insert–> Module"

command from the Visual Basic Editor Menu, we add a blank module to the code. This module will appear with the name "Module1". We then use the

"View–> Properties Window"

EXHIBIT 6.40 "ReadCashFlowFile" module has been installed

command and click on the Properties Window. We can then enter the module name in the "Name" field at the top of the pop-up menu.

When we are done, we will see the new module inserted in the project at the appropriate location as shown in Exhibit 6.40.

Reading the Cash Flow File We now have a specific module into which we can place the VBA subroutines that we will use to open and read the Collateral Waterfall files. We have written the code that will confirm the existence of the target Collateral Cash Flow file. The next code we need to write will locate this file and read its contents into arrays that the BLM can use to populate the Waterfall spreadsheet!

Reading the Assumptions Page Information We will start by writing a subroutine to read the contents of the Assumptions page. This exercise will be laborious but simple! We already have a subroutine that writes the user inputs and some of the collateral selection results to the Assumptions page in each of the report packages. It is named "Write_Assumptions_Report". All we have to do is eliminate any of the references to the inputs from the Program Costs menu and reverse the assignment statements of this code! We will then have a subroutine that reads the contents of an Assumption page and places it into the appropriate variables. To reverse the assignments, simply take this:

```
Cells(15, 2).Value = gCriteriaMinOrigTerm
```

and make it this:

```
gCriteriaMinOrigTerm = Cells(15, 2).Value
```

```
Sub Read_CFInputFileAssumpPage()

    Sheets("Assumptions").Select
    'SECTION I - Program Costs, Selection Critera, Spread Information
    'load the collateral selelction criteria
    gCriteriaMinOrigTerm = Cells(15, 2).Value      'min original term in months
    gCriteriaMaxOrigTerm = Cells(15, 4).Value      'max original term in months
    gCriteriaMinRemTerm = Cells(16, 2).Value       'min remaining term in months
    gCriteriaMaxRemTerm = Cells(16, 4).Value       'max remaining term in months
    gCriteriaMinOrigBal = Cells(17, 2).Value       'min original balance
    gCriteriaMaxOrigBal = Cells(17, 4).Value       'max original balance
    gCriteriaMinRemBal = Cells(18, 2).Value        'min remaining balance
    gCriteriaMaxRemBal = Cells(18, 4).Value        'max remaining balance
    gCriteraMinCoupon = Cells(19, 2).Value         'min gross coupon
    gCriteriaMaxCoupon = Cells(19, 4).Value        'max gross coupon
    gCriteriaMaxLTV = Cells(20, 4).Value           'max LTV ratio
    gCriteraMaxPmtDiff = Cells(21, 4).Value        'allowable difference stated/calc p
    'write the spread information
    i_count = 1
    For irow = 24 To 29
        gCriteriaOKIndex(i_count) = Cells(irow, 2).Value
        gCriteriaMinSpread(i_count) = Cells(irow, 4).Value
        i_count = i_count + 1
    Next irow

    'SECTION II - Prepayment and default assumptions
    'collateral file information
    gfnCollateralFileName = Cells(4, 9).Value
    'load default information
    gDefaultBaseRate = Cells(6, 9).Value
    gDefaultIncrement = Cells(7, 9).Value
    gDefaultLevels = Cells(8, 9).Value
    gDefaultMethod = Cells(9, 9).Value
    'load repayment levels
    gPrepayBaseLevels = Cells(11, 9).Value
    gPrepayIncrement = Cells(12, 9).Value
    gPrepayLevels = Cells(13, 9).Value
```

EXHIBIT 6.41 "Read_ CFInputFileAssumpPage" subroutine

We will call this subroutine "Read_CFInputFileAssumpPage". It is shown in Exhibit 6.41. We will place this code in the newly created "ReadCashFlowsFile" module.

Reading the Cash Flow Vectors from the Collateral Waterfall File With the assumptions captured, we can now move on to the cash flow vectors themselves. The file that contains these cash flows is comprised of a collection of worksheets, each of which represents a unique prepayment and default rate combination. If there were, for example, four prepayment rates combined with five default rates, there would be 20 total (5*4) scenarios. The immediate task is to identify how many of these unique scenarios there are in the workbook and what the names of each of the worksheets that contain them are. Once that has been accomplished, we can approach them in the correct order and load the contents of each scenario into the proper cash flow VBA variable vector.

We will start by using a vital piece of information from the Assumptions page of the Collateral Cash Flow file. These very useful items are:

- The Base Default Rate assumption used.
- The number of default speeds to be evaluated.

■ The incremental step rate for each exclusive level after the Base Default Rate assumption.
■ The above information for the Base Prepayment Rate, the number of prepayment speeds to be used, and the incremental step rate from the Base Prepayment Rate for the remainder of the prepayment rates.

With this information in place, we can construct a list of worksheet names that should appear in the workbook. The names are expressed in the following format:

```
''P-'' & PrepaySpeed & ''% '' & space & ''D-'' & DefaultSpeed
& ''%''
```

Thus a scenario with a prepayment speed of 200 PSA and a default speed of 400 SDA would produce the following worksheet title:

```
''P-200% D-400%''
```

The BAM produces these cash flow scenarios by starting with the initial prepayment rate and then cycling through the number of default rate levels before starting again with the next higher prepayment rate. Once all the default rates have been addressed, it increments the prepayment rate and cycles through the default rates again. If the prepayment interval step was 50 PSA with two steps and the default speed interval step was 25 SDA with three default steps, respectively, we would have six scenarios with the worksheet names seen in Exhibit 6.42.

With the array of worksheet names in hand, we can simply step through the workbook reading the five component cash flow vectors from each of the worksheets.

To accomplish all this, we will create a series of modular-level variables and the following subroutine, "ReadCashFlows_From_File", which is comprised of calls to four other subroutines. The first call, to the subroutine "Read_CFInput FileAssumpPage", reads the contents of the Assumptions page of the file into a series of global variables and arrays. This gathers all the information we have and gives us a context into which to place the cash flow scenarios that are on the following pages. The second subroutine, "ReDim_SetUp_Prepay_Default_Levels", uses the information from the Assumptions page to determine how many prepayment and default levels have been specified and the number of resultant scenarios. The

EXHIBIT 6.42 Table of worksheet and scenario names derived from prepayment and default speeds

Scenario Number	Prepay Speed	Default Speed	Scenario and Worksheet Title
1	200 PSA	400 SDA	"P-200% D-400%"
2	200 PSA	425 SDA	"P-200% D-425%"
3	200 PSA	450 SDA	"P-200% D-450%"
4	250 PSA	400 SDA	"P-250% D-400%"
5	250 PSA	425 SDA	"P-250% D-425%"
6	250 PSA	450 SDA	"P-250% D-450%"

```
Option Explicit

Dim mNumberSheetsCnt    As Integer    'number of sheets counted in workbook
Dim mNumberSheetsCalc   As Integer    'number calc based on pre * def scens
Dim mCFSheetName()      As String     'names of the worksheets
Dim prate               As Double     'current prepayment rate
Dim drate               As Double     'current default rate
Dim read_cfs            As Boolean    'OK to read the CFs?
Dim iscen               As Integer    'nth scenaro
Dim ip                  As Integer    'prepayment case loop counter
Dim id                  As Integer    'default cases loop counter
Dim icol                As Integer
Dim irow                As Integer
'==================================================================
'
'
'
'==================================================================
Sub ReadCashFlows_From_File()

    Workbooks.Open Filename:=gPathwayCFFiles & gfnCollatCFFileName
    Call Read_CFInputFileAssumpPage
    Call ReDim_SetUp_Prepay_Default_Levels
    Call SetUp_CashFlow_WorksheetNames
    Call Read_CashFlows_FromWorksheets
    ActiveWorkbook.Close

End Sub
```

EXHIBIT 6.43 Module-level variables and the "ReadCashFlows_From_File" subroutine

third subroutine call, "SetUp_CashFlow_WorksheetNames", uses the information just obtained to create the series of worksheet names. As the model writes the cash flows into the output file we will need to sequentially, and in a specific order, select the proper worksheet to read the cash flows from. In the last subroutine call to "Read_CashFlows_FromWorksheets", we read the contents of each of the worksheets into a set of five arrays. We will later use the contents of these arrays to populate the Liabilities Waterfall Model. See Exhibit 6.43.

We are familiar with the form and function of the subroutine that reads the Assumptions page, "Read_CFInputFileAssumpPage", and do not need to revisit it. The next step is to use some of the information obtained by this subroutine to determine the number of prepayment/default scenarios and the specific combinations of speeds used for both factors. We determine the number of prepayment speeds and the number of default levels to be used in the scenarios. The product of these speeds and levels tells us the number of total scenarios. This task is performed by the "ReDim_SetUp_Prepay_Default_Levels" subroutine shown in Exhibit 6.44.

We now know the number of prepayment speeds and their individual values and the number of default levels and their individual levels. This information can now be used to determine the total number of scenarios and what specific combinations of prepayment/default activity are used for each scenario. The subroutine uses this information first to calculate the total number of expected scenarios. This number is compared to the number of cash flow worksheets actually present in the workbook. If there is a match, we can be fairly well assured that we will find the data we want. Next it uses the individual prepayment speeds and default levels to construct a vector of worksheet names. The "SetUp_CashFlow_WorksheetNames" subroutine can be seen in Exhibit 6.45.

```
Sub ReDim_SetUp_Prepay_Default_Levels()

    'prepayment levels
    ReDim gPrepayRate(1 To gPrepayLevels) As Double
    For ip = 1 To gPrepayLevels
        If ip = 1 Then
            gPrepayRate(ip) = gPrepayBaseLevels
        Else
            gPrepayRate(ip) = gPrepayRate(ip - 1) + gPrepayIncrement
        End If
    Next ip
    'default levels
    ReDim gDefaultRate(1 To gDefaultLevels) As Double
    For id = 1 To gDefaultLevels
        If id = 1 Then
            gDefaultRate(id) = gDefaultBaseRate
        Else
            gDefaultRate(id) = gDefaultRate(id - 1) + gDefaultIncrement
        End If
    Next id

End Sub
```

EXHIBIT 6.44   "ReDim_SetUp_Prepay_Default_Levels" subroutine

```
Sub SetUp_CashFlow_WorksheetNames()

Dim i_name  As Integer

    'read the Cash Flow Report
    'compare the number of sheets counted versus calculated, remember that
    '  you need to subtract the 1 from the count number for the assumptions
    '  page, the rest would be cash flow worksheets
    mNumberSheetsCnt = ActiveWorkbook.Sheets.Count - 1
    mNumberSheetsCalc = gDefaultLevels * gPrepayLevels
    read_cfs = False
    If mNumberSheetsCnt = mNumberSheetsCalc Then read_cfs = True
    If read_cfs Then
        'build the list of names
        ReDim mCFSheetName(1 To mNumberSheetsCalc) As String
        i_name = 1
        prate = gPrepayBaseLevels
        For ip = 1 To gPrepayLevels
            drate = gDefaultBaseRate
            For id = 1 To gDefaultLevels
                ' name the sheets using the prepayment and default parameters
                mCFSheetName(i_name) = "P-" & (prate * 100) & "%" & _
                                    " D-" & (drate * 100) & "%"
                drate = drate + gDefaultIncrement
                i_name = i_name + 1
            Next id
            prate = prate + gPrepayIncrement
        Next ip
    Else
        'error some scenarios missing
    End If

End Sub
```

EXHIBIT 6.45   "SetUp_CashFlow_WorksheetNames" subroutine

```
Sub Read_CashFlows_FromWorksheets()

    Call Erase_All_CFComponents 'clear the current array contents
    Call Redim_All_CFComponents 'redim the arrays
    If read_cfs Then
        iscen = 0
        For ip = 1 To gPrepayLevels
            For id = 1 To gDefaultLevels
                iscen = iscen + 1
                Sheets(mCFSheetName(iscen)).Select
                If id = 1 And ip = 1 Then
                    gBeginCollateral = Cells(14, 11).Value
                End If
                For irow = 14 To (PAY_DATES + 14)
                    If Cells(irow, 11).Value > 0.01 Then
                        gAmortPrin(ip, id, irow - 13) = Cells(irow, 13).Value
                        gPrepaidPrin(ip, id, irow - 13) = Cells(irow, 14).Value
                        gDefaultPrin(ip, id, irow - 13) = Cells(irow, 15).Value
                        gCoupIncome(ip, id, irow - 13) = Cells(irow, 18).Value
                        gRecoverPrin(ip, id, irow - 13) = Cells(irow, 19).Value
                    End If
                Next irow
            Next id
        Next ip
    End If

End Sub
```

EXHIBIT 6.46 "Read_CashFlows_FromWorksheets" subroutine

All the preparatory work has now been accomplished. All that is left to do is to visit each worksheet of the Collateral Waterfall file in turn and copy the contents of the worksheet into a series of global cash flow arrays that are available to receive them. With the cash flows assigned into the arrays and the capture of the beginning collateral pool balance, we have all the information we need to populate the liabilities waterfall. The subroutine in Exhibit 6.46, "Read_CashFlows_FromWorksheets", performs this last task.

We will copy one column of the worksheet that represents one component of the cash flow stream into a separate position in an array. The five arrays that we will assign the cash flows to are dimensioned to:

```
(1 to Prepayment Levels, 1 to Default Levels, 1 to PAY_DATES)
```

We will place the scheduled amortization of principal in the array "gAmortPrin", prepayments of principal in "gPrepaidPrin", defaulted principal in "gDefaultPrin", coupon cash flows in "gCoupIncome", and recoveries of principal in "gRecover-Prin".

We will also need to write two small pieces of support code. These subroutines perform the useful functions of re-dimensioning the arrays and clearing them of their previous values before loading the new cash flows into them. See Exhibit 6.47.

Modify the BLM Main Program To finish this task, we now need to insert the call to the subroutine "ReadCashFlows_From_File" into the main program, "Base_Liabilities_Model", as shown in Exhibit 6.48.

```
' ===============================================================
'
'
' ===============================================================
Sub Erase_All_CFComponents()

    ' Cashflow components variables
    Erase gPrepaidPrin
    Erase gDefaultPrin
    Erase gAmortPrin
    Erase gCoupIncome
    Erase gRecoverPrin

End Sub
' ===============================================================
'
'
' ===============================================================
Sub Redim_All_CFComponents()

    ' Cashflow components variables
    ReDim gPrepaidPrin(1 To gPrepayLevels, 1 To gDefaultLevels, 1 To PAY_DATES) As D
    ReDim gDefaultPrin(1 To gPrepayLevels, 1 To gDefaultLevels, 1 To PAY_DATES) As D
    ReDim gAmortPrin(1 To gPrepayLevels, 1 To gDefaultLevels, 1 To PAY_DATES) As Dou
    ReDim gCoupIncome(1 To gPrepayLevels, 1 To gDefaultLevels, 1 To PAY_DATES) As Dc
    ReDim gRecoverPrin(1 To gPrepayLevels, 1 To gDefaultLevels, 1 To PAY_DATES) As D

End Sub
```

EXHIBIT 6.47 "Erase_All_CFComponents" subroutine and the "Redim_All_
CFComponents" subroutine

We are now done building the BLM! Let us see just how good, or lucky, we are.
Let the testing begin!

TESTING THE COMPLETED BASE LIABILITIES MODEL

While we will assume that we have done everything correctly, we need to be sure! We
will now put the model through a testing cycle. Remember, no reasonable amount
of time spent on testing is ever wasted. It is imperative that you test you models prior

```
Sub Base_Liabilities_Model()

    Application.DisplayAlerts = False      'turn off warning messages
    'read and verify inputs
    Call ErrCheck_All_Menus                'error check all menu entries
    Call Read_All_Menu_Input               'read menu entries into variables
    'read cash flows from a file and run the model
    gMainFileName = ActiveWorkbook.Name
    Call ReadCashFlows_From_File           'open and read collateral cash flows
    Call Load_and_Run_the_Waterfall        'loads scenario cfs, runs the model
    'write the report package
    Call Write_Waterfall_Report_Package    'waterfall reports by scenario
    Call Write_Matrix_Report_Package       '4 matrix reports
    Call Write_Scenario_Report_Package     'single scenario reports
    'exit the program
    Sheets("Main Menu").Select
    Application.DisplayAlerts = True        'turn message displays back on
    Application.StatusBar = False

End Sub
```

EXHIBIT 6.48 "Base_Liabilities_Model" with the call to "ReadCashFlow_From_File"

to release and use by others. You need to be assured that the model will perform the request tasks and produce the expected results. Do not damage the credibility and reputations of your coworkers, subordinates, or yourself by letting what might appear to be obvious errors remain undetected.

Having said all of that, we can be somewhat more economical in testing this program than a model that was a completely new development effort. Why? The original Structuring Model was extensively tested after its creation. We have hundreds if not thousands of cases to compare the new, now-split program to, and we can be sure that the test cases are correct if they match the previously validated results!

Running the Model

Now that we have both the BAM and the BLM (we hope) complete, we can begin testing. A starting test would be to run a single case with a range of scenarios through the BAM starting from scratch with a collateral file, applying the standard selection criteria, and generating the collateral cash flows for a number of prepayment and default scenarios. We will then have the BLM read the Cash Flow Waterfall report produced by the BAM and apply the cash flows to the existent liabilities structure. Fortunately we have already performed the first half of this test in Chapter 5.

We have a Collateral Cash Flow file named "ReadCFTest_Waterfall" that contains 25 scenarios. These are created from the following conditions:

	Base Rate	Step Increment	# of Steps
Prepayment Rate	200 PSA	50	5
Default Rate	400 SDA	50	5

This will create a distribution of conditions from "P-200% D-400%" on the low end of activity to "P-400% D-600" on the high activity end of the spectrum. With these differences we will see a set of significantly varied structure responses by the liabilities. It should be a good test.

Comparing the Results

To generate the results, we will move the "ReadCFTest_Waterfall" file to the "cffiles" directory and then enter its name in the appropriate field of the Main Menu of the BLM. We will make sure that the inputs to the Program Costs Menu and the Rates and Dates Menu are the same as the inputs we used when we modeled these scenarios using the current Structuring Model. We will select all the report packages for output. The Liabilities Waterfall report package will be the one we will first examine because it has the most detail. If there is a problem, it will be easier to find the differences on these reports than on the Matrix Summary or the Single Scenario reports.

We then run the model and compare the results.

On the Web site you will find three sets of files, the first generated by the current Structuring Model, the second by the BAM, and the third by the BLM. Exhibit 6.49 shows the cross-references you can use to verify the results.

EXHIBIT 6.49   Output verification files on the Web site

	Current Structuring Model	Base Asset Model	Base Liabilities Model
Ineligible Collateral Reports	Full	Full	No
Eligible Collateral Reports	Full	Full	No
Eligible Collateral Data File	Full	Full	No
Waterfall Reports	Full	Partial	Full
Matrix Summary Reports	Full	Partial	Full
Single Scenario Reports	Full	Partial	Full

The files for the Structuring Model have the prefix "TestCombined", the files for the BAM have the prefix "BaseCollat", and files for the BLM have the prefix "BaseLiab".

To quickly verify the results of the BAM and BLM to the Structuring Model, we can start with the high-level reports: the Matrix Summary reports. A comparison of these reports reveals some very small discrepancies between the report sets; all differences are less than $2. All these reports display summary scenario data. If there are only rounding errors present, we can feel very confident that the Waterfall and Single Scenario reports produced by the bifurcated models will match those of the Structuring Model. A quick examination of the report sets indicates that they do. We can therefore consider the first major development effort a success. We now have two verified models to use as the development platforms for our future modeling efforts.

ON THE WEB SITE

There is a chapter comments file, "**Chapter06_Comments.xls**".

There are 12 interim versions of the work-in-progress Base Asset Model, named "**BaseLiabModel_1.xlsx**" through "**BaseLiabModel_11.xlsx**", which correspond to Steps 1 through 11 in the BLM creation process.

The report template files that have be edited for the BAM are as follows:

- "**lwmMatrixTemplate.xlsx**". Matrix Summary report package template
- "**lwmScenarioTemplate.xlsx**". Single Scenario report package template
- "**lwmWaterfallTemplate.xlsx**". Cash Flow Waterfall report template

Three sets of output files were generated in the testing process. These files are:

1. "**TestCombined.zip**". This file contains the full output file set of the Structuring Model. It was run using the Structuring Model, the "portfolio_comb.xls" collateral file, and templates associated with the Structuring Model.
2. "**BaseAsset.zip**". This file contains the BAM output package run with the same assumptions and portfolio data file used in the Structuring Model run above.

3. **"BaseLiabilities.zip".** These reports were run using the BLM and the Waterfall Cash Flow report produced by the BAM.

The first set of output files consisting of six files was generated by the current Structuring Model and has the prefix "TestCombined". The second set of output files was generated by the BAM and has the prefix "BaseCollat". The third set generated by the BLM has the prefix "BaseLiab".

There is a more detailed explanation of these files on the Web site itself.

## CHAPTER 7

Establishing the Model Environment

OVERVIEW

In this chapter we will create the external environment that will organize and house the models and their attendant data, template, and output files that we are about to create in Chapters 8 through 17. The delineation and early establishment of a directory structure to hold our models and their supporting files is extremely important! I am personally amazed that in every modeling book that I have ever read, this aspect of modeling is universally ignored! It is as if the models existed independent of time and space, floating around in a modeling Nirvana. In this modeling Nirvana all input information is effortlessly and immediately available to the model. This Nirvana not only embraces the inputs of the model but also extends to its results as well! After the model has completed its run and the output has been produced, this information is assumed to effortlessly and unerringly find its way to safe and secure location, nestled in a universally available location!

Alas, this is not the case in the real world. The world that you and I and the programs we create live in is a very, very different world. If you are not careful, do not plan ahead, and do not create a well-organized, logical, and ruthlessly enforced directory system to house your model, you dramatically increase the chances of problems occurring. Some of these problems may be small, annoying, or simply embarrassing. Lost or overwritten input files or model output is low on the problem scale. Using the wrong input data and not discovering it until after the runs of the model have been distributed to a client is on the life-threatening end of the scale.

Fortunately for us, establishing a directory environment is neither laborious nor mentally taxing. The important thing is to *just do it*! It also helps to do it early enough in the model development process that it frames your thinking and actively helps you to organize the models and their supporting files.

Last I would like to say that this is a short but important chapter. It will yield a highly leveraged return if you invest a small amount of time and energy to understand the concepts. If the content is self-evident to you, all the better! If it is not, stick with these principles until they become routine work habits, and you will avoid much distress and misery. Remember, Murphy's Law has a terrible and almost inexhaustible patience to wait until just the right time to strike. Pay attention here, and your visitations by that phenomenon will be both infrequent and mild.

DELIVERABLES

The modeling knowledge deliverables for this chapter are:

- Understanding why we need an established directory environment for the models before we start down the path of development.
- How to set up the directory system we will need to manage our development effort in the following chapters.

UNDER CONSTRUCTION

In this chapter we will construct an external environment in which we will develop and store our models, their supporting files, and their output.

IMPORTANCE OF A STANDARDIZED DIRECTORY STRUCTURE

The advantages of having a standardized directory environment for the model where its supporting files reside is substantial. Specifically these include:

- The concept of "a place for everything and everything in its place." This system places files in clear and appropriately named directories. Models are in model directories. Files containing input are in input directories, with subdirectories by input types. The output of the models is in output directories segregated by the type of model run that produced the output or by the intended audience or both.
- The ability to quickly locate any file you need because the directory system essentially is a filing system for all the files of the system.
- Greatly lessened chances of overwriting or misplacing files.
- A standard directory system is devised for each model group. You will find that it is easier to train new personnel than it would be if the directory system was one with an individually idiosyncratic (or no) structure.

CREATING DIRECTORIES AND DEFINING THEIR FUNCTIONS

This is not rocket science! All programs, from the smallest Excel spreadsheet all the way up to massive trading and valuation systems, share three common elements. These elements are *inputs* to the program, the *program* itself, and the *output* of the program. That is all there is to it! Some programs or models contain all three elements in a single file. Some programs use hundreds, thousands, or even tens of thousands of files, but, in the end, they all consist of the same three-part paradigm.

Operating Directories

Our basic organizational structure will therefore be predicated along these three elements. We will need a directory to store the inputs to the model, the model or models themselves, and a place, which will be neither of the two aforementioned places, to put the results of the model.

The complexity and specificity to which we develop these directories will be driven by two factors: (1) the scope and complexity of the model system and (2) common sense. If the model we are developing requires three input files, a simple, single "data" directory may be all we need. Conversely, if the model requires tens or even hundreds of files to be accessed before and during a routine run, a more robust directory system may be called for. It might then be obvious that a much more detailed, tiered, and specific directory structure will be required. Even in this case, however, common sense may override the obvious choice. What if the model requires 200 input data files but each has an identical format and all are broadly similar in content? Given a collection of files with these characteristics, a single directory might be quite adequate from an organizational standpoint!

The operating directories of the model environment are:

- **Data directory.** Holds all input data in files or data bases needed to run the model.
- **Models directory.** Holds the Base Models, the Intermediate Models under development, and the Representative Line Generator program.
- **Output directory.** Holds all output from the models and programs.
- **Templates directory.** Holds all template files used by the models.
- **Valuation directory.** Holds all valuation runs of the securities of the deal in either the primary or secondary markets.

Administrative Directories

Once we move away from the operation of the model itself, we will also need a series of directories for administrative, regulatory, and backup purposes. These directories are as much for our own sense of self-preservation as they are for anything else. The reasons that many developers do not create these types of "supporting" directories are:

- They are not enlightened or experienced enough to see the advantages of doing so.
- They are not compelled to do so by their firms or others, such as regulatory bodies.
- They are lazy.
- They are obstructionist.
- They are any combination or, worse yet, *all* of the above.

These administrative directories serve a number of important functions:

- **Backup directory.** Holds "protected" copies of the models. These model versions are verified and segregated and are not accessible by the user communities.
- **Validation directory.** Holds programs and input/output files used in the model validation process.

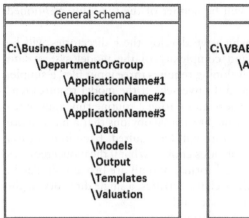

EXHIBIT 7.1   Directory Structure (Level One)

- **Documentation directory.** Holds the model documentation material.
- **Training directory.** Holds any training versions of the model, case studies, and instructional material.

Directory Map

Using the above schema, the initial directory system would look like the schema in Exhibit 7.1. Here the "BusinessName" directory level is the organization acronym for your unit. The Mortgage Backed Securities Unit might be assigned an "MBS" business designation while an Asset Backed Securities Unit might be assigned "ABS". Immediately under the business unit directory designation would be the specific product line directory or departmental subgroup. In a securitization unit, this might be arranged by product, such as Auto, Boat, or HELOC. As the product line that we are building these models is based on residential mortgage backed securities analysis, "Mort" might be an appropriate directory name. Immediately underneath the product line level would be each of the "operational" directories. All "administrative" directories would be grouped under a single "Admin" directory. Exhibit 7.1 displays both a generic organizational pattern (on the left) and the directory structure we will use for this book (on the right). You will need to create these directories to hold the models and files from the Web site so you might as well set them up on your computer at this time You will need to follow this directory pattern exactly if you do not wish to have to modify any of the directory and file pathways in the models later.

Let us look at the structure of the directory sections and what they contain.

OPERATING DIRECTORIES

The following directories are our set of operating directories. We may create more operating directories later, but these will provide the model with a solid initial framework.

```
\Data
        \CFs
        \Collat
        \DemoInputs
        \GeoInputs
        \RepLine
        \ReportSelect
        \SelectCrit
        \StateInfo
                \StateFlags
                \StateMaps
        \Structure
```

EXHIBIT 7.2 Data Directory (Level Two)

Data Directory

The Data directory will hold all of the input files and databases needed by the model. It will include the collateral files containing the loan-by-loan collateral data files and any files containing collateral selection criteria that we may create during the model run process. It will also include any files originally created or subsequently modified that contain the amortization assumptions the Collateral Cash Flow Generator (CCFG) needs to perform it calculations or the structuring input files needed by the Liabilities Waterfall Model (LWM). The major divisions in the Exhibit 7.2 contain the following:

- **"CFs"**. This is the directory that will contain the cash flow files produced by the CCFG. These files will be use by the LWM as its "sources" of funds.
- **"Collat"**. This directory will hold the collateral data files.
- **"DemoInputs"**. This directory holds the evaluation and penalty criteria that are assessed to the loans to determine their default rates and their market value decline risks.
- **"GeoInputs"**. This directory contains the prepayment, default rate, recovery lag period, and market value decline curves for each state and Metropolitan Statistical Areas (MSA) of the United States. These curves are used to generate the collateral cash flows when using the Geographic Methodology.
- **"RepLine"**. This directory contains the specification files that determine the "buckets," or classes, that the collateral will be aggregated into if Rep Lines are to be used.
- **"ReportSelect"**. This directory contains files in which we can specify various configurations of report packages. These files are then read by the model, alleviating the need to enter the report specifications one by one in the menus of the model.
- **"SelectCrit"**. This directory contains files that hold financial, demographic, geographic, and geographic concentration criteria. As with the report specification files above, these files serve to make the selection criteria process more efficient

by storing the contents and specifics of our selection criteria. These files can be selected directly from the models and will load the criteria directly into the model bypassing, the need to enter each criterion manually.

■ **"StateInfo".** This directory contains two subdirectories that hold a set of 50 files each. These file sets are state maps and state flags. We will use them in the "presentation" and PowerPoint report packages.

■ **"Structure".** This directory contains LWM structure input files that specify all information needed by the LWM to create a bond structure for the model.

See Exhibit 7.2.

At this point you are probably wondering just how many directory levels we are going to create! This is a valid concern. The longer directory and pathway names to files become, the more there is a chance for error. The easiest way to avoid unwieldy pathway names is to keep the subdirectory names small. Sometimes this is easier said than done. Do not sacrifice clarity for brevity! If the abbreviated name of a subdirectory becomes so short that even you, its creator, have trouble recognizing it, you could be laying the groundwork for future difficulties. If we were to examine the entire pathway name from the top of the "C" drive to a file containing one of the state flag images (under the above schema), it would look like this:

``C:\ABS\Mort01\Data\StateInfo\StateFlags\CT_Flag.jpg''

This pathway is still of manageable length and clear as to the hierarchical progression from main directory to subdirectory.

Model Directory

The Model directory will contain the two Basic Models that we created in Chapters 5 and 6. These are the Basic Asset Model (BAM) and the Basic Liabilities Model (BLM).

The Model directory will also contain the intermediate level models we will build in the following chapters. These models will be designed and built in Chapters 8 through 16. The successor to the BAM will be an improved CCFG model. The successor to the BLM will be the Liabilities Waterfall Model, LWM. In addition, the Model directory will also contain the code of the collateral Representative Line Generator (RLG) program. While the RLG program is not strictly a model, it is an integral part of the new model group and will be included in this directory. See Exhibit 7.3.

Output File Directory

The Output directory contains all the output produced by the models stored in either the Base or Intermediate directories and by the RLG program. As we use these programs, we will generate, and have to save, more and more output.

In the suggested schema, the directory structure is specifically oriented to the names of the deals that you are working on. The name of our deal is "Mort_01_ 2010". Anything related to that deal goes into that subdirectory. That is all there is to it. Once the output is deposited in the deal specific directory, you can then be

```
\Models
    \Base
        \BAM
        \BLM
    \Intermediate
        \CCFG
                \ChapterVersions
        \LWM
        \RLP
```

EXHIBIT 7.3   Model directory

concerned with type of scenario generated the reports. Alternatively, you could add other subdirectories if you needed to segregate special-purpose reports by audience. If the deal is nonpublic, it is a regulatory requirement to supply all investors with the same material information. In this case it is critical to closely track all model output sent to every investor to be sure of meeting this information sharing requirement. See Exhibit 7.4.

In the example in Exhibit 7.4, we have outlined the directory system that you will need to organize and store the reports that we will produce in Chapter 20. If you intend to produce these reports or simply to download them from the Web site, you will need to establish this directory system on your own computer.

Template Directory

The Template directory contains all template data input or output report files used by any of the models. It also contains any template files needed by Access. There are

```
\Output
    \Mort_01_2010
        \CollatAnalysis
            \Run_NoSelect
            \Run_01InitCriteria
            \Run_02FinCriteria
            \Run_03GeoSelect
            \Run_04GeoConcen
            \Run_05GeoMethodCFs
            \Run_06DemoMethodCFs
            \Run_07PowerPointPres
        \LWMAnalysis
            \DemoMethodBase
            \DemoMethodStress
            \GeoMethodBase
            \GeoMethodStress
```

EXHIBIT 7.4   Output directory

four major subdirectories under the Template directory. Of these four, two of them contain an additional 14 directories between them. The directories are:

- **"DataInputs"**. Contains the template files for the major data input files.
    - **"Collat"**. Contains the template file for the collateral data file.
    - **"RepLine"**. Contains the template files for the representative line aggregation criteria sets. These are the groupings that the Rep Line generator uses to condense the collateral data.
    - **"Structure"**. Contains the template for the LWM structure inputs.
- **"Reports"**. Contains 11 subdirectories for the various report files of the CCFG and LWM models that we will build in Chapters 8 to 16.
    - **"Assumptions"**. Contains the template file for the Assumption report of the model run. This report lists every assumption made in the particular model run that it is associated with.
    - **"CashFlows"**. Contains two report template files. The first is for the cash flows produced by the CCFG that are used as inputs by the LWM. The second is the Single Scenario report that summarizes each of the unique prepayment/default scenarios produced by the CCFG.
    - **"CollatElig"**. Contains three eligible collateral report files. The first is the user-defined stratification reports, the second is the cross-tabulation reports, and the third is the eligible collateral list report.
    - **"CollatInelig"**. Contains the reports listing the ineligible collateral. This consists of Base and the User-specified Ineligible Collateral reports.
    - **"Demo"**. Contains the template file for the Demographic reports.
    - **"DemoRisk"**. Contains the template file for the Demographic Methodology Risk factors report.
    - **"Geo"**. Contains the reports for all geographic collateral reports. These are the geographic loan listing report, the State and Metropolitan Statistical Area geographic template reports, and the Geographic Concentration report.
    - **"InitScreen"**. Contains the template for the Initial Data Screening Results report.
    - **"LiabPerfrom"**. Contains the 11 templates for the various output reports of the LWM.
    - **"LiabStructure"**. Contains the template for the liabilities structure inputs file.
    - **"PowerPoint"**. Contains the template report file for the PowerPoint reports we will build in Chapter 19.
- **"RepSpecs"**. Contains the template files that are used to set up the reporting specifications for the collateral stratification and cross-tabulation reports. The analyst can enter the specifications for up to 50 stratification and 50 cross-tabulation reports. The file is then read by the model, avoiding the need to enter the specifications by hand.
- **"SelectCriteria"**. Contains the template files used to build a financial and a geographic selection criteria file. These files, much like the files in the "RepSpecs" directory above, are used to enter the financial and geographic selection using a file containing many assumptions as opposed to entering each assumption manually.

```
\Templates
    \DataInputs
        \Collat
        \RepLine
        \Structure
    \Reports
        \Assumption
        \CashFlows
        \CollatElig
        \CollatInelig
        \Demo
        \DemoRisk
        \Geo
        \InitScreen
        \LiabPerform
        \LiabStructure
        \PowerPoint
    \RepSpecs
    \SelectCriteria
```

EXHIBIT 7.5 Template directory

See Exhibit 7.5.

Valuation Directory

The last, but certainly not least, among the operating directories is the Valuation directory. We will not undertake to develop a valuation model in this book. It is, however, highly likely that we eventually develop a model to perform pricing of the securities created by the deal in the secondary market. If we are called upon to provide secondary market valuation, we will place the results of those activities here.

ADMINISTRATIVE DIRECTORIES

The following directories are administrative in nature. They help support the product but do not contribute directly to the issuance, valuation, or trading of the securities. In that we will not be actively employing directories of this type in this book, we have not included them in the directory exhibits of this chapter.

Backup Directory

The "Backup" directory contains the critical, read-only copies of all of the files, models, and supporting programs necessary to re-create the system. If models or data files are damaged, we can come here, copy the critical files from this directory, and proceed onward. It should be noted that this is *not* the directory in which Audit or Risk Department "Gold Copies" of the model are kept. These copies are the base benchmark copies of the model that form the organization level backup, not the local backups, and as such need to be segregated from the developed/user community of the model.

When we talk of the "Backup", we do not mean the following:

- Automated system-wide backup performed by the Computing and Information Services group of your firm on an hourly, daily, weekly, or monthly basis.
- Any type of backups run on demand from software packages at the machine or department levels.

These files are just "working backups" for your interday work effort. It is your immediate "go to" set of replacement files if something goes wrong in the middle of the day with the latest change you just put in the model. It is essentially your mental health insurance directory.

Validation Directory

This subdirectory hold sets of benchmark output files based on the previous versions of the model. You need to consult these files each time you make changes to the model. You will write file comparison programs to parse the cash flow and waterfall performance output from the previous model against that of the current model. These files are essential in that they serve as a sanity check to compare the latest version of the model to its immediate predecessor.

Documentation Directory

The "Documentation" subdirectory holds all the online documentation material and electronic copies of any hard-copy documentation as we may see fit to create or as may be required by any of the internal or external control groups.

Training Directory

We have not elected to create a "Training" subdirectory, but we may do so at some later date if the distribution of the models becomes more general. We would place training versions of the model or perhaps even scripted versions of the model in this directory.

If the model is in widespread use by a large community, we can create this directory and populate it with training versions of the model. We can then train people until they have reached a minimum proficiency or knowledge level and can be let loose with the real model on an actual deal.

CREATING NEW DIRECTORIES FOR THE MODEL AS WE NEED THEM

Having said all of the above, it is necessary to add one more thought at this point. No directory system is static. You will need to add or delete directories as circumstances and the passage of time dictates. The general rule is to keep the structure as clean as possible and maintain what any reasonable person would consider a logical organizational structure. I have a very useful rule of thumb in this regard. If you think that you could sit down and explain the organizational structure of your directory system to a reasonably intelligent high school student, it is probably fine!

Think about what you are doing in response to new situations before you leap in. If it involves a major reorganization, make sure that you sit down and step through it with someone else. You will be surprised how many times you will discover a potential misstep just by talking through the process with someone else.

ON THE WEB SITE

There is no material on the Web Site for this chapter.

PART Two

Building the New Assets Model

Chapter 8: Designing the New Collateral Cash Flow Generator

In this chapter we lay out the development goals for the new asset model, the Collateral Cash Flow Generator (CCFG). These include:

- Addition of UserForms to most menus of the CCFG to improve flexibility and to handle more complex choices across many more options and items.
- Allowing the CCFG to analyze multiple collateral files.
- The conceptual introduction of two new prepayment/default methodologies: a Geographic based approach and a Demographic based approach.
- The ability to select collateral by Metropolitan Statistical Areas.
- The plan for a significantly expanded report package.
- The creation and use of representative collateral records: "Rep Lines."

Chapter 9: Writing the CCFG Menus and Data Sheets

This chapter begins the design implementation phase. We will build all the menus of the CCFG in this chapter. We learn how to construct UserForms and embed them into the menus of the CCFG. We learn how to create and design the UserForm VBA support code. We will also examine the use of Data sheets. These are worksheets within the model that hold key collections of data. By linking the menus and this data, we allow for rapid, efficient modification of various menu functions and inputs.

Chapter 10: Writing the Collateral Data Handling Code

In this chapter we develop the portions of the CCFG that will read the collateral information into the model and perform the initial data screening processes. We will build the VBA modules that will allow us to analyze multiple collateral pools. We will also build the record screening VBA subroutines that will perform and report the results of the Initial Screening process. Last we will develop a collateral Rep Line generator.

Chapter 11: Writing the Collateral Selection Code

In this chapter we will develop the capability to specify multiple collateral selection criteria sets for use with multiple collateral files. We will also develop the reporting function for eligible and ineligible collateral. Finally we will write the ability to specify, compute, solve, and report on geographic concentration issues.

Chapter 12: Writing the Collateral Cash Flow Amortization Code

In this chapter we expand the capabilities of the CCFG building upon the existing subroutines of the Base Asset Model (BAM) in respect to new mortgage types. These are hybrid adjustable-rate mortgages (HARMs) and floating- and fixed-rate balloon mortgages. We will also implement the VBA code necessary for the use of both the Geographic and Demographic Prepayment/Default Methodologies. We will also write the reporting code for the various reports associated with these methodologies.

Chapter 13: Writing the CCFG Reporting Capability

In the final chapter of the section we will finish the construction of the remaining report generation capabilities of the CCFG. We will also fully implement the CCFG Editor and Report Menu. This menu will allow us to import preconfigured files with various report and format options.

CHAPTER **8**

Designing the New Collateral Cash Flow Generator

OVERVIEW

In this chapter we will present detailed design plans for the new Collateral Cash Flow Generator (CCFG). Starting with the Base Asset Model (BAM), we will consider the changes in the information processing, computational, and reporting challenges that the completed CCFG will have to face.

The challenges include:

- An increase in the quantity of collateral and the number of portfolios we will need to analyze
- An increase in the variety and complexity of the collateral
- A more varied and flexible collateral eligibility test process
- A more complex cash flow calculation process
- A more detailed and extensive reporting package

The first challenge we will consider is the increase in the number of individual pieces of collateral and the use of multiple collateral portfolios contributing their cash flows to an individual deal. The combination of these increases in both the individual size of each of the records and the number of loans in the collateral portfolio and collective size is one that the CCFG will need to address. The BAM currently performs well for portfolios from 3,500 to 5,000 loans. If the number of loans and/or the number of portfolios increases dramatically, we may need to consider alternative computation strategies. We will also need to build a Representative Line Generator (RLG). This program will be used to produce the aggregate groupings of collateral that are a reporting requirement for any public mortgage deal. A Representative Line (Rep Line) is a group of individual loans that share similar or identical financial and demographic characteristics. Depending on the degree of homogeneity in the representative line, it can be used for descriptive (low commonality), statistical (medium commonality), or financial amortization calculations (highest commonality) analysis and reporting. Each grouping should be easily identifiable by its salient characteristics, and the representative lines as a whole should immediately present interested parties with an overall picture, at a glance, as to the composition of the collateral pool supporting the deal.

The second challenge we will be faced with is an increase in the complexity of the collateral. This will be found in the expansion of the CCFG to amortize three additional classes of mortgages: hybrid adjustable-rate mortgages (HARMs) and fixed- and floating-rate balloon mortgages. The HARM type of mortgage combines various features of both fixed- and floating-rate mortgages. Balloon mortgages allow the mortgagor to make payments lower than what is needed to fully amortize the principal balance of the loan. At the expiration of the original term of the loan, any remaining balance is paid off in a lump, or "balloon," payment.

The third challenge is the need to develop more flexible and detailed collateral selection criteria. We must also plan for the fact that we will have multiple collateral portfolios. We may wish to apply the same criteria to different portfolios, or different criteria to different portfolios, or different criteria to the same portfolio (although the last option can be used only when running the model in Batch Mode). We will need to keep track of each of these selection activities and be able to segregate the results of multiple efforts in at least the same level of detail now available in the BAM.

The fourth challenge will be to design a computational framework that makes efficient use of the existing VBA framework and at the same time accurately calculates the cash flows of the new collateral types. In addition to the new amortization patterns, we will be implementing major changes to how we look at the inputs to those calculations. We will expand our available analytical options from the current use of single-speed, portfolio level estimates of prepayment and default activity and augment them with two other approaches. The first is the use of individual loan risk-adjusted performance curves based exclusively on geographically specific estimates. The second approach is based on the individual financial and demographic characteristics of the loans. It borrows some of its assumptions from the geographic approach method (prepayment and recovery lag assumptions) but then uses the demographic profile of the loan to determine the default rate and the market value decline percentage of the loan. When we finish with the amortization calculations, we will need to segregate the resultant cash flows at either the pool level (one pool per deal) or separately at the sub-portfolio level (up to five different sub-portfolios).

The final challenge to the new CCFG will be to report all of this activity in a proper form and with the necessary detail (or lack thereof) to the people who need to know it! In this effort we will keep in mind that the BAM produces reports that are primarily analytical reports. These analytical reports have two salient features: They are highly detailed and quite Spartan in format. The audiences of these reports are the people performing the analytical studies on the deal. The new CCFG will produce a wider range of reports. These reports will address the information needs of a variety of internal and external constituencies. We will therefore add an additional level to the reporting packages based on the expanded audiences of these reports. The additional report group is the "Presentation Group" level designed for managers or external parties such as rating agencies, investors, and regulatory agencies.

Addressing each of these challenges will require significant effort! We will be able to use the BAM as a starting point, but only a starting point. We are lucky to have it as a *base*, but it is only that. Our task in this chapter is to anticipate, in as much detail as possible, the changes we will make and what we want the final product to look like. In this chapter we will outline the content and roles of the new reports and menus, lay out the steps in amortizing the new collateral types, look at the organization of data of the model, and examine calculation sequences. It is critical to plan this work in as detailed a manner as possible before we start the process of building the new CCFG in Chapters 9 to 13.

The more we plan now, the more efficient that process will be.

DELIVERABLES

The modeling knowledge deliverables for this chapter are:

- Understand the value of detailed planning for a large-scale development such as that we are about to undertake.
- Understand the design changes necessitated by large collateral aggregations and multiple portfolios.
- Conceptualize the creation of more flexible and robust collateral selection processes that may have to function in a multiple portfolio environment.
- Conceptualize the collateral amortization on an individual loan level and on a multiple portfolio level. This will include the organization and integration of Metropolitan Statistical Area (MSA) performance data at an individual loan level.
- Design the new report packages. This will include the ability to control format and content appropriate to specific audiences, and will specifically differentiate between working and presentation report packages.
- Design the new layouts of the menus for the CCFG.

UNDER CONSTRUCTION

We will not undertake any programming development of the CCFG in this chapter. We will, however, have a brief foray into the world of VBA UserForms. We will outline the steps for producing a UserForm for the Geographic Selection Menu. In the rest of the chapter, we will plan the appearance and functionality of the CCFG. Once this design work is done, we will have a clear idea of exactly what implementation approach we will take.

IMPROVING THE CCFG MENUS: CONVERSION TO USERFORMS

One of the most significant and visible changes in the new CCFG will be the introduction of the use of Excel UserForms in the menus. UserForms will allow us to create menus in the CCFG with a much higher level of complexity and efficiency than the menus of the BAM.

UserForms allow for a wider degree of freedom in expressing choices and also allow the analyst to pack a considerably greater amount of information in a given menu. The increase in complexity results from the number of action or choice combinations that can be specified by the analyst. UserForms have features, such as OptionButtons, that allow us to specify a range of combination actions that would be difficult to implement in a standard Excel menu. In addition to various button functions, UserForms allow us to display lists of choices and to quickly and easily select one or multiple items from them. We will see this feature used repeatedly in the new Collateral Selection Menu and the Geographic Selections Menu.

Menus Containing UserForms

This is *not* a book about the science of designing user interfaces. The emphasis in this discussion will be on designing a menu interface that allows significantly more flexibility to address the increasingly complex tasks we now face. As a result, the menus we will implement in Chapter 9, "Writing the CCFG Menus and Datasheets," will be practical and designed to offer the analyst just enough flexibility to get the job done without drowning ourselves in choices.

Example of a Simple UserForm   In the following sections we will look at the appearance and organization of a simple UserForm. This UserForm is a component of the Geographic Selection Menu. It is one of six UserForms that can be displayed by clicking on various buttons on that menu.

Geographic Selection Menu   The Geographic Selection Menu is displayed in Exhibit 8.1. This menu contains a total of six buttons that will display UserForms when clicked. Three of these buttons, contained in the uppermost section of the menu, call UserForms that are used to either include or exclude states and MSAs from the collateral. An MSA is a significant population concentration whose inhabitants share related political and economic ties. These lists consist of geographic regions, states, and MSAs that can be checked off quickly and easily to affect our selection choices. The next button that displays a UserForm is in the middle section of the menu. It allows us to specify collateral concentration limits for states and major MSAs. The fifth and sixth buttons that display UserForms are found in the lower portion of the menu. One of these buttons is employed to specify which of the selection tests we

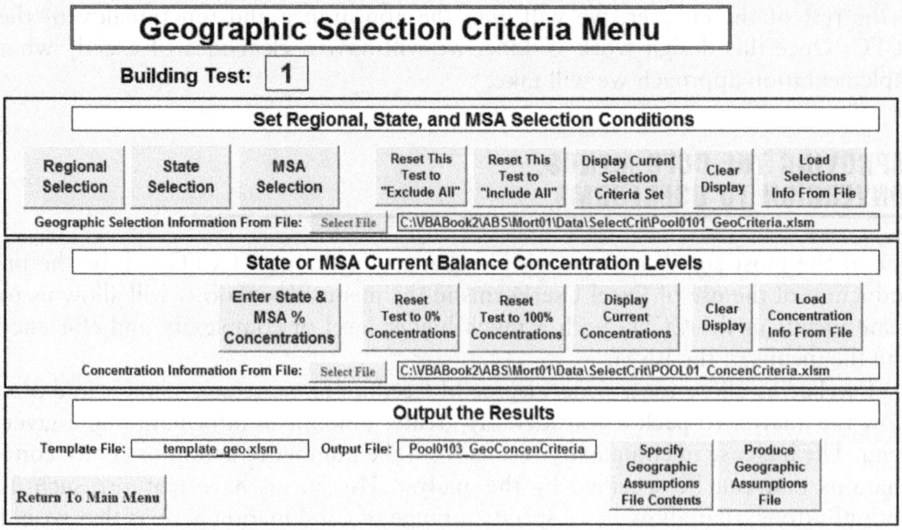

EXHIBIT 8.1   CCFG Geographic Selection Menu

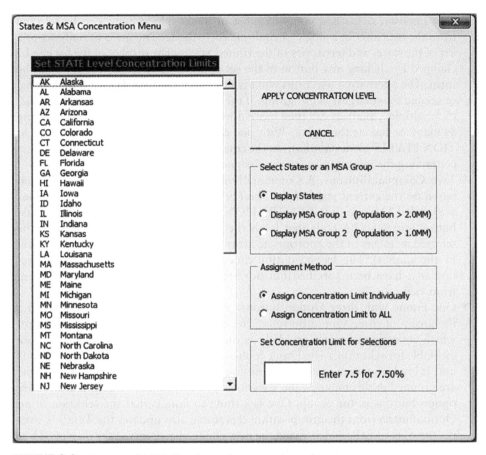

EXHIBIT 8.2 States and MSA UserForm Concentration submenu

wish to write to an Assumptions file. The other allows us to select all the tests created or indicate individual tests from a list. These geographic inclusion and concentration tests will then be written to a file. You should immediately note that this menu consists of only four fields (all used to enter file names) and no less than 17 buttons. This is in marked contrast to the existing Geographic Selection Menu of the BAM, which has 54 fields and 15 buttons (most of them used only to control the display of the menu). If you have forgotten what that menu looks like in the BAM, see Exhibit 2.5. See Exhibit 8.1.

State and MSA Concentration Limit UserForm The UserForm displayed in Exhibit 8.2 was created to set the collateral concentration limits. This UserForm is displayed by clicking the button "Enter State and MSA % Concentrations". Moving from left to right and from top to bottom, this UserForm consists of the following controls:

- **One TextBox.** A TextBox is an Object into which you can enter a text message in the UserForm. The first item on this menu is a header over a ListBox (see the immediately following bullet point) informing us of the content of the displayed list. It says "Set STATE Level Concentration Limits".

- **One ListBox.** A ListBox contains a list of items. These items can be selected from the list either in a single or multiple entry mode. The list is initially set to a list of the states and territories of the United States. The display of the list can be changed by clicking any button in the set of OptionButtons to the right on the form. The alternative selections will display either the first (largest populations) or second (next largest) MSA group. If the selection criteria for the ListBox is set to "multiple", analysts can then move down the line of displayed items selecting as many or few as they wish. With one click on the "APPLY CONCENTRA-TION LEVEL" CommandButton, the concentration limit is loaded into an array containing the information for the designated concentration test.
- **Two CommandButtons.** A CommandButton tells the model to take an action based on the current state of the UserForm contents. These CommandButtons are labeled "APPLY CONCENTRATION LEVELS", and "CANCEL". The first button initiates VBA code that loads the specified concentration limit into the selected members of the appropriate array of states or MSAs (after confirmation by the analyst). The second button cancels any entries in the displayed selection that have been specified but not yet applied and removes the UserForm from view.
- **One Frame with three OptionButtons.** The Frame is the outline surrounding the group of three OptionButtons. These are the OptionButtons that control which collection of states or MSAs is displayed in the ListBox (and therefore available for selection). The Frame looks very innocuous in this context, but it is not! It binds the three OptionButtons into a single group. When OptionButtons are grouped in this manner, the selection of one immediately deselects all other option buttons in the group. One last thing to note is that the selection of an OptionButton from the group within this frame also updates the TextBox over the top of the ListBox identifying the now changed contents of the displayed list.
- **One Frame with two OptionButtons.** Once again a Frame is used to group a set of OptionButtons. These OptionButtons control the scope to which the concentration limit is applied to members of the list. The selection can be directed to individual members of the list or the list as a whole. This is useful when a universal base value or a universal ceiling value has to be assigned to large groups of items. It is also useful when a preponderance of the items on the list need to assume a specific value while a few do not. Simply apply the majority level in the "ALL" mode and then apply the exceptions in the "Individual" mode.
- **One Frame and one TextBox.** The third and last Frame of the UserForm contains a TextBox used to input the value of the concentration limit. It is this concentration limit value that will be applied to the selected geographic areas. The Frame in this case does not perform a grouping function but instead serves only to visually separate this TextBox from the other groups of items in the UserForm.

UserForms have a total of 16 different building blocks that we can select to construct in almost any configuration we think will get the job done. This UserForm employs just five of those controls: CommandButtons, OptionButtons, ListBoxes, TextBoxes, and Frames. By employing a small number of subcomponents, we were able to construct a very useful menu subpage. This UserForm allows us to easily assign many more state and MSA concentration limits in far less time than using a conventional menu.

Linking the UserForm with the CCFG   We are able to link the actions taken on the UserForm directly to VBA subroutines that will perform these actions. Later, in Chapter 9, we will examine the procedures to link the actions that you take when you make an entry to a TextBox, select an item from the contents of a ListBox, or click on an OptionButton or a CommandButton.

Suffice it to say that there are clear and easily managed steps to link the User-Forms that we will create to each of the actions of the UserForm itself. What is even better is that the vast majority of the code that we develop to support the actions of the UserForm is contained in special VBA modules directly associated with the form itself. UserForms can also be exported between different programs. Thus the feature that allows us to embed the VBA code in a UserForm and *move it along with* the UserForm itself becomes doubly valuable!

New Menus

The new CCFG is a more powerful model than the BAM and will therefore require a more robust set of menus. We will need to provide the analyst with a set of menus that will allow for the specification of operations that are not possible in the BAM. In addition, we will need to extend the capabilities of certain functions that already exist.

Main Menu   The Main Menu is the strategic base from which we launch the activity sequence of the entire model. The Main Menu lists all the steps needed to run the CCFG and presents the analyst with a series of buttons to sequentially access each of the menus needed to successfully complete the tasks at hand. We will step from one menu to another, delineating our specific instructions that will trigger the activities needed to complete the processing, computational, and reporting actions of the model. A series of CommandButtons will direct the analyst (most likely us) to the appropriate menu controlling that process. We will then make our entries into the menu, finally returning to the Main Menu to run the program. See Exhibit 8.3.

The buttons and activities in the order they appear on the Main Menu are as follows:

1. "Set Model Run Options". Use the Run/Output Options Menu to set the tasks that you wish the model to perform and what assumptions files or collateral portfolios to use.
2. "Identify Collateral Data Files". Use the Collateral Pool Menu to specify either a pool level data file or a combination (up to five) of sub-portfolio level data files to use in the analysis.
3. "Define Geographic Selection Criteria". Set loan selection criteria based on the properties location in state level and/or MSA level geographic entities. Set the current balance concentration limits for any or all of these entities if available.
4. "Define Fin/Demo Selection Criteria". Establish the tests for collateral eligibility based on either financial or demographic loan criteria, or both.

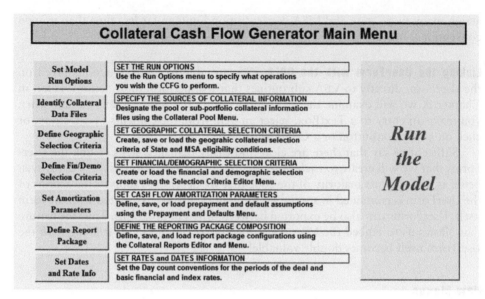

EXHIBIT 8.3 Main Menu

5. **"Set Amortization Parameters"**. Select one of three Prepayment/Default methodologies: Uniform Speed, Geographic, or Demographic. If either the Geographic or the Demographic Methodology is chosen, enter a set of stress factors, if desired. Finally enter the name of the file that you wish to write the finished cash flows to.
6. **"Define Report Package"**. Select the combinations of the reports you wish to produce and in what format you wish to produce them.
7. **"Set Dates and Rates Info"**. Set the day count conventions and the Index Rate projections you wish to use.

Run/Output Options Menu   The information displayed on this menu was originally part of the Main Menu of the BAM. See Exhibit 8.4.

The model will perform five activities. These activities are:

1. **Perform the initial loan record data screening tests.** These tests examine each loan record and report missing, inappropriate, or data that are expressed in an incorrect format.
2. **Apply the financial and demographic collateral selection tests.** These tests determine the eligibility of the collateral on a loan-by-loan basis by applying analyst-defined tests of the financial and demographic characteristics of the loan.
3. **Apply geographic state and MSA selection tests.** These tests determine the eligibility of collateral based on its geographic location.
4. **Apply geographic concentration limits.** These tests determine the amount of eligible collateral that can be included in the overall collateral pool based on the percentage of current balances by geographic entity as a percentage of the total pool current balance.

CCFG Run/Output Options Menu

Pool or Sub Portfolio	Collateral File Name	Initial Loan Record Data Screening Tests	Apply Financial and Demographic Tests	Apply Geographic (State & MSA) Tests	Apply Geographic Concentration Limits	Produce Elligible Collateral Cash Flows
	Run Option Code =>	1	2	3	4	5
		REQUIRED		OPTIONAL		
			Collateral Selction Processes			Collateral Cash Flow Files
#0	C:\VBA_Book2\Code\data\CollateralPool\Pool01Test1.xlsm		N	N		
#1	No File Selected		1	1		
#2	No File Selected	Y	1	1	Y	N
#3	No File Selected		1	1		
#4	No File Selected		1	1		
#5	No File Selected		1	1		

Remember: Enter the names of the collateral files in the CollatPoolMenu! This menu will pick them up from there.

| Return To Main Menu | To avoid having either the Financial/Demographic Selection tests (column 2) or the Geographic Selection tests (column 3) run against the collateral enter a "N" for "No" in these fields instead of a collateral selection test set number. |

EXHIBIT 8.4 Run/Output Options Menu

5. **Produce eligible collateral cash flows.** This file contains month-by-month cash flows of the eligible collateral for all prepayment and default condition cases calculated by the model.

Collateral Pool Menu The Collateral Pool Menu is a menu that has no functional counterpart in the BAM. This menu will tell the CCFG where the collateral of the deal is to be found. Unlike the BAM, the CCFG is capable of using more than one data file as the source of collateral information. When more than one file is used, they will be referred to as sub-portfolio files. These files can be combined into a single collateral file called the pool file. There is only a single pool file for a given model run. The CCFG can either operate against a single pool file or a collection of sub-portfolio files, but *not* both.

The role of this menu is to allow the analyst to specify a single pool level file or up to five sub-portfolio files that will comprise the collective collateral of the deal. The menu will also allow us to perform two other important functions. The first of these is to designate a file name and pathway and to combine the sub-portfolios listed on the menu into a single pool level file. The second is to create a pool level file from those pieces of collateral that have passed the base eligibility tests. The functions will be triggered by two CommandButtons.

The pool and sub-portfolio collateral files entered on this menu will be read by the Run/Output Options Menu. This menu identifies to the CCFG which groups of collateral we will use as the beginning collateral of the deal. After we have created the Financial and Geographic Selection Criteria sets, we will be able to apply them to the various collections of collateral at our disposal. In the BAM, this was a trivial issue in that we only had a single Financial Selection Criteria set, a single Geographic Selection Criteria set, and a single pool level collateral portfolio. Here we need to provide the analyst with the ability to perform these assignments so that we are free to apply whatever set of criteria we have created against whatever collateral portfolio is present. In a most complex case, with five sub-portfolios, we could be

CCFG Collateral Pool Menu		

		Collateral File Name
Collateral Pool #1	Select File	C:\VBA_Book2\Code\data\CollateralPool\Pool01Test1.xlsm
Sub Portfolio #1	Select File	No File Selected
Sub Portfolio #2	Select File	No File Selected
Sub Portfolio #3	Select File	No File Selected
Sub Portfolio #4	Select File	No File Selected
Sub Portfolio #5	Select File	No File Selected

	Pool Level File Name
Create Pool File From Sub-Portfolios?	C:\VBA_Book2\Code\data\CollateralPool\NewTestPoolFrom01_05.xls

	Initial Data Screening File Name
Create Initial Data Screening Report?	InitialDataRep.xls

Return To Main Menu	Create Pool File From Sub-Portfolios

EXHIBIT 8.5   Collateral Pool Menu

applying unique Financial Selection Criteria sets and unique Geographic Selection Criteria sets against each of the sub-portfolios in a single model run.

The purpose of the Collateral Data File Menu is to allow the analyst to efficiently evaluate combinations of collateral data with the aim of assembling the most efficient aggregate pool of collateral for use in the deal. See Exhibit 8.5.

Financial/Demographic Selection Criteria Editor Menu   The Financial/Demographic Selection Criteria Editor Menu will allow the analyst to create and save into designated sets a series of Financial Selection Criteria sets, each comprised of up to 20 individual tests based on the financial and demographic characteristics of the loans of the asset pool. See Exhibit 8.6.

The characteristics of the Financial Selection Criteria Editor accessed by this menu will be as follows:

1. The analyst can create a maximum of five Financial Selection Criteria sets of selection conditions. Once created, they can be entered into the Run/Output Options Menu and be applied to the pool or designated sub-portfolios. A single Financial Selection Criteria set can be applied against a single sub-portfolio, or several, or all of them. Different Financial Selection Criteria sets may be applied against each of the designated sub-portfolios.
2. Each Financial Selection Criteria set can contain a maximum of 20 individual selection tests.
3. The Financial Selection Criteria set test parameters can include any data item in the collateral file to include all obligor demographic parameters as well as all financial and underwriting criteria items.
4. Six different types of financial criteria tests can be specified. The tests range from very simple to moderately complex. This complexity range is designed to provide the analyst with a range of test types that will serve to cover all test conditions needed in the selection process.

CCFG Financial/Demographic Selection Criteria Editor Menu

Return To Main Menu	**Type 1: Single Condition Test** Example: Orginal Term LE 480
	Type 2: Minimum/Maximum Test Example: Original Term GE 180 AND Original Term LE 480

Type 3: Single Condition Test Combined With Minimum/Maximum
Example: PropertyType EQ 1 AND [Original Term GE 180 OR Original Term LE 480]

Type 4: Single Criteria Item, Multiple Values Selection
Example: PropertyType EQ 1 OR PropertyType EQ 5 OR PropertyType EQ 6 OR PropertyType EQ 8

Type 5: Joint Minimum/Maximum Test
Example: [OriginalTerm GE 120 AND OriginalTerm LE 480] AND [PropertyType EQ 3 OR PropertyType EQ 4]

Type 6: Two Criteria Table Test
Example: [Index EQ 1 AND Spread GE 2%] OR [Index EQ 2 AND Spread GE 1.5%] OR [Index EQ 3 AND Spread GE 4%]

Assign Test Set (Limit 5 Sets) and Test Number (Limit 20 Tests) Within Set

Set: 1   **Test:** 5   **File:** Pool100Loans_FinSelTests.xls

Assign Test Set, Test Number, and Enter Test Type

Test Type 1 Single Condition Test	Test Type 2 Min/Max Test	Test Type 3 Single Test & Min/Max Test	Test Type 4 Single Criteria Multiple Values	Test Type 5 2 Joint Min/Max Tests	Test Type 6 2 Criteria Table Test

Printing, Saving and Reading Test Sets			Removing A Test or Test Set	
Print This Test Set	Write Test Sets To File	Read Test Sets From File	Delete Test	Delete Test Set

EXHIBIT 8.6 Financial/Demographic Selection Criteria Editor Menu

The first section of the menu describes the logical structure of the tests.

The second section of the menu allows the analyst to identify the set number, test number, and, if necessary, the file name into which the Financial Selection Criteria set is to be saved. The analyst will specify the Financial Selection Criteria set identifier number and the individual test number within that criteria set on the face of the menu prior to the creation of the test. If the Financial Selection Criteria set is to be reused at a future date, it can be saved to the file designated in the input field "File:".

The third section of the menu contains six CommandButtons. Each of the buttons, when clicked, displays a unique special-purpose UserForm designated for one particular test type. The UserForm used in the construction of a Type 2 test is shown in Exhibit 8.7.

The fourth section of the menu will contain a series of CommandButtons that will allow the analyst to perform the following tasks:

- Print the tests of the currently designated Financial Selection Criteria set.
- Write the currently designated Financial Selection Criteria sets to a file. This includes not only the currently specified sets but all sets in the active model.
- Read a previously created Financial Selection Criteria set file into the CCFG.
- Delete the contents of a test. The test deleted will be the test whose Set number and Test number are currently displayed in those fields in section 2 of the menu.
- Delete an entire Financial Selection Criteria set. The set deleted will be the one whose number is displayed in the Set field of section 2 of the menu.

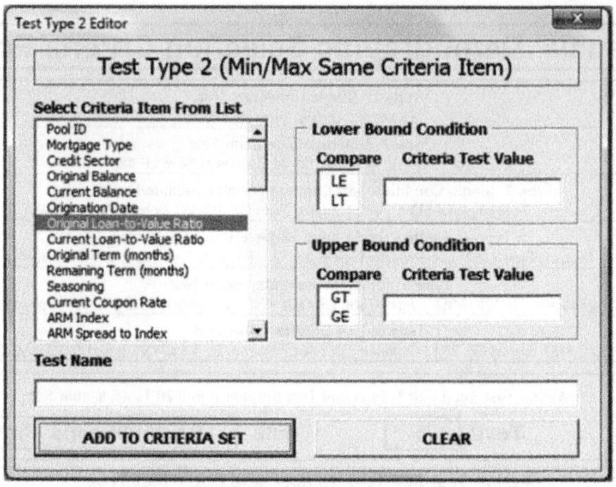

EXHIBIT 8.7 UserForm for a Type 2 Financial Criteria Selection test

Geographic Selection Menu The Geographic Selection Menu (GSM) of the CCFG will be significantly more detailed than that contained in the BAM. We will need to incorporate a number of features that are wholly absent from the existing model and extend some of the features that are already there.

Introducing Metropolitan Statistical Areas to the Selection Process The major change in the GSM will be the inclusion of the largest 150 MSAs. An MSA is a concentrated urban population center and any of the surrounding economically, demographically, or politically linked locales. All of the rating agencies employ the use of MSAs to assess benefits or penalties in the estimation of future default rates and market value decline estimations. In most of these models, only the most populous 25 to 50 MSAs are specifically analyzed to produce a benefit/penalty assessment. Our model is not solely constructed to mirror rating agency criteria. We may wish to single out a particular MSA that is not in the top 50 for special treatment in our estimated loss analysis. Some smaller MSAs located in states that have the most challenging mortgage environments, such as California, Pennsylvania, Nevada, Michigan, and Florida, may also be of specific interest to us. We may wish to include these areas with a particular penalty or exclude them altogether from the portfolio.

States and Other Regions We continue to include the national, regional, and state level selection features in the menu. The challenge now will be to provide the analyst with an effective manner of specifying complex and overlapping selections with the least amount of work and in the clearest means possible.

The national selection switch is useful for including or excluding all the states and MSAs in a single operation. For example, if we wanted to run a stratification report package for just the state of California, we can *exclude* all states and MSAs and then in a second operation simply *include* the state of California and its MSAs. Building this capability into the GSM saves us the trouble of deselecting long lists of states and MSAs individually.

In a similar manner, we should allow the analyst to select the following combinations:

- The national level.
- All states at a regional level.
- Include the state and include all MSAs at the state level.
- Include the state and exclude all MSAs at the state level.
- Exclude the state but include the MSAs of the state.
- Exclude both the state and all of its MSAs.

If a loan is in an included state and its MSA is not in the list of MSAs that can be individually included or excluded, it will be included as part of the state's territory.

Balance Concentration Limits   A second GSM feature will be the provision for the analyst to specify a current balance concentration limit. This concentration limit seeks to avoid undue concentration of risk in a specific geographic location. The repercussions of localized natural disasters or of economic impacts are mitigated by dispersion. Not putting all of your eggs in one basket is a centuries-old adage. We will need to make provisions for the analyst to be able to specify particular concentration limits, expressed as a percentage of the total portfolio, for either state or MSAs.

Here is another area where UserForms will provide us a convenient means of achieving our design goal. We will want to design a menu that will allow the analyst to specify a precise percentage concentration and then apply it to any number of states and MSAs.

Assumptions Trace Reports   We will also need to provide the analyst with a set of working reports that can be displayed in a screen in the model or written to a file that reflect the current state of the selection set by entries to the GSM.

Menu Organization and Structure   The GSM will be organized into three sections. The first section will allow the analyst to construct the Geographic Selection Criteria set. The second section will allow the analyst to construct a set of concentration limits for state and MSA entities. The third section of the menu will allow the analyst to specify the contents of a Geographic Selection Criteria file and save the current set of completed tests to it. See Exhibit 8.8.

In the first section of the GSM, the analyst will see three buttons, each of which serves a different purpose in the geographic selection process. The first triggers geographic selections at the regional levels (a collection of states), the second at the state level (states and their constituent MSAs), and the third at the MSA level (individual MSAs). Each of these buttons will, when clicked, display a purpose-specific UserForm that can then be used to select/deselect various combinations of states and MSAs. See Exhibit 8.9 for the UserForm displayed when the "Select State" button is clicked.

To the right of these three buttons on the GSM will be placed a series of five utility buttons to allow the analyst to perform the following tasks. See Exhibit 8.8:

- **"Reset this Test to 'Exclude All' "**. This button sets all states and MSAs to excluded, that is, all collateral from anywhere is ineligible. This feature is useful

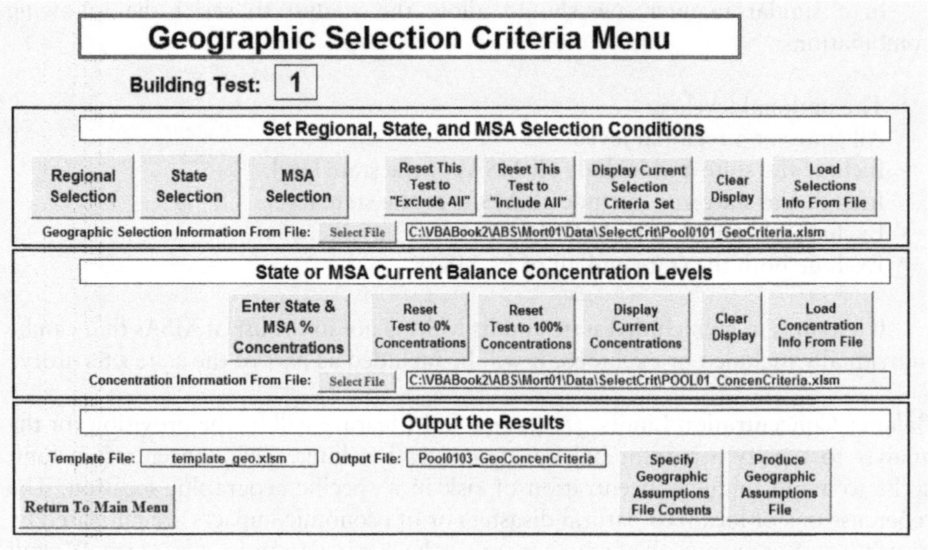

EXHIBIT 8.8 Geographic Selection Menu

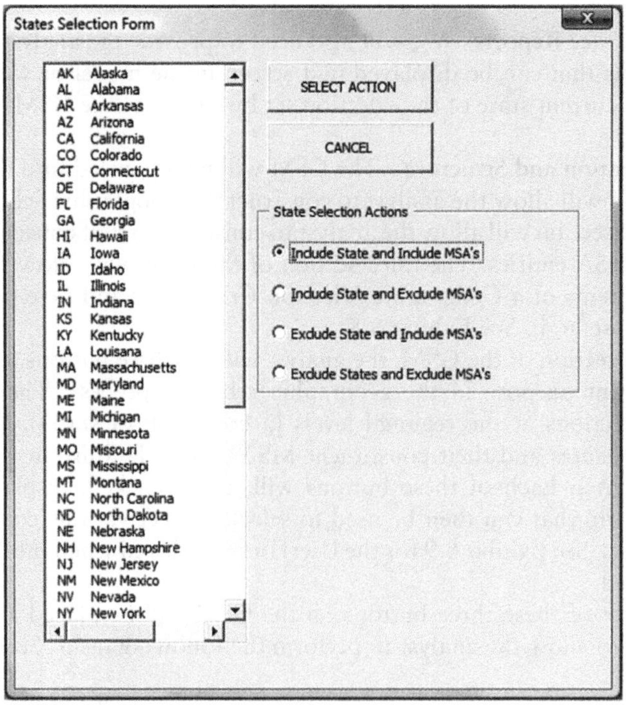

EXHIBIT 8.9 "Select State" UserForm

if an analysis of all loans from one state only is desired. Every other state and MSA is effectively turned "off" and then the analyst uses one of the action buttons to select the state or MSA to be turned "on".

■ **"Reset this Test to 'Include All'"**. The exact opposite of the above; all collateral from any state or MSA is eligible.
■ **"Display Current Selection Criteria Set"**. Allows the currently indicated Geographic Selection set to be displayed to the "Geo Selection" worksheet.
■ **"Clear the Display"**. Clears the GeoSelect worksheet of its displayed content.
■ **"Load Selections Info From File"**. Loads a previously created set of assumptions from the file designated in the "Geographic Selection Information From File:" field below the buttons of this section.

The second section of the menu will be designed to facilitate the setting of geographic concentration limits at the state and MSA level. There is a single Geographic Concentration UserForm whose display is triggered by the "Enter State and MSA % Concentrations". See Exhibit 8.10.

Utility buttons for the Geographic Concentration section of the GSM will also be provided. They follow a one-to-one correspondence with the buttons of the Geographic Selection section. The analyst will be able to set all of the states and MSAs as either completely excluded due to concentration or completely included. This is accomplished by the first two buttons, "Reset Test to 0% Concentrations" and "Reset Test to 100% Concentrations". In the first instance, the concentration limits of all

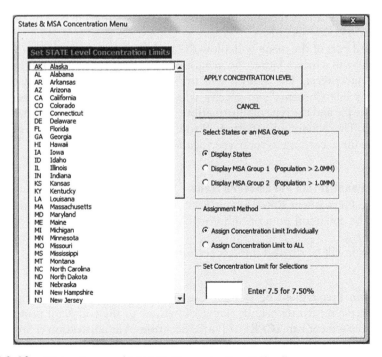

EXHIBIT 8.10 "Enter State and MSA % Concentrations" UserForm

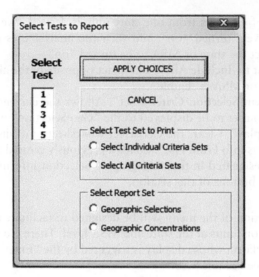

EXHIBIT 8.11   "Specify Geographic Assumptions File Content" UserForm

states and MSAs are set to 0% of the total collateral of the asset pool. That condition says that any concentration over 0% is unacceptable. (It deems all collateral ineligible on the basis of geographic location.) The second sets the concentration limits to 100% of the total collateral of the deal, making all collateral eligible regardless of location or size. The remaining utility buttons serve the same purpose as those in the Geographic Selection section.

The third part of the menu will allow the analyst to specify the form and content of a file that will capture either the geographic selection criteria or the geographic concentration criteria. The analyst will use the first button, "Specify Geographic Assumptions File Contents", to specify which of the tests (or all of them) are to written to the file and the type of information, Selection Criteria sets or Concentration Criteria sets. The second utility button, "Produce Geographic Assumptions File", will produce the file according to these specifications. See Exhibit 8.11.

Cash Flow Amortization Parameters Menu   This menu allows the analyst to specify one of three Prepayment Rate/Default Rate methodologies and criteria that will be applied to the collateral pool or Sub-Portfolios of the deal on a loan-by-loan basis. See Exhibit 8.12.

The menu will be divided into six sections. They are as follows:

1. **"Uniform Prepayment & Default Curves"** . Application of a pairing of uniform prepayment rate/default rate assumptions to the collateral using the constant prepayment rate (CPR) or Public Securities Administration (PSA) attrition methodologies at either a pool or sub-portfolio level. This methodology ignores differences in amortization characteristics of different mortgage types, borrower demographics, underwriting criteria, and geographic location.

CCFG Cash Flow Amortization Parameters Menu

Uniform Prepayment & Default Curves

	Method	Base Speed	Step Increment	# of Steps
Prepayment Rate:				
Default Rate:				
Recovery Lag Period:		(months)		
Market Value Decline:		(% of Original Appraisal)		

(Note: Prepayment/Default Method codes: 1=CPR or 2=PSA)

Specify Methodology

Uniform:	
Geographic:	
Demographic:	X
Apply Stress:	X

Return To Main Menu

(Note: Apply Stress to Geographic or Demographic methodologies ONLY!)

Geographic Specific Prepayment, Default, MVD, and Recovery Lag Curves

File Name

Geographics Assumptions File | Select File |

Demographic Methodology Factor Weighting File

File Name

Demo Assumptions File | Select File | C:\VBA_Book2\Code\data\DemoCalcInputs\DemoMethodInputs.xlsm

Stress Factors Range - % of Base Prepayment/Default Speeds

	Base	Increment	# Steps
Prepayment:	100%	25%	2
Defaults:	100%	25%	2

(Note: Stress Levels applied against Geographic and Demographic Prepayment methodologies ONLY!)

Write Cash Flow Output File

Cash Flow Output File |

View Cash Flow Output File

Cash Flow File | Select File |

EXHIBIT 8.12   Cash Flow Amortization Parameters Menu

2. **"Specify Methodology"**. Here the analyst tells the CCFG which of the three approaches will be used. Stress cases can be selected for use in the model runs employing the Geographic or Demographic methodologies only.

3. **"Geographic Specific Prepayment, Default, MVD, and Recovery Lag Curves"**. This section allows the selection of a Geographic Methodology file. The file contains a series of mortgage balance attrition curves based solely on the geographic location of the property. These attrition curves are assumptions in regard to default rates, prepayment rates, recovery lag periods, and market value decline factors. These curves will specify conditions monthly for the next five years and then level off to a constant rate for the remainder of the life of the mortgage. While considering geographic location and local conditions, this methodology still ignores differences in amortization characteristics of different mortgage types, borrower demographics, and underwriting criteria

4. **"Demographic Methodology Factor Weighting File"**. The Demographic Methodology uses the geographic location of the mortgage to determine the prepayment assumptions and the recovery lag periods to be applied to each loan. It then diverges from the Geographic Methodology by analyzing a number of factors concerning the borrowers' economic characteristics, their mortgage and property types, and the underwriting criteria used to create the loan. Two different sets of these factors are used to determine the default rate assumptions and the market value decline factors on a loan-by-loan basis.

5. **"Stress Factors Range—% of Base Prepayment/Default Speeds".** This section applies a range of specified stresses to the inputs of both the Geographic and Demographic Methodologies.

6. **"Write Cash Flow Output File, View Cash Flow Output File" Section.** Allows the analyst to designate the name of the Cash Flow output file to be created by the model run. Alternatively it allows the analyst to open and examine a previously created Cash Flow file.

Reports Editor and Menu   The Reports Editor and Menu, See Exhibit 8.13, will be designed to allow the analyst to perform the following tasks:

- Specify the states and MSA for inclusion in the Geographic report package.
- Specify the number and content of any Custom Stratification reports to be produced.
- Specify the number and content of any Cross Tabulation reports to be produced.
- Select all other reports from those available to the CCFG.

The menu will be divided into three major parts.

Geographic Reports Editor   This portion of the Reports Editor and Menu allows the analyst to select a series of geographically specific reports about the collateral. Specific reports can be generated for the collateral contained in each state and MSA entity. These report elections will be entered into the model by the use of a UserForm. The

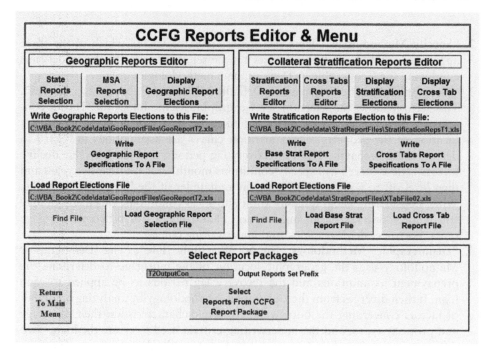

EXHIBIT 8.13   Reports Editor and Menu

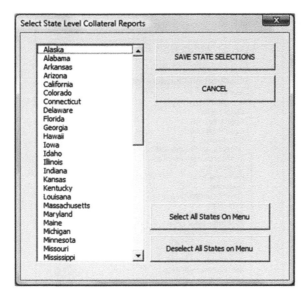

EXHIBIT 8.14   Geographic States Editor UserForm

reporting elections can be saved to a file and also displayed so that the analyst can confirm any of the choices made. Files of report selections can be loaded into the model by specifying their pathway and using the "Find File" CommandButton on the menu. The two buttons of this section will produce UserForms for state and MSA report selections respectively. The Geographic States Editor UserForm is seen in Exhibit 8.14.

Collateral Stratification Reports Editor   This portion of the Reports Editor and Menu allows the analyst to specify two different types of stratification reports in addition to the standard set automatically produced by the CCFG. The first report type is an analyst-selected univariate stratification report. The second type of stratification report is a bivariate grid that aggregates collateral by two specific shared characteristics. The report specifications for both types of reports can be saved to a file and also displayed to a report screen of the model, which allows the analyst to confirm that the specified parameters and formats are correct. The report specification UserForms are displayed in Exhibit 8.15 and 8.16.

Select Report Packages Section   This portion of the menu will allow the analyst to specify a unique prefix that will be attached to all output files of this model run. In addition, clicking on the CommandButton "Select Reports From CCFG Report Package" will display all the other available reports. A CommandButton to return to the Main Menu s provided as a convenience to the analyst. See Exhibit 8.17.

IMPROVING THE CCFG DATA-HANDLING CAPABILITIES

The analysis of residential mortgage portfolios requires significantly more data than used by the BAM. We will therefore need to make several significant changes to the BAM to arrive at a finished CCFG that will handle the mortgage analysis we will need to perform.

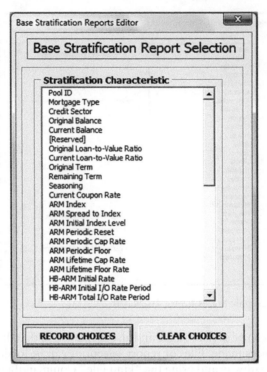

EXHIBIT 8.15   Base Stratification Report Selection UserForm

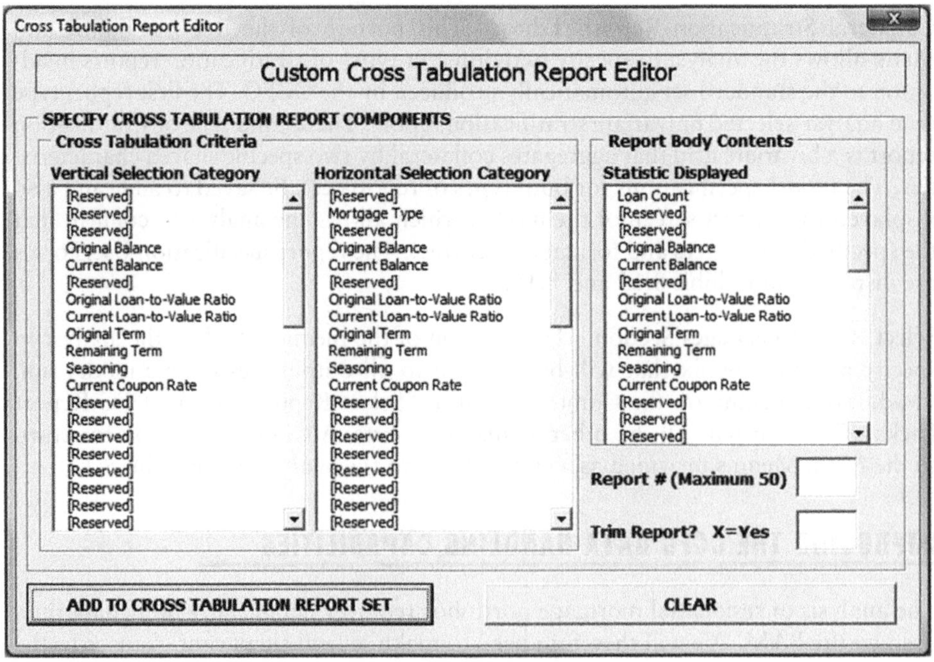

EXHIBIT 8.16   Custom Cross Tabulation Report Editor UserForm

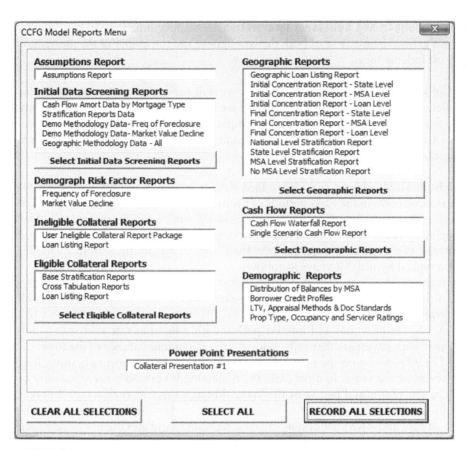

EXHIBIT 8.17 CCFG Model Report Package Menu UserForm

New Data

The new data that we need to address with the CCFG falls into two broad categories:

1. **Additional obligor and collateral information**
   a. **New collateral types.** The CCFG will need to amortize a number of loan types that have payment terms and conditions unlike those the BAM can now accommodate.
   b. **New obligor and property information.** The CCFG will need to accept and process information about the obligor and the property that is specific to risk analysis for residential mortgages.
2. **Macroeconomic loss and payment assumptions.** The CCFG will need to include prepayment, delinquency, default, and loss information in a more detailed manner than now implemented in the BAM. This is primarily driven by the need to step one level deeper into geographic-specific assumptions, moving downward from the state to the MSA levels.

Additional Obligor and Collateral Information   This new information will help us to form a general assessment of both the willingness and the ability of the mortgagor to pay off indebtedness.

New Collateral Types   The first thing that we will need to change is the layout of the collateral data files. In the existing model we needed to analyze and amortize only simple fixed-rate mortgages (FRMs) and simple adjustable-rate mortgages (ARMs). In the CCFG we will need to tackle three additional types of mortgages that are in widespread use. These are:

1. **Hybrid ARMs.** These are ARMs that have a rate lock, or interest-only (IO) period, or both, in the early periods of the mortgage and then after a set period of time convert to a standard ARM. At the conversion period the mortgage holder begins to make a fully amortizing payment consisting of both principal and interest that then fully amortizes the loan over its remaining period. Examples of a typical hybrid ARM are as follows:
   ▪ A five-year IO period with a fixed rate.
   ▪ A five-year IO period with a floating-rate coupon level that resets once each year.
   ▪ A 20-year principal and interest period with a floating rate that resets each year with payments that fully amortize the remaining balance of the loan.
   ▪ The IO period with the rate lock can range in term across one, two, three, five, seven, or ten years. In most cases the remaining IO period is the remainder of the ten-year initial period of the loan, although this can vary across different programs.
2. **Fixed-rate and ARM balloon mortgages.** Balloon mortgages are not widely seen but can still crop up in portfolios from time to time. In a typical balloon mortgage, only a portion of the original balance is amortized by the monthly payment. In a 30/20 balloon mortgage, the payment is based on the monthly coupon rate, which may be either fixed or floating, and the principal component needed to fully amortize the mortgage over a 30-year period. The actual term of the mortgage is, however, only 20 years. This means that at the end of the 20-year period, there will be a significant remaining current balance that was not amortized. The remaining balance then becomes due as a "balloon payment" at that time.

These new loan amortization types have somewhat more complex payment patterns than the loan collateral of the portfolios we have modeled so far. To provide the model with the information that it requires to correctly amortize these new loan types, we will need to include additional information in the collateral data file. We will list these additional data items in the section "Contents of the Expanded Collateral Data File" later in the chapter. We will explain these items and their roles in the amortization calculations of these types of collateral in Chapter 12, "Writing the Collateral Cash Flow Amortization Code."

New Obligor and Property Information   The current BAM makes almost no use of obligor, underwriting, servicing, or property description information. This

Risk Factor	Low Risk	High Risk
Loan Factors		
Mortgage Type	Fixed Rate	Hybrid-ARM
Credit Sector	Prime	Sub-Prime
Original Balance	Median	High
Current Balance	Less than original balance	Less than original balance
Original Loan-to-Value Ratio	Below 80%	Above 80%
Current Loan-to-Value Ratio	Below 60%	Above 100%
Original Term (months)	180 months	360 months
Seasoning	Greater than 24 months	Less than 12 months
Current Coupon Rate	Fixed rate	Teaser rate
Original Appraisal Type	Walk Through	Tax Estimate
Collateral Characteristics		
Property Type	Condo	2nd Home
Occupancy Code	Owner	Non-Owner
Financing Purpose	Purchase	Equity Take-Out; Debt Consol
State Code	Not CA, FL, or NV	CA, FL, NV, MI
MSA Code	Major MSA	Not Major MSA
Borrower & Other		
Self-employed	Not CA, FL, or NV	Yes
FICO Score	780	650
Mortgage Debt-to-Income Ratio	35%	40%
Total Debt-to-Income Ratio	45%	90%
Escrow	Yes, Taxes & Insurance	No
Third Party Confirmation	Yes	No
Origination Documentation	Full	No income, no assets
Servicier Rating	Excellent	Poor

EXHIBIT 8.18 Mortgage and Mortgagor risk factor comparison

information is of vital importance in the analysis of residential mortgage portfolios. There is a wide range of risk factors when one considers the possible combinations of borrowers and mortgage types. See Exhibit 8.18.

This additional loan information is valuable to us for a number of reasons. When looking at the credit risk of a mortgage borrower, the analyst is concerned with two separate and distinct credit concerns. The first concern is the *capacity* of the borrower to repay the loan; the second concern is the *willingness* of the borrower to repay the loan.

Obviously, the worst-case scenario from the lender's point of view is low borrower capacity coupled with low borrower willingness. In a nutshell, this situation may pertain to the following scenario:

- The borrower has poor credit and a spotty job history.
- The property has depreciated in value and now has a lower market value than the balance of the loan.
- The borrower has just experienced a payment reset resulting in an increase in the monthly payment of over 200%.
- There are a large number of properties similar to that owned by the borrower for sale in the immediate vicinity, dramatically lowering the probability of limiting losses by a quick sale.

The obverse of this disaster is a borrower who exhibits high capacity and high willingness to repay. This could be described in the following (and highly contrasted) scenario:

- The borrower has a long and stable history of employment both within his or her industry and also in the company the borrower is currently employed by. The borrower has had a history of progressive promotions and exhibits a continued growth in disposable income.
- The borrower has both a low debt-to-income ratio and a low mortgage debt-to-income ratio. These ratios have dropped steadily ever since the borrower was granted the loan ten years earlier.
- The borrower has a considerable equity position, over 50%, in the property.
- The property is well maintained and has had a series of economically valuable additions built onto it over the last five years, all of which the borrower paid for through savings, not adding any second mortgage debt.
- The property is in a desirable, well-established neighborhood with an excellent school system and a low inventory of homes for sale.

We can see that the use of the incremental financial, property, economic, and demographic information can be quite revealing as to the credit risks we face with these two very different situations.

Macroeconomic Loss and Payment Assumptions   The third type of enhanced data-handling capability of the CCFG will be the use of curves that specify mortgagor behavior over time. In the BAM, there is a single assumption for such factors as default rate, prepayment rate, recovery lag period, and market value decline that are applied uniformly to each piece of collateral in the portfolio. In the CCFG, we will adjust loss rates based on geographic location of the property, borrower characteristics, and the type of loan in question. Instead of a single value for a loss rate, a projection of base default rates will be specified for each piece of collateral. Market value decline factors will be projected on property location in the case of the Geographic Methodology and property location and borrower/property profile information in the case of the Demographic Methodology.

If a loan is situated in an MSA for which prepayment, default, recovery period, and market value decline curves have been specified, these will form the basis of the loss analysis. If the loan is located outside of an MSA or is in an MSA for which no idiosyncratic data are available, it will be evaluated using a state level set of assumptions. These assumptions will be in the form of a month-to-month, five-year set of values that will be applied to the cash flows monthly as they are calculated. In Exhibit 8.4 we see a set of assumptions for the recovery lag period for the MSA of Buffalo, New York, and the MSA of New York City–Northern New Jersey–Long Island. As you can see, the expected recovery lag period will vary significantly, depending on the location of the property and the number of months from now that the default occurs. See Exhibit 8.19.

Contents of the Expanded Collateral Data File   Having said the above, we will now turn to the contents of the data file and its supporting information. The listing of the format of the collateral data file is shown in Exhibit 8.20. The name, format,

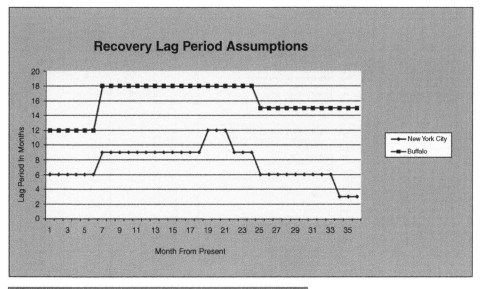

MSA	State	Name	Population
35620	NY	New York-Northern New Jersey-Long Island	19,006,798
15380	NY	Buffalo-Niagara Falls	1,124,309

EXHIBIT 8.19   Recovery period lag assumptions next three years

and explanation of each of the data items are displayed. In addition, a grid showing what data items are considered in the adjustments to frequency of foreclosure and severity of loss is also provided to the right of the exhibit. As mentioned earlier, we will go into far more depth about these items in Chapters 9 through 13 as we begin to integrate the information into all phases of the CCFG.

State and Metropolitan Statistical Area Data   As mentioned above, the model will also support a collection of files that will contain state and MSA specific mortgagor and economic behavior assumptions. When a property falls into an MSA that has specific assumptions available, those assumptions will be used in the default and severity calculations. If the property lies outside of an MSA or if it is in an MSA that does not have specific assumptions, the state level assumptions will be used.

State and MSA level curves will be provided for the following items:

- **Base prepayment rates.** These assumptions are based entirely on the geographic location of the property.
- **Recovery lag period assumptions.** These assumptions are based entirely on the geographic location of the property.
- **Base default rates.** These rates will be determined by property location in the case of the Geographic Methodology and by borrower and other demographic data in the Demographic Methodology.
- **Market value decline assumptions.** These rates will be determined by property location in the case of the Geographic Methodology and by borrower and other demographic data in the Demographic Methodology.

Collateral Data File Record Format

Field	Data Field Name	Visual Basic Data Type	Data Field Description	Used in Amortization Calculation	Used in Stratification Reporting	Used in Calculation of Frequency of Foreclosure	Used in Calculation of Severity of Loss Calculations
1	Pool ID	Integer	Number of collateral portfolio		X		
2	Mortgage Type	Integer	See Table		X	X	X
3	Credit Sector	Integer	See Table		X		X
4	Original Balance	Float	Initial principal mortgage balance		X	X	
5	Current Balance	Float	Current principal mortgage balance	X	X		X
6	Origination Date	Long	Date of loan origination		X		
7	Original Loan-to-Value Ratio	Float	Original balance / original appraisal		X		
8	Current Loan-to-Value Ratio	Float	Current balance / current appraisal		X		X
9	Original Term (months)	Integer	Original term of the mortgage in months	X	X		X
10	Remaining Term (months)	Integer	Remaining term of the mortgage in months	X	X		
11	Seasoning	Integer	Original term less remaining term	X	X		X
12	Current Coupon Rate	Float	Coupon rate for FRM; Current ARM Coupon	X	X		
13	ARM Index	Integer	See Table	X	X		
14	ARM Spread to Index	Float	Spread to index	X			
15	ARM Initial Index Level	Float	Current index rate level	X			
16	ARM Periodic Reset	Float	Number of months between interest resets	X			
17	ARM Periodic Cap Rate	Float	Highest limit of change in fully indexed rate	X			
18	ARM Periodic Floor	Float	Lowest limit of change in fully indexed rate	X			
19	ARM Lifetime Cap Rate	Float	Highest limit of fully indexed rate	X			
20	ARM Lifetime Floor Rate	Float	Lowest limit of fully indexed rate	X			
21	HB-ARM Initial Rate	Float	Initial locked rate	X			
22	HB-ARM Initial I/O Rate Period	Integer	Number of months initial locked rate	X			
23	HB-ARM Total I/O Rate Period	Integer	Number of months I/O period only	X			
24	HB-ARM Recast Term	Integer	Number of months for full amortization calculation	X			
25	BALLOON Amortization Period	Integer	Number of months for amortization calculation	X			
26	BALLOON Period	Integer	Month of balloon payment period	X			
27	Original Appraisal Value	Float	Appraisal value to time of mortgage origination		X		
28	Current Appraisal Value	Float	Appraisal value at the current time		X	X	
29	Original Appraisal Type	Integer	See Table		X		
30	Current Appraisal Type	Integer	See Table		X		
31	Property Type	Integer	See Table		X	X	
32	Occupancy Code	Integer	See Table		X	X	
33	Financing Purpose	Integer	See Table		X	X	X
34	State Code	Alpha	State postal code	X	X	X	X
35	MSA Code	Long	Metropolitan Statistical Area code	X	X	X	X
36	Zip Code	Long	Postal Zip code		X		
37	Self-employed	Integer	Yes=1, No=0			X	
38	Number of years in position	Integer	Years in current pay grade and responsibilities			X	
39	First Time Homeowner	Integer	Yes=1, No=0			X	
40	Number of Payments in Arrears	Integer	Number of monthly payments in arrears				X
41	Amount payments in Arrears	Float	Amount of payments in arrears				X
42	FICO Score	Integer	Fair-Issacs credit score			X	
43	Mortgage Debt-to-Income Ratio	Float	Mortgage P&I, plus insurance and taxes to income			X	
44	Total Debt-to-Income Ratio	Float	Mortgae plus consumer debt to income			X	
45	Bankruptcy	Integer	See Table			X	
46	Escrow	Integer	See Table			X	
47	Third Party Confirmation	Integer	See Table			X	
48	Origination Documentation	Integer	See Table			X	
49	Servicier Rating	Integer	See Table			X	
50	Day Count Convention of the Loan	Integer	See Table	X			

EXHIBIT 8.20   Expanded collateral data file format

In the process of calculating the cash flows of a piece of collateral, the model will perform the following steps.

Step 1. Read all the collateral and borrower information from the collateral data file.

Step 2. If the Geographic or Demographic Methodology has been selected, match the loan to its most immediate geographic entity.

Step 3. Read the prepayment rate assumption curves and the recovery lag period assumptions that match the geographic location of the property.

Step 4. If the Geographic Methodology is selected, apply the default rate and the market value decline factors for the geographic entity in which the property resides. If the Demographic Methodology is selected, determine the default rate and market value decline assumptions based on mortgage type, collateral characteristics, borrower demographics, servicing efforts, and underwriting criteria of the loan.

Step 5. Calculate and aggregate the cash flows of the loan into the collective cash flows of the pool or sub-portfolio.

We have now reviewed the contents of the collateral data file. Now let us look at how the model needs to handle the information at the next step up: the file level.

Use of Multiple Collateral Files

In the BAM we had a single collateral data file and, from it, based on our assumptions for each specified scenario, we produced a single set of cash flows. In the CCFG we will need to expand our capabilities and build in the ability to analyze and output the information from multiple collateral data files in the same model run.

We will need to do this because it is not uncommon to build a collateral pool from a series of collateral sub-portfolios.

Sub-Portfolio Specific Selection Criteria   We will need to specify sub-portfolio level–specific collateral selection criteria for each of the collateral data files that we wish to assess for inclusion in the final pool or pools that will go into the deal.

Sub-Portfolio Specific Stratification Reports   We may also want to look at the structure and contents of the sub-portfolios in a more detailed and exhaustive manner. We may need to assess the incremental risk to the deal of the inclusion of one or more of these collateral collections.

Sub-Portfolio Specific Cash Flows   We will want to measure both the timing and the magnitude of the individual cash flow contribution of each of the collateral data files to the aggregate cash flows of the deal. We will also need to display and store the cash flow components of each of the sub-portfolios under consideration for inclusion in the final aggregate pool of the deal.

Representative Lines: Uses and Limitations

The CCFG may well be dealing with portfolios that consist of thousands or tens of thousands of loans. When we include information about the collateral in the offering memorandum or prospectus, we will need a way to present the contents of the portfolios without listing each of the loans individually. To do this we will develop a feature in the CCFG to aggregate and display portfolio Rep Lines.

What Is a Rep Line?   A representative line is a statistical representation of a group of loans that have been grouped together by a set of common characteristics. The idea behind the concept of the Rep Line is to allow someone who is either unwilling or unable to conduct a loan-by-loan analysis of the portfolio to use an aggregated representative loan. This aggregated loan will consist of the average of the component loans it is comprised of. It will, if carefully constructed, yield approximately the same cash flows in terms of timing and magnitude that the summed period-by-period amortization of the constituent individual loans would produce.

Rep lines are most accurate if the degree of aggregation is limited to a few key characteristics. These are:

- **Type of loan must match.** Do not mix FRMs with ARMs and standard ARMs with hybrid ARMs.

- **Payment characteristics must match exactly.** This is especially true of more complex mortgage types with many amortization parameter inputs, such as those found in ARMs and hybrid ARMs.
- **Original term.** As one of the most critical inputs that determine the amortization characteristics of a loan the original terms should be exact.
- **Seasoning.** In regard to age, loans should be grouped within a narrow range of 3, 6, or 12 months based on the original term and type of the loan.
- **Coupon,** a narrow spread of coupons, usually less than 2%, often less than 0.5% for large portfolios

If the portfolio is large enough you may also wish to match loans by additional factors such as:

- Geographic characteristics, such as state and MSA
- Property type
- Occupancy code
- Fair Isaacs Corporation credit score range

Designing a Rep Line Generator   There are two basic approaches to designing a Rep Line Generator. They can be categorized as follows (with no pejorative intended in the use of either of the terms):

1. Garbage compactor
2. Bucket filler

In the first approach, that of the garbage compactor, the Rep Line Generator simply tries to come up with the best grouping it can give the collateral portfolio at hand. It groups first by loan type, then by term, then by seasoning, and last by coupon. The guidelines are a series of ranges for inclusion. For example, the grouping criteria for original term might be 120, 240, 300, 360, and 480 months. Within that grouping, seasoning may be every 12 months, and coupon spreads may be 3% intervals. The program simply sorts the portfolio and starts compacting as best it can with what is there.

The second approach is to designate a number of "buckets" of predetermined characteristics and simply match the collateral with the buckets, instead of manufacturing the aggregation criteria on the fly as in the compactor approach. The bucket approach is the method we will use in this model. The bucket approach is more widely employed as it is generally applied against portfolios with known characteristics, the loans of which have been originated by issuers following a set of product guidelines and therefore producing sets of broadly similar loans.

There are two approaches with bucket method. The first is to group the loans more loosely in fewer buckets; the second is to group them more tightly in a greater number of buckets. Rep Line construction tends to be more accurate with more buckets than less, as we will see in Chapter 10 when we revisit this subject in detail. However, many times the optimal solution is very specific buckets when we have large concentrations of a particular type of loan in our portfolio and more loosely when the characteristics of the loans are more dissimilar. It may even be wise to bucket across loan characteristics and geographic characteristics with special buckets designed just for that purpose. This is especially true if we are faced with

Rep Line Groupings -- 15 Yr, Hybrid ARMs
Fixed I/O Period 1 or 2 years; Floating I/O Period 4 or 3 Years; Fully Amortizing Thereafter
Bucket Approach -- Tight Criteria

Rep Line Number	Original Term Range	Seasoning Range	Index Type	Spread to Index Range	Fixed I/O Period	Floating I/O Period	Floating Amort Period	Floating Reset Period	Periodic Reset Cap	Periodic Reset Floor	Lifetime Reset Cap	Lifetime Reset Floor
1	180	1 to 6	LIBOR	0% to 2%	12	48	120	12	ANY	ANY	ANY	ANY
2	180	1 to 6	LIBOR	2% to 4%	12	48	120	12	ANY	ANY	ANY	ANY
3	180	1 to 6	LIBOR	4%+	12	48	120	12	ANY	ANY	ANY	ANY
4	180	6 to 12	LIBOR	0% to 2%	12	48	120	12	ANY	ANY	ANY	ANY
5	180	6 to 12	LIBOR	2% to 4%	12	48	120	12	ANY	ANY	ANY	ANY
6	180	6 to 12	LIBOR	4%+	12	48	120	12	ANY	ANY	ANY	ANY
7	180	13 to 24	LIBOR	0% to 2%	12	48	120	12	ANY	ANY	ANY	ANY
8	180	13 to 24	LIBOR	2% to 4%	12	48	120	12	ANY	ANY	ANY	ANY
9	180	13 to 24	LIBOR	4%+	12	48	120	12	ANY	ANY	ANY	ANY
10	180	25 to 36	LIBOR	0% to 2%	12	48	120	12	ANY	ANY	ANY	ANY
11	180	25 to 36	LIBOR	2% to 4%	12	48	120	12	ANY	ANY	ANY	ANY
12	180	25 to 36	LIBOR	4%+	12	48	120	12	ANY	ANY	ANY	ANY
13	180	37 to 60	LIBOR	0% to 3%	12	48	120	12	ANY	ANY	ANY	ANY
14	180	37 to 60	LIBOR	3%+	12	48	120	12	ANY	ANY	ANY	ANY
15	180	61 to 120	LIBOR	0% to 3%	12	48	120	12	ANY	ANY	ANY	ANY
16	180	61 to 120	LIBOR	3%+	12	48	120	12	ANY	ANY	ANY	ANY
17	180	121 to 180	LIBOR	0% to 3%	12	48	120	12	ANY	ANY	ANY	ANY
18	180	121 to 180	LIBOR	3%+	12	48	120	12	ANY	ANY	ANY	ANY
19	180	1 to 6	LIBOR	0% to 2%	24	36	120	12	ANY	ANY	ANY	ANY
20	180	1 to 6	LIBOR	2% to 4%	24	36	120	12	ANY	ANY	ANY	ANY
21	180	1 to 6	LIBOR	4%+	24	36	120	12	ANY	ANY	ANY	ANY
22	180	6 to 12	LIBOR	0% to 2%	24	36	120	12	ANY	ANY	ANY	ANY
23	180	6 to 12	LIBOR	2% to 4%	24	36	120	12	ANY	ANY	ANY	ANY
24	180	6 to 12	LIBOR	4%+	24	36	120	12	ANY	ANY	ANY	ANY
25	180	13 to 24	LIBOR	0% to 2%	24	36	120	12	ANY	ANY	ANY	ANY
26	180	13 to 24	LIBOR	2% to 4%	24	36	120	12	ANY	ANY	ANY	ANY
27	180	13 to 24	LIBOR	4%+	24	36	120	12	ANY	ANY	ANY	ANY
28	180	25 to 36	LIBOR	0% to 2%	24	36	120	12	ANY	ANY	ANY	ANY
29	180	25 to 36	LIBOR	2% to 4%	24	36	120	12	ANY	ANY	ANY	ANY
30	180	25 to 36	LIBOR	4%+	24	36	120	12	ANY	ANY	ANY	ANY
31	180	37 to 60	LIBOR	0% to 3%	24	36	120	12	ANY	ANY	ANY	ANY
32	180	37 to 60	LIBOR	3%+	24	36	120	12	ANY	ANY	ANY	ANY
33	180	61 to 120	LIBOR	0% to 3%	24	36	120	12	ANY	ANY	ANY	ANY
34	180	61 to 120	LIBOR	3%+	24	36	120	12	ANY	ANY	ANY	ANY
35	180	121 to 180	LIBOR	0% to 3%	24	36	120	12	ANY	ANY	ANY	ANY
36	180	121 to 180	LIBOR	3%+	24	36	120	12	ANY	ANY	ANY	ANY

EXHIBIT 8.21   Rep Lines for "tight" bucket approach for concentrations

balance concentrations in particular states or MSAs. Exhibits 8.21 and 8.22 display a set of buckets for 15-year, hybrid ARMs that have either a one-year or two-year fixed IO period, the remainder of the first five years on the loan, a floating IO period, followed by a fully amortizing remaining ten-year period.

Exhibit 8.21 is an example of a set of tight buckets while Exhibit 8.22 is an example of looser buckets. We might use the Rep Line definitions in Exhibit 8.21 if we had a concentration of these loans, say 20% or greater, in our collateral pool. If they constituted a smaller amount of the collateral, say less than 5%, the larger bucket approach in Exhibit 8.22 would be appropriate.

Remember one thing: Just because you set up Rep Lines does not mean that you will always have collateral to fill them! There are some computational penalties attached to having more Rep Lines than fewer. In the end, it can still be very much a judgment call as to how many Rep Lines are enough!

IMPROVING THE CCFG COLLATERAL SELECTION PROCESS

We have already touched on a number of the new features of the collateral selection process when we covered the design changes planned for various menus of the

Rep Line Groupings -- 15 Yr, Hybrid ARMs
Fixed I/O Period 1 or 2 years; Floating I/O Period 4 or 3 Years; Fully Amortizing Thereafter
Bucket Approach -- Loose Criteria

Rep Line Number	Original Term Range	Seasoning Range	Index Type	Spread to Index Range	Fixed I/O Period	Floating I/O Period	Floating Amort Period	Floating Reset Period	Periodic Reset Cap	Periodic Reset Floor	Lifetime Reset Cap	Lifetime Reset Floor
1	180	1 to 12	LIBOR	0% to 4%	12	48	120	12	ANY	ANY	ANY	ANY
2	180	13 to 24	LIBOR	0% to 4%	12	48	120	12	ANY	ANY	ANY	ANY
3	180	25 to 36	LIBOR	0% to 4%	12	48	120	12	ANY	ANY	ANY	ANY
4	180	36 to 60	LIBOR	0% to 4%	12	48	120	12	ANY	ANY	ANY	ANY
5	180	61 to 120	LIBOR	0% to 4%	12	48	120	12	ANY	ANY	ANY	ANY
6	180	120+	LIBOR	0% to 4%	12	48	120	12	ANY	ANY	ANY	ANY
7	180	1 to 12	LIBOR	0% to 4%	24	36	120	12	ANY	ANY	ANY	ANY
8	180	13 to 24	LIBOR	0% to 4%	24	36	120	12	ANY	ANY	ANY	ANY
9	180	25 to 36	LIBOR	0% to 4%	24	36	120	12	ANY	ANY	ANY	ANY
10	180	36 to 60	LIBOR	0% to 4%	24	36	120	12	ANY	ANY	ANY	ANY
11	180	61 to 120	LIBOR	0% to 4%	24	36	120	12	ANY	ANY	ANY	ANY
12	180	120+	LIBOR	0% to 4%	24	36	120	12	ANY	ANY	ANY	ANY

EXHIBIT 8.22   Rep Lines for a "loose" bucket approach where collateral type is de minimis

model. As stated previously, there will be three major changes to the structure of the collateral selection process:

1. **The ability to specify, retain, and load an Initial Collateral Data Screening Process.** The function of these tests is to immediately identify and remove from the portfolio collateral records that are ambiguous, damaged, incomplete, or grossly unsuitable. Building this capability into the CCFG will greatly improve the efficiency of the model by eliminating collateral that we cannot possibly use later in the structuring process. It reduces the size of the portfolio, sometimes in quite a significant manner. Smaller portfolios require shorter processing time in the model and are easier to error check if we need to as we work on the deal.
2. **The ability to create additional criteria tests using a Selection Criteria Design Menu.** We need to provide the analyst with the ability to construct a series of tests utilizing the key parameters of the financial and demographic characteristics of the loan record. We will provide the analyst with the ability to create up to 20 of these tests, per test set, from 6 different test type formats.
3. **The ability to store the tests created in (2) above in a criteria file.** This file can contain up to five sets of different collateral tests. There can be up to 20 individual tests in each of the ten sets.

Initial Data Screening Tests

This test set will determine the following for each loan in the collateral file based on its mortgage type:

- Are any data missing that are critical to the amortization calculations of this loan type?
- Is any demographic information missing, illegible, or does any have an unreasonable value?
- Are any financial data missing, illegible, or do any have an unreasonable value?

Development of an Initial Data Screening Test Set

A Initial Data Screening Test set will be able to be selected and stored in a file that will be loaded into the model at the election of the analyst. This set of tests will contain general balance, coupon, term, type, spread, basis, and collateral demographic tests.

It will be designed as a set of universal selections for all portfolios to eliminate collateral that is damaged, inconsistent, or grossly unsuitable for inclusion in a securitization. These tests are designed to check data integrity and accuracy and do not relate, except in a very general way, to the optimization of the portfolio selection process.

Ability to Create and Save Criteria Sets

We will create a menu in which we assemble and save into specific selection sets individual selection criteria tests. The types of tests that can be constructed using this menu are:

- **Single-Condition test**
  OriginalTerm LE 480
- **Minimum/Maximum test**
  OriginalTerm GE 180 AND OriginalTerm LE 480
- **Single-Condition test with Minimum/Maximum test**
  OriginalBalance LE 2000000 AND [OriginalTerm GE 180 AND OriginalTerm LE 480]
  - Single Criteria with Multiple Values
  - PropertyType EQ 1 OR
  - PropertyType EQ 3 OR PropertyType EQ 4 OR
  - PropertyType EQ 9 OR PropertyType EQ 12
- **Joint Minimum/Maximum test**
  [OriginalTerm GE 180 AND OriginalTerm LE 480] AND [CurrentBalance GT 5000 AND Current Balance LE 5000000].
- **Two Criteria Table test**
  [Index EQ 1 AND Spread GE 2.0%] OR
  [Index EQ 2 AND Spread GE 1.5%] OR
  [Index EQ 4 AND Spread GE 4.0%]

The analyst will build the selection criteria set by specify up to 20 individual tests for each set. The sets will then be saved and can be applied individually against any selected collateral data file.

Dynamic Ability to Address Concentration Issues

A feature that would be a *very* useful addition to the CCFG would be an automated concentration limits calculator that would winnow out collateral to automatically achieve compliance with the stated concentration limits of a particular parameter.

The exclusion of the concentrated collateral would be directed by a series of simple rules. These rules might consist of the following:

- Sort all loans for state or MSA by balance.
- Determine amount of balance over-concentration for state or MSA.
- Select largest loan balance first, if the balance of the loan is less than the over-concentration of the geographic entity subtract the balance over-concentration amount.
- Deem the loan ineligible.
- Continue selecting loans from the largest to the smallest until a loan is found whose balance exceeds the current over-concentration.
- Move to the bottom of the loan list. Repeat the process of subtracting loan balances until the smallest loan exceeds the remaining over-concentration balance.
- Select one last loan to reduce the over concentration balance to below the target overconcentration balance and stop.

The model would, by following these selection criteria, exclude collateral pieces until the concentration of loans in the portfolio reached an acceptable level.

IMPROVING THE CCFG CASH FLOW GENERATION PROCESS

We will improve the cash flow generation process in two ways:

1. Expanding the number of collateral types the model can address by adding hybrid ARMs and Balloon mortgages.
2. Using loan-specific geographic and demographic information to determine amortization attrition factors.

New Mortgage Amortization Capabilities

We will expand the CCFG to be capable of amortizing three additional mortgage types. We have given an overview of these types along with an amortization example earlier in the chapter so we will only mention them is passing here. These types are:

1. **Hybrid ARMs.** These hybrids will all have a fixed coupon rate IO period of up to ten years. Some have fixed lower rates for a portion of the first ten years. After the ten-year period, they convert to a fully amortizing plain vanilla ARM.
2. **Balloon mortgages.** These mortgages allow the mortgagor to pay a reduced payment based on a longer term than the actual stated term of the mortgage. The remaining unamortized principal balance is then due upon the last date of the mortgage term in the form of a balloon or bullet payment.

Adding Prepayment and Default Methodologies

A major improvement in the new CCFG will be the implementation of two new approaches to modeling prepayments of principal, principal default rates, market value decline factors, and recovery lag periods.

Overview of the Existing Methodology (Uniform Speed) The current model uses a prepayment and default methodology best described as the Uniform Speed Methodology. The Uniform Speed Methodology applies a constant prepayment rate and a constant default rate to *all* loans in the portfolio. The geographic location of the loan within a state or MSA is not a factor in the prepayment or default rate estimations. In addition, demographic characteristics of the loan, the financial and credit profile of the borrower, the characteristics of the property, the underwriting criteria applied at the issuance of the loan, and the competency and aggressiveness of the servicing effort are also ignored. The two new methodologies, the Geographic Methodology and the Demographic Methodology, employ a significantly different approach.

First New Approach: Geographic Methodology In the Geographic Methodology, all default and prepayments assumptions are contained in a series of analyst-created files. An assumption file in the Geographic Methodology is specified on the CCFG Cash Flow Amortization Parameters Menu and targeted for use with either the portfolio as a whole (at the pool level), or to a specific subset of the pool (at the sub-portfolio level). The assumptions of the particular file selected are then applied *only* to that portion of the portfolio that the analyst indicates on the menu. The file contains a total of four worksheets, each of which has a listing of national level (1 vector), state level (54 vectors), and MSA level (150 vectors) of data. Each of these vectors contains geographically specific assumptions for that particular geographic entity. A total of five years of monthly assumptions followed by a long-term rate estimate is included for each of the national, state, and MSA geographic entity. There are four worksheets in the file:

1. Prepayment rate estimates by geographic region
2. Default rate estimates by geographic region
3. Recovery period lags estimates by geographic region
4. Market value decline estimates by geographic region

The Geographic Methodology will then match the loan to the appropriate geographic entity and employ the assumptions for that area in the cash flow amortization calculations. If the loan is missing information as to MSA or state location, the model will default to the next larger geographic region. Thus if a loan is in the New York City MSA, that set of assumptions are used. If the state is indicated as New York and the MSA code of the loan is unavailable or irrelevant (the loan is not located in *any* New York state MSA), the state level assumptions are applied. This will also happen if the MSA where the loan is located lacks a set of specific assumptions. If the state level information is missing, the national level assumptions will be applied.

This methodology, while a significant improvement over that of the Uniform Speed Methodology, still ignores the significant differences that can arise between two different pieces of collateral. These issues are addressed by the Demographics Methodology.

Second New Approach: Demographic Methodology   The Demographic Methodology is both similar and dissimilar to the Geographic Methodology. As with the Geographic Methodology, the prepayment and recovery lag period information is determined exclusively by the geographic location of the property.

The Demographic Methodology parts company with the Geographic Methodology at the subject of determining the default rates and market value decline assumptions. In the Demographic Methodology, the demographic characteristics of each piece of collateral are examined in determining the probability of borrower default and the severity of that default. The model assigns a series of penalties for borrower, underwriting, servicing, property, and loan characteristics. Each characteristic can either add to or, in some cases, diminish the overall risk score. Based on the individual loan record information, a total risk score for default rate and a separate one for market value decline are derived. The aggregate default or market value decline risk score is then compared to a table, and corresponding assumption is derived.

The factors involved in the calculation of the default rate risk are:

- Mortgage loan amortization characteristics
- Credit sector of the loan (Prime, Alt-A, etc.)
- Original balance
- Current balance
- Seasoning
- Property type code
- Occupancy status code
- Purpose of the financing code
- State location code
- MSA location code
- Borrower employment status
- Number of years borrower in current employment position
- First-time homeowner code
- FICO score
- Mortgage debt-to-income ratio
- Total indebtedness debt-to-income ratio
- Bankruptcy condition code
- Tax and insurance escrowing conditions code
- Third-party confirmation of borrow data code
- Documentation criteria of underwriting code
- Rating of the mortgage servicer code

The factors involved in the calculation of the market value decline risk factor percentage are:

- Mortgage loan amortization characteristics
- Credit sector of the loan (Prime, Alt-A, etc.)

- Current balance
- Current loan-to-value amount
- Seasoning
- Property type code
- Occupancy status code
- Purpose of the financing code
- State location code
- MSA location code
- Number of monthly payments in arrears
- Rating of the mortgage servicer code

These factors are then added to a national level base rate to determine the loan-specific assumption. These assumptions are then applied across the remaining life of the loan.

To recap, the steps of the Demographics Methodology are as follows:

1. Determine the geographic location of the collateral.
2. Read the prepayment assumptions based on geographic location.
3. Read the recovery lag period based on geographic location.
4. Calculate the default rate risk factor based on individual loan demographics.
5. Calculate the market value decline percentage based on the individual loan demographics.

It can be seen that the development of both the Geographic and the Demographic Methodologies in the model will significantly increase its sophistication and capabilities.

IMPROVING THE CCFG REPORT GENERATION PROCESS

One of the major changes between the BAM and the CCFG is a significant improvement in the number, scope, and complexity of the report packages produced by the CCFG. We will significantly expand both the types of reports and their appearances.

Organization of the CCFG Report Package

The reports of the CCFG will be organized along six major divisions. These are the following:

1. **Assumptions report.** This report will hold all the assumptions necessary to replicate the run of the model. The Assumptions report will be a separate stand-alone report file but will be linked to the reports files of the model run by an analyst-designated report name prefix. The Assumptions file will consist of seven individual sub-reports. These reports will hold all the information needed to replicate the model run, as they will contain the contents of the all the CCFG menu inputs. These are:
   a. Run/Output Options Menu
   b. Collateral Pool Menu

    c. Prepayment/Default Menu

    d. User Financial Selection Criteria

    e. Geographic Selection Menu

    f. Geographic Concentration Menu

    g. Rates and Dates Menu

2. **Initial Data Screening reports.** These reports are new to the CCFG. They develop a picture of what the raw data of the file looks like before we do any other analysis. The reports tell us how many of the records are illegible, have illegal values, or are incomplete. The reports present the results of the data sufficiency tests for various calculation and stratification activities we may wish to perform later. These tests are as follows:

    a. Missing, illegible, or illegal data items

    b. Data sufficiency to perform Geographic Methodology

    c. Data sufficiency to perform Demographic Methodology

    d. Data sufficiency to amortize the loan (by loan type)

    e. Data sufficiency to calculate the Demographic Methodology frequency of foreclosure risk analysis

    f. Data sufficiency to calculate the Demographic Methodology market value decline rate

    g. Risk factor contributions for Demographic Methodology

3. **Demographic Risk Factors reports.** These reports display the amount of risk attributable to either the financial or the demographic characteristics of each loan. These weightings are used to derive a raw score from which the frequency of foreclosure and the market value decline numbers are generated. These two factors are then employed in the Demographic Cash Flow Calculation Methodology.

    a. **Frequency of Foreclosure Risk report.** Risk factor weightings for demographic methodology frequency of foreclosure

    b. **Market Value Decline Risk report.** Risk factor weightings for market value declines percentages

4. **Ineligible Collateral reports.** This section is broadly similar to the capabilities of the BAM, although it is now modified to report on up to five sets of User Defined Financial Selection Criteria tests. As with the BAM Ineligible Collateral package, it produces three reports. These are:

    a. **Single Criteria Loan report.** A listing of all loans that failed a specific criterion, by that criterion

    b. **Loan Listing report.** A listing of each ineligible loans and displaying the conditions of ineligibility

    c. **Summary Exception report.** An aggregation of all loans that have failed a specific pattern of eligibility tests.

5. **Eligible Collateral reports.** This set of reports is very heavily focused on the geographic characteristics of the collateral. It has a much more sophisticated stratification reporting system, allowing for wider choice and analyst-driven configurations of up to 50 reports. It consists of the following reports:

    a. **Custom Defined Stratification reports.** The analyst can specify configurations of up to 50 Base Stratification reports.

    b. **Cross Tabulation reports.** Up to 50 Cross Tabulation reports can be specified. Each report constructs a matrix of two collateral data. The contents of the body are selected independently.

    c. **Loan Listing report.** Listing of all eligible loans, one by one with their amortization, demographic, financial, credit, and underwriting characteristics displayed.

6. **Geographic reports.** This set of reports describes the geographic characteristics of the individual and aggregate collateral collections at national, state, MSA, and individual loan levels.

    a. **Geographic Loan Listing report.** Individual loans listed by MSA/state/national locations.

    b. **Geographic Concentration reports.** There are six of these reports altogether. The first three describe the composition of the collateral portfolio prior to any selection activity to address concentration limit overages. The next three reports display the composition of the collateral after the concentration selections have been completed. Both the pre- and post-concentration reports can be selected at the state, MSA or individual loan listings levels.

    c. **Geographic Stratification reports.** These four reports produce a geographically stratified presentation of the collateral at the national, state, and MSA level. In addition to the MSA level reports, a separate report listing all collateral not associated with any MSA for each state can be produced.

7. **Collateral Cash Flow reports.** This report package contains individual waterfall reports for each prepayment/default scenario run by the model.

    a. **Cash Flow Waterfall report.** This report contains the cash flows for each period of the model. Each prepayment and default rate scenario combination is on its own worksheet. This report is used as the input cash flow report for the Liabilities Waterfall Model.

    b. **Single Scenario Cash Flow report.** This report contains a presentation report summary of each unique cash flow waterfall. It displays a summary section of the total cash flows by type, an annual schedule, and a line graph of the data.

8. **Demographic reports.** These reports are specifically designed to display the key financial and demographic characteristics of the eligible collateral at the MSA level by state, items related to borrower credit, property valuation methods, and property type and servicing. These are presentation-formatted reports. The reports are:

    a. **Collateral Distribution by State with MSA detail report.** This report displays the distribution of the collateral for all MSAs of the state and all non-MSA collateral.

    b. **Borrower Credit report.** This report contains frequency distributions and accompanying graphs of borrower mortgage debt-to-income and total-debt-to-income ratios, FICO scores, financing purpose, bankruptcy histories, and the ratio of first-time homeowners.

    c. **Valuation Criteria report.** This report contains information as to the valuation for the collateral. It has frequency distributions and graphs of the original and current loan-to-value ratios, the original and current appraisal methods, and the loan documentation standards at origination.

    d. **Property Type and Occupancy report.** This report contains the frequency distributions and graphs of the property types of the collateral and their owner occupancy characteristics.

Rationale behind the CCFG Report Package

These reports are constructed to provide three perspectives on the content of the collateral portfolio. The three reporting needs this report package address are data integrity, financial and geographic suitability and cash flow amortization. Let us look at each in turn.

Data Integrity   The first goal is to improve our immediate perspective of the data. We need to answer two immediate questions as early as we can in the collateral examination process. These questions are how many records does the file consist of, and how many are immediately available in a form that can be used by the model? These reports are the outcome of the initial data screening process. The results of the initial data screening process is our immediate picture of the contents and suitability of the collateral data even before we begin the financial and geographic selection processes. These reports are the ones in Report Group 2, the "Initial Data Screening reports."

Financial and Geographic Suitability   These reports tell us how much of the collateral whose data integrity is sufficient to allow it to be used by the full range of the CCFG analytical operations is desirable for the deal at hand. It is the collateral collection that meets the specific needs of *this* deal. It is the collateral that has and, almost as important, has not, survived the financial and geographic selection process.

We need to be able to report on the collateral that has failed the criteria tests. This task is addressed by the reports of Report Group 4, The "Ineligible Collateral reports." We also need to know that the collateral that has passed these tests has met all or requirements. We need to have the reports to prove it, if necessary! These are the reports of Report Group 5, the "Eligible Collateral reports." This group contains all the User Defined Stratification and Cross Tabulation reports as well as the Geographic Selection, Listing, and Concentration reports.

Cash Flow Amortization   This final set of reports describes the characteristics of the amortized cash flows of the eligible collateral for each of the prepayment/default scenarios we have produced. It identifies the cash flow calculation methodology used,Uniform Speed, Geographic, or Demographic,and displays the period-by-period component cash flows of the collateral.

These reports are the two members of Report Group 7, the Cash Flow Waterfall report and the Single Scenario Cash Flow report. The last, but far from least, member of this group is the Assumptions report of Report Group 1. It is the cash flow amortization support file that will allow us at a later date to both preserve the conditions of the model run that produced the cash flows and serve as a launching point if we need to defend or replicate them.

Development of the CCFG Report Package

The initial development of the CCFG report package will be in VBA using Excel template files. Later in the Report Package development process we will incorporate Access and then finally PowerPoint.

Initial Steps   In the following chapters we will address the tasks of building the CCFG as we have stated in this design chapter. In Chapter 13, "Writing the CCFG

Reporting Capability," we will concentrate our major report development efforts. In between the current chapter and Chapter 13 lies a lot of ground. It is too much ground, in fact, to defer all discussion of report writing until we reach Chapter 13.

We will therefore introduce a number of reports in these intervening chapters. These reports will tend to be basic in nature and simple to organize and produce. We will save the complex reports for detailed analysis in Chapter 13. In that chapter we will look at how to organize and write the VBA code for the more difficult reports. These reports will be characterized by conditional formatting (the contents of the data determine the appearance of the report) and by more complex aggregation and calculation sequences.

The four immediate steps that we can take to lay the groundwork for the process to come are as follows:

1. Determine how many VBA modules we will need and what their names are. (We will segregate the VBA code that produces each of the report in its own module. This will allow us to export the report writing code to other models if we need to. It also avoids any problems associated with disentangling the VBA from other parts of the model when we do use it elsewhere.)
2. Determine the names of the template files and their general formats.
3. Designate the names of the Public Constants for each of the report templates we will create.
4. For developmental planning purposes, we should also develop a table of all of the prospective reports and a list of their functions. We can then work through this list as we build the report package, checking them off as we complete them.

See Exhibit 8.23 and Exhibit 8.24.

Report Package of the Collateral Cash Flow Generator

Model Function / Report Name / Sub Report	Report Function	CCFG VBA Module "Report " +	Public Constant Variable Name	Template Name	Chapter Discussed
Enter Run Time Assumptions					
Assumptions Report	Run time assumptions of the model	Assumptions	ASSUMPTIONS_FILE_NAME	AssumptionsTemplate	Chapter 12
Data Screening					
Initial Data Screening Report Package					
Missing, Illegible or Illegal Values Data	Checks data record for unusable data	DataScreenInit	INIT_DATA_SCREEN_TEMPLATE	InitDataScreenTemplate	Chapter 10
Geographic Loss/Prepay Methodology	Data screen for Geographic Methodology	DataScreenInit	INIT_DATA_SCREEN_TEMPLATE	InitDataScreenTemplate	Chapter 10
Demographic Loss/Prepay Methodology	Data screen for Demographic Methodology	DataScreenInit	INIT_DATA_SCREEN_TEMPLATE	InitDataScreenTemplate	Chapter 10
Cash Flow Amortization Criteria	Data screen for cash flow amortization by type	DataScreenInit	INIT_DATA_SCREEN_TEMPLATE	InitDataScreenTemplate	Chapter 10
Frequency of Default Calculation Criteria	Data screen for Frequency of Foreclosure calculations	DataScreenInit	INIT_DATA_SCREEN_TEMPLATE	InitDataScreenTemplate	Chapter 10
Market Value Decline Calculation Criteria	Data screen for Market Value Decline calculations	DataScreenInit	INIT_DATA_SCREEN_TEMPLATE	InitDataScreenTemplate	Chapter 10
Risk Report - Demographic Methodology	Risk factors weighting report for Demo Method	DataDemoRisk	COLLAT_DEMO_RISKS_TEMPLATE	DemoRiskFactorsTemplate	Chapter 10
Reporting Ineligible Collateral					
Ineligible Collateral Report Package					
Single Criteria Exceptions Reports	Ineligible collateral list by single criteria	CollatIneligUser	COLLAT_USER_INELIG_TEMPLATE	UserIneligCollatTemplate	Chapter 11
Loan Listing Exception Report	Ineligibility conditions per loan	CollatIneligUser	COLLAT_USER_INELIG_TEMPLATE	UserIneligCollatTemplate	Chapter 11
Summary Exception Report	Loans by unique pattern of ineligibility conditions	CollatIneligUser	COLLAT_USER_INELIG_TEMPLATE	UserIneligCollatTemplate	Chapter 11
Reporting Eligible Collateral					
Eligible Collateral Reports					
User Defined Stratification Reports	Set of up to 40 user defined startification reports	CollatEligStratBase	BASE_STRAT_REPORTS_TEMPLATE	BaseStratReportTemplate	Chapter 13
Cross Tabulation Reports	Stratification by 2 user defined data fields	CollatEligCrossTabs	CROSSTABS_REPORTS_TEMPLATE	CrossTabsReportTemplate	Chapter 13
Loan Listing Report	Eligible Collateral Listing by amortization type	LoanListing	LOANLIST_REPORTS_TEMPLATE	LoanListingTemplate	Chapter 13
Geographic Loan Listing Report	Eligible Collateral geograpic listing summary report	GeoLoanList	GEO_LOANLIST_TEMPLATE	GeoLoanListTemplate	Chapter 11
Geographic Concentration Report Package					
Concentration Report - National Level	Loan Listing of selected States within National Level	GeoConcentration	GEO_CONCEN_TEMPLATE	GeoConcenTemplate	Chapter 11
Concentration Report - State Level	Loan listing of MSA's within States	GeoConcentration	GEO_CONCEN_TEMPLATE	GeoConcenTemplate	Chapter 11
Concentration Report - MSA Level	Loan listing by individual MSAs	GeoConcentration	GEO_CONCEN_TEMPLATE	GeoConcenTemplate	Chapter 11
Geographic Stratification Reports					
National Level Stratification Report	National Stratification Report	GeoStratification	GEO_STRATS_STATE_TEMPLATE	GeoStartStateTemplate	Chapter 13
State Level Stratification Report	State Stratification Report	GeoStratification	GEO_STRATS_STATE_TEMPLATE	GeoStartStateTemplate	Chapter 13
No MSA Level Stratification Report	Non-MSA Collateral Stratification Report	GeoStratification	GEO_STRATS_STATE_TEMPLATE	GeoStartStateTemplate	Chapter 13
MSA Level Stratification Report	MSA Collateral Stratification Report	GeoStratification	GEO_STRATS_MSA_TEMPLATE	GeoMSAStateTemplate	Chapter 13
Reporting Cash Flows					
Cash Flow Waterfall Report	Per period cash flows for all scenarios	CollatEligCFs	CASHFLOW_REPORT_TEMPLATE	CashFlowOutputTemplate	Chapter 12
Presentation Reports					
Single Scenario Cash Flow Report	Summary of Performance, single page report	SingleScenarioCFs	CF_SINGLE_SCENARIO_TEMPLATE	CFSingleScenarioTemplate	Chapter 12
Portfolio Presentation Report	Presentation report package collateral structure	PortPresentation	PRESENT_PORTFOLIO_TEMPLATE	PortfolioPresentTemplate	Chapter 13

EXHIBIT 8.23 Report Package of the Collateral Cash Flow Generator

```
'CCFG REPORT PACKAGE
Public Const DIR_TEMPLATE_REP = CODE_DIRECTORY & "template_report\"
'assumptions
Public Const ASSUMPTIONS_FILE_TEMPLATE = "AssumptionsTemplate"
'data screening
Public Const INIT_DATA_SCREEN_TEMPLATE = "InitDataScreenTemplate"
Public Const COLLAT_DEMO_RISKS_TEMPLATE = "DemoRiskFactorsTemplate"
'ineligible collateral reporting
Public Const COLLAT_USER_INELIGIBLE_TEMPLATE = "UserIneligCollatTemplate"
'eligible collateral reporting
Public Const BASE_STRAT_REPORTS_TEMPLATE = "BaseStratReportsTemplate"
Public Const CROSSTABS_REPORTS_TEMPLATE = "CrossTabsReportsTemplate2"
Public Const LOANLIST_REPORTS_TEMPLATE = "LoanListingTemplate"
Public Const GEO_LOANLIST_TEMPLATE = "GeoLoanListTemplate"
Public Const GEO_CONCEN_TEMPLATE = "GeoConcenTemplate"
Public Const GEO_STRATS_STATE_TEMPLATE = "GeoStateStratTemplate"
Public Const GEO_STRATS_MSA_TEMPLATE = "GeoMSAStratTemplate"
'reporting cash flows
Public Const CASHFLOW_REPORT_TEMPLATE = "CashFlowOutputTemplate"
'presentation reports
Public Const PRESENT_PORTFOLIO_TEMPLATE = "PortfolioPresentTemplate"
Public Const CF_SINGLE_SCENARIO_TEMPLATE = "CashFlowSingleScenTemplate"
```

EXHIBIT 8.24   Constant Variable declarations for the Report Template files

Looking Ahead: PowerPoint Presentations from VBA   In the future we will build
the capability of generating PowerPoint presentations directly from the results of
the model run. To accomplish this, we will combine the capabilities of VBA and
PowerPoint. The VBA will select, format, cut, and transfer specific model outputs to
a PowerPoint file. Here they will be additionally manipulated by programmatically
editing the PowerPoint presentation using purpose-built VBA subroutines. We will
address the use of VBA/PowerPoint programming in Chapter 20.

IMPROVING THE CCFG MESSAGING PROCESS

Along with other improvements to the CCFG, we will add to the ability of the program to communicate to us both directly and indirectly. These improved communication capabilities will involve having the CCFG produce more progress messages
than the current BAM does and provide more information within the messages that
it does generate.

A second improvement is to have the CCFG generate messages that are sent
using MS Outlook to our e-mail address. We can then easily monitor the progress of
the program on long model runs without the necessity of being physically present!
We can also automate the distribution of reports and other model output to prepare
lists of investors, rating agencies and other interested parties! We will address these
issues in Chapter 21.

ON THE WEB SITE

There is a "**Chapter08_Comments.doc**" file on the Web site.

There is a file named "**Chapter08_MenuGeographic.xls**" on the Web site. This
file contains a working version of the new Geographic Selection and Concentration
Menu that employs UserForms.

You will also find a template of the expanded format of the collateral data file
named "**Chapter08_CollateralDataFile**".

## CHAPTER 9

Writing the CCFG Menus and Data Sheets

OVERVIEW

In this chapter we will implement the menus for the Collateral Cash Flow Generator (CCFG). We will use Excel, VBA code, and UserForms that will allow these menus to interact with the other parts of the model.

One of the most significant and visible changes in the new CCFG will be the introduction of Excel UserForms in a number of the menus. UserForms allow for a wider degree of freedom in expressing choices and also have the benefit of allowing the analyst to pack more information in a given menu. This additional flexibility results from the increase in the number of menu features and component combinations that can be specified by the analyst. UserForms have a number of features, such as OptionButtons, that allow the analyst to specify a range of combination actions that would be difficult to implement in a standard Excel/VBA menu. In addition to various button functions, UserForms allow the analyst to display lists of choices and to quickly and easily select one or multiple items from them. We will see this feature used repeatedly in the new Collateral Selection Criteria Menu and the Geographic Selections Menu.

DELIVERABLES

The modeling knowledge deliverables for this chapter are:

- Understanding basic menu design.
- Understanding how to construct menus using VBA and Excel Worksheets.
- Learning how to work with UserForms, VBA, and Excel.
- Learning the features of the UserForm Editor.
- Learning the most common of the various types of UserForm components, such as ListBoxes, ComboBoxes, TextBoxes, CommandButtons, OptionButtons, CheckBoxes, and Frames.
- Learning how the UserForm Editor can be employed to create UserForm VBA support code that performs error checking, messaging, computations, and data transfer from the UserForm to the model.

UNDER CONSTRUCTION

In this chapter we will build the following menus and their entire supporting User-Form, VBA, and Excel infrastructure:

- Main Menu
- Run Options Menu
- Rates and Dates Menu
- Geographic Selection Criteria Menu
- Collateral Financial Selection Criteria Menu
- Collateral Pool and Sub-Portfolio Menu
- Cash Flow Amortization Parameters Menu
- Collateral Reports Editor and Menu

We will create a series of modules to hold the VBA code to perform data verification and error checking. These modules will correspond to the above menus. We will prefix their names with "MenuSupport_" followed by the name of the menu they are connected to. We will also write any of the code that we need to support the UserForms that are embedded in the respective menus. As you will see, most of the VBA code that supports a UserForm resides within it, but some does not. These modules will also house that code. As we develop the subroutines for managing the menus and their attendant data, we will need to be especially careful to adhere to the practice of placing prefixes on the names of the subroutine names. This will allow us to quickly and easily identify the general role of the subroutine and where to find it.

There is a lot to do in this chapter. Much of the menu-building techniques that employ only Excel and VBA will be familiar to those of you who have read my earlier volume, *A Fast Track to Structured Finance Modeling, Monitoring, and Valuation: Jump Start VBA* (John Wiley & Sons, 2008). The development of menus containing embedded UserForms will be a new subject, however. We will need to learn how to use a new editor, the UserForms Editor. We will learn how to assemble a completed UserForm from a number of UserForm component elements each with a different function, appearance, and data capability. We will employ these UserForms where we have menus that require large amounts of data or a more demanding series of decisions than are normally handled by an Excel/VBA menu alone.

MENUS AND USERFORMS

As mentioned earlier, this is not a book about the science of designing user interfaces. The emphasis of this chapter will be focused on designing a menu interface that allows significantly more flexibility to address the complex tasks we now face. As a result the menus we will implement in this chapter will be practical and designed to offer the analyst just enough power to get the job done without drowning him in choices.

Sixteen types of subcomponents can be placed in a UserForm. We will employ, on average, from four to eight of these components in each of the UserForms that we will create. In some cases we may employ as few as four or five of these components when we want to present the analyst with a simple choice. In other instances we will choose a wider array of subcomponents to implement a combination of formatting and selection components to frame the actions the analyst can take and provide an efficient way of manipulating the model environment.

A Simple UserForm Tutorial

Creating a UserForm is a fairly straightforward matter. Once you have created your two or three dozen UserForms, you will become quite adept at the process! In case you had not noticed, the preceding statement was made tongue in cheek! Nevertheless, although the process of creating a UserForm and its supporting VBA code may seem laborious at first, I highly recommend that you keep your spirits up and resolve to bravely plow through the process. UserForms can add a lot of power to your menus. In addition, they may be the only practical solution to the need to specify a complex series of conditions that the model must operate upon. One outstanding advantage to employing UserForms is that they allow a designer to present large amounts of information without consuming large amounts of space on the face of the menu.

How to Operate the UserForm Editor Before we can build a UserForm we need to know how to operate the UserForm Editor. This editor has many similarities to the Visual Basic Editor, but it also has some unique features. In this section we will go through a step-by-step approach to how to run the Editor, show you how to create the visual portion of the UserForm, how to create the VBA code that allows it to run, and how to get it to interact with the CCFG.

Open the UserForm Editor from Excel From any Excel Worksheet, use the same command that you would use to enter the VBA Editor: "Alt+F11". Once inside the VBA Editor, right click the mouse on the "Insert" tab in the Editor header section; a list will be displayed. This list has three items: "UserForm", "Module", and "Class Module". Select the "UserForm" option. See Exhibit 9.1.

Select the "UserForm" Option from the "Insert" Tab When you click on the "User-Form" choice in the menu, several things will happen. The first is that a subscreen labeled "UserForm1" will appear on the right side of the VBA Editor window. It is into this initially blank area that you will add any of the various UserForm elements to make a completed form. In addition to this working area, an icon for the User-Form Toolbox will now appear on the left of the screen, usually over the Project window. This menu contains 16 icons, each of which is an Object that you can add to the blank "UserForm1". Directly under the caption for the Project window you will now note that there are three active icons displayed. Starting with the leftmost, we can position the cursor over the icon to discover its function. Moving left to right we see that the captions are "View Code", "View Object", and "Toggle Folders". See Exhibit 9.2.

View Code Icon If you click on the "View Code" icon, the UserForm Editor creates a module that is part of the UserForm, *not* part of the model, to place any VBA code that we need to write to help the UserForm do its job. You will notice that a subroutine named "UserForm_Click" has appeared. It is void, without any code.

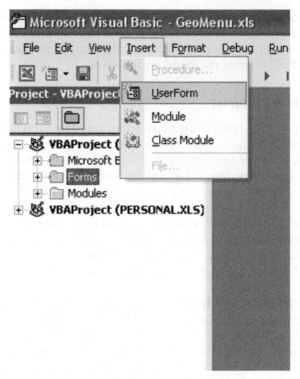

EXHIBIT 9.1   Visual Basic Editor for UserForms

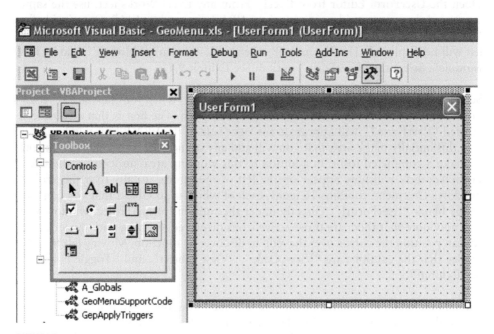

EXHIBIT 9.2   Initial Display after Clicking on "UserForm" in the "Insert" tab

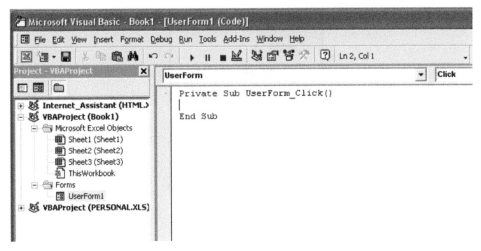

EXHIBIT 9.3   Clicking on The "View Code" icon in the "Project- VBA Project" window.

We will add code later as we need to do so, but for the moment we will leave it blank. The name indicates that if the analyst clicks anywhere on the UserForm, the code in this subroutine will be activated. If you wish to employ the UserForm in other projects, you can simply drag and drop it to the other workbook, and all the supporting VBA code you have written in the UserForm will accompany the form to its new home! See Exhibit 9.3.

Toggle Folders Icon   In Exhibits 9.4(a) and 9.4(b) you will see the effects of clicking on the "Toggle Folders" icon. In this Excel application we have three Excel

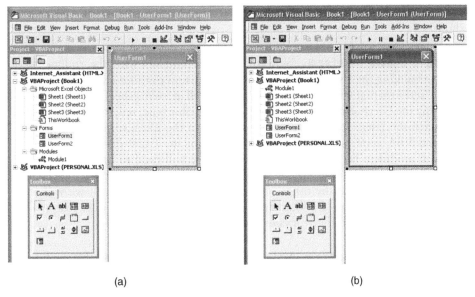

(a)   (b)

EXHIBIT 9.4   Project Window (a) before and (b) after clicking on the "Toggle Folders" icon

EXHIBIT 9.5   UserForm Toolbox Menu

Worksheet Objects, two UserForm Objects, and one VBA Module Object. In the initial condition of the Project Window display, we see that these Objects are displayed under separate folder icons. After we click on the "Toggle Folders", they are displayed in alphabetical order in a single list.

UserForm Toolbox   This small menu contains a series of icons that can be selected and dragged into the UserForm. There are 16 items on this list. Placing the cursor over any item on the list will identify each of these icons. Although there are 16 of these command structures that can be used in the construction of a UserForm, a typical UserForm will employ no more than 6 or 7 types of Objects. They are, in order from left to right, top to bottom, Select, Objects, Labels, TextBox, ComboBox, ListBox, CheckBox, OptionButton, ToggleButton, Frame, CommandButton, TabStrip, MultiPage, ScrollBar, SpinButton, and Image.

In the tutorial immediately following we will use a Label, TextBox, OptionButton, Frame, and CommandButton Objects to build our first UserForm. See Exhibit 9.5.

Creating a Simple UserForm   Now that we are familiar with the rudiments of moving around in the UserForm Editor, we can start on our first UserForm! We will build a UserForm that will allow us to designate a cell in a worksheet of the workbook containing the UserForm and turn its background color blue, red, or yellow. We will then attach the UserForm to a CommandButton in the Excel spreadsheet. We will also build VBA code both in the VBA modules of the Excel program and in the UserForm modules. To accomplish this project we will need to create a UserForm and give it a title. Next we will create two Frames (one to group the color choices with OptionButtons and the other containing TextBoxes into which we will enter the cell location). Finally we will add a pair of CommandButtons either to apply the choices we have made to the worksheet or to cancel the action.

Step 1: Insert a New UserForm, Add a Label Object   Enter the Visual Basic Editor; select the "Insert->UserForm" command. This will bring up a new UserForm and the UserForm Toolbox menu. Note that a new icon has appeared in the Project Explorer Window named "Forms". If this is the first UserForm to be added, the

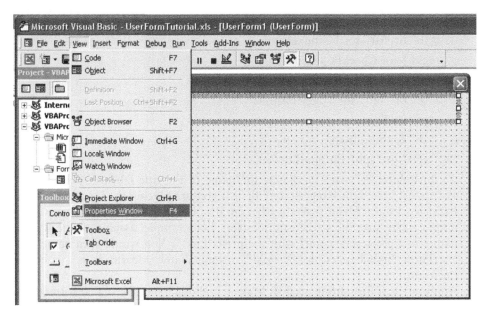

EXHIBIT 9.6   Creating a new UserForm, adding a Label Object

name of the new form will be "UserForm1". Begin by adding the first Object to the UserForm. Click on the Label icon in the Toolbox. Add controls to the new UserForm by selecting them from the UserForm Toolbox. When you click on any of the icons in the UserForm Toolbox Menu, a "+" will appear on the UserForm and the symbol of the control feature will appear next to it. You can then drag the "+" to trace the size of the control feature in the UserForm work area. We will start by adding a Label control feature to the UserForm. Although temporarily obscured by the View drop down menu, the new highlighted box is the Label Object that now has an identifying notation "Label1". If we were to create a series of Label Objects, the UserForm Editor would number them sequentially for us. See Exhibit 9.6.

Step 2: Using the Properties Window to Edit the Label   Once we have created an Object and placed it in the UserForm, we can edit its properties to meet the appearance and functional needs of the form. Using the "View=>Properties Editor" command, it is possible to see all of the editable properties of the form you have just created. You can make entries into the fields of the Properties Window, and the changes will immediately appear in the Object. There are three things you should do immediately after creating an Object. See Exhibit 9.7.

1. **Rename the Object to have a unique name.** To do this you select the "(Name)" property at the top of the editor. Enter a new name for the Object. Try to follow the same guidelines you would for a variable name. Use mixed-case notation and prefix the Object name with an identifier to tell yourself and others what type of Object it is. For the most commonly used Objects, the prefixes are:

   "lab" for Labels

   "tb" for TextBoxes

"cmbx" for ComboBoxes

"lb" or "lst" for ListBoxes

"ckb" for CheckBoxes

"ob" for OptionButtons

"tg" or "tgb" for ToggleButtons

"fr" for Frames,

"sb" for ScrollBars

"spn" or "spb" for SpinButtons

In Exhibit 9.7 we will change the name of the title label, now displayed as "Label1" to "labChangeColorTitle". If you are placing the UserForm in an Excel worksheet Menu that already contains a coding identifier for its Range names, make sure the UserForm does too. For example, assume all the Range names in a given menu start with the prefix "m3". You would then name this UserForm "m3ChangeColorTutorial" to immediately identify it as related to the menu.

2. **Apply any text formatting needed.** Make a preliminary choice of text formatting to maintain a uniform style across all of your UserForms. This is especially true of Labels, TextBoxes, and Frames. See Exhibit 9.7.

3. **Enter any default setting or values.** Make sure you enter them at this time so you do not forget latter. We will discuss default values and how to declare them later in this chapter.

Step 3: Add a Frame with Three OptionButtons for the Color Choices We are now building the first part of the UserForm that will directly communicate with the

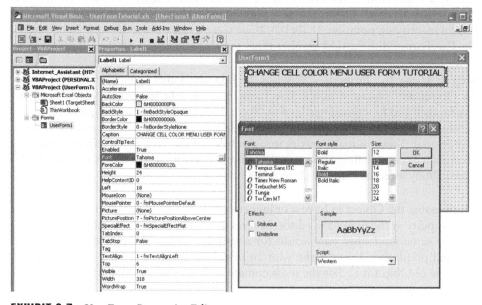

EXHIBIT 9.7 UserForm Properties Editor

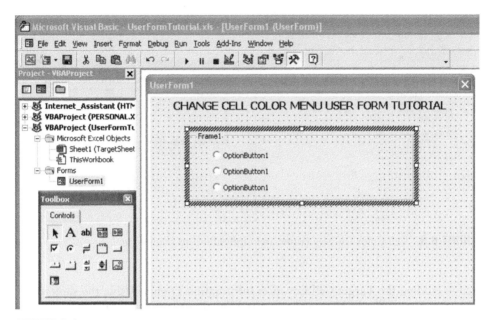

EXHIBIT 9.8 Adding a Frame and three OptionButtons

model. Now create three OptionButtons, one for each of the color choices. Before we do this, however, we will first create a Frame Object to place them in.

Why are we wasting our time with a Frame? It appears to just be an outline in the UserForm. Appearances can be deceiving! A Frame is one of the most powerful Objects in UserForms because Frames have the ability to group all the Objects that you put within them into a single collection. Thus when we place the three Option buttons inside the Frame, we will discover that checking any one of them to the "Selected" position immediately sets all the others in the Frame to "Unselected".

Now select the Frame Object from the Toolbox and draw it large enough to contain three OptionButtons. We will rename the Frame from its default name of "Frame1" to "frColorChoices". We will also change its "Caption" property from "Frame1" to "Cell Color Choices".

We can now add the OptionButtons. We will click on the Toolbox and draw an OptionButton Object inside of the Frame boundaries. We only need to create a single OptionButton item; we can then select it and, by using Ctl-C and Ctl-P, quickly make two copies of it. Notice that the caption for all three of the OptionButtons is "OptionButton1". If you examine each of them in the Properties Window, you will see that they are named OptionButton1, OptionButton2, and OptionButton3 that identifies them as three separate and distinct Objects. See Exhibit 9.8.

We will now change the captions and the names of each of these buttons. Their names will now be "obColorBlue", "obColorRed", and "obColorYellow". Their captions will be set to "BLUE", "RED", and "YELLOW", respectively. We have now finished all we need to do to allow the user to specify color; next we will turn to identifying the cell location. See Exhibit 9.9.

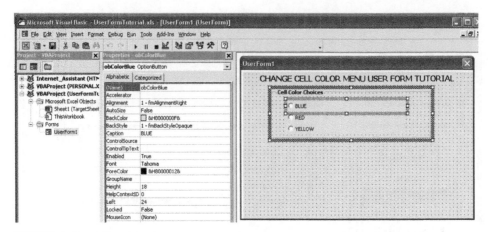

EXHIBIT 9.9   Cell Color Choices Frame and OptionButtons ready to go

Step 4: Adding the Target Cell Location Information Frame   Using the same steps as in Step 3, we will add a Frame Object and this time place a pair of TextBoxes and a pair of Labels to identify them into the Frame. This Frame will contain two fields that will allow the analyst to input the row and column location of the cell.

We will use TextBoxes because they are the most convenient way to move numbers and text information from the face of the UserForm into its supporting VBA code. We will name the Frame "frCellLocation" and give it a caption name of "Location of Cell to be Changed". We will name the TextBoxes "tbRowLocation" and "tbColLocation", and caption them "Row" and "Column". We need to remember that these are TextBoxes and as such the values that they will bring into the VBA code in back of the UserForm will be in a String variable format. We will need to convert them from a String format to an Integer, Long or Double format before we can use them. See Exhibit 9.10.

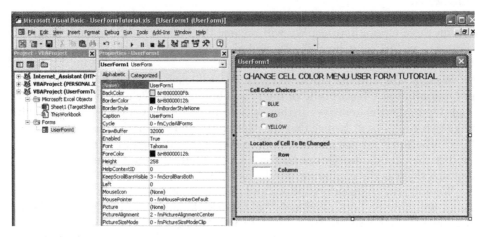

EXHIBIT 9.10   Frame containing the cell location fields

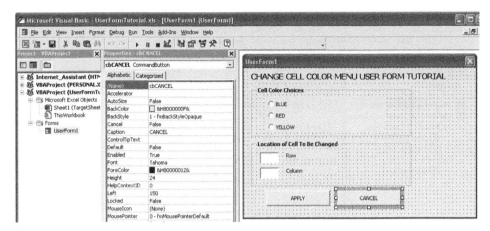

EXHIBIT 9.11 "APPLY" and "CANCEL" CommandButtons

Step 5: Adding the CommandButtons The final Objects that we will add to the UserForm are a pair of CommandButtons. CommandButtons are used when you want the UserForm to initiate an action. We will add the minimum number of buttons possible. One button will do something and the other will do nothing. The first one, which we will caption "Apply", will trigger cell color changing action. The second button, captioned "Cancel", will perform no action other than to unload the UserForm and thereby cancel any entries we have made to it. See Exhibit 9.11.

We will name these buttons "cbApply" and "cbCancel" and give them the captions "APPLY" and "CANCEL".

Step 6: Giving the UserForm a Name and Title The last step we will take is to click on "UserForm1" and, working in the Properties window, change its name to "ufChangeColorMenu" and change its caption to "ChangeCellColorMenu". With this done we are ready to turn to writing the menu support code in VBA.

Step 7: Creating the Subroutine Calls from the UserForm To create subroutine calls from the UserForm screen to the UserForm code, we simply click each of the Objects in the UserForm that we want to create a subroutine from. This will be each of the three OptionButtons, both of the TextBoxes, and both of the CommandButtons. The UserForm Editor now automatically creates subroutine calls from each of these Objects. After clicking on the two CommandButtons, two subroutine calls are created, both private, and using the format:

```
Private Sub (Name of CommandButton)''_''Click()]
```

Thus the APPLY CommandButton with the property Name "cbApply" generates the subroutine call

```
Private Sub cbApply_Click()
```

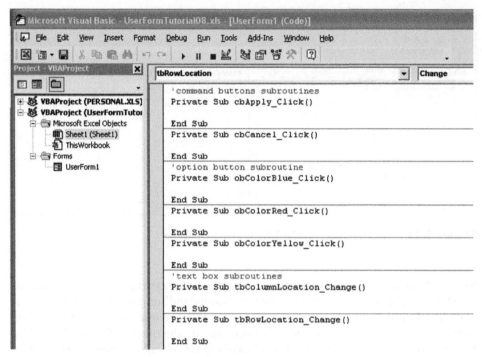

EXHIBIT 9.12   Initial subroutine calls created by the UserForm Editor

The same format is followed for each of the OptionButtons whose calls are also suffixed with "_Click". When we get to the call created for the TextBoxes, however, we see that here the suffix is changed to "_Change". That means that the subroutine will be called anytime the value in the TextBox is changed and the cursor leaves the box.

Since we will not be initiating any actions by clicking on the Frames or the Labels of the UserForm, we can stop here. See Exhibit 9.12 for a listing of the calls that can now be viewed by selecting the "View Code" editor option icon.

Step 8: Writing the User Menu Support Code into the Subroutine Calls   We now have everything in place to begin the process of writing the menu support code. We need the code to perform three tasks:

1. Read the color specified by the analyst in the Cell Color Choices frame. We will do this by assigning a color value to each of the OptionButtons and recording that color as the current choice when the button is clicked. (We already know what the color codes are because we recorded a macro while changing the color of the cells and read the codes for blue, red, and yellow as "5", "3", and "6", respectively!)

2. Determine the row and column location of the cells. We can find out these two numbers by capturing the values when the contents of the two TextBoxes are changed. Remember that the value will come in as a String, and we will convert it to a numeric value before using it.

3. Choose to apply the contents of the variable values to the Excel Worksheet or cancel the activity and deactivate the menu.

To accomplish Step 1 above, all we need do is assign a variable to hold the value of the color based on the OptionButton that was just clicked. We will create a variable "CellColorIndex" and assign either "5", "3", or "6" to it when the OptionButton for that color is clicked. This is the VBA statement for the color red:

```
CellColorIndex = 3
```

To accomplish Step 2 above we need to read the value from the TextBox Object. Once we have the text value, we need to change it to numeric form and store it in either a row location or column location variable that we will use later when designating the cell for the color change. We will create three variables, "answer" to hold the value of the TextBox, "CellRowLoc" to store the row location, and "CellColLoc" to store the column location. "CellColLoc" can be typed as an Integer, but "CellRowLoc" needs to be typed as a Long. This is because the maximum number of rows in an Excel worksheet, 65,536, exceeds the maximum value of the Integer variable type, which is 32,767. We need to remember to use the "Val" function to convert the contents of the variable "answer" from a string to a numeric.

On to Step 3! Putting all of this activity together is the role of the "cbApply_Click" subroutine. Here we will combine the indicated color with the cell location and, when we are done, hide the menu. To accomplish this we will assign the indicated color and location information to a Cell Object in the following manner:

```
Cells(row,col).Interior.ColorIndex = color
```

In the "cbApply_Click" subroutine the code looks like this:

```
Cells(CellRowLoc,CellColLoc).Interior.ColorIndex = _
    CellColorIndex
```

Alternatively, if we decide, after the menu has been displayed, to do nothing, we simply hide the menu, thereby not applying any of the choices that we entered. We can do this with the statement:

```
ChangeColorMenu.Hide
```

After filling in the blank subroutine with all this code, we arrive at the set of variables and subroutines seen in Exhibit 9.13.

Step 9: Writing the VBA Code in the Model Module to Call the UserForm   We now need to write a mechanism to open the UserForm from the Excel model. All that the subroutine needs to do is to apply the "Show" method to the UserForm. We can do this with the command:

```
(Name of UserForm).Show
```

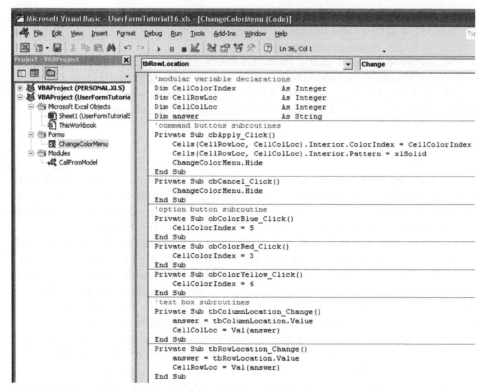

EXHIBIT 9.13   Completed Menu support code

or, in this case,

```
ChangeColorMenu.Show
```

We will place this single line of VBA code into a subroutine named "Load-ChangeColorMenu". We will then create a CommandButton on the Excel Worksheet and, once it is in place, left click on it. We will select the "Assign Macro" option and click on "LoadChangeColorMenu". This is the only VBA code we need to display the UserForm. *One important point: This subroutine needs to reside in a VBA module of the Excel Workbook and* not *in the UserForm VBA code.* You already know how to do this as we trigger standard VBA subroutines from CommandButtons on various menus to perform different tasks in the model. See Exhibit 9.14.

Step 10: Testing the Change Cell Color Menu and Its Support Code   The next to the last step in the process is to test the menu and its associated support code. We compile this code the same way we do the other VBA code of the model that is contained in the Module sections. Use the "Debug=>CompileVBAProject" option. If there are any syntax errors, they will be displayed just as they are routinely displayed for standard VBA code in modules.

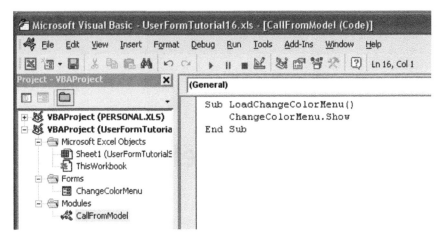

EXHIBIT 9.14 "LoadChangeColorMenu" subroutine

If one of the Color Choice Frame OptionButtons is checked and if there are valid row and column values in the row and column location variables, we will observe the results shown in Exhibits 9.15 and 9.16.

Step 11: Building Error Checking Code into the UserForm   Are we finished? Not quite. If the menu is going to be part of a large system, especially one that has been in existence for some time, we have another task to complete. We need to be sure that this menu blends into the crowd and looks just similar menus. To ensure that the appearance of our newly created UserForm is consistent with the UserForms already resident in the existing application, we may need to change the size and font of the

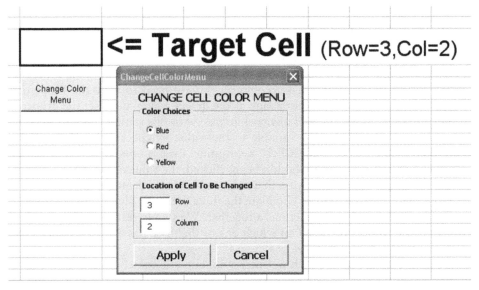

EXHIBIT 9.15   Change Cell Color Menu displayed with inputs

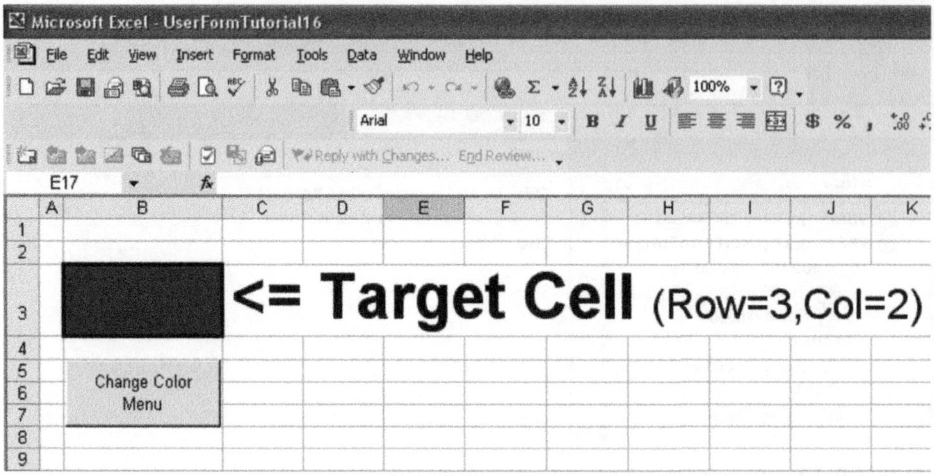

EXHIBIT 9.16 After the Apply CommandButton

labels, the positions of the CommandButtons (right side, left side, or center?), and any other similar formatting conventions currently in use.

You can see some evidence of a movement toward format standardization in the earlier exhibits of UserForms in this chapter. One of the conventions is to have the captions of the OptionButtons and the TextBoxes as similar as possible. You will notice in Exhibit 9.12 that the initial captions for the OptionButtons in the Color Choices Frame were "BLUE", "RED", and "YELLOW". These have subsequently been changed to conform to the mixed-case "Row" and "Column" labels in the Location Frame.

With all the values filled in, everything went well in our first round of testing. In the second round of testing, we did not fare so well! The next test consisted of leaving all of the options in the Color Choices Frame unchecked. When we then hit the Apply button, the designated cell reverted to white, the default color. How can we prevent this from happening? We can designate one of the three OptionButtons as the default value. When the menu is displayed for the first time, this button will always display as "selected". To accomplish this we need to view the Properties Window of the button we wish to assign as the default value. If we set the property "Value" to TRUE the menu will always initialize with this setting. We can then set the value of the "ColorIndex" variable to this value by checking all three of the OptionButtons in the "cbApply_Click" subroutine. Even if none of the buttons has been clicked prior to the Apply button being clicked, the value of the default button value will be TRUE and we will use that color, which is the default choice. In fact, if we adopt this approach, we can eliminate the three "obColorBlue", "obColorRed", and "obColorYellow" click functions altogether. We simply read the values of each and assign the color code based on which one of the three has a TRUE value, since only one can! See Exhibit 9.17.

The third test is one in which we enter a nonnumeric value, or make no entry at all, into either the row or column TextBox. Lacking a row and column location to modify, the program does not know which cell to change. This will also cause the

```
cbCancel                                    ▼   Click

    Option Explicit

    'modular variable declarations
    Dim CellColorIndex        As Integer   'color code
    Dim CellRowLoc            As Long      'row location of cell
    Dim CellColLoc            As Integer   'col location of cell
    Dim answer                As String    'response from text box
    Dim go_ok                 As Boolean   'continue to process?
    Dim msgPrompt             As String    'message box prompt
    Dim msgTitle              As String    'message box title
    Dim msgButton             As Integer   'message box button configuration
    Dim msgResult             As Integer   'message box response to process
    Dim err_case              As Integer   'numeric value of error condition (summation)
    Dim msgTotal              As String    'total message to be displayed

    'command buttons subroutines
    Private Sub cbApply_Click()

        'read the three Option Button values and assign the color
        If obColorBlue.Value Then CellColorIndex = 5
        If obColorRed.Value Then CellColorIndex = 3
        If obColorYellow.Value Then CellColorIndex = 6

        'error check the values of the row and colun inputs
        go_ok = True
        Call ErrorCheck_RowColLocAlpha
        If go_ok Then ErrorCheck_RowColLocLimits

        'assign the color
        If go_ok Then
            Cells(CellRowLoc, CellColLoc).Interior.ColorIndex = CellColorIndex
            Cells(CellRowLoc, CellColLoc).Interior.Pattern = xlSolid
            ChangeColorMenu.Hide
        End If

    End Sub
```

EXHIBIT 9.17   Default testing for Color Choice OptionButtons value

program to fail. To circumvent this problem we need to do two checks. The first is to test if the row or column entry in the TextBoxes can be converted to a numeric. The second test is to determine if the value input into the TextBox Object is a numeric that is an appropriate value for either a row or column designation.

We will construct the first test to determine if the value of the row and column location input into the TextBoxes is indeed a numeric. We can determine this by using the "Val" function. If the variable sent to this function cannot be converted to a numeric value the Val function will return "0" which stands for FALSE. This indicates that the string in the TextBox cannot be successfully converted to a numeric value. Since there is not a valid "0th" row or column, this becomes our error value for the numeric test. We will set the Boolean variable "go_ok" to FALSE. If this is the case, we do not have a valid cell location and we just skip the rest of the actions in the "cbApply_Click" subroutine.

The second error test we need to apply is a check for the reasonableness of the entry value in the location TextBoxes. We can do this by comparing the converted "answer" value against a limit of 256 for a column location input and 65,536 for a row location value. If the row and column entries have not triggered an error condition and set the "go_ok" variable to FALSE, we will now perform this test.

```
(General)                                              ▼    ErrorCheck_RowColLocLimits

    Private Sub ErrorCheck_RowColLocAlpha()

        'msg box alpha in column location
        If CellColLoc = 0 Then
            msgTitle = "Alpha Value in the Col Location"
            msgPrompt = "Enter a number between 1 and 256" & vbCrLf & vbCrLf
            msgResult = MsgBox(msgPrompt, vbOKCancel + vbExclamation, msgTitle)
            go_ok = False
        End If

        'msg box alpha in row location
        If go_ok And CellRowLoc = 0 Then
            msgTitle = "Alpha Value in the Row Location"
            msgPrompt = "Enter a number between 1 and 65,536" & vbCrLf & vbCrLf
            msgResult = MsgBox(msgPrompt, vbOKCancel + vbExclamation, msgTitle)
            go_ok = False
        End If

    End Sub

    Private Sub ErrorCheck_RowColLocLimits()

        'value too large
        If CellColLoc > 256 Or CellRowLoc > 65636 Then
            msgTitle = "Row or Column Values Too Large"
            msgPrompt = "Row <= 65536 and Column <= 256" & vbCrLf & vbCrLf
            msgResult = MsgBox(msgPrompt, vbOKCancel + vbExclamation, msgTitle)
            go_ok = False
        End If

    End Sub
```

EXHIBIT 9.18   Error checking subroutines for the row and column location values

If we find a value that exceeds either limit, we will produce an error message. See Exhibits 9.18 and 9.19.

Alternative Approach to the Task of Color Selection   In the above example User-Form, we need to build a menu that allows the analyst to choose between three colors. For this, three OptionButtons in a single Frame are perfectly adequate and indeed the most efficient way to build the menu. This approach rapidly begins to become inefficient if we move from 3 choices to 10. It becomes totally unmanageable if we move from 10 choices to 40, the number of colors in the Excel Worksheet palette. If we need to accommodate a larger number of choices, we need to discard the OptionButton approach and employ a ListBox Object. A ListBox is one of the Objects on the UserForm Toolbox Menu (it is the rightmost symbol in the topmost row). To add a ListBox, do what you would do with any other Object in the menu: Simply click on it and then on the UserForm.

In Exhibit 9.20 we see the revised UserForm Menu with the Frame and Option-Buttons removed and the ListBox Object added. The important properties we need to set for a ListBox are its name, the list of items it will contain, whether we can select a single option or multiple options from the list, and a default display value we would like the list to initialize to.

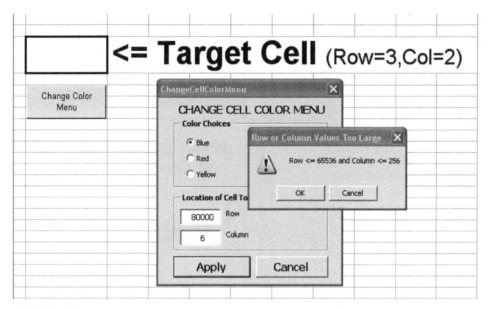

EXHIBIT 9.19   Error message for row column location reasonableness check

We already know how to rename an Object from its default designation by using the (Name) entries in the Properties Editor window. We next need to create the list of items to be displayed on an Excel Worksheet and set the ListBox property to reference that location. We do this in one of two ways. The ListBox property "Row Source" needs the name of the Excel Worksheet and the set of cells containing the information. In this example we have created a worksheet named "ColorList" and have listed the colors of the visible spectrum plus infrared and ultraviolet at either end. These entries occupy the cells A1:A9 in the worksheet. We can set the value of the "Row Source" property either by referencing the cells directly or by placing them in a range and referencing them by the Range name. Thus either:

```
ColorList!A1:A9
```

or

```
ColorList!ColorListSelection
```

is a valid designation. See Exhibit 9.20.

To restrict the analyst to a single choice, we next click on the property "Multi-Select". Here we will utilize the default setting of "fmMultiSelectSingle" to restrict the analyst to a single selection from the list. (If we need to design a ListBox with a multiple selection capability, we would specify the "fmMultiSelectMulti" alternative for this property.)

The final property we will designate is a default value that appears as the selected item of the list when it is initially displayed. To do this we merely select the property "Text" and click on the item of the list we wish to designate as the default value.

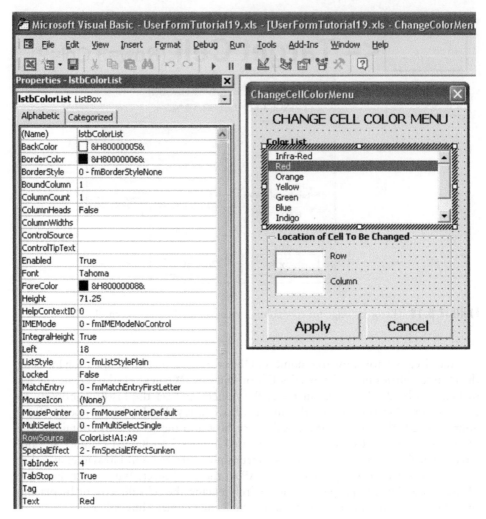

EXHIBIT 9.20   Using a ListBox for multiple choice alternatives

Now that we have the ListBox in place, we will need to be able to identify what choices have been made by the analyst when the "Apply" action is taken. Each ListBox has a number of properties that help us decipher the entries from the list. The first is the ".ListCount" property, which tells us how many items are in the ListBox. This count starts at 0 so in the case of the Color List in our example, the value of "lstbColorList.ListCount" would be 8. We can then loop through the ".Selected" property, a Boolean array, that will read TRUE if the element of the ListBox was selected and FALSE if it was not. Thus if the color Orange, the third item in the list, having the array location of 2, was selected, "lstbColorList.Selected(2)" would be TRUE. Once we have identified the array location, we add 1 to the array value to indicate the true location in the list on the Excel Worksheet. We now have the choice indicated by the analyst!

We will see this feature used where we have large lists to choose from, especially in the Geographic Collateral Eligibility Selection Menus that follow.

Conclusion   We now have a basic knowledge of UserForms and how to design and write their support code. Let us see how we can apply these simple principles to the UserForms we will employ in the CCFG.

MENUS OF THE CCFG

We can now begin to build the menus of the CCFG. Our approach to this problem will be to address the menus in the order that it would be logical to *use* them when running the model. Keeping this idea in mind, we would then step through the modeling exercise by using the menus in the following manner.

- **Main Menu.** On the Main Menu, we will work our way through a list of activities needed to set up a model run. A set of CommandButtons will direct us to other menus of the CCFG.
- **Run Options Menu.** This menu will present us with a series of actions that we can have the model perform against a collateral pool containing up to five sub-portfolios. These actions can include creating collateral tests, performing collateral selection activities, reporting the results of those activities, producing collateral files of eligible and/or ineligible collateral, specifying amortization criteria, amortizing the collateral, producing a cash flow files, selecting specific reporting choices from a template file collection, and, last, producing a collateral reporting package from the results.
- **Geographic Selection Criteria Menu.** Specify the geographic selection tests for up to five sub-portfolios of loans. This will include specifications to include/exclude collateral on a regional, state, and Metropolitan Statistical Area (MSA).
- **Financial Selection Criteria Editor.** Use this menu to create up to five sets of collateral selection criteria based on financial or demographic characteristics of the collateral.
- **Collateral Pool and Sub-Portfolio Menu.** This menu will allow us to select how many (none, some, all) of the collateral sub-portfolios will be subject to a criteria selection process based on either a financial and demographic basis or on a geographic basis, or both.
- **Cash Flow Amortization Parameters Menu.** This menu allows us to enter our choice of three different prepayment/default methodologies. These are a Uniform, Demographic or Geographic Methodologies.
- **Reports Editor and Menu.** This menu will allow us to specify a report package for the collateral pools and each of the collateral sub-portfolios.

We will now examine the information that each of these menus will provide the model. We will also try to design these menus so that the data from the environment combined with our own choice of options can be transmitted to the model in the most efficient, effective, and clear manner possible. One last note before we begin. Remember that there are five more chapters following this one that focus on the implementation of the CCFG. Our goal in this chapter is to provide a working design, complete with supporting VBA or UserForm support code that conveys the information from the data sources—*and only that*! It is sufficient in this chapter to, for example, have the Geographic Selection Menu provide the CCFG with a coherent set of selection criteria from which the model can then *later* perform the selection activity. The actual selection criteria processing code will be addressed in detail in Chapter 11, "Writing the Collateral Selection Code." This is also true of the VBA subroutines of the CCFG that will perform processing tasks, such as selecting the collateral data files, reading and processing collateral pool financial/demographic data, applying the prepayments and defaults assumptions in the amortization process, and writing the collateral report package. These activities lie considerably beyond the scope of a chapter on menus. The goal in this chapter is to provide the menu interface to allow the information needed by the model to be accessed by the CCFG and then translated into a form the model can make use of in its various operations!

MAIN MENU

The Main Menu is the topmost menu of the CCFG.

Purpose of the Menu

The Main Menu is the launching pad for all activity taken by the analyst. It is the place from which we will visit the other subordinate menus to establish the conditions under which the model will operate and which operations it will perform.

Structure of the Menu

The Main Menu contains a series of CommandButtons that the CCFG user can employ to navigate across the system. See Exhibit 9.21. The button notations are straightforward and are aligned in the sequential order of a typical model run.
    The steps in a typical CCFG model run are:

Step 1. Enter the Run Options that you wish the CCFG model to perform.
Step 2. Specify the Collateral Data files of the collateral sub-portfolios that will comprise the pool.
Step 3. If the sub-portfolios are to be subjected to a collateral selection process, specify:
 ■ The geographic selection criteria.
 ■ The financial and demographic selection criteria.
Step 4. Perform the selection process and report the results.
Step 5. Stipulate the cash flow valuation criteria in the form of prepayment, default, and recovery rates. The Market Value Decline (MVD) rate is also specified at this time. These can consist of either:
 ■ MSA or state level performance curves.
 ■ A base default rate assumptions with adjustments based on loan types and demographics.
 ■ A uniform assumption applied to all the collateral.
Step 6. Designate the report package and produce it.

Collateral Cash Flow Generator Main Menu

Set Model Run Options	**SET THE RUN OPTIONS** Use the Run Options menu to specify what operations you wish the CCFG to perform.	
Identify Collateral Data Files	**SPECIFY THE SOURCES OF COLLATERAL INFORMATION** Designate the pool or sub-portfolio collateral information files using the Collateral Pool Menu.	
Define Geographic Selection Criteria	**SET GEOGRAPHIC COLLATERAL SELECTION CRITERIA** Create, save or load the geograhic collateral selection criteria of State and SMA eligibility conditions.	*Run*
Define Fin/Demo Selection Criteria	**SET FINANCIAL/DEMOGRAPHIC SELECTION CRITERIA** Create or load the financial and demographic selection create using the Selection Criteria Editor Menu.	*the*
Set Amortization Parameters	**SET CASH FLOW AMORTIZATION PARAMETERS** Define, save, or load prepayment and default assumptions using the Prepayment and Defaults Menu.	*Model*
Define Report Package	**DEFINE THE REPORTING PACKAGE COMPOSITION** Define, save, and load report package configurations using the Collateral Reports Editor and Menu.	
Set Dates and Rate Info	**SET RATES and DATES INFORMATION** Set the Day count conventions for the periods of the deal and basic financial and index rates.	

EXHIBIT 9.21   Main Menu

Operation of the Menu

The Main Menu is probably the simplest menu of the entire CCFG in terms of both its content and the VBA support code behind it. The role of the Main Menu is simply to provide a framework from which all of the other more detailed menus can be accessed. Once we have used these much more complicated and detailed menus to specify the model's operational parameters and to indicate the actions we wish it to perform, we then run the model.

Thus each of the seven buttons to the left-hand side of the menu allows the analyst to immediately access a subordinate menu. When all the entries to these menus have been completed, we simply return to the Main Menu to run the program. The support code for the Main Menu is displayed in Exhibit 9.22.

We will now turn our attention to the other subordinate menus of the CCFG and learn their layouts and features, so we know what to do when we arrive at them from the Main Menu!

RUN OPTIONS MENU

The role of the Run Options Menu is to allow the analyst to communicate to the CCFG the range of actions that need to be taken on each of the sub-portfolios in the collateral set of the deal for this model run. The deal collateral pool can have up to five component collateral sub-portfolios. When the CCFG performs the collateral selection process or, for any matter, ANY of the processes, it will perform them working at the sub-portfolios level only. Only upon conclusion of all activities conducted on the collateral of the sub-portfolios will the results be rolled up into the pool level.

```
'======================================================================
' MAIN MENU
'======================================================================

'======================================================================
' Button macro calls from the Main Menu
'======================================================================
Sub RunCCFG()
    Call CCFG_Model
End Sub
Sub MainMenu_RunOptionsMenu()
    Sheets("RunOptionsMenu").Select
End Sub
Sub MainMenu_CollateralPoolMenu()
    Sheets("CollatPoolMenu").Select
End Sub
Sub MainMenu_GeoCriteriaEditorMenu()
    Sheets("GeoSelectMenu").Select
End Sub
Sub MainMenu_FinDemoCriteriaEditorMenu()
    Sheets("FinSelectMenu").Select
End Sub
Sub MainMenu_CFAmortizationMenu()
    Sheets("PrepayDefaultMenu").Select
End Sub
Sub MainMenu_ReportEditorMenu()
    Sheets("ReportsEditorMenu").Select
End Sub
Sub MainMenu_RatesAndDatesMenu()
    Sheets("RatesDatesMenu").Select
End Sub
```

EXHIBIT 9.22 Support code for the Main Menu

Description of the Run Time Options

The complete potential range of activities that the CCFG can perform against any of the sub-portfolios is listed on the Run Options Menu. The tasks are also in the order that the CCFG would perform them in a standard model run, moving from left to right.

The list of run options that would be performed as part of a complete, all-inclusive collateral selection process consists of the following:

1. **Apply Initial Data Screening tests.** This run option screens the collateral for illegal, illegible, or missing, data in each of the collateral loan records. An example of each would be:
   ■ **Illegal.** The remaining term of the loans is greater than the original term of the loan. The property type, occupancy code, or any other demographic information has a code that is not recognized; that is, property type code can assume a value of 1 through 6 and the code in the record is 23.
   ■ **Illegible.** There is an alphabetic symbol in a field that can only have numeric values.
   ■ **Missing.** A datum in the record is simply not present, or the record information is not complete enough to provide the elements necessary for a risk assessment or amortization calculation to be performed.

2. **Apply Financial and Demographic tests.** Perform the collateral selection process using the constraints input by the analyst in the Financial Selection Criteria Editor. These eligibility tests are stored in up to five sets, each set of can contain a maximum of 20 individual tests.
3. **Apply Geographic Area tests.** Perform the collateral eligibility tests based on basis of geographic location. As with the financial selection tests above, the analyst can create a maximum of five sets of geographic location criteria tests. The analyst, in the Geographic Selection Criteria Menu, creates these test sets.
4. **Apply Geographic Concentration tests.** These tests are performed at the pool level after the collateral selection process in the sub-portfolios is complete and the aggregate pool collateral is finalized. It is also specified on the Geographic Selection Criteria Menu.
5. **Eligible Collateral Cash Flow Waterfall file.** This option produces a Cash Flow Waterfall file for use by the Structuring Model. The file will also contain a single worksheet for each of the sub-portfolios delineating their component cash flows.

The layout of the Run Options Menu is displayed in Exhibit 9.23.

Requirements of the Run Options Menu

The requirements of the Run Options are straightforward. The first and foremost requirement is simply to accept the analyst inputs and get them into VBA variables that the CCFG can make use of. Before the information can be transferred to the VBA, we need to create a number of Ranges in the Excel Menu itself. The use of Ranges will make it significantly easier to maintain and modify the menu if we need to do so in the future. After the information on the menu has been made available to the CCFG in a series of Ranges, we can read the information from the Ranges and error check it. Once it is error checked and we are sure that it is in a form we can use, we will load it into VBA arrays that we will pass around the CCFG to control the sequence and scope of the computational activity of the model. These arrays will have one position for each of the five sub-portfolios that comprise the pool of collateral.

Range Names of the Run Options Menu

The Run Options Menu will be assigned the following Range names:

- "m02CollatBaseTest". This Range covers the column of responses under the "Initial Loan Record Data Screening Tests", Run Option 1.
- "m02CollatSelectFinGeoTest". This Range covers the three columns of responses under the "Apply Financial and Demographic Tests" and "Apply Geographic (State & MSA) Tests", Run Options 2 and 3.
- "m02CollatSelectGeoConTest". This Range covers the column under the "Apply Geographic Concentration Limits", Run Option 4.
- "m02WriteCFFiles". This Range covers the column of responses under "Produce Eligible Collateral Cash Flows", Run Options 5.

CCFG Run/Output Options Menu

Pool or Sub Portfolio	Collateral File Name	Collateral Selection Processes				Collateral Cash Flow Files
Run Option Code =>		REQUIRED	OPTIONAL			
		1	2	3	4	5
		Initial Loan Record Data Screening Tests	Apply Financial and Demographic Tests	Apply Geographic (State & MSA) Tests	Apply Geographic Concentration Limits	Produce Eligible Collateral Cash Flows
#0	C:\VBA_Book2\Code\data\CollateralPool\Pool01Test1.xlsm	Y	N	N	Y	N
#1	No File Selected		1	1		
#2	No File Selected		1	1		
#3	No File Selected		1	1		
#4	No File Selected		1	1		
#5	No File Selected		1	1		

Remember: Enter the names of the collateral files in the CollatPoolMenu! This menu will pick them up from there.

Return To Main Menu

To avoid having either the Financial/Demographic Selection tests (column 2) or the Geographic Selection tests (column 3) run against the collateral enter a "N" for "No" in these fields instead of a collateral selection test set number.

EXHIBIT 9.23 Run Options Menu

```
'==================================================================
'RUN OPTIONS MENU
'==================================================================
Public gPortActive(0 To NUM_PORTS)   As Boolean   'is this portfolio active?
Public gROInitDataTest               As Boolean   'apply base collat screening
Public gROApplyFinDemo()             As Boolean   'apply fin/demo test
Public gROApplyGeoSelect()           As Boolean   'apply geo test
Public gROTestSetFinDemo()           As Integer   'apply fin/demo test
Public gROTestSetGeoSelect()         As Integer   'apply geo test set
Public gROApplyGeoConcen             As Boolean   'apply geo concentration?
Public gROCFWaterfall                As Boolean   'write cf waterfall file
```

EXHIBIT 9.24 Declaration of the Run Option arrays

You will notice that each of the Range names in the Run Option Menu has a prefix of "m02". This is the identifying prefix for this menu. (The prefix "m01" was reserved for use in the Main Menu.) We will prefix all of the Ranges in the menus with a "m(number)" designation. This serves to group them in the Names Editor in Excel and also allows us to quickly identify the Ranges that are being used in each menu of the CCFG.

Making the Choices Available to the CCFG

With the Range names in place on the menu, we can next declare the VBA arrays that will hold the menu information that the CCFG will read from their contents.

We will declare these arrays in the "A_Globals" module as shown in Exhibit 9.24. When we declare these arrays, we will prefix them with "gRO", which indicates that they are global in scope and variables that support the Run Options Menu.

Error Checking Inputs

Before we rush off to load the contents of the Run Options Menu into the arrays that we just created, we should pause for a moment and consider error checking the inputs before we let the CCFG tear into them. We may have inputs that are in the wrong format, say String data type formats when they should be Integer or Double data type formats, or vice versa. They may exceed the value limits that are acceptable, say a selection test set number greater than five for Run Options 2 or 3. We need to stop them at the gate (so to speak)! We will do so by error checking them *before* we read them into the arrays of the CCFG.

To do this we will need to read the values and test the formats of the menu inputs while they are still contained in the Ranges, prior to assigning them to the VBA arrays. We will need to design the following tests:

- Tests to determine that the entries for Run Options 2 and 3 the Selection Test set designations are numeric in form.
- Tests to determine that the above are also within the limits of from "N", "NO", or "No" (take no action), to "5", the largest value allowed since we are currently limited to five test sets.

```
Sub MainProgram_errCheck_AllMenus()
    Call errRunOptionsMenu
    Call errCFAmortizationMenu
End Sub
```

EXHIBIT 9.25   "errCheck_AllMenus" subroutine

- We also want to inform the analyst if any of the Run Options have been elected that are specified to be applied to nonexistent sub-portfolios. It would not be a good thing for the analyst to believe analysis is being performed when it is not!

To begin the process, we will add a line to the subroutine responsible for managing the entire error checking process for all the menus of the CCFG. This is the "errCheck_AllMenus" subroutine. See Exhibit 9.25.

"errRunOptionsMenu" Subroutine   This subroutine is the controlling subroutine for all the error checking that will be performed on the Run Options Menu. It is broken into two parts. The upper part of the subroutine performs the first two tests, one for numeric entries in the Selection Set fields and the second that these entries are between zero and the maximum number of selection sets allowed. The lower portion of the subroutine then checks that we are not performing actions against nonexistent sub-portfolios.

The first step in the process is to determine if we are using pool level data or a collection of sub-portfolio files. We next call the subroutine "RunOptions_RedimArrays" that, based on the pool versus sub-portfolio determination, re-dimensions all the Run Option Menu arrays listed in Exhibit 9.24. After the arrays are dimensioned, we next set the Boolean variable "mPrintErrMsg" to FALSE (no error messages to print as of now)! We next initialize the array "OptSelected" to FALSE (no options selected as yet).

We next call the subroutine "errRunOpts_OptSelActivePorts". This subroutine first checks to see if the pool or sub-portfolio is active and then checks that the fields of the menu for the selected items are non-NULL. If they are the value of the variable, "mPrintErrMsg" is set to TRUE, and the "OptSelected" array value also is set to TRUE, indicating that there is a problem with this particular menu entry. Based on the entries in the "OptSelected" array, the subroutine "errRunOpts_SetPortsMsgBody" now builds a series of error messages, displays them in a TextBox message to the screen, and halts the execution of the CCFG. A very convenient feature of UserForms is that all the VBA code that we build to support the form itself becomes part of the form. We may decide to reuse a particular UserForm in another application. Any support code in the VBA section of the UserForm is included in the exported module. We would not have to rebuild any of the code contained in the exported module; it is ready to run!

If all of the fields are non-NULL, we will still need to test some of them for non-numeric content and, if the field content IS numeric, that the values are between one and five. We will first call the subroutine "errRunOpts_InitTestSetErrorArrays" that initializes two arrays, "mInvalidTest" for the numerics test results and "msgLarge" to test that the entry is greater the maximum number of selection sets (now five).

```
Sub errRunOptionsMenu()

    'set the number of portfolios based on what type of data we have
    If gPoolLevelData Then
        BegPort = 0: EndPort = 0
    Else
        BegPort = 1: EndPort = NUM_PORTS
    End If
    'dimension all the global arrays
    Call RunOptions_RedimArrays
    'assume we don't have to print the error message
    mPrintErrMsg = False
    'check that one run option is selected for the Pool or each active
    ' Sub-Portfolio
    '0 index is for Pool Level data only
    For iport = 0 To NUM_PORTS
        OptSelected(iport) = False
    Next iport
    Call errRunOpts_OptSelActivePorts    'locate any errors in the selection grid
    If mPrintErrMsg Then Call errRunOpts_SetPortsMsgBody
    'first we will check that the numeric block of inputs for the collateral
    '   selection criteria test sets are all under the maximum value
    'this test is for Run Options 2, and 3 only
    Call errRunOpts_InitTestSetErrorArrays    'initialize terror detection array
    Call errRunOpts_TestSetNonNumeric        'non-numerc entries for test sets
    Call errRunOpts_TestSetNumTooLarge       'invalid collateral test set number
    If mPrintErrMsg Then Call errRunOpts_SetCollatPortMsgBody

End Sub
```

EXHIBIT 9.26 "errRunOptionsMenu" subroutine

The subroutine "errRunOpts_TestSetNonNumeric" now tests options 2 and 3 to determine if the contents of the fields are numeric. After these tests are completed, the subroutine "errRunOpts_TestSetNumTooLarge" next tests to see if they exceed the maximum test set limit. If either of these subroutines detects a nonnumeric or illegal entry, the "mPrintErrMsg" is set to TRUE. If this is the case, the subroutine "errRunOpts_SetCollatPortMsgBody" will produce the appropriate error messages, place them in a TextBox, and display them to the screen. Execution of the CCFG then ends.

You will note that, in keeping with our policy of identifying related subroutines, all of the subroutines in this group have the prefix "errRunOpts". This identifies them as error checking code directed to the Run Options Menu. See Exhibit 9.26.

We will now look at some of these subroutines in more detail.

"errRunOpts_InitTestSetErrorArrays" Subroutine   This subroutine simply initializes the two arrays we will use to record the test results for the nonnumeric tests and then tests if the value of the Selection Criteria Test Set is greater than the maximum tests that number of available selection criteria test the model can currently accommodate. The variables "mInvalidTest" and "mLarge" capture the results of the aforementioned tests respectively. See Exhibit 9.27.

"errRunOpts_TestSetNonNumeric" Subroutine   Now that we have something to store the results of the error testing, we can proceed to perform it. The first set of tests will be to check that all of the entries to the Run Option 2 and 3 columns are

```
Sub errRunOpts_InitTestSetErrorArrays()

    'initialize the error grid -- this grid records either the occurance of a
    '  non-numeric entry into one of the collateral selection test sets or a
    '  test set number that exceeds the max test set value
    For ip = BegPort To EndPort
        For itest = 1 To 2
            mInvalidTest(ip, itest) = False
            msgLarge(ip, itest) = False
        Next itest
    Next ip

End Sub
```

EXHIBIT 9.27   "errRunOpts_InitTestSetErrorArrays" subroutine

numeric. If they are not, we will record this fact in the "mInvalidTest" array and use the contents of that array later to construct our error message.

This subroutine works its way, line by line, down the Ranges of the Run Options Menu, testing each of the values in the rows. If it finds a nonnumeric entry, it stores it as TRUE in the corresponding location in the array "mInvalidTest". See Exhibit 9.28.

```
Sub errRunOpts_TestSetNonNumeric()

    'read through each of the portfolios based on the type of data as
    '  determined above
    For ip = BegPort To EndPort
        'financial/demographic selection test set fields
        mInvalidTest(ip, 1) = True
        If Range("m02CollatSelectFinGeoTest").Cells(ip + 1, 1) = "N" Or _
            Range("m02CollatSelectFinGeoTest").Cells(ip + 1, 1) = "No" Or _
            Range("m02CollatSelectFinGeoTest").Cells(ip + 1, 1) = "NO" Then
                mInvalidTest(ip, 1) = False
                gROApplyFinDemo(ip) = False
        Else
                mInvalidTest(ip, 1) = _
                (IsNumeric(Range("m02CollatSelectFinGeoTest").Cells(ip + 1, 1)) _
                    = False)
                If mInvalidTest(ip, 1) = False Then gROApplyFinDemo(ip) = True
        End If
        'read the geographic selection test set fields
        mInvalidTest(ip, 2) = True
        If Range("m02CollatSelectFinGeoTest").Cells(ip + 1, 2) = "N" Or _
            Range("m02CollatSelectFinGeoTest").Cells(ip + 1, 2) = "No" Or _
            Range("m02CollatSelectFinGeoTest").Cells(ip + 1, 2) = "NO" Then
                mInvalidTest(ip, 2) = False
                gROApplyGeoSelect(ip) = False
        Else
                mInvalidTest(ip, 2) = _
                (IsNumeric(Range("m02CollatSelectFinGeoTest").Cells(ip + 1, 2)) _
                    = False)
                If mInvalidTest(ip, 1) = False Then gROApplyGeoSelect(ip) = True
        End If
    Next ip

    'set the "print error message" trigger if any of the mInvalidTest
    '  variables are TRUE
    For ip = BegPort To EndPort
        If mInvalidTest(ip, 1) Or mInvalidTest(ip, 2) Then mPrintErrMsg = True
    Next ip

End Sub
```

EXHIBIT 9.28   "errRunOpts_TestSetNonNumeric" subroutine

"errRunOpts_TestSetNumTooLarge" Subroutine   Next we will test all entries made in the Range "m02CollatSelectFinGeoTest" to ensure that any test set numbers entered are between the limits of zero and "NUM_POOLS" or "NUM_PORTS" (currently a value of 5). If any values violating this limit are found, the corresponding array positions of the array "msgLarge" are set to TRUE.

The first determination the subroutine makes is to establish if any other testing is needed at all! If the analyst has entered "N", "No", or "NO" in the field, the option is inactive and we do not have to test the value of the selection set at all. If the value in the field is numeric, we do need to test to determine if there is a valid entry. As we did in the prior subroutine, we will test all the values of the "msgLarge" array to see if any of them have been set to TRUE, that is, an error has been detected. If there is an error condition indicated, we will set the value of the variable "PrintHeader" to TRUE. This will alert the CCFG that we will be producing error messages at a later time and that we need to assemble and display an error message to the analyst. See Exhibit 9.29.

"errRunOpts_SetCollatPortMsgBody" Subroutine   We have now completed both sets of tests related to the numeric entries in the Collateral Selection Process section of the Run Options Menu. With the error condition information in hand, we can now translate this information into an intelligible error message and, if needed, inform the analyst of the problems that we have detected.

In the beginning of the subroutine, we set the value of the variable "test_set" as the limit that we will use to evaluate the entries of the Range against. Next we construct the components of an error message. Depending on the error conditions detected, we will then build the complete error message from these pieces. See Exhibit 9.30.

```
Sub errRunOpts_TestSetNumTooLarge()

Dim MaxTest         As Integer
Dim iChoice         As Integer

    'is the selecion test set # requested on the menu is <= 0 or > 5?
    MaxTest = NUM_PORTS
    For ip = BegPort To EndPort
        For iChoice = 1 To 2          '1 = fin select, 2 = geo select
            'financial selection menu entry
            If Range("m02CollatSelectFinGeoTest").Cells(ip + 1, iChoice) <> "N" Or _
               Range("m02CollatSelectFinGeoTest").Cells(ip + 1, iChoice) <> "No" Or _
               Range("m02CollatSelectFinGeoTest").Cells(ip + 1, iChoice) <> "NO" Then
                        msgLarge(ip + 1, iChoice) = False
            Else
                If mInvalidTest(ip, 1) = False Then
                    If Range("m02CollatSelectFinGeoTest").Cells(ip + 1, iChoice) > MaxTest Or _
                       Range("m02CollatSelectFinGeoTest").Cells(ip + 1, iChoice) < 0 Then
                            msgLarge(ip + 1, iChoice) = True
                    End If
                End If
            End If
        Next iChoice
    Next ip
    'check to see if we need to print the message box with errors
    For ip = BegPort To EndPort
        If msgLarge(ip + 1, 1) Or msgLarge(ip + 1, 2) Then
            mPrintErrMsg = True  'there is at least one error in the set
        End If
    Next ip

End Sub
```

EXHIBIT 9.29   "errRunOpts_TestSetNumTooLarge" subroutine

```
Sub errRunOpts_SetCollatPortMsgBody()

Dim itests              As Integer

    mNumTestSet = NUM_PORTS
    'Error message components
    msgHeader = "RUN OPTIONS MENU INPUT ERROR MESSAGES " & vbCrLf & vbCrLf
    msgInfo(1) = "Pool Level Data" & vbCrLf
    msgInfo(2) = "Sub-Portfolio Level Data" & vbCrLf
    msgInfo(3) = "Selection Set Entries Must be Numeric and Between 1 and " & _
                    mNumTestSet & " " & vbCrLf
    msgPort = " Portfolio #"
    'non-numeric error messages
    msgNonNum(1) = " Collateral Selection Set Non Numeric" & vbCrLf
    msgNonNum(2) = " Geographic Selection Set Non Numeric" & vbCrLf
    'numeric entry too large error messages
    mLarge(1) = " Collateral Selection Set Too Large" & vbCrLf
    mLarge(2) = " Geographic Selection Set Too Large" & vbCrLf

    msgBody = ""            'set the error message string to NULL
    If mPrintErrMsg Then
        'write the customized message box header based on Pool
        ' or Sub-Portfolios
        If gPoolLevelData Then
            msgBody = msgBody & msgHeader & msgInfo(1) & msgInfo(3) & vbCrLf
        Else
            msgBody = msgBody & msgHeader & msgInfo(2) & msgInfo(3)
        End If
        'construct the remainder of the message
        For ip = BegPort To EndPort
            For itests = 1 To 2
                If mInvalidTest(ip, itests) Then    'nonnumeric entry
                    msgBody = msgBody & msgPort & ip & vbCrLf
                    If itests = 1 Then msgBody = msgBody & msgNonNum(1)
                    If itests = 2 Then msgBody = msgBody & msgNonNum(2)
                End If
                If msgLarge(ip, itests) Then        'numeric entry too large
                    msgBody = msgBody & msgPort & ip & vbCrLf
                    If itests = 1 Then msgBody = msgBody & mLarge(1)
                    If itests = 2 Then msgBody = msgBody & mLarge(2)
                End If
            Next itests
        Next ip
        'write the message and end the program
        Sheets("RunOptionsMenu").Select
        msgResult = MsgBox(msgBody, cMsgButtonCode1, msgTitle)
        End
    End If

End Sub
```

EXHIBIT 9.30   "errRunOpts_SetCollatPortMsgBody" subroutine

The variable that will become the *entire* error message is "msgBody". This variable will start with a null value and then will have various members of the error message components appended to it. The loop goes through its processes and in the end produces an error message similar to that seen in Exhibit 9.31.

"errRunOpts_OptSelActivePorts" Subroutine   Just before we enter this subroutine from the "errRunOptionsMenu" subroutine, we initialize an array to record the results of our test results. These tests will check to see if the analyst has entered at least one Run Options into the rows for each sub-portfolio that is active.

This subroutine employs a looping structure that runs from one to five for the sub-portfolios. If any entry is found, the condition of the "OptSelect" variable for

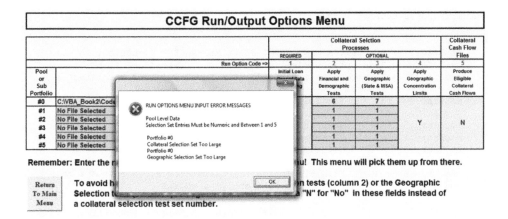

EXHIBIT 9.31 Error message

that portfolio is set to TRUE. At the end of the If..Then blocks, we will test to see if the "OptSelect" variable has retained its initial setting of FALSE. If it has, it means that there are *no* Run Options checked for this sub-portfolio. It therefore sets the "PrintHeader" variable to TRUE, meaning that we will have to produce an error message. See Exhibit 9.32.

```
Sub errRunOpts_OptSelActivePorts()

Dim ientry          As Integer  'test counter for the six entries

    'check the inputs by the number of Pool or Sub-Portfolio entities
    'because we are dealing with checking only the ranges of the menu here we
    ' need to increment the beginning and ending portfolio loop counters by 1;
    ' thus Pool Level data is in the first position of the Range and the
    ' Sub-Portfolios are in positions 2 to 6.
    For ip = BegPort + 1 To EndPort + 1
        If gPortActive(ip - 1) Then     'gPortActive dimensioned 0 to NUM_PORTS
            For ientry = 1 To 6
                mError(ientry, ip) = False     'no errors detected yet
            Next ientry
            'check Base Test entry
            If Range("m02CollatBaseTest").Text = "" Then mError(1, ip) = True
            'check Financial/Geographic Election Test entries
            If Range("m02CollatSelectFinGeoTest").Cells(ip, 1).Text = "" Or _
                Range("m02CollatSelectFinGeoTest").Cells(ip, 2).Text = "" Then _
                    mError(2, ip) = True
            'check Geographic Concentrations Test entry
            If Range("m02CollatSelectGeoConTest").Text = "" Then _
                    mError(3, ip) = True
            'test to see if any error were detected, if yes, print message later
            For ientry = 1 To 3
                If mError(ientry, ip) = True Then
                    mPrintErrMsg = True     'at least entry is wrong
                    OptSelected(ip) = False 'this sub-portfolio is wrong
                    Exit For
                End If
            Next ientry
        End If
    Next ip

End Sub
```

EXHIBIT 9.32 "errRunOpts_OptSelActivePorts" subroutine

```
Sub errRunOpts_SetPortsMsgBody()

    'Error message components
    msgHeader = "RUN OPTION MENU INPUT ERROR MESSAGES " & vbCrLf & vbCrLf
    msgInfo(1) = "Run Options missing for the Pool specified" & vbCrLf
    msgInfo(2) = "Run Options missing for the Sub-Portfolios specified" & _
            vbCrLf
    msgPort = " for Sub-Portfolio #"
    'components of the Run Options Menu
    msgEntry(1) = "      Base Test entry" & vbCrLf
    msgEntry(2) = "      Financial/Geographic Selections Test entry" & vbCrLf
    msgEntry(3) = "      Geographic Concentrations Test entry" & vbCrLf
    msgEntry(4) = "      Selection Results Files entry" & vbCrLf
    msgEntry(5) = "      Eligible/Ineligible Collateral Files entry" & vbCrLf
    msgEntry(6) = "      Cash Flows File entry" & vbCrLf

    msgBody = ""                    'initialize the contents of the error message
    If mPrintErrMsg Then
        If gPoolLevelData Then       'Pool Level data only
            msgBody = msgBody & msgHeader & msgInfo(1)
            For irow = 1 To 6
                If mError(1, irow) Then msgBody = msgBody & msgEntry(irow)
            Next irow
        Else
            'will print out messages by each of the Sub-Portfolios
            For ip = 2 To NUM_PORTS + 1
                If gPortActive(ip - 1) And (OptSelected(ip - 1) = False) Then
                    msgBody = msgBody & " " & msgPort & ip & vbCrLf
                    For irow = 1 To 6
                        If mError(ip, irow) Then _
                            msgBody = msgBody & msgEntry(irow)
                    Next irow
                End If
            Next ip
        End If
        'print the message and end the program
        Sheets("RunOptionsMenu").Select
        msgResult = MsgBox(msgBody, cMsgButtonCode1, msgTitle)
        End
    End If

End Sub
```

EXHIBIT 9.33   "errRunOpts_SetPortsMsgBody" subroutine

"errRunOpts_SetPortsMsgBody" Subroutine If the "PrintHeader" is TRUE, we have an error condition arising from the subroutine "errRunOpts_OptSel ActivePorts". We therefore need to be informed of which active sub-portfolios are lacking any selected Run Options. This subroutine will now read each of the five members of the "OptSelected" arrays and produce a one-line error message for each pool/portfolio combination lacking entries. See Exhibit 9.33.

Reading the Run Options Menu Inputs

After wading through all this error checking code, it is almost anticlimactic when we finally get to read the now-vetted data. The subroutine that we will employ for this purpose will be "RunOptions_ReadMenu". We will place a call to this subroutine into the "MainProgram_ReadAllMenuInputs" subroutine in the "A_MainProgram"

```
Sub MainProgram_ReadAllMenuInputs()

    Call RunOptions_ReadMenu

End Sub
```

EXHIBIT 9.34   "MainProgram_ReadAllMenuInputs" subroutine

module. In the 'RunOptions_ReadMenu" subroutine, we will use a simple loop to pass through the now-screened Range contents and load their contents into the set of "gRO" arrays that we declared earlier. Next we will use a nested For..Next loop to read the information from the Ranges into the VBA arrays. See Exhibits 9.34, 9.35, and 9.36.

Other Remarks

The structure and use of Ranges by this menu is fairly typical of a complex VBA Menu. We will not be covering all of the menus of the CCFG in this amount of detail. We will, however, next look at a pair of complex menus that employ UserForms. These two menus will be the only other menus that we will discuss at this level of specificity. You can examine the support code of the other menus of the CCFG that are on the Web site.

COLLATERAL POOL MENU

Having all the selection criteria, cash flow calculation, or reporting subroutines in the world built into the CCFG will not help us if we do not have any data available

```
Sub RunOptions_RedimArrays()

Dim NumberOfPortfolios  As Integer  'if PoolLevel then "0", else NUM_PORTS
Dim StartPortfolio      As Integer  'first position to store run time options

    'set the data initialization field read counters
    If gPoolLevelData Then
        StartPortfolio = 0      'just the pool information in the 0th position
        NumberOfPortfolios = 0 'a single portfolio in the zeroth position
    Else
        StartPortfolio = 1                  'dimension from 1 to NUM_PORTS
        NumberOfPortfolios = NUM_PORTS 'five sub-portfolios
    End If
    'redimension based on the number of possible Pool or Sub-Portfolio entities
    ReDim gROApplyFinDemo(StartPortfolio To NumberOfPortfolios) As Boolean
    ReDim gROApplyGeoSelect(StartPortfolio To NumberOfPortfolios) As Boolean
    ReDim gROTestSetFinDemo(StartPortfolio To NumberOfPortfolios) As Integer
    ReDim gROTestSetGeoSelect(StartPortfolio To NumberOfPortfolios) As Integer

End Sub
```

EXHIBIT 9.35   "RunOptions_RedimArrays" subroutine

```
Sub RunOptions_ReadMenu()

    Sheets("RunOptionsMenu").Select
    Range("A1").Select
    'read the program runtime options selections
    If gPoolLevelData Then
        'if Pool Level Data read just the first line of the menu
        If gROApplyFinDemo(0) Then _
            gROTestSetFinDemo(0) = Range("m02CollatSelectFinGeoTest").Cells(1, 1)
        If gROApplyGeoSelect(0) Then _
            gROTestSetGeoSelect(0) = Range("m02CollatSelectFinGeoTest").Cells(1, 2)
    Else
        'if Sub-Portfolio Data loop through the 2nd through the 6th lines of the menu
        For ip = 1 To NUM_PORTS
            If gPortActive(ip) Then
                If gROApplyFinDemo(ip) Then _
                    gROTestSetFinDemo(ip) = _
                        Range("m02CollatSelectFinGeoTest").Cells(ip + 1, 1)
                If gROApplyGeoSelect(ip) Then _
                    gROTestSetGeoSelect(ip) = _
                        Range("m02CollatSelectFinGeoTest").Cells(ip + 1, 2)
            End If
        Next ip
    End If
    gROInitDataTest = _
        UCase(Range("m02CollatBaseTest").Cells.Cells.Value2(1, 1)) = "Y"
    gROApplyGeoConcen = _
        UCase(Range("m02CollatSelectGeoConTest").Cells.Cells.Value2) = "Y"
    gROCFWaterfall = _
        UCase(Range("m02WriteCFFiles").Cells.Cells.Value2(1, 1)) = "Y"

End Sub
```

EXHIBIT 9.36 "RunOptions_ReadMenu" subroutine

for it to work on. The Collateral Pool Menu gives us the platform from which to specify the data files that constitute up to five sub-portfolios of collateral.

Purpose of the Menu

The purpose of this menu is to allow us to specify either one pool level data file or up to five sub-portfolio file pathways we will use in the deal. It will also serve to identify these portfolios by their order in the list, which will come in handy when and if we want to examine their eligibility statistics and their cash flows.

The final product that this menu will pass to the CCFG will be an array named "gPortNames". This array will contain the names of the five files from which we will read collateral information.

Layout of the Menu

With the exception of the Main Menu, the Collateral Pool Menu is the least complex menu in the CCFG. To operate the menu, simply click on each of the "Select Pool" CommandButtons. You will see the File Open dialog window. However, instead of opening the file you select, the File Open dialog window will record the pathway of the file and return the complete file pathway to the menu. Then at the point that you wish to open the file, the CCFG will read these file pathways. Using the techniques in the VBA support code of this menu, we can completely

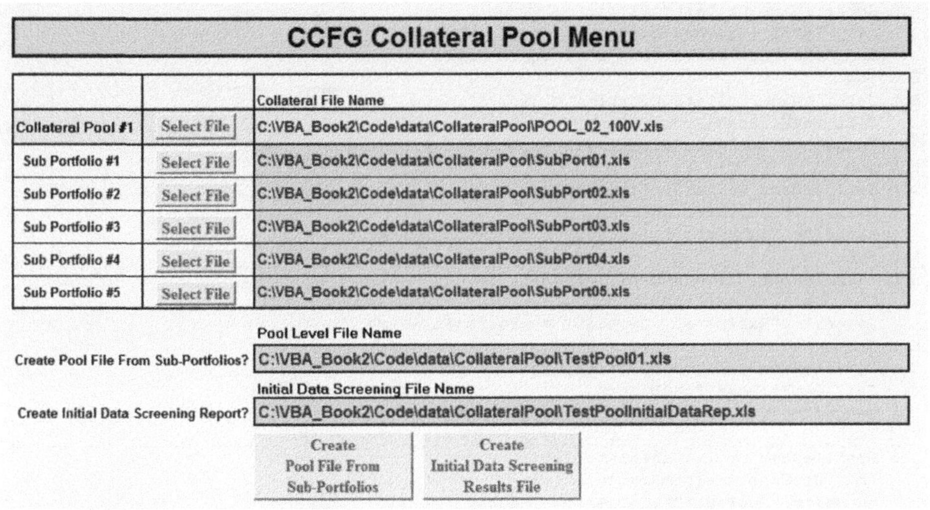

EXHIBIT 9.37 Collateral Pool Menu

eliminate the possibility of misspelling or typographical error for the model analyst! See Exhibit 9.37.

Operation of the Menu

The menu has two sections.

The uppermost section allows the analyst to specify either a pool level collateral file name and its pathway, or up to five sub-portfolio collateral file names and their pathways.

The lower half allows the analyst to do two things:

1. Create a pool level collateral file from the collection of sub-portfolio files displayed below it. The file is given the name and file pathway shown in the entry field "Create Pool File From Sub-Portfolios?"
2. Generate the results report of the Initial Data Screening process and write it to the file name and pathway specified in the field "Create Initial Data Screening Report?".

Filename and Pathway Section When any of the buttons of the menu are clicked, a specific subroutine named "GetFilenameFromButton" is called. This subroutine returns the name of the file selected in the Open File dialog window. The file name is then passed to the calling subroutine. That subroutine assigns the file name pathway to the correct Range cell in the menu where it is then displayed. See Exhibits 9.38 and 9.39.

Create Pool File and Initial Data Screening Report Section There are two fields and two buttons in the lower portion of the menu. The uppermost field is paired with the leftmost button. This feature allows the analyst to combine the contents

```
Sub GetFileName_CollatPool1()
    Call GetFilenameFromButton
    Range("m07CollatPool") = gButtonFileName
End Sub
Sub GetFileName_CollatSubPortfolio1()
    Call GetFilenameFromButton
    Range("m07SubPorts").Cells(1) = gButtonFileName
End Sub
Sub GetFileName_CollatSubPortfolio2()
    Call GetFilenameFromButton
    Range("m07SubPorts").Cells(2) = gButtonFileName
End Sub
Sub GetFileName_CollatSubPortfolio3()
    Call GetFilenameFromButton
    Range("m07SubPorts").Cells(3) = gButtonFileName
End Sub
Sub GetFileName_CollatSubPortfolio4()
    Call GetFilenameFromButton
    Range("m07SubPorts").Cells(4) = gButtonFileName
End Sub
Sub GetFileName_CollatSubPortfolio5()
    Call GetFilenameFromButton
    Range("m07SubPorts").Cells(5) = gButtonFileName
End Sub
```

EXHIBIT 9.38   CommandButton code

of how many sub-portfolio level files are listed above to be combined into a single pool level file whose name is entered into the first field. The CommandButton calls the subroutine "CollatData_WritePoolLevelDataFile". The code of this subroutine resides in the "CollatData_ReadFileInfo" module. This is a very simple piece of code that can be seen on the Web site in the version of the CCFG for this chapter. We will not review this code at this time.

The second field and the rightmost button are a pair. This feature allows the analyst to produce a report displaying the results of the Initial Data Screening process

```
' ===============================================================================
'
' ===============================================================================
Sub GetFilenameFromButton()

    'List of acceptable files
    Filter = "Excel Files (*.xls), *.xls"
    FilterIndex = 1
    Title = "Select a File to Read"
    'get the file name
    FileName = Application.GetOpenFilename _
            (FileFilter:=Filter, FilterIndex:=FilterIndex, _
            Title:=Title)
    'if cancelled
    If FileName = False Then
        MsgBox "No file selected"
        FileName = "No File Selected"
        Exit Sub
    End If
    'if OK
    MsgBox "You selected " & FileName

End Sub
```

EXHIBIT 9.39   "GetFileNameFromButton" subroutine

for the current set of collateral. The report will be written to the file name and file pathway specified in the field "Create Initial Data Screening Report?". The subroutine activated by this CommandButton is "RepInitScreen_MainWriteReport". This subroutine resides in the "Report_CollatDataScreenInit", and we will look at it in some detail in Chapter 10. We will therefore not look at it here.

COLLATERAL GEOGRAPHIC SELECTION CRITERIA MENU

The Geographic Criteria Selection Menu is one of the most important menus of the CCFG. With the current housing crisis, the old saw of "Location, Location, and Location!" has assumed a relevance that in many cases outweighs all of the other collateral demographics combined.

Purpose of the Menu

The purpose of the Geographic Criteria Selection Menu is to allow the analyst of the model the ability to precisely and efficiently select those states and MSA whose properties will be either included or excluded from the collateral portfolio. A second function of the menu is to allow the specification of concentration limits as to the total percentage of current principal balance of the entire portfolio that will be eligible for inclusion in the finished portfolio. The analyst will be given a menu that allows any state or group of states to be assigned a percentage limit of the total portfolio current balance as its concentration limits. Such concentration limits can also be assigned to members of the two sets of the largest MSAs.

We are currently allowing the analyst to specify a maximum of five collateral sub-portfolios. Given the potential for significant differences between these component portfolios, we will allow the analyst to specify up to five sets of selection criteria. This will then provide the analyst with the ability to design a selection set that is unique to each of the sub-portfolios, should the need arise. Each piece of collateral has a state level geographic designation, and many will have MSA level designations. What we therefore need to end up with at the end of the menu session is a set of five checklists, one for each collateral sub-portfolio that tells the CCFG which states and MSA are eligible, of the eligible ones, which have concentration limits, and what are the percentage amounts of the user specified concentration limits are

Geographic Selection and Concentration Issues   Why do we need this menu at all? We need this menu because concentrations of *any* type, but especially geographic concentrations, can dramatically increase risk. This risk may be the result of either man-made or natural phenomena. One such case of economic risk effects would be a state, collection of associated MSAs, or a single large MSA that contains a predominant industry. A particularly relevant example of the risks of concentrated economic effects can be found in the geographic entities of the New York City–Northern New Jersey–Southwestern Connecticut super MSA and their surrounding states. These MSAs are all suffering economic effects from the contraction of the Wall Street financial community layoffs. An example of both long- and short-term effects of a natural disaster is the aftermath of Hurricane Katrina or the 2010 British Petroleum "Deepwater Horizon" oil spill disaster. Extensive portions of the Gulf states' littoral regions have yet to recover, from the effects of Katrina alone, and the MSA of New Orleans will need the most time to fully recover.

General concentration limits also need to be applied to very large states just because of their size. Underperforming or damaged areas of very large states tend to produce ripple effects in other, not directly affected portions of the same state. By their very size, these large states also exert significant effects on the surrounding states with smaller economies that are directly dependent on the health of their larger neighbor to support them. An example of this is the state of California and its relationship with its economic neighbors Arizona, Nevada, New Mexico, Oregon, and Utah, or that of the state of New York, Connecticut, and New Jersey.

How to Manage the Selection Process   The Geographic Criteria Selection Menu is designed to present the analyst with a top-down approach to the task of specifying both the factors of general geographic eligibility and concentration. The hierarchy of this selection approach is:

National Level => State Level => MSA Level

Let us look at the task of specifying eligibility first. The model analyst can specify collateral for inclusion or exclusion at each of the levels listed above. The results of the state level and MSA level selections are recorded in the vectors that we will later use in the selection process itself. Why are we bothering to provide the model with the ability to select or deselect collateral at a national level if we are not recording the results of those specific actions? The answer is *analyst convenience*! If the analyst wishes to include 46 of the 54 state level entries, it is far easier to include all 54 state level units by using the national level selection and then deselect the unwanted 8 state level units in a second subsequent action. You will have deduced from the above that all of the selections made to construct a given criteria set are cumulative in nature. We will therefore need to provide a way to hold the pending selections until the analyst decides to apply them to the current set of existing selections already in place for that set (if any).

Final Product of the Menu Sent to the CCFG   When the selection process is complete, the menu and its supporting code will have populated a collection of up to five sets of selection criteria, each of which can be assigned to a sub-portfolio or a single set that would be applied to pool level data. (This is not to say that a given criteria selection set could not be assigned to more than one or even to all of the sub-portfolios, if that is what is desired!) Each of these criteria sets will contain the specifications for the eligibility of the state level and the four MSA Level elections of the analyst. These five vectors (one state level and four MSA levels) will contain the model users' choices as to geographic inclusion or exclusion. Three additional vectors (one state level and two MSA levels) will hold the Concentration Limits information. See Exhibit 9.40.

The Geographic Selection vectors will be declared as variable type Boolean. Either the collateral from a given state or MSA will be allowed to be included as eligible collateral in the portfolio, or it will not. The second set of three vectors will contain the concentration percentage limits, usually ranging from a high of

Output of Geographic Criteria Selection Menu

Role	Vector Name	Type	Size
Eligibility Status			
State	gFinalStatusStates	Boolean	54
MSA Group 1 (Greater Than 2.0MM Population)	gFinalStatusMSASet1	Boolean	29
MSA Group 2 (1.0MM to 2.0MM Population)	gFinalStatusMSASet2	Boolean	23
MSA Group 3 (1.0MM to 0.5MM Population)	gFinalStatusMSASet3	Boolean	49
MSA Group 4 (Under 0.5MM + Population)	gFinalStatusMSASet4	Boolean	49
Concentration Limits			
State	gFinalConcenStates	Double	54
MSA Group 1 (Greater Than 2.0MM Population)	gFinalConcenMSASet1	Double	29
MSA Group 2 (1.0MM to 2.0MM Population)	gFinalConcenMSASet2	Double	23

EXHIBIT 9.40   Table of Geographic Selection Criteria vectors

25.0% down to as little as 1%, of the amount of the aggregate current balances of that state or MSA that can be included in the collateral pool. This percentage is the limit, net of all ineligible collateral discarded from the pool, for either eligibility or concentration reasons. These vectors will be declared as variable type "Double".

If we can design the Geographic Criteria Selection Menu to populate all of these vectors in accordance with the desires of the analyst, we will then be able to employ this information in the collateral selection process. Our challenge is to translate the analyst choices in the menus and UserForms into the contents of these eight vectors so the CCFG can get to work.

Organization of the Menu

The organization of the Geographic Selection Criteria Menu is divided into three major sections:

1. **Geographic Eligibility section.** This section, entitled "Set Regional, State, and MSA Selection Conditions", allows the analyst to specify which state level and MSA level designations are eligible for inclusion in the deal. Any collateral regardless of its financial or other demographic characteristics will be considered ineligible if the geographic selection choices deem it excluded.
2. **Geographic Concentration section.** This section of the menu, entitled "State or MSA Current Balance Concentration Levels", allows the analyst to set Concentration Limits information at the state and MSA level.
3. **Report/File Writing section.** This section entitled "Output the Results", allows the analyst to produce a listing of any or all of the Selection sets (maximum of five).

See Exhibit 9.41.

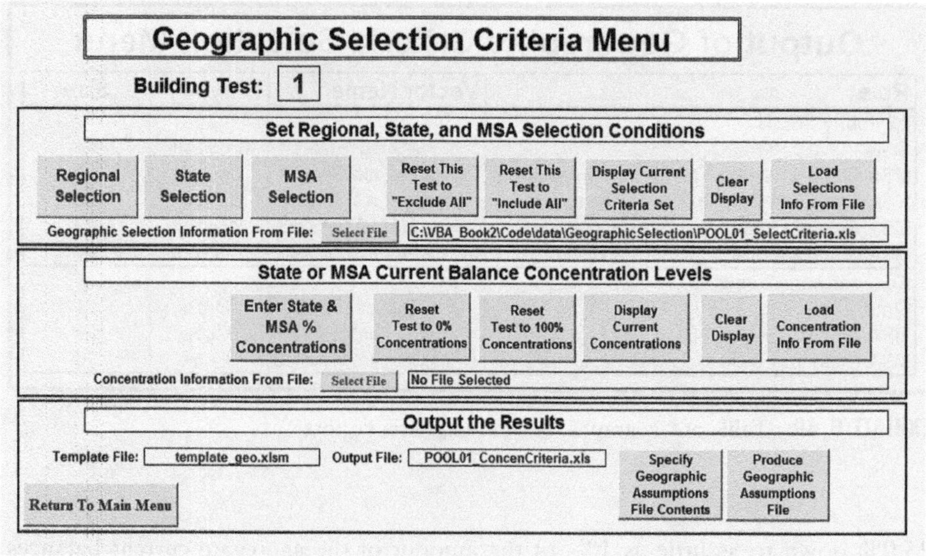

EXHIBIT 9.41 Geographic Selection Criteria Menu

Building a Test Set This menu needs to convey to the rest of the CCFG both the eligibility criteria and the concentration criteria input by the analyst. These criteria are specified at the state level and the MSA level. We need to be able to build up to five of these geographic selection criteria sets so that, in the most involved case, the analyst is in a position to apply unique selection criteria against each of the collateral sub-portfolios.

Geographic Selection The first part of the menu allows the analyst to specify the geographic eligibility conditions of the model for the indicated selection set. It has a pair of specification buttons to allow eligibility criteria to be set at the regional, state, and MSA levels. These are the three leftmost buttons. It also has a total of five utility buttons to the right of the menu. These buttons allow the analyst to set all state level and MSA level elections to Include or Exclude (which means the collateral from all states and MSAs is either completely eligible or completely ineligible). We can also display the criteria that we have elected for any of the tests, clear the currently displayed criteria, or load a file containing a set of all our geographic selections.

We need to do the following to build each of the geographic eligibility criteria sets:

- Identify the number of the set we are constructing. This number will be from 1 to 5, the maximum number of possible test sets.
- Specify the state level criteria for the test set.
- Specify the MSA level criteria for the test set.

The most efficient manner in which to do this is to allow the analyst to make a series of broadly applied elections and then follow this broad specification by a process of fine-tuning with more limited specifications to round out the details thereby completing the set. Prior to this we have mentioned the facility of having a national level selection capability. This allows us to set the criteria for a large group and subsequently tailor our specifications by choosing the opposite action for some portion of the population.

When it comes to state level and MSA level information, we can employ the same principles on a smaller scale. The model analyst may legitimately wish to take any of the flowing actions at the state level

- Include the state and include all of the MSAs within the state.
- Include the state and exclude all of the MSAs within the state.
- Exclude the state and exclude all of the MSAs within the state.
- Exclude the state and include all of the MSAs within the state.

At the MSA level, the model analyst can perform the following operations:

- Include all of the MSAs in an MSA group.
- Include some MSAs in an MSA group.
- Exclude all of the MSAs in an MSA group.
- Exclude some of the MSAs in an MSA group.

As mentioned before, we will make each subsequent selection action override the current set of selection criteria for the portion of the criteria affected by the current changes. We want to end up with all states except California included, and San Francisco included but all other MSAs excluded. An example of a sequence of these steps on the state of California and the MSAs of San Francisco, and the other 15 California MSA's would be:

- **Step #1: Select at the state level.**
  - Action: Include all states and MSAs.
  - Selection: No selection needed. With this CommandButton all states and MSAs are automatically included.
  - Result: CA—Included; San Francisco MSA—Included; remaining 15 California MSAs—Included.
- **Step #2: Select at the state level.**
  - Action: Exclude state and MSAs.
  - Selection: State of California only. The above action will exclude California and all MSAs within it.
  - Result: CA—Excluded; San Francisco MSA—Excluded; remaining 15 California MSAs—Excluded
- **Step #3: Select at the MSA level.**
  - Action: Include San Francisco MSA only.
  - Selection: San Francisco MSA only.
  - Result: CA—Excluded; San Francisco MSA—Included; remaining 15 California MSAs—Excluded.

By using each of the subsequent levels of detail, we were able to quickly and clearly achieve the configuration we desired.

Geographic Concentration   The second part of the menu allows the analyst to specify the Concentration Limits of the model for the indicated selection set. It also allows the analyst to use buttons for the following purposes:

- Display the limits that we have elected for the selected tests.
- To set all the elections of the test back to 100% (all collateral eligible).
- To set the elections of the test to 0% (all collateral ineligible).
- To clear the currently displayed limits.
- Or to load a file containing a set of concentration limits.

Concentration limits can be set in a similar pattern to that used in the geographic eligibility example above. Here the task is simpler in that only the two largest sets of MSAs are included for specific concentrations. By specifying a Concentration Limit at the national level, the analyst has specified a baseline concentration for all states simultaneously.

Specific state level and MSA level concentration limits can then be entered by selecting individual states and MSA's from a UserForm Menu and setting the percentage limits as desired. Remember that you cannot specify a higher concentration for any entity than the concentration limit of the next higher entity to which it belongs. Thus if there is a concentration limit for all California collateral of 20%, the sum of all the California collateral, MSAs and non-MSA based, must be less than 20%.

Report and File Writing   The third section of the menu allows us to specify a template file and a file name and then write the contents of all of the geographic selection eligibility and concentration criteria to it.

Operation of the Overall Menu

Having decided what we need to put into the menu, how we want it to work, and what we want it to produce, we can begin to create it. In this section you will not see any new UserForm techniques so we will not discuss how the UserForms are constructed. We will, however, closely examine the menu support code and the organization of the Excel and UserForm Menus.

There are two levels of menus here. The first is the Excel portion that the modeler employs to display the UserForms, run the model, and control the storage of the input selection criteria and its subsequent presentation by the model. This code is contained in the VBA modules of the model.

Once we display a UserForm and start working with it, we enter the second level of the menu. All the menu support code for the UserForm that is currently displayed is contained in the UserForm Object itself. This second level is the collection of UserForms in which the modeler expresses the state and MSA level criteria selections and where they are assigned to the Global variable arrays. It is these Global arrays that the CCFG will subsequently use in the collateral selection process. Mirroring this dichotomy of action, we will find that in the first two selections of the menu there is a clear separation of two sets of buttons. The CommandButtons that contain the words "Region", "State", or "MSA" are positioned to the left of the centerline of the menu. The remaining CommandButtons positioned to the right side of the menu are not used in specifying criteria but are used instead for display and data manipulation purposes.

Last, at the bottom of the menu in the third region, the menu deals with saving the results of the criteria specification process in a file. By making elections to the UserForm that will appear when we click on the "Specify Geographic Assumption File Contents" button, we can specify which of the criteria sets we would like to save to a file. This file contains the current status of any or all of the five criteria selection sets that we have indicated we wish to save at the time of the creation of the file. By specifying its name and clicking either the "Load Selections Info From File" or the "Load Concentration Info From File" buttons, we can subsequently read the information in the geographic eligibility and concentration limits file back into the model. We therefore save ourselves the time and trouble of creating these criteria in the future. This is also a handy feature to have if you have created one set of criteria and wish to modify the original set with a series of small changes. In that case you would read the data file in, modify the criteria in the menu, and save it as another file under a different name.

Operation of the Geographic Eligibility Portion of the Menu

There are two distinct and clearly different sets of operations that comprise the Geographic Eligibility section of the menu. The first are those UserForms and their supporting VBA code that allow us to specify the criteria. The second are a set of data management and display functions that allow us to load and display the criteria we have either created in the past or are creating in the moment. We will now examine each of these activities and how the menu accomplishes them.

Creating the Geographic Selection Criteria   There are three selection buttons— "Regional Selection", "State Selection", and "MSA Selection" in the uppermost portion of the menu. They are used in the creation of the selection criteria sets. Each of these buttons displays a unique UserForm that allows the input of inclusion/exclusion conditions at the state level and the MSA level, respectively.

Displaying the UserForms   Each of the three "Selection" buttons enumerated above has a VBA macro assigned to it. These macros reside in the VBA modules of the CCFG model because they are called from the CCFG model and not from within the UserForm itself. They each perform a single function: They display the appropriate UserForm by appending the "Show" method of the UserForm Object. As mentioned earlier, once we have displayed the UserForms, all activity that takes place will be controlled by the VBA code attached to each UserForm Object and not by the VBA contained in the modules of the CCFG model. See Exhibit 9.42. Let us start with the "State Selection" CommandButton, which activates the UserForm named "m3StatesSelection"; see Exhibit 9.43.

States Selection UserForm and Its VBA Code   The role of the States Selection User-Form is to allow for the inclusion (or exclusion) of the collateral of a designated state, group of states, or all states. In addition to this, the analyst also has the option of

```
'===========================================================================
' Display the User Form for National and Regional Level Selection
'===========================================================================
Sub GeoSelect_RegionalSelectButton()
    m3RegionalSelection.Show
End Sub
'===========================================================================
' Display the User Form for State Level Selection
'===========================================================================
Sub GeoSelect_StateSelectButton()
    m3StatesSelection.Show
End Sub
'===========================================================================
' Display the User Form for MSA Level Selection
'===========================================================================
Sub GeoSelect_MSASelectButton()
    m3MSAGroupSelection.Show
End Sub
'===========================================================================
' Display the User Form for setting Concentration Limits
'===========================================================================
Sub GeoSelect_Concentrations()
    m3ConcentrationLimits.Show
End Sub
'===========================================================================
' Display the User Form for Report Writing
'===========================================================================
Sub GeoSelect_ReportWriter()
    m3ReportTests.Show
End Sub
```

EXHIBIT 9.42 VBA Subroutines that display the Selection UserForms from the menu

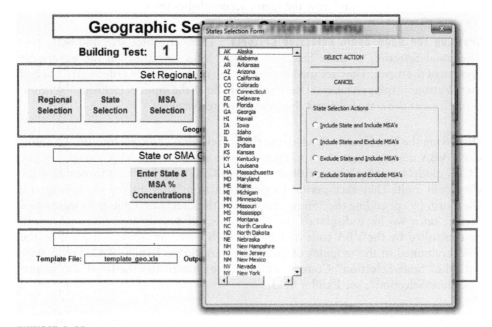

EXHIBIT 9.43 UserForm "m3StateSelection"

selecting whether the MSAs located within the states should be themselves included or excluded.

The menu is comprised of a ListBox containing all of the states of the United States and an additional four territories. These territories are the District of Columbia, the Marinas Islands, the Virgin Islands, and Puerto Rico. There is a Frame that contains four OptionButtons listing the various choices of inclusion and exclusion for the states and their MSAs. Last there are a pair of CommandButtons that can be used to either record the choices or cancel the selection process. We will now examine how to build the VBA menu support code inside of the UserForm module to get everything working the way it should. Our objective will be to correctly translate the choices that we have made on the States Selection UserForm into the contents of the "gFinalStatusStates" array and the four arrays that will hold the status of the MSA groups "gFinalStatusMSASet1, 2, 3, and 4".

If we think of the organization of the menu itself, we will see that most of the action of the VBA will be focused around what happens when we click on the "Select Action" CommandButton. At that point we will need to combine two sets of information. The first is the number of states selected from the ListBox, and the second is the information from one of the OptionButtons as to what status we will assign to the selected states and their MSAs.

Starting with the items of the ListBox, we will need to determine which item, set of items, or no items have been selected. Remember, we can have a situation where the analyst clicks the "Select Action" button without a single state selected from the list, and everything is fine. This case would arise if the OptionButton setting were either "Include All States" or "Exclude All States". If, however, the "Select Action" CommandButton was clicked with no states currently selected from the list with the other two OptionButton checked other than the include or exclude all options, we would have an obvious error condition. Keeping the above remarks in mind, we can see that when we click on the "Select Action" CommandButton, the program must perform the following steps to correctly express our selections:

Step 1. Determine what test number (1 to 5) we are currently working on so that we place all the selection information in the test we think we are specifying it for!

Step 2. If this is the first time into the menu, correctly initialize all the setting for the states and MSAs of this particular test number.

Step 3. We need to determine if, based on the active OptionButton, a choice from the state list needs to be made. If the OptionButton is not either "Include All States and Include MSA's" or "Exclude All States and Exclude MSA's", we need to confirm that at least one state has been selected from the list. If no states have been selected, we need to issue an error message and stop the selection process by hiding the UserForm.

Step 4. If we meet the requirements of Step 3, we now need to determine which of the OptionButtons is active. This will tell us if we will be including or excluding the selected state(s) and their member MSAs. We will need to set a variable to record what those elections are for both the state and MSAs involved.

Step 5. We will now opt to be safe rather than sorry. We will produce a message to the analyst stating what choice was made in the OptionButton section and also produce a list of the states selected. If the analyst then confirms these selections, we will proceed. If not, we will hide the UserForm.

Step 6. If everything is okay at this point and the analyst has confirmed the choices as indicated, we can now apply these choices by recording them in the appropriate "gFinalStatus****" arrays.

Each of these steps will require a subroutine or two to be called from the code that will be activated when the "Select Action" button is clicked. Let us start with that subroutine and work our way through the above tasks.

"SelectActionButton_Click" Subroutine The subroutine "SelectActionButton_Click", see Exhibit 9.44, opens by selecting the "GeoMenu" Worksheet so that the UserForm will be displayed over the contents of that page. Next the subroutine reads the value of the Range "m3TestNumber", which is the index of the Geographic Selection test that we are working on. Any and all changes based on the selections in this action will now be recorded to that particular test. We have now completed Step 1 above.

Next we call the subroutine "States_CheckInitialStatus"; see Exhibit 9.45. This subroutine is designed to determine if this is the first time any action has been taken

```
Private Sub SelectActionButton_Click()

    Sheets("GeoSelectMenu").Select      'make this menu the active one
    gGeoCriteriaTest = Range("m3TestNumber")
    Call States_CheckInitialStatus
    Call States_CheckSomeSelectionMade
    Call States_SetSelectionActionCode
    If go_ok Then
        Call States_SetActionCode
        'print out the confirm message
        msg = ""
        For icnt = 0 To StateChoices.ListCount - 1
            If StateChoices.Selected(icnt) Then _
                msg = msg & StateChoices.List(icnt, 0) & "    " _
                        & StateChoices.List(icnt, 1) & vbCrLf
        Next icnt
        'produce the confirmation message
        Call States_ProduceSelectionResultsMsgBox
        If go_ok Then
            'user has confirmed choices log them in
            For icnt = 0 To StateChoices.ListCount - 1
                If StateChoices.Selected(icnt) Then _
                    gWasSelectedStates(gGeoCriteriaTest, icnt + 1) = True
            Next icnt
            Call GeoSelect_ApplyStateTriggers
        Else
            Call GeoSelect_MenuNoSelectionActionTaken(CODE_STATES)
        End If
    End If
    'put down the user form
    Unload m3StatesSelection

End Sub
```

EXHIBIT 9.44 "SelectActionButton_Click" subroutine

```
Sub States_CheckInitialStatus()

    ' first time in setting up the test set all to INCLUDED
    gGeoFirstTimeAnywhere = gGeoFirstTimeAnywhere + 1
    If gGeoFirstTimeAnywhere = 1 Then
        Call GeoSelect_InitGeoSelectShell(INIT_ALL, INCLUDE_GEO)
        Call GeoSelect_InitGeoConcenShell(INIT_ALL)
        Call GeoSelect_ReadGeoData
    End If
    Sheets("GeoSelectMenu").Select

End Sub
```

EXHIBIT 9.45 "States_CheckInitialStatus" subroutine

on this or any other of the Geographic Selection UserForms. If the value of the Integer variable "gFirstTimeAnywhere" is "0", then this is the first time that any UserForm has been called; if it is greater than "0", it means that a UserForm has been called and we have, at some point previously, initialized the values of the state and MSA selection codes to TRUE. If, however, the value of "gFirstTimeAnywhere" is "0", then we will initialize all of the Geographic Selection tests and all of the Geographic Concentration limits. These actions are performed by the subroutines "GeoSelect_InitGeoSelectInclude" and "GeoSelect_InitializeGeoConcen0Pct" and "...100Pct"; see Exhibits 9.46 and 9.47. With these actions we will have completed Step 2.

We now need to determine if the selections made by the analyst are correct and can be processed by the UserForm and sent onward to the VBA arrays of the CCFG. In all of the four options, we will need to determine if any of the states on the list have been selected prior to hitting the "Select Action" Button. We will use the subroutine "States_CheckSomeSelectionMade" to make this determination; see Exhibit 9.48. In this subroutine we will first set the Boolean variable "go_ok" to TRUE. If we find a problem while in this subroutine, we will assign "go_ok" to FALSE. This will truncate any more processing of the selections when we return to the calling subroutine. The next thing we will do is determine if the OptionButton selected represents a choice that requires at least one member on the list of states be selected. We can do this by testing the values of the buttons. We will then test the four OptionButton values. If any are true, then we absolutely need at least one state to be selected from the list. The name of the ListBox is "StateChoices". One of the properties of "StateChoices" is "ListCount", which tells us how many items are in the ListBox. Be *careful* here! The index of all ListBoxes begin with "0"; therefore, a list with five members will be numbered 0 to 4. We can use the "ListCount" property to set up a loop to examine each of the members of the list one by one. The ListBox also contains a property called "Selected". If the third member of the list has been selected, the "StatesChoices. Selected(2)" array element will be TRUE. Note again the indexing offset. The third item in the list has an index of (2) because the array starts at (0). Upon finding the first selected item, we are finished. We set a Boolean variable named "ListBoxItemsSelected" to TRUE and immediately exit the subroutine. If we cannot find a single selected member of the ListBox, we set "go_ok" to FALSE, print an error message, and return to the calling subroutine. This completes Step 3! See Exhibit 9.48.

```
Sub GeoSelect_InitGeoSelectInclude()

    For itest = StartLoop To EndLoop
        'National/Regional Level to Include
        For mRegion = 1 To NUM_REGIONS
            gWasSelectedRegions(itest, mRegion) = False
            gFinalStatusRegions(itest, mRegion) = "Inc\Inc"
        Next mRegion
        'State Level to Include
        For mState = 1 To NUM_STATES
            gWasSelectedStates(itest, mState) = False
            gFinalStatusStates(itest, mState) = True
        Next mState
        'MSA Levels to Include
        For mMSA = 1 To NUM_MSA_SET1
            gWasSelectedMSASet1(itest, mMSA) = False
            gFinalStatusMSASet1(itest, mMSA) = True
        Next mMSA
        For mMSA = 1 To NUM_MSA_SET2
            gWasSelectedMSASet2(itest, mMSA) = False
            gFinalStatusMSASet2(itest, mMSA) = True
        Next mMSA
        For mMSA = 1 To NUM_MSA_SET3
            gWasSelectedMSASet3(itest, mMSA) = False
            gFinalStatusMSASet3(itest, mMSA) = True
        Next mMSA
        For mMSA = 1 To NUM_MSA_SET4
            gWasSelectedMSASet4(itest, mMSA) = False
            gFinalStatusMSASet4(itest, mMSA) = True
        Next mMSA
    Next itest
    'Display an initialization message to inform the user
    If StartLoop = EndLoop Then _
        Call GeoSelect_InitMsg(INCLUDE_GEO, itest - 1)

End Sub
```

EXHIBIT 9.46   "GeoSelect_InitGeoSelectInclude" subroutine

We now have three steps done and three steps to go. If the value of the variable "go_ok" is TRUE (everything is fine so far!), we can now begin the process of recording our choices. The next thing we have to do is to determine by the state of the OptionButtons what type of selection activity we are engaged in. We will call the subroutine "States_SetActionCode", and based on which one of the four OptionButtons is currently the active one, we will set the value of the "gActionState" and "gActionMSA" variables. See Exhibit 9.49.

If the value of "go_ok" is FALSE, we will fall past the main processing code of the subroutine all the way to the bottom and unload the UserForm, removing it from view. Before we process the selections made in the menu, we wish to have the analyst confirm that they are correct. We will therefore build a message with the selection contents and ask the analyst to confirm its contents. To produce this message, we will loop through the "StateChoices" ListBox elements and, starting with a blank message, append each of the members of the "StatesChoices" list that have been

```
Sub GeoSelect_InitGeoConcen0Pct(test_trigger As Integer)

    Call GeoSelect_InitGeoLoopControls(test_trigger)
    For itest = StartLoop To EndLoop
        For mState = 1 To NUM_STATES
            gFinalConcenStates(mState) = 0#
        Next mState
        For mMSA = 1 To NUM_MSA_SET1
            gFinalConcenMSASet1(mMSA) = 0#
        Next mMSA
        For mMSA = 1 To NUM_MSA_SET2
            gFinalConcenMSASet2(mMSA) = 0#
        Next mMSA
    Next itest
    'Display an initialization message to inform the user
    If StartLoop = EndLoop Then Call GeoConcen_InitMsg(itest - 1, PCT_ZERO)

End Sub
Sub GeoSelect_InitGeoConcen100Pct(test_trigger As Integer)

    Call GeoSelect_InitGeoLoopControls(test_trigger)
    For itest = StartLoop To EndLoop
        For mState = 1 To NUM_STATES
            gFinalConcenStates(mState) = 1#
        Next mState
        For mMSA = 1 To NUM_MSA_SET1
            gFinalConcenMSASet1(mMSA) = 1#
        Next mMSA
        For mMSA = 1 To NUM_MSA_SET2
            gFinalConcenMSASet2(mMSA) = 1#
        Next mMSA
    Next itest
    'Display an initialization message to inform the user
    If StartLoop = EndLoop Then Call GeoConcen_InitMsg(itest - 1, PCT_100)

End Sub
```

EXHIBIT 9.47 "GeoSelect_InitGeoConcen0Pct" and "GeoSelect_InitGeo Concen100Pct" subroutines

```
Sub States_CheckSomeSelectionMade()

    'make sure at least one box is checked
    go_ok = True
    msg = ""
    ListBoxItemsSelected = False
    For icnt = 0 To StateChoices.ListCount - 1
        If StateChoices.Selected(icnt) Then
            ListBoxItemsSelected = True
            Exit Sub
        End If
    Next icnt
    If Not ListBoxItemsSelected Then
        MsgBox "ERROR: NO STATES SELECTED" & vbCrLf
        go_ok = False
    End If

End Sub
```

EXHIBIT 9.48 "States_CheckSomeSelectionMade" subroutine

```
Sub States_SetActionCode()

    If obStateIncStateIncMSA Then
        gActionState = True
        gActionMSA = True
    End If
    If obStateIncStateExcMSA Then
        gActionState = True
        gActionMSA = False
    End If
    If obStateExcStateIncMSA Then
        gActionState = False
        gActionMSA = True
    End If
    If obStateExcStateExcMSA Then
        gActionState = False
        gActionMSA = False
    End If

End Sub
```

EXHIBIT 9.49   "State_SetActionCode" subroutine

selected. With the message in hand, we can display it and let the analyst respond. To produce the message, we will use the "States_ProduceSelectionResultsMsgBox" subroutine. In this subroutine we will restate the Selection Option elected and then list under it all the states selected. See Exhibits 9.50 and 9.51.

If the analyst confirms the selections as displayed in the message, we will then proceed to apply them; if not, then the variable "go_ok" will be set to FALSE. If the analyst declines to confirm the selections, we will print an error message using the subroutine "GeoSelect_MenuNoSelectionActionTaken" and unload the UserForm, ending the selection process. See Exhibit 9.52.

```
Sub States_ProduceSelectionResultsMsgBox()

Dim mChoice        As String

    'based on the choice indicated, produce introductory message
    If obStateIncStateIncMSA Then _
            mChoice = "Include State and Include MSA's: " & vbCrLf & msg
    If obStateIncStateExcMSA Then _
            mChoice = "Include State and Exclude MSA's: " & vbCrLf & msg
    If obStateExcStateIncMSA Then _
            mChoice = "Exclude State and Exclude MSA's: " & vbCrLf & msg
    If obStateExcStateExcMSA Then _
            mChoice = "Exclude State and Exclude MSA's: " & vbCrLf & msg
    'print the message box
    msgTitle = "State Selections Confirmation Listing"
    msgPrompt = "Carefully confirm your selections" & vbCrLf & vbCrLf & mChoice
    msgResult = MsgBox(msgPrompt, gMsgButtonCode1, msgTitle)
    If msgResult = 1 Then go_ok = True
    If msgResult = 2 Then go_ok = False

End Sub
```

EXHIBIT 9.50   "States_ProduceSelectionResultsMsgBox" subroutine

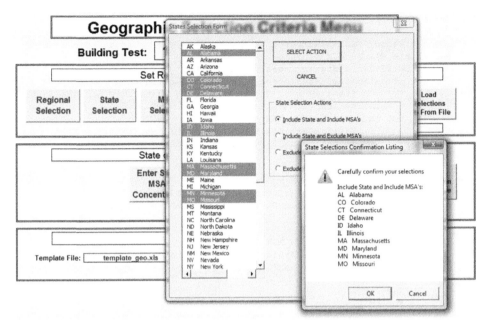

EXHIBIT 9.51 Selection confirmation message

These actions now complete Steps 4 and 5! Only one step remains. We are finally in a position to record the choices from the menu into the five arrays that will be used by the CCFG in the collateral selection process. In the subroutine "GeoSelect_ApplyStateTriggers", we finally record our choices from the UserForm! We will loop through each of the states and record the state level selection. Next we

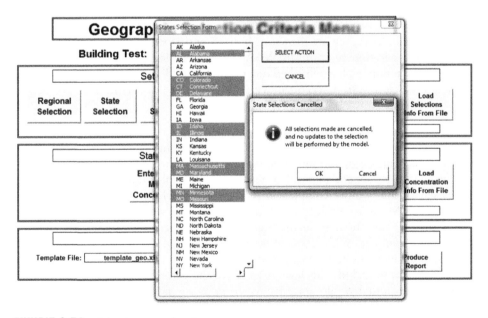

EXHIBIT 9.52 Selection cancel action message

```
Sub GeoSelect_ApplyStateTriggers()

    itest = Range("m03TestNumber")   'just to make the notation more compact
    For iState = 1 To NUM_STATES
        If gWasSelectedStates(itest, iState) Then
            gFinalStatusStates(itest, iState) = gActionState
            'if the state code of MSA matches this state then set the action
            '  code against the MSA
            For iMSA = 1 To NUM_MSA_SET1
                If gDataStates(iState, 1) = gDataMSASet1(iMSA, 2) Then
                    gFinalStatusMSASet1(itest, iMSA) = gActionMSA
                End If
            Next iMSA
            For iMSA = 1 To NUM_MSA_SET2
                If gDataStates(iState, 1) = gDataMSASet2(iMSA, 2) Then
                    gFinalStatusMSASet2(itest, iMSA) = gActionMSA
                End If
            Next iMSA
            For iMSA = 1 To NUM_MSA_SET3
                If gDataStates(iState, 1) = gDataMSASet3(iMSA, 2) Then
                    gFinalStatusMSASet3(itest, iMSA) = gActionMSA
                End If
            Next iMSA
            For iMSA = 1 To NUM_MSA_SET4
                If gDataStates(iState, 1) = gDataMSASet4(iMSA, 2) Then
                    gFinalStatusMSASet4(itest, iMSA) = gActionMSA
                End If
            Next iMSA
        End If
    Next iState

End Sub
```

EXHIBIT 9.53 "GeoSelect_ApplyStateTriggers" subroutine

will compare the state code of the MSAs, one group after another, to the state code of the current state. If they are the same, indicating that the MSA is in the state, we will adjust the selection action of the MSA accordingly. See Exhibit 9.53.

   With this action we have finished one round of building a Geographic Selection set using the Select State UserForm. We will now turn our attention to the Select MSA UserForm.

MSA Level Selection UserForm and Its VBA Code   The MSA Selection Menu is broadly similar in design and function to the State Selection Menu. In one sense this menu is more complex and in another way it is less complex than the State Selection Menu. This menu is more complex in that the MSA Selection Menu allows us to specify which MSAs we wish to include/exclude from a set of four lists, instead of a single list, as was the case in the States Selection Menu. It is, however, not as complex as it could be. While some of the largest of the MSAs—New York City, Los Angeles, and Chicago—have multiple smaller sub-MSAs contained within them, we have chosen not to include this level of detail in the current release of the model. It is less complex in that we do not have to worry as we did with the States Selection Menu about assigning selection code not only to the items on the displayed list but to other hidden items (the MSAs of the state) as well.

The structure of the MSA Selection Menu is similar to that of the States Selection Menu. There is a ListBox containing a series of items from which we can choose either single or multiple entries. There are two groups of OptionButtons each contained in Frames to segregate their actions. Finally there are two CommandButtons, "APPLY CHOICES" and "CANCEL"—the same options we had in the States Selection Menu. The salient difference between the States Selection Menu and the MSA Selection Menu is the use of a single ListBox feature to display one of four series MSAs instead of a single list of states. How do we manage multiple lists in a single menu? (Very carefully!) We will concentrate on getting familiar with this feature of UserForms when we discuss this menu. The other features of this menu are very broadly similar to the States Selection Menu and will be left to the reader. Here we will concentrate only on the aspects of the VBA support code in the UserForm module that relate to the issues of multiple lists.

Managing Multiple Lists in a Menu   The ability to specify the inclusion and exclusion of mortgages at the MSA level is critical for any market environment. Most of this focus will be on the larger MSAs in Lists 1 and 2. The smaller MSAs in Lists 3 and 4 are provided so that the model analyst can single out the hot spots of severe default activity and exclude collateral from those areas (if that is desired).

There are two challenges in this multiple list menu. The first is how to quickly and efficiently display the contents of the four MSA lists and how to ensure that the selections made in the MSA Selection Menu are correctly recorded and available to the CCFG later.

Controlling the Display of Multiple Lists in a Menu   The key to controlling the display of multiple lists in a single ListBox of a menu lies in our ability to programmatically adjust the Properties of the ListBox Object. To allow the ListBox to display multiple lists, we will first create, position, and label the set of four OptionButtons on the menu. We will contain the OptionButtons in a Frame entitled "Display MSA Group". Next we will give each of the OptionButtons a standardized name so that they will be easy to identify in the VBA Menu support code. We will name these buttons "obDisplayMSAGrp1" to "obDisplayMSAGrp4". Next we will click on each of the buttons. Inside the UserForm module, a subroutine called "obDisplay MSAGrp1_Click" is automatically created by this action. There is as yet no VBA code in this subroutine, so there is no current effect of clicking on the OptionButton to which it is attached. See Exhibit 9.54.

The key property that we will need to programmatically control to correctly display the MSA Group 1 List is the property that directs the ListBox to the data it is to display. This is the property "RowSource". In a ListBox that displays a single list, the Range containing the items that the ListBox will can be declared once, in the Properties Editor, at the time of the creation of the ListBox and never changed again.

```
Private Sub obDisplayMSAGrp1_Click()

End Sub
```

EXHIBIT 9.54   Blank subroutine call created by clicking on OptionButton "obDisplayMSAGrp1"

```
'=========================================================================
' Load the MSA Groups Into the List Box
'=========================================================================
Private Sub obDisplayMSAGrp1_Click()
    lbMSAGroup.RowSource = "GeoReport!MSAGroup1"
    lbListBoxTitle.Caption = "        GROUP 1 Metropolitan Statistical Areas"
    mSetDisplayed = CODE_MSA_1
End Sub

Private Sub obDisplayMSAGrp2_Click()
    lbMSAGroup.RowSource = "GeoReport!MSAGroup2"
    lbListBoxTitle.Caption = "        GROUP 2 Metropolitan Statistical Areas"
    mSetDisplayed = CODE_MSA_2
End Sub

Private Sub obDisplayMSAGrp3_Click()
    lbMSAGroup.RowSource = "GeoReport!MSAGroup3"
    lbListBoxTitle.Caption = "        GROUP 3 Metropolitan Statistical Areas"
    mSetDisplayed = CODE_MSA_3
End Sub

Private Sub obDisplayMSAGrp4_Click()
    lbMSAGroup.RowSource = "GeoReport!MSAGroup4"
    lbListBoxTitle.Caption = "        GROUP 4 Metropolitan Statistical Areas"
    mSetDisplayed = CODE_MSA_4
End Sub
```

EXHIBIT 9.55   "_Click" subroutines for each of the four MSA Group lists

In this case we wish to redirect the "RowSource" property each time the analyst clicks on one of the "Display MSA Group" buttons. To effect this reassignment, we will change the designated Range that the ListBox currently has as its "RowSource" depending on which OptionButton is clicked. After the button is clicked, we will also want to change the contents of the menu title to correctly reflect the MSA list currently displayed. Last we need to record for our own use an identifier of which of the four MSA Groups is currently displayed so that we can map the analyst selections to the correct MSA Group in the VBA code. See Exhibit 9.55.

Recording the MSA Selection Assignments   We have solved the first part of the problem. We can present multiple MSA lists in the same ListBox and identify which of them is the current one displayed. Now we need to correctly identify the choices made on the menu and store them in the appropriate arrays for use by the CCFG at a later time. The key to this task is the identification variable that holds the identity of the displayed MSA Group. The variable "mSetDisplayed" was assigned a value by using one of four Constants, "CODE_MSA_1" to "CODE_MSA_4". With this variable pointing the way, we can easily perform a number of steps, such as:

- Identifying the correct group in selection, confirmation, and cancellation messages to the analyst.
- Directing the selection assignment values to the arrays that will hold them, "gFinalStatusMSASet1" to "gFinalStatusMSASet4".

Displaying Lists with Multiple Fields   There is a final difference in the presentation formats of the States Selection Menu and the MSA Selection Menu. The MSA Selection Menu presents three items in the ListBox, while the States Selection Menu displays only one. The States Selection Menu displays the common name for the states on the list. The MSA Selection Menu displays the MSA numeric code, the two-letter postal code of the state of the MSA, and the name of the MSA.

This listing difference is the result of the Range that is designated as the value of the "RowSource" property of the ListBox that we discussed above. The Ranges in each of the assignment statements in Exhibit 9.51 contain multiple columns. There is one other issue that you need to be sensitive to when using multiple columns in a ListBox. You need to make sure that the columns of the ListBox are sufficiently sized to completely display the data of the list. One way you can assure yourself that they are is by setting the column widths of the ListBox at the time you create it. Alternatively you can programmatically adjust them as the program is running, depending on what is being displayed in the ListBox at the time. (We do this in the Geographic Concentration Limits Menu we will discuss next.) The ListBox property that controls the width of the column displays is appropriately named "ColumnWidths". The widths of the columns are expressed in points, separated by semicolons. In the case of the MSA Group ListBox, there are three columns with widths of 30, 20, and 150 points, respectively. See Exhibit 9.56.

This ends the discussion of the portions of the Geographic Menu that allows for the selection of states and MSA. We will next look at how we organize and present these data. We will also discuss how we can make these data available to the model analyst so we will have a clear understanding of the contents of each of the selection tests.

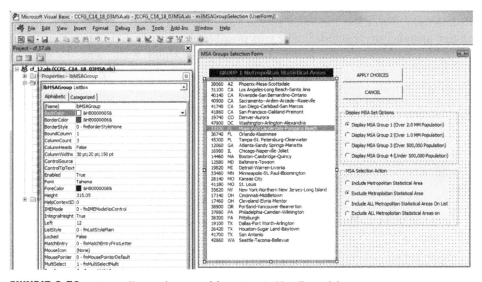

EXHIBIT 9.56   Controlling column width setting in UserForm Menus

```
Sub GeoSelect_InitGeoSelectShell(test_trigger As Integer, _
                            test_action As Integer)
    Call GeoSelect_InitGeoLoopControls(test_trigger)
    Select Case test_action
        Case Is = INCLUDE_GEO: Call GeoSelect_InitGeoSelectInclude
        Case Is = EXCLUDE_GEO: Call GeoSelect_InitGeoSelectExclude
    End Select
End Sub
```

EXHIBIT 9.57   "GeoSelect_InitGeoSelectShell" subroutine

Selection Criteria Management Process   We will now look at the features of the
menu that allow us to effectively manage the Geographic Selection Criteria sets that
we have created above.

Reporting and Utility Buttons and Their Code   There are four buttons that manipulate either the data or the contents of the geographic eligibility selection
criteria.

The first two of these buttons are the "Reset This Test to "Include All"" and
"Reset This Test to "Exclude All"" buttons. The VBA support code activated by
this button writes all the states and MSA eligibility settings to TRUE. This makes all
of the collateral eligible for inclusion in the portfolio regardless of its state or MSA.
The subroutine called by this button is named "GeoSelect_InitGeoSelectShell". See
Exhibit 9.57. The role of this subroutine is to determine if a single selection set or all
selection sets are to be initialized to either "Include" or "Exclude". The first action of
the subroutine is to call "GeoSelect_InitGeoLoopControls". See Exhibit 9.58. Based
on the value of the variable "test_trigger" passed to this subroutine, either a single
selection set or all selection sets will be set to the indicated action. With the limits
of the action established, the subroutine now employs a "Select..Case" statement
to determine, based on the value of the variable "test_acton", if the set is to be
set to "Include" or "Exclude". The two possible choices are the subroutines "Geo
Select_InitGeoSelectInclude" or "...Exclude". See Exhibit 9.59. Why do we not

```
Sub GeoSelect_InitGeoLoopControls(test_trigger As Integer)

    'find out if this is a single or multiple test initialization
    ' and set the loop beginning and ending values
    Select Case test_trigger
        Case Is = INIT_SINGLE
            StartLoop = Range("m03TestNumber")
            EndLoop = Range("m03TestNumber")
        Case Is = INIT_ALL
            StartLoop = 1
            EndLoop = NUM_GEO_TESTS
    End Select

End Sub
```

EXHIBIT 9.58   "GeoSelect_InitGeoLoopControls"

```
Sub GeoSelect_InitGeoSelectExclude()
    For itest = StartLoop To EndLoop
        'National/Regional Level to Include
        For mRegion = 1 To NUM_REGIONS
            gWasSelectedRegions(itest, mRegion) = False
            gFinalStatusRegions(itest, mRegion) = "Out\Out"
        Next mRegion
        'State Level to Include
        For mState = 1 To NUM_STATES
            gWasSelectedStates(itest, mState) = False
            gFinalStatusStates(itest, mState) = False
        Next mState
        'MSA Levels to Include
        For mMSA = 1 To NUM_MSA_SET1
            gWasSelectedMSASet1(itest, mMSA) = False
            gFinalStatusMSASet1(itest, mMSA) = False
        Next mMSA
        For mMSA = 1 To NUM_MSA_SET2
            gWasSelectedMSASet2(itest, mMSA) = False
            gFinalStatusMSASet2(itest, mMSA) = False
        Next mMSA
        For mMSA = 1 To NUM_MSA_SET3
            gWasSelectedMSASet3(itest, mMSA) = False
            gFinalStatusMSASet3(itest, mMSA) = False
        Next mMSA
        For mMSA = 1 To NUM_MSA_SET4
            gWasSelectedMSASet4(itest, mMSA) = False
            gFinalStatusMSASet4(itest, mMSA) = False
        Next mMSA
    Next itest
    'Display an initialization message to inform the user
    If StartLoop = EndLoop Then _
        Call GeoSelect_InitMsg(EXCLUDE_GEO, itest - 1)
End Sub
```

EXHIBIT 9.59   "GeoSelect_InitGeoSelectExclude" subroutine

just call "GeoSelect_InitGeoSelectInclude" or "...Exclude" directly? The "Geo Select_InitializeGeoSelection" subroutine can perform its duties in one of two ways. It can either initialize a single selection criteria test value or all five of the selection criteria test sets. The action taken depends on the value of the subroutine's single argument. This argument is set by one of the two Constant variables, "INIT_ALL" and "INIT_SINGLE". If we choose to send the argument "INIT_SINGLE", the loop controls are set by the "GeoSelect_InitializeGeoLoopControls" subroutine. It will set the variables so that they will start and stop the initialization processes on the same test number; refer to Exhibit 9.58. The loop executes once, initializing that particular test only. This action is appropriate when we are setting the criteria from one of the buttons of the Geographic Selection Menu. This is not the only time in the execution of the CCFG that we need to take such an initialization action. Each time the model is run for the first time, we will need to initialize all the geographic selection settings. In this case we need to reset all of the selection sets so we pass the subroutine the "INIT_ALL" argument. It then initializes all five of the selection tests. We will use this feature when we are first entering the selection UserForms so that we do not carry any old values with us. At the conclusion of this activity,

```
Sub GeoSelect_InitMsg(incSwitch As Integer, test_set As Integer)

Dim msgTitle        As String
Dim msgPromptAll    As String
Dim msgPrompt01     As String
Dim msgPrompt02     As String
Dim msgPrompt03     As String
Dim msgPrompt04     As String
Dim msgPrompt05     As String
Dim msgPrompt06     As String
Dim msgPrompt07     As String
Dim msgResult       As Integer

    msgPrompt01 = "For Selection Test #" & test_set & vbCrLf
    msgPrompt02 = "All Regions set to Inc\Inc, " & vbCrLf
    msgPrompt03 = "All States set to Include  " & vbCrLf
    msgPrompt04 = "All MSA's set to Include"
    msgPrompt05 = "All Regions set to Exc\Exc, " & vbCrLf
    msgPrompt06 = "All States set to Exclude  " & vbCrLf
    msgPrompt07 = "All MSA's set to Exclude"
    'selection is cancelled no action taken
    msgTitle = "All Regional, State, and MSA Initialization Complete"
    msgPromptAll = msgPrompt01
    Select Case incSwitch
        Case Is = INCLUDE_GEO:
            msgPromptAll = msgPromptAll & msgPrompt02 & msgPrompt03 & msgPrompt04
        Case Is = EXCLUDE_GEO:
            msgPromptAll = msgPromptAll & msgPrompt05 & msgPrompt06 & msgPrompt07
    End Select
    msgResult = MsgBox(msgPromptAll, gMsgButtonCode2, msgTitle)

End Sub
```

EXHIBIT 9.60 "GeoSelect_InitMsg" subroutine

the model produces a short message to confirm that the initialization has in fact been effected. This message is produced by the "GeoSelect_InitMsg" subroutine. See Exhibit 9.60.

The second of these buttons is the "Display Current Selection Criteria Set". When the model analyst clicks on this button, the settings of the current Geographic Selection Criteria are displayed on the "GeoReport" Worksheet. The subroutine that performs this work is "GeoSelect_PrintOutStatusByPortfolio". This subroutine reads the number of the currently selected criteria test, selects the "GeoReport" Worksheet, and fills it with the current settings of the indicated test number. See Exhibits 9.61 and 9.62.

The third of the buttons is the "Clear Display" button. This button clears the "GeoReport" Worksheet of its current contents by calling the "GeoSelect_ClearStatusOnGeoMenu" subroutine that sets all the fields to blank. Keep in mind that this subroutine only clears the display of the report and leaves the contents of the arrays that hold the criteria specifications intact. See Exhibit 9.63.

The fourth and last of the utility buttons allows the model analyst to open a previously written collateral eligibility file and read its contents into the any or all of the selection criteria arrays in the model. This is the "Load Selections Info From File" button. When clicked, this button activates the

Collateral Selection Triggers - Geographic Report

Triggers Only   Criteria Test = 3

Regions
2 National; 7 Regions

#	Status	Code	Regional Name
1	Inclinc	NE	New England
2	Inclinc	MA	Mid-Atlantic
3	Inclinc	SE	South East
4	Inclinc	MD	Midwest
5	Inclinc	SW	South West
6	Inclinc	NW	North West
7	Inclinc	TR	Territories

States & Territories
50 States and 4 Territories

#	Status	Code	State Name
1	INCLUDED	AK	Alaska
2	INCLUDED	AL	Alabama
3	INCLUDED	AR	Arkansas
4	INCLUDED	AZ	Arizona
5	OUT	CA	California
6	OUT	CO	Colorado
7	OUT	CT	Connecticut
8	INCLUDED	DE	Delaware
9	INCLUDED	FL	Florida
10	INCLUDED	GA	Georgia
11	INCLUDED	HI	Hawaii
12	INCLUDED	IA	Iowa
13	INCLUDED	ID	Idaho
14	INCLUDED	IL	Illinois
15	INCLUDED	IN	Indiana
16	INCLUDED	KS	Kansas
17	INCLUDED	KY	Kentucky
18	INCLUDED	LA	Louisana

MSA Set 1
Metropolitan Statistical Areas Over 2.0 MM Population

#	Status	Code	State	Metropolitan Area	Population
1	INCLUDED	38060	AZ	Phoenix-Mesa-Scottsdale	4,281,899
2	OUT	31100	CA	Los Angeles-Long Beach-Santa Ana	12,872,808
3	OUT	40140	CA	Riverside-San Bernardino-Ontario	4,115,871
4	OUT	40900	CA	Sacramento-Arden-Arcade-Roseville	2,109,832
5	OUT	41740	CA	San Diego-Carlsbad-San Marcos	3,001,072
6	OUT	41860	CA	San Francisco-Oakland-Fremont	4,274,531
7	OUT	19740	CO	Denver-Aurora	2,506,626
8	INCLUDED	47900	DC	Washington-Arlington-Alexandria	5,358,130
9	INCLUDED	33100	FL	Miami-Fort Lauderdale-Pompano Beach	5,414,772
10	INCLUDED	36740	FL	Orlando-Kissimmee	2,054,574
11	INCLUDED	45300	FL	Tampa-St. Petersburg-Clearwater	2,733,761
12	INCLUDED	12060	GA	Atlanta-Sandy Springs-Marietta	5,376,285
13	INCLUDED	16980	IL	Chicago-Naperville-Joliet	9,569,624
14	INCLUDED	14460	MA	Boston-Cambridge-Quincy	4,522,858
15	INCLUDED	12580	MD	Baltimore-Towson	2,667,117
16	INCLUDED	19820	MI	Detroit-Warren-Livonia	4,425,110
17	INCLUDED	33460	MN	Minneapolis-St. Paul-Bloomington	3,229,878
18	INCLUDED	28140	MO	Kansas City	2,002,047
19	INCLUDED	41180	MO	St. Louis	2,816,710
20	INCLUDED	35620	NY	New York-Northern New Jersey-Long Island	19,006,798
21	INCLUDED	17140	OH	Cincinnati-Middletown	2,155,137
22	INCLUDED	17460	OH	Cleveland-Elyria-Mentor	2,088,291
23	INCLUDED	38900	OR	Portland-Vancouver-Beaverton	2,207,462
24	INCLUDED	37980	PA	Philadelphia-Camden-Wilmington	5,838,471
25	INCLUDED	38300	PA	Pittsburgh	2,351,192
26	INCLUDED	19100	TX	Dallas-Fort Worth-Arlington	6,300,006
27	INCLUDED	26420	TX	Houston-Sugar Land-Baytown	5,728,143
28	INCLUDED	41700	TX	San Antonio	2,031,445
29	INCLUDED	42660	WA	Seattle-Tacoma-Bellevue	3,344,813

MSA Set 3
Metropolitan Statistical Areas Gre

#	Status	Code	State	Metropolit
1	INCLUDED	30780	AR	Little Rock-l
2	OUT	12540	CA	Bakersfield
3	OUT	23420	CA	Fresno
4	OUT	33700	CA	Modesto
5	OUT	37100	CA	Oxnard-Tho
6	OUT	44700	CA	Stockton
7	OUT	17820	CO	Colorado S
8	OUT	14860	CT	Bridgeport-!
9	OUT	35300	CT	New Haven
10	INCLUDED	14600	FL	Bradenton-!
11	INCLUDED	15980	FL	Cape Coral-
12	INCLUDED	29460	FL	Lakeland-W
13	INCLUDED	37340	FL	Palm Bay-N
14	INCLUDED	12260	GA	Augusta-Ri
15	INCLUDED	26180	HI	Honolulu
16	INCLUDED	19780	IA	Des Moines
17	INCLUDED	14260	ID	Boise City-N
18	INCLUDED	48620	KS	Wichita
19	INCLUDED	12940	LA	Baton Rouc
20	INCLUDED	44140	MA	Springfield
21	INCLUDED	49340	MA	Worcester
22	INCLUDED	38860	ME	Portland-Sc
23	INCLUDED	24340	MI	Grand Rapi
24	INCLUDED	27140	MS	Jackson
25	INCLUDED	24660	NC	Greensborc
26	INCLUDED	36540	NE	Omaha-Cou
27	INCLUDED	10740	NM	Albuquerqu
28	INCLUDED	10580	NY	Albany-Sch
29	INCLUDED	39100	NY	Poughkeep

EXHIBIT 9.61 "GeoReport" Worksheet (with the selection criteria from Test#3 displayed)

```
Sub GeoSelect_PrintOutStatusByPortfolio()

    'regional info first
    Sheets("GeoSelection").Select
    itest = Range("m03TestNumber")
    For mRegion = 1 To NUM_REGIONS
        Range("RegionsSet1Data").Cells(mRegion, 1) = _
            gFinalStatusRegions(itest, mRegion)
    Next mRegion
    'State Information
    For mState = 1 To NUM_STATES
        If gFinalStatusStates(itest, mState) Then      'status
            Range("StatesSet1Data").Cells(mState, 1) = "INCLUDED"
        Else
            Range("StatesSet1Data").Cells(mState, 1) = "OUT"
        End If
    Next mState
    'MSA Sets
    For iset = 1 To MSA_SEL_SETS
        Select Case iset
            Case Is = 1: EndLoop = NUM_MSA_SET1: DRange = "MSASet1Data"
            Case Is = 2: EndLoop = NUM_MSA_SET2: DRange = "MSASet2Data"
            Case Is = 3: EndLoop = NUM_MSA_SET3: DRange = "MSASet3Data"
            Case Is = 4: EndLoop = NUM_MSA_SET4: DRange = "MSASet4Data"
        End Select
        For mMSA = 1 To EndLoop
            ActHere = False
            Range(DRange).Cells(mMSA, 1) = "OUT"
            Select Case iset
                Case Is = 1: If gFinalStatusMSASet1(itest, mMSA) Then ActHere = True
                Case Is = 2: If gFinalStatusMSASet2(itest, mMSA) Then ActHere = True
                Case Is = 3: If gFinalStatusMSASet3(itest, mMSA) Then ActHere = True
                Case Is = 4: If gFinalStatusMSASet4(itest, mMSA) Then ActHere = True
            End Select
            If ActHere Then Range(DRange).Cells(mMSA, 1) = "INCLUDED"
        Next mMSA
    Next iset

End Sub
```

EXHIBIT 9.62   "GeoSelect_PrintOutStatusByPortfolio" subroutine

"GeoSelect_ReadGeoSelectionReportsFile" subroutine seen in Exhibit 9.64. The subroutine reads the file name in the Range "m03SelectDataFileName" and appends it with a pathway to the "data" directory. There it opens the file and reads the data. This file has the identical format of the "GeoReport" Worksheet with a single worksheet for each of the five possible tests. This criteria file may have been written with as few as one or as many of five separate criteria test sets. The subroutine determines how many worksheets are in the file and which of the selection criteria test sets they represent.

Operation of the Geographic Concentration Section

The Geographic Concentration Limits section of the menu is organized in a broadly similar manner to that of the Geographic Selection Criteria section. It contains a single button that allows us to display a UserForm into which we can specify concentration limits for both state- and MSA level entities. There is also a collection of

```
Sub GeoSelect_ClearStatusOnGeoReport()

    'regional info first
    Sheets("GeoReport").Select
    For mRegion = 1 To NUM_REGIONS
        Range("RegionsSet1Data").Cells(mRegion, 1) = ""
    Next mRegion
    'state information
    For mState = 1 To NUM_STATES
        Range("StatesSet1Data").Cells(mState, 1) = ""
    Next mState
    'clears MSA set 1-4
    For iset = 1 To MSA_SEL_SETS
        Select Case iset
            Case Is = 1: EndLoop = NUM_MSA_SET1: DRange = "MSASet1Data"
            Case Is = 2: EndLoop = NUM_MSA_SET2: DRange = "MSASet2Data"
            Case Is = 3: EndLoop = NUM_MSA_SET3: DRange = "MSASet3Data"
            Case Is = 4: EndLoop = NUM_MSA_SET4: DRange = "MSASet4Data"
        End Select
        For icnt = 1 To EndLoop
            Range(DRange).Cells(icnt, 1) = ""
        Next icnt
    Next iset

End Sub
```

EXHIBIT 9.63 "GeoSelect_ClearStatusOnGeoMenu" subroutine

criteria management CommandButtons that mirror those in the Geographic Selection portion of the menu. See Exhibit 9.65 and 9.66.

State and MSA Concentration Menu This menu follows the same general plan as the two UserForm Menus of the Geographic Selection section we have previously examined. There are, however, two key differences between them and the UserForms of this menu. The first difference is that the format of the data displayed in the ListBox changes. If we are displaying a list of states, we have a two-column format of the state postal code and the state name; if we are displaying MSA information, we are displaying a three-column format of MSA code, the state postal code of the MSA, and the name of the MSA. Earlier in the MSA Selection Menu, we modified the "RowSource" property of the ListBox to display different MSA lists. We will now modify other property values of the ListBox to reformat it dynamically as the program is running. The second change in menu design is that we will allow the analyst to enter a value, in the form of a concentration limit, for the selected states and MSAs of the ListBox. With these two exceptions, all of the VBA Menu support code in the UserForm module for this menu should be understandable if you compare it to the two previously examined UserForm Menus of the Geographic Selection section.

Changing the Contents and Format of the ListBox Unlike the preceding two User-Form Menus we have examined, the ListBox of this menu will need to display two sets of different data. The first is a listing of state information while the second is a

```
Sub GeoSelect_ReadGeoSelectionReportFile()

Dim data_select_file    As String    'output filename input by user
Dim icount              As Integer

    'open the file
    data_select_file = Range("m03SelectDataFileName")
    Workbooks.Open FileName:= _
        DATA_DIRECTORY & GEOSELECT_SUBDIR & data_select_file
    TargetString = "GeoReport-Test"
    Call GeoSelect_FindAllSheetsPresentInFile(TargetString)

    For itest = 1 To NUM_GEO_TESTS
        If gSheetIsHere(itest) Then
            sheet_name = TargetString & itest
            Sheets(sheet_name).Select
            For mRegion = 1 To NUM_REGIONS 'Read Region Level settings
                gFinalStatusRegions(itest, mRegion) = _
                    Range("SelectRegions").Cells(mRegion, 1)
            Next mRegion
            For mState = 1 To NUM_STATES  'Read State Level settings
                If Range("SelectStates").Cells(mState, 1) = "INCLUDED" Then
                    gFinalStatusStates(itest, mState) = True
                Else
                    gFinalStatusStates(itest, mState) = False
                End If
            Next mState
            For iset = 1 To MSA_SEL_SETS    'Read the 4 sets of MSA Level settings
                Select Case iset
                    Case Is = 1: EndLoop = NUM_MSA_SET1: DRange = "SelectMSA1"
                    Case Is = 2: EndLoop = NUM_MSA_SET2: DRange = "SelectMSA2"
                    Case Is = 3: EndLoop = NUM_MSA_SET3: DRange = "SelectMSA3"
                    Case Is = 4: EndLoop = NUM_MSA_SET4: DRange = "SelectMSA4"
                End Select
                For mMSA = 1 To EndLoop
                    Select Case iset
                        Case Is = 1:
                            If Range(DRange).Cells(mMSA, 1) = "INCLUDED" Then
                                gFinalStatusMSASet1(itest, mMSA) = True
                            Else
                                gFinalStatusMSASet1(itest, mMSA) = False
                            End If
                        Case Is = 2:
                            If Range(DRange).Cells(mMSA, 1) = "INCLUDED" Then
                                gFinalStatusMSASet2(itest, mMSA) = True
                            Else
                                gFinalStatusMSASet2(itest, mMSA) = False
                            End If
                        Case Is = 3:
                            If Range(DRange).Cells(mMSA, 1) = "INCLUDED" Then
                                gFinalStatusMSASet3(itest, mMSA) = True
                            Else
                                gFinalStatusMSASet3(itest, mMSA) = False
                            End If
                        Case Is = 4:
                            If Range(DRange).Cells(mMSA, 1) = "INCLUDED" Then
                                gFinalStatusMSASet4(itest, mMSA) = True
                            Else
                                gFinalStatusMSASet4(itest, mMSA) = False
                            End If
                    End Select
                Next mMSA
            Next iset
        End If
    Next itest
    ActiveWorkbook.Close

End Sub
```

EXHIBIT 9.64 "GeoSelect_ReadGeoSelectionReportFile" subroutine

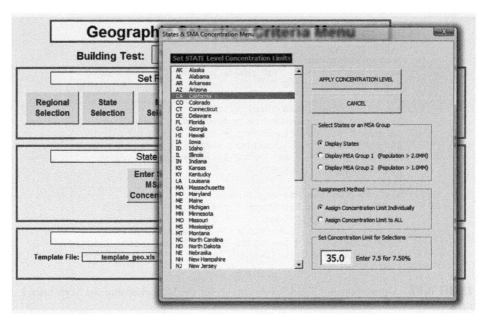

EXHIBIT 9.65 State list displayed

listing of MSA information. The state information has two columns of information to display while the MSA information has three columns. One of the fields in the MSA listing, the MSA name, is, as a rule, much longer that the names of the states. This will require that we redistribute the space of the ListBox to accommodate longer names. Most important, we will need to do this based on the election made in the set

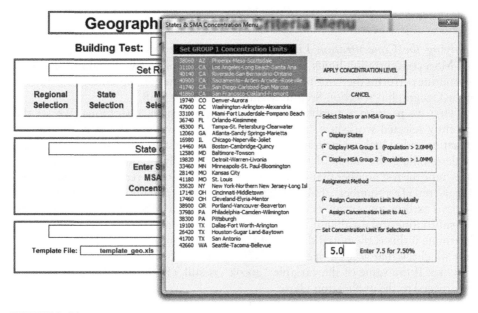

EXHIBIT 9.66 MSA list displayed

```
Private Sub obDisplayMSAGroup1_Click()
    lbConcentrations.RowSource = "GeoReport!MSAGroup1"
    lbConcentrations.ColumnCount = 3
    lbConcentrations.ColumnWidths = "30 pt; 20 pt; 150 pt;"
    Label1.Caption = "   Set GROUP 1 Concentration Limits   "
    mSetDisplayed = CODE_MSA_1
End Sub
Private Sub obDisplayMSAGroup2_Click()
    lbConcentrations.RowSource = "GeoReport!MSAGroup2"
    lbConcentrations.ColumnCount = 3
    lbConcentrations.ColumnWidths = "30 pt; 20 pt; 150 pt;"
    Label1.Caption = " Set GROUP 2 Concentration Limits    "
    mSetDisplayed = CODE_MSA_2
End Sub
Private Sub obDisplayStates_Click()
    lbConcentrations.RowSource = "GeoReport!MSAGroup1"
    lbConcentrations.ColumnCount = 2
    lbConcentrations.ColumnWidths = "20 pt; 150 pt;"
    Label1.Caption = " Set STATE Level Concentration Limits"
    mSetDisplayed = CODE_STATES
End Sub
```

EXHIBIT 9.67 OptionButton "_Click" Subroutines for the States List and the MSA Lists 1 and 2

of OptionButtons that control the contents of the ListBox. This means that we will need to do this from the "_Click" subroutines tied to the OptionButtons. Luckily we are now familiar with the procedure of changing the setting inside the UserForm Properties Editor to achieve this.

We will need to change the number of columns, the column width, the source from which the ListBox contents are accessed, and the title of the menu depending on which of the display OptionButtons is clicked. The code to effect these changes is shown in Exhibit 9.67.

Applying the Concentration Limit Elections The process of applying the state and MSA concentration limits falls to the "cbApplyChoices_Click" subroutine. This subroutine performs the same pattern of operations as the corresponding subroutines in the Geographic Selection Section Menus. See Exhibit 9.68.

First we perform a number of setup, or housekeeping, operations. We set the currently selected worksheet to "GeoMenu", then determine if this is an exercise in setting individual concentration limits or limits for the entire state or MSA list by determining the status of the "obAssignIndividually" OptionButton. Next we determine the test number that we will record the limits for by reading the value of the Range "m03TestNumber". Following that we read the contents of the Concentration Limits TextBox converting its contents from a string to a numeric by the use of the Val subroutine and dividing it by 100 to express it as a percentage. Next we need to determine if this is the initial display of the menu and initialize the test if necessary. Last we check that at least one item has been selected from the list if it is necessary to do so. If the value of the variable "go_ok" is still TRUE (everything went fine), we proceed to the application phase.

In the application phase, we need to know which group, the States List or MSA List 1 or 2, is the active list that we will now apply the concentration limit to. Calling the "CON_GetCodeGroupDisplayed" subroutine will set the variable "mSetDisplayed" based on the condition of the three display OptionButtons. We next build the conformation list message. Here we need to have two display formats based on whether we are looking at state or MSA data. The message is constructed and displayed by the "CON_ProduceSelectionResultsMsgBox" subroutine. If the model analyst indicates that the concentration limits are to be applied, we then proceed to call either the "CON_AssignIndividualConLevel" subroutine or the "CON_AssignALLConLevel" subroutine. If the model user elects not to confirm the assignments, we print the cancellation message.

At the end of these activities, the menu is unloaded and that round of the specification exercise is complete.

```
Private Sub cbApplyChoices_Click()

Dim a As String

    Sheets("GeoSelectMenu").Select      'make this menu the active one
    'see if this is an individual or group assignment
    If obAssignIndividually Then mAssignIndividual = True
    gGeoCriteriaTest = Range("m03TestNumber")
    a = tbConcentrationLimit.Value
    gConLevel = Val(a) / 100
    Call CON_CheckInitialStatus
    Call CON_CheckSomeSelectionMade
    If go_ok Then
        Call CON_GetCodeGroupDisplayed  'which group is displayed?
        'cycle through the displayed list
        'construct and print out the confirm message
        msg = ""
        For icnt = 0 To lbConcentrations.ListCount - 1
            If lbConcentrations.Selected(icnt) Then
                If obDisplayMSAGroup1 Or obDisplayMSAGroup2 Then
                    msg = msg & lbConcentrations.List(icnt, 0) & "      " _
                        & lbConcentrations.List(icnt, 1) & ", " _
                        & lbConcentrations.List(icnt, 2) & vbCrLf
                Else 'states message
                    msg = msg & lbConcentrations.List(icnt, 0) & "      " _
                        & lbConcentrations.List(icnt, 1) & vbCrLf
                End If
            End If
        Next icnt
        Call CON_ProduceSelectionResultsMsgBox
        If go_ok Then
            If mAssignIndividual Then
                Call CON_AssignIndividualConLevel
            Else
                Call CON_AssignALLConLevel
            End If
        Else
            Call GeoSelect_MenuNoSelectionActionTaken(mSetDisplayed)
        End If
    End If
    'put down the user form
    Unload m3ConcentrationLimits

End Sub
```

EXHIBIT 9.68 "cbApplyChoices_Click" subroutine

Concentration Criteria Management Process The four buttons of this section are so similar in form and function to those described in detail in our discussion of the Geographic Selection portion of the menu above that readers will quickly grasp the reason for any differences in the supporting code. For that reason, and for the highly desired goal of brevity (where possible), we will not review them in detail.

FINANCIAL SELECTION CRITERIA MENU

Aside from the geographic selection process, there are other financial and demographic features of a piece of collateral that may make it undesirable or even impossible to include in a securitization. We need to create an ability for the analyst to specify various eligibility conditions based on the non-geographic characteristics of a loan.

Purpose of the Menu

The purpose of the menu is to allow the model user an effective and efficient vehicle for creating a series of collateral eligibility tests based on the financial and demographic characteristics of a loan. To address this need we will create a menu with a series of specialized function UserForms. Each of these UserForms will allow us to create a specific type of collateral eligibility test. We will activate them in the same manner we did in the Geographic Selection Menu by using CommandButtons on the Excel Menu of the model. Each of these UserForms will allow the analyst to create eligibility tests using any of the data found in the Collateral Data file. We can create up to five sets of Selection Criteria, each set having up to 20 individual tests. This allows the model user the ability to build a specifically tailored set of selection criteria for each of the five sub-portfolios of the collateral pool.

Final Product of the Menu

How do we translate the contents of the specialized UserForms of the Selection Criteria Menu into a form that can be later used by the CCFG to perform the collateral screening process? The essence of all of the tests consists of three components. These are:

1. **The data used in the test:** for example, the amortization pattern, occupancy status, or property structure code.
2. **The test value that we wish to compare against the contents of the collateral record.** This typically might be a large current balance loan limit of, say, $2,000,000.
3. **The type of operation action we will employ in the test.** These can be "Equal To", "Not Equal To", "Greater Than", "Greater Than or Equal To", and so on.

There are a myriad of combinations in which the data items, values, and test operators can be strung together. The six combinations that are shown in the menu can address a wide range of collateral eligibility conditions. Nevertheless, all of them can be constructed (or reconstructed) if we know the type of test we are applying, the constituent data items, test operators, and test values. We will need to have one other important piece of information, and that is the order in which the items, operators, and test values were entered so that we can correctly construct the appropriate tests using them when the time comes to do so.

Fortunately we can easily accomplish this through the use of a small number of VBA arrays that we will populate based on the model users' inputs to the various specialized UserForms. In addition to the contents of the items, operators, and values, we will need to know what type of test it is and, to make the looping operations of the model more efficient, if the test in question is "active." The term "active" in this context means "Do the arrays contain information for this test or are they void?" It would also be quite convenient if we had a description of the test for use in reporting when the results of the selection process are made known!

We can create arrays to hold all of this information quite economically. Recall one of the facts from the detailed analysis that we just concluded on the UserForm module code of the Geographic Selection Menu. When we use ListBoxes of whatever length, we can determine the nth location that the selected item(s) occupy in the lists. By storing these index locations, we can quickly "reassemble" the test from components of the list based on their locations in it. Thus we know that a value of 5 in the array that holds the item information identifies "Current Balance", but the same value stored in the operators array for the test means "Equal To"!

To this end we will create seven arrays to hold all of the information we will need to reconstruct the selection criteria tests input by the model user. Remember, we must provide for up to five test sets each containing up to 20 tests. The arrays are:

1. **"gSCEditType"**. Holds the type of test (values 1 through 6) for each of the tests.
2. **"gSCEditItems"**. Holds the index location of the data item on the list of all data items that is to be used in the test. Thus a value of 5 means we will be comparing the value of the "Current Balance" to whatever test criteria we establish. In the six tests the maximum number of "items" we will need is three (in Test Type 3).
3. **"gSCEditOpers"**. Holds the operators to be used in the test. There are six members of the operators list, "Less Than", "Less Than or Equal To", "Greater Than", "Greater Than or Equal To", "Equal To", and "Not Equal To". The maximum number of operators used by a test type is ten, used by Test Type 6.
4. **"gSCEditValues"**. These are the test values that we will compare our collateral data value against to determine eligibility status. The maximum number of values we will need is ten, used by Test Type #6.
5. **"gSCTestName"**. This is the model users' description of the test.
6. **"gSCSetActive"**. This is an array of Boolean variables that will tell us if specifications have been entered for this test set as a whole.
7. **"gSCTestActive"**. This is an array of Boolean variables that will tell us if specifications have been entered for a particular test in a set.

The corresponding portions of the Financial Selection Criteria tests represented by the above arrays are shown in Exhibit 9.69. The declarations of the arrays are shown in Exhibit 9.70.

Financial/Demographic Information Criteria Test Set Report

Set: 1

Test #	Test Type	Test Conditions							
1	1	[Current Balance	LT	2500000	]				
2	2	[Original Balance	LE	5000	AND	[Original Balance	GE	2750000]	
3	3	[Credit Sector	EQ	1	] AND				
		[Current Coupon Rate	LE	0.035	OR	[Current Coupon Rate	GE	0.17]	
4	4	[Mortgage Type	EQ	1	OR				
		Mortgage Type	EQ	2	OR				
		Mortgage Type	EQ	4	OR				
		Mortgage Type	EQ	5	OR				
		Mortgage Type	EQ	6	]				
5	5	[Property Type	LE	5	AND	[Property Type	GE	2] AND	
		[Current Loan-to-Value Ratio	LE	0.9	AND	[Current Loan-to-Value Ratio	GE	0.5]	
6	6	[Original Term (months)	EQ	360	AND	Remaining Term (months)	GT	300] OR	
		[Original Term (months)	EQ	240	AND	Remaining Term (months)	GT	200] OR	
		[Original Term (months)	EQ	180	AND	Remaining Term (months)	GT	150] OR	
		[Original Term (months)	EQ	120	AND	Remaining Term (months)	GT	108] OR	
		[Original Term (months)	EQ	60	AND	Remaining Term (months)	GT	54]	

Key to Selection Criteria Test Components

Original Term (months)	= gSCEditItems
EQ	= gSCEditOperators
360	= gSCEditValues

EXHIBIT 9.69 Financial Selection schema

Layout of the Menu

The Selection Criteria Editor Menu has four sections. See Exhibit 9.71. These are, from top to bottom, left to right:

1. **Test Description section.** This section describes the format and general content of each of the six test types that can be created by the model user employing the CommandButtons at the bottom of the menu.
2. **Test Set Specification section.** This section contains three fields. The first allows the analyst to specify the test set in which to place the test about to be created, the second the individual Test number within that set, and a file name for use with the topmost three Utility buttons.
3. **UserForm Selection Test Editor buttons.** This section contains six Command-Buttons that activate UserForms that are used to construct the types of collateral selection tests described on the face of the menu above.
4. **Utility Button section.** This section of the menu contains five CommandButtons, divided into two groups. These buttons perform various utility roles in managing the selection criteria to make life easier for the analyst. The first set allows the analyst to list the criteria test that has been created (so it can be viewed as a whole), save the tests of the set to a file, and, after the file has been created, load the saved selection criteria from a file back into the model. The second set of buttons allows the analyst to delete either a single selection criteria test or an entire selection criteria test set.

```
'the next set of arrays start with a "0 to" notation, the "0" is when a Pool
' structure is involved in the analysis not a sets of Sub-Portfolios, the
' maximum number of Sub-Portfolios is 5.
Public gSCEditType(0 To NUM_PORTS, 1 To NUM_SEL_TESTS) As Integer                        'type of test
Public gSCEditItems(0 To NUM_PORTS, 1 To NUM_SEL_TESTS, 1 To MAX_SEL_ITEMS) As Integer   'items in test
Public gSCEditOpers(0 To NUM_PORTS, 1 To NUM_SEL_TESTS, 1 To MAX_SEL_OPERS) As Double    'operators in test
Public gSCEditValue(0 To NUM_PORTS, 1 To NUM_SEL_TESTS, 1 To MAX_SEL_VALUE) As Double    'values in test
Public gSCEditTestName(0 To NUM_PORTS, 1 To NUM_SEL_TESTS) As String                     'test name
Public gSCSetActive(0 To NUM_PORTS) As Boolean                                           'is set active?
Public gSCTestActive(0 To NUM_PORTS, 1 To NUM_SEL_TESTS) As Boolean                      'is test active?
```

EXHIBIT 9.70   Financial Selection Criteria Menu global variable declarations

CCFG Financial/Demographic Selection Criteria Editor Menu

Type 1: Single Condition Test
Example: Orginal Term LE 480

Type 2: Minimum/Maximum Test
Example: Original Term GE 180 AND Original Term LE 480

Type 3: Single Condition Test Combined With Minimum/Maximum
Example: PropertyType EQ 1 AND [Original Term GE 180 OR Original Term LE 480]

Type 4: Single Criteria Item, Multiple Values Selection
Example: PropertyType EQ 1 OR PropertyType EQ 5 OR PropertyType EQ 6 OR PropertyType EQ 8

Type 5: Joint Minimum/Maximum Test
Example: [OriginalTerm GE 120 AND OriginalTerm LE 480] AND [PropertyType EQ 3 OR PropertyType EQ 4]

Type 6: Two Criteria Table Test
Example: [Index EQ 1 AND Spread GE 2%] OR [Index EQ 2 AND Spread GE 1.5%] OR [Index EQ 3 AND Spread GE 4%]

Assign Test Set (Limit 5 Sets) and Test Number (Limit 20 Tests) Within Set

Set: 1   Test: 6   File: SaveTheseTests.xls

Assign Test Set, Test Number, and Enter Test Type

Test Type 1 Single Condition Test	Test Type 2 Min/Max Test	Test Type 3 Single Test & Min/Max Test	Test Type 4 Single Criteria Multiple Values	Test Type 5 2 Joint Min/Max Tests	Test Type 6 2 Criteria Table Test

Printing, Saving and Reading Test Sets

Print This Test Set	Write Test Sets To File	Read Test Sets From File

Removing A Test or Test Set

Delete Test	Delete Test Set

EXHIBIT 9.71 Financial Selection Criteria Menu

Operation of the Menu

Test Specification Fields The primary role of the Test Specification section is to identify to the CCFG which of the selection criteria tests, by Test Set number and by Test Number within the Test Set, is being created. If any information needs to be read in from or written out to a file, the Test Set File field is available to specify the file name as needed. See Exhibit 9.72.

Selection Criteria UserForm Menus We will not review the VBA code that resides in the User Modules of each of the Test Criteria UserForms shown below. The code is designed to channel the inputs of the analyst from the forms to the various VBA global arrays described previously. The ListBoxes in each of the forms contain a full listing of all the datum of the collateral data file. The operators are also selected from ListBoxes while the Test values are input into a series of Test boxes. These values are then parsed for reasonableness and correct data form (no String inputs allowed for data that are numeric in nature!).

Let us start with Test Type 1, the most simple of the six types. See Exhibit 9.73. Here we need only to specify a single item, a single operator, and a single value. This

Assign Test Set (Limit 5 Sets) and Test Number (Limit 20 Tests) Within Set

Set: 3   Test: 1   File: SaveTheseTests.xls

EXHIBIT 9.72 Test Specification fields

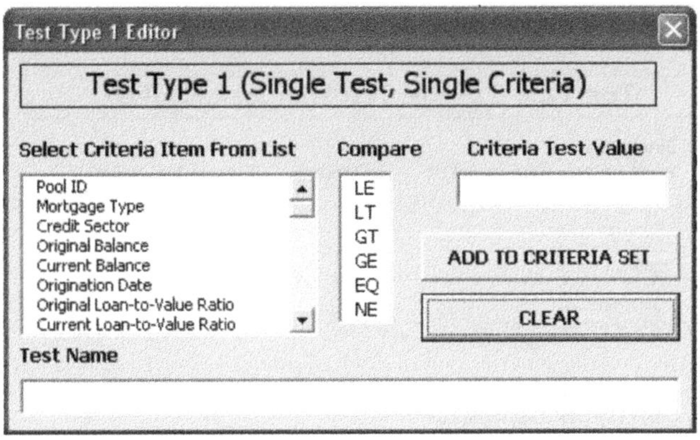

EXHIBIT 9.73 Single-condition test

type of test is usually referred to as a single-tail test. We test an item against a value that serves as a limit.

Test Type 2 performs the function of a two-limit test. The most common form of this test is the Min/Max test. See Exhibit 9.74. The item must be greater that one value and less that another. A single item serves for both sides of the test.

For example:

```
Original Term >= 120 and Original Term <= 480
```

Test Type 3 combines what is usually a Min/Max Test Type 2 with a single-condition test. See Exhibit 9.75. It serves to first identify a set of loans in the first clause of the test (by property type, occupancy code, loan-to-value ratio, etc.) with a range test. For example, we may wish to place a term limit on investor-owned properties. We can use the first part of the test to identify that set of properties by occupancy type and then place the term or balance limits using the second part of the test.

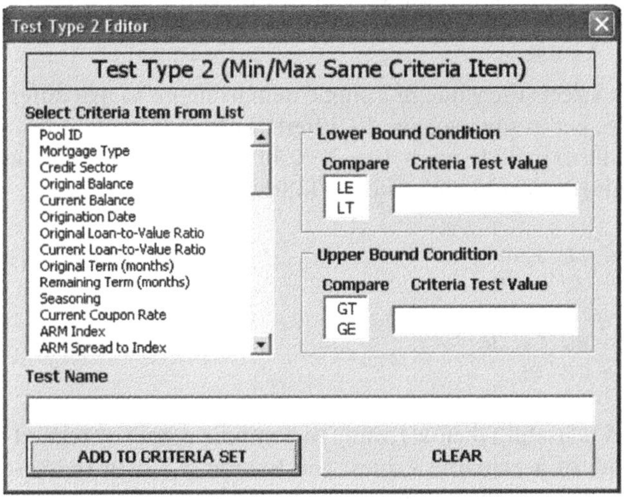

EXHIBIT 9.74 Minimum/Maximum test

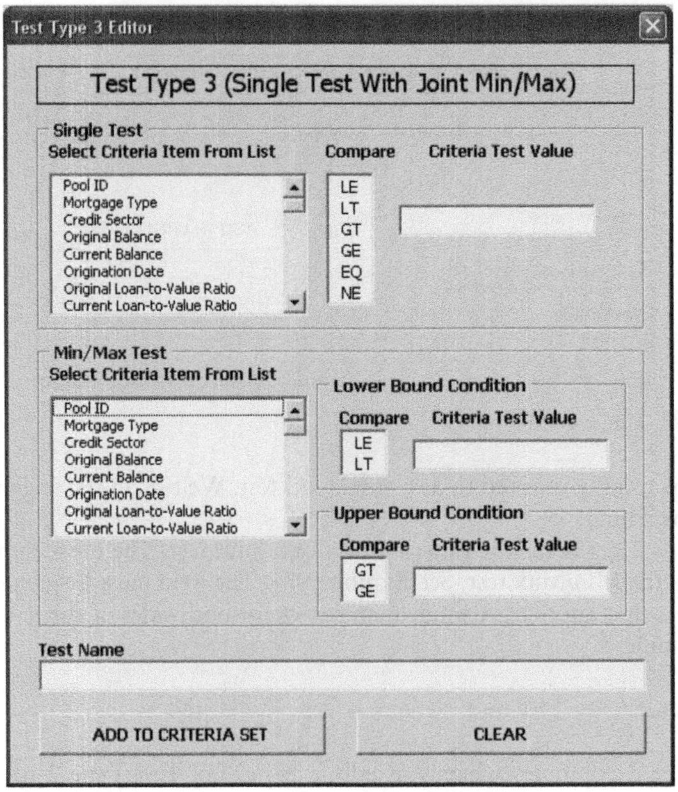

EXHIBIT 9.75   Single-condition with Joint Minimum/Maximum

For example:

```
Occupancy Code = 3 (non-owner occupied) AND
Current Balance >= 10,000 AND Current Balance <= 750,000
```

Test Type 4 selects the value of a single item using up to five different operators. See Exhibit 9.76. Let us say we have 20 different property type codes, with the value 1 to 20. We want to include types 1 to 3, 5, 11, 14, and everything greater than or equal to 18. This test would look like the following:

```
Property Type LE 3 OR
Property Type EQ 5 OR
Property Type EQ 11 OR
Property Type EQ 14 OR
Property Type GE 18
```

Test Type 5 is useful when we want to combine a pair of related variables that each has a range of acceptable values. See Exhibit 9.77. In the case of balances, we may want to limit both the upper and lower limits of the current and original balance. The lower limit will serve to eliminate from the portfolio small-balance

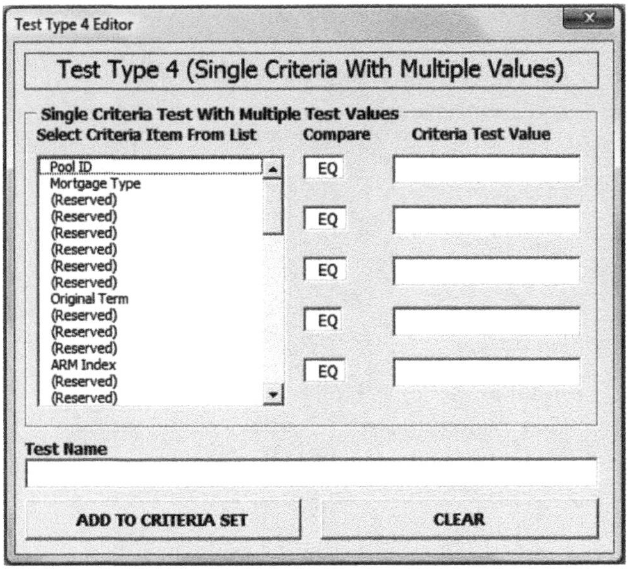

EXHIBIT 9.76 Single-criteria Multiple Values Selection test

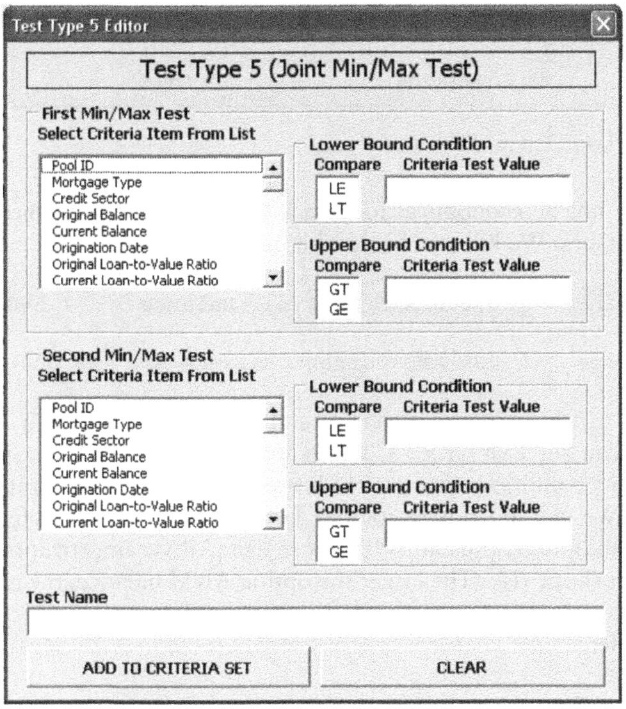

EXHIBIT 9.77 Joint Minimum/Maximum test

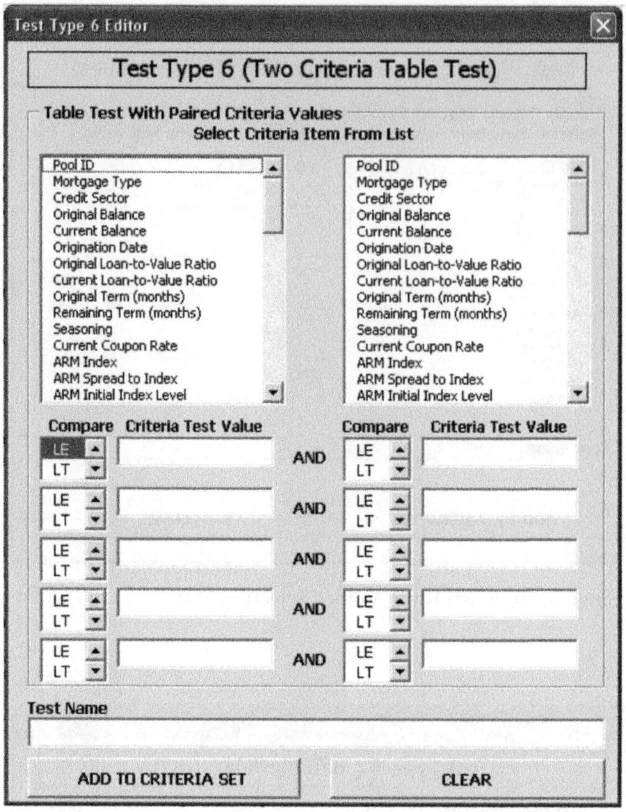

EXHIBIT 9.78 Two Criteria Table test

loans that may not be economical to service while the upper balance will address concentration issues. We kill two birds with one stone thus:

```
Original Balance > 10,000 AND Original Balance <= 1,500,000
AND
Current Balance > 5,000 AND Current Balance <= 750,000
```

Test Type 6, for example, is very useful when dealing with a series of tests in a tabular form. See Exhibit 9.78. For example, we may have maximum current balance eligibility conditions that are predicated on the loan amortization pattern of the mortgage. We may be able to tolerate larger loan balances on fixed rate loans as opposed to an option adjustable-rate mortgage (ARM) amortization pattern that carries payment shock risk. The larger the option ARM balance, the greater the risk of default due to a large payment reset differential will be.

For example:

```
Mortgage Type EQ 1 AND Original Balance < 2,000,000 OR
Mortgage Type EQ 2 AND Original Balance < 1,500,000 OR
Mortgage Type EQ 3 AND Original Balance < 700,000 OR
Mortgage Type EQ 4 AND Original Balance < 500,000 OR
Mortgage Type EQ 5 AND Original Balance < 300,000
```

EXHIBIT 9.79 Menu Utility Function CommandButtons

Menu Utility Functions There are five Utility Function CommandButtons. They are positioned in the upper right of the menu. One prints out all the tests of a single Test set to a worksheet of the CCFG. Two either write the tests to or read the tests from a file. The last two either delete the current individual test or the entire currently indicated Test set. The code for all of these Utility buttons is very straightforward and will not be reviewed in detail at this time. This is Excel menu support code and is contained in the VBA menu support modules, NOT in the UserForm VBA code modules. See Exhibits 9.79, 9.80, and 9.81.

```
Sub FinSelect_PrintSelectionCriteriaReport()

    Call FinSelect_TestAndSetIsNumericsCheck(ISNUMERIC_SET_ONLY)
    If gIsNumericFail Then Exit Sub
    iset = Range("m09CollatSelectSet")
    Range("m09CollatSelectSet") = iset
    'see if we need to read the selection item names
    gReadFinancialNames = gReadFinancialNames + 1
    If gReadFinancialNames = 1 Then
        Call FinSelect_ReadDataItemNames
        Sheets("FinCriteriaReport").Select
    End If
    'clear the contents from the existing report
    Call FinSelect_ClearReportWorksheet
    'write the test set indicated
    irow = 9
    For itest = 1 To NUM_SEL_TESTS
        If gSCTestActive(iset, itest) Then   'is this an active test/
            Cells(irow, 1).Value = itest
            Cells(irow, 2).Value = gSCEditType(iset, itest)
            Cells(irow, 3).Value = "["
            Select Case gSCEditType(iset, itest)
                Case Is = 1: Call FinSelect_WriteTestType1
                Case Is = 2: Call FinSelect_WriteTestType2
                Case Is = 3: Call FinSelect_WriteTestType3
                Case Is = 4: Call FinSelect_WriteTestType4
                Case Is = 5: Call FinSelect_WriteTestType5
                Case Is = 6: Call FinSelect_WriteTestType6
            End Select
            irow = irow + 2     'put a blank line between tests
        End If
    Next itest

End Sub
```

EXHIBIT 9.80 "FinSelect_PrintSelectionCriteriaReport" subroutine

```
Sub FinSelect_WriteTestType3()

    'first line
    Cells(irow, BRACKET_COL1).Value = "["
    Cells(irow, ITEM_COL1).Value = gFinSelNames(gSCEditItems(iset, itest, 1))
    Cells(irow, OPER_COL1).Value = gFinSelOperators(gSCEditOpers(iset, itest, 1))
    Cells(irow, VALUE_COL1).Value = gSCEditValue(iset, itest, 1)
    Cells(irow, BRACKET_COL2).Value = "]"
    Cells(irow, 21).Value = "AND"
    FinSelect_FormatReportCells (ITEM_COL1)
    FinSelect_FormatReportCells (OPER_COL1)
    FinSelect_FormatReportCells (VALUE_COL1)
    'second line
    irow = irow + 1
    Cells(irow, BRACKET_COL1).Value = "["
    Cells(irow, ITEM_COL1).Value = gFinSelNames(gSCEditItems(iset, itest, 2))
    Cells(irow, OPER_COL1).Value = gFinSelOperators(gSCEditOpers(iset, itest, 2))
    Cells(irow, VALUE_COL1).Value = gSCEditValue(iset, itest, 2)
    Cells(irow, 21).Value = "OR"
    Cells(irow, ITEM_COL2).Value = gFinSelNames(gSCEditItems(iset, itest, 2))
    Cells(irow, OPER_COL2).Value = gFinSelOperators(gSCEditOpers(iset, itest, 3))
    Cells(irow, VALUE_COL2).Value = gSCEditValue(iset, itest, 3)
    Cells(irow, BRACKET_COL3).Value = "]"
    FinSelect_FormatReportCells (ITEM_COL1)
    FinSelect_FormatReportCells (OPER_COL1)
    FinSelect_FormatReportCells (VALUE_COL1)
    FinSelect_FormatReportCells (ITEM_COL2)
    FinSelect_FormatReportCells (OPER_COL2)
    FinSelect_FormatReportCells (VALUE_COL2)

End Sub

Sub FinSelect_WriteTestType4()
    Cells(irow, BRACKET_COL1).Value = "["
    For icnt = 1 To 5
        Cells(irow, ITEM_COL1).Value = gFinSelNames(gSCEditItems(iset, itest, 1))
        Call FinSelect_FormatReportCells(ITEM_COL1)
        Cells(irow, OPER_COL1).Value = _
                            gFinSelOperators(gSCEditOpers(iset, itest, icnt))
        Call FinSelect_FormatReportCells(OPER_COL1)
        Cells(irow, VALUE_COL1).Value = gSCEditValue(iset, itest, icnt)
        Call FinSelect_FormatReportCells(VALUE_COL1)
        If icnt < 5 Then
            Cells(irow, 21).Value = "OR"
            irow = irow + 1
        End If
    Next icnt
    Cells(irow, BRACKET_COL2).Value = "]"
End Sub
```

EXHIBIT 9.81   "FinSelect_WriteTestType(n)" subroutine

In Exhibit 9.82 we see the format of the Criteria Test Set report exhibiting the print format for each of the Test types. This is the report is produced for a single Test set when the "Print This Test Set" CommandButton is clicked. The report appears on the "SelCriteriaReport" worksheet of the CCFG.

From this point forward we will assume that the reader has become familiar with the differences between the use of VBA code in modules and in UserForm modules. We will no longer take detailed looks at the menu support code. Instead we will focus on the purpose and general function of the remaining menus and what information they are expected to provide the CCFG so that it may complete its analysis.

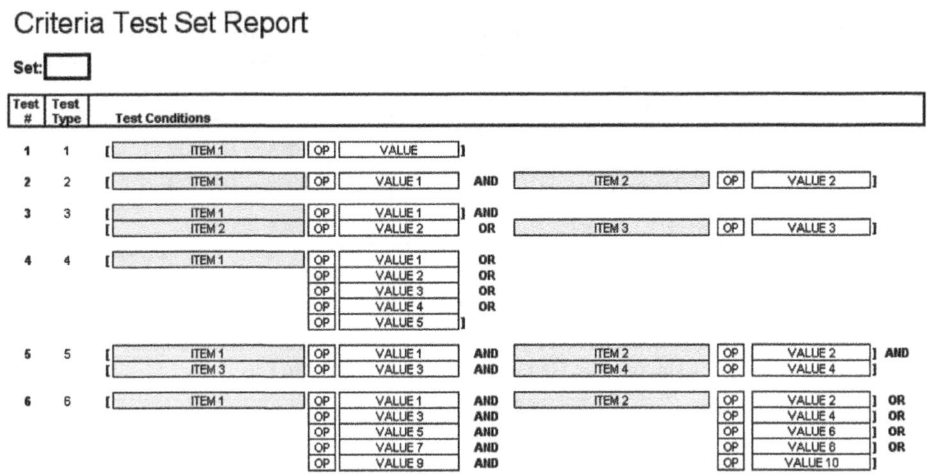

Criteria Test Set Report

Set: [   ]

EXHIBIT 9.82 Criteria Test Set report

CASH FLOW AMORTIZATION PARAMETERS MENU

The Cash Flow Amortization Parameters Menu is one of the most important menus of the CCFG. In this menu we will establish the fundamental criteria regarding the collateral amortization assumptions.

Purpose of the Menu

The purpose of the Cash Flow Amortization Parameters Menu is to allow the model user to select among three mutually exclusive sets of prepayment and default modeling methodologies. These methodologies are:

1. **Uniform prepayment and default curves.** In this methodology a single prepayment and single default curve is applied to all loans in a particular scenario regardless of their amortization type or other financial and demographic features.
2. **Geographic-specific curves.** In this methodology the CCFG reads a file that contains a series of prepayment, default, recovery rate, and market value decline curves based on either the state or the MSA of the collateral. These curves can be further modified by the specification of stress levels.
3. **Demographic/Financial Factors.** In this approach each of the loans is assigned a series of cumulative, multiplicative risk factors that determine the default rate and the severity of the default. This information is stored in a single file that the CCFG can access to obtain the factor information.

Layout of the Menu

The Cash Flow Amortization Parameters Menu is comprised of five sections. Three of these sections are used to specify the assumptions for a particular prepayment and default approach, one is used to specify stress factor sensitivities, and the last is used

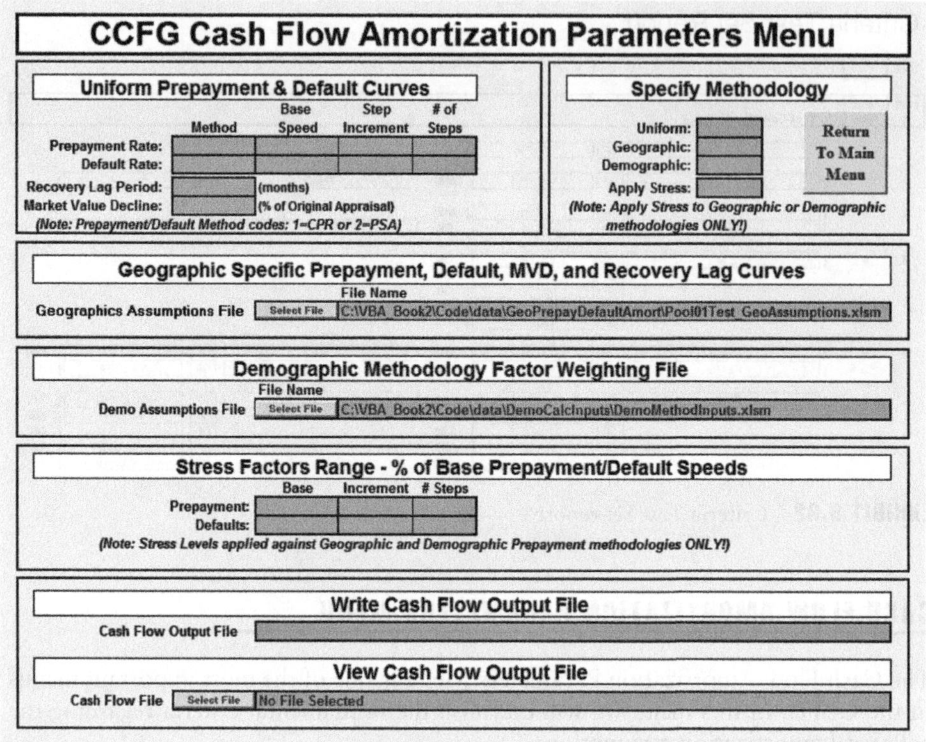

EXHIBIT 9.83　　Cash Flow Amortization Parameters Menu

to specify which of the three approaches is to be applied and if sensitivity analysis is desired. See Exhibit 9.83.

Operation of the Menu

The operation of the menu is dependent on which of the three methodologies is elected by the model analyst. We will look at an example of the inputs needed for each of the methodologies.

Uniform Prepayment and Default Curve Method　　To apply this methodology the model analyst needs to specify the ten inputs of the "Uniform Prepayment and Default Curve" section of the menu. The entries related to the prepayment and default assumptions require four entries each. See Exhibit 9.84. These are as follows:

1. **Prepayment and default methodology.** The analyst can specify either the Public Securities Administration (PSA) methodology or constant percentage rate (CPR) methodology. Note: *Do not* mix methodologies! Use either CPR or PSA but *never* both in the same analysis. Here the methodology is set to "2", "PSA".
2. **Base prepayment or default rate.** In Exhibit 9.84 the analyst has defined the base prepayment rate as 100% and the base default rate as 150%.

CCFG Cash Flow Amortization Parameters Menu

Uniform Prepayment & Default Curves

	Method	Base Speed	Step Increment	# of Steps
Prepayment Rate:	2	100.00%	50.00%	5
Default Rate:	2	150.00%	100.00%	5

Recovery Lag Period: 18 (months)
Market Value Decline: 45% (% of Original Appraisal)
(Note: Prepayment/Default Method codes: 1=CPR or 2=PSA)

Specify Methodology

Uniform: X
Geographic:
Demographic:
Apply Stress:
(Note: Apply Stress to Geographic or Demographic methodologies ONLY!)

Return To Main Menu

Geographic Specific Prepayment, Default, MVD, and Recovery Lag Curves

File Name
Geographics Assumptions File [Select File]

Demographic Methodology Factor Weighting File

File Name
Demo Assumptions File [Select File]

Stress Factors Range - % of Base Prepayment/Default Speeds

	Base	Increment	# Steps
Prepayment:			
Defaults:			

(Note: Stress Levels applied against Geographic and Demographic Prepayment methodologies ONLY!)

Write Cash Flow Output File

Cash Flow Output File

View Cash Flow Output File

Cash Flow File [Select File] No File Selected

EXHIBIT 9.84 Uniform curve methodology entries

3. **Step increment.** This is the sensitivity step up in rate that you would like the model to run. If the base rate is 100% PSA and you enter 50% in this field, the model will increment the 100% PSA rate by 50% PSA for each of the number of steps indicated.

4. **Number of steps.** This field allows the analyst to specify the number of steps to apply the step increment discussed above. If the number of steps is input as 5, the base prepayment rate is 100% PSA, and the step increment is 50% PSA, the model will run five prepayment scenarios of 100% (the base rate), 150%, 200%, 250%, and 300% PSA *for each* of the specified default scenarios. Thus if you specify five default steps (the maximum number of steps is 10 for both prepayments or defaults) and four prepayment steps, the model will generate 20 sets of cash flows.

Next we need to specify the recovery lag period. This period is the length of time (in months) it takes the mortgage servicing group to recover title to the property, restore the property to serviceable condition, and sell it. In Exhibit 9.84 this is set to 18 months.

Last we need to specify the market value decline. This input represents our best estimate of the ultimate decline in the value of the property between the value of the original appraisal and the final sales price at disposal. This exhibit should also include all seizure, repair, preparation, servicing, and selling expenses included in the process of liquidating the property. In this case we have set the market value decline percentage to 45% of the original property appraisal.

The last thing we need to do is to tell the model that this is the methodology we will employ by placing an "X" in the "Uniform" choice field in the "Specify Method" section of the menu. Note: Any entries in the "Stress Factors Range" section of the menu will be ignored. When this methodology is employed, sensitivity runs (if any) are assumed to be included in the multiple scenario prepayment/default combinations specified by the analyst.

Geographic Specific Curve Methodology   In this methodology the model user selects a file that contains a set of pre-described prepayment, default, recovery lag period, and market value decline factors. These factors are described at both the state and MSA levels. The model will read the geographic information for each loan by its geographic location and its amortization type and apply the appropriate set of attrition curves.

The fields of this menu allow the analyst to specify the entire pathway to the file by using the same technique employed in the collateral data file section previously discussed. The analyst need only click on the field to display the "Open" command window, navigate to the file, and select it. The entire file pathway and file name will appear in the window. See Exhibit 9.85. This will tell the program to apply this attrition file against the pool or sub-portfolio.

If you want to generate a sensitivity analysis for the portfolio you can also enter a base rate, step increment, and number of steps for either the prepayment or default curves contained in the file or both. You will note that these rates do not have a methodology label attached to them. They are methodology independent. If you specify the base as 100%, the step increment as 25%, and the number of steps as 5, the model will apply 100%, 125%, 150%, 175%, and 200% of the specified curves. Again, remember that if you specify 5 prepayment steps (the maximum allowed) and 5 default steps (again, the maximum allowed), the model will generate 25 cash flow scenarios!

The last step in using the Geographic Specific methodology will be to check the "Geographic" selection in the "Specify Method" section of the model, and then "Apply Stress" if you wish the sensitivities to be generated.

Demographic/Financial Factor Weighting Methodology   The third methodology, the Demographic/Financial Factor Weighting Methodology, requires the model user to specify a single assumptions file and, if desired, a set of "Stress Factor" section inputs. In this methodology each of the loans is assigned a risk factor based on its individual demographic and financial characteristics. These risk factors are cumulative in nature and determine the probability of default and the severity of default when it occurs. See Exhibit 9.86.

Stress factors can be applied when employing this methodology. A more detailed discussion of the factor compositions and their application will be presented in Chapter 12. After loading in the Demographic/Financial Factors file name, you need to select the methodology "Demographic" in the "Specify Menu" section of the menu.

CCFG Cash Flow Amortization Parameters Menu

Uniform Prepayment & Default Curves

	Method	Base Speed	Step Increment	# of Steps
Prepayment Rate:				
Default Rate:				
Recovery Lag Period:		(months)		
Market Value Decline:		(% of Original Appraisal)		

(Note: Prepayment/Default Method codes: 1=CPR or 2=PSA)

Specify Methodology

Uniform:	
Geographic:	X
Demographic:	
Apply Stress:	X

Return To Main Menu

(Note: Apply Stress to Geographic or Demographic methodologies ONLY!)

Geographic Specific Prepayment, Default, MVD, and Recovery Lag Curves

File Name

Geographics Assumptions File [Select File] C:\VBA_Book2\Code\data\GeoPrepayDefaultAmort\Pool01Test_GeoAssumptions.xlsm

Demographic Methodology Factor Weighting File

File Name

Demo Assumptions File [Select File]

Stress Factors Range - % of Base Prepayment/Default Speeds

	Base	Increment	# Steps
Prepayment:	100%	25%	4
Defaults:	100%	50%	5

(Note: Stress Levels applied against Geographic and Demographic Prepayment methodologies ONLY!)

Write Cash Flow Output File

Cash Flow Output File [CF_TestPool03Geographic]

View Cash Flow Output File

Cash Flow File [Select File] No File Selected

EXHIBIT 9.85 Geographic Specific Curve Methodologies

COLLATERAL REPORTS MENU

The final menu of the CCFG is the Collateral Reports Editor and Menu.

Purpose of the Menu

This menu serves four purposes. These are:

1. **Specify Geographic Reports Contents.** Allow the model user to specify the contents of a geographic report package, save those specifications to a file, revise them as necessary, and load the specifications from the file at model run time.
2. **Create Stratification Reports.** Create, save, and reload files containing analyst-specified stratification reports.
3. **Create Cross-Tabulation Reports.** Create, save, and reload files containing analyst-specified cross-tabulation reports.
4. **Select Standard Report Packages.** Select standardize pool level report packages, such as the Matrix Summary report, the Cash Flow Detail report, the Single Scenario Cash Flow report, the Base Stratification report, and so on.

CCFG Cash Flow Amortization Parameters Menu

Uniform Prepayment & Default Curves

	Method	Base Speed	Step Increment	# of Steps
Prepayment Rate:				
Default Rate:				
Recovery Lag Period:		(months)		
Market Value Decline:		(% of Original Appraisal)		

(Note: Prepayment/Default Method codes: 1=CPR or 2=PSA)

Specify Methodology

Uniform:	
Geographic:	
Demographic:	X
Apply Stress:	X

Return To Main Menu

(Note: Apply Stress to Geographic or Demographic methodologies ONLY!)

Geographic Specific Prepayment, Default, MVD, and Recovery Lag Curves

File Name

Geographics Assumptions File   [Select File] C:\VBA_Book2\Code\data\GeoPrepayDefaultAmort\Pool01Test_GeoAssumptions.xlsm

Demographic Methodology Factor Weighting File

File Name

Demo Assumptions File   [Select File] C:\VBA_Book2\Code\data\DemoCalcInputs\DemoMethodInputs.xlsm

Stress Factors Range - % of Base Prepayment/Default Speeds

	Base	Increment	# Steps
Prepayment:	100%	25%	4
Defaults:	100%	50%	5

(Note: Stress Levels applied against Geographic and Demographic Prepayment methodologies ONLY!)

Write Cash Flow Output File

Cash Flow Output File   [CF_TestPool03Demographic]

View Cash Flow Output File

Cash Flow File   [Select File] [No File Selected]

EXHIBIT 9.86   Demographic/Financial Factor Methodologies

Layout of the Menu

The layout of the Collateral Report Editor and Menu follows the functionality described above. See Exhibit 9.87.

The Collateral Report Editor and Menu consists of three parts.

1. **Geographic Reports Menu.** In this section of the menu, model users can specify which state or MSA level reports they would like to produce. There are two buttons in the left side of the report. Each will produce a UserForm that will allow the specification of state or MSA reports respectively. See Exhibits 9.88 and 9.89.
2. **Collateral Stratification Reports Editor.** This section of the menu allows the analyst to create and order a series of stratification reports based on most of the data items found in the collateral data file. The analyst can select either a single-criterion Base Stratification report or a two-parameter Cross-Tabulation report. Clicking on the buttons will display UserForms into which these reports and their contents can be specified. See Exhibit 9.90. A typical single level stratification report would be a sort by loan type with the content of the report current balance. An example of a Cross-Tabulation report would be loan type by property type with the content of the report current balance.

CCFG Reports Editor & Menu

Geographic Reports Editor

State Reports Selection	MSA Reports Selection	Display Geographic Report Elections

Write Geographic Reports Elections to this File:

C:\VBA_Book2\Code\data\GeoReportFiles\GeoReportT2.xls

Write Geographic Report Specifications To A File

Load Report Elections File

C:\VBA_Book2\Code\data\GeoReportFiles\GeoReportT2.xls

Find File	Load Geographic Report Selection File

Collateral Stratification Reports Editor

Stratification Reports Editor	Cross Tabs Reports Editor	Display Stratification Elections	Display Cross Tab Elections

Write Stratification Reports Election to this File:

C:\VBA_Book2\Code\data\StratReportFiles\StratificationRepsT1.xls

Write Base Strat Report Specifications To A File | **Write Cross Tabs Report Specifications To A File**

Load Report Elections File

C:\VBA_Book2\Code\data\StratReportFiles\XTabFile02.xls

Find File	Load Base Strat Report File	Load Cross Tab Report File

Select Report Packages

Output Reports Set Prefix

Return To Main Menu

Select Reports From CCFG Report Package

EXHIBIT 9.87 Collateral Reports Editor and Menu

Select State Level Collateral Reports

Alaska
Alabama
Arkansas
Arizona
California
Colorado
Connecticut
Delaware
Florida
Georgia
Hawaii
Iowa
Idaho
Illinois
Indiana
Kansas
Kentucky
Louisana
Massachusetts
Maryland
Maine
Michigan
Minnesota
Missouri
Mississippi

SAVE STATE SELECTIONS

CANCEL

Select All States On Menu

Deselect All States on Menu

EXHIBIT 9.88 State level Geographic Reports Menu UserForm

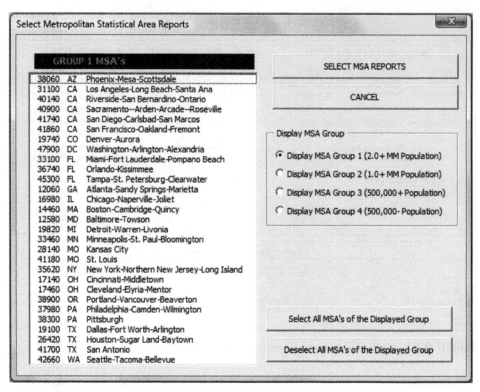

EXHIBIT 9.89   MSA level Geographic Reports Menu UserForm

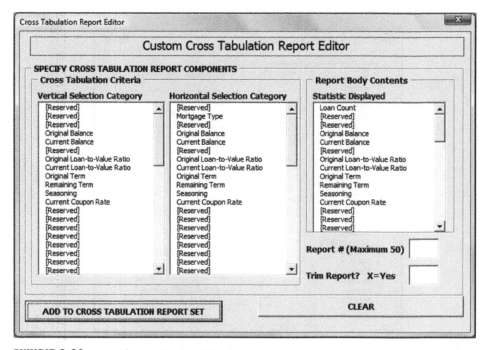

EXHIBIT 9.90   Stratification Report Editor UserForm

3. **Select Report Packages.** This section allows the analyst to select which of the customized and standardized report packages are to be produced during the model run. These 30 reports are contained in a number of various template files. Many of these reports are represented as individual worksheets in a single report template file workbook. The analyst will be able to select any of these reports. If the reports are contained in a multiple report workbook, the unselected portions of the workbook will be deleted. The reports are listed below beneath their groups.

Assumptions Report Group
- Assumptions Report

Data Screening and Sufficiency Reports
- Cash Flow Amortization Criteria by Mortgage Type
- Stratification Reports Data Sufficiency Report
- Demographic Methodology Frequency of Foreclosure Data Report
- Demographic Methodology Market Value Decline Data Report
- Geographic Methodology Calculation Factors Report

Demographic Risk Factors Reports
- Frequency of Foreclosure Risk Factors
- Market Value Decline Risk Factors Report

Ineligible Collateral Reports
- User Ineligible Collateral Reports Package
- Ineligible Loan Listing Report

Eligible Collateral Reports
- Base Stratification Reports
- Cross-Tabulation Reports
- Eligible Loan Listing Report

Geographic Reports
- Geographic Loan Listing Report
- Geographic Initial Concentration Report—State Level
- Geographic Initial Concentration Report—MSA Level
- Geographic Initial Concentration Report—Loan Level
- Geographic Final Concentration Report—State Level
- Geographic Final Concentration Report—MSA Level
- Geographic Final Concentration Report—Loan Level
- Geographic Stratification Report—National Level
- Geographic Stratification Report—State Level
- Geographic Stratification Report MSA—Loan Level
- Geographic Stratification Report Non-MSA—Loan Level

Cash Flow Reports
- Collateral Cash Flow Waterfall Inputs Report
- Cash Flow Report—Single Scenario Report

Portfolio Demographic Reports
- Distribution of Balances by MSA
- Borrower Credit Profiles
- Loan-To-Value, Appraisal Methods, and Documentation Standards
- Property Types, Occupancy, and Servicing Ratings

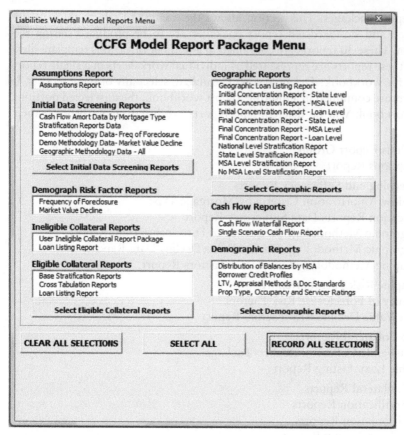

EXHIBIT 9.91   Model Report Package UserForm

The CommandButton labeled "Select Reports From CCFG Report Package" activates the Model Report Package UserForm. This form contains a series of ListBoxes corresponding to the eight report groups listed previously. The contents of these ListBoxes reference various ranges of the "DataReportList" Worksheet on the CCFG. See Exhibits 9.91 and 9.92.

Operation of the Menu

In the first section of the Collateral Reports Editor and Menu, the analyst can specify from a complete list of geographical entities a list of any or all of them upon which collateral reports will be produced. The second section of the menu allows the analyst to custom design a series of univariate stratification reports or bivariate cross-tabulation reports. In the third section of the menu, "Select Report Packages", the model provides the analyst with the menu capabilities to specify which, if any, of these reports are to be created at the end of the collateral analysis run of the CCFG.

Geographic Reports Editor   In this section of the menu, the analyst can display either of the Geographic Selection UserForms seen in Exhibits 9.86 and 9.87. Once

Collateral Cash Flow Generator Report Title List

Assumptions Report

Offset		
0	1	Assumptions Report

Initial Data Screening Report Package

Offset		
1	1	Cash Flow Amort Data by Mortgage Type
	2	Stratification Reports Data
	3	Demo Methodology Data- Freq of Foreclosure
	4	Demo Methodology Data- Market Value Decline
	5	Geographic Methodology Data - All

Demographic Methodology Risk Factor Reports

Offset		
6	1	Frequency of Foreclosure
	2	Market Value Decline

Ineligible Collateral Reports

Offset		
8	1	User Ineligible Collateral Report Package
	2	Loan Listing Report

Eligible Collateral Reports

Offset		
10	1	Base Stratification Reports
	2	Cross Tabulation Reports
	3	Loan Listing Report

Geographic Reports

Offset		
13	1	Geographic Loan Listing Report
	2	Initial Concentration Report - State Level
	3	Initial Concentration Report - MSA Level
	4	Initial Concentration Report - Loan Level
	5	Final Concentration Report - State Level
	6	Final Concentration Report - MSA Level
	7	Final Concentration Report - Loan Level
	8	National Level Stratification Report
	9	State Level Stratification Report
	10	MSA Level Stratification Report
	11	No MSA Level Stratification Report

Cash Flow Reports

Offset		
24	1	Cash Flow Waterfall Report
	2	Single Scenario Cash Flow Report

Demographic Reports

Offset		
26	1	Distribution of Balances by MSA
	2	Borrower Credit Profiles
	3	LTV, Appraisal Methods & Doc Standards
	4	Prop Type, Occupancy and Servicer Ratings

Set the Offset Number to the sum of the reports before the beginning of the current set. Progress down the left hand column and then down the right hand column.

Return To
Reports Editor
Menu

EXHIBIT 9.92 "DataReportList" Worksheet

309

the analyst has made his or her selections, the results are stored in a set of five arrays. The state level elections are stored in "gRepMenuGeoStates" and the elections of the various MSA groups are stored in "gRepMenuGeoMSASet1" through "gRep-MenuGeoMSASet4". If we wish to save the report elections, we can write them to a report file whose format is that of the "GeoReportWriter" Worksheet of the model. This sheet is also used to display the report selection choices.

This Report Elections file can then be reloaded into the CCFG at a later date, with the elections of the file modified and then overwritten if desired. Alternatively, the report contents can be saved under a different file name, and any changes to the original assumption set can be saved to a new file. The current state of the selected Geographic Reports can also be displayed in an Excel Worksheet of the model by clicking on the "Display Report Set" button.

The VBA code that supports the states and MSA UserForms is very similar to that of the Geographic Selections menu UserForm code. The VBA code contained in the module "MenuSupport_ReportsMenu" is also very similar to the code that we have previously examined in the menu support operations of the Geographic Selection Menu. We will therefore refer readers to the CCFG model on the Web site to familiarize themselves with these subroutines.

Collateral Stratification Reports Editor   The Collateral Stratifications Report Editor section of the menu allows the analyst to call up a UserForm as described in Exhibit 9.88. The analyst can then describe the two selection criteria for the report and the report content criteria that will be aggregated based on the conjunction of the selection criteria. These elections constitute all that is needed to describe the format and structure of a set of custom stratification reports. The ability to save these specifications to a file, read these specifications back into the model, and modify and save alternative configurations of the reports selection set is identical to the functionality of the Geographic Reports Editor.

There is one critical difference between the election of geographic reports and those of customized stratification reports. In certain cases a specification of certain parameters of the Stratification Report Editor will produce multiple level reports. For example, if the elections of Mortgage type and Current Balance are given as the Primary and Secondary sort criteria respectively, and Current Balance is elected as the Report Contents, a multiple level report will be generated. The report title will be "Current Balances by Current Balance Distribution by Loan Type". This means that the report will have five substratifications, each in the same format of the total Current Balances by Current Balance Range, corresponding to each of the unique values of the loan type. This aspect of the Report Writer will be discussed in more detail in Chapter 13.

The contents of the ListBoxes of the UserForm displaying the available Horizontal and Vertical Selection categories and the Report Body statistic displayed are read from the "CrossTabReportInfo" Worksheet. The use of such data worksheets is a critical factor in the management of complex UserForms containing multiple ListBox Objects. It allows us to quickly add or subtract list elements by merely entering the data into the appropriate referenced locations on the Excel Worksheets. You will also note that in addition to supplying the UserForm ListBox Objects with their contents, the worksheet also provides the CCFG with information as to the number

Cross Tabulation Report Package Formatting Guidelines Table

	Data Vertical Items	Horizontal Items	Report Body	Cross Tabulation Report Formatting Inputs			
				# Values	Interval Value	Template Used	Dollar Weighted
1	[Reserved]	[Reserved]	Loan Count				False
2	[Reserved]	Mortgage Type	[Reserved]	6	1	Label	
3	[Reserved]	[Reserved]	[Reserved]				
4	Original Balance	Original Balance	Original Balance	39	10,000	Dollar	False
5	Current Balance	Current Balance	Current Balance	39	10,000	Dollar	False
6	[Reserved]	[Reserved]	[Reserved]				
7	Original Loan-to-Value Ratio	Original Loan-to-Value Ratio	Original Loan-to-Value Ratio	40	5.00%	Percent200	True
8	Current Loan-to-Value Ratio	Current Loan-to-Value Ratio	Current Loan-to-Value Ratio	40	5.00%	Percent200	True
9	Original Term	Original Term	Original Term	30	12	Month12	True
10	Remaining Term	Remaining Term	Remaining Term	30	12	Month12	True
11	Seasoning	Seasoning	Seasoning	40	3	Month3	True
12	Current Coupon Rate	Current Coupon Rate	Current Coupon Rate	20	0.50%	Percent10	True
13	[Reserved]	[Reserved]	[Reserved]				
14	[Reserved]	[Reserved]	[Reserved]				
15	[Reserved]	[Reserved]	[Reserved]				
16	[Reserved]	[Reserved]	[Reserved]				
17	[Reserved]	[Reserved]	[Reserved]				
18	[Reserved]	[Reserved]	[Reserved]				
19	[Reserved]	[Reserved]	[Reserved]				
20	[Reserved]	[Reserved]	[Reserved]				
21	[Reserved]	[Reserved]	[Reserved]				
22	[Reserved]	[Reserved]	[Reserved]				
23	[Reserved]	[Reserved]	[Reserved]				
24	[Reserved]	[Reserved]	[Reserved]				
25	[Reserved]	[Reserved]	[Reserved]				
26	[Reserved]	[Reserved]	[Reserved]				
27	Original Appraisal Value	Original Appraisal Value	Original Appraisal Value	39	10,000	Dollar	True
28	Current Appraisal Value	Current Appraisal Value	Current Appraisal Value	39	10,000	Dollar	True
29	Original Appraisal Type	Original Appraisal Type	[Reserved]	7	1	Label	
30	Current Appraisal Type	Current Appraisal Type	[Reserved]	7	1	Label	
31	Property Type	Property Type	[Reserved]	10	1	Label	
32	Occupancy Code	Occupancy Code	[Reserved]	4	1	Label	
33	Financing Purpose	Financing Purpose	[Reserved]	6	1	Label	
34	State Code	[Reserved]	[Reserved]	54	1	State	
35	MSA Code	[Reserved]	[Reserved]	151	1	MSA	
36	[Reserved]	[Reserved]	[Reserved]				
37	Self-employed	Self-employed	[Reserved]	10	1	Label	
38	Number of years in position	Number of years in position	[Reserved]	8	1	Label	
39	First Time Homeowner	First Time Homeowner	[Reserved]	3	1	Label	
40	[Reserved]	[Reserved]	[Reserved]				
41	[Reserved]	[Reserved]	[Reserved]				
42	FICO Score	[Reserved]	FICO Score	23	25	FICO	True
43	Mortgage Debt-to-Income Ratio	Mortgage Debt-to-Income Ratio	Mortgage Debt-to-Income Rat	20	5.00%	Percent100	True
44	Total Debt-to-Income Ratio	Total Debt-to-Income Ratio	Total Debt-to-Income Ratio	20	5.00%	Percent100	True
45	Bankruptcy History	Bankruptcy History	[Reserved]	5	1	Label	
46	Escrow Provisions	Escrow Provisions	[Reserved]	5	1	Label	
47	Third Party Doc Due Diligence	Third Party Doc Due Diligence	Third Party Doc Due Diligence	6	1	Label	True
48	Origination Document Package	Origination Document Package	[Reserved]	7	1	Label	
49	Servicier Rating	Servicier Rating	Servicier Rating	5	1	Label	True
50	[Reserved]	[Reserved]	[Reserved]				

EXHIBIT 9.93   "CrossTabReportInfo" worksheet

of values for the item, the interval value of the stratification, format of the data, and whether the aggregated statistic in the report body is to be dollar weighted or not. See Exhibit 9.93.

Due to the large number of Cross Tabulation reports that can be specified by the analyst (50), it seems only fair, and prudent, to allow for a review mechanism of the currently described report criteria. The analyst can display the current configurations of all described Cross Tabulation sheets by clicking on the CommandButton labeled "Display Cross Tab Elections". The CCFG will then read the contents of the various arrays that hold the Cross Tabulation report information and populate the "CrossTabReport" worksheet. See Exhibit 9.94.

Select Reports Packages   The final section of this menu is the "Select Report Packages" section. This section contains two items: a data input field and a

Report Writer -- Cross Tabulation Reports

Report Number	Vertical Criteria Name	Item #	Horizontal Criteria Name	Item #	Body Criteria Name	Item #	Trim Report
1	Current Balance	5	Mortgage Type	2	Loan Count	1	X
2	Current Balance	5	Mortgage Type	2	Original Balance	4	X
3	Current Balance	5	Mortgage Type	2	Current Balance	5	X
4	Current Balance	5	Mortgage Type	2	Original Loan-to-Value Ratio	7	X
5	Current Balance	5	Mortgage Type	2	Current Loan-to-Value Ratio	8	X
6	Current Balance	5	Mortgage Type	2	Original Term	9	X
7	Current Balance	5	Mortgage Type	2	Remaining Term	10	X
8	Current Balance	5	Mortgage Type	2	Seasoning	11	X
9	Current Balance	5	Mortgage Type	2	Current Coupon Rate	12	X
10	Current Balance	5	Mortgage Type	2	Original Appraisal Value	34	X
11	Current Balance	5	Mortgage Type	2	Current Appraisal Value	35	X
12	Current Balance	5	Mortgage Type	2	FICO Score	49	X
13	Current Balance	5	Mortgage Type	2	Mortgage Debt-to-Income Ratio	50	X
14	Current Balance	5	Mortgage Type	2	Total Debt-to-Income Ratio	51	X
15	Current Balance	5	Mortgage Type	2	Third Party Doc Due Diligence	54	X
16	Current Balance	5	Mortgage Type	2	Servicier Rating	56	X
17	State Code	41	Mortgage Type	2	Loan Count	1	X
18	State Code	41	Mortgage Type	2	Original Balance	4	X
19	State Code	41	Mortgage Type	2	Current Balance	5	X
20	State Code	41	Mortgage Type	2	Original Loan-to-Value Ratio	7	X
21	State Code	41	Mortgage Type	2	Current Loan-to-Value Ratio	8	X
22	State Code	41	Mortgage Type	2	Original Term	9	X
23	State Code	41	Mortgage Type	2	Remaining Term	10	X
24	State Code	41	Mortgage Type	2	Seasoning	11	X
25	State Code	41	Mortgage Type	2	Current Coupon Rate	12	X
26	State Code	41	Mortgage Type	2	Original Appraisal Value	34	X
27	State Code	41	Mortgage Type	2	Current Appraisal Value	35	X
28	State Code	41	Mortgage Type	2	FICO Score	49	X
29	State Code	41	Mortgage Type	2	Mortgage Debt-to-Income Ratio	50	X
30	State Code	41	Mortgage Type	2	Total Debt-to-Income Ratio	51	X
31	State Code	41	Mortgage Type	2	Third Party Doc Due Diligence	54	X
32	State Code	41	Mortgage Type	2	Servicier Rating	56	X
33	MSA Code	42	Mortgage Type	2	Loan Count	1	X
34	MSA Code	42	Mortgage Type	2	Original Balance	4	X
35	MSA Code	42	Mortgage Type	2	Current Balance	5	X
36	MSA Code	42	Mortgage Type	2	Original Loan-to-Value Ratio	7	X
37	MSA Code	42	Mortgage Type	2	Current Loan-to-Value Ratio	8	X
38	MSA Code	42	Mortgage Type	2	Original Term	9	X
39	MSA Code	42	Mortgage Type	2	Remaining Term	10	X
40	MSA Code	42	Mortgage Type	2	Seasoning	11	X
41	MSA Code	42	Mortgage Type	2	Current Coupon Rate	12	X
42	MSA Code	42	Mortgage Type	2	Original Appraisal Value	34	X
43	MSA Code	42	Mortgage Type	2	Current Appraisal Value	35	X
44	MSA Code	42	Mortgage Type	2	FICO Score	49	X
45	MSA Code	42	Mortgage Type	2	Mortgage Debt-to-Income Ratio	50	X
46	MSA Code	42	Mortgage Type	2	Total Debt-to-Income Ratio	51	X
47	MSA Code	42	Mortgage Type	2	Third Party Doc Due Diligence	54	X
48	MSA Code	42	Mortgage Type	2	Servicier Rating	56	X
49							
50							

EXHIBIT 9.94   "CrossTabReport" worksheet

CommandButton. The data field accepts the Outputs File prefix that will be attached to all report files generated in this run of the CCFG. The CommandButton displays the UserForm seen in Exhibit 9.91.

The "Model Report Package Menu" UserForm contains seven ListBoxes and seven CommandButtons. The ListBoxes and four of the CommandButtons are grouped in a single Frame Object. Outside of the Frame we find the remaining three CommandButtons.

The role of this UserForm is to make the selection of the reports as simple as possible for the analyst and to correctly convey those choices to a set of Boolean variables. The list of Boolean variables is *not* in an array. The structure that we are going to read the choices of the analyst made from the UserForm *is* an array. Our challenge is to keep the two lists—the selections from the ListBoxes of the UserForm, and the VBA array that will carry those choices to where we will assign them to the Boolean variables—in agreement.

```
Private Sub cbSelectAllInitData_Click()
   'Initial Data Screening Reports
   For irep = 0 To lbInitDataRepList.ListCount - 1
      lbInitDataRepList.Selected(irep) = True
   Next irep
   For irep = 2 To 8
      gCCFGReps(irep) = True
   Next irep
End Sub
```

EXHIBIT 9.95 "cbSelectAllInitData_Click" subroutine

Making the Selection Process Easy! Let us look at the first solve the simpler of the two tasks first. To aid the analyst in the selection process, we will provide two sets of CommandButtons focused against this issue. The first are the four CommandButtons within the Frame. They will operate against the ListBoxes with four or more reports. There is therefore a "Select (Group) Report" CommandButton under each of the following ListBoxes:

- Initial Data Screening Reports
- Geographic Reports
- Eligible Reports
- Demographic Reports

Each of these buttons will select the entire list within the ListBox. In addition to these buttons, we will also supply the analyst with two additional selection CommandButtons outside of the Frame containing the ListBoxes. These are "Clear All Selections" and "Select All". When a report has been selected, the appropriate element of the "gCCFGReps" array is set to TRUE; when it is deselected, it is set to FALSE. We will need a collection of very brief subroutines to support these buttons. An example of a report set subroutine, the one for the Initial Data Screening reports, can be seen in Exhibit 9.95. The subroutine for the "Clear All" CommandButton can be seen in Exhibit 9.96.

You will note that each subroutine clears each of the members of the ListBoxes at the same time it is setting all (or some) of the members of the "gCCFGReps" array to either TRUE or FALSE. This is immediately apparent in the "cbSelect AllInitData_Click" subroutine and less so in the "cbClearAllReportsButton_Click" subroutine. In the latter, another subroutine performs the assignments to the "gCCFGReps" array. Its name is "ReportsMenu_SetAllSelections".

```
Private Sub cbClearAllReportsButton_Click()
   Call ReportsMenu_SetAllSelections(False)
   For irep = 1 To TOTAL_REP_NUM
      gCCFGReps(irep) = False
   Next irep
End Sub
```

EXHIBIT 9.96 "cbClearAllReportsButton_Click" subroutine

```
Private Sub cbRecordAllReportsButton_Click()

    'Check each of the 8 List Boxes for the entries made, we will error check
    ' for entries made into the [Reserved] fields of the Initial Data,
    ' Geographic and Demographic List Boxes
    Call SelectReport_ReadOffsetValues

    'Assumption Report
    If lbAssumptRepList.Selected(0) Then gCCFGReps(mOffset(1) + 1) = True
    'Initial Data Screening Reports
    For irep = 0 To lbInitDataRepList.ListCount - 1
        If lbInitDataRepList.Selected(irep) Then _
            gCCFGReps(irep + 1 + mOffset(2)) = True
    Next irep
    'Demographic Risk Factor Reports
    For irep = 0 To lbDemoRiskRepList.ListCount - 1
        If lbDemoRiskRepList.Selected(irep) Then _
            gCCFGReps(irep + 1 + mOffset(3)) = True
    Next irep
    'Ineligible Collateral Reports
    For irep = 0 To lbIneligRepList.ListCount - 1
        If lbIneligRepList.Selected(irep) Then _
            gCCFGReps(irep + 1 + mOffset(4)) = True
    Next irep
    'Eligible Collateral Reports
    For irep = 0 To lbEligRepList.ListCount - 1
        If lbEligRepList.Selected(irep) Then _
            gCCFGReps(irep + 1 + mOffset(5)) = True
    Next irep
    'Geographic Reports
    For irep = 0 To lbGeoRepList.ListCount - 1
        If lbGeoRepList.Selected(irep) Then _
            gCCFGReps(irep + 1 + mOffset(6)) = True
    Next irep
    'Cash Flow Reports
    For irep = 0 To lbCFRepList.ListCount - 1
        If lbCFRepList.Selected(irep) Then _
            gCCFGReps(irep + 1 + mOffset(7)) = True
    Next irep
    'Demographic Reports
    For irep = 0 To lbDemoRepList.ListCount - 1
        If lbDemoRepList.Selected(irep) Then _
            gCCFGReps(irep + 1 + mOffset(8)) = True
    Next irep
    'error check the entries for [Reserved] selections
    Call errCheck_CCFGReportMenuUserForm
    'we are done, put down the user form
    Unload m15CCFGReportsMenu

End Sub
```

EXHIBIT 9.97   "cbRecordsAllReportsButton_Click" subroutine

Matching the Menu Selections to the "gCCFGReps" Array   Once all the selections are made, we then click on the "Record All Selections" CommandButton. This button calls the subroutine "cbRecordAllReportsButton_Click" that performs three activities. It first reads the values of the offset number fields on the "DataReportList" Worksheet. Next, using this information, it then reads the state, (selected/deselected), of each of the elements of all of the ListBoxes. Last it performs a set of assignments to the "gCCFGReps" array.

It employs the values of the Offset values input on the "DataReportList" Worksheet to synchronize the ListBox contents to the elements of the "gCCFGReps" array. See Exhibit 9.97.

The sole remaining menu support activity we have is to match the report election values contained in the "gCCFGReps" array to the set of Boolean variables we will use to trigger the report production process. See Exhibit 9.98.

This action concludes the menu construction phase of the CCFG development process.

```
Sub RepMenu_ReadReportPackageElections()

    For irep = 1 To TOTAL_REP_NUM
        Select Case irep
            'assumptions report list box
            Case Is = 1:  gRepMenuAssumptions = gCCFGReps(irep)      'assumptions report
            'initial data screening list box
            Case Is = 2:  gRepMenuCFAmort = gCCFGReps(irep)          'cash flow amort
            Case Is = 3:  gRepMenuScreenStrat = gCCFGReps(irep)      'screen strats
            Case Is = 4:  gRepMenuScreenDemoFOF = gCCFGReps(irep)    'screen demo method
            Case Is = 5:  gRepMenuScreenDemoMVD = gCCFGReps(irep)    'screen demo method
            Case Is = 6:  gRepMenuScreenGeo = gCCFGReps(irep)        'screen geo method
            'demographic risk measurements reports
            Case Is = 7:  gRepMenuDemoRiskFOF = gCCFGReps(irep)      'demo FOF factors
            Case Is = 8:  gRepMenuDemoRiskMVD = gCCFGReps(irep)      'demo MVD factors
            'ineligible collateral list box
            Case Is = 9: gRepMenuIneligUser = gCCFGReps(irep)        'user crit
            Case Is = 10: gRepMenuLoanListInelig = gCCFGReps(irep)   'loan-by-loan data
            'eligible collateral list box
            Case Is = 11: gRepMenuStratBasic = gCCFGReps(irep)       'basic strat package
            Case Is = 12: gRepMenuCrossTab = gCCFGReps(irep)         'cross tabs package
            Case Is = 13: gRepMenuLoanListElig = gCCFGReps(irep)     'loan-by-loan data
            'geographic reports list box
            Case Is = 14: gRepMenuGeoLoanList = gCCFGReps(irep)      'geo loan listing
            Case Is = 15: gRepMenuGeoInitConState = gCCFGReps(irep)  'init con - states
            Case Is = 16: gRepMenuGeoInitConMSA = gCCFGReps(irep)    'init con - MSAs
            Case Is = 17: gRepMenuGeoInitConLoan = gCCFGReps(irep)   'init con - loan
            Case Is = 18: gRepMenuGeoFinConState = gCCFGReps(irep)   'fin con - states
            Case Is = 19: gRepMenuGeoFinConMSA = gCCFGReps(irep)     'fin con - MSAs
            Case Is = 20: gRepMenuGeoFinConLoan = gCCFGReps(irep)    'fin con - loan
            Case Is = 21: gRepMenuGeoAllUSRep = gCCFGReps(irep)      'geo US strats
            Case Is = 22: gRepMenuGeoStatesRep = gCCFGReps(irep)     'geo States strats
            Case Is = 23: gRepMenuGeoMSARep = gCCFGReps(irep)        'geo MSAs strats
            Case Is = 24: gRepMenuGeoNoMSARep = gCCFGReps(irep)      'geo No MSA strats
            'cashflows list box
            Case Is = 25: gRepMenuCFEligible = gCCFGReps(irep)       'elig collat CFs
            Case Is = 26: gRepMenuSingleScen = gCCFGReps(irep)       'single scen CFs
            'demographic reports list box
            Case Is = 27: gRepMenuDemoBalances = gCCFGReps(irep)     'MSA bals by State
            Case Is = 28: gRepMenuDemoCredit = gCCFGReps(irep)       'credit factors
            Case Is = 29: gRepMenuDemoLTV = gCCFGReps(irep)          'LTV, appraisals
            Case Is = 30: gRepMenuDemoPropType = gCCFGReps(irep)     'property type
        End Select
    Next irep
    gRepMenuPrefix = Range("m15RepPrefix")

End Sub
```

EXHIBIT 9.98 "RepMenu_ReadReportPackageElections" subroutine

ON THE WEB SITE

There is one new version of the CCFG model, "**CCFG_Chapter09**". This is the current stage of development of the model containing all of the Excel menus, the UserForms called by them, the UserForm control VBA code, and the VBA code that supports the error checking and data handling for the menus. There is also a simple Excel UserForm tutorial program "**UserFormTutorial**". This is the small program developed at the beginning of the chapter.

## CHAPTER 10

Writing the Collateral Data Handling Code

OVERVIEW

In this chapter we will write the VBA code that will move the contents of either a pool level file or a series of sub-portfolio level data files into the VBA arrays of the Collateral Cash Flow Generator (CCFG). We will need to identify the data files to be opened, open them, determine the number of records in the file, and finally read the valid records into the VBA arrays. We want to end up with all the collateral information in a single array, whether we have read it from a file at the pool level or a collection of files at the sub-portfolio level. We will be able to preserve the identity of the sub-portfolio information in the aggregated pool level file because the sub-portfolio number is one of the fields in the collateral record.

The second task in preparing the collateral data for use by the CCFG involves the initial data screening activity. In this activity we will perform a number of tasks to determine the legibility, reasonableness, and completeness of the contents of each of the loan records. What do we mean when we use these terms in regard to the collateral data? "Legibility" means the same as it does when we speak of any form of written communication: Are we able to read the contents of the text, and does it make sense to us? Here we are referring to values in the collateral file that are undecipherable in the context of what we expect to find. An example of this would be missing or illegally formatted data. For example, it is hard to calculate the monthly payment of a loan with an original balance of either " " or "60 Days". An original balance needs to be a number. This leads us to the next issue, that of data reasonableness. An original balance number needs not only to *be* a number, but it needs to have a reasonable value. A reasonable value of an original balance is $100,000, not –$50 or $0. Last we have the concept of completeness. "Completeness" applies not to any single piece of data but to the minimum collection of data that will be sufficient to perform an analytical or computational task. Thus, using the earlier example of original balance to compute a payment for a fixed-rate mortgage, we need the following:

- Original balance
- Term of the mortgage in months
- Coupon rate
- Frequency of payment

If we have all of these data in a legible and reasonable form, we can complete the monthly payment calculation. The loan record is therefore "complete" in regard to this task. In this chapter we will organize and create a series of initial data screening tests to determine various issues relating to these three concerns with the data.

The third task we will undertake in this chapter is the construction of a Representative Line Generator Program (RLGP). This program will use the "bucket" approach in its aggregation process. A series of bucket definitions are established from a specification grid file, and the eligible collateral of the deal is then matched to the most appropriate group. The weighted average maturity (WAM), weighted average coupon (WAC), the sums of the original and current balances, and other descriptive statistics are computed for the group. These results as well as a description of the aggregation parameters are then written to a Representative Line (Rep Line) Report.

DELIVERABLES

The deliverables for this chapter are:

- The format for the expanded mortgage data file.
- The various subroutines needed to open either a single or a set of collateral data files depending on whether the information is in the form of a single pool or a series of sub-portfolios.
- The initial data screening process code. These subroutines will determine the legibility, reasonableness, and completeness of each of the records of the collateral data files.
- A series of reporting subroutines that will produce a report package of the results of the initial data screening activities.
- The RLGP. This program will utilize files with pre-specified aggregation guidelines to construct a series of Rep Lines of the collateral of the deal.

UNDER CONSTRUCTION

In this chapter we will build a series of file and data handling VBA subroutines to read the collateral data file information into the program. We will also create a new module to hold data file specific Constant variable declarations. These modules and subroutines are:

- **"A_Constants" module.** We will create a series of Constant variables to help us access and track the contents of both the collateral data files and the "gLoanData" array in which we will store the information on the collateral characteristics. We will add these Constants, one for each of the fields in the collateral data record, to the "A_Constants" module. We will then use these Constant variables to manage the layout of the collateral pool and sub-portfolio files. If we need to reconfigure these files in the future, we can simply change the value of the Constant variable for any data item in the file format. This will also immediately effect the change across all references to that Constant in the

CCFG so that we will not need to run down all individual references to it in the code. We will also set up a series of Constant variables to help us track and record the results of the initial data screening activities.

- **"A_Globals" module.** We will create the sub-portfolio VBA data arrays needed to hold the contents of the collateral data files and declare additional variables to hold the total current principal balances and number of records for each of the sub-portfolios. We will also create an array to reflect the integrity of each of the collateral records in regard to the results of the initial data screening activity. This array will hold the error conditions, if any, of each piece of collateral. From these indicators we can determine to what analytical activities the record may be put based on the eligibility, reasonableness, and completeness of the information contained within it.

- **"CollatData_ReadFileInfo" module.** This module will hold the subroutines necessary to open the pool level or sub-portfolio level data files and read their contents into a single master data array. These subroutines include:

  - **"CollatData_ReadCollateralFiles" subroutine.** Determines if we are reading data from a pool or collection of sub-portfolios. Call the appropriate subroutines based on that determination. Also calls a subroutine to produce a pool level collateral data file (if needed).

  - **"CollatData_ReadPoolDataFile" subroutine.** Reads the collateral data from a pool level file.

  - **"CollatData_ReadSubPortDataFiles" subroutine.** This subroutine reads the sub-portfolio data files from the collateral pool menu and opens them. Then, using the subroutines listed below, it reads their contents, verifies the information, and stores the vetted information in VBA arrays.

  - **"CollatData_ReadDataFileContents" subroutine.** Reads the information in the designated data files and places it in a VBA array for use by the CCFG.

  - **"CollatData_WritePoolLevelDataFile" subroutine.** Writes a pool level collateral data file if requested by the user. The subroutine will combine the contents of up to five sub-portfolio files to a single pool level file.

- **"CollatData_InitialDataScreening" module.** This module will hold the subroutines necessary to perform the initial data screening activity and report on the legibility, reasonableness, and completeness of the data. The subroutines will produce eight error code results for each piece of collateral and three "completeness" indicators. The error codes are:

- **Initial data screening score.** Missing or illegible data.

- **Amortization score.** Error conditions in the data that will not allow a cash flow calculation to be performed for the loan.

- **Stratification report score.** Error conditions that will not allow full use of the loan in stratification analysis and reporting.

- **Frequency of foreclosure score.** Error conditions that will not allow the use of the loan in the Demographic Methodology of default analysis.

- **Market value decline (MVD) score.** Error conditions that will not allow the use of the loan in the Demographic Methodology of default and prepayment analysis.

- **Geographic score.** Error conditions that will not allow the use of the loan in the Geographic Methodology of default, prepayment, MVD, and recovery lag analysis.

- **Demographic score.** Error conditions that will not allow the use of the loan in the Demographic Methodology of default and MVD analysis.
- **Overall score.** Error score that tells us if the record is complete for all tests, reporting and calculation activities.
- **"Z_UtilitiesSubroutines" module.** This new module will contain our first general utility subroutine. Its role is to translate a two-letter standard state postal code, such as "CT", into its numerical position in the list of state postal arrays (which is 7).
- **RLGP.** This program will use prespecified aggregation parameters to produce a Rep Line report for the eligible collateral of the deal. The program stands outside of the CCFG and produces rep lines that can be amortized by the CCFG. It uses the "bucket" approach to aggregate collateral into a series of predefined categories.

MANAGING MULTIPLE PORTFOLIO FILES

The CCFG we are about to build has three fundamental differences from its predecessor, the Base Asset Model (BAM). The first difference is that the size of the anticipated collateral portfolio will be much larger. The collateral pool for the deal may contain anywhere from three to ten times the number of records we processed in the BAM.

The second difference is that the data set for each of the collateral records is substantially larger. Not only is it larger, it is *significantly* larger, having expanded from the initial 26 items to nearly double its size to 50 items! This format change will impact how we develop the VBA code to read and store this information. We have already discussed one of these changes. It is the creation of an extensive set of Constant variables used to describe each field of this expanded record format. This increase in the amount of information we have in regard to each piece of collateral will allow us to expand the scope of our analysis. We will be able to produce more and detailed information about our collateral pool. We will now have a much more complete picture of the demographic and geographic makeup of the pool of obligors. We will be able to apply more sophisticated and individualized credit risk analysis as it relates to personal credit history of the mortgagees of the pool. It will prove invaluable in the use of the Demographic and Geographic Prepayment/Default Methodologies as opposed to the somewhat simplistic Uniform Methodology of the existing BAM. In addition to this, the CCFG will be expanded to handle an additional number of mortgage types having more complex amortization patterns.

The third and most visible change is that we will allow the user to designate up to five different sub-portfolios of collateral and have the option of combining them into a single collateral pool. We have two approaches available to us for dealing with the challenge of multiple portfolios. The first approach would be to read the information from each of the five sub-portfolios, segregating it by sub-portfolio and then treating each of these data collections as a separate entity. The second would be to combine all of the collateral into a single pool level array but retain the ability to identify the individual loans by their original sub-portfolio. In this approach we will not lose any information if we tag each of the loans with its sub-portfolio of origin before we begin the aggregation process. We then have the convenience of working with a single unified array that contains all of the data in a single location without giving up the ability to report based on its sub-portfolio of origin. We will adopt this latter approach, that of a single combined pool, as we develop the VBA code below.

Expanded Data Set

As mentioned above, one of the obvious differences in the BAM and the new CCFG is the increased amount of data (almost double on a per-record basis) that the CCFG will have to handle.

Nearly all of the data fields from the BAM are included in the data record layout for the CCFG. There is, however, a considerable amount of new information here that we should examine before proceeding further in the process. It is always prudent to determine the minimum amount of critical information the model needs. Remember, you do not have to find a use for every piece of information just because it is in the file! The first thing that we are going to do is to reexamine the list of the data fields of the records format that we will be using. See Exhibit 10.1.

We will now review this information and group the data by its function.

Balance Information Balance information relates to the original and current balances of the mortgage and any other associated balances and amounts including payment levels. This would include the following fields of the record:

- Fields 4 and 5: Original and current balance
- Fields 7 and 8: Original and current loan-to-value ratios
- Fields 29 and 30: Original and current appraisal value information fields
- Fields 40 and 41: Number and amount of payments in arrears

Rate Information Rate information tells us the *current* coupon level of the mortgage. This information is found in field 12. (We will discuss the other coupon-related information in the record when we discuss the items for the adjustable rate mortgages below.)

Tenor Information Tenor information relates to all elements of time. Thus we have:

- Field 6: Origination date of the mortgage
- Fields 9, 10, and 11: Original and remaining terms and seasoning (age) of the loan
- Field 50: Day count convention of the mortgage

Amortization Information The amortization information for various new mortgage types is one of the greatest contributors to the increase in the size of the collateral record. While there were no additional fields needed for either fixed-rate or standard adjustable rate mortgages (ARMs), this was not the case for hybrid adjustable rate mortgages (HARMs) and balloon mortgages. We will review these types now.

Standard Adjustable Rate Mortgages Standard ARMs—those without any special features such as teaser rates, interest-only periods, and optional payment arrangements—were found in the BAM.

Collateral Data File Record Format

Field	Field Name	Type	Description
1	Pool ID	Integer	Number of collateral portfolio
2	Mortgage Type	Integer	See Table
3	Credit Sector	Integer	See Table
4	Original Balance	Float	Initial principal mortgage balance
5	Current Balance	Float	Current principal mortgage balance
6	Origination Date	Long	Date of loan origination
7	Original Loan-to-Value Ratio	Float	Original balance / original appraisal
8	Current Loan-to-Value Ratio	Float	Current balance / current appraisal
9	Original Term (months)	Integer	Original term of the montgage in months
10	Remaining Term (months)	Integer	Remaining term of the montgage in months
11	Seasoning	Integer	Original term less remaining term
12	Current Coupon Rate	Float	Coupon rate for FRM; Current ARM Coupon
13	ARM Index	Integer	See Table
14	ARM Spread to Index	Float	Spread to Index
15	ARM Initial Index Level	Float	Current Index rate level
16	ARM Periodic Reset	Float	Number of months between interest resets
17	ARM Periodic Cap Rate	Float	Highest limit of change in fully indexed rate
18	ARM Periodic Floor	Float	Lowest limit of change in fully indexed rate
19	ARM Lifetime Cap Rate	Float	Highest limit of fully indexed rate
20	ARM Lifetime Floor Rate	Float	Lowest limit of fully indexed rate
21	HB-ARM Initial Rate	Float	Initial locked rate
22	HB-ARM Initial I/O Rate Period	Integer	Number of months initial locked rate
23	HB-ARM Total I/O Rate Period	Integer	Number of months I/O period only
24	HB-ARM Recast Term	Integer	Number of months for full amortization calculation
25	BALLOON Amortization Period	Integer	Number of months for amortization calculation
26	BALLOON Period	Integer	Month of balloon payment period
27	Original Appraisal Value	Float	Appraisal value to time of mortgage origination
28	Current Appraisal Value	Float	Appraisal value at the current time
29	Original Appraisal Type	Integer	See Table
30	Current Appraisal Type	Integer	See Table
31	Property Type	Integer	See Table
32	Occupancy Code	Integer	See Table
33	Financing Purpose	Integer	See Table
34	State Code	Alpha	State postal code
35	MSA Code	Long	Metropolitan Statistical Area code
36	Zip Code	Long	Postal Zip code
37	Self-employed	Integer	Yes=1, No=0
38	Number of years in position	Integer	Years in current pay grade and responsibilities
39	First Time Homeowner	Integer	Yes=1, No=0
40	Number of Payments in Arrears	Integer	Number of monthly payments in arrears
41	Amount payments in Arrears	Float	Amount of payments in arrears
42	FICO Score	Integer	Fair-Issacs credit score
43	Mortgage Debt-to-Income Ratio	Float	Mortgage P&I, plus insurance and taxes to income
44	Total Debt-to-Income Ratio	Float	Mortgae plus consumer debt to income
45	Bankruptcy	Integer	See Table
46	Escrow	Integer	See Table
47	Third Party Confirmation	Integer	See Table
48	Origination Documentation	Integer	See Table
49	Servicier Rating	Integer	See Table
50	Day Count Convention of the Loan	Integer	See Table

EXHIBIT 10.1   Collateral data file record format

These mortgages require the data found in Fields 13 to 20. These fields specifically are:

- Fields 13, 14, and 15: Index information. These fields include the index from which the loan floats, its spread to the index, and the initial index rate level.
- Fields 16, 17, 18, 19 and 20: Coupon reset conditions. These fields describe the terms for the frequency that the loan resets its coupon and the periodic (short-term) and lifetime (long-term) limits of coupon fluctuation as defined by various caps and floors.

Hybrid Adjustable Rate Mortgages   Hybrid mortgages allow the mortgagor an interest-only payment period at the beginning of the loan usually at a below-market or "teaser" rate. Fields 21 to 24 describe the incremental information needed to amortize this type of mortgage. See a discussion of this mortgage type in Chapter 8.

- Field 21: Initial "teaser" coupon rate.
- Fields 22 and 23: Field 22 delineates the interest-only period at the teaser rate. Field 23 sets the term of the following interest-only period at the market rate.
- Field 24: The recast term is the amortization term upon conclusion of the interest-only period over which the loan now performs exactly like a standard ARM and fully amortizes its principal.

Balloon Mortgages   Balloon mortgages require two data fields that other mortgages do not. Balloon mortgages allow the mortgagor to pay a lower principal amortization amount in the monthly payment over the life of the mortgage. The mortgagor may pay a 30-year amortization payment on a balloon mortgage with an original term of only 20 years. The decreased amount of the principal component of the payment is therefore insufficient to fully amortize the original principal balance over the term of the loan. The remaining principal balance that is unpaid at the maturity date of the loan is retired in a single, usually very large, "balloon" payment.

- Field 25: Amortization period. This is the term that is used to set the principal component of the regular monthly payment. An example would be a balloon mortgage that set the principal payment as if the loan was fully amortizing over 30 years when the loan has a maturity date of 20 years.
- Field 26: Balloon period. This is the period of the payment schedule that the balloon payment is made to retire all remaining principal balance that is outstanding at the time.

Property Information   These fields relate to a description of the physical property that secures the mortgage and its use.

- Field 29 and 30: Original and current appraisal type. Appraisal methods come in many forms, from the exhaustive walk-through with comparable value comparison to an estimate from tax assessment numbers.
- Fields 31 and 32: Property type and occupancy code. These fields list the type of property, such as single family, multifamily, planned unit development, condo, co-op, or mixed use commercial and residential (this list is not exhaustive by any means). For occupancy code, the fields cover owner occupied, non-owner occupied, vacation, and so forth.
- Field 33: Financing purpose. Why was the loan taken out? To what use are the proceeds of the mortgage to be applied?
- Fields 34, 35, and 36: Property location. What state, Metropolitan Statistical Area (MSA), or zip code is the property located in?

Borrower Credit Information   These data measure of the ability and in some cases the willingness of the borrower to make the mortgage payments in a full and timely manner.

- Fields 37 and 38: Borrower employment history. Is the borrower self-employed, or does he or she work for others? If employed by others, what is his or her job stability (how many years in the field and how many years in that position)?
- Field 39: First-time homeowner. Is this the first time the borrower has had a mortgage? Also a first-time homeowner is generally faced with incremental expenses, such as the purchase of large appliances for the home in the first year of occupation.
- Field 42: Fair Isaacs Corporation (FICO) score of the borrower. This covers general creditworthiness as assessed by a third-party credit agency.
- Field 43: Mortgage debt-to-income ratio. What is the ratio of the mortgage payment to gross household income?
- Field 44: Total debt-to-income ratio. This is the ratio of all other debt, credit cards, auto loans, student loans, home equity loans, and personal loans combined with the mortgage payments divided by gross household income.
- Field 45: Bankruptcy history. Has the borrower ever been bankrupt? Is so what was the disposition of the bankruptcy action?

Servicing Information   The last category is the servicing category. If problems arise will there be a quick and effective response?

- Fields 46: Escrow arrangements. Does the borrower escrow taxes, taxes and insurance, or nothing? Escrowing significantly decreases the chance that the property will be seized for nonpayment of taxes.
- Field 47: Third-party documentation review. Were all the legal and credit documents reviewed by a third party for completeness and accuracy? This could become critical in the case of a foreclosure or recapture event. What is the quality of documents to start out with? Do the documents adhere to standard forms ad agreements?
- Field 48: Origination documentation. Was a complete documentation package, including credit reports, appraisal, employment confirmation, income information, and legal loan documents prepared? Was the title history of the property searched and insured?
- Field 49: Servicer rating. What is the capability and track record of the servicer who will have to respond to problems with the loan? Do they have local knowledge of the economic and legal conditions relating to the locale of the property? Is their staffing and experience reflected in fast response times that limit losses and damage to the property?

New Global Constant Variables

As we can see from the above listing, this is a lot of information! One of the first things that we are going to do is to create a series of global Constant variables.

Each of these variables will correspond to a data item in the collateral record, and the value of the global Constant will be equal to the *n*th location of the data in the file. We will immediately use these Constants in this chapter, and we will also find them performing a critical role when we begin writing the collateral financial selection process VBA code in Chapter 11. You will also notice the declaration of a separate Constant variable at the top of Exhibit 10.2. The Constant is named "DATA_FILE_FIELDS" and indicates the number of fields in the data fields and the "gLoanData" array. See Exhibit 10.2.

```
Public Const DATA_FILE_FIELDS = 50    'total data items in a record

Public Const FD_POOLID = 1            'sub-portfolio ID number
Public Const FD_MORTTYPE = 2          'mortgage amortization type
Public Const FD_CREDITSECT = 3        'credit sector
Public Const FD_ORIGBAL = 4           'original balance
Public Const FD_CURRBAL = 5           'current balance
Public Const FD_ORIGDATE = 6          'origination date
Public Const FD_ORIGLTV = 7           'original LTV
Public Const FD_CURRLTV = 8           'current LTV
Public Const FD_ORIGTERM = 9          'original term (months)
Public Const FD_REMTERM = 10          'remaining term (months)
Public Const FD_SEASON = 11           'seasoning (months)
Public Const FD_CURRRATE = 12         'current coupon rate
Public Const FD_ARMINDEX = 13         'ARM index ID number
Public Const FD_ARMSPRD = 14          'ARM spread to index
Public Const FD_ARMORIGLEV = 15       'ARM initial index level
Public Const FD_ARMPERRESET = 16      'ARM periodic reset interval (months)
Public Const FD_ARMPERCAP = 17        'ARM period cap
Public Const FD_ARMPERFLR = 18        'ARM periodic floor
Public Const FD_ARMLIFCAP = 19        'ARM lifetime cap
Public Const FD_ARMLIFFLR = 20        'ARM lifetime floor
Public Const FD_HBAORIGLEV = 21       'Hybrid ARM initial locked rate
Public Const FD_HBAORIGPERIOD = 22    'Hybrid ARM initial locked period
Public Const FD_HBAIOPERIODS = 23     'Hybrid ARM total IO months
Public Const FD_HBARECASTPR = 24      'Hybrid ARM recast payment (months)
Public Const FD_BALAMORTPER = 25      'Balloon pmt level amortization (months)
Public Const FD_BALFINALPER = 26      'Balloon final payment period
Public Const FD_ORIGAPP = 27          'original appraisal
Public Const FD_CURRAPP = 28          'current appraisal
Public Const FD_ORIGAPPTYPE = 29      'original appraisal type
Public Const FD_CURRAPPTYPE = 30      'current appraisal type
Public Const FD_PROPTYPE = 31         'property type
Public Const FD_OCCPCODE = 32         'occupancy code
Public Const FD_FINPURPOSE = 33       'financing purpose
Public Const FD_STATECODE = 34        'state code (numeric 1 to 54)
Public Const FD_MSACODE = 35          'metropolitan statistical area code
Public Const FD_ZIPCODE = 36          'postal zip code
Public Const FD_EMPLOY = 37           'self-employed
Public Const FD_YRSPOST = 38          'years employed at position
Public Const FD_FIRSTHOME = 39        'first time home owner
Public Const FD_ARREARSNUM = 40       'number of payments in arrears
Public Const FD_ARREARSAMT = 41       'amount in arrears
Public Const FD_FICO = 42             'Fair-Issacs score
Public Const FD_MDBTTOINC = 43        'mortgage debt-to-income ratio
Public Const FD_TDBTTOINC = 44        'total debt-to-income ratio
Public Const FD_BANKRUPTCY = 45       'in bankruptcy
Public Const FD_ESCROW = 46           'escrow stipulations
Public Const FD_THIRDPARTY = 47       'third party due diligence
Public Const FD_ORIGDOCS = 48         'origination documentation quality
Public Const FD_SERVERATE = 49        'loan servicer rating
Public Const FD_DAYCOUNT = 50         'interest calculation day count (30/360)
```

EXHIBIT 10.2 Constant variables of the data file

New Global Variables

As discussed previously, we will declare the pool level collateral data array and the five sub-portfolio level arrays as separate entities. We will need to have variables to move the names of the pool or sub-portfolio files from the menus to the VBA subroutines where we can use them to open files. We will name these variables "gfn-PoolName" and "gfnSubPort", and we will make the latter an array to accommodate up to five different sub-portfolio names. At some point we will want to aggregate the contents of the sub-portfolios into a single pool. We will create the Boolean variable "gCreatePoolFromSubs" to tell the CCFG what we want to do and the variable "gfnPoolDataFileName" to hold the name of the pool level collateral data file to be created. Once the loans have been read from the collateral files, we will need variables to tell us if they have passed the various screening processes we will subject them to. The array "gLoanOK", with a position for each loan, is a Boolean array. If the loan has passed all the initial data screening tests and the following financial and geographic selection tests, we will set this variable TRUE . If not, it will be set to FALSE and excluded from the eligible collateral of the deal. It will be extremely convenient to know exactly how many loans we have as we loop through these various operations; we will store that information in "gTotalLoans". One of the largest, and certainly the most important, array we will create is the "gLoanData" array. Dimensioned to the number of loans and the number of loan data fields, this array will contain all the static collateral data of the CCFG.

The last declarations in the exhibit are two arrays, "gLoanScreen" and "gLoan-Select". These arrays will hold the results of the initial data screening activity and the financial/geographic selection activities, respectively. We will populate these arrays with the sum of any error codes that are generated when we test the data of the collateral files. See Exhibit 10.3.

Reading Sub-Portfolio Files

The first task of this chapter is to design and write the VBA code that will transfer the information from either a pool level or a series of sub-portfolio level collateral data files into a single unified pool level. This array can then be easily accessed by

```
'================================================================================
' COLLATERAL DATA FILE VARIABLES
'================================================================================
'input file names
Public gfnPoolName              As String     'pool level input name
Public gfnSubPort(1 To NUM_PORTS) As String   'Collateral sub-portfolios files
'variables for creating a Pool Level file from the sub-portfolios
Public gCreatePoolFromSubs      As Boolean    'create a Pool Level File
Public gfnPoolDataFileName      As String     'pool level data file name (output)
'variables used in the data aggregation process
Public gLoanOK()                As Boolean    'is loan OK to read from file?
Public gTotalLoans              As Long       '# of loans in each sub-portfiolio
Public gLoanData()              As Double     'all data Pool or SubPorts
'initial data screening results arrays
Public gLoanScreen()            As Long       'all loans screening scores
Public gLoanSelect()            As Long       'all loans selection scores
```

EXHIBIT 10.3 Global variable declarations

all parts of the CCFG. This single VBA array will become the main repository of information concerning the collateral. It can be used by the collateral screening, selection, and cash flow amortization code of the CCFG. While such an accomplishment may seem prosaic, it is an important part of model building and performance. The key difference we face is that we have to read and merge up to five files in the CCFG whereas we had a single file in the BAM. Let us see how we can tackle this problem.

The steps in the process are straightforward.

Step 1. We must identify whether we are reading a single pool level file or a series of sub-portfolio level files.

Step 2. We must find and open the data files.

Step 3. We must perform error checking on the contents of the records. Since all the data should be in a numeric format, a good first test is to confirm that this is the case and check for any missing data. We will also determine if the key reporting, demographic, and cash flow amortization data are present and sufficiently complete for a record to be considered valid and usable.

Step 4. We must assign specific error codes based on the data of the collateral record. After the error checking, we can tag any of the records based on our discoveries. Although a record may not be perfect, it may contain all the information necessary for one process while incomplete for another. We will then write these indicators for each of the loans to separate arrays so that we can later consult the status of the record and use it appropriately.

That is the task list. Let us turn the concept into VBA code.

Identifying the Pool Level or Sub-Portfolio Level Files In Chapter 9 we designed the menus of the CCFG.

The collateral data file menu was designed to allow the user to indicate up to five sub-portfolio level collateral data files that could be combined, at the user's discretion, to form a pool level collateral data file. The complete pathways of the data files are displayed in the fields of the menu. We need only read the file pathway and name from the fields of the menu to have all the information we need to access the files and read the data from them. See Exhibit 10.4. In this set of subroutines, each one is assigned to a different "Select File" button on the menu. The Command-Buttons of the menu calls the subroutine "GetFilenameFromButton". This nifty little subroutine fools VBA into thinking you are trying to perform an "Open File" operation but instead returns the file pathway and name of the file you select in the dialog window that it provides. You can maneuver within the dialog box to any directory location you desire. Then select the file and click on the "Open" button in the lower right. This subroutine totally eliminates the need for any manual entry of file pathways, a proverbial and constant source of annoyance and error. See Exhibit 10.5.

We now have the file pathway information transferred from the menu into a series of Ranges on the menu screen that we can read into a set of VBA variables at a later time.

```
' ==========================================================================
'
' ==========================================================================
Sub GetFileName_CollatPool1()
    Call GetFilenameFromButton
    Range("m7Pool1") = FileName
End Sub
Sub GetFileName_CollatSubPortfolio1()
    Call GetFilenameFromButton
    Range("m7Pool1SubPort").Cells(1) = FileName
    gfnSubPort(1) = FileName
End Sub
Sub GetFileName_CollatSubPortfolio2()
    Call GetFilenameFromButton
    Range("m7Pool1SubPort").Cells(2) = FileName
    gfnSubPort(2) = FileName
End Sub
Sub GetFileName_CollatSubPortfolio3()
    Call GetFilenameFromButton
    Range("m7Pool1SubPort").Cells(3) = FileName
    gfnSubPort(3) = FileName
End Sub
Sub GetFileName_CollatSubPortfolio4()
    Call GetFilenameFromButton
    Range("m7Pool1SubPort").Cells(4) = FileName
    gfnSubPort(4) = FileName
End Sub
Sub GetFileName_CollatSubPortfolio5()
    Call GetFilenameFromButton
    Range("m7Pool1SubPort").Cells(5) = FileName
    gfnSubPort(5) = FileName
End Sub
```

EXHIBIT 10.4 CCFG collateral data file menu support code

Opening the Sub-Portfolio Files The "CollatData_ReadCollateralFiles" is the highest-level subroutine in the module and is designed to be the traffic cop that handles all the operations specified on the menu. The first operation it performs is to check if the "gStatePostal" array, which contains the two-letter postal code for each state, is populated. To perform this check, it reads the first element of the array and if it is " " or NULL, we can safely assume that the rest of the array is similarly

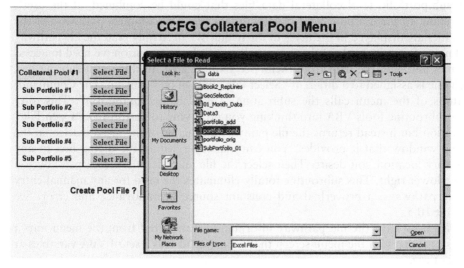

EXHIBIT 10.5 "Select a File" window displayed

```
Sub CollatData_ReadCollateralFiles()

    'if the postal codes array is void populate it at this time
    If gStatePostal(1) = "" Then
        For istate = 1 To NUM_STATES
            gStatePostal(istate) = Range("StatesSet1Data").Cells(istate, 2)
        Next istate
    End If
    'test if this is Pool or Sub-Portfolio data and react accordingly
    If gPoolLevelData Then
        gfnPoolName = Range("m7CollatPool")
        Call CollatData_ReadPoolDataFile
    Else
        For icollat = 1 To NUM_PORTS          'read the Sub-Portfolio file names
            gfnSubPort(icollat) = Range("m7SubPorts").Cells(icollat)
        Next icollat
        Call CollatData_ReadSubPortDataFiles
    End If

End Sub
```

EXHIBIT 10.6 "CollatData_ReadCollateralFiles" subroutine

unpopulated. If this is the case, the subroutine then reads the postal codes from the second column of the Range "StatesSet1Data" on the "DataGeographic" worksheet. We will need this postal code array to convert the two-letter codes contained in the files into a numeric index when we read the collateral data files into arrays later in this process. See Exhibit 10.6.

Pool or Sub-Portfolio Files?   The next step is to determine if we will be reading the collateral data from a single pool level collateral file or from up to five sub-portfolio level data files. We test the Boolean variable "gPoolLevelData" to see if it is TRUE, indicating a pool level file, or FALSE, indicating we will read the sub-portfolio level files. How do we know the state of "gPoolLevelData"? Thankfully, this determination has already been performed by the subroutine "MainProgram_FindActivePoolOrSubPorts" called from the main program. If the content of the pool level file pathway field is either blank or shows the message "No File Selected", a pool level data file is either unavailable or not needed. We will therefore assume that we are to read all the sub-portfolio fields as an alternative. You will also note that the subroutine also sets the elements of a Boolean array named "gPortActive" at the same time. If we have pool level data, the 0th element of the array is set to TRUE while the first to the fifth elements of the array are set to FALSE. If we have sub-portfolio level files, the 0th element of the "gPortActive" array is set to FALSE and each of the five elements of the array are set to TRUE if a corresponding sub-portfolio has been indicated. See Exhibit 10.7.

"CollatData_ReadCollateralFiles" Subroutine   If there is a valid file pathway in the "Collateral Pool #1" field, we will read the pool level file, and only that file, ignoring the entries in the sub-portfolio level file fields of the menu. At the bottom of the subroutine we can see the choice between reading a pool level collateral data file with the subroutine "CollatData_ReadPoolDataFile" or a series of sub-portfolio level collateral data files using the "CollatData_ReadSubPortDataFiles". See Exhibit 10.7.

```
Sub MainProgram_FindActivePoolOrSubPorts()

    'DETERMINE IF WE ARE PERFORMING A MODEL RUN WITH POOL LEVEL DATA OR DATA
    ' FROM SUB-PORTFOLIOS
    If Range("m07CollatPool") = "No File Selected" Or _
        Range("m07CollatPool") = "" Then
        'no Pool Level file specified, we are dealing with a collection of
        ' sub-portfolios
        gPoolLevelData = False
        gPortActive(0) = False
        gSubPortLevelData = True
        For iport = 1 To NUM_PORTS
            gPortActive(iport) = True
            If Range("m07SubPorts").Cells(iport) = "No File Selected" Or _
                Range("m07SubPorts").Cells(iport) Then
                    gPortActive(iport) = False
            End If
        Next iport
    Else
        'Pool Level file specified, ignore the sub-portfolios
        gPoolLevelData = True
        gPortActive(0) = True
        gSubPortLevelData = False
        For iport = 1 To NUM_PORTS
            gPortActive(iport) = False
        Next iport
    End If

End Sub
```

EXHIBIT 10.7 "MainProgram_FindActivePoolOrSubPorts" subroutine

"CollatData_ReadPoolDataFile" Subroutine If we are reading a pool level file, we call the subroutine in Exhibit 10.8. The subroutine opens the file name and pathway stored in the variable "gfnPoolName". It next selects the worksheet named "Loan Information". It starts at the location of the first row containing data, the value of the Constant variable, "FIRST_DATA_ROW", and counting down the rows of the worksheet increments the variable "current_row" for each line of the worksheet that contains a non-NULL column "A" field. Upon encountering the NULL field, it breaks out of the "Do..While" loop. It then transfers its current count to the global "gTotalLoans" variable we declared earlier in Exhibit 10.3. It now re-dimensions a series of four arrays using the value of "gTotalLoans" and other Constant variables. These arrays are:

- "gLoanOK". This array tells us the overall disposition of the loan based on the screening and selection tests applied to it. It was discussed earlier in the chapter.
- "gLoanData". This array will hold the contents of the collateral data file or files.
- "gLoanScreen". This array will hold the results of the initial data screening process.
- "gLoanSelect". This array will hold the results of the geographic, demographic, and financial selection process as well as the results of the geographic concentration tests.

```
Sub CollatData_ReadPoolDataFile()

    'open the Pool Level file
    iloan = 0
    Workbooks.Open FileName:=gfnPoolName
    current_row = FIRST_DATA_ROW
    Sheets("LoanInformation").Select
    Range("A1").Select
    'count the number of loans in the file
    Do While Cells(current_row, 1).Value <> ""
        current_row = current_row + 1
    Loop
    gTotalLoans = current_row - 3    '2 header rows and 1 false count
    'redimension the data arrays based on the number of total loans
    ReDim gLoanOK(1 To gTotalLoans) As Boolean
    ReDim gLoanData(1 To gTotalLoans, 1 To DATA_FILE_FIELDS) As Double
    ReDim gLoanScreen(1 To gTotalLoans, 1 To TOTAL_SCREEN_SCORES) As Long
    ReDim gLoanSelect(1 To gTotalLoans, 1 To TOTAL_SELECT_SCORES) As Long
    Call CollatData_ReadDataFileContents(gTotalLoans + 2, iloan)
    ActiveWorkbook.Close

End Sub
```

EXHIBIT 10.8 "CollatData_ReadPoolDataFile" subroutine

With these arrays in place, we are now ready to read the data and apply whatever screening or selection tests we wish. See Exhibit 10.8.

"CollatData_ReadSubPortDataFiles" Subroutine If, instead of reading the data from a single pool level collateral file, we are reading a series of sub-portfolio level files, we call the subroutine in Exhibit 10.9. The task of this subroutine is to open each of the selected sub-portfolio files, count the number of records in each, sum the number of records in each of the files selected for inclusion, add the per-file total to a running grand total, and then close the file. After all the selected files have been read, we can engage in the process of re-dimensioning the four arrays we just spoke of above. The one complication we face here is that of determining how many loan records we will have in the combined "gLoanData" array.

The upper portion of the subroutine consists of a "For..Next" loop that opens each of the valid sub-portfolio level collateral data file pathways. It then counts the number of records in the file and stores this number in the variable "SumLoansIn-Files". Upon conclusion of the loop, we now know the total number of active records in the combined number of sub-portfolio files that have been selected. We re-dimension the arrays "gLoanOK", "gLoanData", "gLoanSelect", and "gLoan-Screen" as we did when we read a pool level data file.

With these arrays in place, the lower portion of the subroutine then reopens each of the selected sub-portfolio files and reads their contents using the "Collat-Data_ReadDataFileContents" subroutine.

"CollatData_ReadDataFileContents" Subroutine Pool level data or a series of sub-portfolio level data files are all the same to the subroutine "Collat-Data_ReadDataFileContents"! The subroutine takes two arguments: (1) the number

```vba
Sub CollatData_ReadSubPortDataFiles()

Dim LoansInFile(1 To NUM_PORTS)     As Long       '# of loans in Sub-Portfolio
Dim SumLoansInFiles                 As Long       'total loans in all Sub-Portfolios
Dim SubPortSelect(1 To NUM_PORTS) As Boolean      'is Sub-Portfolio selected?

    'open each of the files, count the records and sum them
    SumLoansInFiles = 0
    For subport = 1 To NUM_PORTS
        LoansInFile(subport) = 0
        If gfnSubPort(subport) = "No File Selected" Or gfnSubPort(subport) = "" Then
            SubPortSelect(subport) = False
        Else
            SubPortSelect(subport) = True
            Workbooks.Open FileName:=gfnSubPort(subport)
            'count the number of loans in the file
            current_row = 3
            Do While Cells(current_row, 1).Value <> ""
                current_row = current_row + 1
            Loop
            LoansInFile(subport) = current_row - 3  '2 header rows and 1 false count
            SumLoansInFiles = SumLoansInFiles + LoansInFile(subport)
            ActiveWorkbook.Close
        End If
    Next subport
    ReDim gLoanOK(1 To SumLoansInFiles) As Boolean
    ReDim gLoanData(1 To SumLoansInFiles, 1 To DATA_FILE_FIELDS) As Double
    ReDim gLoanScreen(1 To SumLoansInFiles, 1 To TOTAL_SCREEN_SCORES) As Long
    ReDim gLoanSelect(1 To SumLoansInFiles, 1 To TOTAL_SELECT_SCORES) As Long

    'populate the arrays with the information of the data files
    gTotalLoans = SumLoansInFiles
    iloan = 0
    For subport = 1 To NUM_PORTS
        If SubPortSelect(subport) Then
            'open the subportfolio file
            Workbooks.Open FileName:=gfnSubPort(subport)
            Sheets("LoanInformation").Select
            current_row = FIRST_DATA_ROW
            Range("A1").Select
            'read the loan data. if there are damaged records discard them and
            '  write only records without any non-numeric data to the gLoanData
            '  array
            Call CollatData_ReadDataFileContents(LoansInFile(subport) + 2, iloan)
            ActiveWorkbook.Close
        End If
    Next subport

End Sub
```

EXHIBIT 10.9   "CollatData_ReadSubPortDataFiles" subroutine

of loans in the file that is now open, and (2) the number of the individual loan we are about to read. See Exhibit 10.10.

Whether we are calling this subroutine with the idea of reading a single pool level or a collection of sub-portfolio level files, we now have the VBA arrays sized for the exact number of records in the file or files. However, we may find that some of these records contain information that is missing or in an unacceptable form that will present problems for us when we try to transfer the information to the VBA arrays. We will therefore split the data file reading process into two distinct parts. We will set up a large "For..Next" loop to run through all the records of the now-opened file. Within this loop we create two additional loops that will move

```
Sub CollatData_ReadDataFileContents(row_stop As Long, iloan As Long)

Dim dLoanDataItem    As Double   'double precision form of cell contents
Dim sLoanDataItem    As String   'string form of cell contents
Dim sStateCode       As String   'string State Postal Code

    'first check that all the inputs are numeric mark as rejected any records that
    ' have non-numeric data anywhere, except when the field of the record is blank.
    iloan = 1
    For irow = FIRST_DATA_ROW To row_stop

        gLoanOK(iloan) = False
        'check all data fields in the record for non-numeric content
        For iparm = 2 To DATA_FILE_FIELDS
            If iparm <> FD_STATECODE Then dLoanDataItem = Cells(irow, iparm).Value
            sLoanDataItem = Trim(Cells(irow, iparm).Value)
            If sLoanDataItem <> "" Then
                If iparm <> FD_STATECODE Then 'skip if state id code (alpha)
                    If (IsNumeric(dLoanDataItem)) = False Then
                        gLoanData(iloan, iparm) = ERROR_VALUE         '-99.99
                    End If
                End If
            Else
                gLoanData(iloan, iparm) = ERROR_VALUE         '-99.99
            End If
        Next iparm

        'load the data into the gLoanData array
        For iparm = 1 To DATA_FILE_FIELDS
            Select Case iparm
                Case Is = FD_POOLID             'sub-portfolio field
                    If gPoolLevelData = False Then gLoanData(iloan, iparm) = subport
                Case Is = FD_STATECODE          'convert postal alpha to numeric
                    sStateCode = Cells(irow, iparm).Value
                    gLoanData(iloan, iparm) = _
                                Utility_ConvertStateAlphaToNumeric(sStateCode)
                Case Else:                      'all other fields
                    gLoanData(iloan, iparm) = Cells(irow, iparm).Value
            End Select
        Next iparm
        Cells(1, 1).Value = iloan
        iloan = iloan + 1   'increment the write position

    Next irow

End Sub
```

EXHIBIT 10.10   "CollatData_ReadDataFileContents" subroutine

through the loan record on a field-by-field basis. The task, performed by the first of these interior "For..Next" loops, is to check the data for illegible or missing items. The second loop immediately below it transfers the data from the data file to the VBA arrays.

Checking for Legible Data   Let us look at the first "For..Next" loop. This loop runs through each of the data fields of the loan record. The first test it performs is to determine that it is NOT reading the "FD_STATECODE" field. This field, currently the 34th of the record, is known to contain alphabetic data in the form of a two-letter postal code. We know that this field, unique among all other fields in the record, *is not numeric*! We therefore avoid subjecting its contents to the

"IsNumeric" test that follows in the same line. If the current field is NOT the state code field, we will read the contents into the variable "dLoanDataItem". This variable is a "dummy" array meant to hold the value of the field until we decide what to do with it. On the next line we will copy the contents of the field into yet another dummy variable, this one, declared in a String data format, is named "sLoanDataItem". We next check the contents of the "sLoanDataItem" to see if it is NULL. If it is, that field of the loan record is blank. We then branch to the "Else" cutoff and assign the datum the "ERROR_VALUE". If the value of "sLoan-DataItem" is not NULL, we proceed to test the contents of the field in its double form, stored in the variable "dLoanDataItem". We run the value of the variable "gLoanDataItem" through the "IsNumeric" test and see what pops out. We use the "If..Then" test:

```
If (IsNumeric(dLoanDataItem)) = False Then
```

To determine if the contents are numeric. If they are *not* numeric, then the first part of the test "IsNumeric(dLoanDataItem)" will read FALSE. The entire expression then evaluates to:

```
If False = False Then
```

which equals TRUE! The contents of the field are therefore *not* numeric and are assigned the value of the Constant variable "ERROR_VALUE". This completes the work of screening the data record for missing and illegible fields!

Writing Collateral Data into the "gLoanData" Array We will now turn to the lower "For..Next" loop of the subroutine. Here we will transfer the information from the data file into the "gLoanData" array. The "gLoanData" array is the mother lode of information about the collateral that will, from this point on, be continually used by almost every subroutine until the end of the run of the CCFG. You would think that we had completed all the testing in the upper loop of this subroutine, but a small part remains. To load the contents of "gLoanData", we still have to worry about two exceptions to the rule. The first is the pool identification number, and the second is converting the state postal code to a numeric format. Aside from these two fields, we can transfer the contents of the record into the "gLoanData" field with any further ado. If we are dealing with a pool level data file, the concept of retaining the identity of the file from whence the loan originated is meaningless (everything came from one file!). If we are dealing with a series of sub-portfolios, we may be asked to apply separate sets of selection tests against the loans of different sub-portfolios. Preserving the number of the file that the loan originated from is therefore essential. The first test in the lower loop is to determine if the collateral is from a pool or not. If it is not, we will record the number of the file in the file "FD_POOLID", the first field in the "gLoanData" array. The second task, that of converting the alphabetic postal codes to a numeric, will be handled by a special-purpose subroutine. This function, named "Utility_ConvertStateAlphaToNumeric", compares the alphabetical state code, such as "NY" or "CA", to a list of all postal codes and returns its ordinal rank in the list. Thus "CT", Connecticut, is assigned the value of "7". If we are not dealing with either a postal code or a pool ID number, all other fields are read into the "gLoanData" array at this point.

One final point: Remember, the assignment of the "ERROR_VALUE" occurs in the "gLoanData" array, *not the data file*! This preserves the contents of the data file so that we can examine the problem data fields in the format we received them! Remember also that just reading the contents of the data file into the "gLoanData" array does not indicate that the data have been determined to be either usable or valid. The data could be in a numeric format and have completely unreasonable values. In fact, this is more often the case than is not. To avoid bad data causing future unpleasantness, we will, in a short while, look at the initial data screening process.

Building a Pool Level Collateral Array

Having concluded the task of populating the "gLoanData" array with the contents of the selected file or files, we now can move on to another task that can be performed by the CCFG from the "CollatDataMenu". If the user has elected to read the data from the collection of sub-portfolio collateral data files, he or she may wish to combine the contents of the sub-portfolio files into the much more convenient format of a pool level collateral data file.

To accomplish this, we need to perform the following steps:

Step 1. Determine if the user wants the pool level file created.
Step 2. Determine the file name we are to write the data to.
Step 3. Open a collateral data file template file and rename it to the file name entered by the user.
Step 4. Populate the file with the contents of the "gLoanData" array.
Step 5. Close and save the newly created pool level file.

The subroutine "CollatData_WritePoolLevelDataFile" performs all of these steps with the exception of the first two, which, as we have seen, are addressed in the "CollatData_ReadCollateralFiles" subroutine. See Exhibit 10.11.

INITIAL DATA SCREENING

Just getting the data into the "gLoanData" array is not enough! We now need to attempt to make an initial estimate of how much of the data is useful. We will use these data for five major tasks:

1. **Cash flow amortization.** Each of the five mortgage types will require its own unique set of data to perform a cash flow amortization calculation.
2. **Stratification reporting.** We will need to have as complete as possible information on a variety of amortization, other financial, geographic, demographic, and servicing/credit characteristics of each of the loans.
3. **Frequency of foreclosure estimates.** We will need a specialized subset of the pool level data to estimate the potential default rate of the portfolio. These data will

```
Sub CollatData_WritePoolLevelDataFile()

    'open the data file template file
    gfnPoolDataFileName = Range("m07CollatPoolFileName")
    Workbooks.Open FileName:=DIR_TEMPLATE_UTIL & COLLAT_FILE_TEMPLATE
    'save as the Pool Level data file name specified on the menu
    ActiveWorkbook.SaveAs FileName:=gfnPoolDataFileName
    'write the data
    iloan = 1
    For irow = FIRST_DATA_ROW To (FIRST_DATA_ROW + gTotalLoans - 1)
        Cells(irow, 1).Value = iloan
        For iparm = 2 To DATA_FILE_FIELDS
            Cells(irow, iparm).Value = gLoanData(iloan, iparm)
        Next iparm
        Cells(1, 1).Value = iloan
        iloan = iloan + 1
    Next irow
    ActiveWorkbook.Save
    ActiveWorkbook.Close

End Sub
```

EXHIBIT 10.11   "CollatData_WritePoolLevelDataFile" subroutine

concentrate on the creditworthiness of the borrower, the type of property, its economic use, and the origination and servicing efforts that have and can be made in regard to the particular loan in question.

4. **Market value decline calculations.** We will need a similar set of selected data to estimate the loss due to a foreclosure action. These are the location of the property, the amount of current arrearage, the type of loan, and the original purpose of the financing.

5. **Geographic prepayment/default methodologies.** We will need to check that each record has a valid state and MSA code. We will need these codes to select specific prepayment, foreclosure rate, MVD percentages, and recovery lag period estimates based on the location of the property.

Goal of the Screening Process

We have already screened the information contained in the collateral data files for missing or illegible entries—why do we need to do more? The screening that we have performed to date only addresses the first of the three factors, legibility, and does not address the issues of reasonableness and completeness.

Reasonableness   We now need to make sure that the data, or at least as much as we can set up tests for, is "reasonable" in nature. Broadly stated, that means that the values are ones that are reasonable to expect to occur for the loan record in question. For example, there are ten possible values that the property type field can assume. These are the integers numbered 1 to 10. The CCFG is configured to act on this range of values, either explicitly through the use of "Select..Case" statements or implicitly through the format of reports. We therefore need to make sure that values less than 0 or greater than 10 are not present in the "gLoanData" array for this field. (We would not like the program to malfunction or, worse yet, appear to run successfully, and produce erroneous output!) Remember, we want to invest time and energy now, averting as many problems as we can, before we run the model and find our time and effort wasted! There is nothing more frustrating than having models crash at or near the end of lengthy run times, especially if this occurs as you are about to leave the office for the day or when you are under a deadline to an investor, rating agency, or regulatory body!

Balance Example   In addition to prescribing limits to lists of data values, such as the example of property type, just discussed, we need to also set limits on other values that have no specific range of values. An example of this are the factors of current balance and seasoning. Although we may wish to make as much of the collateral we have on hand eligible for inclusion in our deal, we need to establish upper and lower bounds for the current balance of the loans we will accept. A set of such bounds might well be $1,000 to $2,000,000. Loans with current balances either lower than $1,000 or greater than $2,000,000 are de facto ineligible collateral and should be screened out early in the process. Small-balance loans may not be worth the cost of servicing, and it might well be more economical to write them off than to service them. In addition, a small-balance loan may also have a very limited remaining life over which to contribute cash flows to the deal. Large-balance loans present a different set of problems. Let us say we have a total portfolio of $500 million in current balances consisting of 7,500 loans. Within this portfolio we have two loans with current balances of $5 million, three loans of $4 million, ten loans of $3 million, and ten loans in the range of $2 million to $3 million. In this case we have a minimum of $72 million in current balances representing 14.4% of the balances concentrated in 0.33% of the number of loans. If anything happens to this small number of loans, the collateral cash flows of the deal could be severely diminished! At worst we would probably be required to post a specifically targeted loss reserve against this high-balance group!

Loan Seasoning   Regarding loan seasoning, we would want to place a minimum and maximum limit for related reasons. We would want a three-month minimum, if not a six-month minimum, lower bound for seasoning—especially if the mortgagor is a first-time homeowner. Why? When people purchase a new home, they also need to purchase many other things. Some of these purchases take the form of appliances, furniture, and other home furnishings. In addition, many people are "stretched" financially with the purchase of their first home. Budgets are tight and, in uncertain economic times, subject to disruption. There is historically a spike of defaults in the first year of homeownership. Setting a minimum seasoning allows some of the earlier defaulters to be excluded from the deal collateral pool. A maximum limit on seasoning also serves to keep low remaining term loans out of the portfolio. We do not want a lot of our collateral paying off early in the life of the deal.

Other Tests   Other reasonableness tests include those dealing with interest rates, coupon reset periods, teaser rates, and the like. Excluding collateral with atypical or outlying values (probably reflective of predatory lending practices, poor credit underwriting, or both) can prevent avoidable trouble from being brought into the collateral pool.

Completeness   The concepts of legibility and reasonableness deal with individual collateral data points; the concept of completeness deals with a specific *collection* of data fields. These collective data fields provide the CCFG with the specific inputs it needs to perform a certain task. A specific task, such as calculation of cash flows for a fixed-rate mortgage type, requires six data inputs. If all of these data items are present (not missing from the record), in the correct numeric form, and within whatever reasonableness bounds we establish, the record can be said to be complete. It is, however, complete for that specific task *only*! Just because a record is complete for task A does not mean it is complete for task B! The amortization parameters for a HARM consist of 18 data items. Of these 18 items, all 6 are needed to amortize a fixed-rate loan and to be present as a subset of the 18 total fields. While a collateral record containing 17 valid data fields is not complete for a HARM, it may well be complete for a fixed-rate mortgage if the missing data item is not one of the 6 required by that mortgage type.

We will need to measure completeness in each collateral record for the following tests:

- **Amortization cash flow calculations (by mortgage types).** This can range between 6 data inputs for fixed-rate mortgages and 18 others for HARMs.
- **Stratification reports.** There are 21 data inputs needed to allow the record to be analyzed without any restrictions across the full range of stratification and cross-tabulation collateral reports.
- **Geographic Prepayment/Default Methodology.** There are three data inputs needed to determine the prepayment, default, MVD, and recovery lag periods.
- **Demographic Prepayment/Default Methodology.** There are 21 data inputs needed to determine the frequency of foreclosure rate and 11 data inputs to determine the market value decline percentage factor.

To slightly complicate matters, if we have elected to employ the Demographic Prepayment/Default Methodology, the record needs to be complete for both the frequency of foreclosure input set *and* the market value decline set simultaneously. Fortunately for us, the two sets share seven data items in common, somewhat increasing the chances that we will meet both of the requirements!

Exclusion Screening   There is one last form of initial data screening we need to consider: exclusion screening. A decision may be made that collateral with a certain characteristic(s) be perfunctorily excluded from the pool. We need to make provision in the initial data screening for a quick and easy way to exclude this mortgage type among the other five types.

A somewhat more complex issue arises if we want to exclude multiple mortgage types. Let us suppose that we wish to exclude all ARMs as a group. This would mean the exclusion of mortgage types with the following codes:

- "2": standard ARMs
- "3": hybrid ARMs
- "5": standard ARMs (balloon payments)

We need to provide whoever is using the model (keeping in mind that it may be us!) an easy and foolproof way of implementing such a selection.

Reporting Above all, lest we forget, it is not enough simply to perform the initial data selection; we need to be able to record and analyze the results of the activity for the edification of ourselves and others! That means that we will need to develop a method of not just reporting that a collateral record is unusable. We will also need to display what is wrong from the standpoint of missing or illegible data, unreasonable or excluded values, and incompleteness for specific critical tasks. Above all, we need to allow the user to set up these criteria in an easily accessible manner that will be transparent, flexible, and manageable over the life of the model.

Creating the Initial Data Screening and Error Code Data Table

To meet the requirements of the CCFG to provide the user with an easily accessible method of stipulating all of the screening requirements, we will design something resembling a pseudo menu. This is a data table that will contain all the criteria needed to perform the various tests. These tests are:

- **Reasonableness tests.** This will include a minimum and maximum value for every data field that needs to be screened in the collateral record.
- **Cash flow amortization tests.** One test for each mortgage type. The table will include the fields to be tested and their corresponding error codes for tracking the specific problems in the record.
- **Stratification report tests.** For each data field that can be used in the stratification or the cross-tabulation report packages.
- **Demographic Methodology frequency of foreclosure.** For each required data field and error codes.
- **Demographic Methodology market value decline.** For each required data field and error codes.
- **Geographic Methodology.** For each required data field and error codes.

The contents of this data table will be read into a series of VBA arrays at the inception of the screening process. We will create an Excel Worksheet for the table and name it "DataInitialScreening". See Exhibit 10.12.

Creating the "gLoanScreen" Array

The ultimate goal of the initial data screening process is to have a series of scores that will tell us in no uncertain terms if each piece of prospective collateral has passed the screening process. If a piece of collateral has not passed, we will need to be able to backtrack through the tests and determine *exactly* what the deficiencies of the data for that record are and if we will be restricted in using the loan for certain purposes. For example, a piece of collateral may have all its amortization criteria in place but lack data critical for both the Geographic and Demographic Methodology prepayment and default methods. It would be possible to use this collateral only if we were running the Uniform prepayment method.

Initial Data Screening Criteria and Error Codes

#	Data Item Names	Min Value	Max Value	Fixed Rate	Stand ARM	Hybrid ARM	Fixed Balloon	ARM Balloon	Strat Reports Datum	Freq Of Fore Datum	MVD Datum	Geo Datum
1	Pool ID			1	1	1	1	1	1	1	1	
2	Mortgage Type	1	5	2	2	2	2	2	2	2	2	
3	Credit Sector	1	5						4	4	4	
4	Original Balance	10,000	2,000,000						8		8	
5	Current Balance	1,000	2,000,000						16			1
6	Origination Date											
7	Original Loan-to-Value Ratio	0%	100%	4	4	4	4	4	32			
8	Current Loan-to-Value Ratio	0%	140%	8	8	8	8	8	64		16	
9	Original Term	60	360						128			
10	Remaining Term	6	360						256			
11	Seasoning	3	60						512	8		
12	Current Coupon Rate	2.00%	15.00%	16	16	16	16	16	1,024	16		
13	ARM Index	1	2		32	32		32	2,048			
14	ARM Spread to Index	1.00%	7.00%		64	64		64				
15	ARM Initial Index Level				128	128		128				
16	ARM Periodic Reset	1	3		256	256		256				
17	ARM Periodic Cap Rate	0.10%	5.00%		512	512		512				
18	ARM Periodic Floor	0.10%	5.00%		1,024	1,024		1,024				
19	ARM Lifetime Cap Rate	0%	15%		2,048	2,048		2,048				
20	ARM Lifetime Floor Rate	2%	10%		4,096	4,096		4,096				
21	HB-ARM Initial Rate	2%	15%			8,192						
22	HB-ARM Initial I/O Rate Period	3	60			16,384						
23	HB-ARM Total I/O Rate Period	3	180			32,768						
24	HB-ARM Recast Term	3	12			65,536						
25	BALLOON Amortization Period	60	360				32	8,192				
26	BALLOON Period	60	360				64	16,384				
27	Original Appraisal Value								4,096			
28	Current Appraisal Value								8,192			
29	Original Appraisal Type	1	7						16,384			
30	Current Appraisal Type	1	7						32,768			
31	Property Type	1	10						65,536	32		2
32	Occupancy Code	1	8						131,072	64		
33	Financing Purpose	1	8						262,144	128		
34	State Code	1	54						524,288	256	32	4
35	MSA Code	0	99999						1,048,576	512	64	8
36	Zip Code										128	
37	Self-employed	1	3							1,024		
38	Number of years in position	1	8							2,048		
39	First Time Homeowner	1	3							4,096		
40	Payments in Arrears											
41	Amt Payments in Arrears										256	
42	FICO Score	450	800							8,192	512	
43	Mortgage Debt-to-Income Ratio	0%	100%							16,384		
44	Total Debt-to-Income Ratio	0%	100%							32,768		
45	Bankruptcy History	1	5							65,536		
46	Escrow Provisions											
47	Third Party Doc Due Diligence	1	5							131,072		
48	Origination Document Package	1	6							262,144		
49	Servicer Rating	1	7							524,288		
50	Day Count Convention	1	2	32	8,192	131,072	128	32,768		1,048,576		

Note: The "Test For Excluded Values / Executed Values" column and the Excluded Values columns 1–10 are blank (shaded) for all rows. The Fixed Rate, Stand ARM, Hybrid ARM, Fixed Balloon, and ARM Balloon columns are grouped under the heading "Amortization Data Screening Tests."

Data Item Names (reference):

1 Pool ID
2 Mortgage Type
3 Credit Sector
4 Original Balance
5 Current Balance
6 Origination Date
7 Original Loan-to-Value Ratio
8 Current Loan-to-Value Ratio
9 Original Term
10 Remaining Term
11 Seasoning
12 Current Coupon Rate
13 ARM Index
14 ARM Spread to Index
15 ARM Initial Index Level
16 ARM Periodic Reset
17 ARM Periodic Cap Rate
18 ARM Periodic Floor
19 ARM Lifetime Cap Rate
20 ARM Lifetime Floor Rate
21 HB-ARM Initial Rate
22 HB-ARM Initial I/O Rate Period
23 HB-ARM Total I/O Rate Period
24 HB-ARM Recast Term
25 BALLOON Amortization Period
26 BALLOON Period
34 Original Appraisal Value
35 Current Appraisal Value
36 Original Appraisal Type
37 Current Appraisal Type
38 Property Type
39 Occupancy Code
40 Financing Purpose
41 State Code
42 MSA Code
43 Zip Code
44 Self-employed
45 Number of years in position
46 First Time Homeowner
47 Payments in Arrears
48 Amt Payments in Arrears
49 FICO Score
50 Mortgage Debt-to-Income Ratio
51 Total Debt-to-Income Ratio
52 Bankruptcy History
53 Escrow Provisions
54 Third Party Doc Due Diligence
55 Origination Document Package
56 Servicer Rating
57 Day Count Convention

EXHIBIT 10.12 Initial data screening and error code data table

```
'initial data screening scores stored in the gLoanScreen array
Public Const REC_OKFORALL = 0          'record data ok
Public Const TOTAL_SCREEN_SCORES = 8   'number of test sets for initial screening
Public Const FD_SCREEN_FORMAT = 1      'data in the fields correctly formatted
Public Const FD_SCREEN_AMORT = 2       'cash flow amortization data screening score
Public Const FD_SCREEN_STRAT = 3       'strat report data screening score
Public Const FD_SCREEN_FOF = 4         'default rate data screening score
Public Const FD_SCREEN_MVD = 5         'market value decline data screening score
Public Const FD_SCREEN_GEO = 6         'geographic information scrrening
Public Const FD_SCREEN_ALL_OK = 7      'complete in all regards
Public Const FD_SCREEN_DEMO_OK = 8     'complete for Demographic prepay/default
```

EXHIBIT 10.13   Initial data screening Constant variables

To this end we will declare an array "gLoanScreen" that will contain the screening results for each loan we test. We will establish this array to contain eight scores for each condition of eligibility we need. We will define each of these tests with a Constant variable so that they will be easily identifiable. These definitions will be placed in the "A_Constants" module. See Exhibit 10.13.

The inline comments for these variables are fairly straightforward. You will notice, however, two things. The first is that there does not appear to be a "reasonableness" score. The second is that two of the scores do not appear to relate to specific tests but instead to a collection of tests. You may have expected an entry such as:

```
Public Const FD_SCREEN_REASON = 1 'value between Min/Max limits?
```

A "reasonableness" error score does not exist independent of the other scores we have defined here. A record that has unreasonable values will fail the minimum/maximum range test and trigger an error condition in the "FD_SCREEN_FORMAT" field.

There are six individual scores that relate to specific error conditions in the record. These are:

1. **"FD_SCREEN_FORMAT"**. This error field indicates if the record is legible and has reasonable values in its fields.
2. **"FD_SCREEN_AMORT"**. This error field contains a score that indicates whether all of the requite information needed to calculate a cash flow amortization is present in the loan record.
3. **"FD_SCREEN_STRAT"**. This field indicates if the record is complete from the standpoint of all data necessary to perform stratification and cross-tabulation reports.
4. **"FD_SCREEN_FOF"**. This error field indicates if the data items needed to calculate the frequency of foreclosure under the Demographic Methodology are present.
5. **"FD_SCREEN_MVD"**. This error field indicates if the data items needed to calculate the MVD under the Demographic Methodology are present.
6. **"FD_SCREEN_GEO"**. This error field indicates if the data items needed to determine the assumptions to be applied when using the Geographic Methodology are present.

There are two last "compound scores" that complete the list. These are scores that are constructed from other scores. The first is "FD_SCREEN_ALL_OK" and the second is "FD_SCREEN_DEMO_OK".

These scores will assume the values of either "0" for FALSE or "1" for TRUE. If and only if all six of the individual scores listed above are "0" (no errors present, data fully usable) will the "FD_SCREEN_ALL_OK" value of the record be set to "1", TRUE. If any of these tests is greater than "0", it means that the screening process has detected one or more errors and the record is not complete for use in every aspect of aggregation or calculation.

The second score, "FD_SCREEN_DEMO", is set to "1", TRUE, only if both "FD_SCREEN_FOF" and "FD_SCREEN_MVD" are both "0" (no errors). This certifies that the record is complete for use in the Demographic Prepayment/Default Methodology.

Why do we create these composite scores? We create them because it is easier, more concise, and clearer in the code to test a single value than it is to test a set of multiple values! By building the composite score from the component scores at the point of testing, we assure ourselves that everything is included and we do not need to reassemble the composite to make multiple tests throughout the program (potentially avoiding logic mistakes by failing to include a component). We still have the components available and can use them in special situations, but the composites are safer and more concise for many of the computational and reporting decisions we need to make.

Note on Error Codes

The rightmost ten columns of the body of the "Initial Data Screening Criteria" contain a series of numbers that represent the error codes associated with the tests of each data item. The column titled "Fixed Rate" under the "Amortization Data Screening Types" section contains six of these codes. As you may now have noted, the error codes all appear to be sequential powers of 2. The first error code for any mortgage type is equal to 1, which is 2 to the 0th power followed by 2, 2 to the 1st power; 4, 2 to 2nd power; and so forth up to the number of tests. If the first cash flow amortization datum needed by the mortgage type is either missing or unusable in its current format, the error score for the loan, contained in the array "gLoanScreen(iloan, FD_SCREEN_AMORT)", is increased from "0", its starting value, to "1". If the second piece is missing, the error score would be again incremented, this time by "2" to a total of 3.

If in the case of a fixed-rate mortgage type, we have six data. The range in the values of these error scores is from "0", no error scores assigned, to "63", all data had errors 1+2+4+8+16+32 = 63. If the error score lies between "1" and "63", we know that some of the data we need for the calculation is not available. But we also know more than that! For any score between "1" and "63", the aggregate error score will also immediately reveal to us *which* of the data are unusable. Each error score between these two ranges corresponds to a unique pattern of error. For example, a score of "22" is comprised of 2+4+16 = 22. In this case, the 2nd, 3rd, and 5th data are missing or unusable. If the score was "9", the constituents would be 1+8 = 9, the 1st and 4th data missing!

To perform the screening process, we will identify which of the data is needed to checked for each of the calculation or reporting processes, assign a unique error value to each datum, and finally sum these error values on a loan-by-loan basis if we discover unusable data. Once this process is complete, we will have a series of six error scores, one for each of the data format, the cash flow amortization, the stratification reports, the default rate calculation, the MVD assignment, and the Geographic Methodology information. From these six component error scores, we will derive two composite error scores, and the process will be complete!

WRITING THE SCREENING PROCESS VBA CODE

We will now begin the process of stepping through the initial data screening process. We will create a separate VBA module for this code and name it "CollatData_ InitialDataScreening". The master or most senior subroutine that governs the steps that the CCFG will take to execute the process is "InitScreen_BasicScreeningMain". This subroutine consists of three major phases. The first is the initialization process where we initialize the "gLoanScreen" array and then read the data from the "Initial Data Screening Criteria" sheet. The second and third phases are contained in a "For..Next" loop that moves through the collateral one loan at a time. The second phase is the determination of each of the component screening scores. When this process is complete, the third phase of the subroutine determines the values of the two composite screening scores. You will note that this subroutine and all the subroutines in this module begin with the prefix "InitScreen". See Exhibit 10.14.

Setting Up the VBA Arrays to Hold the Criteria

Before we begin the process of reading the information from the "Initial Data Screening Criteria" data table, we need to create a collection of VBA arrays to store the values. Inasmuch as all the subroutines that we will create to perform the screening process are contained in the module "CollatData_InitialDataScreening", we will declare this set of arrays as module-level arrays. By reading the comments to the right of each variable declaration, we can easily identify those portions of the data table that will be placed into that specific array. All of these arrays are declared to be "1 to DATA_FILE_FIELDS", the number of fields, 50, in current loan record. See Exhibit 10.15.

Phase 1: Initialization and Reading the Data Table

Three subroutines are needed in this phase of the process. This first subroutine simply initialized the "gLoanScreen" array setting all of its elements to "0". This subroutine was called while we were still in the main program. See Exhibit 10.16.

With the screening error array initialized, we now proceed to enter the information that we will use to conduct the screening tests. If we look at the data table in Exhibit 10.12, we can see that the table is broken into six regions, moving

```
Sub InitScreen_BasicScreeningMain()

    If gROInitDataTest Then
        'initialize the screening scores, read all the test criteria
        ' and the error codes associated with them
        Call InitScreen_ReadAllErrorCodes  'reads error codes for screening tests
        Call InitScreen_ReadTestCriteria   'read test value for itmes that have them
        For iloan = 1 To gTotalLoans
            'screen each of the loans for any missing data, for the minimum amorti-
            ' zation calculation parameters, from the stratification report infor-
            ' mation, and lastly for the inputs for the Demographic prepay/default
            ' methodology
            Call InitScreen_MissingOrDamaged
            Call InitScreen_CFAmortParamters
            Call InitScreen_ScreenData(FD_SCREEN_STRAT)
            'Demographic Perepayment/Default Methodology inputs
            Call InitScreen_ScreenData(FD_SCREEN_FOF)   'screen FOF calc inputs
            Call InitScreen_ScreenData(FD_SCREEN_MVD)   'screen the MVD data
            Call InitScreen_ScreenData(FD_SCREEN_GEO)   'screen the geo method inputs
            'Remember!! gLoanScreen of "ALL_OK", DEMO_OK" do NOT contain error
            ' scores. if these items are equal to 0 it means the record is
            ' OK.  Failing the formatting and amortizations conditions are absolute
            ' show stoppers and we will set the gLoanOK to False.  We cannot use
            ' these loans for anything if the data formats are bad or if the
            ' amortization information is illegible of missing.
            If gLoanScreen(iloan, FD_SCREEN_FORMAT) > 0 Or _
               gLoanScreen(iloan, FD_SCREEN_AMORT) > 0 Or _
               gLoanScreen(iloan, FD_SCREEN_STRAT) > 0 Or _
               gLoanScreen(iloan, FD_SCREEN_FOF) > 0 Or _
               gLoanScreen(iloan, FD_SCREEN_MVD) > 0 Or _
               gLoanScreen(iloan, FD_SCREEN_GEO) > 0 Then
                    If gLoanScreen(iloan, FD_SCREEN_FORMAT) > 0 Or _
                       gLoanScreen(iloan, FD_SCREEN_AMORT) > 0 Then
                        gLoanOK(iloan) = False
                    End If
              Else
                    'good for all purposes
                    gLoanScreen(iloan, FD_SCREEN_ALL_OK) = REC_OKFORALL
                    gLoanOK(iloan) = True
            End If
            'check if the loan is complete for the purposes ofthe Demographic
            ' prepay/default method
            If gLoanScreen(iloan, FD_SCREEN_FOF) = 0 Or _
               gLoanScreen(iloan, FD_SCREEN_MVD) = 0 Then
                    'good for demo prepay/default
                    gLoanScreen(iloan, FD_SCREEN_DEMO_OK) = REC_OKFORALL
            End If
        Next iloan

    End If

End Sub
```

EXHIBIT 10.14 "InitScreen_BasicScreeningMain" subroutine

from left to right:

1. Data field number and datum name columns (2)
2. Minimum/Maximum value columns (2)
3. Exclusion test flag, exclusion values columns (11)
4. Amortization component test columns, arranged by mortgage type from "Fixed Rate" to "ARM Balloon" (6)
5. Stratification reports, frequency of foreclosure, market value decline, and geographic columns (4)
6. Data field number and datum name columns (2) (repeated)

```
'table contents of the "DataInitialScreening" worksheet
'Min/Max test active for this datum?
Dim tActiveMinMax(1 To DATA_FILE_FIELDS)              As Boolean
'Min/Max test values
Dim tTestMinMax(1 To DATA_FILE_FIELDS, 1 To 2)       As Double
'Excluded Values tests active?
Dim tActiveExTest(1 To DATA_FILE_FIELDS)             As Boolean
'Excluded Values table
Dim tActiveExVal(1 To DATA_FILE_FIELDS, 1 To 10)     As String
'Stratification Reports error codes
Dim tSTRATErrCode(1 To DATA_FILE_FIELDS)             As Long
'Freq of Foreclosure error codes
Dim tFOFErrCode(1 To DATA_FILE_FIELDS)               As Long
'Mkt Value Decline error codes
Dim tMVDErrCode(1 To DATA_FILE_FIELDS)               As Long
'Geographic info error codes
Dim tGEOErrCode(1 To DATA_FILE_FIELDS)               As Long
'amortization calc error codes
Dim tAmortErrCode(1 To DATA_FILE_FIELDS, 1 To NUM_MORT_TYPES) As Long
```

EXHIBIT 10.15   VBA arrays containing screening criteria and error code values

For the CCFG to have the information the user has provided to perform the initial data screening correctly, we must read into VBA arrays the contents of regions 2, 3, 4, and 5. We will do that using two arrays. The first will read the Minimum/Maximum and Exclusion information, regions 2 and 3, while the second will read regions 4 and 5.

Minimum/Maximum and Excluded Codes Information   The subroutine "InitScreen_ ReadTestCriteria" reads in the Minimum/Maximum criteria tests for all of the data. The first array that is assigned a value in this subroutine is the "tActiveMinMax"

```
Sub MainProgram_InitLoanEligibilityScores()

   For iloan = 1 To gTotalLoans
    'overall eligibility score
    gLoanOK(iloan) = True
    'data sufficency screening scores
    gLoanScreen(iloan, FD_SCREEN_FORMAT) = 0     'data format score
    gLoanScreen(iloan, FD_SCREEN_AMORT) = 0      'cf amort data score
    gLoanScreen(iloan, FD_SCREEN_STRAT) = 0      'strat data score
    gLoanScreen(iloan, FD_SCREEN_FOF) = 0        'freq fore data score
    gLoanScreen(iloan, FD_SCREEN_MVD) = 0        'MVD data screening score
    gLoanScreen(iloan, FD_SCREEN_GEO) = 0        'SOL data screening score
    gLoanScreen(iloan, FD_SCREEN_ALL_OK) = REC_OKFORALL     'assume its good
    gLoanScreen(iloan, FD_SCREEN_DEMO_OK) = REC_OKFORALL    'good for demo
    'financial, geographic and geographc concentration scores
    gLoanSelect(iloan, FD_CALCFINSELECT) = 0     'financial selection criteria
    gLoanSelect(iloan, FD_CALCGEOSELECT) = 0     'geographic selection criteria
    gLoanSelect(iloan, FD_CALCGEOCONCEN) = 0     'geographic concentration
   Next iloan

End Sub
```

EXHIBIT 10.16   "MainProgram_InitLoanEligibilityScores" subroutine

array. This array is a Boolean and is initialized to FALSE, then set to TRUE if there is a value in the Minimum field. In the data sheet the values of the Minimum/Maximum reasonableness tests are stored in the Range "m10InitScreenMinMax". This range contains two columns one for the minimums and the other for the maximums. Both these columns are read into the VBA array "tTestMinMax".

In the second "For..Next" loop below, we will record from fields of the data table, in the excluded values information, all the values that will automatically deem a loan ineligible. The first piece of information tells us whether there are ANY excluded values for this data field. We discover this fact by testing the appropriate cell in the Range ("m10ExcludedValuesTest"). If this field is non-NULL, then there are excluded values for this data field and we need to read the next set of fields to the right to find out how many values are excluded. If we find any non-NULL cells in the Range "m10ExcludedValues", we will record the corresponding value position in the "tActiveExValues" array. You will note that nested "For..Next" loop that reads these values terminated at the value of the Maximum test. This prevents us from reading values for this data field that do not exist. See Exhibit 10.17.

Error Codes for Amortization, Stratification, Demographic, and Geographic Tests
With the various test criteria now in hand, all that remains before we can write the screening code itself is to write the code to read the error codes sections of the table. The error codes are broken into two main groups: those associated with the amortization data requirements of the loans and those concerned with everything else! In the subroutine "InitScreen_ReadAllErrorCodes", we can transfer this information into the VBA arrays by using a "For..Next" loop to read the contents of a series of Ranges in the data sheet. All the amortization error codes are contained in the

```
Sub InitScreen_ReadTestCriteria()

    'reads the contents of the "DataInitialScreening" worksheet to find the
    ' minimum/maximum data values for each of the fields.
    'it also reads the range that contains the excluded values and the range of the
    ' amortization error codes.
    For irow = 1 To DATA_FILE_FIELDS
        'minimum/maximum test conditions and test flags
        tActiveMinMax(irow) = False          'initialize min max test array
        If Range("m10InitScreenMinMax").Cells(irow, 1) <> "" Then
            tActiveMinMax(irow) = True
            tTestMinMax(irow, 1) = Range("m10InitScreenMinMax").Cells(irow, 1)
            tTestMinMax(irow, 2) = Range("m10InitScreenMinMax").Cells(irow, 2)
        End If
        'read the excluded values array
        tActiveExTest(irow) = False          'initialize excluded values test array
        If Range("m10ExcludedValuesTest").Cells(irow) <> "" Then
            tActiveExTest(irow) = True
            For icol = 1 To tTestMinMax(irow, 2)
                tActiveExVal(irow, icol) = _
                                  Range("m10ExcludedValues").Cells(irow, icol)
            Next icol
        End If
    Next irow

End Sub
```

EXHIBIT 10.17   "InitScreen_ReadTestCriteria" subroutine

```
Sub InitScreen_ReadAllErrorCodes()

    For irow = 1 To DATA_FILE_FIELDS
        'reads the contents of the Amortization Data Screening Test table
        For icol = 1 To NUM_MORT_TYPES
            tAmortErrCode(irow, icol) = Range("m10ErrCodesAmort").Cells(irow, icol)
        Next icol
        'Stratification data error codes, Freq of Foreclosure and
        ' Market Value Decline data codes
        tSTRATErrCode(irow) = Range("m10ErrCodesStrat").Cells(irow)
        tFOFErrCode(irow) = Range("m10ErrCodesDefRate").Cells(irow)
        tMVDErrCode(irow) = Range("m10ErrCodesMVD").Cells(irow)
        tGEOErrCode(irow) = Range("m10ErrCodesGeo").Cells(irow)
    Next irow

End Sub
```

EXHIBIT 10.18 "InitScreen_ReadAllErrorCodes" subroutine

Range "m10ErrCodesAmort". This range is a table of 50 rows, one for each data field, and six columns, one for each mortgage type. We will store these codes in the array "tAmortErrCode". Each of the other four component tests—stratification, frequency of foreclosure, MVD, and Geographic Methodology prepayments—are read into individual arrays from their corresponding Ranges on the data sheet. See Exhibit 10.18.

Phase 2: Screening the Individual Records

All the test criteria specifications are read from the "Initial Data Screening Criteria" data sheet and in VBA arrays inside the CCFG where we can use them. Time to begin the screening process.

Screening the Missing/Damaged Data   The screening phase will address the issues of missing or non-numeric format data. The subroutine loops through each data field of the collateral record and tests to see if its value is equal to "ERROR_VALUE", a constant set to –99.99. If it finds such a value, it stops, assigns the number of the item as the error code, and drops immediately out of the loop. This is the only error code that does not use the powers of two schema. Why? There are currently 50 data fields in the record. Using the "powers of 2" methodology would result in unwieldy error codes, specifically over 144 quadrillion! The final step is to assign the value of the variable "mErrorScore" to the "gLoanScreen" array in the "FD_SCREEN_FORMAT" cell for this loan.
    See Exhibit 10.19.

Screening Cash Flow Amortization Data   The subroutine "InitScreen_CFAmort Parameters" now screens the record data to determine if there are any data deficiencies that will prevent us from performing the cash flow amortization calculations for the type of mortgage that the record represents. The outermost "For..Next" works its way through the record on a field-by-field basis. We set the variable "mtype" to the type of mortgage of the record found in the second record field, "FD_MORTTYPE". This assures us that we are pointed at the correct column of error codes in the "tAmortErrCode" array that we populated earlier. If the *n*th field that the loop is

```
Sub InitScreen_MissingOrDamaged()

    'screens record for error value in the record, stops on the first one found and quits
    mErrorScore = 0                             'damaged or missing data
    mtype = gLoanData(iloan, FD_MORTTYPE)
    For irow = 1 To DATA_FILE_FIELDS
        If gLoanData(iloan, irow) = ERROR_VALUE Then
            'check for an error value in the data field first
            mErrorScore = mErrorScore + irow
            Exit For
        End If
    Next irow
    gLoanScreen(iloan, FD_SCREEN_FORMAT) = mErrorScore

End Sub
```

EXHIBIT 10.19   "InitScreen_MissingOrDamaged" subroutine

currently working in has an error code associated with the field, the subroutine first checks for the ERROR_VALUE number, –99.99 in the field. If the error value is found, we add the error code to the running error code total stored in the variable "mErrorScore" and move to the next field.

If the contents of the field pass the "ERROR_VALUE" test, we next test to see if there is a reasonableness check on this field. This is indicated by the fact that the field value in the array "tActiveMinMax" will be TRUE. If it is, we will now test to determine if the field value falls between the Minimum/Maximum Range in the criteria array "tTestMinMax". If it does not fall within the Range of values, the error code for the field is added to "mErrorScore" and we proceed to the next field.

We have one test remaining. The value in the field may not be an error value, and it may fall comfortably between the minimum and maximum acceptable values, but we still need to test to see if it is an excluded value. We first check the array "tActiveExTest" to determine if this field HAS an Excluded Values test. If it does, we will now loop through the array "tActiveExVal" to determine if the record field has the value of one of the excluded test items.

The final step is to assign the value of the variable "mErrorScore" to the "gLoan-Screen" array in the "FD_SCREEN_AMORT" cell for this loan. See Exhibit 10.20.

Screening for Stratification, Frequency of Foreclosure, Market Value Decline, and Geographic Completeness   We have determined the completeness of the amortization information of each record in the prospective pool. We will now move on to determine the completeness of the record for the other four purposes we may need to apply to its contents.

The "InitScreen_ScreenData" subroutine can handle the screening processes for each of these completeness tests. It is very similar in layout and logic to the "InitScreen_CFAmortParameters" subroutine we just examined. The key difference is that this subroutine takes an argument. That argument is the cell number in the array "gLoanScreen" that the subroutine will populate with the computed error code.

We use a series of "Select..Case" statements for three purposes in this subroutine. The first is to set the variable "errCodeTest". Using the value of the "data_type" variable passed into the subroutine, we correctly branch to the error code array of the appropriate test. If "data_type" is equal to "FD_SCREEN_STRAT", we know that we

```
Sub InitScreen_CFAmortParameters()

    mErrorScore = 0                             'damaged or missing data
    mType = gLoanData(iloan, FD_MORTTYPE)
    For irow = 1 To DATA_FILE_FIELDS
        If tAmortErrCode(irow, mType) > 0 Then        'need to check this one!
            If gLoanData(iloan, irow) = ERROR_VALUE Then
                'check for an error value in the data field first
                mErrorScore = mErrorScore + tAmortErrCode(irow, mType)
            Else
                'if the record field is not missing or damaged then conduct the
                ' min/max test and additional check that the record does not
                ' contain an "excluded" value.
                trigger = False
                If tActiveMinMax(irow) Then
                    'test for a min/max limit
                    If gLoanData(iloan, irow) < tTestMinMax(irow, 1) Or _
                        gLoanData(iloan, irow) > tTestMinMax(irow, 2) Then
                      trigger = True
                      'within the min/max limit test for an excluded value
                      If trigger = False Then
                          'is the excluded value test active?
                          If tActiveExTest(irow) Then
                              tValue = gLoanData(iloan, irow)
                              For icol = 1 To tTestMinMax(irow, 2)
                                  If tActiveExVal(irow, icol) = "X" Then
                                      trigger = True
                                  End If
                              Next icol
                          End If
                      End If
                    End If
                End If
                If trigger = True Then
                    mErrorScore = mErrorScore + tAmortErrCode(irow, mType)
                End If
            End If
        End If
    Next irow
    gLoanScreen(iloan, FD_SCREEN_AMORT) = mErrorScore

End Sub
```

EXHIBIT 10.20   "InitScreen_CFAmortParameters" subroutine

need to set the value of "errCodeTest" to the appropriate value of "tSTRATErrCode" array.

Once we have the correct "errCodeTest" value, we can check if it is non zero, indicating that we need to test the field. If we find an "ERROR_VALUE" in the field, we use a second "Select..Case" statement to assign the error code value to "mErrorScore". If, as before, when we were dealing with the amortization parameter completeness test, we pass this test, we next perform the reasonableness tests. If we subsequently fail either the Minimum/Maximum tests or the Excluded Value tests, we employ the third "Select..Case" statement to assign the appropriate error code.

When we have finished testing all the appropriate fields of the record and we exit the "For..Next" loop, we will use a fourth and final "Select..Case" statement to assign the final error score to the appropriate test position in the "gLoanScreen" array. See Exhibit 10.21.

```
Sub InitScreen_ScreenData(dataType As Integer)

Dim errCodeTest      As Long              'dummy error check

    mErrorScore = 0                                  'damaged or missing data
    For irow = 1 To DATA_FILE_FIELDS
        Select Case dataType
            Case FD_SCREEN_STRAT:    errCodeTest = tSTRATErrCode(irow)
            Case FD_SCREEN_FOF:      errCodeTest = tFOFErrCode(irow)
            Case FD_SCREEN_MVD:      errCodeTest = tMVDErrCode(irow)
            Case FD_SCREEN_GEO:      errCodeTest = tGEOErrCode(irow)
        End Select
        If errCodeTest > 0 Then          'need to check this one!
            'check for an error value in the data field first
            If gLoanData(iloan, irow) = ERROR_VALUE Then
                Call InitScreen_IncrementErrorScore(dataType)
            Else
                'if record field not missing or damaged then conduct the min/max
                ' test and that the record does not contain an "excluded" value.
                trigger = False
                If tActiveMinMax(irow) Then
                    'test for a min/max limit
                    If gLoanData(iloan, irow) < tTestMinMax(irow, 1) Or _
                        gLoanData(iloan, irow) > tTestMinMax(irow, 2) Then
                        trigger = True
                        'within the min/max limit test for an excluded value
                        If trigger = False Then
                            If tActiveExTest(irow) Then 'excluded value test active?
                                tValue = gLoanData(iloan, irow)
                                For icol = 1 To tTestMinMax(irow, 2)
                                    If tActiveExVal(irow, icol) = "X" Then
                                        trigger = True
                                    End If
                                Next icol
                            End If
                        End If
                    End If
                End If
                'increment the error score if excluded score found
                If trigger = True Then
                    Call InitScreen_IncrementErrorScore(dataType)
                End If
            End If
        End If
    Next irow
    Select Case dataType             'assign the error score to the record
        Case FD_SCREEN_STRAT:    gLoanScreen(iloan, FD_SCREEN_STRAT) = mErrorScore
        Case FD_SCREEN_FOF:      gLoanScreen(iloan, FD_SCREEN_FOF) = mErrorScore
        Case FD_SCREEN_MVD:      gLoanScreen(iloan, FD_SCREEN_MVD) = mErrorScore
        Case FD_SCREEN_GEO:      gLoanScreen(iloan, FD_SCREEN_GEO) = mErrorScore
    End Select

End Sub
```

EXHIBIT 10.21   "InitScreen_ScreenData" subroutine

Phase 3: Building the Composite Scores

With all of the component error checking completed, we now turn to the final task of the initial data screening process. Once again we are back in the "InitScreen_BasicScreeningMain" subroutine. We will now assemble the composite screening scores. The first, the "FD_SCREEN_ALL_OK" is set to "1", TRUE, if all of the screening component test scores are also TRUE.

The second composite score, "FD_SCREEN_DEMO_OK", is set to "1", TRUE, if both the "FD_SCREEN_FOF" and "FD_SCREEN_MVD" scores are TRUE. With these activities complete, the initial data screening process is complete!

WRITING THE INITIAL DATA SCREENING REPORTS

We now have the VBA code to assess the contents of the collateral data information, have run it, and calculated the loan-by-loan error scores for each of the six data requirements. We have no way of knowing, unless we are monitoring the process using the debugger or progress messages, how many loans are in a usable condition! We can remedy this problem through the construction of a set of fairly straightforward reports that will have the advantages of being informative, easy to read, and, best for us, easy to implement!

Structure of Report Package

We will construct a report package that will consist of five component reports. These reports are:

- Mortgage Amortization Criteria (five reports by mortgage type)
- Stratification and Cross Tabulation Data
- Default Rate Parameters
- Market Value Decline Parameters
- Geographic Prepayment/Default Methodology Parameters

For each of these reports we will display the following results:

- How many loans have incomplete or unusable data
- Loan ID number of each of these loans
- Individual data that are missing or unusable
- A key to identify each of the datum in the report header
- For the cash flow amortization process, reports by specific mortgage type
- Total error score for each of the loans as a check of the screening process

The format of one of the Mortgage Amortization Criteria reports is shown in Exhibit 10.22. It is for the data requirements of a standard ARM-type mortgage that uses 14 data in its calculation. See Exhibits 10.22 and 10.23.

Writing a Mortgage Amortization Criteria Report

To review the code that produces the above report for a standard ARM mortgage type, we start with the "RepInitScreen_MainWriteReport". This subroutine will be the highest-level subroutine for the group of subroutines that produce the entire report package. This subroutine begins by checking each of the five "gRepMenu***" to determine if any of the reports in this file have been selected for production. If at least one of them is selected, the operation of the subroutine proceeds apace; if not, it branches to the end of the subroutine and we move on. If at least one of the five reports

Initial Data Screening Report
Standard ARM Loan Collateral Only

Test Table:

1 = Original Balance	4 = Remaining Term	7 = Spread to Index	10 = Periodic Coupon Cap	13 = Lifetime Coupon Floor
2 = Current Balance	5 = Coupon	8 = Initial Index rate	11 = Periodic Coupon Floor	14 = Day Count Convention
3 = Original Term	6 = ARM Index	9 = Periodic Reset Interval	12 = Lifetime Coupon Floor	

Number of Loans: 14

Line Number	Loan Number	Total Score	1	2	3	4	5	6	7	8	9	10	11	12	13	14
			1	2	1	0	1	1	1	2	2	2	0	1	1	0
									Incomplete Data Fields of the Record							
1	20	6,657	X													
2	56	134		X	X			X	X	X	X	X		X	X	
3	77	1,010		X			X			X	X	X				

EXHIBIT 10.22 Sample standard ARM data screen report

352

Test	Error Score	Loan # 20	Loan # 56	Loan # 77
1 = Original Balance	1	1		
2 = Current Balance	2		2	2
3 = Original Term	4		4	
4 = Remaining Term	8			
5 = Coupon	16			16
6 = ARM Index	32			32
7 = Spread to Index	64			64
8 = Initial Index rate	128		128	128
9 = Periodic Reset Interval	256			256
10 = Periodic Coupon Cap	512	512		512
11 = Periodic Coupon Floor	1,024			
12 = Lifetime Coupon Floor	2,048	2,048		
13 = Lifetime Coupon Floor	4,096	4,096		
14 = Day Count Convention	8,192			
	Total	6,657	134	1,010

EXHIBIT 10.23 Example error code computation matrix

is selected, the subroutine populates an array named "mTestValues" that contains the list of the powers of 2 up to the maximum number of tests, 21. We will later use the values contained in this array to "decode" the aggregate error score for each record that contains a non-zero error code. Next the subroutine opens the template file assigned to the Constant variable "INIT_DATA_SCREEN_TEMPLATE". This file is stored in the template directory for reports. The subroutine then renames it to the file pathway we entered in the "Create Initial Data Screening Report?" field of the CCFG Collateral Pool Menu. Once the file is saved, we are now ready to write the report package. We accomplish this task via the use of the five subroutine calls immediately following the "Save..As" command in the subroutine. Each of these subroutines produces the reports for one of the data screening processes. The call that produces the Mortgage Amortization Criteria report is the first of these lines as indicated by the comment. See Exhibit 10.24.

At this point we should also declare the Constant variables that we will need to write some of these reports. We will create a single Constant variable for each of the individual component error code reports. We will place these declarations in the "A_Constants" module. See Exhibit 10.25.

We now have the template file opened and saved to the report name. The next subroutine, "RepInitScreen_WriteReports", will direct the CCFG to the correct report-writing subroutine needed for the specific report currently being called. The role of this subroutine is two-fold. The first role is to produce the report (if it has been selected), by calling the appropriate report-writing subroutine. In this case, that subroutine is "RepInitScreen_WriteMortgageTypeScreenRep". The second role is to delete any worksheets that will not be used if the report is not selected. In this case, the subroutine will delete the five Cash Flow Amortization Criteria worksheets: "FixedRate", "StandardARMS", "HybridARMs", "BalloonsFixed", and "BalloonsARMs". Since this report group has been selected, we will now find the specific mortgage type report within the group. See Exhibit 10.26.

```
Sub RepInitScreen_MainWriteReport()

Dim itest    As Integer  'loop counter

    'only perform if there is at least one report selected
    If gRepMenuCFAmort Or gRepMenuScreenStrat Or gRepMenuScreenDemoFOF Or _
        gRepMenuScreenDemoMVD Or gRepMenuScreenGeo Then
        'initialize the mTestValues array
        mTestValues(1) = 1
        For itest = 2 To DATA_MAX_TESTS
            mTestValues(itest) = mTestValues(itest - 1) * 2
        Next itest
        'open the template file
        mFileName = Range("m07InitScreenFileName")
        mPathName = DIR_TEMPLATE_REP & INIT_DATA_SCREEN_TEMPLATE
        Workbooks.Open FileName:=mPathName
        'save as the financial selection test file name
        ActiveWorkbook.SaveAs FileName:=OUTPUT_DIRECTORY & gRepMenuPrefix & mFileName
        'call the reporting subroutines
        Call RepInitScreen_WriteReports(1)   'cf amortization info by type
        Call RepInitScreen_WriteReports(2)   'stratification rep info
        Call RepInitScreen_WriteReports(3)   'demo method FOF
        Call RepInitScreen_WriteReports(4)   'demo method MVD
        Call RepInitScreen_WriteReports(5)   'geo method
        ActiveWorkbook.Close
        gRepMenuAssumptions = True
    End If

End Sub
```

EXHIBIT 10.24   "RepInitScreen_MainWriteReport" subroutine

Finding the Report for This Mortgage Type   The subroutine that produces the Mortgage Amortization Criteria Completeness Test report is the most complex reporting subroutine in this module. It is the one that will produce the five mortgage-type screening reports. This subroutine has a very high commonality of code and function to the subroutines that address the stratification reports, frequency of foreclosure, MVD, and Geographic Methodology reports. These reporting subroutines should therefore be easy to understand after we have walked through the mortgage amortization reporting subroutine! Given length constraints, they will not be considered in individual detail here.

The "RepInitScreen_WriteMortgageTypeScreenRep" subroutine consists of a single large "For..Next" loop that cycles through each of the five mortgage types. See Exhibit 10.26. The first action it takes on each iteration of the "For..Next" loop is to set a utility variable that counts the number of collateral records written into each of the reports (if any records are found to have errors) to "1". It next calls the

```
'number of data sufficency tests for selection and reporting requirements
Public Const DATA_TESTS_STRAT = 21       'stratification tests data
Public Const DATA_TESTS_DEFRATE = 21     'default rate calculation tests
Public Const DATA_TESTS_MKTVALDEC = 12   'market value decline tests
Public Const DATA_TESTS_GEOMETHOD = 3    'geographic methodolgy
Public Const DATA_MAX_TESTS = 21         'maximum # of tests for all above
```

EXHIBIT 10.25   Constant variable declarations to support the report writing subroutines

```
Sub RepInitScreen_WriteMortgageTypeScreenRep()

    For mRep = 1 To NUM_MORT_TYPES
        lCount(mRep) = 0
        mRec = 1                    'start the record count at one
        Call RepInitScreen_SetupMortgageTypeAmortSufficencyReport
        'write the loan type specific report
        Sheets(mTargetWorksheet).Select
        For iloan = 1 To gTotalLoans
            mAmortErr = gLoanScreen(iloan, FD_SCREEN_AMORT)
            If mAmortErr > 0 Then 'screening problem
                If gLoanData(iloan, FD_MORTTYPE) = mMortgageType Then
                    lCount(mRep) = lCount(mRep) + 1
                    Range(mReport).Cells(mRec, 1).Value = iloan
                    Range(mReport).Cells(mRec, 2).Value = mAmortErr
                    Call DecodeScreeningScore(mAmortErr, mNumTests)
                    For mDataItems = 1 To mNumTests
                        If mTestResult(mDataItems) = 1 Then _
                            Range(mReport).Cells(mRec, 2 + mDataItems).Value = "X"
                    Next mDataItems
                    Select Case mRep
                        Case Is = MORTTYPE_FIXED_RATE
                            Call RepInitScreen_WriteFIXEDCriteria
                        Case Is = MORTTYPE_STAND_ARM
                            Call RepInitScreen_WriteSARMCriteria
                        Case Is = MORTTYPE_HYBRID_ARM
                            Call RepInitScreen_WriteHARMCriteria
                        Case Is = MORTTYPE_BAL_FIXED
                            Call RepInitScreen_WriteBFIXEDCriteria
                        Case Is = MORTTYPE_BAL_ARM
                            Call RepInitScreen_WriteBARMCriteria
                    End Select
                    mRec = mRec + 1
                End If
            End If
        Next iloan
        Call RepInitScreen_DeleteUnusedMortAmortReps
        ActiveWorkbook.Save
    Next mRep

End Sub
```

EXHIBIT 10.26 "RepInitScreen_WriteMortgageTypeScreenRep" subroutine

subroutine "RepInitScreen_SetupMortgageTypeReport". This subroutine, based on the value of the "mReportNum", the *n*th loop, selects one of the six mortgage types and initializes four variables that will be critical in producing the reports. The first variable, "mTargetWorksheet", is assigned the name of the worksheet into which the report will be written. The second variable, "mMortgageType", is set to the number of the mortgage type to be reported on. The third variable, "mNumTests", is set to the number of data that have been tested and whose contents will be displayed in the report. The fourth variable, "mReport", holds the name of the Range in the report template file worksheet into which the data and the test results are to be written. See Exhibit 10.27. The first subroutine in Exhibit 10.27 contains the code that is activated if there are no loans of a particular mortgage type. In this case the worksheet for that mortgage type is simply deleted. After these assignments have been

```
Sub RepInitScreen_SetupMortgageTypeAmortSufficencyReport()

    'set up the reporting parameters based on loan type
    Select Case mRep
        Case Is = MORTTYPE_FIXED_RATE
            mTargetWorksheet = "FixedRate"
            mMortgageType = MORTTYPE_FIXED_RATE
            mNumTests = DATA_TESTS_FIXED
            mReport = "ReportFixedRate"
        Case Is = MORTTYPE_STAND_ARM
            mTargetWorksheet = "StandardARMs"
            mMortgageType = MORTTYPE_STAND_ARM
            mNumTests = DATA_TESTS_SARM
            mReport = "ReportStandardARM"
        Case Is = MORTTYPE_HYBRID_ARM
            mTargetWorksheet = "HybridARMs"
            mMortgageType = MORTTYPE_HYBRID_ARM
            mNumTests = DATA_TESTS_HARM
            mReport = "ReportHybridARM"
        Case Is = MORTTYPE_BAL_FIXED
            mTargetWorksheet = "BalloonsFixed":
            mMortgageType = MORTTYPE_BAL_FIXED:
            mNumTests = DATA_TESTS_BALL_FIX:
            mReport = "ReportBalloonFixed"
        Case Is = MORTTYPE_BAL_ARM
            mTargetWorksheet = "BalloonsARMs":
            mMortgageType = MORTTYPE_BAL_ARM:
            mNumTests = DATA_TESTS_BALL_ARM:
            mReport = "ReportBalloonFloat"
    End Select

End Sub
```

EXHIBIT 10.27 "RepInitScreen_SetupMortgageTypeAmortSufficencyReport"
subroutine

completed, the "RepInitScreen_SetupMortgageTypeAmortSufficencyReport" sub-routine next selects the correct worksheet report template in the file based on the value of the "mTargetWorksheet" variable. We can now begin to write the report. A "For..Next" loop that will examine each of the loans in the collateral pool now begins to loop through the loans one by one.

The subroutine now performs two tests in quick succession. The first checks the "CF_SCREEN_AMORT" position of the "gScreenLoan" array to determine if there are any screening problems with this loan. If the value of this field for the current loan is "0", there were no problems with the amortization data for this loan. If this is the case, the loop moves on to the next loan. If the amortization error score for the loan is greater than "0", there was a screening problem with the data. A second test is now made to determine if the type of loan matches this type of report. If the loan type is appropriate to the current report being produced, we now need to display the contents of the record and the fields that failed the legibility, missing data, or reasonableness test. We will present this information in two separate sections of the report. Doing this will allow us to identify the data fields with error conditions and the values that triggered those conditions.

Populating the Report We now begin writing the contents of the collateral record to the report. The first field is the ID number of the record. The second field is the total error score contained in the "FD_SCREEN_AMORT" field of the "gLoanScreen" array for this record.

Writing the Error Code Section We now need to take the total score and deconstruct it into its constituent individual error score components. This task is performed by the "DecodeScreeningScore" subroutine. This subroutine takes two arguments as input. The first is the total error score and the second is the number of tests. The value of the "mNumTests" variable, which we assigned earlier in the "RepInitScreen_SetupMortgageTypeAmortSufficencyReport", subroutine is critical to the deconstruction process for two reasons. First, it determines the maximum number of error conditions. Second, and as important as the first, it directly determines the values of each of the successive error codes that we will subtract from the total code to determine the constituent error scores contained within it. (If you need to review this process, see the example in Exhibit 10.23.) This subroutine will deconstruct the aggregate error score into its constituent scores by successively trying to subtract the error scores from it. The end product of this process is the "mTestResult" array whose elements will have been assigned a "1", TRUE, if there is an error for that test, and "0", FALSE, if there is not. See Exhibit 10.28.

All the hard work is now done. We can now display the contents of the "MTestResult" array to display which of the data fields triggered the error condition followed in the report by the values of the fields of the record itself.

Writing the Collateral Record Values All that remains to be done is to write the contents of the record. In that we know the number of the loan and the data fields particular to each mortgage type, this is easily accomplished. There is a "Select..Case" statement that branches the subroutine into one of six choices based on the mortgage

```
Sub DecodeScreeningScore(ScreenScore As Long, NumTests As Integer)

Dim iloop   As Integer

    For iloop = NumTests To 1 Step -1
        mTestResult(iloop) = 0                        'set datum point to OK
        If ScreenScore >= mTestValues(iloop) Then
            mTestResult(iloop) = 1                    'set datum point to NOT OK
            ScreenScore = ScreenScore - mTestValues(iloop)  'adjust the running score
        End If
    Next iloop

End Sub
```

EXHIBIT 10.28 "DecodeScreeningScore" subroutine

```
Sub RepInitScreen_WriteSARMCriteria()
    Range(mReport).Cells(mRec, 17).Value = gLoanData(iloan, FD_ORIGBAL)
    Range(mReport).Cells(mRec, 18).Value = gLoanData(iloan, FD_CURRBAL)
    Range(mReport).Cells(mRec, 19).Value = gLoanData(iloan, FD_ORIGTERM)
    Range(mReport).Cells(mRec, 20).Value = gLoanData(iloan, FD_REMTERM)
    Range(mReport).Cells(mRec, 21).Value = gLoanData(iloan, FD_CURRRATE)
    Range(mReport).Cells(mRec, 22).Value = gLoanData(iloan, FD_ARMINDEX)
    Range(mReport).Cells(mRec, 23).Value = gLoanData(iloan, FD_ARMSPRD)
    Range(mReport).Cells(mRec, 24).Value = gLoanData(iloan, FD_ARMORIGLEV)
    Range(mReport).Cells(mRec, 25).Value = gLoanData(iloan, FD_ARMPERRESET)
    Range(mReport).Cells(mRec, 26).Value = gLoanData(iloan, FD_ARMPERCAP)
    Range(mReport).Cells(mRec, 27).Value = gLoanData(iloan, FD_ARMPERFLR)
    Range(mReport).Cells(mRec, 28).Value = gLoanData(iloan, FD_ARMLIFCAP)
    Range(mReport).Cells(mRec, 29).Value = gLoanData(iloan, FD_ARMLIFFLR)
    Range(mReport).Cells(mRec, 30).Value = gLoanData(iloan, FD_DAYCOUNT)
End Sub
```

EXHIBIT 10.29   RepInitScreen_WriteSARMCriteria subroutine

type in question. In the case that we have chosen, that of a standard ARM mortgage, it will take the second case condition, that of:

```
Case Is = MORTTYPE_STAND_ARM: Call RepInitScreen_WriteSARMCriteria
```

After the error code section has been written on the left half of the report, this subroutine will write the values of the record on the right half of the report. The standard ARM amortization calculations need 14 inputs. The values of these 14 fields are entered into the report by the subroutine "RepInitScreen_WriteSARMCriteria". See Exhibit 10.29.

The "RepInitScreen_SetupMortgageTypeReport" subroutine now increments the record counter by 1 and completes the loop for this individual loan. After all the loans have been examined by the "For..Next" loop, the worksheet is saved, completing the report for this mortgage type. The "RepInitScreen_SetupMortgageTypeReport" subroutine now moves on to the next mortgage type until all five types have been reported.

The "RepInitScreen_SetupMortgageTypeReport" subroutine now transfers control back to the "RepInitScreen_MainWriteReport" subroutine that called it. The "RepInitScreen_MainWriteReport" now writes other initial data screening error reports, saves the workbook to which the report was written and the process is complete.

Writing the Market Value Decline Report

The remaining four reports of the initial data screening process results are designed to produce only a single report each. These reports are virtually identical in form and substance to the Mortgage Amortization Criteria reports. We will choose the least complicated of the four, the Market Value Decline Screening report, as an example for all of them. The format of this report is identical to that of the fixed-rate mortgage report we just examined. The only difference is the number of fields that are being checked and which of the record fields we are checking. See Exhibit 10.30.

Initial Data Screening Report
Market Value Decline Calculation Data Only

1 = Mortgage Type
2 = Credit Sector
3 = Original Balance
4 = Current Loan-to-Value

5 = Seasoning
6 = Financing Purpose
7 = State Code
8 = Metropolitan Statistical Area Code

9 = Payments in Arrears (Amount)
10 = Payments in Arrears (Number)
11 = Servicer Rating

		Number Of Loans Per Condition										
Number of Loans		0	0	0	0	0	0	0	0	0	0	0
0												
		Incomplete or Missing Data Fields of the Record										
Line #	Total Score	1	2	3	4	5	6	7	8	9	10	11
Loan Number												

Line #	Loan Number	Total Score	1 Mortgage Amort Type Code	2 Mortgage Credit Sector Code	3 Original Balance	4 Current Loan To Value Ratio	10 Payments in Arrears $	11 Servicer Rating
					0	0	0	
1								
2								
3								
4								
5								
6								
7								
8								
9								
10								
11								
12								

EXHIBIT 10.30 Market Value Decline Screening report

```
Sub RepInitScreen_WriteMarketValueDeclineScreenRep()

    mRec = 1
    mReport = "ReportMVD"
    Sheets("MarketValueDeclineData").Select
    For iloan = 1 To gTotalLoans
        mMVDerr = gLoanScreen(iloan, FD_SCREEN_MVD)
        If mMVDerr > 0 Then 'screening problem
            Cells(mRec + 10, 2).Value = mRec
            Cells(mRec + 10, 3).Value = iloan
            Cells(mRec + 10, 4).Value = mMVDerr
            Call DecodeScreeningScore(mMVDerr, DATA_TESTS_MKTVALDEC)
            For mDataItems = 1 To DATA_TESTS_MKTVALDEC
                If mTestResult(mDataItems) = 1 Then _
                    Cells(mRec + 10, 4 + mDataItems).Value = "X"
            Next mDataItems
            Call RepInitScreen_MVDScreeningDataValues
            mRec = mRec + 1
        End If
    Next iloan
    ActiveWorkbook.Save

End Sub
```

EXHIBIT 10.31 "RepInitScreen_WriteMarketValueDeclineScreenRep" subroutine

In that the VBA code does not have to choose between six different report alternatives, the subroutine that produces this report, "RepInitScreen_WriteMarket-ValueDeclineScreenRep", is much more straightforward. We see, however, the same processing pattern.:

1. First we select the report worksheet into which we will write the report.
2. Second, the main loop of the subroutine runs through the collateral and selects only those whose error code for the Market Value Decline Methodology inputs is positive, indicating there are problems with that record.
3. Third, the error code is sent to be decoded and the values in the "mTestResults" are checked to indicate which of the fields contain the problem items.
4. Fourth, the values of the record needed to calculate the market value decline statistic are written into the report by the "RepInitScreen_MVDScreening DataValues" subroutine.
5. Finally, with the last of the records examined the report is saved.

See Exhibit 10.31.

WRITING THE DEMOGRAPHIC METHODOLOGY RISK REPORTS

Aside from the initial data screening, we have also determined if each of the records has sufficient data to be used in the Demographic Prepayment/Default Methodology. There are two unique calculations to this methodology. The first is the frequency of foreclosure estimate and the second in the market value decline estimate. Both of these estimates are based on the demographic profile of the record. There can be a wide variance in these risk profiles, and it would be helpful if we had a report that would display the overall risk rating for each of these scores. It would be even more useful to be able to analyze the risk rating for each of the loans individually and to determine the contribution of each risk factor to the overall rating. The next set of reports does just that.

Risk Reporting

After the initial data screening process has been completed, we have, it is hoped, identified the collateral records that appear to be complete and valid. This does not necessarily mean that all of the records that pass the initial data screening process will end up in the deal. There are still the financial, demographic, and geographic tests that the collateral needs to pass in order to be deemed eligible. We will also develop a report that addresses the risk levels of each loan in regard to the Demographic Loss/Prepayment Methodology. This report package contains two reports whose format and content is very similar to the report set that we just examined.

Reports of the Demographic Risk Package   The Risk Reporting package is different from the initial data screening process reports above that identified damaged or inappropriate data values. This report package contains individual risk reports that list the various component contributions of a number of data items to two distinct risk scores. These risk scores are then applied against a table to determine the frequency of foreclosure and the market value decline applied to a particular loan. All the data items in the report are valid. The purpose of the report is to provide us with an understanding of, and an ability to trace, the aggregate risk scores that will determine a loan's frequency of foreclosure (FOF) and MVD risk score. The report formats are similar to the initial data screening reports with one important difference. In the section "Data Fields" of the initial data screening reports, we were content to tag each of the damaged or unacceptable fields with an "X". In these reports we will print the risk weighting of the data item. Thus, in the case of the MVD, there will be a raw score in each of the columns corresponding to the data fields area of the initial data screening report. The sum of these scores is the raw MVD Risk score that is then compared to a table to determine the MVD to apply to the loan. This allows us to quickly and easily check the risk characteristics for any loan in the portfolio and to compare it to other loans if need be. Below the component risk scores are the values of each of the fields of the record used in the MVD Risk score determination. These data items, the values that determine the raw risk score components, and the scores themselves can be seen in Exhibit 10.32.

Demographic Risk Profile Example   The format of the Market Value Decline Risk report is displayed containing two loans that could not be more different. The first is a standard fixed-rate loan, the second a HARM whose property has now declined in value until the current loan to value (LTV) is 110%. The first loan is current in its payments, and the second is between 60 and 75 days delinquent. The disparity of risk scores is also seen in the credit sector, seasoning, and financing purpose fields. The total raw scores are 1 for the first loan and 105 for the second. These scores result in a multiplier factor of 50% for the first loan and 105% for the second. That means that if the base MVD rate for both locations in Connecticut and California

Risk Factors Reports

Market Value Decline Calculation Data Only

1 = Mortgage Type
2 = Credit Sector
3 = Original Balance
4 = Current Loan-to-Value
5 = Seasoning
6 = Property Type
7 = Occupancy Code
8 = Financing Purpose
9 = State Code
10 = Metropolitan Statistical Area Code
11 = Payments in Arrears (Number)
12 = Servicer Rating

DISTRIBUTION OF MARKET VALUE DECLINE MULTIPLIER FACTORS

>+15%	+15%	+10%	0%	5%	10%	20%	30%	40%	50%	60%	70%	80%	90%	100%	100%+
									26.3%						73.7%

Line #	Loan Number	MVD %	Total Score	5%	10%	20%	30%	40%	50%	60%	70%	80%	90%	100%	100%+
									Raw Scores						
				1	2	3	4	5	6	7	8	9	10	11	12
1	1	50%	105	1	-4	5	-5	1	0	0	2	0	0	0	1
2	2	105%	105	10	7	0	10	5	0	0	15	0	0	25	8

	1	2	3	4	5	6	7	8	9	10	11	12
	Mortgage Amort Type Code	Mortgage Credit Sector Code	Original Balance	Current Loan To Value Ratio	Seasoning	Property Type	Occupancy Code	Financing Purpose	State Code	MSA Code	Days in Arrears #	Servicer Rating
	Fixed	Prime	125,000	55%	78	Single Fam	Owner	Purchase	CT	None	0	Excellent
	HARM	Sub-Prime	350,000	110%	18	Single Fam	Owner	Investment	CA	31100	60	Poor

(Original Balance total: 475,000)

EXHIBIT 10.32 Market Value Decline Risk Factors report: upper header section of exhibit is the left side of the report, lower section of exhibit is the right side

were –20%, the MVD factor for loan 1 would be $(-20\%*50\%) = -10\%$ and for loan 2 it would be $(-20\%*105\%) = -21\%$, which is quite a difference. See Exhibit 10.32.

This report is produced in conjunction with the other Demographic Risk Factor report that assigns the multiplier for FOF rates. This code is in the "Report_CollatDataDemoRisk" module.

Writing the Reports

The main subroutine that produces the two Demographic Risk Factor reports is "RepDemoRisk_MainWriteReport". This subroutine begins by first checking the two report request variables, "gRepMenuDemoRiskMVD" and "gRepMenuDemoRisk-FOF". If the value of either of these Boolean variables is TRUE at least one of the reports from this group has been selected for production. The subroutine then opens the template file for the Demographic Risk Factor report and renames it. The template file contains two worksheets. One is the template for the FOF risk factors and the other is for the MVD factors. If we have gotten to this point in the code, it means that at least one, and probably both, of the reports has been selected for production. The subroutine will now call special-purpose subroutines to produce each of these Demographic Risk Factor reports. It starts with the Default Rate Risk report, which checks the report request variable "gRepMenuDemoRiskFOF". If the value of this variable is TRUE, we call the subroutine "DemoRiskRep_WriteDefaultRateRiskReport". If the value of the variable is FALSE, the subroutine deletes the template worksheet from the file. The subroutine then tests the "gRepMenuDemoRiskMVD" variable to determine if it should produce the Demographic Risk Market Value Decline report. See Exhibit 10.33.

Producing the Market Value Decline Risk Report To produce this report, the CCFG program now calls the "DemoRiskRep_WriteMarket ValueDecline RiskReport" subroutine. See Exhibit 10.34.

```
Sub RepDemoRisk_MainWriteReport()

    If gRepMenuDemoRiskMVD Or gRepMenuDemoRiskFOF Then
        mPathName = DIR_TEMPLATE_REP & COLLAT_DEMO_RISKS_TEMPLATE
        Workbooks.Open FileName:=mPathName                    'open template file
        mFileName = "DemoRiskReport"
        ActiveWorkbook.SaveAs FileName:=OUTPUT_DIRECTORY & gRepMenuPrefix & mFileName
        'call the reporting subroutines
        'demographic FOF data
        If gRepMenuDemoRiskFOF Then
            Call DemoRiskRep_WriteDefaultRateRiskReport
            Else
            Sheets("DefaultRateData").Delete
        End If
        'demographic MVD data
        If gRepMenuDemoRiskMVD Then
            Call DemoRiskRep_WriteMarketValueDeclineRiskReport
            Else
            Sheets("MarketValueDeclineData").Delete
        End If
        ActiveWorkbook.Close
        gRepMenuAssumptions = True
    End If

End Sub
```

EXHIBIT 10.33 "RepDemoRisk_MainWriteReport" subroutine

```
Sub DemoRiskRep_WriteMarketValueDeclineRiskReport()

    mRec = 1
    mReport = "ReportMVD"
    Sheets("MarketValueDeclineData").Select
    For icol = 1 To MVD_DIST_COLS
        mMVDDist(icol) = 0
    Next icol
    For iloan = 1 To gTotalLoans
        If gLoanScreen(iloan, FD_SCREEN_MVD) = 0 Then 'no screening problems
            Range(mReport).Cells(mRec, 1).Value = iloan
            Range(mReport).Cells(mRec, 2).Value = gMVDRate(iloan)
            Range(mReport).Cells(mRec, 3).Value = gMVDTotal(iloan)
            For iItems = 1 To DATA_TESTS_MKTVALDEC
                If iItems <> 10 Then
                    Range(mReport).Cells(mRec, 3 + iItems).Value = _
                        gMVDScore(iloan, iItems)
                End If
            Next iItems
            Call DemoRiskRep_WriteMVDScreeningDataValues
            Call DemoRiskRep_BuildMVDDistribution
            mRec = mRec + 1
        End If
    Next iloan
    For icol = 1 To MVD_DIST_COLS
        Cells(9, icol + 5).Value = mMVDDist(icol)
    Next icol
    ActiveWorkbook.Save

End Sub
```

EXHIBIT 10.34 "DemoRiskRep_" subroutine

Before the subroutine does anything else, it initializes the elements of the array "mMVDDist" to "0". This array holds the count of each slice of the MVD rates we will print in the "Distribution of Market Value Decline Factors" section of the report. The subroutine next loops through all the loans of the portfolio array. It tests each to determine if the MVD data score is "0", meaning that the record is complete and contains reasonable values. Next it prints the loan number, the final MVD factor, and the total MVD Raw score. The final MVD factor is the fully adjusted MVD base factor corresponding to the raw score read from the MVD table in Exhibit 10.32 modified by the geographic MVD multipliers displayed in Exhibit 10.34. The MVD raw score is the sum of all the component raw scores in the columns 1 to 10 of that section. The subroutine then calls the subroutine "DemoRiskRep_WriteMVDScreeningDataValues". This subroutine fills in the right side of the report. Notice the references to the array "gRFLabels". Here the subroutine is printing out the text labels for the various collateral data field codes. For example, the field "Servicer Rating", "FD_SERVERATE", has six numeric codes, 1 to 6. These represent, in order, "No Data", "Poor", "Fair", "Average", "Good", and finally "Excellent". The value for this field in the first record is "6" and in the second record "2". The report therefore prints out "Excellent" and "Poor" respectively. See Exhibit 10.35.

The last action inside of the loop is to call the subroutine "DemoRiskRep_Build-MVDDistribution" which is not displayed here, that will populate the "mMVDDist"

```
Sub DemoRiskRep_WriteMVDScreeningDataValues()

    Range(mReport).Cells(mRec, 16).Value = _
                    gRFLabels(FD_MORTTYPE, gLoanData(iloan, FD_MORTTYPE))
    Range(mReport).Cells(mRec, 17).Value = _
                    gRFLabels(FD_CREDITSECT, gLoanData(iloan, FD_CREDITSECT))
    Range(mReport).Cells(mRec, 18).Value = gLoanData(iloan, FD_ORIGBAL)
    Range(mReport).Cells(mRec, 19).Value = gLoanData(iloan, FD_CURRLTV)
    Range(mReport).Cells(mRec, 20).Value = gLoanData(iloan, FD_SEASON)
    Range(mReport).Cells(mRec, 21).Value = _
                    gRFLabels(FD_PROPTYPE, gLoanData(iloan, FD_PROPTYPE))
    Range(mReport).Cells(mRec, 22).Value = _
                    gRFLabels(FD_OCCPCODE, gLoanData(iloan, FD_OCCPCODE))
    Range(mReport).Cells(mRec, 23).Value = _
                    gRFLabels(FD_FINPURPOSE, gLoanData(iloan, FD_FINPURPOSE))
    Range(mReport).Cells(mRec, 24).Value = _
                    gStatePostal(gLoanData(iloan, FD_STATECODE))
    If gLoanData(iloan, FD_MSACODE) = 0 Then
        Range(mReport).Cells(mRec, 25).Value = ""
        Else
        Range(mReport).Cells(mRec, 25).Value = gLoanData(iloan, FD_MSACODE)
    End If
    If gLoanData(iloan, FD_ARREARSNUM) = 0 Then
        Range(mReport).Cells(mRec, 26).Value = ""
        Else
        Range(mReport).Cells(mRec, 26).Value = gLoanData(iloan, FD_ARREARSNUM)
    End If
    Range(mReport).Cells(mRec, 27).Value = _
                    gRFLabels(FD_SERVERATE, gLoanData(iloan, FD_SERVERATE))

End Sub
```

EXHIBIT 10.35 "DemoRiskRep_WriteMVDScreeningDataValues" subroutine

array. Upon exiting the loop we will immediately print this array into the header of the reports, and we are finished!

BUILDING A REPRESENTATIVE LINE GENERATOR PROGRAM

In the second half of this chapter, we will build a representative line, or "Rep Line," generator program. A Rep Line generator serves to aggregate loans that share similar or more rarely, identical characteristics. The rules of the aggregation process are specified prior to running the program in one of two ways. The first method is to place the parameter guidelines in a file and have the program develop the logic based on the stipulations presented. The second is to create a series of predefined "buckets" of the most commonly encountered collateral and have the sorting and aggregation logic already in place. We will adopt the second of these methods in the interest of brevity. I know you all want this book to go on forever, but it just cannot. We have to be mature and draw the line somewhere!

What Are Rep Lines?

What are Rep Lines and, more importantly, why should we go through all this trouble to create them?

A Rep Line is a dollar-weighted statistical aggregation of a collection of individual collateral agreements whose constituent collateral members share common characteristics, such as amortization pattern, coupon, spread, term, seasoning, payment options, or any other identifying or distinguishing characteristics. Having said this, we should immediately add that this is a very broad definition. In fact, this definition is so broad as to be almost nebulous. Rep Lines are probably better understood in terms of how they are used and where they are displayed.

Uses of Rep Lines   A Rep Line is most commonly used to address one or both of the following issues.

- To summarize the contents of a collateral file when it is difficult, burdensome, or unnecessary to provide a listing of all the collateral of the deal on a loan-by-loan basis
- To provide first-level amortization information to any interested investor, regulatory, or credit rating party with the modeling and analytical capabilities to conduct a proxy cash flow analysis. This means that the Rep Line must include all of the key amortization characteristics of the collateral.

Let us take a look at the first point. The intent in producing a collection of Rep Lines in these circumstances is to portray, in a summarized and compact form, as much information concerning the collateral pool as possible without undue distortion. This distortion is caused by any incongruities in the aggregation process. The greater the homogeneity of the constituent pieces of collateral in any particular Rep Line, the more accurately that Rep Line portrays the characteristics of the group. Obviously if a Rep Line were composed of a collection of loans with identical characteristics, it would be indistinguishable from a single loan that had the same balance, payment conditions, term, and coupon level of the members of the line. Conversely if we were to combine all five types of mortgages that can be amortized by the CCFG into a single Rep Line, we would introduce a wide range of distortion. Combining a group of various tenor hybrid ARMs with long-term 30- or 40-year fixed-rate mortgages would yield significantly different characteristics for the aggregate Rep Line than our previous example.

In regard to the second point, that of providing the Rep Lines as guidance to the amortization characteristics of the collateral, we must be even more careful. Here not only is the absolute magnitude of the collateral cash flows calculated from the Rep Line information important but the nuances of the timing and relative components of those cash flows are critical as well. Why do we care whether the relative proportions of scheduled principal, prepaid principal, defaulted principal, and coupon income are as close to those produced when amortizing the Rep Line as opposed to amortizing its constituent loans? We care because many of the liabilities structures in common use segregate these cash flows between different classes of notes or allocate the components differently depending on the amortization conditions of the liability structure itself. Changes in the amount or timing of these components can affect the amortization of the various debt classes of the liability structure. If the changes are large enough, they can result in significant differences in retirement patterns of the liability classes.

Thus when Rep Lines are used as proxies for a loan-by-loan description of the portfolio and are intended to serve as a guide to the cash flow generation characteristics of the deal collateral, we need to exercise caution not to inadvertently provide

HOMOGENEOUS COLLATERAL				HETEROGENEOUS COLLATERAL			
	Mortgage #1	Mortgage #2	Rep Line #1		Mortgage #3	Mortgage #4	Rep Line #2
Mortgage Type	Fixed Rate	Fixed Rate	Fixed Rate	Mortgage Type	Fixed Rate	Fixed Rate	Fixed Rate
Original Balance	100,000	100,000	200,000	Original Balance	300,000	50,000	350,000
Current Balance	95,344	96,201	191,544	Current Balance	86,947	49,703	136,649
Coupon	5.0000%	5.2500%	5.1256%	Coupon	4.1250%	8.7500%	5.8072%
Original Term	360	360	360.000	Original Term	120	360	207.294
Remaining Term	324	329	326.511	Remaining Term	30	350	146.392
Seasoning	36	31	33.489	Seasoning	90	10	60.902
Aggregate CF	173,930	181,675	342,105	Aggregate CF	91,656	137,673	153,844
Difference			-13,500	Difference			-75,485
Difference %			-3.946%	Difference %			-49.066%
Timing Difference			17,427	Timing Difference			228,335
Difference %			5.094%	Difference %			148.420%

EXHIBIT 10.36 Comparison of Rep Lines cash flows with homogeneous versus heterogeneous collateral

misleading information. In this case we would want to define the conditions for inclusion of a particular piece of collateral in any given Rep Line in a much more precise and restricted manner than we would if we were only interested in information presentation. We would have to also be careful to provide a summary of all relevant parameters of the loan necessary for a complete and accurate amortization calculation to be performed.

What Does a Rep Line Look Like? The following is an example of two Rep Lines, one of homogeneous collateral and the other of heterogeneous collateral. See Exhibit 10.36.

This example is shamelessly created to emphasize the dangers inherent in careless Rep Line construction. Here we can dramatically see the results of combining closely related pieces of collateral with similar characteristics versus collateral of strongly divergent characteristics. These Rep Lines are constructed of the simplest type of mortgage, a fixed-rate, level payment amortization type. Both scenarios assume no prepayment or default activity. Such activity would only exacerbate differences so we have ignored it in this example.

Rep Line #1 is composed of two virtually identical pieces of collateral. They have identical original balances; the difference in seasoning is only five months; and the coupons are only 0.25% apart. As a result, their cash flow streams are virtually identical and vary by a minuscule degree. The difference of amortizing the loans under the Rep Line assumption versus each mortgage separately and then combining the results is 3.946% of the aggregate cash flows. More telling is the difference in the timing of the cash flows. This statistic is the sum of the absolute values of the two (undiscounted) cash flows. This means that if there are any differences, either positive or negative, they contribute to the sum value of the statistic. The timing difference is $17,427, which represents 5.094% of the aggregate Rep Line cash flows.

Effects of Mismatched Collateral   There is a completely different story when we look at the difference between the cash flows of the two component mortgages that comprise Rep Line #2 and the Rep Line itself. Here we see huge differences! Why? The mortgages that compose Rep Line #2, while both fixed-rate, level payment mortgages, are different in every other feature. Mortgage #3 has an original term of 120 months and is heavily seasoned. It is so heavily seasoned that it has only 30 payments left in its life. Mortgage #4 has an original term of 360 months and is seasoned a mere 10 months. It has 350 more payments left in its lifetime. The combined balance of Rep Line #2 is $136,649, two-thirds of which is contributed from Mortgage #3. The remaining term of the Rep Line is 146 months, 116 months greater than the remaining term of Mortgage #3! We will thus see the Rep Line generating cash flows from these balances for nearly 10 years after Mortgage #3 has been retired. The timing difference is not only perturbed by the duration of the cash flows but also by the magnitude. Mortgage #3 has a remaining balance not quite twice that of Mortgage #4, as already noted, but, more significantly, it will retire this balance in 30 months, a feat that will require a rather large monthly payment. In the early part of the Rep Line #2 amortization curve, it will be amortizing a balance only a third larger over a remaining term of 146 months, nearly five times the duration of Mortgage #3's remaining life. This means that the absolute size of Mortgage #3's monthly payment alone will swamp the Rep Line #2 payments, immediately building up a large timing difference. In fact, this timing difference exceeds the aggregate Rep Line payments! If you wish to view these schedules in detail, they are available on the Web site in a file named "RepLineCF_Example.xls".

How to Construct Rep Lines

A variety of methods can be used to construct a set of Rep Lines from a collateral pool. These fall into a two-by-two matrix. See Exhibit 10.37.

Exact Matching   The simplest, safest, and also, unfortunately, the rarest approach to building Rep Lines is to rely on *exact* matching. Exact matching would require that, with the exception of the current and original balances, all other characteristics

	Purpose for Which the Rep Lines Will Be Utilized	
	To Provide Descriptive Information	To Provide Amortization Information
Homogeneous	Loose Bucket Approach	Tight Bucket Approach
Heterogeneous	Loose Compactor Approach	Tight Compactor Approach

Collateral Composition Characteristics

EXHIBIT 10.37   Rep Line construction parameters

of the collateral that comprise the Rep Line *would need to be identical!* Does this ever happen on this plane of reality? Surprisingly, the answer is a qualified "Yes"! This situation can arise when a bank or other financial institution or a mortgage company partners with a builder. The builder needs to be large enough to launch and complete hundreds or thousands of housing units in a relatively short period of time, say two years. This scenario assumes that the credit characteristics and financial demographics of the borrowers would prejudice them toward a particular type of mortgage with similar payment characteristics. This then sets the stage for circumstances in which hundreds or thousands of mortgages would be originated with the same rates, terms, and other financial characteristics over a restricted period of time. While unusual, this is not completely beyond the realm of possibility, especially if you are dealing with collateral pools issued en masse in boom years, such as period of 2003 to 2006. Here you might have several hundred million dollars of balances described by two or three dozen Rep Lines.

Interval Grouping Across Selected Parameters   If we cannot apply the exact matching approach of our Rep Line dreams, what can we do? All Rep Lines do not have to result in the train wreck that we witnessed in Rep Line #2 of Exhibit 10.31!

The VBA code examples we are about to look at that implement the Rep Line Generator program show the logic for aggregating 15-, 20-, and 30-year hybrid ARMs. In these mortgage types, the critical parameters are, in order, pairing of index and original term, the initial interest payments only period, seasoning, and, last, the spread to the index. Why these terms and why in this order? As we have seen above, the size of the monthly payments as determined by the amortization term of the loan *have a large impact as to the magnitude of the payment itself*. Whether the loan is still in the interest-only (IO) payment period is critical. There is a big difference between a loan that is paying a teaser rate in an IO period and one that is paying a fully loaded spread plus index coupon combined with a fully amortizing principal payment. Next is the seasoning of the loan, which determines where it is in the IO teaser period, IO index plus spread period, of the fully amortizing payment period. Last is the spread to the index itself. Exhibit 10.38 displays the complete table of buckets for the 15-year original term hybrid ARM mortgage type.

BUILDING THE REP LINE GENERATOR PROGRAM

We know what Rep Lines are. We know that the more homogeneous the collateral that comprises a Rep Line, the more accurate it will be for both descriptive and amortization purposes. How do we put this knowledge into practice?

The steps in building a Rep Line Generator program are:

Step 1. Determine how many types of collateral you are going to include in the Rep Line generation process.

Step 2. Determine for each class of collateral the key parameters that the aggregation should be based on. If the purpose is descriptive, these may include demographic information; if it is for amortization, it will focus primarily on financial terms. Note: If demographics have a significant impact on probability of default, they should be included. A specific example is the difference

15 Yr, Hybrid ARM's
Fixed I/O Period 1, 2, or 3 Years;
Floating I/O Period 5 Years
Fully Amortizing Thereafter

Rep Line Number	Original Term Range	Seasoning Range	Index Type	Spread to Index Range	Fixed I/O Period
449	180	1 to 6	LIBOR	0% to 2%	12
450	180	1 to 6	LIBOR	2% to 4%	12
451	180	1 to 6	LIBOR	4%+	12
452	180	6 to 12	LIBOR	0% to 2%	12
453	180	6 to 12	LIBOR	2% to 4%	12
454	180	6 to 12	LIBOR	4%+	12
455	180	13 to 24	LIBOR	0% to 2%	12
456	180	13 to 24	LIBOR	2% to 4%	12
457	180	13 to 24	LIBOR	4%+	12
458	180	25 to 36	LIBOR	0% to 2%	12
459	180	25 to 36	LIBOR	2% to 4%	12
460	180	25 to 36	LIBOR	4%+	12
461	180	37 to 60	LIBOR	0% to 3%	12
462	180	37 to 60	LIBOR	3%+	12
463	180	61 to 120	LIBOR	0% to 3%	12
464	180	61 to 120	LIBOR	3%+	12
465	180	121 to 180	LIBOR	0% to 3%	12
466	180	121 to 180	LIBOR	3%+	12
467	180	1 to 6	LIBOR	0% to 2%	24
468	180	1 to 6	LIBOR	2% to 4%	24
469	180	1 to 6	LIBOR	4%+	24
470	180	6 to 12	LIBOR	0% to 2%	24
471	180	6 to 12	LIBOR	2% to 4%	24
472	180	6 to 12	LIBOR	4%+	24
473	180	13 to 24	LIBOR	0% to 2%	24
474	180	13 to 24	LIBOR	2% to 4%	24
475	180	13 to 24	LIBOR	4%+	24
476	180	25 to 36	LIBOR	0% to 2%	24
477	180	25 to 36	LIBOR	2% to 4%	24
478	180	25 to 36	LIBOR	4%+	24
479	180	37 to 60	LIBOR	0% to 3%	24
480	180	37 to 60	LIBOR	3%+	24
481	180	61 to 120	LIBOR	0% to 3%	24
482	180	61 to 120	LIBOR	3%+	24
483	180	121 to 180	LIBOR	0% to 3%	24
484	180	121 to 180	LIBOR	3%+	24
485	180	1 to 6	LIBOR	0% to 2%	36
486	180	1 to 6	LIBOR	2% to 4%	36
487	180	1 to 6	LIBOR	4%+	36
488	180	6 to 12	LIBOR	0% to 2%	36
489	180	6 to 12	LIBOR	2% to 4%	36
490	180	6 to 12	LIBOR	4%+	36
491	180	13 to 24	LIBOR	0% to 2%	36
492	180	13 to 24	LIBOR	2% to 4%	36
493	180	13 to 24	LIBOR	4%+	36
494	180	25 to 36	LIBOR	0% to 2%	36
495	180	25 to 36	LIBOR	2% to 4%	36
496	180	25 to 36	LIBOR	4%+	36
497	180	37 to 60	LIBOR	0% to 3%	36
498	180	37 to 60	LIBOR	3%+	36
499	180	61 to 120	LIBOR	0% to 3%	36
500	180	61 to 120	LIBOR	3%+	36
501	180	121 to 180	LIBOR	0% to 3%	36
502	180	121 to 180	LIBOR	3%+	36

EXHIBIT 10.38   Rep Line group table for 15-year hybrid adjustable rate mortgages

in payment behaviors between owner-occupied properties and those that are not. In these examples, we will concentrate solely on the financial characteristics of the loans due to space considerations.

Step 3. Decide if you want the Rep Line Generator to build its own sorting and aggregation criteria based on the composition of the collateral pool (a process known affectionately as garbage compacting). An alternative is to describe a number of pre-designated buckets into which we will aggregate the collateral into these preexisting criteria classes (known as bucketing). Note: This program will adopt the latter approach.

Step 4. Since we are using the bucketing approach, we will design a set of logic switches to funnel the collateral into the appropriate buckets and aggregate it there.

Step 5. Compute the Rep Line statistics for each aggregation. These will vary depending on whether the purpose is descriptive or computational. If it is for the purposes of developing an amortization schedule, we will need to include in the Rep Line statistics every single amortization parameter germane to the particular mortgage type.

Step 6. Write out the resultant collection of Rep Lines.

To facilitate the above, we can employ the general menu format of the CCFG collateral pool menu. This will allow us to specify the pool level or sub-portfolio level collateral data files with an additional file pathway field for the finished Rep Line report file. An "Action" button to kick off the program completes the menu. See Exhibit 10.39.

Rep Line Bucket Specification Tables

With the above admonitions still fresh in our memory, we will now examine a table of specifications for a 15-year original term, hybrid ARM mortgage type. We will

Representative Line Generator Program

		Collateral File Name
Collateral Pool	Select File	C:\VBA_Book2\Code\data\CollateralPool\SubPort01RepLine.xls
Sub Portfolio #1	Select File	C:\VBA_Book2\Code\data\portfolio_add.xls
Sub Portfolio #2	Select File	C:\VBA_Book2\Code\data\portfolio_comb.xls
Sub Portfolio #3	Select File	C:\VBA_Book2\Code\data\portfolio_orig.xls
Sub Portfolio #4	Select File	C:\VBA_Book2\Code\data\Data3.xls
Sub Portfolio #5	Select File	No File Selected

Representative Line File Name C:\VBA_Book2\Code\data\RepLineExample01.xls

Run the Rep Line Generator

EXHIBIT 10.39 Menu of the Rep Line Generator

assume that all loans of this type have the London Interbank Offering Rate (LIBOR) as their index. As noted above, it will be this index and the original term parameter of the loans that form the first selection criteria of these mortgages. The next is the IO payment period, then seasoning, and, last, the spread to the index. The table for this mortgage type consists of 54 distinct Rep Lines, or buckets.

Ordering the Aggregation Criteria   You will notice that the order of these specifications is not random. The order of the specification criteria starts with the most general and works toward the most specific. In essence for this table of 15-year hybrid ARMs, the original term and the index characteristics do not change over the length of the table. They have one value and one value only: the combination of original term of 180 months and an index of LIBOR. The next specification criterion, the fixed IO period, assumes three values over the length of the table: 12, 24, and 36 months. The next specification criterion, seasoning, changes seven times. It assumes the value of less than 6, 12, 24, 36, 60, 120, and 180 months. Last, the most changeable criterion is the spread to the index, which changes 21 times, three times for each of the seasoning values.

Assigning the Data   If we keep to this schema, we can implement a quick and foolproof method of assigning each piece of collateral its appropriate Rep Line bucket number. We will establish the starting values of each bucket for all of the tables of the Rep Line Generator. We do this by assigning a value to a set of Constant variables, one for each individual table we construct. These values are displayed in Exhibit 10.40. Each of these values will form the starting point of the bucketing process. We can start with the beginning table number—in the case of 15-year hybrid ARMs, it is 449—and then add to this number a series of offsets based on the other specification criteria and the characteristics of the individual loan. For example, if we have a 15-year hybrid ARM indexed to LIBOR, our bucket count is set initially to 449. If the value of the next specification criterion, the fixed rate IO period, is 24, we would add 18 to the current bucket count to bring it to 467. If the seasoning of the loan is 40 months, we would next add 12, the start of the seasoning interval of "37 to 60" months. This would increase the bucket count to 479. If the spread to the index was less than 3%, we would add zero; if it was greater than 3%, we would

```
Public Const FIXED_RATE_BUCKET_15Y = 1        'fixed rate buckets 15y OT
Public Const FIXED_RATE_BUCKET_20Y = 81       'fixed rate buckets 20y OT
Public Const FIXED_RATE_BUCKET_30Y = 161      'fixed rate buckets 30y OT
Public Const FLOAT_RATE_BUCKET_15Y = 225      'floating rate buckets 15y OT
Public Const FLOAT_RATE_BUCKET_20Y = 305      'floating rate buckets 20y OT
Public Const FLOAT_RATE_BUCKET_30Y = 385      'floating rate buckets 25y OT
Public Const HYB_ARM_BUCKET_15Y = 449         'hybrid arm buckets 15y OT
Public Const HYB_ARM_BUCKET_20Y = 503         'hybrid arm buckets 20y OT
Public Const HYB_ARM_BUCKET_30Y = 583         'hybrid arm buckets 30y OT
Public Const BALLOON_FIXED_BUCKET_20Y = 703   'fixed balloon buckets 20yr OT
Public Const BALLOON_FIXED_BUCKET_30Y = 831   'fixed balloon buckets 30yr OT
Public Const BALLOON_ARM_BUCKET_20Y = 959     'arm balloon buckets 20yr OT
Public Const BALLOON_ARM_BUCKET_30Y = 1039    'arm balloon buckets 30yr OT
Public Const MAX_BUCKETS = 1246               'ending bucket number
```

EXHIBIT 10.40   Beginning values for each Rep Line table by mortgage type and original term

```
Sub MainProgram_RepresentativeLineGenerator()

    'populate the alpha state potal code array
    For istate = 1 To NUM_STATES
        gStatePostalAlpha(istate) = Range("m2PostalCodes").Cells(istate)
    Next istate
    'read the menu and determine if we are creating lines for a single portfolio
    '   or a collection of up to five sub-portfolios
    If Range("CollateralPoolName") = "No File Selected" Or _
        Range("CollateralPoolName") = "" Then
        For icollat = 1 To NUM_PORTS
            gfnSubPort(icollat) = Range("SubPortfolioNames").Cells(icollat)
        Next icollat
        Call CollatData_ReadSubPortDataFiles
    Else
        gfnPoolName = Range("CollateralPoolName")
        Call CollatData_ReadPoolDataFile
    End If
    'find the rep line bucket for each loan and assign it to the array
    '   gLoanBucket(by loan) and a list of the number of loans in each of
    '   the loan buckets gBucketList
    ReDim gLoanBucket(1 To gTotalLoans) As Long
    ReDim gLoanRepLine(1 To gTotalLoans, 1 To DATA_FILE_FIELDS) As Double
    For iloan = 1 To gTotalLoans
        Call RepLine_AssignBucketNumber(iloan)
    Next iloan
    'calculate the statistics of each of the loans so that we can larter build
    '   the rep lines from them based on their bucket numbers
    Call RepLine_CalculateLoanLevelStatistics
    Call RepLine_Aggregator           'based on bucket numbers aggregate the rep lines
    Call RepLine_WriteRepLineReport   'write report package for financial/demographic
    Call RepLine_DemographicData      'produce the demographic reports
    ActiveWorkbook.Close              'close the report file

End Sub
```

EXHIBIT 10.41   "MainProgram_RepresentativeLineGenerator" subroutine

add 1 to arrive at a final bucket count of either 479 or 480. This is the table location corresponding to a loan with these characteristics!

We will now look at the code to implement the aggregation of each piece of collateral into a specific bucket. We first need to get the information concerning the characteristics of the collateral in a form where the Rep Line Generator can work on it. To accomplish this, we will use copies of the subroutines that we developed to support the collateral pool menu. Since they are now familiar to us, we do not need to review them in detail. We are now ready to begin the process of building the Rep Lines. See Exhibit 10.41.

Storing the Rep Line Aggregation Results   After reading the collateral pool or subportfolio data into the Rep Line Generator, our next step will be to create an array to hold the Rep Line bucket designation of each of the loans. Once we have identified which bucket each of the loans belongs in, we can identify the number of buckets that actually have loans assigned to them, calculate their Rep Line statistics, and aggregate the results. We will dimension the array "gLoanBucket" to the number of total loans of the collateral pool, and we will record the bucket assignments in this array. We will also dimension an array named "gRepLineData", which will hold the statistics of each of the individual Rep Lines. This array will have one row for each loan and a total of 26 columns, the value of the public Constant "BALFINALPER", the value of the balloon final payment period. Why did we stop at this parameter? This parameter is the last of the amortization criteria parameters that we will need to consider in building the Rep Line. If we capture all the information up to and including these data, we will have the complete set of criteria we need to perform amortization calculations with any of the resultant Rep Lines! We will revisit this subject shortly.

Finding the Target Rep Line   In the subroutine "RepLine_AssignBucketNumber", we will begin the process of determining the Rep Line that each of the loans will reside in. In this process, because we are using a schema of predetermined criteria, we are able to quickly and efficiently determine just where each of the loans will end up. In the following exhibits we will consider a 15-year hybrid ARM mortgage type. In Exhibit 10.40, a "Select..Case" statement branches to one of five choices based on mortgage types. The 15-year fixed-rate mortgage type is first in the list. The bucket numbers run from 1 to 80. The 20- and 30-year fixed-rate mortgage types will have bucket numbers between 81 to 160 and 161 to 240, respectively. The second mortgage type is the standard ARM, which contains three Rep Line tables for 15-, 20-, and 30-year mortgages. The lowest bucket number a standard ARM mortgage can assume is 225 and the highest is 448. By the time we get to the hybrid ARM mortgage type, 448 prior Rep Lines have already been described. There are now an additional 254 Rep Lines for the hybrid ARMs. This means that if the mortgage type is a hybrid ARM, it will end up with a Rep Line number of between 449 and 702. We will initially assign the loan in question, which we know to be a hybrid ARM, the base Rep Line number of 449. From that point, as we indicated in our discussion of the Rep Line table structures above, based on individual specification criteria of the loan we are examining, we will increment this Rep Line assignment to reflect its position in the order of the tables.

Once we have determined the Rep Line number for this loan, we will assign it to the nth position of the "gLoanBucket" array to associate it with this loan. Next we will increment the nth position of another array, named "gBucketList". This array is dimensioned to the number of total Rep Line buckets we have for all five mortgage types, a total of 1,588. The "gBucketList" array starts with all of its members set to zero. As we find a loan that meets the criteria for the 275th Rep Line bucket, we will increment "gBucketList(275)" by 1. Thus by the end of the assignment process we will have two arrays, the first, "gLoanBucket", telling us what Rep Line the loan has been assigned to and "gBucketList" telling us which of the Rep Lines have loans assigned to them and how many loans are in each. See Exhibit 10.42.

Rep Line Assignment Example   Returning to our earlier example of a 15-year hybrid ARM, we know that the beginning bucket number for all mortgages of this type is 449 and its final bucket assignment must fall between 449 and 702. We now enter the subroutine "RepLine_HybridARMDesignator". Upon arriving in this subroutine, we see that we have another "Select..Case" statement that will now branch us into one of three other subroutines based on the value of the original term parameter of this loan. The choices are original terms of 180, 240, and 360. It is here, at the initial determination that we have a 15-year hybrid ARM, that the

```
Sub RepLine_AssignBucketNumber(iloan As Long)

    gBucket = 0
    Select Case gLoanData(iloan, FD_MORTTYPE)
        Case Is = MORTTYPE_FIXED_RATE:    Call RepLine_FixedRateDesignator(iloan)
        Case Is = MORTTYPE_STAND_ARM:     Call RepLine_ARMDesignator(iloan)
        Case Is = MORTTYPE_HYBRID_ARM:    Call RepLine_HybridARMDesignator(iloan)
        Case Is = MORTTYPE_BALLOON_FIXED: Call RepLine_BalloonDesignatorFixed(iloan)
        Case Is = MORTTYPE_BALLOON_ARM:   Call RepLine_BalloonDesignatorARM(iloan)
    End Select
    'record the rep line bucket of this loan
    gLoanBucket(iloan) = gBucket
    'increment the bucket count for this loan
    gBucketList(gBucket) = gBucketList(gBucket) + 1

End Sub
```

EXHIBIT 10.42   "RepLine_AssignBucketNumber" subroutine

first increment to the "gBucket" variable occurs. Based on its original term of 180 months, the "gBucket" count is incremented by the value of the Constant variable "HYB_ARM_BUCKET_15Y". This sets the value to an initial level of 449. We will now examine the values of the fixed IO period, the seasoning, and the spread to the index to determine the final "gBucket" variable value. We will now call a series of three additional subroutines to round out the bucket count assignment process. See Exhibit 10.43.

We will now examine the value of the IO period, the seasoning, and the spread parameters of this loan to complete the assignment process.

For this case we will use the example advanced above:

- The loan has an IO period of 24.
- The loan is seasoned 40 months.
- The loan has a spread to LIBOR of 3.5%.

```
Sub RepLine_HybridARMDesignator(iloan As Long)

    Select Case gLoanData(iloan, FD_ORIGTERM)
        Case Is <= 180:
            gBucket = gBucket + HYB_ARM_BUCKET_15Y
            Call RepLine_HybridArmIOPeriodOnly(1, iloan)
            Call RepLine_HybridARMSeasoning(1, iloan)
            Call RepLine_SpreadOffset(36, 180, iloan)
        Case Is <= 240:
            gBucket = gBucket + HYB_ARM_BUCKET_20Y
            Call RepLine_HybridArmIOPeriodOnly(2, iloan)
            Call RepLine_HybridARMSeasoning(2, iloan)
            Call RepLine_SpreadOffset(36, 240, iloan)
        Case Is <= 360:
            gBucket = gBucket + HYB_ARM_BUCKET_30Y
            Call RepLine_HybridArmIOPeriodOnly(3, iloan)
            Call RepLine_HybridARMSeasoning(3, iloan)
            Call RepLine_SpreadOffset(36, 360, iloan)
    End Select

End Sub
```

EXHIBIT 10.43   "RepLine_HybridARMDesignator" subroutine

We first call the "RepLine_HybridARMIOPeriodOnly" subroutine. We pass this subroutine two values: the number of the loan and the case based on original term. With an "icase" value of "1", based on the fact that the original term of the mortgage is 180 months, and with an IO period of 24, we will increment the "gBucket" value by 18 to $449 + 18 = 467$.

Next we call the "RepLine_HybridARMSeasoning" subroutine. Again we pass the "icase" variable with a value of "1". Since the loan is 40 months seasoned, we add 12 to the "gBucket" value, increasing its cumulative value from 467 to $467 + 12 = 479$.

Our last subroutine call will adjust the "gBucket" value based on its spread of 3.5%. We now call the subroutine "RepLine_SpreadOffset". We need to supply this subroutine with three values to correctly determine the effect of the spread value. The first two values relate to the seasoning cutoffs that reference different spread values. If the hybrid ARM is less than 36 months old, we will increment the "gBucket" value based on a three-tier spread distribution; if the seasoning is greater than 36 months, we will use a two-tier gradation. In our example, the seasoning of the loan is 40 months so it will fall into the latter of the two tests. If the spread to the index is greater than 3%, we will increment the "gBucket" value by 1; if it is less than 3%, we will increment it by zero. The spread is 3.5% so we increment the "gBucket" value by 1, resulting in a Rep Line assignment of $479 + 1 = 480$. This corresponds to the value on the chart in Exhibit 10.38! See Exhibit 10.44.

```
Sub RepLine_HybridArmIOPeriodOnly(icase As Integer, iloan As Long)

    Select Case icase
        Case Is = 1
            Select Case gLoanData(iloan, FD_HBAIOPERIOD)
                Case Is <= 12: gBucket = gBucket + 0
                Case Is <= 24: gBucket = gBucket + 18
                Case Is <= 36: gBucket = gBucket + 36
            End Select
        Case Is = 2
            Select Case gLoanData(iloan, FD_HBAIOPERIOD)
                Case Is <= 12: gBucket = gBucket + 0
                Case Is <= 24: gBucket = gBucket + 20
                Case Is <= 36: gBucket = gBucket + 40
                Case Is <= 60: gBucket = gBucket + 60
            End Select
        Case Is = 3
            Select Case gLoanData(iloan, FD_HBAIOPERIOD)
                Case Is <= 12: gBucket = gBucket + 0
                Case Is <= 24: gBucket = gBucket + 20
                Case Is <= 36: gBucket = gBucket + 40
                Case Is <= 60: gBucket = gBucket + 60
                Case Is <= 84: gBucket = gBucket + 80
                Case Is <= 120: gBucket = gBucket + 100
            End Select
    End Select
End Sub
```

EXHIBIT 10.44 "RepLine_HybridARMIOPeriodOnly" subroutine

Representative Line Amortization Parameters By Loan Type

Field	Field Name	Constant	Description	Used in Fixed Rate	Used in Standard ARM	Used in Hybrid ARM	Used in Balloon Fixed	Used in Balloon ARM
4	Original Balance	FD_ORIGBAL	Initial principal mortgage balance	X	X	X	X	X
5	Current Balance	FD_CURRBAL	Current principal mortgage balance	X	X	X	X	X
9	Original Term (months)	FD_ORIGTERM	Original term of the mortgage in months	X	X	X	X	X
10	Remaining Term (months)	FD_REMTERM	Remaining term of the montgage in months	X	X	X	X	X
12	Current Coupon Rate	FD_CURRATE	Coupon rate for FRM; Current ARM Coupon	X	X	X	X	X
13	ARM Index	FD_ARMINDEX	See Table			X		
14	ARM Spread to Index	FD_ARMSPRD	Spread to Index		X	X		X
15	ARM Initial Index Level	FD_ARMORIGLEV	Current Index rate level		X	X		X
16	ARM Periodic Reset	FD_ARMPERRESET	Number of months between interest resets		X	X		X
17	ARM Periodic Cap Rate	FD_ARMPERCAP	Highest limit of change in fully indexed rate		X	X		X
18	ARM Periodic Floor	FD_ARMPERFLR	Lowest limit of change in fully indexed rate		X	X		X
19	ARM Lifetime Cap Rate	FD_ARMLIFCAP	Highest limit of fully indexed rate		X	X		X
20	ARM Lifetime Floor Rate	FD_ARMLIFFLR	Lowest limit of fully indexed rate		X	X		X
21	HB-ARM Initial Rate	FD_HBAORIGLEV	Initial locked rate			X		
22	HB-ARM Initial I/O Rate Period	FD_HBAIOPERIOD	Number of months initial locked rate			X		
23	HB-ARM Total I/O Rate Period	FD_HBSIOPERIOD	Number of months I/O period only			X		
24	HB-ARM Recast Term	FD_HBARECASTPR	Number of months for full amortization calculation			X		
25	BALLOON Amortization Period	FD_BALAMORTPER	Number of months for amortization calculation				X	X
26	BALLOON Period	FD_BALPERIOD	Month of balloon payment period				X	X

EXHIBIT 10.45   Table of amortization criteria by loan type

The above process will continue until each loan in the pool has been assigned a Rep Line number in the array "gLoanBucket". We will have also fully populated the "gBucketList", which will now be a frequency distribution of the allocation of every loan in the entire pool. From this array we now know which Rep Lines have loans in them and which do not.

Building the Lines

In the section above we have accomplished two critical tasks. Every loan is now associated with a Rep Line, and we know which of the Rep Lines are active. Let us put this knowledge to use!

Each of the loan types that we have in the pool requires a different set of amortization criteria to be added to the Rep Line so that we can use these different criteria to generate cash flows with the aggregated information. The table listed in Exhibit 10.45 indicates by loan type just which of these parameters we will need to prepare for the respective loan types.

Having now identified which parameters we need to produce for a Rep Line, let us begin the process. The subroutine "RepLine_CalculateLoanLevelStatistics" begins this process by initializing all the array elements of "gLoanRepLine"—the pool level array that will hold the computed Rep Line statistics—to zero. Next we will use a "Select..Case" statement that will branch based on the mortgage type of the loan to a subroutine specifically configured to perform the calculations we need to populate the Rep Line. See Exhibit 10.46.

Staying with the mortgage type hybrid ARMs, we are directed to the subroutine "RepLine_HybridARMStatistics". Here we will compute the necessary statistics that this individual loan will contribute to its Rep Line. If we refer back to the items listed in Exhibit 10.19, we can see that all but two of these items—item 4, the original

```
Sub RepLine_CalculateLoanLevelStatistics()

    'clear the represenatative line statistics on a loan-by-loan basis
    For iloan = 1 To gTotalLoans
        For iparm = 1 To DATA_FILE_FIELDS
            gLoanRepLine(iloan, iparm) = 0#
        Next iparm
    Next iloan
    'calculate the rep line stats by mortgage type based on data requirements
    For iloan = 1 To gTotalLoans
        cbal = gLoanData(iloan, FD_CURRBAL)
        Select Case gLoanData(iloan, FD_MORTTYPE)
            Case Is = MORTTYPE_FIXED_RATE:      Call RepLine_FixedRateStatistics
            Case Is = MORTTYPE_STAND_ARM:       Call RepLine_FloatRateStatistics
            Case Is = MORTTYPE_HYBRID_ARM:      Call RepLine_HybridARMStatistics
            Case Is = MORTTYPE_BALLOON_FIXED:   Call RepLine_BalloonStatisticsFixed
            Case Is = MORTTYPE_BALLOON_ARM:     Call RepLine_BalloonStatisticsARM
        End Select
    Next iloan

End Sub
```

EXHIBIT 10.46 "RepLine_CalculateLoanLevelStatistics" subroutine

```
Sub RepLine_HybridARMStatistics()

    Call RepLine_CalcStandardARMStatistics
    'weighted average initial rate
    gLoanRepLine(iloan, FD_HBAORIGLEV) = gLoanData(iloan, FD_HBAORIGLEV) * cbal
    'weighted average initial rate months
    gLoanRepLine(iloan, FD_HBAIOPERIOD) = gLoanData(iloan, FD_HBAIOPERIOD) * cbal
    'weighted average months I/O only
    gLoanRepLine(iloan, FD_HBAIOTOTAL) = gLoanData(iloan, FD_HBAIOTOTAL) * cbal
    'weighted average months fully amortizing
    gLoanRepLine(iloan, FD_HBARECASTPR) = gLoanData(iloan, FD_HBARECASTPR) * cbal

End Sub
```

EXHIBIT 10.47   "RepLine_HybridARMStatistics" subroutine

balance, and item 13, the index from which the loan floats—needs to be weighted by the current balance of the loan for inclusion in the Rep Line. These subroutines now perform that task. It also records the original and remaining balance for the purposes of averaging these statistics later. See Exhibits 10.47 and 10.48.

Streamlining the Rep Line List   With the statistics in hand, we can now build the Rep Lines themselves. We will start the process from the subroutine "RepLine_Aggregator". This subroutine call two subroutines to perform the task. We already have an array "gBucketList" that contains the loan count for each Rep Line. We may have thousands of buckets in this list yet only several dozen may contain collateral. Rather than have to search through the entire list each time we

```
Sub RepLine_CalcStandardARMStatistics()

    'original/current balances
    gLoanRepLine(iloan, FD_ORIGBAL) = gLoanData(iloan, FD_ORIGBAL)
    gLoanRepLine(iloan, FD_CURRBAL) = gLoanData(iloan, FD_CURRBAL)
    'WAOT & WARM - current balance weighted original & remaing term
    gLoanRepLine(iloan, FD_ORIGTERM) = gLoanData(iloan, FD_ORIGTERM) * cbal
    gLoanRepLine(iloan, FD_REMTERM) = gLoanData(iloan, FD_REMTERM) * cbal
    'WAC - current balance weighted coupon
    gLoanRepLine(iloan, FD_CURRRATE) = gLoanData(iloan, FD_CURRRATE) * cbal
    'WAS - weighted average spread
    gLoanRepLine(iloan, FD_ARMSPRD) = gLoanData(iloan, FD_ARMSPRD) * cbal
    'weighted average current index
    gLoanRepLine(iloan, FD_ARMORIGLEV) = gLoanData(iloan, FD_ARMORIGLEV) * cbal
    'weighted average months to reset
    gLoanRepLine(iloan, FD_ARMPERRESET) = gLoanData(iloan, FD_ARMPERRESET) * cbal
    'weighted average periodic cap
    gLoanRepLine(iloan, FD_ARMPERCAP) = gLoanData(iloan, FD_ARMPERCAP) * cbal
    'weighted average periodic floor
    gLoanRepLine(iloan, FD_ARMPERFLR) = gLoanData(iloan, FD_ARMPERFLR) * cbal
    'weighted average lifetime cap
    gLoanRepLine(iloan, FD_ARMLIFCAP) = gLoanData(iloan, FD_ARMLIFCAP) * cbal
    'weighted average lifetime floor
    gLoanRepLine(iloan, FD_ARMLIFFLR) = gLoanData(iloan, FD_ARMLIFFLR) * cbal

End Sub
```

EXHIBIT 10.48   "RepLine_CalcStandardARM" statistics subroutine

```
Sub RepLines_BuildListOfActiveBuckets()

    'read the rep line bucket count for each of the buckets, if there are more
    '   than zero loans, record this bucket number in the active que
    ReDim gActiveBuckets(1 To MAX_BUCKETS) As Long
    iactive = 0
    For ibucket = 1 To MAX_BUCKETS
        If gBucketList(ibucket) > 0 Then
            iactive = iactive + 1
            gActiveBuckets(iactive) = ibucket
        End If
    Next ibucket
    ReDim Preserve gActiveBuckets(1 To iactive) As Long
    gTotRepLines = iactive

End Sub
```

EXHIBIT 10.49   "RepLines_BuildListOfActiveBuckets" subroutine

want to perform a bucket-specific operation, we will compress this list to an array called "ActiveBuckets", which will be an array that contains only the numbers of the active Rep Line buckets. We do this using the "RepLines_BuildListOfActiveBuckets" subroutine. See Exhibit 10.49.

Calculation of the Dollar-Weighted Results   We can now loop through each of the loans of the pool using only the Rep Lines designated in the "ActiveBucket" array! We transfer the information that we just computed at the loan-by-loan level and then stored in the "gLoanRepLine" array to the appropriate position in the "gRepLine" array. When we have completed loading in all the data, we need only average each of the active statistics by the aggregate current balance of the Rep Line, and we are finished. *Remember!* At this point all of the information in the "gRepLine" array is dollar weighted but not dollar averaged! It is in effect the numerator of the Rep Line items that has yet to be divided by the denominator that is aggregate current balance. Once we have divided all of the accumulated dollar-weighted balances in the "gRepLine" array by the Rep Line aggregate current balance, we will place the results in the array "gRepLineFinal". We can then report the results of the Rep Line computation or save them to a file or both. See Exhibit 10.50.

Writing the Rep Line Report

Having assembled the Rep Lines, we now need to report them! We will print them out in a series of mortgage-type-specific reports. Due to the fact that the information requirements to amortize each of the mortgages types is different, we will need five different report formats. The report format for the hybrid ARM report is shown in Exhibit 10.51.

Rep Line Template Files   To populate these reports, we will first open the template file "RepLineReportTemplate.xls", and save it to the file pathway entered in the "Representative File name Field" of the Main Menu. Once the report file is saved, we begin the process by initializing the current print line variables. These variables

```
Sub RepLines_AggregateRepLines()

    ReDim gRepLine(1 To gTotRepLines, 1 To DATA_FILE_FIELDS) As Double       'raw data
    ReDim gRepLineFinal(1 To gTotRepLines, 1 To DATA_FILE_FIELDS) As Double  '$ wghted

    For iloan = 1 To gTotalLoans
        For iRepLine = 1 To gTotRepLines
            If gLoanBucket(iloan) = gActiveBuckets(iRepLine) Then
                'we have matched a loan to the nth active bucket
                gRepLine(iRepLine, FD_COUNT) = gRepLine(iRepLine, FD_COUNT) + 1
                For iparm = 2 To DATA_FILE_FIELDS
                    gRepLine(iRepLine, iparm) = _
                        gRepLine(iRepLine, iparm) + gLoanRepLine(iloan, iparm)
                Next iparm
            End If
        Next iRepLine
    Next iloan
    'convert to current balance weighted averages
    For iRepLine = 1 To gTotRepLines
        gRepLineFinal(iRepLine, FD_COUNT) = gRepLine(iRepLine, FD_COUNT)       'loan count
        gRepLineFinal(iRepLine, FD_ORIGBAL) = gRepLine(iRepLine, FD_ORIGBAL)  'orig balance
        gRepLineFinal(iRepLine, FD_CURRBAL) = gRepLine(iRepLine, FD_CURRBAL)  'curr balance
        'all other aggregate statistics
        For iparm = FD_ORIGTERM To DATA_FILE_FIELDS
            If gRepLine(iRepLine, iparm) > 0# Then
                gRepLineFinal(iRepLine, iparm) = _
                    gRepLine(iRepLine, iparm) / gRepLine(iRepLine, FD_CURRBAL)
            End If
        Next iparm
    Next iRepLine

End Sub
```

EXHIBIT 10.50 "RepLines_AggregateRepLines" subroutine

keep track of the next available line for output in each of the five Rep Line reports. We can now loop through the array "gActiveBuckets" that holds the numbers of all the active Rep Lines. A "Select..Case" statement matches the number of the "gActiveBuckets" array position to a series of Constant variables. These Constant variables each delineate the maximum value the five sets of Rep Line buckets for each mortgage type. For example, "FLOAT_RATE_BUCKET_15Y - 1" is the maximum value of any fixed-rate loan Rep Line as it is one less than the beginning of the lowest number standard ARM Rep Line. Based on the routing of the "Select..Case" statement the particular reporting subroutine is called for the appropriate mortgage type. After all the Rep Lines have been output, the workbook is saved and closed completing the reporting process. See Exhibit 10.52.

Recording the Rep Line   Let us take a look at one of the mortgage-type-specific "Write" subroutines called by the "RepLine_WriteRepLineReport" subroutine. All of the mortgage types share the same common six data fields at the beginning of the Rep Line. These are aggregate original and current balances, and current balance weighted original term, remaining term and current coupon level. In addition to this, the standard ARMs and hybrid ARMs share many of the same fields that are common to all forms of ARMs. The first 14 data items of these mortgages are common across both types. This allows us to conveniently group them in a

Rep Line Number	2 Mortgage Type	3 Number of Loans	4 Aggregate Original Balance	5 Aggregate Remaining Balance	6 Average Original Term	7 Average Remaining Term	8 Average Spread	9 Reset Rate	10 Reset Pmt	11 Periodic Coupon Floor	12 Periodic Coupon Cap	13 Lifetime Coupon Cap	14 Lifetime Coupon Floor	15 HARM Initial Rate	16 HARM Initial Rate Months	17 HARM I/O Months	18 HARM Amort Months	23 # of State
1																		
2																		
3																		
4																		
5																		
6																		
7																		
8																		
9																		
10																		
11																		
12																		
13																		
14																		

EXHIBIT 10.51 Hybrid ARM Rep Line report

```
Sub RepLine_WriteRepLineReport()

    mFileName = Range("RepLineFileName")          'rep line report pathway
    'open the rep line template file and save it to the report name
    Workbooks.Open FileName:=TEMPLATE_DIRECTORY & REP_LINE_SUBDIR & _
                                      REP_LINE_FILE_TEMPLATE
    ActiveWorkbook.SaveAs FileName:=mFileName
    'initialize the starting print row for the reports
    mPrintLineFixed = REPLINE_REPORT_START
    mPrintLineSARM = REPLINE_REPORT_START
    mPrintLineHARM = REPLINE_REPORT_START
    mPrintLineBallFixed = REPLINE_REPORT_START
    mPrintLineBallARM = REPLINE_REPORT_START
    'loop by active replines
    For iline = 1 To gTotRepLines
        Select Case gActiveBuckets(iline)
            Case Is <= FLOAT_RATE_BUCKET_15Y - 1
                Call WriteRepLine_FixedRateStatistics
            Case Is <= HYB_ARM_BUCKET_15Y - 1
                Call WriteRepLine_FloatRateStatistics
            Case Is <= BALLOON_FIXED_BUCKET_30Y - 1
                Call WriteRepLine_HybridARMStatistics
            Case Is <= BALLOON_ARM_BUCKET_20Y - 1
                Call WriteRepLine_BalloonFixedStatistics
            Case Is <= MAX_BUCKETS
                Call WriteRepLine_BalloonARMStatistics
        End Select
    Next iline
    ActiveWorkbook.Save

End Sub
```

EXHIBIT 10.52 "RepLine_WriteRepLineReport" subroutine

subroutine that will report these "core" ARM fields. We will call this subroutine "WriteRepLine_BaseARMInfo". We can then call this from the output subroutines for the standard and hybrid ARM types. This makes the code clearer and saves us having to repeat these instructions in each of the ARM reporting subroutines. See Exhibits 10.53 and 10.54.

```
Sub WriteRepLine_HybridARMStatistics()

    Sheets("HybridARM").Select
    Call WriteRepline_BaseARMInfo(mPrintLineHARM)
    'teaser rate level
    Cells(mPrintLineHARM, 16).Value = gRepLineFinal(iline, FD_HBAORIGLEV)
    'teaser rate period
    Cells(mPrintLineHARM, 17).Value = gRepLineFinal(iline, FD_HBAIOPERIOD)
    'I/O months
    Cells(mPrintLineHARM, 18).Value = gRepLineFinal(iline, FD_HBAIOTOTAL)
    'amortizing months
    Cells(mPrintLineHARM, 19).Value = gRepLineFinal(iline, FD_HBARECASTPR)
    mPrintLineHARM = mPrintLineHARM + 1

End Sub
```

EXHIBIT 10.53 "WriteRepLine_HybridARMStatistics" subroutine

```
Sub WriteRepline_BaseARMInfo(line_num As Integer)

    Cells(line_num, 2).Value = gActiveBuckets(iline)              'rep line number
    Cells(line_num, 3).Value = gRepLineFinal(iline, FD_COUNT)     'loan count
    Cells(line_num, 4).Value = gRepLineFinal(iline, FD_ORIGBAL)   'total orig bal
    Cells(line_num, 5).Value = gRepLineFinal(iline, FD_CURRBAL)   'total curr bal
    Cells(line_num, 6).Value = gRepLineFinal(iline, FD_ORIGTERM)  'WAOT
    Cells(line_num, 7).Value = gRepLineFinal(iline, FD_REMTERM)   'WARM
    Cells(line_num, 8).Value = gRepLineFinal(iline, FD_CURRRATE)  'WAC
    Cells(line_num, 9).Value = gRepLineFinal(iline, FD_ARMSPRD)   'spread
    Cells(line_num, 10).Value = gRepLineFinal(iline, FD_ARMORIGLEV)  'current index
    Cells(line_num, 11).Value = gRepLineFinal(iline, FD_ARMPERRESET) 'reset months
    Cells(line_num, 12).Value = gRepLineFinal(iline, FD_ARMPERCAP)   'periodic cap
    Cells(line_num, 13).Value = gRepLineFinal(iline, FD_ARMPERFLR)   'periodic floor
    Cells(line_num, 14).Value = gRepLineFinal(iline, FD_ARMLIFCAP)   'lifetime cap
    Cells(line_num, 15).Value = gRepLineFinal(iline, FD_ARMLIFFLR)   'lifetime floor

End Sub
```

EXHIBIT 10.54   "WriteRepLine_BaseARMInfo" subroutine

Rep Line Demographic Information

The final addition to the Rep Line Generator program will be to add a small number of demographic information reports to the output package. What problem do we address by doing this? Have we not done enough already? Yes and no. Yes in that we have provided ourselves (and others) with a basic but functional Rep Line Generator. It gives us all we need to amortize the cash flows for each of the mortgage types. Is that not enough? No, in that we need to have demographic information available to help us determine the credit risks of any particular Rep Line. Let us consider the case of a single fixed-income Rep Line. It constitutes 16% of the aggregate current balance of the collateral pool. It consists of 6,500 mortgages whose coupons are between 5% and 6%, have 360-month original terms and have between 36 to 48 months of seasoning. Now let us look at three factors—the geographic distribution, original versus current appraisal, and owner occupancy code. We will now hypothesize two dramatically different demographic profiles for the mortgages of this Rep Line.

- Case 1. Geographic concentration. In this case, 42% of the current balance is in Florida, 16% is in Nevada, and 9% is in Michigan (all states with extremely high default rates). On average, the current appraisals are 25% lower than the original appraisal values, although the Florida and Nevada loans range in the 30% to 50% down range. A total of 55% of the Rep Line occupancy code is "Non-Owner Occupied", indicating a degree of speculative purchasing.
- Case 2. Geographic concentration is spread over 42 states, and the largest geographic concentration is California with 7.2% of the current balances. The current appraisals are running on average 12% lower, although 1,148 of the loans are actually showing less than 5% MVDs. Over 94% of the current balances are from properties that are owner occupied.

These two cases are deliberately constructed to emphasize how two Rep Lines can have the identical amortization characteristics yet possess diametrically opposed credit characteristics. Highlighting the extreme differences that can change the basic

Representative Line Demographic Report -- Original and Current Appraisal Methods
Loan Count and Current Balances

Report Line Number	Rep Line Number	Total Loans	Original Total Dollars	Current Total Dollars	Original Appraisal Method										Current Appraisal Method									
					Full Walk-Thru		Partial Walk-Thru		Drive By		Tax Records		Unknown		Full Walk-Thru		Partial Walk-Thru		Full Drive-By		Tax Records		Unknown	
Totals→		80	17,060,000		Count	Dollars	Count	Dollars	Count	Dollars	Count	Dollars	Count	Dollars	Count	Dollars	Count	Dollars	Count	Dollars	Count	Dollars	Count	Dollars
					11	1,530,000	2	240,000	1	470,000	6	1,250,000	16	1,995,000	37	7,577,500	27	3,900,000	6	517,500	14	1,440,000		
1	45	1	690,000	517,500			1	690,000															1	517,500
2	60	2	1,540,000	1,155,000	2	1,540,000											1	420,000	1	735,000				
3	61	15	1,670,000	1,252,500	12	1,370,000	3	300,000							1	67,500	2	150,000	5	480,000	2	150,000	5	405,000
4	62	1	60,000	45,000			1	60,000															1	45,000
5	68	1	80,000	60,000			1	80,000									1	60,000						
6	69	8	770,000	595,000	6	610,000	2	160,000							1	67,500	2	145,000	3	210,000			2	172,500
7	70	2	90,000	67,500	2	90,000											1	22,500	1	45,000				
8	147	1	40,000	30,000									1	40,000			1	30,000						
9	148	1	620,000	465,000									1	620,000			1	465,000						
10	149	14	2,890,000	2,167,500	11	2,100,000					1	470,000	2	320,000	5	952,500	2	240,000	5	825,000			2	150,000
11	150	8	300,000	225,000	4	40,000	1	60,000					1	200,000	1	30,000	1	150,000	1	45,000				
12	156	8	730,000	547,500	4	300,000	1	120,000	2	240,000			1	70,000	1	45,000	2	127,500	3	270,000			2	105,000
13	157	3	180,000	135,000	2	120,000	1	60,000											2	90,000			1	45,000
14	197	4	1,900,000	1,425,000	4	1,900,000									1	255,000	1	1,170,000						
15	211	4	1,220,000	915,000	4	1,220,000											4	915,000						
16	212	2	400,000	300,000	2	400,000									1	90,000	1	97,500	1	202,500				
17	213	7	3,230,000	2,422,500	7	3,230,000									1	30,000	5	2,212,500	1	120,000				
18	214	4	630,000	472,500	4	630,000											3	442,500						
19	215	12	2,730,000	2,047,500	12	2,730,000									3	412,500	3	525,000	2	742,500	4	367,500		
20	216	1	60,000	45,000	1	60,000											1	45,000						
21	219	1	120,000	90,000	1	120,000											1	90,000						
22	221	3	260,000	195,000	3	260,000											1	60,000	2	135,000				
23	223	3	280,000	210,000	3	280,000											3	210,000						
24	224	1	60,000	45,000	1	60,000									1	45,000								

EXHIBIT 10.55 Original and Current Appraisal Method report

mortgagor behaviors using just three demographic aspects should sensitize you to the need to look deeper before just generating numbers in a model! When it comes time to make estimates as to how to apply prepayment and default criteria, we are best served by having demographic information available at a Rep Line level.

Original/Current Appraisal Report   There are two demographic reports in the Rep Line Generator. One is a Geographic Distribution report and the other is an Original/Current Appraisal report. The subroutines that produce these reports are located in the "RepLineCallcStatsDemographics" module. In Exhibit 10.55 we see the report that contrasts both the type of appraisal and the appraisal values of the original appraisal versus the current appraisal for the Rep Lines we generated earlier.

This report is produced by the "RepLine_ProduceAppraisalStatistics" subroutine seen in Exhibit 10.56. This subroutine both aggregates the report data and prints the report. It calls a single processing subroutine, "RepLine_AggregateAppraisal Balances", to prepare the report contents. From that point on its organization and structure are easy to follow; we will forgo a detailed discussion of it at this time. Suffice it to say that it sorts the current and original appraisal values by the Rep Lines already established earlier and by the appraisal method. This gives us, at a glance, an

```
Sub RepLine_ProduceAppraisalStatistics()

    'declare the array and remember the arrays are automatically cleared by ReDim
    ReDim gAppOrigType(1 To gTotRepLines, 1 To APPRAISAL_TYPES) As Long
    ReDim gAppCurrType(1 To gTotRepLines, 1 To APPRAISAL_TYPES) As Long
    ReDim gAppOrigDollars(1 To gTotRepLines, 1 To APPRAISAL_TYPES) As Double
    ReDim gAppCurrDollars(1 To gTotRepLines, 1 To APPRAISAL_TYPES) As Double

    'get the statistics by apprisal type; original and current
    Call RepLine_AggregateAppraisalBalances
    'write the report
    start_row = 6
    Sheets("AppraisalInfo").Select
    For iline = 1 To gTotRepLines
        Cells(start_row + iline, 2).Value = gActiveBuckets(iline)
        data_point = 1
        For icol = 6 To 14 Step 2
            If gAppOrigType(iline, data_point) > 0 Then _
                Cells(start_row + iline, icol).Value = _
                                        gAppOrigType(iline, data_point)
            If gAppOrigType(iline, data_point) > 0 Then _
                Cells(start_row + iline, icol + 1).Value = _
                                        gAppOrigDollars(iline, data_point)
            If gAppCurrType(iline, data_point) > 0 Then _
                Cells(start_row + iline, icol + 10).Value = _
                                        gAppCurrType(iline, data_point)
            If gAppCurrDollars(iline, data_point) > 0 Then _
                Cells(start_row + iline, icol + 10 + 1).Value = _
                                        gAppCurrDollars(iline, data_point)
            data_point = data_point + 1
        Next icol
    Next iline
    Calculate
    Call RepLine_TrimAppraisalDemoReport(start_row, iline)

End Sub
```

EXHIBIT 10.56   "RepLine_ProduceAppraisalStatistics" subroutine

```
Sub RepLine_AggregateAppraisalBalances()

    'get the statistics by apprisal type; original and current
    For iloan = 1 To gTotalLoans
      For ibucket = 1 To gTotRepLines
        If gLoanBucket(iloan) = gActiveBuckets(ibucket) Then
          For itest = 1 To 2
            If itest = 1 Then
              itype = gLoanDemo(iloan, DEMO_ORIGAPPTYPE)
              gAppOrigType(ibucket, itype) = gAppOrigType(ibucket, itype) + 1
              gAppOrigDollars(ibucket, itype) = _
              gAppOrigDollars(ibucket, itype) + gLoanDemo(iloan, DEMO_ORIGAPP)
            Else
              itype = gLoanDemo(iloan, DEMO_CURRAPPTYPE)
              gAppCurrType(ibucket, itype) = gAppCurrType(ibucket, itype) + 1
              gAppCurrDollars(ibucket, itype) = _
              gAppCurrDollars(ibucket, itype) + gLoanDemo(iloan, DEMO_CURRAPP)
            End If
          Next itest
          Exit For
        End If
      Next ibucket
    Next iloan

End Sub
```

EXHIBIT 10.57   "RepLine_AggregateAppraisalBalances" subroutine

immediate assessment of how much faith we can put in the current appraisal values based on their method and the relative market value of the properties since the time of their purchase. See Exhibit 10.57.

ON THE WEB SITE

CCFG Model   File "CCFG_Chapter10.xls" contains the VBA code to read both pool level and sub-portfolio level data files and combine the sub-portfolio level data files into a pool level data file if desired by the user.

Initial Data Screening   File "Chapter10_DataScreeningTables.xls" contains the data requirement tables for the cash flow amortization calculations, the stratification reports, the default rate estimate, and the MVD calculation.

File "InitDataScreenTemplate.xls" is the template file for the initial data screening results report package.

File "Pool01_01New" is the collateral pool which has passed the data initial screening tests.

File "CollateralFile Template" is the template file for all collateral portfolios.

File "DemoRiskFacorsTemplate" is the template file for the report that displays the financial/demographic risk factors of all loans of the portfolio on an individual basis.

Representative Line Generator Model   The file named "RepLineCF_ Example.xls" displays the monthly cash flows for the table in Exhibit 10.36.

The Rep Line Generator model, is contained in file **"RepLineGenerator.xls"**.

The Rep Line tables file, which contains the specifications for each of the five mortgage types, is the file **"Chap10_RepLinesTables.xls"**.

The Rep Line template report file is the file named **"RepLineReport Template.xls"**.

## CHAPTER 11

Writing the Collateral Selection Code

OVERVIEW

In this chapter we will write the VBA code of the collateral selection processes and interface it with the menus and the menu support code that was developed in Chapter 9. We will also make immediate use of the code that we just implemented in Chapter 10, the subroutines that move the collateral data into the Collateral Cash Flow Generator (CCFG) model.

This selection process has four major tasks. These are, in the general order of their performance in the model: the Initial Data Screening activity, the Financial/ Demographic Selection activity, the Geographic Selection activity, and the Geographic Concentration Selection activity.

We have already discussed in detail and implemented the code for the Initial Data Screening process in Chapter 10. The task of the Initial Data Screening Selection is to identify and eliminate outlier collateral. This collateral data contains missing, illegible, or blatantly unacceptable financial or demographic values that render it prima facie ineligible for inclusion in the deal. An example would be a standard fixed rate mortgage whose current balance is greater than its original balance. Another example would be a mortgage of any type that was more than two payments or 60+ days in arrears at the time it is being considered for inclusion in the deal. As we have extensively discussed this process in Chapter 10, we will concentrate on the other three collateral selection processes in this chapter.

The Financial Selection tests will allow us to employ the six types of financial test types, discussed in Chapter 10, to specify collateral that, while containing consistent and complete data, is not economically desirable to include in the collateral pool.

The Geographic Selection tests will allow us to deem ineligible collateral based on the location of the property. This specification may be entered at the regional, state, or Metropolitan Statistical Area (MSA) levels via the menus and UserForms created in Chapter 10.

Last, the Geographic Concentration tests will enforce limits as to the extent of geographically clustered collateral. These clusters may represent an unacceptable risk from the standpoint of several factors. Among these factors are regional, state, and local economic conditions; legislative changes; environmental conditions, or a simple need to diversify the portfolio to dampen other unforeseen geographically correlated risks.

When we have completed the chapter, we will have the framework in place to search through, identify, segregate, and assign eligibility (and ineligibility) codes to each piece of collateral from our initial portfolio holdings. The remaining eligible collateral will be the collection of loans that we will then amortize to produce the cash flows of the deal.

DELIVERABLES

There are six major deliverables in this chapter. They are, in the order we will discuss them:

1. **Building the Financial Selection code** that will allow us to specify up to five sets of selection tests, apply them to the collateral, and record the results of the selection process.
2. **Building the Geographic Selection code** that will allow us to select collateral based on its state or MSA location. Collateral that is deselected in this process will be assigned ineligibility codes so that we can later identify it in the calculation and reporting phases of the model runs.
3. **Building the Geographic Concentration code** that will allow us to specify a percentage limit of the amount of current balance collateral allowable from either a state or MSA. This code will deem ineligible any collateral that exceeds the collective amount from the designated area when expressed as a percentage of the total portfolio.
4. **Building the Ineligible Collateral report code.** This code will produce a multiple report package that displays a listing of each Financial/Demographic Criteria test and the loans that failed that particular test, a listing of each individual ineligible loan, and a listing of all of the unique ineligibility combinations.
5. **Building the Geographic Loan Listing report code** that summarizes the collateral by MSA, state, and national levels.
6. **Building the Geographic Concentration report code.** This code displays the cumulative concentration, from individual loans, to MSA groups, and finally to State Level aggregations.

UNDER CONSTRUCTION

In this chapter we will develop the code that will tie together the work of Chapters 9 and 10. This code will take the inputs from the selection process menus developed in Chapter 9 and apply these criteria and tests to the collateral data of the portfolio files read into the CCFG by the code we developed in Chapter 10. The VBA code of this chapter will apply these tests, translated from the inputs from three of the menus that we developed in Chapter 9—the Financial Selection Criteria Editor Menu, Geographic Selection Criteria Editor Menu, and the Geographic Concentration Editor Menu—into a set of selection tests for the collateral. It will perform these tests, assigning error and eligibility codes as needed to the collateral of the portfolio, on a loan-by-loan basis.

The results of these four selection processes will allow us to identify those loans that are eligible for inclusion in the deal. It will also allow us to confirm that the data of these loan records are complete and consistent enough to perform the next step in the structuring process, that of producing the cash flows of the mortgages. The development effort of this chapter will also provide all the information that we will need to produce a series of detailed reports regarding the eligibility status of each piece of collateral. These reporting subroutines, which we will develop in Chapter 13, will read the collateral ineligibility conditions of each of the loans. Using the contents of these arrays, the report writer portion of the CCFG will then produce either specific case or summary survey reports of the ineligible collateral.

We will create or modify the following modules:

- "A_Constants" module. We will add a series of new Constants that will describe new directory and subdirectory pathways. These will be used to locate collateral files or criteria files and to route the output of the selection process. We will also add a series of constant filed designators for the "gLoanData" array that will carry the "ERROR_CODES" for each of the financial and geographic selection processes subroutines.
- "CollatData_FinancialSelection" module. This module contains a total of ten subroutines. The most important are:
  - The "FinSelect_FinancialCriteriaSelectionMain" subroutine that determines whether we are dealing with a pool or a collection of sub-portfolios.
  - The "FinSelect_ApplyCriteriaTest" selects the correct Selection Criteria test set to apply to the collateral.
  - A group of six "FinSelect_Apply[Test Type Name]Test" subroutines, one for each type of selection criteria test. These subroutines perform tests based on the criteria supplied from the subroutine next mentioned.
  - "FinSelect_AssignTestCriteriaConditions" subroutine loads the test conditions for the particular test to be performed in the form of the data points of the loan to be tested, the operations on that data, and the values it is to be tested against.
- "CollatData_GeographicSelection" module. This module contains the subroutines that will translate the inputs from the Geographic Menu to a series of eligibility conditions. These conditions are then applied to the collateral portfolio based on its state or MSA location. This module will also contain the collection of subroutines that will apply the Geographic Concentration Limits of the portfolio based on the constraints we entered in the "States and MSA Concentration" UserForm.
- "Report_CollatIneligUser" module. This module contains the code that produces the Ineligible Collateral Report Package.
- "Report_GeoLoanList" module. This module contains the code used to produce the Geographic Loan Listing Report Package.
- "Report_GeoConcentration" module. This module contains the code used to produce the loan level, MSA level, and state level geographic concentration reports.

BUILDING THE CODE

We will now build the code that will perform each of these selection functions. We will approach them in the order that the CCFG will apply them.

The first set of selection code to be applied to the collateral is the Initial Data Screening process code. We developed this code in Chapter 10 and can therefore immediately move on to the first of the three remaining processes, the Financial Selection process code. Here we will learn how to write the VBA code to establish, organize, and apply the test sets we can create from our menu inputs. Development of the Geographic Selection Criteria tests will then follow. This code will allow us to eliminate collateral with unsuitable state and MSA locations. Last we will develop the Geographic Concentration Criteria that will impose current balance concentrations across selected state and MSA locations.

FINANCIAL AND DEMOGRAPHIC SELECTION CODE

The most extensive and involved of the four selection criteria processes is the financial and demographic selection tests. In the other three test processes, we apply a single set of test criteria to the collateral of the deal as a whole. This is *not* the case when we are dealing with this selection process. As you recall from the "CCFG Financial/ Demographic Selection Criteria Editor" Menu and again in the "CCFG Program Run Options" Menu in Chapter 9, we allow the analyst of the model to specify up to five distinct sets of selection test sets. On the "CCFG Run Options" Menu, we can designate a specific criteria test set to be applied to a specific pool level of sub-portfolio level collection of collateral.

Not only are we faced with a series of test sets but we also have six unique types of tests that can be formulated and applied to a piece of collateral for any given test in the test set. One of our first tasks is therefore is to match the correct test set to the appropriate pool or sub-portfolio. Next we must identify the type of test that is to be applied from the six available test types. Finally we must correctly populate the test with all the information it needs to function. This information consists of:

- The fields of the collateral record that are to be tested.
- The operators "<", "<=", and so forth that we will apply in the tests.
- The value or set of values that the test will compare against the value in the collateral record.

Last we must assign the correct error code score to the collateral field "FD_CALCFINSELECT" if the record fails any of the tests in the test set. The highest-level subroutine in the "CollatData_FinancialSelection" module is "FinSelect_FinancialCriteriaSelectionMain". It is here that the Financial and Demographic Selection process begins.

"FinSelect_FinancialCriteriaSelectionMain" Subroutine

This subroutine performs the following tasks:

- It determines whether we have a pool level collateral portfolio or a collection of sub-portfolios.
- Tests each loan to determine if it is not already ineligible for some other reason.

See Exhibit 11.1.

```
Sub FinSelect_FinancialCriteriaSelectionMain()

    'there are two possible cases, 1) its Pool Level data or 2) its Sub-Portfolio
    ' Level Data  if it is Pool Level data we will use only a single test set,
    ' the 0th Test Set
    'if it is sub-portfolio we need to match the Sub-Portfolio number with the
    ' correct Selection Criteria Test Set number
    If gPoolLevelData Then
        If gROApplyFinDemo(0) Then
            iSubPort = 0
            mSet = gROTestSetFinDemo(0)
            For iloan = 1 To gTotalLoans
                If gLoanScreen(iloan, FD_SCREEN_ALL_OK) = REC_OKFORALL Then
                    Call FinSelect_ApplyCriteriaTests(mSet)
                End If
            Next iloan
        End If
    Else
        For iloan = 1 To gTotalLoans
            If gLoanScreen(iloan, FD_SCREEN_ALL_OK) = REC_OKFORALL Then
                iSubPort = gLoanData(iloan, FD_POOLID)    'sub-port ID of loan
                mSet = gROTestSetFinDemo(iSubPort)          'test set for this subportfolio
                Call FinSelect_ApplyCriteriaTests(mSet)
            End If
        Next iloan
    End If
    'if loans have failed the collateral selection test set the gLoanOK
    ' array to reflect their ineligibility
    For iloan = 1 To gTotalLoans
        If gLoanSelect(iloan, FD_CALCFINSELECT) > 0 Then gLoanOK(iloan) = False
    Next iloan

End Sub
```

EXHIBIT 11.1   "FinSelect_FinancialCriteriaSelectionMain" subroutine

"FinSelect_ApplyCriteriaTests" Subroutine

This subroutine performs the next set of tasks in the process:

- Determines if the test set containing the financial selection test is active. It consults the setting of the variable "gSCActive" for each set to determine if the analyst wishes to apply the tests of the set to this collateral.
- Determines the number of tests in the test set.
- Determines if the test within this test set is active.
- Selects which one of the six testing subroutines to call based on the type of test.
- Calls the particular test-type subroutine to perform the test on the collateral.

See Exhibit 11.2.

Translating the Eligibility Tests into VBA Code

Once we have reached the appropriate test-type subroutine, we still have a fair amount of work to perform before we can administer the test. We need to populate the framework of the test with its collateral data, the operators of the test, and the test values to be compared to the values accessed from the collateral data fields.

```
Sub FinSelect_ApplyCriteriaTests(mSet As Integer)

    'we now know the Selection Test Set is either 0 for a Pool Level selection
    ' activity or is a number between 1 and 5 for the Sub-Portfolio Level
    ' selection activity. Cycle through the tests of the set, check to see it
    ' the test is active, load the test criteria based on the type of Test
    ' that is next in the Test Set.
    If gSCSetActive(mSet) Then
        For itest = 1 To NUM_SEL_TESTS
            If gSCTestActive(mSet, itest) Then
                Select Case gSCEditType(mSet, itest)
                    Case Is = SINGLE_TEST
                        Call FinSelect_ApplySingleConditionTest(mSet, itest)
                    Case Is = MINMAX_TEST
                        Call FinSelect_ApplyMinimumMaximumTest(mSet, itest)
                    Case Is = SINGLEMINMAX_TEST
                        Call FinSelect_ApplySingleWithMinMaxTest(mSet, itest)
                    Case Is = SINGLEMULTI_TEST
                        Call FinSelect_ApplySingleCriteriaMultiValueTest(mSet, itest)
                    Case Is = JOINTMINMAX_TEST
                        Call FinSelect_ApplyJointMinMaxTest(mSet, itest)
                    Case Is = TWOCRITTABLE_TEST
                        Call FinSelect_ApplyTwoCriteriaTableTest(mSet, itest)
                End Select
            End If
        Next itest
    End If

End Sub
```

EXHIBIT 11.2   "FinSelect_ApplyCriteriaTests" subroutine

Upon completion of the test itself, and if the collateral record has failed the test, we need to assign an error code value to its "FD_CALCFINSELECT" field.

To accomplish the task of populating the test, we will use the "FinSelect_ AssignTestCriteriaConditions" subroutine. See Exhibit 11.3.

The "FinSelect_AssignTestCriteriaConditions" subroutine populates the test with the designated collateral data, test operators, and test comparison values for each of the particular tests in the test set. Based on the test set and the number and type of the individual test, this subroutine loads the test values from a series of arrays. Depending on the type of test, this subroutine will load as few as 3 inputs (for Test Type 1) or as many as 22 (for Test Type 6). In that we have discussed how these arrays are created from the inputs to the "CCFG Financial/Demographic Selection Criteria Editor" Menu, we do not need to review them at this time. If you are not clear on this part of the process, review the sections in Chapter 9 that address this menu.

After the conditions and contents of the test have been established, we can now perform the test! Based on the results, if the collateral fails the test, we will need to assign an error code. This task is performed by the subroutine "FinSelect_ IncrementIneligTotal". You will note that in this case, for the first time, the value of the error code value of the test is computed rather than assigned through the use of a Constant. This is because all the error codes are solely dependent on the nth position of the individual test in the test set. We do not know, nor do we *need* to know, what

```
Sub FinSelect_AssignTestCriteriaConditions(iTestSet As Integer, iTest As Integer)

    Select Case gSCEditType(iTestSet, iTest) 'tests for the type of test
        Case Is = SINGLE_TEST:
            mDataItem(1) = gSCEditItems(iTestSet, iTest, 1)
            mOperator(1) = gSCEditOpers(iTestSet, iTest, 1)
            mTestValue(1) = gSCEditValue(iTestSet, iTest, 1)
        Case Is = MINMAX_TEST:
            mDataItem(1) = gSCEditItems(iTestSet, iTest, 1)
            mOperator(1) = gSCEditOpers(iTestSet, iTest, 1)
            mOperator(2) = gSCEditOpers(iTestSet, iTest, 2)
            mTestValue(1) = gSCEditValue(iTestSet, iTest, 1)
            mTestValue(2) = gSCEditValue(iTestSet, iTest, 2)
        Case Is = SINGLEMINMAX_TEST:
            mDataItem(1) = gSCEditItems(iTestSet, iTest, 1)
            mDataItem(2) = gSCEditItems(iTestSet, iTest, 2)
            mOperator(1) = gSCEditOpers(iTestSet, iTest, 1)
            mOperator(2) = gSCEditOpers(iTestSet, iTest, 2)
            mOperator(3) = gSCEditOpers(iTestSet, iTest, 3)
            mTestValue(1) = gSCEditValue(iTestSet, iTest, 1)
            mTestValue(2) = gSCEditValue(iTestSet, iTest, 2)
        Case Is = SINGLEMULTI_TEST:
            mDataItem(1) = gSCEditItems(iTestSet, iTest, 1)
            For iTest2 = 1 To 5
                mOperator(iTest) = gSCEditOpers(iTestSet, iTest, iTest2)
                mTestValue(iTest) = gSCEditValue(iTestSet, iTest, iTest2)
            Next iTest2
        Case Is = JOINTMINMAX_TEST:
            mDataItem(1) = gSCEditItems(iTestSet, iTest, 1)
            mDataItem(2) = gSCEditItems(iTestSet, iTest, 2)
            For iTest2 = 1 To 4
                mOperator(iTest) = gSCEditOpers(iTestSet, iTest, iTest2)
                mTestValue(iTest) = gSCEditValue(iTestSet, iTest, iTest2)
            Next iTest2
        Case Is = TWOCRITTABLE_TEST:
            mDataItem(1) = gSCEditItems(iTestSet, iTest, 1)
            mDataItem(2) = gSCEditItems(iTestSet, iTest, 2)
            For iTest2 = 1 To 10
                mOperator(iTest) = gSCEditOpers(iTestSet, iTest, iTest2)
                mTestValue(iTest) = gSCEditValue(iTestSet, iTest, iTest2)
            Next iTest2
    End Select

End Sub
```

EXHIBIT 11.3   "FinSelect_AssignTestCriteriaConditions" subroutine

the contents or conditions of the test were, only its position in the test set. If it were the first test the value of the error code would be given by the formula:

```
error_code = 2 ^ (1-1) which is error_code = 2^0th = 1
```

If the current test were the 12th in the series, the formula would read as follows:

```
error_code = 2 ^ (12-1) which is error_code = 2^11th = 1,024
```

See Exhibit 11.4.

```
Sub FinSelect_IncrementIneligTotal(iTest As Integer)
    gLoanData(iloan, FD_CALCFINSELECT) = gLoanData(iloan, FD_CALCFINSELECT) + (2 ^ (iTest - 1))
End Sub
```

EXHIBIT 11.4   "FinSelect_IncrementIneligTotal" subroutine

```
Sub FinSelect_ApplySingleConditionTest(mSet As Integer, itest As Integer)

    mResult(1) = False
    Call FinSelect_AssignTestCriteriaConditions(mSet, itest)
    'each case is based on the value of the first operator
    Select Case mOperator(1)
        Case Is = 1
          If gLoanData(iloan, mDataItem(1)) <= mTestValue(1) Then mResult(1) = True
        Case Is = 2
          If gLoanData(iloan, mDataItem(1)) < mTestValue(1) Then mResult(1) = True
        Case Is = 3
           If gLoanData(iloan, mDataItem(1)) >= mTestValue(1) Then mResult(1) = True
        Case Is = 4
           If gLoanData(iloan, mDataItem(1)) > mTestValue(1) Then mResult(1) = True
        Case Is = 5
           If gLoanData(iloan, mDataItem(1)) = mTestValue(1) Then mResult(1) = True
        Case Is = 6
           If gLoanData(iloan, mDataItem(1)) <> mTestValue(1) Then mResult(1) = True
    End Select
    If mResult(1) Then Call FinSelect_IncrementIneligTotal(itest)

End Sub
```

EXHIBIT 11.5 "FinSelect_ApplySingleConditionTest" subroutine

Now we will look at a range of Financial Selection Tests from the simplest to the most complex.

Building a Simple Test: Test #1

The most simple test type is Test Type #1, "SINGLE_TEST". This test compares the value of a single collateral data record field to a single test value using a single test operator. An example of this type of test designed to eliminate high balance loans might be:

gLoanData(iloan, FD_CURRBAL) $<=$ 1,000,000

In this case we only need to populate the test with three operators from the "FinSelect_AssignTestCriteriaConditions" subroutines and perform the test. See Exhibit 11.5.

The "FinSelect_ApplySingleConditionTest" subroutine accepts the assigned test collateral data location in the collateral data in the array "mDataItem" in location "1" as it is the only collateral data needed. Likewise the test value is contained in the array "mTestValue(1)". The test is then performed using a "Select..Case" statement to branch the test to the correct test operator, a choice of either "$<$", "$<=$", "$>$", "$>=$", " $=$ " or "$<>$". Once the test result is calculated, it is assigned to "MTestResult(1)", and the error code value is calculated and added to the value of the "FD_CALCFINSELECT" collateral record file.

Building a Moderate Test: Test #3

A slightly more complicated test is that of Test Type #3, the "SINGLEMINMAX_TEST". Here the general form of the test is a single-criterion test (Test Type #1), combined with a minimum/maximum value test. This test could be written as:

```
       (X < TestValue(1)) AND
(Y > TestValue(2) AND Y < TestValue(3))
```

The two "AND" operators are fixed and not at the discretion of the analyst to modify, but the two "<" operators and the ">" operator can be set by the analyst to any of the six operator values we saw earlier. In this case the "FinSelect_ AssignTestCriteriaConditions" subroutine would choose the third case in the "Select..Case" statement and assign a total of three "TestValues" using the "mTestValue" array and two collateral data field values using the "mDataItem" array. See Exhibit 11.6.

```
Sub FinSelect_ApplySingleWithMinMaxTest(mSet As Integer, itest As Integer)

    Call FinSelect_AssignTestCriteriaConditions(mSet, itest)
    mResult(1) = False    'result of single type test
    mResult(2) = False    'result on minimum value test
    mResult(3) = False    'result of maximum value test
    'PART #1
    'Single Type Test
    Select Case mOperator(1)
      Case Is = 1
        If gLoanData(iloan, mDataItem(1)) <= mTestValue(1) Then mResult(1) = True
      Case Is = 2
        If gLoanData(iloan, mDataItem(1)) < mTestValue(1) Then mResult(1) = True
      Case Is = 3
        If gLoanData(iloan, mDataItem(1)) >= mTestValue(1) Then mResult(1) = True
      Case Is = 4
        If gLoanData(iloan, mDataItem(1)) > mTestValue(1) Then mResult(1) = True
      Case Is = 5
        If gLoanData(iloan, mDataItem(1)) = mTestValue(1) Then mResult(1) = True
      Case Is = 6
        If gLoanData(iloan, mDataItem(1)) <> mTestValue(1) Then mResult(1) = True
    End Select
    'PART #2 -- Minimum Maximum Test
    'Minimum condition of the test
    Select Case mOperator(2)
      Case Is = 1
        If gLoanData(iloan, mDataItem(2)) <= mTestValue(2) Then mResult(2) = True
      Case Is = 2
        If gLoanData(iloan, mDataItem(2)) < mTestValue(2) Then mResult(2) = True
    End Select
    'Maximum condition of the test
    Select Case mOperator(3)
      Case Is = 1
        If gLoanData(iloan, mDataItem(3)) > mTestValue(3) Then mResult(3) = True
      Case Is = 2
        If gLoanData(iloan, mDataItem(3)) >= mTestValue(3) Then mResult(3) = True
    End Select
    'If the single test condition is TRUE, and if the value violates either the
    'minimum or maximum condition then we have an ineligiblity condition
    If (mResult(1) And (mResult(2) Or mResult(3))) Then
        Call FinSelect_IncrementIneligTotal(itest)
    End If

End Sub
```

EXHIBIT 11.6 "FinSelect_ApplySingleWithMinMaxTest" subroutine

Building a Complex Test: Test #6

The last and most complex test, that of Test Type #6, takes the form of a table of paired tests in which two different data items from the collateral record are tested by a set of up to ten test values. The general form of the test is as follows:

```
((X = TestValue(1)) AND (Y <= TestValue(2))) OR
((X = TestValue(3)) AND (Y <= TestValue(4))) OR
((X = TestValue(5)) AND (Y <= TestValue(6))) OR
((X = TestValue(7)) AND (Y <= TestValue(8))) OR
((X = TestValue(9)) AND (Y <= TestValue(10)))
```

A practical application of this type of test is to exclude large balance mortgages from the pool by their mortgage type as follows:

```
((MortgageType = 1) AND (CurrentBalance <= 1500,00)) OR
((MortgageType = 3) AND (CurrentBalance <= 2000000)) OR
((MortgageType = 5) AND (CurrentBalance <= 1250000)) OR
((MortgageType = 7) AND (CurrentBalance <= 2000000)) OR
((MortgageType = 9) AND (CurrentBalance <= 1000000))
```

Here, however, we need to populate the test with two collateral data field items, ten test values, and then determine the two test operators for each of the clauses of the test (which we will evaluate on a one-by-one basis). See Exhibit 11.7.

FINANCIAL COLLATERAL SELECTION PROCESS REPORTING

After the collateral records have been subjected to the Financial/Demographic Screening process, we can now proceed to reporting the results!

Ineligible Collateral Report Package

The Ineligible Collateral Report package is one of the largest report packages of the CCFG. It contains a total of 23 individual reports. These are:

- **Financial/Demographic Selection Criteria Report.** This report lists all of the financial/demographic selection criteria that we created at the beginning of the selection process. It is identical in form and content to the "FinCriteriaReport" worksheet that we use to display the tests of the various selection criteria sets within the CCFG.
- **Individual Ineligibility Reports.** There are 20 Individual Ineligibility reports in the template. This number corresponds to the maximum number of criteria. Each report is a list of loans that have failed that individual test. As we have seen, a loan can fail more than one test in the selection process. In that case the loan will be listed on each of the individual test criteria reports that it has failed. Each of these reports is a separate worksheet in the report file and is named "Inelig#".

```
Sub FinSelect_ApplyTwoCriteriaTableTest(iTestSet As Integer, iTest As Integer)

Dim ipart              As Integer     'nth clause of test
Dim found_first_clause As Boolean     'found the first stage test

   Call FinSelect_AssignTestCriteriaConditions(iTestSet, iTest)
   For ipart = 1 To 5
      'set the assumption that the collateral passes the test
      test_fails = False         'overall test is false, collateral eligible
      mResult(1) = False         'clause 1 of each test
      mResult(2) = False         'clause 2 of each test
      found_first_clause = False 'test has been conducted for this loop
      'select case based on the comparison oeprator of the first clause
      Select Case mOperator(ipart)
         Case Is = 1:
            If gLoanData(iloan, mDataItem(1)) <= mTestValue(ipart) Then
               found_first_clause = True:  mResult(1) = True
               Call FinSelect_TestSecondCondition(ipart)
            End If
         Case Is = 2:
            If gLoanData(iloan, mDataItem(1)) < mTestValue(ipart) Then
               found_first_clause = True:  mResult(1) = True
               Call FinSelect_TestSecondCondition(ipart)
            End If
         Case Is = 3:
            If gLoanData(iloan, mDataItem(1)) >= mTestValue(ipart) Then
               found_first_clause = True:  mResult(1) = True
               Call FinSelect_TestSecondCondition(ipart)
            End If
         Case Is = 4:
            If gLoanData(iloan, mDataItem(1)) > mTestValue(ipart) Then
               found_first_clause = True:  mResult(1) = True
               Call FinSelect_TestSecondCondition(ipart)
            End If
         Case Is = 5:
            If gLoanData(iloan, mDataItem(1)) = mTestValue(ipart) Then
               found_first_clause = True:  mResult(1) = True
               Call FinSelect_TestSecondCondition(ipart)
            End If
         Case Is = 6:
            If gLoanData(iloan, mDataItem(1)) <> mTestValue(ipart) Then
               found_first_clause = True:  mResult(1) = True
               Call FinSelect_TestSecondCondition(ipart)
            End If
      End Select
      If found_first_clause Then
         If mResult(1) And mResult(2) Then test_fails = True   'ineligible
         If test_fails Then Exit For                           'exit loop
      End If
   Next ipart
   'assign the ineligibiltiy tag
   If test_fails Then Call FinSelect_IncrementIneligTotal(iTest)

End Sub
```

EXHIBIT 11.7 "FinSelect_ApplyTwoCriteriaTableTest" subroutine

- **Loan Listing Exception Report.** This report lists all ineligible loans and provides a set of columns, much like those of the Initial Data Screening report package that tick off each of the criteria tests that the loan has failed to pass. In addition to the grid of up to 20 ineligibility conditions, additional information is provided concerning the loan. These fields describe the loan to help in spotting patterns of ineligibility conditions.

Financial/Demographic Information Criteria Test Set Report

Set: 1

Test #	Test Type	Test Conditions								
1	1	Current Balance	LT	2500000						
2	2	Original Balance	GT	5000	AND	Original Balance	LE	2750000		
3	3	Credit Sector	EQ	1	AND					
		Current Coupon Rate	LE	3.50%	OR	Current Coupon Rate	GE	17.00%		
4	4	Mortgage Type	EQ	1	OR					
		Mortgage Type	EQ	2	OR					
		Mortgage Type	EQ	4	OR					
		Mortgage Type	EQ	5	OR					
		Mortgage Type	EQ	6						
5	5	Property Type	LE	5	AND	Property Type	GE	2	AND	
		Current Loan-to-Value Ratio	LE	90.00%	AND	Current Loan-to-Value Ratio	GE	50.00%		
6	6	Original Term (months)	EQ	360	AND	Remaining Term (months)	GT	300	OR	
		Original Term (months)	EQ	240	AND	Remaining Term (months)	GT	200	OR	
		Original Term (months)	EQ	180	AND	Remaining Term (months)	GT	150	OR	
		Original Term (months)	EQ	120	AND	Remaining Term (months)	GT	108	OR	
		Original Term (months)	EQ	60	AND	Remaining Term (months)	GT	54		

EXHIBIT 11.8   Financial/Demographic Selection Criteria Report

■ **Summary Ineligibility Report.** This report groups all ineligible collateral by its unique pattern of individual ineligible conditions. Summary statistics for the groups are presented to the right of the report.

We will look at the preparation of these reports in the order presented above.

Financial/Demographic Selection Criteria Report

This report is nothing more than the in-model report that we use to review the selection test sets we have constructed. See Exhibit 11.8.

This report is written by a variation of the subroutine that populates the in-model report. In this subroutine the calling subroutine passes the argument of "iport". This allows the "RepUserInelig_PrintSelectionCriteriaReport" subroutine to associate the pool or sub-portfolio to the correct selection criteria set based on the inputs from the Run Options Menu. The elections of the analyst entered into the Run Options Menu designating the Financial Selection Criteria set to use is stored in the variable "gROTestSetFinDemo". All we need to do is to match the value in "gROTest-SetFinDemo(iport)" to the set number and we can print out the appropriate set of selection criteria! You will note from that point forward the subroutine makes use of the test-specific reporting subroutines we developed in the Financial Selection module. See Exhibit 11.9.

Preparatory Work   In that there is a possibility that we may have to create multiple Ineligible Collateral Report Packages, one for each sub-portfolio, we need to do a bit of preparation before we immediately start writing reports.

In the subroutine "RepUserInelig_MainWriteReports", the main subroutine for the Ineligible Collateral reporting process will do just that. This subroutine manages the Ineligible Collateral reporting process from start to finish. See Exhibit 11.10.

```
Sub RepUserInelig_PrintSelectionCriteriaReport()

    Call FinSelect_TestAndSetIsNumericsCheck(ISNUMERIC_SET_ONLY)
    If gIsNumericFail Then Exit Sub
    Cells(4, 2) = mTestSet
    'see if we need to read the selection item names
    gReadFinancialNames = gReadFinancialNames + 1
    If gReadFinancialNames = 1 Then
        Call FinSelect_ReadDataItemNames
        Sheets("FinCriteriaReport").Select
    End If
    'clear the contents from the existing report
    Call FinSelect_ClearReportWorksheet
    'write the test set indicated
    irow = 9
    For itest = 1 To NUM_SEL_TESTS
        If gSCTestActive(mTestSet, itest) Then   'is this an active test/
            Cells(irow, 1).Value = itest
            Cells(irow, 2).Value = gSCEditType(mTestSet, itest)
            Cells(irow, 3).Value = "["
            Select Case gSCEditType(mTestSet, itest)
                Case Is = 1: Call FinSelect_WriteTestType1
                Case Is = 2: Call FinSelect_WriteTestType2
                Case Is = 3: Call FinSelect_WriteTestType3
                Case Is = 4: Call FinSelect_WriteTestType4
                Case Is = 5: Call FinSelect_WriteTestType5
                Case Is = 6: Call FinSelect_WriteTestType6
            End Select
            irow = irow + 2      'put a blank line between tests
        End If
    Next itest

End Sub
```

EXHIBIT 11.9 "RepUserInelig_PrintSelectionCriteriaReport" subroutine

```
Sub RepUserInelig_MainWriteReports()

    If gRepMenuIneligUser Then
        Call RepUserInelig_SetActiveWorkbooksTag  'determine # of active workbooks
        Call RepUserInelig_PrepareWorkbooks       'configure workbooks
        For iport = 0 To NUM_PORTS
            mMaxFailedTestSelect = 0
            If mActiveSubPortReps(iport) Then
                Workbooks.Open FileName:=mIneligReportName(iport)
                Call RepUserInelig_WriteSelectionResultsReport(iport)
                If iport = 0 Then Exit For
            End If
            ActiveWorkbook.Save
            ActiveWorkbook.Close
        Next iport
        gRepMenuAssumptions = True
    End If

End Sub
```

EXHIBIT 11.10 "RepUserInelig_MainWriteReports" subroutine

```
Sub RepUserInelig_SetActiveWorkbooksTag()

    If gPoolLevelData Then
        mActiveSubPortReps(0) = True              'pool is active
        For iport = 1 To NUM_SEL_TESTS
            mActiveSubPortReps(iport) = False     'all sub-portfolios inactive
        Next iport
    Else
        mActiveSubPortReps(0) = False             'pool is inactive
        For iport = 1 To NUM_PORTS
            If gROTestSetFinDemo(iport) > 0 Then  'test if sub-portfolio is active
                mActiveSubPortReps(iport) = True
            End If
        Next iport
    End If

End Sub
```

EXHIBIT 11.11   "RepUserInelig_SetActiveWorkbooksTag" subroutine

Before we do another thing we should first check if any of the following activities are necessary at all! We resolve this important question by checking the value of the variable "gRepMenuIneligUser" to determine if we are going to produce the reports containing the information generated by this process. If we are not requesting this report, we immediately branch out of the entire selection process subroutine! If we *are* going to produce the report, then the next subroutine call is to the "RepUser-Inelig_SetActiveWorkbooksTag" subroutine, which establishes if we are going to report on pool versus sub-portfolio level data. If we have pool level data, it will set the value of the 0th element in the array "mActiveSubPortReps" to TRUE and the remaining elements 1 to 5, representing the sub-portfolios, to FALSE. If we do not have pool level data, it will set the 0th element of the array to FALSE and then test each of the five sub-portfolios to determine which of them are active. From this we will know if we need a single Ineligible Collateral report package for pool level data or a number of reports for various sub-portfolios. See Exhibit 11.11.

Once we have made this determination, we next call the subroutine "RepUser Inelig_PrepareWorkbooks". Based on the pool versus sub-portfolio determination made in "RepUserInelig_SetActiveWorkbooksTag", we can now set up as many Ineligible Collateral Selection report packages as we need. This subroutine performs a series of fairly obvious steps. These are:

1. Makes sure that the arrays containing the names and codes of the states and MSA geographical entities have been read and are stored in the VBA arrays of the CCFG where we can get at them.
2. Assigns the pathway to the Ineligible Collateral Report Package template file to the variable "tempFile" (much easier to read later below)!
3. Makes the determination between pool level and sub-portfolio level collateral files based on the value of the variable "gPollLevelData".
4. If the data is at the pool level, then the model opens the template file and renames it to a "POOL_" prefix. We next customize the template file for the expected pool level selection criteria.
5. It loads the selection criteria test names contained in the array "gSCEditTest Name" into the various worksheets of the report package as needed.
6. If there are fewer than the full complement of 20 selection tests, the subroutine "RepUserInelig_DeleteUnusedSingleTestSheets" deletes the unused Individual

Ineligibility Report sheets. It also removes the references to these individual tests from the two summary reports.

7. The subroutine "RepUserInelig_PrintSelectionCriteriaReport" is called to print the Selection Criteria Tests as we have seen above.

8. The finished workbook is now ready to have reports written to it. It is saved and then closed.

9. If at Step 2 above the data are determined to be in a series of sub-portfolios, each with potentially different selection criteria sets, the subroutine tests each sub-portfolio in turn. Using the values contained in the array "mActiveSubPortReps", it will create a separate Ineligible Collateral report package file for each active sub-portfolio. These are sequentially created, edited, saved, and closed in the same sequence of steps just described for the pool level file.

Due to length constraints we will not specifically review either of the editing subroutines "RepUserInelig_DeleteUnusedSingleTestSheets" or "RepUserInelig_PrintSelectionCriteriaReport" (although readers are invited to do so on their own!). The "RepUserInelig_PrepareWorkbooks" subroutine is in Exhibit 11.12.

Building a "Traffic Cop" Subroutine to Run Things   A single or collection of Ineligible Collateral Report Packages have now been customized and are available to write our reports to. Having already disposed of the first report in the workbook, the Financial/Demographic Selection Criteria Report above, we can proceed immediately to the preparation of the Individual Ineligibility reports. These reports list any loan that has failed the particular test represented by the report.

We may now have up to 20 Individual Ineligibility reports to write, plus the Loan Listing Exception report and the Summary Ineligibility report! To manage this process we need a subroutine to play the role of traffic cop. When you are writing large report packages, a subroutine much like the one you are about to see is a valuable tool. You can use it to loop thorough a collection of similar or dissimilar reports based on how you wish the completed report package to be configured. It also serves as the main framework on which to base the sequencing of calls to each subroutine that produces a specific report. Its general organizational form is a loop with a "Select..Case" statement inside of it. The general form is as follows:

```
Sub WriteReportPackage
    For iReport = 1 to LARGE_NUM_REPORTS
        Select Case iReport
            Case <= 20: Call Write_ReportType1
            Case <= 22: Call Write_ReportType2
            Case <= 26: Call Write_ReportType3
            Case <= LARGE_NUM_REPORTS: Call Write_ReportType4
        End Select
    Next iReport
End Sub
```

The subroutine "RepUserInelig_WriteSelectionResultsReport" is exactly this type of subroutine, and we will design it to populate the reports of the Ineligible Collateral report packages we have just created. See Exhibit 11.13.

```
Sub RepUserInelig_PrepareWorkbooks()

Dim rep_suffix          As String    'identifying report suffix
Dim tempFile            As String    'pathway of the template file

    'CONSTRUCTS AND CONFIGURES THE USER SELECTION CRITERIA TEMPLATE FILES AND SAVES
    ' THEM.  UNUSED SINGLE TEST SHEETS ARE DELETED AND THE LOAN LISTING AND SUMMARY
    ' REPORTS ARE REFORMATTED.  THE SELECTION CRITERIA FOR THIS SET IS PRINTED ON AN
    ' ASSUMPTIONS PAGE.
    'see if we need to read the selection item names
    gReadFinancialNames = gReadFinancialNames + 1
    If gReadFinancialNames = 1 Then
        Call FinSelect_ReadDataItemNames
        Sheets("FinCriteriaReport").Select
    End If
    If gRepMenuIneligUser Then
        tempFile = DIR_TEMPLATE_REP & COLLAT_USER_INELIGIBLE_TEMPLATE
        If gPoolLevelData Then
          'POOL LEVEL DATA ONLY
          Workbooks.Open FileName:=tempFile
          rep_suffix = "POOL_"
          mIneligReportName(0) = _
              OUTPUT_DIRECTORY & gRepMenuPrefix & rep_suffix & "IneligCollat"
          ActiveWorkbook.SaveAs FileName:=mIneligReportName(0)
          'find the user specified financial criteria test set to the POOL
          Call RepUserInelig_DetermineActiveTestsPerSet
          mTestSet = gROTestSetFinDemo(0)                'criteria set of this pool
          Call RepUserInelig_AddTestNamesToWorksheets
          Call RepUserInelig_DeleteUnusedSingleTestSheets
          Call RepUserInelig_PrintSelectionCriteriaReport
          ActiveWorkbook.Save
          ActiveWorkbook.Close
        Else
          'SUB-PORTFOLIO LEVEL DATA ONLY
          Call RepUserInelig_DetermineActiveTestsPerSet
          For iport = 1 To NUM_PORTS
              If mActiveSubPortReps(iport) Then
                  Workbooks.Open FileName:=tempFile
                  'set up the file, contruct report name prefix, name it and save
                  rep_suffix = "SUBPORT_" & iport
                  mIneligReportName(iport) = _
                      OUTPUT_DIRECTORY & gRepMenuPrefix & rep_suffix & _
                      "IneligCollat"
                  ActiveWorkbook.SaveAs FileName:=mIneligReportName(iport)
                  mTestSet = gROTestSetFinDemo(iport)    'criteria set this sub-port
                  Call RepUserInelig_AddTestNamesToWorksheets
                  Call RepUserInelig_DeleteUnusedSingleTestSheets
                  Call RepUserInelig_PrintSelectionCriteriaReport
                  ActiveWorkbook.Save
                  ActiveWorkbook.Close
              End If
          Next iport
        End If
    End If

End Sub
```

EXHIBIT 11.12   "RepUserInelig_PrepareWorkbooks" subroutine

This subroutine performs the following steps:

1. For the pool or sub-portfolio being reported on, it immediately determines the largest error code present in any of the loans in the portfolio. Subroutine "RepUserInelig_FindMaximumErrorScore" is called to perform this test. This subroutine will also quite usefully return a Boolean variable, "mOneFailedTest Select". If this variable is set to TRUE, there is at least one ineligible loan in this

```
Sub RepUserInelig_WriteSelectionResultsReport(iport As Integer)

    'determine the maximum error code for the portfolio
    Call RepUserInelig_FindMaximumErrorScore(iport)
    Call RepUserInelig_FindActiveIneligReports(iport)
    'report workbook is now prepared, print the ineligible collateral reports
    mTotalIneligReps = USER_SELECT_REPORTS
    If mOneFailedTestSelect Then 'at least one loan failed!
        'open the prepared template report
        Workbooks.Open FileName:=mIneligReportName(iport)
        For i_sheet = 1 To mTotalIneligReps + 2
            Select Case i_sheet
                Case Is <= mTotalIneligReps      'individual ineligibility report
                    If mActiveIneligReports(i_sheet) Then
                        sheet_name = "Inelig" & i_sheet
                        Sheets(sheet_name).Select
                        Range("A1").Select
                        Call RepUserInelig_WriteIndCriteriaReport(iport, i_sheet)
                    Else
                        Sheets(sheet_name).Delete
                    End If
                Case Is = mTotalIneligReps + 1   'loan listing report
                    Sheets("IneligALL").Select
                    Call RepUserInelig_WriteLoanListingReport(iport)
                Case Is = mTotalIneligReps + 2   'summary report
                    Sheets("IneligSUM").Select
                    Call RepUserInelig_WriteSummaryReport(iport)
            End Select
        Next i_sheet
        ActiveWorkbook.Save
        ActiveWorkbook.Close
    End If

End Sub
```

EXHIBIT 11.13 "RepUserInelig_WriteSelectionResultsReport" subroutine

portfolio. If not, we can save ourselves a lot of work immediately by skipping the entire reporting activity!

2. The subroutine "RepUserInelig_FindActiveIneligReports" is now called. This subroutine determines how many loans have failed to pass each ineligibility test. It counts these loans, by test, and stores them in the array "mErrorTestCount".

3. If at least one loan in the portfolio is ineligible, it opens the prepared Ineligible Collateral Report Package for the pool or sub-portfolio based on the value of "iport".

4. It will now loop through the number of Individual Reports+2. The "+2" is to accommodate the Loan Listing Exception Report and the Summary Ineligibility Report at the end of the report package.

5. Based on the value of the loop, it will select the appropriate worksheet into which it will write the report. It may be one of the Individual reports, "Inelig1" to "Inelig20", or "IneligAll" for the Loan Listing report, or "IneligSUM" for the Summary Ineligible Report.

6. If the value of the "i_sheet" counter in the loop is less than or equal to the maximum number of Individual Reports, it will call "RepUserInelig_WriteIndividual CriteriaReport"; at "+1" it will call "RepUserInelig_WriteLoanListingReport"; and at "+2" it will call "RepUserInelig_WriteSummaryReport".

7. After the last report is written, it will save and close the workbook, now a completed Ineligible Collateral Report Package!

We are now ready to turn to the VBA subroutine that will write these three types of reports.

Individual Ineligibility Reports

In the subroutine "RepUserInelig_WriteSelectionResultsReport", we can see that the first 20 times through the main loop, we will be writing, or determining if we should be writing, an Individual Ineligibility report. We will check the array "mActiveIneligReports(n)" where *n* is the value of the loop from 1 to 20. If the value of the array cell is TRUE, we have loans that have failed this test. We therefore select the sheet "Inelig(n)" upon which to write the report. If the value is FALSE, we do not need to write this report and we will delete it.

We call "RepUserInelig_WriteIndCriteriaReport" if the "i_sheet" counter is less than the value of the variable "mTotalIneligReps". The task of this subroutine is to populate the report displayed in Exhibit 11.14. The uppermost set of report columns display the right side of the report while the lower portion exhibits the left side.

The subroutine "RepUserInelig_WriteIndCriteriaReport" employs a single large loop to populate an Individual Criterion report. As we enter the subroutine, we will immediately assign the column locations to two variables. These are named, rather prosaically, "Col1" and "Col2". These two variables are the inputs for a small utility function that will draw a light line across the bottom of every fifth record we write to the report. These are called "sight lines," and they are a nice touch to any report. They help the reader keep track of what line they are looking at in wide or lengthy

Single Criteria Ineligibility Report
INELIGIBLE-6 Financing Purpose Purchase or Refinance

Count	Loan Number	Pool or Sub-Port Number	Loan Type	Selection Criteria #1	Selection Criteria #2	Current Coupon	Current Loan Balance	Original Loan Balance	Current Loan-To-Value Ratio	Original Loan-To-Value Ratio	Remain Term	Original Term
553							147,093,242	147,941,610				
1	7	0	SARM	Financing Purpose	NA	5.350%	82,632	83,200	83%	85%	354	360
2	12	0	SARM	Financing Purpose	NA	5.225%	134,106	135,100	80%	81%	178	180
3	14	0	SARM	Financing Purpose	NA	4.975%	93,030	93,600	76%	77%	355	360
4	20	0	SARM	Financing Purpose	NA	4.975%	288,370	292,700	73%	75%	234	240
5	32	0	SARM	Financing Purpose	NA	5.225%	431,202	432,200	83%	81%	358	360
6	56	0	SARM	Financing Purpose	NA	4.975%	193,754	194,700	76%	75%	356	360
7	67	0	SARM	Financing Purpose	NA	4.975%	948,607	955,600	70%	72%	354	360
8	72	0	SARM	Financing Purpose	NA	5.475%	81,147	81,600	72%	72%	355	360
9	75	0	SARM	Financing Purpose	NA	5.350%	187,163	187,800	85%	85%	357	360
10	80	0	SARM	Financing Purpose	NA	5.100%	333,810	335,000	79%	78%	357	360

Season	Current Appraisal Value	Current Appraisal Type	Original Appraisal Value	Original Appraisal Type	Property Type	Occupancy Code	State	Statistical Metropolitan Area
			191,815,000					
6	99,000	Walk Through	98,000	Walk Through	Single Fam	Owner	CA	
2	168,000	Outside	167,000	Walk Through	Single Fam	Owner	NY	
5	122,000	No Data	121,000	Walk Through	Single Fam	Owner	CA	
6	397,000	Walk Through	392,000	Walk Through	Single Fam	Owner	RI	Providence-New Bedford-Fall River
2	519,000	Outside	532,000	Walk Through	Single Fam	Owner	MO	Kansas City
4	256,000	Drive By	261,000	Walk Through	Single Fam	Owner	NY	
6	1,349,000	Outside	1,330,000	Walk Through	Single Fam	Owner	CA	Los Angeles-Long Beach-Santa Ana
5	112,000	Outside	114,000	Walk Through	Single Fam	Owner	OH	Dayton
3	219,000	Walk Through	222,000	Walk Through	Single Fam	Owner	HI	Honolulu
3	422,000	Drive By	431,000	Walk Through	Single Fam	Owner	OH	

EXHIBIT 11.14   Single Criterion Ineligibility report (left side of report (top), right side of report (bottom))

reports. Next we construct the Range name that we will be writing the body of the report to. In that we may have up to 20 Single Criterion Ineligibility Reports (SCIRs), we have assigned a different range name to each of the report worksheets in the Ineligible Collateral Report Package. Thus the contents of the first SCIR will be written into the Range "IndBody1", the second SCIR into "IndBody2", and so on to the 20th report. This will make it easy for us to modify these reports in that we will be able to add or subtract columns without changing the Range name references in the report writing subroutine.

The bulk of the rest of the subroutine is simply the transfer of the information from the ineligible record to the report. As we enter the loop that will examine each of the loans, we will check to see that the value "gLoanOK" is FALSE, that the loan is ineligible, and that it belongs to the pool or sub-portfolio of this report. We can compare the value of the loan record's "FD_POOLID" field to make this determination. Next we need to determine that this record has failed this particular SCIR test. In the subroutine "RepUserInelig_FindActiveIneligReports", we populated the array "mSelectionTag". This array is Boolean in type and has one row for each loan and a column for each Single Criteria test. If the loan has failed the test, the array location of the test is set to TRUE. An "If" statement now tests the cell location for this loan that is the column location of the test. If the "mSelectionTag" array location is TRUE, we write the record to the file. Also note that a number of columns of the report reference the array "gRFLabels". This allows us to place a label in the field instead of a numeric code. It is easier to understand the contents of the field "Property Type" if the content of the report field is "Single Fam" rather than "2"! The fields with label output are the following:

1 Mortgage Type

16 Current Appraisal Type

18 Original Appraisal Type

19 Property Code

20 Occupancy Code

21 State Postal Code (2-letter U. S. Postal Service abbreviation)

22 MSA Location Name (if the loan is in an MSA)

After writing the loan information an "If" test checks if the row number we just finished is divisible evenly by five. This is the "irow Mod 5 = 0" test. It then increments the row counter by one for the next record and completes the loop. See Exhibit 11.15.

Loan Listing Exception Report

Having completed the group of SCIRs, we now need a different type of report to clarify a portion of the ineligibility picture of the portfolio. Each of these reports tells us the loans that have failed a particular eligibility criterion. This is useful; otherwise we would not have gone through the trouble to construct the report! It does not, however, give us the "big picture." A loan may have failed 2, 3, 5, or even all 20 of the tests. We would only know this by painstakingly combining all the SGIRs and

```
Sub RepUserInelig_WriteIndCriteriaReport(iport As Integer, rep_num As Integer)

Dim mRange       As String
Dim tSet         As Integer

    irow = 1                              'print position in the range
    col1 = "B": col2 = "W"                'beg/end column to draw guideline
    mRange = "IndBody" & rep_num
    tSet = gROTestSetFinDemo(iport)
    'Run through the portfolio for the exceptions
    For iloan = 1 To gTotalLoans
        If mSelectionTag(iloan, rep_num) And gLoanData(iloan, FD_POOLID) = iport Then
            If mSelectionTag(iloan, rep_num) Then   'read the sel_tag for a match
                Range(mRange).Cells(irow, 1) = irow
                Range(mRange).Cells(irow, 2) = iloan
                Range(mRange).Cells(irow, 3) = gLoanData(iloan, FD_POOLID)
                Range(mRange).Cells(irow, 4) = _
                        gRFLabels(FD_MORTTYPE, gLoanData(iloan, FD_MORTTYPE))
                'Selection Criteria
                Range(mRange).Cells(irow, 5) = _
                    gFinSelNames(gSCEditItems(tSet, rep_num, 1))
                If IsNumeric(gSCEditItems(tSet, rep_num, 2)) Then
                    If gSCEditItems(tSet, rep_num, 2) <> 0 Then
                        Range(mRange).Cells(irow, 6) = _
                                gFinSelNames(gSCEditItems(tSet, rep_num, 2))
                    Else
                        Range(mRange).Cells(irow, 6) = "NA"
                    End If
                Else
                    Range(mRange).Cells(irow, 6) = "NA"
                End If
                'Loan data
                Range(mRange).Cells(irow, 7) = gLoanData(iloan, FD_CURRRATE)
                Range(mRange).Cells(irow, 8) = gLoanData(iloan, FD_CURRBAL)
                Range(mRange).Cells(irow, 9) = gLoanData(iloan, FD_ORIGBAL)
                Range(mRange).Cells(irow, 10) = gLoanData(iloan, FD_CURRLTV)
                Range(mRange).Cells(irow, 11) = gLoanData(iloan, FD_ORIGLTV)
                Range(mRange).Cells(irow, 12) = gLoanData(iloan, FD_REMTERM)
                Range(mRange).Cells(irow, 13) = gLoanData(iloan, FD_ORIGTERM)
                Range(mRange).Cells(irow, 14) = gLoanData(iloan, FD_SEASON)
                Range(mRange).Cells(irow, 15) = gLoanData(iloan, FD_CURRAPP)
                Range(mRange).Cells(irow, 16) = _
                        gRFLabels(FD_CURRAPPTYPE, gLoanData(iloan, FD_CURRAPPTYPE))
                Range(mRange).Cells(irow, 17) = gLoanData(iloan, FD_ORIGAPP)
                Range(mRange).Cells(irow, 18) = _
                        gRFLabels(FD_ORIGAPPTYPE, gLoanData(iloan, FD_ORIGAPPTYPE))
                Range(mRange).Cells(irow, 19) = _
                        gRFLabels(FD_PROPTYPE, gLoanData(iloan, FD_PROPTYPE))
                Range(mRange).Cells(irow, 20) = _
                        gRFLabels(FD_OCCPCODE, gLoanData(iloan, FD_OCCPCODE))
                Range(mRange).Cells(irow, 21) = _
                        gStatePostal(gLoanData(iloan, FD_STATECODE))
                Range(mRange).Cells(irow, 22) = _
                        Utility_MSANameFromMSANumericCode(iloan)
                If irow Mod 5 = 0 Then
                    Call Utility_DrawLineUnderRowRange(col1, col2, irow + 10)
                End If
                irow = irow + 1
            End If
        End If
    Next iloan

End Sub
```

EXHIBIT 11.15   "RepUserInelig_WriteIndCriteriaReport" subroutine

sorting through them. To avoid that messy and annoying task, we have the Loan Listing Report.

The role of the Loan Listing Report is to produce a loan-by-loan list of each loan that has an ineligibility condition and report the particular pattern to us. Thus we can tell, at a glance for any loan that is ineligible, how many Selection Criteria tests it has failed. The format of the Loan Listing report is shown in Exhibit 11.16. The header section lists each of the test conditions for the 20 possible SCIRs. On the left side of the report there is a section of 20 narrow columns under the header "Ineligibility Conditions". If a loan has failed any of the SCIR tests, a "1" is placed in the appropriate column. This will serve to identify the number and pattern of the ineligibility conditions of the loan. We will also know how many loans have failed a particular test because the report sums the number of "1"'s in each of the columns and places it in the second line of the "Ineligibility Conditions" section. The center and right side of the report contains 17 data fields that display a selection of the individual loan's demographic and financial information. A sample of six different loans subjected to six criteria tests is displayed on the top in Exhibit 11.16.

The subroutine "RepUserInelig_WriteLoanListingReport" populates the Loan Listing report. Its organization is broadly similar to the SCIR format except we now have the grid that displays the individual ineligibility conditions for each of the loans in addition to the loan information at the right of the report. If you look at Exhibit 11.16 (top), you will see the header of the report displaying 17 test conditions and the grid below indicating which of the tests these ten loans failed. Note the column total that tells us how many loans have failed each of the criteria.

Now let us look at the VBA that produces this report. There are four different Ranges on the report. These are in order from left to right:

1. "**ALLCount**". Column B, the *n*th loan of the report.
2. "**ALLLoanNum**". Column C, the loan number of the item.
3. "**ALLGrid**". Columns D to W, the single criterion that has made the loan ineligible.
4. "**ALLBody**". Columns X to AN, the 17 columns of financial and demographic information to help us identify the loan.

All of the output statements of the subroutine will concentrate on these four Ranges. As with the "RepUserInelig_WriteIndCriteriaReport" subroutine, the main structure of "RepUserInelig_WriteLoanListingReport" is that of a single large "For..Next" loop that runs through all of the loans of the portfolio. It performs two tests: (1) Is the loan in the correct portfolio? and (2) Is the loan ineligibility score greater than zero? If the answer to both of these tests is TRUE, we output the loan to the report. You will note that in regard to this report, we do not need to test if the loan has violated any particular Single Criteria test as we did with the Individual Ineligibility report. *Any* ineligibility condition qualifies a loan to be written to the report, somewhat simplifying matters.

We write the value of the variable "irow" into the "Total Loans Rejected" column. The cell at the top of the column has a "max" function that will return the highest number in the column telling us how many records we have written. We then enter the Loan ID number in "ALLLoanNum" Range. Next we print out the results of each of the SCIRs in the "ALLGrid" Range. As we loop through each of

Loan Listing Exception Report
Individual Loan Ineligibility Conditions

Ineligibility Condition Reference

Condition	Description
1 = Current Balance 25,000 to 1,000,000	7 = Bankruptcy Never or Discharged
2 = Current Loan-to-Value LE 95%	8 = Third Party Due Diligence Better Than "Poor"
3 = Original Appraisal Not "Walk Through"	9 = Full or Partial Documentation, No Alt-A
4 = Property Type Known, Not Multi-Family	10 = Servicing Rating Better Than "Poor"
5 = Occupancy Type No Seasonal	11 = Mortgage Debt-to-Income LE 45%
6 = Financing Purpose Purchase or Refinance	12 = Total Debt-to-Income LE 75%
13 = Seasoning Greater Than 1 Month	
14 = No Alt-A, No Sub-Prime	
15 = Original Loan-to-Value LE 85%	
16 = Cannot be in a Delinquent Status	
17 = Original Term > 180 Months	

Total Loans Rejected	Loan Number	1	2	3	4	5	6	7	8	9	10	11	12	13	14	15	16	17	18	19	20
1985		259	0	0	60	65	553	237	67	101	17	427	314	310	0	258	46	495	0	0	0
	1					1															
	3						1											1			
	7						1											1			
	12						1											1			
	14						1														
	15							1													
	20						1	1			1										
	21								1					1			1				
	23															1					
	25																				

Loan Financial and Demographic Information

1 Mortgage Type	2 Credit Sector	3 Current Balance	4 Original Balance	5 Current Coupon	6 Remaining Term	7 Current LTV	8 Original LTV	9 Current Appraisal Amount	10 Original Appraisal Amount	11 Property Type	12 Occupancy Code	13 Financing Purpose	14 Mortgage Debt-to-Income	15 Total Debt-to-Income	16 State Code	17 MSA Location
		291,612,595	293,424,640					379,312,000	381,128,000							
SARM	Prime	80,719	83,200	5.225%	172	75%	78%	108,000	107,000	Single Fam	Owner	Refinance	37.5%	60.4%	NY	New York-Northern New Jersey-Long Island
SARM	Prime	144,185	145,300	4.725%	178	82%	81%	176,000	179,000	Single Fam	No Data	Purchase	20.3%	44.3%	PA	Pittsburgh
SARM	Prime	82,632	83,200	5.350%	354	83%	85%	99,000	98,000	Single Fam	Owner	Restructure	39.1%	46.2%	CA	
SARM	Prime	134,106	136,100	5.225%	178	80%	81%	168,000	167,000	Single Fam	Owner	Restructure	39.0%	52.5%	NY	
SARM	Prime	93,030	93,600	4.975%	355	76%	77%	122,000	121,000	Single Fam	Owner	Restructure	40.7%	66.1%	CA	
SARM	Prime	150,711	151,200	5.600%	357	84%	85%	180,000	178,000	Mult 2	Owner	Purchase	39.9%	62.6%	CA	Stockton
SARM	Prime	288,370	292,700	4.975%	234	73%	75%	397,000	392,000	Single Fam	Owner	Restructure	32.0%	36.6%	RI	Providence-New Bedford-Fall River
SARM	Prime	361,901	362,700	5.850%	239	84%	85%	430,000	427,000	Single Fam	Owner	Purchase	39.1%	61.6%	TX	San Antonio
SARM	Prime	123,858	124,300	5.100%	357	87%	89%	142,000	140,000	Single Fam	Owner	Purchase	42.9%	54.4%	NY	New York-Northern New Jersey-Long Island
SARM	Prime	171,051	172,200	5.475%	354	76%	78%	224,000	222,000	Single Fam	Owner	Purchase	36.5%	65.4%	CA	

EXHIBIT 11.16 Loan Listing report (left side of report (top), right side of report (bottom))

```
Sub RepUserInelig_WriteLoanListingReport(iport As Integer)

    col1 = "B":  col2 = "AN"            'report width in columns
    irow = 1                            'inital print position inside the ranges
    For iloan = 1 To gTotalLoans
        If gLoanData(iloan, FD_POOLID) = iport Then
            If gLoanSelect(iloan, FD_CALCFINSELECT) > 0 Then
                Range("ALLCount").Cells(irow, 1) = inelig_loan
                Range("ALLLoanNum").Cells(irow, 2) = iloan
                ''write the contents of the grid section "1" or ""
                For icol = 1 To mTotalIneligReps
                    Range("ALLGrid").Cells(irow, icol) = ""
                    If mSelectionTag(iloan, icol) Then _
                                        Range("ALLGrid").Cells(irow, icol) = 1
                Next icol
                'write the financial information
                Range("ALLBody").Cells(irow, 1) = _
                        gRFLabels(FD_MORTTYPE, gLoanData(iloan, FD_MORTTYPE))
                Range("ALLBody").Cells(irow, 2) = _
                        gRFLabels(FD_CREDITSECT, gLoanData(iloan, FD_CREDITSECT))
                Range("ALLBody").Cells(irow, 3) = gLoanData(iloan, FD_CURRBAL)
                Range("ALLBody").Cells(irow, 4) = gLoanData(iloan, FD_ORIGBAL)
                Range("ALLBody").Cells(irow, 5) = gLoanData(iloan, FD_CURRRATE)
                Range("ALLBody").Cells(irow, 6) = gLoanData(iloan, FD_REMTERM)
                Range("ALLBody").Cells(irow, 7) = gLoanData(iloan, FD_CURRLTV)
                Range("ALLBody").Cells(irow, 8) = gLoanData(iloan, FD_ORIGLTV)
                Range("ALLBody").Cells(irow, 9) = gLoanData(iloan, FD_CURRAPP)
                Range("ALLBody").Cells(irow, 10) = gLoanData(iloan, FD_ORIGAPP)
                Range("ALLBody").Cells(irow, 11) = _
                        gRFLabels(FD_PROPTYPE, gLoanData(iloan, FD_PROPTYPE))
                Range("ALLBody").Cells(irow, 12) = _
                        gRFLabels(FD_OCCPCODE, gLoanData(iloan, FD_OCCPCODE))
                Range("ALLBody").Cells(irow, 13) = _
                        gRFLabels(FD_FINPURPOSE, gLoanData(iloan, FD_FINPURPOSE))
                Range("ALLBody").Cells(irow, 14) = gLoanData(iloan, FD_MDBTTOINC)
                Range("ALLBody").Cells(irow, 15) = gLoanData(iloan, FD_TDBTTOINC)
                Range("ALLBody").Cells(irow, 16) = _
                        gStatePostal(gLoanData(iloan, FD_STATECODE))
                Range("ALLBody").Cells(irow, 17) = _
                        Utility_MSANameFromMSANumericCode(iloan)
                If irow Mod 5 = 0 Then _
                    Call Utility_DrawLineUnderRowRange(col1, col2, irow + 15)
                irow = irow + 1
            End If
        End If
    Next iloan

End Sub
```

EXHIBIT 11.17   "RepUserInelig_WriteLoanListingReport" subroutine

the 20 tests, we first clear the cell; if the loan is positive for the ineligibility condition, we place a "1" in the cell. Last we print the financial and demographic information into the "ALLBody" Range. Note that we will again make use of the contents of the "gRFLabels" array to place descriptive content into some of the nonnumeric fields of this section of the report. See Exhibit 11.17.

Summary Ineligibility Report

The remaining report of the Ineligible Collateral Report Package is the Summary Ineligibility Report. The role of the Loan Listing report was to provide us with a picture of the ineligibility patterns of the collateral at the loan-by-loan level. The role of Summary Ineligibility Report is to do so at the pool or sub-portfolio levels. This report contains what can be considered ineligible collateral "Rep Line." Each line on this report is the sum of all loans in the collateral pool that share the *exact* ineligibility pattern. The report then aggregates the principal balances, coupons, weighted lives, and other summary statistics concerning each of these collective lines.

The challenge in producing this report is managing the aggregation process. We need to find the number of unique ineligibility patterns, aggregate the collateral information, and then sort the results. The format of the report presents one Rep Line per line in the report, sorted by the total ineligibility score. We will use a small number of Ranges to divide the report into manageable segments and then populate each of the segments in turn. These Ranges are:

- "SUMCode": Column B: the unique ineligibility code for that report record.
- "SUMGrid": Columns C to V: the unique combination of single criterion that have made the loan ineligible.
- "SUMBody": Columns W to AD: the collective or dollar-weighted financial statistics for the report line.

The Summary Ineligibility Report shares a number of format characteristics with the Loan Listing report. The left-side header section of the report lists the descriptions of the tests we have created. The grid section below it displays the combination of failed Individual Ineligibility tests that comprise this report line. The right side of the report displays the aggregated statistics for the loans conforming to the ineligibility pattern. The layout of the report can be seen in Exhibit 11.18. There are four unique ineligibility patterns—6, 13, 121, and 150—displayed in the grid section of the report.

Let us lay out the steps necessary to produce the Summary Ineligibility report:

1. Determine if there are *any* ineligibility scores across all the loans of the portfolio.
2. Determine how many unique scores there are.
3. Determine the lowest and the highest values of the scores.
4. Build a list of all the unique ineligibility scores.
5. Sort the ineligibility scores in low to high order.
6. Search all the ineligible loans of the pool or sub-portfolio and aggregate their contents, counting the number of loans per unique ineligibility code.
7. Output the results to the Summary Ineligibility report.

Steps 1 through 6 will be performed by the subroutine "RepUserInelig_FindActiveIneligibilityScores". This subroutine will call other subroutines in turn. "RepUserInelig_FindActiveIneligibilityScores" is called just as we enter the "RepUserInelig_WriteSummaryReport" subroutine. We will look at the VBA that performs these operations in the order of the above list; then we will return to "RepUserInelig_WriteSummaryReport" when all of the other tasks are complete.

As we enter "RepUserInelig_FindActiveIneligibilityScores", the subroutine sets up an array named "mRawScoresList" and dimensions it to the number of loans in the portfolio. This will allow us to record all of the unique ineligibility scores even if every loan in the portfolio is ineligible and has a score unique from every other loan. Next it initializes the variables "CurNumScores" that will hold the number of

Summary Ineligibility Report
Contracts Grouped By Unique Ineligibility Combinations

	Ineligibility Condition Reference		
1 = Current Balance 25,000 to 1,000,000	7 = Bankruptcy Never or Discharged	13 = Seasoning Greater Than 1 Month	
2 = Current Loan-to-Value LE 95%	8 = Third Party Due Diligence Better Than "Poor"	14 = No Alt-A, No Sub-Prime	
3 = Original Appraisal Not "Walk Through"	9 = Full or Partial Documentation, No Alt-A	15 = Original Loan-to-Value LE 85%	
4 = Property Type Known, Not Multi-Family	10 = Servicing Rating Better Than "Poor"	16 = Cannot be in a Delinquent Status	
5 = Occupancy Type No Seasonal	11 = Mortgage Debt-to-Income LE 45%	17 = Original Term > 180 Months	
6 = Fin Purpose Purchase or Refinance	12 = Total Debt-to-Income LE 75%		

Unique Ineligibility Code	Ineligibility Condition																				Number of Loans
	1	2	3	4	5	6	7	8	9	10	11	12	13	14	15	16	17	18	19	20	
	152	0	0	41	60	103	47	40	29	14	54	48	32	0	34	14	38	0	0	0	2,378
1	1																				149
8	1							1													39
16	1			1	1																29
17	1				1																2
24	1			1	1																2
32	1			1	1	1															322
33	1				1																25
40	1			1		1															4

Total Current Balance	Weighted Average Coupon	Weighted Average Rem Term	Weighted Average Orig Term	Weighted Current LTV	Total Current Appraisal	Total Original Appraisal
703,276,380					924,245,000	929,049,000
125,350,873	5.186%	337.63	341.29	75.5%	169,618,000	170,681,000
10,321,127	5.227%	350.23	354.29	78.5%	13,206,000	13,256,000
5,969,792	5.249%	344.51	348.51	79.8%	7,506,000	7,591,000
3,050,794	4.819%	356.25	360.00	78.8%	3,875,000	3,923,000
272,371	5.245%	312.26	316.82	66.9%	410,000	416,000
77,152,253	5.174%	336.49	340.37	78.5%	98,752,000	99,237,000
17,496,870	5.060%	333.09	335.84	74.6%	24,855,000	24,987,000
1,489,640	5.151%	354.34	360.00	85.1%	1,752,000	1,778,000

EXHIBIT 11.18 Summary Ineligibility report format

unique scores and "MaxScoreFound" to record the largest score found. With these variables in hand we can begin the process.

We next use a loop that examines each loan in turn. As we enter the loop, we first determine if the loan belongs to the correct portfolio for this report. If it does not, we move to the next loan. We next check if the loan has a total ineligibility code greater than zero. If it does, we need to compare its code to the existing list of codes we have developed so far. We set a Boolean switch "IsUnique" to TRUE. We next assign the ineligibility score of the loan to the variable "IneligValue" to make the logic of the subroutine easier to read. We now read the value of "CurNumScores". If it is zero, this is our first ineligibility score, and we assign it to position number "1" in our search position. Since it is the only code in the queue, we need not compare it to any of the others to determine if it is unique or not. By definition it must be unique! We will compare all subsequent codes to the existing members of the list. If the codes are unique, we record them and increase the unique code count by "1". When we have finished with the last loan in the portfolio, we transfer the unique loan count held in the local variable "CurNumScores" to the modular variable "mNumUniqueIneligScores". In this process we have also determined the maximum ineligibility score and placed its value in the variable "MaxScoreFound". This completes Steps 1 through 4 of the process. See Exhibit 11.19.

```
Sub RepUserInelig_FindActiveIneligibilityScores(iport As Integer)

Dim icell            As Integer  'array counter
Dim IsUnique         As Boolean  'new ineligibility code is unique
Dim IneligValue      As Long     'ineligibility score
Dim CurNumScores     As Double   'current number of scores in array
Dim MaxScoreFound    As Long     'maximum score found so far

    ReDim mRawScoresList(1 To gTotalLoans) As Long      'list of unique raw scores
    'if an active score add to the list, (if score isn't there already)
    CurNumScores = 0     'current number of unique ineligibilty scores
    MaxScoreFound = 0    'largest ineligible score recorded
    For iloan = 1 To gTotalLoans
        IneligValue = gLoanSelect(iloan, FD_CALCFINSELECT)
        If gLoanData(iloan, FD_POOLID) = iport And IneligValue > 0 Then
            IsUnique = True       'assume we will find a match and discard
            If IneligValue > 0 Then
                If CurNumScores = 0 Then
                    mRawScoresList(1) = IneligValue
                    CurNumScores = 1
                Else
                    'see if this score is already anywhere on the list
                    For icell = 1 To CurNumScores
                        If IneligValue = mRawScoresList(icell) Then IsUnique = False
                    Next icell
                    'it is new to the list add it to the last current list position
                    If IsUnique Then
                        CurNumScores = CurNumScores + 1
                        mRawScoresList(CurNumScores) = IneligValue
                    End If
                End If
                If IneligValue > MaxScoreFound Then MaxScoreFound = IneligValue
            End If
        End If
    Next iloan
    mNumUniqueIneligScores = CurNumScores
    'populates the mSortScoresList with sorted unique code
    Call RepUserInelig_SortListOfIneligCodes(CurNumScores, MaxScoreFound)
    'gets a loan count for each of the unique code
    Call RepUserInelig_AccumulateByIneligCodes(CurNumScores, iport)

End Sub
```

EXHIBIT 11.19   "RepUserInelig_FindActiveIneligibilityScores" subroutine

We next call the subroutine "RepUserInelig_SortListOfIneligCodes" to sort the scores. This is a fairly simple subroutine, and we do not need to examine it in detail. It does, however, complete Step 5 on our list.

With the unique scores in order, it then becomes a straightforward task simply to move down the line of loans and accumulate each according to its unique ineligibility code. The final Step 6 of the process is performed by the "RepUserInelig_AccumulateByIneligCodes" subroutine. We now have almost everything we need to write the summary report. See Exhibit 11.20.

After all of these efforts we are now, finally, ready to produce the Summary Ineligibility report. The form of this subroutine is substantially similar to that of the subroutine that produces the Loan Listing report. There is a large loop. Instead of looping through the ineligible loans of the portfolio, we loop instead through the list of unique ineligibility codes. As we print each record, we place the pattern of failed individual tests in the "SumGrid" Range followed by the summary statistics

```
Sub RepUserInelig_AccumulateByIneligCodes(NumScores As Double, iport As Integer)

Dim iscore      As Integer
Dim TestScore   As Long
Dim IneligValue As Long

    For iscore = 1 To NumScores
        mSortScoresList(iscore, 2) = 0          'set record count to zero
    Next iscore

    For iloan = 1 To gTotalLoans
        IneligValue = gLoanSelect(iloan, FD_CALCFINSELECT)
        If gLoanData(iloan, FD_POOLID) = iport And IneligValue > 0 Then
            'we have a bad one!
            For iscore = 1 To NumScores
                If mSortScoresList(iscore, 1) = IneligValue Then Exit For
            Next iscore
            'item 2 number of loans
            mSortScoresList(iscore, 2) = mSortScoresList(iscore, 2) + 1
            'item 3 aggregate current balance
            mSortScoresList(iscore, 3) = mSortScoresList(iscore, 3) + _
                gLoanData(iloan, FD_CURRBAL)
            'item 4 weighted average coupon
            mSortScoresList(iscore, 4) = mSortScoresList(iscore, 4) + _
                (gLoanData(iloan, FD_CURRBAL) * gLoanData(iloan, FD_CURRRATE))
            'item 5 weighted average remaining term
            mSortScoresList(iscore, 5) = mSortScoresList(iscore, 5) + _
                (gLoanData(iloan, FD_REMTERM) * gLoanData(iloan, FD_CURRBAL))
            'item 6 weighted average original term
            mSortScoresList(iscore, 6) = mSortScoresList(iscore, 6) + _
                (gLoanData(iloan, FD_ORIGTERM) * gLoanData(iloan, FD_CURRBAL))
            'item 7 weighted average loan-to-value
            mSortScoresList(iscore, 7) = mSortScoresList(iscore, 7) + _
                ((gLoanData(iloan, FD_CURRBAL) / gLoanData(iloan, FD_CURRAPP)) _
                * gLoanData(iloan, FD_CURRBAL))
            'item 8 total current appraisal value
            mSortScoresList(iscore, 8) = mSortScoresList(iscore, 8) + _
                gLoanData(iloan, FD_CURRAPP)
            'item 9 total original appraisal value
            mSortScoresList(iscore, 9) = mSortScoresList(iscore, 9) + _
                gLoanData(iloan, FD_ORIGAPP)
        End If
    Next iloan

End Sub
```

EXHIBIT 11.20 "RepUserInelig_AccumulateByIneligCodes" subroutine

for each record in the "SUMBody" Range. The only thing of note is that the "RepUserInelig_AccumulateByIneligCodes" accumulates just the numerators of all the dollar-weighted statistics. We need to divide these numerators by the total current balance of the record group for this particular failure pattern, that constitutes the denominator of the fraction, to complete the process. With this report, the Ineligible Collateral Report Package is complete! See Exhibit 11.21.

Parting Note

We have paid particular attention to the VBA code that has produced the Initial Data Screen Report Package, the Demographic Risk Factors Report, and the Ineligible

```vba
Sub RepUserInelig_WriteSummaryReport(iport As Integer)

Dim RepRangeName(1 To 3)        As String   'range names for the reports
Dim TestTag(1 To NUM_SEL_TESTS) As Boolean  'settings of the individual tests
Dim WorkValue                   As Long     'current inelig score being decoded
Dim ilevel                      As Integer  'generic loop counter

    col1 = "B":   col2 = "AD"
    'go forward to the max score find all loans with this unique score
    irow = 1                        'initial print position in the ranges
    Call RepUserInelig_FindActiveIneligibilyScores(iport)
    For iscore = 1 To mNumUniqueIneligScores
        Range("SUMCode").Cells(irow) = mSortScoresList(iscore, 1)
        'decode the total score into individual components
        WorkValue = mSortScoresList(iscore, 1)
        For ilevel = mTotalIneligReps To 1 Step -1
            TestTag(ilevel) = False
            If WorkValue >= mErrorTestComp(ilevel) Then
                TestTag(ilevel) = True
                WorkValue = WorkValue - mErrorTestComp(ilevel)
                If WorkValue = 0 Then Exit For
            End If
        Next ilevel
        'print out the test pattern that constitutes this unique line
        For icol = 1 To mTotalIneligReps
            If TestTag(icol) Then Range("SUMGrid").Cells(irow, icol) = 1
        Next icol
        ' 1=loan count, 2=current balance, 3=WAC, 4=WARM, 5=WAOM, 6=WA-LTV
        ' 7=current appraisal, 8=original appraisal
        Range("SUMBody").Cells(irow, 1) = mSortScoresList(iscore, 2)
        Range("SUMBody").Cells(irow, 2) = mSortScoresList(iscore, 3)
        Range("SUMBody").Cells(irow, 3) = _
                mSortScoresList(iscore, 4) / mSortScoresList(iscore, 3)
        Range("SUMBody").Cells(irow, 4) = _
                mSortScoresList(iscore, 5) / mSortScoresList(iscore, 3)
        Range("SUMBody").Cells(irow, 5) = _
                mSortScoresList(iscore, 6) / mSortScoresList(iscore, 3)
        Range("SUMBody").Cells(irow, 6) = _
                mSortScoresList(iscore, 7) / mSortScoresList(iscore, 3)
        Range("SUMBody").Cells(irow, 7) = mSortScoresList(iscore, 8)
        Range("SUMBody").Cells(irow, 8) = mSortScoresList(iscore, 9)
        If irow Mod 1 = 0 Then
            Call Utility_DrawLineUnderRowRange(col1, col2, irow + 15)
        End If
        irow = irow + 1
    Next iscore

End Sub
```

EXHIBIT 11.21   "RepUserInelig_WriteSummaryReport" subroutine

Collateral Report Package. This was done to familiarize you with the techniques common to almost all Excel/VBA report writing techniques.

GEOGRAPHIC SELECTION CODE

In contrast to the Financial and Demographic Selection process, the Geographic Selection process may seem a bit anticlimatic. Unlike the situation pertaining to the Financial Selection process, we have only a single set of Geographic Selection criteria

```
'the final selection status of the regions, states, and MSA groups
Public gFinalStatusRegions(1 To NUM_GEO_TESTS, 1 To NUM_REGIONS)    As String
Public gFinalStatusStates(1 To NUM_GEO_TESTS, 1 To NUM_STATES)      As Boolean
Public gFinalStatusMSASet1(1 To NUM_GEO_TESTS, 1 To NUM_MSA_SET1)   As Boolean
Public gFinalStatusMSASet2(1 To NUM_GEO_TESTS, 1 To NUM_MSA_SET2)   As Boolean
Public gFinalStatusMSASet3(1 To NUM_GEO_TESTS, 1 To NUM_MSA_SET3)   As Boolean
Public gFinalStatusMSASet4(1 To NUM_GEO_TESTS, 1 To NUM_MSA_SET4)   As Boolean
```

EXHIBIT 11.22 Geographic Selection status arrays

that are applied to all the loans without reference to whether they are at the pool level or the sub-portfolio level. There are three levels of increasingly specific Geographic Selection criteria moving from the multiple state regions, to single states, down to individual MSAs. A regional selection specification serves to select or deselect collateral at the level either single states or single MSAs (although there may be many of them in a given region). The results of such an election is, however, no different from selecting each of the component entities separately one at a time. Thus in the end what we are left with is the task of applying two and only two sets of Geographic Selection triggers, the first for individual state entities and the second for individual MSAs.

Translating Geographic Selections into VBA Code

The CCFG model allows us to select, or deselect, any of the loans in the collateral pool on the basis of either its state location or its MSA location (if it is in an MSA!). The information that designates which of the states and MSAs are eligible for inclusion is contained in five arrays, the first for state level information and the following four arrays for MSA information. See Exhibit 11.22.

The construction of these arrays and the code and methods used to populate them were discussed extensively in the section on the "Geographic Selection Criteria Menu" in Chapter 9. These are all Boolean data–type arrays, and each location of the array corresponds to a unique state or MSA. All we need to do is to match the state or MSA code to that of the collateral loan record and we can immediately determine its eligibility status!

Performing Geographic Selection Process

The main subroutine of the Geographic Selection process is the "GeoSelect_ GeographicEligibilityTesting" subroutine. This subroutine performs three tasks.

1. It reads the set of MSA codes from the "GeoData" worksheet of the CCFG. Why do we have to do this? We need to do this to be able to compare the MSA codes of the collateral loan record that are in numeric form with the list of MSA codes that we have read in (up to this point) as String-typed variables. With a set of separate arrays, we can easily compare the MSA code in the collateral loan record with the MSA code in the *n*th position of any of the MSA set arrays.
2. It applies the state level Geographic Selections.
3. It applies the MSA level Geographic Selections.

See Exhibit 11.23.

```
Sub GeoSelect_GeographicEligibilityTesting()

    Call GeoSelect_ReadMSACodesAsDoubles     'read the sets of MSA codes
    'If this is Pool Level data apply the conditions of the 0th test set
    If gPoolLevelData Then
        If gROApplyGeoSelect(0) Then          'is geo selection requested?
            mGeoSelectCase = gROTestSetGeoSelect(0)
            For iloan = 1 To gTotalLoans
                If gLoanScreen(iloan, FD_SCREEN_DEMO_OK) = 1 Then
                    gLoanSelect(iloan, FD_CALCGEOSELECT) = 0  'geo error to 0
                    'determine eligibility at a State level
                    Call GeoSelect_ApplyGeoCritStates(gLoanData(iloan, FD_STATECODE))
                    'determine eligibility at a MSA level
                    If gLoanData(iloan, FD_MSACODE) <> 0 Then
                        Call GeoSelect_ApplyGeoCritMSAs(gLoanData(iloan, FD_MSACODE))
                    End If
                End If
            Next iloan
        End If
    Else
        'Sub-Portfolio data, sub-port code is assigned to the records
        For iloan = 1 To gTotalLoans
            'if the damaged score is 1 the record is complete in all respects
            If gLoanScreen(iloan, FD_SCREEN_DEMO_OK) = 1 Then
                gLoanSelect(iloan, FD_CALCGEOSELECT) = 0
                mGeoSelectCase = gROTestSetGeoSelect(gLoanData(iloan, FD_POOLID))
                If gROApplyGeoSelect(mGeoSelectCase) Then 'is this case active?
                    'determine eligibility at a State level
                    Call GeoSelect_ApplyGeoCritStates(gLoanData(iloan, FD_STATECODE))
                    'determine eligibility at a MSA level
                    If gLoanData(iloan, FD_MSACODE) <> 0 Then _
                        Call GeoSelect_ApplyGeoCritMSAs(gLoanData(iloan, FD_MSACODE))
                End If
            End If
        Next iloan
    End If
    'adjust the gLoanOK status for loans deselected through this process
    For iloan = 1 To gTotalLoans
        If gLoanSelect(iloan, FD_CALCGEOSELECT) > 0 Then gLoanOK(iloan) = False
    Next iloan

End Sub
```

EXHIBIT 11.23 "GeoSelect_GeographicEligibilityTesting" subroutine

Applying the State Level Geographic Selections

The state level selections are contained in the VBA array "gFinalStatusStates". The subroutine receives the value of the nth position of the state code of the collateral loan record from the calling subroutine. If the value of the nth element of the "gFinalStatusStates" array is the same as the value of the nth value of the "gLoanData(iloan, FD_STATECODE)" field of the collateral loan record, then selection action is applied. If the value of the nth location of the "gFinalStatusStates" array is TRUE, the loan is eligible and the "If" test ends in an "Exit Sub" command, immediately terminating the action. If the value of the array position is FALSE, the collateral loan record is deemed ineligible. The error code "ERROR_CODE_STATE" with a value of "1" is assigned to the "gLoanData(iloan, FD_CALCGEOSELECT)" field. See Exhibit 11.24.

```
Sub GeoSelect_ApplyGeoCritStates(STATE_CODE As Double)

    If gFinalStatusStates(mGeoSelectCase, STATE_CODE) Then Exit Sub
    gLoanSelect(iloan, FD_CALCGEOSELECT) = _
            gLoanSelect(iloan, FD_CALCGEOSELECT) + ERR_CODE_STATE

End Sub
```

EXHIBIT 11.24   "GeoSelect_ApplyGeoCritStates" subroutine

Applying the MSA Level Geographic Selections

We face a slightly more complicated problem when we perform the Geographic Selection action at the MSA level. Here we must take the value for the MSA code of the loan and compare it against not one but four distinct arrays to find a match (if there is one). Once we determine the appropriate MSA array element, the subroutine will either immediately exit if the MSA is considered geographically eligible or assign an error code "ERROR_CODE_MSA" with a value of "2" to the gLoanData(iloan, FD_CALCGEOSELECT) field if it is not. See Exhibit 11.25.

With these operations the Geographic Selection process is complete.

GEOGRAPHIC CONCENTRATION CODE

The fourth and final selection process of this chapter is the Geographic Concentration Selection process. Here we will manage the size of the portfolio to meet the specifications of the Geographic Concentration guidelines as entered into the "States and MSA Concentration Menu" UserForm of the CCFG model. This UserForm records the state level as well as the MSA level Geographic Concentration limit constraints. Our task is to devise a series of subroutines that will quickly and accurately manage the portfolio to those simultaneous limits.

The Geographic Concentration limits are stored for the states and the first two MSA sets that contain the 52 largest MSAs of the United States. These data are kept in the arrays shown in Exhibit 11.26.

How Do We Set Concentration Limits?

Concentration limits are expressed as percentages that a collection of collateral may assume as a portion of the entire portfolio that contains it. If we are assigned a concentration limit of 15% within a portfolio that contains $100 million, the collective sum of all members of the group of loans upon which the concentration limit is levied cannot exceed $15 million. If there was a second concentration limit based on other characteristics of 6%, the collateral with those characteristics could not exceed an aggregate balance of $6 million.

Let us assume that we initially have a situation broadly similar to the one above. The aggregate current balances of the portfolio consists of $1 billion. Within the portfolio we have three major concentrations of collateral, the state of California, the state of Florida, and the MSA of "New York–Northern New Jersey–Long Island". These three entities have $110 million, $80 million, and $50 million of current balance collateral between them. The concentration limit for California is 9%,

```
Sub GeoSelect_ApplyGeoCritMSAs(MSA_code As Double)

    'churn through the four sets of MSA code groups until you find a match
    For mMSA = 1 To NUM_MSA_SET1
        If mMSASet1Codes(mMSA) = MSA_code Then
            If gFinalStatusMSASet1(mGeoSelectCase, mMSA) Then Exit Sub
            gLoanSelect(iloan, FD_CALCGEOSELECT) = _
                        gLoanSelect(iloan, FD_CALCGEOSELECT) + ERR_CODE_MSA
            Exit Sub
        End If
    Next mMSA
    For mMSA = 1 To NUM_MSA_SET2
        If mMSASet2Codes(mMSA) = MSA_code Then
            If gFinalStatusMSASet2(mGeoSelectCase, mMSA) Then Exit Sub
            gLoanSelect(iloan, FD_CALCGEOSELECT) = _
                        gLoanSelect(iloan, FD_CALCGEOSELECT) + ERR_CODE_MSA
            Exit Sub
        End If
    Next mMSA
    For mMSA = 1 To NUM_MSA_SET3
        If mMSASet3Codes(mMSA) = MSA_code Then
            If gFinalStatusMSASet3(mGeoSelectCase, mMSA) Then Exit Sub
            gLoanSelect(iloan, FD_CALCGEOSELECT) = _
                        gLoanSelect(iloan, FD_CALCGEOSELECT) + ERR_CODE_MSA
            Exit Sub
        End If
    Next mMSA
    For mMSA = 1 To NUM_MSA_SET4
        If mMSASet4Codes(mMSA) = MSA_code Then
            If gFinalStatusMSASet4(mGeoSelectCase, mMSA) Then Exit Sub
            gLoanSelect(iloan, FD_CALCGEOSELECT) = _
                        gLoanSelect(iloan, FD_CALCGEOSELECT) + ERR_CODE_MSA
            Exit Sub
        End If
    Next mMSA

End Sub
```

EXHIBIT 11.25   "GeoSelect_ApplyGeoCritMSAs" subroutine

for Florida is 7%, and for New York City is 3%. This means that we have, at the current size of the portfolio, a limit of $90, $70, and $30 million for the three geographic entities.

If we then attempt to reach the concentration limits by subtracting $20 million from the California loans, $10 million from the Florida loans, and $20 million from the NYC-MSA loans, we will remove a total of $50 million from the portfolio in total. This will leave us with our original target balances of $90, $70, and $30 million. Will we have addressed the concentration issues?

Surprisingly enough (but *not* for those of you thinking ahead), we will have failed! The concentration levels for California, Florida, and New York City will have declined from 15%, 9%, and 5% to their current levels of 9.47% for Cal-

```
Public gFinalConcenStates(1 To NUM_STATES)      As Double   'concentration limits at state level
Public gFinalConcenMSASet1(1 To NUM_MSA_SET1)   As Double   'concentration limits for MSA set 1
Public gFinalConcenMSASet2(1 To NUM_MSA_SET2)   As Double   'concentration limits for MSA set 2
```

EXHIBIT 11.26   Geographic Limit Arrays for states and 52 largest MSAs

ifornia, 7.37% for Florida, and 5.16% for the NYC-MSA. Close but no cigar! Why? The obvious reason is that by removing these loans, the aggregate balance of the entire portfolio declined simultaneously by $50 million, lowering its balance to $950 million. With the new denominator in effect, we have missed our goal. How can we circumvent this problem and arrive at our correct target concentration limits? The answer is to use an iterative process employing either "Do..While" or "Do..Until" loop structures. In this manner we can iteratively resize the portfolio and zero in on the solution in a step-by-step manner.

On the Web site you will find a small portfolio file named "GeoConcenPortfolio". This file consists of 100 loans. There are nine states represented and three MSAs within this portfolio. The total current balance of the loans total $31,731,738. To facilitate this example, the number of loans has been keep small and the total current balance of the portfolio has been enhanced by the inclusion of two very large loans, one for $10 million and another of $15 million, which will not be subject to constraints. This test file has been made available so that any reader who wishes to step through the geographic concentration code may do so with a manageable size portfolio to look at. The examples, balances, and loan counts in the exhibits below have been drawn from this file. If you step through the geographic concentration VBA subroutines in the "CollatData_GeographicSelection" code using the VBA Debugger, you should observe the exact results seen below.

The steps that the process will follow are:

1. Set the required concentration limits for any of the entities of the portfolio that are subject to such limits. In this portfolio that is the state of California and three MSAs: Los Angeles, CA, Riverside, CA, and New York City, NY. The concentration limits are established as follows:

State of California	10%
MSA Los Angeles, CA	5%
MSA Riverside, CA	5%
MSA New York City, NY	5%

2. Sum all the eligible collateral of the portfolio. In our example portfolio this amounts to $31.731 million.
3. Calculate the aggregate actual current balances for any state or MSA that has a concentration limit. In our initial portfolio configuration these are as follows:

State of California	$4,217,760
MSA Los Angeles, CA	$2,421,852
MSA Riverside, CA	$1,465,338
MSA New York City, NY	$2,127,485

4. Calculate the initial target concentration limits based on the aggregate balance. These are therefore:

State of California	$3,173,178
MSA Los Angeles, CA	$1,586,589
MSA Riverside, CA	$1,586,589
MSA New York City, NY	$1,586,589

5. Find the sum of the differences between the aggregate current balances of these entities in the portfolio and the concentration target limits shown in Step 4 above.

State of California	$1,044,581
MSA Los Angeles, CA	$ 835,262
MSA Riverside, CA	$ −121,250
MSA New York City, NY	$ 540,896

We therefore have concentration overages in the state of California and in the MSAs of Los Angeles and New York City. The MSA of Riverside does not have a concentration issue at the moment based on the initial size of the portfolio. We will call these amounts concentration overages. They will become the initial targets for the elimination of current balance amounts from the three entities that currently exceed their concentration limits.

6. Remove however many loans from each of the entities (by declaring them ineligible collateral based on geographic concentration issues alone) to bring the group totals below the target levels. We will begin by removing the largest loans first, a process that will also help reduce the large loan concentration problem (if any) of our portfolio. It may happen that the balance of the largest loan in the portfolio is greater than the amount that we need to reduce the balances of the entity. In this case we will reverse the process and start with the smallest loan balances, working up the ladder until we have eliminated enough current balances to meet our goals.

7. We next recalculate the balances for the total portfolio, the state of California, and the three MSAs with concentration limits.

8. Compute the new concentration limits based on the totals from Step 7.

9. Test these new concentration percentages against the required concentration percentages. If all of the concentration limits fall below these required limits, we are finished. If not, we repeat the process until they do.

Stepping through the Sample Portfolio Example

We will now work through this process with the sample portfolio contained in the file "CollatData_GeographicSelection".

Initial Portfolio Configuration   In Exhibit 11.27 we can see the initial configuration of the sample portfolio and the effects of the first round of overconcentration selections. The total portfolio is $31.7 million; this aggregate balance results in concentration limits of $3.174 million for the state of California and $1.586 million for each of the three MSAs: Los Angeles, CA, Riverside, CA, and New York City, NY. The state of California, the MSA of Los Angeles, CA, and the MSA of New York City, NY, have positive concentration overages. These amounts are $1.044 million, $0.835 million, and $0.540 million, respectively. The MSA of Riverside does not have a concentration positive overage; it is therefore within its concentration limit.

The process will first address concentration issues in the MSAs. Metropolitan Statistical Areas are addressed first in the process in that elimination of any balance in an MSA that resides within a state that has an overconcentration will simultaneously remove the now-ineligible loan from both the state and MSA concentration totals. This is the case with all loans that are within the MSA of Los Angeles. Elimination

Portfolio Balance:	$31,731,783		Individual Loans By Geographic Entity							
			State of California		MSA Los Angeles, CA		MSA Riverside, CA		MSA New York City, NY	
Balances:			Loans: 12		Loans: 2		Loans: 8		Loans: 4	
California	$ 4,217,760		Balances: 3,085,166		Balances: 1,563,128		Balances: 1,465,338		Balances: 1,530,081	
Los Angeles, CA	$ 2,421,852		ID	Balance	ID	Balance	ID	Balance	ID	Balance
Riverside, CA	$ 1,465,338		84	887,404	84	887,404	40	285,245	62	847,159
New York City, NY	$ 2,127,485		81	675,724	81	675,724	83	283,743	89	266,187
			40	285,245	56	359,345 X	86	277,963	98	214,911
Target Concentrations:			83	283,743	52	274,611 X	41	266,010	5	201,825
California	$ 3,173,178	10%	86	277,963	87	60,994 X	57	152,460	53	176,530 X
Los Angeles, CA	$ 1,586,589	5%	41	266,010	4	55,317 X	94	71,261	73	148,750 X
Riverside, CA	$ 1,586,589	5%	57	152,460	47	44,852 X	31	66,634	71	146,379 X
New York City, NY	$ 1,586,589	5%	94	71,261	54	43,018 X	26	62,022	96	125,746 X
			31	66,634	76	20,587 X				
Concentrations Overages:			26	62,022						
California	$ 1,044,581		65	56,700						
Los Angeles, CA	$ 835,262		85	55,886						
Riverside, CA	$ (121,250)		2	50,137 X						
New York City, NY	$ 540,896		46	37,087 X						
			19	36,211 X						
Post Elimination Balances:			1	29,569 X						
California	$ 3,085,166	10.26%	59	28,138 X						
Los Angeles, CA	$ 1,563,128	5.20%	8	25,224 X						
Riverside, CA	$ 1,465,338	4.88%	3	11,617 X						
New York City, NY	$ 1,530,081	5.09%	X = Ineligible due to concentration issues							

EXHIBIT 11.27   Initial concentrations

of any loans in Los Angeles will immediately lower the concentration percentage of the state of California.

The model will therefore address the MSAs first. The first MSA on the list is Los Angeles, CA. The overage amount for Los Angeles is $835,262. This is the minimum amount of balances we must declare ineligible within the MSA to bring it into initial compliance with the 5% concentration limit. Following the practice of looking first to the largest loan balances, we select loan #84 with a balance of $887,404. Unfortunately, that loan exceeds the concentration overage amount of $835,262 and we will need to bypass it. We will now start with the other end of the loan schedule, the low-balance loans. Working our way up from the bottom, we find that we need to declare ineligible loans #76, #54, #47, #4, #87, #52, and finally #56. This is a total balance of $858,724. This balance meets the requirement of eliminating the overage amount of $835,262. We are finished with Los Angeles. The next MSA in line is Riverside, CA. Riverside has a negative overage amount; therefore, no concentration adjustments need to be made to its loans. The final MSA is New York City, NY. This MSA has a positive concentration overage amount of $540,896. As with the case of Los Angeles, we find that the largest balance loan exceeds the overage amount ($847,159 versus $540,896), and we will again need to start from the bottom of the loan balances upward. Loans #96, #71, #73, and #53, for a total of $597,404, will be declared ineligible. New York City is now in compliance with its 5% concentration limit with a total $1,530,081 in balances.

We now look to the state of California. The balance of the state of California has been decreased by the loan balances declared ineligible when we were adjusting the MSA of Los Angeles. As a result, the beginning schedule of the California loans does not contain any of the Los Angeles collateral already declared ineligible. The seven loans that were declared ineligible when we culled the Los Angeles MSA are missing from the beginning schedule of the state of California loans. The state of California overage has been adjusted downward by the $858,724 that we have removed from

Portfolio Balance:	$30,057,671		Individual Loans By Geographic Entity							
			State of California		MSA Los Angeles, CA		MSA Riverside, CA		MSA New York City, NY	
Balances:			Loans:	11	Loans:	1	Loans:	8	Loans:	3
California	$ 3,141,051		Balances:	2,465,328	Balances:	887,404	Balances:	1,465,338	Balances:	1,328,256
Los Angeles, CA	$ 1,563,127		ID	Balance	ID	Balance	ID	Balance	ID	Balance
Riverside, CA	$ 1,465,338		84	887,404	84	887,404	40	285,245	62	847,159
New York City, NY	$ 1,530,080		40	285,245	81	675,724 X	83	283,743	89	266,187
			83	283,743			86	277,963	98	214,911
Target Concentrations:			86	277,963			41	266,010	5	201,825 X
California	$ 3,005,767	10%	41	266,010			57	152,460		
Los Angeles, CA	$ 1,502,883	5%	57	152,460			94	71,261		
Riverside, CA	$ 1,502,883	5%	94	71,261			31	66,634		
New York City, NY	$ 1,502,883	5%	31	66,634			26	62,022		
			26	62,022						
Concentrations Overages:			65	56,700						
California	$ 135,285		85	55,886						
Los Angeles, CA	$ 60,244									
Riverside, CA	$ (37,545)									
New York City, NY	$ 27,197									
Post Elimination Balances:										
California	$ 2,465,328	8.45%								
Los Angeles, CA	$ 887,403	3.04%								
Riverside, CA	$ 1,465,338	5.02%								
New York City, NY	$ 1,328,256	4.55%					X = Ineligible due to concentration issues			

EXHIBIT 11.28   Concentrations after first adjustments

the Los Angeles concentration. The revised state of California overage target is now ($1,044,581 – $858,724), or $185,757.

In that the overage is smaller than the first large loan, we will again drop to the bottom of the schedule and work our way upward. In this process we will declare ineligible loans #3, #8, #59, #1, #19, #46, and #2.

The ending concentration percentages are now recalculated against the reduced portfolio balance of $30,057,671 and found to be 10.26% for the state of California, 5.20% for Los Angeles, 4.88% for Riverside, and 5.08% for New York. California, Los Angeles, and New York City are therefore still in violation of their concentration limits, and we must repeat the process.

First Elimination of Overconcentrated Loans   Exhibit 11.28 displays the effect of the second iteration of the concentration adjustment process. The starting balance of the now-reduced portfolio is $30.057 million. This results in a $3.005 concentration limit for the state of California and $1.502 million concentration limits for each of the three MSAs. The concentration overages are now $135,285 for the state of California, $60,244 for the MSA of Los Angeles, CA, $(37,545) for the MSA of Riverside, CA, and $27,197 for New York City, NY.

The model will again start with the MSA of Los Angeles. Unfortunately, we only have two loans left, one with a balance of $88,7404 and the second with one of $675,724, to address an overage of $60,244! We will therefore select the smaller of the two loans, #81, and eliminate it. (This will have the unintended benefit to the state of California concentration overage of $135,285 by immediately turning it into a $(540,439) overage.) With the elimination of this one loan, both Los Angeles and California are immediately in compliance with their respective concentration limits.

The MSA of Riverside, CA, is still in compliance at the beginning of this model pass so it is ignored for the time being. The next MSA on the list is New York City, NY. New York City has a $27,197 overage. As in the prior case with Los Angeles,

Portfolio Balance:	$29,180,122		Individual Loans By Geographic Entity							
			State of California		MSA Los Angeles, CA		MSA Riverside, CA		MSA New York City, NY	
Balances:			Loans: 11		Loans: 1		Loans: 7		Loans: 3	
California	$ 2,465,327		Balances: 2,403,306		Balances: 887,404		Balances: 1,403,317		Balances: 1,328,256	
Los Angeles, CA	$ 887,404		ID	Balance	ID	Balance	ID	Balance	ID	Balance
Riverside, CA	$ 1,465,338		84	887,404	84	887,404	40	285,245	62	847,159
New York City, NY	$ 1,328,256		40	285,245			83	283,743	89	266,187
			83	283,743			86	277,963	98	214,911
Target Concentrations:			86	277,963			41	266,010		
California	$ 2,918,012	10%	41	266,010			57	152,460		
Los Angeles, CA	$ 1,459,006	5%	57	152,460			94	71,261		
Riverside, CA	$ 1,459,006	5%	94	71,261			31	66,634		
New York City, NY	$ 1,459,006	5%	31	66,634			26	62,022 X		
			65	56,700						
Concentrations Overages:			85	55,886						
California	$ (452,684)									
Los Angeles, CA	$ (571,602)									
Riverside, CA	$ 6,332									
New York City, NY	$ (130,750)									
Post Elimination Balances:										
California	$ 2,403,306	8.25%								
Los Angeles, CA	$ 887,403	3.05%								
Riverside, CA	$ 1,403,317	4.82%								
New York City, NY	$ 1,328,256	4.56%	X = Ineligible due to concentration issues							

EXHIBIT 11.29 Concentrations after second adjustments

we will kill a fly with a sledgehammer by declaring ineligible the lowest-balance loan remaining in the New York City group, #5, with a balance of $201,825! This is unfortunate and wasteful, but there is no alternative when using this approach.

Last we test the state of California. With the adjustment made to the Los Angeles, CA, loan set (mentioned above), we have corrected the concentration overage of California. This brings all entities into compliance with the concentration ratios for the moment.

We have one problem, however. With these eliminations, over $875,000 in balances, the aggregate balance of the portfolio has now fallen to $29,180,122. At this balance the target dollar concentration for the three MSAs is $1.459 million. The MSA of Riverside, CA, with a balance of $1.465, now violates this constraint! Riverside, which we have been able to safely ignore up until now, has unexpectedly become a concentration problem!

Second Elimination of Overconcentrated Loans   In the final iteration of the process we now need to address the overconcentration issue of Riverside. The Riverside MSA is now a mere $6,332 overconcentrated. We will select the lowest balance loan in the Riverside group, #26, in the amount of $62,022, and declare it ineligible.

With the elimination of this loan, the concentration balances of the state of California, 8.25%, and the MSAs of Los Angeles, Riverside, and New York City, at 3.05%, 4.82%, and 4.56%, are all within the prescribed limits. See Exhibit 11.29.

Having stepped through the process on paper, let us now translate it into VBA code!

Geographic Concentration Calculation Subroutines

The main subroutine for the Geographic Concentration Selection Criteria process is "GeoConcen_ApplyConcentrationLimits". This subroutine steps through the

```
Sub GeoConcen_ApplyConcentrationLimits()

Dim ConcenOK      As Boolean

    If gROApplyGeoConcen Then
        ReDim mConMSAIndex(1 To gTotalLoans) As Integer      'MSA index # by loan
        ReDim mConEligible(1 To gTotalLoans) As Boolean      'is loan eligible?
        ReDim gLoanPreConTest(1 To gTotalLoans) As Boolean   'loan status pre con
        ReDim gLoanPostConTest(1 To gTotalLoans) As Boolean  'loan status post con
        For iloan = 1 To gTotalLoans
            gLoanPreConTest(iloan) = gLoanOK(iloan)
        Next iloan
        'Step #0
        'reads the MSA codes as doubles, so that we can use them in comparison
        '  and buckets later in the process,  the arrays are mMSASet1Codes to
        '  mMSASet2Codes
        Call GeoSelect_ReadMSACodesAsDoubles
        Call GeoConcen_BuildCombinedMSAList     'builds sequential list of MSAs
        Call GeoConcen_AssignLoansMSAIndex      'finds nth MSA loan is in (or not)
        'set the terminal condition of the loop to false (unsatisfied criteria)
        ConcenOK = False
        Do While ConcenOK = False         'loop until all criteria are satisfied
            'Step #1 - get the current eligible collateral balances
            Call GeoConcen_AssignEligibilityCode 'determine currently elig loans
            Call GeoConcen_CalcExistingBalances  'determine the existing concen
            'Step #2 - calculate target balances (post concentration) by state
            '  and MSA
            Call GeoConcen_CalculateTargetBalances
            'Step #3 - determine the over concentrations (in dollars) of each
            '  entity that has a concentration limit, and the portfolio sum of
            '  these overages
            ConcenOK = GeoConcen_TestForCompletedConcentrations
            If ConcenOK = False Then
                'Step #4 - remove the excess collateral from the states and
                '  the MSA's.
                Sheets("ConcenWorksheet").Select
                Call GeoConcen_AdjustMSABalances
                Call GeoConcen_AdjustStateBalances
            End If
        Loop
        'if loans are deemed ineligible for concentration puposes reflect this
        '  in the gLoanOK array status
        For iloan = 1 To gTotalLoans
            If gLoanSelect(iloan, FD_CALCGEOCONCEN) > 0 Then gLoanOK(iloan) = False
            gLoanPostConTest(iloan) = gLoanOK(iloan)
        Next iloan
    End If

End Sub
```

EXHIBIT 11.30   "GeoConcen_ApplyConcentrationLimits" subroutine

process just described. See Exhibit 11.30. The subroutine is composed of two distinctly different areas. The first is a series of initialization subroutines that set up certain necessary arrays for the selection process. The second region is contained entirely within the "Do..While" loop controlled by the variable "ConcenOK". This variable is initialized to FALSE, indicating that our compliance with the specified concentration limits is either unknown or not met. We will not know if we are in compliance with the limits until we have, at a minimum, determined the initial concentration limits for any state or MSA that has had such limits earlier specified for it.

The comments contained in this subroutine divide the process into five steps. These are numbered Step #0, all the preliminary setup processes, to Steps #1 to #4, the steps that perform the actions that we have just taken in the concentration sizing exercise shown in Exhibits 11.13 to 11.15.

Immediately after we have tested the variable "gROApplyGeoConcen" to determine if we are going to produce the Geographic Concentration reports, you will see the declaration of four arrays. The first is "mConMSAIndex", which holds the MSA index position of the loan in the list of 150 MSAs. If the loan is not in an MSA, the value of "MConMSAIndex" is "0". This is important as we will use that value to list and aggregate all non-MSA collateral at different points throughout the CCFG. The second array is the "mConEligible" array. This array is Boolean and indicates if the loan is acceptable for use in the concentration-sizing activities that lay ahead. If the loan is already deemed ineligible collateral for any other reason, we cannot use it in the concentration-sizing activity. Why? The initial geographic concentration ratios are computed using only eligible collateral. All loans deemed ineligible for any other reasons lie outside the eligible portfolio. Including them or excluding them will have no effect on the balances and proportions of the various geographic concentrations within the eligible portfolio! The next two variables, "gLoanPreConTest" and "gLoanPostConTest", are used to differentiate between the status of each individual loan prior to and immediately on the conclusion of the concentration sizing activity. If the loan has a value of TRUE in the "gLoanPreConTest" array at the beginning of the process and one of FALSE in the "gLoanPostConTest" at the end of the process, we know it has been deemed ineligible due to concentration issues. The values of these variables will also be the basis for being able to produce the preselection versus postselection concentration reports. With these important recording variables in place, we can now properly begin the concentration sizing exercise.

Step #0 includes three distinct processes. The first is to read all of the numeric codes for the MSAs. There are a total of 140 individual MSAs. The concentration parameters UserForm only allows selections to be made to the largest 52 of these MSAs. These are the MSAs in sets 1 and 2. The model will read the numeric codes for these MSAs so it can later use them to identify the collateral of those MSAs that need to be considered in the concentration adjustment process. These codes are stored in the array "mConMSACodes". The second component of Step #0 is to set the concentration limits of these MSAs into a separate array named "mConMSALimit". Here they will be available to the model for the calculation of the Target Concentration amounts. The third step is to assign each loan that has an MSA code attached to it a corresponding index number based on the MSA code of the loan. For example, the MSA of Phoenix-Mesa-Scottsdale, code 38060, is the first on the combined MSA1 and MSA2 list. Any loan that had the 38060 code would therefore be assigned an index value of 1. New York City is 20th on the list, and any loan from that MSA would have an index value of 20. The index is stored in the array "mConMSAIndex", which is 1, to "gTotalLoans" in length. See Exhibit 11.31.

With these arrays established, we are ready to begin the concentration selection process. If we are going to determine the concentration levels present in the collateral pool, we need to know the balance of the aggregate portfolio and the balance of each state and MSA entity contained in that pool. This is the task of the next step, Step #1. Before we begin to aggregate the collateral by portfolio, state, and MSA levels, we need to assure ourselves that the collateral contained in these balances

```
'===================================================================================
' STEP #0
'===================================================================================
Sub GeoConcen_BuildCombinedMSAList()

    'combine the MSA numeric codes for the first two sets of MSA (the 52 largest)
    ' into a single list.  Assign the concentration limits for any of the MSA's
    ' that have a limit set to this new combined list.
    mIndex = 1
    For mMSA = 1 To TOT_CON_MSA
        If mMSA <= NUM_MSA_SET1 Then
            mConMSACodes(mMSA) = mMSASet1Codes(mMSA)
            mConMSALimit(mMSA) = gFinalConcenMSASet1(mMSA)
        Else
            mConMSACodes(mMSA) = mMSASet2Codes(mIndex)
            mConMSALimit(mMSA) = gFinalConcenMSASet2(mIndex)
            mIndex = mIndex + 1
        End If
    Next mMSA

End Sub
'===================================================================================
'
'===================================================================================
Sub GeoConcen_AssignLoansMSAIndex()

    'if a loan is NOT in one of the top 52 largest MSA codes it is assigned a
    ' 0 Index.  if a loan is in one of the top 52 MSAs it is assigned an index
    ' between 1 and 52
    For iloan = 1 To gTotalLoans
        MSA_code = gLoanData(iloan, FD_MSACODE)
        'if zero forget about it; if non-zero match to index
        If MSA_code = 0 Then
            mConMSAIndex(iloan) = 0      'loan not in any MSA, set index to zero
        Else
            'loop through the list of the 52 largest MSA codes if the loan falls
            ' into one of these assign it the index location on the combined list
            mConMSAIndex(iloan) = 0                   'default value
            For mMSA = 1 To TOT_CON_MSA
                If MSA_code = mConMSACodes(mMSA) Then
                    mConMSAIndex(iloan) = mMSA        'nth in the table
                    Exit For
                End If
            Next mMSA
        End If
    Next iloan

End Sub
```

EXHIBIT 11.31   "GeoConcen_BuildCombinedMSAList" and "GeoConcen_AssignLoansMSAIndex" subroutines

is eligible collateral only. This role is performed by the first subroutine inside the "Do..While" loop, "GeoConcen_AssignEligibilityCode". This subroutine loops through each piece of collateral and determines that it is eligible by testing its Base Selection Criteria score, its Financial Criteria score, its Geographic Selection score, and last its Geographic Concentration score. If all of these scores are "0", the collateral is eligible. See Exhibit 11.32.

Once we have determined what of the collateral is still eligible, we are able to begin the summation process for the portfolio as a whole and the state and MSA entities.

```
'=================================================================
' STEP #1
'=================================================================
Sub GeoConcen_AssignEligibilityCode()        'determine currently eligible loans

    'loan must have a 0 score for Base, Financial, Geographic and Concentration
    ' selection to be eligible collateral
    For iloan = 1 To gTotalLoans
        If gLoanSelect(iloan, FD_CALCFINSELECT) = 0 And _
           gLoanSelect(iloan, FD_CALCGEOSELECT) = 0 And _
           gLoanSelect(iloan, FD_CALCGEOCONCEN) = 0 Then
                mConEligible(iloan) = True
        End If
    Next iloan

End Sub
```

EXHIBIT 11.32   "GeoConcen_AssignEligibilityCode" subroutine

This process is performed by the subroutine "GeoConcen_CalcExistingBalances." This subroutine calls three other subroutines to perform the three specific tasks. See Exhibit 11.33.

As you should know, this subroutine and all of the others we will now discuss are contained inside the "Do..While" loop whose operation is governed by the value of the variable "ConcenOK". If this variable, of type Boolean, is ever reset to the value TRUE from its initial value of FALSE, we will know that we have achieved all the desired concentration levels and can terminate the concentration selection process.

Step #2 involves calculating each of the target balance dollar amounts for any of the states and MSAs that have had concentration limits set for them. The concentration limits that we entered in the UserForm Menu "States and MSAs Concentration Menu" were stored in the arrays "gFinalConceLimitStates", "gFinalConcenMSASet1", and "gFinalConcenMSASet2". The contents of the last two arrays were then transferred to the array "mConMSALimit" as we have seen above. These concentration limits are multiplied by the portfolio balance to arrive at the concentration dollar limits for each of the states or MSAs. See Exhibit 11.23. The target balances for each of the states and MSAs that have concentration limits are stored in the variables "mConTargetBalStates" and "mConTargetBalMSAs". These target balances are then subtracted from the current balances of the states and MSAs stored in the arrays "mConCurBalStates" and "mConCurBalMSA" to determine the concentration overages. See Exhibit 11.34.

The overage is the collateral balance that exceeds the concentration limit. The overages for the states and the MSAs are stored in the arrays "mConOverBalStates" and "mConOverBalMSA", respectively. The positive overages are summed into the variable "mTotalOverage". If the total concentration overage for the portfolio is less than $10, we have met all of our concentration requirements and have finished the process. We indicate this by setting the value of the function to TRUE. When we reemerge into the master subroutine, "GeoConcen_ApplyConcentrationLimits", it will then bypass any of the concentration adjustment code and terminate the concentration adjustment process. See Exhibit 11.35.

```
Sub GeoConcen_CalcExistingBalances()
    Call GeoConcen_SumPortfolioBalance   'sum balances of all eligible loans
    Call GeoConcen_SumBalancesAllStates  'sum balances by state code
    Call GeoConcen_SumBalancesAllMSAs    'sum balances by MSA code
End Sub
'==============================================================================
Sub GeoConcen_SumPortfolioBalance()
    'sum all currently eligible loans to determine the base portfolio balances
    ' from which to calculate the State and MSA concentration percentages
    mPortSum = 0
    For iloan = 1 To gTotalLoans
        If mConEligible(iloan) Then mPortSum = _
                mPortSum + gLoanData(iloan, FD_CURRBAL)
    Next iloan
End Sub
Sub GeoConcen_SumBalancesAllStates()
    'initialize the current concentratios to 0%
    For mState = 1 To NUM_STATES
        mConCurBalStates(mState) = 0#
    Next mState
    'sum the loan into a state specific bucket
    For iloan = 1 To gTotalLoans
        mState = gLoanData(iloan, FD_STATECODE)
        If mConEligible(iloan) Then
            mConCurBalStates(mState) = _
                mConCurBalStates(mState) + gLoanData(iloan, FD_CURRBAL)
        End If
    Next iloan
End Sub
Sub GeoConcen_SumBalancesAllMSAs()

Dim MSAIndex        As Integer  'nth MSA in the list if 52

    'initialize the balance arrays for each of the MSAs
    For mMSA = 1 To TOT_CON_MSA
        mConCurBalMSA(mMSA) = 0
    Next mMSA
    'sum by the MSA code
    For iloan = 1 To gTotalLoans
        MSA_code = gLoanData(iloan, FD_MSACODE) 'loan level MSA code
        'if zero forget about it; if non-zero match to index
        If MSA_code <> 0 Then
            If mConEligible(iloan) Then
                'assign loan on the basis of the MSA index
                MSAIndex = mConMSAIndex(iloan)
                mConCurBalMSA(MSAIndex) = _
                    mConCurBalMSA(MSAIndex) + gLoanData(iloan, FD_CURRBAL)
            End If
        End If
    Next iloan

End Sub
```

EXHIBIT 11.33 "GeoConcen_CalcExistingBalances" and portfolio, state, and MSA summation subroutines

If we have not arrived at a stopping criteria (all concentration limits meet), we will proceed on to Step #4 to adjust the balances of the states or MSAs that need it. The main subroutines for this process are named "GeoConcen_AdjustStateBalances" and "GeoConcen_AdjustMSABalances". These subroutines will sequentially address each of the overconcentrated states and MSAs. To set up the process by which we

```
' ====================================================================================
' STEP #2
' ====================================================================================
Sub GeoConcen_CalculateTargetBalances()

    'calculate the target concentration dollars by states and MSA's as a
    ' percentage of the total eligible collateral of the portfolio. If there is
    ' no concentration limit for the state or MSA set to zero (all loans eligible).
    For mState = 1 To NUM_STATES
        If gFinalConcenStates(mState) = 0 Then
            mConTargetBalState(mState) = 0
        Else
            mConTargetBalState(mState) = mPortSum * gFinalConcenStates(mState)
        End If
    Next mState
    For mMSA = 1 To TOT_CON_MSA
        If mConMSALimit(mMSA) = 0 Then
            mConTargetBalMSA(mMSA) = 0
        Else
            mConTargetBalMSA(mMSA) = mPortSum * mConMSALimit(mMSA)
        End If
    Next mMSA

End Sub
```

EXHIBIT 11.34 "GeoConcen_CalculateTargetBalances" subroutine

```
' ====================================================================================
' STEP #3
' ====================================================================================
Function GeoConcen_TestForCompletedConcentrations()

    'we now now the target concentrations in dollars for states and MSAs and we
    ' also know the current balances in each of those states and MSA's. we will
    ' know find the differences between the current balances and the targets based
    ' on the current size of the portfolio.
    'for each state
    For mState = 1 To NUM_STATES
        If mConTargetBalState(mState) > 0 Then
            mConOverBalStates(mState) = _
                mConCurBalStates(mState) - mConTargetBalState(mState)
        Else
            mConOverBalStates(mState) = 0
        End If
        If mConOverBalStates(mState) > 0 Then _
                mTotalOverage = mTotalOverage + mConOverBalStates(mState)
    Next mState
    'for each MSA
    For mMSA = 1 To TOT_CON_MSA
        If mConTargetBalMSA(mMSA) > 0 Then
            mConOverBalMSAs(mMSA) = mConCurBalMSA(mMSA) - mConTargetBalMSA(mMSA)
        Else
            mConOverBalMSAs(mMSA) = 0
        End If
        If mConOverBalMSAs(mMSA) > 0 Then _
            mTotalOverage = mTotalOverage + mConOverBalMSAs(mMSA)
    Next mMSA
    If mTotalOverage < 10# Then GeoConcen_TestForCompletedConcentrations = True

End Function
```

EXHIBIT 11.35 "GeoConcen_TestForCompletedConcentrations" function

```
Sub GeoConcen_AdjustStateBalances()

Dim clear_rows          As Long

    clear_rows = gTotalLoans
    For mState = 1 To NUM_STATES
        'find the states with a difference between the actual and targeted bals
        If mConOverBalStates(mState) > 0# Then
            'write out the balances
            Call GeoConcen_ClearLoanSchedule(clear_rows)
            irow = 1
            For iloan = 1 To gTotalLoans
                If gLoanData(iloan, FD_STATECODE) = mState Then
                    If mConEligible(iloan) Then 'eligible collateral only
                        Range("m18GeoConcentration").Cells(irow, 1) = iloan
                        Range("m18GeoConcentration").Cells(irow, 2) = _
                            gLoanData(iloan, FD_CURRBAL)
                        irow = irow + 1
                    End If
                End If
            Next iloan
            clear_rows = irow
            Calculate                               'calcs number of loans
            Call GeoConcen_SortLoanSchedule         'sorts the loan schedule
            Call GeoConcen_ReadLoanSchedule         'reads the loan schedule
            'drop loans as needed
            Call GeoConcen_CullLoanSchedule(ERR_CODE_STATE_CONCEN)
        End If
    Next mState

End Sub
```

EXHIBIT 11.36   "GeoConcen_AdjustStateBalances" subroutine

will cull the overconcentrated balances, we need to have a sorted list, from largest to smallest, of the loan balances for the entity to know how many loans are in the list. To build this list, we will print out the eligible loans for the state and MSA on the "ConcenWorksheet" worksheet. Here we can use a recorded macro contained in the subroutine "GeoConcen_SortLoanSchedule" to sort the loan list. We will then read the list into a VBA array named "mPortSort" using the "GeoConcen_ReadLoanSchedule". This array will contain the loan number of the collateral loan record and its current balance. Once this array is complete, we can employ the "GeoConcen_CullLoanSchedule" to remove the loans that constitute the overconcentration amount for the entity.

In that the two "Adjust***Balances" subroutines are virtually identical, we do not need to look at them both. In Exhibit 11.36 we see the code for the "GeoConcen_AdjustStateBalances" subroutine. It follows each of the steps in the process described immediately above and prepares the loan list of the state for the culling process. The list is ordered from high balance to low balance. The "GeoConcen_CullLoanSchedule" subroutine then has all the information it needs, in the proper order, to begin the overconcentration ineligibility assignment process.

The final step in the process is to eliminate the overconcentrated loan balances from the list of the target state or MSA entity. The process is divided into two parts. The first part is the top-down approach and the second is the bottom-up approach.

```
Sub GeoConcen_CullLoanSchedule(err_code As Integer)

Dim loop_trigger    As Boolean   'trigger to terminate Do While loops
Dim StateID         As Integer   'state postal ID nth in list
Dim LoanBal         As Double    'curr bal of loan to be deemed ineligible
Dim LoanID          As Long      'id number of loan to be deemed ineligible

    'cull out the over target concentration balance; start with the biggest
    ' first until they are larger than the required reduction amount, then
    ' switches over to the smallest loans next until the total indicated
    ' reduction has been acheived.
    'establish the target amounts and running amount variables for this entity
    Call GeoConcen_SetReductionTargetAmounts(err_code)
    'CULL OF LARGER BALANCE LOANS
    'start with the large balance loans first, render them ineligible until
    ' taking the next loan makes the overage amount go negative, stop there,
    ' move to small balance loans
    Call GeoConcen_CullLargeLoans(err_code)
    'CULL OF SMALL BALANCE LOANS
    'having gone as far as we can with the large loans above we now turn to the
    ' small loans.  we will use the same approach but from the bottom up, deeming
    ' each loan ineligible until we have driven the value of the mRunningOverage
    ' variable to zero or below zero.
    Call GeoConcen_CullSmallLoans(err_code)

End Sub
```

EXHIBIT 11.37   "GeoConcen_CullLoanSchedule" subroutine

The subroutine begins by reading the largest loan in the group and comparing its balance to that of the concentration overage. If the largest loan is greater than the overage amount, the subroutine abandons the top-down approach and switches to the bottom-up approach. In this approach the subroutine begins with the smallest balance loan and works its way up the list until the overage for the entity is reduced to below zero. As each loan is eliminated, loans that are members of MSAs also have their balances subtracted from the aggregate balance of the state to which they belong.

The "GeoConcen_CullLoanSchedule" subroutine manages the overall process. When we are working with the largest loans first, the subroutine "GeoConcen_CullLargeLoans" does the processing. This continues until the largest surviving loan is larger than the remaining balance of loans to be removed. The call then shifts to the subroutine "GeoConcen_CullSmallLoans" that works its way up from the smallest loans of the schedule. When overage has been reduced below zero, the rather unimaginatively named variable "loop_trigger" is set to TRUE and the respective "Do..While" loop terminates. See Exhibits 11.37, 11.38, and 11.39.

INTRODUCTION TO GEOGRAPHIC REPORTING

One of the major areas of interest is the characteristics of the geographic dispersion of the loans. We need to know where they are, how many are in each location, and the accompanying demographics of these subpopulations. To this end the CCFG has a number of Geographic reports that seek to meet this need.

```
Sub GeoConcen_CullLargeLoans(err_code As Integer)

Dim loop_trigger    As Boolean   'trigger to terminate Do While loops
Dim StateID         As Integer   'state postal ID nth in list
Dim LoanBal         As Double    'curr bal of loan to be deemed ineligible
Dim LoanID          As Long      'id number of loan to be deemed ineligible

    'CULL OF LARGER BALANCE LOANS
    'start with the large balance loans first, render them ineligible until
    ' taking the next loan makes the overage amount go negative, stop there,
    ' move to small balance loans
    irow = 1
    loop_trigger = False
    Do While loop_trigger = False
        LoanID = mPortSort(irow, 1)
        LoanBal = mPortSort(irow, 2)
        If mRunningOverage - LoanBal >= 0# Then
            'deselect the loan - set the error code for geo over-concentration
            gLoanSelect(LoanID, FD_CALCGEOCONCEN) = _
                gLoanSelect(LoanID, FD_CALCGEOCONCEN) + err_code
            mConEligible(LoanID) = False
            'decrease the running total for this State or MSA
            mRunningOverage = mRunningOverage - LoanBal
            If err_code = ERR_CODE_MSA_CONCEN Then
                'this entity is an MSA, we need to net the ineligble loan
                ' balance from the overage of the state containing the MSA also
                ' to avoid double counting
                StateID = gLoanData(LoanID, FD_STATECODE)
                If mConCurBalStates(StateID) > 0 Then
                    mConCurBalStates(StateID) = _
                                    mConCurBalStates(StateID) - LoanBal
                    mConOverBalStates(StateID) = _
                                    mConOverBalStates(StateID) - LoanBal
                End If
            End If
            irow = irow + 1
        Else
            'this loan would drive the running overage negative, we are done!
            loop_trigger = True
        End If
    Loop

End Sub
```

EXHIBIT 11.38   "GeoConcen_CullLargeLoans" subroutine

Geographic Loan Listing Report

The first Geographic Report that we will examine is the Geographic Loan Listing Report. This report is designed to produce a list of all the eligible and ineligible collateral of the portfolio based on its state and MSA location. The individual loans are then listed under their MSA location or, if they are not in an MSA, under the state location. A basic demographic profile of each loan is also produced. While both the Basic and the Cross Tabulation Stratification Reports are available to the CCFG analyst, these reports suffer from their strengths. This is to say that their outstanding ability to give us the big picture comes at the expense of allowing us to bore down to the loan-by-loan detail of the collateral at the state and MSA level of detail.

```
Sub GeoConcen_CullSmallLoans(err_code As Integer)

Dim loop_trigger     As Boolean   'trigger to terminate Do While loops
Dim StateID          As Integer   'state postal ID nth in list
Dim LoanBal          As Double    'curr bal of loan to be deemed ineligible
Dim LoanID           As Long      'id number of loan to be deemed ineligible

    'CULL OF SMALL BALANCE LOANS
    'having gone as far as we can with the large loans above we now turn to the
    ' small loans.  we will use the same approach but from the bottom up, deeming
    ' each loan ineligible until we have driven the value of the mRunningOverage
    ' variable to zero or below zero.
    irow = mNumPortSort                     'starting row is last row of the schedule
    loop_trigger = False
    Do While loop_trigger = False
        LoanID = mPortSort(irow, 1)
        LoanBal = mPortSort(irow, 2)
        If mRunningOverage - LoanBal >= 0# Then
            'deselect the loan - set the error code to geo over-concentration
            gLoanSelect(LoanID, FD_CALCGEOCONCEN) = _
                gLoanSelect(LoanID, FD_CALCGEOCONCEN) + err_code
            mConEligible(LoanID) = False
            mRunningOverage = mRunningOverage - LoanBal
            'net it from the state concentration total number
            If err_code = ERR_CODE_MSA_CONCEN Then
                StateID = gLoanData(mPortSort(irow, 1), FD_STATECODE)
                If mConCurBalStates(StateID) > 0 Then
                    mConCurBalStates(StateID) = _
                        mConCurBalStates(StateID) - LoanBal
                    mConOverBalStates(StateID) = _
                        mConOverBalStates(StateID) - LoanBal
                End If
            End If
            irow = irow - 1
        Else
            loop_trigger = True      'deselect this last loan, we are finished
            gLoanSelect(LoanID, FD_CALCGEOCONCEN) = _
                gLoanSelect(LoanID, FD_CALCGEOCONCEN) + err_code
            mConEligible(LoanID) = False
            If err_code = ERR_CODE_MSA_CONCEN Then
                StateID = gLoanData(LoanID, FD_STATECODE)
                If mConCurBalStates(StateID) > 0 Then
                    mConCurBalStates(StateID) = _
                        mConCurBalStates(StateID) - LoanBal
                    mConOverBalStates(StateID) = _
                        mConOverBalStates(StateID) - LoanBal
                End If
            End If
        End If
    Loop

End Sub
```

EXHIBIT 11.39 "GeoConcen_CullSmallLoans" subroutine

Format of the Geographic Loan Listing Report   The Geographic Loan Listing report allows us to view all individual loans with their specific amortization, balance,
borrower, and demographic detail. The fields of the report are as follows.

1. Postal Code and Common Name of the State
2. MSA Code and MSA Designation

3. Aggregate current balances by State and MSA areas
4. Number of loans by State and MSA areas

At the individual loan level:

5. Original Loan-to-Value Ratio
6. Current Loan-to-Value Ratio
7. Original Term
8. Remaining Term
9. Seasoning
10. Current Coupon Rate (Fixed or Index+Spread)
11. Original Appraisal Amount
12. Current Appraisal Amount
13. Property Type
14. Occupancy Code
15. Finance Purpose
16. Mortgage-to-Income Ratio
17. Total Debt-to-Income Ratio

See Exhibit 11.40.

VBA Code for the Geographic Loan Listing Report   This report looks quite involved, and I am sure that you think that you are about be tortured with hundreds of lines of VBA code. Surprise! This is a very compact report in regard to the VBA that produces and then performs its formatting operations. It is an excellent example how a little VBA can go a long way.

"RepGeoLoanList_MainWriteReports" Subroutine   The subroutine "RepGeoLoan List_MainWriteReports" is the main subroutine for the Geographic Loan Listing Report. Once again, as is our standard practice in all reporting subroutines, we will first check if the report has been requested by the analyst for production in this run of the CCFG. If it has, the subroutine immediately calls a series of subroutines that load the contents of several MSA information lists. The subroutine "Utility_ReadStateAndMSAInfo" populates a list of state postal codes as well as MSA numeric codes and names. The subroutine "RepGeoLoan List_ReadStateMSAInformation" also populates an array that tells us how many MSAs there are in each state and the numerical order of their codes. This subroutine reads all the MSA information associated with each state. The last subroutine, "RepGeoLoanList_SetMSAIndex", populates an array "gMSAIndex" that contains the index location of the MSA of the loan. If the loan is not associated with an MSA it assigns the value of "0" to that loan's MSA index.

"RepGeoLoanList_MainWriteReports" then opens the report template file, renames it, and saves it. It then calls the subroutine "RepGeoLoanList_WriteLoanList" to write the report and format it. After that it saves and closes the completed report file. See Exhibit 11.41.

"RepGeoLoanList_WriteLoanList" Subroutine   This subroutine aggregates the loan data by both state and MSA levels and produces the report for those states that have been selected.

Eligible Collateral Loan List By Geographic Region
With State and Metropolitan Statistical Area Totals

Postal Code	State Name	MSA Code	Metropolitan Statistical Area	#Loans State	#Loans MSA	Loan ID#	Original Balance	Remain Balance	Mort Type	Original Docs	Orig LTV	Current LTV	Orig Term	Remain Term	Season	Current Coupon	Original Appraisal	Current Appraisal	Property Type	Occupancy Code	Finance Purpose	% Mort D to I	% Total D to I
							State Balance / MSA Balance	State Balance / MSA Balance													State Totals & Dollar Weighted Statistics / Metropolitan Statistical Area Totals & Dollar Weighted Statistics / Individual Loan Information		
AK	Alaska			7			1,455,300	1,424,935			83.5%	102.6%	360.0	342.8	17.2	5.267%	438,718	376,198				38.3%	60.9%
			0 Loans With No MSA Designated			1502	73,086	73,086	SARM	Full	83%	112%	360	352	8	5.850%	88,440	81,900	Single Fam	Owner	Purchase	52%	83%
						3550	147,900	144,502	SARM	Partial	67%	134%	360	340	20	5.475%	221,850	194,200	Single Fam	Owner	Purchase	21%	37%
						4655	142,000	136,953	SARM	Partial	83%	93%	360	331	29	5.225%	170,400	127,800	Single Fam	Non-Owner	Purchase	46%	82%
					Totals 3		363,600	354,541			76.5%	113.9%	360.0	339.0	21.0	5.456%	480,690	403,900				37.1%	64.0%
		11260	Anchorage			663	638,400	630,316	SARM	Full	83%	106%	360	349	11	5.350%	766,080	670,400	Condo	Owner	Refinance	34%	51%
						2839	178,400	170,801	SARM	Full	91%	69%	360	327	33	4.975%	196,240	117,800	Single Fam	Owner	Purchase	48%	79%
						4731	186,700	184,829	SARM	Full	91%	103%	360	352	8	4.850%	205,370	190,000	Muti 2	Non-Owner	Purchase	46%	72%
						4763	88,200	84,448	SARM	Full	83%	94%	360	325	35	5.350%	105,840	79,400	Single Fam	Owner	Purchase	42%	58%
					Totals 4		1,091,700	1,070,393			85.9%	98.8%	360.0	341.1	15.9	5.204%	1,273,530	1,057,600				38.6%	59.9%
AL	Alabama			48			13,510,700	13,245,964			84.2%	105.3%	825.3	310.4	14.9	5.219%	781,047	683,622				45.1%	64.6%
			0 Loans With No MSA Designated			494	107,000	102,294	SARM	Full	83%	122%	360	326	34	4.975%	128,400	125,200	Muti 2	Owner	Purchase	50%	53%
						1341	182,800	179,007	SARM	Full	87%	97%	360	343	17	5.100%	210,220	173,500	Single Fam	Owner	Refinance	56%	64%
						1552	177,400	174,650	SARM	Full	91%	73%	360	348	12	4.725%	195,140	126,900	Muti 2	Owner	Refinance	42%	75%
						1691	57,700	57,099	SARM	Full	91%	106%	300	294	6	4.850%	63,470	60,300	Single Fam	Owner	No Data	49%	81%
						1829	354,900	350,799	SARM	Alt A	83%	115%	360	351	9	4.725%	425,880	404,600	Muti 2	Owner	Purchase	51%	58%
						2085	169,900	168,023	SARM	Full	91%	95%	360	351	9	4.975%	186,890	158,900	Single Fam	Non-Owner	Refinance	40%	76%
						2479	959,700	924,212	SARM	Full	87%	78%	360	328	32	5.600%	1,103,655	717,400	Single Fam	Owner	Refinance	59%	81%
						2710	77,600	76,733	SARM	Full	87%	116%	180	177	3	5.100%	89,240	89,300	Single Fam	Owner	Purchase	34%	63%
						2965	545,400	540,029	SARM	Full	83%	118%	300	294	6	5.225%	654,480	638,200	Single Fam	Owner	Purchase	55%	82%
						4035	86,900	84,483	SARM	Full	80%	103%	360	337	23	5.225%	108,625	86,900	Single Fam	Owner	Refinance	49%	71%
						4238	183,100	181,533	SARM	Full	87%	110%	360	353	7	4.975%	210,565	200,100	Single Fam	Seasonal	Purchase	35%	46%
						4448	990,300	979,458	SARM	Full	80%	126%	180	177	3	5.350%	1,237,875	1,237,900	Single Fam	No Data	Purchase	46%	53%
						4863	77,700	76,963	SARM	Full	83%	109%	300	294	6	5.475%	93,240	84,000	Condo	Owner	Purchase	46%	65%
					Totals 13		3,970,400	3,895,284			84.5%	105.3%	300.8	287.1	13.7	5.240%	4,707,680	4,103,200				50.1%	67.4%
		13820	Birmingham-Hoover			589	1,042,700	1,032,240	SARM	Full	80%	123%	300	294	6	5.100%	1,303,375	1,270,800	Single Fam	Owner	Refinance	36%	40%
						696	68,200	67,650	SARM	Full	87%	119%	360	349	11	5.475%	79,005	80,600	Single Fam	Owner	Purchase	31%	49%

EXHIBIT 11.40 Geographic Loan Listing Detail Report

```
Sub RepGeoLoanList_MainWriteReports()

    If gRepMenuGeoLoanList Then
        'read state lists that contain MSA codes and names
        Call GeoSelect_ReadGeoData
        Call Utility_ReadStateAndMSAInfo
        Call RepGeoLoanList_ReadStateMSAInformation
        ReDim gMSAIndex(1 To gTotalLoans) As Integer
        Call RepGeoLoanList_SetMSAIndex
        'write the Geographic Loan List
        Workbooks.Open FileName:=DIR_TEMPLATE_REP & GEO_LOANLIST_TEMPLATE
        ActiveWorkbook.SaveAs FileName:= _
            OUTPUT_DIRECTORY & gRepMenuPrefix & "GeoLoanList"
        Sheets("LoanListing").Select
        Call RepGeoLoanList_WriteLoanList 'write the eligible loan listing report
        Range("A1").Select
        ActiveWorkbook.Save
        ActiveWorkbook.Close
        gRepMenuAssumptions = True
    End If

End Sub
```

EXHIBIT 11.41   "RepGeoLoanList_MainWriteReports" subroutine

The first call is to the "RepGeoLoanList_AggregateCollat" subroutine. See Exhibit 11.42. This subroutine in turn calls two other subroutines that focus on aggregating the MSA and state collateral information, respectively. The aggregation is performed using the state index of the loan, found in "gLoanData(iloan, FD_STATECODE", and the index of the MSA numeric code, found in "gLoanData(iloan, FD_MSACODE)". The aggregated balances are placed in two arrays, "mStateInfo" and "mMSAInfo". In addition, the subroutine populates the arrays "mStateCount" and "mMSACount". These two arrays hold the total number of loans for each of the states and MSAs, respectively. With the data aggregated, we can now begin to write the report.

The report-writing code consists of a series of nested "For..Next" loops. The outermost of these loops run through each of the states. The next innermost "For..Next"

```
Sub RepGeoLoanList_AggregateCollat()

    Erase mStateInfo                'erase prior state information
    Erase mMSAInfo                  'erase prior MSA information
    For iloan = 1 To gTotalLoans
        istate = gLoanData(iloan, FD_STATECODE)
        If IsNumeric(gLoanData(iloan, FD_MSACODE)) Then
            iMSA = gLoanData(iloan, FD_MSACODE)
            Else
            iMSA = 0
        End If
        mStateCount(istate) = mStateCount(istate) + 1
        mMSACount(iMSA) = mMSACount(iMSA) + 1
        Call RepGeoLoanList_AggregateStateInfo
        Call RepGeoLoanList_AggregateMSAInfo
    Next iloan

End Sub
```

EXHIBIT 11.42   "RepGeoLoanList_WriteLoanList" subroutine

loop runs through each of the MSAs within the state, and the last, most interior "For..Next" loop, cycles through the "gLoanData" array, testing each loan to determine if it belongs to the state/MSA combination currently being reported.

The outermost "For..Next" loops through each of the 54 state level entities. It tests each one in turn to determine if that state has been selected for inclusion in this report. The election to place a state in the report is made by clicking on the "States Report Selection" button in the "Geographic Reports Editor" section of the "CCFG Reports Editor & Menu". The UserForm attached to the button appears and any or all states can be selected from the menu. The program now reads the current report line. This line will become the first line for the state section, where we will print the name of the state and the total information when we have it. We will record this row position in the spreadsheet in the "mStateTotalRow" variable. We then print the postal code and the common name of the state in the first two columns of this line of the report. We will add the totals and the dollar-weighted statistics when we have completed the search process some time latter.

We now enter the MSA loop. We then record the now-current row in the "iMSA" variable as the location for the totals statistic line for the current MSA. You will note that this loop runs from "0th" iteration of the loop to the number of MSAs in the state, the value of "gByStateMSATotal". On the "0" loop, the subroutine is looking for all loans that do not have an MSA associated with them. After that it moves through the MSAs of the states in their numerical code order. The MSA information, code, and name are added to the report. Before entering the loan-by-loan search loop, we check to see if there *are* any balances in the current MSA. If there are, we will search for the loans whose "FD_MSACODE" field value matches the current MSA code. Since each MSA code is unique, we do not have to also match the "FD_STATECODE" field. If we find a match, we print out the loan. We also increment the "runCount" variable by 1. If the value of the "runCount" variable equals the value of the "mMSACount" variable for this MSA, we have found all of the loans in this MSA and we exit the loan-by-loan loop.

When the loan-by-loan loop is completed, the subroutine "RepoGeoLoanList_WriteMSATotals" prints the totals statistics to the report at the previously recorded "mMSATotalRow" location. When all the MSAs for the state have been examined, the state totals statistics are output by the "RepGeoLoanList_WriteStateTotals" subroutine.

At the conclusion of the state loop, the report is formatted by the "RepGeoLoanList_ReformatReport" subroutine. See Exhibit 11.43.

"RepGeoLoanList_Reformat" Report During the entire time of the production of the report, state totals line, the MSA total lines, and the individual loan information lines are being added to the sheet. Although there are indentation differences and the formats of the lines are somewhat different, the report would be greatly improved by some judicious formatting. This is provided by the "RepGeoLoanList_ReformatReport" subroutine. You will note that if the line of the report contains state level totals, information there will be a state postal code (a String format) in Column 1 of the report. If the line is an MSA totals information line, it contains the MSA code (a Numeric) in Column 1. If it is an individual loan report line Column 1 is blank. We can use this information as the trigger conditions to format. We want to impose the following formats:

```
Sub RepGeoLoanList_WriteLoanList()

Dim runCount          As Long 'number of loans in the MSA
Dim noRow             As Integer 'row count for loans not in an MSA

    'Aggregate the collateral portfolio information by state and MSA
    Call RepGeoLoanList_AggregateCollat
    'write out the report body for states that have been selected
    irow = 10
    For istate = 1 To NUM_STATES
        'determine if the State has been selected from the User Form menu we do not
        ' print any records for non-selected States.  This is because the user may
        ' wish to run the report on a single state for presentation purposes.  We
        ' would then have 53 other States when we don't want/need them!
        If gRepMenuGeoStates(istate) Then
            mStateTotalRow = irow         'record the State totals row
            If istate > 1 Then Call RepGeoList_StateLineSpacer(irow - 1)
            Cells(irow, 1).Value = gDataStates(istate, 1) '1=state postal code
            Cells(irow, 2).Value = gDataStates(istate, 2) '2=state common name
            If istate = 1 Then
                Call RepGeoList_StateHeaderFormat(irow)
                Else
                Call RepGeoList_StateHeaderFormat(irow)
            End If
            irow = irow + 1              'increment to the first print row
            For iMSA = 0 To gByStateMSATotal(istate)
                runCount = 0
                irow = irow   'record the MSA totals row
                If iMSA > 0 Then
                    Cells(irow, 1).Value = gByStateMSACodes(istate, iMSA) 'MSA code
                    Cells(irow, 2).Value = gByStateMSANames(istate, iMSA) 'MSA name
                    Else
                    Cells(irow, 1).Value = 0        'some loans at not in an MSA
                    Cells(irow, 2).Value = "Loans With No MSA Designated"
                End If
                Call RepGeoList_MSAHeaderFormat(irow)
                'don't look for loans in MSA's that don't have any!
                If iMSA = 0 Then
                    'find all loans with same state code but 0 for MSA code
                    For noRow = 1 To TOT_DTI
                        mNOMSAInfo(noRow) = 0
                    Next noRow
                    For iloan = 1 To gTotalLoans
                        If gLoanData(iloan, FD_MSACODE) = iMSA And _
                            gLoanData(iloan, FD_STATECODE) = istate Then
                                Call RepGeoLoanList_WriteIndividualLoanData
                                Call RepGeoLoanList_AggregateNOMSAInfo
                                runCount = runCount + 1
                        End If
                    Next iloan
                    Call RepGeoLoanList_WriteNOMSATotals  'loans with NO MSA totals
                    Call RepGeoList_MSATotalsFormat(irow - 1)
                Else
                    If mMSAInfo(iMSA, CURR_BAL) > 0 Then
                        For iloan = 1 To gTotalLoans
                            If gLoanData(iloan, FD_MSACODE) = _
                                    gByStateMSACodes(istate, iMSA) Then
                                Call RepGeoLoanList_WriteIndividualLoanData
                                runCount = runCount + 1
                                'exit if you got them all
                                If runCount = mMSACount(iMSA) Then Exit For
                            End If
                        Next iloan
                    End If
                    Call RepGeoLoanList_WriteMSATotals     'MSA total line output
                    Call RepGeoList_MSATotalsFormat(irow - 1)
                End If
            Next iMSA
            Call RepGeoLoanList_WriteStateTotals         'State total line output
        End If
        stopRow = irow   'current last row of the report
    Next istate
    'report conten is complete, reformat and save
    stopRow = irow      'last row of the report
    Call RepGeoLoanList_ReformatReport

End Sub
```

EXHIBIT 11.43 "RepGeoLoanList_AggregateCollat" subroutine

- State Totals line = Bold, 12 pitch
- MSA Totals line = Bold, 11 pitch
- Loan line = Regular, 10 pitch
- Between the last entry of the previous state and the State Totals line of a new state we will insert a blank blue line.
- In the total lines themselves, we wish to express certain columns of dollar-weighted statistical results to one decimal place. These will be the original and current loan-to-values (LTVs), the original and remaining terms, seasoning, and the mortgage and total debt-to-income ratios.

Employing some recorded macro code and then stripping it down, we end up with the formatting subroutine in Exhibit 11.44 that gets the job done just as we desire. See Exhibit 11.44.

```
Sub RepGeoLoanList_ReformatReport()
    For irow = 10 To 10000
        If Cells(irow, 5) > 0# And Trim(Cells(irow, 6).Value) = "" Then
            'orig and current LTV
            Range("H" & irow & ":I" & irow).Select
            Selection.NumberFormat = "0.0%"
            'terms
            Range("J" & irow & ":L" & irow).Select
            Selection.NumberFormat = "0.0"
            'debt to income
            Range("S" & irow & ":T" & irow).Select
            Selection.NumberFormat = "0.0%"
        End If
    Next irow
End Sub
Sub RepGeoList_StateLineSpacer(irow As Long)
    Range("A" & irow & ":T" & irow).Select
    With Selection.Interior
        .Pattern = xlSolid
        .ThemeColor = xlThemeColorAccent1
        .TintAndShade = 0.799981688894314
    End With
End Sub
Sub RepGeoList_StateHeaderFormat(irow As Long)
    Range("A" & irow & ":T" & irow).Select
    Selection.Font.Bold = True
    Rows(irow & ":" & irow).Select
    With Selection.Font
        .Name = "Calibri"
        .Size = 12
    End With
End Sub
Sub RepGeoList_MSATotalsFormat(irow As Long)
    Cells(irow, 2).Value = "Totals"
    Range("B" & irow).Select
    With Selection
        .HorizontalAlignment = xlRight
    End With
    Range("A" & irow & ":T" & irow).Select
    Selection.Font.Bold = True
End Sub
Sub RepGeoList_MSAHeaderFormat(irow As Long)
    Range("A" & irow & ":B" & irow).Select
    Selection.Font.Bold = True
End Sub
```

EXHIBIT 11.44 "RepGeoLoanList_ReformatReport" subroutine

Geographic Concentration Reports

The format and contents of the three Geographic Concentration reports are directly related to the formating and reporting VBA code that we just developed for the Geographic Loan Listing Report.

Loan, MSA, and State Level Geographic Concentration Report Formats   The Geographic Concentration Report Package (GCRP) consists of three reports of varying degrees of details. These are, from most specific to most general:

1. Loan Level Geographic Concentration Report
2. Metropolitan Statistical Area Level Geographic Concentration Report
3. State Level Geographic Concentration Report

The Loan Level report provides concentration statistics at the state level, the MSA level in which the loan resides, and the loan itself. The MSA Level report contains concentrations on all active MSAs in the state and the state itself. It also contains a "synthetic" MSA comprised of all loans that do not have an MSA code or are not in an MSA. The State Level report provides state level concentration statistics only.

The GCRP template file consists of the above three reports. They share 80%+ formatting, but we will have to write a different subroutine to produce each of them. The reason for this will become clear shortly. The layout of the most complex of the three reports, the Loan Level report, displays a high degree of commonality with the Geographic Loan Listing Report. See Exhibit 11.45.

This report consists of 22 columns broken into four sections. These sections are:

1. Geographic Regional Section
   1 State/MSA code column
   2 State/MSA name column
2. % Balances Section
   3 % National Balances (% that State, MSA, or Loan is of National balance)
   4 % State Balances (% that MSA or Loan is of State balance)
   5 % MSA Balances (% Loan is of MSA balance)
3. Loan Count and Dollar Balances Section
   6 Loan Count column for National, States, and MSAs
   7 Original Balance column for States and MSAs
   8 Current Balance column for National, States, and MSAs
4. Demographics and Credit Section
   9 Mortgage Type column (Loan Listing report only)
   10, 11 Original and Current Loan-to-Value Ratios columns
   12, 13, 14 Original and Remaining Terms, and Seasoning columns
   15 Current Coupon column
   16, 17 Original and Current Appraisal columns

Concentration Report By Geographic Region
Individual Loans With State and Metropolitan Statistical Area Totals

Postal Code (State / MSA)	State Name / Metropolitan Statistical Area	% State Balances	% MSA Balances	% Loan Balances	# Loans State / MSA / Loan ID #	State MSA Original Balance	State MSA Remain Balance	Mort Type	Orig LTV	Current LTV	Orig Term	Remain Term	Season	Current Coupon	Original Appraisal	Current Appraisal	$ Avg FICO	% First Home	% Self Employed	% Mort D to I	% Total D to I
USA	National				4,599	1,372,464,300	1,345,023,360		83%	106%	320.9	312.4	13.06	5.167%	1,628,801,045	1,424,643,500	702.7	27%	46%	44%	64%
AK	Alaska	0.11%			7	1,455,300	1,424,935		84%	103%	352.49	342.84	17.159	5.267%	1,754,220	1,461,500	673.2104	42.9%	28.6%	38%	61%
0	Loans With No MSA Designated	0.03%	24.88%		3	363,600	354,541		75%	114%	351.03	339	21.003	5.456%	480,690	403,900	695.7113	66.7%	0.0%	37%	64%
		0.01%		20.61%	1502	73,700	73,086	SARM	83%	112%	360	352	8	5.850%	88,440	81,900	700	Yes	No	52%	83%
		0.01%		10.14%	3550	147,900	144,502	SARM	67%	134%	360	340	20	5.475%	221,850	194,200	680	Yes	No	21%	37%
		0.01%		9.61%	4655	142,000	136,953	SARM	83%	93%	360	331	29	5.225%	170,400	127,800	710	No	No	46%	82%
11260	Anchorage	0.08%	75.12%		4	1,091,700	1,070,393		86%	99%	352.97	344.11	15.886	5.204%	1,273,530	1,057,600	665.7576	25.0%	50.0%	39%	60%
		0.05%		44.23%	663	638,400	630,316	SARM	83%	106%	360	349	11	5.350%	766,080	670,400	670	Yes	Yes	34%	51%
		0.01%		11.99%	2839	178,400	170,801	SARM	91%	69%	360	327	33	4.975%	196,240	117,800	670	No	No	48%	79%
		0.01%		12.97%	4731	186,700	184,829	SARM	91%	103%	360	352	8	4.850%	205,370	190,000	650	No	No	46%	72%
		0.01%		5.93%	4763	88,200	84,448	SARM	83%	94%	360	325	35	5.350%	105,840	79,400	660	No	No	42%	58%
AL	Alabama	0.98%			48	13,510,700	13,245,964		84%	105%	318.88	310.4	14.856	5.219%	16,079,965	13,948,200	728.6886	31.3%	31.3%	45%	65%
0	Loans With No MSA Designated	0.29%	29.41%		13	3,970,400	3,895,284		83%	105%	295.12	287.13	13.68	5.240%	4,707,680	4,103,200	737.3941	30.8%	30.8%	50%	67%
		0.01%		0.77%	494	107,000	102,294	SARM	83%	122%	360	326	34	4.975%	128,400	125,200	710	Yes	No	50%	53%
		0.01%		1.35%	1341	182,800	179,007	SARM	87%	97%	360	343	17	5.100%	210,220	173,500	700	Yes	No	56%	64%
		0.01%		1.32%	1552	177,400	174,650	SARM	91%	73%	360	348	12	4.725%	195,140	126,900	680	No	No	42%	75%
		0.00%		0.43%	1691	57,700	57,099	SARM	91%	106%	300	294	6	4.850%	63,470	60,300	750	No	No	49%	81%
		0.03%		2.65%	1829	854,900	850,799	SARM	83%	115%	360	351	9	4.725%	425,880	404,600	710	Yes	No	51%	58%
		0.01%		1.27%	2085	169,900	168,023	SARM	91%	95%	360	351	9	4.975%	186,890	158,900	690	No	Yes	40%	76%
		0.07%		6.98%	2479	959,700	924,212	SARM	87%	78%	360	328	32	5.600%	1,103,655	717,400	810	No	Yes	59%	81%
		0.01%		0.58%	2710	77,600	76,733	SARM	87%	116%	180	177	3	5.100%	89,240	89,300	720	No	No	34%	63%
		0.04%		4.08%	2965	545,400	540,029	SARM	83%	118%	300	294	6	5.225%	654,480	638,200	730	No	Yes	55%	82%
		0.01%		0.64%	4035	86,900	84,483	SARM	80%	103%	360	337	23	5.225%	108,625	86,900	730	No	Yes	49%	71%
		0.01%		1.37%	4238	183,100	181,533	SARM	87%	110%	360	353	7	4.975%	210,565	200,100	790	No	No	35%	46%
		0.07%		7.39%	4448	990,300	979,458	SARM	80%	126%	180	177	3	5.350%	1,237,875	1,237,900	710	Yes	No	46%	53%
		0.01%		0.58%	4863	77,700	76,963	SARM	83%	109%	300	294	6	5.475%	93,240	84,000	640	No	No	46%	65%
13820	Birmingham-Hoover	0.23%	23.40%		16	3,152,600	3,099,440		82%	109%	306.48	299.56	12.178	5.180%	3,834,830	3,388,400	726.6806	37.5%	25.0%	41%	57%
		0.08%	7.79%	33.30%	589	1,042,700	1,032,240	SARM	80%	123%	300	294	6	5.100%	1,303,375	1,270,800	720	Yes	No	36%	40%
		...	...	...	...	...	...	...	...	...	...	...	...	...	...	...	...	...	...	...	...

Section headers spanning the statistical columns: State Totals & Dollar Weighted Statistics; Metropolitan Statistical Area Totals & Dollar Weighted Statistics; Individual Loan Information.

EXHIBIT 11.45 Geographic Concentration Report: Loan Level

18 Dollar-Weighted FICO Score column

19 Dollar-Weighted First Time Homeowner column ($Yes)/($Total)

20 Dollar Weighted Self Employed column ($Yes)/($Total)

21, 22 Mortgage and Total Debt-to-Income Ratio columns

The format for the State Level Concentration Report forgoes columns 5, the % MSA Balances column, and 9, the Mortgage Type column, since these fields cannot be displayed on a report that has MSA as its lowest level of detail. The State Level drops the % State Balances column in addition to the other columns mentioned previously. Note that in the column entitled "First Time Homeowner" we have a dollar-weighted percentage number as the display statistics. This parameter is expressed in a "No Data", "Yes", or "No" response, as is the field next to it "Self Employment?". How can we dollar-weight two such parameters? First-time homeowners are higher-risk mortgagors. They are generally transitioning from a rental arrangement and need to buy many things to set up housekeeping. They have generally put a substantial amount of their savings in the down payment and are in a condition of illiquidity known as being house poor. If there is an employment disruption due to unemployment, illness, death, or other conditions that could draw on the remaining funds of the household, a default could result. Therefore, the risk conditions would be either "Yes" or "No Data" in which case we would need to assume that the missing condition is actually an unreported "Yes." We will therefore sum the balances at risk, these being designated as current balances of all "Yes" and "No Data" loans, and divide that sum by the total current balances from the same loans. In this case we find that for California as a whole, 90.57% of the current principal balances of the portfolio are at some level of incremental risk due to first-time home ownership. See Exhibit 11.46 for the MSA Level and the State Level Geographic Concentration Reports. To make comparisons easier, the California concentration information has been included on all three reports.

Geographic Concentration Report Package Template File   The GCRP uses the template file "GeographicConcenTemplate". It consists of three worksheets, one for the Loan, MSA, and State Level Reports. The spreadsheets are named:

- "LoanLevelListing"
- "MSALevelListing"
- "StateLevelListing"

The main GCRP subroutine opens the template file, renames it, and saves it. The three reports are written directly to these worksheets, and the CGRP is saved and closed ending the process.

Steps to Producing the Individual Loan Level Report   The steps in producing the Individual Loan Listing Report using the "RepGeoCon_MainWriteReports" subroutine are:

1. Call the subroutine "RepGeoCon_MainWriteReports". We need to load a number of arrays with state and MSA information. We want this information

Concentration Report By Geographic Region
State and Metropolitan Statistical Area Totals

Postal MSA Code	MSA Code	State Name / Metropolitan Statistical Area	% State Balances	% MSA Balances	# Loans State	# Loans MSA	Orig Balance	Curr Balance	Orig LTV	Current LTV	Orig Term	Remain Term	Season	Current Coupon	Original Appraisal	Current Appraisal	S Avg FICO	%First Home	%Self Employed	%Mort D to I	%Total D to I
USA		National			4,832		1,253,636,600	1,228,399,945	83.0%	97.5%	321.3	312.7	15.2	5.169%	1,488,969,760	1,298,769,200	702.0	26.53%	45.80%	43.76%	63.60%
CA		California	10.2%		686		128,135,900	125,569,172	84.6%	97.4%	321.1	312.5	15.2	5.184%	152,280,005	133,168,500	704.2	25.66%	45.80%	44.13%	63.93%
	0	Loans With No MSA Designated	7.6%	73.9%		451	94,727,400	92,847,162	82.9%	95.6%	315.5	307.0	14.9	5.184%	112,653,640	99,827,000	707.3	27.05%	44.35%	44.26%	63.41%
12540		Bakersfield	0.3%	2.8%		19	3,606,100	3,549,415	85.6%	95.7%	315.5	307.2	15.0	5.051%	4,248,315	3,807,100	658.0	47.37%	31.58%	42.33%	66.14%
23420		Fresno	0.2%	2.4%		15	3,806,100	2,955,671	80.4%	87.6%	346.5	338.7	13.6	5.266%	3,785,020	3,483,100	698.1	40.00%	20.00%	47.12%	71.88%
31100		Los Angeles-Long Beach-Santa Ana	2.3%	22.8%		161	29,207,900	28,609,097	80.2%	95.9%	344.8	334.3	17.8	5.402%	34,598,360	30,111,000	703.1	28.57%	46.58%	44.78%	63.39%
33700		Modesto	0.1%	0.8%		6	975,800	955,681	83.2%	91.2%	275.1	270.2	8.8	5.276%	1,224,145	1,009,200	748.8	33.33%	66.67%	44.78%	64.58%
37100		Oxnard-Thousand Oaks-Ventura	0.2%	1.8%		14	2,255,400	2,213,977	86.7%	95.5%	329.0	319.9	16.1	5.276%	2,412,200	2,472,100	731.3	21.43%	57.14%	40.98%	72.34%
40140		Riverside-San Bernardino-Ontario	1.0%	9.5%		61	12,137,200	11,919,560	85.4%	97.6%	329.0	319.9	17.0	5.191%	14,218,250	12,541,000	697.6	19.67%	40.98%	44.87%	61.20%
40900		Sacramento-Arden-Arcade-Roseville	0.4%	4.3%		32	5,827,900	5,400,748	84.8%	105.1%	334.4	324.7	17.0	5.194%	6,556,645	5,385,300	702.7	18.75%	46.88%	46.88%	61.20%
41500		Salinas	0.1%	0.6%		4	799,500	786,669	81.8%	93.1%	354.0	345.7	17.3	5.358%	796,045	859,300	679.4	22.58%	54.84%	54.84%	59.71%
41740		San Diego-Carlsbad-San Marcos	0.5%	4.8%		31	6,173,200	6,080,633	85.0%	97.9%	316.6	327.3	17.2	5.197%	7,225,445	6,381,300	710.7	23.19%	52.17%	52.17%	54.19%
41860		San Francisco-Oakland-Fremont	1.1%	10.3%		69	13,135,000	12,955,649	85.1%	97.9%	327.3	333.7	15.7	5.137%	15,449,390	13,900,300	669.6	14.81%	44.44%	42.40%	67.57%
41940		San Jose-Sunnyvale-Santa Clara	0.5%	4.6%		37	5,854,400	5,735,052	81.6%	88.2%	332.3	307.2	15.7	5.425%	6,813,170	5,841,600	733.8	16.67%	33.33%	42.40%	63.47%
42060		Santa Barbara-Santa Maria-Goleta	0.1%	1.3%		6	1,616,000	1,597,335	87.2%	118.4%	352.1	302.4	8.4	5.425%	1,982,935	1,858,700	655.3	16.67%	33.33%	33.33%	68.63%
42220		Santa Rosa-Petaluma	0.0%	0.3%		2	592,400	583,803	87.2%	110.3%	352.1	341.6	18.4	5.227%	451,230	330,300	715.1	50.00%	50.00%	50.00%	63.43%
44700		Stockton	0.2%	1.7%		11	2,174,600	2,179,215	87.5%	110.3%	352.5	342.7	17.3	5.261%	2,490,665	1,985,900	731.8	18.18%	45.45%	42.46%	64.84%
46700		Vallejo-Fairfield	0.1%	1.1%		8	1,419,100	1,390,770	82.6%	93.1%	337.0	328.5	15.3	5.009%	1,729,170	1,553,100	711.8	25.00%	37.50%	40.71%	61.67%
47300		Visalia-Porterville	0.1%	0.7%		4	853,600	843,650	83.6%	83.4%	269.8	266.0	7.3	4.924%	1,020,940	1,012,500	741.5	25.00%	50.00%	43.11%	72.89%
CO		Colorado	1.8%		70		23,090,300	22,620,304	85.0%	94.0%	322.3	314.7	13.4	5.240%	27,330,100	24,632,700	704.9	25.71%	52.86%	44.86%	64.49%
	0	Loans With No MSA Designated	0.9%	51.0%		42	11,752,600	11,533,431	79.7%	91.1%	350.0	341.8	14.8	5.093%	14,693,680	13,200,600	718.5	33.33%	52.38%	42.45%	60.32%
17820		Colorado Springs	0.1%	6.0%		6	1,381,200	1,365,650	84.0%	86.4%	306.7	302.3	7.9	5.321%	1,645,640	1,597,600	663.4	33.33%	50.00%	50.00%	59.59%
19740		Denver-Aurora	1.3%	68.5%		43	15,773,800	15,487,598	86.5%	95.8%	313.4	305.7	13.4	5.288%	18,337,610	16,434,800	703.5	20.93%	53.49%	46.36%	66.48%
CT		Connecticut	1.5%		72		18,416,100	18,041,952	84.4%	96.9%	327.2	318.3	15.7	5.220%	21,946,100	19,198,800	701.7	26.39%	58.33%	44.77%	63.94%
	0	Loans With No MSA Designated	0.9%	59.3%		38	10,889,000	10,705,719	84.3%	93.6%	318.3	310.6	13.1	5.386%	12,767,000	11,585,200	726.3	21.05%	57.89%	43.22%	58.48%
14860		Bridgeport-Stamford-Norwalk	0.2%	16.7%		14	3,063,900	3,010,303	78.6%	89.0%	342.5	334.9	13.7	5.084%	3,937,220	3,599,800	698.1	14.29%	57.14%	43.05%	66.99%
25540		Hartford-West Hartford-East Hartford	0.5%	33.6%		24	6,213,400	6,067,969	86.7%	106.7%	327.6	317.0	18.4	5.242%	7,196,390	5,856,000	681.4	29.17%	62.50%	43.11%	63.57%
35300		New Haven-Milford	0.3%	20.0%		15	3,694,300	3,610,820	83.6%	91.9%	324.7	316.0	16.9	5.051%	4,428,950	4,006,400	702.2	40.00%	53.33%	51.24%	67.61%

Concentration Report By Geographic Region
State Totals

Postal Code	State Name	% State Balances	# Loans	Original Balance	Current Balance	Orig LTV	Current LTV	Orig Term	Remain Term	Season	Current Coupon	Original Appraisal	Current Appraisal	S Avg FICO	% First Home	% Self Employed	% Mort D to I	% Total D to I
USA	National		4,832	1,253,636,600	1,228,399,945	83%	98%	321.3	312.7	15.2	5.169%	1,488,969,760	1,298,769,200	702.0	26.5%	45.8%	43.8%	63.6%
AK	Alaska	0.12%	7	1,455,300	1,424,935	84%	100%	352.5	342.8	17.2	5.267%	1,754,220	1,461,500	673.2	42.9%	28.6%	38.3%	60.9%
AL	Alabama	1.08%	47	13,502,400	13,237,779	84%	100%	318.9	310.4	14.9	5.219%	16,067,515	11,936,300	728.7	31.9%	31.9%	45.1%	64.6%
AR	Arkansas	0.58%	26	7,238,600	7,099,750	86%	99%	317.1	308.9	14.4	5.280%	8,443,175	7,421,100	716.1	23.1%	38.5%	40.7%	62.5%
AZ	Arizona	2.56%	117	32,080,800	31,505,105	86%	97%	327.3	319.5	13.7	5.127%	37,285,905	33,509,400	714.4	28.2%	55.6%	44.3%	66.0%
CA	California	10.22%	686	128,135,900	125,569,172	85%	97%	321.1	312.5	15.2	5.184%	152,280,005	133,168,500	704.2	25.7%	45.6%	44.1%	63.9%
CO	Colorado	1.84%	70	23,090,300	22,620,304	85%	94%	322.3	314.7	13.4	5.240%	27,330,100	24,632,700	704.9	25.7%	52.9%	44.9%	64.5%
CT	Connecticut	1.47%	72	18,416,100	18,041,952	84%	97%	327.2	318.3	15.7	5.220%	21,946,100	19,198,800	701.7	26.4%	58.3%	44.8%	63.9%
DE	Delaware	0.00%																
FL	Florida	8.25%	366	103,367,100	101,306,330	85%	97%	315.4	307.0	14.8	5.170%	122,131,245	107,090,500	701.2	24.6%	45.1%	43.9%	63.7%
GA	Georgia	2.62%	129	32,847,500	32,209,989	85%	95%	331.6	323.0	15.2	5.229%	39,064,960	34,547,700	677.0	25.6%	41.1%	44.5%	61.4%
HI	Hawaii	0.42%	24	5,246,700	5,170,858	84%	97%	329.1	323.0	11.0	5.249%	6,232,605	5,457,200	698.8	25.0%	33.3%	45.2%	59.4%
IA	Iowa	0.55%	20	6,941,500	6,802,436	85%	95%	342.5	333.7	15.9	5.091%	8,208,525	7,322,700	712.8	25.0%	40.0%	41.1%	67.1%
ID	Idaho	0.21%	9	2,681,300	2,617,681	86%	99%	351.5	343.1	18.7	4.971%	3,128,885	2,666,100	733.5	33.3%	33.3%	46.9%	66.0%
IL	Illinois	5.01%	228	62,864,600	61,596,639	84%	97%	324.7	316.0	15.3	5.160%	75,428,390	65,581,900	703.6	32.5%	45.2%	43.0%	62.3%

EXHIBIT 11.46 Geographic Concentration Report: MSA and State Levels

available so that we can easily associate a particular MSA with the state that it is situated in, or find out the number and codes of the MSAs in a particular state. We will also want to establish index locations for the MSAs and their appropriate states, such as "the 12th MSA is in the 5th State", or "the 9th State contains the 31st to the 45th MSAs". We will also calculate the total current balance amount of eligible collateral in the portfolio at this time

2. We test the variable "mCollatTag" to determine if the reports requested are pre- or post-concentration activity reports. Based on this determination we check to see if any of the three—state, MSA, or loan level—reports of this type have been selected. If they have, we set the "go_ok" variable to TRUE.

3. We now test the "go_ok" variable. If it TRUE, appropriate reports have been requested and we will proceed to write them. If it is FALSE, no reports are selected and we exit the process altogether.

4. We now enter a loop that runs from 1 to 3. This loop will trigger the production of the loan level, MSA level and state level reports (if they have been selected). The first time through the loop we will perform all of the aggregation and calculation methods needed to provide complete information for all three of the reports.

5. We call the subroutine "RepGeoCon_EraseAllAggregationArrays". This clears out any totals from previous CCFG model runs.

6. We then set the MSA index for all loan in the pool. This matches the MSA codes of the collateral to the nth position of those codes in the MSA code list.

7. We now aggregate the collateral by MSA and state levels. The subroutine "RepGeoCon_AggregateCollat" performs the three-level aggregations at the MSA, state, and national levels. This subroutine must evaluate the settings of the "mCollatTag" to determine what collateral will be included in the statistics. If the election is for a report displaying initial concentrations, all collateral is aggregated. If the setting is "1", final concentrations, only eligible collateral is aggregated. At the same time, since we have now calculated the amount of collateral in each of the 54 states and 150 MSAs, we can calculate the loan, MSA, and state level concentration percentages. We will also compute all of the MSA and state level averages and totals for the demographic and credit data columns of the report. A count of the number of loans in each state and MSA is also made at this time.

8. We then exit the calculation loop and call the subroutine "RepGeoCon_WriteReports". Based on the conditions of the model run and if the report selected is either pre- or postconcentration test, we set up an Excel template file to receive the reports. We will open, rename, and save the template file. Next we will delete the two unnecessary reports. If the state level report is selected, the MSA and loan level template report worksheets for those reports will be deleted. These operations are performed by the subroutine "RepGeoCo_SetUp Workbook".

9. With the workbook prepared and available, we will now be directed to one of three different reporting subroutines based on the type of report: loan, MSA, or state level.

10. To call the particular reporting subroutine, we will need, in this case, "RepGeoCon_WriteLoanListing".

11. Write the national total current balance report line.

12. Loop through all states. Report on those selected in the UserForm of the Geographic Reports Menu subsection of the CCFG Reports Editor and Menu. For each selected state, first write the state totals line.
13. For each selected state, first write the report line summarizing all loans in the state without an MSA code.
14. Write the first MSA report line. The MSAs are alphabetically arranged within their states.
15. Search the "gLoanData" array for all loans with a MSA code matching the current code, and print these records and their concentration statistics calculated in Step #7 to the report. Write out each loan as it is found. When we find the last loan of the MSA, we break out of the loop. We will start with all loans with an MSA code of "0", the MSA code of loans *not* situated in an MSA. Next we proceed to the loans within specific MSAs.
16. Continue until we have exhausted the MSAs in the state and the selected states in the state menu list.
17. Save the completed GCRP and close the file.

GCRP VBA Code The VBA code that produces the GCRP resides in the module named "Report_GeoConcentration". The structure of the code of the highest-level subroutine "RepGeoCon_MainWriteReports" is virtually identical to the subroutine that produces the Geographic Loan Listing Report. It reads the geographic information concerning the states and MSA and then makes the same determination as to what reports to produce. Once these tasks are accomplished, it cycles through the reporting sequence three times, performing all calculation and aggregation activities on the first loop of that process. Each of these loops activates a series of subroutines that are report specific but that share a very high degree of commonality with not only each other but also with the VBA code that built the Geographic Loan Listing report package. In that the Loan Level Listing report is the most involved, we will examine the VBA code that produces it, in lieu of the MSA or state level report. We will not look at each and every subroutine that produces that report, but we will look at the critical ones closely.

The key challenge in producing the GCRP is to keep the relationships between Loan = MSA = State in correct hierarchical order and to be able to link relation of State = MSA and MSA = State.

"RepGeoCon_MainWriteReports" Subroutine This subroutine is the master subroutine for the process of producing the Geographic Concentration Reports. See Exhibit 11.47.

The subroutine "RepGeoCon_MainWriteReports" begins by calling the subroutine "GeoSelect_ReadGeoData". This subroutine loads a series of arrays with the state and MSA level identification information, such as postal codes, names, and rank order locations in various lists.

The subroutine next calls "Utility_ReadStateandMSAInfo". This subroutine populates three arrays:

1. "gMSACodes". Contains the 150 MSA five-digit numeric code numbers.
2. "gMSANames". Contains the 150 MSA names.
3. "gStatePostal". Contains the two-letter postal code for each state and territory.

```
Sub RepGeoCon_MainWriteReports(mCollatTag As Integer)

    go_ok = False
    ReDim gMSAIndex(1 To gTotalLoans) As Integer
    Call GeoSelect_ReadGeoData
    Call Utility_ReadStateAndMSAInfo
    Call RepGeoCon_ReadStateMSAInformation

    If mCollatTag = COLLAT_PRECON Then
        'check for initial concentration reports requested
        If gRepMenuGeoInitConLoan Or gRepMenuGeoInitConState Or _
            gRepMenuGeoInitConMSA Then go_ok = True
    Else
        'checkfor final concentration reports requested
        If gRepMenuGeoFinConLoan Or gRepMenuGeoFinConState Or _
            gRepMenuGeoFinConMSA Then go_ok = True
    End If

    If go_ok Then
        For irep = 1 To 3
            If irep = 1 Then
                'erase all geo concentration aggregation arrays
                Call RepGeoCon_EraseAllAggregationArrays
                Call RepGeoCon_SetMSAIndex   'finds MSA index in State/MSA list
                'aggregate the collateral and calculate the concetration balances
                ReDim ConcenLoan(1 To gTotalLoans, 1 To 3) As Double
                Call RepGeoCon_AggregateCollat(mCollatTag)
            End If
            Call RepGeoCon_WriteReports(mCollatTag, irep)
        Next irep
        gRepMenuAssumptions = True
    End If

End Sub
```

EXHIBIT 11.47   "RepGeoCon_MainWriteReports" subroutine

The third subroutine call is to "RepGeoCon_ReadStateMSAInformation" that populates the arrays:

- **"mStateMSANumber".** The number of MSAs in each state.
- **"mStateMSACode".** The list of MSA codes for each state.
- **"mStateMSAName".** Names of the MSAs in each of the states.
- **"gMSAStatesByCode".** Postal code of each state associated with each MSA.
- **"gMSAStatesIndex".** The index position of the state in the state list associated with the MSA code.

With these tasks completed, we now proceed by checking the status of the variable "mCollatTag", which is passed into it from the Main Program. The value of this variable will tell us if we are reporting an initial—"mCollatTag" = COL-LAT_PRECON—or a final—"mCollatTag" = POST_CONCEN—concentration report. After determining the type of data we are presenting, we need to check the report variables that tell us which reports data levels to produce. Only if at least one of the following three variables—"gRepMenuInitConLoan", "gRepMenuInit ConMSA", or "gRepMenuInitConState"—is TRUE will we produce any reports. If they are all FALSE, we set the variable "go_ok" to FALSE and bypass the rest of the subroutine. Conversely if we had entered the subroutine and the value of "mCollatTag" is not equal to "COLLAT_PRECON", we would check the report request variables for the Final Concentration reports to see how to proceed. In either case, if "go_ok" is set to TRUE, we proceed. We now have all the basic reference data in hand, and we know what type of reports we are being asked to produce. Our next step is to perform two more housekeeping tasks before we can begin the process constructing the reports. The first task is to clear all residual balances from any prior model run that may interfere with the calculation process. The second is to tie each of the loans to a particular MSA or set the loan's MSA code to zero if it is not associated with an MSA.

"RepGeoCon_SetMSAIndex" Subroutine A call to the subroutine "RepGeoCon_EraseAllAggregationArrays" will accomplish the first task. A call to the subroutine "RepGeoCon_SetMSAIndex" will accomplish the second. See Exhibit 11.48. This subroutine matches the MSA code of the loan to a table of MSA codes in the array "gMSACode". It then puts the index position of the MSA code it has found that matches the loan-specific MSA in the array "gMSAIndex". The array uses a set of step cutoffs to speed up the search process.

"RepGeoCon_AggregateCollat" Subroutine We must now aggregate the collateral by its MSA/non-MSA and state levels. The subroutine "RepGeoCon_Aggregate Collat" performs this task. We need to pass it an argument delineating the type

```
Sub RepGeoCon_SetMSAIndex()

Dim startRow        As Integer 'break the list into 10 segments to speed up search

    'run through the list, find a match between the codes and immediately exit
    ' the loop.  The list is 150 names long so we have set up a "divide and
    ' conquer" helper based on the State code of the loan.
    For iloan = 1 To gTotalLoans
        If gLoanOK(iloan) Then
            Select Case gLoanData(iloan, FD_STATECODE)
                Case Is < 5:  startRow = 1        'pre California
                Case Is < 7:  startRow = 10       'pre Connecticut
                Case Is < 10: startRow = 28       'pre Georgia
                Case Is < 16: startRow = 45       'pre Kansas
                Case Is < 22: startRow = 59       'pre Michigan
                Case Is < 29: startRow = 70       'pre Nebraska
                Case Is < 35: startRow = 90       'pre Ohio
                Case Is < 38: startRow = 102      'pre Pennsylvannia
                Case Is < 43: startRow = 115      'pre Texas
                Case Else:    startRow = 131      'Texas to end of list
            End Select
            'search a smaller part oft he total list
            For iMSA = startRow To TOTAL_MSAS
                If gLoanData(iloan, FD_MSACODE) = gMSACodes(iMSA) Then
                    gMSAIndex(iloan) = iMSA
                    Exit For
                End If
            Next iMSA
        End If
    Next iloan

End Sub
```

EXHIBIT 11.48 "RepGeoCon_SetMSAIndex" subroutine

of collateral, either preconcentration or postconcentration, upon which we wish the reports to be based. The subroutine determines if we are aggregating pre- or postconcentration data, sums the total balances of the eligible loans of the portfolio, records the loan to its MSA group, and then performs a series of aggregation calculations at the national, state, and MSA levels. It also runs a subroutine that aggregates all the collateral of each state that lies outside of the MSAs of the state.

If the value of the variable "mCollatTag" is "COLLAT_PRECON", the subroutine will aggregate all the collateral of the portfolio regardless of eligibility status. This report is named the "Initial Concentration Report" and is designed to display the entire contents of the portfolio without regard to the any deletions caused by the various selection processes. If the value of the "mCollatTag" variable is "COLLAT_POSTCON", only eligible collateral, collateral whose "gLoanOK(iloan)" value is TRUE, will be aggregated. This collateral makes up the contents of the Final Concentration report.

See Exhibit 11.49.

"RepGeoCon_AggregateStateInfo" Subroutine   Exhibit 11.50 is the subroutine that aggregates data at the state level.

```
Sub RepGeoCon_AggregateCollat(mCollatTag As Integer)

    gTotalPortfolio = 0
    For iloan = 1 To gTotalLoans
        go_ok = False
        If mCollatTag = COLLAT_PRECON Then
            If gLoanPreConTest(iloan) Then go_ok = True
        Else
            If gLoanPostConTest(iloan) Then go_ok = True
        End If
        If go_ok Then
            gTotalPortfolio = gTotalPortfolio + gLoanData(iloan, FD_CURRBAL)
            istate = gLoanData(iloan, FD_STATECODE)
            If IsNumeric(gLoanData(iloan, FD_MSACODE)) Then
                iMSA = gMSAIndex(iloan)
            Else
                iMSA = 0
            End If
            If iMSA > 150 Then
                go_ok = True
            End If
            mStateCount(istate) = mStateCount(istate) + 1
            mMSACount(iMSA) = mMSACount(iMSA) + 1
            Call RepGeoCon_AggregateNationalInfo
            Call RepGeoCon_AggregateStateInfo
            Call RepGeoCon_AggregateNoMSAInfo
            Call RepGeoCon_AggregateMSAInfo
        End If
    Next iloan
    Call RepGeoCon_CalcConcentrations

End Sub
```

EXHIBIT 11.49   "RepGeoCon_AggregateCollat" subroutine

```
Sub RepGeoCon_AggregateStateInfo()

    mStateInfo(istate, LOAN_CT) = mStateInfo(istate, LOAN_CT) + 1
    mStateInfo(istate, ORIG_BAL) = _
                mStateInfo(istate, ORIG_BAL) + gLoanData(iloan, FD_ORIGBAL)
    mStateInfo(istate, CURR_BAL) = _
                mStateInfo(istate, CURR_BAL) + gLoanData(iloan, FD_CURRBAL)
    mStateInfo(istate, ORIG_LTV) = mStateInfo(istate, ORIG_LTV) + _
                (gLoanData(iloan, FD_ORIGLTV) * gLoanData(iloan, FD_CURRBAL))
    mStateInfo(istate, CURR_LTV) = mStateInfo(istate, CURR_LTV) + _
                (gLoanData(iloan, FD_CURRLTV) * gLoanData(iloan, FD_CURRBAL))
    mStateInfo(istate, ORIG_TERM) = mStateInfo(istate, ORIG_TERM) + _
                (gLoanData(iloan, FD_ORIGTERM) * gLoanData(iloan, FD_CURRBAL))
    mStateInfo(istate, REM_TERM) = mStateInfo(istate, REM_TERM) + _
                (gLoanData(iloan, FD_REMTERM) * gLoanData(iloan, FD_CURRBAL))
    mStateInfo(istate, SEASON) = mStateInfo(istate, SEASON) + _
                (gLoanData(iloan, FD_SEASON) * gLoanData(iloan, FD_CURRBAL))
    mStateInfo(istate, CURR_COUP) = mStateInfo(istate, CURR_COUP) + _
                (gLoanData(iloan, FD_CURRRATE) * gLoanData(iloan, FD_CURRBAL))
    mStateInfo(istate, ORIG_APP) = _
                mStateInfo(istate, ORIG_APP) + gLoanData(iloan, FD_ORIGAPP)
    mStateInfo(istate, CURR_APP) = _
                mStateInfo(istate, CURR_APP) + gLoanData(iloan, FD_CURRAPP)
    mStateInfo(istate, FICO_NUM) = mStateInfo(istate, FICO_NUM) + _
                (gLoanData(iloan, FD_FICO) * gLoanData(iloan, FD_CURRBAL))
    'if a first time home owner increment by one
    If gLoanData(iloan, FD_FIRSTHOME) = 2 Then
        mStateInfo(istate, FIRST_HOME) = mStateInfo(istate, FIRST_HOME) + 1
    End If
    'if self employed increment by 1
    If gLoanData(iloan, FD_EMPLOY) = 2 Then
        mStateInfo(istate, SELF_EMPLOY) = mStateInfo(istate, SELF_EMPLOY) + 1
    End If
    mStateInfo(istate, MORT_DTI) = mStateInfo(istate, MORT_DTI) + _
                (gLoanData(iloan, FD_MDBTTOINC) * gLoanData(iloan, FD_CURRBAL))
    mStateInfo(istate, TOT_DTI) = mStateInfo(istate, TOT_DTI) + _
                (gLoanData(iloan, FD_TDBTTOINC) * gLoanData(iloan, FD_CURRBAL))

End Sub
```

EXHIBIT 11.50   "RepGeoCon_AggregateStateInfo" subroutine

"RepGeoCon_CalcConcentrations" Subroutine   The collateral has now been aggregated and the concentration percentages are calculated for each loan, MSA, and state. This action is performed by the last subroutine call to the "RepGeo-Con_CalcConcentrations" subroutine. This subroutine calculates the loan level concentration ratios first, the MSA level ratios next, and finally the state level ratios. We need to calculate the following concentration percentages by level:

- **Loan level.** Concentrations against national, state, and MSA levels.
- **MSA and NoMSA level.** Concentrations against national and state levels.
- **State level.** Concentrations against national level.

See Exhibit 11.51.

After this work has been completed, we are ready to begin the report output process, and the subroutine "RepConGeo_SetUpWorkbook" is called. The GCRP

```
Sub RepGeoCon_CalcConcentrations()

Dim iMSALoop    As Integer
Dim msaCBAL     As Double
Dim stateCBal   As Double

    'loan level concentrations first
    For iloan = 1 To gTotalLoans
        iMSA = gMSAIndex(iloan)
        iState = gLoanData(iloan, FD_STATECODE)
        msaCBAL = mMSAInfo(iMSA, CURR_BAL)
        stateCBal = mStateInfo(iState, CURR_BAL)
        ConcenLoan(iloan, PCT_NAT) = _
                gLoanData(iloan, FD_CURRBAL) / gTotalPortfolio
        If msaCBAL > 0# Then
            ConcenLoan(iloan, PCT_MSA) = _
                            gLoanData(iloan, FD_CURRBAL) / msaCBAL
            Else
            ConcenLoan(iloan, PCT_MSA) = 0#
        End If
        If stateCBal > 0# Then
            ConcenLoan(iloan, PCT_STA) = _
                            gLoanData(iloan, FD_CURRBAL) / stateCBal
            Else
            ConcenLoan(iloan, PCT_STA) = 0#
        End If
    Next iloan

    'MSA level concentrations
    For iMSALoop = 1 To TOTAL_MSAS
        'national level concentration of MSA
        ConcenMSA(iMSALoop, PCT_NAT) = _
                    mMSAInfo(iMSALoop, CURR_BAL) / gTotalPortfolio
        'state level concentration of msa
        stateCBal = mStateInfo(gMSAStatesIndex(iMSALoop), CURR_BAL)
        If mStateInfo(gMSAStatesIndex(iMSALoop), CURR_BAL) > 0 Then
            ConcenMSA(iMSALoop, PCT_STA) = _
                        mMSAInfo(iMSALoop, CURR_BAL) / stateCBal
        Else
            ConcenMSA(iMSALoop, PCT_STA) = 0#
        End If
    Next iMSALoop

    'there is only one non-MSA collection of loans per state so we
    '   can process them in the in the State concentraion loop
    'State and No MSA level concentrations
    For iState = 1 To NUM_STATES
        stateCBal = mStateInfo(iState, CURR_BAL)
        'national concentation for state
        ConcenState(iState) = stateCBal / gTotalPortfolio
        'national concentration fo no MSA loans
        ConcenNoMSA(iState, PCT_NAT) = _
                        mNOMSAInfo(iState, CURR_BAL) / gTotalPortfolio
        'state level concentration for non MSA loans
        If stateCBal Then
            ConcenNoMSA(iState, PCT_STA) = _
                        mNOMSAInfo(iState, CURR_BAL) / stateCBal
        Else
            ConcenNoMSA(iState, PCT_STA) = 0#
        End If
    Next iState
    'loans with no MSAs
    For iloan = 1 To gTotalLoans
        If gMSAIndex(iloan) = 0 Then
            msaCBAL = mNOMSAInfo(gLoanData(iloan, FD_STATECODE), CURR_BAL)
            ConcenLoan(iloan, PCT_NAT) = _
                        gLoanData(iloan, FD_CURRBAL) / gTotalPortfolio
            If msaCBAL > 0# Then
                ConcenLoan(iloan, PCT_MSA) = _
                            gLoanData(iloan, FD_CURRBAL) / msaCBAL
                Else
                ConcenLoan(iloan, PCT_MSA) = 0#
            End If
        End If
    Next iloan

End Sub
```

EXHIBIT 11.51 "RepGeoCon_CalcConcentrations" subroutine

template file is opened, renamed, and saved. If any of the "gRepMenuInit**" or "gRepMenuFin**" variables are FALSE, the unneeded worksheets for those reports are deleted from the template file.

"RepGeoCon_WriteReports" Subroutine   The aggregation and calculation activities are now complete. All that remains is to produce the appropriate reports. This process is initiated by the "RepGeoCon_WriteReports" subroutine. Using the value of the "mCollatTag" variable, it calls two other subroutines. The "RepGeoCon_SetUpWorkbook" subroutine formats the report template file for the specific report type that is to be written. The "RepGeoCon_Write***Listing" subroutines then produce the specific report. These subroutines are specialized for loan, MSA, or state levels of reporting detail. See Exhibit 11.52.

"RepGeoCon_SetUpWorkbook" Subroutine   This subroutine determines what level of reporting detail is to be produced, names the report template file based on the value of the "mCollatTag" variable and the reporting level, and then deletes the two unnecessary reports. See Exhibit 11.53.

With the report template file prepared, we can now write the report itself.

"RepGeoCon_WriteLoanListing" Subroutine   The subroutine begins by writing the national level balance on the first line of the report. It was this balance that was used earlier by the "RepGeoCon_CalcConcentrations" to calculate all the national concentration statistics. The subroutine now enters the outer loop. This loop checks each of the states in turn and, if the state has been selected, reports its statistics on the report. See Exhibit 11.54.

The next line printed on the report is the state level line. This is the first "complete" line of the report that fills all of the columns of the line with the exception of the state and MSA concentration percentages and the Mortgage Type field. This report line is produced by the subroutine "RepGeoCon_WriteStateAllData". This subroutine reads the value of the variable "ireport" and adjusts the print locations of the data based on the report file format—loan, MSA, or state—that is currently displayed. After the state information line has been printed, the row counter is advanced by one and the subroutine enters the inner loop.

The purpose of this loop is to find all of the MSAs for the state that we just reported, list their MSA statistics, and then list all individual loans within the MSA. The inner loop will cycle once for each MSA that is in the state. We have earlier loaded an array, "mStateMSANumber", with the number of MSAs in each of the states. We will use the value of this variable to determine the number of times this loop will operate.

We note that the loop is configured to run from "0" to the number of MSAs in this particular state. Why? Why not "1" to the number of MSAs? If you recall, we can have a situation where some number of loans may be missing their MSA codes or are legitimately situated outside of an MSA. These form the "NoMSA" group. If there are loans in this sort of "NULL" MSA, we will have already aggregated their balances and calculated their concentrations against state and national levels.

```
Sub RepGeoCon_WriteReports(mCollatTag As Integer, irep As Integer)

Dim rWritten     As Boolean   'was a report just written

    rWritten = False
    Select Case mCollatTag
        Case Is = COLLAT_PRECON
            Select Case irep
                Case Is = 1
                    If gRepMenuGeoInitConLoan Then
                        Call RepGeoCon_SetUpWorkbook(mCollatTag, irep)
                        Call RepGeoCon_WriteLoanListing: rWritten = True
                    End If
                Case Is = 2
                    If gRepMenuGeoInitConMSA Then
                        Call RepGeoCon_SetUpWorkbook(mCollatTag, irep)
                        Call RepGeoCon_WriteMSAListing: rWritten = True
                    End If
                Case Is = 3
                    If gRepMenuGeoInitConState Then
                        Call RepGeoCon_SetUpWorkbook(mCollatTag, irep)
                        Call RepGeoCon_WriteStateListing: rWritten = True
                    End If
            End Select
        Case Is = COLLAT_POSTCON
            Select Case irep
                Case Is = 1
                    If gRepMenuGeoFinConLoan Then
                        Call RepGeoCon_SetUpWorkbook(mCollatTag, irep)
                        Call RepGeoCon_WriteLoanListing: rWritten = True
                    End If
                Case Is = 2
                    If gRepMenuGeoFinConMSA Then
                        Call RepGeoCon_SetUpWorkbook(mCollatTag, irep)
                        Call RepGeoCon_WriteMSAListing: rWritten = True
                    End If
                Case Is = 3
                    If gRepMenuGeoFinConState Then
                        Call RepGeoCon_SetUpWorkbook(mCollatTag, irep)
                        Call RepGeoCon_WriteStateListing: rWritten = True
                    End If
            End Select
    End Select
    If rWritten Then
        Range("A1").Select
        ActiveWorkbook.Save
        ActiveWorkbook.Close
    End If

End Sub
```

EXHIBIT 11.52 "RepGeoCon_WriteReports" subroutine

```
Sub RepGeoCon_SetUpWorkbook(mCollatTag As Integer, irep As Integer)

Dim file_prefix     As String

    If irep = 1 Then file_prefix = "Loan"
    If irep = 2 Then file_prefix = "MSA"
    If irep = 3 Then file_prefix = "State"
    'write the Geographic Loan List
    Workbooks.Open FileName:=DIR_TEMPLATE_REP & GEO_CONCEN_TEMPLATE
    If mCollatTag = COLLAT_PRECON Then
        ActiveWorkbook.SaveAs FileName:= _
            OUTPUT_DIRECTORY & gRepMenuPrefix & file_prefix & _
            "InitGeoConcenReport"
    Else
        ActiveWorkbook.SaveAs FileName:= _
            OUTPUT_DIRECTORY & gRepMenuPrefix & file_prefix & _
            "FinalGeoConcenReport"
    End If
    Select Case irep
        Case Is = 1
            Sheets("MSALevelListing").Delete
            Sheets("StateLevelListing").Delete
        Case Is = 2
            Sheets("StateLevelListing").Delete
            Sheets("LoanLevelListing").Delete
        Case Is = 3
            Sheets("LoanLevelListing").Delete
            Sheets("MSALevelListing").Delete
    End Select

End Sub
```

EXHIBIT 11.53   "RepGeoCon_SetUpWorkbook" subroutine

An "If..Then..Else" statement,

```
If iMSALoop > 0 Then
```

asks if this is the 0th loop, the "NoMSA" loop. The first time through the inner
loop it is and we will branch to the lower half of the test and prepare to print
the "NoMSA" data. The first subroutine call to "RepGeoCon_WriteNoMSATotal"
writes the summary concentration, balance, and demographic information for the
group of loans without MSA codes. If there are no loans in the "NoMSA" category
it will place the message:

```
''No Collateral for this MSA''
```

in column 3 of the report. If there are loans for the "noMSA" group we need to
find them and display them on the report. This task is performed by the "Rep-
GeoCon_WriteNoMSALoansAllData" subroutine. This subroutine cycles through
the loans of the portfolio. It will check eligible collateral only and compares the
"FD_STATECODE" of the record to the value of the outer state loop. If there is a
match the loan is from the correct state, if the loan also has "0" as the value of its
"FD_MSACODE" field we will print it out. This process continues until we have
found all of the loans from this NoMSA. We know how many loans are in this
group because we have stored the number of NoMSA loans for each state in the

```
Sub RepGeoCon_WriteLoanListing()

    irow = 10
    Sheets("LoanLevelListing").Select
    Call RepGeoCon_WriteNationalTotals(LOAN_REPORT)
    For istate = 1 To NUM_STATES
        If gRepMenuGeoStates(istate) Then
            'irow = irow + 1
            Call RepGeoList_StateLineSpacer(irep)
            'if the state has been selected write the State Level totals
            Call RepGeoCon_WriteStateAllData(LOAN_REPORT)
            For iMSALoop = 0 To gByStateMSATotal(istate)
                If iMSALoop > 0 Then
                    For icnt = 1 To TOTAL_MSAS
                        If gMSACodes(icnt) = gByStateMSACodes(istate, iMSALoop) Then
                            iMSA = icnt
                            Exit For
                        End If
                    Next icnt
                    Cells(irow, 1).Value = gByStateMSACodes(istate, iMSALoop) 'MSA code
                    Cells(irow, 2).Value = gByStateMSANames(istate, iMSALoop) 'MSA name
                    Call RepGeoCon_WriteMSATotals(LOAN_REPORT) 'MSA total line output
                    Call RepGeoCon_FormatMSATotalsLine
                    Call RepGeoCon_WriteConcens(MSA_TOTALS)
                    Call RepGeoCon_WriteMSALoansAllData
                Else
                    Cells(irow, 1).Value = 0          'some loans at not in an MSA
                    Cells(irow, 2).Value = "Loans With No MSA Designated"
                    Call RepGeoCon_WriteNoMSATotals(LOAN_REPORT) 'MSA total line output
                    Call RepGeoCon_FormatMSATotalsLine
                    Call RepGeoCon_WriteConcens(NOMSA_TOTALS)
                    Call RepGeoCon_WriteNoMSALoansAllData
                End If
            Next iMSALoop
        End If
    Next istate
    'report content is complete, reformat and save
    stopRow = irow        'last row of the report

End Sub
```

EXHIBIT 11.54 "RepGeoCon_WriteLoanListing" subroutine

array "mNoMSACount" earlier in the aggregation process! Once we have found the last loan, we break out of the loop. The presentation for the "NoMSA" loans is complete. See Exhibit 11.55.

The next loop of the inner loop takes us to the first MSA for the state, or it may terminate the loop. (Remember that the states of Delaware, Montana, North Dakota, South Dakota, Vermont, West Virginia, and Wyoming do not have any MSAs in the top 150 list. Any loan in these states will perforce be a NoMSA loan.) If the state has one or more MSAs, we will now visit them in turn.

We first need to find the location of the current MSA in the list of overall MSAs. If the value of the loop counter "iMSALoop" is "1", the value of the first element in the "mStateMSACode(istate,iMSALoop)" is the first MSA code for that state. In the example shown in Exhibit 11.46, the state of California, this MSA is Bakersfield with a MSA code of 12540. The loop will move through the full list of MSAs and find that the Bakersfield MSA is the 10th MSA in the overall list. The value of 10 is now assigned to the variable "iMSA". This is a key determination as it now allows us to directly access all the information that is stored by MSA Index number, in this case, 10.

```
Sub RepGeoCon_AggregateNoMSAInfo()

    'aggregates by state, for loans with no MSAs
    If gLoanData(iloan, FD_STATECODE) = istate And _
        gLoanData(iloan, FD_MSACODE) = 0 Then
        mNoMSACount(istate) = mNoMSACount(istate) + 1
        mNOMSAInfo(istate, LOAN_CT) = mNOMSAInfo(istate, LOAN_CT) + 1
        mNOMSAInfo(istate, ORIG_BAL) = _
                mNOMSAInfo(istate, ORIG_BAL) + gLoanData(iloan, FD_ORIGBAL)
        mNOMSAInfo(istate, CURR_BAL) = _
                mNOMSAInfo(istate, CURR_BAL) + gLoanData(iloan, FD_CURRBAL)
        mNOMSAInfo(istate, ORIG_LTV) = mNOMSAInfo(istate, ORIG_LTV) + _
                (gLoanData(iloan, FD_ORIGLTV) * gLoanData(iloan, FD_CURRBAL))
        mNOMSAInfo(istate, CURR_LTV) = mNOMSAInfo(istate, CURR_LTV) + _
                (gLoanData(iloan, FD_CURRLTV) * gLoanData(iloan, FD_CURRBAL))
        mNOMSAInfo(istate, ORIG_TERM) = mNOMSAInfo(istate, ORIG_TERM) + _
                (gLoanData(iloan, FD_ORIGTERM) * gLoanData(iloan, FD_CURRBAL))
        mNOMSAInfo(istate, REM_TERM) = mNOMSAInfo(istate, REM_TERM) + _
                (gLoanData(iloan, FD_REMTERM) * gLoanData(iloan, FD_CURRBAL))
        mNOMSAInfo(istate, SEASON) = mNOMSAInfo(istate, SEASON) + _
                (gLoanData(iloan, FD_SEASON) * gLoanData(iloan, FD_CURRBAL))
        mNOMSAInfo(istate, CURR_COUP) = mNOMSAInfo(istate, CURR_COUP) + _
                (gLoanData(iloan, FD_CURRRATE) * gLoanData(iloan, FD_CURRBAL))
        mNOMSAInfo(istate, ORIG_APP) = _
                mNOMSAInfo(istate, ORIG_APP) + gLoanData(iloan, FD_ORIGAPP)
        mNOMSAInfo(istate, CURR_APP) = _
                mNOMSAInfo(istate, CURR_APP) + gLoanData(iloan, FD_CURRAPP)
        mNOMSAInfo(istate, FICO_NUM) = mNOMSAInfo(istate, FICO_NUM) + _
                (gLoanData(iloan, FD_FICO) * gLoanData(iloan, FD_CURRBAL))
        'if a first time home owner increment by one
        If gLoanData(iloan, FD_FIRSTHOME) = 2 Then _
            mNOMSAInfo(istate, FIRST_HOME) = mNOMSAInfo(istate, FIRST_HOME) + 1
        If gLoanData(iloan, FD_EMPLOY) = 2 Then _
            mNOMSAInfo(istate, SELF_EMPLOY) = mNOMSAInfo(istate, SELF_EMPLOY) + 1
        mNOMSAInfo(istate, MORT_DTI) = mNOMSAInfo(istate, MORT_DTI) + _
                (gLoanData(iloan, FD_MDBTTOINC) * gLoanData(iloan, FD_CURRBAL))
        mNOMSAInfo(istate, TOT_DTI) = mNOMSAInfo(istate, TOT_DTI) + _
                (gLoanData(iloan, FD_TDBTTOINC) * gLoanData(iloan, FD_CURRBAL))
    End If

End Sub
```

EXHIBIT 11.55   "RepGeoCon_AggregateNoMSAInfo" subroutine

We now immediately write the MSA code and MSA name in the first two columns of the report. We next call "RepGeoCon_WriteMSATotals", the subroutine that will fill in the rest of the MSA level statistics for this line. We next call "RepGeoCon_WriteConcens", which fills in the MSA level concentration percentages in columns 3 and 4 of the report. All that remains is to find all the loans that have 12540 in their "FD_MSACODE" field. We do *not* need to check for the state code as MSAs are unique to their states. We will break out of the loan-by-loan loop when we have found the last loan in the MSA, again using the MSA loan count value we calculated during the aggregation phase. Refer to Exhibit 11.55 to follow this process.

We now loop through the rest of the MSAs of the state. When we have finished with the current state, we pass to the outer loop and test the succeeding states in turn. Once we complete the outer state loop, we have finished writing the body of the report. We then call a formatting subroutine "RepGeoCon_ReformatReportLoan".

This subroutine visits each line of the report and formats it based on whether it is a state, MSA, or loan level report line. The control then passes back to the calling subroutine, "RepGeoCon_MainWriteReports". We loop twice more, producing the MSA and State Level Geographic Concentration reports, and the package is complete.

Parting Thought   The Geographic Concentration report is a very dense report. It combines very detailed information at the individual loan level with very condensed information at the MSA and state levels. It has a complex format that combines both numeric and string format data. While you may never build a report identical to this one, the ability to organize summary and detail data on the same report in such a manner is widely applicable to a myriad of applications.

For example, the state/MSA/loan combination might be replaced by "SalesDistrict/SalesTerritory/Salesperson" or "ProductLine/Product/ResultsSummary". I would like to inform everyone who reads this book that the purpose of reviewing these reports in the detail that we do in this chapter is *not* to teach you to program *any specific report* that we will present in this book. It is to teach you to *how to think* about the best ways to organize and present this type of data. Look at the features of the VBA language used and how these reports are generated predicated on the use of those features. Generalize the process, do not memorize the example and attempt to apply it specifically (where it might not belong). I want you to recognize that all of these reports are really all-purpose in nature. Be ready to apply the broad techniques you see here to be an effective, efficient, and capable professional able to solve the problems you will be called upon to analyze.

ON THE WEB SITE

There is a chapter comments file, "Chapter11Comments".

The "CCFG_Chapter11" model contains all of the code of this chapter.

The report template files for the report packages of the chapter are:

- "UserIneligCollatTemplate". Ineligible Collateral report package.
- "BaseIneligCollateralTemplate". Base Collateral Eligibility report package.
- "FinSelectCriteriaTemplate". Financial/Demographic Selection Criteria data file.
- "GeoSelectCriteriaTemplate". Geographic Selection Criteria data file.
- "LoanListing Template". Loan Listing Report template file.
- "GeoLoanListTemplate". Geographic Loan Listing report template.
- "GeoConcenTemplate". Geographic Concentration report template.

There are also two completed criteria specification report files:

- "BaseStratReps". Report specification input file.
- "StateRep02". Geographic selection criteria input file.

## CHAPTER 12

Writing the Collateral Cash Flow Amortization Code

OVERVIEW

In this chapter we will write the VBA code to perform the collateral cash flow amortization calculations for three additional mortgage types. These are hybrid adjustable-rate mortgages (HARMs) and fixed- and adjustable-rate balloon mortgages (balloons). We will use as our base code the VBA code from the existing Base Asset Model (BAM) modules.

We will then integrate these new mortgage types with the existing mortgage types in the cash flow amortization code that computes the effects of prepayment and default activity. Here we will add two additional prepayment/default approaches. The first, the Geographic Methodology, will use a collection of geographically specific prepayment, default, market value decline (MVD), and recovery lag assumption curves based on the location of the property. The second, the Demographic Methodology, will compute a frequency of foreclosure statistic and a severity of loss estimate based on the financial, property, and credit demographics of the collateral and the borrower.

Last we will develop a VBA module to display and store the resultant cash flows of the portfolios for each of the prepayment/default scenarios we have generated. These results can either be displayed on a report screen or written to a cash flow file for use by the Liabilities Waterfall Model (LWM).

DELIVERABLES

There are four major deliverables in this chapter. They are, in the order we will discuss them:

1. VBA code to amortize hybrid ARMs and both fixed-rate and ARM balloon payment mortgage types.
2. VBA code implementing a geographically specific prepayment and default activity driven amortization analysis.
3. VBA code implementing a financial, property type, and demographically driven default model.

4. VBA code that will populate a report screen in the model and/or a cash flow template file to display and store the pool- or sub-portfolio level calculation results.

UNDER CONSTRUCTION

We will begin by adding a number of global variables to the "A_Globals" module and a number of global Constant variables to the "A_Constants" module. We will create subroutines to amortize the three new mortgage types. With the code to deal with the new mortgage types in place, we will then reorganize the existing Uniform Methodology, segregating all of its code into a separate module. Next we will then create two new modules to hold the VBA code of the Geographic and Demographic Prepayment/Default methodologies. We will preface all the modules that facilitate the cash flow amortization calculation process with the name "CollatCF_" so that we can more easily identify them.

The following modules will be created or expanded:

- "A_Constants" module. We will add a series of new Constants that will describe a number of values that we will use in the data handling and prepayment and default calculations.
- "A_Globals" module. We will add all the global variables we need to support the Uniform, Geographic, and Demographic methodologies and their attendant file-handling tasks.
- "CollatCF_CFGenerator" module. This module is the controlling module that will initialize the arrays and variables we will need to use in the cash flow calculation process. It will also translate the inputs of the Collateral Cash Flow Generator (CCFG) Cash Flow Amortization Parameters Menu into the choices the CCFG will make to implement the selected prepayment and default methodologies.
- "CollatCF_MethodUniform" module. This module implements the Uniform Methodology. In this methodology the user specifies Base Rates for both the prepayment and default assumptions and an accompanying series of steps of a fixed increment. These speeds are then applied to each piece of collateral regardless of its geographic or demographic characteristics. This module contains the VBA code that calculates the principal prepayments, defaults of principal, and recoveries of defaulted principal components for this method.
- "CollatCF_MethodGeographic" module. This module implements the Geographic Methodology in which each piece of collateral is matched to a set of geographically specific prepayment and default assumptions. In addition to the prepayment and default assumptions, recovery lag periods and MVDs are also specified at the national, state, and Metropolitan Statistical Area (MSA) levels. These assumptions specify the collateral behavior month-by-month for a five-year period with a long-term rate specified thereafter.
- "CollatCF_MethodDemographic" module. This module implements the Demographic Methodology. In this methodology the prepayment and recovery lag assumptions are determined as in the Geographic Methodology. The default rate and the MVD assumptions are determined by two specific and different

combinations of demographic characteristics. The specific demographics of each loan determine the individual default rate and MVD assumptions.

- **"CollatCF_CalcFactorsCoupon" module.** This module contains the VBA code that calculates the coupon cash flow component for each of the loan types.
- **"CollatCF_CalcFactorsPrincipal" module.** This module contains the VBA code that calculates the scheduled principal amortization component for each of the loan types.
- **"CollatCF_CalcFactorsPreDef" module.** This module contains the VBA code that calculates the principal prepayments, defaults of principal, and recoveries of defaulted principal components for each of the loan types.
- **"Report_Assumptions" module.** This module contains the code for the Assumptions report package.
- **"Report_CollatEligCFs" module.** This module contains the code needed to produce the collateral cash flow output file. It will open a template file, write all the assumptions used in the cash flow calculations, and create a separate worksheet for each of the unique cash flow scenarios generated by the CCFG. We will also add some code that will allow us to view the newly created cash flow file directly from the CCFG.

QUICK REVIEW OF EXISTING CF GENERATION CODE

The current code is housed in two modules. The names of these modules and the roles that they play in the generation of the collateral cash flows are:

- **"CollateralCFGenerator".** This module contains the VBA code that performs the Uniform Methodology and a second method, the User Defined Attrition method. It contains the VBA code that produces the coupon cash flows, the scheduled principal amortization amounts, and the recoveries of defaulted principal.
- **"CollateralPreDefCals".** This module contains the VBA code that sets up the prepayment and default speeds for the Uniform method and the allocations of the loss in the User Defined method. It also converts the prepayment and default speeds into monthly factors so that they can be applied to the balances of the loans to produce the monthly cash flows.

Capabilities of the Current Code

The capabilities of the current code can be described as a combination of the types of mortgage payment types that can be amortized and the amortization methodologies that are available to be applied to them.

The current mortgage types accommodated by the existing VBA code are:

- Fixed-rate, level-payment mortgages up to 480 months of remaining term.
- Floating-rate, variable-payment mortgages. These instruments have a variable coupon that is the combination of a fixed spread to an index. This combined coupon level is subject to a regular periodic reset action. Upon reset, the resultant new coupon level is subject to limitation based on the existence of both periodic coupon floors and caps and lifetime floors and caps.

The current prepayment and default methodologies are:

- Uniform prepayment and default curves based on the Public Securities Administration (PSA) prepayment methodology or the Constant prepayment rate (CPR). This is to say that a constant rate, such as 100% PSA or 6% CPR is input by the user. This rate then remains at a Uniform rate, (hence the name of the methodology) for each month of the model. There is a provision to model a series of rates beginning with the specification of a base rate, which is then increased by a constant step increment over a specified number of steps. An example of this would be 100% PSA, incremented by 20% PSA for ten increments. This would result in the model evaluating the collateral cash flows at a series of 100%, 120%, 140% ... 280% PSA.
- A User-Defined Percentage Default Rate Methodology in which a fixed percentage of the aggregate principal of the portfolio will default over a series of years (up to 30 years), based on a specified annual percentage of the total defaults rate. For example, the aggregate percentage of defaulted principal will be 25% of the beginning balance of the portfolio. The distribution pattern will be 1%, 2%, 2%, 5%, 5%, 10%, 10%, 15%, 3%, 2%, and then 1.5% for the next 20 years. This means that 25% (total defaults) times 1% (first-year defaults) times (1/12) monthly proration, or $(.25^*.015^*(1/12))$ of the initial principal balance of the pool will default in the first month of the deal.

In the CCFG we will retain the Uniform Methodology but discard the User Defined Methodology. This was done to allow us more pages to discuss newer and more relevant methodologies.

Calculation of the Monthly Cash Flows

The calculation of the cash flows produces the following mortgage components: defaulted principal, scheduled amortization of principal, coupon income, prepayments of principal, and recoveries of defaulted principal. This approach develops, on a loan-by-loan basis, a series of vectors that express the dollar amounts of these components as a percentage of the original balance of the mortgage. In this methodology, the model constructs a series of vectors for each loan into which are placed the decimal expression of the cash flow components.

For a detailed discussion of this methodology, see the Web chapter material, particularly Web Chapter 12.1, "Computation of Basic Mortgage Cash Flows."

ADDING NEW MORTGAGE TYPES

In this section we will lay out our approach to integrating three new mortgage amortization types into the existing VBA code. These types are:

1. Hybrid adjustable-rate mortgages
2. Fixed-rate balloon mortgages
3. Floating-rate balloon mortgages

Hybrid Adjustable Rate Mortgages

Hybrid adjustable-rate mortgages have the following amortization characteristics:

1. **Initial interest-only (IO) period.** In this period, ranging from 1 to 10 years, the mortgage has a combination of a fixed/floating interest-only payment. In the case of HARMs with short IO periods, such as one-, two-, three-, or five-year IO periods, the initial rate is fixed over the entire period. In the case of longer IO periods, such as seven or ten years, a portion of the IO period will be fixed while a portion will float. If the loan has a floating-rate structure, it will be fully indexed. The term "fully indexed" means that the full coupon rate is used (i.e., index rate + spread).

2. **Amortization period.** Upon the conclusion of the IO period, the mortgage switches to become fully amortizing, with a fixed or floating coupon for the remaining term. The payment will amortize its remaining balance as if it were a fixed- or floating-rate loan with its current balance being equivalent to the original balance at the end of the IO period and the payment amount sufficient to completely retire that balance by the end of the remaining term. If it is floating rate, it will be subject to periodic and lifetime floors and caps in regard to its fully indexed rate. If the mortgage is a fixed-rate loan, its payments will be level and identical to a fixed-rate loan of the same remaining term.

HARM Amortization Sequence   The calculation steps in computing the amortization of a hybrid ARM are:

1. **IO period or amortization period determination.** Determine if the loan is in the IO period or in the fully amortizing period. We make this determination based on the current seasoning of the loan versus the length of the IO period. If the seasoning is greater than the term of the IO period, we are in the fully amortizing period; if it is not, we are in the IO period.

2. **IO period determination.** If we are in the IO period, we must now determine if the mortgage has a fixed/floating rate split in the IO period. For mortgages with IO periods less than five years, we will *always* be in the fixed-rate IO period. For mortgages with IO periods greater than five years, we need to compare the seasoning of the loan to the length of the IO fixed-rate period. If it exceeds the fixed-rate IO period, then we are in the floating-rate IO period.

3. **IO period fixed-rate portion.** Apply the coupon rate to the outstanding balance. No scheduled amortization of principal is received. Prepayments of principal, defaults of principal, and recoveries of defaulted principal are calculated.

4. **IO period floating-rate portion.** Apply the current fully indexed floating coupon rate to outstanding balance. No payments of scheduled amortization of principal. Prepayments, defaults, and recoveries are calculated.

5. **Fully amortizing period.** The amortization characteristics are calculated as if the loan were a fully amortizing fixed- or floating-rate loan over the period of the remaining term. Thus the last 20 years of the payment stream for a fixed-rate HARM with a 10-year IO period followed by a 20-year fully amortizing period is identical to that of a 20-year fixed-rate loan. The payment amount is determined by the current balance of the loan at the beginning of the fully amortizing period.

HARM Amortization Implementation Code   Based on the above procedure, we
will implement the amortization calculation of a HARM mortgage by creating
a number of new subroutines or modifying and adding to some of our existing
subroutines. Before we start writing any additional code, we will create two
new VBA modules. The first will be named "CollatCF_CalcFactorsCoupon" and
the second, "CollatCF_CalcFactorsPrincipal". We will move all subroutines that
perform the calculation of the coupon income from any mortgage type into the
first of these modules and any VBA code that performs the calculation of scheduled
amortization of principal into the second. This will therefore leave the module
"CollatCF_CalcFactorsPreDef" the exclusive domain of all the prepayment and
default of principal calculations. We will place any code that calculates recoveries
in this module also as they are related to the defaults of principal.

   We will visit each of the subroutines discussed below in the order in which they
are called in the Uniform, Geographic, and Demographic methodologies. Inasmuch,
as you will see later, we will not need to modify the prepayment or default calculation code (merely where these subroutines receive their starting values), we will
concentrate on coupon income and the scheduled amortization of principal.

"CollatCF_CalcMonthlyCoupFactors" Subroutine   The first subroutine, "Collat
CF_CalcMonthlyCoupFactors", is the highest-level code that begins the coupon income component cash flow calculation. This subroutine loops through each loan of
the collateral portfolio and directs the flow of the program based on task-specific
subroutines (based on mortgage type) that calculate the coupon cash flows.

   The "Select..Case" statement tests the "FD_MORTTYPE" field of the loan
record and branches to the appropriate subroutine when it finds a match for one of
the six Constant variables that delineate the loan type values. See Exhibit 12.1. Here

```
Sub CollatCF_CalcMonthlyCoupFactors()

    Call CollatCF_PrepayDefaultProgressMsg(4)
    If gValidateCoupTraceSwitch Then
      ReDim gValidateCoupTrace(1 To gTotalLoans, 1 To PAY_DATES, 1 To 4) As Double
    End If
    For iloan = 1 To gTotalLoans
        'set day count convention 1, 2, or 3
        mDayCntType = gLoanData(iloan, FD_DAYCOUNT)
        rterm = gLoanData(iloan, FD_REMTERM)
        Select Case gLoanData(iloan, FD_MORTTYPE)
            Case Is = MORTTYPE_FIXED_RATE:
                Call CollatCF_CalcCoupFactorsFixed(1, rterm)
            Case Is = MORTTYPE_STAND_ARM
                Call CollatCF_CalcCoupFactorsARMStandard(1, rterm)
            Case Is = MORTTYPE_HYBRID_ARM:
                Call CollatCF_CalcCoupFactorsARMHybrid
            Case Is = MORTTYPE_BALLOON_FIXED:
                Call CollatCF_CalcCoupFactorsFixed(1, rterm)
            Case Is = MORTTYPE_BALLOON_ARM
                Call CollatCF_CalcCoupFactorsARMStandard(1, rterm)
        End Select
    Next iloan

End Sub
```

EXHIBIT 12.1   "CollatCF_CalcMonthlyCoupFactors" subroutine

```
Sub CollatCF_CalcCoupFactorsARMHybrid()

    itrace = 1
    'Which portion of the coupon determination period is the loan in?
    '1) Determine if the loan is in a FIXED rate period
    Call CollatCF_LoadARMFixedRateInterestPeriod
    '2) Determine if the loan is in the ADJUSTABLE rate portion,
    '   past the end of the fixed rate period set the initial rate to the
    '   current index rate and the spread of the loan
    '2.1) determine the starting period of the ARM only period
    Call CollatCF_DetermineARMStartPeriod
    '2.2) fill the periods from the current period to the end of the remaining
    '     term with the adjustable rate coupon levels calculated from index +
    '     spread and possibly modified by caps and floors.
    Call CollatCF_CalcCoupFactorsARMStandard(mStartARMPeriod, _
         gLoanData(iloan, FD_REMTERM))

End Sub
```

EXHIBIT 12.2 "CollatCF_CalcCoupFactorsARMHybrid" subroutine

we will add the tests for the three new loan types in the "Select..Case" statement. These are the choices for the new mortgage types, "MORTTYPE_HYBRID_ARM" (hybrid ARMs) and the two types of balloon mortgages, fixed and floating rates, respectively labeled "MORTTYPE_BALLOON_FIXED" and MORTTYPE_ BALLOON_ARM".

"CollatCF_CalcCoupFactorsARMHybrid" Subroutine   Once we have selected the correct coupon calculation subroutine based on the HARM type, we can compute the coupon cash flows. To do this we will need to determine if the HARM is in the IO period. If it is in the IO period, we then need to determine whether it is in the fixed- or floating-coupon phase (if it has one). Finally we need to determine when the loan enters the fully amortizing phase and how long in its final maturity.

We can see that this subroutine determines these questions by calling a special-purpose subroutine to answer each one. We will be examining each of these subroutines in turn. See Exhibit 12.2.

"CollatCF_LoadARMFixedRateInterestPeriod" Subroutine   The job of this subroutine is to determine if the HARM is in the fixed-rate portion of the IO period. The subroutine compares the seasoning of the loan in field "FD_SEASON" with the length of the HARM's fixed IO period given in field "FD_HBAORIGPERIOD" of the loan record. If it is in the fixed IO period, it next determines how many months are remaining in that period. It then fills the array "gMonthlyCoupLevels" with the current coupon rate of the loan found in field "FD_CURRRATE". See Exhibit 12.3.

"CollatCF_DetermineARMStartPeriod" Subroutine   With the fixed-rate portion of the coupon cash flows now disposed of, we can advance to the floating-rate portion of the loan. At this point it does not matter whether the loan is in the IO floating period or the fully amortizing floating period. We will be calculating a floating-rate coupon cash flow in either case. We already have made the determination that the loan is either in or not in the fixed rate IO period and stored this condition in the

```
Sub CollatCF_LoadARMFixedRateInterestPeriod()

    mInFixedPeriod = False
    If gLoanData(iloan, FD_SEASON) < gLoanData(iloan, FD_HBAORIGPERIOD) Then _
        mInFixedPeriod = True
    'assign the fixed rate coupon for the remainder of the fixed rate period
    If mInFixedPeriod Then
        'how many months of fixed rate is left
        mFixedRateMonths = _
            gLoanData(iloan, FD_HBAORIGPERIOD) - gLoanData(iloan, FD_SEASON)
        For im = 1 To mFixedRateMonths
            gMonthlyCoupLevels(iloan, im) = gLoanData(iloan, FD_CURRRATE) * _
                            gDayFactors(im, mDayCntType)
        Next im
    End If

End Sub
```

EXHIBIT 12.3 "CollatCF_LoadARMFixedRateInterestPeriod" subroutine

variable "mInFixedPeriod" in the immediately preceding subroutine. If we are not already in the floating-rate portion of the loan, we calculate the start of the floating rate period and store it in the variable "mStartARMPeriod". If we are already in the floating-rate period, we set this variable to "1". By setting "mStartARMPeriod" to "1", the subroutine will immediately assign the floating-rate interest levels at the fully indexed rate. See Exhibit 12.4.

"CollatCF_CalcCoupFactorsARMStandard" Subroutine   To complete the coupon assignment process, we will assign the fully indexed rate to all remaining periods of the loan. This subroutine accomplishes that task using the value of the "mStartARM-Period" as the first period and determining the appropriate fully indexed interest rate for all remaining periods. It begins by finding the index number of the floating-rate coupon schedule to use. This is the value of the variable "ifloat". The value of "ifloat" is 1 for the prime rate and 2 for LIBOR (the London Interbank Offering Rate). In a fully developed model, we would have to provide for as many as a dozen index rates to fully address the loans of a diverse portfolio, but for now we will limit ourselves to these two. The user is allowed to enter five different pathways for each of the two indexes. The monthly values of these indexes (and their alternative pathways) are displayed in the "RatesDatesMenu" worksheet.

Having determined the correct index, the subroutine now applies the spread of the loan to it. The spread is found in the field "FD_ARMSPD". With the initial period

```
Sub CollatCF_DetermineARMStartPeriod()

    If mInFixedPeriod Then
        'still have some amount of time left in the fixed rate period
        mStartARMPeriod = _
          (gLoanData(iloan, FD_HBAORIGPERIOD) - gLoanData(iloan, FD_SEASON)) + 1
    Else
        'loan is past the fixed rate period of the loan
        mStartARMPeriod = 1
    End If

End Sub
```

EXHIBIT 12.4 "CollatCF_DetermineARMStartPeriod" subroutine

```
Sub CollatCF_CalcCoupFactorsARMStandard(BegPeriod As Double, EndPeriod As Double)

    'fill the periods from the current period to the end of the remaining term
    '  with the adjustable rate coupon levels calculated from index+spread and
    '  possibly modified by caps and floors.
    ifloat = gLoanData(iloan, FD_ARMINDEX)
    'set the initial rate to the current index rate and the spread of the loan
    beg_rate = gIndexLevels(1, ifloat) + gLoanData(iloan, FD_ARMSPRD)
    gMonthlyCoupLevels(iloan, 1) = beg_rate * gDayFactors(iperiod, mDayCntType)
    For im = BegPeriod To EndPeriod
        If (gLoanData(iloan, FD_SEASON) + im - 1) Mod _
            gLoanData(iloan, FD_ARMPERRESET) = 0 Then
            'this is a coupon reset month, load the computed rate into "now_rate"
            '  variable.  this rate is provisional and may be revised subject to
            '  the terms of the coupon caps and floors of the loan
            now_rate = gIndexLevels(im, ifloat) + gLoanData(FD_ARMSPRD)
            Call CollatCF_TestCouponCapsFloors
            Call CollatCF_LoadValidationPathway
            'apply the adjusted rate to the current coupon rate array
            gMonthlyCoupLevels(iloan, im) = _
                now_rate * gDayFactors(iperiod, mDayCntType)
            'the value of the current coupon rate no resets the beg period rate
            beg_rate = now_rate
        Else
            'it is not a reset month, load the current coupon
            gMonthlyCoupLevels(iloan, im) = _
                beg_rate * gDayFactors(iperiod, mDayCntType)
        End If
    Next im

End Sub
```

EXHIBIT 12.5   "CollatCF_CalcCoupFactorsARMStandard" subroutine

fully indexed rate in hand, the model now needs to determine three questions in each of the succeeding monthly periods:

1. Is this an ARM reset period?
2. If it is, is the newly reset fully indexed rate within the limits of the periodic caps and floors for the reset period?
3. If it is, is the newly reset fully indexed rate within the limits of the lifetime floors and caps for the loan?

The remaining calls of the subroutine check for these conditions and adjust the coupon levels accordingly. See Exhibit 12.5.

These calculations have now accomplished all we need to do (for the present) in regard to calculating the coupon income cash flow of the loan. We can now turn to the determination of the monthly scheduled amortization of principal.

"CollatCF_CalcScheduledAmortFactors" Subroutine   The first subroutine we will call in this calculation process is the highest subroutine in the process and is the subroutine that corresponds to "CollatCF_CalcMonthlyCoupFactors" discussed above in the coupon income calculation process. It is the main switching station that controls the flow of the calculation sequence and directs it to the appropriate specialized subroutine based on the value of the "FD_MORTTYPE" field of the loan record. It chooses from between six different principal calculation options based on a match between the "FD_MORTTYPE" field of the loan and the "Select..Case" Constant variable value.

```
Sub CollatCF_CalcScheduledAmortFactors()

    're-dimension the per period scheduled amortization cf's
    ReDim gLoanAmortFactors(1 To gTotalLoans, 1 To PAY_DATES)
    Call CollatCF_PrepayDefaultProgressMsg(5)
    For iloan = 1 To gTotalLoans
      If gLoanOK(iloan) Then
        mDayCntType = gLoanData(iloan, FD_DAYCOUNT)
          Select Case gLoanData(iloan, FD_MORTTYPE)
            Case Is = MORTTYPE_FIXED_RATE
                Call CollatCF_CalcFixedRateSchPrin(iloan)
            Case Is = MORTTYPE_STAND_ARM
                Call CollatCF_CalcStandARMSchPrin(iloan)
            Case Is = MORTTYPE_HYBRID_ARM
                Call CollatCF_CalcHybridARMSchPrin(iloan)
            Case Is = MORTTYPE_BAL_FIXED
                Call CollatCF_CalcFixBalSchPrin(iloan)
            Case Is = MORTTYPE_BAL_ARM
                Call CollatCF_CalcSARMBalSchPrin(iloan)
          End Select
      End If
    Next iloan
    Call CollatCF_PrepayDefaultProgressMsg(99)

End Sub
```

EXHIBIT 12.6   "CollatCF_CalcScheduledAmortFactors" subroutine

In the case of the HARMS, it chooses the third option:

```
MORTTYPE_HYBRID_ARM
```

and calls the subroutine "CollatCF_CalcHybridARMSchPrin". See Exhibit 12.6.

"CollatCF_CalcHybridARMSchPrin" Subroutine   This subroutine is divided into two portions. The first test determines if the HARM is in any part of the IO period. The second portion tests if it is in the fully amortizing portion of the loan payment stream. If the loan is in the IO period, no scheduled principal is received. Therefore, the value of the periods of the loan in the "gLoanAmortFactors" array are set to "0.0".

If the loan is in the fully amortizing portion of its payment stream, the principal is calculated using the coupon factors generated by the subroutines just discussed above. The per-period scheduled amortization factor is calculated using by subtracting the ratio of the quantities of:

```
1 - ((remaining period discount factor - current period discount
factor)/ (remaining period discount factor - current period - 1
discount factor))
```

See Exhibit 12.7.

```
Sub CollatCF_CalcHybridARMSchPrin(iloan As Long)

Dim RemPeriods     As Double   'remaining term periods
Dim IOPeriods      As Integer  'interest only periods

    IOPeriods = gLoanData(iloan, FD_HBAIOPERIODS)
    'INTEREST ONLY PHASE
    'test if the loan is in the I/O period. if it is there is no principal
    '   payment, set factors to 0.
    If gLoanData(iloan, FD_SEASON) < IOPeriods Then
        For mPeriods = 1 To (IOPeriods - gLoanData(iloan, FD_SEASON))
            gLoanAmortFactors(iloan, mPeriods) = 0#   'no principal component!
        Next mPeriods
    End If
    'PRINCIPAL AMORTIZATION PHASE
    'first we need to determine the starting position of the amortization
    '   sequence. Is the loan at the very beginning of the full payment phase
    '   (having just finished the I/O period assignments above), or is it
    '   already into the full payment phase?
    If gLoanData(iloan, FD_SEASON) < IOPeriods Then
        'we just filled the I/O period months with zeros above therefore
        '   advance the starting period to first principal pay month.
        mStart = IOPeriods + 1
        RemPeriods = gLoanData(iloan, FD_REMTERM) - IOPeriods
        mResetStart = IOPeriods
    Else
        'the loan is already out of the I/O periods, amortize principal
        '   as if it were a Standard ARM the reset sequence will start with
        '   the seasoning.
        mStart = 1
        RemPeriods = gLoanData(iloan, FD_REMTERM)
        mResetStart = gLoanData(iloan, FD_SEASON)
    End If
    'with the starting time period in place we can calculate the remaining
    '   principal amortization factors
    For mPeriods = mStart To RemPeriods
      If mPeriods = 1 Then Call CollatCF_CalcDiscountFactors(RemPeriods)
      'if its a reset period recalculate the factor sets
      If (mResetStart + mPeriods - 1) Mod gLoanData(iloan, FD_ARMPERRESET) = 0 Then
        Call CollatCF_CalcDiscountFactors(RemPeriods - mPeriods)
      End If
      mBaseDiscFactor = mDiscFactors(RemPeriods)
      gLoanAmortFactors(iloan, mPeriods) = _
            1 - ((mBaseDiscFactor - mDiscFactors(mPeriods)) / _
              (mBaseDiscFactor - mDiscFactors(mPeriods - 1)))
    Next mPeriods

End Sub
```

EXHIBIT 12.7 "CollatCF_CalcHybridARMSchPrin" subroutine

Fixed-Rate and ARM Balloon Mortgages

Balloon mortgages were originally designed to allow mortgagors an affordable monthly payment and to provide them a specific amount of time over which their equity position in the property would increase before the final due date of the loan. As such, the monthly payment of the mortgage is predicated on a longer original term than the stated term of the mortgage. For example, a balloon mortgage with a 20-year original term will have the principal component of the mortgage payment set to a 30-year amortization schedule.

At the balloon period, always the final payment month of the mortgage, the entire outstanding principal balance of the mortgage is then due. In Exhibit 12.8 there

360-Month Original Term					
Coupon	5 Yrs	10 Yrs	15 Yrs	20 Yrs	25 Yrs
4.50%	$91,322	$80,295	$66,491	$49,212	$27,582
5.00%	$91,982	$81,539	$68,137	$50,937	$28,863
5.50%	$92,604	$82,730	$69,738	$52,645	$30,155
6.00%	$93,188	$83,866	$71,292	$54,331	$31,454
6.50%	$93,735	$84,948	$72,797	$55,994	$32,759
7.00%	$94,247	$85,976	$74,251	$57,629	$34,066

240-Month Original Term				180-Month Original Term			
Coupon	5 Yrs	10 Yrs	15 Yrs	Coupon	5 Yrs	7 Yrs	10 Yrs
4.50%	$83,021	$61,446	$34,438	4.50%	$74,300	$62,110	$41,643
5.00%	$83,766	$62,621	$35,484	5.00%	$75,035	$62,993	$42,518
5.50%	$84,489	$63,780	$36,533	5.50%	$75,759	$63,867	$43,395
6.00%	$85,190	$64,923	$37,586	6.00%	$76,471	$64,734	$44,271
6.50%	$85,870	$66,049	$38,642	6.50%	$77,170	$65,591	$45,148
7.00%	$86,527	$67,157	$39,698	7.00%	$77,857	$66,438	$46,023

EXHIBIT 12.8 Final balloon payments across a Range of fixed coupons and an original balance of $100,000

are three tables of balloon balances outstanding at the repayment period. In the uppermost table, the payment is set to 360 months. A list of coupon rates runs down the vertical axis of the table while the balloon periods run across the horizontal axis. Coupon rates are fixed from inception to the balloon period. The original principal balance of the loan was $100,000. Thus for a 6% coupon with a ten-year balloon payment, the balloon amount due in the 120th month would be $83,866. If we drop the interest rate to 5% and extend the balloon payment to 20 years, the amount due in the 240th month balloon payment would be $50,937. The other two tables represent balloon payments due at various time horizons for an amortization payment level of 20 and 15 years. Balloon payment amounts are also based on a fixed-coupon rate and an original balance of $100,000. See Exhibit 12.8.

The coupon payments of the mortgage are unaffected. At the conclusion of the original term, any principal balance remaining is "ballooned" in the last payment of the mortgage. Balloon mortgages can have original terms as short as 5 years or as long as 30 years. In the cases of shorter-term balloon mortgages, the coupon rates are generally lower than market rates due to the short period of time to principal payback.

The inputs for a balloon mortgage are therefore:

- Original term
- Remaining term
- Coupon rate, or in the case of a balloon ARM, an index and the spread to the index, and both periodic and lifetime coupon rate floors and caps
- Amortization period to be applied in setting the principal component of the monthly payment

Fixed-Rate Balloon Mortgage Amortization Sequence The amortization of a fixed-rate balloon mortgage is:

- **Regular payment phase.** In this phase the mortgagor makes a level payment consisting of the coupon income at a fixed rate applied against the outstanding balance of the loan. The principal component of the payment is based on an amortization schedule of a longer period than the stated original balance. This results in an unamortized principal balance on the last payment date of the loan and a principal component based on a longer period than the stated original balance.
- **Balloon payment phase.** On the last period of the stated original term, the regular coupon payment is made and any outstanding principal balance of the mortgage is retired.

Fixed-Rate Amortization Implementation Code Based on the above we will implement the amortization calculation of a fixed-rate balloon mortgage by developing the following subroutines.

"CollatCF_CalcMonthlyCoupFactors" Subroutine We will need to add the choice to select the fixed-rate balloon mortgage type. We have already designated this type as "MORTTYPE_BALLOON_FIXED" and have previously added it to the fifth case in the "Select..Case" statement.

"CollatCF_CalcCoupFactorsFixed" Subroutine In this subroutine we will not need to change a single thing as the calculation of the coupon income for a fixed-rate mortgage and a fixed-rate balloon mortgage is identical.

"CollatCFs_CalcScheduledAmortFactors" Subroutine In this subroutine we need to enter a "Select..Case" choice for the fixed-rate balloon mortgage. We have already designated this type as "MORTTYPE_BALLOON_FIXED", and we will now add it as the fourth case in the "Select..Case" statement. To view this subroutine, see Exhibit 12.6.

"CollatCF_CalcFixedBalSchPrin" Subroutine In this subroutine we will need to modify the amortization calculation process calculations from the case of a fixed-rate mortgage in two respects:

1. We need to reflect that the time periods we will use for the calculation of the per-period incremental discount factors are now predicated from a longer time period than the stated original term of the loan. Thus we need to make use of the value stored in the "FD_BALAMORTPER" field of the loan record. This will set the discount factors to the longer amortization term than the stated original term.
2. We will need to test if the balloon payment period has arrived and then retire all of the remaining principal balance of the mortgage. This value for this period is stored in the "FD_BALFINALPER" field of the loan record.

See Exhibit 12.9.

```
Sub CollatCF_CalcFixBalSchPrin(iloan As Long)

    For mPeriods = 1 To gLoanData(iloan, FD_REMTERM)
        If mPeriods = 1 Then _
            Call CollatCF_CalcDiscountFactors(gLoanData(iloan, FD_BALAMORTPER))
        mBaseDiscFactor = mDiscFactors(gLoanData(iloan, FD_BALAMORTPER))
        If mPeriods = gLoanData(iloan, FD_BALFINALPER) Then
            gLoanAmortFactors(iloan, mPeriods - 1) = 1#
            Exit For
            Else
            mBaseDiscFactor = mDiscFactors(gLoanData(iloan, FD_BALAMORTPER))
            gLoanAmortFactors(iloan, mPeriods) = 1 - _
                ((mBaseDiscFactor - mDiscFactors(mPeriods)) / _
                (mBaseDiscFactor - mDiscFactors(mPeriods - 1)))
        End If
    Next mPeriods

End Sub
```

EXHIBIT 12.9   "CollatCF_CalcFixedBalSchPrin" subroutine

ARM Balloon Mortgage Amortization Sequence   The amortization of an adjustable-rate balloon mortgage is:

- **Regular payment phase.** In this phase the mortgagor makes a payment consisting of the coupon income at a fully indexed floating rate. This fully indexed rate is subject to the same events of periodic coupon level resets as specified in the documentation of the loan. The reset fully indexed rate will be subject to the limitations or adjustments necessary to allow it to conform with both its periodic and lifetime caps and floors. As with the fixed-rate balloon mortgage the principal component of the payment is based on an amortization schedule of a longer period than the stated original balance. This results in an unamortized principal balance on the last payment date of the loan.
- **Balloon payment phase.** On the last period of the stated original term, the regular coupon payment is made and any outstanding principal balance of the mortgage is retired.

ARM Amortization Implementation Code   Based on the above we will implement the amortization calculation of an ARM balloon mortgage by developing the following subroutines.

"CollatCF_CalcMonthlyCoupFactors" Subroutine   We will need to add the choice to select the adjustable-rate balloon mortgage type. We have already designated this type as "MORTTYPE_BALLOON_ARM", and we will now add it as the fifth case in the "Select..Case" statement. See Exhibit 12.1.

"CollatCF_CalcCoupFactorsARMStandard" Subroutine   As in the above case of the fixed-rate balloon mortgages, we will not need to change a single thing as the calculation of the coupon income for an adjustable-rate mortgage and a adjustable-rate balloon mortgage is identical. See Exhibit 12.5.

```
Sub CollatCF_CalcSARMBalSchPrin(iloan As Long)

Dim BallAmortPer        As Double  'balloon amortization term

    BallAmortPer = gLoanData(iloan, FD_BALAMORTPER)
    For mPeriods = 1 To gLoanData(iloan, FD_REMTERM)
        If mPeriods = 1 Then _
            Call CollatCF_CalcDiscountFactors(BallAmortPer)
        If mPeriods = gLoanData(iloan, FD_BALFINALPER) Then
            gLoanAmortFactors(iloan, mPeriods - 1) = 1#
            Exit For
        Else
            'if its a reset period recalculate the factor sets
            If (gLoanData(iloan, FD_SEASON) + mPeriods - 1) Mod _
                gLoanData(iloan, FD_ARMPERRESET) = 0 Then
                Call CollatCF_CalcDiscountFactors(BallAmortPer - mPeriods)
            End If
            mBaseDiscFactor = mDiscFactors(BallAmortPer)
            gLoanAmortFactors(iloan, mPeriods) = 1 - _
                ((mBaseDiscFactor - mDiscFactors(mPeriods)) / _
                (mBaseDiscFactor - mDiscFactors(mPeriods - 1)))
        End If
    Next mPeriods

End Sub
```

EXHIBIT 12.10   "CollatCF_CalcStandARMBalSchPrin" subroutine

"CollatCF_CalcScheduledAmortFactors" Subroutine   In this subroutine we need to enter a "Select..Case" choice for the floating-rate balloon mortgage. We have already designated this type as "MORTTYPE_BALLOON_ARM", and we will now add it as the sixth case in the "Select..Case" statement. See Exhibit 12.6.

"CollatCF_CalcStandARMBalSchPrin" Subroutine   As was the case with the fixed-rate balloon mortgages, we need to modify the calculation of the ARM balloon mortgages to reflect the difference in principal amortizing term and stated original term and the payment of the final balloon principal payment. Using the same two fields of the loan record that we employed for this purpose earlier, we now have the VBA code in Exhibit 12.10.

NEW PREPAYMENT AND DEFAULT METHODOLOGIES

Having completed the task of expanding the scope of mortgage instruments that can be amortized by the CCFG, we will now turn to the development of the new prepayment and default methodologies. In this effort we will first review the existing methodology, the Uniform Methodology. In a nutshell, this methodology applies a combination of default and prepayment rates to measure the sensitivity of the collateral cash flows to various fluctuations away from our base case default and prepayment speed assumptions. The virtues of the Uniform Methodology are also its vices. It is simple to understand and easy to program and use.

It is due to this simplicity that results of the Uniform Methodology is of limited value.

The foremost limitation of the approach is that it does not differentiate any specific risk attached at the loan level. The Uniform Methodology is completely indifferent as to the question of geographic location and its attendant problem of geographic concentrations. Furthermore, and to compound the effects of the geographic myopia, it ignores the individual differences of property, lending process, servicing capabilities, and credit risk demographics of the borrowers. All of these factors have significant and immediate impact on both the rate that the loans can be expected to default and the severity of the losses that will result when they do.

In modeling terms, however, it is a good basic starting framework. It is a framework, moreover, that we can build on to advance our modeling efforts to encompass the inclusion of geographic and demographic material in our analysis. These more advanced techniques will allow us to address more specifically most if not all of the limitations in data and process we have enumerated in our discussion above.

The Uniform Methodology has one other value to the individual first starting out into this area of financial modeling. Its simplicity allows us to see the basic organization and processes that we will employ in a more complex modeling effort. We can use the existing Uniform methodologies as a springboard and a learning tool when we move on to develop the Geographic and Demographic methodologies later in the chapter.

UNIFORM METHODOLOGY

We will now review the steps of the Uniform Methodology. We will look at the organization of the calculation inputs and the sources of the data, and how the amortization is performed. This is the code of the BAM that we segregated from the preceding combined model back in Chapter 5. As such, we will look at this methodology from a structural approach and not a line-by-line code approach. Our discussion of this methodology will be limited to understanding it as a springboard to the development of the more complete Geographic and Demographic approaches of the next two sections of this chapter.

Steps of the Uniform Methodology

The steps in the Uniform Methodology are as follows:

1. Read the inputs of the user from the CCFG Cash Flow Amortization Parameters Menu. The inputs we will need are the Prepayment/Default methodology (single monthly mortality [SMM] rate, CPR, PSA, or Public Securities Administration Standard Default Assumptions Curve [SDA]), the base prepayment and default speeds, the number of step increments for both, and the size of the step increments. We will also need a uniform recovery lag period (RLP) assumption and a uniform MVD assumption.
2. Propagate the matrix of prepayment and default speeds to be applied against the base cash flow assumptions. Thus if the base prepayment rate is 100 PSA with five step increments of 100 PSA each, we will evaluate prepayment speeds

of 100, 200, 300, 400, and 500 PSA. If this is combined with a base default rate of 50 SDA with four step increments of 50 SDA each, we will evaluate default rates of 50, 100, and 150 SDA. This will in the end give us a total of 15 pairings of prepayment speeds with default rates.

3. Develop a set of prepayment and default factor vectors. These factors will contain the monthly decimal (percent of outstanding principal balance) and attrition factors for each of the prepayment and default speeds. We then have these available to apply later on a loan-by-loan basis.

4. Amortize the collateral. This will require a four-nested looping structure. They will loop through the collateral portfolio starting by prepayment cases, then by default rates, then by loan-by-loan basis, and finally by period-by-period basis. This process will generate the individual loan cash flows using the vectors we created in Step 3 above.

5. Calculate losses and recoveries of defaulted principal. Apply the uniform MVD assumptions against the equity positions of the individual loans to determine the severity of loss. Having determined the gross losses, apply the recovery lag period to correctly time the receipt of the recoveries of defaulted principal.

6. Aggregate the specific components of the loan cash flows. These would be the period-by-period defaulted principal amounts, payments of coupon income, scheduled amortization, and prepayments of principal. Last record the lagged recoveries of defaulted principal from earlier periods.

Basic Structural Approach of the Uniform Methodology

To accomplish the steps above, the Uniform Methodology focuses on the population of two sets of vectors. The first of these sets of vectors concerns the per-period factors for the various cash flows of the collateral on a monthly basis. These factors are derived as a series of decimal expressions that can be applied on a period-by-period to determine each of the cash flow components from any of the pieces of collateral. The application of these decimal factors against the outstanding balances of the individual collateral pieces results in the dollar cash flows we can expect from the collateral in that period.

Factor Arrays The decimal factor vectors are produced by a series of single-purpose subroutines, each of which addresses itself to the creation of a single type of decimal vector. A table listing the decimal factor arrays and the subroutines that create them is shown in Exhibit 12.11. An example of the type of subroutine is

COMPUTATION OF CASH FLOW VECTORS		
Cash Flow Component	VBA "Factor" Vector	Subroutine
Coupon Income	gDayFactors(Period,DayCntType) * Coupon	CollatCF_CalcMonthlyCoupFactors
Scheduled Amortization	gLoanAmortFactors(loan, time)	CollatCFs_CalcScheduledAmortFactors
Prepayents of Principal	gPrepayRate(1 to PrepaySteps)	CollatCF_CalcMonthlyCPRFactors
Defaults of Principal	gDefaultRate(1 to DefaultSteps)	CollatCF_CalcMonthlyCPRFactors
Recoveries of Defaults	gRecover	CollatCF_CalcPrincipalRecoveries

EXHIBIT 12.11 Table of cash flow component array code

```
Sub CollatCF_CalcDiscountFactors(RemTerm As Double)

Dim run_factor      As Double       'current period discount factor
Dim itime           As Integer      'loop counter for periods

    mDiscFactors(0) = 1#
    run_factor = 1#
    For iperiod = 1 To RemTerm
        mBaseDiscFactor = 1 + gMonthlyCoupLevels(iloan, iperiod)
        run_factor = run_factor * mBaseDiscFactor
        mDiscFactors(iperiod) = run_factor
    Next iperiod

End Sub
```

EXHIBIT 12.12 "CollatCF_CalcDiscountFactors" subroutine

shown in Exhibit 12.12. It is the subroutine "CollatCF_CalcDiscountFactors" that calculates the scheduled amortization decimal factors for a fixed-rate loan.

Cash Flow Arrays   Once the above decimal arrays have been created, it is a very straightforward matter to produce the monthly cash flows; all we need to do is multiply the monthly factors by the outstanding dollar amounts of the loans in any given period. We need to be careful, especially when using prepayment or default calculation methodologies that are sensitive to seasoning effects, but aside from that, the process is simplicity itself! See Exhibit 12.13 for the table of cash flow arrays and the corresponding subroutines that produce them. Exhibit 12.14 shows the subroutine that produces the scheduled amortization cash flows for the scheduled amortization cash flow array.

Finishing Up the Cash Flow Calculation Process

To finish the process we only need to correctly aggregate the loan-by-loan cash flows into the correct pool or sub-portfolio level scenarios. Again it is important to emphasize that the cash flows in the Uniform Methodology are differentiated solely by the unique combination of prepayment speed and default rate.

These cash flows and their attendant assumptions can then be written to a file or an Access database. They can then be applied as inputs, along with the collateral balances, to any liabilities structure created in a separate model. There is a Web

COMPUTATION OF CASH FLOW AMOUNTS		
Cash Flow Component	Cash Flow Vector	Subroutine
Coupon Income	gCoupIncome	CollatCF_CalcCouponPayments
Scheduled Amortization	gAmortPrin	CollatCF_CalcScheduledAmortization
Prepayents of Principal	gPrepaidPrin	CollatCF_CalcPrincipalPrepayments
Defaults of Principal	gDefaultPrin	CollatCF_CalcDefaultEffects
Recoveries of Defaults	gRecoverPrin	CollatCF_AccumulateCFComponents

EXHIBIT 12.13   Table of cash flow arrays

```
Sub CollatCF_CalcScheduledAmortization(iloan As Long, iperiod As Integer)

    gLoanPrinRet = 0#
    If gLoanCurBal > 1# Then
        gLoanPrinRet = gLoanCurBal * gLoanAmortFactors(iloan, iperiod)
        gLoanCurBal = gLoanCurBal - gLoanPrinRet
        Else
        gLoanPrinRet = gLoanCurBal
        gLoanCurBal = 0#
    End If

End Sub
```

EXHIBIT 12.14 "CollatCF_CalcScheduledAmortization" subroutine

chapter, Chapter 12.2 "The Uniform Methodology," that deals in detail with the Uniform Methodology if you wish to read further.

Taking the Next Steps in Development

Given the framework of the Uniform Methodology, it then becomes a fairly straight-forward proposition to transition the model to an alternative analytical approach employing geographic and demographic inputs.

In the Uniform Methodology we assign a series of monthly prepayment speeds to the factor array for prepayment speeds. These speeds are then converted into decimal attrition factors, and the resultant factors are then employed to calculate the cash flows. If the prepayment methodology is CPR, or PSA after the 60th month, the input is a Constant amount. The model looks to the contents of the speeds input to produce the decimal factor and that factor to produce the cash flows. If a different (and perhaps varying), series of prepayment speeds were contained in the vector (as is the case when the PSA methodology is in its first 60 months), the model will still perform in the same way. Clearly it is a simple step then to think one step further. The prepayment rate may also vary because of other conditions rather than due only to the conventions of the methodology. Thus the successive monthly values of the prepayment speed array could be the product of:

- A specialized analysis (regression studies)
- Historical data (prepayment history of like mortgage types)
- Our own best guess (I hope not!)
- The product of statistical selection (Monte Carlo perhaps)

It really does not make any different to the calculation structure how the initial prepayment speeds are derived, as long as they are congruent with valid values (i.e., not negative, etc.). While we always run the risk of Garbage In = Garbage Out, the calculation methodology is blind to the validity of the assumptions at this level of detail.

Thus we can easily take the next step to the use of geographic- or demographic-based prepayment and default estimates. Instead of entering a single value for the prepayment speed of all loans in the collateral pool, we can immediately progress to a more specifically derived set of estimates. Just as the Uniform Methodology will handle a ramping set of PSA prepayment method speeds, it should be quite capable of computing the prepayments from a varied set of prepayment speed estimates over, say, the next five years based on the location of the property and the type of mortgage.

Now we can simply use various characteristics of the loan, such as its geographic location or the demographics of its borrower, to determine a more individualized set of prepayment and default assumptions. We will move from the one-size-fits-all approach of the Uniform Methodology to the special-orders-don't-upset-us! approach of a geographically/demographically tailored approach.

To implement the alternative approaches, we will need to develop a way of finding, accessing, and loading the loan-by-loan specific information. This information will include prepayment, default, MVD, and recovery lag inputs the model will need to replace those of the Uniform Methodology approach. We will read some of these directly from a collection of files generated by our own or other research groups. Others we may be asked to use by the rating agencies or even prospective investors. We will not go into the processes that create these files. The processes and programs—such as the multiple linear regression studies that produce the factor analysis that links demographic characteristics of the borrower to default rate, for example—lie outside the scope of this book. We will assume that the information available to us is valid and contained in either Excel files or Access databases. From this starting point we will look at the code that implements first a strictly geographic approach to prepayment/default estimation and then one that combines a mix of geographic and demographic approaches.

GEOGRAPHIC METHODOLOGY

The Geographic Methodology replaces the portfolio-level assumptions used by the Uniform Methodology with a series of specific assumptions that are applied on a loan-by-loan basis determined by the geographic location of the loan. These assumptions are loan-by-loan specific and consist of individual sets of monthly assumptions based solely on the location of the loan.

Moving to a File-Based System

The Geographic Methodology replaces the specification by the user of prepayment and default behaviors from to the CCFG Cash Flow Amortization Parameters Menu with a set of files containing geographic-specific assumptions.

A Geographic Assumptions file, or sets of files, is constructed by the user in which the prepayment rate assumptions, default rate assumptions, MVD assumptions, and recovery lag assumptions of the collateral are stored. These sets of assumptions are differentiated by, from most local to most general, MSAs, state levels, and finally a national level. If the geographic information cannot identify a loan as being in a particular MSA, its treatment is defaulted to the state level; if the state-level information is missing, it is defaulted to the national assumptions. These assumption sets can be constructed independently of each other and can be specified to pertain to any pool or any of the sub-portfolios by using the "Select File" buttons in the Geographic section of the CCFG Cash Flow Amortization Parameters Menu. A single file can be applied to one or several collateral sub-portfolios.

The assumptions in the file are then matched to the geographic location of the collateral and applied on a loan-by-loan basis. The assumptions are in the form of five years of short-term month-to-month rates and terms whereupon the file shifts over to a longer-term level rate from the 61st month onward. We can fill the existing prepayment and default rate vectors with these assumptions and modify the MVD and recovery lag information to be read on a period-by-period basis. At this point all of the assumptions will filter through the remaining cash flow calculation and aggregation subroutines.

Let us now descend from this high-level discussion to its implementation in the model.

Setting the Groundwork

The first step in adding both the Geographic and Demographic Methodologies to the CCFG will be to create a very high-level master subroutine that will determine which of the three methodologies, Uniform, Geographic, or Demographic, the user has selected. This subroutine will also prepare the model for the cash flow calculations by performing tasks essential to all of them in common.

"CollatCF_ComputeCollateralCashflows" Subroutine   As stated above, we have now moved to a model that, instead of a single prepayment and default methodology, allows the user a choice of three different approaches. With three choices, the first task we need to accomplish is to develop a topmost subroutine that can perform some useful activities in preparing the model to execute our choice. This subroutine will be the master subroutine for the cash flow calculation sequence. It will perform the following roles:

- Establish the set of working arrays that hold the prepayment, default, MVD, and recovery lag assumptions. This will be affected by using the "ReDim" statement that will establish the dimensions of the arrays required for the type of prepayment/default analysis selected.
- Establish the set of arrays that hold the results of the forthcoming cash flow calculations. Again we will use the "ReDim" command to size these arrays based on the methodology choice of the user. Using this command also has the side benefit of erasing all data from any previous runs of the model.
- Correctly branch the model to the appropriate methodology, Uniform, Geographic, or Demographic.

The "CollatCF_ComputeCollateralCashflows" subroutine performs these tasks. See Exhibit 12.15.

"CollatCF_RedimAllCashflowArrays" Subroutine   The subroutine "CollatCF_ComputeCollateralCashflows" first calls the subroutine "CollatCF_RedimAllCash-FlowArrays" to establish the number and size of the vectors that will hold the competed cash flow calculations. These arrays will hold the aggregated component collateral portfolio cash flows on a month-by-month basis. Clearing these arrays is

```
Sub CollatCF_ComputeCollateralCashflows()

    If gROCFWaterfall Then
        'setup all the cash flow arrays section
        ReDim gMonthlyCoupLevels(1 To gTotalLoans, 1 To PAY_DATES) As Double
        're-dimension the arrays that will be receiving results
        Call CollatCF_CalcPortTotal
        Call CollatCF_RedimAllCashFlowArrays
        Call CollatCF_RedimAllPrepayDefaultArrays
        Sheets("Main Menu").Select
        gCalcComplete = 0
        'PREPAYMENT AND DEFAULT METHODOLOGY SELECTION
        If gMethodUniform Then Call CollatCF_ApplyUniformMethodology
        If gMethodGeographic Then Call CollatCF_ApplyGeographicMethodology
        If gMethodDemographic Then Call CollatCF_ApplyDemographicMethodology
    End If

End Sub
```

EXHIBIT 12.15   "CollatCF_ComputeCollateralCashflows" subroutine

an immediate priority when starting any new run of the model to avoid the reten-
tion of information of computed results from a previous run. The arrays will hold
the coupon income, the scheduled amortization of principal, principal prepayments,
principal defaults, and the recoveries of defaulted principal.

Note that this subroutine is divided into two sections. The first is the code
that is executed when the Uniform Methodology is selected. Here the arrays
are dimensioned to the number of prepayment speeds, by the number of default
rates, by the periods. In the second case, that of either the Geographic or Demographic methodologies, the arrays are dimensioned to the number of stress levels
for both prepayments and defaults. In the case that no stress factors are applied
("mApplyStress = FALSE") then the dimensions of the arrays are set to 1. This is because with no stress steps, we can run only the Base Prepayment Speed in conjunction
with the Base Default Rate. See Exhibit 12.16.

"CollatCF_RedimAllPrepayDefaultArrays" Subroutine   The   second   subroutine
that "CollatCF_ComputeCollateralCashflows" calls is "CollatCF_RedimAllPrepay
DefaultArrays". This subroutine dimensions all the arrays needed to provide for
any inputs needed in the prepayment and default calculations and the arrays that
will hold the speeds that we will assign to each of the loans. Again, as with the
"CollatCF_RedimAllCashFlowArrays" subroutine, the number and size of the vectors that the model will need to store the information required to assign the prepayment speeds and default rates the model will use varies widely by the methodology
selected. In the case of the Uniform Methodology, there are 11 arrays. In the case of
either the Geographic or Demographic Methodology, 13 arrays are required.

These arrays are the ultimate result of the calculation process, and it is vital that
we re-dimension them to the correct number of prepayment and default cases we
wish to produce before initiating another run of the model. Again, as noted above,
by re-dimensioning the arrays, we will also reinitialize all of their members to zero.

Note that the subroutine is divided into two cases. The first is the Uniform Methodology while the other addresses the Geographic and Demographic

```
Sub CollatCF_RedimAllCashFlowArrays()

    'UNIFORM METHOD
    'Uniform method allows the input of a base rate, increment, and number of steps for both default and
    '    prepayment rates.  The increment is additive, NOT MULTIPLICATIVE, as with the Geographic and
    '    Demographic approaches below.  A base rate of 10% CPR with 5 steps of 2% results in the following
    '    speeds, 10%, 12%, 14%, 16% and 18%.
    If gMethodUniform Then
        'Uniform method cash flows are determined by the number of prepayment and default steps specified
        ReDim gPrepaidPrin(1 To gPrepayLevels, 1 To gDefaultLevels, 1 To PAY_DATES) As Double
        ReDim gDefaultPrin(1 To gPrepayLevels, 1 To gDefaultLevels, 1 To PAY_DATES) As Double
        [7 lines of code omitted]
        ReDim gTotCoupIncome(1 To gPrepayLevels, 1 To gDefaultLevels) As Double
        ReDim gTotRecoverPrin(1 To gPrepayLevels, 1 To gDefaultLevels) As Double
    End If
    'GEOGRAPHIC METHOD
    'Geographic method uses base geographic prepayment and geographic default speed vectors that are
    '    assigned based on the location of the property.  Stresses to both prepayments and defaults are
    '    applied by entering the base rate, increment, and # of steps. (see Apply Stress below.)
    'DEMOGRAPHIC METHOD
    'Demographic method uses a scoring system based on the characteristics of the borrower to determine
    '    a base default rate.  The prepayment speeds are determined by the property location as in the
    '    geographic method above.  Both the prepayment and default rates can be stressed.  (see Apply
    '    Stress section below)
    'APPLY STRESS
    'Both the prepayment rate determined by the properties location, and its default rate determined
    '    by its location when using the geographic method, or the borrowers demographic characteristics
    '    when using the demographic method can be stressed.
    '    Stress levels are specified by indicateing the base rate as a percentage multiplier, the number
    '    of stress streps, and the incfrement of each stress step.  For example with a 80% Base Rate, 5
    '    steps, and an increment of 10% the results will be 80%-90%-100%-110%-120% of the Base Rate.  If
    '    the Base Default Rate is 10% CPR the applied rates will be 8%, 9%, 10%, 11%, and 12% CPR.
    If gMethodGeographic Or gMethodDemographic Then
        If gMethodApplyStress Then
            'by stress steps for both prepayments and defaults
            ReDim gPrepaidPrin(1 To gPrepayStressSteps, 1 To gDefaultStressSteps, 1 To PAY_DATES) As Double
            ReDim gDefaultPrin(1 To gPrepayStressSteps, 1 To gDefaultStressSteps, 1 To PAY_DATES) As Double
            [9 lines of code omitted]
            ReDim gPrepayStressFactor(1 To gPrepayStressSteps) As Double
            ReDim gDefaultStressFactor(1 To gDefaultStressSteps) As Double
        Else
            'no stress steps applied -- a single scenario
            ReDim gPrepaidPrin(1 To 1, 1 To 1, 1 To PAY_DATES) As Double
            ReDim gDefaultPrin(1 To 1, 1 To 1, 1 To PAY_DATES) As Double
            [9 lines of code omitted]
            ReDim gPrepayStressFactor(1) As Double
            ReDim gDefaultStressFactor(1) As Double
        End If
    End If

End Sub
```

EXHIBIT 12.16   "CollatCF_RedimAllCashFlowArrays" subroutine

Methodologies simultaneously. In the section concerning the Uniform Methodology, we can see that the arrays are dimensioned as to the number of prepayment and default cases we wish to run. These in turn are determined by our entries in the Prepayment Step Increments and Default Step Increments fields of the CCFG Cash Flow Amortization Parameters menu.

In the case of the Geographic and Demographic Methodologies, we do not have the same structure of step increments we see in the Uniform Methodology. Instead we have something that is virtually analogous. These are the Stress Factor "# of Steps". If we indicate that we wish three levels of stress applied to the prepayment Base Stress Rate and two to the Base Stress Rate for defaults, we will be evaluating a total of six distinct cases. However, we have to allow for a special case and that is the condition that applies when the user wishes *no stresses* applied to the Geographic or Demographic Methodology assumptions. In this case we have a single dimension array of the unmodified base case assumptions. The model appropriately dimensions the arrays, and we are ready to go on to the next step of the process.

```
Sub CollatCF_RedimAllPrepayDefaultArrays()

    If gMethodGeographic Or gMethodDemographic Then
        'UNIFORM SPEED METHODOLOGY ARRAYS (THESE ARRAYS ARE NOT NEEDED)
        ReDim gMonthlyPrepayRate(1 To gPrepayStressSteps, 1 To PAY_DATES) As Double
        ReDim gMonthlyDefaultRate(1 To gDefaultStressSteps, 1 To PAY_DATES) As Double
        'GEOGRAPHIC OR DEMOGRAPHIC METHODOLOGY ARRAYS
        'These arrays hold the values of the geographic entity id numbers, the geographic prepayment,
        ' geographic specific default rates, geographic market value declines, and geographic recovery
        ' lag arrays that have been read from the file names of the CF Amortization Menu. The last array
        ' tells us if there is a schedule of each type for the state/msa.
        ReDim gGeoCodeTable(1 To GEO_ENTITIES) As Double        'state/MSA numbers
        [5 lines of code omitted]
        ReDim gGeoActive(1 To GEO_ENTITIES, 1 To 4) As Boolean
        'These arrays hold the values that have been assigned to each loan based on the amortization
        '   methodology and its own characteristics
        ReDim gByLoanPrepays(1 To gTotalLoans, 1 To PAY_DATES) As Double
        ReDim gByLoanDefaults(1 To gTotalLoans, 1 To PAY_DATES) As Double
        ReDim gByLoanMVDs(1 To gTotalLoans, 1 To PAY_DATES) As Double
        ReDim gByLoanLags(1 To gTotalLoans, 1 To PAY_DATES) As Double
        'Demographic MVD, MVD adjustment factor, default rates
        ReDim gMVDRate(1 To gTotalLoans) As Double        'base per loan market value decline percentage
        ReDim gMVDPercent(1 To gTotalLoans) As Double     'final per loan market value decline percentage
        ReDim gDefRate(1 To gTotalLoans) As Double        'calculated demographic default rate by loan
    Else
        'UNIFORM SPEED METHOD ARRAYS
        'uniform prepayment and default rates by period, applicable to ALL loans
        ReDim gMonthlyPrepayRate(1 To gPrepayLevels, 1 To PAY_DATES) As Double
        ReDim gMonthlyDefaultRate(1 To gDefaultLevels, 1 To PAY_DATES) As Double
        'GEOGRAPHIC OR DEMOGRAPHIC METHODOLOGY ARRAYS (THESE ARRAYS ARE NOT NEEDED)
        ReDim gGeoCodeTable(1 To 1) As Double
        ReDim gGeoPrepayTable(1 To 1) As Double
        ReDim gGeoDefaultTable(1 To 1) As Double
        ReDim gGeoMVDTable(1 To 1) As Double
        [5 lines of code omitted]
        ReDim gByLoanMVDs(1 To 1) As Double
        ReDim gByLoanLags(1 To 1) As Double
        ReDim gGeoPrepayType(1 To 1) As Integer
        ReDim gMVDRate(1 To 1) As Double
        ReDim gMVDPercent(1 To 1) As Double
        ReDim gDefRate(1 To 1) As Double
    End If

End Sub
```

EXHIBIT 12.17   "CollatCF_RedimAllPrepayDefaultArrays" subroutine

You will further note that we will re-dimension the arrays not needed by the selected model run to the minimum size. This will save a lot of storage in the case of the Uniform Methodology and a small amount of storage if the other methodologies are selected. See Exhibit 12.17.

After clearing and re-dimensioning all of the critical arrays, the model now chooses the prepayment/default cash flow calculation methodology predicated by the users entry in the "Specify Method" section fields of the CCFG Cash Flow Amortization Parameters Menu.

Assigning Loan-Specific Prepayment, Recovery, Default, and MVD Assumptions

Until now all of the activity performed by the subroutine "CollatCF_ComputeCollateralCashflows" and the subroutines called by it has been common to all three of the cash flow calculation methodologies. Now we will assume that the user has selected the Geographic Methodology, and, starting with this methodology's highest subroutine, trace how the choice is translated into cash flows. All of the Geographic Methodology VBA code will be found in the "CollatCF_MethodGeographic" module. The subroutines that produce the period-by-period component cash flows are common to all of the three methodologies. They are contained in the "CollatCF_CFGenerator" module.

"CollatCF_ApplyGeographicMethodology" Subroutine This subroutine is the highest-level subroutine in the Geographic Methodology cash flow calculation approach. It is divided into two functional areas:

1. Setting up the component statistics and information read from the Geographic Methodology assumption files
2. Using this information to produce the cash flows themselves

This subroutine contains no less than 14 calls to other subroutines, and many of those subroutines also call other subroutines. In the remainder of this section, we will examine nearly all of the subroutines one by one to understand the organization and function of the Geographic Methodology.

The first two calls set up the stress-level variables (if needed) so that they can be applied to the assumptions at a later point in the calculation process. The next two subroutines called "CollatCF_LoadGeoInfoToArraysNeeded" and "CollatCF_PopulateLoanByLoanArrays" read the Geographic Assumptions files as designed by the user on the CCFG Cash Flow Amortization Parameters menu. They open the designated assumption files, read the contents into VBA arrays, and use this information to assign the prepayment rates and default speeds to individual loans. The next step is performed by the subroutine "CollatCF_CalcMonthlyCoupFactors" to set the monthly coupon rates. The subroutine "CollatCF_CalcScheduled AmortFactors" then sets the scheduled amortization factor calculations for each of the loans based on the period coupon rates just calculated. With these tasks completed, the setup portion of the Geographic Methodology is complete. The model now has all the cash flow calculation input information needed, and that information is assigned to each individual loan.

The standard cash flow calculation subroutines can now be called from inside of a four-level-deep "For..Next" looping structure. The outermost loop is regulated by the number of Prepayment Stress steps. The second loop is regulated by the number of Default Stress steps. The third loop is regulated by the number of loans in the pool or sub-portfolios, and the innermost loop is that of time, the month-by-month periods of the remaining term of each of the individual loans. When this subroutine completes its run, the Geographic Methodology will be complete. See Exhibit 12.18.

"CollatCF_CalcPrepaymentStressLevels" Subroutine The role of this subroutine is to set the values for the array "gPrepayStressLevels". There are two possible calculation choices. The first is that either the Geographic or the Demographic Methodology has been selected but no stress-level information has been entered. In this case the subroutine sets the number of stress levels to "1" and the stress level to "100%". If there are stress levels specified, the subroutine starts with the base level and creates additional levels based on the increment rate and the number of steps specified by the user. See Exhibit 12.19.

```
Sub CollatCF_ApplyGeographicMethodology()

Dim drate       As Double
Dim prate       As Double

    'SETUP PREPAYMENT AND DEFAULT STRESS LEVELS (IF SPECIFIED)
    Call CollatCF_CalcPrepaymentStressLevels
    Call CollatCF_CalcDefaultStressLevels
    'READ THE ASSUMPTION FILES AND ASSIGN THE ASSUMPTIONS ON A LOAN-BY-LOAN
    '  BASIS BY GEOGRAPHIC LOCATION
    Call CollatCF_LoadGeoInfoToArrays
    Call CollatCF_PopulateLoanByLoanArrays
    'CALCULATE THE PREPAYMENT, DEFAULT, COUPON AND PRIN AMORTIZATION FACTORS
    Call CollatCF_CalcMonthlyCoupFactors    'set coupon factors
    Call CollatCF_CalcScheduledAmortFactors 'set principal factors
    'CASH FLOWS CALCULATION SECTION
    'this loop structure takes all the factor calculations contained in the
    ' various arrays for prepayments, defaults, coupon, sceduled amortzation,
    ' and recoveries and applies then to the balanes of each of individual loans.
    For iprepay = 1 To gPrepayStressSteps
      pstress = gPrepayStressFactor(iprepay)
      For idefault = 1 To gDefaultStressSteps
        dstress = gDefaultStressFactor(idefault)
        For iloan = 1 To gTotalLoans
            If gLoanOK(iloan) And gLoanSelect(iloan, FD_SCREEN_GEO) = 0 Then
                Call Setup_Initial_Loan_Parameters(iloan)
                For iperiod = 1 To gLoanData(iloan, FD_REMTERM)
                    drate = gByLoanDefaults(iloan, iperiod) * dstress
                    Call CollatCF_CalcDefaultEffects(drate)
                    Call CollatCF_CalcCouponPayments(iloan, iperiod)
                    Call CollatCF_CalcScheduledAmortization(iloan, iperiod)
                    prate = gByLoanPrepays(iloan, iperiod) * pstress
                    Call CollatCF_CalcPrincipalPrepayments(prate)
                    Call CollatCF_CalcPrincipalRecoveries(iloan, iperiod)
                    Call CollatCF_SumAllCFComponents(iloan, iprepay, idefault, iperiod)
                Next iperiod
            End If
        Next iloan
        Call Display_Amortization_ProgressMsg(iprepay, idefault)
      Next idefault
    Next iprepay

End Sub
```

EXHIBIT 12.18 "CollatCF_ApplyGeographicMethodology" subroutine

"CollatCF_CalcDefaultStressLevels" Subroutine This subroutine performs the mirror image of the prepayment stress-level subroutine except for that the stress are those applied to the defaults. See Exhibit 12.20.

"CollatCF_LoadGeoAssumptionFilesToArrays" Subroutine This subroutine locates, opens and reads the file designated in the "Geographic Specific Prepayment, Default, Recovery, MVD, and Recovery Lag Curves" section of the menu in the "Geographic Assumptions File" field. This subroutine performs three functions in this order:

1. Reads the names and identification codes of each of the geographic entities. These are National = 0, States = 1 to 54, and MSAs = 1 to 150. The value of the Constant variable "GEO_ENTITIES" is the sum of these three numbers, 155.

```
Sub CollatCF_CalcPrepaymentStressLevels()

    If gMethodApplyStress Then
        If gPrepayStressSteps = 0 Then
            If gPrepayStressBase = 0# Then
                'no entry made, set steps to one, stress level to 100%
                gPrepayStressSteps = 1
                gPrepayStressFactor(1) = 1#
            Else
                For istress = 1 To gPrepayStressSteps
                    If istress = 1 Then
                        gPrepayStressFactor(1) = gPrepayStressBase
                    Else
                        gPrepayStressFactor(istress) = _
                        gPrepayStressFactor(istress - 1) + gPrepayStressIncr
                    End If
                Next istress
            End If
        End If
    Else
        gPrepayStressSteps = 1
        gPrepayStressFactor(1) = 1#
    End If

End Sub
```

EXHIBIT 12.19   "CollatCF_CalcPrepaymentStressLevels" subroutine

2. Regardless of the type of methodology, either Geographic or Demographic, the subroutine now reads the contents of the worksheets containing prepayment and recovery lag information. The assumptions for prepayment rates are contained in the worksheet "GeoPrepay", and the recovery lag period assumptions are in the "GeoRecoveryLag" worksheet of the file.

```
Sub CollatCF_CalcDefaultStressLevels()

    If gMethodApplyStress Then
        If gDefaultStressSteps = 0 Then
            If gDefaultStressBase = 0# Then
                'no entry made, set steps to one, stress level to 100%
                gDefaultStressSteps = 1
                gDefaultStressFactor(1) = 1#
            Else
                For istress = 1 To gDefaultStressSteps
                    If istress = 1 Then
                        gDefaultStressFactor(1) = gDefaultStressBase
                    Else
                        gDefaultStressFactor(istress) = _
                            gDefaultStressFactor(istress - 1) + gDefaultStressIncr
                    End If
                Next istress
            End If
        End If
    Else
        'no entry made, set steps to one, stress level to 100%
        gDefaultStressSteps = 1
        gDefaultStressFactor(1) = 1#
    End If

End Sub
```

EXHIBIT 12.20   "CollatCF_CalcDefaultStressLevels" subroutine

3. If the Cash Flow Calculation Methodology is geographic (not demographic), the
CCFG reads the default rate assumptions from the "GeoDefault" worksheet and
the MVD information from the "GeoMVD" worksheet.

The contents of the file are monthly rates for the first 60 months of the
remaining life of the loan and a uniform rate for all periods thereafter. This
subroutine populates the "gGeoPrepayTable" array with monthly prepay rates,
the "gGeoRecoverLag" array with recovery lag period assumptions (expressed in
months), the "gGeoDefault" array with monthly default rates (CPR method), and
last, the "gGeoMVD" array with monthly MVD estimates. Just remember all that
we are doing at this point is loading a series of geographic assumptions from a series
of files into the model. We have not yet reached the point where we are assigning
these assumptions to the individual loans or using them in any calculations. See
Exhibit 12.21.

```
Sub CollatCF_LoadGeoInfoToArrays()

Dim sRow    As Integer      'start row of data in the assumptions file
Dim arow    As Integer      'current row in the table

    Workbooks.Open FileName:=gGeographicFileName
    'READ THE GEOGRAPHIC ENTITY CODE (common to all tables)
    'READ THE PREPAYMENT AND RECOVERY LAG ASSUMPTIONS
    'These assumptions are common across both the Geographic and Demographic
    ' methodologies read prepayment information
    Sheets("GeoPrepay").Select
    For irow = 1 To GEO_ENTITIES
        'general geographic info common to all 4 schedules
        gGeoStateCode(irow) = Trim(Range("PreStates").Cells(irow).Value)
        gGeoMSACode(irow) = Range("PreCodes").Cells(irow).Value
        'prepayment and recovery lag specific information
        If Trim(Range("PreType").Cells(irow).Value) = "CPR" Then
            gGeoPrepayType(irow) = 1      'CPR method
        Else
            gGeoPrepayType(irow) = 2      'PSA method
        End If
        gGeoActive(irow, GEO_PRE) = Range("ActivePre").Cells(irow).Value
        gGeoActive(irow, GEO_LAG) = Range("ActiveLag").Cells(irow).Value
        For icol = 1 To GEOMTHS
            gGeoPrepayTable(irow, icol) = Range("PreCurve").Cells(irow, icol).Value
            gGeoLagTable(irow, icol) = Range("LagCurves").Cells(irow, icol).Value
        Next icol
    Next irow
    'GEOGRAPHIC METHODOLOGY ONLY - DEFAULT RATES AND MARKET VALUE DECLINES
    'Read the default information and market value information GEOGRAPHIC method
    ' only! The default and market value decline is CALCULATED using property
    ' and mortgagee demographics in the Demographic methodology.
    If gMethodGeographic Then
        For irow = 1 To GEO_ENTITIES
            'default rate and MVD information
            gGeoActive(irow, GEO_FOF) = Range("ActiveFOF").Cells(irow).Value
            gGeoActive(irow, GEO_MVD) = Range("ActiveMVD").Cells(irow).Value
            For icol = 1 To GEOMTHS
                gGeoMVDTable(irow, icol) = Range("MVDCurves").Cells(irow, icol).Value
                gGeoDefaultTable(irow, icol) = Range("DefCurves").Cells(irow, icol).Value
            Next icol
        Next irow
    End If
    ActiveWorkbook.Close

End Sub
```

EXHIBIT 12.21   "CollatCF_LoadGeoInfoToArrays" subroutine

"CollatCF_PopulateLoanByLoanArrays" Subroutine This subroutine is responsible for assigning each loan all of its geographic or demographic prepayment rate, default rate, MVD rate, and recovery lag period data assumptions. It calls seven other subroutines that we will visit individually below. Briefly, the subroutine performs these three functions, in order:

1. Load the geographic prepayment rate assumptions for each of the loans. This is a two-step process. First we must identify which geographic entity the loan lies within. Then, upon making this determination, we match it to the correct set of prepayment assumptions.
2. Load the recovery period lag factor for each of the loans. This is again performed on a purely geographic basis (greatly aided by the fact that we have already identified the geographic entity within which the loan falls) in Step 1 above.
3. Set the default and MVD rates. Here we have a parting of the ways between the Geographic Methodology and the Demographic Methodology. In the Geographic Methodology, we assign these factors based on the geographic location of the loan. In the Demographic Methodology, we assign them based on the demographics of the borrower, the credit characteristics of the loan, the characteristics of the property type, and the due diligence and experience of the underwriters and the loan servicers.

At the conclusion of this very busy subroutine, we will have populated each individual loan with all the prepayment and default assumptions we need to calculate its cash flow performance. See Exhibit 12.22.

Now let us look at each of the subroutines that perform the various component steps of this process!

"CollatCF_FindGeographicEntityIndex" Subroutine The first and obvious task we need to perform in assigning geographic-specific assumptions to individual loans is to identify the geographic entity in which we are going to place the loan to match it to the assignment. In this subroutine the loan is first examined to see if it has an MSA designation and, if so, is matched to it. If the loan lacks a specific MSA designation, we default to the state designation. If the state designation is missing, we default to the national assumption. See Exhibit 12.23.

"CollatCF_LoadGeoPrepaymentAssumptions" Subroutine Having established a geographic reference for the loan, we will now match it to a set of geographically specific prepayment assumptions and load them into the loan array. The argument of the subroutine is the number of the loan that we will assign the geographic-specific prepayment assumptions to. It starts by checking whether the value of the "mGeo Index" for this loan is that of a geographic entity containing prepayment assumptions information. Some MSAs or even states may not have prepayment assumptions entered in the file. Earlier in the subroutine "CollatCF_LoadGeoInfoToArrays", we read a column of values in the worksheets of both the prepayment assumptions and recovery lag assumptions that indicated whether the entity had an active assumption. These indicators (one for each of the 155 entities) were stored in the array "gGeoActive". This array contains a row for each entity and a column for each of the geographic inputs of prepayment, defaults, recovery lag, and MVD. The current

```
Sub CollatCF_PopulateLoanByLoanArrays()

    'match the loans to the specific geographic assumptions
    For iloan = 1 To gTotalLoans
        'SET PREPAYMENT RATES
        'prepayment curve statistics are geographically based and are common
        '  to both geo/demo methods
        Call CollatCF_FindGeographicEntityIndex(iloan, gLoanData(iloan, FD_MSACODE))
        Call CollatCF_LoadGeoPrepaymentAssumptions(iloan)
        'SET RECOVERY CURVES
        'recovery curve statistics are geographically based and are common
        '  to both geo/demo methods
        Call CollatCF_LoadGeoRecoveryLagAssumptions(iloan)
        'SET DEFAULTS AND MARKET VALUE DECLINE RATES
        If gMethodGeographic Then
            'read geographic base default curves from a file
            Call CollatCF_CalcGeoDefaultAssumptions(iloan)
            'read geographic MVD curves from a file
            Call CollatCF_CalcGeoMVDAssumptions(iloan)
            gDefaultMethod = DEFAULTS_CPR        'geographic method is CPR only
        End If
    Next iloan

    If gMethodDemographic Then
        'calculate demographic base default rates
        Call CollatCF_DemoMethodCalcDefRates
        'calculate demographic based MVDs
        Call CollatCF_DemoMethodCalcMVDRates
        gDefaultMethod = DEFAULTS_CPR        'demographic method is CPR only
    End If

End Sub
```

EXHIBIT 12.22   "CollatCF_PopulateLoanbyLoanArrays" subroutine

```
Sub CollatCF_FindGeographicEntityIndex(iloan As Long, MSACode As Double)

    'find the MSA code index position, we can skip the first 54 as they are
    '  states, and start with the MSA codes that begin currently in the 55th
    '  position to the 205th position in the table.
    If gLoanData(iloan, FD_MSACODE) > 0 Then
        For icode = GEO_STATE_COUNT + 1 To GEO_ENTITIES
            If gGeoMSACode(icode) = MSACode Then
                mGeoIndex = icode   'got a match for the MSA code
                Exit For            'get out of Dodge City
            Else
                'in searching the list we are now in MSA values greater than
                '  the target search value since the list is sorted low to high
                '  that means we have NO chance of a match, so we can stop
                '  looking through the table and return the UNKNOWN code
                If gGeoMSACode(icode) > MSACode Then
                    'assign the state code as a default
                    mGeoIndex = gLoanData(iloan, FD_STATECODE)
                    Exit For
                End If
            End If
        Next icode
    Else
        'assign the state code as a default
        mGeoIndex = gLoanData(iloan, FD_STATECODE)
    End If

End Sub
```

EXHIBIT 12.23   "CollatCF_FindGeographicEntityIndex" subroutine

record may be a loan that has an MSA code listed in its record. There may be no specific prepayment assumptions developed for that particular MSA as yet!

In the first test, if the CCFG finds that the geographic entity exists, it establishes the geographic index code as a valid one. We can then assign the prepayment assumption data associated to this geographic location to the loan. If the geographic entity has prepayment information, the value of "mGeoIndex" is assigned to the variable "mWIndex". With this assignment we can ignore all the rest of the selection code and move immediately to apply stresses. If the geographic entity *does not* have a set of prepayment assumptions associated with it, we need to default to the next higher geographic level. If the first value was an MSA-level entity, we will need to default up one level to the state level entity that contains that MSA. If the initial code of the record was a state level entity, we will default to the national level. If the loan fails the first test, we will then apply the second test. This second test determines if the initial failure occurred at the MSA level or the state level. If the value of "mGeoIndex" is greater than that of the greatest state-level geographic code (54, 50 states + 4 territories), the initial level was that of an MSA. The value of the highest state-level entity is contained in the Constant variable "GEO_STATE_COUNT". If the initial level *was that of an MSA code*, that is, greater than 54, then we will first default to state level. We will then provisionally assign the value of the state level code in the field "FD_STATECODE" to the "mWIndex" variable. We now test to see if this state level code is active. If the state-level entity code is active, we do not need to do anything further and we drop out of the decision tree. If the state level code is inactive, we now know that we *must again* default to the next higher level which is the national level and assign the value of "0" to the "mWorkingIndex" variable, completing the process. But what if the initial code was not an MSA but a state level code? All we need to do at that point is to test if the state level is active, assign it if it is, or default up one level to the national level.

Once we have a value assigned to the "mWIndex" variable, we can load the appropriate geographically specific prepayment assumptions. Having identified the correct index associated with the geographic entity, we now have the prepayment assumption vector we need. Using the content of this vector, stored in the array "gGeoPrepayTable", we can compute the monthly prepayment factors and place them in the "gByLoanPrepays" array. This array is organized as "1 to the number of loans, by 1 to the number of periods". The subroutine will use the first 60 months of prepayment assumptions from the file and then fill the remainder of the life of the loan with the long-term prepayment rate found in the 61st column of the assumptions file. See Exhibit 12.24.

"CollatCF_LoadGeoRecoveryLagAssumptions" Subroutine   Of the four major inputs to both the Geographic and the Demographic Methodologies, only the prepayment assumptions and the recovery lag assumptions are used by both methodologies. For this reason we will now examine the VBA code that determines which set of recovery lag assumptions to apply.

This subroutine is virtually identical to the subroutine that we just examined, "CollatCF_LoadGeoRecoveryAssumptions". The first portion of the subroutine will determine what value we will assign to the variable "mWIndex" based on the availability of recovery lag data particular to the geographic location of the loan and the availability of the data themselves. This process of defaulting from MSAs to

```
Sub CollatCF_LoadGeoPrepaymentAssumptions(iloan As Long)

    'if the State Level or MSA is "Active" we are good to go
    If gGeoActive(mGeoIndex, GEO_PRE) Then
        mWIndex = mGeoIndex
    Else
        'tested code is inactive
        If mGeoIndex > GEO_STATE_COUNT Then
            'mGeoIndex was greater than any State Level code, therefore default
            '   to the State Level
            mWIndex = gLoanData(iloan, FD_STATECODE)
            'test to see if the value of the State Level code is active, if not
            '   default to National
            If gGeoActive(mWIndex, GEO_PRE) = False Then
                'it was an inactive state, default to National level
                mWIndex = NATIONAL_DEFAULT
            End If
        Else
            'it was an inactive state, default to National level
            mWIndex = NATIONAL_DEFAULT
        End If
    End If

    'Assign the prepayment rate assumptions to the individual loan
    For iperiod = 1 To PAY_DATES
        If iperiod <= GEOMTHS - 1 Then
            gByLoanPrepays(iloan, iperiod) = _
                1# - (1# - (gGeoPrepayTable(mWIndex, iperiod))) ^ (1 / 12)
        Else
            gByLoanPrepays(iloan, iperiod) = _
                1# - (1# - (gGeoPrepayTable(mWIndex, GEOMTHS))) ^ (1 / 12)
        End If
    Next iperiod

End Sub
```

EXHIBIT 12.24   "CollatCF_LoadGeoPrepaymentAssumptions" subroutine

state levels or state levels to the national level is identical to that described in the "CollatCF_LoadGeoPrepaymentAssumptions" subroutine above.

The recovery lag periods are not stressed so we can ignore the application of a stress factor to them. Upon reading the information from the "gGeoLagTable", we can write it to the "gByLoanLags" array. We will use the information from that array to perform the cash flow calculations. See Exhibit 12.25.

"CollatCF_CalcGeoDefaultAssumptions" Subroutine   We now have the prepayment and recovery lag assumptions loaded into loan-by-loan arrays. The next major process we must address is the association of geographically specific default rate assumptions to each of the loans. In the Geographic Methodology, the steps of this process are identical to those of assigning the prepayment and recovery lag assumptions. First we will determine the availability of the default rate information in the file at the MSA, state, or national levels. Next we will determine if we need to apply stress factors and, if so, how many. Last we will read the geographically appropriate default rate information from the "gGeoDefaultTable", perform the calculation to scale the annual rate to a monthly one, and assign the result to the "gByLoanDefaults" array for use by the model in the cash flow calculations. See Exhibit 12.26.

```
Sub CollatCF_LoadGeoRecoveryLagAssumptions()

    'if the State Level or MSA is "Active" we are good to go
    If gGeoLagTable(mLoanPool, mGeoIndex, 2) = ATTRIT_ACTIVE Then
        mWIndex = mGeoIndex
    Else
        'tested code is inactive
        If mGeoIndex > GEO_STATE_COUNT Then
            'default to State level
            mWIndex = gLoanData(iloan, FD_STATECODE)
            If gGeoLagTable(mLoanPool, mWIndex, 2) = ATTRIT_INACTIVE Then
                'it was an inactive state, default to National level
                mWIndex = 0
            End If
        Else
            'it was an inactive state, default to National level
            mWIndex = 0
        End If
    End If
    'read he recovery period lag information from the array
    For iperiod = 1 To PAY_DATES
        If iperiod < ATTRIT_PERIODS - 1 Then
            gByLoanLags(iloan, iperiod) = _
                gGeoLagTable(mLoanPool, mWIndex, iperiod)
        Else
            gByLoanLags(iloan, iperiod) = _
                gGeoLagTable(mLoanPool, mWIndex, ATTRIT_PERIODS)
        End If
    Next iperiod

End Sub
```

EXHIBIT 12.25 "CollatCF_LoadGeoRecoveryLagAssumptions" subroutine

"CollatCF_CalcGeoMVDAssumptions" Subroutine The fourth and last set of geographically determined inputs to the cash flow calculations are the MVD factors. These factors are stored in the same manner as the prepayment, recovery lag, and default rate information we have just discussed. As is the case with the recovery lag information, the MVD factors are not subject to modification by any stress factors. The default process for missing geographic information is the same. If an MSA does not have specific MVD assumptions, the model will default to the state level. If state level data are lacking, the national level data will be used.

The subroutine will assign to the loan the contents of the appropriate entry in the "gGeoMVDTable" and write it into the "gByLoanMVDs" array for use in the future calculations. See Exhibit 12.27.

Converting the Assumptions to Attrition Factors

We now have the prepayment rate, default rate, recovery lag period, and MVD assumptions assigned to each of the loans based on their geographic location. All of this information is in a form that can be utilized immediately by the cash flow calculation subroutines. We will still need to construct corresponding monthly factors

```
Sub CollatCF_CalcGeoDefaultAssumptions()

    'Find the geographic index of the active geogrphic entity
    If gGeoDefaultTable(mLoanPool, mGeoIndex, 2) = ATTRIT_ACTIVE Then
        mWIndex = mGeoIndex
    Else
        'tested code is inactive
        If mGeoIndex > GEO_STATE_COUNT Then
            mWIndex = gLoanData(iloan, FD_STATECODE)    'default to State level
            If gGeoDefaultTable(mLoanPool, mWIndex, 2) = ATTRIT_INACTIVE Then
                'it was an inactive state, default to National level
                mWIndex = 0
            End If
        Else
            'it was an inactive state, default to National level
            mWIndex = 0
        End If
    End If

    'Assign the default rate assumptions to the inidividual loan
    For iperiod = 1 To PAY_DATES
        If iperiod < ATTRIT_PERIODS - 1 Then
            gByLoanDefaults(iloan, iperiod) = _
                1# - (1# - (gGeoDefaultTable(mLoanPool, mWIndex, iperiod))) _
                ^ (1 / 12)
        Else
            gByLoanDefaults(iloan, iperiod, istress) = _
                1# - (1# - (gGeoDefaultTable(mLoanPool, mWIndex, ATTRIT_PERIODS))) _
                ^ (1 / 12)
        End If
    Next iperiod

End Sub
```

EXHIBIT 12.26   "CollatCF_CalcGeoDefaultAssumptions" subroutine

for the coupon rates and the monthly scheduled principal amortization. When we have these factors in place, we can then quickly and easily determine the monthly cash flow amounts for each of the components. We will use the same subroutines to compute the monthly coupon factors and the monthly scheduled amortization of principal factors. The subroutines are "CollatCF_CalcMonthlyCoupFactors" and "CollatCF_CalcScheduledAmortFactors".

Calculating the Monthly Cash Flows

With all the factor arrays populated, we are ready to calculate the cash flows under the Geographic Methodology. We will be able to use two of the subroutines we wrote for the Uniform Methodology without modifying them. These two are used in the calculation of the coupon income cash flow and the amounts of scheduled amortization of principal amounts.

We will now enter the same four level nested "For..Next" structure to compute the cash flows as we did in the Uniform Methodology. The outermost loop contains the prepayment levels, followed by default levels, then the individual loan-by-loan level, and finally the period-by-period level. We will assign the values of the prepayment stress and default stress levels immediately after entering each of these

```
Sub CollatCF_CalcGeoMVDAssumptions(iloan As Long)

    'if the State Level or MSA is "Active" we are good to go
    If gGeoActive(mGeoIndex, GEO_MVD) Then
        mWIndex = mGeoIndex
    Else
        'tested code is inactive
        If mGeoIndex > GEO_STATE_COUNT + 1 Then
            'default to State level
            mWIndex = gLoanData(iloan, FD_STATECODE)
            If gGeoActive(mWIndex, GEO_MVD) = False Then
                'it was an inactive state, default to National level
                mWIndex = NATIONAL_DEFAULT
            End If
        Else
            'it was an inactive state, default to National level
            mWIndex = NATIONAL_DEFAULT
        End If
    End If
    'read the market value decline information from the array
    For iperiod = 1 To PAY_DATES
        If iperiod <= GEOMTHS - 1 Then
            gByLoanMVDs(iloan, iperiod) = gGeoMVDTable(mWIndex, iperiod)
        Else
            gByLoanMVDs(iloan, iperiod) = gGeoMVDTable(mWIndex, GEOMTHS)
        End If
    Next iperiod

End Sub
```

EXHIBIT 12.27 "CollatCF_CalcGeoMVDAssumptions" subroutine

loops. These stress levels are then applied against the monthly prepayment and default factors in the innermost portion of the loops. The current per-period values of the arrays "gByLoanPrepays" and "gByLoanDefaults" are adjusted for these stress levels and then sent to the appropriate subroutines. These subroutines "CollatCF_CalcPrincipalPrepayments" and "CollatCF_CalcDefaultEffects" then compute the dollar amounts prepaid and defaulted from the loan for that monthly period.

DEMOGRAPHIC METHODOLOGY

The Demographic Methodology differs from the Uniform and the Geographic Methodologies in that it incorporates the use of borrower, underwriting, property type, and loan servicing activities demographic information in its loss calculations. Various sets of the contents of the loan record are used to determine an adjustment factor that is applied to either the base default rate assumption or the base severity of loss assumption.

In the case of the determination of the multiplier of the base default rate, the Demographic Methodology looks at such factors as the underwriting standards and practices of the lender and the creditworthiness of the borrower. It also adjusts the adjustment score for the type of loan the borrower has taken. In loans that involve fixed coupon and therefore fixed payment amounts, the default risks are low. In the case of loans types in which there can be larger fluctuations in the amounts of the monthly payment, such as HARMs, the loan type can exert a significant impact on the adjustment factor. In the case of the severity of loss factor, the balance of the loan relative to its issuance amount, the underwriting criteria, and the rigorousness of the servicing effort are critical factors in assigning the adjustment factor.

A Disclaimer and a Warning

One thing should be said before continuing much further into a discussion of the Demographic Methodology. As it is applied in the real world, this methodology is critically dependent on the analysis of mind-numbingly vast amounts of data by complicated and computationally intense statistical models. These statistical analysis approaches are either proprietary in nature or are "black boxed" in the case of the rating agencies. The recapitulation of these analysis methods and results is clearly far beyond the scope of and length restrictions of this book. (In fact, a study of these methodologies and their attendant research papers would make a very interesting full-length book!) As a result, we will simply assign a weight to each of the factors that is commonly used in the analysis. This method is a gross simplification of the multiple linear regression approach, which, de facto, simultaneously weights all of these factors to arrive at the adjustment number. In this chapter and in the model, not the process, or the component weightings, or the resulting adjustment factors should be taken to have any real-world applicability.

A review of the factors that contribute to either the default rate adjustment factor or the severity of loss adjustment factor can be found in Chapter 8, "Designing the New Collateral Cash Flow Generator."

Code for the Demographic Methodology

Having issued our warning, we will now take a quick glance at the VBA code that will provide a very crude proxy for an implementation of the Demographic code. In an actual application the model would feed all of the loan characteristics into a black-box subroutine provided by the rating agency. Another alternative would be to submit the prospective collateral to the rating agency for evaluation and receive the individual loan default rates and severity of loss in return.

"CollatCF_ApplyDemographicMethodology" Subroutine   This subroutine is the primary subroutine of the Demographic Methodology calculation approach. Its structure is very similar to the approach of the Geographic Methodology. The divergence will occur when we determine the severity of loss percentages and the default rates on a loan-by-loan basis. The sequence of operations and structure of this subroutine is very similar to that of the Geographic Methodology subroutine described above.

The subroutine begins by re-dimensioning four arrays that will hold the demographic factor weighting we will apply later on to determine the default rate and the MVD rate. The two variables "gDefRateTotal" and "gMVDTotal" will hold the total demographic scores for each of the loans in the portfolio. The "gDefRateScore" and "gMVDScore" arrays hold the collection of individual scores for each of the parameters of the two methods.

The first two subroutine calls set up the default and prepayment stress levels for the run. The next call is to the subroutine "CollatCF_LoadGeoInfoToArrays". See Exhibit 12.21. This subroutine loads the prepayment and recovery lag period assumptions from geographic files.

As with the Geographic Methodology, the Demographic Methodology now calls the two subroutines that read the stress-level inputs from the CCFG Cash Flow Amortization Parameters menu. The default rate and MVD factors derived for the individual characteristics of the loans will be further adjusted by this set of stress rates. This application of stress to the corresponding base rate assumptions is identical to the approach in the Geographic Methodology.

The next call is to the subroutine "CollatCF_LoadGeoInfoToArrays", which determines the prepayment and recovery lag characteristics of the loans based on their geographic locations only.

The call to "CollatCF_DemoMethodReadRiskFactors" now opens a file containing the current risk factors for the constituent parameters of the default rate estimate and the MVD factor estimate. From this file we will read four sets of scores that we will later apply to the loans on a loan-by-loan basis. These factors are the components of the total demographic score of the loan for both the default rate and the MVD rate estimates.

"CollatCF_PopulateLoanByLoanArrays" is now called. We have already examined this subroutine in the Geographic Methodology discussion. It, however, calls two other subroutines we have *not* looked at. These are the two that set the default rate, "CollatCF_DemoMethodCalcDefRates" and "CollatCF_Demo MethodCalcMVDRates". These two subroutines assemble the raw scores for the two rates and then, using a lookup table, set the default rate and MVD for the individual loan based on them.

With the default rate and the MVD rate now set, the remaining subroutine calls are identical to those of the Uniform and Geographic methodologies. See Exhibit 12.28.

Let us then start with the first of these Demographic Methodology subroutines and follow the process to its completion.

"CollatCF_DemoMethodReadRiskFactors" Subroutine   This is the first uniquely Demographic Methodology subroutine. Its purpose is to open a file containing a series of assumptions and factor weightings used to ultimately determine the multiplier that we will apply to the base default and MVD rate assumptions. The subroutine opens the current Demographic Methodology assumptions file. It then calls three other subroutines to read the various geographic and demographic factors used in the analysis. See Exhibit 12.29.

"CollatCF_DemMethodReadGeoPenalties" is the first subroutine called by "CollatCF_DemoMethodReadRiskFactors". Its task is to read two schedules of multipliers, one for states and the other for individual MSAs. These multipliers will be applied to the total raw scores accumulated by the combination of credit and demographic characteristics of the loans. The subroutine accesses the "StateGeoPenalty" and the "MSAGeoPenalty" worksheets of the assumptions file. The two columns of default rate and MVD rate multipliers are read from each. If a loan is in a particular

```
Sub CollatCF_ApplyDemographicMethodology()

Dim drate        As Double
Dim prate        As Double

    'INITIALIZE THE DEMOGRAPHIC DEFUALT RATE AND MVD SCORE ARRAYS
    ReDim gDefRateTotal(1 To gTotalLoans) As Integer
    ReDim gMVDTotal(1 To gTotalLoans) As Integer
    ReDim gDefRateScore(1 To gTotalLoans, 1 To DATA_TESTS_DEFRATE) As Integer
    ReDim gMVDScore(1 To gTotalLoans, 1 To DATA_TESTS_MKTVALDEC) As Integer
    'SETUP PREPAYMENT AND DEFAULT STRESS LEVELS
    Call CollatCF_CalcPrepaymentStressLevels
    Call CollatCF_CalcDefaultStressLevels
    'READ THE ASSUMPTION FILES AND ASSIGN THE ASSUMPTIONS ON A LOAN-BY-LOAN
    ' BASIS BY GEOGRAPHIC LOCATION
    Call CollatCF_LoadGeoInfoToArrays
    Call CollatCF_DemoMethodReadRiskFactors
    Call CollatCF_PopulateLoanByLoanArrays
    'CALCULATE THE PREPAYMENT, DEFAULT, COUPON AND PRIN AMORTIZATION FACTORS
    Call CollatCF_CalcMonthlyCoupFactors      'coupon payment factors
    Call CollatCF_CalcScheduledAmortFactors 'scheduled principl factors
    'CASH FLOWS CALCULATION SECTION
    For iprepay = 1 To gPrepayStressSteps        'loop by prepayment stress
      pstress = gPrepayStressFactor(iprepay)
      For idefault = 1 To gDefaultStressSteps    'loop by default stress
        dstress = gDefaultStressFactor(idefault)
        For iloan = 1 To gTotalLoans
          If gLoanOK(iloan) And gLoanSelect(iloan, FD_SCREEN_DEMO_OK) = 0 Then
            Call Setup_Initial_Loan_Parameters(iloan)
            For iperiod = 1 To gLoanData(iloan, FD_REMTERM)
              drate = gByLoanDefaults(iloan, iperiod) * dstress
              Call CollatCF_CalcDefaultEffects(drate)
              Call CollatCF_CalcCouponPayments(iloan, iperiod)
              Call CollatCF_CalcScheduledAmortization(iloan, iperiod)
              prate = gByLoanPrepays(iloan, iperiod) * pstress
              Call CollatCF_CalcPrincipalPrepayments(prate)
              Call CollatCF_CalcPrincipalRecoveries(iloan, iperiod)
              Call CollatCF_SumAllCFComponents(iloan, iprepay, idefault, iperiod)
            Next iperiod
          End If
        Next iloan
        Call Display_Amortization_ProgressMsg(iprepay, idefault)
      Next idefault
    Next iprepay

End Sub
```

EXHIBIT 12.28   "CollatCF_ApplyDemographicMethodology" subroutine

MSA, it is assigned the risk factor multiplier for that MSA. If it is not within an MSA on the list, it receives the state-level multiplier. See Exhibits 12.30 and 12.31.

"CollatCF_DemMethodReadRiskFactorValues" is the second subroutine called by "CollatCF_DemoMethodReadRiskFactors". This subroutine reads a table consisting of the set of collateral record fields that are used in the calculation of the default rate and the MVD rate risk total raw score. This table contains a series of valuable inputs to the CCFG:

- The individual demographic risk factor parameters.
- A notation indicating which of the two processes, Geographic or Demographic Methodology, that are employed in the calculations. In many instances the data is used in both.

```
Sub CollatCF_DemoMethodReadRiskFactors()

    'reads the Demographic Methodology Risk Factor File
    'this file contains four worksheets containing all of the demographic risk
    '  factor information. They are the following:
    '  StateGeoPenalties = state geo penalty multiplier for FOF/SOL rates
    '  MSAGeoPenalties = MSA geo penalty multiplier for FOF/SOL rates
    '  RiskFactors = table of test values and raw score fisk factors
    '  RiskTable = table that translates raw risk scores into risk multiplier
    '    for both default rates and market value decline rates
    Workbooks.Open FileName:=gDemoRiskFactorFileName
    'geographic penalties by state/territory & MSA
    Call CollatCF_DemoMethodReadGeoPenalties
    'table of data items used as risk factors
    Call CollatCF_DemoMethodReadRiskFactorValues
    'tables to convert raw scores to demographic multipliers
    Call CollatCF_DemoMethodReadRiskTable
    ActiveWorkbook.Close

End Sub
```

EXHIBIT 12.29   "CollatCF_DemoMethodReadRiskFactors" subroutine

- The raw scores assigned to each of the values that the data can assume. An example would be the value of the occupancy code of record.
- The Constant variable name the field is identified by.
- The number of values for the parameter.
- The search value associated with the record value.
- The raw score associated with the value in the collateral record field based on the search value.
- The type of search used to find the risk value.

There are two ways to find the penalty associated with a risk factor on this table. The first is matching, identified with an "M". In a matching search, a parameter will have a discrete value, say "5". The CCFG simply sequentially tests each of the fields of the parameter up to and including its limit. If it finds a "5", we have an identical match. If the "5" occurs in the 5th position of the "Risk Factor Sort Points" section, we will assign the value found in the corresponding "Risk Factor Weights" section of the table. For the parameter "Occupancy Code", a value of "5" would result in a risk weight factor of 4 being added to the raw score of the loan.

The second search is on non-discrete values and is carried out by finding the cumulative position that the value of the record field falls into on the table. These tests are designated with a "C" in the "Type Sort" column of the table. The value is assigned the highest position it exceeds, a process of rounding up. Therefore, if a particular loan has a current loan-to-value (LTV) of 92.5%, it would be assigned risk factor sort point "6". This point would carry a risk weight factor of 5. See Exhibit 12.32.

The subroutine itself uses a "For..Next" loop to loop through all the cells of the table. Various Ranges are used to segregate the data of the table and arrange it into columnar arrays. These Ranges and their contents are:

- **"RiskFactorIndex"**. The index number of the collateral data field. This is a very helpful piece of information as we can use it to identify the specific parameters

Default Rate and Market Value Decline Rate Geographic Multipliers
State/Territories

Index	Postal Code	Common Name	Default Multiplier	MVD Multiplier
0	NT	National	1.3374	1.2024
1	AK	Alaska	1.2512	1.1507
2	AL	Alabama	1.0825	1.0495
3	AR	Arkansas	1.0361	1.0217
4	AZ	Arizona	1.2015	1.1209
5	CA	California	1.0803	1.0482
6	CO	Colorado	1.0947	1.0568
7	CT	Connecticut	1.0048	1.0029
8	DE	Delaware	1.2629	1.1577
9	FL	Florida	1.1897	1.1138
10	GA	Georgia	1.2141	1.1284
11	HI	Hawaii	1.3017	1.1810
12	IA	Iowa	1.1144	1.0687
13	ID	Idaho	1.0754	1.0453
14	IL	Illinois	1.1399	1.0839
15	IN	Indiana	1.3381	1.2029

Default Rate/Market Value Decline Rate
Metropolitan Statistical Areas 1–50

Index	MSA Code	Common Name	Default Multiplier	MVD Multiplier
1	38060	Phoenix-Mesa-Scottsdale	1.0366	1.0439
2	31100	Los Angeles-Long Beach-Santa Ana	1.0797	1.0956
3	40140	Riverside-San Bernardino-Ontario	1.1612	1.1934
4	40900	Sacramento--Arden-Arcade--Roseville	1.3385	1.4062
5	41740	San Diego-Carlsbad-San Marcos	1.3390	1.4068
6	41860	San Francisco-Oakland-Fremont	1.1339	1.1607
7	19740	Denver-Aurora	1.1208	1.1450
8	47900	Washington-Arlington-Alexandria	1.0888	1.1066
9	33100	Miami-Fort Lauderdale-Pompano Beach	1.0863	1.1036
10	36740	Orlando-Kissimmee	1.2623	1.3148
11	45300	Tampa-St. Petersburg-Clearwater	1.1840	1.2208
12	12060	Atlanta-Sandy Springs-Marietta	1.2235	1.2683
13	16980	Chicago-Naperville-Joliet	1.2920	1.3503
14	14460	Boston-Cambridge-Quincy	1.1141	1.1370
15	12580	Baltimore-Towson	1.0238	1.0285

EXHIBIT 12.30   "StateGeoPenalty" worksheet and MSA "GeoPenalty" worksheet formats

```
Sub CollatCF_DemoMethodReadGeoPenalties()

    'geographic penalties by state/territory
    For irow = 0 To NUM_STATES
        'loop = 0 is the National base rate
        gStatesDefRateMulti(irow) = _
            Range("StatesDefRateMultiplier").Cells(irow + 1)
        gStatesMVDRateMulti(irow) = _
            Range("StatesDefRateMultiplier").Cells(irow + 1)
    Next irow
    'geographic penalties by MSA
    For irow = 1 To TOTAL_MSAS
        gMSADemoCodes(irow) = Range("MSACodes").Cells(irow)
        gMSADefRateMulti(irow) = Range("MSADefRateMultiplier").Cells(irow)
        gMSAMVDRateMulti(irow) = Range("MSADefRateMultiplier").Cells(irow)
    Next irow

End Sub
```

EXHIBIT 12.31 "CollatCF_DemoMethodReadGeoPenalties" subroutine

we need to assess for risk purposes. It allows us to use a "For..Next" loop to hunt through all of the data fields and test only the ones identified here.

- **"RiskFactorUsedDef"**. Collateral data fields used in the default rate estimations.
- **"RiskFactorUsedMVD"**. Collateral data fields used in the MVD estimations.
- **"RiskFactorCount"**. Maximum number of search levels for this risk factor.
- **"RiskFactorSort"**. The method of finding the correct risk factor, "M" for matching, "C" for cumulative.
- **"RiskFactorSortPoints"**. The sorting points for the search to determine which raw score to choose from the "Risk Factor Weights" portion of the table.
- **"RiskFactorRawScores"**. The raw scores of the "Risk Factor Weights" portion of the table.

We will place the values of these Ranges into a series of global VBA variables that share the common prefix "gDemoRisk".

See Exhibit 12.33.

"CollatCF_DemMethodReadRiskTable" is the third subroutine called by "CollatCF_DemoMethodReadRiskFactors". This subroutine reads the table from the worksheet "Risk Table". We will use the values of this table to match the total raw rate risk scores to determine the appropriate default rate and MVD rates for each of the loans individually. If the base default rate for the Demographic Methodology is 6% CPR, a loan with a raw risk score of 105 will draw a 95% default rate modifier, adjusting the default rate downward to 5.7% CPR. The subroutine needs to read the raw score cutoff for the default rate ladder and the MVD rate ladder and the corresponding multipliers for each of the levels. We will also read from the table the maximum value for default rates, 15%, and the maximum MVD value, 70%. If the calculated values for the default rate or the MVD rate exceed this value, they will be capped at the levels stated in the table. See Exhibits 12.34 and 12.35.

We now have all the assumptions we need to perform the Demographic Methodology risk assessment and assign the loan-by-loan default rate and MVD rates.

Demographic Methodology Factor Weights

Index	Data Name	Def Factor	MVD Factor	Variable Name	# of Values	Risk Factor Sort Points										Risk Factor Weights										Type	Sort
						#1	#2	#3	#4	#5	#6	#7	#8	#9	#10	#1	#2	#3	#4	#5	#6	#7	#8	#9	#10		
2	Mortgage Type	X	X	FD_MORTTYPE	6	1	2	3	4	5						1	2	10	7	12						M	M
3	Credit Sector	X	X	FD_CREDITSEC	3	1	2	3								-4	7	5								M	M
4	Original Balance	X	X	FD_ORIGBAL	7	20	40	80	125	250	500	500				5	4	3	2	1	0	-1				C	C
8	Current LTV Ratio	X	X	FD_CURRLTV	11	50%	70%	75%	80%	90%	95%	100%	110%	125%	125%	-5	-4	-2	2	3	5	7	10	15	20	C	C
11	Seasoning	X	X	FD_SEASON	6	12	24	36	48	60	60					6	5	2	1	0	1					C	C
38	Property Type	X	X	FD_PROPTYPE	10	1	2	3	4	5	6	7	8	9	10	0	0	5	2	6	8	10	12	25	10	M	M
39	Occupancy Code	X	X	FD_OCCPCODE	8	1	2	3	4	5	6	7	8			12	0	4	8	4	12	6	8			M	M
40	Financing Purpose	X	X	FD_FINPURPOSE	6	1	2	3	4	5	6					18	2	6	12	15	18					M	M
44	Self-employed	X		FD_EMPLOY	10	1	2	3	4	5	6	7	8	9		10	10	8	6	8	0	1	2	3		M	M
45	# of years in position	X		FD_YRSPOST	8	99	1	2	5	10	15	20				12	12	10	8	4	2	1	0			C	C
46	First Time Homeowner	X		FD_FIRSTHOME	3	1	2	3								2	5	0								M	M
47	# of Pmts in Arrears		X	FD_ARREARSNUM	8	9999	0	30	45	60	75	90	90			15	0	10	20	25	30	40	50			C	C
49	FICO Score	X		FD_FICO	7	0	550	600	650	700	725	750				8	4	-5	1	-1	-2	-3				C	C
50	Mortgage D-to-I Ratio	X		FD_MDBTTOINC	10	10%	20%	30%	40%	50%	60%	70%	80%	90%	90%	-10	-7	-5	-5	0	4	8	20	30	40	C	C
51	Total D-to-I Ratio	X		FD_TDBTTOINC	10	10%	20%	30%	40%	50%	60%	70%	80%	90%	90%	-5	-4	-3	0	2	8	10	15	20	30	C	C
52	Bankruptcy	X		FD_BANKRUPTCY	5	1	2	3	4	5						5	-5	0	5	10						M	M
53	Escrow	X		FD_ESCROW	5	1	2	3	4	5						6	6	2	4	0						M	M
54	3rd Party Confirmation	X		FD_THIRDPARTY	6	1	2	3	4	5	6					10	8	4	2	1	0					M	M
55	Origination Docs	X		FD_ORIGDOCS	7	1	2	3	4	5	6	7				12	-2	2	8	4	4	12				M	M
56	Servicier Rating	X	X	FD_SERVERATE	6	1	2	3	4	5	6					8	8	4	2	1	0					M	M

EXHIBIT 12.32 Demographic Methodology factor weights table

```
Sub CollatCF_DemoMethodReadRiskFactorValues()

    'table of data items used as risk factors
    Sheets("RiskFactors").Select
    For irow = 1 To RTABLE_ROWS
        gDemoRiskItemIndex(irow) = Range("RiskFactorIndex").Cells(irow)
        gDemoRiskUsedDef(irow) = False
        If Range("RiskFactorUsedDef").Cells(irow) = "X" Then _
            gDemoRiskUsedDef(irow) = True
        gDemoRiskUsedMVD(irow) = False
        If Range("RiskFactorUsedMVD").Cells(irow) = "X" Then _
            gDemoRiskUsedMVD(irow) = True
        gDemoRiskCount(irow) = Range("RiskFactorCount").Cells(irow)
        gDemoRiskSortMethod(irow) = Range("RiskFactorSort").Cells(irow)
        For icol = 1 To 10
            gDemoRiskValues(irow, icol) = _
                Range("RiskFactorSortPoints").Cells(irow, icol)
            'expand the original balance cutoff figures by $1,000s
            If irow = 3 Then gDemoRiskValues(irow, icol) = _
                gDemoRiskValues(irow, icol) * 1000#
            gDemoRiskRawScores(irow, icol) = _
                Range("RiskFactorRawScores").Cells(irow, icol)
        Next icol
    Next irow

End Sub
```

EXHIBIT 12.33 "CollatCF_DemoMethodReadRiskFactorValues" subroutine

The subroutine "CollatCF_DemoMethodPopulateLoanByLoanArrays" is now called on to perform these tasks.. This subroutine then calls "CollatCF_DemoMethodCalcDefRates" to calculate the default rates and "CollatCF_DemoMethodCalcMVDRates" to calculate the MVD rates. These subroutines are *very*

Demographic Methodology Multiplier Based on Raw Risk Factor Weights

	Default Rate Raw Total	Default Rate Multiplier	MVD Raw Total	MVD Multiplier
1	0	25.0%	0	50.0%
2	20	50.0%	25	70.0%
3	35	75.0%	50	90.0%
4	50	90.0%	55	92.5%
5	75	92.5%	60	95.0%
6	100	95.0%	65	97.3%
7	125	97.5%	70	100.0%
8	150	100.0%	80	102.5%
9	175	102.5%	85	105.0%
10	200	105.0%	90	110.0%
11	250	110.0%	95	115.0%
12	270	115.0%	100	120.0%
Cap		15%		70%

EXHIBIT 12.34 Demographic Methodology multiplier table

```
Sub CollatCF_DemoMethodReadRiskTable()

    'tables to convert raw scores to demographic multipliers
    Sheets("RiskTable").Select
    For irow = 1 To FTABLE_ROWS
        gDemoFinalDRCutoff(irow) = Range("RawScoreDefRate").Cells(irow)
        gDemoFinalDRMulti(irow) = Range("MultiplierDefRate").Cells(irow)
        gDemoFinalMVDCutoff(irow) = Range("RawScoreMVD").Cells(irow)
        gDemoFinalMVDMulti(irow) = Range("MultiplierMVDRate").Cells(irow)
    Next irow
    gDemoFinalDRCap = Range("CapDefRate")
    gDemoFinalMVDCap = Range("CapMVDRate")

End Sub
```

EXHIBIT 12.35 "CollatCF_DemoMethodReadRiskTable" subroutine

similar in their logic and differ only in the number and types of parameters that they assess in their calculation sequences. Each solely uses the information from the Demographic Methodology Factor table in the process of arriving at the final raw scores. In light of these strong similarities, we will visit only one of these subroutines in detail.

"CollatCF_DemoMethodCalcDefRates" Subroutine This subroutine is the highest-level subroutine that works to assemble the composite default rate raw score. It performs eight steps to arrive at the adjusted default rate for the loan.

Step #1. Sets the base default rate. The base default rate for all loans is currently stored in the Constant "BASE_DEFAULT_RATE" and is set at 6%.

Step #2. Build the default rate raw score. Loops through the portfolio loan by loan, and then each loan record field by field. It initializes the variable "tRaw Score" to zero. As the inner "For..Next" loop visits each file in the collateral record, the subroutine test whether the value of the loop counter "irow" is one of the fields used in the default rate calculation. If the "gDemo RiskUsedDef(irow)" value is TRUE, it will evaluate the risk factor for the loan in regard to this field. It next reads the following information:

- The index value of the field
- The value of the field in the collateral loan record
- The type of sort/search method—either "M" for matching or "C" for cumulative
- The number of values in the risk table to be searched

A "Select..Case" statement next determines, based on the value in the "gDemoRiskSortMethod", what branch to pursue to find a match using all of the above information in the cumulative search. Within the search choice the subroutine runs down the number of choices for this field, finds the match, and assigns the risk weight to the running total of the "tRawScore" variable.

Step #3. Record the raw score for this field. The subroutine now records the raw risk score assigned to this field. The subroutine "CollatCF_RecordDef

ComponentRawScore" places the raw score in the "gDefRateScore" array for this loan so that we have a trace of how the score was accumulated and can print it out at a future date.

Step #4. Assign the geographic multiplier for the loan. The subroutine "CollatCf_SetGeoDefMultiplier" looks up the geographic state or MSA default rate multiplier based on the state or MSA field information of the loan. If the loan does not have an MSA code, the state code is used as a default.

Step #5. Assign the base rate multiplier. The subroutine "CollatCF_SetDefault RateByRawScore" now sets the default rate multiplier based on the raw score. This assignment is made on the values we read into the CCFG from the Demographic Methodology Multiplier Table.

Step #6. Adjust the base default rate by the multiplier.

Step #7. Test the adjusted rate against a default rate cap. The adjusted rate which is the product of the base rate and the multiplier is subject to a cap of 80% CPR.

Step #8. Assign the cap-adjusted default rate to the loan default speed array for the remaining life of the loan.

See Exhibit 12.36.

With the end of this section we have completed the process of generating the cash flows. *Now that we have them, whatever shall we do we them?* The answer: Put them in a nice file format that makes them accessible to the Liabilities Waterfall Model (LWM) or any other analytical model we wish to use them with!

REPORTING THE RESULTS OF THE CASH FLOW CALCULATIONS

Writing the Cash Flow File

This is the last step in the process! Having done all this heavy lifting to produce the cash flow files, it would be a pity if they were not usable. To make these cash flows accessible to the LWM and other programs, we must write them to a well-organized and documented file. It is vitally important that we include with the cash flows as much information as we have in regard to any assumptions that were used to create them. This is important for two obvious reasons:

1. We want to be able to quickly and clearly identify these cash flows from others based on the assumption set used to generate them.
2. If necessary we may need to validate, or even replicate, these cash flows using other programs or to demonstrate that they are correct.

Writing the Cash Flow Scenarios to a File   To create the cash flow files, we will need to perform the following steps, in order:

1. Have an available template file that contains worksheets to record not only each of the individual cash flow scenarios but also each set of assumptions that were used to produce the cash flows themselves.

```
Sub CollatCF_DemoMethodCalcDefRates()

Dim BaseDEFRate        As Double    'starting geographic default facotr
Dim ifactor            As Integer   'loop factor

    BaseDEFRate = BASE_DEFAULT_RATE 'currently 6% CPR
    For iloan = 1 To gTotalLoans
        gDefRateTotal(iloan) = 0#
        gDefRate(iloan) = 0#
        For irow = 1 To RTABLE_ROWS
            tRawScore = 0#
            'if this data item is need for the calculation of the default rate
            '  demographic/financial multiplier then proceed
            If gDemoRiskUsedDef(irow) Then
                'set up the test parameters for this data item
                dIndex = gDemoRiskItemIndex(irow)    'index of the data item used
                tValue = gLoanData(iloan, dIndex)    'test value of the data item
                tSort = gDemoRiskSortMethod(irow)    'raw score assignment method
                tTries = gDemoRiskCount(irow)        'number of comparison values
                'find the raw score for the value of this test data
                Select Case gDemoRiskSortMethod(irow)
                    Case Is = "M"        'match to a direct match table
                        For ilevel = 1 To tTries
                            If tValue = gDemoRiskValues(irow, ilevel) Then
                                tRawScore = gDemoRiskRawScores(irow, ilevel)
                                Exit For
                            End If
                        Next ilevel
                    Case Is = "C"        'match to cumulative value table
                        For ilevel = 1 To tTries
                            If tValue <= gDemoRiskValues(irow, ilevel) Then
                                tRawScore = gDemoRiskRawScores(irow, ilevel)
                                Exit For
                            End If
                        Next ilevel
                End Select
                gDefRateTotal(iloan) = gDefRateTotal(iloan) + tRawScore
                Call CollatCF_RecordDefComponentRawScores(irow, tRawScore)
            End If
        Next irow
        Call CollatCF_SetGeoDefMultiplier      'sets the geo def multiplier
        Call CollatCF_SetDefRateByRawScore     'sets the fin demo mutiplier
        'adjust base default rate by the fin/demo multipliers and geo multipliers
        gDefRate(iloan) = (BaseDEFRate * gDefRate(iloan) * mDefMultiplier)
        'if the computed rate exceeds the default rate cap,  adjust downward to the
        '  default rate cap
        If gDefRate(iloan) > gDemoFinalDRCap Then gDefRate(iloan) = gDemoFinalDRCap
        'assign the default rate for the remaining life of the loan
        For iperiod = 1 To gLoanData(iloan, FD_REMTERM)
            gByLoanDefaults(iloan, iperiod) = 1# - (1# - (gDefRate(iloan))) ^ (1 / 12)
        Next iperiod
    Next iloan

End Sub
```

EXHIBIT 12.36 "CollatCf_DemoMethodCalcDefRates" subroutine

2. Open the template file and rename it to the user-indicated output file name.
3. Write the assumptions sets into each specific assumption set worksheet page of the file.
4. Create the correct number of cash flow scenario worksheets, one for each scenario, and name them in a consistent and easily identifiable pattern.

5. Output the individual cash flow scenarios into the appropriately named worksheets, place headers as to the prepayment and default speeds, and fill the cash flow schedule.
6. Save and close the workbook after the last scenario has been written.

Writing the Cash Flow File VBA   All the code to perform these functions can be found in the "Report_CollatEligCFs" module. It is very simple and standard VBA output code and quite understandable. The most difficult portion of writing the Cash Flow report file is the preliminary organization of the workbook. The workbook template file contains a single cash flow worksheet. We will need to determine how many copies of this worksheet to make, how to identify them, and then how to populate them with the appropriate cash flows. We will review the code in the light of the above steps and identify how each of the subroutines contributes to the overall task of producing this, the most important report of the CCFG!

The field to enter the cash flow file name is contained in the CCFG Cash Flow Amortization Parameters Menu section named "Write Cash Flow File".

"RepCollatCF_MainWriteReport" Subroutine   This subroutine is the main subroutine for the Cash Flow Report file generation activity. It is broadly similar to many of the other output subroutines that we have created so far. It begins by checking the value of the variable "gRepMenuCFEligible", which was set on the Run Options Menu. This Boolean variable will be TRUE if we want to output the report file and FALSE if we do not. If it is TRUE, the subroutine next checks to see if the file name of the output file has been supplied. If it has not, either the name of the file is set to " " or "No File Selected", and we bypass producing the report.

Next we open the template file that we earlier declared in the "A_Constants" module:

```
Public Const CFWATERFALL_TEMPLATE =
_CFSUBDIR & ''CashFlowOutputTemplate''
```

and save it to the name of the cash flow file we entered on the Cash Flow Amortization Parameters Menu.

With the file now in place, we need to modify it based on the number of cash flow scenarios we wish to write into it. There will be one waterfall schedule for each combination of prepayment/default scenario. The subroutine calls "RepCollatCF_SetupCashFlowOutputFileWorksheets" to set up the required worksheets and name them appropriately. It then saves the workbook, locking the now-complete workbook configuration in place. With the workbook prepared, all that remains is to write the individual cash flow information into the appropriate worksheet based on the prepayment/default scenarios.

This we accomplish by calling three subroutines that are inside a pair of nested "For..Next" loops. These three subroutines perform the following tasks:

- "RepCollatCF_WriteCashFlowWorksheetHeaders". Writes the header content to each of the worksheets so that we can identify the particular scenario.
- "RepCollatCF_WritePeriodicCashFlowComponents". Writes the period-by-period cash flows. These cash flows consist of six components: beginning-period

```
Sub RepCollatCF_MainWriteReport()

    'WRITE CF FILE, 1SHEET/SCENARIO, AND CF AMORTIZATION ASSUMPTIONS PAGE
    If gRepMenuCFEligible Then
       If gCashFlowWriteCFFileName <> "" And gCashFlowWriteCFFileName <> "No File Selected" Then
          If gMethodUniform Then pLevels = gPrepayLevels: dLevels = gDefaultLevels
          If Not gMethodUniform Then pLevels = gPrepayStressSteps: dLevels = gDefaultStressSteps
          Workbooks.Open FileName:=CFWATERFALL_TEMPLATE       'open cash flow waterfall file
          ActiveWorkbook.SaveAs FileName:=OUTPUT_DIRECTORY & gRepMenuPrefix & gCashFlowWriteCFFileName
          Call RepCollatCF_SetupCashFlowOutputFileWorksheets
          isheet = 1
          For ip = 1 To pLevels        'by prepayment levels
            For id = 1 To dLevels      'by default levels
               Sheets(CFSheetName(isheet)).Select              'select scenario worksheet
               Call RepCollatCF_WriteCashFlowWorksheetHeaders(isheet)    'write scenario header info
               Application.Calculation = xlManual              'calculation mode to manual
               Call RepCollatCF_WritePeriodicCashFlowComponents         'write the monthly cash flows
               Call RepCollatCF_TrimAndBorderCFWorksheet       'delete blank report lines
               isheet = isheet + 1                             'advance the sheet counter
               Range("A1").Select                              'cursor to report NW corner
            Next id
          Next ip
          Call RepCollatCF_WriteSummaryMatrixReport            'write the summary matrix report
          Call RepAssumptions_WritePrepayDefaultAssumptions    'cf amortization menu
          Call RepAssumptions_WriteRateAndDatesInformation     'financing rate info
          ActiveWorkbook.Save:  ActiveWorkbook.Close           'close and save workbook
       End If
    End If
    Application.Calculation = xlAutomatic                      'reset calculations to automatic

End Sub
```

EXHIBIT 12.37 "RepCollatCF_MainWriteReport" subroutine

principal balance, scheduled amortization of principal, prepayments of principal, defaulted principal, coupon interest, and recoveries of defaulted principal.
- **"RepCollatCF_TrimAndBorderCFWorksheet".** Trims the worksheet of any unused time period rows at the bottom of the report.

After all of the prepayment/default scenarios have finished printing, the subroutine calls "RepCollatCF_WriteSummaryMatrixReport" to produce the Summary Matrix sheet of the workbook. This report is a one-page summary of all the scenarios of the model run arranged in a matrix. This matrix is defined by "Prepayment Speed" assumptions on the horizontal axis and "Default Speed Assumptions" on the vertical axis. Once this report is populated, it too is trimmed of unused matrix cells.

The workbook is again saved and the subroutine finishes. See Exhibit 12.37.

"RepCollatCF_SetUpCashFlowOutputFileWorksheets" Subroutine The task of this subroutine is to create, name, and save one worksheet in the template file for every unique prepayment and default cash flow waterfall scenario. It begins by calculating the number of scenarios, the product of the number of prepayment levels times the number of default levels. It places this value in the "CFScenarios" variable.

It then calls "RepCollatCF_GenerateWorksheetNames". This subroutine loops through the scenario conditions naming the worksheets. Last the subroutine applies these names to each of the scenario worksheets. This is in the lower portion of the subroutine.

```
Sub RepCollatCF_SetupCashFlowOutputFileWorksheets()

Dim iname        As Integer
     'ADD 1 WORKSHEETS PER PREPAY/DEFAULT SCENARIOS number needed by method:
     'Uniform: defaults*prepays   Geo/Demo Method: def stress * prepay stress
     CFScenarios = pLevels * dLevels
     ReDim mPrepayScenarioSpeed(1 To CFScenarios) As Double
     ReDim mDefaultScenarioSpeed(1 To CFScenarios) As Double
     ReDim mPrepayScenarioStress(1 To CFScenarios) As Double
     ReDim mDefaultScenarioStress(1 To CFScenarios) As Double
     iscen = 1            'scenario counter
     'copy the blank worksheet, add sheets as required; one for each of the
     '  prepay and default scenario combination. Number them at end of workbook.
     Call RepCollatCF_GenerateWorksheetNames
     'ADD 1 WORKSHEET PER SCENARIO, NAME THEM BY PREPAYMENT/DEFAULT SCENARIOS
     iscen = iscen - 1                'correct for last count (not used)
     iname = 1:  scen_copy = CFSheetName(iname) & " (2)"    'set 1st worksheet name
     Sheets("CF-1").Name = CFSheetName(iname)
     For isheet = 5 To iscen + 3
         iname = iname + 1
         Sheets(CFSheetName(1)).Select
         Sheets(CFSheetName(1)).Copy After:=Sheets(isheet - 1)
         Sheets(scen_copy).Select
         Sheets(scen_copy).Name = CFSheetName(iname)
     Next isheet

End Sub
```

EXHIBIT 12.38 "RepCollatCF_SetupCashFlowOutputFileWorksheets" subroutine

The original worksheet "CF-1" is assigned the first name. A loop then moves from "2", the index of the next spreadsheet, to "iscen", the number of scenarios. This loop applies the names stored in the array "CFSheetName". See Exhibit 12.38.

"RepCollatCF_GenerateWorksheetNames" Subroutine   This subroutine performs the vital task of generating names for each of the worksheets of the cash flow reports. Without these names we would find it, difficult, if not impossible, to identify one scenario from the other. The names will also be valuable at a later date when we open these files to read their contents into the LWM. The subroutine is divided into two clearly identifiable parts. The first "If..Then" statement tests if the prepayment/default methodology is "Uniform" or not. This is an important distinction to make early in the process. If the methodology is "Uniform", the prepayment and default assumptions are expressed in speeds; if it is Demographic or Geographic, it is expressed in stress levels of the base speed assumptions.

If the assumptions for the scenarios are generated from the Uniform Methodology, with the prepayment speed of 200 PSA to 300 PSA by 100 PSA and the default rate of 100 SDA to 200 SDA by 50 SDA, the worksheet names will be as follows:

```
P-200% D-100%      P-200% D-150%      P-200% D-200%
P-300% D-100%      P-300% D-150%      P-300% D-200%
```

See Exhibit 12.39.

```
Sub RepCollatCF_GenerateWorksheetNames()

    If gMethodUniform Then
        'Uniform Speed Methodology (prepay by default speeds)
        p_rate = gPrepayBaseLevels
        For ip = 1 To gPrepayLevels
            d_rate = gDefaultBaseRate
            For id = 1 To gDefaultLevels
                ' name the sheets using the prepayment and default parameters
                mPrepayScenarioSpeed(iscen) = p_rate * 100
                mDefaultScenarioSpeed(iscen) = d_rate * 100
                CFSheetName(iscen) = "P-" & (p_rate * 100) & "%" & _
                                     " D-" & (d_rate * 100) & "%"
                d_rate = d_rate + gDefaultIncrement
                iscen = iscen + 1
            Next id
            p_rate = p_rate + gPrepayIncrement
        Next ip
    Else
        'Geographic or Demographic Methodology (prepay stress by default stress)
        For ip = 1 To gPrepayStressSteps
            For id = 1 To gDefaultStressSteps
                ' name the sheets using the prepayment and default parameters
                mPrepayScenarioSpeed(iscen) = gPrepayStressFactor(ip) * 100
                mDefaultScenarioSpeed(iscen) = gDefaultStressFactor(id) * 100
                CFSheetName(iscen) = _
                    "PStress-" & (gPrepayStressFactor(ip) * 100) & "% " & _
                    "DStress-" & (gDefaultStressFactor(id) * 100) & "%"
                iscen = iscen + 1
            Next id
        Next ip
    End If

End Sub
```

EXHIBIT 12.39   "RepCollatCF_GenerateWorksheetNames" subroutine

"RepCollatCF_WritePeriodicCashFlowComponents" Subroutine   With the worksheets created, the headers are now written into each of the sheets. All that remains to be done is to populate the reports with the scenario-specific cash flows. Each of the cash flow components listed below are written to the specific scenario worksheet. Notice that the "Beginning Principal Balance" for the period is computed by using the "Portfolio Total" balance in period 1 and netting from it the successive "Principal Amortization", "Principal Prepayments", and "Principal Default" amounts on a monthly basis. See Exhibit 12.40.

After all of the scenario waterfalls are written, the Matrix Summary report is written, and the Cash Flow report workbook is saved and closed.

Viewing the Cash Flow Files from the CCFG   To be able to view the cash flow files from the CCFG, we will create a field on the CCFG Cash Flow Amortization Parameters Menu that will allow us to open the cash flow file directly by entering it name and clicking on the "Open File" button.

The file name and button will be placed in a section of the menu named "View Cash Flow File". We will create the macro "GetFileName_ViewCFOutputFile" and assign it to the button. Using the button, we can display the file and retain its name in the "View Cash Flow File" field. See Exhibits 12.41 and 12.42.

```
Sub RepCollatCF_WritePeriodicCashFlowComponents()

    For iperiod = 1 To PAY_DATES
      irow = iperiod + 13
      If gCoupIncome(ip, id, iperiod) > 0.01 Or gPrepaidPrin(ip, id, iperiod) > 0.01 Or _
        gDefaultPrin(ip, id, iperiod) > 0.01 Or gRecoverPrin(ip, id, iperiod) > 0.01 Then
        'scheduled amortization
        Cells(irow, CF_AMORTPRIN_COL).Value = gAmortPrin(ip, id, iperiod)
        'calculate beginning principal balance
        If iperiod = 1 Then
            gBegPrinBal(ip, id, iperiod) = gTotalPortfolio
        Else
            'previous balance - (schd amort + prepays + defaults)
            gBegPrinBal(ip, id, iperiod) = gBegPrinBal(ip, id, iperiod - 1) - _
              (gAmortPrin(ip, id, iperiod - 1) + gPrepaidPrin(ip, id, iperiod - 1) + _
              gDefaultPrin(ip, id, iperiod - 1))
        End If
        Cells(irow, CF_BEG_PRIN_COL).Value = gBegPrinBal(ip, id, iperiod)
        Cells(irow, CF_PREPAY_COL).Value = gPrepaidPrin(ip, id, iperiod)  'prepayments
        Cells(irow, CF_DEFAULTS_COL).Value = gDefaultPrin(ip, id, iperiod) 'defaults
        Cells(irow, CF_COUPINCOME_COL).Value = gCoupIncome(ip, id, iperiod) 'coupon
        Cells(irow, CF_RECOVER_COL).Value = gRecoverPrin(ip, id, iperiod)  'recoveries
      Else
        Exit For
      End If
    Next iperiod
    Calculate        'to generate the Pool Factor column statistics

End Sub
```

EXHIBIT 12.40 "RepCollatCF_WritePeriodicCashFlowComponents" subroutine

With the cash flow files successfully written and with a way to painlessly view them, we are finished with this chapter! Congratulations to everyone who took the considerable amount of time to go through the test and the code!

Writing the Single Scenario Report Package

This report is designed to provide the CCFG user with a Single Scenario snapshot of the cash flows of a single prepayment/default combination. This is a presentation-format report. It is meant to be included in reports that are basically aimed at outside audiences. This report sacrifices some detail the monthly cash flows by aggregating it to a set of annual sums. The compensation for this loss of specificity is a gain in compactness and clarity. With the cash flows represented at an annual level, we are able to add a summary table and a graph.

This is the first report that contains an embedded graphic. This graphic is pre-configured to reference the body of the annual cash flow table. Once this table is populated, the graph displays the contents of the table. This is the simplest way of using an embedded graphic. We are simply pointing the graph at a static portion of

```
Sub GetFileName_ViewCFOutputFile()
    Call GetFilenameFromButton
    Range("m8ViewCashFlowFile") = gButtonFileName
    Workbooks.Open FileName:=Range("m8ViewCashFlowFile")
End Sub
```

EXHIBIT 12.41 "GetFileName_ViewCFOutputFile" subroutine

Scenario #8
DemographicMethodology
Prepayment Speed Stress = 150%
Default Rate Stress = 110%

1	2	3	4	5	6	7	8	9	10	11	12
				Collateral Cash Flows							
Month	Beginning Principal Balance	Pool Factor	Regular Amort Principal	Prepaid Principal	Defaulted Principal	Ending Principal Balance Outstanding	Total Principal Retired	Coupon Income	Recoveries of Principal	Total Cash Available	Month
			12,265,727	71,542,581	80,648,001		83,808,308	67,328,615	34,670,456	185,807,379	
1	354,500,000	1.00000	334,278	1,949,750	2,197,900	350,018,072	2,284,028	1,834,907	-	4,118,935	1
2	350,018,072	0.98736	330,052	1,925,099	2,170,112	345,592,809	2,255,151	1,811,708	-	4,066,859	2
3	345,592,809	0.97487	325,879	1,900,760	2,142,675	341,223,494	2,226,639	1,788,803	-	4,015,442	3
4	341,223,494	0.96255	321,759	1,876,729	2,115,586	336,909,421	2,198,488	1,766,187	-	3,964,675	4
5	336,909,421	0.95038	317,691	1,853,002	2,083,838	332,649,890	2,170,693	1,743,857	-	3,914,550	5
6	332,649,890	0.93836	313,674	1,829,574	2,062,429	328,444,212	2,143,249	1,721,810	-	3,865,058	6
7	328,444,212	0.92650	309,708	1,806,443	2,036,354	324,291,706	2,116,152	1,700,041	-	3,816,192	7
8	324,291,706	0.91479	305,793	1,783,604	2,010,609	320,191,701	2,089,397	1,678,547	-	3,767,945	8
9	320,191,701	0.90322	301,927	1,761,054	1,985,189	316,143,531	2,062,981	1,657,326	-	3,720,307	9
10	316,143,531	0.89180	298,109	1,738,789	1,960,090	312,146,542	2,036,899	1,636,372	1,098,950	4,772,221	10
11	312,146,542	0.88053	294,340	1,716,806	1,935,309	308,200,087	2,011,146	1,615,684	1,085,056	4,711,886	11
12	308,200,087	0.86939	290,619	1,695,100	1,910,841	304,303,527	1,985,720	1,595,256	1,071,338	4,652,314	12
13	304,303,527	0.85840	286,945	1,673,669	1,886,682	300,456,231	1,960,614	1,575,088	1,057,793	4,593,495	13
14	300,456,231	0.84755	283,317	1,652,509	1,862,829	296,657,576	1,935,826	1,555,174	1,044,419	4,535,419	14
15	296,657,576	0.83683	279,735	1,631,617	1,839,277	292,906,948	1,911,352	1,535,512	1,031,215	4,478,078	15
16	292,906,948	0.82625	276,198	1,610,988	1,816,023	289,203,738	1,887,187	1,516,099	1,018,177	4,421,462	16
17	289,203,738	0.81581	272,706	1,590,621	1,793,063	285,547,348	1,863,327	1,496,931	1,005,304	4,365,562	17
18	285,547,348	0.80549	269,259	1,570,510	1,770,394	281,937,186	1,839,769	1,478,005	992,594	4,310,368	18
19	281,937,186	0.79531	265,854	1,550,655	1,748,011	278,372,666	1,816,509	1,459,319	980,045	4,255,872	19
20	278,372,666	0.78525	262,493	1,531,050	1,725,911	274,853,213	1,793,543	1,440,869	967,654	4,202,066	20
21	274,853,213	0.77533	259,174	1,511,693	1,704,090	271,378,256	1,770,867	1,422,652	955,420	4,148,939	21
22	271,378,256	0.76552	255,898	1,492,580	1,682,545	267,947,232	1,748,478	1,404,665	943,341	4,096,484	22
23	267,947,232	0.75585	252,662	1,473,710	1,661,273	264,559,587	1,726,372	1,386,906	931,414	4,044,693	23
24	264,559,587	0.74629	249,468	1,455,078	1,640,269	261,214,772	1,704,546	1,369,371	919,638	3,993,556	24

EXHIBIT 12.42 Cash Flow report file

the table containing the statistics we wish to display. In a more advanced configuration, we could embed VBA macros and CommandButton objects in the template file. These CommandButtons could then be linked to the VBA macros to modify the contents of the graph across alternative data sets to change the contents of the graphic display. We could also employ VBA, resident in the report-writing module for this report of the CCFG, to modify the appearance and contents of the graphic.

The first table is the upper left of the Single Scenario report. The second table is the table of annual cash flows. The graph of these cash flows appears to the right of the table. The VBA code for this report is found in the module "Rep_SingleScenarioCFs". It functions in much the same way as the VBA code that sets up the Cash Flow Report file we just examined. It uses the same approach to create a series of worksheets, one for each scenario. Once the worksheets are created, labeled, titled, and saved, the cash flows are written into the second table. Instead of simply writing the monthly cash flows out, we need to first aggregate them to annual totals. This action is performed by the subroutine "RepSingleScen_WriteScenarioDescription". The scenario totals for each of the cash flow components are displayed by the subroutine "RepSingleScen_PopulateCFSummarySection".

The steps in generating the Single Scenario Cash Flow Report package are:

1. Open the template file, rename it to the designated name plus the deal prefix identifier, and save it.
2. Determine the number of individual scenarios to be displayed, and create a scenario worksheet name for each.
3. Create an individual worksheet for each scenario, and apply the worksheet names created in (2) above to each of the worksheets.
4. On each worksheet create three Range names. These Range names will be used in writing the summary and annual cash flow tables and the scenario description.
5. Write the scenario description to each of the worksheet reports.
6. Write each summary scenario cash flows to each worksheet.
7. Write the annual cash flows to each worksheet.
8. Save and close the completed Single Scenario Cash Flow Report package.

This process will produce the Single Scenario Report package with a set of reports configured as the one displayed in Exhibit 12.43.

WRITING THE ASSUMPTIONS REPORT PACKAGE

Now that we have completed all the inputs for the model, we can turn our attention to the Assumptions Report package. The Assumptions report consists of a series of subreports, each of which mimics a menu of the CCFG. If we replicate the menu contents in the Assumptions Report, we will de facto have captured all the data needed by the model to replicate that particular run. This assumes that there are no inputs to the model that do not enter through the menus, and there are not! Producing an Assumptions Report also has the added benefit of recording, in the menu fields, any specialized assumptions sets for financial, geographic, or demographic conditions that we have saved for future use.

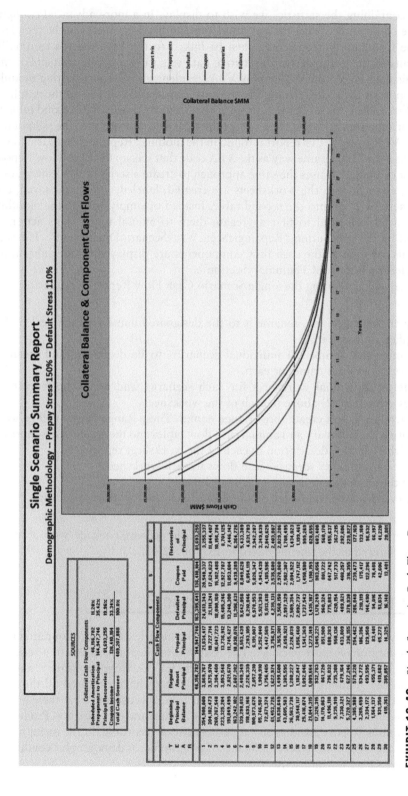

EXHIBIT 12.43 Single Scenario Cash Flow Report

512

Why Do We Need an Assumptions Report?

Although they often are overlooked by those new to the model-building profession, assumptions files are some of the most critical files in the entire report package. Why? Are you a savant, blessed with total recall? Can you remember everything, and I mean everything, down to the last detail of your fourth birthday party? If you have answered yes to the above question, you are either one person in a million, self-delusional, or lying! An alternative is that you may have thought that by answering yes, you would then be directed to skip this section of the chapter!

No such luck! Even if you have a complete and perfect memory, you are probably not the only person on the face of the earth who will use this model! Even if not for yourself, you need to build the capability of producing an all-inclusive Assumptions Report into your model. There will come a time when you will have to modify or recapitulate a run for which you no longer have the output files. When that day comes, and it will come, I assure you, a well-designed and available Assumptions file will count for a lot. It will be the difference between looking competent and assured or disorganized and inefficient. It may well save you time, stress, and embarrassment! You will immediately avoid a task that might have consumed hours or days, over which time you desperately try various combinations of inputs. Instead you will simply enter the contents of the Assumptions Report to re-create the original study. To this end the Assumptions Report must contain all the data needed to run the model, or tell you where to find it. Obviously an Assumptions Report will not help you if you have mismanaged critical files by, say, deleting them. No planning can compensate for carelessness or stupidity. The French mathematical genius Blaise Pascal, one of the founders of probability theory, was once asked why he was a Christian. He replied that acting in a moral and considerate manner to other people was a small price to pay for the infinite payoff of eternity in heaven. Even if he was wrong, he said, it was still the correct bet to place. That is the essence of the role of the Assumptions file!

Organization of the Assumptions Report

The Assumptions Report is a stand-alone report with six worksheets. These work-sheets are replicas of several of the menus of the CCFG and therefore contain exactly the information we seek to capture:

- Run Options Menu
- Collateral Pool Menu
- Cash Flow Amortization Parameters Menu
- Geographic Selections Form
- Geographic Concentration Form
- Financial Criteria Sheet
- Rates and Dates Menu

VBA Code for the Assumptions Reports

All of the VBA code that populates these sheets is contained in the module "Report_Assumptions". The main subroutine for the production of the Assumptions

Report named "RepAssumptions_WriteAllAssumptions" calls a total of seven other subroutines, one for each worksheet in the report.

These subroutine are essentially mirror-image subroutines of some of the subroutines that read the information from the menus in the first place. The original subroutines are scattered across many of the VBA modules that begin with the prefix "MenuSupport". When reading the information into the CCFG from the various menus, the formula would be:

```
''variable = menu input''
```

now we are simply reversing the process and reading the contents of the VBA variables and writing them to the Assumptions Report:

```
''menu input = variable''
```

Run Options Menu Assumptions Worksheet   Let us look at this activity in more detail using the "Run Options" menu inputs as an example. The Assumptions Report contains a worksheet named "RunOptions" into which we will write the run options assumptions of the current run of the model we wish to save. The layout of this worksheet is virtually identical to the "Run Options" menu itself. See Exhibit 12.44.

In the "RepAssumptions_WriteAllAssumptions" subroutine, we have a typical mater report-writing subroutine. The role of the first three lines is to locate the Assumptions Template file by concatenating the values of two VBA Constant variables and combining them with a file open statement:

```
Workbooks.Open FileName: = DIR_TEMPLATE_REP &_
   ASSUMPTIONS_FILE_TEMPLATE
```

This command opens the Assumptions Report template file. The next command saves the file to the file name created by concatenating the value of the deal prefix with that of "_Assumptions". This will, if we have been careful, create a unique name for the Assumptions Report file.

```
AssumptionsFile = OUTPUT_DIRECTORY & gRepMenuPrefix &_
   ''_Assumptions.xls''
ActiveWorkbook.SaveAs FileName: = AssumptionsFile
```

We now have a uniquely named Assumptions Report into which we can write the information we need to preserve concerning thus run. The subroutine now calls seven other subroutines in sequence populating each of the report worksheets in turn. At the conclusion of this activity, the last two commands save and close the workbook, completing the process. See Exhibit 12.45.

The first call of the "RepAssumptions_WriteAllAssumptions" subroutine is to "RepAssumptions_WriteRunOptions". This subroutine populates the "Run Options" worksheet report shown in Exhibit 12.44. The subroutine must make a determination between two possible situations: There is pool level data only, or there are as many as five sub-portfolios. The subroutine first checks if the collateral data

CCFG Run/Output Options Menu

Pool or Sub Portfolio	Collateral File Name	Collateral Selction Processes					Collateral Cash Flow Files
		Run Option Code =>					
		REQUIRED	OPTIONAL				
		1	2	3	4		5
		Initial Loan Record Data Screening Tests	Apply Financial and Demographic Tests	Apply Geographic (State & MSA) Tests	Apply Geographic Concentration Limits		Produce Elligible Collateral Cash Flows
#0							
#1							
#2							
#3							
#4							
#5							

EXHIBIT 12.44 "Run Options" worksheet of the Assumptions Report

515

```
Sub RepAssumptions_WriteAllAssumptions()

Dim AssumptionsFile  As String   'pathway of the assumptions file

    Workbooks.Open FileName:=DIR_TEMPLATE_REP & ASSUMPTIONS_FILE_TEMPLATE
    AssumptionsFile = OUTPUT_DIRECTORY & gRepMenuPrefix & "_Assumptions.xls"
    ActiveWorkbook.SaveAs FileName:=AssumptionsFile
    'WRITE ALL THE STANDARD MODEL RUN ASSUMPTIONS
    Call RepAssumptions_WriteRunOptions                  'run time options
    Call RepAssumptions_WriteCollateralPoolInfo          'collateral pool files
    Call RepAssumptions_WriteUserCollatSelectAssumptions 'base qualifing
    Call RepAssumptions_WriteGeoSelectionAssumptions     'geographic selection
    Call RepAssumptions_WriteGeoConcentrationAssumptions 'geographic concentrations
    Call RepAssumptions_WriteRateAndDatesInformation     'write the rates and dates
    Call RepAssumptions_WritePrepayDefaultAssumptions    'cf amortization menu
    ActiveWorkbook.Save
    ActiveWorkbook.Close

End Sub
```

EXHIBIT 12.45   "RepAssumptions_WriteAllAssumptions" subroutine

is at the pool level. If it is, it sets the beginning print row to 12, the Pool File Name line, and sets the beginning and ending loop counters to zero. The 0th position in the Run Option global arrays—that is, all arrays that begin with "gRO"—are the pool level options, while positions one to five are for sub-portfolio level options. With these parameters in place, the subroutine now writes in three of the Run Options that span either pool or sub-portfolio level data. These are the Initial Data Screening option, the Geographic Concentration option, and the choice of whether to generate a Cash Flow file from the eligible collateral. The subroutine next loops through the other six Run Options and prints them in either the pool level section only or the sub-portfolio level lines. This worksheet report is now complete. See Exhibit 12.46.

```
Sub RepAssumptions_WriteRunOptions()

    Sheets("RunOptions").Select
    Range("A1").Select
    'determine if it is a single pool or up to five sub-portfolios
    If gPoolLevelData Then
        irow = 12: mBeg = 0: mEnd = 0
        Else
        irow = 13: mBeg = 1: mEnd = NUM_PORTS
    End If
    Cells(irow, 4).Value = gROInitDataTest    'initial data screening test
    Cells(irow, 7).Value = gROApplyGeoConcen  'geographic selection tests
    Cells(irow, 12).Value = gROCFWaterfall    'eligible collat CF file
    For iport = mBeg To mEnd
        Cells(irow, 5).Value = gROTestSetFinDemo(iport)   'financial selection set
        Cells(irow, 6).Value = gROTestSetGeoSelect(iport) 'geographic selection set
        Cells(irow, 8).Value = gROReportElig(iport)       'report eligible collat?
        Cells(irow, 9).Value = gROReportInelig(iport)     'report inelig collat?
        Cells(irow, 10).Value = gRODataFileElig(iport)    'write elig collat data
        Cells(irow, 11).Value = gRODataFileInelig(iport)  'write inelig collat data
    Next iport

End Sub
```

EXHIBIT 12.46   "RepAssumptions_WriteRunOptions" subroutine

```
Sub RepAssumptions_WriteGeoConcentrationAssumptions()

    Sheets("GeoConcentration").Select
    Call GeoSelect_PrintOutConcentrations

End Sub
```

EXHIBIT 12.47 "RepAssumption_WriteGeoConcentrationAssumptions" subroutine

```
Sub RepAssumptions_WriteUserCollatSelectAssumptions()

Dim itest          As Integer  'loop for inidividual tests
Dim LastSheet      As Integer  'last worksheet position counter
Dim isets          As Integer  'portfolio loop counter
Dim SetsActive     As Integer  'how many of the user criteria sets are there?

    'how many User Selection Criteria sets are active, create a worksheet for each.
    SetsActive = 0
    LastSheet = 5
    For isets = 1 To NUM_SEL_SETS    'maximum number of user selection criteria sets
        If gSCSetActive(isets) Then 'a criteria set is active for this count
            Sheets("UserSelectionCriteria").Select
            Sheets("UserSelectionCriteria").Copy After:=Sheets(LastSheet)
            Sheets("UserSelectionCriteria (2)").Select
            Sheets("UserSelectionCriteria (2)").Name = "UserSelectCritSet" & isets
            LastSheet = LastSheet + 1
            SetsActive = SetsActive + 1
        End If
    Next isets
    Sheets("UserSelectionCriteria").Delete

    'write the selection criteria sets into the appropriate worksheets
    Call FinSelect_ReadDataItemNames      'read the list of data names for the report
    For isets = 1 To NUM_SEL_SETS
        If gSCSetActive(isets) Then                    'is this an active set?
            Sheets("UserSelectCritSet" & isets).Select
            Call FinSelect_ClearReportWorksheet    'clear the contents
            irow = 9
            For itest = 1 To NUM_SEL_TESTS
                If gSCTestActive(iset, itest) Then  'is this an active test?
                    Cells(irow, 1).Value = itest
                    Cells(irow, 2).Value = gSCEditType(iset, itest)
                    Cells(irow, 3).Value = "["
                    Select Case gSCEditType(iset, itest)
                        Case Is = 1: Call FinSelect_WriteTestType1
                        Case Is = 2: Call FinSelect_WriteTestType2
                        Case Is = 3: Call FinSelect_WriteTestType3
                        Case Is = 4: Call FinSelect_WriteTestType4
                        Case Is = 5: Call FinSelect_WriteTestType5
                        Case Is = 6: Call FinSelect_WriteTestType6
                    End Select
                    irow = irow + 2       'put a blank line between tests
                End If
            Next itest
        End If
    Next isets

End Sub
```

EXHIBIT 12.48 "RepAssumptions_WriteUserCollatSelectAssumptions" subroutine

Other Assumptions Report Worksheets   The remaining worksheets range from the very simple to moderately complex.

Geographic Concentration Assumptions   The most efficient of them is the Geographic Concentration Assumptions worksheet report. In this report we are able to simply call the subroutine "GeoSelect_PrintOutConcentrations" that we use to populate the "GeoConcentration" worksheet of the model. We originally wrote this subroutine so that we could quickly display the concentration limits by state and MSA on a worksheet inside the model. It is, however, perfect for the role of displaying these assumptions here. See Exhibit 12.47.

Financial Criteria Selection Set Assumptions   The most complex Assumptions Report prints out Financial/Demographic Selection Criteria (FSCS) Tests for either a pool or a collection of sub-portfolios. This subroutine "RepAssumptions_ WriteUserCollatSelectAssumptions" is the most complex of the Assumptions Report's subroutines. The upper portion of the report creates up to five different report worksheets with the Assumptions Report file based on how many active sets of FSCS are active. It names each of these worksheets "UserSelectCriteriaSet#", based on whether the set is active or not. It then deletes the original worksheet "UserSelectionCriteria" that it made the copies from.

 It then uses the same set of subroutines that we use to populate the "FinCriteria Report" worksheet in the model. Thus we can see that, even for complex reports, with a little forethought and planning, we can reuse code from the model to write the Assumptions Report preparation activities. See Exhibit 12.48.

ON THE WEB SITE

There is a chapter comments file, "**Chapter 12 Comments.xls**".
 Web Chapter 12.1, "Computation of Basic Mortgage Cash Flows."
 Web Chapter 12.2, "The Uniform Methodology."
 The "**CCFG_Chapter12**" model contains all of the code contained in this chapter.
 There are four cash flow methodology input criteria files, two for the Demographic methodology and two for the Geographic methodology:

- "**DemoMethodInputsBase**". Demographic methodology base case assumptions.
- "**DemoMethodInputsStress**". Demographic methodology stress case assumptions.
- "**POOL01_GeoAssumptionsBase**". Geographic methodology base case assumptions.
- "**POOL01_GeoAssumptionsStress**". Geographic methodology stress case assumptions.

 There are also two report template files:

- "**CashFlowOutputTemplate**". Report template file containing cash flows for all scenarios.
- "**CashFlowSingleScenTemplate**". Report template file for single prepayment/ default scenarios.

## CHAPTER 13

Writing the CCFG Reporting Capability

OVERVIEW

In this chapter we will implement the remaining portion of the report package that we designed in Chapter 8. In Chapters 9 to 12 we have constructed many of the simpler reports. Most of these reports were "list" reports. These reports listed eligible or ineligible collateral, menu inputs, and financial and geographic selection criteria. Others recapped the results of the various Initial Data Screening process tests. They presented the collateral and reported on its completeness and sufficiency. Last we produced the pair of cash flow reports. The first was the Cash Flow Report containing the results of the various scenarios run by the Collateral Cash Flow Generator (CCFG). The second, the Single Scenario Report, was a one-page presentation report combining graphic and tabular information. It summarized the cash flows of a unique combination of prepayment and default speeds.

The reports presented in the earlier chapters when we were building the functionality of the CCFG were of a more straightforward and easily understood nature. The reports in this chapter will require some more thought. Here we will build reports that can be dynamically configured. The User Defined Stratification reports and the Cross Tabulation reports are table driven. We can modify both their UserForms and the choices and configurations of the reports themselves by manipulation of a master table inside the CCFG. The approach to writing the Geographic Stratification Report Package is completely different. Here we will build a series of specialized subroutines and split the report into sections of microtables building one section after another. The Portfolio Presentation Report continues this type of report building but expands it to entire sets of reports each built from a preselected template. The template file contains four report templates. Each time it is opened three of the four templates will be immediately discarded and the fourth will then serve as the basis for the entire package.

It is absolutely critical to remember that the best model in the world—the most accurate, most incisive, and most computationaly exhaustive—is absolutely *worthless* if its findings cannot be packaged in such a manner that they are clearly understood.

Having said all of the above, we can clearly draw a major dichotomy in the reporting aims of the CCFG. The first half of the set of questions that we will have to answer concerns the disposition of the initial collateral. How much was of economic value to the deal, how much could not be used, and what are the potential costs to the deal of the excluded assets. The second set of questions concerns the timing, characteristics, and magnitude of the cash flows produced by that eligible collateral. It is along this divide, the static analysis of the loan-by-loan eligibility and the dynamics of the cash flows, that the reports fall out.

DELIVERABLES

The modeling knowledge deliverables for this chapter are:

- How to organize the output of the CCFG along major divisions.

  The VBA techniques and concept deliverables of the chapter are:

- How to modify the existing code of the Base Asset Model (BAM) to address the reporting needs of the new CCFG.
- How to develop more complex reports using new VBA report-writing techniques.
- How to manipulate Chart and Graph objects using VBA.
- How to write single-purpose report generation VBA subroutines that can be used in different combinations to produce a wide variety of reports of differing size and complexity.

UNDER CONSTRUCTION

In this chapter we will develop the remaining reports of the CCFG.

We will write the VBA code and Excel template files to produce the following reports:

- User Defined Stratification report package
- Cross Tabulation report package
- Loan Listing report
- Geographic Stratification reports for the state and Metropolitan Statistical Area (MSA) levels
- Portfolio Presentation report

To accomplish this task we will add or modify the following modules.

- **"A_Constants"**. We will add a number of report switch Constant variables to this module to help use more clearly route the program during the report production effort.
- **"A_Globals"**. We will need to add additional global arrays that are specific to the various report writing activities. Our first priority will be to group the reports in task-specific modules and declare these variables to be modular variables. However, if the information needs to be incorporated into different sets of reports prepared by different modules, global variables may be more efficient.
- **"Report_CollatEligibleCrossTab"**. The Cross Tabulation report package is a cross-matrix report of any two eligible collateral record fields. An example would be Coupon by Remaining Term. It is a form of two-dimensional stratification to

augment the traditional on field stratification reports. We designed these reports and the UserForms we needed to input our choices in Chapter 9.

- **"Report_CollatEligibleStratBase"**. As with the "Report_CollatIneligible" module (to follow), we will use as our development base the code we have already existing in the BAM that produces the Base Stratification Reports. In addition to these reports, the module will also produce the reports that we have specified in the UserForm "Custom Stratification Report Editor" designed in Chapter 11.
- **"Report_GeoStratification"**. This module produces the national, state, and SMA geographic reports. These reports list the balance, geographic dispersion, and demographic summaries of the collateral by the selected geographic entity.
- **"Report_LoanListing"**. This module produces a listing of eligible collateral records.
- **"Report_PortPresentation"**. This module produces the one and two-page Portfolio Presentation Report for the portfolio.

A Note of Encouragement

Well, that is quite a list! Although at first glance this must seem like an almost insurmountable task of report writing, you will soon see that it is not. If we plan carefully, building the smaller, simpler reports first, we will develop a set of report-writing code blocks that we can string together to make writing the more complex reports *much* easier by the end of the process. Let us get started right away. (Remember, the sooner we start, the sooner we are finished!)

RECAPPING THE CCFG REPORT PACKAGE

The complete CCFG report package consists of 28 reports. These reports fall into six major groups based on the sequence of operations that the CCFG performs. Some of these reports, such as the Assumptions Report we built in Chapter 11, merely repeat the information that we have entered in the model. Others take the collateral record information and sort, segregate, or regroup it. An example of these types of reports are all the collateral reporting reports. Last there are the reports that present the results of the computational operations of the model, the Cash Flow Amortization Reports.

Each of these report groups serves a different function:

- **Assumptions Reports.** These reports preserve the model inputs, including the names of any of the files that we have used to set selection or cash flow amortization criteria.
- **Initial Data Screening Reports.** These reports display the results of the initial data screening. This screening serves two purposes: to weed out collateral records that have damaged or illegible contents and to display those records that have insufficient data for to perform a series of calculations. Specifically these are:
  - Geographic Methodology calculations
  - Demographic Methodology calculations
  - Frequency of default estimates
  - Market value decline estimates

- **Ineligible Collateral Reports.** These reports display the number, amount, and conditions of the ineligible collateral.
- **Eligible Collateral Reports.** These reports describe the financial, credit, demographic, and geographic characteristics of the eligible collateral that will be included in the deal portfolio.
- **Cash Flow Reports.** These reports display the period-by-period cash flows of the eligible collateral for each of the unique prepayment/default scenarios calculated by the CCFG.
- **Performance Reports.** These reports summarize the collective performance of the collateral. They also include a more sophisticated graphics approach that is representative of reports used for external presentations to outside parties, such as rating agencies, regulatory bodies and, most important, investors.

The table of these reports is shown in Exhibit 13.1.

CCFG ACTIVITIES AND REPORTS

In this chapter we will write the VBA code, the template files, the data files, and the information grid spreadsheets we will need to complete each of the remaining five reports. We will also examine the information the report needs to use. This information can come from a number of sources, such as:

- The external collateral data file
- The operations of the model, including selection, sorting, and amortization processes
- Internal Excel worksheets that contain format and name data that are critical to the reporting function

As before, our approach will be to follow the operational steps of the model, examine the reports for each of the processes, explain the need for each of the reports, exhibit a copy of the report, and examine the VBA code that creates the model.

Why do we need the reports that comprise this report package? What will I need to think of in my own future projects? How will you use the VBA, and later Access, products and techniques to build your own individual reports and report groups? Your first assignments may require reports that have appearances and content that look very similar, somewhat similar, or not at all similar, to the reports we have created here. That is *not important*! What is important is that you begin to think of the flow of information from the inputs of the model, through its processes, and finally to its stopping point. What are the critical data that we and other decision makers need to focus on? What is the most clear, least ambiguous, form that we can present it in? How can we use the reports to fully communicate the results of the various model processes? This is where your focus should be over the remainder of the chapter! Remember, however, that the best design plans in the world are useless unless they can be translated into a functional working result. With this in mind, pay attention to the VBA code also!

Report Package of the Collateral Cash Flow Generator

Model Function / Report Name / Sub Report	Report Function	CCFG VBA Module "Report..." +	Public Constant Variable Name	Template Name	Chapter Discussed
Enter Run Time Assumptions					
Assumptions Report	Run time assumptions of the model	Assumptions	ASSUMPTIONS_FILE_NAME	AssumptionsTemplate	Chapter 12
Data Screening					
Initial Data Screening Report Package					
Missing, Illegible or Illegal Values Data	Checks data record for unusable data	DataScreenInit	INIT_DATA_SCREEN_TEMPLATE	InitDataScreenTemplate	Chapter 10
Geographic Loss/Prepay Methodology	Data screen for Geographic Methodology	DataScreenInit	INIT_DATA_SCREEN_TEMPLATE	InitDataScreenTemplate	Chapter 10
Demographic Loss/Prepay Methodology	Data screen for Demographic Methodology	DataScreenInit	INIT_DATA_SCREEN_TEMPLATE	InitDataScreenTemplate	Chapter 10
Cash Flow Amortization Criteria	Data screen for cash flow amortization by type	DataScreenInit	INIT_DATA_SCREEN_TEMPLATE	InitDataScreenTemplate	Chapter 10
Frequency of Default Calculation Criteria	Data screen for Frequency of Foreclosure calculations	DataScreenInit	INIT_DATA_SCREEN_TEMPLATE	InitDataScreenTemplate	Chapter 10
Market Value Decline Calculation Criteria	Data screen for Market Value Decline calculations	DataScreenInit	INIT_DATA_SCREEN_TEMPLATE	InitDataScreenTemplate	Chapter 10
Risk Report - Demographic Methodology					
Frequency of Foreclosure Risk Report	Frequency of Foreclosure risk factors weighting	DataDemoRisk	COLLAT_DEMO_RISKS_TEMPLATE	DemoRiskFactorsTemplate	Chapter 10
Market Value Decline Risk Report	Market Value Decline risk factors weighting	DataDemoRisk	COLLAT_DEMO_RISKS_TEMPLATE	DemoRiskFactorsTemplate	Chapter 10
Reporting Ineligible Collateral					
Ineligible Collateral Report Package					
Single Criterion Exception Reports	Ineligible collateral list by single criterion	CollatIneligUser	COLLAT_USER_INELIG_TEMPLATE	UserIneligCollatTemplate	Chapter 11
Loan Listing Exception Report	Ineligibility conditions per loan	CollatIneligUser	COLLAT_USER_INELIG_TEMPLATE	UserIneligCollatTemplate	Chapter 11
Summary Exception Report	Loans by unique pattern of ineligibility conditions	CollatIneligUser	COLLAT_USER_INELIG_TEMPLATE	UserIneligCollatTemplate	Chapter 11
Reporting Eligible Collateral					
Eligible Collateral Reports					
User Defined Stratification Reports	Set of up to 40 user-defined stratification reports	CollatEligStratBase	BASE_STRAT_REPORTS_TEMPLATE	BaseStratReportTemplate	Chapter 13
Cross Tabulation Reports	Stratification by 2 user-defined data fields	CollatEligCrossTabs	CROSSTABS_REPORTS_TEMPLATE	CrossTabsReportTemplate	Chapter 13
Loan Listing Report	Eligible Collateral Listing by amortization type	LoanListing	LOANLIST_REPORTS_TEMPLATE	LoanListingTemplate	Chapter 13
Geographic Loan Listing Report	Eligible Collateral geographic listing summary report	GeoLoanList	GEO_LOANLIST_TEMPLATE	GeoLoanListTemplate	Chapter 11
Geographic Concentration Report Package					
Concentration Report - National Level	Loan Listing of selected States within National Level	GeoConcentration	GEO_CONCEN_TEMPLATE	GeoConcenTemplate	Chapter 11
Concentration Report - State Level	Loan listing of MSA's within States	GeoConcentration	GEO_CONCEN_TEMPLATE	GeoConcenTemplate	Chapter 11
Concentration Report - MSA Level	Loan listing by individual MSAs	GeoConcentration	GEO_CONCEN_TEMPLATE	GeoConcenTemplate	Chapter 11
Geographic Stratification Reports					
National Level Stratification Reports	National Stratification Report	GeoStratification	GEO_STRATS_STATE_TEMPLATE	GeoStratStateTemplate	Chapter 13
State Level Stratification Report	State Stratification Report	GeoStratification	GEO_STRATS_STATE_TEMPLATE	GeoStratStateTemplate	Chapter 13
No MSA Level Stratification Report	Non-MSA Collateral Stratification Report	GeoStratification	GEO_STRATS_STATE_TEMPLATE	GeoStratStateTemplate	Chapter 13
MSA Level Stratification Report	MSA Collateral Stratification Report	GeoStratification	GEO_STRATS_MSA_TEMPLATE	GeoMSAStateTemplate	Chapter 13
Reporting Cash Flows					
Cash Flow Waterfall Report	Per period cash flows for all scenarios	CollatEligCfs	CASHFLOW_REPORT_TEMPLATE	CashFlowOutputTemplate	Chapter 12
Presentation Reports					
Single Scenario Cash Flow Report	Summary of Performance, single-page report	SingleScenarioCFs	CF_SINGLE_SCENARIO_TEMPLATE	CFSingleScenarioTemplate	Chapter 12
Portfolio Presentation Report	Presentation report package collateral structure	PortPresentation	PRESENT_PORTFOLIO_TEMPLATE	PortfolioPresentTemplate	Chapter 13

EXHIBIT 13.1 Report Package of the Cash Flow Generator

ELIGIBLE COLLATERAL ASSESSMENT PROCESS

We wrote the reports that analyze the collateral that did *not* make it into the deal back in Chapter 11 when we built the selection criteria logic into our model. Now let us turn to the reporting requirements of the eligible collateral, the collateral that *did* make it into the deal. In Chapter 11 we touched on some of the Geographic reports that delineate the content of the eligible collateral portfolio. Here we will expand our analysis of these loans by building stratification reports. The term "stratification" means "to form into layers or groups." What we want to accomplish with the reports that we are about to build is to be able to view the eligible collateral in a one- and two-dimensional stratification.

One-dimensional stratification displays the composition of a group across a range of that groups structure. A common example of a classic stratification table is to display the distribution of current balances in the portfolio. The strata, or layers, are a distribution of cutoff amounts. A typical distribution of current balances might be as follows:

- From $0 to $100,000 by $10,000 (10 layers)
- From $100,000 to $500,000 by $50,000 (8 layers)
- From $500,000 to $1.0 million by $100,000 (5 layers)
- From $1 million to $5 million by $1million (4 layers)

The report would then stratify each loan of the portfolio into one of these 27 layers. It would record aggregate statistics about each layer and present them on a separate line of the stratification report.

The second approach to stratification is to apply a cross-tabulation approach. In this approach two loan characteristics are compared and a matrix is constructed. One of the loan characteristics is stratified along the horizontal axis while the other is stratified along the vertical axis. Either of the loan characteristics can then be placed in the matrix, or you may choose a third loan characteristic. For example, a cross tabulation may select Property Type as the horizontal data, and Current Balance as the vertical data with Current Balance displayed in the cells of the matrix. There are 10 Property Type codes and, if we use the previous example for Current Balances, 27 Current Balance stratification levels. This would produce a 10 by 270, or 270, cell matrix. In each of the cells of the matrix would be the sum of all current balances whose loans fit the criteria for that particular intersection of row and column values. Suppose the property type of a loan was "Single Family", code 2 of Property Types, and the current balance was $210,000, the 12th stratification level. The balance of $210,000 would then be added to the 12th row, 2nd column, of the Cross Tabulation Report.

Having decided on the structure of these reports, we now need to make a judgment as to their content. We have a total of 50 data items. Of these, which shall we choose to produce reports on? For the cross-tabulation fields, what combinations make sense?

We should *not* try to guess as to the particular loan characteristics that we or someone else using the model will need! That approach is sure to lead to frustration and inefficiency. We need to devise a general approach to producing both of the reports that allows anyone to pick from a menu. We already have accomplished this in Chapter 9 when we built the UserForms for the Stratification and the Cross

Tabulation Reports. How do we then translate this idea of flexible report construction into an application that will not give us an undue amount of heartache to implement and maintain?

A Somewhat Different Approach

To answer the last question we need to recognize that we will need to take an entirely new approach to report writing from what we have seen so far in this chapter.

Table-Driven Approach   We are going to develop a report-writing approach that is "table driven." What do we mean by this? A table-driven approach will utilize a table of parameters that will be read by the CCFG and serve as the basis for a series of rules that we will implement in the VBA modules. This table will also be directly linked to the UserForms of the model and will serve as a sort of dictionary of values and formats that the CCFG can utilize in its report-building activity. Why would we adopt this approach?

One immediate advantage is that we can place a considerable amount of data on a single Excel worksheet. We will need to get the report specifications into the model somehow! We have two alternatives. The first is to build a worksheet within the CCFG will hold the information, and the second is to position it in a file or database outside of the CCFG and read it into the model. The amount of information we need to store—less than 1,000 pieces for the Base Stratification reports—does not seem overly onerous. A second advantage is that we will be able to reference this information directly in the CCFG. If, for example, we link a portion of the data worksheet to a UserForm, the List Box objects will update automatically when we change the list in the model. By using a table we will also avoid the use of lengthy blocks of Public Constant variable declarations or some other set of VBA commands to hold the data.

More Sophisticated Template Files   Along with adopting the table approach, we will also make use of more sophisticated report template files. The sets of report template files for the Initial Data Screening process, the Risk Factors reporting, and the Ineligible Collateral Report Package can best be categorized as a collection of blank forms. You get a file full of blank worksheet reports and you fill them in.

In contrast, the Base Stratification report template file will contain a set of proto-reports. We will modify the formats, dimensions, and content of these reports as needed to produce the finished Base Stratification and Cross Tabulation Reports. These modifications will utilize the guidelines from the Stratification Information and the Cross Tabulation Report tables, as well as information contained in the template file itself.

A Report-Writing Swiss Army Knife   I think that you will be surprised how generic this approach to report writing can be. Once you become familiar with both the approach and the process, you will find that it is applicable to any type of report writing you will be faced with. It is also an exercise in creativity. You have an example of a way to combine several features of Excel, VBA, and UserForms to address a task that you will be faced with not once but many times. There is a U.S. Army Special Forces maxim:

"There are no dangerous weapons, there are only dangerous men!"

The truth of this statement is transcendentally clear! People with the warrior spirit fight with what is available; if nothing is available, they find something and turn it into a weapon! This approach to report writing is just that, a tool. Rather than being a particular tool, it is an approach that will help you attack problems in general. It is intended to stimulate you to think in different terms about combining the various pieces of the Microsoft product lines to make Excel, VBA, UserForms, and Access work in new and different ways for you.

Base Stratification Reports

In designing and implementing the Base Stratification Report (BSR) package, we will work with four different and distinct components, each of which contributes to the finished process in its own way. These are:

1. The Stratification Report Package Table
2. The UserForms of the Reports Edit Menu
3. The "BaseStratReportTemplate" file
4. The VBA code in the "Report_CollatEligibleStratBase" module

We will now look at each of these in turn to see how the pieces fit together to produce the report writer we want to end up with.

Stratification Report Package Table   We will start with the Stratification Report Package Table (SRPT). This table is the bedrock upon which we will build the rest of the Base Stratification Report Writer. There are 50 data fields in each loan collateral file. Some loans will have values in almost all of these fields while some will have data in many fewer. With a few exceptions, almost every field is a candidate for use in a BSR. We have said earlier that we will not try to anticipate the use of any particular field or to design field-specific reports. That leaves us with some thinking to do!

Of the 50 fields, we will drop 5 from the list, leaving 45. These 5 are either not used by the CCFG at the present time or are unsuitable for inclusion in a BaseStratification report. They are:

- Field #6: Origination Date (Seasoning and Remaining Term are suitable substitutes)
- Field #36: Zip Code (reporting by zip code not currently implemented)
- Field #40: $ Pmts in Arrears (we will not include any collateral currently showing an arrearage amount)
- Field #41: # Pmts in Arrears (see above)
- Field #50: Day Count Convention (of marginal or little use as a stratification parameter)

Of the remaining 45 data fields, we are faced with the following distribution of data formats:

- Number: 1 field
- Label: 16 fields
- Dollars: 4 fields

- Months: 9 fields
- Percent: 12 fields
- State: 1 field
- MSA entity: 1 field
- FICO: 1 field

To complete a BSR, we will need to provide the report writer with the following items:

- The name of the item that is to be stratified (Current Balances)
- The number of stratification levels for the vertical axis of the report (50)
- The starting and ending values of the stratification ladder. ($0 to $1.25 million)
- The interval value of the stratification ladder ($25,000)
- The form of the stratification values (Dollars)
- If the data format is a label, all label values (Not applicable)
- A suggested template worksheet appropriate to this data (Dollar)
- The column header information for the vertical column (Current Balance)
- The report title ("Stratification by Current Balances")

If we were to construct our SRPT containing this information for the 52 remaining fields, we would end up with a large and formidable table. To display this table, we will need to hide some of the rows and columns, but the structure of the table is still clearly visible. See Exhibit 13.2.

We now have a wealth of report content, format, structure, and title information at our fingertips! We will now mine this mother lode of reporting information to streamline the BSR writing process.

UserForms of the Reports Edit Menu One of the immediate advantages of centralizing all of the information about the formatting and contents of the BSRs is that we can make it immediately available to other processes of the CCFG that are also involved in the report-writing process. The most convenient aspect of this feature is the ability of the UserForms to immediately reference information stored elsewhere in our Excel model.

For example, say that we wanted to change the contents of the BaseBSR's UserForm in the CCFG "Reports Editor and Menu" screen. We want to remove the items "Credit Sector" and "ARM Index" from the UserForm list and add "Origination Date". To effect this change we need only modify the contents of the first column of the SRPT. We do not need to edit the UserForm of the Excel Menu at all. See Exhibits 13.3 and 13.4.

"BaseStratReportTemplate" File We will now construct the BSR Package Template file. This template file, "BaseStratReportsTemplate", consists of ten different worksheet reports. Each of these report worksheets is a generic report for a particular type of BSR that we will apply based on the "Template Used" column of the SPRT. These templates are:

- "Month 3": Three-month intervals from 1 to 180 months
- "Month 12": One-year intervals from 1 to 30 years

Basic Stratification Report Package Formatting Guidelines

Item #	Data Item Names	# Values	Start Value	Interval Value	Data Type	1	2	3	4	5	6	7	8	9	10	Template Used	Column Header #1	Column Header #2	Report Title
1	Pool ID	5	1	1	Number											Label		Pool ID	Stratification by Pool ID
2	Mortgage Type	6	1	1	Label	FIXED	SARM	HARM	Fixed Bal	ARM Bal						Label		Mortgage Type	Stratification by Mortgage Type
3	Credit Sector	3	1	1	Label	Prime	Alt-A	Sub-Prime								Label		Credit Sector	Stratification by Credit Sector
4	Original Balance	100	25,000	25,000	Dollar											Dollar		Original Balance	Stratification by Original Balance
5	Current Balance	100	25,000	25,000	Dollar											Dollar		Current Balance	Stratification by Current Balance
6	[Reserved]	999	999	999	NA											NA			
7	Original Loan-to-Value Ratio	60	5.00%	5.00%	Percent											Percent100		Original LTV Ratio	Stratification by Original Loan-to-Value Ratio
8	Current Loan-to-Value Ratio	60	5.00%	5.00%	Percent											Percent100		Current LTV Ratio	Stratification by Current Loan-to-Value Ratio
9	Original Term	30	12	12	Month											Month12		Original Term	Stratification by Original Term
10	Remaining Term	30	12	12	Month											Month12		Remaining Term	Stratification by Remaining Term
11	Seasoning	60	3	3	Month											Month3		Seasoning	Stratification by Seasoning
12	Current Coupon Rate	80	0.25%	0.25%	Percent											Percent20		Current Coupon Rate	Stratification by Current Coupon Rate
13	ARM Index	2	1	1	Label	LIBOR	1YrTsy									Label		Index Name	Stratification by ARM Index
14	ARM Spread to Index	80	0.25%	0.25%	Percent											Percent20		Spread to Index	Stratification by ARM Spread to Index
15	ARM Initial Index Level	80	0.25%	0.25%	Percent											Percent20		Initial Index Level	Stratification by ARM Initial Index Level
16	ARM Periodic Reset	10	3	3	Month											Month3		Periodic Reset	Stratification by ARM Periodic Reset
17	ARM Periodic Cap Rate	80	0.25%	0.25%	Percent											Percent20		Periodic Cap Rate	Stratification by ARM Periodic Cap Rate
18	ARM Periodic Floor	80	0.25%	0.25%	Percent											Percent20		Periodic Floor	Stratification by ARM Periodic Floor
19	ARM Lifetime Cap Rate	80	0.25%	0.25%	Percent											Percent20		Lifetime Cap	Stratification by ARM Lifetime Cap Rate
20	ARM Lifetime Floor Rate	80	0.25%	0.25%	Percent											Percent20		Lifetime Floor	Stratification by ARM Lifetime Floor Rate
21	HB-ARM Initial Rate	80	0.25%	0.25%	Percent											Percent20		HARM Initial Rate	Stratification by HB-ARM Initial Rate
22	HB-ARM Initial I/O Rate Period	10	3	3	Month											Month3	HARM Int I/O	Period	Stratification by HB-ARM Initial I/O Rate Period
23	HB-ARM Total I/O Rate Period	10	3	3	Month											Month3	HARM Total I/O	Period	Stratification by HB-ARM Total I/O Rate Period
24	HB-ARM Recast Term	4	3	3	Month											Month3	HARM Payment	Recast Term	Stratification by HB-ARM Recast Term
25	BALLOON Amortization Period	30	12	12	Month											Month12		BALL Amort Period	Stratification by BALLOON Amortization Period
26	BALLOON Period	30	12	12	Month											Month12		BALL Final Period	Stratification by BALLOON Period
27	Original Appraisal Value	100	25,000	25,000	Dollar											Dollar		Original Appraisal Value	Stratification by Original Appraisal Value
28	Current Appraisal Value	100	25,000	25,000	Dollar											Dollar		Current Appraisal Value	Stratification by Current Appraisal Value
29	Original Appraisal Type	7	1	1	Label	No Data	Walk Through	Outside	Drive By	Tax Assess	Other	None				Label	Original Appraisal	Type	Stratification by Original Appraisal Type
30	Current Appraisal Type	7	1	1	Label	No Data	Walk Through	Outside	Drive By	Tax Assess	Other	None				Label	Curr Appraisal	Type	Stratification by Current Appraisal Type
31	Property Type	10	1	1	Label	No Data	Single Fam	Multi 2	Condo	Coop	Multi <4	Multi <10	Multi 10+	High Rise	Mixed	Label		Property Type	Stratification by Property Type
32	Occupancy Code	4	1	1	Label	No Data	Owner	Non-Owner	Investment							Label		Occupancy Code	Stratification by Occupancy Code
33	Financing Purpose	6	1	1	Label	No Data	Purchase	Refinance	Restructure	Equity Out	Seasonal					Label		Financing Purpose	Stratification by Financing Purpose
34	State Code	54	1	1	State											State		State Code	Stratification by State Code
35	MSA Code	151	1	1	MSA											MSA		MSA Code	Stratification by MSA Code
36	[Reserved]	999	999	999	NA											NA			
37	Self-employed	10	1	1	Label	No Data	Yes	No								Label		Self-Employed?	Stratification by Self-employed
38	Number of years in position	8	1	1	Label	No Data	LT 1 Yr	LT 2 Yrs	LT 5 Yrs	LT 10 Yrs	LT 15 Yrs	LT 20 Yrs	GE 20 Yrs			Label	Number Yrs in	CurrentPosition	Stratification by Number of years in position
39	First Time Homeowner	3	1	1	Label	No Data	Yes	No								Label	First Time	First Time Homeowner	Stratification by First Time Homeowner
40	[Reserved]	999	999	999	NA											NA			
41	[Reserved]	999	999	999	NA											NA			
42	FICO Score	23	300	25	FICO											FICO		FICO Score	Stratification by FICO Score
43	Mortgage Debt-to-Income Ratio	60	5.00%	5.00%	Percent											Percent100	Mortgage	Debt-to-Inc Ratio	Stratification by Mortgage Debt-to-Income Ratio
44	Total Debt-to-Income Ratio	60	5.00%	5.00%	Percent											Percent100	Total	Debt-to-Inc Ratio	Stratification by Total Debt-to-Income Ratio
45	Bankruptcy History	5	1	1	Label	No Data	Never	Discharged	Filed	Current						Label		Bankruptcy Status	Stratification by Bankruptcy History
46	Escrow Provisions	5	1	1	Label	No Data	None	Tax	Insurance	All						Label		Escrow Account	Stratification by Escrow Provisions
47	Third Party Doc Due Diligence	6	1	1	Label	No Data	Poor	Fair	Average	Good	Excellent					Label		Third Party Doc Due Diligence	Stratification by Third Party Doc Due Diligence
48	Origination Document Package	7	1	1	Label	No Data	Full	Partial	Full	No Income	No Assets	No Inc/Assets				Label	Origination Doc	Document Package	Stratification by Origination Document Package
49	Servicer Rating	5	1	1	Label	Poor	Fair	Average	Good	Excellent						Label		Servicer Rating	Stratification by Servicer Rating
50	[Reserved]	999	999	999	NA											NA			

EXHIBIT 13.2 Base Stratification Report Package Table

528

Basic Stratification Report Package Formatting Guidelines

Data Item Names	Stratification Report Formatting Inputs				Label Table	
	# Values	Start Value	Interval Value	Data Type	1	2
1 Pool ID	5	1	1	Number		
2 Mortgage Type	6	1	1	Label	FIXED	SARM
3 Credit Sector	3	1	1	Label	Prime	Alt-A
4 Original Balance	50	25,000	25,000	Dollar		
5 Current Balance	50	25,000	25,000	Dollar		
6 [Reserved]	999	999	999	NA		
7 Original Loan-to-Value Ratio	20	5.00%	5.00%	Percent		
8 Current Loan-to-Value Ratio	20	5.00%	5.00%	Percent		
9 Original Term	30	12	12	Month		
10 Remaining Term	30	12	12	Month		
11 Seasoning	60	3	3	Month		
12 Current Coupon Rate	80	0.25%	0.25%	Percent		
13 ARM Index	2	1	1	Label	LIBOR	1YrTsy
14 ARM Spread to Index	80	0.25%	0.25%	Percent		
15 ARM Initial Index Level	80	0.25%	0.25%	Percent		

Base Stratification Reports Editor

Base Stratification Report Selection

Stratification Characteristic

Pool ID
Mortgage Type
Credit Sector
Original Balance
Current Balance
[Reserved]
Original Loan-to-Value Ratio
Current Loan-to-Value Ratio
Original Term
Remaining Term
Seasoning
Current Coupon Rate
ARM Index
ARM Spread to Index
ARM Initial Index Level
ARM Periodic Reset
ARM Periodic Cap Rate
ARM Periodic Floor
ARM Lifetime Cap Rate
ARM Lifetime Floor Rate
HB-ARM Initial Rate
HB-ARM Initial I/O Rate Period
HB-ARM Total I/O Rate Period

RECORD CHOICES **CLEAR CHOICES**

EXHIBIT 13.3 Base Stratification Report Table and UserForm before change

- "Percent 20": 0.25% intervals from 0% to 20%
- "Percent 100": 5% intervals from 0% to 100%
- "Label": Label vertical list for up to ten labels
- "Dollar": $25 million intervals from $0 to $1.25 million
- "State": 50 States and 4 U.S. territories
- "MSA": Largest 150 Metropolitan Statistical Areas of the United States

BSR Writer VBA Code All the VBA that supports the report writing activities of the BSR package is located in the module "Report_CollatEligibleStratBase".

"RepBaseStrat_MainWriteReports" Subroutine The main subroutine of the process is "RepBaseStrat_MainWriteReports". This subroutine consists of a "For..Next"

Base Stratification Report Package Formatting Guidelines

Data Item Names	Stratification Report Formatting Inputs				Label Table	
	# Values	Start Value	Interval Value	Data Type	1	2
1 Pool ID	5	1	1	Number		
2 Mortgage Type	6	1	1	Label	FIXED	SARM
3 [Reserved]	3	1	1	Label	Prime	Alt-A
4 Original Balance	50	25,000	25,000	Dollar		
5 Current Balance	50	25,000	25,000	Dollar		
6 Origination Date	999	999	999	NA		
7 Original Loan-to-Value Ratio	20	5.00%	5.00%	Percent		
8 Current Loan-to-Value Ratio	20	5.00%	5.00%	Percent		
9 Original Term	30	12	12	Month		
10 Remaining Term	30	12	12	Month		
11 Seasoning	60	3	3	Month		
12 Current Coupon Rate	80	0.25%	0.25%	Percent		
13 [Reserved]	2	1	1	Label	LIBOR	1YrTsy
14 ARM Spread to Index	80	0.25%	0.25%	Percent		
15 ARM Initial Index Level	80	0.25%	0.25%	Percent		

Base Stratification Reports Editor

Base Stratification Report Selection

Stratification Characteristic

Pool ID
Mortgage Type
[Reserved]
Original Balance
Current Balance
Origination Date
Original Loan-to-Value Ratio
Current Loan-to-Value Ratio
Original Term
Remaining Term
Seasoning
Current Coupon Rate
[Reserved]
ARM Spread to Index
ARM Initial Index Level
ARM Periodic Reset
ARM Periodic Cap Rate
ARM Periodic Floor
ARM Lifetime Cap Rate
ARM Lifetime Floor Rate
HB-ARM Initial Rate
HB-ARM Initial I/O Rate Period
HB-ARM Total I/O Rate Period

RECORD CHOICES **CLEAR CHOICES**

EXHIBIT 13.4 Base Stratification Report Table and UserForm after change

```
Sub RepBaseStrat_MainWriteReports()

    If gRepMenuStratBasic Then
        'read the stratification report specifications page
        Call RepBaseStrat_ReadFormatSpecs
        'open up the template file and rename it to the standard name plus report
        ' package prefix
        Workbooks.Open FileName:=DIR_TEMPLATE_REP & BASE_STRAT_REPORTS_TEMPLATE
        ActiveWorkbook.SaveAs FileName:= _
            OUTPUT_DIRECTORY & gRepMenuPrefix & "UserStratRepTest01"
        'write the reports
        WorksheetCount = 0        'current number of reports in the workbook
        For irep = 1 To DATA_FILE_FIELDS
          If gBaseStratReportChoice(irep) And _
             mRFName(irep) <> "[Reserved]" Then        'report selected?
             'select correct template based on datum type
             Call RepBaseStrat_FindTemplate
             'write report titles and headers
             Call RepBaseStrat_FillInRepHeaders
             'accumulate the balances'accumulate the balances
             Call RepBaseStrat_PopulateStratArrays
             'write the body of the report
             Call RepBaseStrat_WriteStratReportBody
          End If
        Next
        Call RepBaseStrat_DeleteTemplateWorksheets
        ActiveWorkbook.Save
        ActiveWorkbook.Close
        gRepMenuAssumptions = True
    End If

End Sub
```

EXHIBIT 13.5   "RepBaseStrat_MainWriteReports" subroutine

loop that moves through each of the fields of the loan record format and determines
if any of them have been selected for the reporting process. If a data field has been
selected for a BSR, then this subroutine initiates a series of four calls to other subroutines to produce the report. The structure of this subroutine is straightforward
and needs little other comment. See Exhibit 13.5.

"RepBaseStrat_ReadFormatSpecs" Subroutine   We will now trace how each of the
subroutines inside of the loop process the information from the SRPT to make decisions about which template worksheet to use and how to format the data and the
report. The first subroutine called by the "RepBaseStrat_MainWriteReports" subroutine is "RepBaseStrat_ReadFormatSpecs". This subroutine reads the contents of the
SRPT and stores it in a series of arrays for further use later in the report-processing effort. Note that the subroutine does *not* read the ten-column "Label Table" portion of
the SRPT that contains the data labels. These labels, as we have already seen, are used
not only by the BSRs but by other reports as well. Due to this fact, this portion of the
SRPT is read into an array named "gRFLabels" by the subroutine "MainProgram_
ReadAllDataFileLabels" from the Main Program. By placing this information into
an array with Global scope, we will make the information immediately available to
all portions of the program. See Exhibit 13.6.

```
Sub RepBaseStrat_ReadFormatSpecs()

Dim rName    As String    'range name of the Strat Report Format Table
Dim ipos     As Integer   'print counter for vertical sort label titles
Dim ilab     As Integer   'loop counter

    'reads the report formatting and content variables from the worksheet
    '  "StratReportInfo"
    rName = "m51StratReportSpecs"
    For irow = 1 To DATA_FILE_FIELDS
      If Trim(Range(rName).Cells(irow, 1).Value) <> "[Reserved]" Then
        mRFName(irow) = Trim(Range(rName).Cells(irow, 1).Value) 'name of data item
        mRFValues(irow) = Range(rName).Cells(irow, 2).Value     '# of strat value
        mRFStart(irow) = Range(rName).Cells(irow, 3).Value      'begin strat value
        mRFStep(irow) = Range(rName).Cells(irow, 4).Value       'step inteval
        mRFType(irow) = Trim(Range(rName).Cells(irow, 5).Value) 'report type
        If mRFType(irow) = "Label" Then
          For ilab = 1 To 10
            If ilab <= mRFValues(irow) Then
                mRFLabel(irow, ilab) = Trim(Range(rName).Cells(irow, ilab + 5).Value)
            Else
                mRFLabel(irow, ilab) = ""
            End If
          Next ilab
        End If
        mRFTemplate(irow) = Trim(Range(rName).Cells(irow, 16).Value) 'template type
        mRFTitle1(irow) = Trim(Range(rName).Cells(irow, 17).Value)  'column hdr 1
        mRFTitle2(irow) = Trim(Range(rName).Cells(irow, 18).Value)  'column hdr 2
        mRFRepTitle(irow) = Trim(Range(rName).Cells(irow, 19).Value) 'report title
      End If
    Next irow
    'read the list of MSA codes
    mRFMSACodes(1) = 0              'loans with no MSA indicated
    For iMSA = 2 To TOTAL_MSAS + 1
        mRFMSACodes(iMSA) = Range("m50MSACodeList").Cells(iMSA)
    Next iMSA

End Sub
```

EXHIBIT 13.6   "RepBaseStrat_ReadFormatSpecs" subroutine

"RepBaseStrat_FindTemplate" Subroutine   Having retrieved all the information from the SRPT and placed it in arrays where it is ready to use, we turn to the next step of the report-writing process. We open the Base Stratification Template file and save it. Next we enter the main loop of the subroutine. This loop will test each of the data fields to determine if it has been selected for a BSR. If it has, and if the data file name is *not* equal to the string "[Reserved]", an invalid field, the report-writing process begins.

Before we can write a single character into the Template file, we need to select the correct template report worksheet based on the data. The subroutine "RepBaseStrat_FindTemplate" locates the correct template, copies it, and re-names it to "BaseStrat-#", where # is the ordinal number of the data field. See Exhibit 13.7.

"RepBaseStrat_FillInRepHeaders" Subroutine   With the worksheet in place, we now begin to populate it. We next use the information from the SRPT to write all the report-specific headers and the report title. See Exhibit 13.8.

```
Sub RepBaseStrat_FindTemplate()

    'select the appropriate stratification worksheet template for this information
    Select Case mRFTemplate(irep)
        Case Is = "Label":      Sheets("Label").Select
        Case Is = "Dollar":     Sheets("Dollar").Select
        Case Is = "Percent20":  Sheets("Percent20").Select
        Case Is = "Percent100": Sheets("Percent100").Select
        Case Is = "Month3":     Sheets("Month3").Select
        Case Is = "Month6":     Sheets("Month6").Select
        Case Is = "Month12":    Sheets("Month12").Select
        Case Is = "State":      Sheets("State").Select
        Case Is = "MSA":        Sheets("MSA").Select
        Case Is = "FICO":       Sheets("FICO").Select
    End Select
    WorksheetCount = WorksheetCount + 1
    Cells.Select
    Selection.Copy
    Sheets.Add After:=Sheets(Sheets.Count)
    ActiveSheet.Paste
    Sheets("Sheet" & WorksheetCount).Select
    Sheets("Sheet" & WorksheetCount).Name = "BaseStrat-" & irep

End Sub
```

EXHIBIT 13.7 "RepBaseStrat_FindTemplate" subroutine

"RepBaseStrat_PopulateStratArrays" Subroutine With the framework of the report now in place, we need to compute the stratification statistics to populate it. We will call a specific subroutine based on the type of report that we selected earlier to display this particular data item. The subroutine "RepBaseStrat_PopulateStratArrays" uses a "Select..Case" statement to direct the CCFG model flow to the correct aggregation subroutine for these types of data. See Exhibit 13.9.

"RepBaseStrat_WriteLabelReport" Subroutine We will not review each of the ten different types of stratification aggregation subroutines. Their structures are broadly similar. Based on the formatting and sorting criteria data we have read from the SRPT, we already know how many stratification levels and the interval of each level. Some of these stratification criteria are very discrete in nature. Any datum that is displayed in a "Label" report will be distributed across ten or less criteria. In the "Percentage20" report format, there may be as many as 80 stratification levels.

```
Sub RepBaseStrat_FillInRepHeaders()

    'write the first and second report title lines
    Range("B2").Select
    Application.CutCopyMode = False
    ActiveCell.FormulaR1C1 = "Eligible Collateral Report #" & WorksheetCount
    Range("B3").Select
    ActiveCell.FormulaR1C1 = mRFRepTitle(irep)
    'add the stratification criteria range column headers
    Range("B6").Select:  ActiveCell.FormulaR1C1 = mRFTitle1(irep)
    Range("B7").Select:  ActiveCell.FormulaR1C1 = mRFTitle2(irep)

End Sub
```

EXHIBIT 13.8 "RepBaseStrat_FillInRepHeaders" subroutine

```
Sub RepBaseStrat_PopulateStratArrays()

    Select Case mRFTemplate(irep)
        Case Is = "Label":      Call RepBaseStrat_WriteLabelReport
        Case Is = "Dollar":     Call RepBaseStrat_WriteDollarReport
        Case Is = "Percent20":  Call RepBaseStrat_WritePercent20Report
        Case Is = "Percent100": Call RepBaseStrat_WritePercent100Report
        Case Is = "Month3":     Call RepBaseStrat_WriteMonth3Report
        Case Is = "Month12":    Call RepBaseStrat_WriteMonth12Report
        Case Is = "State":      Call RepBaseStrat_WriteStateReport
        Case Is = "MSA":        Call RepBaseStrat_WriteMSAReport
        Case Is = "FICO":       Call RepBaseStrat_WriteFICOReport
    End Select

End Sub
```

EXHIBIT 13.9   "RepBaseStrat_PopulateStratArrays" subroutine

Regardless of the type of report, the entire focus of the logic it contains comes down to the assignment of a value to a single, innocuous-sounding variable, "slot". "Slot" is the stratification level into which we will aggregate the financial data of this loan record. We will pass "slot" on to an accumulator subroutine that will then add the contents of the current record to the running total for that particular stratification level. Let us look at two very different subroutines that perform this function. We will first examine "RepBaseStrat_WriteLabelReport" as an example of a more complicated stratification subroutine and then "RepBaseStrat_WriteDollarReport" as an example of a simpler report.

In "RepBaseStrat_WriteLableReport" we are faced with the task of stratifying any one of 18 different types of data. They range from Mortgage Type, to Adjustable Rate Mortgage Index Type, to Bankruptcy History. One thing that is in our favor is that each of the values in a "Label" type field is a numeric value that represents the "*n*th" label of that datum. In other words if the value of the field "FD_BANKRUPTCY" is equal to "3", we know that the corresponding label is "Discharged". We can then aggregate the financial information across the "Discharged" stratification level on the report.

The "RepBaseStrat_WriteLabelReport" subroutine begins by writing the labels of the particular datum down the side of the report. The subroutine then loops through all loans. There are two special cases that the subroutine must plan for. Of the 18 different data fields that will use the "Label" format stratification report template, two are fields that will have data in them *only* if they are adjustable-rate mortgages. If either of these two data fields has been chosen, we need to qualify the loan before aggregating it. You can see that the subroutine sets a Boolean variable "go_ok" to FALSE. If the datum is the field "FD_ARMINDEX", the index from which the ARM coupon is set, we will test to determine if the mortgage type is one of the adjustable-rate mortgages: a standard, hybrid, or balloon ARM. If the tests are TRUE, "go_ok" is set to TRUE and we continue with the stratification process. If the test is FALSE, the subroutine will use an "If..Then" test to route us around the aggregation subroutine call. The variable "go_ok" will be set to true for all of the other 16 "Label" type data fields by the "Case Else" clause in the "Select..Case" statement.

```
Sub RepBaseStrat_WriteLabelReport()

    Call RepBaseStrat_WriteReportLabels
    For iloan = 1 To gTotalLoans
        'accumulate the information of the loan to the stratification report
        go_ok = False
        Select Case irep
            Case Is = FD_ARMINDEX
                'accumulate only if the mortgage is a variable rate loan
                If gLoanData(iloan, FD_MORTTYPE) = MORTTYPE_STAND_ARM Or _
                    gLoanData(iloan, FD_MORTTYPE) = MORTTYPE_HYBRID_ARM Or _
                    gLoanData(iloan, FD_MORTTYPE) = MORTTYPE_BAL_ARM Then
                        go_ok = True
                End If
            Case Else: go_ok = True
        End Select
        If gLoanScreen(iloan, FD_SCREEN_ALL_OK) = REC_OKFORALL And go_ok Then
            Select Case irep
                Case Is = FD_MORTTYPE:       slot = gLoanData(iloan, FD_MORTTYPE)
                Case Is = FD_CREDITSECT:     slot = gLoanData(iloan, FD_CREDITSECT)
                Case Is = FD_ARMINDEX:       slot = gLoanData(iloan, FD_ARMINDEX)
                Case Is = FD_ORIGAPPTYPE:    slot = gLoanData(iloan, FD_ORIGAPPTYPE)
                Case Is = FD_CURRAPPTYPE:    slot = gLoanData(iloan, FD_CURRAPPTYPE)
                Case Is = FD_PROPTYPE:       slot = gLoanData(iloan, FD_PROPTYPE)
                Case Is = FD_OCCPCODE:       slot = gLoanData(iloan, FD_OCCPCODE)
                Case Is = FD_FINPURPOSE:     slot = gLoanData(iloan, FD_FINPURPOSE)
                Case Is = FD_EMPLOY:         slot = gLoanData(iloan, FD_EMPLOY)
                Case Is = FD_YRSPOST:        slot = gLoanData(iloan, FD_YRSPOST)
                Case Is = FD_FIRSTHOME:      slot = gLoanData(iloan, FD_FIRSTHOME)
                Case Is = FD_BANKRUPTCY:     slot = gLoanData(iloan, FD_BANKRUPTCY)
                Case Is = FD_ESCROW:         slot = gLoanData(iloan, FD_ESCROW)
                Case Is = FD_THIRDPARTY:     slot = gLoanData(iloan, FD_THIRDPARTY)
                Case Is = FD_ORIGDOCS:       slot = gLoanData(iloan, FD_ORIGDOCS)
                Case Is = FD_SERVERATE:      slot = gLoanData(iloan, FD_SERVERATE)
            End Select
            Call RepBaseStrat_AggregateBalances(slot)
        End If
    Next iloan

End Sub
```

EXHIBIT 13.10   "RepBaseStrat_WriteLabelReport" subroutine

If "go_ok" is TRUE and the value of the "gLoanOK" array for this loan is also TRUE, we will next determine the "slot" value for this record in the stratification levels. For all "Label" type data fields, their value is also their "slot," as we pointed out earlier. With the "slot" value in hand, we can now call the subroutine "RepBaseStrat_AccumulateLoanBalances" to populate the appropriate stratification level with the information from this record. See Exhibit 13.10.

"RepBaseStrat_WriteDollarReport" Subroutine The subroutine "RepBaseStrat_WriteDollarReport" is much shorter and simpler. There are only five data that use this report format. Four are dollar amounts, and the last is the FICO score of the borrower. We do not need to do any screening for special cases of data, and we already have the interval for the stratification levels from the SRPT. Thus we see that the determination of the "slot" value is simply dividing the value of the field by the interval value and rounding up the result. See Exhibit 13.11.

```
Sub RepBaseStrat_WriteDollarReport()

Dim amt          As Double    'amount determining stratification level

    For iloan = 1 To gTotalLoans
        If gLoanOK(iloan) Then
            Select Case irep
                Case Is = FD_ORIGBAL: amt = gLoanData(iloan, FD_ORIGBAL)
                Case Is = FD_CURRBAL: amt = gLoanData(iloan, FD_CURRBAL)
                Case Is = FD_ORIGAPP: amt = gLoanData(iloan, FD_ORIGAPP)
                Case Is = FD_CURRAPP: amt = gLoanData(iloan, FD_CURRAPP)
                Case Is = FD_FICO:    amt = gLoanData(iloan, FD_FICO)
            End Select
            slot = Application.RoundUp((amt) / mRFStep(irep), 0)
            Call RepBaseStrat_AggregateBalances(slot)
        End If
    Next iloan

End Sub
```

EXHIBIT 13.11 "RepBaseStrat_WriteDollarReport" subroutine

"RepBaseStrat_AggregateBalances" Subroutine   With the values of the "slot" variable in hand, we now proceed to aggregate the data into the appropriate stratification level. This activity is performed by the "RepBaseStrat_AggregateBalances" subroutine. See Exhibit 13.12.

"RepBaseStrat_WriteStratReportBody" Subroutine   The subroutine "RepBase Strat_WriteStratReportBody" will now print out the report. There are a number of fields on the report—percentages and cumulative percentages of each stratification level—that we cannot compute until we have finished aggregating all of the loans. We will perform these calculations now, as we write the report. Last we will start at the bottom of the report and trim all unused levels from the bottom up. We will not trim unused levels from the body of the report in that it is more useful to visualize the

```
Sub RepBaseStrat_AggregateBalances(interval As Integer)

    mLoanCount(interval) = mLoanCount(interval) + 1
    mLoanBalance(interval) = mLoanBalance(interval) + gLoanData(FD_CURRBAL, iloan)
    mEquityBalance(interval) = _
        mEquityBalance(interval) + (gLoanData(FD_ORIGBAL, iloan) - _
        gLoanData(FD_CURRBAL, iloan))
    mTotAppraisal(interval) = mTotAppraisal(interval) + gLoanData(FD_CURRAPP, iloan)
    mWACSum(interval) = mWACSum(interval) + _
                (gLoanData(FD_CURRBAL, iloan) * gLoanData(FD_CURRRATE, iloan))
    mWASSum(interval) = mWASSum(interval) + _
                (gLoanData(FD_CURRBAL, iloan) * gLoanData(FD_SEASON, iloan))
    mWAOMSum(interval) = mWAOMSum(interval) + _
                (gLoanData(FD_CURRBAL, iloan) * gLoanData(FD_ORIGTERM, iloan))
    mWARMSum(interval) = mWARMSum(interval) + _
                (gLoanData(FD_CURRBAL, iloan) * gLoanData(FD_REMTERM, iloan))
    mTotalCurBal = mTotalCurBal + gLoanData(FD_CURRBAL, iloan)

End Sub
```

EXHIBIT 13.12 "RepBaseStrat_AggregateBalances" subroutine

```
Sub RepBaseStrat_WriteStratReportBody()

Dim StartCol      As Integer      'starting print column
Dim pcol          As Integer      'print column in the worksheet
Dim prow          As Integer      'print row on the worksheet
Dim arow          As Integer      'array row in the aggregation matrix

    mCumPct = 0#
    arow = 1
    StartCol = 5
    If irep = FD_MSACODE Then StartCol = 6
    mRFLastRow = REPORT_FIRST_LINE + mRFValues(irep) - 1
    For irow = REPORT_FIRST_LINE To mRFLastRow
        ' Print out only the active ranges
        If mLoanCount(arow) > 0 Then
            Cells(irow, StartCol + 0) = mLoanCount(arow)
            Cells(irow, StartCol + 1) = mLoanBalance(arow)
            Cells(irow, StartCol + 2) = mLoanBalance(arow) / mTotAppraisal(arow)
            Cells(irow, StartCol + 3) = mLoanBalance(arow) / mTotalCurBal
            mCumPct = mCumPct + (mLoanBalance(arow) / mTotalCurBal)
            Cells(irow, StartCol + 4) = mCumPct
            Cells(irow, StartCol + 5) = mLoanBalance(arow) / mLoanCount(arow)
            Cells(irow, StartCol + 6) = mWACSum(arow) / mLoanBalance(arow)
            Cells(irow, StartCol + 7) = mWAOMSum(arow) / mLoanBalance(arow)
            Cells(irow, StartCol + 8) = mWARMSum(arow) / mLoanBalance(arow)
            Cells(irow, StartCol + 9) = mWASSum(arow) / mLoanBalance(arow)
            Cells(irow, StartCol + 10) = mEquityBalance(arow)
            Cells(irow, StartCol + 11) = mEquityBalance(arow) / mTotAppraisal(arow)
            Cells(irow, StartCol + 12) = mTotAppraisal(arow)
        End If
        arow = arow + 1
    Next
    Call RepBaseStrat_SortGeographicReports
    Call RepBaseStrat_TrimOutputReport
    Call RepBaseStrat_SetAccumulatorsToZero
    irow = 0

End Sub
```

EXHIBIT 13.13 "RepBaseStrat_WriteStratReportBody" subroutine

gaps in the data if these lines are left in. Remember that sometimes what you *do not* see in a stratification report can be as informative as what you do see. Finally the last subroutine call at the bottom of the report "RepBaseStrat_SetAccumulatorsToZero" sets all the amounts in the stratification ladder to zero so that we do not carry any balances over into the next report. See Exhibit 13.13.

Upon returning to the "RepBaseStrat_MainWriteReports" after the loop has completed and we have written the last report, we will call the subroutine "RepBaseStrat_DeleteTemplateWorksheets". This subroutine will delete each of the original template worksheets in the workbook, leaving only our stratification reports. We then save and close the workbook. The BSR package is complete!

Completed Base Stratification Report The following BSR is by FICO scores of borrowers of eligible loans in the portfolio. See Exhibit 13.14.

Cross Tabulation Collateral Reports

The Cross Tabulation Report Package (CTRP) can be thought of as a two-dimensional extension of the BSR package. The CTRP allows the user of the CCFG

Eligible Collateral Report #22

Stratification by FICO Score

FICO Score	Number of Loans	Current Loan Balance	Current Loan LTV	% Current Balances	Cum % Current Balances	Average Loan Balance	WtAvg Current Yield	WtAvg Original Term	WtAvg Remain Term	WtAvg Current Seasoning	Equity Balance	Equity % Appraisal	Total Appraisal
	305	34,632,885									7,440,508		42,073,392
400 to 425													
426 to 450	19	1,681,123	91.0%	4.9%	4.9%	88,480	6.357%	112.4	99.1	13.3	165,735	9.0%	1,846,858
451 to 475	15	1,046,151	78.1%	3.0%	7.9%	69,743	6.651%	101.8	87.6	14.2	292,856	21.9%	1,339,006
476 to 500	18	3,430,480	87.5%	9.9%	17.8%	190,582	6.040%	164.7	156.9	7.7	492,024	12.5%	3,922,503
501 to 525	16	2,037,857	84.4%	5.9%	23.7%	127,366	6.511%	114.6	104.5	10.0	377,286	15.6%	2,415,144
526 to 550	19	2,002,446	74.2%	5.8%	29.4%	105,392	6.455%	102.0	90.2	11.8	696,500	25.8%	2,698,947
551 to 575	17	1,352,450	72.8%	3.9%	33.4%	79,556	6.628%	103.1	87.5	15.7	504,243	27.2%	1,856,693
576 to 600	21	2,592,651	82.1%	7.5%	40.8%	123,460	6.635%	153.1	141.4	11.7	566,857	17.9%	3,159,508
601 to 625	22	2,149,955	76.3%	6.2%	47.0%	97,725	6.600%	104.1	91.5	12.5	666,272	23.7%	2,816,227
626 to 650	14	904,575	79.4%	2.6%	49.7%	64,612	6.648%	121.3	101.3	20.0	234,700	20.6%	1,139,275
651 to 675	19	1,620,495	81.4%	4.7%	54.3%	85,289	6.711%	103.7	86.4	17.3	369,767	18.6%	1,990,263
676 to 700	21	2,385,606	91.3%	6.9%	61.2%	113,600	6.231%	121.2	108.1	13.1	228,417	8.7%	2,614,022
701 to 725	13	3,043,516	93.9%	8.8%	70.0%	234,117	6.153%	149.0	134.4	14.6	198,275	6.1%	3,241,792
726 to 750	9	743,111	76.8%	2.1%	72.2%	82,568	6.459%	109.7	95.4	14.3	224,219	23.2%	967,329
751 to 775	27	3,623,164	71.4%	10.5%	82.6%	134,191	6.387%	110.1	98.6	11.5	1,450,575	28.6%	5,073,739
776 to 800	21	2,659,659	82.6%	7.7%	90.3%	126,650	6.428%	129.3	115.6	13.7	561,939	17.4%	3,221,598
801 to 825	17	2,313,536	84.3%	6.7%	97.0%	136,090	6.245%	160.5	142.7	17.8	431,027	15.7%	2,744,563
826 to 850	17	1,046,110	102.0%	3.0%	100.0%	61,536	6.755%	99.3	86.3	12.9	(20,185)	-2.0%	1,025,925

EXHIBIT 13.14 Base Stratification Report #22: Stratification by FICO scores

537

to specify three data items from the Cross Tabulation UserForm. The first of these becomes the vertical axis and the second the horizontal axis of a matrix, while the third becomes the aggregated data that is the body of the report. In writing the CTRP, we are faced with the same set of logical decisions that we were dealing with in the BSR, just in an additional dimension (the horizontal axis), and with the ability to pick from a list of Report Body content variables.

Thus in our construction of the CTRP report, we are faced with an additional consideration, that of accommodating, both in the report format and in the data selection and aggregation, the second dimension of the report. Whereas with the BSRP we were focused on the determination of the value of the "slot" variable that designated the stratification level, here we will need to determine two "slots," the vertical and the horizontal. In addition, we will have to build a variety of very different horizontal headers for the CTRP in different formats and widely differing lengths.

Cross Tabulation Report Package Infrastructure   As with the BSRP, the CTRP will consist of four elements:

1. The Cross Tabulation Report Package Table.
2. The Cross Tabulation UserForms of the Reports Edit Menu
3. The "CrossTabulationReportTemplate" file
4. The VBA code in the "Report_CollatEligilibleCrossTab" module

We have already examined these elements of the BSRP in some detail. In this section we will concentrate on the differences between the BSRP and the CTRP.

Cross Tabulation Report Package Table   The one feature of the CTRP Table (CTRPT) that is immediately apparent is the number of times the term "[Reserved]" appears in it! We should expect this as we have already seen the contents of these fields appear in the display areas of the Cross Tabulation UserForms designed in Chapter 9. Nonetheless, there are quite a few of them. This is due to the fact that it is unlikely that the model user would need to stratify data along the lines of some of the minor features of adjustable-rate loans. See Exhibit 13.15.

Vertical, Horizontal, and Report Body Selection Columns   What is immediately different from the BSR is that instead of a single column of data fields in the table, we have three: the vertical, the horizontal, and the report body. There are 27 fields that can appear in the vertical selection, 27 that can serve as the horizontal selection, and 16 that can populate the Report Body. Notice that the list of the 27 vertical selection and the 27 horizontal selections are not identical. This is because we are trying to impose some limitations as to the layout and content of the report. For example, the fields state code and MSA code do not appear in the horizontal selection. There are 54 unique state codes and 150 unique MSA codes. Any Cross Tabulation Report will be much more legible and easier to reproduce if these longer list items are constrained to the vertical axis of the report. On a similar note, the selection fields with smaller populations are available only in the horizontal axis. Counterbalancing the longer state and MSA vertical options are the shorter Mortgage Type with five options, and the FICO score with seven. Some of the very short vertical selections are

Cross Tabulation Report Package Formatting Guidelines Table

#	Data / Vertical Items	Horizontal Items	Report Body	Cross Tabulation Report Formatting Inputs — # Values	Interval Value	Template Used	Dollar Weighted?
1	[Reserved]	[Reserved]	Loan Count	6	1		
2	[Reserved]	Mortgage Type	[Reserved]				
3	[Reserved]	[Reserved]	[Reserved]				
4	Original Balance	Original Balance	Original Balance	31	10,000	Dollar	False
5	Current Balance	Current Balance	Current Balance	31	10,000	Dollar	False
6	[Reserved]	[Reserved]	[Reserved]				
7	Original Loan-to-Value Ratio	Original Loan-to-Value Ratio	Original Loan-to-Value Ratio	20	5.00%	Percent100	True
8	Current Loan-to-Value Ratio	Current Loan-to-Value Ratio	Current Loan-to-Value Ratio	20	5.00%	Percent100	True
9	Original Term	Original Term	Original Term	30	12	Month12	True
10	Remaining Term	Remaining Term	Remaining Term	30	12	Month12	True
11	Seasoning	Seasoning	Seasoning	20	3	Month3	True
12	Current Coupon Rate	Current Coupon Rate	Current Coupon Rate	20	0.50%	Percent10	True
13	[Reserved]	[Reserved]	[Reserved]				
	Rows 14 to 32 Not Displayed						
33	[Reserved]	[Reserved]	[Reserved]				
34	Original Appraisal Value	Original Appraisal Value	Original Appraisal Value	31	10,000	Dollar	False
35	Current Appraisal Value	Current Appraisal Value	Current Appraisal Value	31	10,000	Dollar	False
36	Original Appraisal Type	Original Appraisal Type	[Reserved]	7	1	Label	
37	Current Appraisal Type	Current Appraisal Type	[Reserved]	7	1	Label	
38	Property Type	Property Type	[Reserved]	10	1	Label	
39	Occupancy Code	Occupancy Code	[Reserved]	8	1	Label	
40	Financing Purpose	Financing Purpose	[Reserved]	6	1	Label	
41	State Code	[Reserved]	[Reserved]	999	999	State	
42	MSA Code	[Reserved]	[Reserved]	999	999	MSA	
43	[Reserved]	[Reserved]	[Reserved]				
44	Self-employed	Self-employed	[Reserved]	10	1	Label	
45	Number of years in position	Number of years in position	[Reserved]	8	1	Label	
46	First Time Homeowner	First Time Homeowner	[Reserved]	3	1	Label	
47	[Reserved]	[Reserved]	[Reserved]				
48	[Reserved]	[Reserved]	[Reserved]				
49	[Reserved]	FICO Score	FICO Score	7	50	FICO	True
50	Mortgage Debt-to-Income Ratio	Mortgage Debt-to-Income Ratio	Mortgage Debt-to-Income Ratio	20	5.00%	Percent100	True
51	Total Debt-to-Income Ratio	Total Debt-to-Income Ratio	Total Debt-to-Income Ratio	20	5.00%	Percent100	True
52	Bankruptcy History	Bankruptcy History	[Reserved]	5	1	Label	
53	Escrow Provisions	Escrow Provisions	[Reserved]	5	1	Label	
54	Third Party Doc Due Diligence	Third Party Doc Due Diligence	Third Party Doc Due Diligence	6	1	Label	True
55	Origination Document Package	Origination Document Package	Origination Document Package	7	1	Label	
56	Servicier Rating	Servicier Rating	Servicier Rating	6	1	Label	True
57	[Reserved]	[Reserved]	[Reserved]				

EXHIBIT 13.15 Cross Tabulation Report Package Formatting Table

retained in the horizontal selection list. This is true of the data fields of "First Time Homeowner" and "Self Employed". The reasons that these fields are maintained in both the horizontal and the vertical columns are that they frequently are matched with other demographic fields that themselves have a limited number of options. Also one must be careful not to limit useful combination to a single selection column. For example, if both the "Self Employed" and the "First Time Homeowner" data fields were horizontal selection items only, we could not cross-reference them.

Number of Values, Interval Value, and Template Used Columns These columns hold the same type of values for organizing the data that we have used in the BSR and need no additional comment at this time.

"Dollar-Weighted ?" Column This column alerts the CTRP subroutines as to which of the data fields that can be selected to be aggregated in the Report Body need to be dollar weighted. Clearly the purely dollar fields of Original and Current Balance and Original and Current Appraisal Amounts can simply be aggregated and displayed. If we wish to display a dollar-weighted statistic in any position of a CTR, then we need to construct the numerator of the entry by weighting it with the current balance and the denominator for the CTR location by aggregating the current balance. When we write the report, we will divide the denominator by the numerator to obtain the dollar-weighted amount. We will store the numerator values in the array "gCTOutputValue" and the denominator in the array "gCTOutputDollar".

The contents of the column "Dollar Weighted ?" are either TRUE or FALSE and are written to a Boolean-type array named "gCTDolWght".

Cross Tabulation Report UserForm The Cross Tabulation Report UserForm contains a total of three List Boxes and a Text Box. The List Boxes display the vertical, horizontal, and Report Body elections for the report. The Text Box allows the user to input the number of the report. The CCFG is currently configured to accept up to 50 CTR configurations. The UserForm support code returns a set of five arrays to the CCFG:

1. **"gCTVerticalItem"**. The index number of the vertical selection item.
2. **"gCTHorizonItem"**. The index number of the horizontal selection item.
3. **"gCTBodyItem"**. The index item of the Report Body item.
4. **"gCTReportActive"**. Tells us which of the report numbers have selection criteria specified.
5. **"gCTTrimReport"**. Tells us if the user wants the report trimmed of unpopulated row and columns.

The UserForm VBA support code loops through the contents of each of the List Boxes until it finds the selected item and then returns its position in the list. The lists displayed in these boxes are drawn from the CTRPT. This allows us to automatically change the displays in the UserForm by editing the Excel worksheet containing the CTRPT in the CCFG. The UserForm support code subroutine is "AddButton_Click" and is triggered by clicking on the "ADD TO REPORT SET" button. The UserForm is displayed in Exhibit 13.16 and the "addButton_Click" subroutine in Exhibit 13.17.

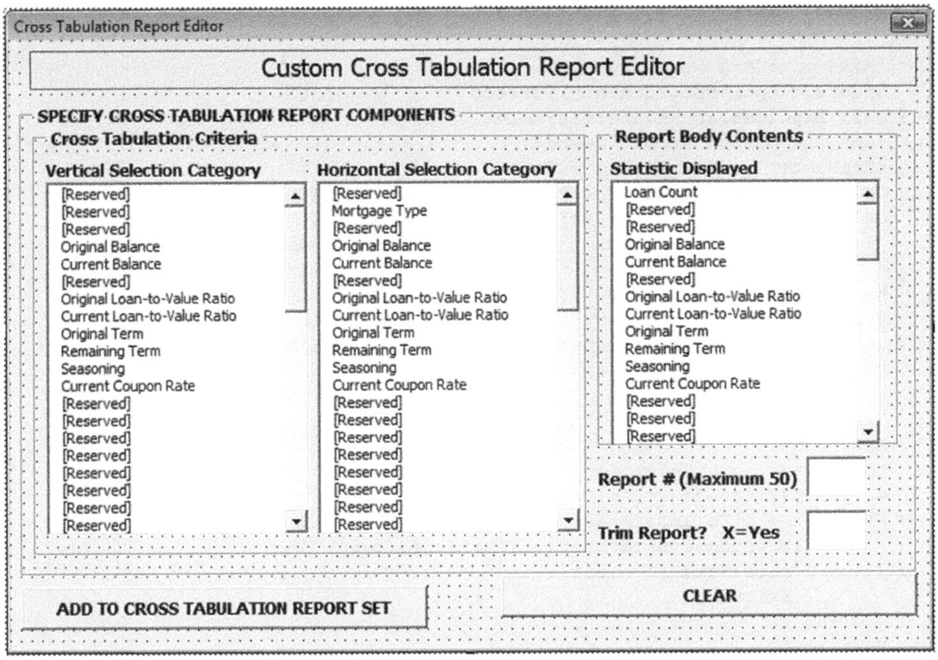

EXHIBIT 13.16 Cross Tabulation Report UserForm

"AddButton_Click" Subroutine The "AddButton_Click" subroutine first reads the contents of the CTRPT to provide itself with the names of the data items that may need to be used later in error messages. It then performs two input error tests in regard to the "Report #" field input. It checks if the entry is numeric and within the values of 1 and "MAX_CROSS_TABS" constant (currently set at 50). It next checks to see if the report number that we have entered is active; if it is, it asks us if we wish to overwrite the existing CTR specification for this test.

Having ascertained that the entry is a valid Report Number, it now employs three separate "For..Next" loops to read through the vertical, horizontal, and Report Body lists. These loops seek to determine the selected choice, if any. You will note that prior to the initiation of the loop search, the variable "mListNum" for each of the lists is set to the value –1. The list numbers for List Box arrays run from "0" to the number of items in the list. If the "mListNum" values remain unchanged, it means that the subroutine could not locate a selected item in that particular list. We will use this variable in an error-checking subroutine later.

If an item from each list was selected, we still need to perform three more tests to ensure that we have a usable CTR specification combination. The first test is to determine that the same item was not selected for both the vertical and horizontal data item. The second is that none of the selections are of a restricted nonvalid data field currently labeled "[Reserved]" in the CTRPT. The third is that a selection was indeed made from each of the List Box items. See Exhibit 13.17.

"errCheck_CrossTabUserForm" Subroutine The "errCheck_CrossTabUserForm" contains the VBA code for the five input error tests of the Cross Tabulation Reports

```
Private Sub AddButton_Click()

    'Make sure the worksheet is active
    Sheets("ReportsEditorMenu").Select
    Call RepCrossTab_ReadFormatTable
    'Get the Custom Report Number
    mRepNumber = tbCustomReportNumber
    Call errCheck_CrossTabUserForm(errREPNUM_ILLEGAL)      'illegal report #
    Call errCheck_CrossTabUserForm(errREPNUM_ACTIVE)       'overwrite test?
    'read the selected items from the three List Boxes
    'First Sort Criteria
    mListNum(1) = -1
    For icnt = 0 To lbPrimaryStratCriteria.ListCount - 1
        If lbPrimaryStratCriteria.Selected(icnt) Then
            mListNum(1) = icnt
            Exit For
        End If
    Next icnt
    'Secondary Sort Criteria
    mListNum(2) = -1
    For icnt = 0 To lbSecondaryStratCriteria.ListCount - 1
        If lbSecondaryStratCriteria.Selected(icnt) Then
            mListNum(2) = icnt
            Exit For
        End If
    Next icnt
    'Report Contents Statistic
    mListNum(3) = -1
    For icnt = 0 To lbReportBodyStatistic.ListCount - 1
        If lbReportBodyStatistic.Selected(icnt) Then
            mListNum(3) = icnt
            Exit For
        End If
    Next icnt
    Call errCheck_CrossTabUserForm(errNO_LIST_ENTRY)    'missing entry
    'tranfer the User Form contents into the VBA arrays
    gCTVerticalItem(mRepNumber) = mListNum(1) + 1
    gCTHorizonItem(mRepNumber) = mListNum(2) + 1
    gCTBodyItem(mRepNumber) = mListNum(3) + 1
    Call errCheck_CrossTabUserForm(errTWO_VH_SAME) 'check for a match
    Call errCheck_CrossTabUserForm(errRESERVED)    'reserved field
    gCTReportActive(mRepNumber) = True
    gCTTrimReport(mRepNumber) = False
    If tbTrimReport = "X" Or tbTrimReport = "x" Then
        gCTTrimReport(mRepNumber) = True
    End If
    'we are done, put down the user form
    Unload m15ReportsCrossTabsEditor

End Sub
```

EXHIBIT 13.17 "AddButton_Click" subroutine

UserForm. This subroutine first sets up a series of error messages. Then, depending on the value of the calling argument, it uses a "Select..Case" to choose between five different error tests to call. Each error test will perform a different function and produce a different message.

It is very important that you familiarize yourself with error checking code and employ it rigorously in your modeling efforts. The old saying "A stitch in time saves nine" was never more true than in the case of error checking. The last thing that you

```
Sub errCheck_CrossTabUserForm(errCheck As Integer)

Dim itest                 As Integer

    'some abbreviations to make things easier to read
    If errCheck <> errREPNUM_ILLEGAL Then
        mVItem = gCTVerticalItem(mRepNumber)
        mHItem = gCTHorizonItem(mRepNumber)
        mBItem = gCTBodyItem(mRepNumber)
    End If
    errScore = 0
    'Error message components
    msgTitle = "CROSS TABULATION REPORTS ERROR MESSAGES " & vbCrLf & vbCrLf
    msgInfo(1) = "Illegal Vertical/Horizontal Item Combination" & vbCrLf
    msgInfo(2) = "[Reserved] Field Selected" & vbCrLf
    msgInfo(3) = "Illegal Report Number" & vbCrLf
    msgInfo(4) = "This Report Already Active " & mRepNumber & vbCrLf
    msgInfo(5) = "Missing Vertical/Horizontal/Body Datum Selection" & vbCrLf
    msgBody = ""
    'Put the error message together based on the point of origin
    Sheets("ReportsEditorMenu").Select
    Select Case errCheck
        Case Is = errTWO_VH_SAME:     Call ErrTest_SameItemTwice
        Case Is = errRESERVED:        Call ErrTest_SelectedReservedField
        Case Is = errREPNUM_ILLEGAL:  Call ErrTest_IllegalReportNumber
        Case Is = errREPNUM_ACTIVE:   Call ErrTest_ReportAlreadyActive
        Case Is = errNO_LIST_ENTRY:   Call ErrTest_MissingInputs
    End Select

End Sub
```

EXHIBIT 13.18 "errCheck_CrossTabUserForm" subroutine

want to have happen in the middle of a model run is to have the program crash due to some small value problem or careless input. Study these error-checking subroutines carefully! We will review the "errCheck_CrossTabUserForm" subroutine and one of the specific error-checking subroutines called by it. See Exhibit 13.18.

The first action of the "errCheck_CrossTabUserForm" subroutine is to determine if the current test is the one that validates the Report Number. Why? The next set of statements assigns the values of the data items selected from each of the three List Boxes to a set of abbreviations. We will use these abbreviated variable names for the index locations of the vertical, horizontal, and Report Body selections. We cannot perform this assignment, however, until we are sure the value of the variable "mRepNumber" is valid (both numeric and between 1 and 50). If, for example, a value of 55, a number that exceeds the number of data items in the collateral record, were input into the Report Field the CCFG would use this number to read portions of the array that are dimensioned to be only as large as the number of data fields in the record. It is impossible to use a portion of an array that is beyond the limit of its dimensions. We therefore need to confirm that any input to this field lies within the described boundaries of the collateral data limit we have previously established for numerous arrays.. Without performing this check VBA would immediately crash on the next statement:

```
mVItem = gCTVerticalItem(mRepNumber)
```

due to the fact that the "gCTVerticalItem" is dimensioned from 1 to "MAX_CROSS_TABS",(50), and the assignment would exceed the highest value of the array. If the test is any other than the Report Number validation test, we assign the values to the abbreviations and proceed.

The subroutine then sets up a number of error message box title and headers, one for each of the tests. It also initializes the value of the variable "msgBody" that will form the explanatory portion of the error message we will view if something has gone awry. Based on the value of the argument "errCheck", the subroutine now uses a "Select..Case" statement to choose the appropriate error-checking subroutine to employ. The subroutine is called and the error check is performed. If the condition passes, the error check control returns to the "errCheck_CrossTabUserForm" subroutine and all is well. If the test fails, the specific error-checking subroutine will produce an error message and halt the execution of the program.

"ErrTest_IllegalReportNumber" Subroutine We will now walk through one of these purpose-specific error-testing subroutines. The "ErrTest_IllegalReport Number" subroutine performs two tests. The first is to determine that the input to the Report Number field was numeric, and the second that it was between 1 and the current report maximum of 50.

The first action of the subroutine is to assemble the error header for the message box and add it to the contents of the "msgBody". The contents of msgBody, a String variable, is null since we have just arrived from the calling subroutine where it was initialized to " ". We then perform each of the tests. To keep a record of the conditions that failed, we will concatenate a condition-specific error message to the contents of "msgBody" each time an error is detected. In this case the errors are mutually exclusive; we can be either nonnumeric or out of bounds, but not both. Such is not the case in some of the other error-checking subroutines. In the subroutine that checks for missing data from each of the three List Boxes, we may concatenate as many as three separate error messages to "msgBox" if all the tests fail. Whenever we detect an error message, we will increment the variable "err_score" by "1". If we arrive at the end of the subroutine with an "err_score" greater than zero, we have an error present and need to print an error message. To produce the error message, we call the function "MsgBox". This function takes three arguments:

1. The contents of the message with the box, "msgBody".
2. The type of Response Buttons we want to show in the bottom of the box "cMsgButtonCode1". This Constant variable is set to the following value:

```
vbOKOnly + vbCritical
```

It will display a single button marked "OK" and a "Critical" icon indicating a very serious error condition.
3. The title of the Message Box.

The call to the function will appear as:

```
MsgBox(msgBody, cMsgButtonCode1, msgTitle)
```

The user has only one option: to hit the "OK" button. This returns control to the subroutine. The next VBA statement is "End", which stops the program and

```
Sub ErrTest_IllegalReportNumber()

    msgBody = msgBody & msgInfo(3) & vbCrLf
    If IsNumeric(mRepNumber) = False Then
        msgBody = msgBody & "Report Number is Non-Numeric!" & vbCrLf
        errScore = errScore + 1
    End If
    If mRepNumber < 0 Or mRepNumber > CROSS_TAB_MAX Then
        msgBody = msgBody & "Report Number must be between 1 and " & _
              CROSS_TAB_MAX & vbCrLf
        errScore = errScore + 1
    End If
    If errScore > 0 Then
        msgResult = MsgBox(msgBody, cMsgButtonCode1, msgTitle)
        End
    End If

End Sub
```

EXHIBIT 13.19 "ErrTest_IllegalReportNumber" subroutine

retires the UserForm. See Exhibit 13.19. The error messages produced by this and the other error-checking subroutines are displayed in Exhibit 13.20.

Cross Tabulation Report Package Template File The CTRP Template file consists of eight worksheets containing report formats and another containing a set of column headers for each of the data items that can serve as a horizontal selection. As with the

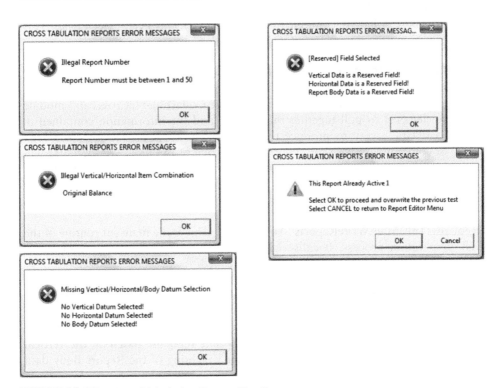

EXHIBIT 13.20 Cross Tabulation Report UserForm error messages

BSR Template file, each of these worksheets is selected, in this case, as needed, based on the vertical selection item. The horizontal selection item is then determined and the set of headers appropriate to that item is copied and pasted from the "Headers" worksheet. Upon the conclusion of the output of an individual report, the CCFG will trim all columns and rows that contain no data from the body of the report. At the conclusion of writing the entire report package, all of the template worksheets that were originally in the CTRP template file are deleted. This leaves behind only the completed reports.

Thus, to complete a CTR, we will need the following items:

- The name of the template file worksheet appropriate for the vertical data selection. There are eight different formats. They are the following:
  - Dollars
  - Percentage range 1 to 100% by 5% intervals
  - Percentage range 0 to 10% in 0.5% intervals
  - A label format
  - A three-month interval format from 0 to 60 months
  - A 12-month format from 0 to 360 months
  - A state format for the 50 states and 4 territories of the United States
  - The 150 largest MSAs
- The selection of column headers for the horizontal selection data item.
- The components of the three parts of the report title, the names of the vertical, horizontal, and Report Body data items.
- The results of the cross-tabulation exercise stored in the "gCTOutputArray".
- If the Report Body data item is dollar weighted, the sum of the dollar weightings and the base dollars to compute the weighted results on a cell-by-cell basis. This information is contained in "gCTOutputDollar" array.

Cross Tabulation Report Writer VBA Code   We have now examined the CTRFT, the CTR UserForm, and the CTR Template file. All that remains is to determine how the various VBA subroutines of the "Report_CollatEligibleCrossTab" module use these elements to pull together these pieces and the information contained in the "gLoanData" array to produce the reports. The CTR process shares a high degree of commonality with the report-writing code of the BSR. We therefore will not trace our way through as many of the subroutines as we did for that report package. We will look at only those parts of the process that relate to the differences between the two report package preparation sequences.

"RepCrossTab_MainWriteReports" Subroutine   This is the main subroutine of the CTR preparation process. It calls eight other subroutines to complete the CTR package. These are, in the order that they are called:

- "RepCrossTab_ReadFormatTable". Reads the contents of the CTRP table. It provides the CCFG with the names of the vertical, horizontal, and Report Body data items; the number of values each can assume or be stratified into; the interval values of those values; the appropriate template based on the vertical data item selection; and the flag for dollar weighting of the Report Body data item.

- ▪ **"RepCrossTab_FindTemplate"**. Finds the appropriate CTR template based on the vertical data item selection.
- ▪ **"RepCrossTab_FillInHeaders"**. Selects among the available horizontal data item selection headers and copies it onto the top of the CTR.
- ▪ **"RepCrossTab_RedimensionCTArray"**. Now that we know the sizes of the vertical and horizontal data item selections, we can redimension the "gCTOutputArray" and the "gCTOutputDollar" arrays.
- ▪ **"RepCrossTab_PopulateOutputArray"**. Performs the cross-tabulation sort with the selected data items. It first populates the "gCTLocArray" that stores the row/column location of each of the loans in the current cross-tabulation matrix. It then aggregates the data item values into the "gCTOutputArray" and the "gCTOutDollar" array, if needed, based on these locations.
- ▪ **"RepCrossTab_WriteReportBody"**. Writes the information from the "gCT-OutputArray" divided by the "gCTOutputDollar", if the data item needs to be dollar weighted, into the selected report template worksheet.
- ▪ **"RepCrossTab_TrimRowsAndCols"**. Trims the unpopulated rows and columns from the report, if requested by the user.
- ▪ **"RepCrossTab_DeleteTemplateWorksheets"**. Deletes all the original CRT Template worksheets after the last report has been written.

See Exhibit 13.21.

"RepCrossTab_PopulateOutputArray"   This subroutine is the first important subroutine called by the "RepCrossTab_MainWriteReports" subroutine. Its purpose is to perform the cross-tabulation activity based on the vertical, horizontal, and Report Body data items selected. It begins the process by calling two subroutines that take the information of each record in the gLoanData array and determining the row and column location of the record based on the data item selected and the values of the row and columns. It places this information in the array "gCTOutputLoc". These two subroutine calls are as follows:

```
'sets the row locations for every piece of loan data
Call RepCrossTab_FindLoanDataRowLocation
'sets the column locations for every piece of loan data
Call RepCrossTab_FindLoanDataColLocation
```

Once the row and column locations have been established, we can now begin the aggregation phase of the cross-tabulation process. The subroutine loops through each of the eligible loans and assigns the row and column location for that loan from the information in the "gCTOutputLoc" array. We now have the matrix location in the CTR. All that remains is to read the values from the selected Report Body data item and aggregate it to this cell location. The large "Select..Case" statement finds the selected Report Body item and reads the amount from the data field in the "gLoanData" array. This amount can now be directly aggregated if it is a pure dollar amount or dollar weighted if it requires that treatment.

The subroutine now reads the value of "gCTDolWght" for the selected Report Body data item. If the value is TRUE, the item is dollar weighted. This is accomplished by multiplying the value in the "gLoanData" record by the current balance amount

```
Sub RepCrossTab_MainWriteReports()

   If gRepMenuCrossTab Then
      'read the stratification report specifications page
      Call RepCrossTab_ReadFormatTable
      'open up the template file and rename it to the standard name plus report
      ' package prefix
      Workbooks.Open FileName:=DIR_TEMPLATE_REP & CROSSTABS_REPORTS_TEMPLATE
      ActiveWorkbook.SaveAs FileName:=OUTPUT_DIRECTORY & gRepMenuPrefix & _
         "CrossTabsFile02Test"
      'write the reports
      WorksheetCount = 0
      For irep = 1 To CROSS_TAB_MAX
         If gCTReportActive(irep) Then
            'these are abbreviations for the field #'s that comprise the items of
            ' this report.  We will use these abbreviation in the indexing of
            ' the formating data to make the VBA statements more legible and
            ' concise.
            mCTVItem = gCTVerticalItem(irep)
            mCTHItem = gCTHorizontalItem(irep)
            mCTBItem = gCTBodyItem(irep)
            'build the report
            Call RepCrossTab_FindTemplate           'select report template
            Call RepCrossTab_FillInHeaders          'write report titles and headers
            Call RepCrossTab_RedimensionCTArray     'redim CTOutput to hold results
            Call RepCrossTab_PopulateOutputArray    'accumulate the balances
            Call RepCrossTab_WriteReportBody        'write the contents of CT matrix
            If gCTTrimReport(irep) Then _
               Call RepCrossTab_TrimRowsAndCols     'trims leading/ending rows/cols
            Erase gCTOutputArray                    'clear the outut array
            Erase gCTOutputLoc                      'clear the data location array
            Erase gCTOutputDollar                   'clear the wght dollar array
         End If
      Next
      'remove blank template sheets from report file leaving only the finished
      ' cross-tabulation report set
      Call RepCrossTab_DeleteTemplateWorksheets
      ActiveWorkbook.Save
      ActiveWorkbook.Close
      gRepMenuAssumptions = True
   End If

End Sub
```

EXHIBIT 13.21 "RepCrossTab_MainWriteReports" subroutine

of the loan. This is then added to the "gCTOutputArray" value for that row/column location. The amount of the current balance of the loan is also accumulated to the row/column location of the "gCTOutputDollar" array. We will then divide the (gCTOutputArray/gCTOutputDollar) to arrive at the weighted average statistic we desire. The subroutine has now provided us with all the cross-tabulated results. See Exhibit 13.22.

"RepCrossTab_FindLoanDataRowLocation" Subroutine In our discussion immediately above, we stated that the subroutine "RepCrossTab_FindLoanData RowLocation" is used to determine the row location of the Report Body selected data item. To perform this action the subroutine refers to the value of the vertical data item selected, "mCTVItem", and then based on that, calls a sorting subroutine based on the type of data for this item. See Exhibit 13.23.

```
Sub RepCrossTab_PopulateOutputArray()

Dim amt      As Double
Dim irow     As Integer
Dim icol     As Integer

    'sets the row  locations for every piece of loan data
    Call RepCrossTab_FindLoanDataRowLocation
    'sets the column locations for every piece of loan data
    Call RepCrossTab_FindLoanDataColLocation
    'populates the gCTOutputArray, and if the data item in the body of the report
    ' needs to be dollar weighted, (which most do), builds the numerator by
    ' multiplying the statistic by the current balance, and the denominator by
    ' accumulating the current balance amouts in the gCTOutputDollar.
    For iloan = 1 To gTotalLoans
        irow = gCTOutputLoc(iloan, 1)    'find the row location of the loan data
        icol = gCTOutputLoc(iloan, 2)    'find the column location of the loan data
        'add loan data to the Cross Tabs matrix based on mRow and MCol values
        Select Case gCTBodyItem(irep)
            Case Is = 1: amt = 1     'loan count per grid square
            Case Is = FD_ORIGBAL:    amt = gLoanData(FD_ORIGBAL, iloan)
            Case Is = FD_CURRBAL:    amt = gLoanData(FD_CURRBAL, iloan)
            Case Is = FD_ORIGLTV:    amt = gLoanData(FD_ORIGLTV, iloan)
            Case Is = FD_CURRLTV:    amt = gLoanData(FD_CURRLTV, iloan)
            Case Is = FD_ORIGTERM:   amt = gLoanData(FD_ORIGTERM, iloan)
            Case Is = FD_REMTERM:    amt = gLoanData(FD_REMTERM, iloan)
            Case Is = FD_SEASON:     amt = gLoanData(FD_SEASON, iloan)
            Case Is = FD_CURRRATE:   amt = gLoanData(FD_CURRRATE, iloan)
            Case Is = FD_ORIGAPP:    amt = gLoanData(FD_ORIGAPP, iloan)
            Case Is = FD_CURRAPP:    amt = gLoanData(FD_CURRAPP, iloan)
            Case Is = FD_FICO:       amt = gLoanData(FD_FICO, iloan)
            Case Is = FD_MDBTTOINC:  amt = gLoanData(FD_MDBTTOINC, iloan)
            Case Is = FD_TDBTTOINC:  amt = gLoanData(FD_TDBTTOINC, iloan)
            Case Is = FD_THIRDPARTY: amt = gLoanData(FD_THIRDPARTY, iloan)
            Case Is = FD_SERVERATE:  amt = gLoanData(FD_SERVERATE, iloan)
        End Select
        'if the data item that makes up the body of the report needs to be dollar
        ' weighted do so at this time
        If gCTDolWght(mCTBItem) Then
            'building the numerator for dollar weighted statistics
            amt = amt * gLoanData(FD_CURRBAL, iloan)
            'building the demoninator for dollar weighted statistics
            gCTOutputDollar(irow, icol) = _
                gCTOutputDollar(irow, icol) + gLoanData(iloan, FD_CURRBAL)
        End If
        'building the denominator
        gCTOutputArray(irow, icol) = gCTOutputArray(irow, icol) + amt
    Next iloan

End Sub
```

EXHIBIT 13.22 "RepCrossTab_PopulateOutputArray" subroutine

We will look at two of these Row Location–finding subroutines, the one for dollars and the one for MSAs.

"RepCrossTab_WriteDollarBasedLocation" If we have a nationally diverse portfolio of home mortgages, we can expect a wide range in the current and original loan balances of the portfolio. We might suspect an even wider range of values in respect to original and current appraisal values.

If we set up a dollar balance table of uniform steps, we find we have an immediate problem. If the initial stratification levels for the low-balance loans, $0 to $200,000,

```
Sub RepCrossTab_FindLoanDataColLocation()

    'call the axis appropriate slotting suproutine to determine the location in
    ' the gCTOutputLoc array for this piece of data.  The use of the "COL_LOC"
    ' constant will place the data by column position.  You will notice that the
    ' State and MSA formats are not available for a column display.
    Select Case gCTTemplate(mCTHItem)
        Case Is = "Label":      Call RepCrossTab_WriteLabelBasedLocation(COL_LOC)
        Case Is = "Dollar":     Call RepCrossTab_WriteDollarBasedLocation(COL_LOC)
        Case Is = "Percent10":  Call RepCrossTab_WritePct10BasedLocation(COL_LOC)
        Case Is = "Percent100": Call RepCrossTab_WritePct100BasedLocation(COL_LOC)
        Case Is = "Percent200": Call RepCrossTab_WritePct200BasedLocation(COL_LOC)
        Case Is = "Month3":     Call RepCrossTab_WriteMonth3BasedLocation(COL_LOC)
        Case Is = "Month12":    Call RepCrossTab_WriteMonth12BasedLocation(COL_LOC)
        Case Is = "FICO":       Call RepCrossTab_WriteFICOBasedLocation(COL_LOC)
    End Select

End Sub
```

EXHIBIT 13.23 "RepCrossTab_FindLoanDataRowLocation" subroutine

is to be meaningful—say, a value of $10,000—we will end up with a prohibitive number of steps by the time we reach stratification levels approaching $1 million. We will thus vary the interval over a series of value ranges for the Dollar Report format. These will now be as follows:

- $0 to $200,000 balances, steps by $10,000
- $200,000 to $500,000 balances, steps by $50,000
- $500,000 to $1,000,000, steps by $100,000
- $1,000,000 and up, steps by $250,000

We can now see now the "RepCrossTab_WriteDollarBasedLocation" subroutine performs this stratification. Based on the value of the variable "BalAmt", a "Select..Case" statement branches to one of three cutoffs. The first is less than $200 million, the second is less than $500 million, and third is everything above $500 million. The subroutine then divides the "BalAmt" by the interval step. For the second and third choices, we must net out the earlier category threshold. To determine the stratification levels for different balances, we see:

```
               $7,000/$10,000 = 0.70 apply round up = 1
              $87,000/$10,000 = 8.70 apply round up = 9
    ($375,000-$200,000)/$50,000 = 3.50 apply round up + 20 = 24
    ($875,000-$500,000)/$100,000 = 3.75 apply round up +26 = 30
($1,375,000-$1,000,000)/$250,000 = 1.50 apply round up +31 = 33
```

See Exhibit 13.24.

"RepCrossTab_WriteMSABasedLocation" We have to perform a very different type of stratification assignment process when dealing with the MSA Cross Tabulation Report. Here we have to match the MSA code contained in a loan record to a list of 150 MSA codes. The MSA codes in the report are sorted first by state code and then numerically by the MSA code within the state. If we simply search the list in sequential order, we could, in the worst case, read 149 MSA codes before finding the match we seek. To speed the process up dramatically, we will read the state code,

```
Sub RepCrossTab_WriteDollarBasedLocation(loc_code As Integer)

Dim BalAmt  As Double

    If loc_code = ROW_LOC Then idata = mCTVItem
    If loc_code = COL_LOC Then idata = mCTHItem
    For iloan = 1 To gTotalLoans
        If gLoanScreen(iloan, FD_SCREEN_ALL_OK) = REC_OKFORALL Then
            'assign the dollar balance based on the variable we are sorting
            Select Case idata
                Case Is = FD_ORIGBAL: BalAmt = gLoanData(iloan, FD_ORIGBAL)
                Case Is = FD_CURRBAL: BalAmt = gLoanData(iloan, FD_CURRBAL)
                Case Is = FD_ORIGAPP: BalAmt = gLoanData(iloan, FD_ORIGAPP)
                Case Is = FD_CURRAPP: BalAmt = gLoanData(iloan, FD_CURRAPP)
            End Select
            'find the sort location
            Select Case BalAmt
                Case Is <= 200000
                    slot = Application.RoundUp(BalAmt / gCTValInt(idata), 0)
                Case Is <= 500000
                    slot = 20 + Application.RoundUp((BalAmt - 200000) / 50000, 0)
                Case Is <= 1000000
                    slot = 26 + Application.RoundUp((BalAmt - 500000) / 100000, 0)
                Case Is <= 2500000
                    slot = 31 + Application.RoundUp((BalAmt - 1000000) / 250000, 0)
            End Select
            gCTOutputLoc(iloan, loc_code) = slot
        End If
    Next iloan

End Sub
```

EXHIBIT 13.24 "RepCrossTab_WriteDollarBasedLocation" subroutine

a numeric value, and then jump the list to the nearest of a series of ordered landing points in the 150-item list.

The "Select..Case" statement reads the state code numeric value and tests one after another of the cases until it arrives at the landing point that is the closest before the value of the current state code. We then search the 15 to 20 MSAs in that interval. We arrive at the exact match and assign the value. In a worst-case scenario, we test ten landing points in the "Select..Case" ladder and then 18 individual MSA to match the 150th MSA, a total of 28 tests versus 149! See Exhibit 13.25.

"RepCrossTab_WriteReportBody"   The Report Body data item has now been aggregated and assigned to the proper row/column location in the cross-tabulation matrix "gCTOutputArray". All that remains is to print out the values into a report. The "RepCrossTab_WriteReportBody" does this. Except for some minor cleanup to the reports performed by the "RepCrossTab_TrimRowsAndCols" subroutine, we are finished.

See Exhibit 13.26.

Pair of Completed Cross Tabulation Reports   The following exhibits display finished Cross Tabulation Reports. The first is a dollar-stratification report that displays current balance ranges while the second is a labels report that presents the MSA in the vertical axis.

```
Sub RepCrossTab_WriteMSABasedLocation(loc_code As Integer)

Dim startRow         As Integer 'break the list into 10 segments to speed up search

    'run through the list, find a match between the codes and immediately exit
    ' the loop.  The list is 150 names long so we have set up a "divide and
    ' conquer" helper based on the State code of the loan.
    For iloan = 1 To gTotalLoans
        If gLoanScreen(iloan, FD_SCREEN_ALL_OK) = REC_OKFORALL Then
            Select Case gLoanData(iloan, FD_STATECODE)
                Case Is < 5:   startRow = 1      'pre California
                Case Is < 7:   startRow = 10     'pre Connecticut
                Case Is < 10:  startRow = 28     'pre Georgia
                Case Is < 16:  startRow = 45     'pre Kansas
                Case Is < 22:  startRow = 60     'pre Michigan
                Case Is < 29:  startRow = 71     'pre Nebraska
                Case Is < 35:  startRow = 91     'pre Ohio
                Case Is < 38:  startRow = 103    'pre Pennsylvannia
                Case Is < 43:  startRow = 116    'pre Texas
                Case Else:     startRow = 132    'Texas to end of list
            End Select
            'search a smaller part of the total list
            If gLoanData(iloan, FD_MSACODE) = 0 Then
                'MSA code missing or non existent
                gCTOutputLoc(iloan, loc_code) = 1
            Else
                For iMSA = startRow To TOTAL_MSAS
                    If gLoanData(iloan, FD_MSACODE) = gCTMSACodes(iMSA) Then
                        gCTOutputLoc(iloan, loc_code) = iMSA + 1
                        Exit For
                    End If
                    'was not found in the loop therefore not on the list
                    gCTOutputLoc(iloan, loc_code) = 1
                Next iMSA
            End If
        End If
    Next iloan

End Sub
```

EXHIBIT 13.25   "RepCrossTab_WriteMSABasedLocation" subroutine

```
Sub RepCrossTab_WriteReportBody()

Dim amt     As Double

    Sheets(mActRepSheetName).Select
    cur_row = 11
    For irow = 1 To gCTNumberRows(irep)
        cur_col = 6
        For icol = 1 To gCTNumberCols(irep)
            'test if this is a dollar weighted data item, if it is divide by
            ' the value of the gCTOutputDollar array to weight the statistic
            If gCTDolWght(irep) Then
                gCTOutputArray(irow, icol) = _
                    gCTOutputArray(irow, icol) / gCTOutputDollar(irow, icol)
            End If
            Cells(cur_row, cur_col).Value = gCTOutputArray(irow, icol)
            cur_col = cur_col + 1
        Next icol
        cur_row = cur_row + 1
    Next irow
    Calculate

End Sub
```

EXHIBIT 13.26   "RepCrossTab_WriteReportBody" subroutine

Cross Tabulation Report #2
Vertical Category = Current Balance
Horizontal Category = Mortgage Type
Report Statistic = Original Balance

Current Loan Balance Range	Totals		1 Fixed Rate	2 Standard ARM	3 Hybrid ARM	5 Fixed Rate Balloon	6 ARM Balloon
	36,150,000 100.00%		12,187,700 33.71%	15,256,500 42.20%	3,869,000 10.70%	2,233,100 6.18%	2,603,700 7.20%
10,001 to 20,000	137,800	0.38%	67,000	24,400	46,400		
20,001 to 30,000	686,200	1.90%	443,100	39,900	63,600	40,800	98,800
30,001 to 40,000	1,311,600	3.63%	675,100	351,200	84,000	144,500	56,800
40,001 to 50,000	2,125,100	5.88%	749,200	1,083,400	173,700	118,800	
50,001 to 60,000	2,714,700	7.51%	888,700	1,363,600	180,400	80,400	201,600
60,001 to 70,000	2,175,100	6.02%	1,003,000	650,700	383,200		138,200
70,001 to 80,000	1,465,400	4.05%	1,030,900	170,600	167,900		96,000
80,001 to 90,000	93,600	0.26%	93,600				
90,001 to 100,000	744,300	2.06%		625,300		119,000	
100,001 to 110,000	382,000	1.06%	271,000	111,000			
110,001 to 120,000	370,200	1.02%	118,400	125,400	126,400		
120,001 to 130,000	537,200	1.49%	409,200			128,000	
130,001 to 140,000	152,500	0.42%		152,500			
140,001 to 150,000	1,779,700	4.92%	894,900	563,200	148,000		173,600
150,001 to 160,000	636,200	1.76%	158,000	313,000	165,200		
160,001 to 170,000	1,739,900	4.81%	806,600	191,700	741,600		
170,001 to 180,000	664,000	1.84%	218,400				445,600
180,001 to 190,000	218,400	0.60%		218,400			
190,001 to 200,000	451,400	1.25%	451,400				
200,001 to 250,000	2,169,900	6.00%	256,000	1,463,100	238,000	212,800	
250,001 to 300,000	3,576,300	9.89%	1,765,800	904,100	609,600	296,800	
300,001 to 350,000	1,426,600	3.95%	743,400	683,200			
350,001 to 400,000	1,558,400	4.31%	403,000	779,200			376,200
400,001 to 450,000	897,000	2.48%		448,500			448,500
500,001 to 600,000	1,136,800	3.14%		568,400			568,400
600,001 to 700,000	1,482,000	4.10%	741,000		741,000		
800,001 to 900,000	4,023,600	11.13%		2,931,600		1,092,000	
1,250,001 to 1,500,000	1,494,100	4.13%		1,494,100			

EXHIBIT 13.27 Cross Tabulation Report dollar stratifications

See Exhibits 13.27 and 13.28.

After the Smoke Has Cleared The Cross Tabulation Report is a widely used and valuable analysis tool. Pay attention to the techniques and how the four pieces of the CTRP were used in tandem to produce the reports. We were able to put together a flexible and powerful report writer using the following:

1 UserForm

222 Lines of UserForm VBA code (counting blank lines and comments)

1 Excel Worksheet containing the CTRP Table

1 Excel report Template file containing 9 worksheets

570 Lines of VBA code (counting blank lines and comments)

Think about how to make all these elements work for you in the future.

Cross Tabulation Report #2
Vertical Category = MSA Code
Horizontal Category = Mortgage Type
Report Statistic = Current Balance

Rank	Code	Metropolitan Statistical Area Name	State	Totals (0)	%	Fixed Rate (1)	Standard ARM (2)	Hybrid ARM (3)	Fixed Rate Balloon (4)	ARM Balloon (5)
				31,603,806	100.00%	10,455,647	13,471,120	3,481,035	1,887,453	2,308,552
						33.08%	42.62%	11.01%	5.97%	7.30%
		No MSA Data or MSA Not on List		4,787,729	15.15%	2,093,543	1,293,525	1,038,326	225,378	136,959
10	12540	Bakersfield	CA	3,245,029	10.27%	809,171	1,018,997	185,365	201,825	1,029,671
11	23420	Fresno	CA	563,307	1.78%	349,721	92,137	66,330	27,891	27,228
12	31100	Los Angeles-Long Beach-Santa Ana	CA	1,222,107	3.87%	937,397	284,711			
13	33700	Modesto	CA	1,610,556	5.10%	435,631	1,157,450	17,476		
14	37100	Oxnard-Thousand Oaks-Ventura	CA	885,863	2.80%	335,342	366,251	35,520		148,750
15	40140	Riverside-San Bernardino-Ontario	CA	2,607,404	8.25%	1,070,568	1,253,093	283,743		
16	40900	Sacramento--Arden-Arcade--Roseville	CA	895,623	2.83%	532,770	362,853			
17	41500	Salinas	CA	808,193	2.56%	121,727	575,835			110,632
18	41740	San Diego-Carlsbad-San Marcos	CA	404,513	1.28%	241,446	133,950	29,117		
19	41860	San Francisco-Oakland-Fremont	CA	1,309,422	4.14%	125,041	1,139,920	44,461		
20	41940	San Jose-Sunnyvale-Santa Clara	CA	671,938	2.13%	50,485	230,974	343,124	47,355	
21	42060	Santa Barbara-Santa Maria-Goleta	CA	402,488	1.27%	199,413	175,847			27,228
22	42220	Santa Rosa-Petaluma	CA	1,359,772	4.30%	498,227	538,245	19,859	126,911	176,530
23	44700	Stockton	CA	1,802,179	5.70%	413,661	1,188,493	160,579	39,445	
24	46700	Vallejo-Fairfield	CA	957,857	3.03%	363,828	101,484	105,707		386,838
25	47300	Visalia-Porterville	CA	1,907,708	6.04%	60,837		675,724	1,171,147	
26	17820	Colorado Springs	CO	824,362	2.61%	517,822	253,223	53,317		
27	19740	Denver-Aurora	CO	714,658	2.26%	66,849	303,752	118,764		225,273
28	14860	Bridgeport-Stamford-Norwalk	CT	926,770	2.93%	39,135	848,191			39,445
29	25540	Hartford-West Hartford-East Hartford	CT	716,842	2.27%	385,667	331,176			
30	35300	New Haven-Milford	CT	465,775	1.47%	216,013	91,633	158,128		
32	14600	Bradenton-Sarasota-Venice	FL	72,114	0.23%	72,114				
33	15980	Cape Coral-Fort Myers	FL	40,090	0.13%	40,090				
34	19660	Deltona-Daytona Beach-Ormond Beach	FL	54,856	0.17%		54,856			
35	27260	Jacksonville	FL	47,501	0.15%				47,501	
36	29460	Lakeland-Winter Haven	FL	47,191	0.15%		47,191			
37	33100	Miami-Fort Lauderdale-Pompano Beach	FL	184,259	0.58%		184,259			
38	34940	Naples-Marco Island	FL	145,496	0.46%			145,496		
39	36100	Ocala	FL	238,255	0.75%	238,255				
40	36740	Orlando-Kissimmee	FL	195,056	0.62%	195,056				
41	37340	Palm Bay-Melbourne-Titusville	FL	1,401,406	4.43%		1,401,406			
42	37860	Pensacola-Ferry Pass-Brent	FL	41,667	0.13%		41,667			
43	38940	Port St. Lucie	FL	45,839	0.15%	45,839				
44	45220	Tallahassee	FL		0.00%					
45	45300	Tampa-St. Petersburg-Clearwater	FL	-	0.00%					

EXHIBIT 13.28 Cross Tabulation Report selected state/MSA stratification

Loan Listing Report

The Loan Listing Report is merely a formatted version of the collateral file. It is produced by the VBA code in the "Report_LoanListing" module. The module contains three subroutines:

1. "RepLoanListing_MainWriteReports". The main subroutine finds the template file, opens it, and saves it under the user-specified name. It then calls the report-writing subroutine "RepLoanListing_FinalLoanStatusReport" that produces two files, one with the eligible and the other with the ineligible collateral. Last it saves and closes the report file.
2. "RepLoanListing_FinalLoanStatusReport". This subroutine produces a listing of either an eligible or ineligible Loan Listing worksheet report.
3. "RepLoanListing_TrimOutputReport". This subroutine trims any unneeded rows from the bottom of the report file after all the loans have been written.

The organization, VBA code, and execution of the report-writing code for the Loan Listing Report is very simple and straightforward. We will not examine it explicitly here.

GEOGRAPHIC/DEMOGRAPHIC REPORTS

Aside from the Base and Cross Tabulation Stratification Report Packages, it is important to address the need to examine the collateral of the portfolio along other lines. One of the major areas of interest is the characteristics of the geographic dispersion of the loans. We need to know where they are, how many are in each location, and the accompanying demographics of these subpopulations. To this end, the CCFG has a number of Geographic Reports that seek to meet this need.

Geographic Stratification Report

The Geographic Stratification Report (GSR) is not so much a single report as it is a collection of microreports, gathered together to make a bigger report. We will hope that the "sum is greater than the parts."

Report Format As just mentioned, the GSR is intended to be a one-page collection of a number of small schedules. Each of these schedules is, in effect, a microreport. Due to their small size and limited scope, each of these component schedules hardly merits a separate worksheet and report name. When they are combined, they can, however, present a very substantial picture of the collateral composition of a given geographic region, either at the state or the MSA level. The component reports, from left to right, top to bottom, of the Geographic Stratification Report are as follows:

1. Current Balances by Property
2. Number of Loans, Current Balances, and % Current Balances, State Total and all MSAs of the State
3. Current and Original Balances and %, by Current Loan, to Value

4. Number of Loans, Current Balances, and % Current Balances by FICO score
5. Number of Loans, Current Balances, and % Current Balances by Bankruptcy History
6. Number of Loans, Current Balances, and % Current Balances by First-Time Homeownership
7. Number of Loans, Current Balances, and % Current Balances by Financing Purpose
8. Cross Tabulation Report, Number of Loans and Current Balances by Occupancy Code and Property Type
9. Cross Tabulation Report, Number of Loans and Current Balances by Servicer Rating and Property Type
10. Cross Tabulation Report, Number of Loans and Current Balances by Escrow Agreement and Property Type
11. Number of Loans, Current Balances, and % Current Balances by Documentation Package
12. Number of Loans, Current Balances, and % Current Balances by Original Appraisal Type
13. Continuation section of Number of Loans, Current Balances, and % Current Balances, for MSAs #5 to #12
14. Continuation section of Number of Loans, Current Balances, and % Current Balances, for MSAs #13 to #16

See Exhibit 13.29.

Geographic Stratification Report Template Files   There are two template files for this report. The first is a state-level report, "GeographicStateStratTemplate" and the second is "GeographicMSAStratTemplate". The layout of the state-level report is displayed in Exhibit 13.26. The MSA-level report shares nearly all of the sub-reports of the state-level report. The upper MSA section is replaced with a distribution of Current Balances by Mortgage Type, while the two lower sections of MSA distributions are, of course, omitted in their entirety.

VBA Code   Almost all of the code in this report-writing package is a simple aggregation subroutine. Having just looked at a lot of much more complicated aggregation VBA code, we will uncharacteristically leave this one to the reader. I will walk you through the subroutine "RepGeoStrat_MainWriteReports" and leave the rest in what I assume are your now increasingly capable hands.

"RepGeoStrat_MainWriteReports" Subroutine   This subroutine contains a loop that executes twice, once to write the state-level GSRs for the selected states and again to write the MSA-level GSRs. In that the templates for these reports are in two separate files, we will open the template files only once we are inside the report-specific subroutine. Once these reports have been completed, they are saved and closed and the loop moves to the next set of reports or terminates. See Exhibit 13.30.

State Name

Property Type

	# of Loans	Current Balance	% Curr Balance
No data			#DIV/0!
Single			#DIV/0!
Multi 2			#DIV/0!
Condo			#DIV/0!
Coop			#DIV/0!
Multi <=4			#DIV/0!
Multi <=10			#DIV/0!
Multi 10+			#DIV/0!
High Rise			#DIV/0!
Mixed			#DIV/0!
Totals	0	0	#DIV/0!

Loan-to-Value Ratios

	Current		Original	
	# Loans	Curr $	# Loans	Curr $
120%+				
110%				
100%				
95%				
90%				
85%				
80%				
75%				
70%				
-70%				
Totals	0	0	0	0

Geographic Distribution by Mortgage Type

Additional MSA's Below

Mortgage Amortization Type	No MSA Indicated			State Level			MSA #1			MSA #2			MSA #3			MSA #4		
	Number of Loans	Curr Balance	% Curr Balance	Number of Loans	Curr Balance	% Curr Balance	Number of Loans	Curr Balance	% Curr Balance	Number of Loans	Curr Balance	% Curr Balance	Number of Loans	Curr Balance	% Curr Balance	Number of Loans	Curr Balance	% Curr Balance
Fixed Rate			#DIV/0!			#DIV/0!			#DIV/0!			#DIV/0!			#DIV/0!			#DIV/0!
Standard ARM			#DIV/0!			#DIV/0!			#DIV/0!			#DIV/0!			#DIV/0!			#DIV/0!
Hybrid ARM			#DIV/0!			#DIV/0!			#DIV/0!			#DIV/0!			#DIV/0!			#DIV/0!
Balloon Fixed			#DIV/0!			#DIV/0!			#DIV/0!			#DIV/0!			#DIV/0!			#DIV/0!
Balloon ARM			#DIV/0!			#DIV/0!			#DIV/0!			#DIV/0!			#DIV/0!			#DIV/0!
Totals	0	0	#DIV/0!	0	0	#DIV/0!	0	0	#DIV/0!	0	0	#DIV/0!	0	0	#DIV/0!	0	0	#DIV/0!

Debt Ratios (Total & Mortgage)

	Debt to Income		Mort to Income	
	# Loans	Curr $	# Loans	Curr $
100%				
90%				
80%				
70%				
60%				
50%				
40%				
30%				
20%				
10%				
Totals	0	0	0	0

FICO Scores

	# of Loans	Current Balance	% Curr Balance
750+			#DIV/0!
700			#DIV/0!
650			#DIV/0!
625			#DIV/0!
600			#DIV/0!
575			#DIV/0!
550			#DIV/0!
525			#DIV/0!
500			#DIV/0!
-500			#DIV/0!
Totals	0	0	#DIV/0!

Bankruptcy History

	# of Loans	Current Balance	% Curr Balance
No Data			#DIV/0!
Never			#DIV/0!
Discharge			#DIV/0!
Filed			#DIV/0!
Current			#DIV/0!
Totals	0	0	#DIV/0!

First Time Homeowner

	# of Loans	Current Balance	% Curr Balance
No Data			#DIV/0!
Yes			#DIV/0!
No			#DIV/0!
Totals	0	0	#DIV/0!

Financing Purpose

	# of Loans	Current Balance	% Curr Balance
No Data			#DIV/0!
Purchase			#DIV/0!
Refi			#DIV/0!
Restruct			#DIV/0!
Equity			#DIV/0!
Invest			#DIV/0!
Totals	0	0	#DIV/0!

EXHIBIT 13.29 State-level Geographic Stratification Report template (upper portion of report)

Property Type By Occupancy Code

Property Type	Owner Occupied		Owner Seasonal		Owner 2nd Home		Non-Owner Rental		No Data	
	Number of Loans	Curr Balance	Number of Loans	Curr Balance	Number of Loans	Curr Balance	Number of Loans	Curr Balance	Number of Loans	Curr Balance
No Data										
Single Family										
Multi 2 Units										
Condo										
Coop										
Multi <= 4 Units										
Multi <= 10 Units										
Multi 10+ Units										
High Rise										
Mixed Use										
Totals	0	0	0	0	0	0	0	0	0	0

Property Type By Servicer Rating

Property Type	Excellent		Very Good		Average		Below Average		Poor		No Data	
	Number of Loans	Curr Balance	Number of Loans	Curr Balance	Number of Loans	Curr Balance	Number of Loans	Curr Balance	Number of Loans	Curr Balance	Number of Loans	Curr Balance
No Data												
Single Family												
Multi 2 Units												
Condo												
Coop												
Multi <= 4 Units												
Multi <= 10 Units												
Multi 10+ Units												
High Rise												
Mixed Use												
Totals	0	0	0	0	0	0	0	0	0	0	0	0

Property Type By Escrow

Property Type	No Escrow		Property Tax Only		Insurance Only		Tax & Insurance		No Data	
	Number of Loans	Curr Balance	Number of Loans	Curr Balance	Number of Loans	Curr Balance	Number of Loans	Curr Balance	Number of Loans	Current Balance
No Data										
Single Family										
Multi 2 Units										
Condo										
Coop										
Multi <= 4 Units										
Multi <= 10 Units										
Multi 10+ Units										
High Rise										
Mixed Use										
Totals	0	0	0	0	0	0	0	0	0	0

Appraisal Type

Appraisal Type	Original		Current	
	Number of Loans	Curr Balance	Number of Loans	Curr Balance
No Data				
Walk Through				
Outside				
Drive By				
Tax Assessment				
Other				
None				
Totals	0	0	0	0

Documentation

Documentation Package	No Escrow	
	Number of Loans	Curr Balance
No Data		
Full Docs		
Partial Docs		
Alt A		
No Income		
No Assets		
No Inc No Assets		
Totals	0	0

ADDITIONAL MSA SECTION

Geographic Distribution by Mortgage Type

Property Type	MSA #5			MSA #6			MSA #7			MSA #8			MSA #9			MSA #10			MSA #11			MSA #12		
	Number of Loans	Curr Balance	% Curr Balance	Number of Loans	Curr Balance	% Curr Balance	Number of Loans	Curr Balance	% Curr Balance	Number of Loans	Curr Balance	% Curr Balance	Number of Loans	Curr Balance	% Curr Balance	Number of Loans	Curr Balance	% Curr Balance	Number of Loans	Curr Balance	% Curr Balance	Number of Loans	Curr Balance	% Curr Balance
Fixed Rate			#DIV/0!			#DIV/0!			#DIV/0!			#DIV/0!			#DIV/0!			#DIV/0!			#DIV/0!			#DIV/0!
Standard ARM			#DIV/0!			#DIV/0!			#DIV/0!			#DIV/0!			#DIV/0!			#DIV/0!			#DIV/0!			#DIV/0!
Hybrid ARM			#DIV/0!			#DIV/0!			#DIV/0!			#DIV/0!			#DIV/0!			#DIV/0!			#DIV/0!			#DIV/0!
Balloon Fixed			#DIV/0!			#DIV/0!			#DIV/0!			#DIV/0!			#DIV/0!			#DIV/0!			#DIV/0!			#DIV/0!
Balloon ARM			#DIV/0!			#DIV/0!			#DIV/0!			#DIV/0!			#DIV/0!			#DIV/0!			#DIV/0!			#DIV/0!
Totals	0	0	#DIV/0!	0	0	#DIV/0!	0	0	#DIV/0!	0	0	#DIV/0!	0	0	#DIV/0!	0	0	#DIV/0!	0	0	#DIV/0!	0	0	#DIV/0!

EXHIBIT 13.29 State-level Geographic Stratification Report template (lower portion of report)

```
Sub RepGeoStrat_MainWriteReports()

    For mGeoSwitch = 1 To 4
        Select Case mGeoSwitch
            Case Is = STATES_REPORT:   Call RepGeoStrat_WriteStatesReport
            Case Is = MSA_REPORT:      Call RepGeoStrat_WriteMSAsReport
            Case Is = NO_MSA_REPORT:   Call RepGeoStrat_WriteNoMSAreport
            Case Is = NATIONAL_REPORT: Call RepGeoStrat_WriteUSReport
        End Select
    Next mGeoSwitch

End Sub
```

EXHIBIT 13.30 "RepGeoStrat_MainWriteReports" subroutine

"RepGeoStrat_WriteStatesReport" Subroutine We will now examine one of the two report-writing subroutines, the "RepGeoStrat_WriteStatesReport". To produce the state-level report, the subroutine performs the following steps.

1. Calls "RepGeoStrat_ReadStateInformation". This subroutine loads a number of arrays with all the information about the state and the MSAs in it that is available on the "MSAReportInfo" worksheet of the CCFG.
2. Finds, opens, and renames the template file "GeographicStateStratTemplate" to the report file name we have designated.
3. Calls "RepGeoStrat_SetupStateLevelWorksheets", which sets up copies of the template state-level report for each selected state and names the spreadsheet using the two-letter postal code of the state.
4. Calls "RepGeoStrat_CreateSheetRangeNames", which sets up a series of worksheet unique range named for each of the subreport sections of the report.
5. Enters a loop that will cycle through the number of selected states.
6. Calls "RepGeoStrat_EraseSingleReportArrays", which erases the arrays that will hold the contents of each of the subreports.
7. Selects the current (loop value) state to report worksheet.
8. Calls "RepGeoStrat_AccumGeoInfo", which aggregates the MSA information for the state MSA list.
9. Calls "RepGeoStrat_IsThereCollateral", which tests to see if there is any collateral for the state. If there is, it performs Steps 10, 11, and 12.
10. Calls "RepGeoStrat_AccumCreditInfo", which aggregates the information for the LTV, Debt Ratio, FICO Scores, Bankruptcy History, Financing Purpose, and Documentation Package subreports.
11. Calls "RepGeoStrat_AccumPropInfo", which aggregates the data for the Property Type and the three Cross Tabulation Reports.
12. Calls "RepGeoStrat_WriteGeoStateReport", which outputs the contents of the arrays to each of the subreports.
13. Calls "RepGeoStrat_NoCollateral", which marks the selected state worksheet to indicate that there is no collateral in this state.
14. Loops to the next selected state.

See Exhibit 13.31.

```
Sub RepGeoStrat_WriteStatesReport()
    If gRepMenuGeoStatesRep Then
        'reads State Level information
        Call RepGeoStrat_ReadStateInformation
        Workbooks.Open FileName:=GEOSTATE_TEMPLATE
        ActiveWorkbook.SaveAs FileName:= _
            OUTPUT_DIRECTORY & gRepMenuPrefix & "GeoStratStateReport"
        Call RepGeoStrat_SetUpAllWorksheets      'one per state sel
        Call RepGeoStrat_CreateStateSheetNameRanges          'names per worksheet
        For iState = 1 To mNumActiveStates
            Call RepGeoStrat_EraseSingleReportArrays 'clear the accumulation arrays
            Sheets(mGeoStratName(iState)).Select   'select the state worksheet
            Call RepGeoStrat_AccumGeoInfo(iState, 0)
            go_ok = RepGeoStrat_IsThereCollateral
            If go_ok Then
                Call RepGeoStrat_AccumCreditInfo(iState, 0)
                Call RepGeoStrat_AccumPropTypeInfo(iState, 0)
                Call RepGeoStrat_WriteGeoStateReport 'write the state report
            Else
                Call RepGeoStrat_MarkWorksheetNoCollateral(iState, 0)
            End If
            Range("A1").Select
        Next iState
        ActiveWorkbook.Save
        ActiveWorkbook.Close
    End If
End Sub
```

EXHIBIT 13.31   "RepGeoStrat_WriteStatesReports" subroutine

The formating and coding techniques in this report are designed to demonstrate how to build separate and distinct subsections to reports and how to manage their calculation and output.

Completed Geographic Stratification Report   Exhibit 13.32 is a completed Geographic Stratification Report at the state level.

PRESENTATION REPORTS

Presentation reports are designed to impress and inform. As such they are usually highly audience specific in both format and content. An example of such a report is presented below. These reports are designed to fit inside of a larger and more comprehensive package. They are not throw-up-on-the-wall reports. Their content and detail are far too dense for a general presentation. These reports would be used in detailed discussions with external parties interested in examining specific facets of a portfolio from the ground up.

Portfolio Presentation Report Package

The Collateral Presentation Report package is a group of four reports that are designed to be placed directly into presentations for external parties. These four reports contain a collection of tabular and graphic displays that summarize various aspects of the collateral pool at a high level of abstraction.

The four reports of the package are:

1. **Distribution of Current Balances by MSA.** This report contains two tables of data and a single graphic. The first table is the state-level distribution of the

Connecticut All Loans

Property Type

	# of Loans	Current Balance	% Curr Balance
No data	1	335,090	2.0%
Single	59	15,014,635	90.2%
Multi 2	1	132,222	0.8%
Condo	2	778,072	4.7%
Coop	2	387,505	2.3%
Multi <=10			0.0%
Multi 10+			0.0%
High Rise			0.0%
Mixed			0.0%
Totals	65	16,647,523	100.0%

Loan-to-Value Ratios

	Current		Original	
	#Loans	Curr $	#Loans	Curr $
120%+	6	1,516,888		
110%	6	1,242,903		
100%	10	2,890,774		
95%	5	850,576	4	807,694
90%	9	3,717,622	14	4,610,483
85%	5	834,082	9	1,188,108
80%	15	3,507,074	31	8,171,925
75%	5	580,164	5	65,073
70%	2	1,305,675	2	1,167,576
-70%	2	201,765	4	636,664
Totals	65	16,647,523	65	16,647,523

Geographic Distribution by Mortgage Type

Mortgage Amortization Type	State Level			No MSA Indicated			Bridgeport-Stamford-Norwalk			Htford-West Hartford-East Hartf			New Haven-Milford		
	Number of Loans	Curr Balance	% Curr Balance	Number of Loans	Balance	% Curr Balance	Number of Loans	Curr Balance	% Curr Balance	Number of Loans	Curr Balance	% Curr Balance	Number of Loans	Curr Balance	% Curr Balance
Fixed Rate			0.0%			0.0%			0.0%			0.0%			0.0%
Standard ARM	65	16,647,523	100.0%	19	5,352,859	100.0%	13	2,830,994	100.0%	21	5,346,223	100.0%	12	3,117,447	100.0%
Hybrid ARM			0.0%			0.0%			0.0%			0.0%			0.0%
Balloon Fixed			0.0%			0.0%			0.0%			0.0%			0.0%
Balloon ARM			0.0%			0.0%			0.0%			0.0%			0.0%
Totals	65	16,647,523	100.0%	19	5,352,859	100.0%	13	2,830,994	100.0%	21	5,346,223	100.0%	12	3,117,447	100.0%

Debt Ratios (Total & Mortgage)

	Debt to Income		Mort to Income	
	#Loans	Curr $	#Loans	Curr $
100%				
90%	1	180,721		
80%	4	1,162,719		
70%	15	5,103,271		
60%	20	3,813,761	2	928,223
50%	10	3,080,657	16	4,429,325
40%	9	2,432,329	19	6,353,815
30%	3	589,518	23	4,419,322
20%	3	334,548	4	407,242
10%			1	109,597
Totals	65	16,647,523	65	16,647,523

FICO Scores

	# of Loans	Current Balance	% Curr Balance
750+	61	14,416,312	86.6%
700			0.0%
650			0.0%
625			0.0%
600			0.0%
575			0.0%
550			0.0%
525			0.0%
500	4	2,331,212	13.4%
-500			0.0%
Totals	65	16,647,523	100.0%

Financing Purpose

	# of Loans	Current Balance	% Curr Balance
No Data	2	335,854	2.0%
Purchase	41	9,719,507	58.4%
Refi	17	5,743,735	34.5%
Restruct	5	858,428	5.2%
Equity			0.0%
Invest			0.0%
Totals	65	16,647,523	100.0%

Bankruptcy History

	# of Loans	Current Balance	% Curr Balance
No Data			0.0%
Never	60	15,469,851	92.9%
Discharge			0.0%
Filed	1	156,989	0.9%
Current	4	1,020,684	6.1%
Totals	65	16,647,523	100.0%

First Time Homeowner

	# of Loans	Current Balance	% Curr Balance
No Data			0.0%
Yes	16	2,745,918	16.5%
No	49	13,901,605	83.5%
Totals	65	16,647,523	100.0%

EXHIBIT 13.32 State-level Geographic Stratification Report (upper portion of report)

Property Type By Occupancy Code

Property Type	Owner Occupied		Owner Seasonal		Owner 2nd Home		Non-Owner Rental		No Data	
	Number of Loans	Curr Balance	Number of Loans	Curr Balance	Number of Loans	Curr Balance	Number of Loans	Curr Balance	Number of Loans	Curr Balance
No Data			1	335,090						
Single Family	3	433,227	46	12,681,844	4	631,267	6	1,268,297		
Multi 2 Units			1	132,222						
Condo			2	778,072						
Coop			2	387,505						
Multi <= 4 Units										
Multi <= 10 Units										
Multi 10+ Units										
High Rise										
Mixed Use										
Totals	3	433,227	52	14,314,732	4	631,267	6	1,268,297	0	0

Property Type By Servicer Rating

Property Type	Excellent		Very Good		Average		Below Average		Poor		No Data	
	Number of Loans	Curr Balance	Number of Loans	Curr Balance	Number of Loans	Curr Balance	Number of Loans	Curr Balance	Number of Loans	Curr Balance	Number of Loans	Curr Balance
No Data							1	335,090				
Single Family	6	2,389,868	6	1,005,430	12	3,998,546	31	6,016,020	4	1,602,751		
Multi 2 Units			1	132,222								
Condo									1	694,087		
Coop	1	144,261			1	243,244	1	83,985				
Multi <= 4 Units												
Multi <= 10 Units												
Multi 10+ Units												
High Rise												
Mixed Use												
Totals	7	2,534,149	7	1,137,652	13	4,241,790	33	6,437,094	5	2,296,838	0	0

Property Type By Escrow

Property Type	No Escrow		Property Tax Only		Insurance Only		Tax & Insurance		No Data	
	Number of Loans	Curr Balance	Number of Loans	Curr Balance	Number of Loans	Curr Balance	Number of Loans	Curr Balance	Number of Loans	Current Balance
No Data									1	335,090
Single Family			7	2,222,143	8	1,726,337	2	1,393,508	42	9,672,647
Multi 2 Units									1	132,222
Condo					1	83,985			1	694,087
Coop					1	243,244			1	144,261
Multi <= 4 Units										
Multi <= 10 Units										
Multi 10+ Units										
High Rise										
Mixed Use										
Totals	0	0	7	2,222,143	10	2,053,565	2	1,393,508	46	10,978,307

Documentation

Documentation Package	No Escrow	
	Number of Loans	Curr Balance
No Data		
Full Docs	60	14,968,852
Partial Docs	3	474,644
Alt A	2	1,204,027
No Income		
No Assets		
No Inc No Assets		
Totals	65	16,647,523

Appraisal Type

Appraisal Type	Original		Current	
	Number of Loans	Curr Balance	Number of Loans	Curr Balance
No Data			3	716,797
Walk Through	65	16,647,523	12	2,643,042
Outside			22	6,238,025
Drive By			23	5,751,861
Tax Assessment			1	132,222
Other			2	778,072
None			2	387,505
Totals	65	16,647,523	65	16,647,523

EXHIBIT 13.32 State-level Geographic Stratification Report (lower portion of report)

number of loans and the current balances by mortgage amortization type. This table is a feature of all four of the reports and serves as a statistical summary of the count and balance information of the eligible collateral from this state. The second table is a listing of all loans in each of the MSAs of the state. The graphic is a pie chart of the MSA balance totals for the state as a whole, including loans with no MSA specified. See Exhibit 13.33 for the blank template of this report and Exhibit 13.46 for the completed report.

2. **Borrower Credit Profile Report.** This report is designed to give a thumbnail sketch of the credit characteristics of the borrower pool of the eligible collateral See Exhibit 13.47. This report contains six tables and six graphics. Besides the mortgage-type summary table at the top of the report, the report contains tables for the following:
   - Current and original balances distributed by mortgage debt and total debt ratios of the borrowers. This table drives two pie charts.
   - Distribution of loan count and current balances by FICO scores. This table has an accompanying pie chart.
   - Distribution of loan count and current balances by financing purpose. This table has an accompanying pie chart.
   - Distribution of loan count and current balances by bankruptcy history. This table has an accompanying pie chart.
   - Distribution of loan count and current balances by first-time homeowner status. This table has an accompanying pie chart.

3. **LTV, Appraisal, and Documentation Standards.** This report is designed to present an overview of the underwriting standards of the eligible collateral. It consists of the following:
   - Distribution of loan count current balance by current and original LTV ratios. There are two pie charts with this table.
   - Distribution of loan count and current balances by original and current appraisal method. There are two pie charts accompanying this table.
   - Distribution of loan count and current balances by origination documentation standards. A pie chart displays the current balance information.

4. **Property Type, with Owner Occupancy or Servicing Rating.** This report looks at the cross-tabulation of property type with either owner occupancy status or servicer rating. There are two tables, each accompanied by a three-dimensional bar chart displaying the current balance cross tabulation values of the tables.

Report Formats   "One picture is worth a thousand words." The formats of two of the reports are presented below. These are the template formats of the "Current Balances by MSA" and the "LTV, Appraisal, and Documentation Standards Report." You will note that all of the tabular and graphic areas of the reports are blank. The tables are blank because we have not populated them as yet. The graphics are blank because they are linked directly to the table information.

Each table shares the common table, "Statewide Current Balances by Collateral Amortization Type," in the upper center of the report. This section of the report is designed to allow the user to establish a broad-stroke picture of:

- How many loans are in the portfolio
- Total loan count and current balances

- Distribution of the loan count and current balances across mortgage types
- Average balances per type
- Balance range, minimum to maximum by type

We will insert the state name in the title box immediately above this schedule. We will also add a state profile map and the state flag to the right and left of the table, respectively.

Balances by MSA Report   This is the configuration of the "Current Balances by MSA" Report prior to the population of the report. See Exhibit 13.33.

LTV, Appraisal, and Documentation Standards Report   This is the configuration of the "LTV, Appraisal Methods, and Documentation Standards" Report prior to the population of the report. See Exhibit 13.34.

With the template files waiting, let us write the VBA code that will populate the various tables we need to drive the report package.

Steps of the Report Package Preparation Process   Blank template files are interesting, but not as interesting as populated statistically and graphically completed reports are. Let us look at the steps we need to populate the Portfolio Presentation Report package. We will then translate these steps into VBA code to accomplish the task.

The steps of preparing the report package are:

1. Load the state and MSA demographic information.
2. Erase the contents of all the aggregation arrays that we will use to populate the various tables of the four reports.
3. Aggregate all the information needed by the tables of each of the four reports. This also includes aggregation at of the state-level data for the "Current Balances by Amortization Type" table at the head of each of the reports. The CCFG will loop through each eligible loan of the portfolio and aggregate the various statistics needed by the report. Report-specific aggregation subroutines are called by a main aggregation subroutine "RepPortPresent_AggregateAllData" for the "Current Balances by Amortization Type" table. This information includes the state-level loan counts, current balances, and minimum and maximum balances by state and by amortization class. Once we have the total loan counts and the totals current balance, we can compute the percentages of each amortization type within the state. Each of the tables in the report has separate VBA arrays that will be fully populated by this subroutine.
4. Loop through a series of steps four times (once for each type of report).
5. Open the template file. This task is performed by the subroutine "RepPort Present_OpenTemplateFileAndSave".
6. Based on what report type we are preparing, delete the other three report template worksheets of the file. Each file we produce will contain the same report format for each of the selected set of reports. Thus on the first pass of the report loop, the pass that produces the "Current Balances by MSA" loop, we will

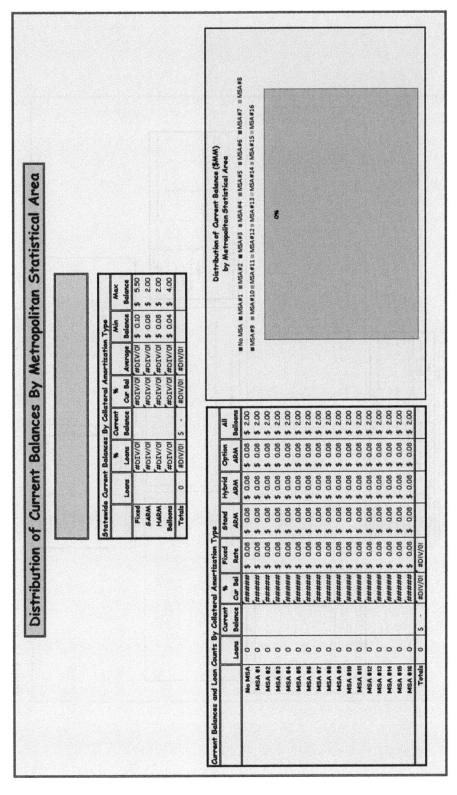

EXHIBIT 13.33 Current Balances by MSA Report template

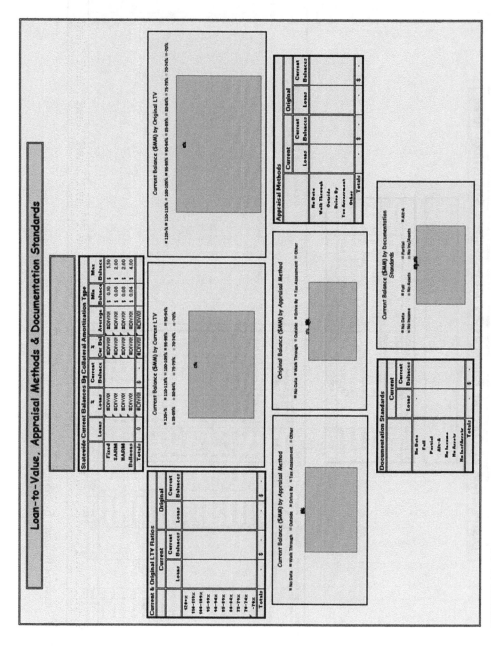

EXHIBIT 13.34 LTV, Appraisal Method and Documentation Standards Report template

delete the other three report template worksheets. This task is performed by the "RepPortPresent_DeleteUnusedTemplateReports" subroutine.

7. Copy the template worksheet and rename the copy for each state selected for the report package. The name of the worksheet will be the two-letter postal code of the state. This task is performed by the subroutine "RepPortPresent_BuildReportFileWorksheets".

8. Enter a series of report worksheet specific Range names into each of the state reports. We will use these to simplify the report writing process. This task is undertaken by the subroutine "RepPortPresent_EnterOutputGridRangeNames".

9. Add the state-level flag and profile map to each of the worksheets.

10. Write the "Current Balances by Amortization Type" table to the top of the report. This task is performed by the "RepPortPresent_WriteMSABalanceReport" subroutine.

11. Write the body of the specific report.

12. Save and close the file for this report type.

13. Loop through the remaining three report types.

We will now write the VBA code to translate these steps into completed reports.

VBA Code The following VBA subroutines are key in the production of the Portfolio Presentation Report.

"RepPortPresent_MainWriteReports" Subroutine The "RepPortPresent_Main WriteReports" subroutine is the master reporting subroutine for the report writing process. This subroutine produces all four of the Demographic Presentation group of reports. As such it begins by checking the four "gRepMenuDemo**" variables to determine that at least one of these reports has been selected for production. If one has been selected of the subroutine continues.

The first two subroutine calls load a series of vectors containing state and MSA names, code numbers, and abbreviations. Next we will make a series of high-level calls to other subroutines that perform the tasks listed in the "Steps" section immediately above. Before anything else is attempted, we must be sure to clear the results of any previous calculations from the arrays we will use to populate the report tables. This task is performed by the subroutine "RepPortPresent_EraseAllArrays". This subroutine simply uses the VBA command "Erase" to clear any values from the aggregation arrays. Step 2 is complete.

The call to the "RepPortPresent_AggregateAllData" subroutine begins the aggregation process. This subroutine and others that are called from it perform Step 3. The main loop of the subroutine now executes four times, once for each of the report types. At the beginning of each loop, a template file is opened based on the value of the loop. The subroutine is "RepPortPresent_OpenTemplateFileAnd-Save". This completes Steps 4 and 5. The subroutine "RepPortPresent_DeleteUnused-TemplateReports" now deletes all template worksheets of the workbook except that designated by the loop control variable value. This completes Step 6. If the loop value is "1", all worksheets other that the "Current Balances by MSA" worksheet are deleted. The "RepPortPresent_BuildReportFileWorksheets" subroutine creates a single report for each selected state. It also calls a series of other subroutines that prepare the state-by-state worksheets to receive the aggregate data. These are formatting subroutines that place the name of the state on the report as well as the flag and map graphics. This completes Steps 7, 8, and 9.

A "Select..Case" now calls one of four different report-writing subroutines. The subroutine "RepPortPresent_WriteBalanceReport" is called if the loop value is "1". It writes the "Current Balances by Amortization Type" table at the top of the report. The statistics that form the contents of the various tables of the reports are aggregated and then written to the report body on a state-by-state basis. This completes Steps 10 and 11. The finished report workbook is saved after all state level reports are written. This completes Step 12. The loop executes three more times, writing the remaining reports, and stops, bringing the report preparation process to an end, Step 13.

See Exhibit 13.35.

"RepPortPresent_EraseAllTableArrays" Subroutine   After we have loaded the geographic information that we will need later in this reporting process, we undertake an equally important task. This task is to erase any trace of data left in the various aggregation arrays that we have created to hold the information we will later write to the tables of the reports. In the process of aggregation, we are most often incrementally adding a new piece of information to an existing sum. The common form of an aggregation calculation is "sum = sum+amount". We need to be careful to immediately reset all our arrays back to zero before we start the reporting process. This avoids the embarrassing effect of aggregating the portfolio to itself over and over again. Without this balance-clearing activity, we can easily fall into this trap in sequential runs of the CCFG in the same session. The "Erase" command is easy to use and will clear the values of all types of data. Using it at this point in the reporting process assures us of getting started with a completely clean slate. See Exhibit 13.36.

"RepPortPresent_AggregateAllData" Subroutine   The next subroutine call to "RepPortPresent_AggregateAllData" is the master subroutine that will aggregate data for all of the arrays that we will later use to write the report tables. The subroutine loops through the portfolio loan-by-loan basis. It is important to perform all of the aggregations in one pass through the loan portfolio. Performing the aggregations as we are writing the reports, with each report individually cycling through the portfolio, is to be avoided at all costs. If we later add another report, or two or six more reports, to the package, centralizing the aggregation process is critical. At the current time we do not allow the user to select an individual report from the package. We do not allow the sole production of the "Current Balances by MSA" report without also producing the other three reports in the same run. We may choose to do this at a later time. Will centralizing the aggregation code hurt us in this case? No. We can easily embed the aggregation code needed by the various reports in a "Select..Case" statement and include/exclude them as we see fit. The key reason we position this subroutine *outside* of the reporting loop is to avoid an incremental computational burden. With this schema, it does not matter how many reports we add to the report package. We will still visit each loan of the portfolio once and only once!

The subroutine calls five other subroutines from within the loan-by-loan loop. The first of these aggregates the statistics that we will need for the "Current Balances by Amortization Type" table that is resident on all four of the reports. The remaining four calls are report specific for each of the reports. We will follow the subroutine chain that produces the "Current Balances by MSA" report. This report, in common

```
Sub RepPortPresent_MainWriteReports()

Dim rep_trigger As Boolean

    If gRepMenuDemoBalances Or gRepMenuDemoCredit Or gRepMenuDemoLTV Or _
       gRepMenuDemoPropType Then
        Call RepPortPresent_EraseAllTableArrays      'erase all data aggregation arrays
        'setup geographic information arrays
        Call Utility_ReadStateAndMSAInfo
        For mState = 1 To NUM_STATES - 4
            Call RepPortPresent_SetupMSAInfoByState
        Next mState
        'aggregate all the data in the reports by making one and one only pass through
        ' the portfolio on a loan by loan basis!
        Call RepPortPresent_AggregateAllData         'aggregates all data for tables
        'loop by the number of geographic presentation reports, there are currently
        ' four formats in the report package.  On each loop the value "mReport" is
        ' used to configure a report file containing a single type of report, one for
        ' each of the states selected on the geographic selection User Form.
        For mReport = 1 To NUM_GEO_PRESENTS
            Select Case mReport
                Case Is = GEOREP_MSA_CURBALS: rep_trigger = gRepMenuDemoBalances
                Case Is = GEOREP_CREDIT:      rep_trigger = gRepMenuDemoCredit
                Case Is = GEOREP_VALUATION:   rep_trigger = gRepMenuDemoLTV
                Case Is = GEOREP_SERVICING:   rep_trigger = gRepMenuDemoPropType
            End Select
            If rep_trigger Then      'write the report (or not)
                'opens template file, saves with the report type in the file name
                Call RepPortPresent_OpenTemplateFileAndSave
                'only one template worksheet is used in each run of the loop
                Call RepPortPresent_DeleteUnusedTemplateReports
                'Add a worksheet for each selected state in the package
                Call RepPortPresent_BuildReportFileWorksheets
                'based on the value of the loop selects either the balances,
                ' credit, valuation or servicing report format and the
                ' appropriate aggregation subroutines
                Select Case mReport
                    Case Is = GEOREP_MSA_CURBALS
                        Call RepPortPresent_WriteBalanceReport
                    Case Is = GEOREP_CREDIT
                        Call RepPortPresent_WriteCreditReport
                    Case Is = GEOREP_VALUATION
                        Call RepPortPresent_WriteValuationReport
                    Case Is = GEOREP_SERVICING
                        Call RepPortPresent_WriteServicingReport
                End Select
                'this particular report set is finished, save, close the worksheet
                ActiveWorkbook.Save
                ActiveWorkbook.Close
            End If
        Next mReport
        gRepMenuAssumptions = True
    End If

End Sub
```

EXHIBIT 13.35   "RepPortPresent_WriteMainReports" subroutine

with the other three reports, contains the "Current Balances by Amortization Type" table. We will also trace how the data for this report is produced.

You will notice that inside the loop, there are a series of assignment statements. The first of these statements assigns the numerical value of the "FD_STATECODE" of the loan to a variable "mState". The second assigns the value of the loan field "FD_CURRBAL" to the variable "cbal". What is the purpose of these assignments? We will use the numerical value of the state code countless times in these aggregation

```
Sub RepPortPresent_EraseAllTableArrays()

    'Current Balances by Amortization Type table
    '(present on all reports)
    Erase mTypeGrid
    'Current Balances by MSA report
    Erase mMSAGrid            'MSA section of the balances report
    'Borrower Credit Profile report
    Erase mDebtRatioGrid      'Mortgage and Total Debt to income
    Erase mFICOGrid           'FICO score table
    Erase mPurposeGrid        'Financing Purpose table
    Erase mBankruptcyGrid     'Bankruptcy History table
    Erase mOwnershipGrid      'First Ownership table
    'LTV, Appraisal, and Documentation Standards
    Erase mLTVGrid                'Current and Original LTV
    Erase mAppraisalGrid          'Current and Original Appraisal Method
    Erase mDocsGrid               'Doocumentations Standards
    'Property Type Report
    Erase mOccGrid            'Ownership/Property Type cross tabulation
    Erase mServeGrid          'Servicer Rating/Property Type cross tabulation

End Sub
```

EXHIBIT 13.36   "RepPortPresent_EraseAllTableArrays" subroutine

subroutines due to the simple fact that all the data are aggregated at the state level! The name of the variable "mState" is short when compared to:

```
''gLoanData(iloan, FD_STATECODE)''
```

It is far more convenient to use as an index notation. In addition to the advantage of brevity, it also has the advantage of clarifying the code. It is a variable name long enough to mean something and still short enough to be handy. Replacing "gLoanData(iloan, FD_CURRBAL)" with the much more convenient "cBal" serves the same purpose. There are 23 uses of the variable "cBal" in the module. Almost all of them involve a variant of the equation:

```
mSomeArray = mSomeArray + cBal
```

where we are simply adding the current balance of the loan to some aggregation variable. You need to be careful when you make use of this practice. Use these types of "abbreviated assignments" with some degree of forethought and discretion. Do *not* overabbreviate! For example, further abbreviation of "mState" could lead to "mS", which could be open to any number of interpretations! However, applied with a little common sense, this practice can help make your code clearer than it would be with the more lengthy (and often repeated) names. In the case of the Property Type report, both tables have the Property Type code of the loan as the horizontal sorting axis. Abbreviating "gLoanData(iloan, FD_PROPTYPE)" to "mPType" also makes a lot of sense here.

At the bottom of this subroutine there is a second loop. This loop computes the report totals and percentages for the "Current Balances By Amortization Type"

```
Sub RepPortPresent_AggregateAllData()        'aggregates all data for tables

Dim imax      As Integer

    Call RepPortPresent_InitializeTypeGrid
    For mloan = 1 To gTotalLoans
       If gLoanScreen(mloan, FD_SCREEN_ALL_OK) = REC_OKFORALL Then
          mState = gLoanData(mloan, FD_STATECODE)
          cbal = gLoanData(mloan, FD_CURRBAL)
          Call RepPortPresent_AggregateAmortTypeGrid     'amort type table
          Call RepPortPresent_AggregateMSAGridTotals     'balance report table
          Call RepPortPresent_AggregateCreditReport      'credit report tables
          Call RepPortPresent_AggregateValuationReport   'valuation report tables
          mPType = gLoanData(mloan, FD_PROPTYPE)
          Call RepPortPresent_AggregateServicingReport   'servicing report
       End If
    Next mloan
    For mState = 1 To NUM_STATES - 4
       Call RepPortPresent_AggregateAmortTypeGridTotals
       'calculate MSA % by state of the state total
       For imax = 1 To mMSAPerState(mState)
          If mPTotal(mState) > 0 Then
             mMSAGrid(mState, imax, 3) = mMSAGrid(mState, imax, 3) / mPTotal(mState)
             Else
             mMSAGrid(mState, imax, 3) = 0#
          End If
       Next imax
    Next mState

End Sub
```

EXHIBIT 13.37   "RepPortPresent_AggregateAllData" subroutine

table. This loop moves state by state, unlike the loop above it that moves loan by loan. Why? At this point, the subroutine calls that have already been completed above have aggregated all the stratified data for the reports. The "Current Balances By Amortization Type" table is the only one that has averages and percentage total figures. To calculate these figures, we need to have a total current balance number for each of the selected states. We will not have this total until we have completed the loan-by-loan loop. By the time we reach the lower state-by-state loop, it is available on a state-by-state level and we can complete the process.

We will now follow the course of the call of this subroutine as it assembles first the "Current Balances By Amortization Type" table and then the table of MSA balances that make up the "Current Balances by MSA" report. See Exhibit 13.37.

"RepPortPresent_AggregateAmortTypeGrid" subroutine This subroutine performs Step 2 of the report preparation process. Its role is to aggregate all the information to populate the standard Report Boxes at the top of each of the reports. This box contains the total collateral of the state distributed by the amortization pattern of the collateral. These patterns are the by-now-familiar fixed-rate, standard ARM, hybrid ARM, and both types of balloon mortgages (fixed and floating rate). The subroutine produces a state-by-state loan count, the total current balances, and the minimum and maximum balance of the loans in each of the five amortization patterns. From these statistics we can then go on to calculate the percentage of loan count, the percentage of current balances, and the average current balance of the loans in each of the amortization patterns. The minimum/maximum values of the

```
Sub RepPortPresent_AggregateAmortTypeGrid()

    'loans from user selected states only!
    If gStateSelect(mState) Then
        'identify the mortage amortization type
        mType = gLoanData(mloan, FD_MORTTYPE)
        'put the fixed and floating balloons in the same line
        If mType >= MORTTYPE_BALLOON_FIXED Then
            mType = MORTTYPE_BALLOON_FIXED
        End If
        mPTotal(mState) = mPTotal(mState) + cBal
        'loan count
        mTypeGrid(mState, mType, 1) = mTypeGrid(mState, mType, 1) + 1
        mPCount(mState) = mPCount(mState) + 1
        'accumulate current balances
        mTypeGrid(mState, mType, 3) = mTypeGrid(mState, mType, 3) + cBal
        'test for the minimum first, and then the maximum
        If cBal < mTypeGrid(mState, mType, 6) Then
            mTypeGrid(mState, mType, 6) = cBal
        End If
        If cBal > mTypeGrid(mState, mType, 7) Then
            mTypeGrid(mState, mType, 7) = cBal
        End If
    End If

End Sub
```

EXHIBIT 13.38 "RepPortPresent_AggregateAmortTypeGrid" subroutine

loans in each category are found by initially setting the maximum value of the loan to zero. If the value of any subsequent loan is found to be greater than zero, the maximum value is overwritten. To find the minimum balances of all of the loans in the category, we simply reverse the process by assigning a very large balance to the initial minimum test value. If the value of the loan is less than the current running minimum, the minimum value is overwritten.

Note that the subroutine only loops through the loans of the portfolio once. It uses the numeric state code as the index by which to aggregate the loan values:

```
mState = gLoanData(mloan, FD_STATECODE)
```

"mState", the nth value of the current state in the overall states list, determines the location in the "mTypeGrid" array that we are to assign this loan (if the state of the loan has been selected for display!). See Exhibit 13.38.

"RepPortPresent_AggregateMSAGridTotals" Subroutine This is the first of the report-specific aggregation arrays that we will populate and later write to a report table. This subroutine aggregates the balances by MSA for each selected state. It also records the current balances of the MSA by the amortization pattern of the loan. To do this it must match the loan to the MSA and record the current balance in the MSA total and then in the appropriate amortization-type subtotal for the MSA.

Earlier we read a number of useful data items concerning MSA into the "m MSAPerState" array and the "mMSAIdNum" arrays. These arrays hold the number of MSAs in each individual state and their respective ID numbers. We can then use a loop to search the list of ID numbers of the MSAs of the state until we find a match between the MSA code of the loan record and the MSA ID code. When we have the match, we place it in the *n*th position of the "mMSAGrid". This array has three dimensions. The first dimension is 1 to the number of states, the second 1 to maximum number of MSAs in a state (16), and the third is the number of columns (8) in the grid. Having determined the correct state and MSA, we need to determine the correct column into which to place the current balance or loan count information. The columns of the "mMSAGrid" array are:

1. Loan count
2. Total current balance by MSA
3. MSA % current balance of the state total current balance
4. Total fixed rate amortization type current balance
5. Total standard ARM amortization type current balance
6. Total hybrid ARM amortization type current balance
7. Total fixed and ARM Balloon amortization type current balance

When we find a match, we can immediately increment column 1 of the "m MSAGrid" by 1, increasing the loan count for this MSA. Next we add the current balance of the loan, "cBal", to column 2. We cannot compute the percentage figure in column 3 until we know the state totals, which, at this point, we do not know. We then aggregate the balance based on the value of the loan type. Keep in mind that fixed-rate amortization loans have a loan-type value of "1", SARMs of "2", HARMs of "3", and fixed and ARM balloons of "4" and "5". We can use this number to immediately determine the column that the current balance by type is to be assigned to! In that we are aggregating both fixed and ARM balloons in the same column of the report, column 8, we will first test to see if the current loan is an ARM balloon. If it is we will assign it the type code of "5", and therefore it will be assigned to the same location as the fixed-rate balloons. Now all we have to do is to add "4" to the loan type number and we have the correct column in which to place the current balance by amortization type! If the loan is a fixed-rate loan with a loan type of "1", we will add "4" and assign it to column "5" of the "mMSAGrid". Thus we have a quick and easy method for making the table assignments in one line of code:

```
icol = itype + 4 mMSAGrid(mState, imatch, icol) = mMSAGrid
  (mState, imatch, icol) + cBal
```

With the balances assigned to the proper loan amortization type column, we have finished the aggregation process for the moment. We will need to revisit it to calculate the contents of the percentage in column 3, but we need the state balance total. When it becomes available, we will complete the process. See Exhibit 13.39.

We now return to "RepPortPresent_AggregateAllData". The CCFG will now continue the aggregation process for the other reports. When the report-specific aggregation activities are complete, we can return to the question of finishing the percentages.

When the loan-by-loan is complete, we have the total balances by state available. The state-by-state balances contained in the array "mPortTotal (1 to

```
Sub RepPortPresent_AggregateMSAGridTotals()

Dim itype   As Integer     'amortization type code for the loan
Dim icode   As Long        'MSA ID number
Dim imatch  As Integer     'matching MSA ID numbe

    itype = gLoanData(mloan, FD_MORTTYPE)
    icode = gLoanData(mloan, FD_MSACODE)
    'loop through all the MSA code for the state and find the match
    For imatch = 0 To mMSAPerState(mState)
        If icode = mMSAIdNum(mState, imatch) Then
            'loan count
            mMSAGrid(mState, imatch, 1) = mMSAGrid(mState, imatch, 1) + 1
            'current balance for the MSA
            mMSAGrid(mState, imatch, 2) = mMSAGrid(mState, imatch, 2) + cBal
            'put the fixed and floating balloons in the same line
            If itype >= MORTTYPE_BALLOON_FIXED Then
                itype = MORTTYPE_BALLOON_FIXED
            End If
            icol = itype + 3
            mMSAGrid(mState, imatch, icol) = mMSAGrid(mState, imatch, icol) + cBal
            Exit For
        End If
    Next imatch

End Sub
```

EXHIBIT 13.39   "RepPortPresent_AggregateMSAGridTotals" subroutine

NUM_STATES)" and the state-by-state loan counts are contained in "mPortCount (1 to NUM_STATES)". In the lower portion of the "RepPortPresent_AggregateAll Data" subroutine, we apply the contents of these two arrays to compute the loan count and current balance percentage statistics. This completes Step 3 of the reporting process.

"RepPortPresent_OpenTemplateFileAndSave" Subroutine   As noted in the previous section, this subroutine selects the template file of the Portfolio Presentation Report package and opens it. The now-open template file is renamed on the basis of the value of the loop counter variable in "RepPortPresent_MainWriteReports", the calling subroutine. This is Step 4 in the process. The subroutine appends "Balances", "Credit", "Valuation", or "Servicing" to the file name based on the report to be produced. See Exhibit 13.40.

"RepPortPresent_DeleteUnusedTemplateReports" Subroutine   We now have an opened template named for the type of reports it will contain. There are, however, four different worksheets in this Report Template workbook. We will use only one of them. From this single report worksheet, we will make as many copies as we need to, one for each state selected for display. We will therefore delete the other three unused sheets. This is Step 5 in the process. See Exhibit 13.41.

"RepPortPresent_BuildReportFileWorksheets" Subroutine   The role of this subroutine is to create a worksheet for each of the selected states. It then names each of the new worksheets with the two-letter postal code of the state. After that it enters

```
Sub RepPortPresent_OpenTemplateFileAndSave()

    Workbooks.Open FileName:=DIR_TEMPLATE_REP & PRESENT_PORTFOLIO_TEMPLATE
    Select Case mReport
        Case Is = GEOREP_MSA_CURBALS: ftitle = "Balances"
        Case Is = GEOREP_CREDIT:      ftitle = "Credit"
        Case Is = GEOREP_VALUATION:   ftitle = "Valuation"
        Case Is = GEOREP_SERVICING:   ftitle = "Servicing"
    End Select
    ActiveWorkbook.SaveAs FileName:= _
        OUTPUT_DIRECTORY & gRepMenuPrefix & "PortPresentReport" & _
        "_" & ftitle

End Sub
```

EXHIBIT 13.40 "RepPortPresent_OpenTemplateFileAndsave" subroutine

the name of the state in the title line of the report. The subroutine then calls two other subroutines that will continue the formatting of the worksheets until they are complete and lacking only the statistical results in their tables. This subroutine and the subroutines it calls complete Steps 6, 7, and 8. See Exhibit 13.42.

"RepPortPresent_EnterOutputGridRangeNames" and "RepPortPresent_EnterMSA BalanceRangeNames" Subroutines The above two subroutines complete the formatting of the Report Template worksheet for an individual state report. The first enters a worksheet-specific range name for the table or tables contained in the report.

The second subroutine selects a pair of clip art files, one that contains a state profile map and a second that contains a state flag and appends them to the report. These clip art files are found in the directories:

```
C:\VBA_Book2\Code\clipart\maps
```

```
Sub RepPortPresent_DeleteUnusedTemplateReports()

Dim DeleteTemplate(1 To NUM_GEO_PRESENTS)  As Boolean
Dim irep        As Integer

    'set all to be deleted
    For irep = 1 To NUM_GEO_PRESENTS
        DeleteTemplate(irep) = True
    Next irep
    'save only the worksheet corresponding to this report loop
    DeleteTemplate(mReport) = False
    For irep = 1 To NUM_GEO_PRESENTS
        If DeleteTemplate(irep) Then Sheets("TemplateRep" & irep).Delete
    Next irep
    Sheets("TemplateRep" & mReport).Select
    Sheets("TemplateRep" & mReport).Name = "Template"
    ActiveWorkbook.Save

End Sub
```

EXHIBIT 13.41 "RepPortPresent_DeleteUnusedTemplateReports" subroutine

```
Sub RepPortPresent_BuildReportFileWorksheets()

    mSheetPosition = 1
    For mState = 1 To NUM_STATES - 4
        If gRepMenuGeoStates(mState) Then
            Sheets("Template").Select
            Sheets("Template").Copy Before:=Sheets(mSheetPosition)
            Sheets("Template (2)").Select
            Call RepPortPresent_EnterOutputGridRangeNames
            Sheets("Template (2)").Name = gStatePostal(mState)
            Call RepPortPresent_InsertStateMapFlag
            Range("G5").Value = gStateName(mState)
            mSheetPosition = mSheetPosition + 1
        End If
    Next mState
    Sheets("Template").Select
    ActiveWindow.SelectedSheets.Delete
    ActiveWorkbook.Save

End Sub
```

EXHIBIT 13.42   "RepPortPresent_BuildReportFileWorksheets" subroutine

and

```
C:\VBA_Book2\Code\clipart\flags
```

These files have the names "XXFlag.xls" and "XXMap.xls", where "XX" is the two-letter postal code of the state. With this accomplished, the only activity remaining is to populate the contents of the amortization-type table at the top of the report and any specialized, report-format-dependent tables in the lower body of the report. See Exhibit 13.43

```
Sub RepPortPresent_EnterOutputGridRangeNames()

    Select Case mReport
        Case Is = GEOREP_MSA_CURBALS: Call RepPortPresent_EnterMSABalanceRangeNames
        Case Is = GEOREP_CREDIT:      Call RepPortPresent_EnterCreditRangeNames
        Case Is = GEOREP_VALUATION:   Call RepPortPresent_EnterValuationRangeNames
        Case Is = GEOREP_SERVICING:   Call RepPortPresent_EnterServicingRangeNames
    End Select

End Sub
'============================================================================
Sub RepPortPresent_EnterMSABalanceRangeNames()

    'Mortgage Type balances grid
    mSampleName = "MortTypeGrid" & mStatePostal(mState)
    ActiveWorkbook.Names.Add Name:=mSampleName, _
            RefersToR1C1:="='Template (2)'!R12C8:R16C14"
    'MSA Balances grid
    mSampleName = "Rep1MSAGrid" & mStatePostal(mState)
    ActiveWorkbook.Names.Add Name:=mSampleName, _
            RefersToR1C1:="='Template (2)'!R23C2:R39C10"

End Sub
```

EXHIBIT 13.43   "RepPortPresent_EnterOutputGridRangeNames" and
"RepPortPresent_EnterMSABalanceRangeNames" subroutines

```
Sub RepPortPresent_InsertStateMapFlag()

Dim iImage          As Integer
Dim mPicture        As Object
Dim mTop            As Double
Dim mLength         As Double
Dim mWidth          As Double
Dim mHeight         As Double

    mMapFileName = gStatePostal(mState) & "Map.wmf"
    mFlagFileName = gStatePostal(mState) & "Flag.jpg"
    mMapPicture = STATE_MAPS_DIR & mMapFileName
    mFlagPicture = STATE_FLAGS_DIR & mFlagFileName
    For iImage = 1 To 2
        If iImage = 1 Then
            Set mPicture = ActiveSheet.Pictures.Insert(mMapPicture)
            With mPicture
                .Top = Range("C5:F13").Top
                .Left = Range("C5:F13").Left
                .Width = (182 / 245) * 150
            End With
        Else
            Set mPicture = ActiveSheet.Pictures.Insert(mFlagPicture)
            With mPicture
                .Top = Range("P5:R13").Top
                .Left = Range("P5:R13").Left
                .Width = (182 / 245) * 225
            End With
        End If
        Set mPicture = Nothing
    Next iImage

End Sub
```

EXHIBIT 13.44   "RepPortPresent_InsertStateMapFlag" subroutine

"RepPortPresent_InsertStateMapFlag" Subroutine This subroutine finds and copies the state profile map and the state flag to the body of the report. The profile map is copied to a Range to the left of the state name field in the title while the flag of the state is copied to its right. With these two graphics in place, we are finished with everything except the tables of the report. From this point the CCFG will select task-specialized subroutine for whichever of the reports it is currently writing. Based on the type of report, it will have to populate as few as two tables or as many as six. In all cases the first table to be populated is the "Current Balances by Amortization Type" table at the top of the report. Subsequent tables are populated based on the type of the report. See Exhibit 13.44.

"RepPortPresent_WriteBalanceReport" Subroutine   By the time we have finally arrived at the point of writing the report, it is almost anticlimactic! All the heavy work is in the past. All the subroutine needs to determine is the following:

1. Is the state selected for reporting?
2. If TRUE to Step 1 above, select the prepared state sheet identified by its postal code. The report worksheet for California would be simply "CA".
3. Write the amortization-type table at the top of the report.

```
Sub RepPortPresent_WriteBalanceReport()

    'write the grid to the report
    For mState = 1 To NUM_STATES - 4
        If gRepMenuGeoStates(mState) Then
            Sheets(gStatePostal(mState)).Select        'get to the correct sheet
            Call RepPortPresent_WriteAmortTypeGrid
            mTargetRange = "Rep1MSAGrid" & gStatePostal(mState)
            For irow = 1 To mMSAPerState(mState) + 1
                'col1=MSA name
                Range(mTargetRange).Cells(irow, 1) = mMSAName(mState, irow - 1)
                If mMSAGrid(mState, irow - 1, 1) > 0 Then
                    'col2=MSA loan count, col3=MSA current balance,
                    'col4=MSA current balance/ State current balance
                    Range(mTargetRange).Cells(irow, 2) = _
                                        mMSAGrid(mState, irow - 1, 1)
                    Range(mTargetRange).Cells(irow, 3) = _
                                        mMSAGrid(mState, irow - 1, 2) / 1000
                    Range(mTargetRange).Cells(irow, 4) = _
                                        mMSAGrid(mState, irow - 1, 2) / mPTotal(mState)
                    'current balances by loan types, col 5 = Fixed, col 6 = SARM,
                    ' col 7 = HARM, col 8 = Balloons
                    Range(mTargetRange).Cells(irow, 5) = _
                                        mMSAGrid(mState, irow - 1, 4) / 1000
                    Range(mTargetRange).Cells(irow, 6) = _
                                        mMSAGrid(mState, irow - 1, 5) / 1000
                    Range(mTargetRange).Cells(irow, 7) = _
                                        mMSAGrid(mState, irow - 1, 6) / 1000
                    Range(mTargetRange).Cells(irow, 8) = _
                                        mMSAGrid(mState, irow - 1, 7) / 1000
                Else
                    For icol = 1 To 7
                        Range(mTargetRange).Cells(irow, 3) = ""
                    Next icol
                End If
            Next irow
        End If
        Call RepPortPresent_TrimMSAGrid
    Next mState

End Sub
```

EXHIBIT 13.45 RepPortPresent_WriteBalanceReport subroutine

4. Set the value of the variable "TargetRange" into which we will write the report contents. In the case of California, it will be "REP1MSAGridCA".
5. Loop through the number of MSAs in the state and print the results for each one. If there are no loans in the MSA, leave the MSA name in place but enter "No Loans Found for this MSA".

See Exhibit 13.45.

Finished Portfolio Presentation Reports

When all the code has stopped, this is what we should have produced! See Exhibits 13.46 and 13.47.

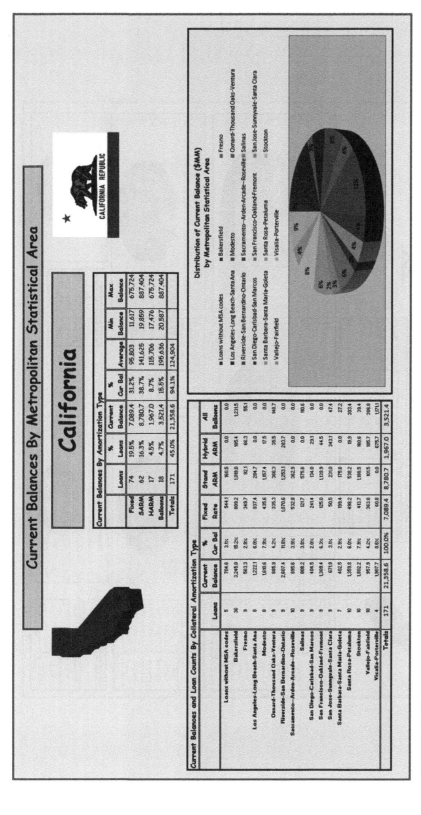

EXHIBIT 13.46 Current Balances by MSA

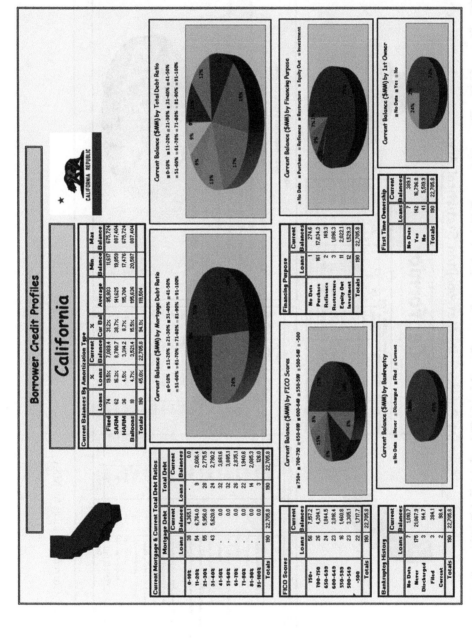

EXHIBIT 13.47 Borrower Credit Profiles Report

ON THE WEB SITE

The following material can be found on the Web Site for this chapter.

Web Chapter File is the "WebCommentsChapter13.wrd"—Web comments chapter.

Program Files There are two collections of program files on the Web site, the final version of the CCFG and the report package template files.

Model File "CCFG_Chapter13"—is the final version of the Collateral Cash Flow Generator.

Template Files The Web site for this chapter contains the following Report Template files:

- "**AssumptionsTemplate.xls**". Template file for the assumptions used to run the model.
- "**CashFlowOutputTemplate.xls**". Template file for the Summary and Detailed Collateral Cash Flow Reports for the eligible collateral.
- "**CrossTabsReportsTemplate.xls**". Template file for the Cross Tabulation Reports.
- "**BaseStratReportsTemplate.xls**". Template report file for the Base Stratification Reports.
- "**GeoStratStateTemplate.xls**". Template file for the State Geographic Stratification Reports.
- "**GeoStratMSATemplate.xls**". Template file for the Statistical Metropolitan Area Geographic Stratification Reports.
- "**PortfolioPresentTemplate.xls**. Template file for the Portfolio Presentation Report.
- "**StateFlags**" directory. A directory containing 50 files each of a state flag.
- "**StateMaps**" directory. A directory containing 50 files each of a state outline map.
- "**CrossTabReportSpecsTemplate**". Input file specifying the Cross Tabulation Reports package.
- "**UserStratReportSpecsTemplate**". Input file specifying the User Specified Stratification Reports package.

Building the New Liabilities Model

Chapter 14: Designing the Liabilities Waterfall Model

In this chapter we lay out the design of the Liabilities Waterfall Model (LWM). This includes the type of Liabilities Structure that we will model, the basic format of the Excel Waterfall Spreadsheet, and all the supporting menus, data sheets, and VBA modules. The VBA modules will locate the cash flows generated by the Collateral Cash Flow Generator (CCFG), load them into the model, trigger the Waterfall Spreadsheet calculations, then capture and report the results.

Chapter 15: Writing the Liabilities Waterfall Model Spreadsheet

In this chapter we write the Excel Waterfall Spreadsheet that is the heart of the LWM. We review each of the sections of the Waterfall Spreadsheet, explain its function in the model, and review the formulas and calculation sequences. This spreadsheet is the vehicle that translates the specifications of the Liabilities Structure legal agreements into an analytical engine.

Chapter 16: Writing the LWM VBA Code

In this chapter we create the VBA modules we need to hold the code that will perform all of the functions required by the LWM that lie outside the Waterfall Spreadsheet itself. This includes importing the cash flows of the CCFG into the model, triggering the calculation sequence, and reporting the results of the various model runs. We will create menus and menu support code as well as all the report generation code needed by the LWM.

Designing the Liabilities Waterfall Model

OVERVIEW

In this chapter we will design the Liabilities Waterfall Model (LWM). The securitization that we are modeling in this chapter includes a large number of the more common features present in many outstanding mortgage-backed securities (MBS) deals. Each deal is different, as evidenced by the wide range of structural features employed in the market since the 1970s. In building the LWM, the reader will get a firm introduction to the basic structures and components of MBS deals. We are really only scratching the surface of the field, however. All of the techniques and methods in this chapter are applicable to a wide range of asset-backed securitization and other structured products modeling.

DELIVERABLES

The modeling knowledge deliverables are:

- Selection of a current MBS deal that is typical of those in the current market environment.
- The overall schema of the LWM.
- The general structure of multi-tranche MBS deals.
- The uses of interest, principal, and recoveries in the waterfall. These uses include payments of fees, swap payments, bond interest, bond principal, loss reimbursement, and residual payments.
- Different forms of enhancement, namely overcollateralization, subordination, excess spread, performance triggers, interest rate swaps, and step-down provisions.
- Performance metrics of the model.

UNDER CONSTRUCTION

In this chapter our deliverable will be the overall plan for the development of the LWM. We will not create the LWM Excel worksheets or any of the VBA code of the model at this time.

STRUCTURE OF THE DEAL: SOURCES AND USES OF FUNDS

The design requirements of the LWM are best visualized if we reduce the modeling of the deal into its most basic components: the Sources of Funds on one side of the equation and the Uses of Funds on the other.

Sources of Funds: The Collateral

The role of the Collateral Cash Flow Generator (CCFG) is to amortize the Collateral Pool of the deal under various assumptions of prepayment, default, recovery lag period, and market value decline assumptions. These assumptions are the components of any of the three cash flow projection methodologies available in the CCFG. These are the Uniform, Geographic, and Demographic Methodologies.

Regardless of the methodology selected by the analyst, the CCFG will need to segregate and account for the amounts of each of the components of the aggregate cash flow streams on a monthly basis. These cash flow components are:

- Defaults of principal
- Scheduled amortization of principal
- Coupon payments
- Prepayments of principal
- Recoveries of defaulted principal

It is critical for us to maintain the identity and amounts of each of these cash flow components. As we will see below, the use of these cash flows by the Liabilities Structure will vary based on the origin of the cash flow itself.

Uses of Funds: The Liabilities Structure

The Uses of Funds by the Liabilities Structure consists of broadly three activities: paying fees, paying the debt service and principal of the bonds, and funding the credit enhancement features of the deal. Before we dive into the finer details of the planned Liabilities Structure, it would be useful to discuss the overall characteristics and mechanics of the structure. These can be described in two words: payment subordination.

Concept of Subordination: Payment Prioritization   First and foremost, subordination places the payment priorities of certain notes beneath those of more senior notes. This prioritization is typically applied to all distributions in the deal, namely interest, principal, and loss reimbursements, although this is not necessarily always the case. When the collateral backing a deal is performing well, all payments due on each of the notes should be made in full. In the event that the mortgage loans are experiencing high delinquencies and losses, it is possible that not all of the bonds will receive their amounts due.

Each note in the deal has a right to a minimum amount of subordination, as determined by that note's Target Subordination Percentage. Generally speaking, the more senior a note is, the higher that note's Target Subordination Percentage. Throughout the life of the deal, the structure will try to maintain each note's subordination level, and thus the principal payment amounts are computed off the Target Subordination Percentages.

Benefits and Use of Subordination in Bond Structures   By prioritizing payments based on seniority, we can ensure that the more senior, higher-credit-quality bonds are paid before the more subordinate, lower-credit, supporting bonds. This will certainly be the case in our model structure, as the Class A senior notes receive principal and interest first. Only after these expenses have been met and funds are still available are the interest and principal expenses paid to any of the Class B subordinate notes.

In addition to payment prioritization, subordination also determines in which order losses, if any, are experienced by the notes. The most senior notes will be the last to be written down (i.e., have their outstanding principal balance decreased by losses of the assets), while the most subordinate notes will be the first. This feature, like the payment priorities, functions to improve the credit quality of the senior notes by making them less susceptible to cash flow variance caused by any adverse effects of poorly performing assets.

Bond Structure   The six bonds in our deal are all floating rate notes (FRNs) where the floating index is LIBOR (London Interbank Offering Rate). Each note accrues interest monthly at a rate of LIBOR plus that note's specified spread above LIBOR. The different spreads are to account for the differing risk profiles of each of the notes. If a note is subordinate to other notes in terms of payments priorities and loss allocation, then the likelihood of experiencing a loss or delay in payments is greater; therefore, an investor in those bonds needs to be compensated for this incremental risk.

Our deal structure will consist of two senior notes (the Class A notes), four subordinated notes (the Class B notes), and an overcollateralization amount. We discuss the characteristics of the different classes at length below.

Fees of the Deal   MBS deals have a number of variable and fixed costs. The most prominent of these fees is the servicing fee. This fee is the amount paid to the servicer of the assets, who is responsible for collecting borrower payments and remitting these payments to the trust for payments to the note holders. The servicer is also usually responsible for producing a monthly servicer report for investors in the securities. The servicing fee is a variable cost, as it is computed off the current outstanding principal balance of the assets for each month of the deal. Other fees include the master servicer fee, trustee fee, structuring fee, swap counter-party fee, and legal fees of the trust.

Senior A1 and A2 Classes   The two Class A notes, A-1 and A-2, are senior to the Class B notes in payment priority and loss allocation. Therefore, if there is not enough cash from the assets to make a full distribution to the Class A notes, the Class B notes will receive no distribution.

However, Class A-1 and A-2 have equal seniority, and as a result neither will take priority in payment preferences over the other. When there is not enough cash to make a full payment to the senior notes, the interest and principal distribution amounts are split pro rata between these two classes. For principal distribution amounts, the cash flows are split proportionally based on each note's outstanding principal balance. With respect to interest distributions, the available interest is split proportionally based on each note's interest due amount. This pro rata distribution for the Class A notes is in contrast to the *sequential* payment structure for the subordinate Class B notes.

Subordinate B1, B2, B3, and B4 Classes   The Class B notes are structured such that payments of interest and principal are made *sequentially*. In other words, each Class B note is senior to those below it. Specifically, Class B-1 receives payments before Class B-2, B-3, and B-4; Class B-2 is above B-3 and B-4 in the payment structure; and so on. Class B-4 is supported only by the overcollateralization amount, and is the most subordinated note in our deal. The Class B-1 note will be paid its due amounts prior to any distribution to Class B-2, B-3, and B-4. Class B-4 will receive principal and interest payments only after all other bonds in the deal have received their payments. The Class B-4 notes will also be the first note to experience losses after the overcollateralization amount has been depleted. Obviously, the Class B-4 notes are the riskiest notes in our deal.

Credit Enhancement Features   In terms of the Class A senior notes, the greatest sources of credit enhancement are those resulting from the existence of the four Class B subordinate notes. As touched on briefly above, the Class B notes act as a buffer for the Class A notes, insulating them from payment shortfalls and losses to principal.

Excess spread (XS) is the amount by which interest received from assets exceeds the all-inclusive debt service of the structure (i.e. fees and interest to the notes). This extra interest can be used to pay down principal to maintain subordination levels or to reimburse losses. Depending on the assets and the interest rate environment, XS can be a substantial source of enhancement, keeping the deal amortization on schedule while the assets are experiencing some losses.

Another source of enhancement is the overcollateralization of the deal. Overcollateralization (OC) acts as a buffer between the assets and the notes. The OC is the amount by which the balance on the assets exceeds that of notes. When the assets experience losses that cannot be fully covered by the XS, the OC amount will shrink to compensate for these losses. If losses persist, the OC will be reduced to zero and the notes will begin taking write-downs in order of reverse seniority.

The other sources of enhancement are purely structural. The first of these is a step-down date. Prior to the step-down date (month 30), the Class A senior notes receive all principal distributions. During this period the Class B subordinate notes receive only interest payments. The senior balance will decrease while the subordinates will remain constant, effectively increasing the percentage of subordination for the senior note.

Another structural enhancement is the existence of a performance trigger. This trigger, driven by the current cumulative net loss percentage, diverts cash to the senior bonds if the assets performance deteriorates past a prescribed level. This works to prevent a scenario where senior notes are adversely affected and the subordinate notes are still receiving cash.

DESIGN ELEMENTS OF THE LWM

There are seven structural elements to the LWM:

1. **Main Menu.** This is an Excel worksheet that will serve as the Main Menu to the LWM. It will allow the user to enter a maximum of five "Cases" for the LWM to run. Each Case will consist of a designated set of files:
   1. Liabilities Structure Input file
   2. Collateral Cash Flow Input file containing up to 25 individual prepayment/default scenarios
   3. Report File Prefix that will be used as an identifier for all output files of that Case
2. **VBA UserForms.** A UserForm will be created to facilitate the section of the LWM Report Package that will be produced at the conclusion of the run of each of the Cases.
3. **Structure Inputs Menu.** This Excel worksheet accepts all the structural inputs from the Structure Inputs File, displaying them and making them available to the LWM Waterfall Worksheet.
4. **Liabilities Waterfall Worksheet.** The Deal waterfall.
5. **Performance Summary Page.** An Excel worksheet that serves as an in-model performance report of the current Deal scenario.
6. **VBA Modules.** These are a series of VBA code modules that will direct the actions of the LWM based on the designations of the user. They will perform the following operations:
   - Declare global variables and Constants.
   - Provide a Main Program
   - Find, open, read into the VBA arrays of the LWM, and close files containing Liabilities Structure inputs.
   - Find, open, read into the VBA arrays of the LWM, and close files containing Collateral Cash Flows.
   - Load the inputs in Liabilities Structure and the Collateral Cash Flows above into the LWM Waterfall Spreadsheet.
   - Trigger the calculation of the LWM for each scenario present in the Collateral Cash Flow File.
   - Capture and store the results of the calculation of the LWM Spreadsheet in VBA arrays or Access databases.
   - Write output report packages containing the LWM calculations results.
7. **Report Template Files.** The template files for the LWM Report Package.

MAIN MENU

As with the CCFG Main Menu, the Main Menu of the LWM will be the control panel of the model. We want to design the LWM such that an analyst is able to evaluate multiple combinations of Sources of Funds, Collateral Cash Flow Input files, in combination with multiple Uses of Funds and Liabilities Structure Input files. Each pairing of a "Sources" cash flow file and a "Uses" structure inputs file will be termed a Case. Keeping in mind that each Collateral Cash Flow Input file can contain up to 25 individual cash flow schedules, we will limit the number of Cases (Sources/Uses file pairings) to five. Thus in a maximum utilization situation the LWM will evaluate a total of 125 individual scenarios, 5 Cases, each containing 25 individual scenarios. We need to keep track of, and to be able to quickly identify, the output of the LWM. We will therefore provide the analyst with the ability to give a unique file prefix for each of the five Cases. This prefix is prepended to all output files generated by running a Case.

In addition, we will build a UserForm into the Main Menu. This UserForm will display a menu of the reports of the LWM Output Package for selection by the analyst.

A last feature will be a set of navigation buttons to allow the analyst to page quickly to any worksheet of the model and then return to the Main Menu. See Exhibit 14.1.

REPORT PACKAGE MENU USERFORM

The Report Package Menu UserForm will be attached to the Main Menu of the LWM. It will be activated by a Command Button from the face of the menu. This is

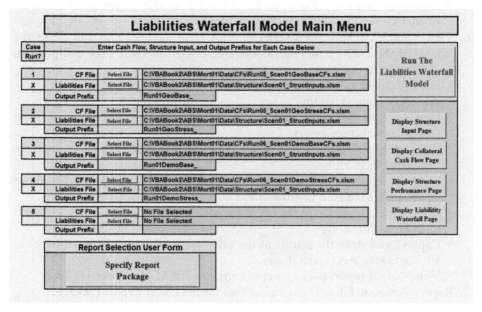

EXHIBIT 14.1   Main Menu of the LWM

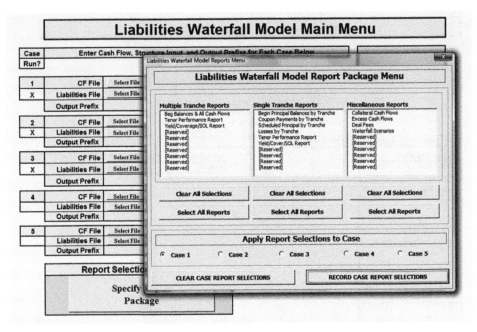

EXHIBIT 14.2   Report Package Menu UserForm

the button labeled "Specify Report Package" in Exhibit 14.1. The Report Package Menu UserForm will allow the analyst to make a selection of any report in the three Report Group List Boxes of the UserForm. These groups are:

1. Multiple Tranche Reports
2. Single Trance Reports
3. Miscellaneous Content Reports

The analyst will be able to perform the following actions from the UserForm:

- Select individual multiple, single, or miscellaneous content reports.
- Deselect individual multiple, single, or miscellaneous content reports.
- Select all reports in any one of the three categories only.
- Deselect all reports in any one of the three categories only.
- Record all selection made.
- Clear all selection made.

The design of the Report Package UserForm is shown in Exhibit 14.2.

STRUCTURE INPUTS MENU

The Structure Inputs Menu displays the inputs to the LWM that will determine the salient characteristics of the Liabilities Structure. These inputs will be read from a Liabilities Structure Input File with a format identical to that of this menu. The

Bond and Structural Inputs

Bond Class Information Table

Bond Class	%	Balance	Index	Spread	Initial Rating
A-1	85.95%	456,535,412.13	Libor (1M)	0.20%	Aaa
A-2	9.55%	50,726,156.90	Libor (1M)	0.25%	Aaa
B-1	1.90%	10,092,114.99	Libor (1M)	0.36%	Aa2
B-2	1.10%	5,842,803.41	Libor (1M)	0.48%	A2
B-3	0.50%	2,655,819.73	Libor (1M)	1.00%	Baa1
B-4	0.50%	2,655,819.73	Libor (1M)	2.20%	Baa3
OC	0.50%	2,655,819.73	NA	NA	NA
Total	100.00%	531,163,946.64			

Program Expenses

Servicer Fee	0.25%
Other Fees	0.02%

File Name Prefix

Scen01_

Interest Rate Swap

Swap	Off
Rate	5.10%
Speed (CPR)	45.00%
Swap Term (yrs)	7

Step Down Characteristics

Period	30
Senior CE %	9.00%
Post Step Down OC %	1.00%

Target Sub %

A	91.00%
B-1	94.80%
B-2	97.00%
B-3	98.00%
B-4	99.00%

Cumulative Realized Loss Trigger

ID	Start	End	%
0	0	24	100.00%
1	25	36	0.15%
2	37	48	0.25%
3	49	60	0.50%
4	61	72	0.70%
5	73	360	0.75%

Cleanup Call %	10%

EXHIBIT 14.3   Structure Inputs Menu

contents of the menu are shown in Exhibit 14.3. These inputs will determine the size, coupon levels, and payment priorities of the bond tranches. They will also describe the various credit enhancement features of the deal structure.

LIABILITIES WATERFALL WORKSHEET

The Liabilities Waterfall Worksheet is the heart of the LWM. It contains the Excel worksheet that fully describes all elements of the deal structure. It is the Liabilities Waterfall Worksheet into which we load with the structure inputs and the collateral cash flows, run, and from which we read the Liabilities Structure performance results.

At its most basic, an MBS waterfall model can be separated into the following two broad sections:

1. **Cash Flow Sources.** This section of the waterfall tracks the cash flows from the pool of assets. These cash flows are broken up into principal, interest, and

recoveries to principal. They are usually tracked separately because they can be used for different and specific purposes in the waterfall.

2. **Uses of Funds.** This section of the waterfall is where all the structural features of the deal are modeled. Using the funds tracked in the Cash Flow Sources section, we model the real-life expected performance of the structure based on the cash flows and structural inputs.

Components of the Waterfall: Sources

The Sources section of the waterfall is further broken down into two subsections: the Collateral Cash Flows section and the Available Cash section.

Collateral Cash Flows Section   This section of the waterfall is populated with either the results of the CCFG or with a simplified one-loan scenario stored in an Excel spreadsheet. In this way it can serve as an alternate cash flow input section. The fields tracked in this section are beginning/ending balances, pool factor, scheduled principal, prepaid principal, defaulted principal, total principal received, coupon income, and recoveries to principal. The pool factor shows the portion of the initial asset balance that is outstanding at the beginning of every month.

Available Cash Section   The values from the Collateral Cash Flows section are further grouped into total interest and total principal + recoveries. These two sums will be employed differently within the deal, and this section can be thought of as the starting point of all payments and distributions that follow. As such, these values are said to come in at the top of the waterfall.

Components of the Waterfall: Uses

The Uses of Funds section of the waterfall model is where all the Liabilities Structure modeling takes place. This section is where we must compute and track the notes and their relationships to the various types of enhancement in the deal. The six sections below fully describe our MBS model:

1. **Structural Fees Section.** Every structure has fixed and variable costs associated with it. Most prominently, the servicer of the assets must be compensated. The servicer fee is computed by multiplying the fee percentage rate by the total amount of assets outstanding at the start of the given period. Other examples of fees are trustee fees, credit guarantee fees, master servicer fees, and so on. Transaction fees are paid before any payments are made to the investors in the structured notes. These fees have the highest priority in the waterfall due to the fact that without the work of the service providers, we would be unable to administer the day-to-day activities of the structure.

2. **Interest Rate Swap Section.** When there is a mismatch between the interest generated from the assets and the interest payments due to the notes, the trust enters into a fixed for floating interest rate swap with the swap counterparty. This section tracks how the available interest after fees is adjusted by the net swap payments.

3. **Principal Distribution Section.** Principal payments to the senior and subordinate classes are bifurcated in this section based on deal stage, senior target subordination percent, and collateral performance triggers.
4. **Interest and Principal Payments Sections.** Once the fees have been paid, distributions are then made to the bond holders in the form of principal and interest payments. How a single bond receives payments is usually different from how other bonds in the deal are paid, and each bond's payment characteristics are described in the deal prospectus.
5. **Balance Tracking Sections.** A section dedicated to keeping track of outstanding bond balances as they are decreased by principal payments and loss allocation.
6. **Credit enhancement features sections.** Sections dedicated to the various forms of credit enhancement incorporated into the structure of the deal.

Structural Fees Section   The first use of interest payments is to pay the deal fees. In our deal we have a servicer fee and another amount due every period that is deemed other fees. The latter is a catchall fee that, like the servicer fee, is computed as a percentage of the beginning period balance, and is intended to encompass such deal costs as trustee fees, master servicer fees, and facility fees.

In our model, fees are paid from interest cash flows off the assets as opposed to principal flows. For each of the two fees we need three columns:

1. **Fee Due.** We first compute the fee amount due by taking the annual fee percentage from the Structure inputs sheets, converting it to a monthly percent and multiplying it by the beginning period asset balance.
2. **Fee Paid.** Once we have the fee due amount, we pay some or hopefully all of it from the amount of interest available. The available amount for the servicing fee is the amount stored in the Total Interest column of the Available Cash section. For the other fees, paid second, the amount available is the total interest less the amount paid to the servicing fee.
3. **Fee Unpaid.** If there is not enough interest to pay the full fee due, we track this in a Fee Unpaid column.

With these six columns we have tracked the fees due, paid and unpaid, for both of the fee types. The amount of interest cash flow available after paying these fees is then considered in the Interest Rate Swap section below.

Interest Rate Swap   When the assets are generating interest at a fixed rate and the notes are owed interest based on a floating rate, the trust would enter into a fixed for floating interest rate swap. In doing so the trust would greatly reduce its interest rate risk. We mentioned briefly above how important excess spread can be as a form of enhancement. Without a swap the excess spread would be far less dependable later in the deal as interest rates change. For example, if the assets are generating interest at a fixed rate of 7.5% and the floating-rate index used to compute interest due to the notes increases significantly, whatever excess spread that existed could shrink drastically. It could even be negative. By entering into an interest rate swap, the trust is required to pay a fixed rate and receives a floating rate payment, essentially converting fixed rate cash flows to floating (for a fee, which we incorporate into other fees). These payments are based on a notional amortization schedule that is established at the beginning of the deal. The notional amount of the swap schedule is an anticipated target principal amortization schedule for the Liabilities Structure. It may or may not occur based on the performance of the collateral in generating cash flows to drive the deal over its life.

Keep in mind that by entering into a swap, the trust gives up any potential financial advantage from a favorable upward movement in the collateral financing benchmark as well. If rates decreased significantly over the life of a deal, then the debt services to the floating-rate notes would be decreased, in effect increasing the excess spread. This is the nature of the hedge, but investors are not typically interested in taking such a large degree of interest rate risk that would accompany holding a security based on 30-year fixed mortgages, for example.

If the loans in our portfolio were pure floating-rate mortgages, we would not have to build a swap into the deal. In our case we are dealing with a portfolio that may contain hybrid adjustable-rate mortgages (ARMs), pure floaters, and balloon loans. Because the majority of deals are securitized by recently issued collateral, there is a period at the beginning of the deal where the hybrid mortgages will be in their fixed rate phase. If our deal is made up of a significant amount of these 3/1, 5/1, and 7/1 hybrid ARMs, their cash flows will be indistinguishable from a fixed rate mortgage over the period of the initial 3, 5, or 7 year interest rate lock. Therefore we could, if the collateral contained a significant number of these loans include a quickly amortizing fixed for floating swap with a termination seven years out.

In the interest rate swap section, we enter four columns to track its effect on the deal:

1. **Swap Notional.** The swap notional is the balance schedule that the swap payment is based off of. This schedule is produced based on the Constant prepayment rate (CPR) amortization assumption from the Structure input sheet along with the swap tenor.
2. **Swap Rate.** This column contains the contractual swap rate used to compute fixed payment the trust is to pay the swap counterparty. This rate is typically set near the initial weighted average interest rate of the notes.
3. **Net Swap Payment.** The fixed payment minus the floating payment due to the trust from the counterparty based on the floating rate index in this case (LIBOR) and the notional schedule. When this amount is negative, it means the trust is receiving cash from the swap counterparty. A positive number signifies a payment to the counterparty by the trust out of the interest cash flows.
4. **Interest Available.** We already used the total interest amount to pay fees. This column reflects the total interest amount from the Available Cash section, less the fees paid and adjusted by the net swap payment.

If we net the total interest against the sum of the fees paid and the net swap payment amount, we are left with the sum of the available interest that will next be used to pay interest due on the notes.

Principal Distribution Section   This small, three-column section of the waterfall is one of the most important. In this section we compute the amount of cash that is going to be applied against the principal balances of the Class A and Class B notes. Literally every single element of the cash flow waterfall somehow factors into the computation of these fields. Once we have these values computed, the distribution of cash is relatively straightforward. There are some key concepts that we need to touch on before computing the senior and subordinate principal distribution amounts.

Step-Down Considerations   In the pre–step-down period of the deal, all of the total principal computed in the Available Cash section is paid to the Class A senior notes. During this stage of the deal, the senior class balances are reduced while the subordinate notes are kept constant (unless reduced due to losses). This has the effect of increasing the senior subordination amount with the goal of arriving at the Class A target subordination percentage as defined on the Structure inputs sheet. Once the step-down date is reached, the subordinate notes can receive cash if performance triggers are satisfied.

Senior Target Subordination Percentage   The "Target Sub %" table on the Structure inputs sheet specifies what each note's target subordination percentage is. For the senior notes, we consider them jointly when computing the subordination amounts. If the Class A target subordination percentage is 91%, then the amount of principal due to the Class A notes is the amount that will make the end of period Class A notes balance equal to 91% of the total asset balance. Since we know the previous Class A note balance and the current end of period asset balance, the principal payment due to maintain the 9% subordination (100% − 91%) is easily computed. Below is an example "Target Sub %" set:

Target Sub %	
A	91.00%
B-1	94.80%
B-2	97.00%
B-3	98.00%
B-4	99.00%

Use of Excess Spread in Principal Distribution   The amount available to make a principal distribution is not simply the amount stored in the Total Principal column in the Available Cash section. Recall that since the asset interest rate is greater than the all-in debt rate, we will more than likely have excess spread after making fee and interest payments. This left-over interest can be used to make principal payments if the Total Principal + Recoveries amount is not enough to maintain/achieve the notes' subordination amounts as defined by the target subordination percentages.

What this means is that in order to compute the total amount of principal distribution for a period, we will already have had to compute all the interest distribution amounts and derive the excess spread amount. If there is no excess spread, then only the Total Principal + Recoveries amount is available to distribute to the notes as principal. If there is spread left over, it can be used for different purposes elsewhere in the waterfall.

Principal Distribution Amounts   To compute the senior and subordinate principal distribution amounts, we need to tie together the above concepts. If the deal is in the period prior to the step down or a trigger has been activated, then all cash principal distribution is directed to the senior notes. When the deal has stepped down and both senior and subordinate notes are receiving principal payments, the amount paid to the senior notes is the amount needed to maintain the Class A Target Subordination %. The principal cash flow that is left after making this payment is the subordinate principal distribution amount.

Principal and Interest Payment Sections The manner in which principal and interest are paid to bond holders can vary tremendously from deal to deal. Our deal has six different bond classes: two senior bonds (A-1 and A-2) and four subordinate bonds (B-1, B-2, B-3, and B-4). In its essence, the senior/subordinate distinction speaks to the payment priority of the bonds.

Priority of Interest Payments   In every period the senior Class A bonds are paid their interest due before Class B bonds are paid any interest at all. In this case, we say that interest is paid *sequentially* from Class A to Class B. If there is not enough cash to make interest payments to all the bonds, then the most subordinated certificate (in our case B-4) will not receive a full interest payment. Depending on how the assets are performing, it may be the case that none of the subordinated certificates receives any interest payments.

In contrast to the sequential interest payments from Class A to Class B, the Class A-1 and A-2 certificates are paid interest pro rata based on the beginning period balance. What this means for Class A interest payments is that if there is not enough cash to pay the full interest due to the Class A certificates, what cash is available is split between Class A-1 and A-2 based on the amount due.

EXAMPLE

In a given period, the amount of interest due to the Class A-1 and A-2 notes, based on their beginning-of-period balances and periodic interest rate, is $90 and $10, respectively. There is only $52 received from the assets as interest payments in this period. After paying fees, there is $50 left to make interest distribution to the notes. In this case, Class A-1 will receive $45 (90/(90+10)*50) and Class A-2 receives $5 (10/(90+10)*50). The Class B notes receive no interest payments this period.

Each of the six interest payment sections has four columns. These columns and their functions are:

1. **Interest Rate.** Displays the periodic (annual) interest rate for the specified note. The values in these columns are sourced from an interest rate tracking section on the far right of the LWM.
2. **Interest Due.** The interest due amount is computed off the interest rate and the beginning-of-period balance of the note. The notes in the interest rate column are quoted on an annual basis, so we must divide by 12 to arrive at a monthly interest rate.
3. **Interest Paid.** The amount of interest paid to a note in a period is the maximum of the amount due and what is available to make the payment.
4. **Interest Allocation Carryforward.** These are the amounts of interest allocated but unpaid to the tranche.

In each of the six interest payment sections, it is essential to keep track of how much interest cash flow is still available, since the interest is paid sequentially. After the Class A notes have been paid their interest, the remaining amount is available to Class B-1. If there is still interest cash flow after Class B-1 is paid, then Class B-2 can receive a distribution, and so on.

Priority of Principal Payments   Principal payments in our deal have the same priority as the interest payments when it comes to making a distribution to the Class A and Class B notes. All principal payments from the assets (including recoveries) are first applied to the Class A notes up to their amount due and then sequentially to the Class B-1, B-2, B-3, and B-4 notes in order of seniority. If there is not enough cash from principal to make full payments to Class A-1 and A-2, then the amount available is split between the two classes pro rata based on the beginning-of-period outstanding principal balance of the notes.

EXAMPLE

In a given period, the Class A-1 and A-2 beginning principal balances are $900 and $100, respectively. The amounts due to the notes are $50 and $5, respectively, making a total amount of due of $55. Only $50 of principal is generated by the assets in this period. In this case, Class A-1 is paid $45 (900/(900+100)*50) and Class A-2 is paid $5 (100/(900+100)*50).

In our modeled deal, the Class A notes cannot experience write-downs. Therefore, since we have already computed the senior principal distribution amount in the Principal Distribution Amounts section, we simply pay the Class A-1 and A-2 notes the maximum of what is due and each class's respective pro rata share of the distribution amount.

The subordinated notes can take write-downs if the assets are performing poorly and all other enhancement (XS and OC) has been exhausted. We therefore need to build in a mechanism for tracking write-downs on the subordinated notes. Remember, if there are losses earlier in the deal, XS available later in the deal, if any, can be used to reimburse some of these losses.

The four columns needed for each Class B principal payment section are:

1. **Principal Paid.** The amount of principal paid is based on the available principal and the class's Target Subordination %.
2. **Loss Allocated.** When losses on the assets exceed the amount of XS and OC, the subordinated notes will have to start taking losses in order of reverse seniority. This column tracks the periodic loss allocated to a note.
3. **Cumulative Loss Allocated.** Tracks the total amount of losses allocated to a class net of any reimbursements it may have participated in.
4. **Loss Reimbursed.** Losses reimbursed from XS in order of seniority.

Balance Tracking Sections This section tracks the end of period balances for the six bonds in our deal. In every period, a bond's balance must decrease by any principal distribution amount or by any amount of loss allocated to the bond class (in the case of subordinated classes). We also track the periodic overcollateralization amount in this section.

Credit Enhancement Features Sections Three forms of credit enhancement need to be managed to some extent in sections toward the end of the LWM.

Target Overcollateralization Section In this section we track the target OC amount throughout the deal. Under usual circumstances the OC amount is stable for the life of the deal. In the later months of the deal, after the notes balances have been significantly reduced through amortization activity the OC Amount has stayed constant. The OC will then, if unadjusted, will become a very significant portion of the entire outstanding note balances. This will draw funds away from the amortization process and create entirely unneeded and disproportional amounts of OC in the deal. At this point the target OC amount is reduced to ensure that the senior notes continue to amortize as expected.

Excess Cash Treatment After paying fees and interest to the notes, there is a possibility that there will still be cash remaining. Actually, our deal was structured in such a way to ensure an excess cash flow. There are three uses of excess spread:

1. **Cover loss.** If there are periodic losses on the assets then, without employing XS, the target subordination percentages would cease to be met. By using XS to further pay down the notes, we can have losses on the assets but still maintain the enhancement enjoyed by subordination amounts.
2. **Reimburse losses.** If the performance of the assets has improved after a period of write-downs, XS can be used to reimburse those losses.
3. **Release.** If the structure does not need to use XS to maintain target subordination percentages and there are no unreimbursed losses, the excess cash flow is released to the residual note holder (in many cases the original owner of the assets).

Trigger Tracking The performance trigger in the deal looks at the cumulative net loss percentage in a given period and compares it against a trigger threshold table on the Structure inputs tab. The threshold changes throughout the deal, as cumulative losses are expected to rise as the deal progresses. Below is an example of the trigger threshold schedule:

Cumulative Realized Loss Trigger			
ID	Start	End	%
0	0	24	100.00%
1	25	36	0.15%
2	37	48	0.25%
3	49	60	0.50%
4	61	72	0.70%
5	73	360	0.75%

If the performance test fails, a mechanism similar to the pre–step-down period process diverts all principal distributions to the Class A senior notes. For tracking the performance trigger state, we will need two columns: one to track the Cumulative Net Loss % throughout the deal and one to test whether the trigger has failed. In the Principal Distribution section, we built a column called "Pre-Step Down or Trigger". This trigger column aggregates the performance trigger and step down behavior into a single trigger.

A second trigger is called the "Clean Up Call" trigger. In addition to the servicing fee discussed above, there are also fixed costs associated with an MBS transaction. Since these fees are fixed, the relative drag of these fees becomes more significant as the magnitude of the collateral cash flows declines through time, prepayments, and defaults as the deal matures. At a certain point it becomes uneconomical to have a small amount of assets in a trust. Most deals set a time where the seller of the assets has the opportunity to repurchase the assets from the trust at par, thus terminating the trust and retiring the notes. The cleanup call is exercisable at a point in time (the cleanup date) or when the outstanding assets drop below a percentage of the initial balance (the cleanup percentage). Our deal has a 10% cleanup call percentage, which is fairly typical of deals of this type. This trigger is tracked alongside the performance trigger.

PERFORMANCE SUMMARY PAGE

The Performance Summary Page worksheet will provide a snapshot of the last scenario calculated by the Liabilities Waterfall Spreadsheet. It will display a variety of summary statistics by bond tranche as well as a summary statement of the components of the collateral cash flows that were the source of funds for the structure.

We will also provide a graphic of the amortization performance of the various bond tranches for the scenario. See Exhibit 14.4.

VBA CODE MODULES

In the VBA environment we will create the following modules to perform the tasks of menu support, inputs importation, managing the calculation process, and reporting.

UserForm Support Code
- "m01LWMReportsMenu". A VBA UserForm module containing the support code for the Report Package Menu UserForm.

VBA Modules of the LWM
- "A_Constants". This module containing all Public Constant variables of the model. It will also contain all the fixed file pathways to the template directories of the LWM directory environment.
- "A_Globals". This module contains all Public variables of the model.
- "A_MainProgram". This module will contain the Main Program module of the LWM.

Performance Results

Collateral Performance

Scheduled Amortization	30,568,305
Prepayments	79,200,566
Total Principal	109,769,471
Defaulted Principal	421,294,476
Gross Loss %	79.33%
Recoveries	360,562,873
Lifetime Severity	14.44%
Interest	85,238,183
Net Swap Payment	0
Total Cash	555,570,527
Total Fees	4,549,437
Asset VAL	38.07
Call Period	71

Model Checks	
Assets	TRUE
Cash In / Cash Out	TRUE

Bond Performance

Class	A-1	A-2	B-1	B-2	B-3	B-4	OC	Total
Initial Balance ($)	456,535,412	50,728,157	10,092,115	5,842,803	2,655,820	2,655,820	2,655,820	531,163,947
Initial Balance (%)	85.95%	9.55%	1.90%	1.10%	0.50%	0.50%	0.50%	100.00%
Total Principal	456,535,412	50,728,157	10,092,115	5,842,803	2,655,820	2,655,820	0	507,261,569
Total Interest	28,408,390	3,037,664	69,843	27,766	10,125	11,617	0	29,885,995
Gross Write Downs	NA	NA	10,092,115	5,842,803	2,655,820	2,655,820	NA	21,246,558
Write Down Reimbursment	NA	NA	10,092,115	4,101,411	0	0	NA	14,193,526
Net Write Downs	NA	NA	0	1,741,392	2,655,820	2,655,820	NA	7,053,032
Yield to Maturity	1.42%	1.47%	0.08%	-7.60%	-99.99%	-99.99%	NA	NA
Yield to Call	1.42%	1.47%	-99.99%	-99.99%	-99.99%	-99.99%	NA	NA
Coverage Ratio NPV	0.00%	0.00%	0.00%	0.00%	0.00%	0.00%	NA	NA
Coverage Ratio FV	0.00%	0.00%	0.00%	0.00%	0.00%	0.00%	NA	NA
Severity of Loss NPV	0.00%	0.00%	99.08%	99.44%	99.45%	89.43%	NA	NA
Severity of Loss FV	0.00%	0.00%	100.00%	100.00%	100.00%	100.00%	NA	NA
VAL (maturity)	48.9	48.9	5.3	3.4	2.1	1.5	NA	NA
VAL (to call)	46.7	46.7	5.3	3.4	2.1	1.5	NA	NA
Duration	3.9	3.9	0.3	0.2	0.1	0.1	NA	NA

Deal Balance %

EXHIBIT 14.4 Performance Summary page

- **"MenuSupportAggAnnCFs"**. This module will aggregate all of the monthly cash flows presented in the report package into annual schedules. This will considerably condense the data and make them easier to display in tables and graphs.
- **"MenuSupport_ErrorChecking"**. The module will contain the error checking/warning menu support code for the Main Menu. It will help the user to avoid errors that could lead to conflicts in file names and incomplete or missing entries for model run information.
- **"MenuSupport_ImportCFsFiles"**. This module will contain the VBA code that reads the contents of Collateral Cash Flow Input files and places the information into VBA arrays. It will also error check all of the inputs on the Assumptions Report attached to the cash flow schedule worksheets of the report. As a part of this process it performs a scan of every number of the file for nonnumeric or missing entries. Last, the code of the module will construct the set of Prepayment and Default Case conditions that identify each particular collateral cash flow scenario to the LWM.
- **"MenuSupport_ImportStructFiles"**. This module contains the VBA code that reads the contents of Liabilities Structure Input files and places them in VBA arrays. The subroutines here perform a series of tests of the content file for data format and reasonableness. In addition, they scan the tranche descriptions of the file to make sure that the structure has no internal subordination inconsistencies.
- **"MenuSupport_WriteStructFiles"**. This module contains the VBA that reads the contents of the Structure Inputs Menu and creates a Liabilities Structure input file that can be later used by the model.
- **"Run_LiabilitesModel"**. This module loads the collateral cash flow information into the LWM, loads the structure inputs, runs the model, and records the calculation results of the LWM.
- **"Run_ReadResultsStructure"**. The subroutines of this module are sequentially integrated with the subroutines contained in the "Run_LiabilitiesModel" module. After the cash flows have been loaded, the spreadsheet calculated, and the results generated and displayed, the subroutines of this module record the results in a series of purpose-specific arrays. These arrays record tenor performance, principal, and coupon paid to the tranches; the uses of excess cash flows; and other structural performance. These are the arrays that we will draw from to produce the reports.
- **"Report_LiabilitesWaterfall"**. This report module captures the entire contents of each of the LWS at the time of the completion of the calculation sequence. The report package consists of a series of one spreadsheet copy for each of the cash flow prepayment/default collateral cash flow scenarios.
- **"Report_MiscWaterfall"**. This report module captures the entire contents of each of the LWS at the time of the completion of the calculation sequence. The report package consists of a series of one spreadsheet copy for each of the cash flow prepayment/default collateral cash flow scenarios.
- **"Report_MiscCFs"**. This module contains the VBA code that produces three reports.
- **Collateral Cash Flows Report.** This report module allows the analyst to display the annual amounts of the six cash flow arrays for any of the 25 scenarios

of a Case. The arrays are the Beginning Period Collateral Principal Balances, Defaults of Principal, Scheduled Amortization of Principal, Coupon Payments, Prepayments of Principal, and Recoveries of Defaulted Principal. The Beginning Period Collateral Principal Balances are plotted on the right axis of the report due to the disparity of size in the cash flows and the collateral pool balances.

- **Excess Cash Flows Report.** This report allows the analyst to select a single scenario of the 25 scenarios of the Case. It displays the five components of excess cash (or overcollateralization). These are the Beginning Period Excess Cash Amount, the Over Collateralization Deficiency, the Over Collateralization Applied, the Over Collateralization Reimbursement, and the Over Collateralization Released (to the investor).

- **Deal Fees Report.** This report displays the annual fee schedule of up to six different scenarios.

- **"Report_MultiTrancheCFs".** This report module presents a single specific cash flow component for each of the tranches of the structure on a single report. The components are Principal Paid, Coupon Expense Paid, Losses Incurred, and the Beginning Period Principal Balance of each tranche.

- **"Report_MultiTrancheTenor".** This report displays a single measure of tenor performance for all of the tranches of the structure on a single page. The tenor measurements are Weighted Average Life to Maturity and to Call, Final Maturity, and Modified Duration.

- **"Report_MultiTrancheReturns".** This report displays a single measure of returns and ratio performances. It contains the Yield to Maturity, the Yield to Call, the Net Present Value, and Future Value Coverage Ratios for each tranche and the Net Present Value and Future Value Severity of Loss statistics for each tranche.

- **"Report_SingleTrancheCFs".** This report displays all cash flow components of a single tranche on the same page. The cash flows are those presented in the MultiTrancheCFs report above.

- **"Report_SingleTrancheTenor".** This report module produces a series of reports, one per tranche, of all of the tenor statistic performances of the tranche across the various cash flow scenarios of the case.

- **"Report_SingleTrancheReturns".** This report displays Yield to Maturity, the Yield to Call, the Net Present Value, and Future Value Coverage Ratios for each tranche, and the Net Present Value and Future Value Severity of Loss statistics for each tranche, one tranche at a time.

- **"Z_ButtonSubroutines".** Support code for all of the LWM buttons. These buttons include the navigation and the "get file" buttons of the Main Menu in addition to the button used to display the Report Selection User Form.

- **"Z_UtilityPrepayDefaultWriter".** This module contains all the formatting code to load the prepayment and default scenario assumptions into each of the reports of the LWM.

- **"Z_UtilitySubroutines".** This module contains a series of general utility subroutines related to report formation, number/letter conversions, and file retrieval activity.

REPORT TEMPLATE FILES

The report template files of the LWM will consist of the following files found in the "C:\VBA_Book2\Code\templates_liab" directory.

Single Tranche Performance Reports

There are two Single Tranche Performance reports. The first one contains cash flow information and the other contains tenor performance of the individual tranches.

Cash Flows Report   There are four Single Tranche Cash Flow Report template files. Each of these files reports a specific cash flow component of a tranche.

1. "TemplateSTCF_AmortBalance". Schedule of annual beginning principal balances by tranche for each scenario of the Case.
2. "TemplateSTCF_PrinPmts". Annual schedule of principal retired by tranche for each scenario of the Case.
3. "TemplateSTCF_CoupPaid". Annual schedule of coupon debt service paid to each tranche for each scenario of the Case.
4. "TemplateSTCF_Losses". Annual schedule of losses included by each tranche for each scenario of the Case.

Too Much of a Good Thing!   There are six bond tranches and up to a maximum of 25 scenarios per Case. This could result in a total of 150 reports generated by a single Case of the model. The model allows for up to five pairings of a Collateral Cash Flow File along with a Liabilities Structure File. Thus five Cases run could produce a single LWM run maximum of 750 individual reports. This quantity of reports quickly becomes unwieldy for the analyst to digest! What we need is a format that allows all the information contained in the various runs to be accessible without actually displaying all of it at one time and overwhelming the model user.

Conditional Displays   The solution to the above problem is to design the template file for each of the Single Tranche Cash Flow reports to allow it to function as a *report writer* as opposed to just a *report file*. We will accomplish this through a combination of report design and VBA programming. We will create a single worksheet for each of the six bond tranches, A-1 and A-2, and B-1 through B-4.

Report Structure   In each of the template files we will divide the report into two distinct areas. The first of these areas is the Display Area. The second is the Data Schedule Area.

In the Display Area, we will group those elements of the report that will be become the finished report. This area will consist of two elements, a table that holds up to 30 years of annual cash flows for a specific tranche and a graph of the contents of the table. The analyst will be able to enter the identification numbers of up to six scenarios (defined by unique prepayment/default combinations) into the header area of the table. The VBA code contained in the template file will then load the specified scenario cash flows from the Data Schedule Area.

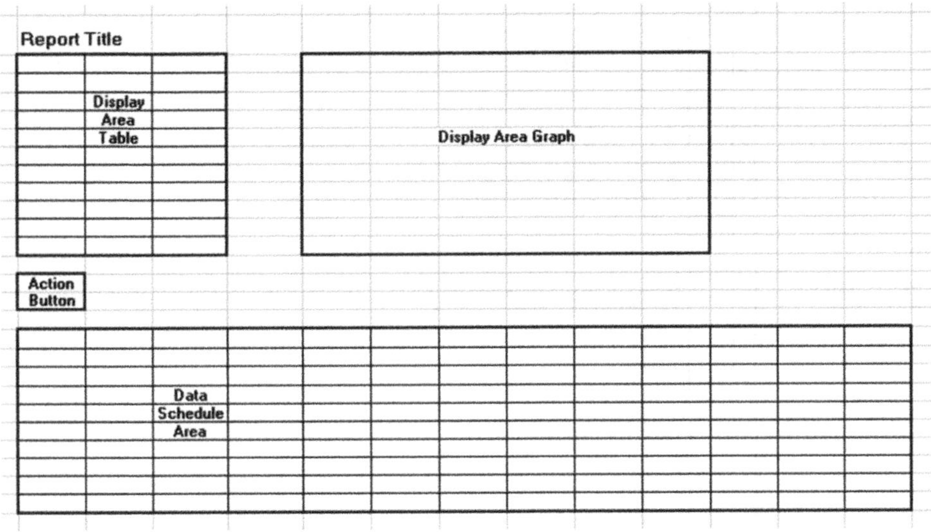

EXHIBIT 14.5   Single Tranche Cash Flow Report schematic

The Data Schedule Area will contain the annually aggregated cash flows for each of the unique scenarios contained in the Case the LWM has just run. This means there can be a possible maximum of 25 of these scenarios. (Remember, the Collateral Cash Flow Generator Program can generate a maximum of 25 collateral cash flow scenarios by combining up to five prepayment and five default speed assumptions.)

A Command Button will be provided to initiate the lookup and loading process of moving the selected cash flows from the Data Schedule Area into the Display Area. The schematic for a Single Tranche worksheet of the file is shown in Exhibit 14.5.

A sample Data Schedule Area is shown in Exhibit 14.6.

A sample Display Area is shown in Exhibit 14.7.

Report Presentation Issues   What we have now accomplished provides the analyst with the ability to format the content of the report in a flexible manner with a very large number of scenario combinations. We have provided for up to six scenarios to be displayed simultaneously in the Display Area of the report. Why six? We want to preserve the visual integrity of the report by balancing the tabular representation of data to the left of the report and the graphic representation of data to the right of the report. If we allow for a larger number of scenarios, say ten, the size of the table will begin to push the graph off the right side of the viewing area of an average screen. We then have two equally unsavory alternatives. We can reduce the size of both the table and the graph (and go blind trying to read them), or maintain the size and force the analyst to page back and forth between them (annoying at best). A larger report may well become illegible when we try to compress it to fit on a single printed page of a presentation.

The use of six scenarios also allows the user to designate a single scenario of the Case as a "Base Case" and subsequently display five other scenarios in juxtaposition to it. What is the advantage of displaying five alternative scenarios? Five scenarios

Tranche A-1 Annual Principal Balances By Scenario

Scenario	1	2	3	4	5	6	7	8	9	10	11	12	13	14	15
Prepay Info	GEO 100%	GEO 100%	GEO 100%	GEO 100%	GEO 100%	GEO 125%	GEO 125%	GEO 125%	GEO 125%	GEO 125%	GEO 150%	GEO 150%	GEO 150%	GEO 150%	GEO 150%
Default Info	DEMO 100%	DEMO 125%	DEMO 150%	DEMO 175%	DEMO 200%	DEMO 100%	DEMO 125%	DEMO 150%	DEMO 175%	DEMO 200%	DEMO 100%	DEMO 125%	DEMO 150%	DEMO 175%	DEMO 200%
1	456,535,412	456,535,412	456,535,412	456,535,412	456,535,412	456,535,412	456,535,412	456,535,412	456,535,412	456,535,412	456,535,412	456,535,412	456,535,412	456,535,412	456,535,412
2	424,633,931	422,535,146	420,446,625	418,368,320	416,300,182	424,907,144	422,826,652	420,756,365	418,696,235	416,646,215	425,193,135	423,130,990	421,078,992	419,037,092	417,005,244
3	390,910,493	386,934,335	383,000,811	379,109,469	375,259,876	391,150,252	387,246,820	383,385,519	379,565,899	375,787,513	391,444,384	387,613,191	383,823,627	380,075,245	376,367,603
4	346,406,091	340,626,192	334,951,293	329,379,468	323,908,843	344,267,093	338,659,519	333,154,895	327,751,322	322,446,935	342,183,248	336,747,505	331,412,663	326,176,851	321,038,234
5	294,115,233	286,010,061	278,328,109	270,647,619	263,245,651	284,204,444	276,996,832	269,993,719	263,189,251	256,577,745	277,471,195	270,597,568	263,922,280	257,439,608	251,144,001
6	243,574,178	233,680,009	224,365,151	215,199,120	206,450,688	218,346,670	209,892,771	201,780,971	193,997,349	186,528,562	205,970,543	198,071,014	190,499,189	183,241,590	176,285,303
7	195,007,747	183,846,187	173,437,007	163,336,450	153,800,915	163,156,298	153,103,863	143,912,468	135,194,705	126,721,515	138,814,621	130,513,604	122,672,764	115,267,318	108,273,851
8	153,868,487	141,928,427	130,916,563	120,371,632	110,534,033	117,068,300	106,526,344	97,004,011	88,097,364	79,561,833	84,085,055	75,932,339	68,355,416	61,315,148	54,771,280
9	119,832,897	107,548,350	96,360,112	85,785,710	76,045,906	79,686,394	69,100,603	59,685,233	51,016,656	42,831,623	41,432,478	34,309,760	28,045,151	22,521,703	17,618,022
10	87,977,889	75,728,623	64,731,887	54,487,736	45,183,643	44,519,895	35,173,619	26,924,240	19,701,662	13,090,041	8,773,513	3,618,700	0	0	0
11	58,340,335	46,522,618	36,393,385	27,373,690	19,545,766	15,817,237	8,311,540	2,007,682	0	0	0	0	0	0	0
12	31,961,100	21,961,099	13,556,120	6,275,956	148,172	0	0	0	0	0	0	0	0	0	0
13	10,995,201	3,121,621	0	0	0	0	0	0	0	0	0	0	0	0	0
14	0	0	0	0	0	0	0	0	0	0	0	0	0	0	0
15	0	0	0	0	0	0	0	0	0	0	0	0	0	0	0
16	0	0	0	0	0	0	0	0	0	0	0	0	0	0	0
17	0	0	0	0	0	0	0	0	0	0	0	0	0	0	0
18	0	0	0	0	0	0	0	0	0	0	0	0	0	0	0
19	0	0	0	0	0	0	0	0	0	0	0	0	0	0	0
20	0	0	0	0	0	0	0	0	0	0	0	0	0	0	0

EXHIBIT 14.6 Single Tranche Cash Flow Report Data Schedule Area (partial)

Tranche A-1 Principal Balances

Scenario Assump	1 G100%-D100%	2 G100%-D125%	5 G100%-D200%	6 G125%-D100%	8 G125%-D150%	20 G175%-D200%
1	456,535,412	456,535,412	456,535,412	456,535,412	456,535,412	456,535,412
2	424,633,931	422,535,146	416,300,182	424,907,144	420,756,365	417,383,318
3	390,910,493	386,934,335	375,259,876	391,150,252	383,385,519	376,967,678
4	346,406,091	340,626,192	323,908,843	344,267,093	333,154,895	319,649,803
5	294,115,233	286,010,061	263,245,651	284,204,444	269,993,719	245,730,818
6	243,574,178	233,680,009	206,450,688	218,346,670	201,780,971	166,062,901
7	195,007,747	183,846,187	153,800,915	163,156,298	143,912,468	93,820,503
8	153,868,487	141,928,427	110,534,033	117,068,300	97,004,011	39,209,208
9	119,832,897	107,548,350	76,045,906	79,686,394	59,685,233	7,314,904
10	87,977,889	75,728,623	45,183,643	44,519,895	26,924,240	0
11	58,340,335	46,522,618	19,545,766	15,817,237	2,007,682	
12	31,961,100	21,961,099	148,172	0	0	
13	10,995,201	3,121,621	0			
14	0	0				
15		0				
16						
17						
18						
19						
20						
21						
22						
23						
24						
25						
26						
27						
28						
29						
30						

Principal Amortization Curves for Selected Scenarios
Geographic Stress Prepayment, Demographic Stress Default Methodology

Legend: G100%-D100%, G100%-D125%, G100%-D200%, G125%-D100%, G125%-D150%, G175%-D200%

EXHIBIT 14.7 Single Tranche Cash Flow Report Data Display Area

are the full complement of a maximum prepayment/default row or column in the CCFG. For example:

- The analyst initially generates 25 collateral cash flow scenarios in the CCFG by inputting a Base Prepayment Rate of 100% Geographic Stress with five Prepayment Stress Increments of 10% each. The base default rate is 100% Demographic with five default stress increments of 20% each.
- The "Base Case" is designated to be 100% geographic prepayments by 100% demographic defaults.
- The analyst could now select any of the five rows or columns of the prepayment/default matrix combinations to compare to the "Base Case" of 100% GEO/100% DEMO. (Note: If either the first row of combinations or the first column of combinations were selected, one would probably elect to deselect the "Base Case" to avoid repetition of displayed results.)

Graphic Format and Notation Practices   The format of the graph is a multiple-series line chart. The Prepayment/Default descriptions of the selected scenarios are presented in the column headers of the table. The abbreviations used are as follows:

1. **PSA** and **CPR:** for the Uniform Methodologies
2. **GEO:** for the Geographic Methodology
3. **DEMO:** for the Demographic Methodology

Prepayment methodology/speeds are given first followed by default methodology/speeds. Thus the abbreviation for the "Base Case" of 100% Geographic Prepayments and 100% Demographic Defaults would be abbreviated to "GEO100%/DEMO100%". This is the identifying label that will be presented in the legend of the graph.

Working from the information above, we will also create a specialized Main Title for the graph. The first line of the title will contain the name of the tranche selected for presentation and the name of the Tenor statistic. The second line of the Main Title will display the Prepayment/Default methodology of the scenario. We could also display the scenario number but, in that the number of the scenario is specific, the particular Case this might be confusing. The Main Title would appear as follows:

"Tranche A-2 Principal Payments for Selected Scenarios
Geographic Prepayment, Demographic Default Methodologies"

This will complete the customized formatting necessary to allow the analyst to quickly and correctly identify the contents of the report.

Tenor Performance Report   The structure and presentation of the Single Tranche Tenor Report is similar to that of the Single Tranche Cash Flows Report in that they both have a Display Area at the top of the template file worksheet. The structural schema of the Single Tranche Tenor Report lacks a Data Schedule Area below it. This is due to the fact that the amount of information in the Single Tranche Tenor Report is dramatically smaller than that required to produce the Single Tranche Cash Flow file. The data in the Data Schedule of the Cash Flows Report can be a maximum of 30 rows by 25 columns, a total 750 datum for a single tranche. A single Case

Tranche A1 - All Tenor Results

Select Tenor Choice = [1]   Load Selected Tenor Results

Select	Tranche	Default	Prepayment Method and Speeds				
			G-100%	G-125%	G-150%	G-175%	G-200%
1	WAL to Maturity	D-100%	5.7	5.5	5.3	5.1	4.9
		D-125%	5.1	4.9	4.8	4.6	4.5
		D-150%	4.7	4.6	4.5	4.4	4.3
		D-175%	4.5	4.4	4.3	4.3	4.2
		D-200%	4.4	4.3	4.2	4.1	4.1
Select	Tranche	Default	G-100%	G-125%	G-150%	G-175%	G-200%
2	WAL to Call	D-100%	5.6	5.4	5.2	5.0	4.8
		D-125%	5.0	4.9	4.7	4.6	4.5
		D-150%	4.7	4.5	4.4	4.3	4.2
		D-175%	4.4	4.3	4.2	4.1	4.1
		D-200%	4.2	4.1	4.1	4.0	3.9
Select	Tranche	Default	G-100%	G-125%	G-150%	G-175%	G-200%
3	Final Maturity	D-100%	0.0	0.0	0.0	0.0	0.0
		D-125%	0.0	0.0	0.0	0.0	0.0
		D-150%	0.0	0.0	0.0	0.0	0.0
		D-175%	0.0	0.0	0.0	0.0	0.0
		D-200%	0.0	0.0	0.0	0.0	0.0
Select	Tranche	Default	G-100%	G-125%	G-150%	G-175%	G-200%
4	Modified Duration	D-100%	0.5	0.4	0.4	0.4	0.4
		D-125%	0.4	0.4	0.4	0.4	0.4
		D-150%	0.4	0.4	0.4	0.4	0.3
		D-175%	0.4	0.4	0.3	0.3	0.3
		D-200%	0.4	0.3	0.3	0.3	0.3

EXHIBIT 14.8 Display Area table: Single Tranche Tenor Performance Report

run of the LWM produces only four tenor data for each scenario. The total amount of data produced for a single tranche in a 25- scenario Case is therefore capped at 100, less than 15% of the data of a full cash flow schedule report. This amount of information can be easily accommodated in a table of quite manageable size in the Display Area of the report. See Exhibit 14.8.

With all four tenor performance statistics in each of the tranche-specific worksheets, we do not need multiple template files as we did in the instance of the Single Tranche Cash Flow reports. All the tenor performance statistics can be displayed in a single table in a single worksheet per tranche.

We can now allow the analyst to make selections of tenor statistics rather than by prepayment/default scenario. The data for all 25 scenarios of the LWM Case can be displayed in a single graph. The contents of the Display Area of the template file consist of a table that is divided into four sections, one for each of the tenor measurements produced by the LWM. There is a single measurement for each of the four tenor statistics in each of the scenarios of the Case. This allows the entire table to consist of four subsections, each having the provision to display 25 results, one from each of the scenarios of the Case, in a relatively compact table to the left side of the Display Area. Due to the small amount of data, we can also modify the display

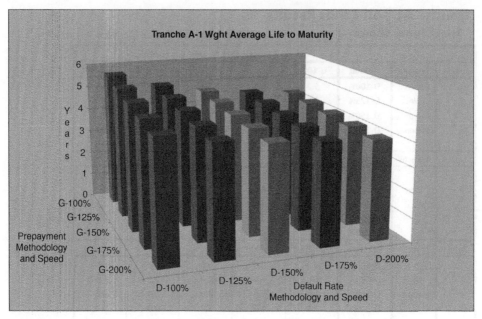

EXHIBIT 14.9 Display Area graph: Weighted Average Life to Maturity data

in the graph to more closely mimic the prepayment/default matrix of the CCFG Prepayment/Default combinations. We will use a 3-D bar graph format to display the full contents of a single sub-section of the Display Area table. See Exhibit 14.9.

In that the grid of the 3-D bar graph defines the data series completely, we can dispense with a legend when using this type of graph. We will, however, use the abbreviation system noted in the Single Tranche Cash Flow section immediately above to identify the row and columns of the matrix. Time periods are on the vertical axis, prepayment methodology/speed is on the left horizontal axis, and the default methodology/speed is on the right horizontal axis.

Multiple Tranche Performance Reports

The structure and composition of the three Multiple Tranche Reports is simply a reversal of the structure of the Single Tranche Reports. In a Single Tranche Report workbook, the worksheets are organized by tranche; in Multiple Tranche Reports, the worksheets of the report are organized by the data items to be displayed. As with the Single Tranche Report, we will look at the Multiple Tranche Cash Flow Report first. The Multiple Tranche Tenor Report will be created to display the tenor performance of all of the tranches in a single worksheet. Each tenor measurement will have its own worksheet.

Cash Flows Report   Unlike the organization of the Single Tranche Cash Flow Report, the Multiple Tranche Cash Flow Report consists of a single report template file named "TemplateMTCFs_All". The template file consists of four individual worksheets, one each for the four cash flows available for presentation. The names of the worksheets in the template file will be:

1. "BegBals". Beginning annual principal balances of the individual bond tranches.
2. "Prin". Total principal retired from the remaining tranche balance for that year.
3. "Coup". Total annual coupon debt service paid to the tranche for that year.
4. "Losses". Total annual losses applied to the tranche for that year.

The Display Area table and graph as shown in Exhibits 14.10 and 14.11.

Display Area   The Display Area consists of a table and graph in common with the other reports. The table contains six columns, one each for the bond tranches of the structure. In that all of the results are from a single scenario, there is only one scenario selection field and a single prepayment/default abbreviation for the contents of the table as a whole.

Annual Beginning Principal Balances

Scenario	1	Assumpt	G100%-D100%			
Tranche	A-1	A-2	B-1	B-2	B-3	B-4
1	456,535,412	50,726,157	10,092,115	5,842,803	2,655,820	2,655,820
2	424,633,931	47,181,548	8,953,727	0	0	0
3	390,910,493	43,434,499	0			
4	346,406,091	38,489,566				
5	294,115,233	32,679,470				
6	243,574,178	27,063,798				
7	195,007,747	21,667,527				
8	153,868,487	17,096,499				
9	119,832,897	13,314,766				
10	87,977,889	9,775,321				
11	58,340,335	6,482,259				
12	31,961,100	3,551,233				
13	10,995,201	1,221,689				
14	0	0				
15						
16						
17						
18						
19						
20						
21						
22						
23						
24						
25						
26						
27						
28						
29						
30						

EXHIBIT 14.10   Multiple Tranche Cash Flow Report Display Area table

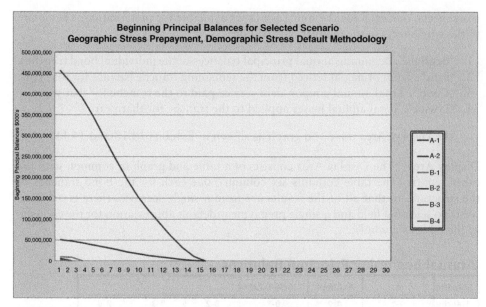

EXHIBIT 14.11   Multiple Tranche Cash Flow Report Display Area graph

All cash flows are either beginning annual balances or annual sums. The main title of the graph consists of the name of the cash flow displayed in the first line and the prepayment/default methodology used in the second.

Data Schedule Area   The Data Schedule Area of each of the worksheets will contain 25 sections, each of which has six columns, one for each of the bond tranches. The prepayment and default methodologies/speeds used to generate the selected scenario are displayed in the header of each of the six column sections. The user selects a single scenario from the Data Schedule Area and its contents are presented in the Display Area of the report.

Tenor Performance Report   The Multiple Tranche Tenor Performance Report consists of four worksheets, one each for the four tenor measurements of each of the bond tranches. The Display Area of the report consists of a table and a graph. There is no Data Schedule Area in these worksheets as all of the information can be contained in the Data Display Area table. The LWM will simply populate the Display Area table with the 25 scenario results for the tenor performance statistic. The analyst will then select the number of the tranche to have the information automatically loaded into the Display Area graph. The graph will be a 3-D bar chart. See Exhibits 14.12 and 14.13.

Waterfall Performance Report

The Waterfall Performance Report will consist of a single worksheet for each of the scenarios of the Case. These scenario-specific worksheets will contain a copy of the entire LWM spreadsheet. They will also include the Sources and Uses check columns

Tenor Report All Tranches - Average Life

Select Tranche Choice = | 1 | **Load Selected Tranche Results**

Select	Tranche	Default	G-100%	G-125%	G-150%	G-175%	G-200%
					Prepayment Method and Speeds		
	A	D-100%	5.7	5.1	4.7	4.5	4.4
	1	D-125%	5.5	4.9	4.6	4.4	4.3
1		D-150%	5.3	4.8	4.5	4.3	4.2
		D-175%	5.1	4.6	4.4	4.3	4.1
		D-200%	4.9	4.5	4.3	4.2	4.1
Select	Tranche	Default	G-100%	G-125%	G-150%	G-175%	G-200%
	A	D-100%	5.7	5.1	4.7	4.5	4.4
	2	D-125%	5.5	4.9	4.6	4.4	4.3
2		D-150%	5.3	4.8	4.5	4.3	4.2
		D-175%	5.1	4.6	4.4	4.3	4.1
		D-200%	4.9	4.5	4.3	4.2	4.1
Select	Tranche	Default	G-100%	G-125%	G-150%	G-175%	G-200%
	B	D-100%	1.3	0.9	0.6	0.5	0.4
	1	D-125%	1.3	0.9	0.6	0.5	0.4
3		D-150%	1.3	0.9	0.6	0.5	0.4
		D-175%	1.3	0.9	0.6	0.5	0.4
		D-200%	1.3	0.9	0.6	0.5	0.4
Select	Tranche	Default	G-100%	G-125%	G-150%	G-175%	G-200%
	B	D-100%	0.8	0.5	0.4	0.3	0.3
	2	D-125%	0.8	0.5	0.4	0.3	0.3
4		D-150%	0.8	0.5	0.4	0.3	0.3
		D-175%	0.8	0.5	0.4	0.3	0.3
		D-200%	0.8	0.5	0.4	0.3	0.3
Select	Tranche	Default	G-100%	G-125%	G-150%	G-175%	G-200%
	B	D-100%	0.5	0.3	0.3	0.2	0.2
	3	D-125%	0.5	0.3	0.3	0.2	0.2
5		D-150%	0.5	0.3	0.3	0.2	0.2
		D-175%	0.5	0.3	0.3	0.2	0.2
		D-200%	0.5	0.3	0.3	0.2	0.2
Select	Tranche	Default	G-100%	G-125%	G-150%	G-175%	G-200%
	B	D-100%	0.3	0.2	0.2	0.1	0.1
	4	D-125%	0.3	0.2	0.2	0.1	0.1
6		D-150%	0.3	0.2	0.2	0.1	0.1
		D-175%	0.3	0.2	0.2	0.1	0.1
		D-200%	0.3	0.2	0.2	0.1	0.1

EXHIBIT 14.12 Multiple Tranche Tenor Performance Report Display Area table

at the far right of the spreadsheets. There are no summary statistics in the Waterfall Performance Report.

One of the key functions of this report is to provide the analyst using the LWM with a fully detailed set of cash flows across all periods of the life of the liabilities waterfall. The Waterfall Performance Report is designed for the analyst and no one else!. It are useful for a variety of purposes, one of the most important of which is model verification activities upon the development of future versions of the model.

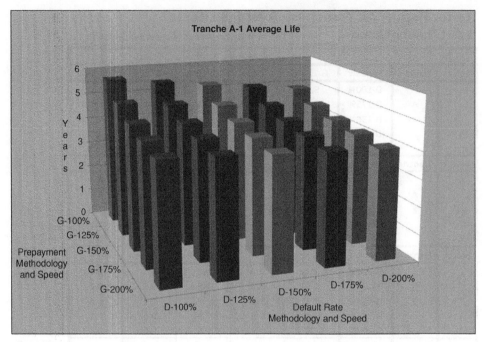

EXHIBIT 14.13   Multiple Tranche Tenor Performance Report Display Area graph

It is also useful for internal validation requirements placed on models by audit and risk groups within the organization.

In that the Waterfall Performance Report is identical to the format of the LWM waterfall spreadsheet, we will defer any discussion of it at this time.

Miscellaneous Reports

In addition to the above reports, the LWM produces three special-purpose reports that will provide the analyst with a picture of the expenses of the deal for up to six scenarios, a report that outlines the amount and application of any excess cash flows of the deal, and a report of the annual collateral cash flows of any single scenario. This last report is provided as a convenience to the model user. The Collateral Cash Flow Generator produces a robust series of analytical reports that can be used in a variety of ways. Most of that descriptive information concerning the collateral is ignored by the LWM. The magnitude and timing of the cash flows are, however, critical to the performance of the Liabilities Structure. Only the net cash flows per period are used in the calculations of the LWM. We therefore provide the analyst with a report that has the look and feel of other LWM reports and that can be included in any report dealing with the performance of the Liabilities Structure.

Deal Fees Report   The Deal Fees report is identical in content to a Single Tranche Cash Flow Report. The workbook contains a single worksheet, "Fees," that allows the analyst to select up to six individual prepayment/default scenarios from those of the Case that is loaded into the Data Schedule Area of the report. The format of the graph is a line format. The data table will identify the selected scenarios using the abbreviations discussed earlier in the chapter in the Single Tranche Report section. These scenario abbreviations will be presented in the legend of the graph. The Data Schedule Area of the worksheet consists of 25 columns, each representing 30 annual totals of the deal expenses by scenario.

Excess Cash Flows Report   The template file for the Excess Cash Flow Report is similar in structure and organization to that of the multiple tranche template files discussed above. A single scenario is selected and the four component cash flows of the Excess Cash Flow section of the LWM are displayed for that scenario. These Excess Cash Flow components are as follows:

- Beginning Period Excess Cash
- Period Over Collateralization Deficiency
- Applied Over Collateralization
- Over Collateralization Loss Reimbursement
- Over Collateralization Released

The form of the graph is a line graph with a legend that identifies the selected scenario using the abbreviation practice outlined above. The Data Schedule Area of the template files consists of 25 sets of five columns for each of the possible CCFG scenarios. See Exhibit 14.14.

Collateral Cash Flows Report   This template report produces a Display Area containing a table and graph of the six components of a single CCFG collateral prepayment/default scenario of the Case run by the LWM. This report is presented as a convenience to the analyst, who may wish to include the collateral cash flows

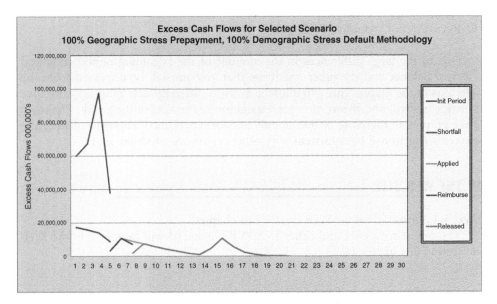

EXHIBIT 14.14   Excess Cash Flows Report Display Area graph

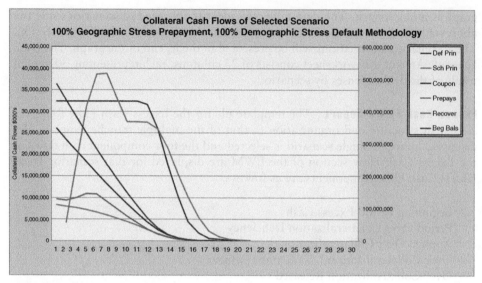

EXHIBIT 14.15   Collateral Cash Flow Report Display Area graph

in the same presentation as the results of the LWM. It allows for a consistency in format between the LWM performance reports and the CCFG results report. The components of the report are:

1. Beginning Period Collateral Principal Balance
2. Defaults of Principal
3. Scheduled Amortization of Principal
4. Coupon Income from Payments
5. Prepayments of Principal
6. Recoveries of Defaulted Principal

Due to the large differences in the amount of the beginning period collateral principal balance and the other five items that amount will be displayed from the right axis of the graph. This will allow it to use a different scale than the other five statistics and will not distort their representation in the field of the graph. The form of the graph will therefore be a dual-axis line format. Abbreviations to identify the selected scenario will be consistent with other reports. See Exhibit 14.15.

ON THE WEB SITE

There is no material on the Web site for this chapter.

The report templates and other Excel/VBA material will be found in the Web site section of Chapter 16.

## CHAPTER 15

Writing the Liabilities Waterfall Model Spreadsheet

OVERVIEW

In Chapter 14 we discussed the design elements of the deal structure we are to implement in our model and the overall design of the Liabilities Waterfall Model (LWM). In this chapter we will examine each of the major sections of the LWM and describe how these features are incorporated into the Excel Waterfall Spreadsheet workbook. As we saw in Chapter 14, the rules that govern the allocation of cash flows in the LWM are complex. Allocations of the incoming collateral cash flows need to be segregated between principal and interest flows and then allocated between the two senior and four subordinate tranches. Much of this chapter will be spent specifically explaining how these allocations are managed by the LWM. The inputs and cell formulas we place in the workbook are primarily committed to tracking the balances of the various note tranches to determine how principal and interest payments, as well as losses, are distributed to them. There is a critical interdependence in the rules governing how each tranche receives its allocation in regard to the current balances and performance of the other tranches. Due to these interactions between tranches, simply moving across the columns of the waterfall spreadsheet from left to right is not necessarily the best way to understand the rules of the structure. A series of decisions need to be made involving precalculating certain amounts and setting various switches to direct the flow of cash to the various Classes and Tranches of the deal. These decision elements are more easily established outside of the linear time flow of the model. A more thoughtful approach is therefore required. We will instead, in explaining the interrelationships and function of the LWM, start by examining some of the basic elements of the structure first. We will then build on these elements as we review the major activity and calculation groups in the spreadsheet itself.

DELIVERABLES

The modeling deliverables for this chapter are:

- The overall schema of the waterfall.
- Conversion of each design element of Chapter 14 into Excel.

- Use of Excel formulas to build the LWM Results worksheet. We will employ some complex array formulas to produce meaningful summary metrics by which to evaluate the deal performance.

UNDER CONSTRUCTION

In this chapter we examine in specific detail the Liabilities Waterfall Model designed in Chapter 14. As mentioned in the Overview section, the strong interdependencies of rules governing the waterfall elements will require us to take a circuitous approach to understanding how everything falls into place. When complete, we should have a clear and precise understanding of how every feature of the waterfall affects the whole of the structure.

DEAL STRUCTURE INPUTS

The deal structure inputs of the LWM fall into six main categories. These are:

1. **Note tranche inputs.** These inputs relate to the balances, percentage of total deal size, and coupon spreads.
2. **Interest rate swap.** Contains inputs relating to the interest rate swap, if any, in the deal. The two inputs include the swap rate and amortization assumption.
3. **Step-down parameters.** These inputs relate to the step-down percentages and the collateral allocation rules governing their distribution after the step down event has occurred.
4. **Credit enhancement inputs.** These include overcollateralization ratios and other items meant to preserve the initial structure of the deal.
5. **Performance trigger inputs.** Performance trigger inputs relate to the creditworthiness of the collateral pool. If the performance of the collateral pool deteriorates due to higher-than-expected default rates, these triggers will alter the cash flow allocation process to preserve the credit characteristics of the senior notes.
6. **Cleanup call parameters.** These parameters relate to the liquidation of the deal in its final stages. They trigger the conditions that will cause the deal to be repurchased by the issuer from the investors when the assets of the deal have declined below a certain fixed percentage.

Let us look at each of these input sets in turn and explain their particular contributions to the overall LWM structure.

Overview of Note Tranche Inputs

Our first step in constructing the LWM is to set up an inputs page for the overall deal structure and Note attributes of each of the tranches. Note inputs consist of initial dollar balances and percentages that each of the Note balances represent at the beginning deal structure. We also need to enter the coupon spread and post step down target subordinate percentages. Remember from Chapter 14 that one of the crucial sources of credit enhancement (CE) for a note is that note's subordinate percentage. The subordinate percentage of a note is the total percentage balance of all note tranches that are subordinate to that particular note tranche in terms of payment priority and loss allocation. These subordination percentages, which come into effect after the step down date, are input on the Structure Menu. We will observe later in this chapter that much of the complexity of the cash allocation rules of the LWM arises from the fact that each Note is entitled to maintain its level of post step down subordination. As a result of this requirement, the rules of the structure strive to constantly balance the allocation of collateral cash flows needed to preserve these initial levels throughout the life of the deal. In our present deal, the Class A-1 and A-2 Notes have an identical level of seniority (i.e., neither has payment priority over the other). We can therefore treat them as if they are a single tranche of Class A certificates for purposes of distributions.

In addition to the Note inputs mentioned above, we will also need to set up elements of the structure such as the swap dynamics, triggers, and cleanup call specifications. Once they are all in place, we can begin implementing the waterfall.

Note Input Table

The Note Input table resides on the Structure worksheet. Our deal is composed of six note tranches. There are two senior classes and four subordinate classes. In addition to these classes, there is also an overcollateralization (OC) amount. From Exhibit 15.1 we see that our assumed deal is modeled on collateral that has an initial starting balance of $500 million.

The initial Note balances are calculated by multiplying the note class percentages and the total beginning principal balance of the assets. These note class percentages are used to calculate the balances of the classes; not the other way around. The formula in cell D5 reads:

```
=C5*TotalBeginPrincipal
```

Note the use of the Range name "TotalBeginPrincipal" in the equation of this cell. It is a practice that we will put into widespread use across the LWM spreadsheet. This

	B	C	D	E	F	G
3	**Bond Class Information Table**					
4	**Bond Class**	**%**	**Balance**	**Index**	**Spread**	**Initial Rating**
5	A-1	85.95%	429,750,000.00	Libor (1M)	0.20%	Aaa
6	A-2	9.55%	47,750,000.00	Libor (1M)	0.25%	Aaa
7	B-1	1.90%	9,500,000.00	Libor (1M)	0.36%	Aa2
8	B-2	1.10%	5,500,000.00	Libor (1M)	0.48%	A2
9	B-3	0.50%	2,500,000.00	Libor (1M)	1.00%	Baa1
10	B-4	0.50%	2,500,000.00	Libor (1M)	2.20%	Baa3
11	OC	0.50%	2,500,000.00	NA	NA	NA
12	Total	100.00%	500,000,000.00			
14	**Program Expenses**					
15	Servicer Fee	0.25%				
16	Other Fees	0.02%				

EXHIBIT 15.1   Note Input table

practice greatly improves legibility of the worksheet formulas. Range names bring clarity to cell equations, especially the longer and more complicated they need to be. The benefits of this practice will become greater and greater the further we advance into the process of building the LWM.

The remainder of the Note Input table includes the floating rate index for the notes (1-month LIBOR [London Interbank Offering Rate] in our case), the spread above this index and the initial rating for each note class.

The input fields for the deal fees are immediately below the Note Input table in cells C15:C16. The Range names for the servicing and other fees fields are "servicerFee" and "otherFees", respectively. See Exhibit 15.1.

Interest Rate Swap Table

The typical use of an interest rate swap (IRS) in securitizations is to match the asset interest rate behavior with that of the liabilities. For example, if the assets were all fixed rate mortgages, any structure supporting floating rate notes would struggle to make payments if the floating rate index rose too far above the set fixed rate of the assets. To protect against this scenario, the trust would enter into an IRS with a swap counterparty to trade a fixed payment for a floating payment based on a determined schedule.

The asset composition we consider in this book is entirely floating rate assets. Similarly, the notes issued by the trust are floating rate notes. We therefore will not be using an IRS in our examples, but we build in the capability to include one if and when we need to model fixed rate assets backed by floating rate notes. If we were modeling a new deal comprised of 7/1 adjustable-rate mortgages (ARMs), the deal would have a seven-year amortizing swap for the first seven years of the deal corresponding to the fixed pay period on the assets.

The three inputs on the Structure page pertaining to the IRS are the "Swap" on/off, "Swap Rate, Speed" (Constant prepayment rate [CPR]), and "Swap Term" fields. The first designates whether or not a swap is active in our deal. The swap rate is the fixed rate that the trust is obligated to pay based on the swap schedule in order to receive the floating rate payment. The next two inputs determine the swap schedule. In building the swap schedule, we only need to derive the beginning of period notional balances. This is done by backing the notional amortization out of the actual amortization from the Collateral Cash Flow Generator (CCFG) outputs and applying the CPR found in the speed input. The swap term sets the expiration of the swap. These inputs are named "swapOnOff", "swapRate", "swapCPR", and "swapTerm". See Exhibit 15.2.

Step Down Characteristics Table

The next step is to provide the user a place to input the step-down characteristics and subordination percentages for the notes. In the initial 30 months of the deal, the senior notes will receive all the principal cash flows of the assets. After this time, provided certain criteria are met, the subordinate notes can begin sharing in the principal distribution.

	A	B	C
17			
18		**Interest Rate Swap**	
19		Swap	Off
20		Rate	5.10%
21		Speed (CPR)	45.00%
22		Swap Term (yrs)	7
23			
24		**Step Down Characteristics**	
25		Period	30
26		Senior CE %	9.00%
27		Post Step Down OC %	1.00%

EXHIBIT 15.2 Interest Rate Swap and Step-Down Characteristics tables

The distribution date immediately following the Step down period is the first month when the subordinate notes can be allocated a share of the principal distribution. The step down provision is specified such that the deal will step down only if, in any period after the step down period, the senior CE percentage is greater than the 9.00% level entered in the table. The CE percentage is the sum of the balances of the Class B certificates and the overcollateralization amount divided by the outstanding collateral balance.

A second step down input parameter is the Post Step Down OC% rate. The post step down OC rate is used to establish a minimum value of dollar overcollateralization. We name these three Ranges (C25:C27) "stepdownPeriod", "stepdownPercent", and "stepdownOCPercent". See Exhibit 15.2.

Target Credit Enhancement Percentages Table

The Target CE Percentages table specifies the degree of subordination for each class of notes that is targeted to maintain in the post-step-down periods of the deal. These percentages are the critical determinants in the allocation of the collateral cash flows to the various note classes of the structure. At each step, the allocation of principal to any note class is calculated by direct reference to these percentages. The five cells in Range C30:C34 are named based on the CE percentages of their respective note classes. These Ranges are, from top to bottom, "ClassAPercentage", "ClassB1Percentage", "ClassB2Percentage", "ClassB3Percentage", and "ClassB4Percentage". Take specific notice of the fact that the senior enhancement percentage, 91.00%, is specified for the Class A notes as a whole, not for its two individual components. See Exhibit 15.3.

Performance Trigger Table

There is a performance trigger in our deal. This trigger is the cumulative loss trigger. This trigger is designed to redirect principal payments (depending on the current amount of cumulative losses minus recoveries or realized losses). Realized losses are losses net of defaulted principal recoveries. The realized losses percentage is

	Target Sub %
A	91.00%
B-1	94.80%
B-2	97.00%
B-3	98.00%
B-4	99.00%

EXHIBIT 15.3   Target CE Percentages table

computed by dividing the cumulative realized dollar losses by the original outstanding balance of the mortgages loans backing the deal. As shown in the table, the threshold trigger percentage levels of cumulative losses in the table rises over the life of the deal. See Exhibit 15.4.

Cleanup Percentage Parameter

In addition to variable fees, such as our servicing fee, deals also have a number of fixed fees. These fees are aggregated into the "Other Fees" input. As the deal matures, the collateral cash flows diminish in direct relationship to the retirement of their principal balances through scheduled amortization, prepayments, and defaults. Fixed fees can form a growing, and potentially debilitating, economic drain on the trust. The cleanup percentage offers a solution to this problem. Eventually the ratio of the current balances of the assets divided by their original principal balance will fall below the value of the cleanup percentage. The seller, at that point, has the option to repurchase the outstanding notes. A typical cleanup percentage level is 10%. This input is in cell C46 and is named "cleanupPercent". See Exhibit 15.4.

With the addition of the cleanup percentage to the Structure sheet, we are now ready to begin modeling the waterfall. In the next section we will discuss the specific roles these inputs play in determining the form and functionality of the deal structure.

Cumulative Realized Loss Trigger			
ID	Start	End	%
0	0	24	100.00%
1	25	36	0.15%
2	37	48	0.25%
3	49	60	0.50%
4	61	72	0.70%
5	73	360	0.75%

Cleanup Call %	10%

EXHIBIT 15.4   Cumulative Realized Loss Trigger and Cleanup Call % tables

BUILDING THE LIABILITIES WATERFALL MODEL

We are now ready to begin the process of building the Liabilities Waterfall Model using the cash flows from the CCFG we built in Chapters 8 through 13. The path we will take through the waterfall model is one of a top-down approach. It is generally true that the activities contained in each of the sections described below depend in part or in whole from those preceding them. These sections will be discussed in the following order:

1. **Collateral cash flows.** These columns receive the collateral cash flows output from the CCFG. This section is the source (along with the IRS) of all sources of cash flows to the deals. These columns are "at the top of the waterfall," all other activities and calculations rely on them to fuel the structure.
2. **Available cash.** Separates the collateral cash flows into principal and interest flows.
3. **Servicing/Other fees.** The first use of interest in the waterfall is for servicing and other fees. The net amount of interest after fees is the amount available to make payments to the bonds used in the interest rate swap section if the swap is active. Otherwise, the interest remaining is available for distributions to the bonds.
4. **Interest rate swap (IRS).** In the case of a fixed/floating swap, if LIBOR has increased or decreased since the beginning of the deal the trustee could receive money from or be required to make a payment to the swap counterparty. The net swap payment is derived and tracked in this section. The net amount of interest after fees is the amount available for distribution to the notes.
5. **End of period balances.** Contains the balances for Class A Notes, Class B Notes, and overcollateralization amount. This is one of the most important sections of the waterfall, as many expenses, fees, and other calculations of periodic cash flows are based on previous end of period balances.
6. **End of period percentages.** A tracking section that looks at each amount of the deal balances that is attributable to each note and to OC expressed as a percentage of the total balance of all notes and the overcollateralization amount.
7. **Target OC amount.** Tracking column for the required amount of OC in each period. This is an important input in the principal distribution sections below.
8. **Trigger tracking.** Tracking section for the cleanup call and realized loss performance trigger.
9. **Interest allocation.** Calculation and payment of interest to all six notes.
10. **Excess spread treatment.** Determines behavior of excess spread, if any, once all fees and interest due have been paid.
11. **Principal distribution amounts.** Calculation of principal available to make payments to the senior (Class A) and subordinated (Class B) Notes.
12. **Principal payments.** Actual amount distributed to each of the Class A and Class B Notes.
13. **Losses.** Losses allocated to and reimbursements made to the subordinated notes.
14. **Excess cash released.** Amount of cash left over after making all payments due for fees, note interest, note principal, and loss reimbursement. This amount is released to the residual Note holder.

15. **Period factors.** A computation column that will be used to calculate duration on the Results page.
16. **Total cash flows.** A section tracking the principal and interest cash flows to each note on a maturity and cleanup call basis.

After we have gone over every section, we will turn to the Results page, where the behavior of the notes and assets in the Waterfall page are condensed down to summary performance statistics.

Collateral Cash Flows Section

The first component of the LWM is the Collateral Cash Flows section. This section contains the periodic cash flows generated by the CCFG.

The first entry in this section is the Beginning Principal Balance in Cell D14 with the Range name "TotalBeginPrincipal". You will recall that we used this Range name in the Structure inputs sheet to compute the dollar balances of each of the note tranches.

The only components of this section that are not directly provided to the LWM by the CCFG are the contents of the Pool Factors, Ending Principal Balance Outstanding, and Total Principal Retired columns. The Pool Factors are computed based on the periodic current balances of the Collateral Pool divided by its beginning principal balance. The formula for the Pool Factor in cell E14 is:

```
=D14/TotalBeginPrincipal
```

This formula is consistent within the entire "E" column and extends to cell E373, which is deal period 360. Throughout the rest of this chapter, you can assume, unless specifically stated otherwise, that the formula in the top-most cell of a column has been copied down the entire column. The ending principal balance outstanding for a period is the previous period's ending principal balance outstanding less the sum of the Regular Amort, Prepaid and Defaulted Principal. The formula in cell I13 (period 0) is simply set to "TotalBeginPrincipal". The formula in cell I14 is:

```
=I13-F14-G14-H14
```

The final computed field in the Collateral Cash Flows section is the Total Principal Retired field, which is computed by taking the sum of the Regular Amort and Prepaid Principal fields.

In our construction of the LWM, we will employ a series of conventions when creating formats and cell equations. You may have noticed in the upper portion of this section that we have built fields into the header area of the LWM. These fields display the sum of the cash flows in the columns of the LWN main body directly underneath them. Note these cash flow total amounts will be used for two different purposes.

First they will assist us in verifying the consistency and accuracy of our model. This spreadsheet will be both large and complicated. Viewing all or even most of it at once will become impossible by the time we have finished. By employing these column totals, we will find the task of matching the "Total Sources of Cash Flows"

		1	2	3	4	5	6	7	8	9	10
						Collateral Cash Flows					
		Beginning Principal Balance	Pool Factor	Regular Amort Principal	Prepaid Principal	Defaulted Principal	Ending Principal Balance Outstanding	Total Principal Retired	Interest Income	Recoveries of Principal
				33,966,264	458,564,426	7,469,310		492,530,690	127,248,263	3,734,609
	0						500,000,000			
	1	500,000,000	1.00000	465,539	9,208,972	150,000	490,175,489	9,674,511	2,555,422	-
	2	490,175,489	0.98035	459,205	9,028,024	147,053	480,541,208	9,487,229	2,505,210	-
	3	480,541,208	0.96108	452,956	8,850,581	144,162	471,093,509	9,303,537	2,455,971	-
	4	471,093,509	0.94219	446,793	8,676,573	141,328	461,828,815	9,123,366	2,407,685	-
	5	461,828,815	0.92366	440,713	8,505,937	138,549	452,743,616	8,946,650	2,360,335	-
	6	452,743,616	0.90549	434,716	8,338,606	135,823	443,834,470	8,773,322	2,313,902	-
	7	443,834,470	0.88767	428,801	8,174,518	133,150	435,098,001	8,603,319	2,268,369	-
	8	435,098,001	0.87020	422,966	8,013,610	130,529	426,530,895	8,436,577	2,223,718	-
	9	426,530,895	0.85306	417,211	7,855,822	127,959	418,129,903	8,273,033	2,179,933	-
	10	418,129,903	0.83626	411,534	7,701,093	125,439	409,891,837	8,112,627	2,136,997	-

EXHIBIT 15.5 Collateral cash flows section

to the "Total Uses of Cash Flows" much easier. We will later employ them in the last section of the LWM, the Sources and Uses Validation section. These summary amounts can help us identify possible modeling errors early in the development process.

Second, we will also use these totals in many of our LWM output reports. If we need to represent the totals of particular columns on the spreadsheet, they are already available! We can also use them in calculations of various financial performance statistics such as average life whose component terms are sums of cash flows over time. See Exhibit 15.5.

Available Cash Section

Once the cash flows have been imported into the spreadsheet, we need to segregate the principal and interest components. We also need to clearly identify the balances available from these two components. Each will be put to use in distinct manners in the waterfall. The role of the Available Cash section is to display the split between all principal cash flows, including recoveries from defaults, and interest cash flows.

The Total Interest amount is simply the coupon payments received from the assets. The Available Principal is the sum of scheduled amortized principal, prepayments of principal, and recoveries of defaulted principal. The formula for Total Principal in cell O14 is:

```
=F14+G14+L14
```

See Exhibit 15.6.

Servicing and Other Fees Section

The expenses incurred in managing a deal take priority over either principal and interest payments to the note holders. It is vitally important to pay the people who are performing the accounting, cash management, and trustee functions first to ensure that these activities are accomplished in a complete and timely manner. Nowhere is

	M	N	O
4			
5	11	12	13
6		Available Cash	
7			
8		Total	Total
9		Interest	Principal
10			(+Recoveries)
11			
12		127,248,263	496,265,299
13	0		
14	1	2,555,422	9,674,511
15	2	2,505,210	9,487,229
16	3	2,455,971	9,303,537
17	4	2,407,685	9,123,366
18	5	2,360,335	8,946,650
19	6	2,313,902	8,773,322
20	7	2,268,369	8,603,319
21	8	2,223,718	8,436,577
22	9	2,179,933	8,273,033
23	10	2,136,997	8,112,627

EXHIBIT 15.6   Available Cash section

this priority of payment more critical than in regard to the servicer fee. Servicers are the best first line of defense for the deal. Their role is to collect the payments; deal with emerging delinquency issues, often by making advances; and work with attorneys to handle defaulted mortgages, manage, repair, and sell foreclosed properties. Therefore before any cash is directed to the notes, the first use of interest payments is directed to pay the servicing fee and the other fees. On the Structure input page, we have entered an annual servicing fee of 0.25% and another fee of 0.02% of the outstanding principal balance of the assets.

The formulas for computing the servicing fees and other fees due in the first month (cells Q14 and T14, respectively) are:

```
=IF(D14>=0.01, servicerFee*D14/12+S13, 0)
=IF(D14>=0.01, otherFee*D14/12+V13, 0)
```

The formulas first check the cell that contains the outstanding principal balance of the assets. If the outstanding principal balance is greater than one cent, the fees are due in the current period. As previously noted, the monthly fees are computed using the beginning of period asset principal balance outstanding. The deal may have carried forward to the current month outstanding fees owed from prior months. If this is the case we will add this amount to the current month's amount due. The servicing fee is paid from the available total interest. If the total interest available exceeds the servicing fee, the fees (and any arrearages) are paid in full. If there are insufficient funds to pay, the servicing fee will pay the total of the Interest Available amount and roll forward the unpaid portion of the servicing fee into the next month.

```
=MIN(Q14,N14)
```

	P	Q	R	S	T	U	V
4							
5	14	15	16	17	18	19	20
6		Servicing Fees					
7							
8		Servicing	Servicing	Servicing	Other	Other	Other
9		Fee	Fee	Fee	Fees	Fees	Fees
10		Due	Paid	Unpaid	Due	Paid	Unpaid
11							
12		5,187,021	5,187,021	-	414,962	414,962	-
13	0						
14	1	104,167	104,167	-	8,333	8,333	-
15	2	102,120	102,120	-	8,170	8,170	-
16	3	100,113	100,113	-	8,009	8,009	-
17	4	98,144	98,144	-	7,852	7,852	-
18	5	96,214	96,214	-	7,697	7,697	-
19	6	94,322	94,322	-	7,546	7,546	-
20	7	92,466	92,466	-	7,397	7,397	-
21	8	90,645	90,645	-	7,252	7,252	-
22	9	88,861	88,861	-	7,109	7,109	-
23	10	87,110	87,110	-	6,969	6,969	-

EXHIBIT 15.7 Servicing and Other Fees section

The amount available to pay the other fees due is adjusted for the amount already paid to cover the servicing fees.

```
=MIN(T14,N14-R14)
```

See Exhibit 15.7.

Interest Rate Swap Section

The interest rate swap is a potential form of credit enhancement in the deal. Under the terms of the swap, the trust is required to pay a fixed interest rate to the counterparty while the counterparty is responsible for a LIBOR-based, variable payment. Therefore, if LIBOR exceeds the fixed rate, the trust will have added cash flow from the interest rate swap. However, if LIBOR drops below the fixed rate, the trust has an additional liability. In our deal the assets and liabilities are both based on LIBOR, so we will not be using the swap functionality.

Both of these payments are based on a swap schedule that is established when the deal is structured. This notional balance amortization schedule is constructed by computing a 0% prepayment amortization schedule of the assets and applying a prepayment assumption. This combination is considered to be the expected target amortization of the asset pool, the "best guess" estimate. The swap schedule is constructed by making a prediction as to how the assets will actually amortize. If the deal does not amortize as predicted, a situation will arise in which the actual balance of the assets has varied from the predicted amortization as represented by the swap schedule.

The three pieces of information needed to compute the net swap payment are the swap notional schedule, current LIBOR, and the fixed rate the trust pays in the swap. The swap notional schedule is computed at each month by referencing the Collateral Cash Flows section and determining what the base-line amortization characteristics of the asset pool are. A prepayment assumption as measured by a Constant prepayment rate (CPR) is then applied to determine the swap notional schedule. The CPR we are using is 45%. Cell X14 is the initial swap notional balance and, as long as the swap is activated, is equal to the initial asset balance ("TotalBeginPrincipal"). The period 1 swap notional balance in cell X15 is computed as:

```
=IF(AND(W15<=swapTerm*12,CW13>0.01,swapOnOff=''On''),
X14-X14*((1-(1-swapCPR)^(1/12)))
 -(X14-X14*((1-(1-swapCPR)^(1/12)))))*(F15/(D15-G15-H15)),0)
```

This formula first checks that the current period is before the swap termination date, the deal is still outstanding, and the swap is active. If these three criteria are met, the current swap notional balance is found by taking the previous swap notional balance less prepays less scheduled principal. The prepaid principal is found by multiplying the CPR input (converted to a monthly number) by the previous swap notional balance. The scheduled payments are applied against the previous balance less the amount that we just calculated as prepays. The periodic scheduled principal paydown is calculated by finding the periodic principal paydown of the actual modeled amortization. As we perform this calculation, we arrive at an accurate idea of how the assets would amortize if they were comprised of the same types of loans, but prepaid (voluntary and involuntary) at 45%.

The fixed rate the trust must pay per the swap agreement is taken from the inputs page, "swapRate". The net swap payment is the difference between LIBOR and the swap rate times the period swap notional balance.

```
=(Y14-DN14)/12*X14
```

Notice that this is quoted as a "payment," so a negative number signifies the swap provider is paying the trust. The Interest Available column represents the interest remaining from column N after paying fees and accounting for the net swap payment.

```
=N14-R14-U14-Z14
```

See Exhibit 15.8.

End of Period Balances Section

One of the most referenced sections of our waterfall spreadsheet is the End of Period Balances section. This section is a key determinant in the following calculations:

- End of period percentages
- Determination of the onset of the step-down provision
- Various triggers
- Sizing of the principal and interest distribution amounts

	W	X	Y	Z	AA
4					
5	21	22	23	24	25
6		Interest Rate Swap			
7					
8		Swap	Swap	Net	Interest
9		Notional	Rate	Swap	Available
10				Payment	
11					
12		45.00%	5.10%	-	121,646,281
13	0				
14	1	-	5.10%	-	2,442,922
15	2	-	5.10%	-	2,394,921
16	3	-	5.10%	-	2,347,849
17	4	-	5.10%	-	2,301,689
18	5	-	5.10%	-	2,256,424
19	6	-	5.10%	-	2,212,035
20	7	-	5.10%	-	2,168,506
21	8	-	5.10%	-	2,125,821
22	9	-	5.10%	-	2,083,963
23	10	-	5.10%	-	2,042,917

EXHIBIT 15.8 Interest Rate Swap section

In this section, we have to be very careful because the end of period balances for the Class A Notes, the Class B Notes, and the OC are all computed somewhat differently.

Class A Balances The Class A Notes cannot experience write-downs in this structure. Delinquency and default activity may decrease the cash flows from the asset pool to the point that the OC is depleted. Continued deterioration of the performance of the asset pool will affect the expectation that the Class B Notes will receive full payment of principal and interest. In this event the OC and the Class B Notes will have had their outstanding balances written down either partially or completely. The Class A Notes, however, will *not* have their balances decreased by further asset underperformance. If we arrive at a position where the Class A Note balance is greater than the outstanding principal balance of the asset pool, the deal is said to be "undercollateralized." Why are no write-downs allowed against Class A balances? At that point there is no credit support remaining in any form, either excess cash, OC, or any outstanding balances of the Class B Notes. Only the Class A Notes remain. Writing down the principal balance has a negative effect on the note holders. If the Class A principal is written down, less interest is paid. The retirement of the remaining Class A Note principal will therefore be accelerated regardless of how much additional cash is available from the collateral after the write-down takes place. If the performance of the collateral pool subsequently recovers the Class A Note holder would receive less money but through attenuated principal and interest payments if the write-downs had occurred.

The formula below is from cell CP13 "Class A-1 Principal Balance" in the LWM. The variable "TotalBeginPrincipal" is the beginning principal balance of the asset pool. The entries at the top of columns "CP" through "CV" are the initial Note

	CO	CP	CQ
4			
5	91	92	93
6			
7		Class	Class
8		A-1	A-2
9		Principal	Principal
10		Balance	Balance
11			
12		85.95%	9.55%
13	0	429,750,000	47,750,000
14	1	420,907,940	46,767,549
15	2	412,237,087	45,804,121
16	3	403,734,158	44,859,351
17	4	395,395,933	43,932,881
18	5	387,219,254	43,024,362
19	6	379,201,023	42,133,447
20	7	371,338,201	41,259,800
21	8	363,627,806	40,403,090
22	9	356,066,913	39,562,990
23	10	348,652,654	38,739,184

EXHIBIT 15.9   Class A End of Period Balances columns

percentages imported from the Structure input sheet. The formula in cell CP13 for period 0 "Class A-1 End of Period Balance" is therefore:

```
=CP$12*TotalBeginPrincipal
```

We have the values of the note percentages from the Structure inputs sheet to place in the appropriate note class fields of row 12 of the balances section. From this point onward, using this beginning balance of the Class A Notes, we compute later-period balances by taking the previous period's balance and subtracting from it the principal retired of the Class A-1 Note in that period. The formula for "Class A-1 End of Period Balances" in all later months is analogous to:

```
=If(CP13<0.01, 0, CP13-AQ14)
```

Column AQ contains the amount of principal retired of the Class A-1 Note. See Exhibit 15.9.

Class B Balances   The computations for the Class B Notes' ending balances are identical to those of the Class A Notes with one exception: The Class B Notes can be written down in any period, and we need to adjust their ending period balances by the amounts of the write-down activity, if any.

The period 0 balance of the Class B-1 Note is computed in an identical manner to that of the Class A-1 Notes described above. In period "0", the beginning balance of the Class B-1 Notes is the product of the value of "TotalBeginPrincipal" variable multiplied by the initial class percentages displayed at the top of the column. Subsequent monthly balances are computed by taking the previous month's Class B-1 ending balance and subtracting from it the principal retired and balances that were

	CR	CS	CT	CU
4				
5	94	95	96	97
6	End of Period Balances			
7	Class	Class	Class	Class
8	B-1	B-2	B-3	B-4
9	Principal	Principal	Principal	Principal
10	Balance	Balance	Balance	Balance
11				
12	1.90%	1.10%	0.50%	0.50%
13	9,500,000	5,500,000	2,500,000	2,500,000
14	9,500,000	5,500,000	2,500,000	2,500,000
15	9,500,000	5,500,000	2,500,000	2,500,000
16	9,500,000	5,500,000	2,500,000	2,500,000
17	9,500,000	5,500,000	2,500,000	2,500,000
18	9,500,000	5,500,000	2,500,000	2,500,000
19	9,500,000	5,500,000	2,500,000	2,500,000
20	9,500,000	5,500,000	2,500,000	2,500,000
21	9,500,000	5,500,000	2,500,000	2,500,000
22	9,500,000	5,500,000	2,500,000	2,500,000
23	9,500,000	5,500,000	2,500,000	2,500,000

EXHIBIT 15.10   Class B End of Period Balances section

written down in that month. The principal paid to Class B-1 is located in column AS. Any Class B-1 write-down amounts are drawn from column AZ. The formula for the Class B-1 End of Period Balance in cell CR14 is:

```
=IF(CR13<0.01,0,CR13-AZ14-BA14)
```

We will discuss how write-down amounts for each class are computed in the LWM later in this chapter. See Exhibit 15.10.

From Exhibit 15.10 we see that the balances of the subordinate notes are constant for the first portion of the deal. In the pre-step-down phase of the deal the Class B Notes receive no principal distribution and can only have their balances decreased by write-downs in a high-loss scenario.

Overcollateralization Balance   The OC balance at the end of each period is the amount by which the total outstanding principal asset balance exceeds the combined note balance of all classes. If this difference is positive—the assets exceed the combined principal balances outstanding of the Notes—the condition of the deal is said to be "overcollateralized." Only subordinated note classes (non-Class A) can experience write-downs. Write downs occur when the amount of note principal outstanding exceeds the amount of outstanding principal balance of the assets. The aggregate amount of the notes must be reduced to equal the balance of the assets. When these write-downs occur, they will reduce the most subordinate note class first. When the principal balance of that note class has been written down to zero, the write-downs will shift to the now newly most subordinate note class. At the beginning of this deal, the most subordinate note class is the Class B-4 Notes. Write-downs will then progress to the Class B-3, then Class B-2, and finally the Class B-1 Notes. At some point, if the asset pool has deteriorated to the point that *all* of the subordinate Note classes have been written down the senior notes will have no support. If there is a further decline in the sum of the outstanding principal balances of the assets below that of the principal balances of the Class A Notes, the deal will not have any other classes to cannibalize through write-down activity. At this point the deal is said to be "under collateralized."

Due to the necessity to balance the OC coverage with write-down activity directed against the subordinate tranches, the calculation of the per-period ending balance is not straightforward. We have to look ahead through the anticipated expenses of the period to arrive at a picture of where we will be in the assets versus notes relationship by the end of the period.

We will anticipate the ending period OC balance by first applying all principal payments to the note classes. If the balance of the notes after these payments is greater than the sum of the principal balance of the asset pool, we will apply write-downs to the existing most subordinate note class. That class will be written down until the asset balance equals the note balance. We will discuss the write-down calculations and their allocation process later in this chapter.

The formula to calculate the end of period OC balance involves the following steps:

1. Determine the current end of period balances for all note classes by taking their prior period ending balances and subtracting their current period principal retirement amounts.
2. Subtract this amount from the current ending of period asset balance.
3. If the net sum of Step 2 is negative (more notes then assets) then there is no OC and the most subordinated note will experience a write-down.
4. If the net of Step 2 is positive display this value as current OC, the deal is over-collateralized.

The formula for OC balance is therefore:

```
=MAX(0,I14-(SUM(CP13:CU13)-SUM(AD14:AE14)))
```

The sum of the columns CP through CU are the end of period balances for the note balances outstanding in the previous period. The columns AD14:AE14 are the current period payments each of the note classes are to receive. (Note the note balances are in row 13 and the principal retirement payment columns are in row 14!) The cell I14 is the current ending period balance of the assets. The value of the OC balance is the maximum of "0" or the difference of the asset balances versus note principal balance. See Exhibit 15.11.

End of Period Percentages Section

Sometimes in large spreadsheets it is useful to compute a few heavily used values in a set of columns and then refer to them from everywhere else rather than repeating these calculations in many formulas across many cells. Another advantage of this approach is that we or anyone else can view the sum, ratio, percentage, or logical condition without the need to dig it out of a longer formula. This is the role of the End of Period Percentages section of the LWM.

	CV	CW
4		
5	98	99
6		
7		
8	OC	Deal Balance
9	Balance	
10		
11		
12	0.50%	
13	2,500,000	500,000,000
14	2,500,000	490,175,489
15	2,500,000	480,541,208
16	2,500,000	471,093,509
17	2,500,000	461,828,815
18	2,500,000	452,743,616
19	2,500,000	443,834,470
20	2,500,000	435,098,001
21	2,500,000	426,530,895
22	2,500,000	418,129,903
23	2,500,000	409,891,837

EXHIBIT 15.11   End of Period OC and Deal Balances

In this section we will compute the percentage that each Note class is of the current outstanding balance of the asset pool. Having these percentages in individual cells will allow us to view them directly. This in turn enhances our ability to "eyeball" the model. It is also useful when we have to trace the effects of these percentages on other calculations in the LWM. We will also add the percentages of the aggregate Class A-1 and A-2 Notes and a separate percentage for the aggregate of the Class B Notes. See Exhibit 15.12.

Target Overcollateralization Amount Section

The calculation of the OC balance for any period is directly dependent on the target OC amount for that period. On the Structure sheet in the step down characteristics table, the last entry is the "Post Step Down OC %", currently set to 1%.

The Target OC Amount column is in "DI" on the LWM worksheet.

The steps in computing the Target OC Amount for the period are:

1. If the sum of all outstanding balances for the note classes is 0, SUM(CP13:CU13), then the Target OC Amount is the current period remaining balance of the asset pool, I14. We are done!
2. If the sum of all outstanding balances for the note classes is greater than 0, there are note balances outstanding! If the current period, DH14, is prior to the advent of the step down period, "stepdownPeriod", the Target OC Amount is the initial OC percentage, "OCPercentage", from the Note Class Information Table (0.50%) multiplied by the beginning principal balance of the asset pool, "TotalBeginPrincipal". We are done!

	DF	DG
4		
5	**108**	**109**
6		
7		
8	Total	Total
9	Senior	Subordinate
10	Percentage	Percentage
11		
12		
13	95.50%	4.00%
14	95.41%	4.08%
15	95.32%	4.16%
16	95.22%	4.25%
17	95.13%	4.33%
18	95.03%	4.42%
19	94.93%	4.51%
20	94.83%	4.60%
21	94.72%	4.69%
22	94.62%	4.78%
23	94.51%	4.88%

EXHIBIT 15.12 Total Senior Percentage and Total Subordinate Percentage

3. If we are past the step down period and no other performance triggers are active, AC14=FALSE, then the Target OC Amount is the greater of either:
   a. The initial OC percentage, "OCPercentage" multiplied by the beginning balance of the assets, "TotalBeginPrincipal" or,
   b. The step down OC percentage, "stepdownOCPercent", multiplied by the ending period outstanding principal balance of the assets, I14.
4. If we are past the step down period and a performance trigger is in effect, we use the previous period's Target OC Amount, DI13.

The formula, for the first period of the deal, located in cell DI14, is:

```
=IF(SUM(CP14:CU14)=0,I15,IF($DH15<=stepdownPeriod,
       OCPercentage*TotalBeginPrincipal,IF(AC14=FALSE,
       MAX(OCPercentage*TotalBeginPrincipal,
       stepdownOCPercent*$I14),DI14)))
```

See Exhibit 15.13.

Trigger Tracking Section

The deal has a cumulative realized loss trigger. This trigger is based on cumulative lifetime net defaults of collateral principal.

Calculation of the Realized Loss Trigger The cumulative realized loss percentage is calculated by dividing the sum of all asset principal defaults net of recoveries by the beginning asset balance. Principal defaults are shown in column H and recoveries

	DH	DI
4		
5	110	111
6		**OC**
7		
8		**Target**
9		**OC**
10		**Amount**
11		
12		
13	0	
14	1	2,500,000
15	2	2,500,000
16	3	2,500,000
17	4	2,500,000
18	5	2,500,000
19	6	2,500,000
20	7	2,500,000
21	8	2,500,000
22	9	2,500,000
23	10	2,500,000

EXHIBIT 15.13 Target OC Amount

of defaulted principal are shown in column L. The formula is in column EC is therefore:

```
=(SUM($H$14:H14)-SUM($L$14:L14))/TotalBeginPrincipal
```

Note in this formula the sums of principal defaults and recoveries are anchored at the first period ($H$14 and $L$14). The anchoring ensures that we consider lifetime amounts for each period.

Applying the Trigger Now that the cumulative realized loss percentage has been calculated, we can test it as well as the cleanup trigger in each period of the deal. As you recall, there is an entry in the Structure worksheet into which we placed a cleanup trigger of 10% ("cleanupPercent"). We now need to design a test to see if the various triggers are active.

Testing the Lifetime Default Rate Trigger The Lifetime Default Rate trigger is set at an initial value and then rises slowly at various intervals over the remaining life of the deal. Here we see that the Lifetime Default Rate trigger is inactive for the first two years of the deal. At the end of that period the cumulative realized loss trigger hurdles start at 0.15% in year 3 and then rise to 0.25%, 0.50%, and 0.70% in years 4, 5 and 6, respectively. At the end of year 6 and for the remaining life of the deal, the rate levels off at 0.75%. The trigger is tested in column DL and the formula is as follows:

```
=IF($EC14>INDEX(Structure!$E$38:$E$43,
   MATCH(CFWaterfall!$DJ14,Structure!$C$38:$C$43,1),1),TRUE,FALSE)
```

The functions INDEX() and MATCH are employed to link the current month of the deal, $DJ14, to the appropriate time period and accompanying loss threshold percent. In the formula you will see that there is a MATCH() function embedded in an INDEX() function as its second argument.

Let us examine the MATCH() function. The MATCH() function takes three arguments:

1. The value to be compared to a list ("DJ14", the current period).
2. The list, usually expressed as a Range, that the value is to be matched to (Structure!$C$38:$C$433. What type of a match is needed? There are three different match option values: (0) for exact, (1) for the greatest value less than or equal to the input, or (−1) the smallest value greater than or equal to the input. In this case we are looking for the greatest value in the lower bound column that is less than or equal to the current period.

The INDEX() function in this form takes three arguments:

1. The Range that we are indexing within, column E, containing the default trigger rates
2. The row number in the Range, determined by the MATCH() function above
3. The column number in the Range (1)

Thus the MATCH() function first determines the correct row. That value becomes the second argument in the INDEX() function. The formula now has all it needs to compare the value in cell EC14, the current period lifetime default rate, to the hurdle as determined by the INDEX() function. If the value in column EC for the period exceeds the hurdle, the trigger is set to TRUE.

Testing the Cleanup Call Trigger   The Cleanup trigger is activated when the current asset balance is less than the cleanup percentage (10%) as entered on the Structure worksheet. The Cleanup Call trigger test is in column DK. In cell E1 is the Pool Factor (surviving original asset principal percentage):

```
=IF(E14<=cleanupPercent,TRUE,FALSE)
```

See Exhibit 15.14.

Interest Allocation Section

Having completed the section of the worksheet that tracks balances, OC, and triggers, we can now address the issues of paying interest and principal to the note holders. Allocation and payment of interest is the more straightforward of the two processes and is far easier to implement than principal payments. The total distribution of interest will depend on interest amounts remaining after paying the note interest due.

There are two basic approaches to the allocation of interest payments. The first is the case where two note classes, Class A-1 and A-2, share seniority and must therefore divide funds available to pay their interest charges between themselves.

	DJ	DK	DL
4			
5	112	113	114
6		Triggers	
7			
8		Cleanup	Default
9		Trigger	Trigger
10			
11			
12		10.00%	
13	0		
14	1	FALSE	FALSE
15	2	FALSE	FALSE
16	3	FALSE	FALSE
17	4	FALSE	FALSE
18	5	FALSE	FALSE
19	6	FALSE	FALSE
20	7	FALSE	FALSE
21	8	FALSE	FALSE
22	9	FALSE	FALSE
23	10	FALSE	FALSE

EXHIBIT 15.14   Cleanup Trigger and Cumulative Realized Loss (Default)Trigger tracking columns

The Class B notes have four separate levels of subordination and therefore allocate and pay their interest charges from the available cash flows sequentially.

Prior to any allocation or payment activities, we must pay all costs and expenses of the deal and the IRS (if there is one). All interest payments to the notes are taken from the available interest payments of the collateral, column N, net of the fees paid and after the swap in column AA. This is the amount available to start making interest payments to the notes.

Interest Payment to Class A-1 and A-2 Notes   The first interest payment is due to the Class A-1 and A-2 Notes simultaneously. These Notes are not subordinated to each other. If there is an insufficient amount of interest remaining to pay the interest due to both of the Class A Notes, each would then receive a pro rata share of the available funds. The pro rata share would be based on their respective amounts of interest due in the period. If there is sufficient interest available to pay the total interest due to the Class A Notes, they receive full payment and the remaining funds are applied to the Class B Notes in order of seniority.

Calculation of Interest Due the Class A-1 Notes   The formula for interest due to the Class A-1 notes is as follows:

```
=IF(OR($D14<0.01,$CP13<0.01),0,$AG14/12*$CP13+$AJ13)
```

The OR operator performs a first check to see if either the current Collateral Pool balance, D14, or the Class A-1 Note principal balance from the previous period,

CP13, is zero. If either of these cases is true, no interest is paid. If there are assets or balances, we will apply the interest rate for the period of the Class A-1 Notes, AG14/12, multiplied by the outstanding principal balance of the Notes. To this amount we will also add in any previously unpaid interest amount for the Class A-1 Notes from a prior period, AJ13. We now know the interest due to the Class A-1 Notes. Now we need to determine if we can pay it!

Calculation of Interest Paid to the Class A-1 Notes The formula for Class A-1 interest paid is:

```
=IF(OR($D14<0.01,$CP13<0.01),0,MIN((AH14/(AH14+AL14))*$AA14,AH14))
```

Once again we first determine with an OR statement if either the current collateral pool balance, D14, or the principal balance of the Class A-1 Notes is zero, CP13. If either case is true, there is no payment of interest to the class. If the OR test returns FALSE the next portion of the formula states that it will pay the minimum of two amounts. The first amount is the pro rata share of the interest remaining based on the interest due to the Class A-1 and A-2 classes, AH14/(AH14+AL14), where AA14 is the Class A-1 interest due and AL14 is the Class A-2 interest due. The second amount is the amount of Class A-1 interest due. This MIN() ensures that if there is not enough interest to make a full payment, then the cash available is split appropriately between the Class A Notes.

Class A-2 Notes Interest Due and Interest Paid Calculations The changes to the preceding Class A-1 formulas to accommodate the calculations of the Class A-2 interest due and interest paid amounts are straightforward. The formula for interest paid to Class A-2, located in column AF, is:

```
=IF(OR($D14<0.01,$CQ13<0.01),0,MIN(AL14/(AH14+AL14)*$AA14,AL14
```

We have simply replaced the Class A-1 interest due amounts and A-2 references in the MIN() formula to compute Class A-2's pro rata share as opposed to Class A-1's. See Exhibit 15.15.

Interest Payment to All Class B Notes All Class B Notes are paid sequentially in the order of their seniority from B-1 to B-4. After we have used the available interest to pay interest on the Class A Notes the Class B Notes receive the remainder. Class B-1 Notes will be paid only if there is available interest remaining after payment of both of the Class A Notes. Let us look at the last Class B Note in the seniority list, the Class B-4, and see how the interest due and interest paid amounts are determined. The Class B-4 Notes will not receive any interest payments until all of the notes with higher seniority receive their payments first. It is the bottommost rung on this structure.

Class B-4 Interest Due Calculation Even though Class B-4 is last in line for payment of interest, this fact does not affect its calculation of interest due. The following formula, in column BZ, we see this to be the case:

```
=IF(OR($D14<0.01,$CU13<0.01),0,BY14/12*CU13+CB13)
```

	AF	AG	AH	AI	AJ
4					
5	30	31	32	33	34
6					Cla
7					
8		A-1	A-1	A-1	A-1
9		Interest	Interest	Interest	Interest
10		Rate	Due	Paid	Carryforward
11					
12			90,336,860	90,336,860	-
13	0				
14	1	5.32%	1,905,225	1,905,225	-
15	2	5.32%	1,866,025	1,866,025	-
16	3	5.32%	1,827,584	1,827,584	-
17	4	5.32%	1,789,888	1,789,888	-
18	5	5.32%	1,752,922	1,752,922	-
19	6	5.32%	1,716,672	1,716,672	-
20	7	5.32%	1,681,125	1,681,125	-
21	8	5.32%	1,646,266	1,646,266	-
22	9	5.32%	1,612,083	1,612,083	-
23	10	5.32%	1,578,563	1,578,563	-

EXHIBIT 15.15   Interest payment to Class A-1

Again the first step is to check the current balance of the collateral pool, D14, and the previous period ending principal balance for this note, CU13. If either is zero, interest due is zero and we are done. If both are positive, the interest due is the product of the monthly coupon rate of the Class B-4, BY14/12, multiplied by the previous period outstanding balance. As with the Class A Notes, if there is any interest unpaid from a prior period, we will add it to the interest due amount at this time, CB13.

Class B-4 Interest Paid Calculation   The formula for Class B-4 interest paid is:

```
=IF($D14<0.01,0,MIN(BZ14,$AA14-$AO14-$AW14-$BG14-$BQ14))
```

If the current collateral pool balance, D14, is greater than zero, we will continue. If not, the interest paid is zero and we are done. As long as Class B-4's balance has not been reduced to zero, either through principal payments or losses, the amount of interest paid is the minimum of the interest due, BZ14, and what is remaining of the interest remaining, AA14, less interest payments on the Class A Notes, AO14, and the three senior Class B Notes, AW14, BG14, and BQ14. See Exhibit 15.16.

Excess Spread Treatment Section

This section determines what happens to the excess spread (XS) that is available after paying interest on all the note classes. It is important in that the XS remaining can be critical in maintaining the OC of the structure. The availability of XS preserves OC by reducing the balances of the note classes through principal payments to the notes.

Recall that we said in Chapter 14 that XS is available to cover losses. If, due to losses, the total principal from the assets is not great enough to maintain the OC of

	BX	BY	BZ	CA	CB
4					
5	74	75	76	77	78
6			Class B-4 Interest		
7					
8		Interest	Interest	Interest	Interest
9		Rate	Due	Paid	Allocation
10					Carryforward
11					
12			942,195	942,195	-
13	0				
14	1	7.32%	15,250	15,250	-
15	2	7.32%	15,250	15,250	-
16	3	7.32%	15,250	15,250	-
17	4	7.32%	15,250	15,250	-
18	5	7.32%	15,250	15,250	-
19	6	7.32%	15,250	15,250	-
20	7	7.32%	15,250	15,250	-
21	8	7.32%	15,250	15,250	-
22	9	7.32%	15,250	15,250	-
23	10	7.32%	15,250	15,250	-

EXHIBIT 15.16 Interest payment to Class B-4

the deal the specified subordination percentages excess spread can be included in the principal payment distribution to pay down the notes. By reducing the amount of aggregate note principal outstanding, enhancement levels can be maintained even when the assets are experiencing losses. Due to these payments, the notes will experience a more rapid amortization. As an immediate and highly beneficial trade-off, they will maintain their initial protection levels. If XS is not enough to cover all losses, then the OC will be reduced and, if losses exceed the OC amount, the subordinated certificates will begin taking losses. We will address mechanics of note losses later in the section dealing with the implementation of principal payments.

The Interim OC Deficiency column tracks the amount of XS in a period that will be used as principal payment in an attempt to maintain enhancement levels. The formulas in this field essentially construct a forward estimate of OC based on the use of principal collections from assets to pay down the notes. The formula for interim OC deficiency, located in column CJ, is:

```
=MAX(0,DI14-(I14-(SUM(CP13:CU13)-O14)))
```

The formula follows the following steps to determine the interim OC deficiency:

1. Total the current beginning period balances for all of the note classes, SUM(CI13:CN13).
2. Subtract the current period principal payments, O14, from this total. This is now the aggregate balance of the notes less anticipated principal payments only.
3. Subtract the sum in Step 2 from the ending period asset balance, I14.
4. We subtract the amount calculated in Step 3 from the required OC amount, DI14.
5. The formula now takes the maximum of the required OC amount in Step 4 or $0 as the interim OC deficiency.

	CH	CI	CJ	CK	CL	CM	CN
4							
5	84	85	86	87	88	89	90
6				Excess Spread Treatment			
7 8 9 10 11		Interest Remaining After Distribution	Interim OC Deficiency	XS Applied to OC	XS Remaining	Losses Reimbursed	Excess Realeased
12		13,696,479	3,727,454	3,727,454	12,461,778	-	12,461,778
13	0						
14	1	226,966	150,000	150,000	76,966	-	76,966
15	2	222,561	147,053	147,053	75,508	-	75,508
16	3	218,242	144,162	144,162	74,079	-	74,079
17	4	214,006	141,328	141,328	72,678	-	72,678
18	5	209,852	138,549	138,549	71,303	-	71,303
19	6	205,779	135,823	135,823	69,956	-	69,956
20	7	201,784	133,150	133,150	68,634	-	68,634
21	8	197,867	130,529	130,529	67,338	-	67,338
22	9	194,026	127,959	127,959	66,067	-	66,067
23	10	190,260	125,439	125,439	64,821	-	64,821

EXHIBIT 15.17 Excess Spread Treatment section

We have now determined the amount of XS needed to be applied to the notes to maintain the required OC of the deal. If this amount is available, it is set aside for inclusion in the principal distribution amount. If after the use of XS to reduce the balance of the notes there is XS remaining, it can be used to reimburse loss. If XS remains after the reimbursement of losses it is paid to the Residual Noteholder. See Exhibit 15.17.

Principal Distribution Amounts Section

In the previous section we calculated the amount of excess spread that is available to be used as a supplement to the principal payments. We will next attack the problem of calculating the senior and subordinate principal payments. We use two columns to track the principal and subordinate principal payments in each period. If there are principal cash flows available, the Class A Notes will receive some principal payments each month. Subordinate Class B Notes, of all tranches, will receive principal distributions only after four conditions are met. These are:

1. There are principal distributions remaining after the payment of principal to the Class A Notes.
2. The step-down month has passed.
3. No performance triggers have been tripped that would direct all principal payments to the Class A Notes.
4. Any Class B Note that is senior to the Class B Note immediately in line to receive a principal distribution has been paid enough principal to maintain its target subordination percentage.

To facilitate testing all of these criteria in an efficient manner, we have added a column to the LWM to track if the deal is in pre-step-down and that, later in the

	AB	AC	AD	AE
5	26	27	28	29
6			Principal Distribution	
8–11		Pre Stepdown or Trigger	Senior Principal Distribution (incl XS for OC def)	Subordinate Principal Distribution (incl XS for OC def)
12		-	477,500,000	22,492,753
13	0	TRUE		
14	1	TRUE	9,824,511	-
15	2	TRUE	9,634,281	-
16	3	TRUE	9,447,699	-
17	4	TRUE	9,264,694	-
18	5	TRUE	9,085,199	-
19	6	TRUE	8,909,146	-
20	7	TRUE	8,736,469	-
21	8	TRUE	8,567,106	-
22	9	TRUE	8,400,992	-
23	10	TRUE	8,238,066	-

EXHIBIT 15.18   Principal distribution amounts

deal, no trigger thresholds are breached. If either of these conditions is in effect, all principal distributions are paid to the senior notes. This structural feature is a major credit enhancement to the Class A Notes. See Exhibit 15.18.

Senior Principal Distribution Amount   The formula for the senior principal distribution amount is:

```
=MIN(CP13+CQ13,IF(AC14,O14+CK14,MIN(O14+CK14,MAX(0,(CP13+CQ13)
  -MIN(I14*ClassAPercentage,I14-DI14)))))
```

Wow! That looks like quite a formidable equation to squeeze into a single cell. Actually, if we take the time to work our way into it, from the outside in, we will find, that with a little patience, it makes perfect sense!

If we look at the structure of the formula, we see that it has this general schema:

```
=MIN(A, IF(B, C, MIN(D, MAX(0, E - MIN(F, G)))))
```

We can unravel it in the following steps:

1. Take the minimum of A. A in this case is "CP13+CQ13", the prior period ending balances of the two Class A senior notes.
2. And, IF (B. The value of B in this case in the cell "AC14" is a Boolean indication that the deal is in pre–step-down mode or that triggers have been tripped. In the case that B is TRUE, we will evaluate C. If B is FALSE we will evaluate MIN(D, MAX(0, E − MIN(F-G))).
3. B is TRUE. The Class A Notes are the only ones that are allowed to receive a principal distribution. The principal distribution is "O14+CK14", Principal + Recoveries from asset cash flows, and Excess Cash available for application to maintain OC.

4. B is FALSE. The principal distribution will be the minimum of D, "O14+CK14", Principal + Recoveries from asset cash flows and Excess Cash available for application to OC. Or the maximum of either zero or the value of E, "CP13+CQ13", the prior period ending balances of the two Class A senior notes minus the minimum of F, ending period principal balance of the assets multiplied by the Class A percentage, or G, the ending period principal balance of the assets minus the target OC amount.

If we talk our way through it, the outermost MIN() function takes the minimum of the outstanding senior note balance and what is due to be paid (which we do not know just yet). Next we check to see if the deal is in the initial 30-month lockout period or if any trigger is active.

If we are in the lockout period, the senior note classes receive all the principal payments. These amounts are the sum of the principal payments and recoveries from the assets plus any amounts of available excess spread determined in the previous section.

If both senior and subordinate notes are receiving principal payments, then we want to pay the seniors enough cash so that their portion of the deal is in agreement with the Class A Target Subordinate % from the Inputs tab. To determine that amount, we look at the previous Class A balances and subtract the product of the Class A Target Subordinate % and the current end of period asset balance. This will give us the total payment required to the Class A Notes to maintain a 10% (100% – 90%) enhancement level.

Last but not least, the innermost MIN() function of the above formula only comes into play toward the end of the deal. At some point, if the cleanup call is not exercised, the required OC dollar amount for the deal will make up an ever-increasing portion of the total deal balance, approaching the dollar amount implied by the 10% senior enhancement. At the point where the OC makes up 10% of the deal, without this MIN() function, the senior notes would start getting less principal payments than the subordinates. To keep the senior pay down consistent, we will add this MIN() function into the formulas for all the principal paid sections.

Subordinate Principal Distribution Amount   The subordinate principal distribution amount is calculated by taking the total amount of principal available less the senior principal payment amount determined above. Class B Notes are paid sequentially with each note's principal payment amount determined by its Target Subordinate % in the same way the Class A distribution was determined above.

Principal Payments Section

The general approach to the application of the Class A and Class B principal distribution amounts is identical to that of the application of the interest paid calculations. Class A Notes will share any principal distribution amounts on a pro rata basis. Class B Notes will receive principal distribution amounts in a sequential manner based on relative seniority from Class B-1 first to Class B-4 last.

Class A-1 Principal Payments   The senior principal distribution amount computed in the previous section is split pro rata between Class A-1 and A-2 based on their

	A-1 Principal Paid	A-2 Principal Paid	Total Class A Principal Paid
	40	41	42	43

Row layout:

	AP	AQ	AR	AS
5	40	41	42	43
6		Class A Principal		
8–11		A-1 Principal Paid	A-2 Principal Paid	Total Class A Principal Paid
12		429,750,000	47,750,000	477,500,000
13	0			
14	1	8,842,060	982,451	9,824,511
15	2	8,670,853	963,428	9,634,281
16	3	8,502,929	944,770	9,447,699
17	4	8,338,225	926,469	9,264,694
18	5	8,176,679	908,520	9,085,199
19	6	8,018,231	890,915	8,909,146
20	7	7,862,822	873,647	8,736,469
21	8	7,710,395	856,711	8,567,106
22	9	7,560,893	840,099	8,400,992
23	10	7,414,259	823,807	8,238,066

EXHIBIT 15.19   Class A Principal payments section

respective beginning of period outstanding balances. The formula for Class A-1 principal payment is:

```
=IF($CP13<0.1,0,MIN($CP13,$AD14*$CP13/SUM($CP13:$CQ13)))
```

First we determine if the balance of Class A-1 is greater than zero. If it is not, the senior principal distribution amount will not be applied. If the Class A-1 balance is positive, we will apply the minimum of the beginning period outstanding Class A-1 Note balance or the Class A-1 pro rata share of senior principal distribution amount for the period. See Exhibit 15.19.

Class B Principal Payments   The subordinate principal payments take place sequentially and are paid such that each note maintains its Target Subordinate % as initially established on the Structure inputs sheet. The principal payment section for Class B-1 demonstrates how, when a deal is performing in accordance with its initially structured expectations, the subordinate notes will begin receiving principal payments in period 31. See Exhibit 15.20.

The formula for the principal payment to Class B-1 is:

```
=MAX(0,MIN($CR13,MIN($AE14,SUM(CP13:CR13)-(AS14)-
  MIN($I14*ClassB1Percentage,I14-$DI14)))))
```

The first test of "Max(0," guarantees that the principal payment cannot be negative. The next Minimum tests the outstanding balance of the Class B-1 Notes, CR13, against an amount we have yet to compute. From this we know, however, that

	AY	AZ	BA	BB	BC
4					
5	49	50	51	52	53
6		Class B-1 Principal			
7					
8		Principal	Loss	Cumulative	Loss
9		Paid	Allocated	Allocated	Reimbursed
10				Loss	
11					
12		9,500,000	-		-
13	0			-	
14	1	-	-	-	-
15	2	-	-	-	-
16	3	-	-	-	-
17	4	-	-	-	-
18	5	-	-	-	-
19	6	-	-	-	-
20	7	-	-	-	-
21	8	-	-	-	-
22	9	-	-	-	-
23	10	-	-	-	-

EXHIBIT 15.20   Class B-1 Principal payments section

the upper limit of the Principal Payment is the entire outstanding balance of the Class B-1 Notes. The next term of the formula "Minimum(AE14," represents the minimum of the subordinate principal payment amount calculated in the previous section. The remainder of the formula is very similar to how the senior principal distribution amount was computed. We start with the beginning of period balances for Class A and Class B-1 Notes, SUM(CI13:CK13). We then subtract from this value the amount we know to have been paid to the senior notes, AS13. This gives us the starting value for computing how much we need to pay Class B-1 in order to maintain its Target Subordination %. The last step is to subtract the Class B-1 balance that we are targeting, which is 94.8% of the end of period asset balance in our example, I14*ClassB1Percentage.

In this way we proceed to compute principal payments for Class B-2, B-3, and B-4. At each step we need to consider the balances and the payments to the notes that are senior in the payment structure to each class that is now in line to receive a principal payment. The formula for Class B-4 principal payment amount is:

```
=MAX(0,MIN($CT13,MIN($AE14-$AZ14-$BJ14,SUM(CP13:CT13)-
   (AS14+AZ14+BJ14)-MIN($I14*ClassB3Percentage,I14-$DI14)))) 
```

This formula shows how we take the end of period balances for the Class A, B-1, B-2, and B-3 Notes and subtract the payments made to these notes to arrive at the starting point for the Class B-4 principal payment. We then use the Class B-4 percentage to find the target subordination amount and calculate the payment need to maintain this subordination. If there is not enough principal, subordinate classes may receive a partial payment or no payment at all.

Recap of the Preceding Sections   We have now seen how principal payments from the assets are distributed in the waterfall. The total liabilities should never be greater than the asset balance, so that every dollar of decreased asset balance, whether by payments or losses, needs to be reflected in a decrease in the balances of the notes and the OC. These declines in notes and OC can occur in various manners. If there is a mortgage loss, excess cash may reimburse these dollar losses in the assets. If excess cash is insufficient OC will be tapped. Once OC has been exhausted, we will turn to the subordinate notes. Beginning with the most subordinate Class B Notes first, Class B-4, and moving up through the B-3, B-2, and finally B-1 classes, we will begin experiencing write-downs. The next section covers how losses are allocated across the subordinate notes.

Losses Section

There are two different activities that we need to perform in regard to modeling losses to the notes attributable to collateral underperformance. We first need to consider how to allocate losses to each of the Class B Notes as they occur and in congruency with their seniority. The second activity that we will model is a process of reimbursement to note classes that have already taken losses earlier in the deal but that now can have the losses repaid by excess cash at a later time. This section is broken into two subsections, each dealing with one of these activities. The first section, immediately following, examines how the loss allocation process will apply loss to each of the note classes. This process will cause us to write down the balances of the subordinate notes of the deal when losses exceed OC and excess cash available to cover them. The second section, examining the reimbursement activity, follows. This section will describe how reimbursements may occur if, after a period of losses, excess cash becomes available. Should losses slow and excess cash becomes plentiful enough to restore all the target subordinate percentages, there may be excess cash to reimburse notes for previous write-downs. Do not confuse the process of reimbursement to the note holders for prior losses with a "write up," an increase in the outstanding principal of the note class. Once a note class has been written down, its outstanding principal balance can *never* increase. This is impossible due to the fact that the total asset principal must equal total liability principal and there is no way for the value of the assets to increase. Reimbursements will instead be viewed as cash flow compensation to the note holders to ameliorate previous losses to principal.

Loss Allocation Section Losses will begin to be allocated to the subordinated, Class B certificates once all of the OC has been exhausted. Recall that the original OC of the deal is the amount by which the asset balance exceeds the balances of the notes. When all the initial OC has been exhausted by the absorption of losses, we will still need a mechanism for maintaining the parity of the deal (i.e., assets = liabilities). Loss allocation is the mechanism that prevents the deal from becoming undercollateralized by lowering the principal balances of the note classes through write-down activity.

Loss Allocation to the Class B-4 Notes The loss allocation columns for each note class are located within the principal distribution sections of each subordinated note. Class B-4 is the first note that would experience losses. This note is the most subordinate of all the note classes. It will experience losses first, without any reference

	CC	CD	CE	CF	CG
4					
5	79	80	81	82	83
6			Class B-4 Principal		
7					
8		Principal	Loss	Cumulative	Loss
9		Paid	Allocated	Allocated	Reimbursed
10				Loss	
11					
12		-	2,500,000		0
13	0			-	
14	1	-	-	-	-
15	2	-	-	-	-
16	3	-	27,023	27,023	-
17	4	-	804,919	831,941	-
18	5	-	782,103	1,614,044	-
19	6	-	759,900	2,373,944	-
20	7	-	113,293	2,487,237	-
21	8	-	12,763	2,500,000	0
22	9	-	-	2,500,000	-
23	10	-	-	2,500,000	-

EXHIBIT 15.21 Class B-4 Principal section

to the other note classes. We do not need to check the status of any of the other note classes prior to a write-down of this class. It will therefore have the most simple allocation formula and is a good starting place to study the allocation process. The scenario modeled in Exhibit 15.21 is one that experiences high losses. The formula for loss allocated to the Class B-4 notes in cell CE14 is:

```
=IF(CV14=0,MIN(CU13-CD14,MIN(0,I14-(SUM(CP13:CU13)-O14-CK14))*-
  1),0)
```

The formula first checks that the OC of the deal has been exhausted, CV14=0; this is a precursor condition to the allocation of *any* losses to the notes of whatever class. If it has, we move to calculate the write-down, if there is OC available, the loss allocation is set to zero. The first MIN() in this formula sets the write-down amount as the minimum of either:

1. The previous month's Class B-4 balance, CU13, minus this month's principal distribution amount, CD14; or
2. The principal write-down amount we have not computed as of yet.

In order to calculate the write-down amount, we now move to the second MIN() statement. The loss allocation will be the minimum of either:

1. "0", the first term of the Minimum statement, which guarantees that the loss allocation will be positive, or
2. The beginning of period asset balance, I14, minus the would-be balance of the notes if there were no write-down taken, SUM(CP13:CU13), less the total

principal available, O14, and less the excess cash applied to the OC. Since if losses are occurring this number will be negative, we multiply it by negative 1 to turn it into a positive number. Being positive, it is greater than "0" above and becomes the loss allocation for the Class B-1 Notes.

The calculation of the loss allocation is somewhat similar to the intermediate OC deficiency amount used in calculating the excess cash applied to notes, and is calculated by taking the previous note balances and subtracting the total principal distribution from the assets and excess cash applied to principal. See Exhibit 15.21.

Loss Allocation to the Class B-1 Notes   If writing down Class B-4's balance to zero does not cover the full amount of the liability principal write-down needed to maintain deal parity, further write-downs will be allocated to additional subordinate notes. Each note needs to take into consideration the write-downs already taken in the period by notes subordinated to it. To illustrate this, the formula for Class B-1 loss allocation is:

```
=IF(CV14=0,MIN(CR13-AZ14,MIN(0,I14-(SUM(CP13:CU13)-O14-CK14-CE14-
  BU14-BK14))*-1),0)
```

This formula is broadly similar to the loss allocation formula for Class B-1. With the Class B-1 Notes, however, we need to add the previous write-downs taken by Class B-2, B-3, and B-4 to correctly perform the allocation. Thus we see the addition of the three terms in the second MIN() statement of CE for the Class B-4 Notes, and BU and BK for the Class B-3 and B-2 Notes, respectively.

Loss Reimbursement   Losses are allocated to the most subordinate Class B Notes first and then work their way up the Class B seniority ladder. Reimbursement of prior-period losses are, as would be expected, are performed in the opposite order. If excess cash is available to pay back write-downs experienced earlier in the deal, we will examine the Class B-1 write-down history first. It is fortunate that it is impossible for a loss allocation and a reimbursement allocation to occur in the same period. This simplifies our task considerably. Any amount of excess cash available to trigger a reimbursement allocation would have already been redirected to attempt to cover any loss incurred in the current period and to restore OC if possible.

Excess Cash Remaining and the Role of Principal Recoveries   In the Excess Spread Treatment section we have a column for XS Remaining. See Exhibit 15.17. This amount is the sum of the interest remaining after the payment of fees, interest on the notes, and principal. The XS Remaining number also includes any excess principal. Why should there be any excess principal in the deal at all? Recoveries of defaulted principal, due to the lag in their receipt, can create instances where the collateral principal cash flows are increased by the receipt of these deferred principal recoveries. All recoveries are included in the principal distribution amount. It is also important to note that excess principal is not included in the XS Applied to OC or in the calculation of interim OC deficiency. Excess principal cash flows and an interim OC deficiency in a period are mutually exclusive; if principal existed to pay down the notes, it would have been already exhausted before considering the redistribution of XS in a high loss period. The formula for XS Remaining is:

```
=(AD14-AS14)+(AE14-AZ14-BJ14-BT14-CD14)+(CI14-CK14)
```

This formula is the sum of:

1. The senior principal distribution, AD14, less the total Class A principal paid, AS14, plus
2. The cash remaining from subordinate principal distribution. This is the subordinate principal distribution, AE14, minus the principal distributions for each of the four Class B notes, AZ14, BJ14, BT14, and CD14, and,
3. The excess cash remaining after covering losses (CI14–CK14).

This value, if nonzero, can be used to reimburse losses.

Reimbursements to the Class B-1 Notes The Class B-1 Principal section was featured previously in Exhibit 15.20. The formula for cumulative allocated loss in a period is the previous cumulative loss, BB13 (hard-coded zero in period 0), plus any loss allocated, BA14, and less any loss reimbursed, BC14. Specifically:

```
=BB13+BA14-BC14
```

The cumulative allocated losses can be interpreted, for sake of calculating reimbursements, as the maximum amount of loss reimbursements possible in a given period. We are then able to calculate the loss reimbursed for Class B-1 with the following formula:

```
=MIN(BB13,CL14)
```

This formula is the minimum of the previous cumulative allocated loss, BB13, and the excess available to make reimbursements, CL14.

Reimbursements to the Class B-4 Notes For reimbursements to the other subordinated certificates, we need to be careful to subtract reimbursements made to senior note classes from the available excess amount. For example, the formula for Class B-4 loss reimbursed is:

```
=MIN(CF13,CL14-BC14-BM14-BW14)
```

The cash available to reimburse Class B-4 losses is the minimum of:

1. The cumulative allocated loss, or
2. The amount of excess cash, CL14, decreased by any amounts already reimbursed to Classes B-1, B-2 and B-3 (in that order), BC14, BN14, BW14.

Excess Cash Released Section

Aside from adding some computation columns to the LWM, we have only to add one more cash flow field: excess cash released. When the deal is performing well and losses are low, there will be excess cash after all payments of fees, interest, and principal. When this occurs, the excess cash will be released to the Residual Note. The holder of the Residual Note is typically the entity that originated the assets and sold them into the trust in the first place. The formula for excess released, located in column CG, is:

```
=CL14-CM14
```

Column CL contains the excess remaining after covering losses with XS. Column CM contains the amount losses reimbursed in the period.

PERIOD FACTORS WORKSHEET

The final section we need to build on the waterfall sheet is one that we will use to calculate the Note performance statistic "Duration" which is modified duration on the Results page. See Exhibit 15.22. Each period factor essentially compounds the periodic interest rates for each note. This section would not be necessary if the notes where fixed rate notes. In that case, the duration formulas would contain a simplified component,

```
1/(1 + (i/12))^n
```

	DU	DV	DW	DX	DY	DZ	EA
4							
5	123	124	125	126	127	128	129
6		Period Factors					
7							
8		Class	Class	Class	Class	Class	Class
9		A-1	A-2	B-1	B-2	B-3	B-4
10		Factor	Factor	Factor	Factor	Factor	Factor
11							
12							
13	0						
14	1	0.9956	0.9955	0.9955	0.9954	0.9949	0.9939
15	2	0.9912	0.9911	0.9909	0.9907	0.9899	0.9879
16	3	0.9868	0.9867	0.9864	0.9861	0.9849	0.9819
17	4	0.9825	0.9823	0.9819	0.9815	0.9799	0.9760
18	5	0.9781	0.9779	0.9775	0.9770	0.9749	0.9701
19	6	0.9738	0.9736	0.9730	0.9725	0.9699	0.9642
20	7	0.9695	0.9692	0.9686	0.9679	0.9650	0.9583
21	8	0.9652	0.9649	0.9642	0.9634	0.9601	0.9525
22	9	0.9610	0.9606	0.9598	0.9590	0.9552	0.9467
23	10	0.9567	0.9563	0.9555	0.9545	0.9504	0.9410

EXHIBIT 15.22 Period Factors section

where i is the annual interest rate and n is the period. The deal is, however, comprised exclusively of floating rate indexed from LIBOR. In that LIBOR continually fluctuates, we will compute these factors considering each prior period.

The array formula for the Class A-1 period factors is:

```
{=PRODUCT(1/(1+DN$14:DN14/12))}
```

Notice the curly brackets ("{}") in the above formula. This signifies that this formula is entered as an array formula and requires the ctrl+shift+enter keystroke. For each period we take the interest rates for each previous period up through the current period and compound using the Excel PRODUCT() function. This has the effect of the "^n" in the fixed rate note formula.

TOTAL CASH FLOWS SECTION

In order to simplify some of the calculation on the Results page, we also create two sections to aggregate the monthly cash flows to each of the bonds. One of these sets of cash flows is comprised of all principal and interest to each note. The other set contains the cash flows to call. The main purpose of these sections is to facilitate the yield calculations on the Results sheet. When calculating yield the zero period cash flow contains the initial outlay of the investment. In our case we are assuming that the notes are purchased at par by the investors, that is 100 cents on the dollar. We therefore enter the initial cost of purchasing each of the notes at par in the zero period cells. The formula in cell EE14 sums the principal and interest cash flows to the Class A-1 Note as follows:

```
=AI14+AQ14
```

See Exhibit 15.23.

RESULTS PAGE WORKSHEET

The Results page of the LWM is separated into three sections. These are the Collateral Performance section, the Note Performance section, and Model Checks section. The Collateral Performance section tracks all cash flows from the assets along with losses, fees, weighted average life, and call period. The Note Performance section contains balances, cash flows, loss behavior, and performance metrics for each note and OC (where applicable). The Model Checks section performs some simple checks to ensure that the cash flows in the model are all accounted for and make sense.

Collateral Performance

The majority of fields in this table have named Ranges that correspond to cells on the LWM worksheet. For example, the formula for scheduled amortization in cell D4 is "=sumPrinRegAmort". This named Range refers to cell F12 on the LWM

	ED	EE	EF	EG	EH	EI	EJ
4							
5	132	133	134	135	136	137	138
6				Total Cash Flows			
7							
8		Class	Class	Class	Class	Class	Class
9		A-1	A-2	B-1	B-2	B-3	B-4
10							
11							
12							
13	0	-429,750,000	-47,750,000	-9,500,000	-5,500,000	-2,500,000	-2,500,000
14	1	10,747,285	1,196,132	43,383	25,667	12,750	15,250
15	2	10,536,879	1,172,713	43,383	25,667	12,750	15,250
16	3	10,330,514	1,149,743	43,383	25,667	12,750	15,250
17	4	10,128,113	1,127,215	43,383	25,667	12,750	15,250
18	5	9,929,601	1,105,120	43,383	25,667	12,750	15,250
19	6	9,734,903	1,083,449	43,383	25,667	12,750	15,250
20	7	9,543,947	1,062,194	43,383	25,667	12,750	15,250
21	8	9,356,661	1,041,348	43,383	25,667	12,750	15,250
22	9	9,172,976	1,020,903	43,383	25,667	12,750	15,250
23	10	8,992,822	1,000,851	43,383	25,667	12,750	15,250

EXHIBIT 15.23 Total Cash Flows to maturity section

"Waterfall" spreadsheet page that is the sum of all scheduled principal received. Likewise for "Prepayments", "Total Principal", "Defaulted Principal", "Recoveries", "Interest" and "Net Swap Payment", we have the corresponding named Ranges "sumPrinPayments", "sumTotalPrincipal", "sumPrinDefaults", "sumPrinRecoveries", "sumInterest", and "sumNetSwapPmt", respectively. The formula for "Total Cash" is the sum of the principal, interest, recoveries, and net swap payments. "Total Fees" references the named Ranges "sumServicerFees" and "sumOtherFees" that correspond to cells R12 and U12 in the LWM worksheet.

In this section we also have a number of computed fields. The "Gross Loss %" is the "Defaulted Principal" divided by the original asset balance, "TotalBeginPrincipal". The "Lifetime Severity" statistic is computed as:

```
1-(Recoveries/Defaulted Principal)
```

The array formula for "Asset Weighted Average Life (WAL)" is:

```
{=SUM((cfBeginBalance-cfEndBalance)*cfPeriod)
 /SUM(cfBeginBalance-cfEndBalance)}
```

On the LWM worksheet we have named Ranges to make reading long and involved formulas easier. The Range "cfBeginBalance" corresponds to the entire Range of beginning principal from period 1 through 360 (D14:D373). A similar Range is defined as "cfEndBalance" (I14:I373). The "Asset WAL" is the weighting by period of the difference between the beginning and ending principal balance. This describes the amount of time, in months, that the principal balances are outstanding on average. This is an excellent indicator of how quickly the assets amortize and is one of the most important metrics to come out of the model.

	B	C	D
4		Collateral Performance	
5		Scheduled Amortization	33,966,264
6		Prepayments	458,564,426
7		Total Principal	492,530,690
8		Defaulted Principal	7,469,310
9		Gross Loss %	1.49%
10		Recoveries	3,734,609
11		Lifetime Severity	50.00%
12		Interest	127,248,263
13		Net Swap Payment	0
14		Total Cash	623,513,562
15			
16		Total Fees	5,601,983
17			
18		Asset WAL	49.80
19		Call Period	115
20			

EXHIBIT 15.24 Collateral Performance Summary section

Another important field to capture is the "Call Period", the first period where the asset balance drops below the "Cleanup Call %" that we set to 10% on the Structure inputs page. After the Call Period, the fees in the deal will usually increase providing further incentive to exercise the call. Due to this fact it is highly likely the call will be exercised as soon as the call period is hit. The formula for the Call Period is:

```
=MATCH(TRUE,cfCallFlag,0)
```

This formula returns the list element number of the first occurrence of TRUE in the Range "cfCallFlag", (DK14:DK373). See Exhibit 15.24.

Note Performance

The Bond Performance table summarizes the performance of each bond in the Class A and Class B groups as well as the OC. In reviewing this table, we will examine the summary fields for Class B-1. The first two values, "Initial Balance ($)" and "Initial Balance (%)", are taken directly from the Structure inputs pages. "Class B-1Total Principal" references the named Range "sumPrinB1" (AS14AZ12:AS373) on the CFWaterfall sheet. The next three fields are set equal to "sumInterestB1", "sumLossB1", and "sumReimbB1". The "Net Write Downs" field is the "Gross Write Down" minus the "Write Down Reimbursements".

Yield to Maturity   The next six values under each of the notes in the Bond Performance table are summary statistics for yield, coverage, and loss severity. To compute yield to maturity and yield to call, we make use of Excel's built-in IRR() (internal rate of return) function and the total cash flow sections included on the waterfall sheet. The formula for Class B-1 yield to maturity in cell G14 is:

```
=IFERROR(IRR(CFWaterfall!EG$13:EG$373,0.01)*12,-0.999)
```

Yield to Call   The inner IRR() function takes as its first argument the Total Cash Flows Range (including initial outlay). The second argument is a guess that Excel uses as a starting point for an iterative process to find the internal rate of return (IRR). We multiply this value by 12 to convert to an annual return number. If a solution cannot be found the IRR function returns an error, in which case we want to show −99.99% as a placeholder. The yield to call is the same formula but computed on the Total Cash Flows to Call section of the "Waterfall" worksheet.

Coverage Ratio   The coverage ratio for a bond is the amount of excess cash flows that have been released from the deal divided by the original balance of the bond and all bonds senior to said bond. We compute this metric on both a present value (PV) and future value (FV) basis. The coverage ratio FV for the Class B-1 Notes is:

```
=sumRelease/SUM(Results!$G$6:I6)
```

which is the total amount of excess cash released to the residual divided by the sum of the Class A-1, A-2 and B-1 original balances. The coverage ratio NPV for Class B-1 is equal to the net present value of the excess cash flows at the debt rate for the Class B-1 Notes divided by the same balance sum. The (array) formula in cell I16 is:

```
{=SUM((CFWaterfall!$CN$14:$CN$373*cfFactorB1))/SUM(Results!$G$6:I6)}
```

Severity of Loss   The severity of loss is the amount of principal not repaid to a note divided by the note's original balance. This is computed by taking the initial balance less any payments that went to reduce principal. Once again we compute NPV and FV values. The formula for severity of loss FV for the Class B-1 is:

```
=ROUND((I$6-sumPrinB1-sumReimbB1)/I$6,6)
```

Here we are rounding the ratio of beginning principal less principal paid and reimbursed loss over the beginning principal. For the NPV calculation, we discount this amount back from the first period where the note balance is reduced to zero to the present period. For Class B-1 we find the appropriate period factor and discount as follows cell (I18):

```
=INDEX(cfFactorB1,MATCH(0,CFWaterfall!CR$14:CR$373,0))*I19
```

For the senior notes we need to change the severity of loss NPV calculation slightly. Remember that the senior notes do not experience write-downs. Therefore in very high-loss scenarios, the senior notes may still be outstanding at the end of the deal when the assets are all paid off. In this scenario the MATCH() function will return an error because the note balances never reach zero. We account for this by hard-coding period 360 when MATCH() returns an error. This Class A-1 formula is:

```
=INDEX(cfFactorA1,IFERROR(MATCH(0,CFWaterfall!CP$14:CP$373,0),
    360))*G19
```

Weighted Average Life The next three values under Class B-1 are the computed additional summary statistics for this class. Notice that there are two different calculations for WAL: to maturity and to call. Notice that similar to yield above, we compute the WAL to maturity and to call. The former is computed assuming the cleanup call is not exercised and the latter assumes the call is exercised at the first opportunity. The array formula for the Class B-1 WAL (maturity) is:

```
{=IF(I$6=0,0,SUM((cfBegBalB1-cfEndBalB1)*cfPeriod)
  /SUM((cfBegBalB1-cfEndBalB1))))}
```

Weighted Average Life to Call We see that WAL for the bonds is computed in the exact same way as for the assets. We have also gone through and named the Ranges that contain the beginning and ending balance for all the notes in the deal, as evidenced by the named Ranges for Class B-1 in the formula above. The outer IF() function addresses the case where we may not be running the full tranche set and are looking at a three subordinate tranche deal, for example.

The array formula for Class B-1 WAL (to call) is:

```
{=IF(I$6=0,0,SUM((cfBegBalB1-cfEndBalB1)*(cfCallFlag=FALSE)*
  cfPeriod+((cfPeriod=resultsCallPeriod-1)*cfEndBalB1*cfPeriod))
  /SUM((cfBegBalB1-cfEndBalB1)*(cfCallFlag=FALSE)+((cfPeriod=
  resultsCallPeriod-1)*cfEndBalB1))))}
```

This formula looks complicated, but it is a simple modification of the WAL (maturity) calculation. Instead of taking the difference between beginning and ending balances for the whole deal, we only use this value up to the call period (i.e., when cfCallFlag = FALSE). In the call period, "resultsCallPeriod", we take as the amortization amount the previous period's end of period balance.

Duration The final metric for Class B-1 is its duration. In this calculation we will use the period factors that we calculated on the waterfall sheet. The array formula for "Class B-1 Duration" is:

```
{=IF(H$6=0,0,SUM((cfIntA2+cfPrinA2)*cfFactorA2*cfPeriod)
  /SUM((cfIntA2+cfPrinA2)*cfFactorA2)/12)}
```

This formula is the weighting by period of the present value of the principal and interest cash flows to Class B-1.

The formulas for the other classes in the deal can be completed making the necessary adjustments to the Class B-1 formulas above. Notice that there are a number of NAs in the Bond Performance section. Some of the summary fields do not apply to all the bonds. For example, the Class A Notes cannot experience loss write-downs, so all the write-down fields are NA for the Class A Notes. Also, what we are calling the "OC/Resid" piece is not really a bond. We have put the total "Residual Release Amount" in the "Total Interest" field for simplicity. See Exhibit 15.25.

	Bond Performance								
	Class	A-1	A-2	B-1	B-2	B-3	B-4	OC	Total
	Initial Balance ($)	429,750,000	47,750,000	9,500,000	5,500,000	2,500,000	2,500,000	2,500,000	500,000,000
	Initial Balance (%)	85.95%	9.55%	1.90%	1.10%	0.50%	0.50%	0.50%	100.00%
	Total Principal	429,750,000	47,750,000	9,500,000	5,500,000	2,500,000	2,500,000	NA	497,500,000
	Total Interest	90,336,860	10,131,766	3,634,137	2,008,319	896,525	942,195	12,461,778	120,411,580
	Gross Write Downs	NA	NA	0	0	0	0	NA	0
	Write Down Reimbursment	NA	NA	0	0	0	0	NA	0
	Net Write Downs	NA	NA	0	0	0	0	NA	0
	Yield to Maturity	5.32%	5.37%	5.48%	5.60%	6.12%	7.32%	NA	NA
	Yield to Call	5.32%	5.37%	5.48%	5.60%	6.12%	7.32%	NA	NA
	Coverage Ratio NPV	1.85%	1.67%	1.64%	1.62%	1.61%	1.60%	NA	NA
	Coverage Ratio FV	2.90%	2.61%	2.56%	2.53%	2.52%	2.50%	NA	NA
	Severity of Loss NVP	0.00%	0.00%	0.00%	0.00%	0.00%	0.00%	NA	NA
	Severity of Loss FV	0.00%	0.00%	0.00%	0.00%	0.00%	0.00%	NA	NA
	WAL (maturity)	47.4	47.4	83.8	78.2	70.3	61.8	NA	NA
	WAL (to call)	43.6	43.6	81.1	78.2	70.3	61.8	NA	NA
	Duration	3.3	3.3	5.7	5.4	4.9	4.3	NA	NA

EXHIBIT 15.25 Bond Performance table

Note Classes Amortization Graph

The amortization of the various note classes is displayed in a graph immediately below the Note Performance table. This graph displays the composition of the deal throughout time by showing the End of Period balance contribution for each of the Class A and B notes and OC. See Exhibit 15.26.

Model Checks

The Model Checks section contains two calculations that check to make sure the model is operating correctly. The first check is the "Assets" check. Here we are making sure that all the fields relating to asset principal amortization (scheduled principal, prepays, and losses) total to the value of "TotalBeginBalance".

The second check, "Cash In / Cash Out", verifies that the entirety of the cash flows from the collateral is accounted for in payments in the waterfall. The formula for this check is:

=ROUND($D$13-$D$15,2)=ROUND(SUM($K$25:$K$26)+$K$28,2)

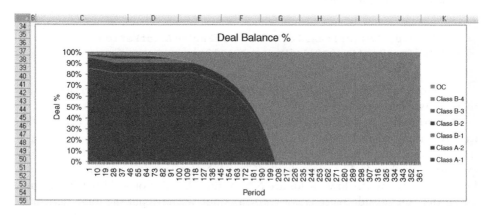

EXHIBIT 15.26 Note Classes Amortization graph

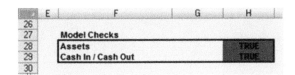

EXHIBIT 15.27 Model Checks section

Total cash minus total fees should be equal to the sum the total principal, total interest (including released cash), and loss reimbursements to the notes. We will also add conditional formatting to these cells so we can notice immediately if one of these checks has failed. This is a critical first level evaluation when an analyst is auditing a deal. See Exhibit 15.27.

ON THE WEB SITE

On the Web site for this chapter you will find a stand-alone Excel workbook containing the complete Liabilities Waterfall Model, "LWM_Chapter15". This workbook consists of four pages:

1. **"Structure"**. Contains the inputs required to drive the performance of the waterfall.
2. **"CFWaterfall"**. The main page of the waterfall workbook. This page contains 360 periods of all cash flows from the assets to liabilities, with many tracking and computation columns included.
3. **"Results"**. A summary page for the waterfall.
4. **"Amort"**. A simple, one-loan amortization example used to test the waterfall during development.

## CHAPTER 16

Writing the LWM VBA Code

OVERVIEW

In this chapter we will augment the Liabilities Waterfall Model (LWM) spreadsheet that we created in Chapter 15 with VBA code. We will use the modules of the existing Base Liabilities Model (BLM) that we created in Chapter 6 to provide a framework for this development. The structure of the deal modeled in the BLM has only a single tranche of liabilities. In our current spreadsheet we have six tranches and a slice of residual overcollateralization. Nevertheless, both the LWM and the BLM share a set of common functionalities that are handled by VBA code. These are:

- Importation of collateral cash flows from files that are designated by the model user and loaded into the spreadsheet model.
- Extraction of the performance results of the Liabilities Structure at the end of each model run. A given cash flow file may have up to 25 individual scenarios comprised of different prepayment and default assumptions. The cash flows of each of these scenarios will produce a unique performance response from the Liabilities Structure.
- Selection and production of a report package to display the results of the LWM runs.

In addition to these functions we will also provide functionality so that of the LWM to specify more than one Liabilities Structure. This feature allows the user to create an input file containing all the specifications of a Liabilities Structure. The LWM will load these files in conjunction with a matching collateral cash flow file and perform a scenario analysis for each set of cash flows.

In the earlier BLM we provided the user with a "Batch Mode" function. We will replace this mode of operation with the ability to create a set of five pairs of files. Each of the sets will contain a collateral cash flow file paired with a Liabilities Structure file and a scenario label name entered by the user. All output files produced by the LWM will be prefixed with this name.

In addition, we will modernize the specification of the report selection. The analyst can now select a combination of reports from a report package UserForm that will be accessible from the Main Menu. We will populate this UserForm from a list of reports maintained on a separate data sheet in the LWM. Thus reports can be easily added to the UserForm in the manner employed in the Stratification and Cross

Tabulation Report UserForms of the Collateral Cash Flow Generator (CCFG). Inside the individual reports we will build a series of VBA subroutines that will allow each report to function as a basic report writer. The analyst will be able to dynamically configure/reconfigure the data displayed in the body of the report. This allows the analyst to specifically tailor the contents of the reports for the analysis needs of the moment.

DELIVERABLES

The modeling knowledge deliverables for this chapter are:

- Building a VBA "shell" model to wrap an existing Excel spreadsheet model.
- Utilizing a system of paired files to provide both collateral cash flow and Liabilities Structure information to the model.
- Development of a UserForm to specify the contents of a reporting package.
- Development of the template file set and the VBA code to produce the reports of the LWM.

UNDER CONSTRUCTION

In this chapter we will be creating an entire VBA model shell to wrap the LWM. This shell will import data containing the collateral cash flows and the Liabilities Structure specifications. It will sequentially run the model matching each of the unique cash flow scenarios against a particular Liabilities Structure, capture the results, and produce a pre-specified reports package. To this end we will re-create, although on a significantly more complex scale, the basic functionality and structure of our earlier BLM.

Menus and Other Excel Worksheets

In the Excel environment we will therefore need to create the following:

- **Main Menu.** A Main Menu to be the "traffic cop" of the LWM. From this menu we will specify the collateral cash flow file names, the Liabilities Structure file names and the output report package prefix names.
- **Structure Inputs Menu.** This menu will be the input point of the model for all structural specifications of the Liabilities Structure.
- **Performance Results Report.** This worksheet is an in-model report of the performance of a single scenario defined by a unique combination of prepayment/default rates.
- **Report Data list.** This worksheet contains the contents of the various report groups of the LWM Report Package UserForm list boxes. It will allow us to quickly and easily update the currently available list of LWM reports.

UserForms and Their Supporting VBA

The LWM will contain a single UserForm with its supporting VBA code contained within it:

- **LWM Report Package UserForm.** This UserForm will allow us to specify the report package of output we wish to produce.
- **"m01LWMReportsMenu".** A VBA UserForm Module containing the support code for the report package UserForm.

VBA Modules of the LWM

The following is a list of modules that will contain the VBA code necessary to manage the input, calculation, and reporting functions of the LWM:

- **"A_Constants".** The module containing all Public Constant variables.
- **"A_Globals".** The module containing all Public variables.
- **"A_MainProgram".** The main program module of the LWM.
- **"MenuSupport_AggAnnCFs".** The module that contains subroutines that convert various related groups of cash flows from monthly frequency to annual total prior to presentation in the reports.
- **"MenuSupport_ErrorChecking".** Error checking/warning menu support code. These error checking routines make sure the analyst has entered complete sets of information regarding the Cases the LWM is asked to run and that there is no duplication of Output File Prefixes.
- **"MenuSupport_ImportCFsFiles".** Reads the contents of the collateral cash flow files previously generated by runs of the CCFG model. This module also contains a series of error checking subroutines that verify the information in the Assumptions Report worksheet of the file is complete. It also formats a series of prepayment and default assumptions labels. These labels are then used to identify the scenarios in the file so that this information can be used to link them with the runs of the LWM that make use of them.
- **"MenuSupport_ImportStructFiles".** This module contains the VBA subroutines that read Liabilities Structure files. These files contain all the Structural Inputs needed by the LWM to describe the Liabilities Structure and to populate the Liabilities Waterfall Worksheet.
- **"MenuSupport_WriteStructFiles".** This module contains the VBA that reads the contents of the Structure Inputs Menu and creates a Liabilities Structure input file that can be later used by the model.
- **"Run_LiabilitiesModel".** Loads the collateral cash flow information into the LWM, loads the structure inputs, runs the model, and captures the results.
- **"Run_ReadResultsStructure".** The subroutines of this module are sequentially integrated with the subroutines contained in the module "Run_Liabilities Model". After the cash flows have been loaded, the spreadsheet calculated, and the results generated and displayed the subroutines of this module record the results in a series of purpose-specific arrays. These arrays record tenor performance, principal, and coupon paid to the tranches, the uses of excess cash

flows, and other structural performance. These are the arrays that we will draw from to produce the reports.

- **"Report_MiscWaterfall"**. This report module captures the entire contents of each of the Liabilities Waterfall Spreadsheets at the time of the completion of the calculation sequence. The report package consists of a series of one spreadsheet copy for each of the cash flow prepayment/default collateral cash flow scenarios.
- **"Report_MiscReports"**. This module contains the VBA code that produces three reports.
    - **Collateral Cash Flows report.** This report module allows the analyst to display the annual amounts of the six cash flow arrays for any of the 25 scenarios of a Case. The arrays are for:
    - The beginning period collateral principal balances, plotted on the right axis of the report due to the disparity of size in the cash flows and the collateral pool balances.
    - Defaults of principal
    - Scheduled amortization of principal
    - Coupon payments
    - Prepayments of principal
    - Recoveries of defaulted principal
    - **Excess Cash Flows report.** This report allows the analyst to select a single scenario of the 25 scenarios of the Case. It displays the five components of excess cash (or overcollateralization). These are the Beginning Period Excess Cash Amount, the Over Collateralization Deficiency, the Over Collateralization Applied, the Over Collateralization Reimbursement, and the Over Collateralization Released (to the investor).
    - **Deal Fees report.** This report displays the annual fee schedule of up to six different scenarios.
- **"Report_MultiTrancheCFs"**. This report module presents a single specific cash flow component for each of the tranches of the structure on a single report. The components are Principal Paid, Coupon Expense Paid, Losses Incurred, and the Beginning Period Principal Balance of each tranche.
- **"Report_MultiTrancheTenor"**. This report displays a single measure of tenor performance for all of the tranches of the structure on a single page. The tenor measurements are Weighted Average Life to Maturity and to Call, Final Maturity, and Modified Duration.
- **"Report_MultiTrancheReturns"**. This report displays a single measure of returns and ratio performance. It contains the Yield to Maturity, the Yield to Call, the Net Present Value, and Future Value Coverage Ratios for each tranche and the Net Present Value and Future Value Severity of Loss statistics for each tranche.
- **"Report _SingleTrancheCFs"**. This report displays all cash flow components of a single tranche on the same page. The cash flows are those presented in the "MultiTrancheCFs" report above.
- **"Report_SingleTrancheTenor"**. This report module produces a series of reports, one per tranche, of all of the tenor statistic performances of the tranche across the various cash flow scenarios of the Case.
- **"Report_SingleTrancheReturns"**. This report displays Yield to Maturity, the Yield to Call, the Net Present Value, and Future Value Coverage Ratios for each

tranche and the Net Present Value and Future Value Severity of Loss statistics for each tranche, one tranche at a time.

- "Z_ButtonSubroutines". Support code for all of the LWM Buttons. These buttons include the navigation and the "get file" buttons of the Main Menu in addition to the button used to display the Report Selection UserForm.
- "Z_UtilityPrepayDefaultWriter". This module contains all the formatting code to load the prepayment and default scenario assumptions into each of the reports of the LWM.
- "Z_UtilitySubroutines". This module will contain a series of general utility subroutines related to report formation, number/letter conversions, and file retrieval activity.

Structure Input Template Files

The LWM will allow the analyst to save the inputs necessary to describe a Liabilities Structure to a file. The template file provided for this activity is:

- "Template_StructureInputs". The template file that contains the Structural Inputs needed by the model.

Report Template Files

The following report template files are used in the production of the LWM results.

Single Tranche Reports The following report template files provide the basis of those reports that present information on a single note tranche:

- "TemplateSTCF_AmortBalance". Schedule of annual beginning principal balances by tranche for each scenario of the Case.
- "TemplateSTCF_PrinPmts". Annual schedule of principal retired by tranche for each scenario of the Case.
- "TemplateSTCF_CoupPaid". Annual schedule of coupon debt service paid to each tranche for each scenario of the Case.
- "TemplateSTCF_Losses". Annual schedule of losses included by each tranche for each scenario of the Case.
- "TemplateSTTenor". Tenor performance statistics report.
- "TemplateSTYield". Yield, coverage ratio, and severity of loss performance statistics report for a single tranche.

Multiple Tranche Reports The following template files form the basis for all reports that contain information on more than one note tranche:

- "TemplateMTCF_All". All cash flows for multiple tranches report template file.
- "TemplateMTTenor". Tenor performance statistics report.
- "TemplateMTYield." Yield, coverage ratio, and severity of loss performance statistics report for multiple tranches.

Miscellaneous Reports   These template files are for reports that are not tranche-specific. They report instead on other aspects of the performance of the Liability Structure that are separate from the performance of the tranches themselves. The Collateral Cash Flows file is provided so that the analyst has access to cash flow information in a similar file format as the Liability Structure output. It is especially helpful when preparing reports containing both liability and asset data to have an asset report that shares the general formatting schema of the majority of the liabilities reports in the presentation.

- "TemplateMiscCollatCFs". A report of the collateral cash flows used in the various scenario model runs.
- "TemplateMiscExcessCFs". Reports on the sources and uses of excess cash flow (overcollateralization) in the structure.
- "TemplateMiscFees". Report template for the Deal Fees report. This report contains the schedule of fee expenses of each scenario of the Case.

Parting Comments

As we examine these reports you will notice that all of them, with the exception of the liabilities waterfall, follow the same layout schema.

Simplicity and Flexibility   The standard configuration that presents a statistical data table to the left of the report and a graph to the right with (or without) the Data Schedule section below is a deliberate choice. It is a simple format to read, and, as you will see, manipulate, by engineering the report template file itself to become a primitive report writer. This allows the analyst a wide range of choices in determining the contents of many of the reports. The composition of the display area table and its accompanying display area graph can be manipulated easily. In most of the reports, simply entering the identifying numbers of the scenarios the analyst wishes to display and clicking on the CommandButton is all that is required to display the report. In that there are no fixed formats for the report contents, any combination of results can be immediately specified and displayed. This is especially useful if you are required to produce special condition runs for regulatory bodies or investors.

Building a Historical Collection of Results   These report formats preserve not only the displayed data but all of the significant data of a run of the LWM. By writing the entire contents of the calculated results of the model run to the output files, we also, de facto, create an audit and testing results corpus. This body of results, if stored, organized and backed up appropriately can provide a valuable collection of results. These results can be used to compare the relative performance of different structures in response to the cash flows of a specific collateral pool. They can also be used for model validation purposes when major changes are made to the model in the future.

Standardization of Reporting Formats   There is another advantage to the standardization of reporting formats. If the output results can be displayed in a relatively restricted number of reporting formats, the supporting VBA code can be generally optimized for these report types. In addition, it becomes easier to create the VBA support subroutines to leverage the similarity of function. This can result in the economies of code as seen in the "Report_MiscCFs" module. In this module we can produce all three miscellaneous cash flow reports simply by installing switches into a set of subroutines shared by each of the reports.

Minimal Amounts of Calculation Subroutines

Unlike the organization of the CCFG, the LWM performs almost none of its calculations in VBA subroutines. The calculations of the LWM take place entirely within the contents of the Excel Liabilities Waterfall spreadsheet.

The only quasi-calculations occur when we need to convert the monthly cash flows and balances of the Liabilities Waterfall spreadsheet from monthly amounts to annual sums. We are at times also required to find and record the beginning period balances of the notes.

VBA REQUIREMENTS OF THE LWM

We touched on the requirements of the VBA code in the Overview section of this chapter. Let us look at them in more detail now.

Managing Menus and Screens

We need to create a Main Menu for the LWM. This menu will help us navigate around the various screens of the model. We will use this menu to enter the names of the collateral cash flow files, the Liabilities Structure files, and to specify the Output File Prefixes that will identify our specific Cases.

The Main Menu will also be the launching point for the LWM Report Package UserForm. This UserForm will allow the analyst to select reports from a list of multi-tranche, single-tranche, or miscellaneous reports.

The menu will also provide the analyst with a small set of navigation buttons to the other spreadsheets of the LWM.

Importation of Cash Flows from CCFG Created Files

One of the most critical tasks of the LWM is the importation of the collateral cash flow information created by the CCFG. The model must read the files, segregate the cash flows into their component scenarios and apply those scenarios in a systemic manner to the Liabilities Waterfall spreadsheet. It needs to:

1. Accept the names of the specific files (up to five) from the user.
2. Find and open the designated file(s).
3. Determine the prepayment/default methodology used to create the contents of the file.

4. Determine the number of scenarios contained in the file.
5. Determine the prepayment and default speeds for each of the scenarios.
6. Store and manage the cash flows so that they are applied to the liabilities waterfall structure in a precise and specific manner.
7. Retain the descriptive information for each of the scenarios for presentation in any reports that are produced.
8. Erase the cash flows of any prior model run before the importation of additional cash flows for subsequent model runs.

Importation of Liabilities Structure Inputs

The importation of the data that describes a Liabilities Structure is much easier than that of a collateral cash flow file. There are many fewer inputs and they all go to a single worksheet in the LWM. The inputs that describe a Liabilities Structure are all written into the "Structure" worksheet. These are in order of left to right, top to bottom:

- Percentage allocation of issuance principal balances by tranche.
- Financing spread to the index by tranche.
- Servicer fee rate (%).
- Step-down parameters:
  - Initial step-down month
  - Initial step-down credit enhancement level
  - Post–step-down credit enhancement level
- Three-month moving average target delinquency trigger percentage.
- Target subordination percentage for each tranche.
- Cumulative realized loss trigger and the various intervals it adjusts over the life of the deal.
- Cleanup trigger percentage for remaining balances.

LWM Reporting Requirements

We will need to create a report package for the LWM. These reports will need to provide output on both the performance of individual tranches and on the performance of the Liabilities Structure as a whole. A collateral cash flow file may contain multiple prepayment/default scenarios. In this case we will have to report the results of each model run and will need to identify in the reports the methodology and the speeds used to generate the set of results.

MENUS OF THE LWM

To optimize the VBA that we will use to support the calculations of the Liabilities Waterfall Model Excel spreadsheet, we will create a Main Menu for the application. In addition to this Excel menu, we will also develop a UserForm. The UserForm will serve as a report selection menu for all reports that comprise the report package of the LWM.

The remaining existing worksheets of the model will serve us well. We can employ them without modification to perform the following critical tasks:

- **"Structure"** worksheet. Entry of the input parameters of the Liabilities Structure.
- **"Results"** worksheet. Performance results of the tranches of the current selected Liabilities Structure.

Main Menu of the LWM

Every program needs a Main Menu or needs to have one of its menus declared as the basic starting point of the model. In this case we will create a Main Menu, as we did earlier for the CCFG, that will serve as the home base for our interaction with the model.

The Main Menu illustrates that the base unit of analysis of the LWM is the "Case". The LWM allows the analyst to describe up to a maximum of five specific Cases. A single Case consists of the following items:

- Collateral cash flows file containing up to a maximum of 25 prepayment and default combination cash flow scenarios.
- Structural Inputs file containing all the information needed to describe a Liabilities Structure.
- Unique Case-specific prefix that will be prepended to all of the output reports.

Throughout the rest of this chapter, when the term "Case" is used, it will describe a specific run of the model that used this combination of information.

Organization of the Main Menu   The Main Menu is divided into four sections. Each of these sections serves a particular purpose in running the LWM. See Exhibit 16.1.

Title Section   This section contains the name of the menu. It is "Liabilities Waterfall Model Main Menu". It may seem painfully obvious to you that every menu or data sheet needs a title to identify itself. This is not, however, the universal perception among model developers, especially inexperienced ones! Many developers fail to name their menus, or, worse, name some but not others. Giving a menu a name not only helps you recognize it but will help others recognize it too! It is especially helpful when you are teaching or assisting others in working with the model. A meaningful name also serves as a guide to the function of the contents of the menu and its place in the overall design and operation of the model.

Case Section   This section allows the analyst to enter the names of up to five sets of files. Each Case contains a Collateral Cash Flows file, a Structural Inputs file, and an Output Prefix unique to that Case. To indicate that the Case is to be run in this operation of the LWM, the analyst enters a "X" in the set of five "Case Run"

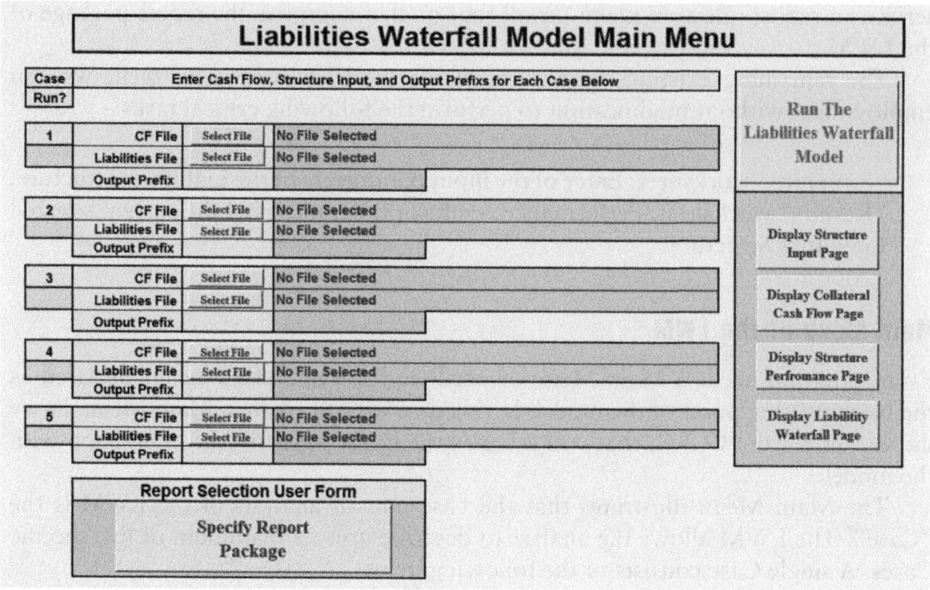

EXHIBIT 16.1   LWM Main Menu

fields at the leftmost side of the model directly under the Case ID number field. The combination of files will then be used in a model run. The Collateral Cash Flow file field and the Structure Inputs file are equipped with a "Select File" Button. As with similar fields in the CCFG, the model user needs only to click on the button in the second field of the section. The button triggers a window display that allows the user to navigate to any directory to select the appropriate file desired. The full pathway of the file is returned to the menu field following the button. See Exhibit 16.2.

Report Selection Section   Clicking on this button will display the LWM Report Selection Menu UserForm. The analyst makes a selection from the report list in the UserForm ListBoxes. These selections are used to trigger the production of the report package.

Navigation Button Section   This section contains a series of buttons that can be used to navigate in the model from the Main Menu to any of the other screens.

A Completed Main Menu   The following is a completed Main Menu. It produces three model runs. There are three pairings of collateral cash flow files and liabilities Structural Inputs files. In the second and third Cases, the same cash flow file will be applied to a different Structural Inputs file. The Output File Prefixes will be "Case001", "Case002", and "Case003". See Exhibit 16.3.

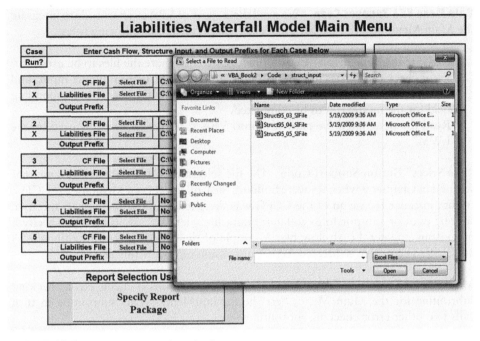

EXHIBIT 16.2 Select File Window display

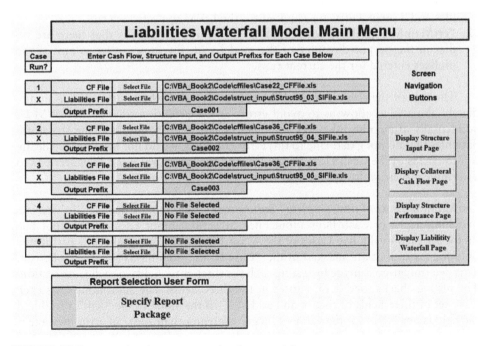

EXHIBIT 16.3 Completed Main Menu for three model runs

Main Menu VBA Support Code   We need three types of VBA support code to integrate the Main Menu into the LWM. This VBA will perform the following roles:

- Activate the "File Select" button functions to designate the files to be used.
- Error check the entries to the Cash Flow Input, the Structural Inputs Input, and the Output File Prefix section. There needs to be an entry in each corresponding field for the model run to be completed.
- Read the designated file pathways into VBA variables that can be used by the LWM.

"File Select" Button Support Code   The file selection button code is the same that we used in Chapter 9 when we were building the Collateral Pool Menu for the CCFG. In that instance the menu of the CCFG was designed to allow the user to specify a specific pool or sub-portfolio collateral data file. Here we are using it to specify a preexisting collateral cash flow file. A sample of the code is given in Exhibits 9.38 and 9.39. The reader is directed to that discussion to review this feature.

Main Menu Error Checking Code   The LWM contains a menu error checking subroutine for the Main Menu, "errCheck_MainMenu". This subroutine in turn calls two other error checking subroutines:

1. **"errMainMenu_RunFilesComplete"**. This subroutine checks that there are entries in the Cash Flow Input File, the Structural Inputs File, and the Output File Prefix sections for each run of the model that contain *any* of these inputs. Both files and a prefix entry are required for the LWM to perform a run.
2. **"errMainMenu_FilesCheckOutput"**. This subroutine checks that there are no files in the output directory of the model with the same prefix as any of the prefixes entered for the current runs.

The role of the specific set of VBA subroutines described in the section immediately above is to allow us to avoid errors at the execution time of the LWM by accidentally attempting to select and load collateral cash flow and the structural data files that do not exist! Due to this error checking, we do not need to specifically test the fields of the Cash Flow Input Files and the Structural Input Files sections to determine if their pathways are valid.

"errMainMenu_RunFilesComplete" Subroutine   This subroutine tests if there is a matching triplet of Cash Flow Input Files, Structural Input Files, and Output File Prefix for each of the five Cases of the Main Menu. This error check is performed *only* for Cases that are marked in the "Case Run?" column as selected to be run. This determination is made by testing each the three entry fields in each Case section. The testing checks for NULL entries in the three fields. The subroutine tests each Case set of three fields of the set and adds "1" to the value of the "icnt" variable if the field is not NULL. If the value of "icnt" is greater than zero, an error message is generated. The subroutine progressively adds the failed Cases to the end of the error message contained in the variable "msgTotal". After the last of the runs are tested, the loop ends and the variable "printMessage" is tested. If it is TRUE, errors were detected and the error message is printed. Program execution stops. If all the file

entries for a given run were present, the Boolean array "activeRun" is set to TRUE for that run. If an error message is produced, this information is of no importance. If, however, all runs pass this test and no errors are detected, the next error checking subroutine will use the values of the "activeRun" array to determine if we need to check for existing output files. See Exhibit 16.4.

```
Sub errMainMenu_RunFilesComplete()

Dim iField       As Integer     'field counter in case inputs set area
Dim goOK         As Boolean     'check that the Case is active
Dim runField     As String      'range name for run option foeld of case

    msgTotal = "MAIN MENU INPUT ERROR MESSAGES " & vbCrLf & vbCrLf & _
               "Missing Collateral Cash Flow File, Structure Inputs File" & _
               vbCrLf & "or Output File Prefix Entry" & _
               vbCrLf & "    For the following model runs: & vbCrLf"
    'determine if any error conditions exist
    printMessage = False                    'no error conditions yet
    For iCase = 1 To MAX_CASES
        goOK = False
        Select Case iCase
          Case Is = 1: runField = Trim(Range("m01Run1"))
          Case Is = 2: runField = Trim(Range("m01Run2"))
          Case Is = 3: runField = Trim(Range("m01Run3"))
          Case Is = 4: runField = Trim(Range("m01Run4"))
          Case Is = 5: runField = Trim(Range("m01Run5"))
        End Select
        If runField <> "" Then goOK = True       'run is selected
        activeRun(iCase) = False
        If goOK Then
          Select Case iCase
            Case Is = 1: mRngString = "m01Case01Inputs"
            Case Is = 2: mRngString = "m01Case02Inputs"
            Case Is = 3: mRngString = "m01Case03Inputs"
            Case Is = 4: mRngString = "m01Case04Inputs"
            Case Is = 5: mRngString = "m01Case05Inputs"
          End Select
          icnt = 0
          'read the three fields of the Case
          For iField = 1 To 3
            If Trim(Range(mRngString).Cells(iField)) = "" Then
                printMessage = True
                msgTotal = msgTotal & "            " & iCase & vbCrLf
                activeRun(iCase) = False
                Exit For
            End If
          Next iField
        End If
    Next iCase
    'print the error message if necessary
    If printMessage Then
        Sheets("MainMenu").Select
        msgResult = MsgBox(msgTotal, cMsgButtonCode1, msgTitle)
        End
    End If

End Sub
```

EXHIBIT 16.4 "errMainMenu_RunFilesComplete" subroutine

"errMainMenu_FilesCheckOutput" Subroutine The second error checking sub-routine is designed to prevent us from overwriting existing files that have the same Output File Prefixes as the prefixes we have entered into the Main Menu for this series of runs. To accomplish this, the subroutine will need to perform the following tasks:

1. Cycle through each of the five Cases.
2. Determine if the model run is active.
3. Read the run number Output File Prefix.
4. Generate a file name for each LWM output file using the Output File Prefix entry for the run.
5. Build a pathway to the Output directory using the above file name.
6. Test if the file exists. If the file is not found, set an error tag for the model run.
7. At the end of the cycle produce an error message of the model runs having prefixes shared by files already in the output directory.

The subroutine "errCheck_BuildPrefixErrorMsg" then assembles the error message from the individual error conditions. As we have just seen earlier, the values of the array "activeRun" are set in the previous error checking subroutine. This may help to speed up the functioning of this error checking process by allowing us to bypass those model runs that are not going to be run by the LWM. See Exhibits 16.5 and 16.6.

Transfer Main Menu Inputs to VBA Arrays The final task of the Main Menu VBA support code is to transfer the contents of the menu into VBA arrays where the LWM can use the information to perform the model runs. The "MainMenu_ReadFileNameInputs" subroutine performs this function. With this VBA code we have finished with the Main Menu. See Exhibit 16.7.

LWM Report Package UserForm

The LWM Report Package Menu is a UserForm that is displayed when activated from the Report Selection Section of the Main Menu. It allows the user of the LWM to designate the contents of the report package that will be produced.

Types of LWM Performance Reports The LWM performance reports fall into three categories: single-tranche, multiple-tranche, and miscellaneous reports. The list of reports available in the model can be managed through entries to and deletions from the contents of the "ReportDataList" spreadsheet. The list on this sheet is the input range for the UserForm list boxes that display the report choices to the user for selection.

The distinctions between the three types of reports are:

- **Single-tranche reports.** Contains information pertaining to the performance of a specific tranche, say the A-1 tranche or the B-3 tranche. The Single Tranche Tenor report contains a series of 3-D column bar charts. Each of these charts displays the tenor performance of the single tranche across each of the cash flow scenarios of the model run (limit 25).

```
Sub errMainMenu_FilesCheckOutput()

Dim iFileNumber          As Integer      'VBA error code

    For irun = 1 To MAX_FILE_NUMBER
        If activeRun(irun) Then
            mFPrefix(irun) = Trim(Range("m01PrefixOutputFile").Cells(irun))
            countExist(irun) = 0        'no existing files found yet
            For irep = 1 To NUM_OUT_FILES
                Call errCheck_GenerateReportName
                outTarget = OUTPUT_DIRECTORY & outFName(irep)
                'open output file and set error condition,
                'default: output file is present
                errFileExist(irun) = True 'assume we found the output file
                On Error GoTo OutputFileErr
                iFileNumber = FreeFile()
                Open outTarget For Input As iFileNumber
                'the file exists, increment the found file count
                If errFileExist(irun) Then
                    countExist(irun) = countExist(irun) + 1
                    Exit For
                End If
            Next irep
        End If
    Next irun
    'construct the error message and display
    Call errCheck_BuildPrefixErrorMsg
    On Error GoTo 0
    Exit Sub

OutputFileErr:
    Select Case Err
        Case Is = 52, 53, 75, 76
            'did not find the file, we are ok
            errFileExist(irun) = False
    End Select
    Resume Next

End Sub
```

EXHIBIT 16.5   "errMainMenu_FilesCheckOutput" subroutine

- **Multiple-tranche reports.** Contains the performance of all the tranches of the deal across a single parameter. An example might be the principal paid for each tranche for the life of the deal; the six amortization curves of a single cash flow scenario.
- **Miscellaneous reports.** Contains all other report types including the waterfall report for each of the cash flow scenarios the model has run from the current collateral cash flow file.

Layout of the LWM Report Package Menu   The LWM Report Package Menu User Form consists of three ListBoxes (each with two CommandButtons) and two additional CommandButtons on the UserForm itself. The ListBoxes are divided to contain all available multiple-tranche, single-tranche, and miscellaneous reports. The analyst may select any, or all, or deselect all of the reports they wish to produce from

```
Sub errCheck_BuildPrefixErrorMsg()

Dim printMessage      As Boolean        'print the error message box

    msgTotal = "MAIN MENU INPUT ERROR MESSAGES " & Chr(13) & Chr(13) & _
              "Output files exist with this prefix" & Chr(13)
    msgLast = "Try changing the output file prefix code" & Chr(13) _
            & "or moving the files to another directory."
    'based on the number of missing/existing files write the compound
    ' error message
    printMessage = False
    For irun = 1 To MAX_FILE_NUMBER
        If countExist(irun) > 0 Then
            'some files with this prefix were found
            msgTotal = msgTotal & _
                " Files with " & mFPrefix(irun) & " prefix exist!" & Chr(13)
            printMessage = True
        End If
    Next irun
    'Print out the results of the error scan
    If printMessage Then
        Sheets("MainMenu").Select
        msgTotal = msgTotal & msgLast
        msgResult = MsgBox(msgTotal, cMsgButtonCode1, msgTitle)
        End
    End If

End Sub
```

EXHIBIT 16.6   "errMainMenu_BuildPrefixErrorMsg" subroutine

```
Sub MainMenu_ReadFileNameInputs()

    'case #1 inputs
    gCFInputFile(1) = Trim(Range("m01Case01Inputs").Cells(1))
    gStructInputFile(1) = Trim(Range("m01Case01Inputs").Cells(2))
    gOutputPrefix(1) = Trim(Range("m01Case01Inputs").Cells(3))
    'case #2 inputs
    gCFInputFile(2) = Trim(Range("m01Case02Inputs").Cells(1))
    gStructInputFile(2) = Trim(Range("m01Case02Inputs").Cells(2))
    gOutputPrefix(2) = Trim(Range("m01Case02Inputs").Cells(3))
    'case #3 inputs
    gCFInputFile(3) = Trim(Range("m01Case03Inputs").Cells(1))
    gStructInputFile(3) = Trim(Range("m01Case03Inputs").Cells(2))
    gOutputPrefix(3) = Trim(Range("m01Case03Inputs").Cells(3))
    'case #4 inputs
    gCFInputFile(4) = Trim(Range("m01Case04Inputs").Cells(1))
    gStructInputFile(4) = Trim(Range("m01Case04Inputs").Cells(2))
    gOutputPrefix(4) = Trim(Range("m01Case04Inputs").Cells(3))
    'case #5 inputs
    gCFInputFile(5) = Trim(Range("m01Case05Inputs").Cells(1))
    gStructInputFile(5) = Trim(Range("m01Case05Inputs").Cells(2))
    gOutputPrefix(5) = Trim(Range("m01Case05Inputs").Cells(3))

End Sub
```

EXHIBIT 16.7   "MainMenu_ReadFileNameInputs" subroutine

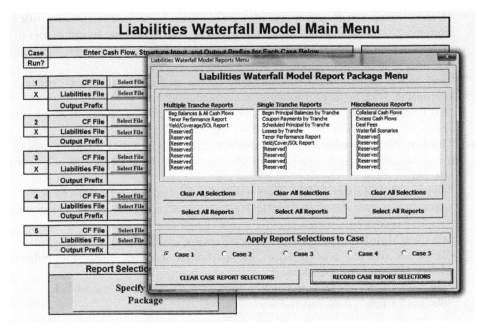

EXHIBIT 16.8 LWM Report Package Menu UserForm

each of the three ListBoxes. Multiple selections are allowed in each ListBox. At any point in the selection process, the analyst can click on either of the two Command Buttons. The first, "Record Report Selection", first checks that none of the choices is "[Reserved]", that is to say, unavailable, reports and that at least one valid report choice was selected. If these two tests are met, the report selections are recorded in a set of VBA arrays and made available to the LWM. If there are illegal entries an appropriate error message is displayed. If the second CommandButton is marked "Clear Report Selections", all report elections are nullified and the UserForm is closed. See Exhibit 16.8.

VBA Support Code of the LWM Report Package Menu The support code for the LWM Report Package Menu UserForm is contained in the UserForm object "m01LWMReportsMenu". This module contains a total of six subroutines that perform the following roles:

- "**AddButton_Click**". Called when the "Record Report Selections" Button is clicked. This subroutine records the entries made in the three ListBoxes transferring them to VBA arrays where we can perform error checking prior to passing them on to the LWM to use. The subroutine also records which of the five Case selections have been recorded so that these elections will be properly matched to the correct LWM run.
- "**ClearButton_Click**". Called when the "Clear Report Selections" Button is clicked. It clears all report selections and the report set flags that indicate if any reports were selected from each of the three groups.

- "UserFormSupport_ReadReportTitles". This subroutine reads the report titles from the "ReportDataList" spreadsheet. We need to read these report names to identify which members of the lists are "[Reserved]", indicating that they are not accessible by the program or have yet to be created.
- "errCheck_LWMReportMenuUserForm". This is the overall error checking subroutine. It calls the two subroutines immediately below.
- "ErrTest_SelectedReservedField". This subroutine checks to see if we have selected a report from the menu that is "[Reserved]".
- "ErrTest_NoReportsSelected". This subroutine checks that at least one report from the total reports available in the combined three ListBoxes has been selected.
- "cbSelectMultiReports", "cbSelectSingleReports", and "cb_SelectMiscReports". Selects all reports from the particular ListBox when the button "Select All Reports" is clicked.
- "cb_ClearMultiReports", "cbClearSingleReports", and "cb_ClearMiscReports". Clears all selected reports from the particular ListBox when the button "Select All Reports" is clicked.
- "obCase1_Click", "obCase2_Click", "obCase3_Click", "obCase4_Click", and "obCase5_Click". Indicates the selected Case.

In the chapters on the development of the CCFG, we have examined numerous examples of UserForm support code. We will therefore confine our examination of this code to the "AddButton_Click" subroutine and the two error checking subroutines: "ErrTest_SelectedReservedField" and "ErrTest_NoReportsSelected". As we have done before, we display the UserForm by writing a one line subroutine that we will assign to the "Specify Report Package" CommandButton on the Main Menu. We will name this macro "ButtonSubs_ReportSelectUserForm". See Exhibit 16.9.

"AddButton_Click" Subroutine   This subroutine is the main subroutine supporting the UserForm. It performs the following tasks:

- Calls a subroutine to read the names of the report lists.
- Reads the ListBoxes to determine which of the report options have been selected.
- Calls a subroutine to read the names of the report lists.
- Records these selections in a VBA array that is specific to each of the report sets.
- Calls the error checking subroutines at the end of the process.

The code fragment immediately below is the first of a set of three "For..Next" loops that peruse the ListBoxes and reads the selection made in each. Here the first element of the array for the Case that is currently selected on the UserForm "mListSelect(iCase,1)" is set to FALSE. This indicates that, as of yet, no report selections have

```
Sub ButtonSubs_ReportSelectUserForm()
    m01LWMReportsMenu.Show
End Sub
```

EXHIBIT 16.9   "ButtonSubs_ReportSelectUserForm" subroutine

been recorded as valid from the contents of the ListBox "lbMultiTrancheRepList" for this Case. The "For..Next" loop will operate through the "ListCount" of the ListBox, that is, the number of items in the list. If the value of the ListBox property ".Selected(irep)" is TRUE, the report line in the ListBox is selected. If it is, we set the corresponding position, "irep+1" in the array "gMultiSelect" to TRUE. Why do we use "irep+1"? You will observe that the initial value of the "irep" loop is "0", not "1". All of the internal arrays of the ListBoxes have an initial value of "0", not "1". If the first item in a ListBox object is selected, this selection would set "lbMultiTrancheRepList.Selected(0)" to TRUE, not "lbMultiTrancheRepList.Selected(1)", which is the second record in the ListBox! You will keep in mind that finding *any* report that is selected will set the value of "mListSelect(iCase,1)" to TRUE. We also set the variable "gCaseReportSelect(1) to "TRUE". This indicates that at least one report has been selected from this ListBox.

```
'Multiple Tranche Reports
mListSelect(iCase, 1) = False
For irep = 0 To lbMultiTrancheRepList.ListCount - 1
   If lbMultiTrancheRepList.Selected(irep) Then
       gMultiSelect(iCase, irep + 1) = True
       mListSelect(iCase, 1) = True
       gCaseReportSelect(1) = True
   End If
Next irep
```

The subroutine utilizes three of above loops and then, with the entry selections detected, transfers them to the three VBA arrays "gMultiSelect", "gSingleSelect", and "gMiscSelect". The contents of these arrays are then examined by the two error checking subroutines (as previously noted). See Exhibit 16.10.

"ErrTest_SelectedReservedField" and "ErrTest_NoReportsSelected" Subroutines These two subroutines check the UserForm selections to determine the following:

1. Have any of the reports with the "[Reserved]" status been selected?
2. Has at least one report been selected from the combined three list boxes?

In "ErrTest_SelectedReservedField", all we need to do is set up three "For..Next" loops, one for each of the ListBoxes. We already know which of the reports in each of the ListBoxes have been selected from the work done in "AddButton_Click" subroutine. We need only compare the selected reports to the list of names read from the "ReportDataList" worksheet by the "UserFormSupport_ReadReportTitles" subroutine earlier. If we find a report with the name "[Reserved]", we create a one-line addition to the error message and append it to the existing error message.

In the "ErrTest_NoReportsSelected" subroutine, we can quickly and easily determine if any of the reports have been selected by testing the values of the "mListSelect" array. If all of them are FALSE, no reports have been selected, and we will inform the user of that. See Exhibit 16.11.

```vb
Private Sub AddButton_Click()

    Sheets("MainMenu").Select    'Make sure the worksheet is active
    iCase = gCaseSelect
    'read the titles of the reports so that we can determine later which are
    ' active reports and which are [Reserved].
    Call UserFormSupport_ReadReportTitles
    'check that we are not about to overwrite any existing set of report
    ' selections for this case
    go_ok = True
    If gCaseReportSelect(iCase) Then
        'case has report selections active - produce an error message
        Call errMsg_DuplicateCaseSelected
        If msgResult = vbOK Then go_ok = True        'overwrite the selections
        If msgResult = vbCancel Then go_ok = False   'don't overwrite selections
    End If
    If go_ok Then
        'read the selected items from the three List Boxes
        'Multiple Tranche Reports
        mListSelect(iCase, 1) = False
        For irep = 0 To lbMultiTrancheRepList.ListCount - 1
            If lbMultiTrancheRepList.Selected(irep) Then
                gMultiSelect(iCase, irep + 1) = True
                mListSelect(iCase, 1) = True
                gCaseReportSelect(1) = True
            End If
        Next irep
        'Single Tranche Reports
        mListSelect(iCase, 2) = False
        For irep = 0 To lbSingleTrancheRepList.ListCount - 1
            If lbSingleTrancheRepList.Selected(irep) Then
                gSingleSelect(iCase, irep + 1) = True
                mListSelect(iCase, 2) = True
                gCaseReportSelect(2) = True
            End If
        Next irep
        'Misc Data Reports
        mListSelect(iCase, 3) = -1
        For irep = 0 To lbMiscDataRepList.ListCount - 1
            If lbMiscDataRepList.Selected(irep) Then
                gMiscSelect(iCase, irep + 1) = True
                mListSelect(iCase, 3) = True
                gCaseReportSelect(3) = True
            End If
        Next irep
        'Error checking performs 2 tests
        'report selected in any othe three groups is not [Reserved]
        'check that at least one entry has been made
        Call errCheck_LWMReportMenuUserForm
    End If
    'we are done, put down the user form
    Unload m01LWMReportsMenu

End Sub
```

EXHIBIT 16.10   "AddButton_Click" subroutine

```
Sub ErrTest_SelectedReservedField()

Dim first_time        As Boolean         'first error detected in any set

    first_time = True
    'Multiple tranche report check for reserved status
    For irep = 1 To MAX_MULTI_REPORTS
        If gLWMRepName1(irep) = "[Reserved]" And gMultiSelect(iCase, irep) Then
            If first_time Then msgBody = msgBody & msgInfo(1) & vbCrLf
            first_time = False
            msgBody = msgBody & _
                "Mutilple Tranche Report is  Reserved" & " =" & irep & vbCrLf
            errScore = errScore + 1
        End If
    Next irep
    'Single tranche report check for reserved status
    For irep = 1 To MAX_SINGLE_REPORTS
        If gLWMRepName2(irep) = "[Reserved]" And gSingleSelect(iCase, irep) Then
            If first_time Then msgBody = msgBody & msgInfo(1) & vbCrLf
            first_time = False
            msgBody = msgBody & _
                "Single Tranche Report is Reserved" & " =" & irep & vbCrLf
            errScore = errScore + 1
        End If
    Next irep
    'Miscellaneous data report check for reserved status
    For irep = 1 To MAX_MISC_REPORTS
        If gLWMRepName3(irep) = "[Reserved]" And gMiscSelect(iCase, irep) Then
            If first_time Then msgBody = msgBody & msgInfo(1) & vbCrLf
            first_time = False
            msgBody = msgBody & _
                "Misc Data Report is Reserved" & " =" & irep & vbCrLf
            errScore = errScore + 1
        End If
    Next irep
    'print the message if there were reports selected that are catagorized
    '  as [Reserved] (not active yet).
    If errScore > 0 Then
        msgResult = MsgBox(msgBody, cMsgButtonCode1, msgTitle)
        End
    End If

End Sub
'=================================================================================
Sub ErrTest_NoReportsSelected()
    If gCaseReportSelect(1) = False And gCaseReportSelect(2) = False And _
       gCaseReportSelect(3) = False Then
        msgBody = msgBody & msgInfo(2) & vbCrLf
        msgResult = MsgBox(msgBody, cMsgButtonCode1, msgTitle)
        End
    End If
End Sub
```

EXHIBIT 16.11   UserForm error checking subroutines

MAIN PROGRAM

The Main Program of the LWM occupies its own module, "A_MainProgram". It is very short, as was the case of the Main Program for the CCFG model. This is due to the fact that only the highest-level subroutines are called from a Main Program. Main Programs should initiate only the most basic of the operational processes of a model. They should call subroutines that are themselves miniature Main Programs for the processes they initiate.

In the LWM, the Main Program calls eight subroutines in total. The first three of these subroutines check the menu inputs made by the analyst. The last five sit inside a loop that processes each of the active Cases of the LMW.

Sequence of the Main Program

The steps of the Main Program are:

1. Suppress the display of warnings and alerts to the screen. If we do not place this statement at the beginning of the Main Program, the program will stop and start at any warning or alert. We would not be able to run the LWM without constantly being in front of it and available to click the "OK" CommandButton on numerous routine warning messages. With the statement in place, the model will ignore all these routine messages and continue its run without interruption or the requirement of human intervention.
2. Error checking of the inputs of the Main Menu. This is the process that we have reviewed earlier in this chapter.
3. Reads the names and pathways of the files of the Main Menu, reads the contents of the report package UserForm.
4. Enters the main loop of the model and cycles through reading the contents of each pair of Structure Inputs and Cash Flow Inputs files.
5. Sets the "go_ok" variable to TRUE. This variable tells the LWM if, after reading either the Structure Inputs file or the Cash Flow Inputs file, the LWM has found any problems with the data. If it has the value greater than zero, then the value of "go_ok" is set to FALSE and no further action is taken on this Case. If "go_ok" evaluates as TRUE, we continue.
6. Open the Liabilities Waterfall Spreadsheet. At the present time there is only one LWM spreadsheet, but this might not always be the case. In the future we may wish to evaluate different structures in the same model run. In that case we may wish to replace the designation of the file opened by the "Workbooks.Open Filename" statement here with that of a variable name. The variable name would be the name of an LWM spreadsheet the analyst selects from the Main Menu. Thus the LWM could access several, or even dozens of Liabilities Structure spreadsheets. We would only need to make sure that the collateral cash flows and the Liabilities Structure inputs were placed in the correct cells in the other waterfall worksheets.
7. Read the Structure Inputs file.
8. If the value of "go_ok" is TRUE after reading the Structure Inputs file, read the Cash Flow Inputs file.
9. If the value of "go_ok" is TRUE after reading the Cash Flow Input file, initiate the calculation sequence of the LWM. For each of the scenarios of the Cash Flow Inputs file, run the LWM.
10. Read the contents of the Cash Flows and Structure Information menu into the LWM.
11. Calculate the spreadsheet using these inputs.

```
Sub Main_LiabilitiesWaterfallModel()

    Application.DisplayAlerts = False 'turn off warning messages
    'error check the menu inputs of the model.  If all entries pass the tests
    ' read the information into the VBA arrays.
    Call ErrCheck_MainMenu              'error check all menu entries
    Call MainMenu_ReadCaseRunFields     'check for selected cases
    Call MainMenu_ReadFileNameInputs    'reads file names into VBA arrays

    'the LWM will now match the collateral cash flow scenarios in each of the
    ' CF files to the corresponding structure input of the Liabilities
    ' Structuring file and capture the results in a series of output reports
    ' prefixed by the report set prefix shown on the Main Menu.
    For iCase = 1 To MAX_CASES
        If gRunThisCase(iCase) Then
            go_ok = True
            Call ImportCFs_Main(iCase)       'open and read collateral cash flows
            If go_ok Then
                'Call Main_OpenWaterfallWorkbook
                Workbooks.Open Filename:= _
                    "C:\VBABook2\ABS\Mort01\Models\WLM_17FINAL07excel.xlsm"
                Call ImportStruct_Main(iCase)    'open and read structure inputs
                Call LoadRunLWM_Main             'loads scenario cfs, runs the model
                Call AggregateAnnualCFs_Main     'sums annual cf arrays from monthly
                ActiveWorkbook.Close             'close the waterfall file
                Call WriteReports_Main(iCase)    'waterfall reports by scenario
            End If
        End If
    Next iCase
    'exit the program
    Sheets("MainMenu").Select               'return to Main Menu screen
    Application.DisplayAlerts = True         'turn message displays back on
    Application.StatusBar = False

End Sub
```

EXHIBIT 16.12   Main Program subroutine of the LWM

12. Read the results of the spreadsheet calculation into a series of output results arrays. These arrays will contain scenario summary statistics, tranche amortization cash flows and balances, and excess cash usage statistics.
13. Based on the selection made on the LWM Report Package UserForm Menu, produce the report package. All reports of this Case run will be prefixed by the Case-specific prefix entered on the Main Menu.
14. Continue through the remaining Cases of the LWM until all have been completed.
15. Return to the Main Menu and end the program.

See Exhibit 16.12.

ERROR CHECKING THE MAIN MENU INPUTS

The first step of the Main Program subroutine of the LWM is to error-check all entries made to the Main Menu. Once these entries have been verified, we can begin the process of importing the data that we will need to run the model. In addition to error checking these entries, the Main Program will also read the contents of the

Report Menu UserForm. This is to ensure that the user has entered a set of reports for the active cases. We examined the purpose and function of this error checking function and the VBA code that performs the tests earlier in this chapter.

IMPORTING THE LIABILITY STRUCTURE INPUTS

We have now determined that all the pathway information is correct and that there are report package prefixes designated for each of the active Cases of the LWM. We will now read in the Liabilities Structure Inputs from the designated file of the first active Case.

Organization of the VBA Code

All the code that we need to accomplish this task is contained in the "MenuSupport_ ImportStructFiles" module. This module contains 17 subroutines. The names and roles of these subroutines are given below.

The Main subroutine for the module is:

"ImportStruct_Main". It calls four other subroutines. One of these subroutines performs a series of error checks on the data of the Structure Inputs file. If the data passes the tests, it is read into a series of VBA arrays for use by the LWM. The data is then read from these arrays into the model spreadsheet by a third subroutine. If the data is found to contain errors, the preceding two steps are bypassed and a fourth subroutine reads the error codes generated and produces a series of error messages to alert the reader to the data problems of the file.

The subroutines that perform the data-checking role are:

- "ErrCheck_NoErrsInStructInputs". A Boolean function that returns either TRUE if no errors are found in the Structure Inputs data file or FALSE if errors are detected. To perform this task, it calls a set of 12 other single-purpose subroutines each of which check for a specific error condition.
  1. "ImportStruct_ErrSAllAreNumerics". Checks that all entries are numeric.
  2. "ImportStruct_ErrSTranchePctLT100". Checks that all individual tranche percentages are less than 100%.
  3. "ImportStruct_ErrSTranchesSum100Pct". Checks that the sum of tranches percentages is 100%.
  4. "ImportStruct_ErrSSubordinationCheck". Checks that the A Class plus the Credit Enhancement Level equal 100%.
  5. "ImportStruct_ErrSSubordinationOrder". Checks that the subordination by class is consistent.
  6. "ImportStruct_ErrSSpreadLevel". Checks that the spreads are reasonable (under a user-defined maximum).
  7. "ImportStruct_ErrSServicerFee". Checks that the servicing fee is reasonable (under a user-defined maximum).
  8. "ImportStruct_ErrSStepDownPeriod". Ensures that the step-down period reasonable (under a user-defined maximum).
  9. "ImportStruct_ErrSLossTriggerPct". Verifies that the loss triggers are in a % format.
  10. "ImportStruct_ErrSLossTriggerCum". Verifies that the loss trigger increases over time.

11. "ImportStruct_ErrSCEPercentage". Checks that the CE % is reasonable (under a user-defined maximum).
12. "ImportStruct_ErrSCleanUpCall". Checks that the cleanup call is reasonable (under 20%).

There is also a subroutine to print any error messages generated by the error checking processes:

1. "ImportStruct_PrintErrors". A subroutine that prints a message of any error conditions in the Structure Inputs file contents.

There are two subroutines that move the structuring parameters from the Structure Inputs files into the LWM:

1. "ImportStruct_ReadFromFile". A subroutine that reads the data from the Structure Inputs file into the VBA arrays of the LWM.
2. "ImportStruct_WriteToModel". A subroutine that reads the data of the VBA arrays of the model into the model spreadsheet.

Key Subroutines

We will now look at each of the key subroutines of the process.

"ImportStruct_Main" Subroutine The Main subroutine of the model is very brief and easy to understand. The subroutine reads the name of the current Case Structuring Inputs file contained in the variable "gStructInputFile(irep)", the current loop of the Main Program. The next step performs error checking of the contents of the file. The subroutine "ErrCheck_NoErrsInStructInputs" performs a series of tests on the contents of the file. If the value returned from "ErrCheck_NoErrsInStructInputs" is TRUE, the data is in error and therefore the value of the variable "go_ok" is set to TRUE. If errors are detected we will create error messages and display them using the "ImportStruct_PrintErrors". If not, we will first call "ImportStruct_ReadFromFile" to transfer the contents of the file into VBA arrays and then the subroutine "Import-Struct_WriteToModel" to transfer them to the LWM input fields of the "Inputs" worksheet. See Exhibit 16.13.

"ErrCheck_NoErrsInStructInputs" Function This function is charged with the task of checking for the form, content, and reasonableness of the Structure Inputs file contents before we read any of them into the VBA arrays of the LWM. It is a

```
Sub ImportStruct_Main(irep As Integer)

    Workbooks.Open Filename:=gStructInputFile(irep)
    go_ok = ErrCheck_NoErrsInStructInputs
    If go_ok Then
        Call ImportStruct_ReadFromFile(irep)
        Call ImportStruct_WriteToModel(irep)
    Else
        Call ImportStruct_PrintErrors
    End If

End Sub
```

EXHIBIT 16.13 "ImportStruct_Main" subroutine

```
Function ErrCheck_NoErrsInStructInputs()

    'initial funtion value
    ErrCheck_NoErrsInStructInputs = True
    'initialize individual error conditions and count
    For itest = 1 To NUM_SERRORS
        mErr(itest) = False
    Next itest
    'run the tests
    Call ImportStruct_ErrSAllAreNumerics        'all entries are numeric
    Call ImportStruct_ErrSTranchePctLT100       'percentages are under 100%
    Call ImportStruct_ErrSTranchesSum100Pct     'sum of tranches is 100%
    Call ImportStruct_ErrSSubordinationCheck    'A Class 100%-CE Level
    Call ImportStruct_ErrSSubordinationOrder    'subordination by class OK
    Call ImportStruct_ErrSSpreadLevel           'spreads are reasonable
    Call ImportStruct_ErrSServicerFee           'servicer fee is reasonable
    Call ImportStruct_ErrSStepDownPeriod        'step down period reasonable
    Call ImportStruct_ErrSLossTriggerPct        'loss triggers are %
    Call ImportStruct_ErrSLossTriggerCum        'loss trigger increases
    Call ImportStruct_ErrSCEPercentage          'CE percentage OK
    Call ImportStruct_ErrSCleanUpCall           'cleanup call ok <20%
    'count up the errors
    For itest = 1 To NUM_SERRORS
        If mErr(itest) Then ErrCheck_NoErrsInStructInputs = False
        Exit Function
    Next itest

End Function
```

EXHIBIT 16.14   "errCheck_NoErrsInStructInputs" subroutine

Boolean function and will therefore return either a TRUE or FALSE indication to the calling subroutine. We will initialize it to TRUE, the assumption that there are no errors present in the data. The function then initializes a Boolean array named "mErr" that has one element for each of the individual tests we will perform. Each element of the array is set to FALSE. These tests are all contained in specific task subroutines that are then called in sequence from this function. A list of these tests and the names of the subroutines responsible for them was presented above. Each of these tests is performed on one or more datum of the Structure Inputs, and if an error condition is detected the value of "mErr(n)" where n is the nth test, is set to TRUE. When the tests have been completed, the elements of the "mErr" array is tested. If any of the elements are found set to TRUE, an error condition, the function itself is set to FALSE and we exit the function. We can exit immediately upon the detection of the first error condition because proceeding with the calculation process of the LWM is an all-or-nothing proposition. Either all the data has to be error free or we cannot proceed. We do not need to concern ourselves with the fact that we have not detected additional errors by leaving the error checking loop upon detection of the first error. If there are additional errors, they will be detected by the "InportStruct_PrintErrors" subroutine at a later point in the process. See Exhibit 16.14 for this subroutine and Exhibit 16.15 for the code of a typical single-test subroutine. The single-test subroutine checks that the sum of the percentage allocation of the tranches totals 100% and sets the value of "mErr(3)" to TRUE if they do not.

"ImportStruct_ReadFromFile" Subroutine   The subroutine "ImportStruct_Read FromFile" is called by the "ImportStruct_Main" subroutine if all the data in the

```
Sub ImportStruct_ErrSTranchesSum100Pct()

Dim pSum          As Double    'sum of tranche %
    'tranche percentages
    pSum = 0
    For irow = 5 To TRANCHES + 5
        pSum = pSum + Cells(irow, 3).Value
    Next irow
    If pSum < 0.99999 Or pSum > 1.000001 Then mErr(3) = True

End Sub
```

EXHIBIT 16.15 "ImportStruct_ErrSTranchesSum100Pct" subroutine

Structure Inputs file passes the error testing process. It performs a series of reads from the data file using the "Cells(row,col).value" notation. These inputs mirror the contents of the "Inputs" worksheet in the LWM. They are placed in a series of modular scope variables. After these variables are populated, the Structure Inputs file is closed. See Exhibit 16.16.

"ImportStruct_WriteToModel" Subroutine Immediately following "ImportStruct_ReadFromFile" is "ImportStruct_WriteToModel". Here we reverse the process we just completed and read the Structure Inputs data from the VBA arrays into the "Inputs" worksheet of the LWM. We will use Range name notation to place the data where it is available. See Exhibit 16.17.

```
Sub ImportStruct_ReadFromFile(irep As Integer)

    'tranche percentages
    For irow = 5 To TRANCHES + 5
        mStructPct(irow - 4) = Cells(irow, 3).Value
        mStructSprd(irow - 4) = Cells(irow, 6).Value
    Next irow
    'other inputs
    mServeFee = Cells(15, 3).Value
    'step down characteristics
    mStepDownPeriod = Cells(18, 3).Value
    mStepDownPct = Cells(19, 3).Value
    mOCPct = Cells(20, 3).Value
    'target subordination
    For irow = 23 To 27
        mTargetSub(irow - 22) = Cells(irow - 22, 3).Value
    Next irow
    'loss trigger table
    For irow = 35 To 40
        mLossTrigBeg(irow - 34) = Cells(irow, 3).Value
        mLossTrigEnd(irow - 34) = Cells(irow, 4).Value
        mLossTrigPct(irow - 34) = Cells(irow, 5).Value
    Next irow
    mCleanUpPct = Cells(42, 3).Value
    ActiveWorkbook.Close

End Sub
```

EXHIBIT 16.16 "ImportStruct_ReadFromFile" subroutine

```
Sub ImportStruct_WriteToModel(irep As Integer)

    Sheets("Structure").Select
    'tranche percentages
    For irow = 5 To TRANCHES + 5
        Cells(irow, 3).Value = mStructPct(irow - 4)
        Cells(irow, 6).Value = mStructSprd(irow - 4)
    Next irow
    'other inputs
    Range("servicerFee") = mServeFee
    'step down characteristics
    Range("stepdownPeriod") = mStepDownPeriod
    Range("stepdownPercent") = mStepDownPct
    Range("stepdownOCPercent") = Cells(20, 3).Value
    'target subordination
    For irow = 23 To 27
        Cells(irow - 22, 3).Value = mTargetSub
    Next irow
    'loss trigger table
    For irow = 35 To 40
        Cells(irow, 3).Value = mLossTrigBeg(irow - 34)
        Cells(irow, 4).Value = mLossTrigEnd(irow - 34)
        Cells(irow, 5).Value = mLossTrigPct(irow - 34)
    Next irow
    Range("cleanupPercent") = mCleanUpPct

End Sub
```

EXHIBIT 16.17   "ImportStruct_WriteToModel" subroutine

"ImportStruct_PrintErrors" Subroutine   The Structure Input file may contain errors that have been identified by the "ErrCheck_NoErrsInStructInputs" subroutine. This subroutine generates a Message Box object that contains a specific list of the data errors found. It works in a manner typical of the other error message generator subroutines we have built in the past. If all error conditions have failed (a highly unlikely event, we hope!), the message shown in Exhibit 16.18 will appear.

IMPORTING THE CASH FLOWS OF THE CCFG

With the Liabilities Structure Input file contents now read into the VBA arrays of the LWM, we next turn our attention to the cash flow scenarios. Unlike the Liabilities Structure inputs, a CCFG output file can contain up to 25 different cash flow scenarios. These scenarios could have been generated with a Uniform, Geographic, or Demographic prepayment/default Methodology. We need to determine the methodology used to create the file (to correctly identify the source of the cash flows in the LWM), the number of cash flow scenarios in the file, and the prepayment/default speeds associated to each cash flow scenario. We need to check the contents of the files for errors as we did with the Structure Inputs file. If the data passes the tests, we will sequentially load each of the cash flow scenarios into VBA arrays for later use by the model.

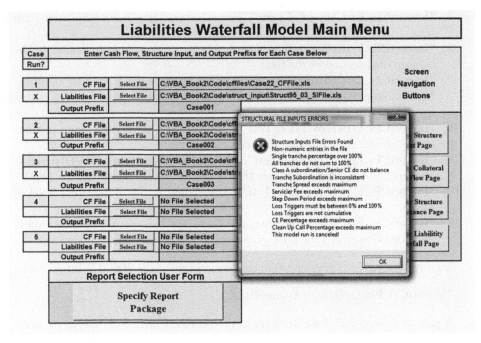

EXHIBIT 16.18 "ImportStruct_PrintErrors" subroutine message box

Organization of the VBA Code

The code that imports the cash flow scenarios produced by the CCFG into the LWM is contained in the VBA module "MenuSupport_ImportCFsFiles". This module contains a total of 17 subroutines that perform the following tasks. The Main subroutine of the module is: **"ImportCFs_Main"**. The main subroutine of the module calls the other five major subroutines. These subroutines perform the error checking, read the assumptions file, determine the number of cash flow scenarios in the file, create a list of worksheet names so they can be read, and transfer the contents of the worksheets into VBA arrays.

The Cash Flow Input file error checking subroutine is:

- **"ErrCheck_NoErrsInCFsInputs"**. This subroutine calls a number of single-purpose subroutines that check the Cash Flow Inputs files for errors and, if they are found, prints a message box detailing the error conditions. These 11 error checking and warning subroutines are:
  1. **"ImportCFs_ErrCFAllAreNumerics"**. All entries that need to be are in numeric form.
  2. **"ImportCFs_ErrCFInvalidUniform"**. An invalid Uniform methodology has been entered.
  3. **"ImportCFs_ErrCFBaseSpeedGTZero"**. The values of the Base Prepayment or Default speeds must be greater than or equal to zero.
  4. **"ImportCFs_ErrCFUniformMaxSteps"**. Too many increment steps have been specified for the Uniform methodology. The maximum number of steps that can be specified is 5.

5. **"ImportCFs_ErrCFStepGTZero"**. The increment step must be greater than zero.
6. **"ImportCFs_ErrCFNoMethodology"**. No methodology is indicated in the assumptions section of the file.
7. **"ImportCFs_ErrCFStressNoInputs"**. The Geographic or Demographic Methodology has been selected with a stress factor indicated but no stress inputs are present.
8. **"ImportCFs_ErrRecoveryLagTest"**. The recovery lag period range test has failed (greater than a user-indicated maximum).
9. **"ImportCFs_ErrMVDRangeTest"**. The market value decline (MVD) percentage range test has failed (greater than a user-indicated maximum).
10. **"ImportCFs_ErrCFStressBaseTest"**. The value of the Base stress level is illegal.
11. **"ImportCFs_ErrCFStressMaxSteps"**. There are too many stress increment steps (maximum is 5 for both prepayment and default stress increments).

A subroutine to read the contents of the Assumptions page of the CF Inputs file is:

- **"ImportCFs_PrepayDefaultAssumpPage"**

A pair of subroutines then determines the prepayment/default speeds or stress levels depending on the methodology that were the inputs used to generate the Cash Flow Input file. These levels are used to identify the various single-scenario worksheets of the Cash Flow Input file to correctly identify the parameters used to generate the cash flows:

- **"ImportCFs_CalcUniformPrepayDefaultLevels"**
- **"ImportCFs_CalcGeoDemoPrepayDefaultLevels"**

A subroutine to generate the Cash Flow Input file target worksheet names based on the above speeds or stress levels is:

- **"ImportCFs_SetUpCFWorksheetNames"**

A subroutine to load the contents of the Cash Flow Input file into the VBA arrays of the LWM is:

- **"ImportCFs_ReadCashFlowsFromWorkbook"**

A subroutine to print a message box of the data error conditions is:

- **"ImportCfs_PrintErrors"**

Key Subroutines

The form and function of the subroutines that are tasked with the importation of the collateral cash flows mirror closely the number and roles of those we just examined in the Structure Inputs importation role. Keeping these similarities in mind, we will be able to spend less time examining all the various actions they perform and concentrate only on the differences between them.

```
Sub ImportCFs_Main(irep As Integer)

    Workbooks.Open Filename:=gPathwayCFFiles & gCFInputFile(irep)
    'error check the contents of the cash flows input file
    go_ok = False
    go_ok = ErrCheck_NoErrsInCFsInputs
    ' if there are no errors, read the data and import into the
    ' VBA arrays of the model
    If go_ok Then
        'no errors detected in the data with these tests
        'read the contents of the assumptions page
        Call ImportCFs_PrepayDefaultAssumpPage
        If gMethodUniform Then
            'generate the prepayment/default speeds
            Call ImportCFs_CalcUniformPrepayDefaultLevels
        Else
            'generate the stress level prepayment/default speeds
            Call ImportCFs_CalcGeoDemoPrepayDefaultLevels
        End If
        'use the speeds/rates calculated above to determine the worksheet names
        Call ImportCFs_SetUpCFWorksheetNames
        'read the cash flows from each of the worksheets of the file
        Call ImportCFs_ReadCashFlowsFromWorkbook
    Else
        'print the cf file input error messages
        Call ImportCFs_PrintErrors
    End If
    ActiveWorkbook.Close

End Sub
```

EXHIBIT 16.19 "ImportCFs_Main" subroutine

"ImportCFs_Main" Subroutine   This subroutine serves as the Main subroutine for the importation of the contents of the Cash Flow Inputs file. The subroutine must perform the steps discussed above. The key difference is that the Main subroutine must read the information of the file and determine the type of prepayment/default methodology used to generate the cash flow scenarios and also the values of those prepayment/defaults speeds/stresses and the number of scenarios contained in the file.

It must then generate the specific worksheet title for each scenario based on the combination of methodology and assumptions of prepayment and default conditions. It needs to create one and only one combination that it will use as a reference lookup label to match to a particular worksheet in the Cash Flow Input file for each scenario.

If the data fails the initial error checking, it must generate a message box with the specific failure conditions as the "ImportStruct_Main" subroutine did. See Exhibit 16.19.

"ImportCFs_PrepayDefaultAssumpPage" Subroutine   If all the data passes the error tests, we can now read it into the VBA variables. We will start with the contents of the Prepayment and Default Assumption Menu page. This page will tell us what methodology was used, Uniform, Geographic, or Demographic. We will also determine, in the case of the Geographic or Demographic Methodologies, if there are stress levels in addition to the base Case. When using the Uniform Methodology, we will need to determine if the prepayment formula was either Public Securities

```
Sub ImportCFs_PrepayDefaultAssumpPage()

    'reading this information will tell us how many collateral cash flow
    ' waterfall inputs we are going to need to read out of the file
    Sheets("PrepayDefault").Select
    'methodologies section
    gMethodUniform = False
    gMethodGeographic = False
    gMethodDemographic = False
    gMethodApplyStress = False
    If Cells(7, 13).Value = "X" Then gMethodUniform = True
    If Cells(8, 13).Value = "X" Then gMethodGeographic = True
    If Cells(9, 13).Value = "X" Then gMethodDemographic = True
    If Cells(11, 13).Value = "X" Then gMethodApplyStress = True
    'Stress Factors Range - % of Base Prepayment/Default Speeds
    ' demographic and geographic methodologies only
    If gMethodUniform Then
        'load default information
        gDefaultMethod = Cells(9, 5).Value
        gDefaultBaseRate = Cells(9, 6).Value
        gDefaultIncrement = Cells(9, 7).Value
        gDefaultLevels = Cells(9, 8).Value
        'load prepayment levels
        gPrepayMethod = Cells(8, 5).Value
        gPrepayBaseLevels = Cells(8, 6).Value
        gPrepayIncrement = Cells(8, 7).Value
        gPrepayLevels = Cells(8, 8).Value
        'number of worksheets
        mNumberSheetsCalc = gDefaultLevels * gPrepayLevels
    Else
        'must be Demographic or Geographic Methodology
        If gMethodApplyStress Then
            gPrepayStressBase = Cells(32, 5).Value
            gPrepayStressIncr = Cells(32, 6).Value
            gPrepayStressSteps = Cells(32, 7).Value
            gDefaultStressBase = Cells(33, 5).Value
            gDefaultStressIncr = Cells(33, 6).Value
            gDefaultStressSteps = Cells(33, 7).Value
            'number of worksheets
            mNumberSheetsCalc = gDefaultStressSteps * gPrepayStressSteps
        End If
    End If

End Sub
```

EXHIBIT 16.20 "ImportCFs_PrepayDefaultAssumpPage" subroutine

Administration (PSA) or Constant prepayment rate (CPR). From the inputs of this screen we will also be able to determine how many prepayment speeds/stress and how many default speeds/stresses were entered and therefore also the number of total cash flow scenarios. See Exhibit 16.20.

"ImportCFs_CalcUniformPrepayDefaultLevels" Subroutine   Using the Base Prepayment/Default rate, the number of Prepayment/Default Increment steps, and the

```
Sub ImportCFs_CalcUniformPrepayDefaultLevels()

    'prepayment levels
    ReDim gPrepayRate(1 To gPrepayLevels) As Double
    For ip = 1 To gPrepayLevels
        If ip = 1 Then
            gPrepayRate(ip) = gPrepayBaseLevels
        Else
            gPrepayRate(ip) = gPrepayRate(ip - 1) + gPrepayIncrement
        End If
    Next ip
    'default levels
    ReDim gDefaultRate(1 To gDefaultLevels) As Double
    For id = 1 To gDefaultLevels
        If id = 1 Then
            gDefaultRate(id) = gDefaultBaseRate
        Else
            gDefaultRate(id) = gDefaultRate(id - 1) + gDefaultIncrement
        End If
    Next id

End Sub
```

EXHIBIT 16.21   "ImportCFs_CalcUniformPrepayDefaultLevels" subroutine

value of the individual Increment step, we can calculate the values of the Prepayment/Default rate combinations and the number of cash flow scenarios present in the file. A similar subroutine "ImportCfs_CalcGeoDemoPrepayDefaultLevels" is used to determine the number of Prepayment/Default scenarios if those methodologies were used to generate the cash flows instead of the Uniform Methodology. See Exhibit 16.21.

"ImportCFs_SetUpCFWorksheetNames" Subroutine   Using the information determined by the subroutines above, we can now create the names of each of the worksheets present in the CCFG Cash Flow Input file. For a Uniform Prepayment/Default Methodology of "PSA", a set of nine speeds might be:

```
P-100 D-100     P-100 D-125     P-100 D-150
P-200 D-100     P-200 D-125     P-200 D-150
```

When electing the Geographic or Demographic Stress Methodology, the names of the worksheets will be in the form of:

```
PS-100% DS-100%     PS-100% DS-125%     PS-100% DS-150%
PS-200% DS-100%     PS-200% DS-125%     PS-200% DS-150%
```

See Exhibit 16.22.

"ImportCFs_ReadCashFlowsFromWorkbook" Subroutine   We now have an array of worksheet names with which to access the various worksheets of the Cash Flow Inputs file. We will first erase the contents of all the cash flow VBA arrays of the LWM. Next we will redimension them to the number of prepayment and default

```
Sub ImportCFs_SetUpCFWorksheetNames()

Dim i_name  As Integer

    'read the Cash Flow Report
    If gMethodUniform Then
        mPLevels = gPrepayLevels
        mDLevels = gDefaultLevels
        Else
        mPLevels = gPrepayStressSteps
        mDLevels = gDefaultStressSteps
    End If
    ReDim mCFSheetName(1 To mNumberSheetsCalc) As String
    i_name = 1
    'set the base prepayment rates, if Geo/Demo multiply by 100
    If gMethodUniform = True Then
        prate = gPrepayBaseLevels
    Else
        prate = gPrepayStressBase * 100#
    End If
    For ip = 1 To gPrepayLevels
        'set the base default rates, if Geo/Demo multiply by 100
        If gMethodUniform = True Then
            drate = gDefaultBaseRate
        Else
            drate = gDefaultStressBase * 100#
        End If
        'generate the sheet name from the methodology, prepay/default speed
        For id = 1 To gDefaultLevels
            If gMethodUniform Then
                mCFSheetName(i_name) = "P-" & prate & " D-" & drate
                drate = drate + gDefaultIncrement
            Else
                mCFSheetName(i_name) = _
                    "PS-" & prate & "% " & "DS-" & drate & "%"
                drate = drate + (gDefaultStressIncr * 100#)
            End If
            i_name = i_name + 1
        Next id
        'incrment the prepayment speed, if Geo/Demo multiply by 100
        If gMethodUniform = True Then
            prate = prate + gPrepayIncrement
        Else
            prate = prate + (gPrepayStressIncr * 100#)
        End If
    Next ip

End Sub
```

EXHIBIT 16.22   "ImportCFs_SetUpCFWorksheetNames" subroutine

scenario combinations in the current Cash Flow Inputs file. The next step is to set up a nested loop of prepayment scenarios by default scenarios. This will cause the innermost commands to execute in the same sequence as the cash flows of the original Cash Flow Inputs file were created and match the set of worksheet names be just created. We then read the contents of the file into the VBA arrays based on their column positions in the worksheets of the Cash Flow Input files. See Exhibit 16.23.

```
Sub ImportCFs_ReadCashFlowsFromWorkbook()

    Call ImportCFs_EraseAllCFComponents 'clear the current array contents
    Call ImportCFs_RedimAllCFComponents 'redim the arrays
    If read_cfs Then
        iscen = 0
        For ip = 1 To gPrepayLevels
            For id = 1 To gDefaultLevels
                iscen = iscen + 1
                Sheets(mCFSheetName(iscen)).Select
                If id = 1 And ip = 1 Then
                    gBeginCollateral = Cells(14, 11).Value
                End If
                For irow = 14 To (PAY_DATES + 14)
                    If Cells(irow, 11).Value > 0.01 Then
                        gBeginBal(ip, id, irow - 13) = Cells(irow, 11).Value
                        gAmortPrin(ip, id, irow - 13) = Cells(irow, 13).Value
                        gPrepaidPrin(ip, id, irow - 13) = Cells(irow, 14).Value
                        gDefaultPrin(ip, id, irow - 13) = Cells(irow, 15).Value
                        gCoupIncome(ip, id, irow - 13) = Cells(irow, 18).Value
                        gRecoverPrin(ip, id, irow - 13) = Cells(irow, 19).Value
                    End If
                Next irow
            Next id
        Next ip
    End If

End Sub
```

EXHIBIT 16.23 "ImportCFs_ReadCashFlowsFromWorkbook" subroutine

LOADING AND RUNNING THE LWM

We now have all of the Structure Inputs and the Cash Flow Inputs read from the various files and stored in VBA arrays accessible by the model. We can now begin the process of running the model by loading them into the LWM spreadsheet.

Organization of the VBA Code

The VBA code that performs the task of loading the inputs into the LWM spreadsheet and running the model is located in the module "Run_LiabilitiesModel". This module contains three subroutines whose function is to manage the sequential execution of the LWM spreadsheet.

The subroutine that controls the inputs of the contents of the VBA arrays containing the Cash Flow Inputs file is:

- ■ **"LoadRunLWM_Main".** This is the main subroutine of the model execution process. It calls the subroutine "LoadRunLWM_LoadIndexRates" that supplies the waterfall worksheet with the benchmark one-month LIBOR (London Interbank Offering Rate). This is the benchmark index upon which the levels of the tranche coupons are set. It then enters a loop of prepayment by default scenarios. Each loop calls the "LoadRunLWM_LoadCashFlows" subroutine that reads a specific cash flow scenario into the waterfall spreadsheet. The Liabilities Waterfall Spreadsheet is then calculated, and the results of the calculations are captured by the "ReadResults_Main" subroutine. See Exhibit 16.24.

```
Sub LoadRunLWM_Main()

    'loads the interest rate index
    Call LoadRunLWM_LoadIndexRates
    irep = 1
    For iprepay = 1 To gPrepayLevels
        For idefault = 1 To gDefaultLevels
            Call LoadRunLWM_LoadCashflows(iprepay, idefault)
            Calculate
            'reads the results of the liabilities waterfall calculation
            Call ReadResults_Main(idefault, iprepay, irep)
            irep = irep + 1
        Next idefault
    Next iprepay

End Sub
```

EXHIBIT 16.24   "LoadRunLWM_Main" subroutine

The subroutine that enters the one-month LIBOR projections used to determine the coupon levels for the tranches on a monthly level. See Exhibit 16.25.

The subroutine that loads the cash flows from each scenario stored in the VBA arrays is:

- "LoadRunLWM_LoadCashFlows". This subroutine clears the contents of the collateral cash flow components and the beginning-period collateral principal balance Ranges. See Exhibit 16.26.

Capturing the LWM Results

All Structure and Cash Flow scenario inputs have been error-checked and read into the LWM VBA arrays. The contents of these arrays have been sequentially entered into the LWM waterfall spreadsheet, the spreadsheet has been calculated, and the results of these calculations are now available to us. We now need to capture them in a series of VBA output arrays and store them so that they are available for the final activity of report writing.

```
Sub LoadRunLWM_LoadIndexRates()

    Application.Calculation = xlCalculationManual
    Sheets("CFWaterfall").Select
    Range("cfFundConduit").ClearContents
    For irow = 1 To PAY_DATES
        Range("cfFundConduit").Cells(irow) = 1 'gFundingIndex(irow)
    Next irow

End Sub
```

EXHIBIT 16.25   "LoadRunLWM_LoadIndexRates" subroutine

```
Sub LoadRunLWM_LoadCashflows(ip As Integer, id As Integer)

    Application.Calculation = xlCalculationManual
    Sheets("CFWaterfall").Select
    'clear the collateral cash flow columns of the waterfall spreadsheet
    Range("cfBeginBalance").ClearContents
    Range("cfPrinRegAmort").ClearContents
    Range("cfPrinPrepayments").ClearContents
    Range("cfPrinDefaults").ClearContents
    Range("cfPrinRecoveries").ClearContents
    Range("cfCoupon").ClearContents
    'write the contents of the VBA arrays into the waterfall spreadsheet
    For irow = 1 To PAY_DATES
        Range("cfBeginBalance").Cells(irow) = gBeginBal(ip, id, irow)
        Range("cfPrinRegAmort").Cells(irow) = gAmortPrin(ip, id, irow)
        Range("cfPrinPrepayments").Cells(irow) = gPrepaidPrin(ip, id, irow)
        Range("cfPrinDefaults").Cells(irow) = gDefaultPrin(ip, id, irow)
        Range("cfPrinRecoveries").Cells(irow) = gRecoverPrin(ip, id, irow)
        Range("cfCoupon").Cells(irow) = gCoupIncome(ip, id, irow)
    Next irow

End Sub
```

EXHIBIT 16.26 "LoadRunLWM_LoadCashFlows" subroutine

Organization of the VBA Code

The VBA code that captures the results of the waterfall spreadsheet calculations is contained in the module "Run_ReadResultsStructure". The output from the model consists of four different types of data:

1. The monthly principal balance outstanding of each tranche.
2. The summary tenor and performance statistics such as average life, final maturity, duration, and loss experience for each tranche.
3. The amounts of interest, principal paid to the tranches on a monthly basis, and the losses allocated to the Class B Notes.
4. The disposition of the excess cash of the deal.

The VBA code that captures the waterfall results may be voluminous and repetitive, but it is also very simple. The subroutines that we will use to capture the data are task-specific to each of the above four sets of output items. We will also prefix all the arrays containing the output data "gOut" to readily identify them. Due to the elementary nature of the VBA code, we will not examine these subroutines but be content with a list of their names and an explanation of their functions.

Key Subroutines

The subroutines responsible for capturing the results of the LWM waterfall spreadsheet model are:

- **"ReadResults_Main"**. The Main subroutine of the process. Calls other subroutines that erase the contents of the VBA results arrays after each scenario is recorded and calls the subroutines that sequentially capture the results of each run of the LWM waterfall spreadsheet. See Exhibit 16.27.

```
Sub ReadResults_Main(ip As Integer, id As Integer, iscen As Integer)

    'if this is the first scenario read in this run erase the existing
    ' contents of the arrays
    If ip = 1 And id = 1 Then
        'clear the current array contents
        Call ReadResults_ClearTrancheStats
        Call ReadResults_ClearTrancheReturns
        Call ReadResults_ClearTrancheCFs
        Call ReadResults_ClearTrancheBalances
        Call ReadResults_ClearExcessCashCFs
        'redimension the arrays
        Call ReadResults_ReDimTrancheStats(ip, id)
        Call ReadResults_ReDimTrancheReturns(ip, id)
        Call ReadResults_ReDimTrancheCFs(ip, id)
        Call ReadResults_ReDimTrancheBalances(ip, id)
        Call ReadResults_ReDimExcessCashCFs(ip, id)
    End If
    'redimension the summary statistics report and the cash flow results
    ' arrays based ont he number of prepayment/default scenario combinations
    'read the summary statistics from the Results worksheet
    Sheets("Results").Select
    Call ReadResults_ReadTrancheStats(ip, id)
    Call ReadResults_ReadTrancheReturns(ip, id)
    'read the cash flows by tranche from the Waterfall worksheet
    Call ReadResults_ReadTrancheCFs(ip, id)
    Call ReadResults_ReadTrancheBalances(ip, id)
    Call ReadResults_ReadExcessCashCFs(ip, id)
    Call ReadResults_ReadWaterfall(iscen)

End Sub
```

EXHIBIT 16.27   "ReadResults_Main" subroutine

- "ReadResults_ClearTrancheStats", "ReadResults_ClearTrancheCFs", "Read Results_ClearTrancheBalances", "ReadResults_ClearTrancheReturns", and "ReadResults_ClearExcessCashCFs". Each of these subroutines erases the contents of the VBA arrays that hold the results of the previous Case of the LWM.
- "ReadResults_ReDimTrancheStats","ReadResults_ReDimTrancheCFs","Read Results_ReDimTrancheBalances", "ReadResults_ReDimTrancheReturns", and "ReadResults_ReDimExcessCashCFs". Each of these subroutines re-dimensions the VBA arrays that hold the results of the previous Case of the LWM.
- "ReadResults_ReadTrancheStats", "ReadResults_ReadTrancheCFs", "Read Results_ReadTrancheBalances", "ReadResults_ReadTrancheReturns", and "ReadResults_ReadExcessCashCFs". Each of these subroutines reads the various portions of the LWM to load the results of the waterfall spreadsheet calculation into the VBA arrays.

REPORTING THE RESULTS

The last step in the operation of the LWM is the production of the selected report package upon conclusion of the analysis of each of the Cases.

LWM Reporting Process

The LWM report generation process is triggered at the conclusion of the model run. How many and what types of reports are generated is determined by the specific inputs the analyst has entered earlier for each individual Case in the Report Package Menu UserForm. The results of these selections are stored in a series of global variables, one for each report set. These are arrays that are dimensioned "1 to number of cases" by "1 to maximum number of reports in each set". They are:

```
'output file selections Single Tranche reports
gSingleSelect(1 To MAX_CASES, 1 To MAX_SINGLE_REPORTS) As Boolean
'output file selections Multiple Tranche reports
Public gMultiSelect(1 To MAX_CASES, 1 To MAX_MULTI_REPORTS) As Boolean
'output file prefixes for Miscellaneous Tranche reports
Public gMiscSelect(1 To MAX_CASES, 1 To MAX_MISC_REPORTS) As Boolean
```

The information contained in these arrays will determine the number and types of reports the LWM will produce for each of the Cases of the model run.

"Reports_Main Subroutine"

The Main program of the LWM calls the "Reports_Main" subroutine that initiates the report generation process as the last step in the major "Cases" loop of the program.

The role of this subroutine is to manage the report generation process. The "Reports_Main" subroutine uses the information in the "gSingleSelect", the "gMulti Select", and the "gMiscSelect" arrays to determine the calls it will subsequently make to the specific-purpose subroutines that will produce the reports.

Current Report Package   The current configuration of the LWM produces the following reports:

- **Single Tranche reports.** Single Tranche report files have a single worksheet for each of the tranches of the Liabilities Structure. This sheet (with the exception of the Cash Flow reports) contains a series of tenor, yield, coverage, or loss statistics. The Cash Flow reports allow the analyst to select up to six different cash flow results from different Case scenarios for display. These results are in annual form, summarized from the monthly schedules produced by the model. The Cash Flow reports are each in a separate Excel Workbook due to their length. The Tenor report and the Yield report are each in a separate workbook. See Chapter 14 if you have any questions as to the contents of the reports.
  - **Single Tranche Cash Flow reports.** A set of four individual report files. There are individual files containing the information about:
    - Beginning period principal balances
    - Principal paid
    - Coupon expense paid
    - Losses to each of the note tranches.
  - **Single Tranche Tenor report.** A report containing four specific page schedules of the Weighted Average Life to Maturity, the Weighted Average Life to Call, the Final Maturity, and the Modified Duration.

- **Single Tranche Yield report.** Contains a schedule of the Average Life to Maturity, the Average Life to Call, the net present value (NPV) and future value (FV) Coverage Ratios and the NPV and FV Severity of Loss statistic.
- **Multiple Tranche reports.** These reports display a single cash flow or statistic for each of the tranches of the Liabilities Structure on a single report. They are, in that regard, the reciprocal organizational schema of the Single Tranche reports. Each of the Single Tranche reports is mirrored in the Multiple Tranche report set. The information items of the reports in regards to the data items and cash flows are identical. In Multiple Tranche reports, the presentation form is organized with the performance data at the worksheet level and the tranche as a portion of the report within the worksheet, whereas the Single Tranche reports are organized to report tranche information at the worksheet level and the various data item details in the tables of the worksheet.
- **Miscellaneous reports.** These reports display a collection of non-tranche data. This data either relates to the deal as a whole or is designed to aid the analyst and is not intended for use by outside parties. The one exception to this rule is the Collateral Cash Flows report.
  - **Deal Fees report.** This report allows the user to select the annual schedule of deal fees paid for up to six scenarios of the Case.
  - **Excess Cash Flows report.** This report displays the five columns of the Sources and Uses of Excess Cash Flows in the Structure for each scenario of a Case.
  - **Collateral Cash Flow report.** This report displays the six components of the balances and cash flows that comprise a single scenario of the Case. The balances are beginning annual balances and the cash flows are annual sums. The accompanying graph plots the balances on the right hand axis, and the cash flows on the left due to the discrepancies in magnitude. The cash flows are Defaulted Principal, Scheduled Amortization of Principal, Coupon Income, Prepayments of Principal, and Recoveries of Defaulted Principal.
  - **Waterfall report.** This report displays the complete Liabilities Waterfall spreadsheet for each of the scenarios of the Case. It is created almost solely for the benefit of the analyst and the model developer. In that it covers every column of the LWM Spreadsheet, it can be very useful for model validation processes, audits, and as a teaching tool.

Report Generation Process   The report generation process begins with the "Reports_Main" subroutine reading the contents of the various single, multiple, and miscellaneous report selections for the current Case.

A purpose-specific subroutine then reads the calculation results of all scenarios of a single Case from the arrays of the LWM where it has been stored after each run of the model. A template file for the report is opened and renamed with the designated Output File prefix for this Case and a standard base name of the report. The contents of the arrays are then written to the report file. Last the various header items, such as the prepayment/default assumptions, that describe the scenarios contained in the report are added. The report is then saved and closed. This process continues until all the reports specified by the analyst for this Case have been completed. See Exhibits 16.28 and 16.29.

Note that in "WriteReports_SingleTrancheReports", four of the six calls are to a single subroutine "Report_STCFsMain". This subroutine produces the four

```
        Sub WriteReports_Main(iCase As Integer)

            Call WriteReports_SingleTrancheReports(iCase)
            Call WriteReports_MultiTrancheReports(iCase)
            Call WriteReports_MiscTrancheReports(iCase)

        End Sub
```

EXHIBIT 16.28 Write "Reports_Main" subroutine

Cash Flow reports. The subroutine that produces the Tenor report is "Report_STCFsTenorMain" and the Yield/Coverage/Loss report is "Report_STCFsReturns Main". You should also remember that each of the single tranche cash flow reports has a unique global Constant variable assigned to it from "SINGLE_PRINBAL" to "SINGLE_RETURN" to help us identify and manipulate the items in the report writing process.

Describing the Reporting Process Six Single Tranche, three Multiple Tranche, and four Miscellaneous reports can be produced for each Case of the LWM. We will not examine the template files and VBA code that produces each of these reports. A number of reports are very similar in both layout and the report writing VBA code that produces them. We will therefore select these representative reports, look at their creation in detail, and comment on those reports that are similar. As an extension of this approach, some of the simpler reports, such as the miscellaneous deal fees, will only be described.

```
Sub WriteReports_SingleTrancheReports(iCase As Integer)

    'Single Tranche Report group
    'beginning annual principal balances
    If gSingleSelect(iCase, SINGLE_PRINBAL) Then _
        Call Report_STCFsMain(iCase, SINGLE_PRINBAL, gNumPre, gNumDef)
    'coupon debt service payments
    If gSingleSelect(iCase, SINGLE_COUPPMT) Then _
        Call Report_STCFsMain(iCase, SINGLE_COUPPMT, gNumPre, gNumDef)
    'scheduled principal payments
    If gSingleSelect(iCase, SINGLE_PRINPMT) Then _
        Call Report_STCFsMain(iCase, SINGLE_PRINPMT, gNumPre, gNumDef)
    'losses by tranche
    If gSingleSelect(iCase, SINGLE_LOSSES) Then _
        Call Report_STCFsMain(iCase, SINGLE_LOSSES, gNumPre, gNumDef)
    'tenor report
    If gSingleSelect(iCase, SINGLE_TENOR) Then _
        Call Report_STTenorMain(iCase, gNumPre, gNumDef)
    'yield/returns report
    If gSingleSelect(iCase, SINGLE_RETURN) Then _
        Call Report_STReturnMain(iCase, gNumPre, gNumDef)

End Sub
```

EXHIBIT 16.29 "WriteReports_SingleTrancheReports" subroutine

VBA Code within Report Files   All of the various report template files of the LWM contain VBA subroutines that help the analyst prepare and select the data that will be displayed in the report. We will also take a cursory look at this code and how these subroutines turn each of the report files into simple de facto report-writing programs. This code allows the analyst to display any of the data produced by the LWM. The majority of the reports allow the analyst to select various individual scenarios and the order of their appearance in the report Display Areas. See Chapter 14 for a discussion of these features.

Single Tranche Reports

We will start our examination of the report generation process of the LWM with a visit to the Single Tranche reports. The orientation of these reports is to display a set of cash flows or performance statistics of a Single Tranche on a single page. To this end, the worksheets of all of these files are organized by tranche and are named "A-1", "A-2", through "B-4". Information specific to that tranche alone is displayed in the report.

In this section we will examine the Cash Flows report and the Tenor report in detail. We will review the code in the LWM that creates the report file and populates it and the VBA code that resides within the report file itself. The Yield/Coverage/Loss report is virtually identical, except for the number of datum, in layout and operation to the Tenor file. For this report we will only comment on the display differences of the report itself.

Single Tranche Cash Flow Reports   The purpose of the Single Tranche Cash Flow (STCF) report is to allow the analyst to display the beginning annual balances of the tranches or the annual sums of principal paid, coupon expense paid, or losses incurred. Each of the reports allows the analyst to select up to six scenarios of the Case and display them in any order desired. The code that opens and creates the file is contained in the LWM. The VBA code that allows for the display of the scenario information is contained in the report file itself (as mentioned above). We will start by examining the layout of the file and then move to the LWM code and finally to the VBA code of the report file itself.

Layout of the File   The layout of the STCF report consists of three distinct areas. These are described in Chapter 14, but we will quickly review them here. The first is the Data Display Area. This area is a table of results that resides in the upper left-hand corner of the STCF. The Data Display Area contains the data that will be displayed in the report graph to the right of it. The data that will populate this table is selected by the analyst from the Data Schedule Area of the report below it. In the Cash Flow report, this area consists of the annual schedule of cash flows or balances from each of the up to 25 different scenarios of the Case. The analyst enters the numbers of the scenarios from the Data Schedule Area and clicks on the CommandButton of the report to load them into the Data Display Area. The values are then immediately displayed in the graph to the right. See Exhibit 16.30.

The analyst enters the scenario numbers that are to be displayed in the row of fields marked "Scenario" at the top of the Display Area. The CommandButton "load Selected Scenarios" is clicked, and the data is copied to the table. In the line

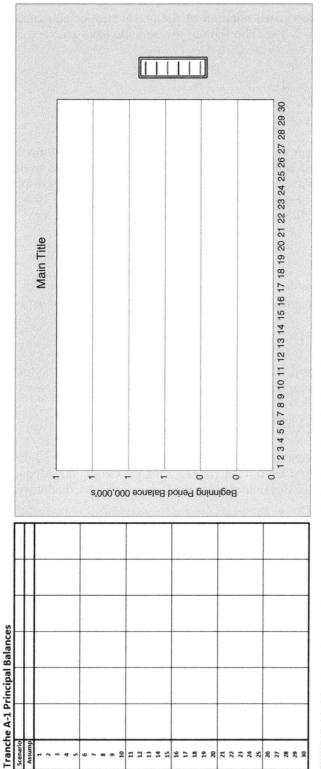

EXHIBIT 16.30 Data Display Area (unpopulated) of a Single Tranche Cash Flows report

"Assump", an abbreviated notation of the prepayment/default conditions of the scenario is presented. The abbreviations for methodologies are:

- Uniform CPR: "C"
- Uniform PSA or SDA: "P"
- Geographic: "G"
- Demographic: "D"

The prepayment and default speeds are given for the Uniform Methodology. For the Geographic and Demographic Methodologies, the stress levels with a "%" appended are displayed. Prepayment methodology and speed are displayed first.

This scenario, employing the Uniform Methodology, with 10% CPR prepayments and 25% CPR defaults would be abbreviated to:

"C10-C25"

A prepayment/default Geographic Methodology scenario of 125% Base Prepayments stress and 175% Base Defaults stress would appear as:

"G125%-G175%"

A prepayment/default Demographic Methodology scenario of 125% Base Prepayments Stress and 175% Base Defaults stress would appear as:

"G125%-D175%"

It should be recalled that in the Demographic Methodology, the prepayment rates of the collateral are still determined using the Geographic Methodology while only the defaults are determined using the Demographic Methodology.

"Report_STCFsMain" Subroutine We will now review the "Report_STCFsMain" subroutine that produces the four different cash flow reports. This subroutine is called four times with a different set of arguments each time depending on the cash flow report content desired. The subroutine performs the typical template preparation operations of opening, renaming, and saving to turn the template file into a ready-to-write report file. The subroutine then selects one of four report-writing subroutines based on the value of the Constant variable in the calling argument of "Report_STCFsMain". These subroutines then load the specific cash flow information into the template file, and the report is complete except for the prepayment/default headers formatting. This information is provided by a utility formatting subroutine that we will review later. See Exhibit 16.31.

"RepSTCFs_WritePrincipalBals" Subroutine With the template file opened, renamed, and saved, we can now write the appropriate data into it. The "RepSTCFs_WritePrinBals" now writes the beginning annual principal balances of the tranches into each of the six worksheets of the report. The structure of the subroutine can be

```
Sub Report_MTCFsMain(iCase As Integer, iPrepays As Integer, _
                     iDefaults As Integer)

    'open the report template file
    Tempfile = "TemplateMTCFs.xlsx"
    Workbooks.Open Filename:=DIR_TEMPLATE_REP & Tempfile
    'get the standard output name for the file
    gMultiTrancheCFsName = "_MTCashFlows.xlsx"
    ActiveWorkbook.SaveAs Filename:= _
        OUTPUT_DIRECTORY & gOutputPrefix(iCase) & gSingleTrancheCFsName
    ActiveWorkbook.Save
    'write the specfic cash flows into the schedule section of the worksheets
    For iCF = 1 To 4
        Select Case iCF
            Case Is = CF_PRINBAL
                Sheets("PrinBal").Select
                Call RepMTCFs_WritePrincipalBals(iPrepays, iDefaults)
            Case Is = CF_COUPAMT
                Sheets("CoupPmts").Select
                Call RepMTCFs_WriteCouponAmounts(iPrepays, iDefaults)
            Case Is = CF_PRINAMT
                Sheets("PrinPmts").Select
                Call RepMTCFs_WritePrincipalAmts(iPrepays, iDefaults)
            Case Is = CF_LOSSES
                Sheets("PrinLosses").Select
                Call RepMTCFs_WriteLossAmts(iPrepays, iDefaults)
        End Select
    Next iCF
    'save and close the report file
    ActiveWorkbook.Save
    ActiveWorkbook.Close

End Sub
```

EXHIBIT 16.31   "Report_STCFsMain" subroutine

summarized as follows:

```
Loop by Tranche
    Select the correct worksheet based on content
    Write the prepayment/default scenario conditions
    Loop by Prepayment Speeds
        Loop by Default Speeds
            Loop by Years
                Write the data for selected tranche
            Next Years
        Next Default Speed
    Next Prepayment Speed
Next Tranche
```

The above pattern will be broadly used for all the reports of the LWM. In the case of the Multiple Tranche reports, the outer Tranche loop will be replaced by a Data Items loop that will loop through the worksheets by the type of data to be presented, instead of the Tranche information. See Exhibit 16.32.

There is an individual subroutine of this type for each of the Single Tranche Cash Flow reports. The one call that may be somewhat unusual is the call to the prepayment/default formatting subroutine. We will look at that subroutine next.

```
Sub RepSTCFs_WritePrincipalBals(iPrepays As Integer, iDefaults As Integer)

    For itran = 1 To TRANCHES - 1
        'select the correct worksheet based on tranche
        Call RepSTCFs_SelectWorksheetByTranche
        'fill in the prepayment and default headers
        Call Report_AddPrepayDefaultInfo(ST_REPORT, SINGLE_PRINBAL)
        'fill in the balances section by tranche
        icol = BEG_SCH_COL
        For ip = 1 To iPrepays
            For id = 1 To iDefaults
                For iyears = 1 To PAY_YEARS
                    'print the contents of the beginning principal balance array
                    irow = BEG_SCH_ROW + iyears - 1
                    Select Case itran
                        Case Is = TRANCHE_A1:
                            Cells(irow, icol).Value = gAnnOutA1BBal(ip, id, iyears)
                        Case Is = TRANCHE_A2:
                            Cells(irow, icol).Value = gAnnOutA2BBal(ip, id, iyears)
                        Case Is = TRANCHE_B1:
                            Cells(irow, icol).Value = gAnnOutB1BBal(ip, id, iyears)
                        Case Is = TRANCHE_B2:
                            Cells(irow, icol).Value = gAnnOutB2BBal(ip, id, iyears)
                        Case Is = TRANCHE_B3:
                            Cells(irow, icol).Value = gAnnOutB3BBal(ip, id, iyears)
                        Case Is = TRANCHE_B4:
                            Cells(irow, icol).Value = gAnnOutB4BBal(ip, id, iyears)
                    End Select
                Next iyears
            Next id
            'advance the column by each prepayment/default combination
            icol = icol + 1
        Next ip
    Next itran

End Sub
```

EXHIBIT 16.32   "ReportSTCFs_WritePrincipalBals" subroutine

Each of the Cash Flow reports needs to be sure that the information concerning a specific tranche is being written to the correct tranche report. A simple subroutine with a "Select..Case" statement will address this issue. When we move to the Multiple Tranche reports, you will see not one but several of these subroutines. Each will call, instead of a tranche-specific worksheet in the report file, a data-specific worksheet. This is indicative of the reciprocity relationship between tranches and data we spoke of earlier. See Exhibit 16.33.

"Report_AddPrepayDefaultInfo"   The subroutine "RepSTCFs_WritePrincipalBals" will, as we have seen, populate the Data Schedule Area of each of the tranche-specific worksheets of the Single Tranche Cash Flow report. This information is of little use to us unless we understand the conditions that were employed to generate the collateral cash flows of the Case they represent. The header section of the Data Schedule Area of the reports provides us with this information—but only if we place it there for the analyst to see!

```
Sub RepSTCFs_SelectWorksheetByTranche()
    'select the correct worksheet based on tranche
    Select Case itran
        Case Is = TRANCHE_A1: Sheets("A1").Select
        Case Is = TRANCHE_A2: Sheets("A2").Select
        Case Is = TRANCHE_B1: Sheets("B1").Select
        Case Is = TRANCHE_B2: Sheets("B2").Select
        Case Is = TRANCHE_B3: Sheets("B3").Select
        Case Is = TRANCHE_B4: Sheets("B4").Select
    End Select
End Sub
```

EXHIBIT 16.33 "RepSTCFs_SelectWorksheetByTranche" subroutine

The "Report_AddPrepayDefaultInfo" subroutine does just that for us. It reads the various prepayment and default information and writes it into the scenario-specific columns of these Cash Flow reports. You will remember that this subroutine and the ones that support it are *not* in the report-writing module, where we would normally expect to find them. The reason for this is the high degree of commonality between the Single and Multiple Tranche reports, and that also extends to a lesser degree to the formats of the Miscellaneous reports. Due to this commonality, it makes sense to centralize the prepayment/default header role and develop a small collection of formatting routines in their own VBA module. In that this collection of subroutines is shared between a number of report-writing subroutines, we can view them as utility code. We will therefore create a module named "Utility_PrepayDefaultWriter" and place this code there.

You will notice that the call to "Report_AddPrepayDefaultInfo" has two arguments, both of which are Public Constants. See Exhibit 16.34. The first argument is the class of report and the second is the type of report. The class of report can assume the value of "ST_REPORT", "MT_REPORT", or "MS_REPORT" for Single Tranche, Multiple Tranche, and Miscellaneous Cash Flow reports, respectively. Within these classes we can then employ the specific Constant variables of the individual reports of that class. The subroutine takes advantage of this relationship to quickly route us to the appropriate formatting subroutine needed by that report. We employ a set of nested "Select..Case" statements to find first the appropriate class and then the appropriate type associated with the current report we are working on.

Once we have completed these two tests, we call the formatting routine. In the case of the Single Tranche Principal Balances Cash Flow report, we need to place the prepayment/default information into the Data Schedule Area. This area provides a four-line header in the Data Schedule table. The first and second line in the scenario column contain the prepayment methodology and speed, the third and fourth the default methodology and speeds, respectively. We have one thing in our favor that makes the task formatting the header section of this report much easier: All the columns are individual scenarios. In addition, we know that the prepayment/default methodologies are consistent across all scenarios. Given that this is the situation, we can immediately fill the two methodology rows with a simple "For..Next" loop. Next we will use a pair of nested prepayment/default loops. We will increment the write position in the report upon each execution of the inner loop. We will

```
Sub Report_AddPrepayDefaultInfo(rClass As Integer, rType As Integer)

    'build the prepayment and default labels
    Call UtilPreDef_DetermineSuffix
    Call UtilPreDef_BuildPreDefLabels
    Call UtilPreDef_LongPreDefLabels
    'copy the labels to the reports
    'classes of reports
    Select Case rClass
        Case Is = ST_REPORT
            Select Case rType
                Case Is = SINGLE_PRINBAL: Call UtilPreDef_Format01
                Case Is = SINGLE_COUPPMT: Call UtilPreDef_Format01
                Case Is = SINGLE_PRINPMT: Call UtilPreDef_Format01
                Case Is = SINGLE_LOSSES:  Call UtilPreDef_Format01
                Case Is = SINGLE_TENOR:   Call UtilPreDef_Format02(4)
                Case Is = SINGLE_RETURN:  Call UtilPreDef_Format02(6)
            End Select
        Case Is = MT_REPORT
            Select Case rType
                Case Is = MULTI_ALLCFS: Call UtilPreDef_Format03(4, 1, 6)
                Case Is = MULTI_TENOR:  Call UtilPreDef_Format04(6, 1)
                Case Is = MULTI_RETURN: Call UtilPreDef_Format04(6, 2)
            End Select
        Case Is = MS_REPORT
            Select Case rType
                Case Is = MISC_COLLAT: Call UtilPreDef_Format03(1, 2, 6)
                Case Is = MISC_EXCESS: Call UtilPreDef_Format03(1, 3, 5)
                Case Is = MISC_FEES:   Call UtilPreDef_Format03(1, 4, 1)
            End Select
    End Select

End Sub
```

EXHIBIT 16.34 "Report_AddPrepayDefaultInfo" subroutine

write the prevailing prepayment/default information as well. If we keep the cash flow scenario generation conditions of prepayments first defaults second, we will be entirely consistent with the ways the scenarios were generated in the CCFG. See Exhibit 16.35.

With these subroutines we can produce all the Single Tranche Cash Flow reports. If we need to add other reports to the collection, we can easily do so using the generalized report-writing structure we have developed here.

VBA Code of the Single Tranche Cash Flow Reports   While we have not completed the discussion of the VBA code supporting the report-writing activities, we should not forget that there is another collection of VBA code inside each of the Single Tranche Cash Flow files themselves. This code facilitates the following tasks when the CommandButton of a report worksheet is clicked:

1. Identifies the particular tranche worksheet that the button call has originated from.
2. Reads the scenario selections made at the top of the Data Display Area table.

```
Sub UtilPreDef_Format01()

    For iSheet = 1 To TRANCHES - 1
        Call UtilPreDef_FindTrancheWorksheet(iSheet)
        For icol = 2 To 26
            Cells(40, icol) = mPLong
            Cells(42, icol) = mDLong
        Next icol
        icol = 2
        For iCnt1 = 1 To gNumPre
            For iCnt2 = 1 To gNumDef
                Cells(41, icol) = gPrepayRate(iCnt1)
                Cells(43, icol) = gDefaultRate(iCnt2)
                icol = icol + 1
            Next iCnt2
        Next iCnt1
    Next iSheet

End Sub
```

EXHIBIT 16.35   "UtilPreDef_Format01" subroutine

3. Based on the input scenario numbers, copies the scenario information from the Data Schedule Area to the Display Area table.
4. Creates the specific prepayment/default assumptions abbreviations for the scenario and writes them to the Display Area table.
5. Creates a Tranche/Data-specific title for the Display Area graph and writes it to the graph of the worksheet.

Identifying the Tranche-Specific Worksheet   When we activate the CommandButton on any of the worksheets, it calls a worksheet-specific subroutine we have linked to it using the "assign Macro" command of the Button Editor. Each subroutine called, such as "STReport_AmortCurvesA1" below immediately selects the worksheet it resides on and then calls several additional subroutines to perform Steps 2 through 5 above. See Exhibit 16.36.

Reading the Display Area Table Scenario Choices   The subroutine "STReport_ReadScenarioChoices" next reads the contents of the scenario choices made by the analyst in the header input section of the Display Area table. See Exhibit 16.37.

Loading the Selected Scenarios   We now know which of the available scenarios have been selected and can now copy the data into the Display Area table from the Data Schedule Area of the worksheet. This task is performed by the subroutine "STReport_LoadTableScenariosToGraph". See Exhibit 16.38.

```
Sub STReport_AmortCurvesA1()
    Sheets("A1").Select
    Call STReport_ReadScenarioChoices
    Call STReport_LoadTableScenariosToGraph
End Sub
```

EXHIBIT 16.36   "STReport_AmortCurvesA1" subroutine

```
Sub STReport_ReadScenarioChoices()
    icol = SCEN_COL
    For inum = 1 To NUM_SCEN
        mScenNums(inum) = Cells(SCEN_ROW, icol).Value
        icol = icol + 1
    Next inum
End Sub
```

EXHIBIT 16.37   "STReport_ReadScenarioChoices" subroutine

```
Sub STReport_LoadTableScenariosToGraph()

Dim baseCol     As Integer   'base column of the table
Dim readCol     As Integer   'current column read position
Dim readRow     As Integer   'current row read position
Dim chartRow    As Integer   'target table row
Dim chartCol    As Integer   'target Table column
Dim writeAmt    As Double    'target amount
Dim writeCol    As Integer   'target amount column
Dim writeRow    As Integer   'target amount row

    baseCol = BEG_COL                   'base column of the full table
    For inum = 1 To NUM_SCEN
        'column to read is the base column + scenario number - 1
        readCol = baseCol + mScenNums(inum) - 1
        'read the prepayment information (speed+method)
        mScenPType(inum) = Cells(SCEN_PSPEED, readCol).Value
        mScenPSpeed(inum) = Cells(SCEN_PSPEED + 1, readCol).Value
        'read the default information (speed+method)
        mScenDType(inum) = Cells(SCEN_DSPEED, readCol).Value
        mScenDSpeed(inum) = Cells(SCEN_DSPEED + 1, readCol).Value
        Call STReport_ConstructAssumptionDesc(inum)
        'read the cash flow table contents for this column
        readRow = BEG_ROW               'base row of the full table $
        writeCol = baseCol              'base column for writing
        writeRow = WRITE_ROW            'base row for writing
        For idate = 1 To PAY_DATES
            'read from the lower master schedule of all 25 scenarios
            writeAmt = Cells(readRow + idate - 1, readCol).Value
            If writeAmt = 0# Then
              'previous writeAmt was zero fill rest of schedule with blanks
              Cells(writeRow + idate - 1, writeCol + inum - 1).Value = ""
            Else
              'write to the upper report schedule
              Cells(writeRow + idate - 1, writeCol + inum - 1).Value = writeAmt
            End If
        Next idate
        'write the abbreviated prepayment/default conditions that were
        ' assembled in the STReport_ConstructAssumptionDesc sub above
        Cells(WRITE_ROW - 1, writeCol + inum - 1).Value = mScenAssumpt(inum)
    Next inum
    'annotate the chart title for the prepayment/default methodologies
    Call STReport_UpdateChartTitle

End Sub
```

EXHIBIT 16.38   "STReport_LoadTableScenariosToGraph" subroutine

```
Sub STReport_ConstructAssumptionDesc(inum As Integer)

Dim ptype    As String    'prepayment methodology abbreviation
Dim dtype    As String    'default methodology abbreviation
Dim pspeed   As String    'prepayment speed as string
Dim dspeed   As String    'default speed as string

    'set the prepayment type abbreviation
    Select Case Trim(mScenPType(inum))
        Case Is = "CPR":    ptype = "C"
        Case Is = "PSA":    ptype = "P"
        Case Is = "GEO":    ptype = "G"
        Case Is = "DEMO":   ptype = "D"
    End Select
    'set the default type abbreviation
    Select Case Trim(mScenDType(inum))
        Case Is = "CPR":    dtype = "C"
        Case Is = "PSA":    dtype = "P"
        Case Is = "GEO":    dtype = "G"
        Case Is = "DEMO":   dtype = "D"
    End Select
    If Trim(mScenDType(inum)) = "GEO" Or Trim(mScenDType(inum)) = "DEMO" Then
        pspeed = mScenPSpeed(inum) * 100#
        dspeed = mScenDSpeed(inum) * 100#
        mScenAssumpt(inum) = ptype & pspeed & "%" & "-" & dtype & dspeed & "%"
    Else
        pspeed = mScenPSpeed(inum)
        dspeed = mScenDSpeed(inum)
        mScenAssumpt(inum) = ptype & pspeed & "%" & "-" & dtype & dspeed & "%"
    End If

End Sub
```

EXHIBIT 16.39   "STReport_ConstructAssumptionDesc" subroutine

Creating the Prepayment/Default Assumption Headers   We next construct the prepayment/default assumptions abbreviations that we need for the Display Area table title areas. This task is performed by the subroutine "STReport_Construct-AssumptionDesc". See Exhibit 16.39.

Creating the Tranche/Data/Assumptions–Specific Headers for the Graph   The last subroutine of the module, "STReport_UpdateChartTitle", reads the tranche, data, and prepayment/default assumptions of the selected scenarios and constructs a content-specific heading for the Display Area graph. See Exhibit 16.40.

Single Tranche Tenor Report   The approaches to writing the Single Tranche Tenor report are broadly similar to those of writing the Single Tranche Cash Flow reports we just reviewed. The crucial difference is that instead of having to report 360 data by 25 scenarios, we need to report only 1 data by 25 scenarios, a considerably less daunting task! We are able to discard the Data Schedule Area of the reports and transfer the data directly from the Display Area table to the graph. As a result of this massive reduction in reported information, we can compress each Tenor report to a single worksheet by tranche. This allows us to place all the Tenor information for each of the reported statistics, the two variations of average life, final maturity, and modified duration, in a single Display Area table. With this greatly reduced file comes

```
Sub STReport_UpdateChartTitle()

Dim sTitle  As String   'full title
Dim p1      As String   'prepayment component
Dim d1      As String   'default component

    ActiveSheet.ChartObjects("Chart 1").Activate
    ActiveChart.ChartTitle.Select
    'base title
    sTitle = "Principal Amortization Curves for Selected Scenarios" & Chr(13)
    'prepayment component
    Select Case Trim(mScenPType(1))
        Case Is = "CPR":  p1 = "Uniform CPR Prepayment, "
        Case Is = "PSA":  p1 = "Uniform PSA Prepayment, "
        Case Is = "GEO":  p1 = "Geographic Stress Prepayment, "
        Case Is = "DEMO": p1 = "Demographic Stress Prepayment, "
    End Select
    'default component
    Select Case Trim(mScenDType(1))
        Case Is = "CPR":  d1 = "Uniform CPR Default Methodology"
        Case Is = "PSA":  d1 = "Uniform PSA Default Methodology"
        Case Is = "GEO":  d1 = "Geographic Stress Default Methodology"
        Case Is = "DEMO": d1 = "Demographic Stress Default Methodology"
    End Select
    'assign the total title
    ActiveChart.ChartTitle.Text = sTitle & p1 & d1
    ActiveSheet.ChartObjects("Chart 1").Activate
    ActiveChart.ChartArea.Select

End Sub
```

EXHIBIT 16.40   "STReport_UpdateChartTitle" subroutine

a few twists in formatting the report prepayment/default assumptions abbreviations. With the extensive discussion of the Cash Flow reports fresh in your mind, you will easily see the similarities of the reports. The Data Display Area table for the Tenor report is shown in Exhibit 16.41.

Single Tranche Yield/Coverage/Loss Report   The process for creating the Yield/Coverage/Loss report is identical to the Tenor report. The only difference is the number of data items, four in the Tenor report as opposed to six in the Yield/Coverage/Loss report.

Multiple Tranche Reports

As we discussed earlier, a Multiple Tranche report presents a specified statistic for a single scenario for all the tranches of the Liabilities Structure in a single report. Due to this fact, the organization of the various Multiple Tranche reports is based on worksheets that are specific to a given *performance measurement* as opposed to the Single Tranche report, which is specific to a particular *tranche*.

In a Single Tranche report, there is a report worksheet for each of the tranches of the Structure. In a Multiple Tranche report, there is a worksheet for each performance statistic to be reported. All cash flow reports are graphically presented using line chart formats. All Tenor and Yield/Coverage/Loss statistics employ a 3-D bar chart format.

Tranche A1 - All Tenor Results

Select Tenor Choice = 1 | Load Selected Tenor Results

Select	Tranche	Default	Prepayment Method and Speed				
			G-100%	G-125%	G-150%	G-175%	G-200%
1	WAL to Maturity	D-100%	5.7	5.5	5.3	5.1	4.9
		D-125%	5.1	4.9	4.8	4.6	4.5
		D-150%	4.7	4.6	4.5	4.4	4.3
		D-175%	4.5	4.4	4.3	4.3	4.2
		D-200%	4.4	4.3	4.2	4.1	4.1
Select	Tranche	Default	G-100%	G-125%	G-150%	G-175%	G-200%
2	WAL to Call	D-100%	5.6	5.4	5.2	5.0	4.8
		D-125%	5.0	4.9	4.7	4.6	4.5
		D-150%	4.7	4.5	4.4	4.3	4.2
		D-175%	4.4	4.3	4.2	4.1	4.1
		D-200%	4.2	4.1	4.1	4.0	3.9
Select	Tranche	Default	G-100%	G-125%	G-150%	G-175%	G-200%
3	Final Maturity	D-100%	0.0	0.0	0.0	0.0	0.0
		D-125%	0.0	0.0	0.0	0.0	0.0
		D-150%	0.0	0.0	0.0	0.0	0.0
		D-175%	0.0	0.0	0.0	0.0	0.0
		D-200%	0.0	0.0	0.0	0.0	0.0
Select	Tranche	Default	G-100%	G-125%	G-150%	G-175%	G-200%
4	Modified Duration	D-100%	0.5	0.4	0.4	0.4	0.4
		D-125%	0.4	0.4	0.4	0.4	0.4
		D-150%	0.4	0.4	0.4	0.4	0.3
		D-175%	0.4	0.4	0.3	0.3	0.3
		D-200%	0.4	0.3	0.3	0.3	0.3

Tranche A-1 Wght Average Life to Maturity

EXHIBIT 16.41 Single Tranche Tenor Report

Multiple Tranche Cash Flows Report   We will first examine the Multiple Tranche
Cash Flow reports and compare it to the Single Tranche report we reviewed above.

Content and Structure of the Report   The Multiple Tranche Cash Flow report is
composed of four worksheets, one for each of the reported performance measurements of the Liabilities Structure. These are the worksheets:

- Beginning annual principal balance by tranche
- Principal balance retired by tranche
- Coupon expenses paid to each tranche
- Losses applied by each tranche (B Class tranches only)

Each worksheet of the report workbook file contains a CommandButton similar
to those found in the Single Tranche report worksheets. Unlike the Single Tranche
reports, the analyst enters a single scenario election, and the cash flow for the selected scenario is displayed for each tranche of the Structure. The Multiple Tranche
Cash Flows report contains a Data Display Area containing a table and a graph.
It also contains a Data Schedule Area beneath the Data Display Area. This Data
Display Area is comprised of 25: six column groups of cash flows, one column for
each of the tranches. (In the case of the Losses report, there are 25 sets of four
columns each in that losses cannot be assigned to the Class A tranches). This block
of six columns (or four columns for Losses) is identified by a single set of four
sets of Prepayment/Default Methodology and speed fields. These fields are over the
first tranche column of each of the 25 sections of the report. See Exhibit 16.42
for a layout of the first three scenario sections of the Data Schedule Area of the
template file.

After the Data Schedule Area is populated by subroutines of the LWM the report
functions in a similar manner to the Single Tranche Cash Flow report. An individual
scenario is selected by the user and the CommandButton is clicked. The subroutines
contained in the report file populate the Display Area and the graph is driven by its
contents.

Populating the Multiple Tranche Cash Flow Report Worksheets   This subroutine
initiates the process of populating the Multiple Tranche Cash Flow report. It first
opens, renames, and save the template file to the designed output file name. The next
step in the process is to sequentially populate the contents of each of the report's
worksheets. A "For..Next" loop selects them and a data type–specific subroutine
writes the particular data item to the appropriate worksheet. See Exhibits 16.43
and 16.44.

As with the Single Tranche Cash Flow report, there is a specific subroutine
to read the prepayment/default criteria contained in the Data Schedule Area. This
subroutine translates the information into the standard abbreviated form used in the
Data Display Area table header section. See Exhibit 16.35.

As in the case of the Single Tranche reports, Multiple Tranche reports all make
use of the utility subroutine "Report_AddPrepayDefaultInfo" to format the Data
Schedule Areas of the report files with the appropriate prepayment and default
methodologies and speeds.

Annual Beginning Principal Balances By Scenario

Scenario	1						2						3					
Tranche	A-1	A-2	B1	B-2	B-3	B-4	A-1	A-2	B1	B-2	B-3	B-4	A-1	A-2	B1	B-2	B-3	B-4
Prepay Info	GEO 100%						GEO 100%						GEO 100%					
Default Info	DEMO 100%						DEMO 125%						DEMO 150%					
1	456,535,412	50,726,157	10,092,115	5,842,803	2,655,820	2,655,820	456,535,412	50,726,157	10,092,115	5,842,803	2,655,820	2,655,820	456,535,412	50,726,157	10,092,115	5,842,803	2,655,820	2,655,820
2	424,633,931	47,181,548	8,953,727	0	0	0	422,535,146	46,948,350	8,915,012	0	0	0	420,446,625	46,716,292	8,876,410	0	0	0
3	390,910,493	43,434,499	0	0	0	0	386,934,335	42,992,704	0	0	0	0	383,000,811	42,555,646	0	0	0	0
4	346,406,091	38,489,566	0	0	0	0	340,626,192	37,847,355	0	0	0	0	334,951,293	37,216,810	0	0	0	0
5	294,115,233	32,679,470	0	0	0	0	286,010,061	31,778,896	0	0	0	0	278,328,109	30,925,345	0	0	0	0
6	243,574,178	27,063,798	0	0	0	0	233,680,009	25,964,445	0	0	0	0	224,365,151	24,929,461	0	0	0	0
7	195,007,747	21,667,527	0	0	0	0	183,846,187	20,427,354	0	0	0	0	173,437,007	19,270,779	0	0	0	0
8	153,868,487	17,096,499	0	0	0	0	141,928,427	15,769,825	0	0	0	0	130,916,563	14,546,285	0	0	0	0
9	119,832,897	13,314,766	0	0	0	0	107,548,350	11,949,817	0	0	0	0	96,360,112	10,706,679	0	0	0	0
10	87,977,889	9,775,321	0	0	0	0	75,728,623	8,414,291	0	0	0	0	64,731,887	7,192,432	0	0	0	0
11	58,340,335	6,482,259	0	0	0	0	46,522,618	5,169,180	0	0	0	0	36,393,385	4,043,709	0	0	0	0
12	31,961,100	3,551,233	0	0	0	0	21,961,099	2,440,122	0	0	0	0	13,556,120	1,506,236	0	0	0	0
13	10,995,201	1,221,689	0	0	0	0	3,121,621	346,847	0	0	0	0	0	0	0	0	0	0
14	0	0	0	0	0	0	0	0	0	0	0	0	0	0	0	0	0	0
15	0	0	0	0	0	0	0	0	0	0	0	0	0	0	0	0	0	0
16	0	0	0	0	0	0	0	0	0	0	0	0	0	0	0	0	0	0
17	0	0	0	0	0	0	0	0	0	0	0	0	0	0	0	0	0	0
18	0	0	0	0	0	0	0	0	0	0	0	0	0	0	0	0	0	0
19	0	0	0	0	0	0	0	0	0	0	0	0	0	0	0	0	0	0
20	0	0	0	0	0	0	0	0	0	0	0	0	0	0	0	0	0	0
21	0	0	0	0	0	0	0	0	0	0	0	0	0	0	0	0	0	0
22	0	0	0	0	0	0	0	0	0	0	0	0	0	0	0	0	0	0
23	0	0	0	0	0	0	0	0	0	0	0	0	0	0	0	0	0	0
24	0	0	0	0	0	0	0	0	0	0	0	0	0	0	0	0	0	0
25	0	0	0	0	0	0	0	0	0	0	0	0	0	0	0	0	0	0
26	0	0	0	0	0	0	0	0	0	0	0	0	0	0	0	0	0	0
27	0	0	0	0	0	0	0	0	0	0	0	0	0	0	0	0	0	0
28	0	0	0	0	0	0	0	0	0	0	0	0	0	0	0	0	0	0
29	0	0	0	0	0	0	0	0	0	0	0	0	0	0	0	0	0	0
30	0	0	0	0	0	0	0	0	0	0	0	0	0	0	0	0	0	0

EXHIBIT 16.42 Data Schedule Area (first three cases) of the Multiple Tranche Cash Flows report

```
Sub Report_MTCFsMain(iCase As Integer, iPrepays As Integer, _
                     iDefaults As Integer)

    'open the report template file
    Tempfile = "TemplateMTCFs.xlsx"
    Workbooks.Open Filename:=DIR_TEMPLATE_REP & Tempfile
    'get the standard output name for the file
    gMultiTrancheCFsName = "_MTCashFlows.xlsx"
    ActiveWorkbook.SaveAs Filename:= _
        OUTPUT_DIRECTORY & gOutputPrefix(iCase) & gSingleTrancheCFsName
    ActiveWorkbook.Save
    'write the specfic cash flows into the schedule section of the worksheets
    For iCF = 1 To 4
        Select Case iCF
            Case Is = CF_PRINBAL
                Sheets("PrinBal").Select
                Call RepMTCFs_WritePrincipalBals(iPrepays, iDefaults)
            Case Is = CF_COUPAMT
                Sheets("CoupPmts").Select
                Call RepMTCFs_WriteCouponAmounts(iPrepays, iDefaults)
            Case Is = CF_PRINAMT
                Sheets("PrinPmts").Select
                Call RepMTCFs_WritePrincipalAmts(iPrepays, iDefaults)
            Case Is = CF_LOSSES
                Sheets("PrinLosses").Select
                Call RepMTCFs_WriteLossAmts(iPrepays, iDefaults)
        End Select
    Next iCF
    'save and close the report file
    ActiveWorkbook.Save
    ActiveWorkbook.Close

End Sub
```

EXHIBIT 16.43   "Report_MTCFsMain" subroutine

```
Sub RepMTCFs_WritePrincipalBals(iPrepays As Integer, iDefaults As Integer, _
                                iCF As Integer)

    Call UtilPreDef_FindCFWorksheet(iCF)
    icol = BEG_SCH_COL
    For ip = 1 To iPrepays
        For id = 1 To iDefaults
            irow = BEG_SCH_ROW
            For iyears = 1 To PAY_YEARS
                Cells(irow, icol + 0).Value = gAnnOutA1BBal(ip, id, iyears)
                Cells(irow, icol + 1).Value = gAnnOutA2BBal(ip, id, iyears)
                Cells(irow, icol + 2).Value = gAnnOutB1BBal(ip, id, iyears)
                Cells(irow, icol + 3).Value = gAnnOutB2BBal(ip, id, iyears)
                Cells(irow, icol + 4).Value = gAnnOutB3BBal(ip, id, iyears)
                Cells(irow, icol + 5).Value = gAnnOutB4BBal(ip, id, iyears)
                irow = irow + 1
            Next iyears
            'advance to next prepay/default section
            icol = icol + 6
        Next id
    Next ip

End Sub
```

EXHIBIT 16.44   "RepMTCFs_WritePrincipalBals" subroutine

Manipulating the Data Inside the Report File   In common with the design features of the Single Tranche reports, Multiple Tranche reports contain VBA subroutines that allow the analyst to specify any of the contents of the Data Schedule Area for display in the Display Area table and graph. These subroutines are very similar to those discussed in detail for the Single Tranche reports and are available in the template files if you wish to peruse them there.

Multiple Tranche Tenor Report   The Multiple Tranche Tenor report consists of a total of four report worksheets, one for each of the tenor performance statistics. Each worksheet consists of a Display Area with a table and graph. The table is horizontally divided into six sections, one for each of the note tranches. Each column has five default speed rows and five prepayment columns in each of the segments. All the tenor information can be accommodated in the Display Area table. The report worksheets do not, therefore, require a Data Schedule Area. The analyst selects the tranche to be displayed, and all scenarios for that tranche that contain data are displayed in the Graph section. To accomplish this, the VBA subroutines of the report file restate the data region that the graph object of the report worksheet looks at as its reference information. The layout of the Tenor Display table can be seen in Exhibit 16.45.

Selection and Display of Report Data   In the Multiple Tranche Tenor report, the analyst enters the number of the tranche whose performance statistic he or she wishes to display in the graph. The CommandButton is clicked and the VBA subroutine linked to the button executes. See Exhibit 16.46 for the subroutine activated from the Average Life to Maturity report worksheet. This button selects the sheet and then calls two other subroutines.

The first subroutine called by the "MTReport_AverageLifeReport" will read the tranche selected and change the chart data reference to the range represented by the tranche in the Display Area table. See Exhibit 16.47.

The final subroutine, "MTReport_UpDateTenorChartTitle", passes the Public Constant "AVERAGE_LIFE" and triggers the creation of a content-specific title for the graph based on tranche, performance statistic, and prepayment/default methodologies and speeds. With that operation, the CommandButton–activated code is complete. You will notice that the prepayment/default information scenario headers of the Data Display Area table are not set by any code in the report template file. This is due to the fact that for Single and Multiple Tenor and Yield reports, four in total, these headers are set by the utility subroutine that resides in the LWM itself.

Multiple Tranche Yield/Coverage/Loss Report   This report is virtually identical to the Multiple Tranche Tenor report just discussed. Interested readers are encouraged to peruse the code at their leisure.

Miscellaneous Reports

The LWM also produces four reports we have placed in the Miscellaneous report category of the Report Selection Menu UserForm. These reports all draw very heavily from the VBA subroutine developed for the Single and Multiple Tranche reports. The Deal Fees, Excess Cash Flows, and Liabilities Waterfall reports are intended more for internal use. The Collateral Cash File report is provided if it is necessary to display

Tenor Report All Tranches – Average Life

Select Tranche Choice = 1 | Load Selected Tranche Results

Select	Tranche		Default	Prepayment Method and Speeds				
				G-100%	G-125%	G-150%	G-175%	G-200%
1	A	1	D-100%	5.7	5.1	4.7	4.5	4.4
			D-125%	5.5	4.9	4.6	4.4	4.3
			D-150%	5.3	4.8	4.5	4.3	4.2
			D-175%	5.1	4.6	4.4	4.3	4.1
			D-200%	4.9	4.5	4.3	4.2	4.1
2	A	2	D-100%	5.7	5.1	4.7	4.5	4.4
			D-125%	5.5	4.9	4.6	4.4	4.3
			D-150%	5.3	4.8	4.5	4.3	4.2
			D-175%	5.1	4.6	4.4	4.3	4.1
			D-200%	4.9	4.5	4.3	4.2	4.1
3	B	1	D-100%	1.3	0.9	0.6	0.5	0.4
			D-125%	1.3	0.9	0.6	0.5	0.4
			D-150%	1.3	0.9	0.6	0.5	0.4
			D-175%	1.3	0.9	0.6	0.5	0.4
			D-200%	1.3	0.9	0.6	0.5	0.4
4	B	2	D-100%	0.8	0.5	0.4	0.3	0.3
			D-125%	0.8	0.5	0.4	0.3	0.3
			D-150%	0.8	0.5	0.4	0.3	0.3
			D-175%	0.8	0.5	0.4	0.3	0.3
			D-200%	0.8	0.5	0.4	0.3	0.3
5	B	3	D-100%	0.5	0.3	0.3	0.2	0.2
			D-125%	0.5	0.3	0.3	0.2	0.2
			D-150%	0.5	0.3	0.3	0.2	0.2
			D-175%	0.5	0.3	0.3	0.2	0.2
			D-200%	0.5	0.3	0.3	0.2	0.2
6	B	4	D-100%	0.3	0.2	0.2	0.1	0.1
			D-125%	0.3	0.2	0.2	0.1	0.1
			D-150%	0.3	0.2	0.2	0.1	0.1
			D-175%	0.3	0.2	0.2	0.1	0.1
			D-200%	0.3	0.2	0.2	0.1	0.1

Tranche A-1 Average Life

EXHIBIT 16.45 Data Display Area: Multiple Tranche Tenor report

```
Sub MTReport_AverageLifeReport()
    Sheets("WALMat").Select
    mTrancheNum = Cells(2, 5).Value
    Call MTReport_ResetChartDataRange
    Call MTReport_UpdateTenorChartTitle(AVERAGE_LIFE)
End Sub
```

EXHIBIT 16.46 "MTReport_AverageLifeReport" subroutine

this information in a format consistent with that of the Single and Multiple Tranche reports discussed previously.

Deal Fees Report   This report presents the annual total deal fees of the Liabilities Structure. The analyst can select up to six scenarios from a Data Schedule Area of up to 25 scenarios of the Case. The cash flows are presented in the Data Display table and an accompanying graph. The report format, the VBA code in the LWM, and the VBA code in the report file are virtually identical to that of any of the Single Tranche Cash Flow reports we discussed ad nausea earlier!

Excess Cash Flows Report   This report and the one following it are very similar in content to any of the Multiple Tranche reports. The analyst selects a single scenario from the Data Schedule Area and a set of multiple cash flows are placed in the Display Area table and graph. There is only a single scenario displayed at a time. In that the data is not tranche specific there is only a single worksheet in the report template file. The report displays the sources and uses of excess cash in any single scenario.

Collateral Cash Flows Report   The Collateral Cash Flows report is provided so that the analyst can present the collateral cash flows of a scenario in a consistent report format as the tranche performance information of the other reports of the LWM package. It is similar to all the Multiple Tranche reports in that a single scenario is selected and graphed. In that this information, like the Excess Cash Flow report discussed immediately above, is *not* tranche-specific, there is a single worksheet in the report workbook.

Liabilities Waterfall Report   The Liabilities Waterfall report produces a report workbook with a single page containing the full copy of the Liabilities Waterfall

```
Sub MTReport_ResetChartDataRange()
    ActiveSheet.ChartObjects("Chart 1").Activate
    Select Case mTrancheNum
        Case Is = 1: ActiveChart.SetSourceData Source:=Range("D5:I10")
        Case Is = 2: ActiveChart.SetSourceData Source:=Range("D11:I16")
        Case Is = 3: ActiveChart.SetSourceData Source:=Range("D17:I22")
        Case Is = 4: ActiveChart.SetSourceData Source:=Range("D23:I28")
        Case Is = 5: ActiveChart.SetSourceData Source:=Range("D29:I34")
        Case Is = 6: ActiveChart.SetSourceData Source:=Range("D39:I44")
    End Select
End Sub
```

EXHIBIT 16.47 "MTReport_ResetChartDataRange" subroutine

Spreadsheet. The report is designed for internal use. It is very helpful for checking new versions of the LWM against other versions when new work has been added. With the full details of the Liabilities Waterfall Spreadsheet available, it is easy to examine the results of model runs in detail. It is also an excellent report for the purposes of creating audit trails and building a corpus of deal-structuring historical information.

OTHER FUNCTIONALITY

Aside from all of the above activities and functionalities of the LWM, there remains one vital capability that we have not yet translated into VBA.

Creating and Saving a Structure Assumptions File

The last capability of the LWM is the ability to create Structural Inputs files from a CommandButton "Create Structure Inputs File" on the Structure worksheet of the model. The analyst enters an output file prefix in the field and clicks the Command-Button. A template file is opened and all the information displayed on the Structure worksheet is copied into a one-page Structure Inputs file that can then be used in the Main Menu of the LWM. The code that performs this task is simple but laborious. See Exhibit 16.48.

The subroutine first calls "WriteStructInputs_ReadWorksheet". This subroutine reads the fields of the Structure Menu into a series of VBA arrays, securing the information for future use. The subroutine next opens a template file, using the Output File Prefix to create the file name. The last step of the process is to

```
Sub WriteStructInputs_Main()

Dim mFileName   As String

    'read the contents of the structure worksheet
    Call WriteStructInputs_ReadWorksheet
    'open the report template file
    Tempfile = "TemplateStructureInputs"
    gStructFNPrefix = Range("StructureFileNamePrefix")
    gStructInputsFileName = "StructInputs"
    mFileName = gStructFNPrefix & gStructInputsFileName
    Workbooks.Open Filename:=LIABSTRUCT_TEMPLATE_SUBDIR & Tempfile
    ActiveWorkbook.SaveAs Filename:=LIABSTRUCT_DATA_SUBDIR & mFileName
    ActiveWorkbook.Save
    'write the contents of the file
    Call WriteStructInputs_WriteStructVariables
    'save and close the report file
    ActiveWorkbook.Save
    ActiveWorkbook.Close

End Sub
```

EXHIBIT 16.48   "WriteStructInputs_Main" subroutine

write the information from the VBA arrays into the template file. The subroutine "WriteStructInputs_WriteStructVariables" performs this task. The Structure Inputs file is now complete. It is saved and closed, ready to be used by the LWM.

ON THE WEB SITE

The following files are on the Web site for Chapter 16.

Web Chapter Blurb "Chapter16_Comments.doc". Chapter comments file.

Model Files "LWM_Chapter16". The final version of the LWM containing all the menus, UserForms, and VBA code described in the chapter.

Data Files The structural inputs for the model are contained in the file "Scen01_StructInputs".

Report Template Files

- "TemplateSTCFAmortBal". Single-tranche annual beginning principal balance schedule template file.
- "TemplateSTCFCoupPmts". Single-tranche coupon expense payments template file.
- "TemplateSTCFLosses". Single-tranche losses to B class tranches template file.
- "TemplateSTCFPrinPmts". Single-tranche principal retirement of note balances template file.
- "TemplateSTTenor". Single-tranche tenor performance statistics template file.
- "TemplateSTYield". Single-tranche yield/coverage/losses template file.
- "TemplateMTCFs". Multiple-tranche cash flows template file.
- "TemplateMTTenor". Multiple-tranche tenor performance statistics template file.
- "TemplateMTYield". Multiple-tranche yield, coverage ratio, and severity of loss performance statistics template file.
- "TemplateMiscCollatCFs". Miscellaneous collateral cash flows template file.
- "TemplateMiscExcessCash". Miscellaneous sources and uses of excess cash report template file.
- "TemplateMiscFees". Deal fees report template file.
- "TemplateWaterfall". Miscellaneous Liabilities Waterfall Spreadsheet report template file.

Other "TemplateStructureInputs". Structural Inputs report template file.

Access, PowerPoint, and Outlook

Chapter 17: Access: An Introduction

This chapter will introduce you to the Access database product. We will learn how to open and save an Access database. We will learn how to create tables within the database, link the database to Excel/VBA and import data from that source. Once the data is within the Access database, we will learn how to write and perform queries against the contents of the tables. We will learn to report the results of the queries. We will build a sample Asset Stratification report using these techniques.

Chapter 18: Implementing Access in the CCFG and the LWM

In this chapter we will implement various Access activities throughout the Collateral Cash Flow Generator (CCFG) and the Liabilities Waterfall Model (LWM).

In the CCFG we will employ Access to:

- Perform the initial data screening process.
- Perform and report the results of the collateral selection for demographic, financial, and geographic items.
- Store the prepayment/default scenario cash flow generation results.

In the LWM we will employ Access to store the performance results of the various note classes.

Chapter 19: Implementing PowerPoint and Outlook in the CCFG

In this chapter we will learn to create PowerPoint presentations using VBA subroutines from within the CCFG. We then create a series of subroutines that will alert various parties via Outlook of the preparation of the reports and distribute copies of the report to selected individuals.

## CHAPTER 17

Access: An Introduction

OVERVIEW

In this chapter we introduce you to Microsoft Access. As we will see in later chapters, certain model functions currently implemented in Excel/VBA are much more easily addressed by the use of Access. As the models are currently implemented, we spend a considerable amount of effort setting up the file structure directories. We do this to make sure that the Excel and crucial to our modeling effort are kept organized and that data integrity is maintained. This type of task is handled easily and intuitively in Access. In this respect, Access can be thought of as a file management system that deals entirely with data.

We begin the chapter by giving a brief overview of what Access is and what kind of tasks it is built to accomplish. We will learn how to open the Access product, how to create a database, import data into the database, build queries to retrieve that data, and finally how to perform calculations and write reports to Excel from the results. In the course of these exercises you will gain a firm foundation in the basic commands and structure of Access. To reinforce the above principals and activities together, this chapter concludes with a production of a simple collateral stratification report. In this example, we will produce the report and read it into an Excel workbook via VBA.

Again, the purpose of this chapter is to teach you the critical concepts, commands, and tools to make your life easier by using Access in the model.

The use of Access will increase the capabilities of our models, simplify their structure, result in more economical code, reduce the complexity of the structural environment needed to support the models, and last but not least make it much easier to maintain and expand the models in the future. In this chapter you will learn a new "language," the language of Access. Beyond the mechanical aspects of Access, we will, more importantly, attempt to impart to you a new way of thinking about how to address data issues in general.

All models are driven by data. Access is a powerful tool, the capabilities of which we only scratch the surface of in this chapter and in the examples in the following chapters. As you use the concepts and techniques you will learn in this book, we hope you see their substantial value. We strongly encourage the interested reader to pick up a book dedicated to Access to learn more!

DELIVERABLES

The general knowledge deliverable in this chapter are:

- What the Access product is and what it is designed to do
- The fundamental objects in Access and how they interact with each other
- The advantages Access offers the modeler as compared to the use of Excel/VBA alone
- How easily the power and flexibility of Access can be expanded through the development of Excel-based VBA code modules

The specific Access knowledge deliverables in this chapter are:

- How to open the Access product
- The structure of Access databases, tables, fields, records, and values
- Seven basic objects of Access: tables, queries, forms, reports, pages, macros, and modules
- How to import data into Access
- How to organize the tables within Access
- How to construct queries to retrieve data from a database
- How to build VBA modules in Excel that interact with Access

UNDER CONSTRUCTION

None of the Access code that we will write in this chapter will become part of either the Collateral Cash Flow Generator (CCFG) or the Liabilities Waterfall Model (LWM). The examples of this chapter will be included in the Web site material for this chapter. On the Web site you will find a working example of the simple Access database coupled with an Excel files that will demonstrate the functionality described later in this chapter. Pay close attention to these examples. They are broadly representative of those that we will later build into both of the models. The basic examples you will see here, with some slight modifications, will be used over and over to move data both in the form of model input information and output results.

BASICS OF ACCESS

Microsoft Access is a relational database management system (RDBMS). The program allows the user to easily create and manage a database. The data in an Access database are organized in an intuitive hierarchy of four levels. These four levels, their descriptions, and an example of each based on the work we do later in the chapter are shown in Exhibit 17.1.

The table object is the structure that contains the organized data of the database. Each database may be comprised of many tables. Each row of the table contains a record, which stores the values for each field of the record. A field is a column in the table that contains the same data information across all of the records of the table.

Level	Description	Example
Database File	The file which houses the data, queries, reports, etc. that allow the user to store and interact with data	A file containing a loan tape and queries that pull information from the tape for presentation and analysis
Table	Object which contains multiple records of related data of multiple types	Loan tape which holds the loan number, balance, interest rate, etc. for multiple borrowers (records).
Field	One column of a table containing data of one type	In our loan tape example loan balance is an example of a field. Each loan (record) will have a balance.
Value	A data point stored in a field of a record in a table	The loan balance corresponding to a single borrower stored in the loan tape

EXHIBIT 17.1 Access data hierarchy

A value is the contents of a single field in a single record. These relationships will become clearer later on in the chapter when we create our own database and tables from scratch.

Access Objects

In Access there are seven types of objects. These objects and their uses are as follows:

1. **Tables.** Store data for use by other objects.
2. **Queries.** Used to return results based on user-supplied criteria; perform computations on data; delete, modify, or append data to a table.
3. **Forms.** Allow for a convenient interface between the user and the data. Used with queries to return formatted data to a form or to add/remove data from a table.
4. **Reports.** Allow the user a way to present data from multiple tables/queries in formatted results.
5. **Pages.** Allow the user to easily publish data to the Web.
6. **Macros.** Used to automate simple tasks (e.g., automatically updating a table or performing data validation).
7. **Modules.** Contain VBA code that can be used to complete tasks and operations within the database or elsewhere in the user's environment (just like Excel-based VBA).

For the purposes of this chapter we will be working almost entirely with simple Access table and query objects. In our finished CCFG and LWM models we will be using Excel/VBA for the computations and reporting based on data housed within Access. Therefore, we will not be spending any time building reports with Access.

At the moment there is no need to publish any of the model results to the Web. We can, however, imagine a situation where we may want to make selected information about our deals available to the general investor community. Such information might consist of updated collateral portfolio data; estimates of the current prepayment, default, and recovery assumptions; or life-to-date performance statistics of the Liabilities Structure of the deal in general.

It is possible to have VBA code modules that reside in the Access database and that perform many of the tasks we are achieving with Excel/VBA modules now. Later in the chapter we will use Excel/VBA code that queries the database and returns the results to an Excel spreadsheet. Alternatively, however, we could just as easily write code in an Access module which writes that data to Excel.

Getting Started With Access

Each of the following sections of this chapter will familiarize you with the fundamental concepts and operations of Access. You will also be taught how to utilize the capabilities of Access to enhance the efficiency, speed, and power of Excel/VBA applications.

The chapter sections will cover the following topics:

- How to open Access and create a new Access file
- The structure and use of Access tables
- How to import data, either by a "Cut and Paste" method or direct import from an Excel table in a workbook
- How to build Access queries to operate on and retrieve data from the database tables you have created and populated
- How to link data across multiple tables and queries
- How to perform numerical operations on the contents of the Access database. Such operations include totaling fields, taking averages, and the like
- How to retrieve query results from Access and import these results into an Excel workbook using VBA

    With that said, let's go!

OPENING ACCESS AND CREATING A DATABASE

In this section we will introduce you to the Access Welcome Screen and show you how to create and save a simple database.

Access Welcome Screen

The first thing we see when we open Access 2007 is the *Getting Started with Microsoft Access* Welcome Screen. See Exhibit 17.2.

The right panel of the Welcome Screen contains a list of recently used databases that you can open directly simply by clicking on them. Access shares this feature with both Excel and Word. A considerable amount of work has been done to make Access 2007 more accessible to the first-time or casual user. In this regard, the Welcome Screen shown in Exhibit 17.2 is heavily populated with an array of database template symbols.

EXHIBIT 17.2 Access Welcome Screen

Creating and Saving a Database

We will not be using any of the Welcome Screen Database templates but instead will start with a blank database by clicking on the "Blank Database" icon in the upper-left corner of the main pane on the Welcome Screen. After choosing the "Blank Database" option, the right panel gives us the option of naming and saving our database. Prior to the release of Access 2007, the file format for Access files was an "mdb" file. With Access 2007, the new standard is the "accdb" file format. Although we are not going to address the various changes that accompany the new file format, we see in Exhibit 17.3 that we are adhering to the new standard.

After saving the database file, we get our first look at an Access database! By default, Access has already constructed our new database by creating a blank table

Blank Database

Create a Microsoft Office Access database that does not contain any existing data or objects.

File Name:

LoanPortfolioExample.accdb

C:\VBA_Book2\ABS\Mort\Training\Access\

[Create]   [Cancel]

EXHIBIT 17.3 Naming and saving "LoanPortfolioExample.accdb"

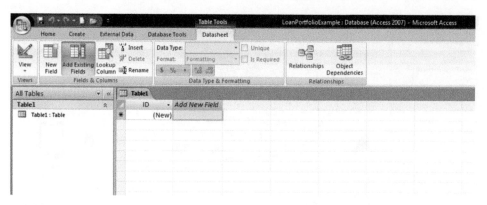

EXHIBIT 17.4   Blank Database with Table1 created

called "Table1". We can examine this new table both in the Navigation Pane region of the screen on the left-hand side of the window and also in the Main Area to the right. See Exhibit 17.4.

The Navigation Pane is the portion of the screen where we will be able to see all of the objects that we have created in our database. Here we will see a listing of all the tables, queries, macros, modules, reports, and other objects of the project. We will use this window in the same manner that we use the "Project Explorer" window in Excel/VBA to navigate among the Excel spreadsheets, VBA modules, and UserForms that comprise our model files. We now also see the Access ribbon immediately above the Navigation Pane and the Main Area. It is this portion of the screen that contains all of the options pertaining to our database. From the ribbon we are able to create and modify objects, retrieve data from other sources, set Access options, and much, much more.

ACCESS TABLES

The main organization unit of a database is its tables. These tables contain the rows (records) and columns (fields) that hold the data of our project. A database may be comprised of a single table or a collection of tables. Let us now look at how we design a table and populate it with data.

Table Design View

There are a variety of methods to view objects in an Access database. In Exhibit 17.4, our newly created "Table1" is opened in what is called "Datasheet View". In this view we are able to add fields and data to "Table1" directly simply by clicking on "Add New Field" and filling in the field values. In some cases you may find that you need to open an Access database and immediately start entering data into it. Far more likely are circumstances in which you have had some time to plan ahead and enter the database creation process more deliberately. In these circumstances you will have time to consider how many fields you will need, a reasonable estimate of how many records the database will probably consist of, and the form of the values

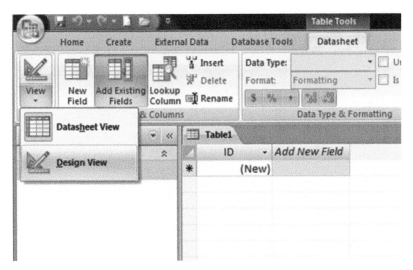

EXHIBIT 17.5 Switch to Design View

in each of the fields. You will have the luxury of planning and forethought. With the essentials of the plan in mind, you will want to build most if not all of the structure (architecture) of the database before *any* of the data is moved into it. Access provides us with a feature called the "Design View" to facilitate this process. See Exhibit 17.5.

Upon entering the Design View, one of the options we are given is the ability to name the currently selected table of the database. In that we have just created the Database, we only have a single table. We will call our first table "tbl_TermRange". Note the use of the prefix "tbl_". We have used prefixes before to designate components of the UserForms we developed for the various menus of the CCFG. As in the case of UserForms, it is important to adopt a naming convention early on in the development of your database and its component objects. As the database is developed and becomes more complex, adherence to a naming convention will make the relationships and interdependencies among the objects of the database clearer and more identifiable. We are lucky to have a fair amount of latitude in this regard as Access does not impose many restrictions on the names of objects. It is therefore possible to have both a report object and a table object with the same name. The lack of naming restrictions can work against us if we are not careful. As a database grows in complexity, a rigorous and clear naming convention is essential. A typical convention is to preface the object name with the object type, such as we did with the table above, "tbl_TermRange". Similarly, query object names are prefaced with "qry_", form object names with "frm_", report object names with "rpt_", and so on. Once we have named our table, we are brought into Design View. See Exhibit 17.6.

The Design View screen is divided into two separate areas:

1. The Field Entry Pane on the top portion of the screen allows us to create new fields and edit existing ones. The Field Name and Data Type are required inputs for any new fields in the table.
2. The Field Properties Pane on the bottom portion of the screen allows you to set the properties of the fields created above.

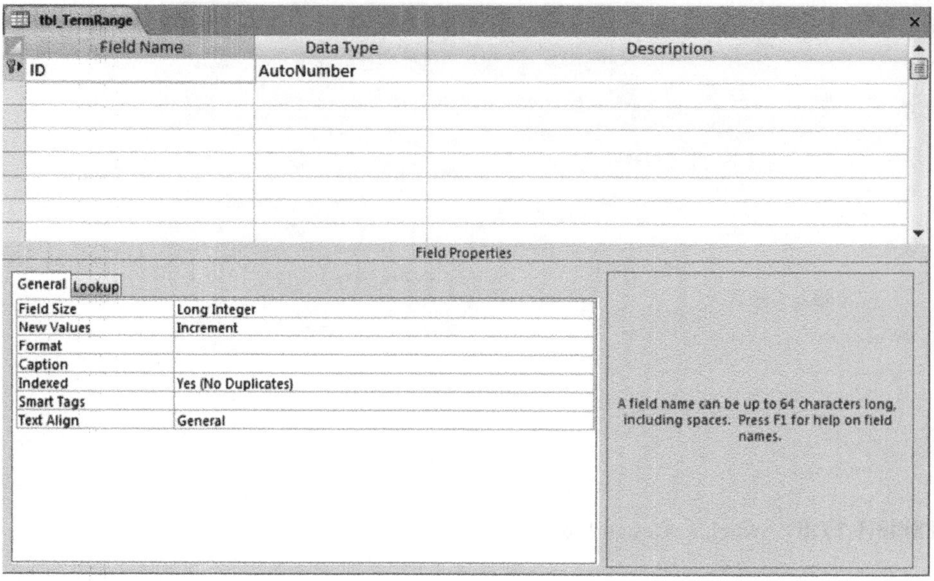

EXHIBIT 17.6   First look at Design View

The Field Properties Pane is broken down into two tabs, General and Lookup. The General tab is where we can edit the display, validation, and structural properties of a field. For example, we could set a field to display as a percentage, give it a default value of 100%, and require the values to be in the range of 0% to 100%. The Lookup tab is for setting up a ListBox or a ComboBox for a field and populating or restricting this field by other lists (tables or queries) in the database.

Adding Data Fields to the Table

We see in Exhibit 17.6 that Access has already automatically created a field called "ID" with Data Type "AutoNumber". You will also notice that there is a key symbol immediately to the left of the "ID" field that signifies that this field is the *primary key* for the table. By designating a field as the primary key for a table, we make an assertion about that field's uniqueness and its necessity. The primary key is the required unique record identifier for a table. Entries in the primary key field, when set, must be present and unique. It is possible to create a table without a primary key, and although this is sometimes not recommended, we will see later there are many situations where this approach is warranted. In that the primary key *is* a unique identifier, the primary key is often the field that is used to link multiple tables to each other. In an Access database containing information on a pool of residential mortgages, we may have over 50 data fields. Some of the fields relate to the type and financial conditions of the mortgage, others to the creditworthiness of the borrowers, some to the demographic information of the property, while the last may relate to the future performance assumptions of the loans in the pools. It may be to our advantage (to make the scope and contents of the mortgage pool data more clear) to treat this information as a set of four separate collections of data. A more likely situation is that

tbl_TermRange	
Field Name	Data Type
ID	Number
LowerBound(>)	Number
UpperBound(<=)	Number

EXHIBIT 17.7   "tbl_TermRange" with fields added

we will have received the data in a series of files. How do we establish a common link between them? If each of these tables has a field representing account numbers of the borrowers and these fields are all designated as primary keys of their tables, we can be sure we are getting a complete and consistent data set when linking these tables based on their primary keys. We therefore have a "fingerprint" that can be used to identify and associate the records of a particular table with records in another table containing the identical account numbers in the corresponding account number field. Thus any number of tables could be linked by the account number, which serves as a unique identifier for each loan and is therefore the natural primary key for all of the tables in this example.

For the table "tbl_TermRange", the table we are currently editing, we will keep the "ID" field as the primary key. The purpose of this table will be to provide upper and lower bounds by which to group data. We will ultimately be interested in grouping mortgage loans by the original and remaining term fields. This table will facilitate those groupings by establishing lower and upper bounds for each "bucket." We will now add two other fields to the table. We will name the first field "LowerBound(>)" and the second field "UpperBound(<=)". Since we know what the contents of these fields will be (we will be entering all these numbers ourselves), we will also confidently change the Data Type of our primary key, the "ID" field, to Number as well. The table in Design View should now look like Exhibit 17.7.

Each of the three fields we have created the "ID", "LowerBound(>)", and "UpperBound(<=)" field—will contain the same integer data. Also, because we will be entering values into this table only once and it is essentially a reference table, we need not take pains to set field properties, such as default values or validations. The properties for the newly added fields in the simple table "tbl_TermRange" are identical and are set as in Exhibit 17.8.

We are now ready to switch the view back to Datasheet View and begin adding values into the records of the "tbl_TermRange" table. We do this by again clicking on the View option on the left side of the Access ribbon. As in all of the Microsoft products, Access will ask if we want to save the changes we have made to the table before moving back to the Datasheet View screen. Upon reentering the Datasheet View screen, the "tbl_TermRange" table should now look like Exhibit 17.9.

GETTING THE DATA IN: ENTERING DATA

We have now opened the Access product, created a table named "tbl_TermRange", designated a field as the primary key for the table, added two additional fields, and described the field properties. We are now ready to begin the data entry phase.

General	Lookup	
Field Size	Long Integer	
Format		
Decimal Places	Auto	
Input Mask		
Caption		
Default Value		
Validation Rule		
Validation Text		
Required	No	
Indexed	No	
Smart Tags		
Text Align	General	

EXHIBIT 17.8   Properties of Upper Bound and Lower Bound Fields

In this phase we will populate two different tables in the database. The first table will consist of a set of term ranges. This is the table that we created in the previous section. We will populate this table by using the first of the data entry methods, "Cut and Paste". Next we will create a table for the collateral loan data called "tbl_DataTape".

Using what we have learned above, we will designate a primary key for the "tbl_DataTape" table. In a later section, after creating a table for the performance properties of each loan in the portfolio, we will join this table to the collateral loan table using their primary keys. Next we will build queries and run these queries against the joined tables in the database. Last we will create the Stratification report from the information returned from the queries and our project will be complete!

Cutting and Pasting Data

Now that we have the initial table of the database, "tbl_TermRange", established, we can begin entering data in it. We have designed this table to contain a collection of ranges through which we are going to sort the original and remaining terms of the mortgages in the pool. This set of term ranges will be the primary criteria we will use to stratify the loan data. In our sample project we have chosen to stratify the contents of the report at yearly intervals. Instead of entering the information describing the stratification groupings one range at a time, we will first create them in an Excel worksheet and then copy them into the "tbl_TermRange" table. We now leave Access for the moment, open a new window, and call up Excel. Exhibit 17.10

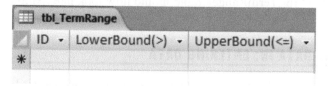

EXHIBIT 17.9   "tbl_TermRange" in Datasheet View

	A	B	C	D
1				
2		**Increment**	12	
3				
4		ID	LowerBound(>)	UpperBound(<=)
5		0	=($B5-1)*$C$2	=($B5)*$C$2
6		1	=($B6-1)*$C$2	=($B6)*$C$2
7		2		
8		3		
9		4		
10		5		
11		6		
12		7		
13		8		
14		9		
15		10		

EXHIBIT 17.10   Building the inputs to "tbl_TermRange" in Excel

shows the simple Excel spreadsheet and formulas we will use to build the table of term ranges.

We already know that the longest-term mortgages in the pool have an original term of 30 years. We must therefore create a set of 31 paired lower/upper bound range limits (one pair needed to include 0 in the ranges). By copying the formulas down to the row containing ID 30, we will generate the pairings we need. The final entry for the lower/upper bound pair will then be 348/360. The first eleven pairs of inputs are shown in Exhibit 17.11.

	A	B	C	D
1				
2		**Increment**	12	
3				
4		ID	LowerBound(>)	UpperBound(<=)
5		0	-12	0
6		1	0	12
7		2	12	24
8		3	24	36
9		4	36	48
10		5	48	60
11		6	60	72
12		7	72	84
13		8	84	96
14		9	96	108
15		10	108	120

EXHIBIT 17.11   Finished inputs for "tbl_TermRange" in Excel

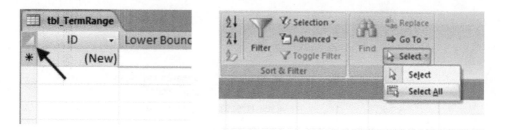

EXHIBIT 17.12   Selecting entire "tbl_TermRange" table in Access

In Excel we now select this table of values from the worksheet and copy it to the Excel clipboard using the "Copy" command. We are interested only in the values of the Excel table, as those are the only inputs we wish to enter into the receiving Access "tbl_TermRange" table. Make sure, therefore, to select only the range values and *not* the field headers when performing the copy. With the contents of the table now in the clipboard, we now switch back to Access. Back in Access, we immediately select the whole "tbl_TermRange" table by clicking on the upper-left corner of the table or by choosing the "Select All" Command from the menu ribbon. See Exhibit 17.12. We now paste the contents of the clipboard into the "tbl_TermRange" table using the "Paste" command of "Ctrl + v".

When we issue the "Paste" command, Access asks us to make sure that we would like to paste 31 records. After answering "Yes", we see that the values of the Excel worksheet are now populating the "tbl_TermRange" table. See Exhibit 17.13. After confirming the table to be accurate and complete, we immediately save the Excel workbook we created as "TermRangeExample.xlsx".

Importing Data from Excel

Our next task is to populate the second Access table, the one that will contain the collateral data information. Here, because of the size of the data set to be entered, we will choose a different method of populating an Access table.

In this approach we will import data directly from an Excel workbook. This data will populate a table named "tbl_DataTape". We will use the term pairs we generated and placed in "tbl_TermRange" and the information we will shortly load into "tbl_DataTape" to produce the stratification report. Exhibit 17.14 shows the 9 data items of the first 25 loans of the pool. This data is in an Excel workbook and has been saved as "LoanPortfolioWorkbook.xlsx".

We will begin the process from Access. First select the "External Data" tab from the menu ribbon. Once in this tab, choose the Excel option with the arrow pointing into it, signifying an import. See Exhibit 17.15.

Steps of Import Process   There are five steps in the process of importing data from an Excel file to an Access Database:

1. Selection of the Excel file containing the data
2. Selection of the specific information from the Excel file

ID	LowerBound(>)	UpperBound(<=)
0	-12	0
1	0	12
2	12	24
3	24	36
4	36	48
5	48	60
6	60	72
7	72	84
8	84	96
9	96	108
10	108	120
11	120	132
12	132	144
13	144	156
14	156	168
15	168	180
16	180	192
17	192	204
18	204	216
19	216	228
20	228	240
21	240	252
22	252	264
23	264	276
24	276	288
25	288	300
26	300	312
27	312	324
28	324	336
29	336	348
30	348	360

EXHIBIT 17.13 Finished Access table "tbl_TermRange"

3. Setting the Data Field properties in the Access table
4. Designation of the Primary Key Field in the Access table
5. Renaming the newly created Access table

Step 1: Selecting the Excel File Access contains a feature called the "Import Spreadsheet Wizard" that opens up to walk us through the data import process. The first step is to identify to Access the target Excel workbook that contains the data—in our case, "LoanPortfolioWorkbook.xlsx". Below the field in which we specify the Excel file pathway, we are presented with three options on how we will store this data in our database. These are:

1. Create a new table for the data.
2. Append the data to a preexisting table.
3. Link an Excel table to our database.

	A	B	C	D	E	F	G	H	I
1	LoanNumber	OrigBalance	CurBalance	InterestRate	OrigTerm	RemTerm	Season	Payment	State
2	1	38,500	37,877	8.350%	120	117	3	474.26	CT
3	2	63,600	63,516	6.600%	300	299	1	433.41	CT
4	3	15,000	14,939	8.820%	360	353	7	118.76	CA
5	4	73,000	70,904	7.330%	120	115	5	860.06	AZ
6	5	212,800	201,391	6.860%	120	111	9	2,455.46	OR
7	6	58,000	57,690	7.990%	300	295	5	447.27	SC
8	7	341,600	338,737	8.920%	300	291	9	2,848.00	FL
9	8	33,000	32,423	7.090%	240	231	9	257.63	CA
10	9	65,000	64,644	7.940%	120	119	1	786.57	NJ
11	10	56,800	56,252	6.840%	180	177	3	505.47	GA
12	11	46,400	45,937	6.180%	300	293	7	304.08	MD
13	12	64,800	64,671	6.670%	240	239	1	489.64	MA
14	13	44,800	44,552	7.790%	120	119	1	538.59	GA
15	14	96,000	93,267	7.490%	120	115	5	1,139.04	IL
16	15	64,800	63,628	6.320%	120	117	3	729.87	NM
17	16	88,800	88,111	8.830%	240	235	5	789.27	VA
18	17	61,600	60,926	8.840%	240	233	7	547.91	NY
19	18	31,800	30,847	6.530%	120	115	5	361.57	NY
20	19	44,800	44,245	6.440%	300	291	9	300.82	CA
21	20	43,400	42,757	8.470%	240	231	9	375.81	TX
22	21	568,400	564,499	6.160%	360	353	7	3,466.53	IN
23	22	56,000	55,922	6.210%	300	299	1	368.03	MO
24	23	61,200	60,986	7.870%	360	355	5	443.53	KY
25	24	75,600	75,527	6.160%	360	359	1	461.07	PA
26	25	76,800	76,586	8.410%	180	179	1	752.23	MN

EXHIBIT 17.14   Partial loan information from "LoanPortfolioWorkbook.xlsx"

We will select the first option. See Exhibit 17.16.

Step 2: Selection of the Data   After clicking "OK", we see that Access does a fine job figuring out which portion of the workbook we are trying to import, at least when the workbook is as simple as the one we are looking at. If the workbook had multiple sheets and/or multiple tables per sheet, we would have to navigate to the table of interest. A useful feature, but one that we will not use with this file, is Access's ability to select target data to import by named Ranges in the workbook. In our case we see the screen shown in Exhibit 17.17 with the "First Row Contains Column Headings" box already checked.

Step 3: Setting the Data Field Properties   In Step 3 we are given the options of renaming any of the data fields, changing the data type of the field, or ignoring the

EXHIBIT 17.15   "Import Data from Excel" option in Access

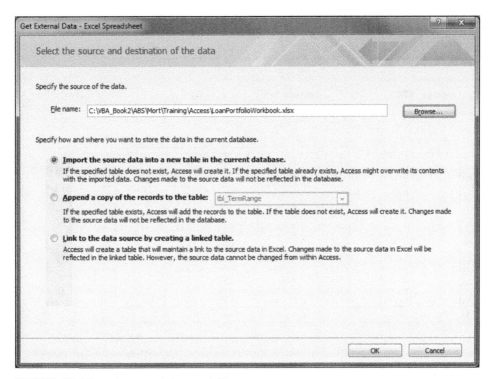

EXHIBIT 17.16 Selection of the Excel file

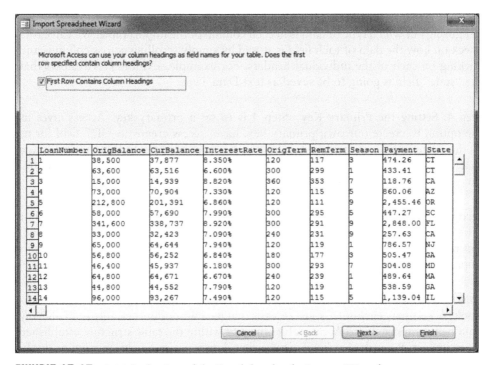

EXHIBIT 17.17 Initial selection of the Excel data by the Import Wizard

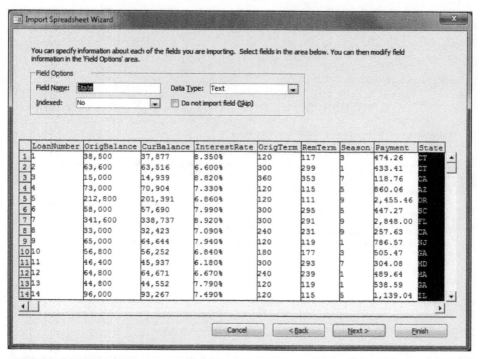

EXHIBIT 17.18   Setting field properties for import data

field altogether in the import. Once again, Access has already done most of the work in figuring out which type of data is in each column of the import table. We can easily check on how the data of each field is stored by simply scrolling across columns and clicking on each of the individual headers. For example, Exhibit 17.18 shows that the "state" field is going to be saved as text Data Type.

Step 4: Setting the Primary Key   Step 4 is to set a primary key. Access gives us the option to create our own primary key, have Access create an "ID" field for us as the primary key, or create a table without a primary key. In this case we know that the "LoanNumber" field is a unique, required identifier for each record, and therefore we should choose this field as our primary key. See Exhibit 17.19.

Step 5: Renaming the New Table   In Step 5 we are given the option to rename our table. To stay consistent with our aforementioned naming convention, we will call this table "tbl_DataTape". We are now ready click the "Finish" button and view our imported data. See Exhibit 17.20.

Import Errors   When importing data from external sources, such as an Excel workbook, Access may encounter some records that it cannot import cleanly or at all. Any data being imported into Access tables must fit within the table structure established upon import. Records that have inconsistent data types in a field, missing or duplicate values in the primary key field, or an inconsistent number of fields for a given

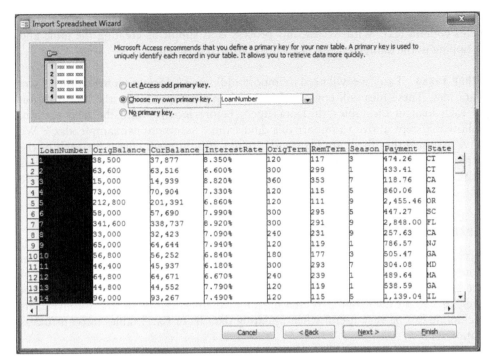

EXHIBIT 17.19 Designation of a primary key

record will produce an error. Any import errors will be written into another table in Access that contains one record for every record that had an error during import, along with an explanation of what the error was. All errors should be investigated in the data source and fixed before re-importing the data to Access.

The import process highlights one of the great advantages of sourcing data out of Access as opposed to Excel: Access has a built-in scrubbing process. With Excel, we would need to do some analysis on the data to make sure that all the account

LoanNumber	OrigBalance	CurBalance	InterestRate	OrigTerm	RemTerm	Season	Payment	State
1	38,500	37,877	8.350%	120	117	3	474.26	CT
2	63,600	63,516	6.600%	300	299	1	433.41	CT
3	15,000	14,939	8.820%	360	353	7	118.76	CA
4	73,000	70,904	7.330%	120	115	5	860.06	AZ
5	212,800	201,391	6.860%	120	111	9	2,455.46	OR
6	58,000	57,690	7.990%	300	295	5	447.27	SC
7	341,600	338,737	8.920%	300	291	9	2,848.00	FL
8	33,000	32,423	7.090%	240	231	9	257.63	CA
9	65,000	64,644	7.940%	120	119	1	786.57	NJ
10	56,800	56,252	6.840%	180	177	3	505.47	GA
11	46,400	45,937	6.180%	300	293	7	304.08	MD
12	64,800	64,671	6.670%	240	239	1	489.64	MA
13	44,800	44,552	7.790%	120	119	1	538.59	GA
14	96,000	93,267	7.490%	120	115	5	1,139.04	IL
15	64,800	63,628	6.320%	120	117	3	729.87	NM

EXHIBIT 17.20 "tbl_DataTape" in Access

numbers were unique and available, all numeric fields contain numbers, and all text fields contain text. With Access, this process is as simple as creating the table and dropping in the data; Access will ensure consistency of data.

Other Tasks Later we will need to import additional information from other Excel data files. These files will contain the modeling assumptions for the amortization of each loan in the table "tbl_DataTape". Before moving onto the next section, follow the steps above to import this data from "AssumptionsExample.xlsx". We have assumed that there are between 150 and 200 different curves for each of the three modeling assumptions (i.e., default, prepay, and recovery). Save this table as "tbl_Assumptions" with the "LoanNumber" field as the primary key. If you have any difficulty, these files and the database can be found on the Web site.

Linking Access and Excel Tables

Access also allows us the option of linking an Excel table to an Access database. In doing so, the data in the linked Access table would reflect any changes that occur in the Excel workbook. To do this, follow the same steps above, making sure to select the "Link to the data source by creating a linked table" option in Step 1 above. This technique can be very useful when updating data from Excel tables into an Access database.

GETTING THE DATA BACK OUT: QUERIES

Now that we have an Access database containing tables, we are able to begin developing and using queries to summarize, select, and manipulate the data.

Basic Query Commands

As the name implies, a query can be thought of as a question posed to a database requesting information about the data stored within it. A simple query may return a set of records in a data set that meet a single criterion. More elaborate queries can select across multiple data fields within multiple tables and other queries and even test computed quantities derived from several fields of a record. For example, we could be interested in seeing only the loans in our portfolio that have the geographic location code of CT. Below is a summary of some of the more commonly used types of queries:

- **Select.** Selects data from one or more tables (or other queries) that fit specific criteria. These are typically used to summarize and filter data.
- **Total.** Runs computations on records and presents the results of these computations as another field in the record. These Access functions mirror the commonly used Excel functions (e.g., sums, conditionals, financial calculations).
- **Action.** These queries allow the user to create new tables, append data, delete data, or update data in a table.
- **Crosstab.** Used more to present data in a specified format. This option is similar in appearance to pivot tables in Excel.

EXHIBIT 17.21   New query with "Show Table" window open

Creating a Query and Adding a Table

Back in our "LoanPortfolioExample" Database, we can select the "Query Design" option from the "Create" tab on the Access ribbon. Access then creates a query and brings up the "Show Table" window. See Exhibit 17.21.

From the "Show Table" window, we are able to select which tables and, eventually, which queries we are going to use to construct the present query. Select table "tbl_DataTape", add it to the query, then close the "Show Table" window.

Access's default query view is called the Query Builder and uses Query by Example (QBE). The idea behind QBE is to create an intuitive and flexible interface by which users can create and edit queries in Access. On the left side of the lower portion of Query Builder, we see the six main QBE options:

1. **Field.** Allows the user to select the fields from the tables/queries shown above.
2. **Table.** Shows which table the field comes from.
3. **Sort.** Allows the user to sort the query results by this field. The three options are ascending, descending, and not sorted.
4. **Show.** A toggle that enables the user to show or not show a field in the query results. In this way, a field that is used to join two tables or to perform calculations can be left out of the query results.
5. **Criteria.** Filter the results by different criteria.
6. **Or.** Allows for entering multiple criteria for a field.

Selecting fields to include in the query is as easy as dragging and dropping the field in the Query Builder. See Exhibit 17.22. You can also add an individual field by double-clicking the field name in the table window or by selecting the field from the "Field" drop-down list.

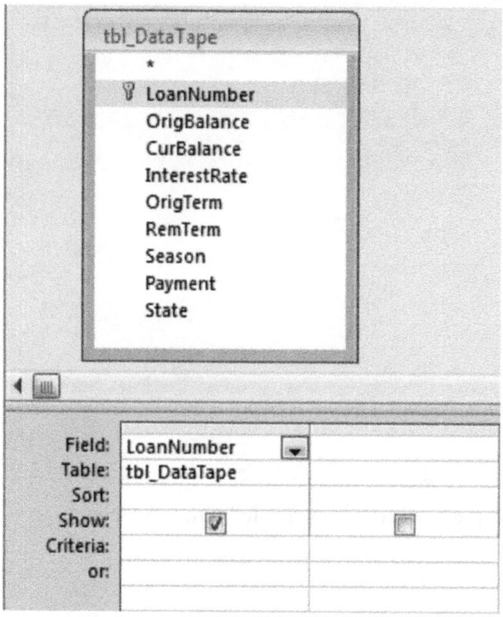

EXHIBIT 17.22   Dragging and dropping a field into the Query Builder

Multiple fields can be selected by holding down the control key while clicking on multiple fields. To select a range of fields from the list, hold down the shift key while clicking on the end points for the range of fields. Additionally, every field from a table can be added to a query by dragging the "*", uppermost in the list, to the Query Builder. To remove a field from the Query Builder, simply click on the top of the column and press the delete key.

Select all the fields from "tbl_DataTape" and drag them down to the Query Builder. Do this individually, not using "*" symbol. We do this so that the names of all of the fields will be displayed and can therefore be operated on individually if need be. Once all the fields have been added to the Query Builder, we can move them around by selecting the field column and dragging the field where we want it to show in the query results. The query we have just constructed is the simplest type of query that selects all records from a table without any filtering or computation.

Running a Query

Once the query has been constructed in the Query Builder, we still need to execute the query to retrieve the results. Click on "Run" (exclamation point!) in the upper-left corner of the Access window to execute the query. The results are shown in Exhibit 17.23.

The records that are returned in the Query View after running the query are identical to the data in the table "tbl_DataTape". This should come as no surprise, seeing that we have not yet filtered the data or applied any computations to it. Before returning to the Query Builder, save this query as "qry_SelectExample" by

LoanNumbe ▾	OrigBalance ▾	CurBalance ▾	InterestRate ▾	OrigTerm ▾	RemTerm ▾	Season ▾	Payment ▾	State ▾
1	38,500	37,877	8.350%	120	117	3	474.26	CT
2	63,600	63,516	6.600%	300	299	1	433.41	CT
3	15,000	14,939	8.820%	360	353	7	118.76	CA
4	73,000	70,904	7.330%	120	115	5	860.06	AZ
5	212,800	201,391	6.860%	120	111	9	2,455.46	OR
6	58,000	57,690	7.990%	300	295	5	447.27	SC
7	341,600	338,737	8.920%	300	291	9	2,848.00	FL
8	33,000	32,423	7.090%	240	231	9	257.63	CA
9	65,000	64,644	7.940%	120	119	1	786.57	NJ
10	56,800	56,252	6.840%	180	177	3	505.47	GA
11	46,400	45,937	6.180%	300	293	7	304.08	MD
12	64,800	64,671	6.670%	240	239	1	489.64	MA
13	44,800	44,552	7.790%	120	119	1	538.59	GA
14	96,000	93,267	7.490%	120	115	5	1,139.04	IL
15	64,800	63,628	6.320%	120	117	3	729.87	NM

EXHIBIT 17.23   Basic Query results

right-clicking on the tab labeled "Query1" at the top of the editor pane and selecting "Save". On the Access ribbon, click on the "Home" tab to change the view back to Design View.

Linking Tables

Our database has two separate tables that contain different information on the same loans, "tbl_Assumptions" and "tbl_DataTape". We would like to be able to view and operate on all of the information in these two tables in a single query. To do so, we need to add "tbl_Assumptions" to "qry_SelectExample". This is done by right-clicking in the empty space in the upper section of the Query Builder and selecting "Show Table". See Exhibit 17.24. Select and add "tbl_Assumptions".

The "LoanNumber" field uniquely identifies each loan in the two tables. We need to link these two tables on their primary key fields that correspond to their respective "LoanNumber" fields. This is accomplished by using a "join". To create a join between these two tables, we will drag the "LoanNumber" field from "tbl_DataTape" onto the "LoanNumber" field in "tbl_Assumptions". See Exhibit 17.25.

Two different join properties can be selected depending on what you are trying to accomplish. To display these properties, right-click on the line joining the two tables and select "Join Properties". See Exhibit 17.26. We see that, as it currently stands, our join will only return records that have matching loan numbers in each table. Records that do not match will be left out completely. This is what is known as an *inner join*. The other type of join is referred to an *outer join*. Outer joins come in two different types: right outer joins and left outer joins. The distinction between the two comes into play later when we discuss Structured Query Language (SQL). The right or left distinction is to show which table in the join shows all the data available for the join field and which shows only results for those records that have a join field match in the other table. From Exhibit 17.26 we see that it is possible to alter this relationship such that all records from one table are returned but only records from the other table that have a matching value in the first are returned.

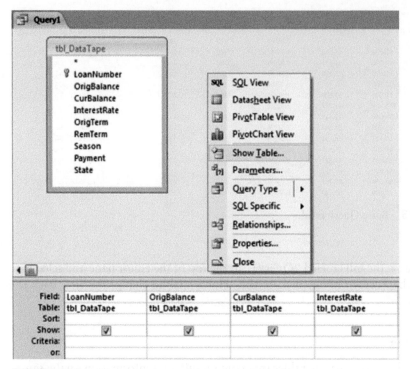

EXHIBIT 17.24 Add "tbl_Assumptions" to "qry_SelectExample"

Now that we have created a linkage between our two tables, we can drag the three modeling assumption fields down from "tbl_Assumptions" and rerun the query. We see that the query view now contains the corresponding fields from "tbl_Assumptions" for each loan in "tbl_DataTape" table. In this query we have pulled together data from two different tables by joining the tables based on a common identifier.

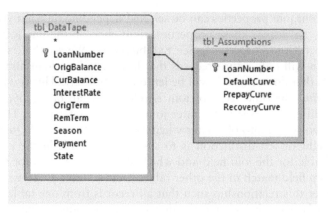

EXHIBIT 17.25 Joining the two tables on the LoanNumber fields

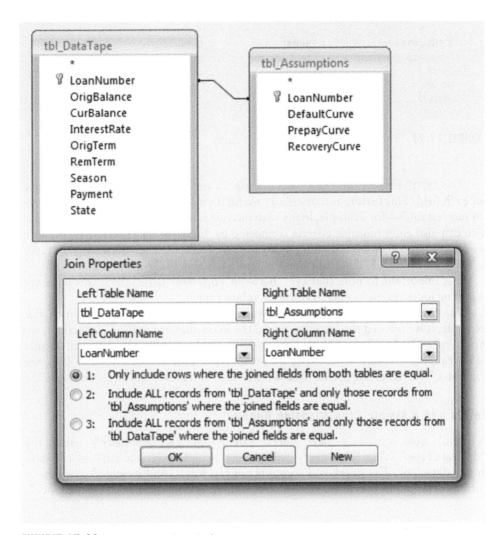

EXHIBIT 17.26   Join Properties window

Adding Criteria to a Select Query

Now that we have the query returning results from our two tables, we want to filter the results to show specific data. To do this, we will enter filtering specifications in the "Criteria" space of the Query Builder. For example, we want to view all the loans on properties in the state of Connecticut. We enter "CT" in the criteria space for the "State" field. See Exhibit 17.27 and rerun the query. The query should return the 99 records that have "CT" in the "State" field.

Let us say that we are primarily interested in high interest rate loans on properties in Connecticut. We can enter ">.085" in the criteria input for the "InterestRate" field. Rerunning this query results in the return of 19 records that are properties based in Connecticut and also have an interest rate greater than 8.5%. A portion of the results are shown in Exhibit 17.28.

Field:	Payment	State	DefaultCurve
Table:	tbl_DataTape	tbl_DataTape	tbl_Assumptions
Sort:			
Show:	✓	✓	✓
Criteria:		"CT"	
or:			

EXHIBIT 17.27   Entering criteria for a field in a query

The "Or:" field in the Query Builder allows the user to enter multiple criteria for each field. This feature is particularly useful if you wanted to set multiple criteria for interest rates—for example, loans with interest rates above 8.5% and below 6%. You can also enter multiple criteria connected by "and" in the criteria bar. Because we are trying to get a bound on interest rates, we could use the "Between" operator as well. See Exhibit 17.29(a) for the first approach and 17.29(b) for the second.

It is important to note that the "Between" operator is inclusive; this is to say that it includes the endpoints in the filter values range.

The "Not" operator is used to filter by the converse of the criteria conditions. For example, if we wanted the query to return the loans that are not in Connecticut, we would type "Not CT" the criteria bar. To select the loans with interest rates outside of the range of 7% to 8% inclusive, we would type "Not Between .07 and .08". See Exhibit 17.30. When we are finished we will save and close "qry_SelectExample".

Totals and a Simple Stratification Query

We will now create a new query called "qry_DataSummary" using the "tbl_DataTape" table. This query will give us a high-level summary of the data in our data tape. The query will compute counts, totals, and weighted averages of various fields in our portfolio. We will first add the "LoanNumber", "OrigBalance",

LoanNumber	OrigBalance	CurBalance	InterestRate	OrigTerm	RemTerm	Season	Payment	State
117	85,200	83,558	8.790%	180	173	7	853.54	CT
569	68,400	67,851	8.950%	180	177	3	691.73	CT
680	257,400	255,419	8.900%	240	235	5	2,299.37	CT
712	55,800	55,536	8.660%	240	237	3	489.91	CT
846	800,100	797,936	8.740%	180	179	1	7,991.86	CT
852	476,100	472,390	8.800%	240	235	5	4,222.55	CT
886	69,300	67,542	8.600%	180	171	9	686.49	CT
911	35,700	35,174	8.520%	240	231	9	310.26	CT
1029	196,100	195,537	8.830%	360	355	5	1,553.94	CT
1217	244,400	244,175	8.800%	300	299	1	2,017.63	CT
1218	130,000	128,244	8.920%	180	175	5	1,312.37	CT
1246	97,500	96,636	8.580%	300	291	9	790.36	CT
1355	138,000	136,850	8.520%	180	177	3	1,360.56	CT
1452	85,200	85,119	8.650%	300	299	1	694.69	CT
1459	466,200	443,401	8.620%	120	111	9	5,810.18	CT
1654	117,000	114,735	8.740%	180	173	7	1,168.66	CT
1677	480,000	462,164	8.920%	120	113	7	6,059.67	CT
1785	290,000	282,861	8.950%	180	171	9	2,932.75	CT
2155	107,800	107,635	8.830%	240	239	1	958.15	CT

EXHIBIT 17.28   Results filtered by state (="CT") and rate (>8.5%)

Field:	CurBalance	InterestRate	OrigTerm
Table:	tbl_DataTape	tbl_DataTape	tbl_DataTape
Sort:			
Show:	✓	✓	✓
Criteria:		> =0.07 And < =0.08	
or:			

(a)

Field:	CurBalance	InterestRate	OrigTerm
Table:	tbl_DataTape	tbl_DataTape	tbl_DataTape
Sort:			
Show:	✓	✓	✓
Criteria:		Between 0.07 And 0.08	
or:			

(b)

EXHIBIT 17.29 Setting multiple criteria for single fields: (a) first approach and (b) second approach

and "CurBalance" fields from "tbl_DataTape" table to the Query Builder. In order to create a high-level summary of the data in the "tbl_DataTape" table, we need to add the "Totals" bar to the Query Builder. This is done by clicking on the "Totals" option under the Design tab. See Exhibit 17.31.

We now see the Totals bar added to the Query Builder below the Table bar. By default, all of the Totals values are set to "Group By". The Group By option controls how the data will be presented after the query has run and which fields computations are calculated across. For example, to sum the balance of Connecticut properties, we set the "State" field as a Group By field. If we click on one of the Totals drop-downs, we will see all of the available options. See Exhibit 17.32. The use of most of these options should be obvious. Here we see a number of familiar Excel-type functions like Sum, Average, Min, Max, and so forth. Two of these options require a brief explanation:

- **Where.** Designates that we plan to add one or more criteria to the fields below.
- **Expression.** In addition to the readily available Totals operations, Access also makes available more complex mathematical, logical, date/time, text, and other functions as well as custom functions that can be used in the same way as inline functions in Excel.

Field:	CurBalance	InterestRate	OrigTerm
Table:	tbl_DataTape	tbl_DataTape	tbl_DataTape
Sort:			
Show:	✓	✓	✓
Criteria:		Not Between 0.07 And 0.08	
or:			

EXHIBIT 17.30 Use of the "Not" operator in a query

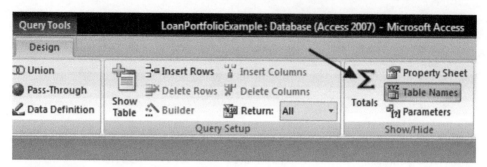

EXHIBIT 17.31   Showing the Totals bar

The first things we will add to the "Totals" query we are building are the "LoanCount", "TotalOrigBalance", and "TotalCurBalance" fields. We will select Count for "LoanNumber" and Sum for both of the balance fields in the Totals bar. We can also enter an alias for each of these fields by entering the desired alias name followed by a colon and the name as it appears in the table/query. The Query Builder will look like Exhibit 17.33. Execute this query to see the results of setting the Totals for these fields. See Exhibit 17.34.

We can also format query results. To do this, return to Design View and click on the "Properties" option next to the Totals option on the Access ribbon to bring up the Properties Sheet. For the two balance totals, choose the "Standard" option under the format bar with two decimals. This change in format immediately clarifies the results of the query Totals. The Property Sheet and the reformatted results are shown in Exhibits 17.35(a) and (b), respectively.

The high-level summary query that we are in the process of constructing will use the total of these balance fields as a component of computing the weighted averages of some of the other fields. To continue adding summary fields to this query, first right-click on one of the fields next to our balances and select the "Build" option. This option will display the "Expression Builder" window where we are able to construct computation expressions for the query. To see all the available functions,

Field:	LoanNumber	OrigBalance
Table:	tbl_DataTape	tbl_DataTape
Total:	Group By ▼	Group By
Sort:	Group By	
Show:	Sum	☑
Criteria:	Avg	
or:	Min	
	Max	
	Count	
	StDev	
	Var	
	First	
	Last	
	Expression	
	Where	

EXHIBIT 17.32   Total options

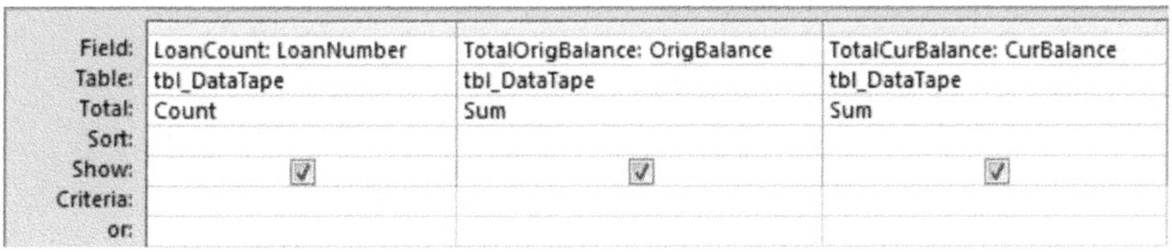

Field:	LoanCount: LoanNumber	TotalOrigBalance: OrigBalance	TotalCurBalance: CurBalance
Table:	tbl_DataTape	tbl_DataTape	tbl_DataTape
Total:	Count	Sum	Sum
Sort:			
Show:	☑	☑	☑
Criteria:			
or:			

EXHIBIT 17.33   Adding loan lount and sum of balances

qry_DataSummary

LoanCount ▾	TotalOrigBalance ▾	TotalCurBalance ▾
2255	552257100	545083059.620001

EXHIBIT 17.34   Results of query for loan count and sum of balances

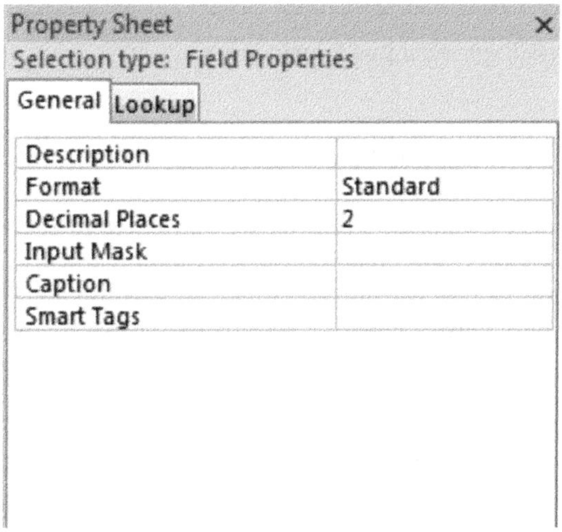

Property Sheet   ✕

Selection type: Field Properties

General | Lookup

Description	
Format	Standard
Decimal Places	2
Input Mask	
Caption	
Smart Tags	

(a)

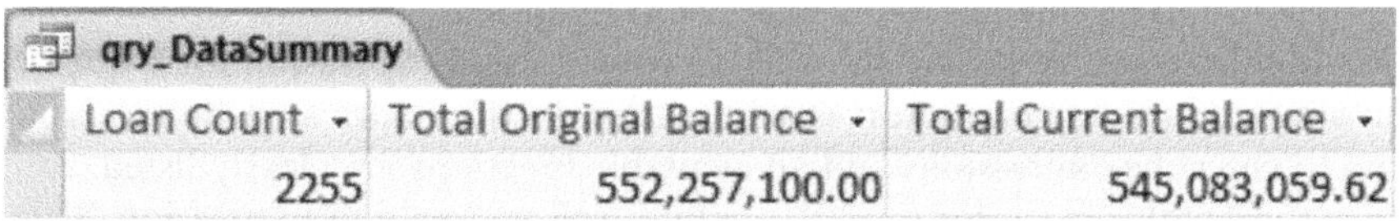

qry_DataSummary

Loan Count ▾	Total Original Balance ▾	Total Current Balance ▾
2255	552,257,100.00	545,083,059.62

(b)

EXHIBIT 17.35   (a) Formatting the query results in the Property Sheet and (b) Formatted query results for "qry_DataSummary"

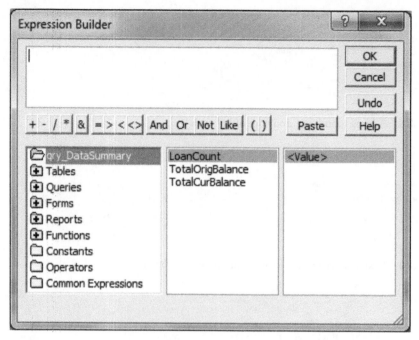

EXHIBIT 17.36   Access Expression Builder window

follow "Functions" → "Built-in Functions" by double-clicking each option. See Exhibit 17.36.

Using the Expression Builder window, we can enter in the formula needed to produce weighted averages. The first weighted average we will compute will be the weighted average interest rate for our portfolio. See Exhibit 17.37.

The formula begins with a block of text to the left of a colon. This text is the alias for the computation results. To the right of the colon is the expression to be evaluated. In our example, the sum of the product of each record's interest rate and current balance is being divided by the sum of the CurBalance field. The numerator is performing the familiar "SUMPRODUCT()" function in Excel. If any of the names of the fields in the expression have embedded spaces, the name must be placed within brackets in the expression.

Click the "OK" button to see the name and expression transfer to the field bar. It is also possible to type changes to the expression right in the field bar. Opening the Expression Builder is not necessary in order to construct an expression for a query, but when you are just starting out, it is a lot easier. In the Expression Builder you have room to enter the expressions and all available functions are clearly listed.

Change the Totals option for our "WAvgInterestRate" field to Expression. This tells the query that we are returning an expression that we have composed in the Expression Builder or in-line at the top of the field. See Exhibit 17.38.

We will now display the Properties Sheet to specify the format for the "WAvgInterestRate" field as a percentage. Executing this query, we now see the weighted average of the interest rate added to the results to the right of the balance totals. See Exhibit 17.39.

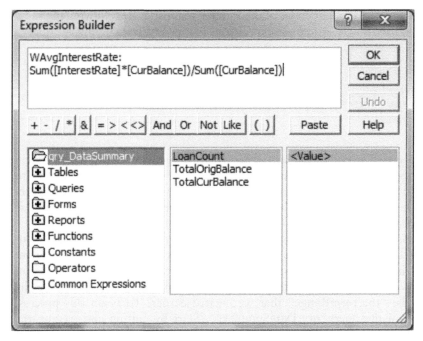

EXHIBIT 17.37 Formula for the "WAvgInterestRate" field entered in Expression Builder

Field:	WAvgInterestRate: Sum([InterestRate]*[CurBalance])/Sum([CurBalance])
Table:	
Total:	Expression
Sort:	
Show:	☑
Criteria:	
or:	

EXHIBIT 17.38 Completed "WAvgInterestRate" field

qry_DataSummary			
LoanCount ▾	TotalOrigBalance ▾	TotalCurBalance ▾	WAvgInterestRate ▾
2255	552,257,100.00	545,083,059.62	7.48%

EXHIBIT 17.39 Query results with "WAvgInterestRate"

We can construct the remainder of the summary statistics by following the same procedures we used above. Add these expressions to the" qry_DataSummary" query:

- WAvgOrigTerm
- WAvgRemTerm
- WAvgSeasoning
- WAvgPayment

These weighted averages express either dollar amounts or months so we will set their formats to "Standard". In this summary there is no meaningful way to summarize the State field, as this is a text field that we cannot weight or aggregate. After the above fields have been added to the query in the same fashion as "WAvgInterestRate", we will save and close"qry_DataSummary" query.

At this point, the "qry_DataSummary" query contains the most basic summary statistics for the loans in our collateral pool. As a next step we may want to see how these statistics are distributed across more specific groupings. As an example, let us produce a stratification report based on original balance using the contents of the "tbl_TermRange" that we created earlier. To begin this process, make a copy of the query"qry_DataSummary". Start by cutting and pasting the query"qry_DataSummary" in the Navigation Pane on the left. Name this new query "qry_OrigTermStrat". Right-click on the new "qry_OrigTermStrat" to open it up in Design View. In order to use "tbl_TermRange", we first need to add it to the Query Editor. Recall from Exhibit 17.24 that this is accomplished by right-clicking in the empty space above the editor and selecting the "Show Table" option. Select the table "tbl_TermRange" and click "OK" to display it next to the "tbl_DataTape" table in the Tables Pane. See Exhibit 17.40.

The stratification divisions in this report are based on the original term pairs in "tbl_TermRange". Add the ' "OrigTerm" field from "tbl_DataTape" to the query

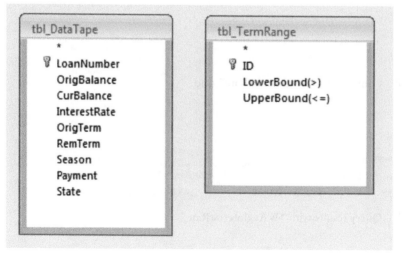

EXHIBIT 17.40 Add "tbl_TermRange" to "qry_OrigTermStrat"

Field:	LowerBound(>)	UpperBound(<=)	OrigTerm	LoanCount: LoanNumber
Table:	tbl_TermRange	tbl_TermRange	tbl_DataTape	tbl_DataTape
Total:	Group By	Group By	Where	Count
Sort:				
Show:	✓	✓	☐	✓
Criteria:				
or:				

EXHIBIT 17.41 Add LowerBound(>), UpperBound(<=), and OrigTerm to the query

by double-clicking on it in the "tbl_DataTape" table. We also need to add "Lower Bound(>)" and "UpperBound(<=)" to the front of the query. See Exhibit 17.41.

The next step is to add the selection criteria to the "OrigTerm" field using range values stored in table "tbl_TermRange". Change the Totals designation for "OrigTerm" to "Where", since the purpose of this field in the query is to aggregate the results with the specified criteria. Notice that when we change to the "Where" option, Access automatically deselects the "Show" box. If you attempt to display a "Where" field, Access will give an error and offer some advice as to how to fix the condition. Next we will add the following to the criteria section for "OrigTerm":

```
>[LowerBound(>)] And <=[UpperBound(<=)]
```

See Exhibit 17.42.

After adding these criteria we will execute the query and examine the results. What are now displayed are results similar to those of "qry_DataSummary" but more specifically aggregated across a range of original terms. From the results we are able to clearly see at a glance how the loan balances are distributed across original term ranges. Also displayed are the weighted averages of the interest rates and terms for each of the original term ranges. By examining these results, we can answer such questions as "How does the interest rate distribution of the 15-year mortgages compare with that of the 20-year mortgages?" See Exhibit 17.43.

It is worth it at this point to take a step back and think about the relative ease of creating this stratification query compared to the amount of work required to complete a similar task in VBA. In VBA, we would begin by setting up an array containing the different original term ranges, identical to ranges in table "tbl_TermRange". Creating a loop, we would need to first count the number of active records in the collateral file. Using this count, we would next read the contents of the file into a series of VBA arrays. At this point we would have two choices. If the data set was small enough, we could sort the contents of the arrays by the selection criteria, the original

Field:	LowerBound(>)	UpperBound(<=)	OrigTerm
Table:	tbl_TermRange	tbl_TermRange	tbl_DataTape
Total:	Group By	Group By	Where
Sort:			
Show:	✓	✓	☐
Criteria:			>[LowerBound(>)] And <=[UpperBound(<=)]
or:			

EXHIBIT 17.42 Adding selection criteria to the stratification query

qry_OrigTermStrat					
LowerBound(>) ▾	UpperBound(<=) ▾	LoanCount ▾	TotalOrigBalance ▾	TotalCurBalance ▾	WAvgInterestRate ▾
108	120	437	113,263,000.00	109,911,220.12	7.45%
168	180	468	122,512,700.00	120,709,252.89	7.51%
228	240	468	111,115,700.00	110,097,495.14	7.48%
288	300	420	93,387,900.00	92,817,038.96	7.53%
348	360	462	111,977,800.00	111,548,052.51	7.45%

EXHIBIT 17.43   Partial results of the query "qry_OrigTermStrat"

term value. If we had hundreds or thousands of loans, we would have to process each loan through a series of "For..Next" or "Do..While" loops. A different number of arrays (or a variable multidimensional array) would have to be used, depending on the stratification field and the data used. We would then have a series of variables to hold the incremental results of the computations and write additional VBA code to compute, format, and output the summary statistics. For examples of this type of process, we refer the reader to the predecessor volume of this work, *Structured Finance Modeling: Structuring, Valuation and Monitoring. A Fast Track Guide to VBA* by William Preinitz (Hoboken, NJ: John Wiley & Sons, 2007). Clearly the use of Access makes this task much more palatable for all concerned.

BASICS OF STRUCTURED QUERY LANGUAGE

Now that we have built queries in Access using Query by Example in the Access Query Builder, we need to take some time to learn what is happening behind the scenes. The Query Builder is Access's way of making database operations more visual. What is actually happening is that every operation and relationship created via QBE is translated into SQL code to be processed. There are some instances where QBE falls short of our desires and is unable to translate certain operations to SQL. One such example is a union query where the results of two queries are combined into one recordset. We will create a number of union queries in Chapter 18.

To get a quick feel for SQL, double-click on the "qry_SelectExample" query we built earlier. It is first displayed in the Datasheet View. The astute reader may have noticed that under the View options there are more options than Datasheet or Design. One of these options is SQL View. Select this option to see how the "qry_SelectExample" query appears in SQL. Exhibit 17.44 shows the SQL script with some formatting to make it easier to read.

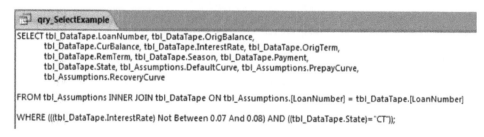

```
qry_SelectExample

SELECT tbl_DataTape.LoanNumber, tbl_DataTape.OrigBalance,
       tbl_DataTape.CurBalance, tbl_DataTape.InterestRate, tbl_DataTape.OrigTerm,
       tbl_DataTape.RemTerm, tbl_DataTape.Season, tbl_DataTape.Payment,
       tbl_DataTape.State, tbl_Assumptions.DefaultCurve, tbl_Assumptions.PrepayCurve,
       tbl_Assumptions.RecoveryCurve

FROM tbl_Assumptions INNER JOIN tbl_DataTape ON tbl_Assumptions.[LoanNumber] = tbl_DataTape.[LoanNumber]

WHERE (((tbl_DataTape.InterestRate) Not Between 0.07 And 0.08) AND ((tbl_DataTape.State)="CT"));
```

EXHIBIT 17.44   "qry_SelectExample" in SQL

This may seem like *very* messy code at first, but once you identify the keywords in the SQL statement, what is going on becomes more obvious. Access automatically capitalizes the SQL keywords for us, and, even more fortunately for us, SQL is a readable, intuitive programming language.

From Exhibit 17.44 we can immediately identify three words displayed in all capital letters: SELECT, FROM, and WHERE. These three keywords are the foundation of every SQL statement. The code that follows the SELECT keywords designates the fields of our query. These are more or less the column headers that we will see when executing the query. The FROM keyword designates the tables or queries that we make available to our current query in which the SELECT fields reside. The WHERE clause sets constraints on our query. A fourth keyword in Exhibit 17.44 is the AND keyword. This allows us to a multiple constraints.

To be more specific, in Exhibit 17.44 we see that the loan number from the data file, along with many other fields, is included in the results. The syntax for this is as follows:

```
SELECT tableName.fieldName''.
```

If there are any spaces in these names, they must be enclosed in brackets for them to be SQL readable. Next we see how the join that we created earlier is expressed in SQL. The syntax for this join is as follows:

```
FROM table1 INNER JOIN table2 ON table1.field1 = table2.field2.
```

The INNER JOIN, as opposed to an OUTER JOIN, is to show that we are only interested in records in "table1" and "table2" where there is a matching "field1" and "field2". All other records will be left out. The WHERE clause is where we are able to set constraints on the query results. For the query "qry_SelectExample", we last looked at loans in the state of Connecticut and that had an interest rate not between 7% and 8%.

Luckily for us, SQL is an easily readable language! It is meant to be very bare bones. The more commonly used keywords in SQL, along with a brief explanation, are given in Exhibit 17.45.

SELECT	**Shows the fields that are going to be represented in the query. The SELECT keyword is required and starts off a SQL statement.**
FROM	Designates which tables the fields in the SELECT statement derive from. A FROM clause must accompany a SELECT statement.
WHERE	Sets the criteria for the fields in the SELECT statement. The WHERE statement designates how the query results are filtered.
AND	Allows for multiple criteria in a single query. The AND statements are continuations of the first condition in the WHERE clause.
GROUP BY	Designates which fields the query results will be grouped by.
ORDER BY	Designates how the query results will be ordered. Similar to the familiar Sort option in Excel.

EXHIBIT 17.45   Common SQL keywords in a select query

```
┌─────────────────────────────────────────────────────────────────────┐
│ ⊞  qry_OrigTermStrat                                                  │
├─────────────────────────────────────────────────────────────────────┤
│ SELECT tbl_TermRange.[LowerBound(>)],                                 │
│        tbl_TermRange.[UpperBound(<=)],                                │
│        Count(tbl_DataTape.LoanNumber) AS [Loan Count],                │
│        Sum(tbl_DataTape.OrigBalance) AS [Total Original Balance],     │
│        Sum(tbl_DataTape.CurBalance) AS [Total Current Balance],       │
│        Sum([InterestRate]*[CurBalance])/Sum([CurBalance]) AS [WAvg Interest Rate], │
│        Sum([OrigTerm]*[CurBalance])/Sum([CurBalance]) AS [WAvg Original Term], │
│        Sum([RemTerm]*[CurBalance])/Sum([CurBalance]) AS [WAvg Remaining Term], │
│        Sum([Season]*[CurBalance])/Sum([CurBalance]) AS [WAvg Seasoning] │
│                                                                       │
│ FROM tbl_DataTape, tbl_TermRange                                      │
│                                                                       │
│ WHERE (((tbl_DataTape.OrigTerm)>[LowerBound(>)] And (tbl_DataTape.OrigTerm)<=[UpperBound(<=)]))  │
│                                                                       │
│ GROUP BY tbl_TermRange.[LowerBound(>)], tbl_TermRange.[UpperBound(<=)]; │
└─────────────────────────────────────────────────────────────────────┘
```

EXHIBIT 17.46 "qry_OrigTermStrat" in SQL view

There are certainly other keywords in SQL that can be utilized to achieve specific results. For our purposes these five keywords are critical and are usually enough to get simple jobs done.

To see a slightly more complicated example in SQL, close the query "qry_SelectExample" and open the query "qry_OrigTermStrat" in SQL view. See Exhibit 17.46.

One of the new keywords we see is AS. This is how we assign aliases in SQL. If it were not for the aliases, the query results would show the formulas we built in their entirety as the name of the field. One other thing to notice is that the computations we built in the Query Builder are clearly visible in the SQL editor. Next, as we should expect, the WHERE and accompanying AND clauses set up the term bounds for our query. The final line in Exhibit 17.46 specifies how the results are grouped.

QBE is usually quicker and less daunting than SQL to those deterred by pure code. As you can see, the raw SQL code behind QBE is not necessarily much more complicated than building a query in the Query Builder. This is fortunate for us because we will be interacting with Access primarily through VBA, and the VBA editor knows nothing of QBE. As we will see next, using VBA to connect to and retrieve results from Access is as easy as converting SQL to a string variable in the VBA editor and specifying where to output the results.

Writing Query Results to Excel Using VBA

We are now ready to show how VBA code modules in an Excel workbook can communicate with a database to retrieve query results. We will start by creating an Excel workbook called "TermStratOutput.xlsm". The first step is to create spaces on "Sheet1" to hold the database path and the query. Enter "Database" and "Query" into cells B2 and B3, respectively. Next, enter the full file path of the Access data in cell C2 ("C:\VBA_Book2\ABS\Mort\Training\Access\LoanPortfolioExample.accdb") and "qry_OrigTermStrat" into cell C3. See Exhibit 17.47.

Next we are going to give Range names to both of these inputs to make our VBA code easier to read. Assign the Range name "dataBase" to cell C2 and the Range

◢	A	B	C	D	E	F
1						
2		Database	C:\VBA_Book2\ABS\Mort\Training\Access\LoanPortfolioExample.accdb			
3		Query	qry_OrigTermStrat			
4						

EXHIBIT 17.47   Setup for "qry_OrigTermStrat" Access output

name "query" to cell C3. We will also want to designate the cell to which the output will be sent. Assign the Range name to cell C5 "queryOutput".

Connecting to the Database

In Office 2007, the preferred way to access external data is through the ActiveX Data Object (ADO). The ADO object library contains many useful methods for accessing and manipulating external data. The first steps in doing so are to open the VBA editor, create a new module ("Module1"), and add the reference to the latest version of the library. In this case that is "Microsoft ActiveX Data Objects 6.0 Library". You can find this reference by selecting "Tools" > "References" in the VBA editor. See Exhibit 17.48.

By using ADO we can access many different data sources in addition to an Access database (e.g., Oracle, MySQL, text files). Each of these different data sources requires a different bit of code in order to connect to it. The connection string, as it is called, also changes depending on which version of Excel you are using.

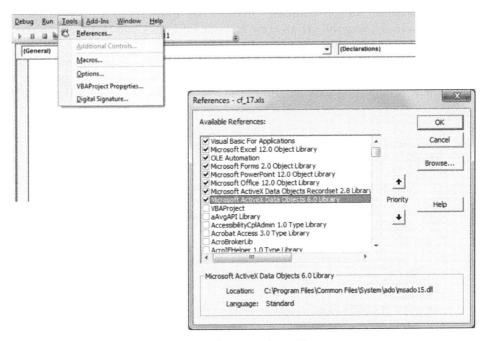

EXHIBIT 17.48   Adding a reference to the ADO object library

The first step is to create a module that will contain our global variable. Create a module and rename it "A_Globals" in the Properties Window (press F4 or find it under the View option up top). In our current example, the only global variable we need is the database connection object: "gCon". This global variable is defined as:

```
Global gCon As ADODB.Connection 'database connection
```

This is the connection to our ADO database (ADODB). We make this a global variable because typically there will be multiple subroutines that make use of this connection to access external data at multiple times in the program execution. It is important for this connection to be closed when it is not in use, and the subroutine that is utilizing the connection will be where the VBA code to close the connection is located.

The next step is to create a module that will contain the "ConnectToDatabase" and "DisconnectFromDatabase" subroutines. In the VBA editor, create a new module and name it "Z_UtilitySubroutines". In the "Z_UtilitySubroutines" module, enter the code as it appears in Exhibit 17.49.

Within the "ConnectToDatabase" subroutine, the first step is to set "gCon", the ADODB connection object, to a new ADODB connection object. The next step is to connect to our database using the connection string. The "Provider" input is specific to Excel 2007. If you are using Excel 2003, the provider portion of the connection string will be "Provider=Microsoft.Jet.OLEDB.4.0;". You also will not need the "Persist Security Info" portion of the statement with that version. Unfortunately, finding the correct connection string for your version of Excel may take a little digging, but the methods of the connection that we are using are the same.

We see from Exhibit 17.49 that the data source references the full file path that we stored in named Range "dataBase" in our Excel spreadsheet. If the file path is entered incorrectly, you will get an error message informing you that the path you are using to try to connect to the file is not a valid file path.

The "DisconnectFromDatabase" subroutine closes the database connection and sets the variable to "Nothing". We will see in the following section that each subroutine that is importing data from the database will run "ConnectToDatabase"

```
Sub ConnectToDataBase(dataSource As String)
    Set gCon = New ADODB.Connection
    With gCon
        .ConnectionString = "Provider=Microsoft.ACE.OLEDB.12.0;" & _
                            "Data Source = " & dataSource & ";" & _
                            "Persist Security Info = False;"
        .Open
    End With
End Sub
```

```
Sub DisconnectFromDatabase()
    gCon.Close
    Set gCon = Nothing
End Sub
```

EXHIBIT 17.49   "ConnectToDataBase" and "DisconnectFromDataBase" subroutines

immediately before making the request to the database and will run "disconnect" as early as possible. It is generally good practice not to keep the data stream open for any longer than is necessary. This is especially important when other users may be using the same data source.

Retrieving Data Using ADODB

Once we have the connection subroutine in place, we are ready to retrieve the query results from our Access database and return these to Excel. At this point, create another module and name it "ReturnRecordset". In this module we will place the code that clears the output space, executes the query, and outputs the results back to Excel. The code required is reproduced in Exhibit 17.50.

First we have to dimension a recordset object that will store the query results. Next we will execute a bit of code that clears the output space. The choice of 100 in the "Resize()" method is somewhat arbitrary. If we were expecting a larger data set, we would probably have to make more space. In this example 20 would suffice. The next step is to call the "ConnectToDatabase" subroutine, which is housed in the "Z_UtilitySubroutines" module. Running this subroutine will establish a connection to the database specified in named Range "dataBase" in the Excel workbook.

Now we are finally ready to start working with the recordset object that we have dimensioned in VBA memory for the time being. Of course, if we want to see a list of properties and methods available with respect to a certain type of object, we simply have to type the name of the object followed by a period. See Exhibit 17.51.

```
Sub returnAccessQuery()

Dim i   As Integer            'iterator over fields
Dim rs  As ADODB.Recordset    'recordset object

    'Clear the output region
    Range("queryOutput").Resize(100, 100).Clear
    'Connect to the database
    ConnectToDataBase (Range("dataBase"))
    'Execute the query and store in recordset rs
    Set rs = gCon.Execute(Range("query"))
    'Output the column headers
    For i = 0 To rs.Fields.Count - 1
        Range("queryOutput").Offset(0, i).Value = rs.Fields(i).Name
    Next i
    'Output recordset rs
    Range("queryOutput").Offset(1, 0).CopyFromRecordset rs
    'Clean up
    Set rs = Nothing
    DisconnectFromDatabase

End Sub
```

EXHIBIT 17.50   "returnAccessQuery" subroutine

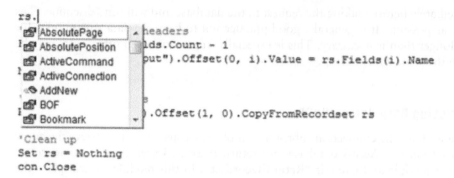

```
rs.|
    AbsolutePage        headers
    AbsolutePosition    lds.Count - 1
    ActiveCommand       put").Offset(0, i).Value = rs.Fields(i).Name
    ActiveConnection
    AddNew
    BOF
    Bookmark            ).Offset(1, 0).CopyFromRecordset rs
'Clean up
Set rs = Nothing
con.Close
```

EXHIBIT 17.51   Accessing the methods and properties of the recordset object

The first occurrence of a recordset method is in setting the upper bound of the For loop. The following statements can be easily puzzled out. The ".Fields()" call returns a collection of all the fields in the recordset. This collection has a method called "count" that counts the elements in the collection. Using these two in concert on our recordset returns the number of fields, or columns, of the results.

Once we have the field count, we are able to access each field individually to retrieve its name. The field collection is indexed with the first element at position 0. This is the reason why the loop runs from 0 to "rs.Fields.Count − 1". We loop through the fields, retrieving their names and outputting them to their appropriate spot in the Excel workbook.

Now that we have all the columns set up, we are ready to output the entire recordset. This is done simply by calling the "CopyFromRecordset" method on the appropriate Range object. The following couple of lines of code are merely cleanup. Since we have finished retrieving data from our Access database, we can break the connection we created between Access and Excel VBA. It is also best practice to set all objects to empty once they have fulfilled their purpose. This cleanly reallocates memory back to the program. Exhibit 17.52 shows the results of running "returnAccessQuery()".

In the example above, because we had already created the query "qry_OrigTermStrat" in our Access database, we were able to call this query directly.

	A	B	C	D	E	F	G
1							
2		Database	C:\VBA_Book2\ABS\Mort\Training\Access\LoanPortfolioExample.accdb				
3		Query	qry_OrigTermStrat				
4							
5		LowerBound(>)	UpperBound(<=)	LoanCount	TotalOrigBalance	TotalCurBalance	WAvgInterestRate
6		108	120	437	113263000	109911220.1	0.074514686
7		168	180	468	122512700	120709252.9	0.075114016
8		228	240	468	111115700	110097495.1	0.074832852
9		288	300	420	93387900	92817038.96	0.07527455
10		348	360	462	111977800	111548052.5	0.074508653
11							

EXHIBIT 17.52   Results of the "returnAccessQuery()" subroutine

```
Sub returnAccessQuery2()

Dim i       As Integer              'iterator over fields
Dim rs      As ADODB.Recordset      'recordset object
Dim str_sql As String               'SQL execution string

    'Clear the output region
    Range("queryOutput").Resize(100, 100).Clear
    'Connect to the database
    ConnectToDataBase (Range("dataBase"))
    'Construct SQL string
    str_sql = _
      "SELECT tbl_TermRange.[LowerBound(>)], " & _
          "tbl_TermRange.[UpperBound(<=)], " & _
        "Count(tbl_DataTape.[LoanNumber]) " & _
          "AS [LoanCount], " & vbCrLf & _
        "Sum(tbl_DataTape.[OrigBalance]) " & _
          "AS [TotalOrigBalance], " & vbCrLf & _
        "Sum(tbl_DataTape.[CurBalance]) " & _
          "AS [TotalCurBalance]," & vbCrLf & _
        "Sum([InterestRate]*[CurBalance])/Sum([CurBalance]) " & _
          "AS [WAvgInterestRate], " & vbCrLf & _
        "Sum([OrigTerm]*[CurBalance])/Sum([CurBalance]) " & _
          "AS [WAvgOriginalTerm], " & vbCrLf & _
        "Sum([RemTerm]*[CurBalance])/Sum([CurBalance]) " & _
          "AS [WAvgRemTerm], " & vbCrLf & _
        "Sum([Season]*[CurBalance])/Sum([CurBalance]) " & _
          "AS [WAvgSeasoning]" & vbCrLf & _
      "FROM tbl_DataTape, tbl_TermRange" & vbCrLf & _
      "WHERE (((tbl_DataTape.[OrigTerm]) > [LowerBound(>)] And " & _
          "(tbl_DataTape.[OrigTerm]) <= [UpperBound(<=)]))" & vbCrLf & _
      "GROUP BY tbl_TermRange.[LowerBound(>)], tbl_TermRange.[UpperBound(<=)]"
    'Execute the query and store in recordset rs
    Set rs = gCon.Execute(str_sql)
    'Output the column headers
    For i = 0 To rs.Fields.Count - 1
        Range("queryOutput").Offset(0, i).Value = rs.Fields(i).Name
    Next i
    'Output recordset rs
    Range("queryOutput").Offset(1, 0).CopyFromRecordset rs
    'Clean up
    Set rs = Nothing
    DisconnectFromDatabase

End Sub
```

EXHIBIT 17.53 Changing "returnAccessQuery()" to account for a custom SQL string

Later on we will see that it is critical to be able to construct a query entirely in VBA that is then executed against a database. This becomes important when queries are variable, changing depending on user input. Exhibit 17.53 shows how the previous module would be modified had we not had a custom-built query already in the database. This may look daunting at first, but it is really just the contents of SQL View for the query "qry_OrigTermStrat" with some additional formatting. When building queries in VBA, we need to be very careful to preserve formatting. Just as in VBA, if there are errant characters or missing spaces in SQL code, the program will return an error. Spaces, carriage returns ("vbcrlf"), and indentations are all used to keep the SQL execution statements Access- and user-readable.

CONCLUDING REMARKS

In this chapter we got our first look at Microsoft Access and familiarized ourselves with some of the objects and interactions among these objects, which we will employ later in our model. We showed how data can be imported, manipulated, and formatted. Once we were comfortable using Access's Query by Example in the Query Builder, we switched over to see how QBE is translated into SQL. Finally, we showed how VBA can be used to retrieve from Access to a recordset and return its contents to an Excel worksheet.

ON THE WEB SITE

The Web site material for this chapter is composed of five files.

- "LoanPortfolioExample.accdb". Access files contain tables and queries built and used as examples in the chapter.
- "LoanPortfolioWorkbook.xlsx". Excel file containing a simplified sample portfolio imported into the "tbl_DataTape" Access table.
- "TermRangeExample.xlsx". Excel workbook used to build the data pasted into the "tbl_TermRange" Access table.
- "AssumptionsExample.xlsx". Excel workbook containing an example set of loan-level modeling assumptions for the loans in "tbl_DataTape".
- "TermStratOutput.xlsm". Macro-enabled workbook containing code that manages the database connection and imports data into the workbook from Access tables.

CHAPTER 18

Implementing Access in the CCFG and LWM

OVERVIEW

In this chapter we will implement Access across many of the major input and output functions of the Collateral Cash Flow Generator Model (CCFG) and the Liabilities Waterfall Model (LWM). The foundation for our Access activities as they pertain to the CCFG will be the creation of an all-inclusive database to hold the widely disparate information that the CCFG needs to function. This database will hold everything from the collateral information at the beginning of the process to the completed cash flow scenarios at the end of a successful run. The database will replace the collection of data and template files that we currently use to drive the model. We will no longer need to track file names and data sets, store pathway information in a collection of Constant variables, or go looking for input and output files to avoid duplicative effort.

Once we have built in Access functionality to select and amortize a portfolio, we will move over to the LWM, where we will show how cash flow results from the CCFG can be brought into the LWM. With the CCFG results in the LWM, we write out the results of our fully realized modeling runs to an LWM results database.

The information in our CCFG Access database will fall into three major clusters. Each is based on the role the information plays in the process of turning raw collateral data into diversified sets of stressed cash flows. The first, and most important (since everything proceeds from it), is the loan-by-loan collateral data. The second are the sets of financial, demographic, and geographic tests we will apply against the collateral during the initial and subsequent screening processes to determine its eligibility for inclusion in the deal. Last are the resultant individual and aggregate collateral cash flows of the surviving collateral that we will later apply to our selected debt structure using the LWM.

We will use Access to store, display, and apply all the data for each of the three sets of information listed above. By the end of this chapter you will be amazed to see the advantages in speed, simplicity, power, and flexibility that Access brings to the model construction and development process. This is particularly true when we look at the amount of infrastructure (Constant variables and file pathway designations) that we can compress or eliminate.

Due to space limitations, the Access-based CCFG workbook that is the result of this chapter is in a sense an abridged model. We will be able to amortize a pool of collateral that has been error-checked, filtered by geographic criteria, and restricted to a set of financial conditions. During these processes we will store various assumption sets and results in an Access database directly from the LWM VBA routines.

DELIVERABLES

The general knowledge deliverables in this chapter are:

- We will learn to use a database product such as Access to improve the control, strength, flexibility, and efficiency of your models.

  The specific Access knowledge deliverables in this chapter are:

- We will learn how to design and create a large Access database for the storage of large amounts of various types of information.
- We will learn how to create and link various special-purpose data tables within the database and customize them to hold information such as collateral data, eligibility tests, and completed cash flows.
- We will learn how to store, display, and read into the CCFG the contents of these various tables.
- We will learn how to populate an Excel spreadsheet with data stored in recordset objects.
- We will learn how to retrieve data from Excel named Ranges and store it in Access database tables.

UNDER CONSTRUCTION

In this chapter we will see how we can replace almost all of the file-based and VBA-driven data handling functionality in the model. Broadly this will include all collateral data itself and the entire analyst input assumptions and modeling criteria. We make changes to both the CCFG and the LWM workbooks. Both portions of the model will be accompanied by an Access database file, each of which contains multiple tables pertaining to the modeling.

Changes to CCFG   The VBA modules affected are:

- "A_MainProgram". Changing which subroutines are called in the CCFG. Altering subroutines that read inputs from the Run Options Menu to use drop-down boxes as opposed to Excel ranges. The subroutines affected are: "CCFG_Model" and "MainProgram_FindActivePoolOrSubPorts".
- "A_Constants". Removing the file and template pathways for loan-level and assumption files. Adding the "DATABASE_FULLPATH" Constant to store the location of the Access file. Adding the "INITDATASCREEN_TEMPLATE_ ACCESS" Constant to store the Access-applicable Initial Data Screening template.
- "A_Globals". Removing the global variables dedicated to the loan-level file position variables. Adding the ADODB connection object definition.

- **"MenuSupport_RunOptions"**. Altering subroutines to read data from newly formatted menu. Subroutines affected are: "RunOptions_ReadMenu", "err RunOpts_TestSetNonNumeric", "errRunOpts_TestSetNumTooLarge", and "errRunOpts_OptSelActivePorts".
- **"CollatCF_WriteCFsToDB"**. New module. Contains "writeCFsToACCESS" subroutine for pulling cash flow data from global arrays and storing them in an Access table.
- **"CollatData_GetPortfolio"**. New module. Replaces selection subroutines under "CollatData" heading.
- **"CollatData_FinancialSelection"**. Removed; encompassed by module "Collat Data_GetPortfolio".
- **"CollatData_GeographicSelection"**. Removed; encompassed by "CollatData_ GetPortfolio".
- **"CollatData_InitialDataScreening"**. All previous code removed and replaced with Access-based VBA implementation.
- **"MenuSupport_CollateralPool"**. Changed to retrieve sub-portfolios from and write combined portfolios to Access. The "CollateralData_BuildPoolFileFrom SubPorts" subroutine is removed and replaced with "addPortfolioToDB".
- **"MenuSupport_FinancialSelect"**. Revised to write financial selection sets to and read presaved sets from. Access tables as opposed to Excel template files. The following four subroutines have been changed: "FinSelect_Write SelectionCriteriaFile", "FinSelect_ReadDataItemNames", "FinSelect", "Read SelectionCriteriaFile", and "FinSelect_DeleteTestSet". A function call "Test SetToSQL" has been added to this module.
- **"MenuSupport_GeographicSelect"**. Revised to write geographic selection sets to, and read presaved sets from Access tables as opposed to Excel template files. The following five subroutines have been changed:
  1. "GeoSelect_WriteGeoSelectionCriteriaReport"
  2. "GeoSelect_WriteCriteriaBody"
  3. "GeoSelect_WriteConcentrationReport"
  4. "GeoSelect_ReadGeoSelectionReportFile"
  5. "GeoSelect_ReadGeoConcentrationReportFile"
  The following three subroutines have been added: "writeRegions ToDB", "writeStatesToDB", and "writeMSAsToDB". The subroutine "Geo Select_FindAllSheetsPresentInFile" has been removed.
- **"MenuSupport_RunOptions"**. Changed to read inputs from drop-down boxes on "RunOptionsMenu" worksheet as opposed to Excel Ranges. The revised sub-routines are: "RunOptions_ReadMenu", "errRunOpts_TestSetNonNumeric", "errRunOpts_TestSetNumTooLarge", "errRunOpts_OptSelActivePorts".
  All Reporting modules remain unchanged.
- **"Z_UtilitySubroutines"**. We add two subroutines to assist with the Access portions of the model. These are: "ConnectToDataBase" and "DisconnectFrom Database".

The Excel worksheets with code affected are:

- **"RunOptionsMenu"**. Code behind the worksheet populates ComboBoxes residing on the worksheet with information from Access.

- **"CollatPoolMenu"**. Code behind the worksheet populates ComboBoxes residing on the worksheet with information from Access. CommandButton code changed to call Access subroutines.

Changes to LWM

- **"A_Constants"**. We add two Constants needed hold the full paths of the two databases used to retrieve and write data. Once again the "CCFG_Data.accdb" location is stored in "DATABASE_FULLPATH" while the new database file, "LWM_Data.accdb", is stored in "LWM_FULLPATH".
- **"A_Globals"**. We will create two connections to different databases. We create two global ADODB connection objects: "gConCCFG" and "gConLWM".
- **"Z_UtilitySubroutines"**. Contains the "ConnectToDatabase" and "Disconnect-FromDatabase" subroutines. These subroutines require some modification from the CCFG versions to account for two ADODB connection objects.
- **"Structure" worksheet**. Contains code pertaining to the control objects embedded on the worksheet. These subroutines will populate the drop-down, check its entry, and attach code to the CommandButtons calling the subroutines of the modules below.
- **"ReturnCashFlows"**. Contains the code that populates the waterfall worksheet with the chosen scenario cash flows. This is accomplished with three subroutines: "getCFs", "getCFsAmortSheet", and "getCFsDatabase".
- **"LWMAccessSubs"**. Contains subroutines that handle the loading of the inputs and results to the database tables. This is also where we place the code that allows the loading of a batch of results for a set of inputs.

The Access file created to house the inputs and results of LWM is called "**LWM_Data.accdb**". This database contains tables for data pertaining to model inputs and results.

In addition to the above code modules, we also will add a spreadsheet to the workbook named "**DB Format**". Within this sheet we create five named Range tables that are appended to the appropriate tables in the "LWM_Data.accdb" file.

ACCESS AND THE COLLATERAL CASH FLOW GENERATOR

The Access implementations in the CCFG will perform analyst input criteria storage, data importation, and data exportation for the following activities of the CCFG:

- **Collateral Portfolio** data at the individual loan level collateral data. These processes also entail reading the names of Pool and Sub-Portfolio collateral collections and merging Sub-Portfolios into Pool level collateral collections if required.
- Storing and managing the **Run Option Elections** of the CCFG.
- In the **Initial Data Screening** section, we test the collateral data for incomplete or damaged records. These tests read the individual loan records by loan type for amortization calculation parameters, for stratification report parameters, and for the credit, financial, and demographic information used to estimate frequency of foreclosure and market value decline rates.
- Storing, managing, applying, and displaying the **Financial Selection Criteria Sets**. There selection criteria sets are broken into two distinct sets. The **Base Criteria**

set is a set of tests that relate to all collateral regardless of type and are used to determine the first tier of eligibility. There are 22 individual tests in the Base Criteria Test set. You will remember that the **Custom Financial Criteria Test** sets can be designated for either the Pool Level collateral data or for each of the five sets of Sub-Portfolio data. There can be up to 5 (one for each Sub-Portfolio), Custom Financial Criteria Test Sets each containing 20 individual tests.

- Storing, managing, applying, and displaying the **Geographic Selection Criteria Test** sets. Geographic Criteria Test sets for the 54 States/Territories and 150 Metropolitan Statistical Areas (MSAs).
- **Monthly Collateral Cash Flows** by scenario. These monthly cash flows are comprised of the following components: period, initial current balance, scheduled amortization of principal, coupon payments, prepayment of principal, principal defaults, recoveries of defaulted principal, and floating rate index vector.

Following you will find a series of major chapter sections devoted to each of the topics.

COLLATERAL PORTFOLIO DATA

As stated earlier, we will construct one large Access database to store all of the data, assumptions, and results of the operation of the CCFG. The first step in the process is, of course, to read the collateral information. We need to identify both the amortization and the demographic characteristics of each of the loans and have this information readily available. In the non-Access model, we are currently using a set of subroutines from the module "CollatData_ReadFileInfo" to open various Excel files and read in the information.

The portion of the Access database we design that is specifically dedicated to the tasks of reading and storing the collateral data will contain:

- All the loan-by-loan collateral information for either one Pool or up to five Sub-Portfolios.

Aggregation and retrieval functions for:

- All collateral record-by-record Pool level and Sub-Portfolio level information.
- Merging Sub-Portfolio information to form a Pool.

Just a Minute!

While we may want to rush off immediately and create a database and begin writing Access code, we need to do some planning first! You should at a minimum engage in research as to the following issues:

- How much data the model will use and what is the form of the data that will go into the tables.
- Aside from data, how the database will store other information, such as selection assumptions and eligibility criteria.
- What data will the rest of the modeling use and how much is there.

You should outline each of the major groups of information and make sure you know where all the information is and how its various pieces used by the model relate to one another. Once you have a clear layout of the overall number of tables, the information that they are to contain, the form of that information, and the uses it will be put through, you are ready to proceed.

Database Design

The first step in the introduction of Access to the CCFG is to create the database. We will use a single database to contain all the information needed by the model. A single Access file will hold all the data tables pertaining to the CCFG. The full file pathway and name of the CCFG database is:

```
''C:\VBABook2\ABS\Mort\Models\Databases''
```

Once we create the Access database, our first task will be to transfer the contents of the collateral data files into one of its component tables. To do this we will need to import the Pool file or alternatively up to five Sub-Portfolios into Access. We will then modify the "CollatPoolMenu" sheet so we can use it to view the Access tables containing this information directly through the use of drop-down boxes (i.e., ActiveX Comboboxes) embedded in the worksheet.

These changes will enable us to create unique portfolios from various combinations of these collateral data groups. Before we begin the process, you will need to download the portfolio data files from the Web site. There are six portfolio files in total: one Pool and five Sub-Portfolios.

With these files in hand, we can open up the newly created CCFG database. We will select the "Blank Database" option from the Welcome Screen. We will begin by importing the data in the Excel file "MainPort.xlsx" to a table called "tbl_MainPort". Exhibits 18.1(a) and 18.1(b) show the two main steps in creating and saving data to table "tbl_MainPort".

In Exhibit 18.1(b) we set the "AccountNumber" field as the primary key. The AccountNumber is a unique identifier for any loan across all of the Pool or Sub-Portfolio files. If this was not the case, we could create a unique identification element for each loan. Continue by importing the five Sub-Portfolios in the same manner. The "AccountNumber" will be the primary key for each table. Use a consistent naming convention (e.g., "tbl_SubPort1" for sub-portfolio 1). We will see the importance of this naming convention shortly. Upon conclusion of this process, the Navigation Pane in our CCFG database should appear as in Exhibit 18.2.

We will also need to create a table that will hold all of the portfolios that we will create in the future. The structure of this table will be identical to the other portfolio tables but with the addition of the "PortfolioName" text field. To create this table, cut and paste "tbl_MainPort" using the "Structure Only" option and name the new table "tbl_PORTFOLIOS". Open "tbl_PORTFOLIOS" in Design View and remove the primary key from the "AccountNumber" field by right-clicking the field. To add a field to the table above the "AccountNumber" field, right-click on "Account Number" and choose "Insert Rows". Name the new field "PortfolioName" and set the field type to "Text". Save and close table "tbl_PORTFOLIOS".

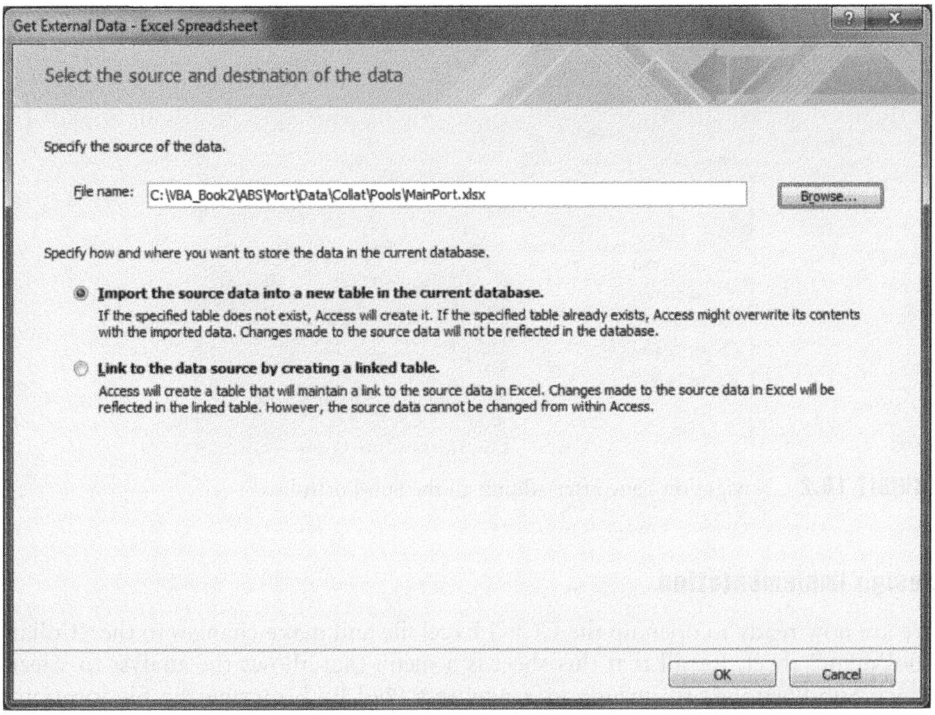

(a)

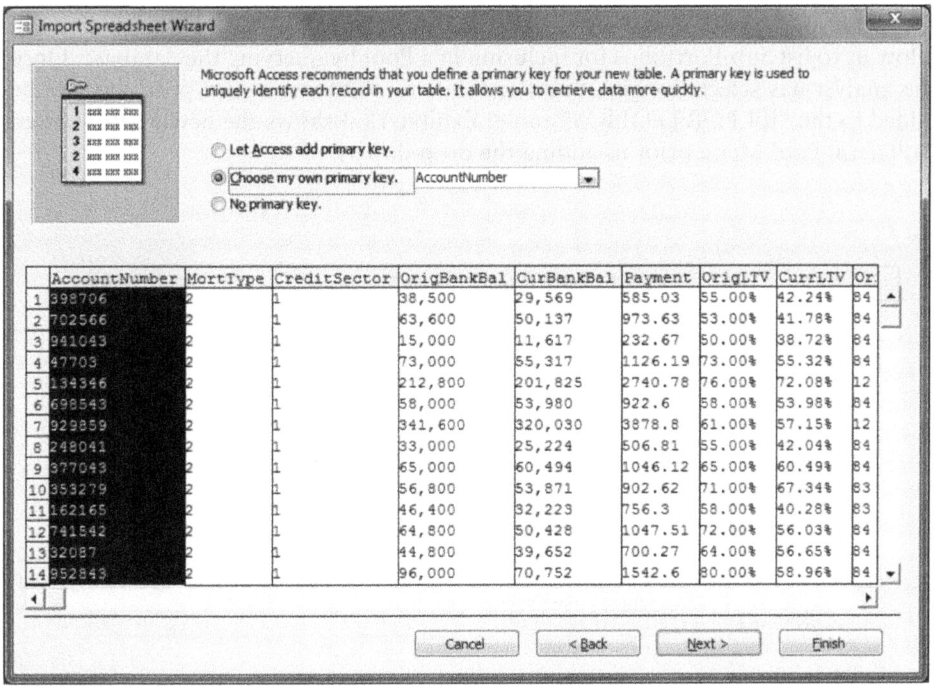

(b)

EXHIBIT 18.1 (a) Selecting "MainPort.xlsx" for import in "tbl_MainPort" and (b) setting the Account Number field as the primary key for "tbl_MainPort"

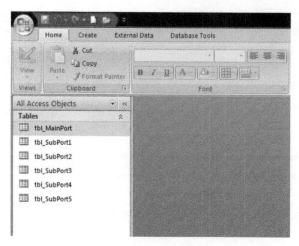

EXHIBIT 18.2   Navigation Pane after adding all the Sub-Portfolios

Design Implementation

We are now ready to open up the CCFG Excel file and make changes to the "Collat PoolMenu" sheet. Recall that this sheet is a menu that allows the analyst to select which Sub-Portfolios to include in a new test Pool by browsing the file location. The analyst then designates the name and path for the Pool that will be created by clicking the "Create Pool File From Sub-Portfolios" Button. Our first modification to the menu will be to embed a series of drop-down control objects. These objects will allow us to list Sub-Portfolios for inclusion in a Pool by querying the database. Once the analyst has selected which Sub-Portfolios to combine, a new portfolio can be added to the "tbl_PORTFOLIOS" table. Exhibit 18.3 shows the newly reformatted Collateral Pool Menu prior to adding the drop-downs.

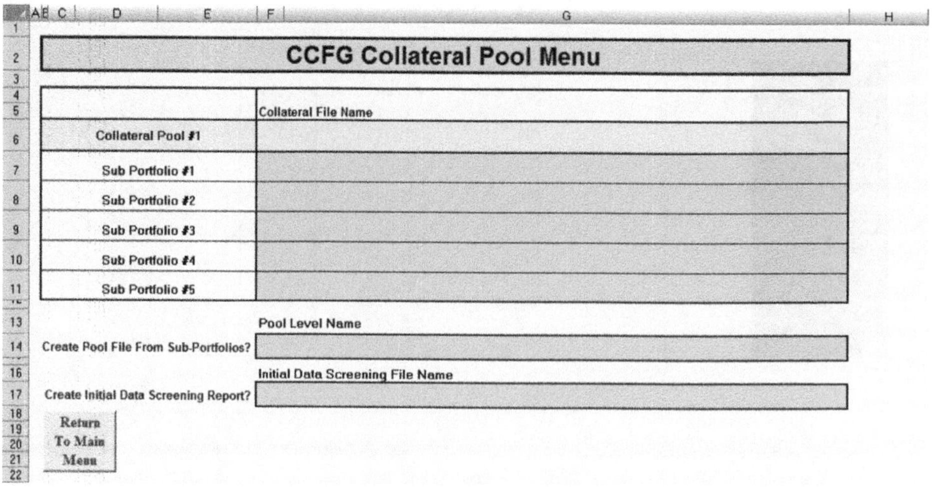

EXHIBIT 18.3   Reformatted "CollatPoolMenu" worksheet

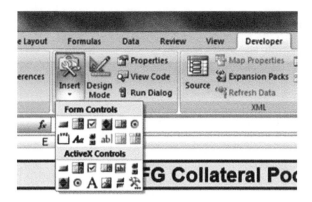

EXHIBIT 18.4 Inserting an ActiveX ComboBox to "CollatPoolMenu" worksheet

We are now ready to start adding the drop-down boxes to select Sub-Portfolios. From the Developer tab on the Excel ribbon, select "Insert". Click on the ComboBox option under the ActiveX Controls. See Exhibit 18.4.

The mouse pointer will change to crosshairs, and we can now draw a ComboBox on the menu. Position the crosshairs in the upper left-hand corner of the space to the right of the cell containing the label "Collateral Pool #1". See Exhibit 18.5. Size the ComboBox to the boundaries of the cell.

Modifying the Combo Box   In Chapter 9 we added control structures to UserForms. As seen in Exhibit 18.5, Excel also allows us to add control objects (with backing VBA code if need be) to worksheets. We will now rename the new ComboBox. Click the "Design" icon on the Developer tab then right-click the control object and select "Properties". "Properties" allows us to rename the ComboBox and change its appearance and behaviors. We will name this first ComboBox "cmb_MainPort". Once the ComboBox has been renamed change the "BackStyle" property to "fmBackStyleTransparent" and the "BackColor" property to the appropriate color to preserve the formatting of the worksheet.

See Exhibit 18.6.

At this point we are ready to open up the VBA editor (Alt+F11) and begin adding code that will manipulate the contents of the ComboBox we just added. We now need to add a couple of Constants and a subroutine to our project that will allow us to connect to the database.

Adding Connection Constants and Subroutines   To make it easier for the CCFG to find the Access database, we will now add a Constant variable named

	Collateral File Name	
Collateral Pool #1		▾
Sub Portfolio #1		

EXHIBIT 18.5 "CollatPoolMenu" with the first ComboBox added

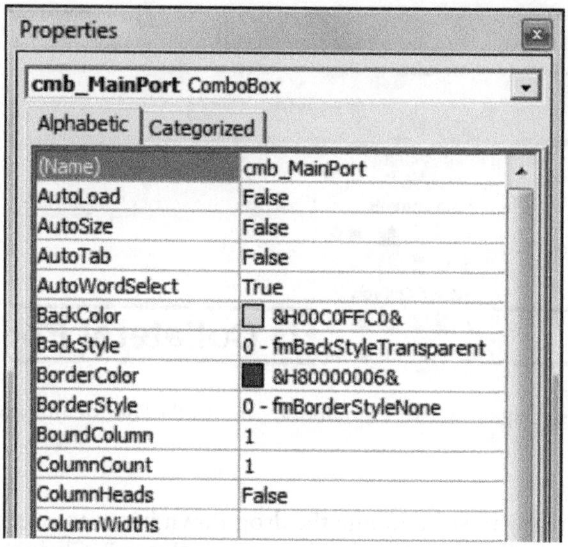

EXHIBIT 18.6 "cmb_MainPort" properties

"DATABASE_FULLPATH" to the major directories section of our "A_Constants" VBA module.

```
Public Const DATABASE_FULLPATH = DATA_DIRECTORY & ''Databases\CCFG_Data.accdb''
```

Next we will add a global variable for the connection to the database. This same connection variable will be used whenever we connect to our database. We will add this global variable under the "Public Variables" section of the "A_Globals" module.

```
Public gCon As ADODB.Connection 'database connection
```

The "ADODB" portion of the variable's type declaration should auto-capitalize when you enter the declaration. If it does not, you have not yet added the ADODB reference in this workbook. None of these Access-based modules will work without this reference added. To add it, select "Tools>References" from the menu in the VBA editor and add the reference to "Microsoft ActiveX Data Objects 6.0 Library" (or if not 6.0, the latest version available). See Exhibit 17.48 for a guide to how this is done. Now we are ready to add the subroutines that will connect us to and disconnect us from the database. The connection subroutine takes as a variable the database location. This will give us the flexibility to switch data sources, if necessary, by changing the Constant "DATABASE_FULLPATH". These subroutines should then be placed in the module "Z_UtilitySubroutines". See Exhibit 18.7.

Building Functionality for the ComboBoxes In the VBA editor, double-click on the "CollatPoolMenu" worksheet to be brought into the code window. As with UserForms, we can now add code governing the control objects of this worksheet. Clicking the object drop-down at the top left of the editor displays the objects that

```
Sub ConnectToDataBase(dataSource As String)
    Set gCon = New ADODB.connection
    With gCon
        .ConnectionString = "Provider=Microsoft.ACE.OLEDB.12.0;" & _
                            "Data Source = " & dataSource & ";" & _
                            "Persist Security Info = False;"
        .Open
    End With
End Sub

Sub DisconnectFromDatabase()
    gCon.Close
    Set gCon = Nothing
End Sub
```

EXHIBIT 18.7   Connection subroutines

we can add event code to. See Exhibit 18.8(a). Now select "cmb_MainPort" from the drop-down. Next select the event drop-down to the right of the object drop-down to see all the event methods available to the ComboBox object. See Exhibit 18.8(b).

This process is virtually identical to adding functionality to control objects on UserForms. Simply select the object and event desired from the drop-down menus.

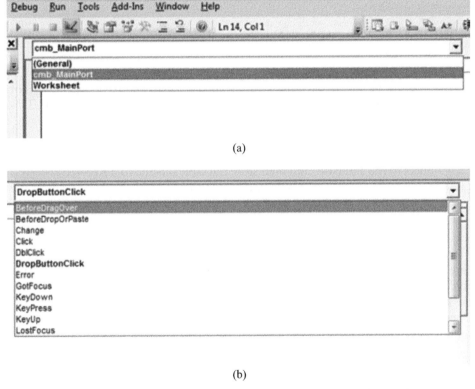

(a)

(b)

EXHIBIT 18.8   (a) Object drop-down box and (b) Method drop-down for "cmb_MainPort" subroutine

```
Private Sub cmb_MainPort_DropButtonClick()

Dim rs As ADODB.Recordset    'recordset object

    'Step 1:  Initialize the control object
    Do While cmb_MainPort.ListCount <> 0
        cmb_MainPort.RemoveItem 0
    Loop
    'Step 2:  Connect to the database and store schema
    ConnectToDataBase (DATABASE_FULLPATH)
    Set rs = gCon.OpenSchema(adSchemaTables)
    'Step 3:  Find portfolio names from schema
    Do While Not rs.EOF
        If InStr(1, rs.fields("TABLE_NAME").Value, "Port") Then
            cmb_MainPort.AddItem rs.fields("TABLE_NAME").Value
        End If
        rs.MoveNext
    Loop
    cmb_MainPort.AddItem "Empty"
    'Clean up
    Set rs = Nothing
    DisconnectFromDatabase

End Sub
```

EXHIBIT 18.9   Populating the "cmb_MainPort" control object

We want to be able to click the "cmb_MainPort" field and have the contents of the ComboBox populated with the portfolio table names from the database. This requires three steps:

1. Initialize the control object, "cmb_MainPort".
2. Connect to the database, and then store the table schema to a RecordSet object.
3. Loop through the recordset object, checking the "TABLE_NAME" field for the substring "Port". If it finds "Port", then add this table name to the ComboBox.

See Exhibit 18.9. The "OpenSchema()" recordset method allows us a way to retrieve from the database information about the database structure. We are interested here in retrieving the names of all the tables in the database. We will pass the variable "adSchemaTables" to the "OpenSchema()" method. By doing so we have all the table names, plus other information on the table objects, stored in a recordset. Once this recordset is populated, we loop over the table names looking for tables that contain the substring "Port". Here we see the importance of sticking to a specific naming convention when building database objects. In this example, our naming convention allowed us to easily filter the database tables when reproducing the results in a ComboBox. As our project grows in scope and complexity, following this practice will help us to stay organized and keep the code easy to understand.

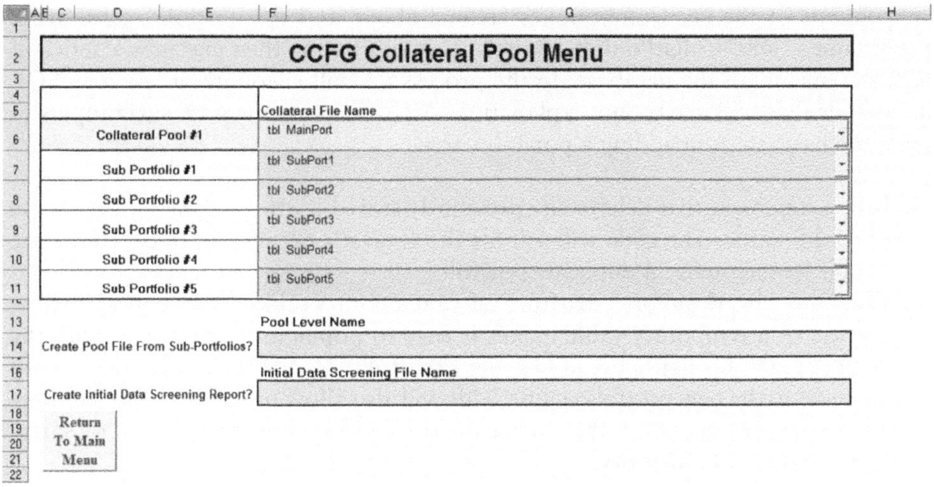

EXHIBIT 18.10 "CollatPoolMenu" worksheet with ComboBoxes added

Now switch back to the Excel workbook and click the "cmb_MainPort" ComboBox. The tables imported earlier are displayed in the ComboBox list. We will now create ComboBoxes for the five Sub-Portfolio fields. Create "cmb_SubPort1", "cmb_SubPort2", and so forth, on the worksheet. Repeat the code for "cmb_Port1", being careful to update the object names. The "CollatPoolMenu" sheet with all the ComboBoxes is shown in Exhibit 18.10.

The final task is to add an error trap. We want to prevent the analyst from entering a portfolio name in the drop-down box that is not part of the list. We create a "Lost Focus" event for each of the ComboBoxes. The code pertaining to "cmb_MainPort" is shown in Exhibit 18.11. This code uses the "ListIndex" property of the control object to return which element of the list is selected. As with lists in UserForms, this index begins at the "0th" position. If the text of the ComboBox is not part of the list, then "ListIndex" returns a value –1 (not on the list anywhere!). If this is the case, we employ a Message Box to inform the analyst of this condition and set the text to "Empty".

Adding a Portfolio to "tbl_PORTFOLIOS" We will now write the code that creates a portfolio in "tbl_PORTFOLIOS" from the inputs of "CollatPoolMenu" worksheet. A CommandButton on the worksheet will call a subroutine that takes as its input

```
'Ensure the selection is from the drop-down list
Private Sub cmb_MainPort_LostFocus()
    If cmb_MainPort.ListIndex = -1 Then
        MsgBox "Selection not part of list."
        cmb_MainPort.Value = "Empty"
    End If
End Sub
```

EXHIBIT 18.11 Error-trapping code for "cmb_MainPort"

the contents of the six ComboBoxes created above and the portfolio name from a cell named "m07CollatPoolFileName". This subroutine then executes a series of SQL statements on the database. In the process we will encounter a few new SQL commands that will need some explanation. After checking the worksheet inputs in VBA, the basic steps in adding a portfolio are:

1. Run a statement that deletes any previously stored portfolio data with the same portfolio name. The code will ask for the analyst's permission to overwrite the data if we encounter a duplicate portfolio.
2. Copy the "tbl_MainPort" structure into a temporary table. As we will see below, the use of a temporary table makes it easy to populate the first field with the correct portfolio name by adding the "Portfolio Name" field with the default value set to the new portfolio name. This will also allow us to detect any database errors prior to accessing the master portfolio table. This added level of safety helps ensure data integrity.
3. Add the main portfolio designated on the worksheet to the temporary table, "tbl_tempPortTable". We add this table outside of the loop that adds the Sub-Portfolios because we are assuming the analyst must select a main portfolio in order to complete this task.
4. Loop to determine if a sub-portfolio has been selected for inclusion in the Pool. For each Sub-Portfolio found, add the loans contained in the table to "tbl_tempPortTable".
5. Transfer the contents of "tbl_tempPortTable" to "tbl_PORTFOLIOS" along with the portfolio name.

This subroutine is located in the "MenuSupport_CollateralPool" module. The subroutine definition, variable declaration, and input checks are shown in the first section of Exhibit 18.12. We will call these setup activities our Step 0 Phase! In Step 0.1 we populate an array that holds the names of the Sub-Portfolios. This makes it possible for us to easily loop through these inputs. Step 0.2 checks to make sure a main portfolio has been selected. If this is not the case, the analyst is alerted and the program is terminated by the "End" statement. Step 0.3 checks if the same Sub-Portfolio has been selected multiple times. This check is performed by a pair of nested "For..Next" loops. These loops check each element of the "subPorts" array against all subsequent elements. In Step 0.4, if (and only if) the inputs pass these checks, we finally connect to the database.

What follows is the portion of the subroutine that checks to see if a portfolio of the same name as the one we are trying to add is already in "tbl_PORTFOLIOS". If it is, then we have to delete the records corresponding to this portfolio name before proceeding. This is one of our first complicated database processes in VBA. Let us take our time to really understand what is going on! Two blocks of code comprise the next step of the process. These are numbered Step 1.1 to Step 1.2. See Exhibit 18.13.

In Step 1.1 we ask for the "PortfolioName" field to be returned from "tbl_PORTFOLIOS" when the "PortfolioName" field matches the value stored in the "portName" input. Without the GROUP BY clause in the execution string, the query would return the "PortfolioName" field for every record where the "PortfolioName" equals "portName". By grouping, we reduce the number of records returned to only the unique records. This query will return either an empty record

```
Sub addPortfolioToDB(portName As String, mainPort As String, _
                    subPort1 As String, subPort2 As String, _
                    subPort3 As String, subPort4 As String, _
                    subPort5 As String)

Dim i          As Integer       'iterator
Dim j          As Integer       'iterator
Dim str_sql    As String        'SQL execution string
Dim subPorts() As Variant       'sub-portfolio variant array
Dim rs         As ADODB.Recordset 'recordset object
Dim dupResult  As Integer       'duplicate results user reply
    'Step 0.1:  Sub-portfolio array
    subPorts = Array(subPort1, subPort2, subPort3, subPort4, subPort5)
    'Step 0.2:  Check for main portfolio selected
    If mainPort = "Empty" Then
        MsgBox "You must specify a collateral pool."
        End
    End If
    'Step 0.3:  Check to see if the same portfolio is selected multiple times
    For i = 0 To UBound(subPorts) - 1
        For j = i + 1 To UBound(subPorts)
            If subPorts(i) = subPorts(j) And subPorts(i) <> "none" Then
                MsgBox "Same portfolio selected more then once.  Please revise."
                End
            End If
        Next j
    Next i
    'Step 0.4:  Connect to database
    ConnectToDataBase (DATABASE_FULLPATH)
```

EXHIBIT 18.12 Subroutine "addPortfolioToDB", Part 0

```
'Step 1.1:  Check to see if porfolio already exists in db
Set rs = gCon.Execute( _
    "SELECT [PortfolioName] FROM tbl_PORTFOLIOS " & vbCrLf & _
    "WHERE [PortfolioName] = '" & portName & "'" & vbCrLf & _
    " GROUP BY [PortfolioName]")

If Not (rs.BOF And rs.EOF) Then
    dupResult = MsgBox("Portfolio " & portName & _
                    " already exists in the database.  Proceed?", _
                    vbOKCancel, "Duplicate Porfolio")
    If dupResult = 2 Then
        MsgBox "Please rename the portfolio."
        GoTo dontOverwritePortfolio
    End If
End If

'Step 1.2 Delete this portfolio duplicate in the master portfolio table
gCon.Execute ( _
    "DELETE * FROM tbl_PORTFOLIOS " & _
    "WHERE [PortfolioName] = '" & portName & "'")
```

EXHIBIT 18.13 Subroutine "addPortfolioToDB", Part 1

set if "portName" is not found in the "PortfolioName" field of "tbl_PORTFOLIOS" or a recordset with a single record returned if it finds a match for our "portName".

Step 1.2 now checks to see if the record set is empty by checking to see if the recordset cursor is pointing to the beginning and end of the recordset at the same time. If this is the case, then there were no records returned from our query (i.e., no duplicate portfolio name was found in the database). If a duplicate name is found, the analyst is asked, via a Message Box, if he or she wishes to allow the subroutine to overwrite the table records with a matching portfolio name or not. If the analyst selects "OK", then the operation continues and runs the DELETE query. Translated, this statement says: "Delete everything from "tbl_PORTFOLIOS" where the entry in the "PortfolioName" field is equal to the value of 'portName'." If the analyst selects "Cancel", then the code is rerouted to VBA statement label "dontOverwritePortfolio". At this point the database connection is closed and the subroutine is ended.

A quick word should be said about the formatting of SQL execution statements in VBA. In the previous code and in most subsequent Access-related VBA exhibits, you will see many occurrences of the string "vbCrLf". The string "vbCrLf" stands for "carriage return left" and is a holdover from the ancient days of manual typewriters. One of the authors (Preinitz) remembers these antique mechanisms quite clearly! To throw the typing carriage to the left is to end the current line, and that is exactly what this symbol does! It serves to tell the VBA compiler that we have completed a line and to start a new one in the string variable. This is true even when a series of commands ending in this string is held together by continuation line symbols "–".

As the SQL execution strings grow in length and complexity, it is very easy to make a simple mistake, such as forgetting a necessary space or a single quote around strings (as in the "[PortfolioName] = 'portName' " statement). The best way to check for these types of problems is to store the execution string in a variable and subsequently output its contents to the Immediate Window of the VBA Debugger using "debug.Print()". Once in the Immediate Window and with the string nicely formatted, it is easier to tell what is going wrong. If it is still not clear what is causing the error, it is helpful to paste the string into the query SQL View within Access. Access will give an error message to point you in the right direction.

The second, third, fourth, and fifth steps in adding a new portfolio to "tbl_PORTFOLIOS" are shown in Exhibit 18.14. In Step 2.1 we first make sure that "tbl_tempPortTable" is cleared out of the database if it already existed. This is achieved by using a DROP TABLE command. If the table does not exist and we attempt to delete it, we will get an error, hence the "On Error Resume Next" line before the execution and the error reset line after. The "On Error Resume Next" forces the program to continue despite the presence of an error condition. Obviously everyone should be careful to use "On Error Resume Next" sparingly, but in this case it makes sense because trying to delete a table and not finding it is not really an error in our program. We expect a temporary table to not be found in the database, and we want to proceed in either event.

In Step 2.2 the code copies the structure of the table specified by variable "main Port" into "tbl_tempPortTable" by using the SELECT INTO statement with the peculiar criterion of "WHERE 0<>0". If the table that is being selected into does not exist, then it is created, and since we just deleted "tbl_tempPortTable" if it already existed, we know this to be the case. Obviously, there are no records that fit the condition of 0<>0 so no records are copied over, but the structure will be copied

```
'Step 2.1: Remove tbl_tempPortTable if it already exists
On Error Resume Next
gCon.Execute ("DROP TABLE " & "tbl_tempPortTable")
On Error GoTo 0
'Step 2.2: Copy the structure of mainPort to tbl_tempPortTable
gCon.Execute ( _
    "SELECT * INTO tbl_tempPortTable" & vbCrLf & _
    "FROM " & mainPort & vbCrLf & _
    "WHERE 0 <> 0")
'Step 2.3: Add PortfolioName field to the table w/ default portName
gCon.Execute ( _
    "ALTER TABLE tbl_tempPortTable" & vbCrLf & _
    "ADD " & "[PortfolioName] VARCHAR(100) DEFAULT " & portName)
'Step 3:  Add the first portfolio
gCon.Execute ( _
    "INSERT INTO tbl_tempPortTable" & vbCrLf & _
    "SELECT " & mainPort & ".*" & vbCrLf & _
    "FROM " & mainPort)
'Step 4: Loop through sub-portfolios and add if selected
For i = 0 To 4
    If subPorts(i) <> "Empty" Then
        gCon.Execute ( _
            "INSERT INTO tbl_tempPortTable" & vbCrLf & _
            "SELECT " & subPorts(i) & ".*" & vbCrLf & _
            "FROM " & subPorts(i))
    End If
Next i
'Step 5: Insert tbl_tempPortTable into tbl_AllPortfolios
gCon.Execute ( _
    "INSERT INTO tbl_PORTFOLIOS" & vbCrLf & _
    "SELECT tbl_tempPortTable.*" & vbCrLf & _
    "FROM tbl_tempPortTable")

'Delete tbl_tempPortTable
gCon.Execute ( _
    "Drop Table tbl_tempPortTable")

dontOverwritePortfolio:
    'Clean-up
    DisconnectFromDatabase
    Set rs = Nothing

End Sub
```

EXHIBIT 18.14   Steps 2 through 5 of subroutine "addPortfolioToDB"

over. In Step 2.3 the ALTER TABLE statement adds the "PortfolioName" field to "tbl_tempPortTable" and sets its default value to the value stored in "portName". In setting a default value, any record added to the table that does not have a portfolio pame specified will have the "PortfolioName" field set to the default. On account of this, in Steps 3 and 4 we will not need to specify a portfolio name.

In Step 3 we insert the main portfolio into "tbl_tempPortTable". This statement reads, "Select everything from mainPort and insert these records into "tbl_tempPortTable". In Step 4 we do the same for the Sub-Portfolios where a portfolio is specified.

Finally in Step 5 we insert "tbl_tempPortTable" in its entirety into "tbl_SUBPORTFOLIOS". We do this in the same way that we added data to the

```
Private Sub cmd_WritePortfolioToDB_Click()
    Call addPortfolioToDB( _
        Range("m07CollatPoolFileName").Value, _
        cmb_MainPort.Value, _
        cmb_SubPort1.Value, _
        cmb_SubPort2.Value, _
        cmb_SubPort3.Value, _
        cmb_SubPort4.Value, _
        cmb_SubPort5.Value)
End Sub
```

EXHIBIT 18.15 Subroutine call from CommandButton on "CollatPoolMenu"

temporary table. Next, since we do not need "tbl_tempPortTable" anymore, we remove it from the database. Last the necessary cleanup and the error-catching code from the data validation forms the final lines of the subroutine.

Adding the "Write Portfolio to DB" CommandButton The final task is to add the code to the "Write Portfolio to Database" Button on the "CollatPoolMenu" worksheet that calls the "addPortfolioToDB" subroutine we have just examined. (We do not want all that hard work to go to waste just because we have no easy way to initiate its actions!) This code resides in the "CollatPoolMenu" worksheet code. See Exhibit 18.15. The inputs for the subroutine are read from the contents of the ComboBox items of the worksheet using the ".Value" property of each of the objects.

Let us test our new code by loading our first test portfolio to the database. On "CollatPoolMenu" select the main Pool or the Sub-Portfolios from the database. Name the new portfolio "PortfolioAll". Execute the code by clicking on the "Write Porfolio to Database" Button. Open the CCFG database and open table "tbl_PORTFOLIOS". You should see the table populated with the 2880 records with "PortfolioName" equal to "PortfolioAll". See Exhibit 18.16.

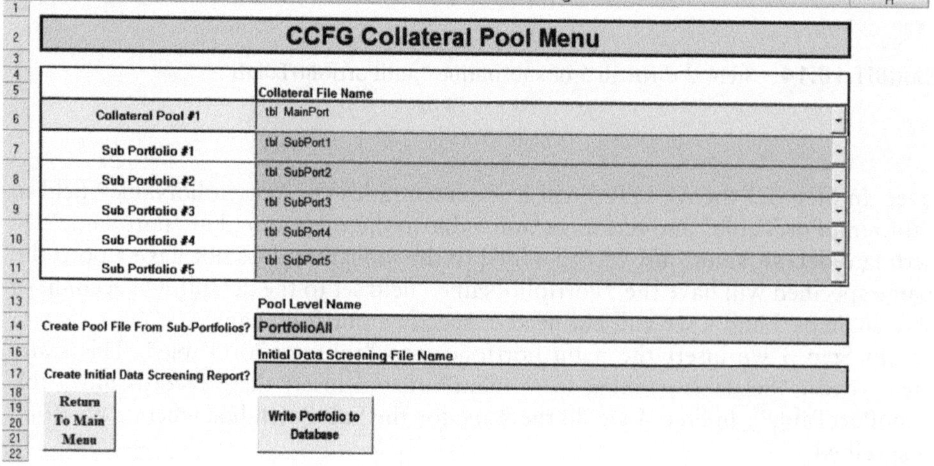

EXHIBIT 18.16 Inputs for "PortfolioAll"

GEOGRAPHIC SELECTION CRITERIA

Once we have the collateral data in the model, we will want to perform a series of selection processes against it to determine how much and what types of collateral are eligible for inclusion in our deal. We will start with transitioning the geographic selection process into Access and then proceed on to geographic concentrations and finally to the financial selection process. To implement the geographic selection process in Access, the database will need to include:

- Tables containing the regional-, state/territorial-, and MSA-level selection criteria options
- Tables containing every geographic selection test defined by the analyst as they apply to regions, states/territories, and MSAs
- Tables containing test concentration limits for states and MSAs

Database Design

As we did at the beginning of the collateral data–handling process in the prior section, we need to transfer information from existing Excel tables to an Access database table in order to make it available to the Access functions we will now write. Specifically we need one table containing regional information, one for states/territories, and one for the MSAs. The contents of these tables will be populated from the tables on the "GeoSelection" sheet in the CCFG workbook. The region table, "tbl_Regions", will have four fields: "ID", "Status", "Code", and "RegionalName". Once the table is created, the data can be copied from the "GeoSelection" sheet and pasted directly into the Access table. The table "tbl_Regions" is shown in Exhibit 18.17.

Next we need to create a table that will contain the state-level information, "tbl_States". This table will contain three fields: "ID", "Code", and "StateName". This table can be populated with the states that are also on the "GeoSelection" spreadsheet (omitting the Status column). A portion of "tbl_States" is shown in Exhibit 18.18.

For the MSA table we need six fields: "MSAGroup", "ID", "Code", "State", "MetropolitanArea", and "Population". All the MSAs are stored in the same table with the appropriate "MSAGroup" designated for each MSA. Construct each table in

tbl_Regions			
ID	Status	Code	RegionalName
1		NE	New England
2		MA	Mid-Atlantic
3		SE	South East
4		MD	Midwest
5		SW	South West
6		NW	North West
7		TR	Territories

EXHIBIT 18.17 Table "tbl_Regions"

tbl_States		
ID	Code	StateName
1	AK	Alaska
2	AL	Alabama
3	AR	Arkansas
4	AZ	Arizona
5	CA	California
6	CO	Colorado
7	CT	Connecticut
8	DE	Delaware
9	FL	Florida
10	GA	Georgia
11	HI	Hawaii
12	IA	Iowa
13	ID	Idaho

EXHIBIT 18.18   Table "tbl_States"

Excel (one for each MSA), and cut and paste these to the newly created "tbl_MSAs".
A portion of "tbl_MSAs" is shown in Exhibit 18.19.

Design Implementation

Now that all the geographic data tables have been transferred to Access tables, we can
begin using this data in our VBA code. The purpose of the following two subsections
is to replace the routines in the CCFG where geographic criteria are loaded to template files with an Access-based data storage system. The two subroutines that will
be changed are "GeoSelect_WriteCriteriaBody", which presently reads data from

tbl_MSAs					
MSAGroup	ID	Code	State	MetropolitanArea	Population
1	1	38060	AZ	Phoenix-Mesa-Scottsdale	4281899
1	2	31100	CA	Los Angeles-Long Beach-Santa Ana	12872808
1	3	40140	CA	Riverside-San Bernardino-Ontario	4115871
1	4	40900	CA	Sacramento--Arden-Arcade--Roseville	2109832
1	5	41740	CA	San Diego-Carlsbad-San Marcos	3001072
1	6	41860	CA	San Francisco-Oakland-Fremont	4274531
1	7	19740	CO	Denver-Aurora	2506626
1	8	47900	DC	Washington-Arlington-Alexandria	5358130
1	9	33100	FL	Miami-Fort Lauderdale-Pompano Beach	5414772
1	10	36740	FL	Orlando-Kissimmee	2054574
1	11	45300	FL	Tampa-St. Petersburg-Clearwater	2733761
1	12	12060	GA	Atlanta-Sandy Springs-Marietta	5376285
1	13	16980	IL	Chicago-Naperville-Joliet	9569624

EXHIBIT 18.19   Table "tbl_MSAs"

global arrays into a template file, and "GeoSelect_ReadGeoSelectionReportFile", where data was retrieved from a template file to populate the same global arrays. Once these routines are converted to Access, we will have freed ourselves of the template/directory structure pertaining to this portion of the model.

Loading Geographic Scenarios to the Database   Before writing the code to write, store, and retrieve geographic selection scenarios in the database, we need to create the three tables that will contain the regional, state, and MSA criteria for each analyst-created test. These tables will be called "tbl_GeoScensRegions", "tbl_GeoScensStates", and "tbl_GeoScensMSAs", respectively. The three scenario tables are going to have a structure identical to their "tbl_Regions", "tbl_States", and "tbl_MSAs" counterparts with an added field called "Test" to hold the test number. See Exhibit 18.20 for the design of these tables. Note that there are no primary keys set for any of these tables.

tbl_GeoScensRegions

Field Name	Data Type
Test	Number
ID	Number
Status	Text
Code	Text
RegionalName	Text

tbl_GeoScensStates

Field Name	Data Type
Test	Number
ID	Number
Code	Text
StateName	Text

tbl_GeoScensMSAs

Field Name	Data Type
Test	Number
MSAGroup	Number
ID	Number
Code	Number
State	Text
MetropolitanArea	Text
Population	Number

EXHIBIT 18.20   Geographic scenario table design

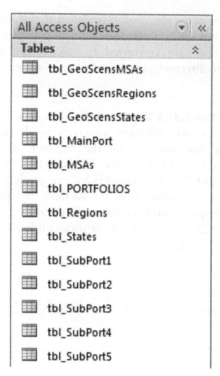

All Access Objects

Tables

- tbl_GeoScensMSAs
- tbl_GeoScensRegions
- tbl_GeoScensStates
- tbl_MainPort
- tbl_MSAs
- tbl_PORTFOLIOS
- tbl_Regions
- tbl_States
- tbl_SubPort1
- tbl_SubPort2
- tbl_SubPort3
- tbl_SubPort4
- tbl_SubPort5

EXHIBIT 18.21   Current table list in the CCFG database

Just to check on our table building progress, we can take a quick peek at the Navigation Pane of "CCFG_Data.accdb" database. If everything has gone right, we should have 13 tables in the database at this point! See Exhibit 18.21.

Let us take a moment to review how the analyst will create geographic selection tests. On the "GeoSelectMenu" worksheet in the CCFG workbook, there are three CommandButtons that bring up three different UserForms, each allowing the analyst to make selections based on region, state, or MSA. Once inside any of these UserForms, when the analyst chooses "Select Action", the choices made within the UserForm are stored in the following global arrays:

- "gFinalStatusRegions"
- "gFinalStatusStates"
- "gFinalStatusMSASet1"
- "gFinalStatusMSASet2"
- "gFinalStatusMSASet3"
- "gFinalStatusMSASet4"

Once the analyst is satisfied with the edits made to these global arrays, he or she would have previously stored the Test scenario in a template file by clicking the "Produce Geographic Assumptions File" Button, which calls "GeoSelect_WriteGeoSelectionCriteriaReport". This subroutine would then call "GeoSelect_WriteCriteriaBody". We are now going to change this subroutine so that the Test set is stored in tables in "CCFG_Data.accdb". We then must also edit the way in which the CCFG retrieves these tests by modifying the "GeoSelect_ReadGeoSelection ReportFile" procedure. We create three subroutines that are called by the "GeoSelect_WriteCriteriaBody" subroutine. These subroutines and their purposes are:

1. **"writeRegionsToDB(testNum As Integer)".** Takes as its one argument the test number to be pulled from the global array "gFinalStatusRegions" and stored in "tbl_GeoSensRegions". This writes the inclusion flags (e.g., "Inc/Inc") for each of the regions.
2. **"writeStatesToDB(testNum As Integer, idSet As String)".** Takes as its one argument the test number and another containing a string of State IDs (corresponding to the "ID" field in "tbl_States") that are to be included in the test.
3. **"writeMSAsToDB(testNum As Integer, idSet As String, msaGroup As Integer)".** Takes a test number, a list of MSA IDs, and the MSA Group number corresponding to the IDs. This subroutine will handle database writing for all four MSA groups.

Create "writeRegionsToDB" Subroutine For a given test number, supplied as an input to the "writeRegionsToDB" subroutine, there are five steps needed to transfer the contents of the "gFinalStatusRegions" to "tbl_GeoSensRegions". These five steps are shown in Exhibit 18.22.

The first step in this subroutine is to do a bit of setup. In Step 1, after connecting to the database, we delete any duplicate tests that already exist in "tbl_GeoSensRegions". We are once again going to use a temporary table, so we delete this table if it already exists. In Step 2 we copy over the entirety of "tbl_Regions" into the temporary table. At this point we have a copy of the regions table in the temporary table.

In Step 3 we update the Status field in "tbl_tempGeoSensRegions" with the contents of the "gFinalStatusRegions" array. We do this by looping over all the regions using Constant "NUM_REGIONS" and update the records of the table based on the loop counter "mRegions". So when mRegion = 2, we update the "Status field" for the record in the temp table with corresponding "ID" of 2. The SQL statement in Exhibit 18.22, without the necessary VBA formatting, is:

```
UPDATE tbl_tempGeoScensRegions
SET [Status] = gFinalStatusRegions(testNum,mRegion)
WHERE [ID] = mRegion.
```

In Step 4 we take the temp table and add a column for "Test". The SQL statement for this is:

```
ALTER TABLE tbl_tempGeoScensRegions
ADD [Test] INT.
```

This will add a field called "Test" that is of integer type. We then set the value of "Test" equal to the input "testNum" using an update query similar to the one above.

In Step 5 the entire contents of "tbl_ tempGeoScensRegions" is updated to the scenarios table "tbl_GeoScensRegions". After this is updated we delete the

```
Sub writeRegionsToDB(testNum As Integer)

    'Step 1:  Delete dupe tests and temp table
    ConnectToDataBase (DATABASE_FULLPATH)
    gCon.Execute ("DELETE * FROM tbl_GeoScensRegions " & _
                    "WHERE [Test] = " & testNum)
    On Error Resume Next
    gCon.Execute ("DROP TABLE " & "tbl_tempGeoScensRegions")
    On Error GoTo 0
    'Step 2:  Copy structure of tbl_Regions to temp table
    gCon.Execute ( _
        "SELECT * INTO tbl_tempGeoScensRegions" & vbCrLf & _
        "FROM tbl_Regions")
    'Step 3:  Update status field in temp table based on global array
    For mRegion = 1 To NUM_REGIONS
        gCon.Execute ( _
            "UPDATE tbl_tempGeoScensRegions" & vbCrLf & _
            "SET [Status] = " & Chr(34) & _
                gFinalStatusRegions(testNum, mRegion) & Chr(34) & _
            " WHERE [ID] = " & mRegion)
    Next mRegion
    'Step 4:  Add Test field to temp table and set to testNum input
    gCon.Execute ( _
        "ALTER TABLE tbl_tempGeoScensRegions" & vbCrLf & _
        "ADD [Test] INT")
    gCon.Execute ( _
        "UPDATE tbl_tempGeoScensRegions" & vbCrLf & _
        "SET [Test] = " & testNum)
    'Step 5:  Update tbl_GeoScensRegions with contents of temp table
    gCon.Execute ( _
        "INSERT INTO tbl_GeoScensRegions" & vbCrLf & _
        "SELECT *" & vbCrLf & _
        "FROM tbl_tempGeoScensRegions")
    'Delete tbl_tempPortTable
    gCon.Execute ( _
        "Drop Table tbl_tempGeoScensRegions")

    DisconnectFromDatabase

End Sub
```

EXHIBIT 18.22   "writeRegionsToDB" subroutine

temp table and disconnect from the database. As an example, the contents of "tbl_GeoScensRegions" after storing a single test are shown in Exhibit 18.23.

Create "writeStatesToDB" Subroutine   The subroutine to write the state selections to the database is simpler than the Region subroutine. In addition to the "test-Num", "writeStatesToDB" also takes a string input that lists which states are included in the Test. The list contains the IDs corresponding to the "ID" field in "tbl_States". For each Test, "tbl_GeoScensStates" will contain only the states that are to be included in the Geographic Selection Scenario. The form of the "idSet" input is "(id1,id2,id3,...)", so it is ready to be incorporated into the criteria for the database query. The subroutine is shown in Exhibit 18.24.

tbl_GeoScensRegions				
Test	ID	Status	Code	RegionalNar
1	1	Inc\Inc	NE	New England
1	2	Inc\Inc	MA	Mid-Atlantic
1	3	Inc\Inc	SE	South East
1	4	Inc\Inc	MD	Midwest
1	5	Inc\Inc	SW	South West
1	6	Inc\Inc	NW	North West
1	7	Inc\Inc	TR	Territories

EXHIBIT 18.23   Table "tbl_GeoScensRegions"

```
Sub writeStatesToDB(testNum As Integer, idSet As String)

    'Step 1:  Delete dupe tests and temp table
    ConnectToDataBase (DATABASE_FULLPATH)
    gCon.Execute ("DELETE * FROM tbl_GeoScensStates " & _
                  "WHERE [Test] = " & testNum)
    On Error Resume Next
    gCon.Execute ("DROP TABLE " & "tbl_tempGeoScensStates")
    On Error GoTo 0
    'Step 2:  Populate temp table with contents of the
    'tbl_States table where the ID is in the input idSet
    gCon.Execute ( _
        "SELECT * INTO tbl_tempGeoScensStates" & vbCrLf & _
        "FROM tbl_States" & vbCrLf & _
        "WHERE [ID] in " & idSet)
    'Step 3:  Add Test field and set to input testNum
    gCon.Execute ( _
        "ALTER TABLE tbl_tempGeoScensStates" & vbCrLf & _
        "ADD [Test] INT")
    gCon.Execute ( _
        "UPDATE tbl_tempGeoScensStates" & vbCrLf & _
        "SET [Test] = " & testNum)
    'Step 4:  Update tbl_GeoScensStates with contents of temp table
    gCon.Execute ( _
        "INSERT INTO tbl_GeoScensStates" & vbCrLf & _
        "SELECT *" & vbCrLf & _
        "FROM tbl_tempGeoScensStates")
    'Delete temp table
    gCon.Execute ( _
        "Drop Table tbl_tempGeoScensStates")

    DisconnectFromDatabase

End Sub
```

EXHIBIT 18.24   "writeStatesToDB" subroutine

tbl_GeoScensStates			
Test	ID	Code	StateName
1	1	AK	Alaska
1	2	AL	Alabama
1	6	CO	Colorado
1	8	DE	Delaware

EXHIBIT 18.25 Table "tbl_GeoScensStates"

In Step 1 we delete any records with "Test" equal to "testNum" from "tbl_GeoScensStates". We also delete the temporary table if it already exists. In Step 2, instead of copying the entire states table over as we did for the regions table, we only copy the records where the ID matches one of the IDs in the "idSet" input. The SQL portion of the code is:

```
SELECT * INTO tbl_tempGeoScensStates
FROM tbl_States
WHERE [ID] in idSet
```

Remember that the idSet will look something like "(1,2,6,8)", in which case the only records copied over to the temp table would be for the corresponding states (AK, AL, CO, and DE).

Once the temporary table is populated with the included states, we then add the "Test" field and set its value to "testNum" in Step 3. Next, in Step 4, the contents of the temporary table are updated to "tbl_GeoScensStates" and the temporary table is deleted. An example state test set is shown in Exhibit 18.25.

Create "writeMSAsToDB" Subroutine The "writeMSAsToDB" subroutine is nearly identical in function to that of the states. The only difference is that instead of copying over the matching IDs in "tbl_MSAs", we only want to copy over those records where the "MSAGroup" field is equal to the input "msaGroup". The SQL statement in Step 2 now appears as:

```
SELECT * INTO tbl_tempGeoScensMSAs
FROM tbl_MSAs
WHERE [ID] in idSet
AND [MSAGroup] = msaGroup
```

The "writeMSAsToDB" subroutine is shown in Exhibit 18.26.

Edit "GeoSelect_WriteCriteriaBody" Subroutine Now that we have created the three subroutines that load the region, state, and MSA selections to the database, we need to edit the subroutine that calls these subroutines. The first half of "GeoSelect_WriteCriteriaBody" is shown in Exhibit 18.27.

This subroutine is passed the Test number as "itest", which it eventually passes on to the three subroutines created above. We also see in Exhibit 18.27 the declaration of the two included ID strings for states and MSAs ("stateIDs" and

```
Sub writeMSAsToDB(testNum As Integer, idSet As String, msaGroup As Integer)

    'Step 1:  Delete dupe tests and temp table
    ConnectToDataBase (DATABASE_FULLPATH)
    If msaGroup = 1 Then
        gCon.Execute ("DELETE * FROM tbl_GeoScensMSAs " & _
                        "WHERE [Test] = " & testNum)
    End If
    On Error Resume Next
    gCon.Execute ("DROP TABLE " & "tbl_tempGeoScensMSAs")
    On Error GoTo 0
    'Step 2:  Populate temp table with contents of the
    'tbl_MSAs table where the ID is in the input idSet
    'and where MSA Group equals input msaGroup
    gCon.Execute ( _
        "SELECT * INTO tbl_tempGeoScensMSAs" & vbCrLf & _
        "FROM tbl_MSAs" & vbCrLf & _
        "WHERE [ID] in " & idSet & _
        " AND [MSAGroup] = " & msaGroup)
    'Step 3:  Add Test field and set to input testNum
    gCon.Execute ( _
        "ALTER TABLE tbl_tempGeoScensMSAs" & vbCrLf & _
        "ADD [Test] INT")
    gCon.Execute ( _
        "UPDATE tbl_tempGeoScensMSAs" & vbCrLf & _
        "SET [Test] = " & testNum)
    'Step 4:  Update tbl_GeoScensMSAs with contents of temp table
    gCon.Execute ( _
        "INSERT INTO tbl_GeoScensMSAs" & vbCrLf & _
        "SELECT *" & vbCrLf & _
        "FROM tbl_tempGeoScensMSAs")
    'Delete temp table
    gCon.Execute ( _
        "Drop Table tbl_tempGeoScensMSAs")

    DisconnectFromDatabase

End Sub
```

EXHIBIT 18.26 "writeMSAsToDB" subroutine

"msaIDs"). In order to output the regional selections to the database, the subroutine simply calls "writeRegionsToDB".

Before calling "writeStatesToDB", we must first create the included ID string "stateIDs". This is done by looping over the states from 1 to "NUM_STATES" and inspecting the contents of "gFinalStatusStates". If the value stored in element ("itest", "mState") of the array is TRUE, then the ID, represented by "mState", is appended to the "stateIDs" string. Once all the elements of the array have been checked, the next "If. .Then" block checks to see if *any* states were selected. If so, we clean up the string by removing the dangling space and comma at the end of the string. If not, we set "stateIDs" equal to the placeholder value "-999". The only thing left to do is tack on the parentheses and call "writeStatesToDB" with the appropriate inputs.

The MSA portion of "GeoSelect_WriteCriteriaBody" subroutine is similar to the States section, but we must create an included ID string and call "writeMSAsToDB" for each of the four MSA groups. The second half of "GeoSelect_WriteCriteriaBody" is shown in Exhibit 18.28.

```
Sub GeoSelect_WriteCriteriaBody(itest As Integer)

Dim stateIDs         As String    'list of action state IDs
Dim msaIDs           As String    'list of action SMA IDs

    'Regions
    Call writeRegionsToDB(itest)

    'States
    'Generate State ID list
    For mState = 1 To NUM_STATES
        If gFinalStatusStates(itest, mState) Then
            stateIDs = stateIDs & mState & ", "
        End If
    Next mState
    'Edit ID string and call writeStatesToDB
    If Len(stateIDs) Then
        stateIDs = Left(stateIDs, Len(stateIDs) - 2)
    Else
        stateIDs = "-999"
    End If
    stateIDs = "(" & stateIDs & ")"
    Call writeStatesToDB(itest, stateIDs)
```

EXHIBIT 18.27   Regions and States portions of "GeoSelect_WriteCriteriaBody" subroutine

Retrieving Geographic Scenarios from the Database   Now that we have a way to store geographic selection tests in the database, we need a way to repopulate the global array when an analyst chooses the "Load Selections Info From File" option on the "GeoSelectMenu" sheet. This button calls the "GeoSelect_ReadGeoSelectionReportFile" subroutine, so this is where all the edits below will take place.

To repopulate the global arrays, we build SQL strings that query the scenario sables populated by the above subroutines to return the IDs and statuses ("Inc/Inc" for segions, "INCLUDED" or "OUT" for states and MSAs) for a specified Test number. These query views will then be stored in a recordset that is looped over to populate the global arrays. Once we have the queries established, it is easy to populate the arrays.

The query for the regions is by far the simplest and is constructed as follows:

```
SELECT [ID], [Status]
FROM tbl_GeoScensRegions
WHERE [Test] = varTest
ORDER BY [ID]
```

This query is pretty easily deciphered. We want the ID and Status of all records in "tbl_GeoScensRegions" where the "Test" number is "varTest". The results are going to be ordered based on the "ID" field. The resultant recordset can easily be looped over to see which regions are set to "Inc/Inc", "Inc/Exl", and so forth. Notice that the above code is shown as it will appear in the VBA editor without the necessary formatting. The string "varTest" is a placeholder that will be replaced by the actual Test number stored on the "GeoSelectMenu" sheet.

```
'MSA Sets
For iset = 1 To MSA_SEL_SETS
    msaIDs = ""
    Select Case iset
        Case Is = 1: EndLoop = NUM_MSA_SET1
        Case Is = 2: EndLoop = NUM_MSA_SET2
        Case Is = 3: EndLoop = NUM_MSA_SET3
        Case Is = 4: EndLoop = NUM_MSA_SET4
    End Select
    For mMSA = 1 To EndLoop
        Select Case iset
            Case Is = 1
                If gFinalStatusMSASet1(itest, mMSA) Then
                    msaIDs = msaIDs & mMSA & ", "
                End If
            Case Is = 2
                If gFinalStatusMSASet2(itest, mMSA) Then
                    msaIDs = msaIDs & mMSA & ", "
                End If
            Case Is = 3
                If gFinalStatusMSASet3(itest, mMSA) Then
                    msaIDs = msaIDs & mMSA & ", "
                End If
            Case Is = 4
                If gFinalStatusMSASet4(itest, mMSA) Then
                    msaIDs = msaIDs & mMSA & ", "
                End If
        End Select
    Next mMSA
    If Len(msaIDs) Then
        msaIDs = Left(msaIDs, Len(msaIDs) - 2)
    Else
        msaIDs = "-999"
    End If
    msaIDs = "(" & msaIDs & ")"
    Call writeMSAsToDB(itest, msaIDs, iset)
Next iset

End Sub
```

EXHIBIT 18.28 MSA portion of "GeoSelect_WriteCriteriaBody" subroutine

The query for states is probably one of the most complex we have seen so far. It is constructed as follows:

```
SELECT [ID], 'OUT' as Status
FROM tbl_States
WHERE [ID] NOT IN
    (SELECT [ID]
    FROM tbl_GeoScensStates
    WHERE [Test] = varTest)
UNION
SELECT [ID], 'INCLUDED' as Status
FROM tbl_States
WHERE [ID] IN
    (SELECT [ID]
    FROM tbl_GeoScensStates
    WHERE [Test] = varTest)
ORDER BY [ID]
```

This query contains two separate subqueries joined by the keyword UNION. Each of the subqueries contains another subquery. The first query returns a view that is composed of an "ID" field and a field called "Status" that contains only the word "OUT". IDs that appear in this query are the IDs that are in "tbl_States" but are "NOT IN" the following subquery:

```
SELECT [ID]
FROM tbl_GeoScensStates
WHERE [Test] = varTest
```

The subquery returns all the state IDs stored within "tbl_GeoScensStates" for a given test. So, in short, the top query gives a list of IDs and "OUT" for all States that were not included in the supplied "Test" number. Once again we see the use of string "varTest" as a placeholder.

The second query does the converse of the first one. It returns the list of state IDs and "INCLUDED" for all IDs that are in "tbl_States" and in the subquery results. If two queries have the same fields in their results, the two views can be stacked on top of one another by using a UNION. The result will be a complete list of states and a "Status" column containing "INCLUDED" or "OUT". This format is readily looped over to repopulate that global state array.

The query for MSAs is similar to that for states but with the added constraint of "varMSA" for the "MSAGroup". This query is constructed as follows:

```
SELECT [ID], 'OUT' as Status
FROM tbl_MSAs
WHERE [ID] NOT IN
    (SELECT [ID]
    FROM tbl_GeoScensStates
    WHERE [Test] = varTest
    AND [MSAGroup] = varMSA)
UNION
SELECT [ID], 'INCLUDED' as Status
FROM tbl_MSAs
WHERE [ID] IN
    (SELECT [ID]
    FROM tbl_GeoScensStates
    WHERE [Test] = varTest
    AND [MSAGroup] = varMSA)
ORDER BY [ID]
```

Edit "GeoSelect_ReadGeoSelectionReportFile" Subroutine   Now that we understand the queries that are going to be used, we can begin editing the subroutine. We first need to dimension and set the string variables for the three queries. This part of the subroutine is shown in Exhibit 18.29. We see in Exhibit 18.29 the "itest"

```
Sub GeoSelect_ReadGeoSelectionReportFile()

Dim str_sql_Reg          As String              'SQL string for Regions
Dim str_sql_Sta          As String              'SQL string for States
Dim str_sql_MSA          As String              'SQL string for MSAs
Dim rs                   As ADODB.Recordset     'recordset object

    itest = Range("m03TestNumber")

    str_sql_Reg = "SELECT [ID], [Status] " & _
                  "FROM tbl_GeoScensRegions " & _
                  "WHERE [Test] = varTest " & _
                  "ORDER BY [ID]"

    str_sql_Sta = "SELECT [ID], 'OUT' as Status" & vbCrLf & _
                  "FROM tbl_States" & vbCrLf & _
                  "WHERE [ID] NOT IN " & _
                  "   (SELECT [ID] FROM tbl_GeoScensStates " & _
                  "   WHERE [Test] = varTest)" & vbCrLf & _
                  "UNION" & vbCrLf & _
                  "SELECT [ID], 'INCLUDED' as Status" & vbCrLf & _
                  "FROM tbl_States" & vbCrLf & _
                  "WHERE [ID] IN " & _
                  "   (SELECT [ID] FROM tbl_GeoScensStates " & _
                  "   WHERE [Test] = varTest)" & vbCrLf & _
                  "ORDER BY [ID]"

    str_sql_MSA = "SELECT [ID], 'OUT' as Status" & vbCrLf & _
                  "FROM tbl_MSAs" & vbCrLf & _
                  "WHERE [ID] NOT IN " & _
                  "   (SELECT [ID] FROM tbl_GeoScensMSAs " & _
                  "   WHERE [Test] = varTest " & _
                  "   AND [MSAGroup] = varMSA)" & vbCrLf & _
                  "AND [MSAGroup] = varMSA" & vbCrLf & _
                  "UNION" & vbCrLf & _
                  "SELECT [ID], 'INCLUDED' as Status " & vbCrLf & _
                  "FROM tbl_MSAs" & vbCrLf & _
                  "WHERE [ID] IN " & _
                  "   (SELECT [ID] FROM tbl_GeoScensMSAs " & _
                  "   WHERE [Test] = varTest " & _
                  "   AND [MSAGroup] = varMSA)" & vbCrLf & _
                  "AND [MSAGroup] = varMSA" & vbCrLf & _
                  "ORDER BY [ID]"

    str_sql_Reg = Replace(str_sql_Reg, "varTest", itest)
    str_sql_Sta = Replace(str_sql_Sta, "varTest", itest)
    str_sql_MSA = Replace(str_sql_MSA, "varTest", itest)
```

EXHIBIT 18.29 Query strings of
"GeoSelect_ReadGeoSelectionReportFile" subroutine

variable set to the "GeoScenSelect" spreadsheet Range "m03TestNumber". After setting up the "str_sql" strings, we replace the substring "varTest" with the contents of "itest".

After connecting to the database, we move on to populate the region and state global arrays based on the contents of the recordset. Before doing so we first check to make sure that this test set has been saved. This is done by checking if the cursor for the region recordset is pointing at the beginning and end of file at the same time. If so, the query returns no results, and we therefore know that the test has yet to be

```
ConnectToDataBase (DATABASE_FULLPATH)
'Regions
Set rs = gCon.Execute(str_sql_Reg)
'Check to see that test has been saved; if not exist routine
If rs.EOF And rs.BOF Then
    MsgBox "This test has not yet been saved to the database."
    GoTo cleanup
End If
'Loop over recordset and populate global array
For mRegion = 1 To NUM_REGIONS 'Read Region Level from rs
    gFinalStatusRegions(itest, mRegion) = _
                rs.Fields("Status").Value
    rs.MoveNext
Next mRegion
'States
Set rs = gCon.Execute(str_sql_Sta)
'Loop over recordset and populate global array
For mState = 1 To NUM_STATES
    If rs.Fields("Status").Value = "INCLUDED" Then
        gFinalStatusStates(itest, mState) = True
    Else
        gFinalStatusStates(itest, mState) = False
    End If
    rs.MoveNext
Next mState
```

EXHIBIT 18.30   Population of region and state global arrays

saved. Once we are sure that there is data loaded for the specified test number, we loop over the regions and states, populating the global arrays as we go. This portion of the subroutine is shown in Exhibit 18.30.

As we have seen many times above, the program flow for the MSA's code portion is similar to the state's process, but with the added complexity of looping over the four different MSA groups. The MSA code is shown in Exhibit 18.31.

GEOGRAPHIC CONCENTRATION CRITERIA

In the previous section we saw how we can use Access to improve the effectiveness and clarity of the VBA code supporting the Geographic Selection Criteria tests. We will now turn to what is essentially a subset of the geographic selection activity—the setting of Geographic concentrations. Geographic concentrations determine what percentage of the total final eligible collateral of the portfolio a specific state or MSA can contribute. In the previous section when we excluded a particular state or MSA, we essentially set its concentration limit to 0%. The UserForm from the menu that allows us to establish concentration limits for states and MSAs is very similar to those used in setting the Geographic Selection Criteria. The main difference is that the last two sets of the smaller MSAs, Sets #3 and #4, which contain a total of 98 of the 150 MSAs, have been dropped.

```
'MSAs
For iset = 1 To MSA_SEL_SETS
'Replace varMSA substring based on iset
    Set rs = gCon.Execute(Replace(str_sql_Sta, "varMSA", iset))
'Set loop counter based on iset
    Select Case iset
        Case Is = 1: EndLoop = NUM_MSA_SET1
        Case Is = 2: EndLoop = NUM_MSA_SET2
        Case Is = 3: EndLoop = NUM_MSA_SET3
        Case Is = 4: EndLoop = NUM_MSA_SET4
    End Select
    For mMSA = 1 To EndLoop
        If rs.Fields("Status").Value = "INCLUDED" Then
            Select Case iset
                Case 1: gFinalStatusMSASet1(itest, mMSA) = True
                Case 2: gFinalStatusMSASet2(itest, mMSA) = True
                Case 3: gFinalStatusMSASet3(itest, mMSA) = True
                Case 4: gFinalStatusMSASet4(itest, mMSA) = True
            End Select
        Else
            Select Case iset
                Case 1: gFinalStatusMSASet1(itest, mMSA) = False
                Case 2: gFinalStatusMSASet2(itest, mMSA) = False
                Case 3: gFinalStatusMSASet3(itest, mMSA) = False
                Case 4: gFinalStatusMSASet4(itest, mMSA) = False
            End Select
        End If
        rs.MoveNext
    Next mMSA
Next iset
cleanup:
    DisconnectFromDatabase
    Set rs = Nothing
End Sub
```

EXHIBIT 18.31   Population of MSA global arrays

The CCFG database will contain a table holding the concentration limits for the set of 54 states and another for the 52 of the largest MSAs, those of MSA sets #1 and #2. There is a single set of concentration limits for each model run. We will want to be able to read, store, retrieve, and display these concentration constraints in the same manner that we were able to handle the Geographic Selection Criteria in the section above. To accomplish these goals we will develop VBA and Access tables quite similar to those used in the section dealing with the region portion of Geographic Selection Criteria tests. The two concentration tables, "tbl_GeoConcStates" and "tbl_GeoConcMSAs", contain the field "Level" in place of the "Status" fields in the previous tables. These columns are populated in temporary tables from the global arrays and are then shifted to the concentration tables in the same way "tbl_GeoScensRegions" was populated in the previous section.

In that these processes and the subroutines that execute them are virtually identical in form and function to the ones in the Geographic Selection Criteria section

```
Sub GeoSelect_WriteGeoSelectionCriteriaReport()

    If gWriteSelectReport Then          'the geo selection is selected
        For itest = 1 To NUM_GEO_TESTS
            If gTestSelectOutput(itest) Then
                Call GeoSelect_WriteCriteriaBody(itest)
            End If
        Next itest
    End If

    If gWriteConcenReport Then          'the geo concentration is selected
        For itest = 1 To NUM_GEO_TESTS
            If gTestSelectOutput(itest) Then
                Call GeoSelect_WriteConcentrationReport(itest)
            End If
        Next itest
    End If

End Sub
```

EXHIBIT 18.32   "GeoSelect_WriteGeoSelectionCriteriaReport" subroutine

above, the reader is invited to view them in the code. Size limitations of the book preclude us from discussing them in detail here.

Once both sections of the Geographic Selection Criteria have been completed, the final step is to edit the code behind the "Produce Geographic Assumptions File" Button on "GeoSelectMenu". Previously, the corresponding code would open up template files and begin adding sheets while iterating over the five possible Geographic Tests. The new code for the "GeoSelect_WriteGeoSelectionCriteriaReport" subroutine appears in Exhibit 18.32. This subroutine is located in the "MenuSupport_GeographicSelect" module.

INITIAL DATA SCREENING CRITERIA

The initial collection of collateral data information was stored in a series of Excel files, one record per row. In that these portfolio files contained a mix of mortgage types, each with characteristics and information specific to it, the files contained fields for all possible data needed by each type. It was also necessary to segregate the Sub-Portfolios based on their origin, not on their collateral compositions. This approach was primarily adopted to allow us to mix and match various collections of collateral regardless of their composition. As a result, any portfolio can, and sometimes does, contain variations of or all of the collateral types.

An alternative approach might have been to provide a method of extracting loans of identical amortization types and building Sub-Portfolios from these collections. We would still need to identify which loans came from which of the original portfolios but this could have been done with a separate Sub-Portfolio ID field.

Had we followed this approach, we would be able to take advantage of Access's ability to require designated fields in a table to have complete and valid values prior to that record being added to the database. As a result, all loans in the database would have had to pass a de facto screening process. For example, the "ResetFrequency" field in the standard adjustable rate mortgages (SARM) table would have been a required field. A SARM cannot be amortized without this piece of information. Access would not allow the addition of a record with a null "ResetFrequency" field value and would return an error message informing us that the record did not fit with the table definition.

In our current schema, the portfolio table contains all acceptable loan types. Lacking the prescreening function of the Access product, we need to perform it ourselves. This section shows how to perform this function using Access tables. We will also create the ability to write the Initial Data Screening Results file that will display the results of the screening process on a loan-by-loan basis.

This routine will run each time the model does. These incomplete records will be deemed ineligible collateral prior to any other selection processes or the calculation of the cash flows. An Access subroutine that will produce report listing these ineligible loans will also be created.

In addition to the information needed to amortize the various loan types, other sets of information may be required depending on the prepayment, default, and recovery assumptions that will be employed. The Initial Data Screening will also need to look at selected collateral record fields to determine if this information is complete. In addition, to provide a full range of stratification reports, another set of information is required. The Access subroutines developed in this section will seek to address all of these data screening issues.

Database Design

To begin, we will first create a table in the database that contains the required fields for each loan type. The number of required fields ranges from 5 for the amortization parameters of a fixed rate loans and up to 22 for a complete set of stratification reports. Once we have created the table, we loop through each of the loans of the portfolio. Loans that fail specific tests will be added to a rejected loan table based on the type of test they have failed.

If we decide to produce reports of these results, VBA will write these ineligible loans to a report file from the Access tables. We will configure the model to allow the Initial Data Screening process to be triggered as a stand-alone activity directly from the "CollatPoolMenu" worksheet.

Database Implementation

We will now create the tables and queries to perform the Initial Data Screening process.

Creating the Required Fields Table "tbl_ReqFields"
The table that contains the loan types and their corresponding required fields looks very similar to tables we have previously created. The "tbl_ReqFields" table is shown in Design View in Exhibit 18.33. It is populated with the field names from "tbl_PORTFOLIOS" corresponding to each loan type. The fields in the exhibit are for a SARM. See Exhibit 18.34.

tbl_ReqFields	
Field Name	**Data Type**
LoanType	Text
TypeNumber	Number
FieldOrder	Number
FieldName	Text

EXHIBIT 18.33　"tbl_ReqFields" in Design View

The entries in this table must be identical to the field names in "tbl_PORTFOLIOS". If there are any incorrectly labeled field names, Access will return an error when we try to execute queries. We can catch these errors early on in the building of SQL execution strings in VBA by outputting the execution strings to the Immediate Window in VBA and pasting the query into a blank Access query in SQL View. If there are misspelled fields, Access will highlight the first of them upon execution. By repeating this process, we can correct all misspellings in our execution strings. This is a prudent and highly recommended step when writing long or complicated execution strings, as the error messages in Access are more instructional than those returned by VBA when executing against an Access database.

The order of the field names in "tbl_ReqFields" is critical because it later designates the field location in the output report. Open the report template file "InitDataScreenTemplateAccess.xlsx"—available on the Web site—to see the fields required for each loan type and the order in which they will appear. Now that we have the "tbl_ReqFields" table created, we will start building queries to perform the data checks and output the results to the Initial Data Screening Report.

tbl_ReqFields			
LoanType	**TypeNumber**	**FieldOrder**	**FieldName**
StandardARM	2	1	OrigBankBal
StandardARM	2	2	CurBankBal
StandardARM	2	3	OrigTerm
StandardARM	2	4	RemTerm
StandardARM	2	5	Coupon
StandardARM	2	6	Index
StandardARM	2	7	Spread
StandardARM	2	8	InitialRate
StandardARM	2	9	ResetRate
StandardARM	2	10	ResetCap
StandardARM	2	11	ResetFloor
StandardARM	2	12	LifeCap
StandardARM	2	13	LifeFloor

EXHIBIT 18.34　Required SARM fields in "tbl_ReqFields"

Writing the Query Code Module   We begin this process by making extensive changes to the "Collat_InitialDataScreening" module. At the top of this module we will create a set of module variables as follows:

```
Dim mPathName    As String          'directory pathway
Dim mthisWBName  As String          'this workbook's name
Dim iType        As Integer         'mort type iterator
Dim rs           As ADODB.Recordset 'recordset object
Dim sheetNames() As Variant         'names of worksheets in report file
Dim rs_array()   As Variant         'output for report file
```

You will note that two of the arrays are dimensioned with the data type variant. The arrays are type variant so that we can employ the "=Array()" syntax when assigning values to the array elements. We can then easily loop through whatever data we have placed in the array.

We will now begin writing the VBA code for the main "InitialScreening" subroutine. This subroutine will take as its three parameters the portfolio name array, the output file name, and a variable indicating if we are to write a report of the screening results. The local variables are an array to hold the various loan amortization types, the various portions of the SQL queries we will build, and a variable to hold the results of the query. Following these variable declarations, the process begins with a pre-check of the output report file name. We want to make sure that the analyst does not unintentionally write over a previous report by selecting the name of an existing file! We will also check the file extension. The first line checks whether the output name has been entered with the file extension included. If this is not the case, this statement will add the required ".xlsx" extension.

A "Do..While" loop then checks whether a report is being output and if the file already exists. If both of these conditions are TRUE, we ask the analyst to input a new file name. If the analyst chooses "Cancel", then the "msgResult" string will be blank and the program will terminate. If a new name has been entered, then we will change the name and check this name against existing files. The "Do..While" loop will continue until the analyst enters a valid file name or chooses to quit. See Exhibit 18.35.

One of the conditions of the "Do..While" Loop is that "fileExists (INITSCRN_SUBDIR& outputName)" is TRUE. The function "fileExists" is an analyst-defined function residing in module "Z_UtilitySubroutines". The method is used to check for existing files in this function is to use the "Dir()" function with the full file path as an input. If the file exists, the function returns a TRUE. This subroutine is:

```
Function FileExists(fname) As Boolean
    FileExists = Dir(fname) <> '' ''
End Function
```

Many of the activities of the "InitialScreening" subroutine should look very familiar. See Exhibit 18.36.

In Step 1 we populate two arrays. The first, "loanTypes", contains a set of each of the tests. All of these tests do not pertain to loan types; the fifth relates to the stratification report data requirements and the sixth and seventh to prepayment and

```
Sub InitialScreening(portName() As String, _
                     outputName As String, _
                     produceReport As Boolean)

Dim loanTypes() As Variant    'loan type array
Dim str_sql     As String     'SQL execution string
Dim str_select  As String     'SQL SELECT clause string
Dim str_where   As String     'SQL WHERE clause string
Dim msgResult   As String     'message result
Dim iPort       As Long       'portfolio name iterator

    If InStr(1, outputName, ".xlsx") = 0 Then outputName = outputName & ".xlsx"
    Do While produceReport And FileExists(INITSCRN_SUBDIR & outputName)
        msgResult = InputBox("Rename the Output File", "File Already Exists")
        If msgResult = "" Then
            End
        Else
            If InStr(1, msgResult, ".xlsx") = 0 Then
                msgResult = msgResult & ".xlsx"
            End If
            outputName = msgResult
        End If
    Loop
```

EXHIBIT 18.35   "InitialScreening" subroutine setup

```
'Step 1: Populate arrays for fields and worksheets
loanTypes = Array("FixedRate", "StandardARM", "HybridARM", _
                  "Balloon", "StratificationData", _
                  "FreqOfForeclosureData", "SeverityOfLossData")
sheetNames = Array("FixedRate", "StandardARMs", "HybridARMs", _
                   "Balloons", "StratificationData", _
                   "FreqOfForeclosureData", "SeverityOfLossData")
'Step 2:  Connect to database and create tbl_IncRecords
ConnectToDataBase (DATABASE_FULLPATH)
On Error Resume Next
gCon.Execute ("DROP TABLE tbl_IncRecords")
On Error GoTo 0
gCon.Execute ( _
        "CREATE TABLE tbl_IncRecords(" & _
            "AccountNumber INT," & _
            "MortType VARCHAR(100)," & _
            "MortTypeNum INT)")
'Step 3: Build the execution strings
For iPort = 0 To UBound(portName)
    For iType = 1 To 7
        Set rs = gCon.Execute( _
                    "SELECT * FROM tbl_ReqFields " & _
                    "WHERE TypeNumber = " & iType & vbCrLf & _
                    "ORDER BY FieldOrder")
        str_select = "SELECT AccountNumber, -999, "
        str_where = "WHERE tbl_PORTFOLIOS.PortfolioName = " & _
                            "'" & portName(iPort) & "' "
        If iType <= 4 Then
            str_where = str_where & "AND tbl_PORTFOLIOS.MortType = " _
                        & iType & " AND("
        Else
            str_where = str_where & "AND("
        End If
```

EXHIBIT 18.36   Steps 1 to 5 of Initial Data Screening process

```
'Step 4: Execution string filtering and formatting required fields
        Do While Not rs.EOF
            str_select = str_select _
                       & "IIf(IsNull(" & rs.Fields("FieldName").Value & "), " _
                       & "'X',''')" _
                       & "as null" & rs.Fields("FieldName").Value & ", "
            str_where = str_where & rs.Fields("FieldName").Value & " is null OR "
            rs.MoveNext
        Loop
        str_select = Left(str_select, Len(str_select) - 2)
        str_where = Left(str_where, Len(str_where) - 3) & ")"
        str_sql = str_select & vbCrLf & "FROM tbl_PORTFOLIOS" & vbCrLf & str_where
        Debug.Print str_sql
'Step 5: Produce report and store incomplete records in tbl_IncRecords
        Set rs = gCon.Execute(str_sql)
        If Not (rs.BOF And rs.EOF) Then
            If produceReport Then
                rs.MoveFirst
                rs_array = Application.WorksheetFunction.Transpose(rs.GetRows)
                If iPort = UBound(portName) Then
                    Call CollatData_WriteInitScreenResultsRep(outputName)
                End If
            End If
            rs.MoveFirst
            Do While Not rs.EOF
                str_sql = "INSERT INTO tbl_IncRecords " & vbCrLf & _
                          "VALUES(" & rs.Fields(0).Value & ", " & _
                          "'" & loanTypes(iType - 1) & "' , " & _
                          iType & ")"
                gCon.Execute (str_sql)
                rs.MoveNext
            Loop
        End If
    Next iType
Next iPort

On Error Resume Next
Workbooks(outputName).Close SaveChanges:=True
On Error GoTo 0

Set rs = Nothing
DisconnectFromDatabase
End Sub
```

EXHIBIT 18.36 *(Continued)*

foreclosure issues. The second array lists the worksheet names of the template report into which we will write the records that have failed the screening tests and the specific conditions of their failure. If there are any spelling errors or omissions in the list of the "loanTypes", the queries will not produce error indications. This is because Access will not recognize the misspelled array elements and ignores them. If the elements of the "sheetNames" array are defined incorrectly, object errors will result when the model looks for sheets in the report file that are not there.

In Step 2 we see the code to delete "tbl_IncRecords" from the database if it already exists followed by the table creation. We create the table by utilizing the CREATE TABLE SQL syntax. This statement creates a table in code the same way we create tables in Access. For "tbl_IncRecords" we assign three fields. The first, "AccountNumber", is an integer type and will contain the account numbers of incomplete records. The next two fields, "MortType" and "MortTypeNum", specify what type of mortgage each loan is by a string and a corresponding type number. This table will hold the loan records that do not pass their respective type criteria.

In Step 3 we employ a "For..Next" loop to iterate through the "portName()" input array. We want to allow the analyst to be able to specify multiple portfolios when running an amortization later in the modeling process. Next we employ another "For..Next" loop to peruse the various loan/report types and build the execution strings. We populate the recordset "rs" with the required fields for the specific loan/report type using the "iType" loop counter. The SELECT and WHERE portions of the execution string are constructed next. These are assigned to the "str_select" and "str_where" variables. In the assignment of the "str_select" variable, we see that in addition to the "AccountNumber" we are also selecting "-999". This is a placeholder used to keep the output formatted in a way that the report template file is expecting. All instances of "-999" will be written over later in the reporting process in the error report file with the cumulative error code. The assignment of the "str_where" variable starts by setting up a filter for "PortfolioName" and then, within the "If Statement", a filter for "MortType". For the stratification, foreclosure, and severity reports, we will look at all mortgages at once, irrespective of type. This is the reason for the "If Statement" setting the mortgage type filter only for reports 1 through 5 (the loan-type reports), as these three reports apply to *all* types of mortgage loans.

In Step 4 we build the remainder of the command string. The "Do..While" loop adds an "IF Statement" to "str_select" for every field name that is stored in recordset "rs". Each of these additions will look something like:

```
If(IsNull(OrigBankBal), ''X'', '''') as nullOrigBankBal
```

For the variable "str_where", we add the check for null fields:

```
OrigBankBal is null OR CurBankBal is null OR...
```

The full execution string will return all records in the portfolio in question where *any* of the required fields for the current "MortType (iType)" are blank, marking those fields with an "X" in the results. This is precisely the format that our report template file is expecting!

In Step 5 we now have a recordset "rs" containing any incomplete loan records for the current value of "MortType" in the correct format to be output to the report. If the size of the record set is greater than zero, we check the value of the Boolean variable "produceReport". If the value of "produceReport" is TRUE, we produce the Initial Screening Report. We then proceed to write out the "AccountNumber", "MortType", and "MortTypeNum" to "tbl_IncRecords".

Writing the Incomplete Data Report File   Next we need to walk through the steps involved in writing the initial screening report. From the subroutine call:

```
Call CollatData_WriteInitScreenResultsRep
```

See Exhibit 18.37 for the VBA code in this subroutine.

In Step 1, we see that the subroutine takes the output file name as an input. We begin the subroutine by declaring a few utility variables. We next open the template file then rename and save this file using the output file name that was passed in as "reportName". This code is executed only if a workbook with the name stored in "reportName" is not already open. In other words, the first time one of the execution statements returns any incomplete records, the output file is initialized.

```
Sub CollatData_WriteInitScreenResultsRep(reportName As String)

Dim wb       As Workbook     'report workbook object
Dim j        As Integer      'formula iterator
Dim dimNum   As Integer      'array dimension for output

    'Step 1: Open workbook and save if not already open
    mthisWBName = ThisWorkbook.Name
    On Error Resume Next
    Set wb = Workbooks(reportName)
    On Error GoTo 0
    If wb Is Nothing Then
        ThisWorkbook.Activate
        mPathName = INITDATASCREEN_TEMPLATE_ACCESS
        Workbooks.Open FileName:=mPathName
        Application.DisplayAlerts = False
        ActiveWorkbook.SaveAs FileName:=OUTPUT_DIRECTORY & reportName
        Application.DisplayAlerts = True
    End If
    'Step 2: Dimension output range and output records array
    dimNum = 1
    On Error Resume Next
    dimNum = UBound(rs_array, 2)
    On Error GoTo 0

    Sheets(sheetNames(iType - 1)).Activate
    With Sheets(sheetNames(iType - 1)).Range("C11")
        If dimNum = 1 Then
            .Resize(dimNum, UBound(rs_array, 1)) = rs_array
        Else
            .Resize(UBound(rs_array, 1), dimNum) = rs_array
        End If
    End With
    'Step 3: Computing the cumulative missing fields score
    Do While Sheets(sheetNames(iType - 1)).Range("C11").Offset(j, 0)
        Sheets(sheetNames(iType - 1)).Range("C11").Offset(j, 1).FormulaArray = _
                "=SUM(IF(RC[1]:RC[25]=" & Chr(34) & "X" & Chr(34) & _
                " ,2^(COLUMN(RC[1]:RC[25])-5)))"
        Sheets(sheetNames(iType - 1)).Range("C11").Offset(j, -1) = j + 1
        j = j + 1
    Loop

End Sub
```

EXHIBIT 18.37   "CollatData_WriteInitScreenResultsRep" subroutine

This is accomplished by using the code "Set wb = Workbooks(reportName)". This assigns the workbook object to an open workbook by passing the name of the workbook. If no such workbook is open, this produces an error condition, hence the "On Error Resume Next" statement. If, after attempting to set the "wb" workbook object, "wb" is still nothing, we enter the "If Statement" block to assign and rename the template file to our current report name.

In Step 2 we need to size the output range in the worksheet of the incomplete records file that we established in Step 1. We first need to determine if the array containing the incomplete loan(s) for the current type contains one loan or multiple loans. If there was only one loan that failed, then this array, "rs_array", is a one-dimensional array. If there are multiple loans that are missing data, then this is a two-dimensional array. Because of this difference we need to deal with these two possibilities in different ways. If "rs_array" is one-dimensional, then the upper bound of the first dimension, found using "UBound(rs_array,1)", contains the number of fields tested for this loan type. Alternatively, if "rs_array" is a two-dimensional array, then "UBound(rs_array,1)" returns the number of loans having failed the test and "UBound(rs_array,2)" returns the number of fields tested.

For Step 2 in Exhibit 18.37, we first set the dimension of the array as 1 by setting the integer variable "dimNum". Next, we change "dimNum" to "UBound(rs_array,2)" if the array has a second dimension. If "rs_array" is a one-dimensional array, this line of code will throw an error. Since we sandwich this statement in the familiar "On Error..." messages, it will not be executed for one-dimensional arrays and "dimNum" will remain equal to 1. We next resize the target range using the "Resize()" function. The first argument in Resize determines the number of cells down the page and the second determines columns right. So in the case of the one-dimensional array, we allot one row down for the one loan and UBound(rs_array,1) columns over. For two-dimensional arrays, we allot UBound(rs_array,1) rows down for the different mortgage loans and "dimNum", set above to UBound(rs_array,2), as the number of fields in the output.

Notice from Step 2 in Exhibit 18.37, we are employing the "sheetsNames()" array that we created and that contains the different worksheet names in the report template. We have also formatted the different sheets in the template file such that all output starts in cell C12.

Finally, in Step 3, we compute the unique score for each of the incomplete records. This is a unique score that is computed based on each missing data item. We display these scores by replacing the cells containing placeholder "-999" with an array formula. The code for this formula is shown below. Within VBA the array formulas are entered in the appropriate Excel cell using the "FormulaArray" property and formula text in R1C1 notation. Once in Excel, the formula will look like this if the record is reported in row 11 of the spreadsheet:

```
=SUM(IF(E11:AC11=''X'',2^(COLUMN(E11:AC11)-5)))
```

The "If" statement in this returns TRUE or FALSE based on whether those cells in the range contain an "X". For the cells marked with an "X", the formula computes a power of 2 based on the cells position on the sheet. The "-5" is an adjustment based on location of the first cell in the range. The formula then sums the result over the specified range of these powers.

After this "Do..While" loop is complete, we have successfully written out the incomplete record results for one of the mortgage types/reports based on "iType". The code is now returned to the Initial Screening subroutine, where we proceed to the next "iType" in the loop in that subroutine. If there are no additional types to check, we close our report workbook and set our objects to nothing using the following code at the end of the Initial Screening subroutine:

```
    On Error Resume Next
    Workbooks(outputName).Close savechanges:=True
    On Error GoTo 0
    Set rs = Nothing
    DisconnectFromDatabase
End Sub
```

Recall that the analyst elects whether to produce an Incomplete Data Report or not. If a report was not created, then attempting to close that report will throw an error. After this we disconnect from the database and end the subroutine.

Installing a CommandButton on the Menu   All that is left is to create a Command-Button on the "CollatPoolMenu" spreadsheet that calls this subroutine with the appropriate inputs. This button is called "cmd_WriteInitialScreeningReport" and resides on the worksheet. The code behind this button, located within the worksheet code, is:

```
Private Sub cmd_WriteInitialScreeningReport_Click()
   Dim portArray() As String

   ReDim portArray(0 To 0)
   portArray(0) = cmb_MainPort.Value
   Call InitialScreening(portArray, _
      Range(''m07InitScreenFileName''), _
      True)
End Sub
```

Notice in the call to the "InitialScreening" subroutine that TRUE is passed as the "produceReport" variable value. Remember that there are two circumstances where this subroutine will be called. The first is from "CollatPoolMenu" sheet, where we are interested only in generating the results of the initial screening report. The second circumstance is immediately before running the cash flows for our portfolio, where we will likely not choose to output the report. In this case the amortization code will first filter out any records with incomplete data that are stored in "tbl_IncRecords" before proceeding with the amortization.

CUSTOM FINANCIAL SELECTION CRITERIA

We have converted two major portions of the selection process to Access in the Geographic Selection and the Initial Data Screening sections. The final portion of the selection process to be converted will be the Custom Financial Selection Criteria processes. We will now add an Access database table that will contain the Custom Financial Selection Criteria Sets (CFSCS). The CCFG allows the analyst to specify up to five of these criteria sets, each of these sets containing up to 20 individual tests each.

In this section we will develop Access functions for:

- Loading, storing, and retrieving the contents of five CFSCS, each with up to 20 individual tests to the database.
- Populating the "FinCriteriaRep" sheet with the contents of our CFSCS.

Database Design

The main challenge in this portion of the modeling will be to translate the contents of the six types of CFSCS tests into an Access database table. Previously we have

tbl_TestConditions			
ID ▾	Condition ▾	ArithOperat ▾	
1	LE	<=	
2	LT	<	
3	GT	>	
4	GE	>=	
5	EQ	=	
6	NE	<>	

tbl_TestParameters		
ID ▾	Condition ▾	DBAlias ▾
1	Pool ID	AccountNumber
2	Mortgage Type	MortType
3	Credit Sector	CreditSector
4	Original Balance	OrigBankBal
5	Current Balance	CurBankBal
6	Origination Date	OrigDate
7	Original Loan-to-Value Ratio	OrigLTV
8	Current Loan-to-Value Ratio	CurrLTV
9	Original Term (months)	OrigTerm
10	Remaining Term (months)	RemTerm
11	Seasoning	Season
12	Current Coupon Rate	Coupon
13	ARM Index	Index
14	ARM Spread to Index	Spread
15	ARM Initial Index Level	InitialRate
16	ARM Periodic Reset	ResetRate
17	ARM Periodic Cap Rate	ResetCap
18	ARM Periodic Floor	ResetFloor

EXHIBIT 18.38   "tbl_TestConditions" and "tbl_TestParameters"

stored these tests in an Excel spreadsheet that has a fixed layout. Much like in the Geographic Criteria Section previously, we will now be moving the Financial Selection Tests from VBA global arrays to an Access tables. The five global arrays that we continue to work with are:

```
Public gSCEditType(0 To NUM_PORTS, 1 To NUM_SEL_TESTS) As Integer
Public gSCEditItems(0 To NUM_PORTS, 1 To NUM_SEL_TESTS, 1 To MAX_SEL_ITEMS) As Integer
Public gSCEditOpers(0 To NUM_PORTS, 1 To NUM_SEL_TESTS, 1 To MAX_SEL_OPERS) As Double
Public gSCEditValue(0 To NUM_PORTS, 1 To NUM_SEL_TESTS, 1 To MAX_SEL_VALUE) As Double
Public gSCEditTestName(0 To NUM_PORTS, 1 To NUM_SEL_TESTS) As String
```

We will need to reference the conditions and parameters of the Financial Tests throughout this process. To simplify the process, we add two tables to our database containing these two sets of information. The contents of table "tbl_TestConditions" and a portion of the table "tbl_TestParameters" are shown in Exhibit 18.38.

Notice in Exhibit 18.38 that both tables have fields that are essentially translation fields. The "ArithOperator" field is the translation of the "Operator" field into its arithmetic equivalent (something SQL understands). The "DBAlias" field translates the parameter value into its equivalent data tape field name. Later in this chapter, when converting Financial Condition Test sets to SQL, we will need a way of converting the Excel spreadsheet names of the loan parameters to database field names. These tables are where we will get these translations.

Database Implementation

As in the sections above, we begin by creating the tables necessary to hold the CFSCS data. The "tbl_FinScens" table will hold all of the sets of tests created by the analyst through the UserForms. This table will closely resemble the "FinancialCriteriaSets" Excel file format but differs in one important aspect: It will hold only a single operator/test value pair per record. We also create a field in the database called

tbl_FinScens	
Field Name	**Data Type**
Set	Number
Test	Number
Test Name	Text
Test Type	Number
Parameter	Text
Operator	Text
Test Value	Number
Index	Number

EXHIBIT 18.39 "tbl_FinScens" in Design View

"Index". This field will hold the order in which an individual criterion was pulled from the arrays. This is especially important when dealing with a test of "Type 6: 2 Criteria Table Test". For this type we build a series of five criteria pairs joined by ORs, and the specific pairings of these criteria are important and need to be tracked as pairs. We will see how we use the Index field later when we construct a SQL clause for a test set. See Exhibit 18.39 for the table design.

Where Matters Stand Now: Using the Existing Code   The entirety of the error-checking code that already exists behind the UserForms and CommandButtons on "FinSelectMenu" can be preserved. The only change we need to make will direct the CommandButtons on the worksheet to use the contents of the database tables as opposed to Excel files. As you will recall, the CommandButton labeled "Print This Test Set" on "FinSelectMenu" reads the information temporarily stored in global arrays and writes these test sets out to the "FinCriteriaReport" sheet. Here they can be inspected prior to committing the test set to a file or, as will be our case, to a database table. As a result we need not make any modifications to these operations because Access does not enter into the process at this point. The two Command-Buttons adjacent to this one, "Write Test Sets to File" and "Read Test Sets From File", will be where we make the most changes.

Reading the Financial Selection Data Items from Database   The financial selection parameters and criteria are stored in the Access tables "tbl_TestParameters" and "tbl_TestCondition". We will utilize these to populate the two global arrays, "gFinSelOperators()" and "gFinSelNames()". We make changes to the "FinSelect_ReadDataItemNames()" subroutine in order to populate the arrays from the database tables. Much of this code should be familiar to us by now, so we will only show it for reference. See Exhibit 18.40.

Writing the Selection Criteria to the DataBase   The VBA code behind the "Write Test Sets To File" Button needs to be changed so the test set is written to the database table instead of to a file. We will implement this in a straightforward and intuitive manner. We need only to change how the tests are retrieved from the global arrays and how they are loaded into the database based on each test's type. We will begin the revisions to the subroutine "FinSelect_WriteSelectionCriteriaFile". See Exhibit 18.41.

```
Sub FinSelect_ReadDataItemNames()

Dim rs As ADODB.Recordset    'recordset object

    ConnectToDataBase (DATABASE_FULLPATH)

    icnt = 1
    Set rs = gCon.Execute("SELECT [Condition] FROM tbl_TestConditions ORDER BY [ID]")
    Do While Not rs.EOF
        gFinSelOperators(icnt) = rs.fields(0).Value
        icnt = icnt + 1
        rs.MoveNext
    Loop
    icnt = 1
    Set rs = gCon.Execute("SELECT [Condition] FROM tbl_TestParameters ORDER BY [ID]")
    Do While Not rs.EOF
        gFinSelNames(icnt) = rs.fields(0).Value
        icnt = icnt + 1
        rs.MoveNext
    Loop
    Set rs = Nothing

    DisconnectFromDatabase
End Sub
```

EXHIBIT 18.40 "FinSelect_ReadDataItemNames" subroutine

```
Sub FinSelect_WriteSelectionCriteriaFile()

Dim str_sql       As String   'SQL execution string
Dim str_base      As String   'base SQL execution string
Dim str_temp      As String   'temp string for exec statment

    Call FinSelect_ReadDataItemNames
    'connect to db and delete tbl_tempFinScens
    ConnectToDataBase (DATABASE_FULLPATH)
    On Error Resume Next
    gCon.Execute ("DROP TABLE tbl_tempFinScens")
    On Error GoTo 0
    'Copy tbl_FinScens structure to temp table
    gCon.Execute ( _
            "SELECT * INTO tbl_tempFinScens" & vbCrLf & _
            "FROM tbl_FinScens" & vbCrLf & _
            "WHERE 0 <> 0")
    'Set up base INSERT VALUES string for use in replace
    str_base = "INSERT INTO tbl_tempFinScens " & _
                "VALUES(varSET,varTEST," & _
                "'varTNAME',varTYPE," & _
                "'varNAME','varOPER', " & _
                "varVALUE,varINDEX)"
```

EXHIBIT 18.41 Revisions to the "FinSelect_WriteSelectionCriteriaFile" subroutine

Very few new are variables needed to be declared in this subroutine because the majority of the information needed to complete the upload is already stored in the global VBA arrays. As we will see shortly, the variables we do declare here are used mainly to keep the code readable and to store portions of the execution strings. Also shown in Exhibit 18.41 are the call to the "FinSelect_ReadDataItems" subroutine and the familiar call to connect to the database. In the next set of commands, we continue the practice of creating a temporary table to store the data before inserting it into the database table "tbl_FinScens". Remember that this will help ensure a certain amount of data integrity as we are building and testing the model.

Writing a Typical Selection Criteria Test We will use the following selection criteria test as an example:

```
[OriginalTerm GE 120 AND OriginalTerm LE 480]
```

as we step through the process of building the command string in the paragraphs ahead. Also assumed is that we are defining and loading Test 1 of Set 1 to the database with the name "OrigTerm120-480". We will enter this test using a test "Type 2: Minimum/Maximum Test". The end result will be an execution string that inserts values into "tbl_tempFinScenTable" by employing the INSERT INTO clause combined with a set of values stored in the VALUES clause. As long as we are careful and build the VALUES portion of the execution string with the fields ordered as they are in the table, we will not need to use the more specific syntax of specifying field names for each value, keeping our code compact.

In Exhibit 18.41 we see initialization of the "str_base" variable. The VALUES clause will contain a value for each of the fields in "tbl_FinScens". When loading a set/test combination, we will use the VBA function "Replace()" to replace the "var" portions of "str_base" with the appropriate values from the global arrays before updating to "tbl_tempFinScens". This will help keep the code very readable, as in each step we can see what is being passed into the execution string via a "Replace()" call. Notice the single quotes around values being updated to string fields, such as "varName" and "varType". We used this replace technique above in the Geographic Selection section.

The main part of the code is placed within two "For" loops, the first of which checks to see which test set is currently active. Once we find the test set, we next loop to find which tests are active. Remember that the number of possible test sets is stored in Constant variable "NUM_PORTS" and is currently set at 5. The total number of tests available per test set ("NUM_SEL_TESTS") is set at 20. Once we find an active test, we are able to enter the second loop and edit the SQL execution string after deleting the current set/test combination from "tbl_FinScens" if it already exists. Next we are ready to start replacing sections of our "str_base" string. See Exhibit 18.42.

We can see how easy it is to tell what is going on when you use "Replace()" to change the different inputs within the VALUES string. First we set "str_sql" to "str_base" with "varSet" replaced with the actual active set number. We then move on to edit "str_sql" by replacing the test number, test name, and test type.

```
For iset = 1 To NUM_PORTS
    If gSCSetActive(iset) Then
        For iTest = 1 To NUM_SEL_TESTS
            If gSCTestActive(iset, iTest) Then
                gcon.Execute ( _
                    "DELETE * FROM tbl_FinScens " & _
                    "WHERE [Set] = " & iset & "AND [Test] =" & iTest)
                str_sql = Replace(str_base, "varSET", iset)
                str_sql = Replace(str_sql, "varTEST", iTest)
                str_sql = Replace(str_sql, "varTNAME", gSCEditTestName(iset, iTest))
                str_sql = Replace(str_sql, "varTYPE", gSCEditType(iset, iTest))
```

EXHIBIT 18.42   Updating "str_sql" with set number, test number, test name and type

Now that we have the first four inputs to the VALUES clause inserted in the "str_sql", we need to replace the field name ("varName"), operator ("varOPER"), value ("varVALUE"), and index values ("varINDEX"). This process varies depending on what test Type we are building. The best way to handle this is with a SELECT CASE statement. The simplest criteria statement is for test "Type 1: Single Condition Test". In this case, we need replace only the four remaining values with the values stored in the global arrays. Because there is only one criterion, and we therefore do not need to worry about order, we set the Index equal to 1. See Exhibit 43a for the VBA code in the SELECT CASE statement.

As an example of the more complicated test Type, let us take a closer look at the VBA code for test "Type 6: 2 Criteria Table Test" in Exhibit 43b. As said before, for this test Type it is critical that we have a way of keeping track of the order of the inputs. For a "Type 6: 2 Criteria Table Test" test, there are two field names stored in the "gSCEditItems" array. For each field name, there are five operators and five corresponding values. In order to get these tests into the database correctly, we place these two "sql_str" statements inside a five-step "For" loop. We use "str_temp" to hold the temporary string state upon entering this node in the SELECT CASE statement. The first execution string is built by replacing "varName" in "str_temp" with the first field for the test. We next replace "varOPER" and "var-VALUE" by employing the "iitem" iterator to retrieve the appropriate values from "gSCEditOpers()" and "gSCEditValue()". We set "varINDEX" equal to:

```
1 + (2 * (iitem - 1))
```

for the first-parameter and

```
2 * iitem
```

for the second-parameter SQL strings. We do this to ensure that the two field values are coupled at each iteration. The first field will have the index values of $(1, 3, 5, 7, 9)$ while the second field will have index values of $(2, 4, 6, 8, 10)$. The index values will be used when reloading the test sets from the database to the global arrays and when constructing the SQL statements for selecting the portfolio.

Once we have looped over all test sets and test numbers, finding all active tests, we update "tbl_FinScens" with the contents of "tbl_tempFinScens" with the following familiar code:

```
gcon.Execute (_
    ''INSERT INTO tbl_FinScens '' & _
    ''SELECT tbl_tempFinScens.* '' & _
    ''FROM tbl_tempFinScens'')
gcon.Execute (''DROP TABLE tbl_tempFinScens'')
```

We can then delete our temporary table from the database and disconnect. When we load the example min/max test, the contents of "tbl_FinScens" appears as in Exhibit 18.44.

Reading a Test Set from the Database   Now that we have the Financial Selection Criteria in the database table, we need to revise the way we load them back into the

```
Select Case gSCEditType(iset, itest)
    Case Is = 1
        str_sql = Replace(str_sql, "varNAME", _
                        gFinSelNames(gSCEditItems(iset, itest, 1)))
        str_sql = Replace(str_sql, "varOPER", _
                        gFinSelOperators(gSCEditOpers(iset, itest, 1)))
        str_sql = Replace(str_sql, "varVALUE", _
                        gSCEditValue(iset, itest, 1))
        str_sql = Replace(str_sql, "varINDEX", "1")
        gCon.Execute (str_sql)
    Case Is = 2
        str_temp = str_sql
        For iitem = 1 To 2
            str_sql = Replace(str_temp, "varNAME", _
                            gFinSelNames(gSCEditItems(iset, itest, 1)))
            str_sql = Replace(str_sql, "varOPER", _
                            gFinSelOperators(gSCEditOpers(iset, itest, iitem)))
            str_sql = Replace(str_sql, "varVALUE", _
                            gSCEditValue(iset, itest, iitem))
            str_sql = Replace(str_sql, "varINDEX", iitem)
            gCon.Execute (str_sql)
        Next iitem
    Case Is = 3
        str_temp = str_sql
        str_sql = Replace(str_temp, "varNAME", _
                        gFinSelNames(gSCEditItems(iset, itest, 1)))
        str_sql = Replace(str_sql, "varOPER", _
                        gFinSelOperators(gSCEditOpers(iset, itest, 1)))
        str_sql = Replace(str_sql, "varVALUE", _
                        gSCEditValue(iset, itest, 1))
        str_sql = Replace(str_sql, "varINDEX", 1)
        gCon.Execute (str_sql)
        For iitem = 2 To 3
            str_sql = Replace(str_temp, "varNAME", _
                            gFinSelNames(gSCEditItems(iset, itest, 2)))
            str_sql = Replace(str_sql, "varOPER", _
                            gFinSelOperators(gSCEditOpers(iset, itest, iitem)))
            str_sql = Replace(str_sql, "varVALUE", _
                            gSCEditValue(iset, itest, iitem))
            str_sql = Replace(str_sql, "varINDEX", iitem)
            gCon.Execute (str_sql)
        Next iitem
        '[32 lines of code for test types 4 and 5]
```

EXHIBIT 43a   SELECT CASE for Financial Scenarios Test Types 1 to 3

```
    Case Is = 6
        str_temp = str_sql
        For iitem = 1 To 5
            str_sql = Replace(str_temp, "varNAME", _
                            gFinSelNames(gSCEditItems(iset, itest, 1)))
            str_sql = Replace(str_sql, "varOPER", _
                            gFinSelOperators(gSCEditOpers(iset, itest, iitem)))
            str_sql = Replace(str_sql, "varVALUE", _
                            gSCEditValue(iset, itest, iitem))
            str_sql = Replace(str_sql, "varINDEX", 1 + (2 * (iitem - 1)))
            gCon.Execute (str_sql)
            str_sql = Replace(str_temp, "varNAME", _
                            gFinSelNames(gSCEditItems(iset, itest, 2)))
            str_sql = Replace(str_sql, "varOPER", _
                            gFinSelOperators(gSCEditOpers(iset, itest, iitem + 5)))
            str_sql = Replace(str_sql, "varVALUE", _
                            gSCEditValue(iset, itest, iitem + 5))
            str_sql = Replace(str_sql, "varINDEX", (2 * iitem))
            gCon.Execute (str_sql)
        Next iitem
End Select
```

EXHIBIT 43b   SELECT CASE for Financial Scenarios Test Type 6

program arrays. This process is essentially the reverse of the above process, where we simply repopulate the global arrays from the database table. We have seen all the elements of this subroutine above and in preceding sections, so we will not reproduce it here. The reader should reference the files on the Web site for this chapter to see how this is accomplished.

Converting a Financial Test to SQL   Now that we have a way of storing test sets in "tbl_FinScens", we need to be able to translate the sets into SQL clauses for use in the CCFG. We create a function call "TestSetToSQL" and place this function within the "MenuSupport_FinancialSelect" module. This function takes as its first of two parameters an integer called "setNum" that corresponds to the test set number. The second parameter, "conOpen", is of type Boolean. What this parameter designates is whether the subroutine calling this function already has the database connection, "gCon", open. It can get confusing when subroutines and functions are all querying or updating to the database, and we have the choice of either creating multiple ADODB connection objects or taking steps to track the state of one connection. We choose the former technique here. The "TestSetToSQL" function, which returns a string, is shown in its entirety in Exhibit 18.45.

For this function we need only to define a recordset object. We next see the "conOpen" parameter being put to use. The connection need be opened only if it has not been opened by the calling subroutine. In the next statement we store the

⊞ tbl_FinScens							
Set ▾	Test ▾	Test Name ▾	Test Type ▾	Parameter ▾	Operator ▾	Test Value ▾	Index ▾
1	1	OrigTerm120-480	2	Original Term (months)	GE	120	1
1	1	OrigTerm120-480	2	Original Term (months)	LE	480	2

EXHIBIT 18.44   "tbl_FinScens" with test saved

```
Function TestSetToSQL(setNum As Integer, conOpen As Boolean) As String

Dim rs      As ADODB.Recordset  'recordset object

    'check if db is open; if not connect
    If Not conOpen Then ConnectToDataBase (DATABASE_FULLPATH)
    'store test set in a rs, order by test and index
    'include in rs the ArithOperator and DBAlias
    Set rs = gCon.Execute( _
        "SELECT tbl_FinScens.*, " & _
            "tbl_TestParameters.DBAlias,tbl_TestConditions.ArithOperator " & vbCrLf & _
        " FROM tbl_FinScens, tbl_TestParameters, tbl_TestConditions" & vbCrLf & _
        "WHERE [Set] = " & setNum & vbCrLf & _
        " AND tbl_FinScens.Parameter = tbl_TestParameters.Parameter" & vbCrLf & _
        " AND tbl_FinScens.Operator = tbl_TestConditions.Condition" & vbCrLf & _
        "ORDER BY [Test], [Index]")
    If rs.EOF And rs.BOF Then GoTo endfunction
    'loop through recordset converting to string based on test type
    Do While Not rs.EOF
        Select Case rs.Fields("Test Type").Value
            Case 1 To 3, 5
                TestSetToSQL = TestSetToSQL & "AND " & rs.Fields("DBAlias") & _
                        " " & rs.Fields("ArithOperator") & _
                        " " & rs.Fields("Test Value") & vbCrLf
                rs.MoveNext
            Case 4
                TestSetToSQL = TestSetToSQL & "AND("
                For itest = 1 To 5
                    TestSetToSQL = TestSetToSQL & "(" & rs.Fields("DBAlias") & _
                        " " & rs.Fields("ArithOperator") & _
                        " " & rs.Fields("Test Value") & ") OR "
                    rs.MoveNext
                Next itest
                TestSetToSQL = Left(TestSetToSQL, Len(TestSetToSQL) - 4) & ")" & vbCrLf

            Case 6
                TestSetToSQL = TestSetToSQL & "AND("
                For itest = 1 To 5
                    TestSetToSQL = TestSetToSQL & "(" & rs.Fields("DBAlias") & _
                        " " & rs.Fields("ArithOperator") & _
                        " " & rs.Fields("Test Value") & " AND "
                    rs.MoveNext
                    TestSetToSQL = TestSetToSQL & rs.Fields("DBAlias") & _
                        " " & rs.Fields("ArithOperator") & _
                        " " & rs.Fields("Test Value") & ") OR" & vbCrLf
                    rs.MoveNext
                Next itest
                TestSetToSQL = Left(TestSetToSQL, Len(TestSetToSQL) - 5) & ")"
        End Select
    Loop
    If Not conOpen Then DisconnectFromDatabase
endfunction:
    Set rs = Nothing
End Function
```

EXHIBIT 18.45   Function "TestSetToSQL"

records of "tbl_FinScens" with test set equal to the "setNum" parameter in our recordset. We are also making use of the "DBAlias" and "ArithOperator" fields from "tbl_TestParameters" and "tbl_TestConditions", respectively. This will make the "TestSetToSQL" statement readable by Access. It is important to notice here that we are ordering by "Test" and by "Index". If we did not explicitly sort the recordset then we would have a difficult time discerning how the records relate to each other in the same test. Now we see the usefulness of the "Index" field in our table. If the recordset is empty, then there is no test set with the specified set number and we can go to the end of the function.

We append text to string "TestSetToSQL" for each test under the designated set number. We translate the records to SQL within the "Do..While" loop. The way the SQL string is created is different for different test Types. Luckily for us, the only tests that require special attention are test Types 4 and 6, where we are creating OR statements as opposed to just AND statements. For test Types 1, 2, 3, and 5, each record will add a line to "TestSetToSQL" in the following format:

```
AND [Parameter] [Operator] [VALUE]
```

For test Type 4, the joining ANDs are switched out for ORs. For test Type 6, we need to combine the two parameters with each other in an extended AND statement that contains five separate AND statements joined by ORs. We place this portion of the code in a FOR statement that runs from 1 to 5. The resulting format of test Type 6 tests is:

```
AND ((([Parameter1] [Operator1:1] [VALUE1:1] AND [Parameter2] [Operator2:1] [VALUE2:1]) OR
([Parameter1] [Operator1:2] [VALUE1:2] AND [Parameter2] [Operator2:2] [VALUE2:2]) OR
([Parameter1] [Operator1:3] [VALUE1:3] AND [Parameter2] [Operator2:3] [VALUE2:3]) OR
([Parameter1] [Operator1:4] [VALUE1:4] AND [Parameter2] [Operator2:4] [VALUE2:4]) OR
([Parameter1] [Operator1:5] [VALUE1:5] AND [Parameter2] [Operator2:5] [VALUE2:5]))
```

The last line in the test Type 6 section removes the dangling OR and replaces it with a ")" to end the AND statement encompassing the four ORs.

If we run "TestSetToSQL" for test set 1 that we created above, the output is as follows:

```
AND OrigTerm >= 120
AND OrigTerm <= 480
```

We can now guess at how we will use the function "TestSetToSQL" in the future. Consider, for example, the following code:

```
''SELECT * '' &
''FROM tbl_PORTFOLIOS '' &
''WHERE PortfolioName = 'port1' '' &
TestSetToSQL(1,TRUE)
```

This would create a SQL select statement retrieving all loans from portfolio "port1" where the criteria represented in the string created by the "TestSetToSQL" function are met. When a portfolio is filtered by a Financial Criteria Set we can simply construct appropriate conditional statements in the query as opposed to looping over every single loan in question for up to 20 tests. This is a clear simplification in both our code and the task of completing the process.

RUN OPTIONS ELECTIONS

For all you faithful readers who have persevered over the large, detailed, and difficult preceding sections of this chapter, we have a surprise! Here is both a short and an easy section. Ordinarily you would think that we would have discussed the Run Options Menu first in the chapter but, because of its brevity and, from what you have learned already, its simplicity, we have saved it until now. Enjoy!

One immediate benefit of using an Access database for storing scenarios and portfolios is the ability to easily populate drop-down boxes when choosing options for the model runs. Before we would have had to either remember what scenarios and portfolios had already been created or periodically check to see what was in the file structure. Granted, this could be accomplished by using file system objects and by opening files to see which scenarios already exist, but the database solution is more elegant and requires far less code. In this section we briefly show how the Run Options Menu is set up to allow selections from the database tables we created in the above sections.

Database Design

In the Collateral Portfolio Data section of this chapter, we learned how to use Access to replace the functionality of the "CollatPoolMenu" spreadsheet to add test portfolios to "tbl_PORTFOLIOS". At this time, to make our lives a bit easier, we add all the Sub-Portfolios to "tbl_PORTFOLIOS" as their own portfolios. To do this, on the "CollatPoolMenu", add the main portfolio and each Sub-Portfolio, one at a time, and call them "MainPort", "SubPort1", "SubPort2", and so on. For the Run Options Menu, we simply need to create multiple drop-down boxes on the spreadsheet that look to the database in order to populate their lists. The different run option selections that will use this technology are Portfolio Selection, Financial Scenario, and Geographic Scenario.

Database Implementation

The first step is to create, name, and format all the drop-down boxes we are going to need. The naming convention we use for the different inputs are:

- "cmb_Port" for the portfolio files
- "cmb_Fin" for the financial/demographic selection tests
- "cmb_Geo" for the geographic selection tests

followed by the appropriate number. The layout of the revised "RunOptionsMenu" is in Exhibit 18.46.

Portfolio Selection Drop-Down Event Code   Now that we have all the drop-downs named and formatted, we need to add the code to populate the lists with the options present in the database tables. We have already seen how this is done when we were dealing with the ComboBoxes in the "Building Functionality for the ComboBoxes" section earlier. The event code behind "cmb_Port" is shown in Exhibit 18.47.

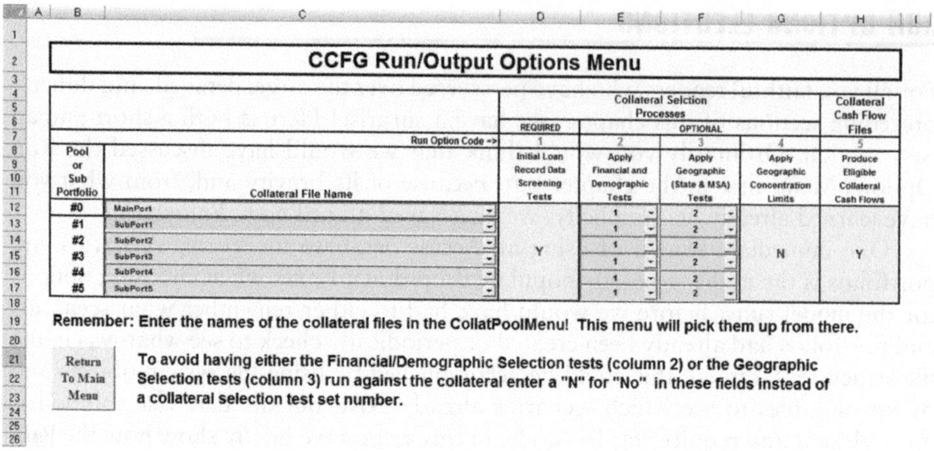

EXHIBIT 18.46   Collateral options on "RunOptionsMenu"

The first step in Exhibit 18.47 is to connect to the database. We then execute a string that selects all unique records in the "PorfolioName" field of "tbl_PORTFOLIOS" and returns these values to a record set. The next step is to clear out the ComboBox list before repopulating it with elements stored in the recordset object. The subroutine shown in Exhibit 18.47 for "cmb_Port" is identical for the other five "cmb_SubPort" objects except that the references to the object must be changed. In that we added all of the Sub-Portfolios to "tbl_PORTFOLIOS", these will all be available to us in the drop-downs.

```
Private Sub cmb_Port_DropButtonClick()

Dim rs As ADODB.Recordset     'recordset object

    ConnectToDataBase (DATABASE_FULLPATH)

    Set rs = gCon.Execute("SELECT DISTINCT [PortfolioName] " & _
                    "FROM tbl_PORTFOLIOS " & _
                    "GROUP BY [PortfolioName] " & _
                    "ORDER BY [PortfolioName]")

    Do While cmb_Port.ListCount <> 0
        cmb_Port.RemoveItem 0
    Loop
    cmb_Port.List = Application.WorksheetFunction.Transpose(rs.GetRows)
    Do While Not rs.EOF
        cmb_Port.AddItem rs.Fields(0).Value
        rs.MoveNext
    Loop
    cmb_Port.AddItem "No File Selected"
    DisconnectFromDatabase
End Sub
```

EXHIBIT 18.47   "cmb_Port" ComboBox

Financial and Geographic Selection Drop-Down Code The subroutines for "cmb_Fin0" and "cmb_Geo0" have over 80% commonality with the portfolio drop-down code we just saw. In the

```
Set rs = gCon.Execute(''SELECT DISTINCT (Portfolio Name) ''&
```

portion, we simply change the arguments from "Portfolio Name" to "Set" and "Test", respectively. For the UNION query used for the Geographic Scenarios drop-downs, in order to pull data from the three different tables, we need to set the recordset using the following execution string:

```
''(SELECT DISTINCT [Test] '' & _
  ''FROM tbl_GeoScensRegions '' & _
    ''GROUP BY [Test]) '' & _
    ''UNION'' & _
    ''(SELECT DISTINCT [Test] '' & _
    ''FROM tbl_GeoScensStates '' & _
    ''GROUP BY [Test]) '' & _
    ''UNION'' & _
    ''(SELECT DISTINCT [Test] '' & _
    ''FROM tbl_GeoScensMSAs '' & _
    ''GROUP BY [Test]) '' & _
    ''ORDER BY [Test]''
```

In the following "Do..While" loop, we need to change the loop control variable from:

```
Do While cmb.Port.ListCount <>0 (for portfolios)
```

to the following:

```
Do While cmb.Fin0.ListCount <>0 (for financial test sets)
Do While cmb.Geo0.ListCount <>0 (for geographic test sets)
```

We will also need to change the list objects in:

```
= Application.WorksheetFunction.Transpose(rs.GetRows)
```

based on the lists appropriate to the drop-down boxes. All these subroutines can be found in the code on the Web site. Remember that all of the code pertaining to these ComboBoxes resides in the "RunOptionMenu" worksheet. When completed, there should be six "DropDownClick" event routines for each of the three inputs.

Once this worksheet is set up, we need to change the subroutines that read these inputs into the model. This is a simple task of changing the portions of the "RunOptions_ReadMenu" subroutine and all the input error-checking subroutines that read inputs from Excel Range objects to read the newly created drop-down boxes.

GENERATING THE LOAN PORTFOLIO

Thus far in this chapter we have converted a number of the model's sections to an Access-based implementation. We saw how to populate "tbl_IncRecords" with loans that fail the initial data screening process for a specified portfolio. We then stored our Geographic and Financial Scenarios in Access tables, with the added step of reinterpreting the Financial Scenario test sets into Access readable strings with the "TestSetToSQL" function. It is now time to tie all these parts together to create the portfolio to be processed by the cash flow engine. When complete, we will see how four subroutines:

```
CollatData_ReadCollateralFiles
InitScreen_BasicScreeningMain
FinSelect_FinancialCriteriaSelectionMain
GeoSelect_GeographicEligibilityTesting
```

can easily be replaced with one Access query! This is a tremendous improvement over the previous methodology, which used one subroutine to read the data and three to further sort and filter the data. After our one Access query, we will have read the correct loans into "gLoanData()", where they are ready to be called on by the "RepGeoCon_CalcPortTotal" and "CollatCF_ComputeCollateralCashflows" subroutines. We will call the subroutine that accomplishes this "getPortfolio ACCESS" and place it within a new module named "CollatData_GetPortfolio".

The "getPortfolioACCESS" subroutine is called from the "CCFG_Model" after all the inputs have been error-checked and read into the global arrays. We can make use of these global arrays inside "getPorfolioACCESS" to assist with program flow. The local variable definitions and some variable initializations are shown in Exhibit 18.48.

Notice from Exhibit 18.48 the use of global variable "gPoolLevelData" and global array "gPortActive" to populate our "ports()" string array that holds all the portfolio names selected in the drop-down boxes on "RunOptionsMenu".

Populating "tbl_CURRENTPORTFOLIO"   The end goal of this subroutine is to populate "gLoanData()" with the loans that will later be used in the collateral cash flow computation. As an intermediate step we store the data in "tbl_CURRENT PORTFOLIO". Before getting to this we first need to run the "InitialDataScreening" on the specified portfolio(s). The following subroutine call accomplishes this:

```
Call InitialScreening(ports, '''', False)
```

As you recall from the Initial Data Screening section above, after running this subroutine, the Access table "tbl_IncRecords" is populated with all the records from the specified portfolio(s) that cannot be used in the amortization or accompanying reports. In Exhibit 18.49 we build the SQL execution strings that filter the loans from the specified portfolios by the incomplete records table, the financial criteria table, and the geographic criteria tables. These filtered results are appended to the "tbl_CURRENTPORTFOLIO" table.

After we take care of the preliminary work of connecting to the database and establishing "tbl_CURRENTPORTFOLIO", we start to build "str_sql". We place

```
Sub getPortfolioACCESS()

Dim ports()          As String              'portfolio name array
Dim begPort          As Long                'beginning port number
Dim endPort          As Long                'ending port number
Dim istate           As Integer             'state iterator
Dim ip               As Long                'portfolio iterator
Dim ws               As Worksheet           'RunOptions worksheet
Dim str_sql          As String              'SQL execution string
Dim rs_loans         As ADODB.Recordset     'recordset object
Dim str_conditions   As String              'financial conditions
Dim str_geo          As String              'geographic selections
Dim iloan            As Long                'loan iterator
Dim iparam           As Long                'parameter iterator

    Set ws = Sheets("RunOptionsMenu")
    If gPoolLevelData Then
        begPort = 0
        endPort = 0
        ReDim ports(0 To 0)
        ports(0) = ws.OLEObjects("cmb_Port").Object.Value
    Else
        begPort = 0
        endPort = 5
        ReDim ports(0 To 5)
        For ip = begPort To endPort
            If gPortActive(ip) Then
                ports(ip) = ws.OLEObjects("cmb_SubPort" & ip).Object.Value
            End If
        Next ip
    End If
```

EXHIBIT 18.48 "getPorfolioACCESS" variables

the SQL string building and execution in a "For" loop that completes once for every portfolio in "ports()". The first step after checking whether the portfolio is active is to check whether, for the given portfolio, a Financial Scenario test set has been specified. If so, we run the function "TestSetToSQL()" on the test set and return the results to "str_conditions". This string will be tacked onto the end of the SQL execution statement we build in the next step.

There are five different filters being applied by the one SQL statement we build in the next step. In order, these are:

1. Portfolio Name
2. Incomplete Records
3. Geographic State Scenario
4. Geographic MSA Scenario
5. Financial Scenario

The first filter is accomplished with a simple WHERE clause. For the Incomplete Records filter, we use the following subquery:

```
SELECT AccountNumber FROM tbl_IncRecords WHERE MortType
    NOT LIKE '%Data'
```

```
Call InitialScreening(ports, "", False)
'connect to db and set up tbl_CURRENTPORTFOLIO
ConnectToDataBase (DATABASE_FULLPATH)
On Error Resume Next
gCon.Execute ("DROP TABLE tbl_CURRENTPORTFOLIO")
On Error GoTo 0
gCon.Execute ( _
        "SELECT * INTO tbl_CURRENTPORTFOLIO" & vbCrLf & _
        "FROM tbl_PORTFOLIOS" & vbCrLf & _
        "WHERE 0 <> 0")
'filter portfolios for inc. records, geo and fin tests
For ip = begPort To endPort
    If gPortActive(ip) Then
'check if fin test is specified on run option menu for each port
        str_conditions = ""
        str_geo = ""
'build financial string conditions string if active
        If gROApplyFinDemo(ip) Then
            str_conditions = TestSetToSQL(gROTestSetFinDemo(ip), True)
        End If
'build string for geographic selection if active
        If gROApplyGeoSelect(ip) Then
            str_geo = "AND (StateCode IN (SELECT Code " & _
                        "FROM tbl_GeoScensStates " & _
                        "WHERE Test = " & gROTestSetGeoSelect(ip) & ")" & vbCrLf & _
                    "OR MSACode IN (SELECT Code " & _
                        "FROM tbl_GeoScensMSAs " & _
                        "WHERE Test = " & gROTestSetGeoSelect(ip) & "))"
        End If
'build full SQL string including conditions and geo selections
        str_sql = _
            "INSERT INTO tbl_CURRENTPORTFOLIO " & vbCrLf & _
            "SELECT * FROM tbl_PORTFOLIOS " & vbCrLf & _
            "WHERE PortfolioName = " & "'" & ports(ip) & "'" & vbCrLf & _
            "AND AccountNumber NOT IN " & _
                        "(SELECT AccountNumber " & _
                        " FROM tbl_IncRecords " & _
                        " WHERE MortType NOT LIKE '%Data')" & vbCrLf & _
            str_geo & vbCrLf & _
            str_conditions
        gCon.Execute str_sql
    End If
Next ip
```

EXHIBIT 18.49   Appending records to table "tbl_CURRENTPORTFOLIO"

This subquery returns a list of account numbers corresponding to loans that failed the initial data screening for their specific loan type. By saying "AND AccountNumber NOT IN...", we are left only with loans that are not in "tbl_IncRecords".

The two global arrays "gROApplyFinDemo" and "gROApplyGeoSelect" are used to control for when no selection criteria were specified. The following subquery is used to filter by states:

```
SELECT Code FROM tbl_GeoScensStates WHERE test
   = gROTestSetGeoSelect(ip)
```

This subquery returns a list of all the states that we included in the test stored in "gROTestSetGeoSelect" for each of the portfolios. By saying "AND StateCode IN..." on this list, we are left only with states included in the test. We use the exact same technique for the MSA scenario.

Once this query is executed, the loan records that are inserted into "tbl_CURRENTPORTFOLIO" have been filtered by the "tbl_IncRecords" table

```
Set rs_loans = gCon.Execute("SELECT * FROM tbl_CURRENTPORTFOLIO")

If rs_loans.EOF And rs_loans.BOF Then
    MsgBox "Selection return no loan results."
    Debug.Print str_sql
    GoTo noloans
End If
'determine the number of loans
gTotalLoans = 0
Do While Not rs_loans.EOF
    gTotalLoans = gTotalLoans + 1
    rs_loans.MoveNext
Loop
'populate the gStatePostal array
If gStatePostal(1) = "" Then
    For istate = 1 To NUM_STATES
        gStatePostal(istate) = Range("StatesSet1Data").Cells(istate, 2)
    Next istate
End If
'populate gLoanData from rs_loans
rs_loans.MoveFirst
ReDim gLoanData(1 To gTotalLoans, 1 To rs_loans.Fields.Count - 1) As Double
iloan = 1
Do While Not rs_loans.EOF
    For iparam = 1 To rs_loans.Fields.Count - 1
        If rs_loans.Fields(iparam).Name = "StateCode" Then
            gLoanData(iloan, iparam) = _
                Utility_ConvertStateAlphaToNumeric(rs_loans.Fields(iparam).Value)
        Else
            If IsNull(rs_loans.Fields(iparam)) Then
                gLoanData(iloan, iparam) = -1
            Else
                gLoanData(iloan, iparam) = rs_loans.Fields(iparam).Value
            End If
        End If
    Next iparam
    iloan = iloan + 1
    rs_loans.MoveNext
Loop
noloans:
    DisconnectFromDatabase
    Set ws = Nothing
    Set rs_loans = Nothing
    End
End Sub
```

EXHIBIT 18.50   Populating "gLoanData()"

and by the financial and geographic criteria, where specified. If we are using Sub-Portfolios, each Sub-Portfolio is filtered in the same way then inserted into "tbl_CURRENTPORTFOLIO". This is the portfolio that is eligible to be amortized with the deal in this scenario.

Populating "gLoanData"   The next step will be to retrieve the loan data from "tbl_CURRENTPORTFOLIOS" to populate "gLoanData()". This portion of the process is similar in function to the original process that uses the Excel files to populate the array. See Exhibit 18.50.

The entire contents of "tbl_CURRENTPORTFOLIO" are stored in the "rs_loans" recordset. After verifying that the selection queries built above return a nonempty recordset, the next "For" loop counts the number of loans in the record-set and stores this number in "gTotalLoans". Next we populate the "gStatePostal" array. After this, the global array is re-dimensioned and the records from "rs_loans" are read into the global array. Once again we are careful to convert the state text identifiers to numerics. Once all the data is loaded into "gLoanData", we can disconnect from the database and set the objects to "Nothing".

This subroutine can now take the place of the four other filtering subroutines in the model. Replace these subroutines with "getPortfolioACCESS()" in the "CCFG_Model()" subroutine call. See the material on the Web site for the changes to the main program subroutine.

MONTHLY CASH FLOWS SCENARIOS

The CCFG, as currently configured, can generate up to 25 scenarios of cash flows. These cash flows will result when the maximum of five prepayment and five default Stress levels are entered for any of the three Cash Flow Amortization Methodologies. Each scenario is comprised of eight individual components having a maximum of 360 monthly periods.

These cash flow components, paired with their global arrays where applicable, are:

1. **Current Period:** "iperiod" (iterator variable)
2. **Beginning of Period Principal:** "gBegPrinBal"
3. **Coupon Income:** "gCoupIncome"
4. **Scheduled Amortized Principal:** "gAmortPrin"
5. **Prepayments of Principal:** "gPrepaidPrin"
6. **Defaulted Principal:** "gDefaultPrin"
7. **Recoveries of Defaulted Principal:** "gRecoverPrin"
8. **Floating Rate Index:** "gIndexLevels"

These cash flows can then be read from the database later for use in running the LWM. To facilitate this in the LWM, we will make sure to key each of the scenarios by the following identifying characteristics:

- **Methodology Used:** Uniform, Geographic, Demographic.
- **Uniform Methodology Scenarios:** Prepayment and Default Speed and Method, Recovery Lag Period assumption, MVD Rate assumption.
- **Geographic Methodology Scenarios:** Table names of the Prepayment, Default, MVD, and Recovery Lag Periods assumption tables used. The Prepayment/Default Stress Rates are applied.
- **Demographic/Financial Scenarios:** Table names of the Prepayment and Recovery Lag assumption files. Either the table of the precomputed Default and MVD risk scores or the tables of values from which those scores were derived. The Prepayment/Default Stress Rates are applied.

Thus a Uniform Methodology scenario would have the following identifying characteristics:

300%/500% PSA Prepayment/ SDA Default Rates

35% MVD

12-month Recovery Lag Period

A Geographic Methodology scenario would have the following identifying characteristics:

Table 2010_2Q (for all assumptions)

125%/200% Prepayment/Default Stress Levels

Finally a Demographic/Financial Methodology scenario would have the following:

Table_2010_2Q (for Prepayment and Recovery assumptions)

Table_2010MVD (for MVD Risk Factors and their weightings)

Table_2010DEF (for Default Rate Risk Factors and their weightings)

125%/200% Prepayment/Default Stress Levels

Database Design

The cash flow runs for each of the three types of cash flow amortization methods will be stored in the same database table. This table is called "tbl_MODELRUNS". It will need to hold the periodic cash flow data for each of the types. Table "tbl_MODELRUNS" is shown in design view in Exhibit 18.51.

The first field will contain a string describing the assumptions for a single modeling run. This will take a different form depending on the type of modeling run and will contain the information described in the previous section. The "Period" field shows in which modeling period each of the cash flows takes place.

tbl_MODELRUNS	
Field Name	**Data Type**
ScenName	Text
Period	Number
BegBalance	Number
SchedPrin	Number
Prepayments	Number
Defaults	Number
CouponIncome	Number
Recoveries	Number
FRNIndexRate	Number

EXHIBIT 18.51   Table "tbl_MODELRUNS" in Design View

Database Implementation

The method by which we update "tbl_MODELRUNS" in the CCFG is very similar to how the Financial Criteria were loaded into "tbl_FinScens". We will first establish strings that are composed of placeholders for all of the values that are to be updated. We then move through the VBA code, updating these base strings at first chance with the appropriate values. As in the Financial Criteria section above, we will use intermediate strings to hold the execution strings during various stages in the process. The real key to this section is to remember where in the program all the relevant data is stored. Once we have the locations, the update is very straightforward.

We create subroutine "writeCFsToACCESS" and store this subroutine in a new module, "CollatCF_WriteCFsToDB". The variables defined in this subroutine include strings used to track the execution strings built below in the code. The global array "gBegPrinBal()" has not yet been populated, so we loop over scenarios and periods to fill in this array. Exhibit 18.52 shows the variable declaration and string initialization of the "str_AmortTypes" and "str_CFs" strings. We identify within these initialized strings the placeholders for database field inputs "ModelRun" (varScenName), "BegBalance" (varBegBal), "SchedPrin" (varPrin), "Prepayments" (varPrepays), "Defaults" (varDefaults), "CouponIncome" (varCoupon), "Recoveries" (varRecov), and "FRNIndexRate" (varIndex). See Exhibit 18.52.

After initializing these strings we connect to the database and set the prefixes for the prepayment and default methodologies used. Of course, these will be used only for model runs under the Uniform Methodology, as the performance under Geographic or Demographic is determined by an input file. After setting these strings, we step into a pair of nested "For" loops iterating over the prepayment and default assumptions. See Exhibit 18.53.

Once inside the "For" loops, the first task is to set the scenario name, depending on the type of modeling run. For a Uniform run, the scenario name will take the following form:

```
UNIFORM / [run name] / [prepay rate] / [default rate] / [recovery lag] / [loss severity]
```

The Geographic or Demographic scenario names take the same format with the exception of the "GEOGRAPHIC" or "DEMOGRAPHIC" prefix:

```
GEOGRAPHIC / [run name] / [assumption table] / [prepay stress] / [default stress]
```

See Exhibit 18.53.

Once we finish setting the scenario name, the remainder of this subroutine makes no distinction as to what type of modeling methodology is used. We simply have to loop over the maximum of 360 periods ("PAY_DATES"), replacing the variable placeholders of the initial strings with the values from the cash flow arrays. The eight replacements occur as follows:

1. "varPer" = "iperiod"
2. "varBegBal" = "gBegBalance(ip, ID, iperiod)"
3. "varPrin" = "gAmortPrin (ip, ID, iperiod)"
4. "varPrepays" = "gPrepaidPrin (ip, ID, iperiod)"
5. "varDefaults" = "gDefaultPrin (ip, ID, iperiod)"

```
Sub writeCFsToACCESS()

Dim str_Prepay      As String    'prepay input string
Dim str_Default     As String    'default input string
Dim str_CFs         As String    'cash flow string; consistent
Dim str_sql         As String    'SQL execution string
Dim str_temp        As String    'intermediate string
Dim str_AmortType   As String    'intermediate string for amort type
Dim scenName        As String    'scenario name
Dim p_rate          As Double    'prepayment rate
Dim d_rate          As Double    'default rate
Dim ip              As Long      'prepay scenario iterator
Dim id              As Long      'default scenario iterator
Dim iperiod         As Long      'period iterator

        'calculate beginning principal balance for all scenarios
    For ip = 1 To gPrepayLevels
        For id = 1 To gDefaultLevels
            For iperiod = 1 To PAY_DATES
                If iperiod = 1 Then
                    gBegPrinBal(ip, id, iperiod) = gTotalPortfolio
                Else
                    gBegPrinBal(ip, id, iperiod) = gBegPrinBal(ip, id, iperiod - 1) - _
                        (gAmortPrin(ip, id, iperiod) + gPrepaidPrin(ip, id, iperiod) + _
                        gDefaultPrin(ip, id, iperiod))
                End If
            Next iperiod
        Next id
    Next ip
    'initial sql strings
    str_AmortType = "INSERT INTO tbl_MODELRUNS VALUES(" & _
                    "'varScenName'," 
    str_CFs = "varPer, varBegBal, varPrin, varPrepays, " & _
                "varDefaults, varCoupon, varRecov, varIndex)"
    ConnectToDataBase (DATABASE_FULLPATH)
    'set prepay/default prefixes
    If gMethodUniform Then
        str_Prepay = "CPR-"
        If gPrepayMethod = 2 Then str_Prepay = "PSA-"
        str_Default = "CPR-"
        If gDefaultMethod = 2 Then str_Default = "PSA-"
        p_rate = gPrepayBaseLevels
        d_rate = gDefaultBaseRate
    End If
```

EXHIBIT 18.52   "writeCFsToACCESS" variables and initial strings

6. "varCoupon" = "gCoupIncome (ip, ID, iperiod)"
7. "varRecov" = "gRecoverPrin(ip, ID, iperiod)"
8. "varIndex" = "gIndexLevels(iperiod,1)"

Finally, after creating the complete cash flows string, we are ready to append this to "str_temp", which is holding the start of the SQL execution string and the scenario name created above. After executing this update string, we move back up to the top of the nested "For" loops to iterate over the default and prepayment scenarios if multiple scenarios were stipulated.

ACCESS IN CCFG REPORTING

Much time has been spent in previous chapters developing reports for various levels of data in the modeling process. In Chapter 13 we built a robust, flexible

```
       For ip = 1 To gPrepayLevels
          For id = 1 To gDefaultLevels
       'create scenario name string base on modeling type
              If gMethodUniform Then
                  scenName = "UNIFORM / " & _
                              gCashFlowWriteCFFileName & " / " & _
                              str_Prepay & (p_rate * 100) & "% (Prepay) / " & _
                              str_Default & (d_rate * 100) & "% (Default) / " & _
                              gRecoveryLagPeriod & " (Lag) / " & _
                              gLossSeverityPct * 100 & "% (MVD)"
                  str_temp = Replace(str_AmortType, "varScenName", scenName)
              ElseIf gMethodGeographic Or gMethodDemographic Then
                  scenName = "GEOGRAPHIC / " & _
                              gCashFlowWriteCFFileName & " / " & _
                              gGeographicFileName(1) & " (File) / " & _
                              gPrepayStressFactor(ip) & "% (Prepay Stress) / " & _
                              gDefaultStressFactor(id) & "% (Default Stress)"
                  str_temp = Replace(str_AmortType, "varScenName", scenName)
       'replace the scen name header if Demographic model run
                  If gMethodDemographic Then
                      str_temp = Replace(str_temp, "GEOGRAPHIC", "DEMOGRAPHIC")
                  End If
              Else
                  DisconnectFromDatabase
                  Exit Sub
              End If
       'delete duplicate scenario names from tbl_MODELRUNS
                  gCon.Execute ("DELETE * FROM tbl_MODELRUNS WHERE ScenName = " & _
                              "'" & scenName & "'")
       'load periodic cash flows to the database
              For iperiod = 1 To PAY_DATES
                  str_sql = Replace(str_CFs, "varPer", iperiod)
                  str_sql = Replace(str_sql, "varBegBal", gBegPrinBal(ip, id, iperiod))
                  str_sql = Replace(str_sql, "varPrin", gAmortPrin(ip, id, iperiod))
                  str_sql = Replace(str_sql, "varPrepays", gPrepaidPrin(ip, id, iperiod))
                  str_sql = Replace(str_sql, "varDefaults", gDefaultPrin(ip, id, iperiod))
                  str_sql = Replace(str_sql, "varCoupon", gCoupIncome(ip, id, iperiod))
                  str_sql = Replace(str_sql, "varRecov", gRecoverPrin(ip, id, iperiod))
                  str_sql = Replace(str_sql, "varIndex", gIndexLevels(iperiod, 1))
                  str_sql = str_temp & str_sql
                  gCon.Execute str_sql
              Next iperiod
              d_rate = d_rate + gDefaultIncrement
          Next id
          p_rate = p_rate + gPrepayIncrement
       Next ip
       DisconnectFromDatabase
   End Sub
```

EXHIBIT 18.53   Setting the scenario name and loading cash flows to the database

Stratification Report Generator. This tool uses data stored in spreadsheets to construct detailed reports through an Excel UserForm interface. In the same way that we used spreadsheets to store information for use in reports, we can use Access to source the data instead. The difficult part is not in retrieving the data but more in what you do with it once you get it. The trick is to represent the results of multiple cash flow runs, data sets, and performance projections in an easy-to-understand, information-rich way.

We will not spend time here going over how to switch over the report writing to pull data from Access as opposed to Excel spreadsheets. Various previous sections give a good introduction to how data is retrieved from Access. In particular, the Initial Data Screening section demonstrated how we can construct a query in such a way as to write recordset results to a spreadsheet in a very specific format, and the techniques used to read data from Access tables to VBA can easily be altered to write directly to a spreadsheet for reporting purposes.

Ultimately, when it comes to reporting results, Excel is far more flexible than Access. Regardless, there are a few types of reports where Access can be utilized effectively. Stratification-style reports are a perfect example of where Access is a natural fit. Recall the ease with which we built an Original Term stratification query in Chapter 17. The amount of VBA code that went into building the Base Stratification Report in Chapter 13 can be easily replaced by a set of custom queries resembling the Original Term query built in Chapter 17. All of the stratification reports built in Chapter 13 could easily be converted in such a way.

It should also be noted that Access contains its own report-building functionality. Unfortunately, because of space considerations, we do not touch on this material here. The interested reader should pick up one of the many Access books available that go more in depth into the query building and report writing features of Access. Bear in mind that the complex, flexible reports built in earlier sections are achieved only with the help of VBA.

ACCESS AND THE LIABILITIES WATERFALL MODEL

At this point in the process we have implemented Access across the CCFG and stored cash flows in the "CCFG_Data.accdb" Access file. These cash flow scenarios are now ready to be read into the LWM, where they will represent the underlying collateral in our securitization. We will start with the LWM Excel file created in Chapter 15 and add VBA code modules to read cash flows from the "CCFG_Data.accdb" database and write LWM results to a new Access file called "LWM_Data.accdb".

CONNECTING THE LWM TO THE CCFG

The VBA code we are building will connect to the CCFG database and the LWM database in the same procedures. Due to this, we need to change the connection and disconnect subroutines. These subroutines, located in the "Z_UtilitySubroutines" module in "LWM_Access.xlsm", are shown in Exhibit 18.54.

It is not too difficult to see what is going on in these subroutines. In the "ConnectToDatabase" subroutine, we open the correct connection object ("gConCCFG" or "gConLWM") based on the connection string that was passed as an argument. We have also now added an argument to the "DisconnectFromDatabase" subroutine. This argument determines which connection object is closed and can take the values of "CCFG" or "LWM".

The subroutines above require the creation of the global connection objects and path Constants. The ADODB connection objects are located in the "A_Globals" module:

```
Public gConCCFG As ADODB.Connection 'CCFG database connection
Public gConLWM As ADODB.Connection 'LWM database connection
```

```
Sub ConnectToDataBase(dataSource As String)
    If dataSource = DATABASE_FULLPATH Then
        Set gConCCFG = New ADODB.Connection
        With gConCCFG
            .ConnectionString = "Provider=Microsoft.ACE.OLEDB.12.0;" & _
                                "Data Source = " & dataSource & ";" & _
                                "Persist Security Info = False;"
            .Open
        End With
    Else
        Set gConLWM = New ADODB.Connection
        With gConLWM
            .ConnectionString = "Provider=Microsoft.ACE.OLEDB.12.0;" & _
                                "Data Source = " & dataSource & ";" & _
                                "Persist Security Info = False;"
            .Open
        End With
    End If
End Sub

Sub DisconnectFromDatabase(con As String)
    If con = "CCFG" Then
        gConCCFG.Close
        Set gConCCFG = Nothing
    ElseIf con = "LWM" Then
        gConLWM.Close
        Set gConLWM = Nothing
    End If
End Sub
```

EXHIBIT 18.54 New connection subroutines

The path Constants for the database are located in the "A_Constants" module:

```
Public Const DATABASE_FULLPATH = _
    ''C:\VBABook2\ABS\Mort\Data\Database\CCFG_Data.accdb''
Public Const LWM_FULLPATH = _
    ''C:\VBABook2\ABS\Mort\Data\Database\LWM_Data.accdb''
```

STRUCTURE WORKSHEET OBJECTS

Once the global variables, Constant variables, and connection subroutines have been added to their appropriate modules, we are ready to add the CCFG scenario ComboBox and the "Load Scenario" CommandButton to the "Structure" worksheet within the LWM workbook.

ComboBox "cmb_CFRunSelect"

The first of the command objects we are to add is a ComboBox that will reflect the scenarios stored within the "tbl_MODELRUNS" table in the CCFG database. The way we accomplish this is very similar to the way we used Access to populate ComboBoxes on the Run Options Menu above. The code resides within

```
Private Sub cmb_CFRunSelect_DropButtonClick()

Dim str_sql As String        'SQL execution string
Dim rs As ADODB.Recordset    'recordset object

    ConnectToDataBase (DATABASE_FULLPATH)
    'get unique scenario names
    str_sql = "SELECT Distinct(ScenName) " & _
              "FROM tbl_ModelRuns " & _
              "ORDER BY ScenName"
    Set rs = gConCCFG.Execute(str_sql)
    'clear the combo box
    Do While cmb_CFRunSelect.ListCount <> 0
        cmb_CFRunSelect.RemoveItem 0
    Loop
    'populate combo box with data from recordset object
    cmb_CFRunSelect.List = Application.WorksheetFunction.Transpose(rs.GetRows)

    cmb_CFRunSelect.AddItem "Amort Sheet"

    DisconnectFromDatabase ("CCFG")
    Set rs = Nothing
End Sub
─────────────────────────────────────────────────────────────────────────
Private Sub cmb_CFRunSelect_LostFocus()

    If cmb_CFRunSelect.ListIndex = -1 Then
        MsgBox "Selection not part of list."
        cmb_CFRunSelect.Value = "Amort Sheet"
        Exit Sub
    End If

End Sub
```

EXHIBIT 18.55   "cmb_CFRunSelect" support code

the "Structure" worksheet. Although we have not yet created the command objects on the worksheet, we can add the supporting code. The two subroutines that support the ComboBox object, "cmb_CFRunSelect", are shown in Exhibit 18.55.

The first subroutine is attached to the "DropButtonClick" event of the ComboBox object. The procedure for populating the ComboBox with available scenario names is as follows:

1. Connect to the database.
2. Populate a recordset object with distinct values of the "ScenName" field in the "tbl_MODELRUNS" table.
3. Clear out all elements of the ComboBox.
4. Set the ComboBox list to the contents of the recordset object.
5. Include the "Amort Sheet" list element to the ComboBox.
6. Disconnect and clean up.

With these six steps we have a ComboBox that is populated only with scenario names that exists in the database table as a result of previously stored model runs (and the "Amort Sheet"). Notice in this subroutine that we are using the "gConCCFG" connection and therefore need to pass "CCFG" as a variable argument

```
Sub getCFs(conOpen As Boolean)
    Application.Calculation = xlCalculationManual
    If Sheets("Structure").cmb_CFRunSelect <> "Amort Sheet" Then
        If Not conOpen Then ConnectToDataBase (DATABASE_FULLPATH)
        Call getCFsDatabase
        If Not conOpen Then DisconnectFromDatabase ("CCFG")
    Else
        Call getCFsAmortSheet
    End If
    Application.Calculation = xlCalculationAutomatic
    Calculate
End Sub
```

EXHIBIT 18.56   "getCFs" subroutine

to the disconnect subroutine. Once again, in typical fashion, we ensure that the analyst can select only an element of the list by employing the "ListIndex = -1" check within the "LostFocus" event code.

CommandButton "cmd_LoadScenario"

The second command object that we will embed on the "Structure" worksheet is a CommandButton that interprets the scenario selected in "cmb_CFRunSelect" and calls the appropriate subroutine to retrieve the cash flows and populate the spreadsheet. The supporting code for this object, located in the "Structure" worksheet code, calls a subroutine located within the "ReturnCashFlows" module:

```
Private Sub cmd_Run_Click()
    Call getCFs(False)
End Sub
```

The "getCFS()" subroutine interprets the contents of the "cmb_CFRunSelect" Combo Box and calls the appropriate subroutine. See Exhibit 18.56. Similar to some of the subroutines built in the CCFG section, we pass a Boolean argument that stipulates whether the calling subroutine already has a connection to the database established. This will be important later in this process when we run multiple scenarios.

Adding Objects to the "Structure" Worksheet

Now that we have the command object support code in place, we switch to Excel and add the objects to the "Structure" worksheet. Recall that we first select the ActiveX Objects from the Insert option under the Developer tab on the Excel ribbon. Once we have the object formatted on the sheet, we right-click on the objects in Design Mode to change their properties. Most important, we need to change the object names to match the supporting code created above. We also designate a field to contain the name of the modeling run or LWM assumption set. This will come into play below when saving these inputs to the database. Name this range (cell E15) "modelName". The "Structure" worksheet with the first two objects embedded and Model Name cell is shown in Exhibit 18.57.

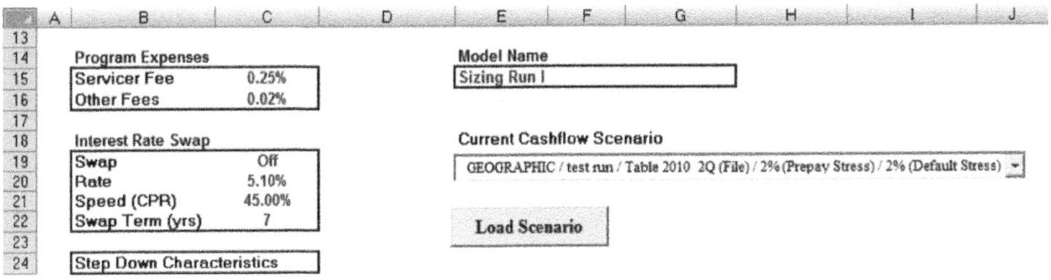

EXHIBIT 18.57 "Structure" worksheet with command object and model run

RETRIEVING THE MONTHLY CASH FLOW SCENARIOS

There are two different sources of cash flows that can be drawn upon, depending on the analyst's scenario selection stored in "cmb_CFRunSelect": the "Amort" worksheet or the CCFG database. These two new subroutines are called from the "getCFs()" subroutine and reside in the "ReturnCashFlows" module.

Cash Flows from the "Amort" Spreadsheet

We still want to allow the analyst to draw cash flows from the "Amort" sheet. The ability to adjust the cash flows in a controlled manner is very valuable during the model testing phase. To facilitate this task we have added a number of named Ranges to the workbook. Some of these were already created in Chapter 15, while others we need to add before proceeding. The full set of named Ranges and corresponding locations is listed below.

On the "CFWaterfall" sheet:

- "cfBeginBalance": cells D14:D373
- "cfPrinRegAmort": cells F14:F373
- "cfPrinPrepayments": cells G14:G373
- "cfPrinDefaults": cells H14:H373
- "cfInterestIncome": cells K14:K373
- "cfPrinRecoveries": cells L14:L373
- "cfFRNIndex": cells DN14:DN373

On the "Amort" sheet:

- "amortBeginBalance": cells K14:K373
- "amortPrinRegAmort": cells N14:N373
- "amortPrinPrepayments": cells M14:M373
- "amortPrinDefaults": cells L14:L373
- "amortInterestIncome": cells O14:O373
- "amortPrinRecoveries": cells P14:P373
- "amortFRNIndex": cells S14:S373

With these Ranges established, the code needed to move the cash flows from the "Amort" sheet to the Collateral Cash Flows section of the "CFWaterfall" sheet is simple. See Exhibit 18.58.

```
Sub getCFsAmortSheet()
    Range("cfBeginBalance").Value = Range("amortBeginBalance").Value
    Range("cfPrinRegAmort").Value = Range("amortPrinRegAmort").Value
    Range("cfPrinPrepayments").Value = Range("amortPrinPrepayments").Value
    Range("cfPrinDefaults").Value = Range("amortPrinDefaults").Value
    Range("cfInterestIncome").Value = Range("amortInterestIncome").Value
    Range("cfPrinRecoveries").Value = Range("amortPrinRecoveries").Value
    Range("cfFRNIndex").Value = Range("amortFRNIndex").Value
End Sub
```

EXHIBIT 18.58   "getCFsAmortSheet" subroutine in the "ReturnCashFlows" module

Cash Flows from Database

If the analyst selects a database scenario from the drop-down list, clicking the "cmd_getScenario" will call the "getCFsDatabase()" subroutine within "getCFs()". This subroutine is displayed in Exhibit 18.59.

We can group together some of the columns that are adjacent to each other in the Collateral Cash Flows section to make the retrieval a bit easier. Take a look at Exhibit 18.51 to recall the design of "tbl_MODELRUNS". The "rs_bal" recordset will contain records from the "BeginBal" field in "tbl_MODELRUNS". Because they are next to each other in the output range, we can use one recordset, "rs_prin", to hold the "SchedPrin", "Prepayments", and "Defaults". The same goes for "rs_IntRecov" in regard to CouponIncome" and "Recoveries" fields. The "FRNIndex" output, which resides on the far right end of the spreadsheet, is stored in "rs_index".

Once we have the recordsets dimensioned, we set the "scenName" string variable equal to the value stored in the "cmb_CFRunSelect" ComboBox. This intermediate step is taken to make the queries more readable. Four different SQL strings are executed against the database to store the cash flow data in the appropriate recordset. In each query we are careful to stipulate ORDER BY "Period" so the results arrive in the correct order. Once the data is stored in the recordsets, we output the results to the spreadsheet making use of the named ranges.

STORING LWM RUN RESULTS IN THE DATABASE

Now that we have a way to load CCFG cash flows into the LWM, we need a way to store the inputs and results. We accomplish this by setting up a collection of output pages upon which the data is organized in the same order as the database tables. To make our lives easier we will use named Ranges to loop over for each of the output tables.

DB Format Worksheet

We need to build a spreadsheet that contains all of the inputs and results of a modeling run in the format that it will be loaded to the database (DB). We break the inputs/results up into the following five tables. All of these tables will also include the analyst-designated name of the model:

1. **"tbl_XL_LWM_Bonds"**. Contains the bond names, percentages, balances, indexes, and ratings from the "Structure" worksheet.

```
Sub getCFsDatabase()

Dim rs_Bal     As ADODB.Recordset  'begin balance
Dim rs_Prin    As ADODB.Recordset  'principal pmts, prepays and loss
Dim rs_IntRecov As ADODB.Recordset 'interest and recoveries
Dim rs_Index   As ADODB.Recordset  'FRN Index
Dim scenName   As String           'scenario name

    scenName = "'" & Sheets("Structure").cmb_CFRunSelect & "'"
    'beginning balance
    Set rs_Bal = gConCCFG.Execute( _
                " SELECT BegBalance " & _
                " FROM tbl_ModelRuns " & _
                " WHERE ScenName = " & scenName & _
                " ORDER BY Period")
    'scheduled prin, prepays and defaults
    Set rs_Prin = gConCCFG.Execute( _
                " SELECT SchedPrin,Prepayments,Defaults " & _
                " FROM tbl_ModelRuns " & _
                " WHERE ScenName = " & scenName & _
                " ORDER BY Period")
    'interest income and recoveries
    Set rs_IntRecov = gConCCFG.Execute( _
                " SELECT CouponIncome,Recoveries " & _
                " FROM tbl_ModelRuns " & _
                " WHERE ScenName = " & scenName & _
                " ORDER BY Period")
    'Floating Rate Note Index
    Set rs_Index = gConCCFG.Execute( _
                " SELECT FRNIndexRate " & _
                " FROM tbl_ModelRuns " & _
                " WHERE ScenName = " & scenName & _
                " ORDER BY Period")
    Range("cfBeginBalance").CopyFromRecordset rs_Bal
    Range("cfPrinRegAmort").CopyFromRecordset rs_Prin
    Range("cfInterestIncome").CopyFromRecordset rs_IntRecov
    Range("cfFRNIndex").CopyFromRecordset rs_Index

    Set rs_Bal = Nothing
    Set rs_Prin = Nothing
    Set rs_IntRecov = Nothing
    Set rs_Index = Nothing
End Sub
```

EXHIBIT 18.59 "getCFsDatabase" subroutine in the "ReturnCashFlows" module

2. **"tbl_XL_LWM_Structure".** Contains the majority of the structural modeling assumptions for a model run. These inputs include fees, swap terms, senior CE percent, and cleanup call behavior.
3. **"tbl_XL_LWM_TargetSub".** Contains the required subordinate percent for each bond.
4. **"tbl_XL_LWM_LossTrigger".** Contains the loss trigger levels throughout the deal.
5. **"tbl_XL_LWM_Results".** Contains the results of the modeling run. This table is populated with the contents of the "Bond Performance" section of the "Results" sheet. Also in this table is the name of the CCFG cash flow run used. This value will be populated with the contents of the "cmb_CFRunSelect" in code.

	A	B	C	D	E	F	G
1							
2		Model Tables					
3							
4		tbl_XL_LWM_Bonds					
5		ModelName	Bond Class	Bond%	Balance	Index	Spread
6		Sizing Run I	A-1	85.95%	145,224,566.42	Libor (1M)	0.200%
7		Sizing Run I	A-2	9.55%	16,136,062.94	Libor (1M)	0.250%
8		Sizing Run I	B-1	1.90%	3,210,316.19	Libor (1M)	0.360%
9		Sizing Run I	B-2	1.10%	1,858,604.11	Libor (1M)	0.480%
10		Sizing Run I	B-3	0.50%	844,820.05	Libor (1M)	1.000%
11		Sizing Run I	B-4	0.50%	844,820.05	Libor (1M)	2.200%
12		Sizing Run I	OC	0.50%	844,820.05		

EXHIBIT 18.60   Bonds output table

The majority of the cells in these tables can be taken directly from their locations on other spreadsheets, but some will require a bit of formatting before they can become linked tables.

Notice that there is no output section dedicated to the cash flows. When building these databases, one thing to try to prevent is redundant data. All of the cash flows are neatly stored in the "tbl_MODELRUNS" table in the "CCFG_Data.accdb" file. Since we are saving the name of the CCFG modeling run in the "tbl_LWM_Results" table, we can easily link results from the two different tables to get a complete picture of what contributed to any particular modeling run.

The first Access-ready table range is shown in Exhibit 18.60.

We can see that this is identical to the first input table on the "Structure" worksheet, aside from the "ModelName" column. The formula in cell C6 is simply "=Structure!B5", and this formula can be copied right on down to the remainder of the table range.

Each of the tables will have as its first column the Model Name from the newly created input on the "Structure" worksheet. Recall that we named this input "model Name", and we can therefore use the formula "=modelName" for all of these tables. When preparing Excel tables that are going to be output to Access, we need to be careful to format the Excel tables as we would format an Access table. This means, of course, that each column needs to have a consistent type. The table Range shown in Exhibit 18.60, including the column headers, is named "tbl_XL_LWM_Bonds". This is the named Range we will use to recognize the tables to be output to Access.

Next we add the other four Excel tables to the "DB Format" spreadsheet. All except for the "tbl_XL_LWM_Results" table can be pulled directly from the "Structure" worksheet. The first portion of the results table is shown in Exhibit 18.61. The contents of this table are drawn from the "Results" page, and because the sourced data is formatted as a table in rows as opposed to columns, we need to transpose it for use on the "DB Format" page. In order to do this we set up the counters on the exterior of the table (e.g., cells A36 and D34) and use an "offset()" formula. The formula in cell D36 is:

```
=IF(OFFSET(Results!$F$5,D$34,$A36)=''NA'',0,OFFSET
  (Results!$F$5,D$34,$A36))
```

	A	B	C	D	E	F
33						
34		tbl_XL_LWM_Results		0	1	2
35		ModelName	ScenName	Class	Initial Balance ($)	Initial Balance (%)
36	1	Sizing Run I	GEOGRAPHIC / test run / Table	A-1	429,750,000.00	85.95%
37	2	Sizing Run I	GEOGRAPHIC / test run / Table	A-2	47,750,000.00	9.55%
38	3	Sizing Run I	GEOGRAPHIC / test run / Table	B-1	9,500,000.00	1.90%
39	4	Sizing Run I	GEOGRAPHIC / test run / Table	B-2	5,500,000.00	1.10%
40	5	Sizing Run I	GEOGRAPHIC / test run / Table	B-3	2,500,000.00	0.50%
41	6	Sizing Run I	GEOGRAPHIC / test run / Table	B-4	2,500,000.00	0.50%
42	7	Sizing Run I	GEOGRAPHIC / test run / Table	OC	2,500,000.00	0.50%
43						

EXHIBIT 18.61 "tbl_XL_LWM_Results" in Excel

Using the counters in column A and row 34, we effectively flip the Results table to make it Access ready. Also in the process we replace the NAs with zeros. If we did not take this step, we would receive an error when trying to link a table that contains numbers and text in the same field.

Moving Data from Excel to Access

Now that we have created and named our five tables in Excel, we are ready to create our new Access database file, "LWM_Data.accdb", and output our results in Excel to Access. Create the new Access file in the location we stored in the "LWM_FULLPATH" Constant in the "A_Constants" module. Open the Access file and choose the "Blank Database" option. When brought into the default "table1", close this table and do not save so we are left with an empty database.

When dealing with large tables in Excel that you wish to transfer to Access tables, sometimes the easiest way to initially set up those tables is to import them to Access. The alternative would be to create the tables from scratch by entering in each field name and corresponding type in Access's Design View. Our "tbl_XL_LWM_Results" table has nineteen fields in total, far too many for this approach. We will therefore import each of our five tables individually and clear the existing contents of these tables so we are left with correctly structured tables containing no data at this point. If you wish to review the steps of this process refer to Exhibits 17.15 through 17.20 in the prior chapter. There is no need to establish a primary key for these tables. When the importation process is complete we should be left with five empty tables in "LWM_Data.accdb" as shown in Exhibit 18.62.

The analyst will have two options to choose from when loading data from the LWM workbook to "LWM_Data.accdb". One option is to load the current scenario to the database. The other is to load every database scenario present in the ComboBox "cmb_CFRunSelect" drop-down list. For either of these options, we need to recognize that each model name (i.e., each set of LWM inputs) can have multiple LWM results associated with it. The multiple results are the result of the fact that each LWM structure can be run with up to 25 different cash flow scenarios. Each cash flow scenario will produce a unique set of liability performance results. Each run of the LWM will therefore produce a single set of modeling assumptions and one result set for each of the scenarios in the CCFG cash flow file selected for that run.

If an LWM model name already exists in the database, the analyst will be given the option to overwrite all data pertaining to the model input set or to just save results for the current scenario with the model name as specified. We will now look

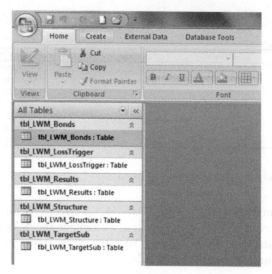

EXHIBIT 18.62   "LWM_Data.accdb" with output tables created

at a set of three subroutines that address the major tasks we need to perform to manage this task.

Building A Trio of Subroutines

In order to best break the overall task of transferring the Excel data into the database we will create three new subroutines. These three subroutines will be called by a main subroutine called "LWMToDatabase" which is responsible for completing the task as a whole. These three subroutines are:

1. **"DeleteModelData".** Deletes all data from all tables where the model name matches the current name. This will be employed when the analyst chooses to overwrite all previously stored model data and repopulate the LWM record anew.
2. **"LWMStructureToDB".** Loads the inputs to the four input database tables by writing the contents of the Excel tables to the Access tables. This subroutine will be called if there are no naming conflicts or after the analyst chooses to delete the model data using "DeleteModelData".
3. **"LWMResultsToDB".** Loads the results data in "tbl_XL_LWM_Results" to "tbl_LWM_Results" after deleting any conflicting model name/scenario records.

"DeleteModelData" subroutine   The "DeleteModelData" subroutine takes as its sole argument a model name. Any record in any of the five tables with matching model name in the "ModelName" field is deleted. The "DeleteModelData" subroutine is shown in Exhibit 18.63.

"LWMStructureToDB" subroutine   The next subroutine we build is the "LWM-StructureToDB" subroutine.

```
Sub DeleteModelData(modelName As String)
    gConLWM.Execute ("DELETE * FROM tbl_LWM_Bonds " & _
            "WHERE [ModelName] = " & modelName)
    gConLWM.Execute ("DELETE * FROM tbl_LWM_LossTrigger " & _
            "WHERE [ModelName] = " & modelName)
    gConLWM.Execute ("DELETE * FROM tbl_LWM_Structure " & _
            "WHERE [ModelName] = " & modelName)
    gConLWM.Execute ("DELETE * FROM tbl_LWM_TargetSub " & _
            "WHERE [ModelName] = " & modelName)
    gConLWM.Execute ("DELETE * FROM tbl_LWM_Results " & _
            "WHERE [ModelName] = " & modelName)
End Sub
```

EXHIBIT 18.63   "DeleteModelData" subroutine

In the "LWMStructureToDB" subroutine, we see two new recordset methods that we have not encountered before: "open()" and "addNew()". With these two methods we are able to open an Access table directly, add a blank record, and pass values in. The way we establish a list of fields and corresponding values for the "addNew()" method is to loop over the four named Range tables in Excel and treat each row in the tables as a record in a data table. For each table we use the code "Range(tblNames(i)).Rows(1))" to get the field names and "Range(tblNames(i)). Rows(j))" to get the values of each record. The "addNew()" function is expecting two one-dimensional arrays as inputs, but because the "Rows()" method on a Range object returns a two-dimensional variant array we have to transpose the results twice to get them formatted correctly. The subroutine is shown in Exhibit 18.64.

"LWMResultsToDB" subroutine   The VBA for the "LWMResultsToDB" subroutine is very similar to "LWMStructureToDB" except we are only updating a single table and run a DELETE statement before uploading the contents of the table to Access. This subroutine is shown in Exhibit 18.65.

Putting the Pieces Together Subroutine "LWMToDatabase"

In this subroutine we accommodate the ability to run one or many scenarios for the same model assumption set. To do this we pass a variable of type Boolean called "allScens" that is true or false depending on what the analyst chooses to do. The process encompasses the following four steps, with some program flow variability based on analyst input:

1. Connect to both databases and populate subroutine variables from objects and inputs on the "Structure" worksheet.
2. Check to see if there is a conflicting modeling set already saved to the database as evidenced by the model name input. If there is a conflict, we give the analyst the option of (a) overwriting all previous stored data, (b) saving only the results, or (c) quitting the program and renaming the model.

```
Sub LWMStructureToDB()

Dim rs            As ADODB.Recordset  'rs table
Dim varFields     As Variant          'field name array
Dim varValues     As Variant          'value array
Dim tblNames      As Variant          'table/range name array
Dim tblNamesXL    As Variant          'table/range name array
Dim i             As Integer          'iterator
Dim j             As Integer          'iterator

    tblNames = Array("tbl_LWM_Bonds", "tbl_LWM_Structure", _
                "tbl_LWM_TargetSub", "tbl_LWM_LossTrigger")
    tblNamesXL = Array("tbl_XL_LWM_Bonds", "tbl_XL_LWM_Structure", _
                "tbl_XL_LWM_TargetSub", "tbl_XL_LWM_LossTrigger")

    Set rs = New ADODB.Recordset

    For i = 0 To UBound(tblNames)
        rs.Open tblNames(i), gConLWM, adOpenKeyset, adLockOptimistic, adCmdTable

        varFields = Application.WorksheetFunction.Transpose( _
                    Application.WorksheetFunction.Transpose( _
                    Range(tblNamesXL(i)).Rows(1)))

        For j = 2 To Range(tblNamesXL(i)).Rows.Count
            varValues = Application.WorksheetFunction.Transpose( _
                        Application.WorksheetFunction.Transpose( _
                        Range(tblNamesXL(i)).Rows(j)))
            rs.addNew varFields, varValues
            rs.Update
        Next j
        rs.Close
    Next i
    Set rs = Nothing

End Sub
```

EXHIBIT 18.64 "LWMStructrueToDB" subroutine

3. Depending on the analyst's response in Step 2, load the structural and modeling inputs to the database.
4. Depending on the analyst's response in Step 2, and depending on whether we are running a single scenario or multiple scenarios, load the cash flows from "CCFG_Data.accdb" (subroutine "getCFs") and save the modeling results to the database with a call to "LWMResultsToDB".

The full subroutine is shown in Exhibit 18.66.

Step #1—Preparation: Connecting, Reading, and Storing In Step 1 we dimension the necessary variables, connect to the databases, and store values in the variables. The "scens" variable is a variant array that holds all the items of the "cmb_CFRunSelect" drop-down box. We use this later when looping over scenarios. We also store the index of the currently selected item in the "scenListNumber" variable. The "modelName" variable is populated with the contents of named Range "ModelName" bookended by single quotes to make it query-ready.

```
Sub LWMResultsToDB(modelName As String, scenName As String)

Dim rs          As ADODB.Recordset 'rs table
Dim varFields   As Variant         'field name array
Dim varValues   As Variant         'value array
Dim i           As Integer         'iterator

    'delete model/scen combination where exists
    gConLWM.Execute ("DELETE * FROM tbl_LWM_Results " & _
                     "WHERE [ModelName] = " & modelName & _
                     " AND [ScenName] = " & scenName)
    Set rs = New ADODB.Recordset

    rs.Open "tbl_LWM_Results", gConLWM, adOpenKeyset, adLockOptimistic, adCmdTable

    varFields = Application.WorksheetFunction.Transpose( _
                Application.WorksheetFunction.Transpose( _
                Range("tbl_XL_LWM_Results").Rows(1)))

    For i = 2 To Range("tbl_XL_LWM_Results").Rows.Count
        varValues = Application.WorksheetFunction.Transpose( _
                    Application.WorksheetFunction.Transpose( _
                    Range("tbl_XL_LWM_Results").Rows(i)))
        rs.addNew varFields, varValues
        rs.Update
    Next i

    rs.Close
    Set rs = Nothing
End Sub
```

EXHIBIT 18.65 "LWMResultsToDB" subroutine

Step #2—Checking the Model Name, Reading the Buttons In Step 2 we check the "tbl_LWM_Bonds" table to see if the current model name already exists in the database tables. We only need to check one table in the database. We will earlier have established the practice of retaining all of the data of a particular model name or none of it. If the model name is present we will find it here; if not, we need look no further. If we find a duplicate model name, the subroutine will display a message box to the user. Three options are presented:

- "Yes". Overwrite all the data corresponding to the model name.
- "No". Save only the results corresponding to the model name.
- "Cancel". End the program in order to have the opportunity to change the existing model name to one not currently found in the database.

The choice is stored in integer variable "dupModelName". The message box is shown in Exhibit 18.67.

The SELECT CASE statement in Step 2 determines the actions the LWM subroutine will take based upon the choice of the analyst from the three options above. These are choices are as follows:

- Case DB_RENAMERUN: This case corresponds to selecting the "Cancel" button. If this is the option elected the program immediately branches to the very last two statements of the subroutine. With nothing to be done all that is required is that we close the database connections and end the subroutine.

```
Sub LWMToDatabase(allScens As Boolean)

Dim modelName        As String           'model name string
Dim scens            As Variant          'array of scenario names
Dim scenName         As String           'single scenario name string
Dim scenListNum      As Integer          'list item number of scenario
Dim dupModelName     As Integer          'msgbox result
Dim rs               As ADODB.Recordset  'recordset object
Dim i                As Integer          'scenario interator
    'Step 1: connect to databases and load in variables from spreadsheet
    ConnectToDataBase (DATABASE_FULLPATH)
    ConnectToDataBase (LWM_FULLPATH)
    scens = Sheets("Structure").cmb_CFRunSelect.List
    scenListNum = Sheets("Structure").cmb_CFRunSelect.ListIndex
    modelName = "'" & Range("modelName").Value & "'"
    'Step 2: check for duplicate model name and request user input
    Set rs = gConLWM.Execute("SELECT Distinct([ModelName]) " & _
                        "FROM tbl_LWM_Bonds " & _
                        "WHERE [ModelName] = " & modelName)
    'if duplicate found ask permission to overwrite
    'if Yes, delete all data for model name and write inputs and results
    'if No, write only results under current model name
    'if Cancel, end program and rename model
    If Not (rs.BOF And rs.EOF) Then
        dupModelName = MsgBox("Model name " & modelName & _
                        " already saved in the database." & vbCrLf & vbCrLf & _
                        "-""Yes"" to delete all data corresponding to this " & _
                        "model name and overwrite." & vbCrLf & vbCrLf & _
                        "-""No"" to save model results" & _
                        " under same model name." & vbCrLf & vbCrLf & _
                        "-""Cancel"" to rename." _
                        , vbYesNoCancel + vbQuestion, "Model Name Exists")

        Select Case dupModelName
            Case DB_RENAMERUN
                MsgBox "Please rename the model."
                GoTo renameModel
            Case DB_DELETEDATA
                Call DeleteModelData(modelName)
            Case DB_UPDATERESULTS
                GoTo updateResultsOnly
        End Select
    End If
    'Step 3: load model inputs to db
    Call LWMStructureToDB
updateResultsOnly:
    'Step 4:
    'if running all scenarios then loop over scens array
    'otherwise just run the current scenListNum item
    If allScens Then
        For i = 0 To UBound(scens, 1) - 1
            Sheets("Structure").cmb_CFRunSelect.Value = scens(i, 0)
            scenName = "'" & Sheets("Structure").cmb_CFRunSelect.Value & "'"
            Call getCFs(True)
            Call LWMResultsToDB(modelName, scenName)
        Next i
    Else
        Sheets("Structure").cmb_CFRunSelect.Value = scens(scenListNum, 0)
        scenName = "'" & Sheets("Structure").cmb_CFRunSelect.Value & "'"
        Call getCFs(True)
        Call LWMResultsToDB(modelName, scenName)
    End If
renameModel:
    DisconnectFromDatabase ("CCFG")
    DisconnectFromDatabase ("LWM")
End Sub
```

EXHIBIT 18.66 "LWMToDatabase" subroutine

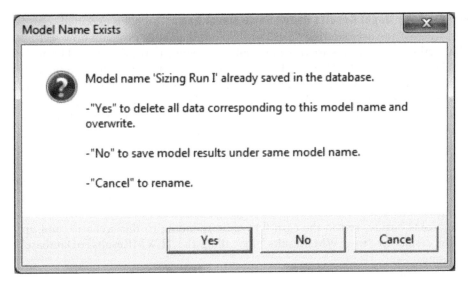

EXHIBIT 18.67 "Model Name Exists" Message Box

- Case DB_DELETEDATA: This case corresponds to selecting the "Yes" button. This is the choice to overwrite the existing model information. Two things will now happen. First we will call the subroutine "DeleteModelData". As mentioned earlier this deletes any information residing in the database associated with the name of the currently designated model run. Having cleared any existing data the subroutine exits the "Select..Case" statement and immediately calls the "LWMStructureToDB" subroutine that completes the process.
- Case DB_UPDATERESULTS: This case corresponds to selecting the "No" button. With this choice we elect to save only the model results and not the structure inputs. The subroutine therefore bypasses the call to subroutine "LWMStructureToDB" and branches to the statement named "updateResultsOnly". See Step 4 for a more detailed discussion of the steps needed to write the results to the database.

To make the SELECT CASE statement more readable we have also added the following three Constant variable to our "A_Constants" module:

```
Public Const DB_RENAMERUN = 2       'Msgbox Cancel
Public Const DB_DELETEDATA = 6      'Msgbox Yes
Public Const DB_UPDATERESULTS = 7   'Msgbox No
```

With these additions we have the user input and program flow portions of the subroutine in place.

Step #3—Overwriting the Existing Model Name Data   Step 3 is executed only if the analyst chooses the "Yes" button to overwrite all data for the indicated model name. If this choice was made, we call the "LWMStructureToDB", as discussed in Step 2, having already deleted the conflicting records inside "Case DB_DELETEDATA" branch of the Select..Case statement.

Step #4—Save Model Results Under Same Model Name   Step 4 is executed regardless of whether the user selected "Yes" or "No" in the above program flow section. In this section the scenarios are run and results are loaded to the database. This is the step where we handle the "Run and Save" versus "Run and Save All" functionality described earlier in this section. If the value of the "allScens" variable that has been passed to the subroutine "LWMToDatabase" is TRUE, we loop over each of the values in the "scens" array. This "For..Next" loop reads the number of LWM results sets and reads each into the "tbl_LWM_Results" table in the database with records identified by the combination of the model name and scenario name, excluding the final "Amort Sheet" value. We leave this scenario choice out because we do not want the database to become cluttered with untraceable scenarios. The "Amort" sheet is for testing the model and not for constructing modeling runs. If we are writing multiple scenarios to the database we change the ComboBox based on the contents of the "scens" array, return the cash flow corresponding to this scenario, and update the results to "tbl_LWM_Results" by calling the "LWMResultsToDatabase" subroutine.

If the value of the variable "allScens" is FALSE we need only write a single scenario. We read the LWM results associated with the scenario indexed by "scenListNum". Notice that the call to the subroutine "getCFs" is passed with the value of its single receiving argument "conOpen" set to TRUE. The value of the arguments of the "getCFs" subroutine determine if the connections to the database are to be opened or closed. This makes it easier to trace the actions and processes of the senior subroutines as they call the subordinate subroutines.

"Structure" Worksheet Final Modifications

Once we have the above code written, the final task is to add the CommandButtons "Run and Save" and "Run and Save All", with supporting code, to the "Structure" worksheet.

New CommandButtons   This particular portion of the finished "Structure" worksheet is shown in Exhibit 18.68.

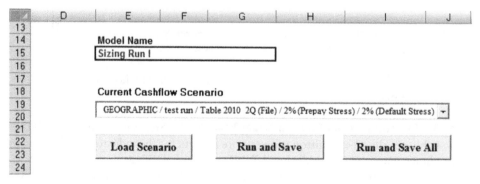

EXHIBIT 18.68   Completed "Structure" worksheet

CommandButton Support Code   The supporting code for these two new buttons is nearly identical. The only difference is that one calls the "LWMToDatabase" subroutine, passing the "allScens" as FALSE, and the other sets it to TRUE. The event subroutines for the three CommandButtons are:

```
Private Sub cmd_Run_Click()
   Call getCFs(False)
End Sub

Private Sub cmd_RunSave_Click()
   Call LWMToDatabase(False)
End Sub

Private Sub cmd_RunSaveAll_Click()
   Call LWMToDatabase(True)
End Sub
```

With this final addition to the "Structure" worksheet supporting code, we have completed the process of linking four components of the Access-based model: "LWM_Access.xlsm", "CCFG_Access.xlsm", "CCFG_Data.accdb", and "LWM_Data.accdb".

CONCLUDING REMARKS

We sincerely hope that you will have seen the advantages of using Access to address this wide variety of activities. There is an enormous amount of new material in this chapter. *Do not be discouraged if you do not understand all of it immediately.* Download the code and the databases from the Web site. Step through the processes in the VBA Debugger until you get comfortable with both the format and the actions of the Access commands. When you build your own Access routines, start simply. We advise that you use one of the simple subroutines in this chapter and begin by making slight modifications to it. Improve your understanding by taking small steps to build confidence. We wish you good luck and success.

Remember the old Roman saying:

"Fortune favors the brave!"

ON THE WEB SITE

The following material is available on the Web site:

Model Files

- "CCFG_Access.xlsm". An Excel workbook containing all of the examples above along with edits to the CCFG referenced in the text.
- "CCFG_Data.accdb". Access file containing all the CCFG tables referenced in the above chapter.

- **"LWM_Access.xlsm".** An Excel workbook building on the Chapter 15 LWM file to include Access functionality.
- **"LWM_Data.accdb".** Access file containing all the LWM tables referenced in the above chapter.

Template File

- **"InitDataScreenTemplateAccess.xlsx"**

Data Files

- **"MainPort.xlsx".** Loan-by-loan data file.
- **"SubPort01.xlsx" to SubPort05.xlsx".** Modeling Sub-Portfolio.

## CHAPTER 19

Implementing PowerPoint and Outlook in the CCFG

OVERVIEW

In this chapter we will explore using Excel/VBA to produce reports in PowerPoint. We will learn how to activate PowerPoint from within the VBA code of the model. We will then select material from the spreadsheets of the model or from reports we generated previously and place it in the PowerPoint presentation. In addition, we will concentrate on a few straightforward examples and demonstrate how you can produce a series of different PowerPoint slides by using a few basic principles of VBA coding. The example will use a PowerPoint presentation template file that contains a series of header slides and exhibit slides to produce a 13-page report.

The second topic of the chapter covers how to send Outlook messages from the model for the purposes of alerting yourself (or anyone else) of the progress of the model or the timing and content of its output. We will also cover how to create Outlook messages that contain attachments so that the results of the model can be communicated to interested parties.

DELIVERABLES

The general knowledge deliverables in this chapter are:

1. A general approach to transferring data from a series of Excel reports into a PowerPoint presentation.
2. How to manipulate existing information, report layouts, and messages to selectively extract various content from Excel files in anticipation of export to a PowerPoint presentation.
3. How to add a new report set to the CCFG.
4. How to manage situations when the analyst has requested a presentation report that cannot be produced with the existing information.
5. How to send both Outlook messages and model results directly from the model to other interested parties.

UNDER CONSTRUCTION

VBA module modifications:

- ■ **"A_Constants"**. Add a series of Public Constants to establish the template files we will need for the new reports. Modify the values of other Constants to reflect the addition of the PowerPoint reports.
- ■ **"A_Globals"**. Add a series of global variables to assist us in integrating the new PowerPoint Presentation Report Package. These will include the variables that indicate that the report has been selected and other variables that convey the choices made in the UserForm as to the content of the report.
- ■ **"A_MainProgram"**. Add a call to the subroutine that writes the PowerPoint Presentation Report Package.
- ■ **"MenuSupport_ReportsMenu"**. Add the menu support code required to manage the UserForm for the PowerPoint presentation we will add to the Reports Menu.
- ■ **"Report_PowerPointPresOne"**. Add a new module with all the VBA code to open PowerPoint, determine if there is sufficient information to produce the report, edit, condense, and reformat the input information for the report, write the report, and then close and save the presentation.

UserForm modifications:

- ■ **"m15PPSingleStateMenu"**. Add a UserForm to select the states for which the PowerPoint presentation is to be produced. We will also add all the UserForm support code of the form.

Menu modifications:

- ■ **CCFG Reports Editor and Menu.** We will add the section for PowerPoint Presentation Reports and add the PowerPoint presentation to the Report Menu UserForm.

Data Sheet modifications:

- ■ **Data Report List.** We will add the PowerPoint presentation as a new report category to this worksheet. This is necessary to preserve the existing schema between this Data Sheet and the CCFG Reports Editor and Menu.

USING POWERPOINT IN THE CCFG

This section will discuss the advantages of integrating the PowerPoint product into the reporting schema of the Collateral Cash Flow Generator (CCFG). This is an interesting process, but it is not so interesting that we should undertake it for its interest alone! If we are to go to the trouble of learning how to join Excel/VBA to PowerPoint, there needs to be clear and compelling reasons to spend the time and effort to do so.

Advantages

The advantages of integrating PowerPoint into the report writing section of the model are compelling. The appearance and versatility of PowerPoint versus a simple Excel worksheet as a presentation delivery vehicle arises from the former's specialization to perform just that role! In this chapter we will teach you how to move blocks of information from the CCFG into a PowerPoint template. The techniques will allow you to transfer various combinations of text, data, and chart information quickly and precisely. You will no longer need to manually cut and paste exhibits from one product to the other. Once you have set up the process using these guidelines and code samples, you will be able to produce a PowerPoint presentation loaded with information in seconds. Another critical reason to use PowerPoint is that the data cannot be modified after the report is produced as it can in Excel. This allows even more standardization of frequently used reports.

Replicable and Reliable   The main advantage to the automation of PowerPoint report production using VBA is replicability combined with reliability. The approach we will take will rely on the use of a template PowerPoint file that is then populated with the text, data, and charts of preexisting Excel reports. If the source data is contained in the targeted Excel files, the VBA report writer will produce your PowerPoint presentation quickly and painlessly.

This approach assumes that you judiciously establish the preconditions necessary for the production of the PowerPoint presentation by having the correct files previously generated by the CCFG in the proper directories where they can be found by the VBA report writer subroutines. If that is the case, you can then design, implement, and run a series of PowerPoint-producing VBA subroutines against this data repository.

Effective and Efficient   The efficiency and effectiveness of this approach goes beyond the immediate time and labor savings of transferring this data from the source Excel files to PowerPoint. If you are in a situation where the need for PowerPoint presentation of deal data is continuous, this approach allows for the immediate standardization of the most frequently used presentations. At first you may choose to replicate the entire presentation into a standardized format. This is especially useful when dealing with investors who require a side-by-side comparative risk approach. With standardized reports, it is much easier to compare not only the differences but also the similarities between successive investment opportunities. As time passes it also allows for the accumulation of a body of reporting histories that share a common style and format. Building this type of report collection can prove an invaluable analytical foundation if the business is engaged in ongoing issuance activity of many deals of the same general type using similar asset Pools and Liabilities Structures.

Templates Files or from Scratch?

One of the first questions we need to resolve before we go any further is that of our basic approach: Do we use a preconfigured template file as the basis for the report writer or do we build the reports dynamically? As you may have already ascertained from the chapter so far, we will use the template approach. Why? We have selected this approach because it is easier to target a specific set of requirements in a report with an established format. As this is only an introduction to the issue, we will keep the first foray into the unknown as clear and simple as possible. This is not to say that the coding techniques and the capabilities that we develop here cannot be broken down and recombined in many different ways! They can! Once you become familiar with the basic approaches of this chapter you will undoubtedly find many more ways of employing them.

We have created a PowerPoint template file that consists of a report header slide, section divider slides, and a number of single-page exhibit slides of different configurations.

Single State Report Package

The report package that we will produce presents information across a series of four categories that outline various characteristics of the loan collateral of an individual state.

Sit Down or Stand Up?　There are basically two types of meetings: sit-down meetings or stand-up meetings. The report package that we will use as the example in this chapter is a sit-down package. In this type of meeting a small group of people, characteristically fewer than six, are meeting to review the presentation in a very detailed manner. As a result the content and format of the PowerPoint slides will not conform to the standard mass visual approach of a projected presentation before an audience of hundreds of people. It will contain a degree of data density that would be incomprehensible in a large-group format. This stems from two reasons. The first is that we would expect the members of the small sit-down meeting to be experts, with a significant amount of shared information and views. The questions arising in such a group will require a tiered approach to the information, ranging from most general to a high level of detail. This requirement will often result with very different content/format on the same page. The second is that viewers are 24 inches away from the report on the conference table in front of them as opposed to tens of feet to tens of yards for a large-audience projection approach. See Exhibits 19.1 and 19.2.

Purpose of the Report　The purpose of the report is fivefold:

1. Comparison of the geographic distribution of the collateral in that selected state to the national distribution of collateral
2. Presentation of the dispersion of the collateral balances within the state itself
3. Stratification of selected credit and underwriting issues
4. Stratification and cross tabulation reports related to Asset Valuation
5. Reports describing the Borrower Demographics of the obligor pool

Structure of the Report Package　The report consists of the following elements:

- A Report Header page
- A Geographic Concentration section header page
- Two Geographic Concentration reports
- An Underwriting section header page

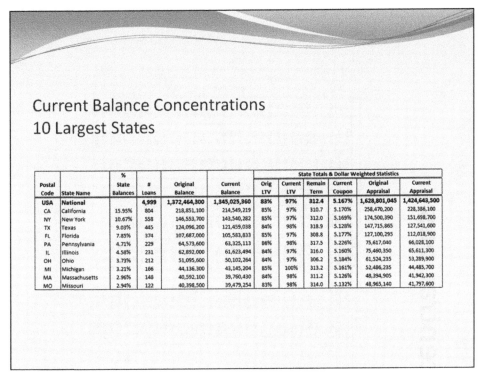

EXHIBIT 19.1 National Geographic Concentration Report (stand up)

- Three reports on debt-to-income ratios
- An Asset Valuation section header page
- Two Valuation reports
- A Borrower Demographics section header page
- A Borrower Demographics Report

National versus State Concentration Section   This section contains three geographic reports. The first is the ranking of the top 30 states by their aggregate current balances in a single data table. The second is the dispersion of current balances by the Metropolitan Statistical Areas (MSAs) within the state.

Underwriting Standards Section   This section contains three reports. The first is the Debt-to-Income Summary Report. This report contains a summary statistical table and two pie charts that display the distributions of Mortgage Debt-to-Income and Total Debt-to-Income. The second report contains two cross tabulation reports of the distribution of National/State Total Debt-to-Income by Fair Isaacs Corporation (FICO) score. The last report contains the same cross tabulations for Mortgage Debt-to-Income statistics.

Valuation Methods and Results Section   This section contains two reports. The first is the Summary Loan-to-Value report. It contains a summary statistics table and a pair of pie charts describing the distribution of Original and Current

Current Balance Concentrations
30 Largest States

Postal Code	State Name	% State Balances	# Loans	Original Balance	Current Balance	Orig LTV	Current LTV	Orig Term	Remain Term	Season	Current Coupon	Original Appraisal	Current Appraisal	$ Avg FICO	% First Home	% Self Employed	% Mort D to I	% Total D to I
USA	National		4,999	1,372,464,300	1,345,025,360	83%	97%	320.9	312.4	15.1	5.167%	1,623,801,045	1,424,648,300	702.7	26.6%	45.6%	43.8%	63.6%
CA	California	15.95%	804	218,851,100	214,549,219	85%	97%	319.0	310.7	14.7	5.170%	258,470,200	228,386,100	706.0	25.9%	45.0%	43.9%	63.3%
NY	New York	10.67%	558	146,553,700	143,540,282	85%	97%	320.8	312.0	15.5	5.169%	174,500,390	151,698,700	709.7	28.7%	41.6%	44.2%	64.2%
TX	Texas	9.03%	445	124,096,200	121,459,038	84%	98%	328.0	318.5	16.3	5.128%	147,715,665	127,541,600	692.4	22.0%	47.5%	44.2%	62.8%
FL	Florida	7.65%	374	107,687,000	105,583,833	85%	97%	317.0	308.8	14.5	5.177%	127,100,295	112,018,900	701.4	24.9%	44.9%	44.0%	63.8%
PA	Pennsylvania	4.71%	229	64,573,600	63,325,113	86%	98%	326.0	317.5	14.9	5.226%	75,617,040	66,028,100	712.4	24.9%	42.8%	43.7%	63.9%
IL	Illinois	4.58%	231	62,892,000	61,623,494	84%	97%	324.7	316.0	15.3	5.160%	75,460,350	65,611,300	703.6	32.0%	45.0%	43.0%	62.3%
OH	Ohio	3.73%	212	51,095,600	50,102,264	84%	97%	314.3	306.2	14.4	5.184%	61,524,235	53,289,900	711.9	29.7%	50.5%	43.8%	63.4%
MI	Michigan	3.21%	166	44,136,300	43,145,204	84%	100%	322.7	313.2	16.9	5.161%	52,486,235	44,485,700	695.4	33.1%	47.0%	42.6%	62.1%
MA	Massachusetts	2.96%	148	40,592,100	39,760,410	84%	98%	320.0	311.2	15.4	5.126%	48,394,955	41,942,300	691.5	28.4%	45.5%	44.6%	65.5%
MO	Missouri	2.94%	122	40,398,500	39,479,254	83%	98%	323.5	314.0	17.1	5.132%	48,965,140	41,797,600	706.7	26.2%	38.5%	44.5%	64.0%
GA	Georgia	2.57%	132	35,240,800	34,580,097	83%	95%	329.3	321.1	14.5	5.237%	41,817,000	37,162,300	680.6	25.8%	40.9%	43.8%	60.1%
AZ	Arizona	2.50%	121	34,265,400	33,652,214	87%	99%	329.0	321.3	13.7	5.093%	39,582,565	35,462,900	712.8	28.1%	55.4%	44.1%	66.5%
NC	North Carolina	2.38%	126	32,641,100	31,972,301	86%	99%	322.9	314.1	15.6	5.186%	38,238,455	33,377,000	693.0	22.2%	52.4%	44.1%	62.4%
DC	Dist of Col	2.32%	114	31,825,100	31,170,193	85%	99%	321.2	312.5	15.4	5.102%	37,801,105	32,416,100	702.9	36.0%	53.5%	43.7%	64.4%
WA	Washington	1.74%	89	23,781,100	23,340,936	85%	94%	311.0	301.6	13.3	5.085%	28,146,355	25,284,700	722.1	29.2%	47.2%	45.4%	65.6%
CO	Colorado	1.68%	70	23,030,300	22,620,304	85%	98%	322.3	314.7	13.4	5.102%	27,130,100	24,632,700	704.9	25.7%	52.9%	44.9%	64.5%
MN	Minnesota	1.54%	72	21,156,600	20,770,715	86%	92%	304.3	296.9	13.1	5.172%	24,847,930	22,870,000	706.8	27.8%	30.6%	44.9%	63.3%
VA	Virginia	1.47%	66	20,220,200	19,797,700	86%	100%	308.9	299.8	15.7	5.265%	23,692,085	20,214,700	682.8	25.8%	47.0%	43.6%	68.3%
OR	Oregon	1.35%	70	18,570,900	18,175,379	85%	98%	322.9	313.7	16.2	5.112%	22,000,195	19,047,900	666.6	18.6%	44.3%	43.2%	62.2%
CT	Connecticut	1.34%	72	18,416,100	18,041,952	84%	97%	327.2	318.3	15.7	5.220%	21,540,100	19,158,600	701.7	26.4%	38.3%	44.8%	63.9%
TN	Tennessee	1.29%	76	17,610,600	17,259,301	85%	92%	307.6	300.2	13.0	5.000%	21,333,640	19,346,700	697.9	26.3%	50.0%	45.2%	70.1%
MD	Maryland	1.20%	54	16,448,400	16,129,355	88%	96%	307.5	299.6	14.0	5.096%	19,248,540	17,178,700	693.1	20.4%	40.7%	41.3%	61.4%
NV	Nevada	1.19%	50	16,281,000	15,976,263	83%	98%	302.2	294.9	13.2	5.113%	19,129,790	17,092,900	667.0	30.0%	32.0%	43.5%	64.7%
IN	Indiana	1.14%	59	15,631,200	15,321,785	87%	102%	316.4	308.2	14.6	5.119%	17,929,530	15,499,900	725.3	33.9%	45.8%	42.0%	63.1%
WI	Wisconsin	1.11%	55	15,178,400	14,916,188	85%	100%	323.1	315.5	13.3	5.273%	18,016,440	15,740,200	680.9	29.1%	47.1%	43.4%	60.9%
AL	Alabama	0.98%	48	13,510,700	13,245,964	84%	100%	318.9	310.4	14.9	5.219%	16,079,965	13,948,200	728.7	31.3%	31.3%	45.1%	64.6%
UT	Utah	0.98%	53	13,371,900	13,136,201	81%	93%	326.7	319.2	13.4	5.183%	16,712,795	14,486,100	707.1	24.5%	49.1%	38.0%	56.9%
LA	Louisiana	0.90%	47	12,440,300	12,168,989	85%	93%	322.4	313.4	16.1	5.086%	14,839,150	13,639,200	701.9	12.8%	40.4%	43.9%	66.6%
SC	South Carolina	0.87%	43	11,862,000	11,660,552	85%	90%	292.0	285.4	11.6	5.103%	13,983,465	13,171,900	703.4	30.2%	53.5%	37.6%	61.0%
KY	Kentucky	0.73%	38	10,072,000	9,849,026	84%	100%	331.4	321.5	17.4	5.242%	12,165,765	9,698,600	721.8	21.1%	36.6%	45.0%	63.5%

EXHIBIT 19.2 National Geographic Concentration Slide 1 (sit down)

Loan-to-Value ratios. The second report describes the distribution of current balances of the collateral by Original and Current Appraisal methods. It contains a summary statistical table, a pair of pie charts, and a combined stratification report.

Borrower Demographics Section The Borrower Demographics section contains four files, one of which is developed for the example. This report outlines the status of First Time Home Ownership. The possible values are "No Data", "Yes", and "No". The report contains a summary statistics table, a graph, a stratification report, and a cross tabulation report.

Null Single State Report Package

In addition to the Single State Report, there is a second report that is produced by the PowerPoint Report Writer subroutines. This is the Null Single State Report Package, the separated-at-birth evil-twin version of the Single State Report.

Purpose of the Report The production of the Single State Report relies on the existence and correct positioning of a series of seven Excel/VBA report files. All of these files are necessary to complete all or some of the sections of the Single State Report. In this exercise we will assume an all-or-nothing approach to the production process. If any of the required information is missing, we will forgo producing any portion of the report (even though there may be sufficient information to create some of the report). We will, with this draconian requirement of total data sufficiency, end up with more cases of complete failure. How do we inform the analysis of the failure criteria that presented the production of the desired report? The answer is simple: Produce a report with a single title page listing the data file conditions that precluded the production of the desired report.

This one-page report lists both the available and missing data files as a guide to what files need to be added/created so the report can be run.

DATA REQUIREMENTS

The data requirements of the Single State Report consist of seven different reports produced by the CCFG. Two of these are National Level reports and five are State Level reports.

Generating the Source Data Files

The seven Excel files we need to generate are:

1. The national level Initial State Geographic Concentration Report named "National_StateInitGeoConcenReport.xlsm".
2. The national level Cross Tabulation Report named "National_CrossTabs.xlsm".
3. The state-level (California) Initial Geographic Concentration Report, named "CA_MSAInitGeoConcenReport.xlsm".
4. The state-level Credit Portfolio Presentation Report named "CA_PortPresent Report_Credit.xlsm".

5. The state-level Valuation Portfolio Presentation Report named "CA_PortPresent Report_Valuation.xlsm".
6. The state-level Cross-Tabulation Report named "CA_CrossTabs.xlsm".
7. The state-level User Stratification Report named "CA_UserStratRep.xlsm".

We will now walk through the CCFG Model settings needed to generate these two sets of reports. We generate the National Level reports first followed by the State Level reports. We will pick the state of California as the victim, oops, I meant to say "subject" of this exercise.

National Level Files   We can generate the two National Level reports by performing the following actions with the CCFG:

1. Start at the "Main Menu". Click the "Set Model Run Options" button. On the "Run Options Menu" we will enter the settings listed below. We will be using the collateral pool file "Pool01_PowerPoint". This pool can be used for this example with any collateral screening.
   a. Initial Loan Data Screening Test = "N".
   b. Apply Initial and Financial and Demographic Tests = "N".
   c. Apply Geographic (State & MSA) Tests = "N".
   d. Apply Geographic Concentration Tests = "N".
   e. Produce Eligible Collateral Cash Flows = "N".
   Click on the "Return To Main Menu" button.
2. From the Main Menu click on the "Identify Collateral Data Files" button. Once in the "CCFG Collateral Pool Menu" we will use the "Select File" feature in the line "Collateral Pool #1" line of the menu to select the following file:

   ''C:\VBA_Book2\ABS\Mort01\Data\Collat\Pool01_PowerPoint.xslm''

   Click on the "Return to Main Menu" button.
3. We will not be performing any collateral eligibility testing on the selected collateral pool file "Pool01_PowerPoint" so we can skip the next two buttons of the "Main Menu", "Define Geographic Selection Criteria" and "Define Fin/Demo Selection Criteria". The PowerPoint presentation file does not display any cash flows so we can also skip the "Set Amortization Parameters" button.
4. Click on the "Define Report Package" button. Once in the "CCFG Reports Editor & Menu", click on the "Select Reports from CCFG Report Package. The UserForm "CCFG Model Reports Menu" will be displayed. Before doing anything else we will want to clear the program of any report elections that might be stored from a prior run of the model. To accomplish this we will first click on the "Clear All Selections" button. Now we will select the two National Level Reports, the PowerPoint presentation report requires a pre-computed input.
   a. In the subsection "Geographic Reports", at the top of the right hand column, select the second report, "Initial Concentration Report—State Level".
   b. In the subsection "Eligible Collateral Reports", the bottommost section of the left hand column, select the second report, "Cross Tabulation Reports".
   c. Click the "Record All Selections" button. The UserForm will be retired and we will be back in the "CCFG Reports Editor & Menu".

5. We will now define what we want to appear on these two reports. We will start with the eligible collateral cross tabulation report first. To specify the particular combination of factors we wish displayed in the cross tabulation reports. We will click on the button "Cross Tabs Reports Editor". Enter the following combinations into the "Custom Cross Tabulation Report Editor" UserForm that will now appear. We need to create two different cross tabulation reports. The specifications of these reports are listed in points a and b below. Select the following sets of three items from left to right:

   a. Report #1: From the column entitled "Vertical Selection Category" select the field "Mortgage Debt-to-Income". From the column entitled "Horizontal Selection Category" select the field "FICO Score". From the column entitled "Statistic Displayed" select the field "Current Balance". Once these selections are complete enter the test number "1" in the "Report # (Maximum 50):" "field and an "X" in the "Trim Report? X=Yes" field. This completes the entries for the first report. We now click on the button "ADD TO CROSS TABULATION REPORT SET". This will record these choices as the parameters that will configure the first Cross Tabulation Report. The UserForm will be retired.

   b. Report #2: Click on the "Cross Tabs Report Editor" button again to redisplay the UserForm and begin the entry for the second report. Using the same procedure as in Step 1 above we will select the field "Total Debt-to-Income" from the "Vertical Selection Category" column, the field "FICO Score" from the "Horizontal Selection Category" column, and last the field "Current Balance" from the "Statistic Displayed" column. Next enter a "2" in the "Report # (Maximum 50):" field and an "X" in the "Trim Report? X=Yes" field. Finally click on the button "ADD TO CROSS TABULATION REPORT SET" to record these entries as those associated with the second cross tabulation report. If we wish to confirm that these report specification entries are correct we can now click on the "Display Cross Tabs Elections" button in the upper right of the screen. The worksheet "CrossTabReportsWorksheet" will appear listing all of the current report selections. Click on the button "Return to Reports Editor menu'

6. Once again in the "CCFG Reports Editor & Menu", we will now set the specifications for the "Initial Concentration Report State Level". In this report we need to list the 10 largest current balance concentrations by state. To accomplish this we will first need to select all of the states for "Inclusion". In the "Geographic Reports Editor" section of the menu in the upper left corner, we will click on the "State Reports Selection" button. The UserForm "Select State Level Collateral Reports" is now displayed. To select all of the states we first must select them from the list and then mark their status as "Included". We are selecting all the states in the menu so we do not need to clear any prior selections that have already been made. We then click on the "Select All States on List" button. The entire contents of the ListBox is now highlighted, indicating that all states and territories have been selected. To set them to "Include" status, we now click on the button at the top right of the UserForm "SET STATES TO INCLUDED." A confirmation message now appears listing the selected states and we will click on the "OK" button to indicate that the displayed selections are correct. The UserForm is then retired. We only have one more step in the report specification process.

7. Once again in the "CCFG Reports Editor & Menu" we will go down to the section "Select Report Packages" Here we will enter "National_" in the "Output Reports Set Prefix" field. This will prefix both the cross tabulation report and the geographic concentration report with this label. The PowerPoint presentation subroutines need to be able to distinguish the National Level data from the State Level data when the report is prepared. This prefix will allow them to do just that. Return to the "Main Menu".
8. Click on the "Run The Model" button.

After the program has run the files will be placed in the general output directory:

```
''C:\VBA_Book2\ABS\Mort01\Output''
```

and will have the names "National_CrossTabs" and "National_StateInitGeo ConcenReport."

State Level Files   We now move on to produce the five State Level Reports required. We will generate these reports by performing the following actions:

1. After the conclusion of the run of the two National Level Reports the CCFG will place us in the "Main Menu". We will be using the same collateral data file "Pool01_PowerPoint" to produce the State Level Reports that we just used to produce the National Level Reports. We therefore do not need to change any of the settings on the "Run Options Menu". They will stay the same as listed in Step 1 in the previous section. We will not need to specify a different collateral file, perform geographic selection and concentration tests or any financial or demographic selection activities. We can therefore ignore all the buttons on the "Main Menu" until we reach the "Define Report Package" button. We will use the reports editor to specify the conditions for each of the five State Level Reports and then run the model.
2. Click on the "Define Report Package" button. This will place us in the "CCFG Reports Editor & Menu". We will now select the five reports we need to produce. First we will clear all report selections from the previous National Level run of the model by clicking on the "CLEAR ALL SELECTIONS" button. In the section of the menu "Select Report Packages" click on the "Select Reports from CCFG Menu". The UserForm "CCFG Model Reports Menu" will now be displayed.
   a. In the subsection "Geographic Reports", in the upper right of the UserForm, select the third report, "Initial Concentration Report—MSA Level".
   b. In the subsection "Eligible Collateral Reports", the last section in the left hand column, select the first and second reports:
      i. "Base Stratification Report"
      ii. "Cross-Tabulation Reports"
   c. In the subsection "Demographic Reports", in the lower right hand column, select the second and third reports:
      i. Borrower Credit Profiles
      ii. "LTV, Appraisal Methods and Doc Standards"

    d. We are now finished selecting the five reports. Click the "RECORD ALL SELECTIONS" button. The UserForm will be retired and we will be back in the "CCFG Reports Editor & Menu".

3. We will now specify the contents of each of the five reports. We will begin with the "Base Stratification Report". On the "CCFG Reports Editor & Menu", click on the button "Stratification Reports Editor." The UserForm "Base Stratification Reports Editor" will be displayed. We will first click on the button "CLEAR CHOICES" to erase any selections from a previous model run. Next we will click on the following report item options in the "Stratification Characteristic" ListBox:
    a. Original Appraisal Type
    b. Current Appraisal Type
    c. First Time Homeowner
       To record our selections we now click on the "RECORD CHOICES" button. The UserForm is then retired. This completes the selection process.

4. We will now make the entries for the cross tabulation reports. We will need to create three of these reports. We will follow the same steps that we did in Step 4 the National Level Reports section above. On the "CCFG Reports Editor & Menu", click on the button "Cross Tabs Reports Editor". The UserForm "Custom Cross Tabulation Report Editor" is now displayed. Create the following three reports:
    a. Report #1: From the "Vertical Selection Category" select the field "Mortgage Debt-to-Income", from the "Horizontal Selection Category" column select the field "FICO Score", and from the column "Statistic Displayed" select the field "Current Balance". After these selections, enter "1" in the "Report # (Maximum 50)" field and an "X" in the "Trim Report? X=Yes" field. When you hit the button "ADD TO CROSS TABULATION REPORT SET" a warning message box will be displayed. Why? We already have a #1 cross tabulation test that we entered from the National Level section above. The CCFG now asks us if we wish to replace this prior #1 test with the currently designated #1 test. We will click "OK" and overwrite the previous test. You will see that this will occur with the second test also. We will also choose to overwrite that test.
    b. Report #2: From the "Vertical Selection Category" column select the field "Total Debt-to-Income", from the "Horizontal Selection Category" column select the field "FICO Score", and from the column "Statistic Displayed" select the field "Current Balance. After these selections, enter "2" in the "Report # (Maximum 50)" field and an "X" in the "Trim Report? X=Yes" field.
    c. Report #3: From the "Vertical Selection Category" column select the field "Current Balance", from the "Horizontal Selection Category" column select the field "First Time Homeowner", and from the column "Statistic Displayed" select the field "Current Balance. After these selection enter "3" in the "Report # (Maximum 50)" field and an "X" in the "Trim Report? X=Yes" field.
       This completes the entries for the cross tabulation reports. When we have finished we can display the three tests using the "Display Cross Tab Elections" button.

5. We will now tell the CCFG what geographic entity we wish the reports to be prepared for. On the "CCFG Reports Editor & Menu", in the section "Geographic

Reports Editor", click on the button "States Report Selection". The UserForm, "Select State level Collateral Reports" will be displayed. Before doing anything else we must clear the selections made in our previous model run when we produced the National Level Reports by selecting all 50 states and 4 territories. To do this we first click on the button "Select All States on List", we then click on the button "SET STATES TO UNINCLUDED", the message box appears and asks us to confirm our selection and we click "OK." All the states in the list are now deselected. The UserForm is then retired. We now click on the "State Reports Selection" button again. The UserForm reappears. We will now select "California" from the list box. Then click on "SET STATES TO INCLUDED" button" to record the choice. A confirmation message box will appear and we will click "OK" to confirm our choice. The UserForm is then retired.

6. When we produce the PowerPoint Presentation Report we will need to identify the reports we have produced so that the CCFG can match them to the selected states. We identified the National Level reports by assigning them a "National_" prefix in the "Output Reports Set Prefix" field of the "Select Report Packages" section of the menu. In this case, for the California report sets we will enter "CA_" (the postal code of the state) in this field. When you are producing these sets of files for later use in constructing the PowerPoint Single State Reports, you must always use the two-letter postal code of the state. This is the file prefix the CCFG model will look for to assemble the data for the finished report.

After you have run the model, we will, as we did with the National Level files, leave the California files in the:

```
''C:\VBA_Book2\ABS\Mort01\Output''
```

directory. That is the location that we will designate the PowerPoint Report subroutines to look for them.

We have generated all the preparatory reports we anticipate needing in the production of the PowerPoint presentation. We will now develop the application to make use of these reports to construct our presentation.

ADDING A NEW CLASS OF REPORTS

The PowerPoint presentations will form a new class of reports for the CCFG. They are different enough to warrant special treatment and placement in the Report Editor and Menu. In addition, before we begin the development of the report- writing VBA code, we will need to make some adjustments to the CCFG to integrate this new type of report into the existing infrastructure of the model itself.

Modifying the CCFG Reports Editor and Menu

We will add a new section to the CCFG Reports Editor & Menu screen. This section will be placed second from the bottom of the menu and will be entitled "Select PowerPoint Presentation Report Contents". Here we will add a button entitled "Single State Collateral Report" for the Single State Report options. This button

CCFG Reports Editor & Menu

Geographic Reports Editor

State Reports Selection	MSA Reports Selection	Display Geographic Report Elections

Write Geographic Reports Elections to this File:

`C:\VBA_Book2\Code\data\GeoReportFiles\GeoReportT2.xls`

Write Geographic Report Specifications To A File

Load Report Elections File

`C:\VBA_Book2\Code\data\GeoReportFiles\GeoReportT2.xls`

Find File	Load Geographic Report Selection File

Collateral Stratification Reports Editor

Stratification Reports Editor	Cross Tabs Reports Editor	Display Stratification Elections	Display Cross Tab Elections

Write Stratification Reports Election to this File:

`C:\VBA_Book2\Code\data\StratReportFiles\StratificationRepsT1.xls`

Write Base Strat Report Specifications To A File	Write Cross Tabs Report Specifications To A File

Load Report Elections File

`C:\VBA_Book2\Code\data\StratReportFiles\XTabFilePP`

Find File	Load Base Strat Report File	Load Cross Tab Report File

Select Power Point Presentation Report Contents

Single State Collateral Report

Select Report Packages

`PPTTest01`   Output Reports Set Prefix

Return To Main Menu	Select Reports From CCFG Report Package

EXHIBIT 19.3   Reports Editor & Menu

will produce a UserForm where we can enter the states we wish to prepare the Single State Presentation Reports for. See Exhibit 19.3.

Adding a UserForm

The UserForm that will be displayed needs to produce a list of all available states upon which we can report. Fortunately we have another UserForm, the "Select State Level Collateral Reports." that is displayed when the button "State Reports Selection" in the upper left corner of the menu is clicked. We can copy not only this UserForm but almost all of the UserForm VBA support code as well. We will name the UserForm "m15PPSingleStateMenu". We will not review this UserForm or its VBA code in any detail here. It is available in the model. The only thing we will note is that its task is to populate a Boolean array named "gPPSingleState", which is dimensioned "1 to NUM_STATES". This array declaration will be placed in the "A_Globals" module.

Modifying the Report Selection UserForm

To allow our analyst to be able to select the Single State Report, we now need to add it to the UserForm displayed when we click on the button "Select Reports from CCFG Menu". We will create a separate Frame object to hold the PowerPoint reports

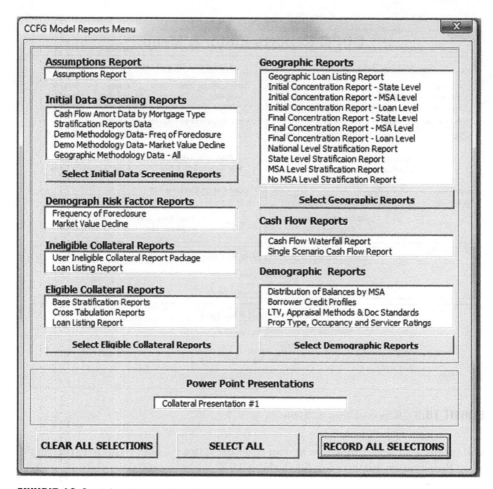

EXHIBIT 19.4   Select Report UserForm

we will eventually develop. This will also serve to visually differentiate this section of the UserForm from the Excel file reports. See Exhibit 19.4.

We also need to add an additional field to the worksheet "DataReportsList". See Exhibit 19.5. If you recall from Chapter 13, "Writing the CCGF Reporting Capability," we use this data sheet to simplify the menu support code for this UserForm. Here we will add an additional field in the right-hand corner of the worksheet and give the new report group its starting report number, "31".

We will also need to add the "PP1RepEditor_ApplyTriggers" subroutine to the UserForm support code for "m15CCFGReportsMenu". This will allow the UserForm support code to recognize the choice we have made on the face of the form in this menu section. See Exhibit 19.6.

Modifying the Reports Menu Support Code

We now need to create the variable that will transfer our choice on the UserForm "CCFG Model Reports Menu" to the VBA program itself. The support code for

Collateral Cash Flow Generator Report Title List

Offset		Assumptions Report
0	1	Assumptions Report

Offset		Initial Data Screening Report Package
1	1	Cash Flow Amort Data by Mortgage Type
	2	Stratification Reports Data
	3	Demo Methodology Data- Freq of Foreclosure
	4	Demo Methodology Data- Market Value Decline
	5	Geographic Methodology Data - All

Offset		Demographic Methodology Risk Factor Reports
6	1	Frequency of Foreclosure
	2	Market Value Decline

Offset		Ineligible Collateral Reports
8	1	User Ineligible Collateral Report Package
	2	Loan Listing Report

Offset		Eligible Collateral Reports
10	1	Base Stratification Reports
	2	Cross Tabulation Reports
	3	Loan Listing Report

Offset		Geographic Reports
13	1	Geographic Loan Listing Report
	2	Initial Concentration Report - State Level
	3	Initial Concentration Report - MSA Level
	4	Initial Concentration Report - Loan Level
	5	Final Concentration Report - State Level
	6	Final Concentration Report - MSA Level
	7	Final Concentration Report - Loan Level
	8	National Level Stratification Report
	9	State Level Stratificaion Report
	10	MSA Level Stratification Report
	11	No MSA Level Stratification Report

Offset		Cash Flow Reports
24	1	Cash Flow Waterfall Report
	2	Single Scenario Cash Flow Report

Offset		Demographic Reports
26	1	Distribution of Balances by MSA
	2	Borrower Credit Profiles
	3	LTV, Appraisal Methods & Doc Standards
	4	Prop Type, Occupancy and Servicer Ratings

Offset		Power Point Presentation
30	1	Collateral Presentation #1

Set the Offset Number to the sum of the reports before the beginning of the current set. Progress down the left hand column and then down the right hand column.

| Return To |
| Reports Editor |
| Menu |

EXHIBIT 19.5 "DataReportsList" worksheet containing all the CCFG report titles

the "m15CCFGReportsMenu" UserForm will set the values of the Boolean array "gCCFGReps". This is the global array through which the information on the User-Form communicates to the CCFG that a particular report has been selected. This array is used in turn to set a number of report-specific variables that are tested by the individual subroutines that write the various reports. We will now create a variable "gRepPPSingleState" of type Boolean and place it with the other report trigger variables in the "A_Globals" module.

```
Public gRepPPSingleState   As Boolean   'PowerPoint single state
```

Finally we need to transfer the information from the "gCCFGReps" arrays to the "gRepPPSingleState" variable. Fortunately we already have a subroutine that does this, "RepMenu_ReadReportPackageElections". We add a new "Case Is = 31" at the end of the "Select..Case" statement and we are ready to go. See Exhibit 19.7. We notice, however, that the number of loops in the "For..Next" loop that contains this code is set to "1 to TOTAL_REP_NUM". We now locate this Public Constant in the "A_Constants" module and change its value from "30" to "31". The CCFG is now ready for the new report.

```
Sub PP1RepEditor_ApplyTriggers()
    For iState = 1 To NUM_STATES
        If lbPPRepStateChoices.Selected(iState - 1) Then _
            gPPSingleState(iState) = True
    Next iState
End Sub
```

EXHIBIT 19.6 "PP1RepEditor_ApplyTriggers" subroutine

```
Sub RepMenu_ReadReportPackageElections()

    For irep = 1 To TOTAL_REP_NUM
        Select Case irep
            'assumptions report list box
            Case Is = 1:  gRepMenuAssumptions = gCCFGReps(irep)       'assumptions report
            'initial data screening list box
            Case Is = 2:  gRepMenuCFAmort = gCCFGReps(irep)           'cash flow amortization
            Case Is = 3:  gRepMenuScreenStrat = gCCFGReps(irep)       'init screen strats
            Case Is = 4:  gRepMenuScreenDemoFOF = gCCFGReps(irep)     'init screen demo method
            Case Is = 5:  gRepMenuScreenDemoMVD = gCCFGReps(irep)     'init screen demo method
            Case Is = 6:  gRepMenuScreenGeo = gCCFGReps(irep)         'init screen geo method
            'demographic risk measurements reports
            Case Is = 7:  gRepMenuDemoRiskFOF = gCCFGReps(irep)       'demo FOF factors
            Case Is = 8:  gRepMenuDemoRiskMVD = gCCFGReps(irep)       'demo MVD factors
            'ineligible collateral list box
            Case Is = 9:  gRepMenuIneligUser = gCCFGReps(irep)        'inelig collat user crit
            Case Is = 10: gRepMenuLoanListInelig = gCCFGReps(irep)    'loan-by-loan data
            'eligible collateral list box
            Case Is = 11: gRepMenuStratBasic = gCCFGReps(irep)        'basic strat package
            Case Is = 12: gRepMenuCrossTab = gCCFGReps(irep)          'cross tabs package
            Case Is = 13: gRepMenuLoanListElig = gCCFGReps(irep)      'loan-by-loan data
            'geographic reports list box
            Case Is = 14: gRepMenuGeoLoanList = gCCFGReps(irep)       'geo loan listing
            Case Is = 15: gRepMenuGeoInitConState = gCCFGReps(irep)   'init con - states
            Case Is = 16: gRepMenuGeoInitConMSA = gCCFGReps(irep)     'init con - MSAs
            Case Is = 17: gRepMenuGeoInitConLoan = gCCFGReps(irep)    'init con - loan
            Case Is = 18: gRepMenuGeoFinConState = gCCFGReps(irep)    'fin con - states
            Case Is = 19: gRepMenuGeoFinConMSA = gCCFGReps(irep)      'fin con - MSAs
            Case Is = 20: gRepMenuGeoFinConLoan = gCCFGReps(irep)     'fin con - loan
            Case Is = 21: gRepMenuGeoAllUSRep = gCCFGReps(irep)       'geo US strats
            Case Is = 22: gRepMenuGeoStatesRep = gCCFGReps(irep)      'geo States strats
            Case Is = 23: gRepMenuGeoMSARep = gCCFGReps(irep)         'geo MSAs strats
            Case Is = 24: gRepMenuGeoNoMSARep = gCCFGReps(irep)       'geo No MSA strats
            'cashflows list box
            Case Is = 25: gRepMenuCFEligible = gCCFGReps(irep)        'elig collat CFs
            Case Is = 26: gRepMenuSingleScen = gCCFGReps(irep)        'single scen CFs
            'demographic reports list box
            Case Is = 27: gRepMenuDemoBalances = gCCFGReps(irep)      'demo - MSA bals by State
            Case Is = 28: gRepMenuDemoCredit = gCCFGReps(irep)        'demo - credit factors
            Case Is = 29: gRepMenuDemoLTV = gCCFGReps(irep)           'demo - LTV, appraisals
            Case Is = 30: gRepMenuDemoPropType = gCCFGReps(irep)      'demo - property type
            Case Is = 31: gRepPPSingleState = gCCFGReps(irep)         'PowerPoint single state
        End Select
    Next irep
    gRepMenuPrefix = Range("m15RepPrefix")

End Sub
```

EXHIBIT 19.7 "RepMenu_ReadReportPackageElections" subroutine

INTRODUCTION TO POWERPOINT IN VBA

We have done all the preparatory work we can. We can now develop the application to make use of these reports to construct our presentation. We will approach the construction of this report application from the top down in the order in which the report writer will execute.

Getting Started

We will first declare a number of variables for the module and then we will write the "Main" subroutine for the module. Once that base is established, we will then write two other high-level subroutines. The first will produce the PowerPoint Presentation

```
'slide numbers in Single State Presentation Report
Const SLIDE_MASTHEAD = 1
Const SLIDE_GEOCON_NAT = 3
Const SLIDE_GEOCON_MSA = 4
Const SLIDE_DTOI_SUM = 6
Const SLIDE_DTOI_TOTAL = 7
Const SLIDE_DTOI_MORT = 8
Const SLIDE_VALCLTV_SUM = 10
Const SLIDE_VALAPP_METHOD = 11
Const SLIDE_1STTIME_HOME = 13
'number of Excel output files needed for presentation data
Const NUM_PPINPUT_FILES = 7
```

EXHIBIT 19.8 Module-level Constants variables declarations

Report and the second the Null Report for states that have been selected but lack all the required data.

Create the PowerPoint Report Module The first thing we need to do is create a separate module to hold the new code. We do this and name it "Report_PPSingleState".

Declare the Module-Level Variables We will now declare variables we will need for the subroutines of the module. The first set of variables will be a collection of Constants, one for the Title Page of the report and other variables for each of the slides that will contain exhibits. The Constants will carry the value of the *n*th location of the slide in the presentation. We will use them to tell the code which PowerPoint slide object we are currently working on and where to direct the content that we will export from the Excel files. The last Constant variable declaration tells the module how many Excel output files we need to check to determine if there is sufficient information to produce this report. See Exhibit 19.8.

The next set of variables is our first encounter with PowerPoint. These variables are used to identify the PowerPoint Application object, the current Presentation object, and the current slide object to the model.

```
Dim PPApp     As PowerPoint.Application   'PowerPoint as application
Dim PPPres    As PowerPoint.Presentation  'PowerPoint file in app
Dim PPSlide   As PowerPoint.Slide         'PowerPoint slide in file
```

The next set of variables is used by the model to locate and determine the identity and, if necessary, the size of the exhibit we are going to import from the Excel files.

```
Dim XslideNumber    As Integer   'slide number in PP to write to
Dim XTextBoxNumber  As Integer   '# of target text box on PP slide
Dim XtotalWide      As Integer   'width of the exhibit
Dim XtotalHigh      As Integer   'height of the exhibit
Dim XfromTop        As Integer   'distance from top of slide
Dim XfromLeft       As Integer   'distance from left border
```

The next set of variables is used by the model to position and size the Excel data on to the face of the PowerPoint slide.

```
Dim XsheetName     As String    'Excel worksheet containing exhibit
Dim XbegCol        As Integer   'beg col of exhibit in Excel
Dim XbegRow        As Integer   'beg row of exhibit in Excel
Dim XrowCount      As Integer   'row width of exhibit in Excel
Dim XcolCount      As Integer   'col count of exhibit in Excel
Dim XChartName     As String    'name of target chart in Excel
```

The next set of variables is used in the process of testing if the requisite Excel output files exist and are in the proper place for use by the report-writing subroutines of the module. They are also used to create error messages.

```
Dim mTestFile(1 To NUM_PPINPUT_FILES)   As String 'Excel output
   file names
Dim mErrors(1 To NUM_PPINPUT_FILES)    As Boolean 'not found file codes
Dim mErrorCnt   As Integer 'total number of Excel files missing
Dim mErrMsg    As String    'combined file error message
```

The last set of variables consists of utility variables that hold information about the particular state being reported upon, for use as loop counters and other incidental uses.

```
Dim gReportFile    As String    'output report file
Dim mFlagPicture   As String    'name of the flag picture
Dim mStateNumNow   As Integer   'number of the current state
Dim mStatePCode    As String    'current state postal code
Dim iState         As Integer   'state counter
Dim iChart         As Integer   'chart counter
Dim irow           As Long      'generic row counter
Dim ifile          As Integer   'file counter
Dim OD             As String    'abbreviation OUTPUT_DIRECTORY
```

There is a great deal of opening and closing of files in this module! In an effort to make the various file opening commands clearer, we will create the variable "OD". This variable will be used as an abbreviation for the Constant "OUTPUT_DIRECTORY". It is hoped that this will make some of these longer commands easier to read.

Create the Main Module Subroutine   Next we create the master report subroutine for the module. We will call this subroutine "PPSingleStateReport_Main". We want this subroutine to perform several tasks. These are:

1. Check to see if the analyst has selected the Single State Report.
2. If "Yes", produce the report; if "No", exit the subroutine.
3. If the report is to be produced, loop through the list of states selection choices contained in the array "gPPSingleState" to determine the states selected.
4. If we find a state selected for reporting, call a subroutine that determines, based on the state postal code and the file requirements of the report, if the requisite Excel report files are available in the "\Output" directory.
5. If the Excel files are available, produce the Single State Report.

```
Sub PPSingleStateReport_Main()

    If gRepPPSingleState Then
        OD = OUTPUT_DIRECTORY
        'read basic state and MSA information
        Call Utility_ReadStateAndMSAInfo
        For iState = 1 To NUM_STATES
            If gPPSingleState(iState) Then
                mStateNumNow = iState
                mStatePCode = gStatePostal(iState)
                Call PPSingleStateRep_CheckForInputFiles
                If mErrorCnt = 0 Then
                    Call PPSingleStateRep_ProduceStateReport
                Else
                    Call PPSingleStateRep_ProduceNULLReport
                End If
            End If
        Next iState
    End If
    Sheets("Main Menu").Select

End Sub
```

EXHIBIT 19.9   "PPSingleStateReport_Main" subroutine

6. If the Excel files are not available, produce the Null Single State Report.
7. When we have tested all state choices contained in the "gPPSingleState" array, exit the loop and return to the Main Menu.

See Exhibit 19.9.

This subroutine is completely composed of VBA that does not interact with PowerPoint. The stage is now set, however, and the action begins shortly!

Writing the Single State Report

When we have located our first selected state, the "Report_PPSingleState" subroutine calls the "PPSingleStateRep_ProduceStateReport" subroutine to begin the report-writing process. See Exhibit 19.10.

The tasks we need this subroutine to perform are:

1. Set the "DisplayAlerts" method in Excel to suppress all warning messages. (This will stop a number of annoying queries from Excel during the file opening and closing activities and not stop the model while the program waits for a reply.)
2. Open up an instance of PowerPoint.
3. Bring the PowerPoint object to the forefront of the display.
4. Find the PowerPoint Single State Presentation Report template file and open it.

```
Sub PPSingleStateRep_ProduceStateReport()

Dim templateFile     As String
Dim PPT              As PowerPoint.Application

    Application.DisplayAlerts = False
    Call CreateFlagSheet
    'create an instance of Power Point
    Set PPApp = CreateObject("Powerpoint.Application")
    PPApp.Visible = True
    templateFile = DIR_TEMPLATE_REP & PP_PRES_ONE_TEMPLATE
    Set PPPres = PPApp.Presentations.Open(templateFile)
    PPPres.SaveAs OD & gRepMenuPrefix & gStateName(iState) & ".ppt"
    'construct the individual reports and place them into the template file
    Call PPSingleStateRep_ReportMastHeadPage
    Call PPSingleStateRep_NationalCollatDist
    Call PPSingleStateRep_StateCollatDistByMSAs
    Call PPSingleStateRep_DebtToIncomeSummary
    Call PPSingleStateRep_DebtToIncomeRatios
    Call PPSingleStateRep_LoanToValue
    Call PPSingleStateRep_AppraisalMethods
    Call PPSingleStateRep_FirstTimeHomeowner
    'finished, close up the template file
    PPApp.ActiveWindow.View.GotoSlide (SLIDE_MASTHEAD)
    Call PPUtility_CloseAndSave
    Call PPUtility_ClosePowerPoint
    Sheets("FlagSheet").Delete
    Application.DisplayAlerts = False

End Sub
```

EXHIBIT 19.10   "PPSingleStateRep_ProduceStateReport" subroutine

5. Save the PowerPoint template file to the name we have selected for the output Single State Presentation Report.
6. Create the title page of the report.
7. Create each of the slides in the presentation by calling a VBA subroutine specific to each.
8. When we have completed the report writing process, select the Title Page slide. (When we open the report file we want this to be the slide to which the report initializes its display.)
9. Save and close the report.
10. Close the PowerPoint Application object.
11. Reset the "DisplayAlerts" method in Excel to resume displaying warnings.

The new feature in this subroutine is the creation of a PowerPoint Application object. The creation of this object allows us to open the PowerPoint template file, make it visible, and save it to the output file name we have entered. Once the PowerPoint Application is active, we can move back and forth between the Excel output files that contain the data that we wish to import into the PowerPoint file and that file itself.

At this point we have opened a PowerPoint file and already ascertained that the Excel output files are present and complete. We are now ready to move the information from Excel to PowerPoint. How do we accomplish this task?

How VBA Places Objects in PowerPoint

To move the information we desire from the Excel output files to the PowerPoint report file, we will employ a small number of VBA subroutines. Each of these subroutines specializes in a different importation task. One copies the contents of an Excel Range, one copies the contents of an Excel Chart object, and the last imports text in a single cell. To perform this task of importation, the subroutine needs to know where the data is coming from and where it is going to.

On the Excel side, we need to be able to tell the subroutine everything it needs to know about how to find the information, identify it, and correctly copy the intended target information. We will pass it this information be using the series of Constant variables we previously declared in Exhibit 19.8. These variables will identify the following pieces of information needed by the subroutine:

- "XsheetName". The Excel worksheet within which the data resides.
- "XbegRow". If we are importing a Range or a piece of Text, this is the lowest number Row in the Range or the Row of the cell containing the Text.
- "XbegCol". This is the leftmost column of the Range or the column of the Text cell. Together with "XbegRow" above, they are the northwest corner of the target region to be copied.
- "XrowCount". The number of Rows in the Range or "1" for Text.
- "XcolCount". The number of Columns in the Range or "1" for Text.
- "XChartName". The name of the Excel Chart object if we are importing a chart.

Once the subroutine has located the Excel object using this information, it then needs to know where we wish to place it in the PowerPoint application. We supply this information by specifying our requirements with the following variables:

- "XslideNumber". The slide number of the PowerPoint file.
- "XTextBoxNumber". If we are placing Text into a Text Box on a slide, the number of the target Text Box. (You can find the Text Box numbers by clicking on the Text Boxes of the slide.)
- "XtotalWide". In the case of Ranges and Charts, the width of the exhibit on the PowerPoint slide.
- "XtotalHigh". In the case of Ranges and Charts, the height of the exhibit on the PowerPoint slide.
- "XfromTop". The location of the exhibit in the number of pixels from the top of the slide.
- "XfromLeft". The location of the exhibit from the left side of the slide.

With this information in hand, the subroutine is ready to find the information in the Excel file and paste it into the PowerPoint presentation.

Excel Ranges The "PPUtility_CopyRange" subroutine copies a Range of cells from an Excel spreadsheet to a location in the PowerPoint presentation. It performs the following steps:

1. Selects the Excel worksheet using the value of the "XsheetName" variable.
2. Using the values of the "XbegRow" and "XbegCol", determines the location of the Range, and using "XrowCount" and "XcolCount", determines the size of the Range. It then selects the now-identified target Range.
3. Checks that the selected area of the worksheet is in fact a named Range. If it is not a Range, it prints an error message and exits the subroutine, ending the importation process before it has begun!
4. Sets the value of the "PPApp" variable to the current PowerPoint Application object. It makes it the "ActivePresentation", the one that will be written to.
5. Sets the "View" setting of the PowerPoint display to slide, displaying the slide in the full window of the application. The subroutine now displays the selected slide based on the value of the variable "XslideNumber".
6. Sets this slide to be the target slide in the ActiveWindow.
7. With everything now in place in the PowerPoint slide, copies the Excel Range using the "Selection.Copy.Picture" command.
8. Copies the Range into the "PPSlide" that we set in Step 6.
9. Last, resizes the copied picture and place it in the correct position on the Power Point slide. The subroutine does this by using the previously declared variable "RangeSizeShape", which is a PowerPoint "ShapeRange" property. The subroutine assigns the "RangeSizeSpecs" properties of ".Width", ".Height", ".Top", and ".Left" by using the values of "XtotalWide", "XtotalHigh", "XfromTop", and "XfromLeft", respectively.

See Exhibit 19.11.

```
Sub PPUtility_CopyRange(sheet As String, StartRow As Integer, _
                        StartCol As Integer, RowCount As Integer, _
                        ColCount As Integer, slide As Integer, _
                        aheight As Integer, awidth As Integer, _
                        atop As Integer, aleft As Integer)

Dim RangeSizeSpecs As PowerPoint.ShapeRange

    Sheets(sheet).Select
    Cells(StartRow, StartCol).Resize(RowCount, ColCount).Select
    ' Make sure a range is selected
    If Not TypeName(Selection) = "Range" Then
        MsgBox "Please select a worksheet range and try again.", vbExclamation, _
            "No Range Selected"
    Else
        'Reference existing instance of PowerPoint
        Set PPApp = GetObject(, "Powerpoint.Application")
        Set PPPres = PPApp.ActivePresentation 'Reference active presentation
        PPApp.ActiveWindow.ViewType = ppViewSlide
        PPApp.ActiveWindow.View.GotoSlide (slide)
        Set PPSlide = PPPres.Slides(PPApp.ActiveWindow.Selection.SlideRange.SlideIndex)
        Selection.CopyPicture Appearance:=xlScreen, Format:=xlBitmap
        PPSlide.Shapes.Paste.Select
        Set RangeSizeSpecs = PPApp.ActiveWindow.Selection.ShapeRange
        RangeSizeSpecs.Width = awidth
        RangeSizeSpecs.Height = aheight
        RangeSizeSpecs.Top = atop
        RangeSizeSpecs.Left = aleft
    End If

End Sub
```

EXHIBIT 19.11 "PPUtility_CopyRange" subroutine

```
Sub PPUtility_CopyChart(sheet As String, chart_name As String, _
                             slide As Integer, _
                             aheight As Integer, awidth As Integer, _
                             atop As Integer, aleft As Integer)

Dim ChartSizeSpecs As PowerPoint.ShapeRange

    Sheets(sheet).Select
    'get to the correct slide
    PPApp.ActiveWindow.ViewType = ppViewSlide
    PPApp.ActiveWindow.View.GotoSlide (slide)
    Set PPSlide = PPPres.Slides(PPApp.ActiveWindow.Selection.SlideRange.SlideIndex)
    ActiveSheet.ChartObjects(chart_name).Activate  'chart name in arguement
    ActiveChart.ChartArea.Copy                          'copy chart object
    ActiveChart.CopyPicture Appearance:=xlScreen, Size:=xlScreen, Format:=xlPicture
    PPSlide.Shapes.Paste.Select
    Set ChartSizeSpecs = PPApp.ActiveWindow.Selection.ShapeRange
    ChartSizeSpecs.Width = awidth
    ChartSizeSpecs.Height = aheight
    ChartSizeSpecs.Top = atop
    ChartSizeSpecs.Left = aleft

End Sub
```

EXHIBIT 19.12   "PPUtility_CopyChart" subroutine

Excel Charts   The "PPUtility_CopyChart" subroutine follows the same general approach as the "PPUtility_CopyRange" subroutine. Because the target Excel Chart object does not need to be identified as a Range before copying and we do not need to declare its size, the process can omit those steps. We therefore need only Step 1 and then Steps 4 to 9 to complete the process. In place of Step 3, the subroutine merely identifies the Chart by its object name and copies it. (You can find the name of the Excel Chart simply by clicking on it and looking in the Range window at the upper left-hand side of the screen.) See Exhibit 19.12.

Excel-Generated Text   The "PPUtility_CopyText" subroutine eliminates Steps 2 and 3. In that the Text copy is limited to writing into a specifically identified Text Box in the PowerPoint slide, it can also skip Step 9, where it resizes and positions the copied picture. The subroutine needs to know the identity of the target Text Box. We supply it in the form of the value of the variable "XTextBoxNumber". See Exhibit 19.13.

PREPARING THE DATA FOR USE

The "PPSingleStateRep_ProduceStateReport" subroutine creates eight slides displaying various exhibits from the Excel output files. These slides are created by a set of special-purpose VBA subroutines that manipulate PowerPoint objects. They are called in the master report writing subroutine in the order shown in Exhibit 19.14.

Each of these subroutines employs a combination of the three "PPUtility_Copy" subroutines to move the targeted exhibits from the Excel output files to a specific PowerPoint slide. As we examine these subroutines, notice that they do not represent only a portion of all of the activity that takes place between the identification of the Excel exhibit and its importation and copying into the slide! In every one of

```
Sub PPUtility_CopyText(sheet As String, rowStart As Integer, _
                       columnStart As Integer, row_count As Integer, _
                       columnCount As Integer, slide As Integer, _
                       textbox As Integer)
Dim Text As String

    Sheets(sheet).Select
    Text = Cells(rowStart, columnStart).Resize(row_count, columnCount).Text
    'Reference existing instance of PowerPoint
    Set PPApp = GetObject(, "Powerpoint.Application")
    'Reference active presentation
    Set PPPres = PPApp.ActivePresentation
    PPApp.ActiveWindow.ViewType = ppViewSlide
    PPApp.ActiveWindow.View.GotoSlide (slide)
    Set PPSlide = PPPres.Slides(PPApp.ActiveWindow.Selection.SlideRange.SlideIndex)
    PPSlide.Shapes(textbox).TextFrame.TextRange = Text

End Sub
```

EXHIBIT 19.13   "PPUtility_CopyText" subroutine

these subroutines that copies a Range exhibit from the Excel output file, there is a
subroutine call that performs the following steps:

1. Copies the worksheet containing the exhibit, renaming the copied worksheet
   "Target" in the Excel output file.
2. Manipulates the exhibit. This manipulation, performed by recorded VBA
   macros, may include some or all of the following actions:
   a. Delete columns or rows of the Range.
   b. Reformat exhibit titles.
   c. Move exhibit titles or headers.
   d. Copy additional exhibits to the same worksheet and merge them.
   e. Reformat the data of the exhibit.
   f. Change the color of the exhibit background.
   g. Remove the Excel guidelines from the background of the exhibit.
   h. Condense or combine data in various columns or rows of the exhibit.
3. When the editing of the Excel Range is complete, it is assigned a Range name on
   the "Target" worksheet so that it is available to be copied.

You can see by this that we can essentially "data mine" the Excel output reports
to produce whatever exhibits we wish to place in the PowerPoint presentation,
provided the data is initially present.

```
'construct the individual reports and place them into the template file
Call PPSingleStateRep_ReportMastHeadPage
Call PPSingleStateRep_NationalCollatDist
Call PPSingleStateRep_StateCollatDistByMSAs
Call PPSingleStateRep_DebtToIncomeSummary
Call PPSingleStateRep_DebtToIncomeRatios
Call PPSingleStateRep_LoanToValue
Call PPSingleStateRep_AppraisalMethods
Call PPSingleStateRep_FirstTimeHomeowner
```

EXHIBIT 19.14   "PPSingleStateRep_ProduceStateReport" subroutine (partial)

FIRST TIME HOMEOWNERS SLIDE

We will not exhaustively examine the creation of each and every slide of the Single State Presentation Report. A finished copy of the report can be found on the Web site for this chapter. We will, however, follow the creation of a single slide, the "First Time Homeowner" slide in the "Borrower Demographics" section of the report. The "PPSingleStateRep_FirstTimeHomeowner" subroutine creates this report. The completed slide is seen in Exhibit 19.15.

This slide is composed of the following items:

- **Summary Statistics table.** This table resides in the Excel output file "CA_Port PresentReport_Credit" file.
- **Pie chart.** From the same file as the Summary Statistics table.
- **Base Stratification report.** This report resides in the Excel output file "CA_User StratRep".
- **Cross Tabulation table.** This report resides in the Excel output file "CA_CrossTabs".

To create this slide, the "PPSingleStateRep_FirstTimeHomeowner" subroutine will open three different files and export three Ranges and a Chart. We will edit one of the Ranges, the User Specified Stratification Report, and locate, copy and position the others.

"PPSingleStateRep_FirstTimeHomeower" Subroutine

The subroutine that we will now examine in detail is broadly representative of each of the report-generating subroutines of this module. If you follow the general flow of this subroutine, you will have no difficulty understanding the other subroutines that also produce slides for the report. The greatest variance is not in the portion of the report preparation that interfaces with the PowerPoint file. It is instead in the VBA that prepares the Range data to be moved to the PowerPoint presentation file. Keeping that in mind, let us look at the subroutine "PPSingleStateRep_FirstTimeHomeower" and analyze the step-by-step process it follows to create its slide. See Exhibit 19.16.

This subroutine has three major divisions of activity. These are specific to the three Excel output files that it must open to find the exhibits that will eventually be imported into the PowerPoint slide. If we move step by step through the activities of the subroutine as it finds, copies, and imports an Excel exhibit into PowerPoint, we will see the pattern of VBA statements discussed in detail below as they manipulate each of the exhibits of the slide. We will place the VBA statement(s) beneath each of the steps. We will choose the third exhibit in the first column of the slide, the Stratification Report, as our example. In the "PPSingleStateRep_FirstTimeHomeower" subroutine, the process of importing this Excel Range begins under the comment

```
!Stratification detail next
```

on the 20th line of the subroutine.

First Time Homeowners

Summary

First Time Ownership

	Loans	Current Balances
No Data		
Yes	205	$ 52,696.5
No	584	$ 149,941.3
Totals	789	$ 202,637.8

Current Balance ($MM) by 1st Owner

■ No Data ■ Yes ■ No

74%   26%

Stratification by First Time Homeowner / **Eligible Collateral Report #22**

Line	First Time Home Owner Category	Number of Loans	Current Loan Balance	Current Loan LTV	Wavg Current Yield	Wavg Original Term	Wavg Remain Term	Total Appraisal
1	No Data							
2	Yes	205	52,696,509	64.4%	5.308%	326.3	311.2	55,692,300
3	No	584	149,941,325	61.8%	5.171%	325.3	310.9	159,501,900
		789	202,637,834					215,494,200

Detail by Balance

Cross Tabulation Report #10
Vertical Category = Current Balance
Horizontal Category = First Time Homeowner
Report Statistic = Current Balance

Current Loan Balance Range	Totals		Yes	No
	202,637,834		52,696,509	149,941,325
			26.01%	73.99%
10,001 to 20,000	135,256	0.07%	58,691	76,535
20,001 to 30,000	96,823	0.05%	24,974	71,848
30,001 to 40,000	208,161	0.10%	106,534	101,827
40,001 to 50,000	423,186	0.21%	97,394	325,792
50,001 to 60,000	1,432,722	0.71%	436,045	996,678
60,001 to 70,000	2,748,560	1.36%	664,383	2,084,177
70,001 to 80,000	2,999,765	1.48%	583,125	2,416,640
80,001 to 90,000	4,156,650	2.05%	1,188,570	2,968,080
90,001 to 100,000	1,883,754	0.91%	385,446	1,498,308
100,001 to 110,000	2,852,384	1.41%	212,511	2,639,873
110,001 to 120,000	2,070,835	1.02%	689,679	1,381,157
120,001 to 130,000	3,402,644	1.68%	626,702	2,775,942
130,001 to 140,000	3,807,706	1.88%	947,123	2,860,584
140,001 to 150,000	6,390,432	3.15%	1,748,341	4,642,091
150,001 to 160,000	5,892,587	2.91%	1,564,518	4,328,069
160,001 to 170,000	7,081,373	3.49%	2,781,015	4,300,358
170,001 to 180,000	5,267,515	2.60%	1,573,429	3,694,088
180,001 to 190,000	7,575,921	3.74%	1,842,996	5,732,925
190,001 to 200,000	7,395,208	3.65%	2,137,241	5,257,967
200,001 to 250,000	6,987,250	3.45%	1,879,408	5,107,842
250,001 to 300,000	11,881,955	5.85%	2,770,390	9,111,566
300,001 to 350,000	8,218,373	4.01%	2,274,401	5,853,972
350,001 to 400,000	7,959,119	3.93%	1,141,053	6,818,065
400,001 to 450,000	4,657,778	2.30%	839,686	3,818,093
450,001 to 500,000	5,168,599	2.64%	2,374,418	3,794,174
500,001 to 600,000	9,389,673	4.63%	1,528,585	7,860,889
600,001 to 700,000	8,636,130	4.24%	2,674,345	5,959,785
700,001 to 800,000	7,314,730	3.56%	2,909,498	4,314,332
800,001 to 900,000	11,095,833	5.48%	1,684,743	9,411,090
900,001 to 1,000,000	19,738,727	9.74%	4,612,638	15,126,089
1,000,001 to 1,250,000	11,795,289	5.82%	3,283,005	8,512,284
1,250,001 to 1,500,000	16,442,815	8.11%	5,462,890	10,979,925
1,500,001 to 1,750,000	4,613,693	2.28%	1,538,427	3,075,266
1,750,001 to 2,000,000	1,955,925	0.97%		1,955,925

EXHIBIT 19.15 First Time Homeowners Report slide

```
Sub PPSingleStateRep_FirstTimeHomeowner()
Dim iChart   As Integer
    'Open the Credit Presentation report
    Workbooks.Open FileName:=OD & mStatePCode & "_PortPresentReport_Credit.xlsm"
    XslideNumber = SLIDE_1STTIME_HOME        'first time homeowner
    XsheetName = mStatePCode                 'Excel target sheet
    'get the table
    XbegRow = 47:        XbegCol = 14         'northwest corner of range
    XrowCount = 7:       XcolCount = 4        'number rows and columns
    XtotalWide = 110:    XtotalHigh = 110     'height and width of the exhibit
    XfromTop = 150:      XfromLeft = 115      'table from left hand margin
    Call PPUtility_CopyRange(XsheetName, XbegRow, XbegCol, _
             XrowCount, XcolCount, XslideNumber, XtotalHigh, _
             XtotalWide, XfromTop, XfromLeft)
    'get the chart
    XChartName = "Chart 6"                    'chart object name
    XtotalWide = 220:    XtotalHigh = 130     'height and width of the exhibit
    XfromLeft = 54                            'northwest corner placement
    XfromTop = 265                            'from the top
    Call PPUtility_CopyChart(XsheetName, XChartName, XslideNumber, _
             XtotalHigh, XtotalWide, XfromTop, XfromLeft)
    ActiveWorkbook.Close
    'Open the User Stratification Report
    Workbooks.Open FileName:=OD & mStatePCode & "_UserStratRep.xlsm"
    Call PPRep06_PrepareExhibit01
    'set the range copy parameters
    XsheetName = "Target"                     'Excel target sheet
    XtotalWide = 145:    XtotalHigh = 70      'height and width of the exhibit
    XfromTop = 410:      XfromLeft = 40       'northwest corner placement
    XbegCol = 1:         XbegRow = 1:         'northwest corner of range
    XrowCount = 9:       XcolCount = 10       'number rows and columns
    'get the material
    Call PPUtility_CopyRange(XsheetName, XbegRow, XbegCol, _
             XrowCount, XcolCount, XslideNumber, XtotalHigh, _
             XtotalWide, XfromTop, XfromLeft)
    ActiveWorkbook.Close
    'Open the Cross tabulation Report
    Workbooks.Open FileName:=OD & mStatePCode & "_CrossTabsChop.xlsm"
    Call PPRep06_PrepareExhibit02
    'set the range copy parameters
    XsheetName = "Target"                     'Excel target sheet
    XtotalWide = 215:    XtotalHigh = 350     'height and width of the exhibit
    XfromTop = 150:      XfromLeft = 425      'northwest corner placement
    XbegCol = 1:         XbegRow = 1          'northwest corner of range
    XrowCount = 44:      XcolCount = 7        'number rows and columns
    'get the material
    Call PPUtility_CopyRange(XsheetName, XbegRow, XbegCol, _
             XrowCount, XcolCount, XslideNumber, XtotalHigh, _
             XtotalWide, XfromTop, XfromLeft)
    ActiveWorkbook.Close
End Sub
```

EXHIBIT 19.16   "PPSingleStateRep_FirstTimeHomeower" subroutine

The steps in the process are:

1. Open the Excel file containing the exhibit we wish to import.

   ```
   Workbooks.Open FileName:=OD & mStatePCode & ''_UserStratRep.xlsm
   ```

2. Perform whatever actions we need to take to prepare the exhibit for use in the PowerPoint presentation. A sample of the possible actions we could apply was

discussed earlier in the Preparing the Data for Use section. In this instance we will perform the following actions to the original format of the report:

```
Call PPRep06_PrepareExhibit01
```

1. Perform a move and copy of the original worksheet containing the stratification report, "BaseStrat-39", to a worksheet named "Target".

```
sheetName = ''BaseStrat-39''
Call MoveAndCopyTargetWorksheet(sheetName)
```

2. Delete column "A" and row 1. (They are blank.)

```
Columns(''A:A'').Select:   Selection.Delete   Shift:=xlToLeft
Rows(''1:1'').Select:      Selection.Delete   Shift:=xlUp
Columns(''M:O'').Select:   Selection.Delete   Shift:=xlToLeft
Columns(''G:I'').Select:   Selection.Delete   Shift:=xlToLeft
```

3. Increase the size of column "C" to 17.29. (This is the most narrow column width that makes the column headers legible.)

```
Columns(''C:C'').ColumnWidth = 17.29
```

4. Delete columns "M" to "O" and columns "G" to "I". (These columns contain report detail unsuitable for the slide; in addition, we need to reduce the exhibit size so it will fit in the first column of the slide.)

```
Columns(''M:O'').Select:   Selection.Delete   Shift:=xlToLeft
Columns(''G:I'').Select:   Selection.Delete   Shift:=xlToLeft
```

5. We now tint the backround of the remaining report to match the Summary Statistics Table at the top of the first column of the PowerPoint presentation.

```
Range(''A1:J10'').Select
With Selection.Interior
   .Pattern = xlSolid
   .PatternColorIndex = xlAutomatic
   .ThemeColor = xlThemeColorAccent5
   .TintAndShade = 0.799981688894314
   .PatternTintAndShade = 0
End With
```

6. We have a two-line header in the report. The first line identifies the number of the stratification report, "#22". We will move this title line from the top of the report and reposition it to the upper right of the report on the same line as the exhibit title, "Stratification by First Time Homeowner". This compacts the exhibit further by eliminating another line! We delete the now-empty title line.

```
Range(``A1'').Select: Selection.Copy
Range(``J2'').Select: ActiveSheet.Paste
Application.CutCopyMode = False
With Selection
    .HorizontalAlignment = xlRight
    .VerticalAlignment = xlBottom
End With
Rows(``1:1'').Select: Selection.Delete Shift:=xlUp
```

7. We now draw a border around the report.

```
Range(``A1:J9'').Select
With Selection.Borders(xlEdgeLeft)
    .LineStyle = xlContinuous
    .Weight = xlThick
End With
With Selection.Borders(xlEdgeTop)
    .LineStyle = xlContinuous
    .Weight = xlThick
End With
With Selection.Borders(xlEdgeBottom)
    .LineStyle = xlContinuous
    .Weight = xlThick
End With
With Selection.Borders(xlEdgeRight)
    .LineStyle = xlContinuous
    .Weight = xlThick
End With
```

8. The last step is to create a Range of the now-reduced report. We will call the Range "App". It does not matter what we call it as we will soon close the file without saving the changes we have made to it. The "PPUtility_CopyRange", however, requires that the object that we are attempting to import be a Range. Making the reduced exhibit a Range removes this potential future problem. We are now done editing the Excel exhibit and can return to the "PPSingleStateRep_FirstTimeHomeowner" subroutine. Then we move the cursor out of the way so its image is not copied within the exhibit!

```
Range(``A1:J9'').Select
target_range = ``=Target!R1C1:R10C9''
ActiveWorkbook.Names.Add Name:=``App'', RefersToR1C1:= _
    target_range
Range(``B10'').Select
```

9. We now set the variables that will tell the "PPUtility_CopyRange" subroutine the location and size of the Excel exhibit and the location and size we wish to import it onto the PowerPoint slide. These variable assignments are:

```
XsheetName = ``Target''              `Excel target sheet
XtotalWide = 145:  XtotalHigh = 70   `height and width
   of the exhibit
```

```
XfromTop = 410: XfromLeft = 40   'northwest corner placement
XbegCol = 1:    XbegRow = 1:      'northwest corner of range
XrowCount = 9:  XcolCount = 10    'number rows and columns
```

10. Everything is now in place. We call the subroutine "PPUtility_CopyRange", and the Excel exhibit is copied onto the selected slide (XslideNumber = SLIDE_1STHOME).

```
Call  PPUtility_CopyRange(XsheetName, XbegRow, XbegCol, _
      XrowCount, XcolCount, XslideNumber, XtotalHigh, _
      XtotalWide, XfromTop, XfromLeft)
```

11. The last step of the process is to close the Excel file "CA_UserStratRep.xlsm". We will *not* save changes to the file. Thus the "Target" worksheet with the edited exhibit is lost, but the original contents of the workbook are preserved for future use.

```
ActiveWorkbook.Close
```

This is the pattern for each of the four Excel exhibits that we will import to the PowerPoint presentation. In fact, the process is far easier for Text and Charts in that we will probably want to copy them in an unmodified format.

This pattern of format and placement is repeated across all the slide preparation subroutines that are called from "PPSingleState_FirstTimeHomeower"!

Not every story has a happy ending (as in this section, where we end up with a beautiful and informative PowerPoint presentation). The next section of the chapter deals with the situation in which we cannot write the Single State Report.

CREATING THE NULL REPORT

Creating the Null Report is significantly easier than preparing the Single State Report. Here our goal is to identify for the analyst which of the requested Single State Reports were not produced and the conditions that precluded their creation.

We have a separate PowerPoint template file for this report named "PPCollat PresentOneNullTemplate". This PowerPoint template file contains only one slide. We will populate this slide with the name of the state and an error message detailing the status of the missing (and found) Excel output files needed to produce the report. The process of producing a "NULL" file begins when the subroutine "PPSingleStateRep_CheckForInputFiles" fails to detect the presence of a full set of files needed to produce the requested Single State Report. This subroutine uses a "For..Next" loop to sequentially search the "Output" file directory for each of the seven required files. The names of these files are stored in the array "mTestFiles". See Exhibit 19.17.

If the value of the variable "mErrorCnt" is greater than 1, we cannot produce the requested report. We therefore branch and call the subroutine

```
Sub PPSingleStateRep_ProduceNULLReport()

Dim templateFile    As String
Dim PPT             As PowerPoint.Application

    Application.DisplayAlerts = False
    Call CreateFlagSheet
    'create an instance of Power Point
    Set PPApp = CreateObject("Powerpoint.Application")
    PPApp.Visible = True
    templateFile = DIR_TEMPLATE_REP & PP_PRES_ONENULL_TEMPLATE
    Set PPPres = PPApp.Presentations.Open(templateFile)
    PPPres.SaveAs OD & gRepMenuPrefix & gStateName(iState) & ".ppt"
    'construct the individual reports and place them into the template file
    Call PPSingleStateRep_SNameToTextBox(SLIDE_MASTHEAD, 1)
    Call PPSingleStateRep_CreateFileErrorMsg
    XslideNumber = SLIDE_MASTHEAD
    XsheetName = "FlagSheet"               'slide # and Excel target sheet
    XfromTop = 1:        XfromLeft = 1     'northwest corner placement
    XbegRow = 3:         XbegCol = 10      'dimensions of the range
    XrowCount = 1:       XcolCount = 1
    XTextBoxNumber = 2
    Call PPUtility_CopyText(XsheetName, XbegRow, XbegCol, XrowCount, _
                    XcolCount, XslideNumber, XTextBoxNumber)
    Call PPUtility_CloseAndSave
    Call PPUtility_ClosePowerPoint
    Sheets("FlagSheet").Delete
    Application.DisplayAlerts = False

End Sub
```

EXHIBIT 19.17   "PPSingleStateRep_ProduceNULLReport" subroutine

"PPSingleStateRep_ProduceNULLReport". This subroutine performs the following steps:

1. Sets the "DisplayAlerts" method in Excel to suppress all warning messages. (This will stop a number of annoying queries from Excel during the file opening and closing activities and not stop the model while the program waits for a reply.)
2. Opens up an instance of PowerPoint.
3. Brings the PowerPoint object to the forefront of the display.
4. Finds the PowerPoint Single State Presentation Report template file and opens it.
5. Saves the PowerPoint template file to the name we have selected for the output Single State Presentation Report.
6. Writes the name of the requested State into Text Box 1 of the slide by calling "PPSingleStateRep_SNameToTextBox".
7. Calls the "PPSingleStateRep_CreateFileErrorMsg" subroutine. This subroutine assembles a multiple-line error message that delineates each file found or missing by the "PPSingleStateRep_CheckForInputFiles" subroutine. See Exhibit 19.18.

```
Sub PPSingleStateRep_CreateFileErrorMsg()

    'we dont need the directory path in the file names so reassign
    mTestFile(1) = "National_StateInitGeoConcenReport.xlsm"
    mTestFile(2) = "National_CrossTabs.xlsm"
    mTestFile(3) = mStatePCode & "_MSAInitGeoConcenReport.xlsm"
    mTestFile(4) = mStatePCode & "_PortPresentReport_Credit.xlsm"
    mTestFile(5) = mStatePCode & "_PortPresentReport_Valuation.xlsm"
    mTestFile(6) = mStatePCode & "_CrossTabs.xlsm"
    mTestFile(7) = mStatePCode & "_UserStratRep.xlsm"
    'error message components
    mErrMsg = "COULD NOT PRODUCE SINGLE STATE REPORT" & vbCrLf
    mErrMsg = mErrMsg & "The following files were missing: " & vbCrLf & vbCrLf
    mErrMsg = mErrMsg & "Directory = " & OD & vbCrLf & vbCrLf
    For ifile = 1 To NUM_PPINPUT_FILES
        If mErrors(ifile) Then
            mErrMsg = mErrMsg & "FOUND   ==>   " & mTestFile(ifile) & vbCrLf
        Else
            mErrMsg = mErrMsg & "MISSING ==>   " & mTestFile(ifile) & vbCrLf
        End If
    Next ifile
    Sheets("FlagSheet").Select
    Cells(3, 10).Value = mErrMsg

End Sub
```

EXHIBIT 19.18   "PPSingleStateRep_CreateFileErrorMsg" subroutine

8. Copies the error message to a single cell in the Excel worksheet "FlagSheet" of the CCFG model. Remember that we have not opened any of the Excel output files (nor will we), so we are still in the CCFG at this time!
9. Specifies the Excel target coordinates of the cell containing the error message. Set the value of the PowerPoint target Text Box to "2". Using the "PPUtility_ CopyText" subroutine, copies the error message from the Excel worksheet.
10. Saves and closes the report.
11. Closes the PowerPoint Application object.
12. Resets the "DisplayAlerts" method in Excel to resume displaying warnings.

A copy of the finished Null Report for a state with some of the Excel output reports missing is shown in Exhibit 19.19.

MS OUTLOOK

There are a number of situations where the analyst may find it useful or even critical to communicate modeling results and project status automatically through automating Outlook with VBA. Consider, for example, a situation where dozens of models are performing monthly performance forecasts using the latest empirical data from the deal servicers in order to better project future performance. In such a situation, probably a large number of people are anticipating the arrival of these updated results and wish to be informed when they become available. In this circumstance it would be critical to inform the various parties as quickly as possible. Having a fully developed manner of automatic notification would be a wonderful additional capability to build into the model.

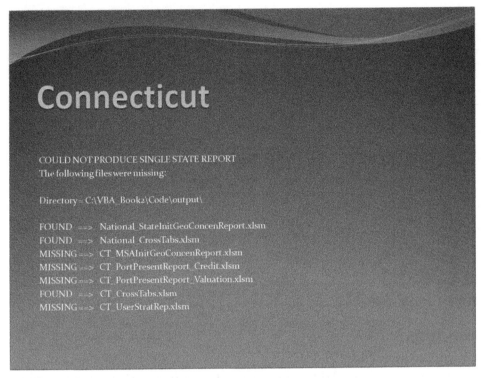

EXHIBIT 19.19   Sample of NULL Report for the state of Connecticut

Another example of a need for this type of communication is when the performance of the forecasting modeling duties is split among multiple parties. It is not uncommon for the analyst in charge of running the collateral to be different from the person evaluating the deal structure and communicating the forecasted results. Obviously, the deal structure analyst cannot complete his or her job until the results of the collateral runs are made available. Thus, immediately notifying all interested parties that new collateral information is available allows the overall process to move forward.

In this section we will construct examples of how to assemble and send email messages with varying levels of detail. Sometimes automated emailing just calls for simple notification messages. Other times reporting files may have to be included as attachments with a high-level summary appearing in the body of the email. Below we produce two different emails:

1. **Alert Email.** The purpose of this email is to alert the concerned parties of a model run completion.
2. **Working Group Email.** This email is sent internally and has attached the full detailed collateral report created in the PowerPoint section previously. This message also contains summary statistics in the body of the email. This summary is useful in providing at-a-glance statistics for individuals not necessarily interested in immersing themselves in the finer points of the collateral analysis.

Structuring Group Alert Email	
Recipients:	structureGroup@bank.com
CC:	collateralGroup@bank.com
BCC:	directorGroup@bank.com
Subject:	New Collateral Files Posted - May2010
Message Body:	Structuring Group, Updated modeling files have been posted to C:\MFIN\RMBS\Output\ for deal RMBS08-1 for the current update period. Please revert back to the Collateral Group with any questions or concerns. Thank you. Regards, Collateral Modeling Group

EXHIBIT 19.20   "MsgTemplate" worksheet with "Alerts" message

Alert Email

In the following example we are assuming that the analyst or group responsible for modeling the collateral side of the effort is distinct from the liabilities/structuring group. To ensure that the structuring group is alerted promptly of recently completed CCFG runs, we will create a subroutine that sends an email alert notifying the group analysts of the newly created modeling data.

The first step is to create and add a new worksheet to the CCFG file that contains the email inputs (e.g., recipients, subject, etc.). Create worksheet "MsgTemplate". The inputs stored on this sheet are exactly what you might envision to be the basic elements of an electronic mail message. See Exhibit 19.20.

This worksheet contains five named Ranges:

1. "Out_AlertReceipt". Cell C3
2. "Out_AlertCC". Cell C5
3. "Out_AlertBCC". Cell C7
4. "Out_AlertSubject". Cell C9
5. "Out_AlertMsgBody". Cell C11

The portions of the email message contained in each of these ranges should be fairly obvious! All inputs are values except the Subject Range. This cell contains a formula that updates the subject line of the email message with the current month. The formula is

```
=''New Collateral Files Posted - '' & TEXT(TODAY(),''MMMyyyy'')
```

where we are using the "TODAY()" function in concert with the "TEXT()" function to format the current date as an "MMMyyyy" string.

```
Option Explicit

Dim mReceiptsTo      As String            'To: string
Dim mReceiptsCC      As String            'CC: string
Dim mReceiptsBCC     As String            'BCC: string
Dim mSubject         As String            'subject string
Dim mMsgBody         As String            'message body
Dim oOutlook         As Outlook.Application  'outlook app object
Dim oMail            As Outlook.MailItem     'mail item object


'================================================================
'
'
'================================================================

Sub OutlookMsg_SendCollatAlertEmail()

    'retrieve inputs from Excel ranges
    mReceiptsTo = Range("Out_AlertReceipt")
    mReceiptsCC = Range("Out_AlertCC")
    mReceiptsBCC = Range("Out_AlertBCC")
    mSubject = Range("Out_AlertSubject")
    mMsgBody = Range("Out_AlertMsgBody")
    'create new Outlook and MailItem objects
    Set oOutlook = New Outlook.Application
    Set oMail = oOutlook.CreateItem(olMailItem)
    'edit the message and send
    With oMail
        .Subject = mSubject
        .To = mReceiptsTo
        .CC = mReceiptsCC
        .BCC = mReceiptsBCC
        .Body = mMsgBody
        .Importance = olImportanceHigh
        .Send
    End With
    'clean up
    Set oMail = Nothing
    Set oOutlook = Nothing

End Sub
```

EXHIBIT 19.21 "OutlookMsg_SendCollatAlertEmail" subroutine

The code necessary to send a message from Outlook is surprisingly simple. In order to have access to the method list of the Outlook application object when typing VBA code, we add the reference to the "Microsoft Outlook 12.0 Object Library". Once this reference is added, the code for sending the Alert Message is straightforward. We create a new VBA module "Outlook_AlertAndWrkGrp" in the CCFG workbook and place this code inside of it. See Exhibit 19.21.

In addition to the string variables containing the contents of the worksheet Ranges, we also dimension the Outlook Application and Mail Item objects. After reading the data inputs from the worksheet named Ranges, we set our Outlook object to a new Outlook Application. We then create an Item of type "olMailItem" within the application and set this object to our "oMail" variable.

Once we have established the necessary object variables, the code that edits the Mail Item object is straightforward. We set the relevant attributes of the Mail Item object with the values from the worksheet. After these are set, we call ".Send" and the Mail Item is on its way! That is all there is to it!

The last step is to insert the call to this subroutine into the flow of the CCFG model. After the CCFG has completed running all the scenarios and producing all

```
Sub OutlookMsg_EmailAlertPermission()

Dim msgResult As Long 'user input

    msgResult = MsgBox( _
            "All cash flow modeling runs have completed successfully." & vbCrLf & _
            "Do you wish to send Email Alert at this time?", vbQuestion + vbYesNo) _
    Debug.Print msgResult

    If msgResult = 6 Then sendCollatAlertEmail

End Sub
```

EXHIBIT 19.22   "OutlookMsg_EmailAlertPermission" subroutine

of the selected reports, the analyst will be asked whether the alert should be sent
out at this time. We create the "userEmailAlertPermission" subroutine that builds
the Message Box and sends the email message if the analyst chooses to do so.
We will place the call to this subroutine in the last position at the bottom of the
"A_MainProgram" module in the CCFG. See Exhibit 19.22.

Working Group Email

The construction of the Working Group Email includes all the features of the Alert
Email above. We add a second message template to the worksheet "MsgTemplate".
See Exhibit 19.23.

Note that in Range "Out_WorkGrpMsgBody" in this worksheet, we have two
substrings with the "var" prefix: "varState" and "varSummary". These two substrings will be replaced within the body of the message with the State of the report
and the Summary Statistics block of results.

Collateral Working Group Email

Recipients:	collateralGroup@bank.com, structureGroup@bank.com
CC:	
BCC:	
Subject:	Collateral Comparative Analysis
Message Body:	Collateral Group, Please find the Collateral Analysis Report for varState attached. SUMMARY: varSummary Regards, John Doe

EXHIBIT 19.23   "MsgTemplate" worksheet with "Working Group" message

```
Sub OutlookMsg_SendCollatStateEmail()

Dim textSummary As String          'state summary data
Dim dataSummary As DataObject      'state summary string
Dim attSource   As String          'attachment string
Dim currState   As String          'current state

    'retrieve inputs from Excel ranges
    mReceiptsTo = Range("Out_WorkGrpReceipt")
    mReceiptsCC = Range("Out_WorkGrpCC")
    mReceiptsBCC = Range("Out_WorkGrpBCC")
    mSubject = Range("Out_WorkGrpSubject")
    mMsgBody = Range("Out_WorkGrpMsgBox")

    'retrieve attachment location and state from program
    attSource = "C:\Users\Home\Documents\Book\Chapter 7\Chap07_FINALExhibits.ppt"
    currState = "Massachusetts"
    'create new Outlook and MailItem objects
    Set oOutlook = New Outlook.Application
    Set oMail = oOutlook.CreateItem(olMailItem)
    'create new data object
    Set dataSummary = New DataObject
    'load data to clipboard
    Range("rngStateSummary").Copy
    dataSummary.GetFromClipboard
    textSummary = dataSummary.GetText
    textSummary = Replace(textSummary, vbTab, " -- ")
    mMsgBody = Replace(mMsgBody, "varState", currState)
    mMsgBody = Replace(mMsgBody, "varSummary", textSummary)
    'edit the message and send
    With oMail
        .Subject = mSubject
        .To = mReceiptsTo
        .CC = mReceiptsCC
        .BCC = mReceiptsBCC
        .Body = mMsgBody
        .Attachments.Add attSource
        .Importance = olImportanceHigh
        .Send
    End With
    'clean up
    Set dataSummary = Nothing
    Set oMail = Nothing
    Set oOutlook = Nothing

End Sub
```

EXHIBIT 19.24 "OutlookMsg_SendCollatStateEmail" subroutine

With this email we will attach the output from our State/National comparative analysis and some summary statistics in the body of the email. We create a subroutine called "OutlookMsg_SendCollatStateEmail" for this purpose. See Exhibit 19.24.

There are four new variables defined in this subroutine. Two of these variables are for the full path of the file that we wish to attach and name of the state that is featured in the report. The other two objects will facilitate our retrieving the target text out of the clipboard once the summary Range has been copied. The "dataSummary" variable is a data object that will reference the information in the clipboard. The "textSummary" variable will contain the "dataSummary" converted to a string. In order to use the DataObject, we reference "Microsoft Form 2.0 Object Library".

We copy the summary Range to the clipboard by using ".Copy". Next we retrieve the table from the clipboard using the "GetFromClipboard" method of the "dataSummary" DataObject. After this we convert the table to a text format and add the extra formatting of replacing the tabs with "–". The "textSummary" string replaces the "varSummary" substring of the "msgBody". Notice that the only line of code needed to add an attachment to the email is

```
.Attachments.Add attSource
```

If necessary, multiple attachments can be added to the email by repeating this line.

As with the Alert Email above, we want to send out the Working Group email only if the analyst chooses to do so. We create a subroutine called "OutlookMsg_EmailWorkGrpPermission" that facilitates this in the same way as the "OutlookMsg_EmailAlertPermission" subroutine.

ON THE WEB SITE

On the Web site you will find the following files:

Model File
- **"CCFG_Chapter19".** This model has the modifications to the menu and the VBA code that comprises the PowerPoint report writer.

Report Template Files
- **"PPCollatPresentOneTemplate.ppt".** The Single State Comparison Report Package.
- **"PPCollatPresentOneNullTemplate.ppt".** The Single State comparison error report template.

Collateral Data File
- **"Pool01_PowerPoint".** This is the collateral data pool that we will use to produce the PowerPoint presentation report.

Model Output Files
- These are required inputs for the PowerPoint Report Writer. These are broken into two categories, the United States National Level reports and the state of California reports.

The National Reports are:

- **"National_StateInitGeoConcenReport.xlsm".** The National Level Initial Geographic Concentration Report. This file contains the State Level Current Balance Concentration reports on the collateral of the pool after it had been subjected to the initial data screening process only.
- **"National_CrossTabs.xlsm".** The National Level Cross Tabulations Report containing the report group listed in the chapter.

The State of California Reports are:

- "CA_MSAInitGeoConcenReport.xlsm". The state of California Initial Geographic Concentration Report.
- "CA_PortPresentReport_Credit.xlsm". The Credit Presentation Report.
- "CA_PortPresentReport_Valuation.xlsm". The Valuation Presentation Report.
- "CA_CrossTabs.xlsm". The Cross Tabulation Report Package.
- "CA_UserStratRep.xlsm". The User-Selected Base Stratification Report Package.

Running the CCFG and the LWM

Chapter 20: Running the Models

In this chapter we will run both the Collateral Cash Flow Generator (CCFG) and the Liabilities Waterfall Model (LWM) with the goal of creating a simplified structured finance deal.

To begin we will use the CCFG to perform the collateral selection process. In this process we will survey the values contained in the records of the collateral data file for completeness and reasonableness. We will produce reports that will tell us how much of the collateral can be used in the deal and what are the specific defects of the ineligible collateral. Having identified all the records of the collateral data file that are legible and complete, we will then eliminate those that are blatantly unsuitable for inclusion in the deal. The collateral represented by these records exhibit demographic or financial characteristics that make them prima facie ineligible for inclusion in the deal. Next we will perform more specific eligibility tests based on financial, demographic, and geographic characteristics. These will include a geographic concentration test. These tests will result in a final eligible collateral pool. We will then generate a series of four cash flow schedules from the final eligible collateral pool. These will consist of a base and stressed Geographic Methodology cash flow analysis and a base and stressed Demographic Methodology cash flow analysis. This will complete the collateral analysis phase.

With the collateral cash flows now in hand, we will turn our attention to the liabilities side of the deal structure. We will use the LWM to input the deal liabilities structure by specify the various note tranches, deal expenses, and payment triggers. We will then run the LWM once for each of the four collateral cash flow schedules and review the results.

Last, we will return to the CCFG and create a PowerPoint presentation of the California collateral in the portfolio.

CHAPTER 20

Running the Models

OVERVIEW

In this chapter we will finally have an opportunity to run the models! The intent of this chapter is to familiarize the reader with the mainstream procedures of working one's way through the settings of the model to produce a set of basic outputs. We will visit each model in the order that you would employ them if you were working on a transaction. We will review the various menu settings and a local approach to producing the results you need.

Remember that all the development activity we have undertaken is wasted if the models cannot address the issues and questions that arise in the business unit. Due to length considerations we will focus on extracts of the reports of the model rather than full reports. We will examine each of the interim results as a step in the process of producing a structured financing as the final goal of our work. Due to this need for overview and brevity, it is highly encouraged that the reader review the menu and data sections of the book (Chapter 9) and become familiar with the contents of the various reports produced by the runs.

Pay particular attention to the sequence of the entries. The approach we will take will be to begin each run of the two models by following the sequence of events described on its Main Menu. We will work our way through each of the special-purpose menus, entering various settings and confirming our elections (where possible) before moving on. After we have completed the model run setup entries, we will perform the model run and review the salient results of the various reports produced.

DELIVERABLES

The modeling knowledge deliverables for this chapter are:

- Becoming familiar with the mechanical aspects of preparing the models for the various analytical tasks involved in producing each run.
- Understanding why various reports or report packages were produced for each run.
- Understanding how each run of the model relates to the overall progression toward the solution of producing a working structured finance deal.

UNDER CONSTRUCTION

There is no model development in this chapter.

RUNNING THE CCFG, ANALYZING THE ASSET SIDE OF THE DEAL

Every deal begins with an analysis of the collateral. Without the collateral there are no collateral cash flows, and without collateral cash flows there is no point in having a liability structure that perforce cannot pay its note holders. We want to build a collateral set that we can be confident has the characteristics, both financial and demographic, to produce the cash flows we require. This means that we will make a diligent and honest attempt to evaluate the risk of the assets that comprise the collateral pool.

Not all assets are equal, which is a matter we touched on when we built the Rep Line Generator in Chapter 10. "A rose by any other name (may not) smell as sweet"! To this end we need to make a determination of the initial Asset Pool to see what kind of a hand we have been dealt. We will do this in the following manner:

0. This is the step before any other steps! It is the beginning of time for the process, the moment just prior to the Big Bang of our analytical process! In this step, before the process can even be said to begin, we examine the contents of the prospective pool collateral. In this step we will *not* apply any screening or selection criteria. We want to view the raw composition of the initial collateral pool in a completely unfiltered state.
1. Apply initial screening criteria to eliminate collateral that is prima facie ineligible. This collateral may have a data record that is illegible, that is missing critical information, or that has characteristics that render it unsuitable for inclusion in our deal.
2. Having eliminated unsuitable collateral, we now select collateral that contains the characteristics that we believe will result in cash flows with dampened volatility. We do this by selecting against financial and demographic characteristics that empirical analysis has shown to contribute to collateral volatility.
3. Next we will examine the survivors of the selection process of Step 2 from the standpoint of geographic location. We may find that collateral from certain states or Metropolitan Statistical Areas (MSAs) has a history of erratic prepayment and/or default performance.
4. We will then address the issue of geographic concentration. Geographic concentration is undesirable as the effects of localized environmental, regulatory, or economic conditions can significantly distort the intrinsic volatility of the asset pool. We do not want all of our eggs in one basket!
5. With the selection process complete, we will now run the collateral through the cash flow projection portion of the model. We will begin by calculating the future estimated cash flows of the collateral pool by employing the Geographic Methodology.

6. Finally we will generate the collateral cash flows using the Demographic Methodology. (See Chapter 13 to refresh your memory of these approaches.)

Remember to pay strict attention to the various menu entries we will make; the files we will create, save, and use; and the steps in each of the above run option sequences. Think about each step, why it is necessary to the process, and the measures we must take to achieve the desired results.

CCFG Run #0: An Unfiltered Assessment

In this step we want to view the collateral in its unvarnished state. We will perform no selection activities. We simply wish to know how much collateral there is, what are its general characteristics, and where it is located.

Preparing the Analysis   To accomplish this we will perform the following steps:

1. Enter the Main Menu.
2. Click on the first button in the column "Set Model Run Options". We will be placed in the CCFG Run/Output Options Menu. Enter an "N" (for "No") in all the fields. This will bypass the initial data screening process, the financial/demographic screening process, the geographic selection process, the geographic concentration sizing process, and finally the calculation of collateral cash flows. When you are finished, the menu should be configured as shown in Exhibit 20.1.
3. Return to the Main Menu by clicking on the "Return To Main Menu" Command-Button in the lower left of the menu. Once back in the Main Menu, click on the "Identify Collateral Data Files" button. This places us in the CCFG Collateral Pool Menu. Click on the "Select" button in the "Collateral Pool #1" line. A window will appear. Navigate to the directory

CCFG Run/Output Options Menu

Pool or Sub Portfolio	Collateral File Name	Initial Loan Record Data Screening Tests	Apply Financial and Demographic Tests	Apply Geographic (State & MSA) Tests	Apply Geographic Concentration Limits	Produce Eligible Collateral Cash Flows
		REQUIRED	OPTIONAL			Collateral Cash Flow Files
Run Option Code =>		1	2	3	4	5
#0	No File Selected		N	N		
#1	No File Selected		N	N		
#2	No File Selected	N	N	N	N	N
#3	No File Selected		N	N		
#4	No File Selected		N	N		
#5	No File Selected		N	N		

Remember: Enter the names of the collateral files in the CollatPoolMenu! This menu will pick them up from there.

Return To Main Menu   To avoid having either the Financial/Demographic Selection tests (column 2) or the Geographic Selection tests (column 3) run against the collateral enter a "N" for "No" in these fields instead of a collateral selection test set number.

EXHIBIT 20.1   CCFG Run/Output Options Menu

<table>
<tr><td colspan="3" align="center">**CCFG Collateral Pool Menu**</td></tr>
<tr><td></td><td></td><td>Collateral File Name</td></tr>
<tr><td>Collateral Pool #1</td><td>Select File</td><td>No File Selected</td></tr>
<tr><td>Sub Portfolio #1</td><td>Select File</td><td>No File Selected</td></tr>
<tr><td>Sub Portfolio #2</td><td>Select File</td><td>No File Selected</td></tr>
<tr><td>Sub Portfolio #3</td><td>Select File</td><td>No File Selected</td></tr>
<tr><td>Sub Portfolio #4</td><td>Select File</td><td>No File Selected</td></tr>
<tr><td>Sub Portfolio #5</td><td>Select File</td><td>No File Selected</td></tr>
<tr><td></td><td colspan="2">Pool Level File Name</td></tr>
<tr><td>Create Pool File From Sub-Portfolios?</td><td colspan="2">C:\VBABook2\ABS\Mort01\Data\Collat\Pool01_04New</td></tr>
<tr><td></td><td colspan="2">Initial Data Screening File Name</td></tr>
<tr><td>Create Initial Data Screening Report?</td><td colspan="2">InitialDataRep.xls</td></tr>
<tr><td>Return
To Main
Menu</td><td align="center">Create
Pool File From
Sub-Portfolios</td><td align="center">Create Eligible
Collateral
Pool File</td></tr>
</table>

EXHIBIT 20.2   CCFG Collateral Pool Menu (pre–file selection)

"C:\VBABook2\ABS\Mort1\Data\Collat". Select the file "Pool01_01New".
This file and its pathway:

```
C:\VBABook2\ABS\Mort1\Data\Collat\Pool01_01New
```

will now appear in the entry field of "Collateral Pool #1". See Exhibits 20.2,
20.3, and 20.4 for "before," "during," and "after" pictures of the process.

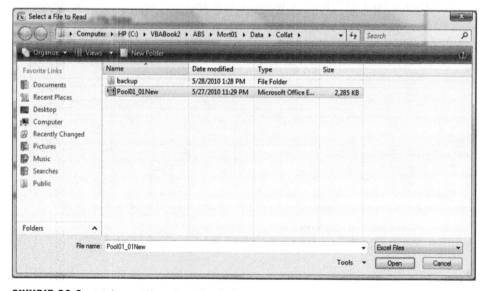

EXHIBIT 20.3   "Select a File to Read" window

		Collateral File Name
Collateral Pool #1	Select File	C:\VBABook2\ABS\Mort01\Data\Collat\Pool01_01New.xlsm
Sub Portfolio #1	Select File	No File Selected
Sub Portfolio #2	Select File	No File Selected
Sub Portfolio #3	Select File	No File Selected
Sub Portfolio #4	Select File	No File Selected
Sub Portfolio #5	Select File	No File Selected

CCFG Collateral Pool Menu

Pool Level File Name

Create Pool File From Sub-Portfolios? C:\VBABook2\ABS\Mort01\Data\Collat\Pool01_04New

Initial Data Screening File Name

Create Initial Data Screening Report? InitialDataRep.xls

Return To Main Menu	Create Pool File From Sub-Portfolios	Create Eligible Collateral Pool File

EXHIBIT 20.4 CCFG Collateral Pool Menu (post–file selection)

4. Return to the Main Menu by clicking the "Return to Main Menu" button. In that we are not performing any selection or computational analysis, we can ignore the next three buttons, "Define Geographic Selection Criteria", "Define Fin/Demo Selection Criteria", and "Set Amortization Criteria", which deal with the geographic selection, the financial/demographic selection, and cash flow amortization processes. Even though we are not performing collateral analysis per se, we do want to discover the contents of the prospective portfolio. To assess the initial state of the collateral, we select a number of basic reports. We will now click on the Reports Menu button "Define Report Package". This will place us in the CCFG Reports Editor & Menu screen. See Exhibit 20.5.

5. We want to develop a broad picture of the collateral. To do this we will run a series of geographic and stratification reports. We will begin by selecting the geographic entities we wish to report on. Click the "State Reports Selection" button in the upper left side of the menu. A UserForm named "Select State Level Collateral Reports" will appear. Click the "Select All States on List" Button, then on the "SET STATES TO INCLUDED". A confirmation message box appears telling us that all states are selected. We are then returned to the CCFG Reports Editor & Menu screen. See Exhibit 20.6.

6. Having selected all the states upon which we wish produce reports, we will now select the MSAs. Click the "MSA Reports Selection" button in the upper left of the menu. A UserForm named "Select Metropolitan Statistical Area Reports" will appear. A frame listing the four MSA groups, located on the right side of the form, will display MSA Group #1 as the initial default selection. Click the "Select All MSA's of the Displayed Group" button, then on the "SET SELECTED MSAs TO INCLUDED". A confirmation message box appears telling us all MSAs in Group #1 have been selected. This will give us a comprehensive overview with individual reports of the 25 largest MSAs in the country. We are then returned to the CCFG Reports Editor & Menu. See Exhibit 20.7.

CCFG Reports Editor & Menu

Geographic Reports Editor

State Reports Selection	MSA Reports Selection	Display Geographic Report Elections

Write Geographic Reports Elections to this File:

`C:\VBABook2\ABS\Mort01\Data\ReportSelect\StateRep02.xls`

Write Geographic Report Specifications To A File

Load Report Elections File

`C:\VBABook2\ABS\Mort01\Data\ReportSelect\StateRep02.xlsm`

Find File	Load Geographic Report Selection File

Collateral Stratification Reports Editor

Stratification Reports Editor	Cross Tabs Reports Editor	Display Stratification Elections	Display Cross Tab Elections

Write Stratification Reports Election to this File:

`C:\VBABook2\ABS\Mort01\Data\ReportSelect\BaseStratReps.xls`

Write Base Strat Report Specifications To A File	Write Cross Tabs Report Specifications To A File

Load Report Elections File

`C:\VBABook2\ABS\Mort01\Data\ReportSelect\BaseStratReps.xlsm`

Find File	Load Base Strat Report File	Load Cross Tab Report File

Select Power Point Presentation Report Contents

Single State Collateral Report

Select Report Packages

Output Reports Set Prefix

Return To Main Menu	Select Reports From CCFG Report Package

EXHIBIT 20.5   CCFG Reports Editor & Menu screen

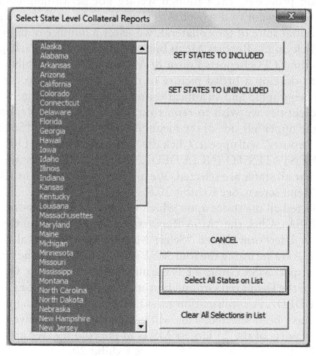

EXHIBIT 20.6   Select State Level Collateral Reports UserForm (with all states selected)

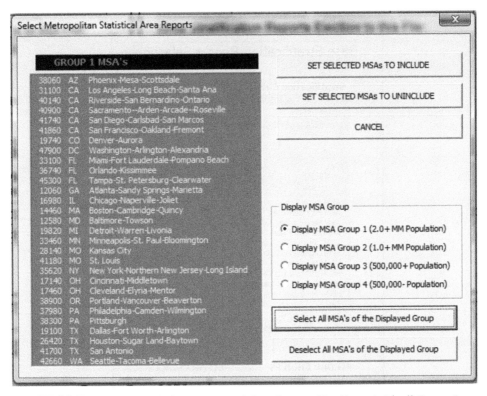

EXHIBIT 20.7 Select Metropolitan Statistical Area Reports UserForm (with all Group 1 MSAs selected)

7. We will now specify the contents of various report packages. We will start with the Base Stratification Reports. Click on the "Stratification Reports Editor" button. It displays a UserForm named "Base Stratification Reports Editor". This UserForm displays all data items in the collateral record that we can select to produce individual stratification reports. We will select the following range of items (first to last inclusive) from the list:
   - Mortgage Type to Current Balance (4 items)
   - Original LTV to ARM Index (7 items)
   - Original Appraisal Value to Servicer Rating (20 items)

   Do not select any "Reserved" fields from the range of entries of the UserForm as they represent items that are unsuitable for inclusion in one-dimensional stratification reports. Reports will not be produced for any "Reserved" field. Click on the "RECORD CHOICES" button. The UserForm will then disappear and we will be back in the CCFG Reports Editor Menu again. To avoid having to go through the process of making these stratification data selections in the future we will now save them to the following file:

   `C:\VBABook2\ABS\Mort01\Data\ReportSelect\BaseStratReports`

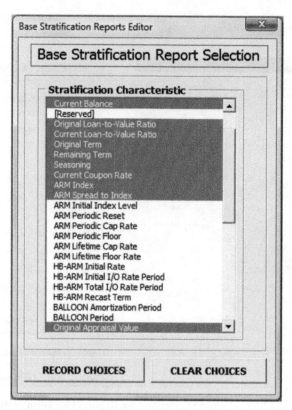

EXHIBIT 20.8   Base Stratification Report Selection UserForm

To accomplish this we enter the above pathway into the field "Write Stratification Reports Elections to this File:" We then click on the button "Write Base Strat Report Specifications To A File" button. This button creates a file that can be read by the CCFG and will allow us to use these specifications without entering the choices again. See Exhibits 20.8 and 20.9.

8. Having specified the report package contents, we will now select the report packages themselves. We click on the "Select Reports From CCFG Report Package" button. The UserForm "CCFG Model Reports Menu" is displayed. As a precaution we will first click on the button "CLEAR ALL SELECTIONS" to initialize the arrays that will hold our report elections. We will select the individual reports as highlighted from the UserForm. When our selections are complete we click on the "RECORD ALL SELECTIONS" button. The UserForm is retired and we are back in the CCFG Reports Editor Menu again. We have one final task ahead of us. Before we leave this menu, we will also enter "Run00_" in the "Output Reports Set Prefix" field to identify this group of files as being associated with this particular run of the model. See Exhibits 20.10 and 20.11. These files are:
   - Basic Stratification Report Package (one report)
   - Geographic Loan Listing Report (one report)

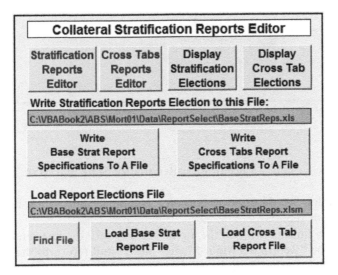

EXHIBIT 20.9   CCFG Reports Editor Menu (Collateral Stratification Reports Editor detail)

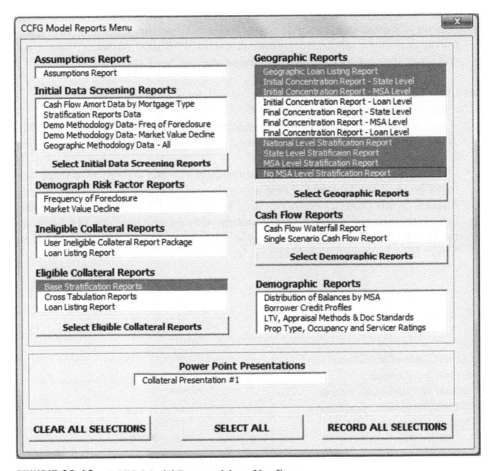

EXHIBIT 20.10   CCFG Model Reports Menu UserForm

Select Report Packages		
	Run00 Output Reports Set Prefix	
Return To Main Menu		Select Reports From CCFG Report Package

EXHIBIT 20.11   "Output Reports Set Prefix" field

- Initial Geographic Concentration Reports for State and MSA levels (two reports)
- Geographic Stratification Reports for National, State, MSA, and non-MSA
  loans (four reports)
9. We are now finished with all the inputs necessary for the first run of the CCFG.
   We click the "Return To Main Menu" button and return to the Main Menu.
   Here we click on the "Run the Model" button. The reports are written into the

        C:\VBABook2\ABS\Mort01\Output

   directory. We will create a subdirectory under this directory named "\Port New"
   for the deal and a subdirectory under that named "Run00_NoSelect" where we
   will move the reports for more permanent storage. See Exhibit 20.12.

Results   The key results of the survey of the collateral are:

- If we look at the National Level stratification report named "Run00_GeoStrat
  NationalReport", we see that we have 5,000 loans with an aggregate current
  balance of $1,302,207,184.
- Opening the "Run00_StateInitGeoConcenReport" file, we see that there are
  loans in 43 of the 50 states. There are no loans in Delaware, Montana, North
  Dakota, South Dakota, Vermont, West Virginia, and Wyoming. As far as the
  U.S. Territories are concerned, we find the following: There are 114 loans in
  the District of Columbia but no loans in the territories of Puerto Rico, the U.S.
  Virgin Islands, and the U.S. Marianas Islands.

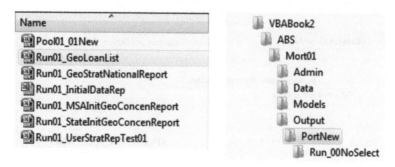

EXHIBIT 20.12   Finished Reports

- From this report we also see that the five largest concentrations of loans are in the states of:
  - California   15.70% $205,594,920
  - New York   10.63% $139,230,474
  - Texas   8.94% $117,048,233
  - Florida   8.04% $105,294,330
  - Illinois   4.78% $ 65,529,029
- Opening the "Run00_MSAInitGeoConcenReport" file, we see that the distribution of loans among MSAs is consistent with a nationally distributed portfolio. This report also provides us with information as to how many loans are not associated with *any* MSA in their state. These loans are found in the line entitled "Loans With No MSA Designated". These are either loans that lie outside of defined MSAs or do not have an MSA coded in their record.
- If we now turn to the "Run00_UserStratRepTest01" file, we can examine the distribution of loans and balances by the characteristics of the various selected data points. In this report each worksheet is a separate report and the number associated with the report "BaseStrat-N" is the ordinal position of the data in the record file. If we look at "BaseStrat-2", mortgage type code, we see that 100% of the loans are standard adjustable rate mortgages (ARMs).
- In worksheet "BaseStrat-3", the "Stratification by Credit Sector" report, we see that 100% of the loans are in the Prime credit sector, there are no Alt-A or subprime loans.
- In worksheet "BaseStrat-11", the "Stratification by Seasoning" report, we see that all of the loans are new, with seasoning ranging from between 1 and 9 months.
- In worksheet "BaseStrat-12", the "Stratification by Current Coupon Rate" report, we see that all of the gross coupons on the loans range from 4.50% to 6.00% with the main cluster between 5.00% and 5.50%.
- In worksheet "BaseStrat-29", the "Stratification by Original Appraisal Type" report, we see that 100% of original appraisal types are "Walk Through".
- In worksheet "BaseStrat-31", the "Stratification by Property Type" report, we see that 84% of the current balances are single family homes.
- In worksheet "BaseStrat-32", the "Stratification by Occupancy Code" report, we see that 86% of the current balances are owner occupied properties.
- In worksheet "BaseStrat-33", the "Stratification by Financing Purpose" report, we see that 88% of the current balances were originated as purchases or refinances, and not as restructured previous mortgages.
- In worksheet "BaseStrat-39", the "Stratification by First Time Homeowner Code" report, we see that 73% of the mortgagors are not first-time homeowners.
- In worksheet "BaseStrat-42", the "Stratification by FICO Score" report, we see that 89% of all households have Fair Isaac Corporation (FICO) scores greater than 600.
- In worksheet "BaseStrat-45", the "Stratification by Bankruptcy History" report, we see that 93% of all households have never declared bankruptcy.
- In worksheet "BaseStrat-46", the "Stratification by Escrow Provisions" report, we see that 70% of the current balances are held by households that escrow both taxes and insurance.

- In worksheet "BaseStrat-48", the "Stratification by Origination Document Package" report, we see that 92% of the current balances are in loans with full documentation packages.
- In worksheet "BaseStrat-49", the "Stratification by Servicer Rating" report, we see that only 0.39% of the current balances reside in loans for which the servicer rating is "Poor".

This would appear to be a portfolio with a number of favorable securitization characteristics. There are, however, some weaknesses in the portfolio as well.

- In worksheet "BaseStrat-5", the "Stratification by Current Balance" report, we see that there are 160 large-balance loans over $1 million. These constitute nearly 15% of the total current balances of the portfolio and will definitely be ineligible.
- In worksheet "BaseStrat-7", the "Stratification by Original Loan-to-Value Ratio" report, we see that 43% of the current balances of the portfolio have an original loan-to-value (LTV) of greater than 80%.
- In worksheet "BaseStrat-8", the "Stratification by Current Loan-to-Value Ratio" report, we see that 39% of the current balances of the portfolio have an original LTV of greater than 80%.
- In worksheet "BaseStrat-33", the "Stratification by Financing Purpose" report, we see that 9% of the current balances list "Restructure" as the financing purpose.
- In worksheet "BaseStrat-38", the "Stratification by Number of Years in Position" report, we see that 60% of the current balances of the portfolio is owed by mortgagors with less than five years in their current employment position.
- In worksheet "BaseStrat-43", the "Stratification by Mortgage Debt-to-Income" report, we see that 46% of the current balances are held by households with mortgage debt greater than 40% of their income.
- In worksheet "BaseStrat-44", the "Stratification by Total Debt-to-Income" report, we see that many of the households have higher-than-average, 70%, total debt to income ratios. A total of 24% of the current balances of the portfolio exceed this level.
- In worksheet "BaseStrat-49", the "Stratification by Servicer Rating" report, we see that in addition to the 0.39% of the current balances of the portfolio serviced by firms with ratings of "Poor", another 20% is serviced by firms with ratings of "Fair".

Note to the reader! We have stepped through the processes of Run #0 (our base starting position) in great detail. If we need to perform identical steps in CCFG Run #1 to CCFG Run #6, we will discuss them in a more abbreviated approach. We will describe the activities of the substep but not necessarily do so with the detailed explanations and specific exhibits. Nevertheless, whenever we take an action to add inputs to a menu, specify selections on UserForms, or perform other activities that we have *not* encountered before, we will step through them in detail.

CCFG Run #1: Initial Criteria Filter

Having performed the first survey of the collateral pool, we will now conduct the initial data screening process. The criteria that we will apply in this run of the CCFG will first test each of the collateral pieces to determine if there is any missing data and if the data present is legible. If the data is present and in a valid format, the next step is to apply a reasonableness test based on values for each of the data items. These reasonableness values can be found on the "DataInitialScreening" worksheet of the CCFG. Upper and lower ranges of acceptable values for many of the data fields of the collateral record are contained in columns "C" and "D" of this worksheet. Each of these data points is used in mortgage amortization calculations, the stratification reports, the components of the Geographic Methodology, or the more data intense Demographic Methodology. It is therefore critical that we are able to assess its form and completeness early in the process of the analysis.

Preparing the Analysis   The steps we need to take to apply these tests are:

1. Return to the Main Menu. From the Main Menu, click the button to access the Run Options Menu. We will now turn on the option to perform the Initial Loan Record Data Screening Tests option. Configure the Run Options Menu to the settings shown in Exhibit 20.13. Click on the "Return to the Main Menu" button.
2. Click on the "Define Report Package" button to enter the CCFG Reports Editor Menu. Use the "State Reports Selection" and the "MSA Reports Selection" buttons to select all states and all the Group 1 MSAs. Follow the same steps as we did in Steps 5 and 6 of CCFG Run #0 previously.
3. We now want to produce the same set of stratification reports that we just examined in CCFG Run #0. If we click on the "Load Base Strat Report to File" button, the CCFG will automatically load the assumptions stored in the file designated in the "Load Report Elections File". We will place the same pathway and file name we saved our selections to earlier in CCFG Run #0. The CCFG will

CCFG Run/Output Options Menu

			Collateral Selection Processes			Collateral Cash Flow Files
		REQUIRED	OPTIONAL			
	Run Option Code ⇒	1	2	3	4	5
Pool or Sub Portfolio	Collateral File Name	Initial Loan Record Data Screening Tests	Apply Financial and Demographic Tests	Apply Geographic (State & MSA) Tests	Apply Geographic Concentration Limits	Produce Eligible Collateral Cash Flows
#0	C:\VBABook2\ABS\Mort01\Data\Collat\Pool01_01New.xlsm		N	N		
#1	No File Selected		N	N		
#2	No File Selected		N	N		
#3	No File Selected	Y	N	N	N	N
#4	No File Selected		N	N		
#5	No File Selected		N	N		

Remember: Enter the names of the collateral files in the CollatPoolMenu! This menu will pick them up from there.

Return To Main Menu	To avoid having either the Financial/Demographic Selection tests (column 2) or the Geographic Selection tests (column 3) run against the collateral enter a "N" for "No" in these fields instead of a collateral selection test set number.

EXHIBIT 20.13   Run/Output Options Menu entries for Run #1

then will load those base stratifications selections contained in this file, thereby saving us the time and effort of entering them individually. It will also serve to ensure that any replication of these collateral selection runs uses a consistent and identifiable set of assumptions, thus ensuring a consistent basis for any future analysis.

4. With the contents of the stratification reports now specified, we will move on to the selection of the remaining reports. We click on the "Select Reports From CCFG Report Packages" button. As before, this action displays the "CCFG Model Reports Menu" UserForm.

   a. Before we do anything else we click the "CLEAR ALL SELECTIONS" button. This ensures that only the reports we now select will be produced and that we will not carry forward any report selections from a previous CCFG run.

   b. We will want to produce all the reports in the report package "Initial Data Screening Reports". We can select all these reports simply by clicking on the button "Select Initial Data Screening Reports" at the bottom of the list of these reports. As was mentioned earlier, these reports are crucial to understanding both the appropriateness and sufficiency of the data in the collateral file.

   c. We then select two reports, the "Base Stratification Report" and the "Loan Listing Report", in the "Eligible Collateral Group". These reports will produce basic stratification report package and a loan-by-loan list of all eligible loans.

   d. To finish we click on the "Select Geographic Reports" button in the right-hand column near the top of the UserForm to select all of the reports of this group. We will then deselect all reports with the "Initial Concentration Report" prefix. We do not need to example geographic concentration reports on a loan-by-loan basis so we will also deselect the "Final Concentration Report—Loan Level" report.

   e. When we have finished, the "CCFG Model Reports Menu" UserForm should reflect the entries of Exhibit 20.14. We click the button "RECORD ALL SELECTIONS" to lock in our choices. The UserForm is then retired.

   f. Before we leave the CCFG Reports Editor & Menu, we will enter "Run01_" into the "Output Reports Set Prefix" field to differentiate these reports from those of the other CCFG runs we will make throughout this chapter

5. Return to the Main Menu by clicking the "Return to Main Menu" button. We are now ready to perform the Initial Data Screening process. Click the "Run the Model" button.

Results   The results of this run fall into two categories:

- **Data Integrity Tests.** These tests determine if the form and values of the data contained in the collateral file are valid and, if they are, whether they contain reasonable data.
- **Data Sufficiency Tests.** These determine if the collateral record contains enough information to be utilized in the Geographic or Demographic Prepayment/Default Methodology calculations.

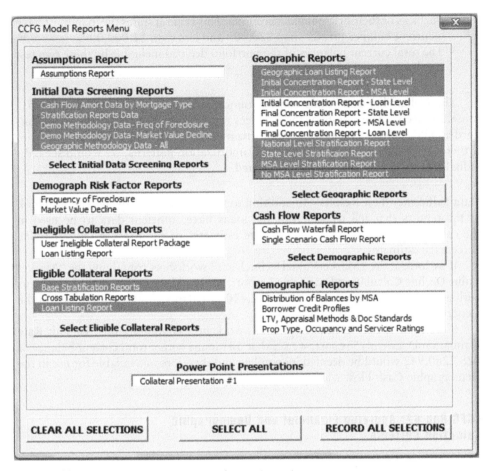

EXHIBIT 20.14 Report Selections, Initial Data Screening run

Data Integrity Test Results   The Initial Data Screening process now determines which pieces of collateral have passed all of our first tests. The results are as follows:

- If we look at the "Run01GeoStratNationalReport", we see that we now have 4,755 loans with an aggregate current balance of $1,096,299,474. A total of 245 loans with an aggregate balance of $205,732,828 have failed the initial data screening process.
- Why were these loans deemed ineligible? Since all the loans are Standard ARMs, we can look at the "StandardARMs" worksheet in the "Run_01InitialDataRep" report file. Here we find that most of these loans have been deemed ineligible for one or more of the following reasons:
  - A total of 241 loans with a current balance of $201,921,772 were deemed ineligible due to the minimum/maximum current loan balance criteria. All of the loans eliminated for this condition would have also been deemed ineligible on the basis of their original balances. An additional 4 loans were rejected on

the basis of their original balance alone. This criteria states the loan must have a current balance greater than $20,000 and less than $1,000,000.

■ The total current balances of the portfolio deemed ineligible by these two test conditions was $205,907,710.

The ineligibility conditions can be found in the report package file "Run01_ InitialDataRep". The results of the balances test are found in the worksheet "StandardARMS", which screens for the amortization information for that type of loan. If there were other mortgages with other amortization patterns, we would see individual reports for each type separately listed.

Data Sufficiency Test Results   In addition to these screening tests, we can also look at the reports that tell us which of the loans have sufficient data to be used in the calculation of either the Default Rate estimates or the Market Value Decline Percentage estimates.

If we look at the "MarketValueDeclineData" worksheet containing the "Market Value Decline Calculation Data Only" report, we would see that a total of 245 loans with a total current balance of $206,962,410 in balances could not be used in the Geographic Cash Flow Methodology.

If we look at the "DefaultRateData" worksheet containing the "Default Rate Estimation Data Only" report, we see that 581 loans with a total current balance of $287,260,942 would be deemed incomplete and therefore unavailable for use in the Demographic Cash Flow Methodology calculation.

CCFG Run #2: Applying Financial and Demographic Selection Criteria

With the Initial Data Screening Reports in hand, we can now apply the Financial/ Demographic Selection Criteria. These criteria are general tests, most of them quite simple, that select against unfavorable financial and demographic characteristics of the individual loans. They attempt to filter out those loans whose underwriting standards are impaired. They are also aimed at borrowers whose demographic or credit characteristics might make them higher-than-normal payment and default risks now and in the future. In addition to these tests, one in particular is necessary: The borrowers' seasoning must exceed one month. This seasoning test demonstrates that the mechanisms for payment processing and surveillance are in place.

Preparing the Analysis   The steps in applying the Financial/Demographic Selection Criteria are:

1. Return to the Main Menu.
2. Click on the "Set Model Run Options" button. On the CCFG Run Options Menu, set the "Apply Financial and Demographic Tests" field in the collateral pool row of the menu to "1". This indicates to the CCFG that it will look to the first set of financial and demographic selection options that we will create next. We will leave the setting of the "Initial Loan Record Data Screening Tests" field set to "Y". With these two settings in place we will select against the portfolio

CCFG Run/Output Options Menu

		Collateral Selction Processes				Collateral Cash Flow Files
		REQUIRED	OPTIONAL			
	Run Option Code =>	1	2	3	4	5
Pool or Sub Portfolio	Collateral File Name	Initial Loan Record Data Screening Tests	Apply Financial and Demographic Tests	Apply Geographic (State & MSA) Tests	Apply Geographic Concentration Limits	Produce Eligible Collateral Cash Flows
#0	C:\VBABook2\ABS\Mort01\Data\Collat\Pool01_01New.xlsm	Y	1	N	N	N
#1	No File Selected		N	N		
#2	No File Selected		N	N		
#3	No File Selected		N	N		
#4	No File Selected		N	N		
#5	No File Selected		N	N		

Remember: Enter the names of the collateral files in the CollatPoolMenu! This menu will pick them up from there.

Return To Main Menu

To avoid having either the Financial/Demographic Selection tests (column 2) or the Geographic Selection tests (column 3) run against the collateral enter a "N" for "No" in these fields instead of a collateral selection test set number.

EXHIBIT 20.15 Run/Output Options Menu entries for Run #2

using both sets of tests. When you complete the inputs to the Run Options Menu, it should appear identical to the entries shown in Exhibit 20.15.

3. Return to the Main Menu.
4. Click on the "Define Fin/Demo Selection Criteria" button. In the CCFG Financial/Demographic Selection Criteria Editor Menu, we will construct a series of tests. These tests will be created using the Criteria Test UserForms that are displayed by clicking the buttons with the headers "Test Type #1" to "Test Type #6". All of the tests we will create for this run will be either Test Type #1 or Test Type #2 tests. Refer to Chapters 9 and 11 for the procedures to follow to construct these tests. When we have completed inputting each of the tests, we will save the tests to a file that we can reload into the CCFG whenever we wish to do so. All of these tests are contained in a file named "FinSelectRun02". Note: This file is available on the Web site and can be downloaded and read into the CCFG. Place the file in the directory

   ```
   C:\VBABook2\ABS\Mort01\Data\SelectCrit\
   ```

   Enter the name of the file in the "File:" field and click on the "Read Test Sets From File" button in the menu section entitled "Printing, Saving and Reading Test Sets". The file will load and you can confirm that the selection information is in the CCFG by clicking on the "Print This Test Set" button in the same section. Upon clicking this button, the CCFG will display the tests on the "FinCriteriaReport" worksheet. See Exhibit 20.16.
5. Return to the Main Menu.
6. Click on the "Define Report Package" button to reach the CCFG Reports Editor & Menu. Through past experience we know that the application of these tests will significantly affect the amount of eligible collateral available to our deal. We will want to know what particular selection tests have the greatest effects. We will therefore select a wider array of reports. For the first time in the process we are in a position to employ the Ineligible Collateral Report Package.

Financial/Demographic Information Criteria Test Set Report

Set: [1]

Return To Financial Selections Menu

Test #	Test Type	Test Conditions						
1	2	Current Balance	GE	25000	AND	Current Balance	LE	1000000
2	1	Current Loan-to-Value Ratio	LE	0.95				
3	1	Original Appraisal Type	EQ	2				
4	1	Property Type	GE	2				
5	2	Occupancy Code	GE	2	AND	Occupancy Code	LE	4
6	2	Financing Purpose	GE	2	AND	Financing Purpose	LE	3
7	2	Bankruptcy	GE	2	AND	Bankruptcy	LE	3
8	1	Third Party Confirmation	GE	2				
9	2	Origination Documentation	GE	2	AND	Origination Documentation	LE	3
10	1	Servicier Rating	GE	2				
11	1	Mortgage Debt-to-Income Ratio	LE	0.45				
12	1	Total Debt-to-Income Ratio	LE	0.75				
13	1	Seasoning	GT	1				
14	1	Credit Sector	EQ	1				
15	1	Original Loan-to-Value Ratio	LE	0.85				
16	1	Number of Payments in Arrears	LE	0.001				
17	1	Original Term (months)	GT	180				

EXHIBIT 20.16 Financial/Demographic Criteria Set 1

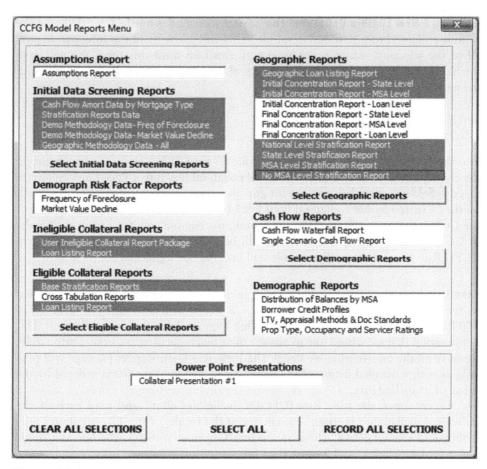

EXHIBIT 20.17 Report Selections, Financial and Demographic Selection Criteria for CCFG Run #2

This package will produce individual test-specific results that list each of the pieces of collateral deemed ineligible on a test-by-test basis.

   a. To select these reports first click the "CLEAR ALL SELECTIONS" button. This action reinitializes all report choices to non-selected.

   b. Next select all the reports of the "Initial Data Screening Reports" section.

   c. Select both of the reports in the "Ineligible Collateral Reports" section.

   d. Next select the "Base Stratification Reports" and the "Loan Listing Report" from the "Eligible Collateral Reports" section.

   e. Replicate the selection of reports we made in CCFG Run #1 in the "Geographic Reports" section.

   f. When the UserForm looks like Exhibit 20.17 click on the "RECORD ALL SELECTIONS" button.

   g. Upon returning to the CCFG Reports Editor & Menu screen we will identify the reports of this run by entering "Run02_" into the "Output Reports Set Prefix" field.

 7. Return to the Main Menu and click the "Run the Model" button.

Creating a New Eligible Collateral File   After Run #2 has finished, we will save the eligible collateral to a new collateral file. This will allow us in the future to bypass all of the selection activities we have performed up until this time. We will save the file by navigating to the CCFG Collateral Pool Menu. Once there, we will enter the name:

```
C:\VBABook2\ABS\Mort01\Data\Collat\Pool01_02New
```

into the "Create Pool File from Sub-Portfolios?" field. While we are not aggregating the contents of a set of Sub-Portfolio Level collateral files into a Pool Level collateral file, this field serves as the reference for any file created from this menu. We now click on the "Create Eligible Collateral Pool File" button. Upon conclusion of this run of the CCFG, the new collateral file, containing the eligible collateral from the results of CCFG Run #1 and CCFG Run #2, will be available for use. When we perform CCFG Run #3, this new collateral file will become our input file.

Results   After the financial and demographic selection criteria have been applied to the Collateral Pool, an additional 2,378 loans with an aggregate balance of $703,276,380 were deemed ineligible! What happened to all of our collateral? This is a question that we would like to answer in as much detail as possible. Fortunately, we have all the information we need! The Ineligible Loan Report Package will provide us with a detailed listing of the disposition of each of the loans ordered by the cause of its ineligibility.

We can open the file "Run_02POOL_IneligibleCollat" and read each of the individual ineligibility reports. A summary of the results of the 17 ineligibility tests is shown in Exhibit 20.18. There are no totals on this summary schedule as a single loan may be ineligible under more than one condition.

If we wish to examine the unique ineligibility combinations for each group of ineligible collateral, we can refer to the "Run02_POOLIneligCollat" file. This file will contain a series of worksheets, one for each of the ineligibility tests, and a listing of each individual loan that failed that test. The worksheet "IneligSUM" contains the report "Summary Ineligibility Report". An extract of this report is displayed on the right side of Exhibit 20.18. This report lists each unique combination of ineligibility criteria and totals all loans that failed this particular set of tests. The extracted section of the report details all unique ineligibility codes that contribute to the balance of $202,324,425, which is the sum of all loans that fail eligibility Test #1. If we look at the left-hand side of the exhibit, we see that 259 loans fail the current balance range test that requires the loan to be greater than $25,000 and less than or equal to $1,000,000. These 259 loans, however, are distributed between 29 different ineligibility test combinations. The bulk of the loans, 149 of them, for a combined current balance of $125,350,873, representing 61.955% of the total, fail this test alone. This report shows us that were we able to dispense with Test #1 altogether we would not recoup the full $202.3 million but rather only $125.4 million in eligible collateral. See Exhibit 20.18.

If we look at the "Run02_GeoStratNationalReport" file we see that our remaining portfolio now consists of 2,622 loans with an aggregate current balance of $598,930,804.

Summary Balances by Test

Ineligibile Loan Count and Balances By Test

Loans may fail multiple test and be reported in more than one test!

Indiv Test #	Failed Test Conditions	# of Loans	Total Current Balance
1	Current Balance 25,000 to 1,000,000	259	202,324,425
2	Current Loan-to-Value LE 95%	0	0
3	Original Appraisal Not "Walk Through"	0	0
4	Property Type Known, Not Multi-Family	60	16,062,638
5	Occupancy Type Not Seasonal	65	18,040,232
6	Financing Purpose Purchase or Refinance	553	147,093,242
7	Bankruptcy Never or Discharged	237	63,552,023
8	Third Party Due Diligence Better Than "Poor"	67	18,379,806
9	Full or Partial Documentation, No Alt-A	101	28,879,949
10	Servicing Rating Better Than "Poor"	17	5,041,046
11	Mortgage Debt-to-Income LE 75%	427	110,400,558
12	Total Debt-to-Income LE 75%	314	81,684,148
13	Seasoning Greater Than 1 Month	310	73,010,883
14	No Alt-A, No Sub-Prime	0	0
15	Original Loan-to-Value LE 85%	258	66,708,248
16	Cannot be in a Delinquent Status	46	12,901,472
17	Original Term > 180 Months	495	120,636,522
	Total Number of Loans Ineligible	2,378	
	Total Current Balance Ineligible		703,276,380

Summary Ineligibility Report (Extract)
All Ineligibility Combinations That Incude Test #1

Ineligibility Condition Reference

1 = Current Balance 25,000 to 1,000,000   8 = Third Party Due Diligence Better Than "Poor"   13 = Seasoning Greater Than 1 Month
4 = Property Type Known, Not Multi-Family   9 = Full or Partial Documentation, No Alt-A   15 = Original Loan-to-Value LE 85%
5 = Occupancy Type Not Seasonal   10 = Servicing Rating Better Than "Poor"   16 = Cannot be in a Delinquent Status
6 = Financing Purpose Purchase or Refinance   11 = Mortgage Debt-to-Income LE 45%   17 = Original Term >= 180 Months
7 = Bankruptcy Never or Discharged   12 = Total Debt-to-Income LE 75%

# of Unique Ineligibility Codes	Code	1	5	6	7	8	9	10	11	12	13	15	16	17	# of Loans	Total Current Balance	Percent Current Balance	Cum Pct Current Balance
		29	3	8	3	2	5	1	4	7	4	5	1	5	259	202,324,425		
1	1	1													149	125,350,873	61.955%	61.965%
2	33	1		1											25	17,496,870	8.648%	70.603%
3	65	1			1										9	7,344,407	3.630%	74.233%
4	4097	1									1				10	6,908,757	3.415%	77.648%
5	2049	1								1					9	4,924,051	2.434%	80.082%
6	65537	1												1	13	4,734,752	2.340%	82.422%
7	16385	1										1			3	3,743,369	1.850%	84.272%
8	257	1					1								5	3,446,620	1.704%	85.976%
9	17	1	1												2	3,050,794	1.508%	87.484%
10	129	1				1									2	2,943,919	1.455%	88.939%
11	65569	1		1										1	3	2,526,933	1.249%	90.188%
12	1025	1							1						4	2,512,810	1.242%	91.429%
13	32769	1											1		2	2,290,293	1.132%	92.561%
14	18433	1								1		1			2	2,117,197	1.046%	93.608%
15	3105	1		1					1	1					2	1,496,713	0.740%	94.348%
16	97	1		1	1										1	1,488,299	0.736%	95.083%
17	49	1	1	1											1	1,405,688	0.695%	95.778%
18	67585	1								1				1	1	1,341,500	0.663%	96.441%
19	4353	1					1				1				1	1,312,421	0.649%	97.090%
20	321	1			1		1								1	1,308,057	0.647%	97.736%
21	2689	1				1		1		1					1	1,305,726	0.645%	98.382%
22	66561	1							1					1	1	1,109,467	0.548%	98.930%
23	3073	1							1	1					6	1,089,502	0.538%	99.468%
24	16641	1					1					1			1	1,020,046	0.504%	99.973%
25	18465	1		1						1		1			1	24,517	0.012%	99.985%
26	289	1		1			1								1	8,618	0.004%	99.989%
27	69633	1									1			1	1	8,170	0.004%	99.993%
28	16417	1		1								1			1	7,665	0.004%	99.997%
29	4113	1	1								1				1	6,393	0.003%	100.000%

EXHIBIT 20.18 Ineligible balances by Financial/Demographic selection criteria with Summary Ineligibility Report extract

CCFG Run #3: Applying Geographic Selection Criteria

Only two other selection tests need to be applied. These are the geographic exclusion selection process and geographic concentration limits sizing selection process. We will address the question of Geographic Selection first as it will have an immediate and inescapable impact on any post-selection concentrations. The Geographic Selection exclusion criteria we will apply are:

- No collateral from any U.S. territory or the District of Columbia
- No collateral from the states of Louisiana or Rhode Island

Preparing the Analysis   We can perform the analysis using the following steps:

1. Return to the Main Menu.
2. Click on the "Set Model Run Options" button. On the CCFG Run Options Menu, we will enter the following settings:
   a. Place an "N" for performing the "Initial Loan Record Data Screening Tests" column and in the "Apply Financial and Demographic Tests" column. We do not now need to repeat these selection actions as they are already reflected in the contents of our new collateral file.
   b. Place a "1" in the column "Apply Geographic (State & MSA) Tests". We will shortly create a series of geographic selection test and save them in a file as we did with the financial/demographic test set we created earlier.
   c. We will perform the Geographic Concentration Selection in CCFG Run #4, so we will place a "N" in that column at this time.
   d. We are still in the collateral selection process and have not arrived at the size of the final portfolio so we will place an "N" in the "Produce Eligible Collateral Cash Flows" column.

   The Run Options Menu entries should look like those of Exhibit 20.19. Return to the Main Menu.

CCFG Run/Output Options Menu

Pool or Sub Portfolio	Collateral File Name	Initial Loan Record Data Screening Tests	Apply Financial and Demographic Tests	Apply Geographic (State & MSA) Tests	Apply Geographic Concentration Limits	Produce Eligible Collateral Cash Flows
		REQUIRED 1	2	OPTIONAL 3	4	Collateral Cash Flow Files 5
#0	C:\VBABook2\ABS\Mort01\Data\Collat\Pool01_01New.xlsm		N	1		
#1	No File Selected		N	N		
#2	No File Selected		N	N		
#3	No File Selected	N	N	N	N	N
#4	No File Selected		N	N		
#5	No File Selected		N	N		

Remember: Enter the names of the collateral files in the CollatPoolMenu! This menu will pick them up from there.

Return To Main Menu	To avoid having either the Financial/Demographic Selection tests (column 2) or the Geographic Selection tests (column 3) run against the collateral enter a "N" for "No" in these fields instead of a collateral selection test set number.

EXHIBIT 20.19   Run/Output Options Menu Settings for Run #3

3. Click on the "Identify Collateral Data Files" button. On the CCFG Collateral Pool Menu, we will enter the name of the new eligible collateral file in the "Collateral Pool #1" field. The directory pathway and name of this file is:

```
C:\VBABook2\ABS\Mort01\Data\Collat\Pool01_02New
```

4. Return to the Main Menu.
5. Click on the "Define Geographic Selection Criteria" button. On the menu we will enter a "1" in the "Building Test:" field. All of our remaining activities in this menu will be in the "Set Regional, State, and MSA Selection Conditions" subsection of the menu.
   a. Click on the second button from the left of the group of five action buttons on the right side of the section, the "Reset This Test to "Include All"" button. This will ensure that all States and MSAs are set to "Eligible". We can now easily set our selection criteria by deselecting the States and MSAs we wish to deem ineligible.
   b. Clicking on the "State Selection" button will display the UserForm named "States Selection Form". The default UserForm display setting for the type of selection we will perform is "Exclude State and Exclude MSAs". This will deem ineligible all collateral from any of the states we subsequently select. We click on the following states on the list:
      ▪ Louisiana
      ▪ Rhode Island
      ▪ District of Columbia
      ▪ Puerto Rico
      ▪ U.S. Virgin Islands
      ▪ Marianas Islands
   c. We now click on the CommandButton of the UserForm "SELECT ACTION". A confirmation message appears, we click on "OK" if we are happy with our selections, and we are finished with this UserForm. See Exhibit 20.20.
6. Upon returning to the Geographic Selection Criteria Menu, we will now click on the "MSA Selection" button. The UserForm "MSA Groups Selection Form" is displayed. This UserForm has an initial default display of MSA Group 1, the 25 largest of the MSAs. Unfortunately, none of our targeted MSAs are in this group. The MSAs we wish to exclude from selection are:
   ▪ Las Vegas, Nevada (MSA Group 2)
   ▪ Trenton, New Jersey(MSA Group 4)
   ▪ Reno, Nevada (MSA Group 4)
      Here we will select MSA Group 2 first, click on Las Vegas and click on the "APPLY CHOICES" button. Next we display MSA Group 4, scroll down to the bottom of the list, click on Trenton and Reno, and finish by clicking on the "APPLY CHOICES" button. After each selection process the UserForm will be retired and you will have to redisplay it using the "MSA Selection" button. When you have finished return to the Main Menu.
7. The final step to specify what we want done in this run of the CCFG is to select the reports. We now move to the CCFG Reports Editor Menu. Here we will select all states and all members of the Group 1 MSA to report on by using

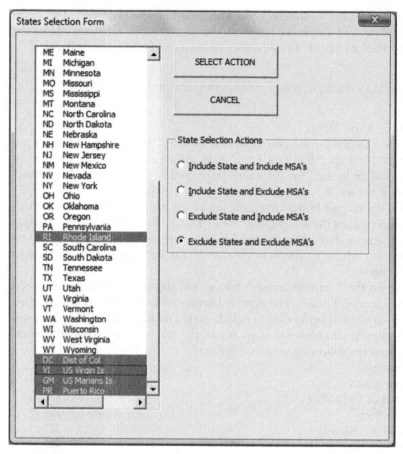

EXHIBIT 20.20 Selecting States for exclusion

the "States Report Selection" and the "MSA Reports Selection" buttons in the "Geographic Report Editor" section of the menu.

a. Clicking on the "States Report Selection" button we display the now familiar "Select States Level Collateral Reports" UserForm. We click the "Select All States on List" button followed by the "SET STATES TO INCLUDED" button.

b. We click on the "MSA Reports Selection" button to display the "Select Metropolitan Statistical Area Reports" UserForm. The MSA Group 1 list is the default display group. We click on the "Select All MSA's of the Displayed Group" button, followed by "SET SELECTED MSAs TO INCLUDE" button.

c. Having told the CCFG what we want to report on, we now need to tell it which reports we wish produced. We will make the following report selections. Clicking on the "Select Reports From CCFG Report Package", we display the "CCFG Model Reports Menu" UserForm. We select only two Initial Concentration Reports, one for states and one for MSAs from the "Geographic Reports" section, as the output for CCFG Run #3. We will need this information immediately following this run for two reasons: to

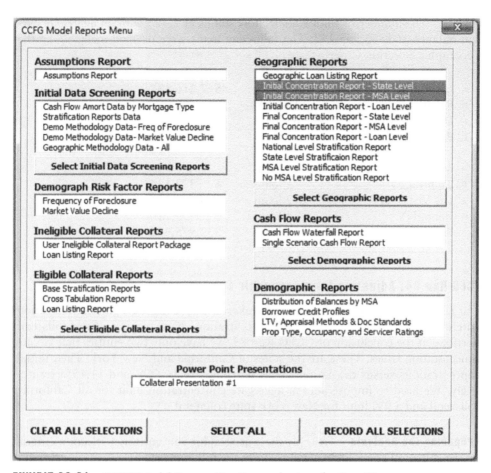

EXHIBIT 20.21 CCFG Model Reports UserForm selections for Run #3

confirm that all collateral from the excluded states and MSAs have indeed been eliminated and to immediately identify any potential geographic concentration issues in the now reconfigured portfolio. We need to correct any concentration issues as the last step in the process prior to calculation the eligible collateral cash flows.

When we have finished, the entries to the Reports UserForm should look like Exhibit 20.21.

8. Upon returning to the CCFG Reports Editor & Menu screen, we will identify the reports of this run by entering "Run03_" into the "Output Reports Set Prefix" field.

9. Return to the Main Menu and click the "Run the Model" button.

Saving the Collateral File   Following the steps that we outlined at the end of CCFG Run #2, we will save the eligible collateral set produced by CCFG Run #3 under the name

C:\VBABook2\ABS\Mort01\Data\Collat\Pool01_03New

Results   The number of eligible loans now stands at 2,493 with an aggregate current balance of $565,955,152. The following loans were deemed ineligible by the Geographic Selection Criteria tests:

■ Louisiana	31 loans	$ 7,216,187
■ Rhode Island	16 loans	$ 4,488,087
■ District of Columbia	64 loans	$16,260,202
■ Puerto Rico	0 loans	-0-
■ U.S. Virgin Islands	0 loans	-0-
■ Marianas Islands	0 loans	-0-
■ Trenton, NJ	2 loans	$ 372,124
■ Las Vegas, NV	12 loans	$ 3,743,341
■ Reno, NV	4 loans	$ 895,710
Totals	114 loans	$32,975,652

CCFG Run #4: Adjusting for Geographic Concentrations

Our last collateral sizing activity is undertaken to meet the geographic concentration criteria limits. Given the geographic concentration characteristics of the collateral portfolio at the conclusion of CCFG Run #3, we have only two entities that violate concentration issues. These are the states of California and New York. Their initial concentrations versus the national-level portfolio are 16.56% and 11.15% respectively. We need to impose a 14% aggregate concentration limit for all California collateral and a 9% limit for New York state collateral.

Preparing the Analysis   To apply these geographic concentration selection criteria on the collateral portfolio, we will perform the following steps:

1. Return to the Main Menu. Click on the "Set Model Run Options" button. On the CCFG Run Options Menu, we will set all options to "N" except for the "Apply Geographic Concentration Limits" column, which we will set to "Y". Return to the Main Menu. See Exhibit 20.22.
2. Click on the "Identify Collateral Data Files" button. On the CCFG Collateral Pool Menu, use the "Select File" feature to find and enter

   ```
   C:\VBABook2\ABS\Mort01\Data\Collat\Pool01_03New
   ```

   as the current collateral data file into the "Collateral Pool #1" field. Return to the Main Menu.
3. Click on the "Define Geographic Selection Criteria" button. On the Geographic Selection Criteria Menu, we will be working exclusively within the section of the menu entitled "State or MSA Current Balance Concentration Levels". Click on the "Reset Test to 100% Concentrations" button. This setting allows any entity to comprise up to 100% of the collateral of the pool; in other words, an unlimited collateral concentration! We will then tell the CCFG which states and MSAs have specific concentration limits.

CCFG Run/Output Options Menu

Pool or Sub Portfolio	Collateral File Name	Collateral Selection Processes					Collateral Cash Flow Files
		REQUIRED	OPTIONAL				
	Run Option Code ⇒	1	2	3	4		5
		Initial Loan Record Data Screening Tests	Apply Financial and Demographic Tests	Apply Geographic (State & MSA) Tests	Apply Geographic Concentration Limits		Produce Eligible Collateral Cash Flows
#0	C:\VBABook2\ABS\Mort01\Data\Collat\Pool01_03New.xlsm		N	N			
#1	No File Selected		N	N			
#2	No File Selected		N	N			
#3	No File Selected	N	N	N	Y		N
#4	No File Selected		N	N			
#5	No File Selected		N	N			

Remember: Enter the names of the collateral files in the CollatPoolMenu! This menu will pick them up from there.

Return To Main Menu | To avoid having either the Financial/Demographic Selection tests (column 2) or the Geographic Selection tests (column 3) run against the collateral enter a "N" for "No" in these fields instead of a collateral selection test set number.

EXHIBIT 20.22 Run/Output Options Menu settings for CCFG Run #4

4. Click on the "Enter State and MSA Concentrations" button. The UserForm "State & MSA Concentration Menu" will be displayed. This UserForm has three display options, one for the states and two more for the two largest MSA Groups 1 and 2. Conveniently it initializes to the State Level. We wish to set two state level concentration levels. These are:
   - California—14% of total portfolio current balances
   - New York—9% of total portfolio current balances

   We will need to enter each of the concentration limits individually as they are at different percentage levels. If the limits for the states were identical, we could simply select both states, enter a single concentration limit. and click the "APPLY CONCENTRATION LEVEL" button. We will select each state separately: Enter 14.0 for California and 9.0 for New York in the "Set Concentration Limit for Selections" input field. The UserForm will convert them to percentage form after error checking. The entry for California can be seen in Exhibit 20.23.

5. Return to the Main Menu. Click on the "Define Report Package" button. In the CCFG Reports Editor & Menu, we will click on the "States Reports Selection" button. When the UserForm "Select State Level Collateral Reports" is displayed, we will click on the button "Select All States On List" and then on the button "SET STATES TO INCLUDED". The UserForm will be retired, and we next click on the "MSA Reports Selection" button. On the User Form "Select Metropolitan Statistical Area Reports", we will click the buttons "Select All MSA's of the Displayed Group" and "SET ALL MSAs TO INCLUDE". The UserForm will be retired.

6. We will next click on the "Select Reports From CCFG Report Package" button. The UserForm "CCFG Model Reports Menu" will be displayed. First click the "CLEAR ALL SELECTIONS" button. Next we will select two reports from the "Geographic Reports" section. These are the "Final Concentration Reports" at the state and MSA levels. These reports will verify that the final concentration target levels have been achieved. Click the "RECORD ALL SELECTIONS" button. The UserForm will be retired. See Exhibit 20.24.

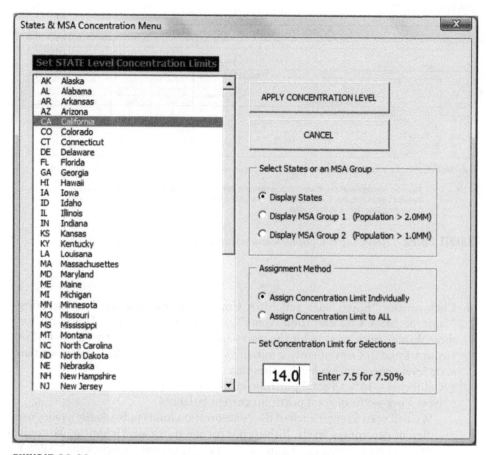

EXHIBIT 20.23   Setting state of California concentration limit

7. Upon returning to the CCFG Reports Editor & Menu screen, we will identify the reports of this run by entering "Run04_" into the "Output Reports Set Prefix" field.
8. Return to the Main Menu and click the "Run the Model" button.

Saving the Collateral File   We will save the eligible collateral set produced by Run #4 under the name

```
C:\VBABook2\ABS\Mort01\Data\Collat\Pool01_04New
```

This is now our final post–selection process collateral pool! We can produce all future runs of the CCFG without any selection processing at all by simply using this file as the eligible collateral data file.

Results   The remaining portfolio now consists of 2,413 loans with an aggregate balance of $531,163,947. The following loans were deemed ineligible to achieve the

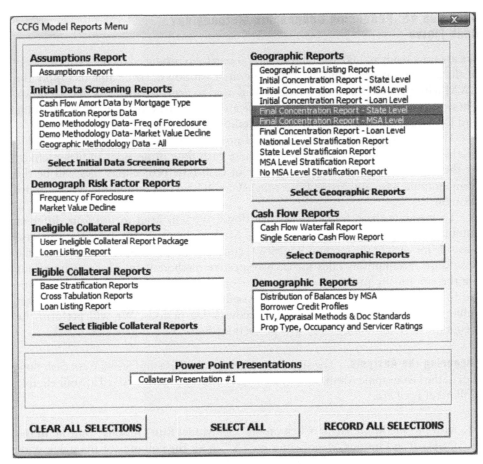

EXHIBIT 20.24 CCFG Model Reports Menu UserForm selections for CCFG Run #4

targeted Geographic Concentration levels:

- California 42 loans $19,411,856
- New York State 38 loans $15,379,350
- Totals 80 loans $34,791,206

If we look at the "Concentration by Geographic Region" report in the file "Run04_StateFinalGeoConcenReport", we see that the above loans were deemed ineligible and removed from the portfolio to achieve the desired balance concentrations in the states of California and New York.

| California | 385 loans | $74,350,492 | 14.00% concentration |
| New York | 259 loans | $47,746,823 | 8.99% concentration |

CCFG Run #5: Producing Geographic Methodology Cash Flows

We are now ready to take the final collateral portfolio produced by the various stages of the selection process and use it to generate cash flows. To be able to supply the LWM with the cash flows required, we will need to generate four sets of cash flows. These four sets will consist of a set of base and stress cases for both the Geographic and Demographic Prepayment/Default Methodologies.

The next two runs of the CCFG will produce the base and stress Geographic Methodology cash flows; we will store these cash flow projections in files prefixed by the name "Run05_". The second pair of cash flow projections files will be the Demographic Base and Stress Case runs. We will give this output file set the prefix "Run06_".

To generate these four sets of cash flows, we will need to use four different combinations of Geographic/Demographic Methodology assumptions files. The Base Case file for each of the methodologies will contain a single set of cash flows using the Base Case Assumptions Files for each respective methodology. These assumptions are the empirically predicted collateral performance. The Stress Case Assumptions file for each methodology contains increased default activity, more severe market value decline percentages, and longer recovery lag periods. We will perform the Geographic Methodology cash flow projections first.

Preparing the Analysis   The steps in generating the Base and Stress Case cash flow files of the Geographic Methodology cash flows once you have arrived at your eligible Collateral Pool are:

1. Move to the Main Menu. Click on the "Set Model Run Options" button. In the CCFG Run Options Menu, enter an "N" in all the columns of the menu with the exception of the last column, "Produce Eligible Collateral Cash Flows", where we will place a "Y". When you have finished, the menu should look like the one in Exhibit 20.25.

CCFG Run/Output Options Menu						
			Collateral Selection Processes			Collateral Cash Flow Files
		REQUIRED	OPTIONAL			
	Run Option Code =>	1	2	3	4	5
Pool or Sub Portfolio	Collateral File Name	Initial Loan Record Data Screening Tests	Apply Financial and Demographic Tests	Apply Geographic (State & MSA) Tests	Apply Geographic Concentration Limits	Produce Eligible Collateral Cash Flows
#0	C:\VBABook2\ABS\Mort01\Data\Collat\Pool01_04New.xlsm		N	N		
#1	No File Selected		N	N		
#2	No File Selected		N	N		
#3	No File Selected	N	N	N	N	Y
#4	No File Selected		N	N		
#5	No File Selected		N	N		

Remember: Enter the names of the collateral files in the CollatPoolMenu! This menu will pick them up from there.

Return To Main Menu	To avoid having either the Financial/Demographic Selection tests (column 2) or the Geographic Selection tests (column 3) run against the collateral enter a "N" for "No" in these fields instead of a collateral selection test set number.

EXHIBIT 20.25   Run/Output Options Menu settings for Run #5

2. Return to the Main Menu. Click on the "Identify Collateral Data Files" button. In the CCFG Collateral Pool Menu, in the "Collateral Pool #1" field, using the "Select File" feature, find the collateral file "Pool01_04New", produced in CCFG Run #4 that we just created. This collateral file will be the file that we will use for all of the following cash flow calculation runs of the CCFG. The entry in the field should read:

```
C:\VBABook2\ABS\Mort01\Data\Collat\Pool01_04New
```

   We will not need to change this file designation for the remaining three cash flow calculation runs of the CCFG.
3. Return to the Main Menu. Click on the "Set Amortization Parameters" button. On the CCFG Cash Flow Amortization Parameters Menu, we will now enter the assumptions we need to generate the collateral cash flows of the Geographic Methodology Base Case (GMBC). In the "Specify Methodology" section of the menu in the upper right-hand corner, place an "X" in the "Geographic:" field. Only one of the three fields, "Uniform:", Geographic:", or "Demographic", can be checked at one time. Thus make sure the other fields are blank. In that this run of the CCFG is a Base Case run instead of a Stress Case run, we will also leave the "Apply Stress:" field blank.
4. We have indicated that the model run is to use the Geographic Methodology. We now need to supply the CCFG with a file containing the Geographic Methodology Base Case assumptions. In the "Geographic Specific Prepayment, Default, MVD, and Recovery Lag Curves" section of the menu, we will use the "Select File" button to designate this file. Find the file named:

```
C:\VBABook2\ABS\Mort01\Data\GeoInputs\GeoAssumptionsBase.xlsm
```

for the Base Case run of the model. When we rerun the model for the Stress Case, we will use the following Stress Case assumptions file:

```
C:\VBABook2\ABS\Mort01\Data\GeoInputs\GeoAssumptionsStress.xlsm
```

5. We will not need to supply the CCFG with a file for the field in the "Demographic Methodology Factor Weighting File" section of the model because this is a Geographic Methodology run and therefore no demographic information is required.
6. We will now set the inputs to the "Stress Factors Range—% of Base Prepayment/Default Speeds".
   a. If we are running a Base Case cash flow projection, we can leave all the fields of the stress factor table blank. The CCFG will not read them unless the "Apply Stress:" field in the "Specify Methodology" section of the menu has been checked above. We will however need to enter a name for the Base Case Geographic Methodology cash flows file we are about to create. This file name will be placed in the "Cash Flow Output File:" field in the "Write Cash Flow Output File" section of the menu. We will name the Base Case cash flow file:

```
Scen01GeoBaseCFs
```

b. After we have completed the Base Case cash flow calculations using the settings above, we run the CCFG again to generate the Geographic Methodology Stress Case (GMSC) cash flow projections. For the GMSC cash flow projections, we are required to generate a total of 25 individual cash flow scenarios. These will consist of a combination of stressed default and prepayment assumptions. We will also generate a baseline cash flow that is at 100% for both the prepayment and default assumptions. Therefore we enter "100%" in both the Base Prepayment and Base Default Rates fields of the menu, "5" each for the number of Prepay and Default Steps fields, "25%" for the "Prepayments: Step Increment" field, and "25%" for the "Default: Step Increment" field.

c. We will now enter a name for the GMSC cash flows file we are about to create. We will name the Stress Case cash flow file:

```
Scen01GeoStressCFs
```

When the entries are complete for the GMSC, the CCFG Cash Flow Amortization Parameters Menu should look like Exhibit 20.26.

7. Return to the Main Menu. Click the "Define Report Package" button. On the CCFG Reports & Editor Menu, click the button "Select Reports From CCFG Report Package". This displays the CCFG Model Reports Menu. Upon entering

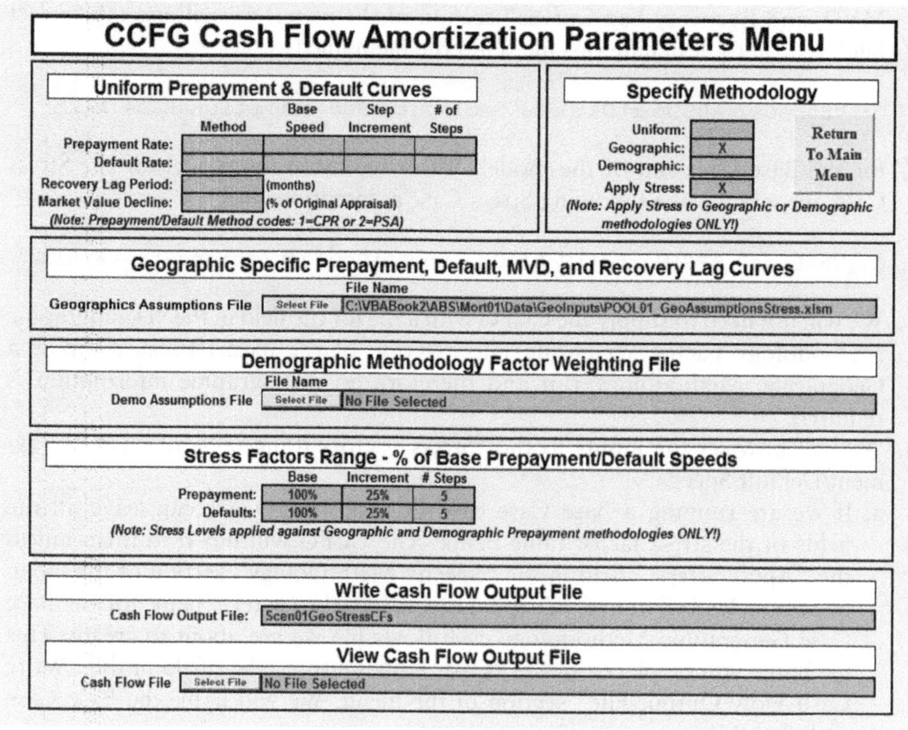

EXHIBIT 20.26 CCFG Cash Flow Amortization Parameters Menu entries for the Stress Case Run #5.

the UserForm, first click on the "CLEAR ALL SELECTIONS" button to clear the form. Here we will select two sets of files. The first set of two files reflect the final geographic concentrations of the portfolio and will be useful to have available if any questions arise concerning geographic dispersion of collateral. Select both the state-level and the MSA-level "Final Concentration Reports" from the "Geographic Reports" section of the UserForm. Next we will select both files in the "Cash Flow Reports" section of the UserForm. These are the "Cash Flow Waterfall Report" and the "Single Scenario Cash Flow Report". When you have completed these selections, the UserForm should look like Exhibit 20.27. Now click on the "RECORD ALL SELECTIONS" button. The UserForm will be retired. On the CCFG Reports Editor & Menu, enter "Run05_" in the "Output Reports Set Prefix" field in the "Select Report Packages" section of the menu.

8. Return to the Main Menu and click the "Run the Model" Button.

Results   The cash flow files that will serve as one of the key input files for the LWM has been produced! We will use the GMBC Cash flow file in LWM Run #1 and the

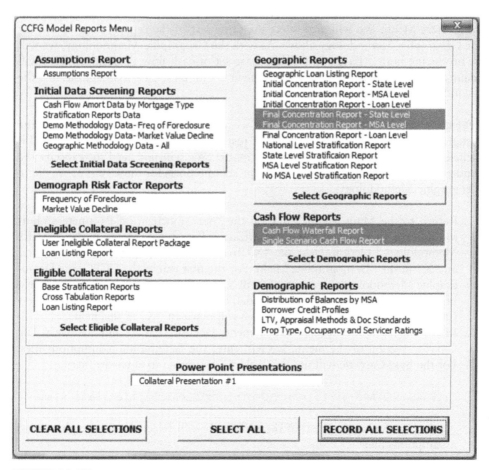

EXHIBIT 20.27   CCFG Model Reports UserForm selections for Run #5

GMSC cash flow file in LWM Run #2. A comparison of the Summary Matrix Report Selections of the Base Case cash flow projections, shown at the upper left, with the each of the 25 Stress Case scenarios is shown in Exhibit 20.28.

In addition to the cash flow file above, we have also produced a set of Single Scenario Summary Reports for the Base Case and each of the 25 Stress Cases. These reports are designed to be single-page summaries that provide a Summary Cash Flow Component Table, an Annual Schedule of Cash Flows, and a graph of the current balance of the pool and the cash flows over time. An example of this report can be seen in Exhibit 20.29. This Single Scenario Report is of the baseline Stress Case Geographic Methodology cash flows, 100% default rate, 100% prepayment rate.

CCFG Run #6: Producing Demographic Methodology Cash Flows

We will now prepare a file of cash flow projections for the eligible collateral pool under the assumptions of the Demographic Prepayment/Default Methodology. As you recall from Chapter 12, the Demographic Methodology draws from both a Demographic Assumptions file and a Geographic Assumptions file. We already have the file pathways for these files entered into the CCFG Cash Flow Amortization Parameters Menu. We will also select the same sets of the reports that we did for the Geographic Methodology above. As with the Geographic Methodology, we will be producing both a Base and a Stress Case set of cash flow projections. This will require two separate runs of the CCFG, the first with Base Case assumptions and the second with Stress Case assumptions.

Preparing the Analysis   The steps that we will take will mirror the steps on the Geographic Methodology CCFG Run #5 just completed. We have some small efficiencies in the Demographic runs of the model. We will not need to respecify the report options, as we will produce the same set of reports for these runs as we did in Geographic Methodology:

1. Return to the Main Menu. Click on the "Set Amortization Parameters" button. On the CCFG Cash Flow Amortization Parameters Menu, in the "Specify Methodology" section, clear the "X" from the "Geographic:" field and enter an "X" in the "Demographic:" field. For the first run of the CCFG, the Demographic Methodology Base Case (DMBC), we will leave the "Apply Stress:" field blank. For the second run of the model, the Demographic Methodology Stress Case (DMSC) cash flow projection, we will place an "X" in this field.
2. In the "Geographic Specific Prepayment, Default, MVD, and Recovery Lag Curves" section of the menu, we will enter the Geographic assumptions files. For the Base Case we will use the "Select File: option to enter the file:

        C:\VBABook2\ABS\Mort01\Data\GeoInputs\GeoAssumptionsBase.xlsm

    For the Stress Case run of the model, we will select the Geographic Stress assumptions file:

        C:\VBABook2\ABS\Mort01\Data\GeoInputs\GeoAssumptionsStress.xlsm

Base Case Geographic

Default Levels	Geographic Methodology
	1
	100.00%
Stress 100.00%	231,735,626
	191,042,818
	422,778,445
	106,385,502
	107,453,187
	313,868,027

Summary Matrix

Collateral Cash Flow Report -- Comparison of Base Case and Stress Case Geographic Cash Flow Results

- Total Scheduled Amortization
- Total Prepayment to Principal
- Total Principal Retired
- Total Defaults of Principal
- Total Recoveries of Principal
- Total Coupon Cashflows

Stress Case Geographic $

Default Levels		Geographic Default Methodology				
		1	2	3	4	5
		100.00%	125.00%	150.00%	175.00%	200.00%
1 Prepay Stress 100.00%		144,374,415	121,470,881	103,543,106	89,244,368	77,645,969
		151,505,961	136,927,042	123,666,059	111,691,047	100,915,983
		295,880,376	258,397,923	227,209,165	200,935,416	178,561,952
		235,283,571	272,766,024	303,954,781	330,228,531	352,601,995
		205,835,962	238,046,924	264,522,241	286,497,756	304,887,812
		249,563,106	226,168,882	205,099,599	186,262,966	169,475,868
2 Prepay Stress 125.00%		128,700,012	109,201,508	93,854,884	81,521,089	71,433,960
		174,135,002	157,616,456	142,655,383	129,165,470	117,024,418
		302,835,015	266,817,964	236,510,267	210,686,559	188,458,368
		228,328,932	264,345,982	294,663,680	320,477,387	342,705,578
		199,348,471	230,162,160	255,780,701	277,302,759	295,527,832
		233,538,422	212,079,086	192,815,582	175,603,995	160,250,081
3 Prepay Stress 150.00%		116,140,793	99,324,352	86,999,068	75,206,128	66,310,014
		193,335,293	175,299,819	159,004,067	144,315,111	131,082,604
		309,476,086	274,624,171	245,003,134	219,521,239	197,392,618
		221,687,861	255,539,776	286,160,812	311,642,708	333,771,329
		193,153,685	222,857,747	247,808,526	268,984,612	287,092,276
		219,619,538	199,872,995	182,177,196	166,360,627	152,229,789
4 Prepay Stress 175.00%		105,881,602	91,207,575	79,495,388	69,936,715	62,000,281
		209,845,236	190,617,455	173,264,140	157,615,047	143,499,145
		315,726,837	281,825,031	252,759,528	227,551,762	205,499,426
		215,437,109	249,338,316	278,404,418	303,612,185	325,664,520
		187,326,750	216,126,787	240,537,265	261,434,981	279,450,413
		207,434,626	189,199,395	172,867,934	158,256,632	145,179,032
5 Prepay Stress 200.00%		97,358,284	84,420,102	74,017,380	65,465,631	58,316,991
		224,208,628	204,038,767	185,840,474	169,414,805	154,576,131
		321,566,913	288,458,868	259,857,855	234,880,437	212,893,122
		209,597,034	242,705,078	271,306,092	296,283,510	318,270,825
		181,887,688	209,932,964	233,891,685	254,555,107	272,491,408
		196,685,913	179,784,665	164,645,788	151,083,187	138,920,525

Stress Case Geographic $ Differences

Default Levels		Geographic Default Methodology				
		1	2	3	4	5
		100.00%	125.00%	150.00%	175.00%	200.00%
1 Prepay Stress 100.00%		87,361,211	110,264,746	128,192,521	142,491,258	154,089,658
		39,536,857	54,115,776	67,376,759	79,351,771	90,126,835
		126,898,068	164,380,522	195,569,279	221,843,029	244,216,492
		(126,898,068)	(164,380,522)	(195,569,279)	(221,843,029)	(244,216,492)
		(98,382,775)	(130,593,736)	(157,069,064)	(179,044,569)	(197,434,625)
		64,304,921	87,699,145	108,768,428	127,605,061	144,392,158
2 Prepay Stress 125.00%		103,035,614	122,534,118	137,880,743	150,214,537	160,301,677
		16,907,816	33,426,362	48,387,435	61,877,348	74,018,400
		119,943,430	155,960,480	186,268,178	212,091,885	234,320,076
		(119,943,430)	(155,960,480)	(186,268,178)	(212,091,885)	(234,320,076)
		(91,895,284)	(122,708,973)	(148,327,514)	(169,849,572)	(188,074,645)
		80,329,605	101,788,941	121,052,445	138,264,031	153,617,946
3 Prepay Stress 150.00%		115,594,833	132,411,275	145,736,559	156,529,498	165,425,613
		(2,292,475)	15,742,999	32,038,751	46,727,707	59,960,214
		113,302,358	148,154,274	177,775,310	203,257,206	225,385,827
		(113,302,358)	(148,154,274)	(177,775,310)	(203,257,206)	(225,385,827)
		(85,700,498)	(115,404,560)	(140,355,338)	(161,531,425)	(179,639,089)
		94,248,489	113,995,032	131,690,830	147,507,400	161,638,238
4 Prepay Stress 175.00%		125,864,025	140,528,051	152,240,238	161,798,911	169,735,345
		(18,802,418)	425,363	17,778,678	33,427,771	47,543,673
		107,051,607	140,953,414	170,018,916	195,226,683	217,279,018
		(107,051,607)	(140,953,414)	(170,018,916)	(195,226,683)	(217,279,018)
		(79,873,563)	(108,673,599)	(133,084,078)	(153,981,794)	(171,997,226)
		106,433,401	124,668,632	141,000,093	155,611,395	168,688,995
5 Prepay Stress 200.00%		134,377,342	147,315,525	157,718,246	166,269,995	173,418,635
		(33,165,810)	(12,995,949)	5,202,344	21,628,013	36,466,687
		101,211,532	134,319,576	162,920,590	187,898,008	209,885,323
		(101,211,532)	(134,319,576)	(162,920,590)	(187,898,008)	(209,885,323)
		(74,434,500)	(102,491,777)	(126,438,498)	(147,101,920)	(165,038,221)
		117,182,114	134,083,362	149,222,239	162,784,840	174,947,502

Stress Case Geographic % Differences

Default Levels		Geographic Default Methodology				
		1	2	3	4	5
		100.00%	125.00%	150.00%	175.00%	200.00%
1 Prepay Stress 100.00%		62.3%	52.4%	44.7%	38.5%	33.5%
		79.3%	71.7%	64.7%	58.5%	52.8%
		70.0%	61.1%	53.7%	47.5%	42.2%
		251.1%	251.7%	280.4%	304.7%	325.3%
		191.6%	221.5%	246.2%	266.6%	283.7%
		79.5%	72.1%	65.3%	59.3%	54.0%
2 Prepay Stress 125.00%		55.5%	47.1%	40.5%	35.2%	30.8%
		91.1%	82.5%	74.7%	67.6%	61.3%
		71.6%	63.1%	55.9%	49.8%	44.6%
		210.7%	243.9%	271.9%	295.7%	316.2%
		185.5%	214.2%	238.0%	258.1%	275.0%
		74.4%	67.6%	61.4%	55.9%	51.1%
3 Prepay Stress 150.00%		50.1%	42.9%	37.1%	32.5%	28.6%
		101.2%	91.8%	83.2%	75.5%	68.6%
		73.2%	65.0%	58.0%	51.9%	46.7%
		204.5%	236.7%	264.0%	287.5%	307.9%
		179.8%	207.4%	230.6%	250.3%	267.2%
		70.0%	63.7%	58.0%	53.0%	48.5%
4 Prepay Stress 175.00%		45.7%	39.4%	34.3%	30.2%	26.8%
		109.8%	99.8%	90.7%	82.5%	75.1%
		74.7%	66.7%	59.8%	53.8%	48.6%
		198.8%	230.0%	256.9%	280.1%	300.5%
		174.3%	201.1%	223.9%	243.3%	260.1%
		66.1%	60.3%	55.1%	50.4%	46.3%
5 Prepay Stress 200.00%		42.0%	36.4%	31.9%	28.3%	25.2%
		117.4%	106.8%	97.3%	88.7%	80.9%
		76.1%	68.2%	61.5%	55.6%	50.4%
		193.4%	223.9%	250.3%	273.4%	293.6%
		169.3%	195.4%	217.7%	236.1%	253.6%
		62.7%	57.3%	52.5%	48.1%	44.3%

EXHIBIT 20.28 Comparison of single GMBC and the 25 scenarios of the GMSC cash flow files

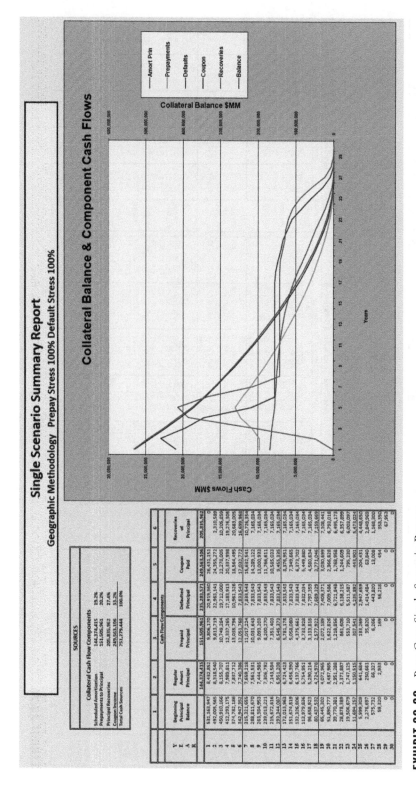

EXHIBIT 20.29 Base Case Single Scenario Report

3. We next need to enter the demographic assumptions files we will use for the DMBC and DMSC runs. In the "Demographic Methodology Factor Weighting File" section of the menu, in the "Demo Assumptions File:" field, we will use the "Select File:" option to enter these files. For the DMBC cash flow projection run, we will use the demographic assumptions file:

```
C:\VBABook2\ABS\Mort01\Data\GeoInputs\DemoMethodInputsBase.xlsm
```

For the DMSC cash flow projection run of the CCFG, we will use the Demographic assumptions file:

```
C:\VBABook2\ABS\Mort01\Data\GeoInputs\DemoMethodInputsStress.xlsm
```

4. In the "Stress Factors Range—% of Base Prepayment/Default Speeds" section of the menu, we will make the same entries as we did when we performed the Geographic Methodology analysis above. For the DMBC cash flow projections, we will leave all the fields of this section blank. For the DMSC cash flow scenario projections. we will enter 100% in both of the "Base" fields, 25% in both of the "Increment" fields, and "5" in both of the "# Steps" fields.
5. In the "Write Cash Flow Output File" section of the menu, in the "Cash Flow Output File:" field, we will enter a file name in which we want to save the DMBC and the DMSC cash flows. We will use the following names:
   - **Base Case:** Scen01DemoBaseCFs
   - **Stress Case:** Scen01DemoStressCFs
6. Return to the Main Menu. Click on the "Define Report Package" button. The CCFG Reports & Editor Menu will now be displayed. For once, we do not have to specify any report options as they will be retained from our earlier Geographic Methodology cash flow runs. All we need to do is enter "Run06_" in the "Output Reports Set Prefix" field in the "Select Report Packages" section of the menu.
7. Return to the Main Menu and click the "Run the Model" button.

Results We have now produced the DMBC and the DMSC cash flow files. A comparison of the DMBC to each of the 25 scenarios of the DMSC can be seen in Exhibit 20.30. We can see in the table that the Demographic Methodology results in significantly greater defaulted principal amounts. However, due to the high credit quality of the collateral and the equity positions of the borrowers, most of the defaulted principal reenters the deal in the form of principal recoveries at the end of the recovery lag period. These recoveries in conjunction with the other principal flows and the coupon income of the portfolio should be sufficient to repay the notes of the Liabilities Structure for the DMBC. Many of the stress scenarios of the DMSC will, however, be another matter.

With the collateral selection process complete and the cash flow projection files available, we are now ready to structure the Liabilities side of the deal!

LIABILITIES SIDE OF THE DEAL

The first step in evaluating the performance of the Liabilities Structure is to establish the inputs that we will use to define the components of the deal.

Summary Matrix

Collateral Cash Flow Report -- Comparison of Base Case and Stress Case Demographic Cash Flow Results

Base Case Demographic

Default Levels	Demographic Methodology
	100.00%
	1
100.00%	116,132,484
	133,108,513
	249,240,997
Stress	281,922,950
100.00%	279,152,790
	229,815,777

Total Scheduled Amortization
Total Prepayment to Principal
Total Principal Retired
Total Defaults of Principal
Total Recoveries of Principal
Total Coupon Cashflows

Stress Case Demographic $
Demographic Default Methodology

Default Levels		1 — 100.00%	2 — 125.00%	3 — 150.00%	4 — 175.00%	5 — 200.00%
1		64,659,614	53,299,192	45,286,765	39,332,457	34,733,837
Prepay		84,882,959	71,224,140	60,814,795	52,669,073	46,160,516
Stress		149,542,573	124,523,332	106,101,560	92,001,530	80,894,354
100.00%		381,621,373	406,640,614	425,062,386	439,162,417	450,269,593
		330,792,481	352,536,015	368,549,276	380,808,340	390,467,318
		155,817,955	134,651,966	118,402,409	105,552,636	95,145,200
2		61,298,879	50,993,192	43,621,273	38,081,681	33,765,043
Prepay		100,468,645	84,858,769	72,850,832	63,379,001	55,759,804
Stress		161,767,524	135,851,961	116,472,105	101,460,682	89,524,847
125.00%		369,396,423	395,311,986	414,691,842	429,703,265	441,639,099
		320,185,382	342,699,844	359,540,102	372,587,251	382,963,591
		149,568,535	129,986,952	114,817,242	102,728,255	92,872,632
3		58,343,594	48,929,611	42,109,782	36,933,478	32,867,198
Prepay		114,565,232	97,337,020	83,972,847	73,365,851	64,763,736
Stress		172,908,827	146,266,631	126,082,629	110,289,328	97,630,933
150.00%		358,255,120	384,897,315	405,081,318	420,874,618	433,533,013
		310,518,813	333,657,965	351,192,123	364,915,169	375,916,873
		143,944,933	125,739,325	111,519,355	100,107,393	90,747,937
4		55,719,275	47,068,368	40,729,337	36,873,922	32,031,479
Prepay		127,402,161	108,820,438	94,297,629	82,685,456	73,236,366
Stress		183,121,436	155,888,796	135,026,965	118,569,378	105,267,835
175.00%		348,042,511	375,275,151	396,136,981	412,604,569	425,896,111
		301,668,279	325,304,743	343,423,599	357,729,381	369,278,900
		138,847,838	121,848,177	108,470,456	97,665,051	88,754,305
5		53,369,263	45,378,287	39,461,539	34,891,740	31,250,613
Prepay		139,160,649	119,439,729	103,920,892	91,439,545	81,232,221
Stress		192,529,912	164,818,016	143,382,431	126,331,285	112,482,835
200.00%		338,634,034	366,345,931	387,781,515	404,832,662	418,681,112
		293,495,647	317,553,891	336,167,202	350,977,163	363,008,436
		134,198,871	118,264,875	105,639,113	95,380,638	86,877,775

Stress Case Demographic $ Differences
Demographic Default Methodology

Default Levels		1 — 100.00%	2 — 125.00%	3 — 150.00%	4 — 175.00%	5 — 200.00%
1		51,472,869	62,833,291	70,845,718	76,800,027	81,398,646
Prepay		48,225,554	61,884,373	72,293,718	80,439,440	86,947,997
Stress		99,698,423	124,717,664	143,139,436	157,239,467	168,346,643
100.00%		(99,698,423)	(124,717,664)	(143,139,436)	(157,239,467)	(168,346,643)
		(61,639,691)	(73,383,225)	(89,396,486)	(101,665,550)	(111,314,528)
		73,997,822	95,163,810	111,413,368	124,263,140	134,670,576
2		54,833,605	65,139,292	72,511,211	78,050,803	82,367,440
Prepay		32,639,868	48,249,744	60,257,681	69,729,512	77,348,709
Stress		87,473,473	113,389,036	132,768,892	147,780,315	159,716,149
125.00%		(87,473,473)	(113,389,036)	(132,768,892)	(147,780,315)	(159,716,149)
		(41,032,592)	(63,547,054)	(80,387,312)	(93,434,461)	(103,810,801)
		80,247,242	99,828,825	114,998,534	127,087,522	136,943,144
3		57,788,889	67,202,873	74,022,702	79,199,006	83,265,285
Prepay		18,543,281	35,771,493	49,135,667	59,752,662	68,344,778
Stress		76,332,170	102,974,365	123,158,368	138,951,668	151,610,063
150.00%		(76,332,170)	(102,974,365)	(123,158,368)	(138,951,668)	(151,610,063)
		(31,366,023)	(54,505,175)	(72,039,333)	(85,762,379)	(96,764,083)
		85,870,843	104,076,451	118,296,422	129,708,383	139,067,839
4		60,413,209	69,064,126	75,403,147	80,258,561	84,101,005
Prepay		5,706,352	24,288,075	38,810,884	50,423,057	59,872,157
Stress		66,119,561	93,352,201	114,214,031	130,681,619	143,973,162
175.00%		(66,119,561)	(93,352,201)	(114,214,031)	(130,681,619)	(143,973,162)
		(22,505,489)	(46,151,953)	(64,270,808)	(78,576,591)	(90,126,110)
		90,967,938	107,967,599	121,345,321	132,150,726	141,061,472
5		62,763,220	70,754,196	76,670,944	81,240,743	84,881,871
Prepay		(6,052,136)	13,668,785	29,187,621	41,668,968	51,876,292
Stress		56,711,084	84,422,981	105,858,565	122,909,712	136,758,162
200.00%		(56,711,085)	(84,422,981)	(105,858,565)	(122,909,712)	(136,758,162)
		(14,342,857)	(38,400,801)	(57,014,412)	(71,824,373)	(83,855,646)
		95,616,906	111,550,902	124,176,664	134,435,138	142,936,002

Stress Case Demographic % Differences
Demographic Default Methodology

Default Levels		1 — 100.00%	2 — 125.00%	3 — 150.00%	4 — 175.00%	5 — 200.00%
1		55.7%	45.9%	39.0%	33.9%	29.9%
Prepay		63.8%	53.5%	45.7%	39.6%	34.7%
Stress		60.0%	50.0%	42.6%	36.9%	32.5%
100.00%		135.4%	144.2%	150.8%	155.8%	159.7%
		118.5%	126.3%	132.0%	136.4%	139.9%
		67.8%	58.6%	51.5%	45.9%	41.4%
2		52.8%	43.9%	37.6%	32.8%	29.1%
Prepay		75.5%	63.8%	54.7%	47.5%	41.9%
Stress		64.9%	54.5%	46.7%	40.7%	35.9%
125.00%		131.0%	140.2%	147.1%	152.4%	156.7%
		114.7%	122.8%	128.8%	133.5%	137.2%
		65.1%	56.6%	50.0%	44.7%	40.4%
3		50.2%	42.1%	36.3%	31.8%	28.3%
Prepay		86.1%	73.1%	63.1%	55.1%	48.7%
Stress		69.4%	58.7%	50.6%	44.3%	39.2%
150.00%		127.1%	136.5%	143.7%	149.3%	153.8%
		111.2%	119.5%	125.8%	130.7%	134.7%
		62.6%	54.7%	48.5%	43.6%	39.5%
4		48.0%	40.5%	35.1%	30.9%	27.6%
Prepay		95.7%	81.8%	70.8%	62.1%	55.0%
Stress		73.5%	62.5%	54.2%	47.6%	42.2%
175.00%		123.5%	133.1%	140.5%	146.4%	151.1%
		108.1%	116.5%	123.0%	128.1%	132.3%
		60.4%	53.0%	47.2%	42.5%	38.6%
5		46.0%	39.1%	34.0%	30.0%	26.9%
Prepay		104.5%	89.7%	78.1%	68.7%	61.0%
Stress		77.2%	66.1%	57.5%	50.7%	45.1%
200.00%		120.1%	129.9%	137.5%	143.6%	148.5%
		105.1%	113.8%	120.4%	125.7%	130.0%
		58.4%	51.5%	46.0%	41.5%	37.6%

EXHIBIT 20.30 Comparison of Demographic Base Case and Stress Cases

924

Setting Up the Structural Inputs

The structure of the deal will consist of five bond tranches as described in Chapters 14 to 16. Refer back to the layout of the Bond and Structural Inputs Menu in Exhibit 14.3, where the inputs of the structure are available in a single-page summary.

Preparing the Analysis   We will use the inputs that we described in Chapter 14. As we described earlier in this chapter, the payment pattern of all of the mortgages in our collateral pool are Standard floating rate mortgages whose coupon rates are indexed to LIBOR. Our financing index is also LIBOR. The Collateral Index is generally three-month or one-year LIBOR and the financing index is one-month LIBOR, so there may be a certain amount of rate risk between the two different LIBOR terms, but we will ignore it for this run of the LWM. What is more important is that we do not have any fixed rate collateral or any hybrid adjustable rate mortgages that begin their lives with a fixed coupon period. We can thus forgo the use of an interest rate swap. We will use the inputs as seen in Exhibit 20.31.

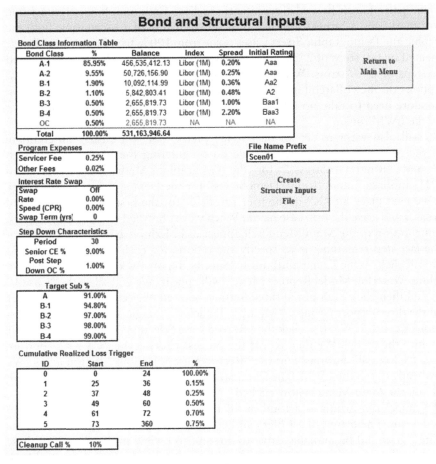

EXHIBIT 20.31   LWM Bond and Structural Inputs Menu

We will enter these criteria into the Structure Inputs Menu and then create a file for use when we run the model. We will name this file "Scen01_StructInputs.xlsm". Using the guidelines of the organization of model environment directories, we will place this file in the subdirectory "C:\VBABook2\ABS\Mort01\Data\Structure". It will be available for use by the model by entering it in the Main Menu. The other inputs needed, the collateral cash flow files, and the prefix of the output files created by each of the model runs can then be matched to the structure file in any combination we choose.

LWM Run: Running the Structure Using Geographic and Demographic Cash Flow Files

We are now ready to set up and run the LWM!

Preparing the Analysis With a file created containing the Structural Inputs and a set of four collateral cash flow files, two using the Geographic Methodology and the other two using the Demographic Methodology, we have everything we need. If you recall, one pair of cash flow files represents the Base Case cash flow set consisting of one scenario and a Stress Case cash flow set consisting of 25 scenarios. Both the Geographic and Demographic Stress Cases range from 100% base Prepayment Rates, incremented by five steps of 25% stress, and 100% base Default Rates, incremented by five steps of 25% stress. When we run the LWM using these files, any Stress assumptions on the collateral are already present and expressed in the cash flows. We therefore need to take no additional steps except to specify the file names for each of the LWM runs.

We will also want to set an output file prefix that will clearly differentiate one of the runs from the other. This we do by entering the names "Run01Geo Base_" and "Run01GeoStress_" for the Geographic Methodology cases and "Run01DemoBase_" and "Run01DemoStress" for the Demographic Methodology cases. We next place an "X" in the four run fields for the first, second, third, and fourth cases and leave the fifth case blank. When we are finished making these entries, the configuration of the Main Menu will appear as in Exhibit 20.32.

The last step remaining is to specify the reports for each of the cases. To do this we will click on the CommandButton "Specify Report Package". The UserForm "Liabilities Waterfall Model Reports Menu" will appear. We will select the "Case 1" Button and then click each of the three buttons marked "Select All Reports" under each of the three Report Groups, "Multiple Tranche", "Single Tranche", and "Miscellaneous Reports". We then click the "Record Case Selections" button to enter our choices into the model. We then repeat the process clicking the "Case #2" button, the three "Select All" buttons, and the "Record Case Selections" button again. We are now ready to run the LWM. The CommandButton "Run the Liabilities Waterfall Model" on the Main Menu is now clicked.

The model run produces a total of 48 reports, 12 each for the four cases in the model run. The listing of all files can be found later in the chapter in "On the Web Site". It would be unmanageable to attempt to review in detail each of these reports for all of the four case runs we have just completed. We will instead look at the annual cash flows and balances of the tranches in a summary statement. We

Liabilities Waterfall Model Main Menu

Run The Liabilities Waterfall Model

Display Structure Input Page

Display Collateral Cash Flow Page

Display Structure Perfromance Page

Display Liability Waterfall Page

Case | **Enter Cash Flow, Structure Input, and Output Prefixs for Each Case Below**

Run?

1			
X	CF File	Select File	C:\VBABook2\ABS\Mort01\Data\CFs\Run05_Scen01GeoBaseCFs.xlsm
	Liabilities File	Select File	C:\VBABook2\ABS\Mort01\Data\Structure\Scen01_StructInputs.xlsm
	Output Prefix		Run01GeoBase_

2			
X	CF File	Select File	C:\VBABook2\ABS\Mort01\Data\CFs\Run05_Scen01GeoStressCFs.xlsm
	Liabilities File	Select File	C:\VBABook2\ABS\Mort01\Data\Structure\Scen01_StructInputs.xlsm
	Output Prefix		Run01GeoStress_

3			
X	CF File	Select File	C:\VBABook2\ABS\Mort01\Data\CFs\Run06_Scen01DemoBaseCFs.xlsm
	Liabilities File	Select File	C:\VBABook2\ABS\Mort01\Data\Structure\Scen01_StructInputs.xlsm
	Output Prefix		Run01DemoBase_

4			
X	CF File	Select File	C:\VBABook2\ABS\Mort01\Data\CFs\Run06_Scen01DemoStressCFs.xlsm
	Liabilities File	Select File	C:\VBABook2\ABS\Mort01\Data\Structure\Scen01_StructInputs.xlsm
	Output Prefix		Run01DemoStress_

5			
	CF File	Select File	No File Selected
	Liabilities File	Select File	No File Selected
	Output Prefix		

Report Selection User Form

Specify Report Package

EXHIBIT 20.32 Main Menu Liabilities Waterfall Model

will choose for the two Stress Cases the most punitive of the Stress Cases, 200% Prepayment Rate and 200% Default Rate.

Results: Geographic Base Case   The first set of results that we will review is the Geographic Methodology Base Case (GMBC). This case is the most generous case of the four that we will examine. Its aggregate collateral cash flows are:

- Total scheduled principal amortization: $231.7 million
- Total prepayments of principal: $191.0 million
- Total recoveries of defaulted principal: $107.5 million
- Total coupon payments: $313.9 million
- **Total collateral cash flows:**   **$844.1 million**

In the Base Case Geographic Methodology, the CCFG projects a total of $108.4 million in principal defaults.

In the GMBC, the principal balances of all of the Bond Classes are fully repaid. A total of $86.9 million in coupon is also paid. There are no losses taken by any of the subordinate tranches of the deal. Both the "A-1" and "A-2" classes receive large ongoing principal payments throughout the early life of the deal, which serve to immunize them in a quick and efficient manner. See Exhibit 20.33.

Results: Geographic Stress Cases   The second set of results that we will review is the Geographic Methodology Stress Case (GMSC). This case is by far the more forgiving of the two Stress Cases, as you will see when we review the Demographic Stress Case. Of the 25 scenarios that comprise the GMSC, the one presented is the most severe. In this Stress Case there is a modeled 200% Prepayment and 200% Default Level rate. The aggregate collateral cash flows are:

- Total scheduled principal amortization: $ 58.4 million
- Total prepayments of principal: $154.8 million
- Total recoveries of defaulted principal: $272.5 million
- Total coupon payments: $139.0 million
- **Total collateral cash flows:**   **$624.6 million**

In the GMSC, the CCFG projects a total of $318.3 million in principal defaults.

In the GMSC, the principal outstanding for all classes is repaid with no net losses. The Class "A-1" and "A-2" notes receive principal payments over the first 13 years of the deal. The Class "B" notes are all written down to zero in year 1 of the deal but then repaid through the use of recovered principal cash flows starting in year 5 for Class "B-1" to year 9 for the Class "B-4" note holders. An aggregate of $36.7 million of debt service is paid to all tranches with the Class "A" notes receiving a full yield and the Class "B" notes receiving coupon payments for only a portion of year 1 before they are written down. As there are no net principal losses, the structure could be deemed "stunned" as opposed to "wounded" or "dead on arrival." Payments are made to the Class "A" tranche holders and the "B" tranche holders wait for repayment predicated on the arrival of recovered defaulted principal through property liquidation and recapture. This will *not* be the case when we visit the Demographic Stress scenario! See Exhibit 20.34.

Base Case Geographic Methodology

Tranche	Beginning Balances A-1	A-2	B1	B-2	B-3	B-4	Principal Payments A-1	A-2	B1	B-2	B-3	B-4	Coupon Payments A-1	A-2	B1	B-2	B-3	B-4	Principal Losses B1	B-2	B-3	B-4
1	456,535,412	50,726,157	10,092,115	5,842,803	2,655,820	2,655,820	24,069,377	2,674,375	0	0	0	0	6,326,538	727,700	159,455	99,328	88,173	90,829	0	0	0	0
2	432,466,035	48,051,782	10,092,115	5,842,803	2,655,820	2,655,820	25,146,276	2,794,031	0	0	0	0	5,978,350	687,651	159,455	99,328	88,173	90,829	0	0	0	0
3	407,319,759	45,257,751	10,092,115	5,842,803	2,655,820	2,655,820	26,720,005	2,968,889	0	0	0	0	5,611,544	645,459	159,455	99,328	88,173	90,829	0	0	0	0
4	380,599,753	42,288,861	10,092,115	5,842,803	2,655,820	2,655,820	28,056,095	3,117,344	0	0	0	0	5,220,624	600,494	159,455	99,328	88,173	90,829	0	0	0	0
5	352,543,659	39,171,518	10,092,115	5,842,803	2,655,820	2,655,820	27,903,209	3,100,357	0	0	0	0	4,820,681	554,491	159,455	99,328	88,173	90,829	0	0	0	0
6	324,640,450	36,071,161	10,092,115	5,842,803	2,655,820	2,655,820	24,529,243	2,725,471	0	0	0	0	4,445,782	511,369	159,455	99,328	88,173	90,829	0	0	0	0
7	300,111,207	33,345,690	10,092,115	5,842,803	2,655,820	2,655,820	20,966,909	2,329,657	0	0	0	0	4,121,130	474,027	159,455	99,328	88,173	90,829	0	0	0	0
8	279,144,298	31,016,033	10,092,115	5,842,803	2,655,820	2,655,820	19,612,926	2,179,214	0	0	0	0	3,835,362	441,157	159,455	99,328	88,173	90,829	0	0	0	0
9	259,531,372	28,836,819	10,092,115	5,842,803	2,655,820	2,655,820	18,912,969	2,101,441	0	0	0	0	3,561,448	409,650	159,455	99,328	88,173	90,829	0	0	0	0
10	240,618,403	26,735,378	10,092,115	5,842,803	2,655,820	2,655,820	18,240,380	2,026,709	0	0	0	0	3,297,292	379,266	159,455	99,328	88,173	90,829	0	0	0	0
11	222,378,022	24,708,669	10,092,115	5,842,803	2,655,820	2,655,820	17,592,687	1,954,743	590,475	341,854	155,388	310,777	3,042,521	349,961	156,429	97,443	85,256	87,382	0	0	0	0
12	204,785,335	22,753,926	9,501,639	5,500,949	2,500,431	2,345,043	16,967,281	1,885,253	787,249	455,776	207,171	414,341	2,796,800	321,698	144,388	89,942	72,338	73,663	0	0	0	0
13	187,818,054	20,868,673	8,714,391	5,045,174	2,293,261	1,930,702	16,361,324	1,817,925	759,133	439,498	199,772	399,544	2,559,830	294,440	132,154	82,321	59,172	59,726	0	0	0	0
14	171,456,730	19,050,748	7,955,257	4,605,675	2,093,489	1,531,158	15,771,587	1,753,399	731,771	423,657	192,571	385,143	2,331,354	268,160	120,358	74,973	46,478	46,286	0	0	0	0
15	155,685,144	17,298,349	7,223,487	4,182,019	1,900,918	1,146,018	15,194,173	1,688,241	704,980	408,146	185,521	371,042	2,111,167	242,894	108,991	67,893	34,244	33,338	0	0	0	0
16	140,490,971	15,610,108	6,518,507	3,773,872	1,715,396	774,973	14,623,968	1,624,885	678,523	392,829	178,559	357,118	1,899,126	218,444	98,044	61,074	22,463	20,867	0	0	0	0
17	125,867,007	13,985,223	5,839,983	3,381,043	1,536,838	417,886	14,053,313	1,561,479	652,046	377,500	171,591	343,182	1,695,173	194,985	87,515	54,515	11,130	8,872	0	0	0	0
18	111,813,694	12,423,744	5,187,937	3,003,542	1,365,247	74,673	13,468,211	1,496,468	624,899	361,783	418,668	74,673	1,499,394	172,465	77,408	48,219	2,225	400	0	0	0	0
19	98,345,483	10,927,276	4,563,038	2,641,759	946,579	0	12,830,307	1,425,590	595,301	344,648	469,975	0	1,312,187	150,932	67,743	42,198	952	0	0	0	0	0
20	85,515,177	9,501,686	3,967,737	2,297,111	476,604	0	11,732,525	1,303,614	544,366	315,159	429,763	0	1,135,813	130,645	58,637	36,526	148	0	0	0	0	0
21	73,782,651	8,198,072	3,423,371	1,981,952	46,841	0	10,666,384	1,185,154	494,899	630,389	46,841	0	977,736	112,463	50,477	29,085	0	0	0	0	0	0
22	63,116,267	7,012,919	2,928,472	1,351,562	0	0	10,183,358	1,131,484	472,488	645,562	0	0	829,394	95,400	42,818	17,895	0	0	0	0	0	0
23	52,932,910	5,881,434	2,455,984	705,000	0	0	9,672,634	1,074,737	448,791	614,136	0	0	688,071	79,144	35,522	7,152	0	0	0	0	0	0
24	43,260,173	4,806,697	2,007,192	90,864	0	0	9,105,735	1,011,748	909,766	90,864	0	0	554,312	63,759	25,641	187	0	0	0	0	0	0
25	34,154,540	3,794,949	1,097,426	0	0	0	8,326,478	925,164	914,998	0	0	0	429,645	49,419	10,572	0	0	0	0	0	0	0
26	25,828,063	2,869,785	182,429	0	0	0	8,161,921	906,880	182,439	0	0	0	313,729	36,086	437	0	0	0	0	0	0	0
27	17,666,141	1,962,905	0	0	0	0	7,554,997	839,400	0	0	0	0	200,681	23,083	0	0	0	0	0	0	0	0
28	10,111,544	1,123,505	0	0	0	0	6,546,052	727,339	0	0	0	0	99,577	11,454	0	0	0	0	0	0	0	0
29	3,565,492	396,166	0	0	0	0	3,565,492	396,166	0	0	0	0	18,536	2,132	0	0	0	0	0	0	0	0
30	0	0	0	0	0	0	0	0	0	0	0	0	0	0	0	0	0	0	0	0	0	0
Totals							456,535,412	50,726,157	10,092,115	5,842,803	2,655,820	2,655,820	71,713,796	8,248,770	2,811,688	1,702,698	1,216,140	1,238,825	0	0	0	2,454,965
Deal Totals							528,508,127						86,931,918									

EXHIBIT 20.33 Base Case Geographic Methodology

Stress Case Geographic Methodology - 200% Prepayment Stress, 200% Default Stress

Tranche	Beginning Balances						Principal Payments						Coupon Payments						Principal Losses			
	A-1	A-2	B1	B-2	B-3	B-4	A-1	A-2	B1	B-2	B-3	B-4	A-1	A-2	B1	B-2	B-3	B-4	B1	B-2	B-3	B-4
1	456,535,412	50,726,157	10,092,115	5,842,803	2,655,820	2,655,820	39,895,265	4,432,807	0	0	0	0	6,217,278	715,133	131,459	51,225	19,611	19,611	10,092,115	5,842,803	2,655,820	2,655,820
2	416,640,147	46,293,350	0	0	0	0	39,951,515	4,439,057	0	0	0	0	5,665,518	651,668	0	0	0	0	0	0	0	0
3	376,688,632	41,854,292	0	0	0	0	51,239,695	5,693,299	0	0	0	0	5,022,811	577,741	0	0	0	0	0	0	0	0
4	325,448,937	36,160,993	0	0	0	0	65,778,732	7,308,748	0	0	0	0	4,200,945	483,207	0	0	0	0	0	0	0	0
5	259,670,205	28,852,245	0	0	0	0	64,169,827	7,129,981	0	0	0	0	3,244,992	373,250	0	0	0	0	-1,630,766	0	0	0
6	195,500,378	21,722,264	0	0	0	0	47,909,373	5,323,264	0	0	0	0	2,448,245	281,606	0	0	0	0	-7,305,842	0	0	0
7	147,591,005	16,399,001	0	0	0	0	34,418,679	3,824,298	0	0	0	0	1,852,754	213,110	0	0	0	0	-1,155,507	0	0	0
8	113,172,327	12,574,705	0	0	0	0	25,475,683	2,830,631	0	0	0	0	1,438,379	165,447	0	0	0	0	0	-5,145,479	0	0
9	87,696,644	9,744,072	0	0	0	0	23,125,288	2,569,476	0	0	0	0	1,092,123	125,620	0	0	0	0	0	-697,324	-2,655,820	-1,884,795
10	64,571,356	7,174,585	0	0	0	0	20,941,767	2,326,863	0	0	0	0	778,151	89,506	0	0	0	0	0	0	0	-771,025
11	43,629,590	4,847,732	0	0	0	0	18,916,194	2,101,799	0	0	0	0	494,123	56,836	0	0	0	0	0	0	0	0
12	24,713,896	2,745,933	0	0	0	0	16,886,328	1,876,259	0	0	0	0	238,562	27,440	0	0	0	0	0	0	0	0
13	7,827,067	869,674	0	0	0	0	7,827,067	869,674	0	0	0	0	32,842	3,778	0	0	0	0	0	0	0	0
14	0	0	0	0	0	0	0	0	0	0	0	0	0	0	0	0	0	0	0	0	0	0
15	0	0	0	0	0	0	0	0	0	0	0	0	0	0	0	0	0	0	0	0	0	0
16	0	0	0	0	0	0	0	0	0	0	0	0	0	0	0	0	0	0	0	0	0	0
17	0	0	0	0	0	0	0	0	0	0	0	0	0	0	0	0	0	0	0	0	0	0
18	0	0	0	0	0	0	0	0	0	0	0	0	0	0	0	0	0	0	0	0	0	0
19	0	0	0	0	0	0	0	0	0	0	0	0	0	0	0	0	0	0	0	0	0	0
20	0	0	0	0	0	0	0	0	0	0	0	0	0	0	0	0	0	0	0	0	0	0
21	0	0	0	0	0	0	0	0	0	0	0	0	0	0	0	0	0	0	0	0	0	0
22	0	0	0	0	0	0	0	0	0	0	0	0	0	0	0	0	0	0	0	0	0	0
23	0	0	0	0	0	0	0	0	0	0	0	0	0	0	0	0	0	0	0	0	0	0
24	0	0	0	0	0	0	0	0	0	0	0	0	0	0	0	0	0	0	0	0	0	0
25	0	0	0	0	0	0	0	0	0	0	0	0	0	0	0	0	0	0	0	0	0	0
26	0	0	0	0	0	0	0	0	0	0	0	0	0	0	0	0	0	0	0	0	0	0
27	0	0	0	0	0	0	0	0	0	0	0	0	0	0	0	0	0	0	0	0	0	0
28	0	0	0	0	0	0	0	0	0	0	0	0	0	0	0	0	0	0	0	0	0	0
29	0	0	0	0	0	0	0	0	0	0	0	0	0	0	0	0	0	0	0	0	0	0
30	0	0	0	0	0	0	0	0	0	0	0	0	0	0	0	0	0	0	0	0	0	0
Totals							456,535,412	50,726,157	0	0	0	0	32,726,723	3,764,341	131,459	51,225	19,611	19,611	0	0	0	0
Deal Totals							507,261,569						36,712,971						0			

EXHIBIT 20.34 Stress Case Geographic Methodology

Results: Demographic Methodology Base Case   The third set of results that we will review is the Demographic Methodology Base Case (DMBC). The DMBC is a much more rigorous Base case that that of the Geographic Methodology. You will note that the DMBC is only slightly better, $12.7 million in total collateral cash flows, than the Stress Case of the Geographic Methodology. Its aggregate collateral cash flows are:

- Total scheduled principal amortization: $ 64.9 million
- Total prepayments of principal: $ 85.2 million
- Total recoveries of defaulted principal: $331.0 million
- Total coupon payments: $156.2 million
- **Total collateral cash flows:** **$637.2 million**

In the Base Case Geographic Methodology, the CCFG projects a total of $331.0 million in principal defaults.

The DMBC scenario is considerably less forgiving than the GMBC and only marginally more robust that the GMSC! Scheduled amortization of principal and principal prepayments collateral cash flows are a fraction of those in the Geographic Methodology Base Case: $150 million total versus $423 million total, thus one methodology produces less than 40% of the cash flows of the other.

In this scenario, the principal balances of all tranches are repaid. The subordinate tranches experience catastrophic write-down activity early in the life of the deal (year 1, in fact) but are later repaid through the realization of the $331 million of recovered principal. In aggregate, all tranches receive $43.2 million in debt service payments, less than half of the monies received in the Geographic Base Case. The Class "A-1" and "A-2" tranches are retired quickly on the basis of recoveries and the redirection of cash flows from the subordinate "B" class tranches.

There are no losses to the "B-1" tranche. The "B-2" tranche incurs an initial loss of $4.14 million in year 1 but is repaid by recoveries of defaulted principal in years 2 and 3. The "B-3" and "B-4" tranches suffer 100% losses in the first year but are then paid in full, again as with the "B-2" tranche by recoveries of defaulted principal in year 3. See Exhibit 20.35.

Results: Demographic Methodology Stress Cases   The last set of results that we will review is the Demographic Methodology Stress Case (DMSC), of 200% Prepayment and 200% Default Stress levels. The DMSC is by far the most parsimonious case of the four cash flow cases we have yet examined. Its aggregate collateral cash flows are:

- Total scheduled principal amortization: $ 30.6 million
- Total prepayments of principal: $ 79.2 million
- Total recoveries of defaulted principal: $360.8 million
- Total coupon payments: $ 85.2 million
- **Total collateral cash flows:** **$555.8 million**

In the GMBC, the CCFG projects a total of $360.8 million in principal defaults.

In respect to the performance of the liabilities structure both the principal balance of the Class "A-1" and "A-2" tranches are fully repaid. All four "B" class tranches

Base Case Demographic Methodology

Tranche	Beginning Balances						Principal Payments						Coupon Payments						Principal Losses			
	A-1	A-2	B1	B-2	B-3	B-4	A-1	A-2	B1	B-2	B-3	B-4	A-1	A-2	B1	B-2	B-3	B-4	B1	B-2	B-3	B-4
1	456,535,412	50,726,157	10,092,115	5,842,603	2,655,820	2,655,820	33,555,895	3,728,433	0	0	0	0	6,270,196	731,220	159,455	85,132	30,812	30,812	0	4,339,232	2,655,820	2,655,820
2	422,979,517	46,997,724	10,092,115	1,703,572	0	0	46,208,375	5,134,264	0	0	0	0	5,706,699	656,404	159,455	25,645	0	0	0	-2,985,428	-2,655,820	
3	376,771,142	41,863,460	10,092,115	1,490,817	0	0	44,311,066	4,923,452	0	0	0	0	5,061,151	582,151	159,455	25,344	0	0	0	-1,153,814	-2,655,820	
4	332,460,077	36,940,009	10,092,115	1,490,817	0	0	45,648,033	5,072,004	0	0	0	0	4,423,088	508,759	159,455	25,344	0	0	0	0	0	0
5	286,812,044	31,868,005	10,092,115	1,490,817	0	0	45,930,627	5,103,403	0	0	0	0	3,773,210	434,008	159,455	25,344	0	0	0	0	0	0
6	240,881,417	26,764,602	10,092,115	1,490,817	0	0	41,162,920	4,573,658	0	0	0	0	3,143,175	361,539	159,455	25,344	0	0	0	0	0	0
7	199,718,496	22,190,944	10,092,115	1,490,817	0	0	38,135,249	4,237,250	0	0	0	0	2,591,954	298,186	159,455	25,344	0	0	0	0	0	0
8	161,583,248	17,953,694	10,092,115	1,490,817	0	0	37,787,644	4,198,605	0	0	0	0	2,046,037	235,342	159,455	25,344	0	0	0	0	0	0
9	123,795,604	13,755,089	10,092,115	1,490,817	0	0	35,605,755	3,956,195	0	0	0	0	1,523,385	175,225	159,455	25,344	0	0	0	0	0	0
10	88,190,049	9,798,894	10,092,115	1,490,817	0	0	32,472,640	3,608,071	0	0	0	0	1,036,740	119,249	159,455	25,344	0	0	0	0	0	0
11	55,717,409	6,190,823	10,092,115	1,490,817	0	0	28,153,196	3,128,133	0	0	0	0	600,085	69,254	159,455	25,344	0	0	0	0	0	0
12	27,564,213	3,062,690	10,092,115	1,490,817	0	0	20,801,884	2,311,320	0	1,490,817	0	0	246,108	28,308	159,455	25,344	0	0	0	0	0	0
13	6,762,329	751,370	10,092,115	1,490,817	0	0	6,762,329	751,370	3,109,166	1,490,817	0	0	24,129	2,775	153,013	16,206	0	0	0	0	0	0
14	0	0	6,982,949	0	0	0	0	0	5,817,694	0	0	0	0	0	62,437	0	0	0	0	0	0	0
15	0	0	1,165,255	0	0	0	0	0	1,165,255	0	0	0	0	0	8,859	0	0	0	0	0	0	0
16	0	0	0	0	0	0	0	0	0	0	0	0	0	0	0	0	0	0	0	0	0	0
17	0	0	0	0	0	0	0	0	0	0	0	0	0	0	0	0	0	0	0	0	0	0
18	0	0	0	0	0	0	0	0	0	0	0	0	0	0	0	0	0	0	0	0	0	0
19	0	0	0	0	0	0	0	0	0	0	0	0	0	0	0	0	0	0	0	0	0	0
20	0	0	0	0	0	0	0	0	0	0	0	0	0	0	0	0	0	0	0	0	0	0
21	0	0	0	0	0	0	0	0	0	0	0	0	0	0	0	0	0	0	0	0	0	0
22	0	0	0	0	0	0	0	0	0	0	0	0	0	0	0	0	0	0	0	0	0	0
23	0	0	0	0	0	0	0	0	0	0	0	0	0	0	0	0	0	0	0	0	0	0
24	0	0	0	0	0	0	0	0	0	0	0	0	0	0	0	0	0	0	0	0	0	0
25	0	0	0	0	0	0	0	0	0	0	0	0	0	0	0	0	0	0	0	0	0	0
26	0	0	0	0	0	0	0	0	0	0	0	0	0	0	0	0	0	0	0	0	0	0
27	0	0	0	0	0	0	0	0	0	0	0	0	0	0	0	0	0	0	0	0	0	0
28	0	0	0	0	0	0	0	0	0	0	0	0	0	0	0	0	0	0	0	0	0	0
29	0	0	0	0	0	0	0	0	0	0	0	0	0	0	0	0	0	0	0	0	0	0
30	0	0	0	0	0	0	0	0	0	0	0	0	0	0	0	0	0	0	0	0	0	0
Totals							456,535,412	50,726,157	10,092,115	1,490,817	0	0	36,447,959	4,192,371	2,132,774	380,422	30,812	30,812	0	0	0	0
Deal Totals						518,844,501												43,215,149				

EXHIBIT 20.35   Base Case Demographic Methodology

932

are completely written down in the first year. By year 10 of the deal, all of the previously written-down principal has been repaid to the Class "B-1" tranche. Partial repayments to the Class "B-2" tranche begin in year 10. This tranche is never fully repaid and has a future value loss of $1.7 million of its original principal balance of $5.8 million. Both the Class "B-3" and "B-4" tranches are written down in full in year 1 without any future repayment, resulting in 100% losses for both tranches. A total of $29.6 million in debt service is paid to the holders of all tranches but less than $120,000 is paid to the Class "B" tranche holders in aggregate. All in all, the DMSC is a very stringent scenario that pulverizes the Class "B" tranches and strips the Class "A" tranches of most of their yield. See Exhibit 20.36.

PREPARING A POWERPOINT PRESENTATION ABOUT GEOGRAPHIC CONCENTRATION

The last exercise of the chapter will be to construct a PowerPoint presentation of the demographics of the California collateral. To accomplish this task we need to revisit the CCFG. There we will prepare a total of seven files: two containing national level data and an additional five containing California specific collateral data.

Report Preparation

The process for the production of a state-specific PowerPoint presentation is, as you will recall from Chapter 19, a twofold process. First we must specify and run the national file needed, then we must specify and run the state-specific information. As this material has been exhaustively described in the previous chapter, we will forgo a step-by-step description of the process at this time. We will, however, direct the reader to the appropriate sections of Chapter 19. For the less adventurous we will provide the files themselves based in the final collateral pool selected above.

Producing the Base Files If you wish to produce the source files of the report yourself, you are directed to Chapter 19, in the "Data Requirements" section. You can follow the instruction steps in the sections "National Level Files" and "State Level Files" to produce the required input files for the CCFG. If you have already done so while reading Chapter 19, congratulations! You are ready to go.

For the less adventurous among you, the files can be found on the Web site. You will need to download them and place them in the following directory:

```
C:\VBABook2\ABS\Mort01\Output
```

You will need the following national level data files: "National_CrossTabs" and "National_StateInitGeoConcenReport".

You will also need the following California files: "CA_CrossTabs", "CA_MSAInitGeoConcenReport", "CA_PortPresentReport_Credit", "CA_PortPresentReport_Valuation", and "CA_UserStratRep".

Stress Case Demographic Methodology - 200% Prepayment Stress, 200% Default Stress

Tranche	Beginning Balances						Principal Payments						Coupon Payments						Principal Losses			
	A-1	A-2	B1	B-2	B-3	B-4	A-1	A-2	B1	B-2	B-3	B-4	A-1	A-2	B1	B-2	B-3	B-4	B1	B-2	B-3	B-4
1	456,535,412	50,726,157	10,092,115	5,842,803	2,655,820	2,655,820	38,765,018	4,307,224	0	0	0	0	6,322,108	715,689	69,843	27,766	11,617	11,617	10,092,115	5,842,803	2,655,820	2,655,820
2	417,770,394	46,418,933	0	0	0	0	40,193,511	4,465,946	0	0	0	0	5,689,767	654,457	0	0	0	0	0	0	0	0
3	377,576,882	43,951,987	0	0	0	0	59,306,249	6,569,583	0	0	0	0	4,984,742	573,362	0	0	0	0	0	0	0	0
4	318,270,833	35,363,404	0	0	0	0	77,943,604	8,660,400	0	0	0	0	4,028,932	463,422	0	0	0	0	0	0	0	0
5	240,327,029	26,703,003	0	0	0	0	84,477,086	9,386,343	0	0	0	0	2,843,489	327,068	0	0	0	0	0	0	0	0
6	155,849,943	17,316,660	0	0	0	0	76,644,648	8,516,072	0	0	0	0	1,692,173	194,640	0	0	0	0	0	0	0	0
7	79,205,295	8,800,588	0	0	0	0	52,325,752	5,813,972	0	0	0	0	742,759	85,435	0	0	0	0	0	0	0	0
8	26,879,542	2,986,616	0	0	0	0	24,893,000	2,765,889	0	0	0	0	202,006	23,235	0	0	0	0	0	0	0	0
9	1,986,543	220,727	0	0	0	0	1,986,543	220,727	0	0	0	0	3,014	347	0	0	0	0	-9,996,128	0	0	0
10	0	0	0	0	0	0	0	0	0	0	0	0	0	0	0	0	0	0	-95,987	-3,259,726	0	0
11			0	0	0	0			0	0	0	0			0	0	0	0	0	-690,121	0	0
12			0	0	0	0			0	0	0	0			0	0	0	0	0	-151,564	0	0
13			0	0	0	0			0	0	0	0			0	0	0	0	0	0	0	0
14			0	0	0	0			0	0	0	0			0	0	0	0	0	0	0	0
15			0	0	0	0			0	0	0	0			0	0	0	0	0	0	0	0
16			0	0	0	0			0	0	0	0			0	0	0	0	0	0	0	0
17			0	0	0	0			0	0	0	0			0	0	0	0	0	0	0	0
18			0	0	0	0			0	0	0	0			0	0	0	0	0	0	0	0
19			0	0	0	0			0	0	0	0			0	0	0	0	0	0	0	0
20			0	0	0	0			0	0	0	0			0	0	0	0	0	0	0	0
21			0	0	0	0			0	0	0	0			0	0	0	0	0	0	0	0
22			0	0	0	0			0	0	0	0			0	0	0	0	0	0	0	0
23			0	0	0	0			0	0	0	0			0	0	0	0	0	0	0	0
24			0	0	0	0			0	0	0	0			0	0	0	0	0	0	0	0
25			0	0	0	0			0	0	0	0			0	0	0	0	0	0	0	0
26			0	0	0	0			0	0	0	0			0	0	0	0	0	0	0	0
27			0	0	0	0			0	0	0	0			0	0	0	0	0	0	0	0
28			0	0	0	0			0	0	0	0			0	0	0	0	0	0	0	0
29			0	0	0	0			0	0	0	0			0	0	0	0	0	0	0	0
30																						
Totals							456,535,412	50,726,157	0	0	0	0	26,408,990	3,037,654	69,843	27,766	11,617	11,617	0	1,741,392	2,655,820	2,655,820
Deal Totals							507,261,569						29,567,487						7,053,032			

EXHIBIT 20.36 Stress Case Demographic Methodology

934

Producing the Geographic Analysis File The steps needed to produce the report are as follows:

1. Go to the Main Menu.
2. Click on the "Set Model Run Options" button. On the CCFG Run/Output Options Menu. Enter "N" into all fields of the menu. Return to the Main Menu.
3. Click on the "Define Report Package" button. On the CCFG Reports Editor and Menu, go to the section entitled "Select PowerPoint Presentation Reports Contents". Click the "Single State Collateral Report" button. The UserForm "PowerPoint Single State Presentation" will be displayed. Select California from the list of states and click on the "SAVE STATE SELECTIONS" button". A message window will appear asking you to confirm your selections. Click "OK", and the message box and UserForm will be retired.
4. In the Menu section "Select Report Packages", click the button "Select Reports from CCFG Report Package". The UserForm "CCFG Model Reports Menu" will be displayed. In the section "PowerPoint Presentations", click on the sole entry in the window, "Collateral Presentation #1". To record your choices, click on the button "Record All Selections". The UserForm will be retired.
5. Return to the Main Menu and click on the "Run the Model" button.

The PowerPoint report will be placed in the "\Output" directory. If you are running a single report, you may also wish to set the report prefix field in the CCFG Model Reports Menu to the two-letter postal code of the state. In this case you would enter "CA_". The file will appear with the prefix followed by the common name of the state.

ON THE WEB SITE

The following files are on the Web site. Please refer to Exhibit 20.37 as a guide to the names and contents of the files.

CCFG Run 0: An Unfiltered Assessment

- "Run00_GeoLoanList"
- "Run00_GeoStratMSAReport"
- "Run00_GeoStratNationalReport"
- "Run00_GeoStratNoMSAReport"
- "Run00_GeoStratStateReport"
- "Run00_MSAInitGeoConcenReport"
- "Run00_StateInitGeoConcenReport"
- "Run00_UserStratReport"

CCFG Run 1: Initial Criteria Filter

- "Run01_GeoLoanList"
- "Run01_GeoStratMSAReport"
- "Run01_GeoStratNationalReport"
- "Run01_GeoStratNoMSAReport"

Report Package of the Collateral Cash Flow Generator

Model Function / Report Name / Sub Report	Report Suffix	Run00	Run01	Run02	Run03	Run04	Run05	Run06	PowerPoint
Data Screening									
Initial Data Screening Report Package									
Missing, Illegible or Illegal Values Data	inside_InitDataRep			2					
Geographic Loss/Prepay Methodology	inside_InitDataRep			2					
Demographic Loss/Prepay Methodology	inside_InitDataRep			2				6	
Cash Flow Amortization Criteria	inside_InitDataRep			2					
Frequency of Default Calculation Criteria	inside_InitDataRep			2					
Market Value Decline Calculation Criteria	inside_InitDataRep			2					
Risk Report - Demographic Methodology									
Frequency of Foreclosure Risk Report	_DemoRiskReport							6	
Market Value Decline Risk Report	DemoRiskReport							6	
Reporting Ineligible Collateral									
Single Criteria Exceptions Reports	POOL_IneligCollat			2					
Loan Listing Exception Report	POOL_IneligCollat			2					
Summary Exception Report	POOL_IneligCollat			2					
Reporting Eligible Collateral									
Eligibile Collateral Reports									
User Defined Stratification Reports	_UserStratReport	0	1	2					
Cross Tabulation Reports	CA or_National CrossTabs								PP
Loan Listing Report	_LoanListingReport		1	2					
Geographic Loan Listing Report									
	GeoLoanList	0	1	2					
Geographic Concentration Report Package									
Concentration Report - National Level									
Concentration Report - State Level	StateIntGeoConcenReport	0	1	2	3	4	5	6	PP
Concentration Report - MSA Level	MSAIntGeoConcenReport	0	1	2	3	4	5	6	PP
Geographic Stratification Reports									
National Level Stratification Report	_GeoStratNationalReport	0	1	2					PP
State Level Stratificaion Report	_GeoStratStateReport	0	1	2					PP
No MSA Level Stratificaion Report	_GeoStratNoMSAReport	0	1	2					PP
MSA Level Stratification Report	_GeoStratMSAReport	0	1	2					PP
Reporting Cash Flows									
Cash Flow Waterfall Report	various by scenario								
Presentation Reports									
Single Scenario Cash Flow Report	_CFScenarioOutput						5	6	
Portfolio Presentation Report	CA_PortPresentReport_*						5	6	PP

Collateral Cash Flow Generator Model Run Prefix Designation

EXHIBIT 20.37 Guide to the Reports of the CCFG

- "Run01_GeoStratStateReport"
- "Run01_MSAInitGeoConcenReport"
- "Run01_StateInitGeoConcenReport"
- "Run01_UserStratReport"

CCFG Run 2: Applying Financial and Demographic Selection Criteria

- "Pool01_02New"
- "Run02_GeoLoanList"
- "Run02_GeoStratMSAReport"
- "Run02_GeoStratNationalReport"
- "Run02_GeoStratNoMSAReport"
- "Run02_GeoStratStateReport"
- "Run02_LoanListingReport"
- "Run02_InitialDataRep"
- "Run02_MSAInitGeoConcenReport"
- "Run02_StateInitGeoConcenReport"
- "Run02_UserStratReport"
- "Run02_POOL_InelgCollat"

CCFG Run 3: Applying Geographic Selection Criteria

- "Pool01_03New"
- "Run03_MSAInitGeoConcenReport"
- "Run03_StateInitGeoConcenReport"

CCFG Run 4: Adjusting for Geographic Concentrations

- "Pool01_04New"
- "Run04_MSAFinalGeoConcenReport"
- "Run04_StateFinalGeoConcenReport"

CCFG Run 5: Producing Geographic Methodology Cash Flows

- "Run05_CFScenarioOutput"
- "Run05_Scen01GeoCFs"
- "Run05_MSAFinalGeoConcenReport"
- "Run05_StateFinalGeoConcenReport"

CCFG Run 6: Producing Demographic Methodology Cash Flows

- "Run06_CFScenarioOutput"
- "Run06_Scen01DemoCFs"
- "Run06_DemoRiskReport"
- "Run06_MSAFinalGeoConcenReport"
- "Run06_StateFinalGeoConcenReport"
- "Run06_PortPresentReport_Balances"
- "Run06_PortPresentReport_Credit"
- "Run06_PortPresentReport_Servicing"
- "Run06_PortPresentReport_Valuation"

CCFG Run 6: Producing a PowerPoint Presentation

- "CA_California"
- "CA_CrossTabs"
- "CA_MSAInitGeoConcenReport"
- "CA_PortPresentReport_Balances"
- "CA_PortPresentReport_Credit"
- "CA_PortPresentReport_Servicing"
- "CA_PortPresentReport_Valuation"
- "CA_UserStratRep"
- "National_CrossTabs"
- "National_StateInitGeoConcenReport"

Setting Up the Structural Inputs

- "Scen01_StructInputs.xlsm"

LWM Run: Running the Structure Using Geographic and Demographic Cash Flow Files

- Refer to Exhibit 20.38 as a guide to the names and contents of the files.

Geographic Analysis Output: Base Case

- "Run01GeoBase_MiscCollatCFS"
- "Run01GeoBase_MiscExcessCFs"
- "Run01GeoBase_MiscFees"
- "Run01GeoBase_MTCashFlows"
- "Run01GeoBase_MTCashFlowsSummary"
- "Run01GeoBase_MTReturns"
- "Run01GeoBase_MTTenor"
- "Run01GeoBase_STCoupAmts"
- "Run01GeoBase_STLosses"
- "Run01GeoBase_STPrinAmts"
- "Run01GeoBase_STPrinBals"
- "Run01GeoBase_STReturns"
- "Run01GeoBase_STTenor"

Geographic Analysis Output: Stress Case

- "Run01GeoStress_MiscCollatCFS"
- "Run01GeoStress_MiscExcessCFs"
- "Run01GeoStress_MiscFees"
- "Run01GeoStress_MTCashFlows"
- "Run01GeoStress_MTCashFlowsSummary"
- "Run01GeoStress_MTReturns"
- "Run01GeoStress_MTTenor"
- "Run01GeoStress_STCoupAmts"
- "Run01GeoStress_STLosses"
- "Run01GeoStress_STPrinAmts"
- "Run01GeoStress_STPrinBals"

Report Package of the Liabilities Waterfall Model

Report Group Name / Report Name	By Tranche	By Scenario	Demographic Methodology		Geographic Methodology	
			Base	Stress	Base	Stress
Single Tranche Reporting						
Amortization Balances Report		x	Run01DemoBase_STPrinBals	Run01DemoStress_STPrinBals	Run01GeoBase_STPrinBals	Run01GeoStress_STPrinBals
Coupon Payments Report		x	Run01DemoBase_STCoupAmts	Run01DemoStress_STCoupAmts	Run01GeoBase_STCoupAmts	Run01GeoStress_STCoupAmts
Losses Report		x	Run01DemoBase_STLosses	Run01DemoStress_STLosses	Run01GeoBase_STLosses	Run01GeoStress_STLosses
Principal Payments Report		x	Run01DemoBase_STPrinAmts	Run01DemoStress_STPrinAmts	Run01GeoBase_STPrinAmts	Run01GeoStress_STPrinAmts
Tenor Report		x	Run01DemoBase_STTenor	Run01DemoStress_STTenor	Run01GeoBase_STTenor	Run01GeoStress_STTenor
Yield Report		x	Run01DemoBase_STReturns	Run01DemoStress_STReturns	Run01GeoBase_STReturns	Run01GeoStress_STReturns
Multiple Tranche Reporting						
Cash Flows Report	x	x	Run01DemoBase_MTCashFlows	Run01DemoStress_MTCashFlows	Run01GeoBase_MTCashFlows	Run01GeoStress_MTCashFlows
Tenor Report	x	x	Run01DemoBase_MTTenor	Run01DemoStress_MTTenor	Run01GeoBase_MTTenor	Run01GeoStress_MTTenor
Yield Report	x		Run01DemoBase_MTReturns	Run01DemoStress_MTReturns	Run01GeoBase_MTReturns	Run01GeoStress_MTReturns
Miscellaneous Reporting						
Collateral Cash Flows		x	Run01DemoBase_MiscCollatCFs	Run01DemoStress_MiscCollatCFs	Run01GeoBase_MiscCollatCFs	Run01GeoStress_MiscCollatCFs
Excess Cash Flows Report		x	Run01DemoBase_MiscExcessCFs	Run01DemoStress_MiscExcessCFs	Run01GeoBase_MiscExcessCFs	Run01GeoStress_MiscExcessCFs
Fees Cash Flows Report		x	Run01DemoBase_MiscFees	Run01DemoStress_MiscFees	Run01GeoBase_MiscFees	Run01GeoStress_MiscFees

EXHIBIT 20.38 Guide to the Reports of the LWM

- "Run01GeoStress_STReturns"
- "Run01GeoStress_STTenor"

Demographic Analysis Output: Base Case

- "Run01DemoBase_MiscCollatCFS"
- "Run01DemoBase_MiscExcessCFs"
- "Run01DemoBase_MiscFees"
- "Run01DemoBase_MTCashFlows"
- "Run01DemoBase_MTCashFlowsSummary"
- "Run01DemoBase_MTReturns"
- "Run01DemoBase_MTTenor"
- "Run01DemoBase_STCoupAmts"
- "Run01DemoBase_STLosses"
- "Run01DemoBase_STPrinAmts"
- "Run01DemoBase_STPrinBals"
- "Run01DemoBase_STReturns"
- "Run01DemoBase_STTenor"

Demographic Analysis Output: Stress Case

- "Run01DemoStress_MiscCollatCFS"
- "Run01DemoStress_MiscExcessCFs"
- "Run01DemoStress_MiscFees"
- "Run01DemoStress_MTCashFlows"
- "Run01DemoStress_MTCashFlowsSummary"
- "Run01DemoStress_MTReturns"
- "Run01DemoStress_MTTenor"
- "Run01DemoStress_STCoupAmts"
- "Run01DemoStress_STLosses"
- "Run01DemoStress_STPrinAmts"
- "Run01DemoStress_STPrinBals"
- "Run01DemoStress_STReturns"
- "Run01DemoStress_STTenor"

Afterword

I hope you have enjoyed the book and that you have found it to be a positive experience.

Last, I hope that you come to enjoy and pursue financial modeling when and where the opportunities present themselves!

"Good Luck and Good Night!"

Exhibits Index

Subject Index

Printed and bound by CPI Group (UK) Ltd, Croydon, CR0 4YY

23/04/2025

14660936-0002